INFORMATION TECHNOLOGY
A Revolutionary Change

INFORMATION TECHNOLOGY
A Revolutionary Change
(In 9 Volumes)

Volume 1
(Digital Opportunities for all)

Editor
RAMESH CHANDRA
Vice-Chancellor, Bundelkhand University, Jhansi (U.P.)

KALPAZ PUBLICATIONS
DELHI–110052

INFORMATION TECHNOLOGY: A REVOLUTIONARY CHANGE
(Information Technology)

Rs. 8000 (Set)
Rs. 900 (Each Volume)

ISBN: 81-7835-201-X (Set)
ISBN: 81-7835-220-6 (Vol. 1)

Published in 2003 in India by
Kalpaz Publications
C-30, Satyawati Nagar
Delhi-110052
E-mail: kalpaz@hotmail.com

Laser Typesetting at: Varsha Graphics, Delhi
Printed at: Mehra Offset Printers, New Delhi

Contents

Contents

Preface

The Information and Communication Technology (ICT) is, in many ways, a unique technology. It has the characteristic of a threshold technology, with the ability to rapidly change the whole structure of society and reshape the way our economy is organised. It permeates every aspect of today's societal activity. Ironically, the very factors that have phenomenally improved productivity by intelligent use of the technology, also risk driving the poor to the periphery, thus creating barriers within and between societies, and could lead to social unrest and tension.Countries and people lacking capacity for ICT will be marginalized in the new economy. New trade barriers will be erected. Moreover, without access to ICT, countries will not be able to benefit from the many innovative ways of addressing poverty and basic needs that these technologies offer.

One reason why the information gap is widening is that the potential of ICT in social and economic development has not been fully understood. There are still too many people in key positions in governments and aid agencies who seem to believe that only when basic needs are met does technology have a role to play. If they were right most of the poor would have to wait forever. The debate must move beyond choosing between ICT and other development needs such as health and education. The issue is not about a trade-off between one or the other, but an understanding that these must go hand in hand. However, technology alone is not enough. Technology must be applied within its social context and that, in many countries, is providing a real challenge. One thing is clear. The new technologies, notably ICT, will bring about major transformations in society.

To bridge the digital divide is both a moral and a social imperative. If we do not succeed, entire regions and hundreds of millions of people will be left behind. The consequences in terms of poverty and deprivation will be devastating. New systems of energy supply and consumption are badly needed. Less polluting and more efficient energy technologies are available, but normally at a higher investment cost than conventional fuels. The international community should play a central role in assisting development country governments in pursuing the goal of digital opportunities for all and to support green technology leapfrogging.

Editor

1

Introduction

The digital convergence of information and communication technologies (ICT) has lessened two long-standing obstacles to communication delay and distance. Ever cheaper, ever more rapid, and ever more varied means of communicating vast amounts of information through the Internet, among other networks, is creating a world in which there is far greater access to information than ever before. Is a "new economy" emerging?

ICT is making access to information more "symmetrical" more people have access to more information whenever and wherever they need it and this is disrupting established economic relations. The effect will be profound changes in the structure of markets and organizations and established patterns of economic behaviour. While much attention has surrounded the volatile new world of the "dot.coms", this is a distraction: the true portent of ICT is how it will transform the "old economy".

Changes in how the economy works will transform the world of work. The creation and loss of jobs, the content and quality of work, the location of work, the nature of the employment contract, the skills required and how often they can be obtained, the organization of work and the functioning and effectiveness of worker and employer organizations all are affected by the emerging era of digital globalization.

Knowledge workers, those who generate ideas and transmit these electronically as "intangible" or "immaterial" products, gain particular advantage in the networking economy: through the Internet and other networking technologies, they have access any time to unlimited amounts of the "raw material" of knowledge creation. Yet there is a knowledge component to all work, and the illiterate farmer can also gain from greater access to information. Nor does networking necessarily mean an increase in knowledge or skill requirements. Unskilled or de-skilled jobs skill polarization in the networking economy also exist.

ICT is a "meta-technology" characterized by pervasive effects on the economy as a whole, and on areas of scientific and technological advance well beyond the ICT sector itself. Barring a disaster scenario, the onrush of information itself is irreversible; however, its course is by no means pre-ordained or pre-determined. This will clearly be a "steerable revolution", in which wise policies and appropriate institutions will be essential toward directing change toward the greatest public good. Passivity will lead to marginalization.

Periods of rapid technological change give rise to innovation and creativity, the outcomes of which cannot be known in advance. One effect of the technologies is clear: work is becoming independent of location and this will change management practices, the nature of the employment contract, and the quality of work. Also, the ability to organize production in "real time" anywhere in the world will no doubt induce changing patterns in the global division of labour.

The digital era has diffused at an astonishing rate. Fifty million people were navigating the Internet within its first four years and their numbers are increasing at a rapid rate. But speed also means disruption and division. Disruption occurs as the inadequacies of existing institutions and regulatory frameworks are exposed to rapid change and new demands. Institutions and organizations that do not adjust risk irrelevance. Technological change always favours the prepared: the world's different speeds of change and different stages of preparedness mean that the existing "digital divides" are certain to widen.

Within countries, the digital divide often has common characteristics. Use of the Internet, for example, is more common among younger than older people, men than women, the more rather than the less educated, urban rather than rural dwellers, and those with higher incomes. One, if not the most significant factor is the level of education, as education itself is related to income and often to location. Girls lag in educational attainment in most countries and, even in wealthy ones, their enrolment in the core courses of the technologies is a small share of boys' enrolment.

Between countries, the divide's features also have common characteristics. Barely 6 per cent of the world's people have ever logged onto the Internet and 85 to 90 per cent of them are in the industrialized countries. The level of national income is strongly related to ICT diffusion and is clearly the distinguishing feature of the divide between industrialized and developing countries.

The cost and availability of telecommunications determines the extent to which the Internet is used, and per capita access costs are most often higher in poorer countries. Coercive governments limit the extent to which information is exchanged, and evidence shows a higher level of Internet usage where political and civil freedoms exist.

Macro-policies and features of the regulatory environment have a determining influence on the degree to which enterprises will adopt new technologies, how they will use them, and whether new enterprises will be created. In general terms, however, it is the incentives that the technologies create at the micro-level and the strong pressure of competition B that will directly determine the economic and employment effects of ICT.

Using ICT lowers costs and can increase productivity economy-wide, including in "old economy" industries. As costs are lowered throughout the economy, some believe that a "new economy" will emerge one characterized by a higher level of potential growth consistent with low inflation. The most that can be said at present is the appearance of a few hopeful signs surrounding the changing price relations associated with ICT. Available evidence does show that electronic markets are more transparent and, through lower transaction costs, appear to result in substantial changes in established price relations. For example, some evidence shows that electronic markets can result in up to 15 per cent lower costs for consumers. It is far more significant that lower costs are also apparent in inter-enterprise or "B2B" transactions across many "old economy" industries. The ICT sector itself is the fastest-growing sector in many industrialized countries. Although the ICT sector usually does not account for much more than 5 per cent of the workforce in any OECD country, the sector's contribution to GDP growth is disproportionately great.

Globalization had already spurred an internal transformation of the enterprise, resulting in changes in the organization of work toward flatter hierarchies and project-based teams. The need for a more rapid response to volatile product markets and declining product life cycles has also been behind the trend toward greater outsourcing. The emerging era of "digital globalization" is accelerating these organizational changes. Enterprises in the most globally competitive industries have experienced both a decline in the time devoted to strategy formulation and a qualitative change in the nature of competitive advantage. "time-to-market" has arisen as a critical competitive asset. This in turn compels companies to rely on the creativity, knowledge, and ability to acquire new knowledge of their core employees.

Evidence shows that major gains in enterprise performance only occur where the use of the new technologies has been combined with wide-ranging changes in work organization. Evidence also shows that the most widespread use of the new technologies exists in enterprises that have adopted the most thorough range of work organization changes, such as the decentralization of decision-making, and the organization of work into semi-autonomous, task-oriented teams.

The fast pace of competition means that, for some highly skilled activities, companies are relying on the external labour market for inputs of temporary duration. The technologies, meanwhile, allow companies to source work independently of location. The outsourcing of needed inputs is accelerated both by the enabling technologies, as well as by competitive pressures. Locations (in both industrialized and developing countries) that have the adequate infrastructure and skills in their labour markets can benefit by participation in new global value chains, in "intangible" product markets such as software development or data processing.

The convergence of "carrier" and "content" industries has resulted in mergers between large firms. At the same time, there are lower barriers to entry in a period of rapidly evolving technologies, in which creativity and innovation matter more than physical plant, physical raw materials, and investment capital. Business start-ups are on the rise.

A world economy integrated in real time carries with it both advantages and new sources of instability. For example, the fortunes of Internet firms and the remuneration of at least some of their workers are unusually dependent on volatile equity markets. Capital markets, meanwhile the most integrated global markets of all through ICT have already proven their ability in recent years to be contributing sources of massive job destruction.

It is also true that value chains integrated in real time create dependencies that, in turn, increase vulnerability to disruption at any stage in the chain. On the one hand, this could prove destabilizing as natural or human-made disturbances anywhere at any one point in a highly integrated chain could have immediate repercussions elsewhere. On the other, another effect of this could well be to increase the leverage that workers and their organizations could bring to bear on the enterprise that employs them.

Finally, a higher level of integration between some developing country locations and industrialized countries could increase the relative exclusion of locations that are not connected. This is another reason why appropriate policies at both international and national levels—involving both the public and private sectors—will be necessary for increasing the gains arising from the use of the technologies.

Productivity growth is greatest in the core ICT sector itself, where, in manufacturing it has resulted in stunning increases in output with nevertheless declining employment. But the employment decline in manufacturing has been more than offset by the rapid growth of new markets and new employment in the service sector, with business and producer services and social services (health, education) claiming the highest share of growth. In France, for example, evidence shows that the negative effects of labour-saving investments in ICT in manufacturing have been largely compensated by job growth in services, business services in particular.

Evidence shows that the countries that have had the greatest growth in "total factor productivity" in the 1990s are those where ICT has been used most widely in the economy. These are also the countries in which employment has grown the most. There is evidence that employment ratios are highest in those countries where the use of ICT is most widespread. Evidence also shows that unemployment has declined most in the small number of countries where Internet use is most widespread, such as Denmark, Finland and Ireland. It is too early to conclude, but there are hopeful signs that the effect of ICT on employment is positive.

Use of the technologies is nevertheless associated with new patterns of job creation and job loss. And despite the hopeful signs of employment creation, it is clear that jobs will also be lost through three main channels obsolescence, automation, and "disintermediation".

ICT replaces old tasks and occupations through automation, such as the telephone switchboard operator. But the technologies also create new tasks and occupations, such as Webpage designers or call-centre workers or a variety of new intermediaries. Consensus reigns on the fact that the highest rates of job creation, job destruction, and job switching occur among the most technologically innovative firms in sectors where overall employment is growing. More generally, ICT creates jobs for occupations in rising demand, such as software programmers, while destroys jobs in those skills in declining demand, such as those associated with analog technologies. Since ICT enables routine tasks to be "codified" and automated as part of the labour-saving increases in productivity that arise with the use of ICT B this, of course, is a source of job loss. Some jobs based on information intermediation travel agents, for example could be lost through more direct access to information or change in function.

Through the Internet and email, when work is independent of location, new ways of working arise. There has been a rise in self-employment. A growing number of "e-lancers" move from enterprise to enterprise or project to project on their own, sometimes for months, sometimes for days. In labour markets that are at the forefront of the digital economy, such as Silicon Valley, the share of self-employed and temporary workers is far higher than the national average. The skill levels and value to the firm of these individuals are high, but the firm specificity of their knowledge is low. In consequence, diversity is increasing in those labour markets where ICT has diffused the most. Although disaggregated data are unavailable, the share of self-employed, temporary and part-time work has been rising in most OECD countries.

The margin of the digital workforce that is mobile has needs that both the reform of existing labour market institutions and the growth of new ones can address. Both public and private employment agencies are extending their range of services beyond the job-matching function to the additional needs of a mobile workforce. While there is substantial variety in the agency work industry, the most advanced companies are not only major providers of career continuity for their temporary workforce, but also providers of skills as well. Trade unions and employer organizations are also offering services to these new independent workers.

The theory that labour markets in the digital era are undergoing profound transformation has some basis in truth. For most people at work, however, there continues to be a surprisingly high degree of employment stability. In 12 out of 16 OECD countries' labour markets, "job tenure", a measure of employment stability, has either remained unchanged during the last decade of the 1990s, or had in fact increased. Even looking more closely at some of the occupations most associated with the "new economy", such as telecommunications workers or those in the distribution sector, job tenure has remained largely unchanged.

Continued employment stability despite an era of fast-paced technological change is not an unreasonable expectation for at least two reasons. First, and as noted earlier, the OECD labour market is ageing. Job tenure always increases with the age of the workforce. A second reason may relate to how ICT and globalization are affecting competitive advantage. As "time-to-market" becomes increasingly important, the organization of work needs to adjust so that a high degree of creativity and a more rapid response to product market pressures can occur. Critical to the new organization of work is the increased need to "tap" the tacit knowledge of the workforce. To do so requires a workplace culture in which trust and experimentation can simultaneously occur. Such behaviours are unlikely to occur between relative strangers in workplaces characterized by a high degree of instability and frequent turnover.

Employment stability is no indication of the absence of change. Labour markets have indeed become more demanding, more diversified, and more turbulent. But most of this turbulence is being internalized with the enterprise, where jobs are indeed changing. Nor does employment stability mean employment security: contracts are changing, stress is on the rise, and there are evidences of employment insecurity perceived by workers up and down the organizational hierarchy.

The places considerable emphasis on the independence of work from any physical location. This is a feature of teleworking from home, but it also refers to the relocation of jobs from industrialized to developing countries, such as "back-office" staff located in call centres, data entry and processing, software development. Work that is independent of location has a growing share of employment in industrialized countries. For example, almost one-fourth of the workforce in the United Kingdom now carries out at least some of its work at home. By 2003, there will be an estimated 1.3 million employed in call centres in the European Union, up from an estimated 670,000 in 2001. Women are often thought to benefit from the new independence of work location.

In some ways, this is clearly the case: working from home, for example, can allow a better accommodation of work and family schedules. But isolation and exclusion from career choices can also occur. Women tend less than men to mix telework with stays at the office. Nor is women's telework as mobile as men's, but concentrated at home. At home, women are more likely to combine telework with family responsibilities, whereas men are more likely to separate the two. Call centres and data processing in developing countries are predominantly female occupations. But data processing, although it may be better than other local labour market alternatives, may not lead to career upgrading. And wages and conditions of work in call centres appear to vary widely. In the best, a new, more informal and more appealing work culture may be apparent; but, in the worst instances, call centres have been called the "sweatshops of the digital era".

One estimate suggests that up to 5 per cent of all service-sector jobs in industrialized countries could be "contestable" by developing countries. This would amount to about 12 million jobs in which relocation to developing countries could occur. For example, in the Caribbean countries, almost 5,000 women were employed in data processing activities in the late 1990s. Such jobs can provide developing countries with an important toehold in global export markets, as well as providing direct employment and foreign exchange earnings. But if the magnitude of the relocation of work is a credible estimate, it implies that the greatest employment potential of ICT for developing countries needs to lie elsewhere. Beyond participation in global value chains through the increasing tradability of services, the technologies offer the chance for purely domestic activities and associated job growth.

Through telecentres, for example, countries such as Bangladesh, India and Senegal and others have been able to create direct employment for thousands of women and men. Over the last four years in India, for example, an estimated 250,000 jobs for women have been created through mobile telephony centres. Such local entrepreneurial activities are likely to have positive externalities on local economies as well. Evidence also shows that women's operation of telecentres increases the participation of women as consumers of these services.

It is clear that ICT is merely a tool, and tools do not substitute for genuine development. ICT, however, offer tools that may accelerate development. Since the principal consequence of ICT is greater access to and use of information, it is precisely those locations that have the least of both where the technologies could have the greatest marginal impact. Telecommunications are positively correlated with economic growth. Even mobile telephony can be a stimulus to local economic development and, in causal terms, some evidence shows that better telecommunications are likely to be a source of economic growth. A widening digital divide may be inevitable, but using the technologies can be beneficial at any level of economic development. The potential welfare gains for developing countries are of three major types are given below:

— Countries with the right mix of skills, infrastructure, and policies could become important locations in global markets for intangible products or ICT products generally. Countries as diverse as Brazil, China, Costa Rica, Israel, Malaysia and Romania have all been able to gain niches in such markets. Some commonalities underlie their success. It is clear, for example, that for maximum gains to emerge, the development of essential ICT skills, including software development, is necessary. Without such skills, the technologies can neither be maintained nor adapted to local usages, from which greater economic advantages are obtained.

— Acceleration of development can occur through the leapfrogging potentials inherent in the technologies, where leapfrogging is defined as the ability to bypass earlier investments in the time or cost of development. Leapfrogging has first of all a technological foundation: through wireless applications, developing countries can bypass more costly and time-consuming investments in fixed-wire telecom infrastructures. In economic terms, leapfrogging can occur through several channels. For example, developing countries have often gained an initial niche in export markets through comparative advantage in cheap, unskilled labour, as is characteristic of the garment industry. Where appropriate skills are available, countries can now bypass this earlier, lower value-added entrance into global markets in favour of greater value-added production. An example is Costa Rica, where the educational level of the workforce was a vital factor in Intel's decision to locate a semiconductor production facility. Small enterprises in developing countries have at least potential access to a global market for both tangible and intangible products. For example, pockets of software development are now occurring in the Philippines and in Viet Nam for clients identified through the Internet. For tangible products, provided that the physical infrastructure is adequate enough for the fulfilment of transactions to occur, countries can find markets for goods in which they have an unassailable competitive advantage, such as products made locally or cultural artefacts. In many cases, leapfrogging refers to advantages at the microeconomic level. For macroeconomic gains to occur requires a range of commercial, trade, investment, telecommunications and other infrastructure policies to be brought to bear on the development potential of ICT. China's strategy is particularly promising in this regard. It has combined previously separate ministries into the Ministry of Information Industries, and established economic zones particularly devoted to the growth of start-up ICT ventures.

— The third welfare gain that could underpin a new development paradigm arises from the possibilities that networking opens up for poverty alleviation. To the extent that ICT can improve aggregate economic growth, this could generate linkages to activities that provide livelihoods for those who are poor. Poor people could also benefit directly through access to the information that the technologies provide or through the potential for greater collective voice and empowerment they allow.

— To the extent that the technologies can make governments more transparent, extend their services more broadly, and at lower cost, the poor could benefit from the improved quality and reach of health, education and social services. This could also create opportunities for women through access to learning, incomes, and greater autonomy. Access to ICT for poor segments of the population is likeliest to occur at the community level. A key focus for expanding such access could be through the improvement of NGO capacities and other local development agencies in, for example, the fields of health care, child welfare, or basic education or nutrition.

ICT and Education

Literacy and education cannot be leapfrogged, yet both are vital for reaping the greatest advantages from the emerging digital era. The promotion of education and literacy generally, and digital literacy in particular, is a challenge facing all countries. Educational differences underlie the different rates of penetration of ICT and Internet usage. For example, the ICT world is often depicted as a world of relatively young men, and the available evidence supports this depiction. Two-thirds of the world's illiterate are girls and women. Nor are girls sufficiently enrolled in the science curricula at the core of the technologies' innovation and use.

In the wealthiest countries, substantial progress has been made in ensuring access to the Internet in school rooms. The European Union's programme, for example, is for 100 per cent "connectivity" in schools by the end of 2001. Access alone is insufficient: teachers need to be trained in the substance of the new technologies and their most effective use. Even in the wealthiest countries, such training is far from thorough, and investments in the pursuit of this objective are often minimal. Obviously, for the majority of the world's people, this objective is distant from reality. In the poorest countries, the main objectives need to continue to be the promotion of literacy and access to general education.

Poorly equipped schools or their absence altogether are most characteristic of the poorest locations. Through their application to distance-learning, the technologies could greatly multiply access to learning opportunities for those who most need them. Distance learning applications, while costly to develop, have low unit costs the more there are people who use them. In such locations, distance learning can be an important complement to existing education providers.

Wealth creation in the wealthiest countries relies less on physical inputs than on knowledge. The frontiers of knowledge itself, however, are rapidly expanding. Two consequences of this are, first, a shift in teaching methodologies away from the transfer of facts to students as passive recipients, and, instead, towards teaching students how to learn and instilling in them the curiosity to do so. In short, how people learn is becoming as important as what they learn. A parallel trend is observable in high tech firms exposed to fast-paced competition. The ability to learn, to transform existing knowledge into new knowledge, is a source of competitive advantage of increasing significance. In such companies, daily learning has become an integral part of the job. Part of such learning relies on the exchange of tacit knowledge among employees.

The adoption of ICT in enterprises is creating two types of skill needs. The first relates to a variety of foundation skills, such as the ability to learn, to communicate, and to analyse and solve problems, all of which are essential to work environments that rely on rapid innovation, and the interpersonal exchange and creation of knowledge. Beyond such skills, however, are the technical skills related to ICT itself, the need for which extends well beyond the ICT sector to the economy as a whole.

Where the technologies are most broadly in use, skill shortages particularly in the technical support skills surrounding both hardware and software applications are acute, if difficult to quantify. This, in turn, is a brake on economic growth for enterprises that would otherwise adopt the technologies' applications more readily. Three problems relating to the skills shortage are of particular significance. The first of these is the debate over labour migration. The availability of technical skills in developing countries could be used to meet the skill needs of industrialized countries.

On the positive side, migrant workers benefit from the greater experience and higher wages that migration can bring, and sending countries can benefit from the remittances their expatriates send home. It is also true that countries such as China, India and Viet Nam have all benefited from the networks their expatriates have created outside the country, and also from the skills and experiences they repatriate when they do return home. For receiving countries, of course, reliance on foreign labour is a way of overcoming skill shortages in the short term.On the negative side, however, the outward migration of the technically skilled can result in a brain drain, depriving developing countries of these scarce skills. For example, possibly all of India's annual graduates in ICT-related core skills could be in demand in industrialized countries. For receiving countries, meanwhile, there are two problems.

— Some evidence suggests that the attractiveness of skilled migrant labour in the United States comes from the lower pay that employers can offer them relative to domestic labour. Additionally, there is concern in both the United States as well as in European Union countries that recourse to foreign labour might detract from the need for the training and retraining of the existing workforce. This is particularly the case where emerging skill shortages coexist with still relatively high unemployment.

— The ageing workforce in many OECD countries. This implies, first of all, that the majority of "tomorrow's workforce" is, in fact, already on the job. The promotion of lifelong learning and the retraining of the existing workforce need therefore to be policy objectives applied to those already at work. Equipping workers with ICT-related skills, therefore, will need to be specifically targeted to the needs of older workers.

— The possibility of a skills polarization emerging as the technologies are taken up by enterprises. On the high end, highly skilled workers using ICT-related skills intensively on the job may have broad career options and command high salaries. But there remain many jobs in the networking economy that are low-skilled and low-paid. The polarization of skills could also reinforce the gender-based segmentation of the labour market.

There are many avenues available to address the greater need for retraining and lifelong learning. Both feature prominently in enterprise training policies, as well as in the strategies of trade unions, and access to learning opportunities increasingly features in national tripartite agreements or at the collective bargaining table. In Singapore, for example, the Critical Enabling Skills Training (CREST) programme will enrol 100,000 trainees in 2001. Germany's tripartite Alliance for Jobs agreed on the creation of training places for 60,000 people in ICT up to 2003. In South Africa, a tripartite training authority in the ICT sector specifically was set up in 2000.

Addressing the skills shortage has resulted in new ways in which training is delivered and new deliverers of that training. Distance-learning is a valuable substitute for classroom instruction. For example, multinational enterprises are increasingly using distance learning applications for their staff worldwide: in an environment of rapid change, lifelong learning has become critical to corporate success, as well as to the employability of workers. Classrooms are a poor substitute for learning vehicles that can be used anywhere, anytime, such as distance-learning. Evidence also suggests that interactive, multimedia formats can often be a more effective means of knowledge retention than classroom lectures. To remedy a worldwide shortage of skills in ICT makes good economic sense and will require both an innovative new range of public/private partnerships as well as investments of human and financial resources.

Will the quality of work and life improve? The networking economy offers genuine potential for striking a better balance between work and family responsibilities, or work and leisure. Work itself has become more rewarding for many in its pay and in its content. The creation and use of knowledge on the job can be inherently more satisfying than the monotony of narrow tasks performed under strict supervision. The independence of work from its location can be liberating not only in spatial terms, but also in the ability to schedule work when desired. The increasing knowledge content of work should favour the equality of women and men in the workforce. Intelligence and creativity are also homogeneously distributed between industrialized and developing countries, or between people with and without physical disabilities. The digital era's potential to improve the quality of work and life is clearly real. But it is not a given. The values, agreements, and institutions of an earlier industrial era are often no longer suited to current trends in working conditions. Gaps in social protection are opening up.

Some of the self-employed, for example, are in disguised self-employment, dependent on an individual employer but without the benefits of an employment contract. Also, as stimulating as work can be in fast-paced, semi-autonomous work teams, not all workers are likely to appreciate the greater risks associated with greater responsibility. These risks extend from the need to keep oneself employable through continuous learning to the greater stress of having simultaneously to manage competing demands, cope with information overload, etc.

An irony of the communications revolution, moreover, is that a sharply higher intensity of virtual communications can go hand in hand with increased isolation. That much work in the digital era can be done anywhere, anytime has meant for some that this is precisely what is occurring, with a consequent blurring of hours or work and hours of leisure. Far from adjusting working needs to the needs of family life, there can be rising pressure to work everywhere and all the time. Older workers could be excluded from the new careers and opportunities created by the technologies, and women, too, as they lag behind men in scientific and technical training.

Addressing the negative consequences of changes in the nature of work has been the key function of industrial relations. In creating a more diversified labour market, however, the diffusion of these technologies renders the effort of collective organization and representation far more difficult. The technologies are associated with smaller units of production and they accelerate both the trend toward outsourcing, as well as the frequent redefinition of who is a core employee and who is not.

Fragmentation in the organization of production, and a continually changing organization of work, are additional challenges to organizing workers in the new economy. The effects of ICT on the quality of life at work have strong potentials in both positive and negative directions. It is clear that the need for worker protection remains and is arguably greater in the context of the disruptive changes that are occurring.

There is evidence of the need for changing attitudes and strategies within the trade union movement to address issues of organizing and the representation of new areas of worker protection. Some international trade secretariats, such as the Union Network International (UNI), have comprehensive strategies and programmes in place for the networking economy. For example, UNI's "online rights for online workers" campaign emphasizes employee representatives' right to corporate email and intranet communications, and the right for privacy and due process in the monitoring of employee communications.

Various of the risks to the quality of life at work are also being addressed by trade unions in their policies, bargaining agreements, or tripartite negotiations. Of these, the right to lifelong learning and access to such opportunities is perhaps the most fundamental, and one where substantial progress is being made. In recognition of the fact that teleworking creates welcome opportunities for some employees but also risks it, too, is an area in which collective bargaining is extensive.

Common features in telework agreements include that it be undertaken voluntarily, that the worker's decision is reversible, and that the pay and employment status of the teleworker are not downgraded. The issue of stress at the workplace is also beginning to enter the bargaining agendas of trade unions. The digital reproduction of intellectual property is a concern of workers in the entertainment and media interests, and a focus of bargaining for journalists.

Trade unions are also addressing the digital divide through expanding access to the new technologies. Both the Swedish LO and the AFL-CIO in the United States, for example, assist in the effort to overcome the within-country digital divide through the provision of low-cost, Internet-connected PCs to members. International trade secretariats are also assisting their affiliates in developing countries to become digitally literate.

However much it may be the case that the present era of technological change presents certain risks to labour market institutions, the technologies can also be of benefit to trade unions and employer organizations. For example, some employer organizations, such as ALMEGA in Sweden, have created an online presence a "virtual employers' organization" allowing them to provide interactive services, individually tailored to members' interests.

The Web allows them to reach out to non-members as well, particularly the new small firms in the new economy. For trade unions, the fundamental aim remains that of organizing the new, more diverse ICT workforce. UNI has targeted the organizing of freelance workers as a priority area, for example. Some trade unions have established organizations especially for the self-employed. In the Netherlands, the Allied Union in the FNV federation created the FNV Zelfstandige Bondgenoten in 1999, the first Dutch trade union specifically for self-employed people.

In the United States, a variant of the "guild model" of organization is being experimented with by a newly formed organization affiliated to the Communication Workers of America: the Washington Alliance of Technology Workers (WashTech) is a new Web-based service provider for agency and directly employed workers in the ICT sector, offering individual services, rather than collective bargaining. Access to information and the collective strength of communication can assist trade unions in redressing imbalances of power in the workplace.

The Internet was the vehicle through which the Seattle protests against the World Trade Organization meeting in 1999 were organized. There are also numerous examples of how the Internet has been used to increase the "symmetry of information" at the bargaining table. Through the Internet, local disputes can "go global". Many trade unions have engaged in "cyber-pickets" to shed light broadly on violations of worker rights and bad industrial relations practices. In a global organization of production that increasingly relies on information flows in real time, giving greater leverage to the voice of workers is a clear possibility.

The issue of policies needed to increase the potential gains of the emerging digital era and lessen the costs of adjustment. The positive potential of the technologies for employment growth, a better quality of life, and as a tool for reinforcing the development agenda is beyond doubt. Not beyond doubt is whether this potential can be translated into reality for the majority of the world's people anytime soon - or whether the risks of change can be avoided. A passive policy stance that leaves to markets alone the direction of change will reinforce divides. It is also the case that the quality of life and work for women and men will be exposed as much to the potential for negative outcomes as positive ones. For all these reasons, social choices and the social institutions through which such choices are moulded are essential to the digital era.

2

Opportunities of Digital Technologies

Information and Communication Technology (ICT) is, in many ways, a unique technology. It has the characteristic of a threshold technology, with the ability to rapidly change the whole structure of society and reshape the way our economy is organised. It is probably not an overstatement to say that the change our economy and technological systems has entered into is of the magnitude of the industrial revolution of the eighteenth century, or even of that of the prehistoric agricultural revolution.

As an interactive technology that fundamentally changes ways and means of communication ICT will also create a cultural revolution, a revolution that could have a significant impact upon the way we perceive ourselves and the world, similar to the impact caused by the Copernican and Darwinian revolutions. However positive the uses of this technology can be if aimed in a sustainable direction, it is important to acknowledge that ICT is not a panacea to the world's environmental and social problems. No matter how we use this technology, our society will continue to have an environmental impact upon the world and social tensions will continue to exist.

There is no such thing as a weightless or friction-less economy: mankind will always need food and shelter, will own material objects, and will need transport for these as well as for itself. All these activities will have an environmental impact. In the same way, ICT will result in new social situations where new actors emerge and new values are shaped. Even if the new society will be more just and equitable, people's views on how society should develop will still differ, as will their influence. Although this might seem obvious, discussions about ICT too often seem to forget that the "new "society is squarely based on the foundation of the traditional society.

When society is transformed from an industrial to an information-based economy, the problems of the industrial society will not vanish, since most parts of this society will still exist, even if in a different form. The information society will be layered atop the industrial society in the same way that the industrial society is layered over the agricultural society. Needless to say, the development of the new form of economy will not take place simultaneously all over the planet, nor look the same everywhere. It is therefore pointless to try and draw a distinct line between the so-called old and new economy, as this blurred line is drawn in time, includes all sectors and contains gradual changes mixed with sudden shifts.

As the infrastructure for this new society begins to come into place, there is, a unique opportunity to shape the whole system in a way coherent to humanity's needs and visions for the future. Thus, while it is important to find the economic, social and environmental triple-win situation today, it is even more important to find in which way to direct development in order to create a structure where most situations have such successful possible outcomes. The complexity of ICT makes it difficult to approach in a traditional manner, which focuses only on the direct impacts of extraction, manufacturing, use, and disposal. It is vital that all due caution be taken when responding to ICT-based challenges.

The impact of ICT must be viewed in a very broad sense, from cultural changes caused by the use of new technologies, to the appearance of new possibilities for shaping a new economy in which production and consumption patterns look fundamentally different.

The impact of E-shopping, for example, cannot be reduced to the computers used for the transactions, or even to the eliminated car trip to the store. Instead, the whole distribution chain must be examined to determine what kind of long term impact this kind of consumption will have on the economy, the development of the infrastructure, as well as upon habits.

To complicate things further, the development of ICT will also create new economic, legal and cultural "meta challenges ". Not only must society learn to think in new ways when working with ICTs, but existing factors, institutions and sectors will have to rearrange themselves.

Some of these participants must abandon areas that they used to dominate, and others must expand their field of responsibility -and obviously new institutions and networks will need to be created during this process.

As the speed of change is so fast, the need for flexible measures and the ability to allow new ideas the room to evolve will be very important. At the same time, a period of rapid change tends to frighten both people and institutions into defensive positions, in which it seems easiest to revert to well-known ways of thinking and well-known ways of work. This creates a challenging situation where the need for new thinking and for new ways of solving probl ns will be confronted with groups trying to protect what they control today, fearful of losing influence in a society with new ground rules and new goals.

It is impossible, and therefore unwise, to try to give a final answer to the question of how to direct ICT development so that it supports sustainable development. Notwithstanding that total solutions have always led societies into dead ends, the rapid change society is going through will make all specific recommendations outdated before they can be applied. A beginning can, however, be made by developing a framework for sustainable ICT development; and in doing that we can hopefully create an atmosphere in which a critical mass of different actors start to move in a sustainable direction.

In an attempt to inspire a discussion about the prerequisite for a sustainable framework where ICT is a part of the solution instead of the problem, this text will go through three steps. First, we will look at two overarching questions that must be discussed by all actors in society. After that, four sustainable ICT principles will be introduced as a guide for drafting long term strategies in different areas, including the private and public sector, as well as civil society. Finally, seven strategic areas for ICT are presented, focusing attention on a number of strategic challenges. Progress in these areas, or lack of it, will be an indicator of whether the use of ICT is contributing to a society that moves in a sustainable direction or not.

Before discussing ICT and democracy, it is helpful to step back and look at the original meaning of democracy. The word derives from the Greek word demokratia, a combination of demos, "people ",and kratos, "rule ". Hence, democracy strictly means rule by the many instead of by the few, based on the belief that everyone in society should have the same basic rights and freedoms and that people should be free to govern themselves. Today most democratic nations are representative democracies, where the people elect public officials, with the expectation that the latter act according to the desires of the people. Popular sovereignty is still supposed to be at the heart of democracy, with the wishes of the people supreme, and not the individual leaders, political parties or groups with money and power.

Many of the trends seen today contrast the manner in which democracy is ensured with new challenges. For example, many large corporations grow fast and already have significantly more resources than many developing countries, the technological development is fast and complex, new ways of communication are dominated by certain participants within society, and there are multiple threats to the planet that cannot be solved on a local or national level. Democracy and the democratic framework needs to evolve to be able to face such supranational issues.

With the growth of ICT, all societies, whether democratic or not, have been given a new context. The opportunities and challenges for democracy are significant, and of different kinds, which may be divided for convenience into three different groups: the first relative to the technological and economical situation, the second to information and knowledge, and the third to the cultural environment.

An important technological and economic challenge, and one that is frequently mentioned in the context of democracy, is access to the technological tools that help find information and communicate. If ICT is to be used as a democratic medium, every citizen must have easy and affordable access to ICT-enabled products. At the global level, the need for action is obvious. International negotiations affecting everyone on this planet are frequently developed in different drafts that are circulated, discussed and commented on over the Internet. This has created a situation where anyone who wants to take part in the development of the global framework, including the development of ICT, must have access to ICT. At the same time, it is obvious that many of those who really need to be a part of these discussions do not have access to ICT.

One of the groups excluded from these discussions are the world's poorest countries. Their biggest problem, however, is usually not access to ICT, but the lack of capacity to process all the information to which it gives access. This is partly due to their lack of ICT infrastructure and equipment, but also to the lack of other basic resources. When looking at exclusion from an individual perspective, it becomes clear that we must go beyond the country and state perspective when addressing excluded groups. Small and medium size enterprises, small scale farmers, the unemployed, young people, ethnic minorities, and those with values difficult or impossible to assess in monetary terms, are all groups that have difficulty participating in the discussions that shape the global framework due to their exclusion. Many of these groups come from economically disadvantaged countries, but far from all.

In a global society, with many challenges facing humanity, it is difficult to envisage a situation where democracy is the guiding principle without ensuring that each and everyone can make their voice heard. With ICT becoming a necessary tool for influencing and participating in the development of the policies and organisations that will shape the future, as well as a tool for sharing information between citizens, universal highspeed access must be placed high up on the international agenda.

Naturally, traditional basic needs must also be addressed. However, instead of treating access and the ability to communicate as a luxury, as is frequently the case today, it must be considered as a fundamental pillar of any serious development policy.

A second, less frequently discussed but no less important challenge for democracy is linked to the rapid technological development of ICT. ICT is an integrated part of a broader technological development, including tailor-made chemicals, biotechnology, robotics, quantum computing and nanotechnology.

New groundbreaking innovations can be expected to come out of research laboratories in the near future, with others already available on a large scale. A key challenge is how to democratically aim the development of these technologies in a direction that support sustainable development. With an economy that demands fast and high rates of return, incentives increase to put new technologies on the market before properly discussing and assessing their social and environmental impact. The use of ICT could, if used in the right way, facilitate and speed up proper assessment of new technologies, as well as a broader discussion of the current technological development.

Today there are good arguments for the current system from a traditional economic perspective, such as economy of scale, but for democratic reasons incentives should be considered that even out the market for other, less complex and locally developed solutions. This is not to say that centralised high-tech solutions could not have an important part to play, but that other approaches also should be encouraged in order to find sustainable solutions.

The broad introduction of ICT has already fundamentally changed the ways information is used, processed and disseminated. Historically, political and economic systems used to work within a timeframe of a few years and sometimes months.

During the Industrial Age, elections and annual reports were the events around which the important decisions of modern democracies have revolved. This limited timeframe has, however, often proven inadequate to deal with many of the challenges that affect nature and future generations, especially when looking years, decades, or even centuries ahead. As ICT spreads through all levels of society, the pace of economic and political decisions has accelerated even further.

Today reactions on the stock market and opinion polls pressurise many groups into using time frames of weeks, days or even hours. The introduction of information technology over the last few years has for example made it possible for global financial markets and others to react and act within minutes, or even seconds, to different events around the planet. Thus, when something happens that affects the economy, the large financial and economic actors usually react in a matter of minutes, followed by the media, then by a political decision in response to the media and pressure from different groups, followed by another market reaction, then by another media reaction.

The need for rapid response increases as the social changes accelerate and different groups try to process new information. In this situation, it is easy to portray the potential responses to the challenges in a dichotomised manner, since there is little time for reflection. This trend is frequently encouraged by the mass media, where a simple and overly dramatic approach built on familiar and well-known ideas is often considered the best. In a democratic society that must take decision regarding complex questions with far reaching consequences this is, however, a dangerous tendency, as it discourages dialogue and the understanding of different and new perspectives.

Sometimes the actual social and environmental implications do not even influence the process where the different actors try to foresee the next move of the other actors without checking out what the real implications are. As the real world is influenced by the reactions on the market, political decisions and how media portray reality, today's society is in a situation where the relation between fiction and reality often are difficult to understand. Some would even claim that it is impossible to uphold the traditional idea of a difference between the real and the virtual. ICT solutions need to be democratically encouraged so as to create a situation where actors with different perspectives can meet, and where the general public can get information about what these different groups decide upon, whilst reflecting both sides of the debate.

Historically, democratic societies have been organised around certain geographical boundaries, where nations, states and corporations exist. However, modern democracy is a relatively recent invention, and has not been around for more than 200 years, even if the concept that a free people should govern itself has been in existence for more than 2000 years. The current structure of society, including representative democracy, is something that to a great extent was created as a response to the industrialisation process that took place during the last two centuries, and was thus imposed from above on nations and states that had evolved from feudalistic concepts.

Globalisation has brought many changes to current institutions. Many new challenges requiring a solution are global or regional. A large number of transnational corporations have become increasingly powerful, and may act with little concern for national borders. An increasing number of individuals are also part of different international networks, through their profession or personal interest.

In many cases, traditional borders today can be said to be of little or no interest - and where there is no national context, a culture is created in which people's identity and interests do not necessarily coincide with national or local geographical boundaries. In this situation, it is not surprising that the role of the existing structures, including democratically elected governments, are now being questioned.

Many groups trying to achieve specific objectives, in environmental, social and other matters, have also shifted their attention from democratically elected institutions and have turned towards large corporations. By its fundamentally networked nature, ICT brings people together and enables groups to meet their objectives without necessarily going through the traditional democratic structures. This could potentially enhance democracy in the future, but could also undermine the current structures that are intended to guarantee democratic development, without replacing it with a new democratic structure.

Many special interest groups have clear and specific objectives, such as human rights, certain environmental problems, or in the case with corporations, profit. Of these groups, very few are engaged in broader issues that deal with the future of our democracy.

The result is that many of these factors, in most cases unintentionally, erode the old democratic structures without replacing them with new democratic structures. Another challenge relates to the kind of information that ICT helps to spread. So far, those economies wherein most hardware and software used for ICT are developed have focused on satisfying mainly material needs.

These material needs are satisfied thanks to two types of information: first, "coping information ",the kind of information needed for basic survival; second, "helping information ",i.e. how to survive in the most efficient way. This last kind of information has ripened to an extreme extent in the current economic system, coming to include almost all economic information that perceives individuals as customers for any nebulous product.

"Empowering information "is required in order to build relationships between people, and to facilitate the development of human beings in everyday life. There is also a need for "edifying information " or "wisdom ".This last category includes more reflective and transcending experiences, ethical or philosophical information that has to do with moral and ethical questions.

A society needs all these different kinds of information, and different structures for distributing them. Unfortunately, the different kinds of information are often considered as dichotomous, when they should be looked upon as complementary.

Food, shelter and other basic necessities are a pre-requirement to having time to consider questions about relationships and the meaning of life. However, in materialistic societies, moral and ethical questions often end up neglected. It is interesting to observe that specific cultures with much less material welfare than western society seem to have developed further in regard to perceptions of non-material and consumerist issues. If a sustainable democratic society is to evolve, which includes time for reflection upon ethical questions, an economic system is required that can deliver enough material goods for all as well as give room to broader human development.

There is no "right " answer when it comes making choices for tomorrow's society, and there is a significant need for democratic arenas in which to discuss the choices faced. Fora and platforms should be created where different stakeholders can meet and discuss the opportunities and challenges that ICT brings on all different levels; local, national, regional, and global.

In the process of developing the new democratic framework, we must not limit ourselves to the traditional structures: instead, different networks should be created, focusing on different areas, creating global clearinghouses for ideas and needs. At the same time, existing democratic institutions should be consistently respected, whilst developing the current system into a structure that can cope with new challenges.

Mankind's primary focus in many regions is no longer simply upon survival. Unfortunately, the way in which this situation was achieved is far from perfect, and the rest of the world cannot develop along the same path if an ecological and social disaster is to be avoided. The fact is that if every human alive today consumed natural resources and emitted carbon dioxide at the same rate as the average American, German or Frenchman, at least another two earths would be required for this to be sustained for any length of time.

As new technologies evolve, the possibility for a highly integrated global economy has emerged. However, economic development in different parts of the globe will naturally not be a carbon copy of western societies industrialisation process. The question then is what will global, regional and local development look like in an economy where the material needs of the world's population are met within the carrying capacity of the planet. It is in this dynamic and complex situation that ICT can play a crucial role.

Approaching the question of ICTs role for a sustainable economy, two points must be kept in mind. First, there should be a balance between marginal changes and structural changes when trying to direct current economy in a sustainable direction. Secondly, ICT must be used in a flexible way, depending on the specific situation, in order to meet very different needs in different parts of the word, while still working in an economy where the interdependence is high.

ICT has the capacity to dematerialise certain products, such as CDs and books, and turn them into services delivered by electrons instead of atoms. ICT can also make many current processes more efficient by supporting more and better information. The way information is processed and shared opens up new possibilities to pooling problem-solving capacities. New ways to monitor different processes could also open up new ways of responding more accurately and faster to problems as they emerge. These would be important steps forward, but are still insufficient to achieve long term sustainable development for all people on this planet.

Marginal improvements in the existing system must therefore be complemented by structural changes. This is even more crucial as some marginal improvements in evidence today are counterproductive. Instead of being a step towards sustainability, these counterproductive marginal improvements lead to dead ends where resources are wasted in bolstering a system that cannot be further improved.Many of ICTs most important contribution to sustainability will therefore take place when it contributes to a structural shift of our current economy, requiring a new use of ICT in our infrastructure systems like transport, housing, agriculture and energy production. In order to reap the full potential of ICT there must also be a progress away from the industrial perspective where human beings are reduced to being either a part in a production chain or a consumer.

In a post-industrial society, human beings should be seen as creative citizens with dreams and visions, and the economy as nothing more than a tool to realise these dreams and visions. When it is said that politics are dead or that we have reached the end of history, it might be of some relevance in the context of the old structures of the modern industrial society, but when looking at ICT and the future beyond the industrial society, nothing could be more wrong.

The chance for change must be seen in today's context, where ICT is being developed in societies that still seem unwilling to move away from a single minded focus on "more ". GDP growth is still widely used as a measure of development and progress, although there is a clear need to further qualify what "more "is required. Even if there are attempts to improve the current growth paradigm, most institutions still encourage increased consumption and more production relentlessly, and do so without any tools separating desirable growth from unwanted and negative developments.

It is clear that in western countries, the emphasis must be shifted away from providing more material goods to providing better and smarter services. In this process. The economic system must be modified, with new indicators providing a more correct picture of the state of society than do today's "compasses ",such as Gross Domestic Product (GDP). With networked technology providing more and better information about the state of the economy, there is also less need for simplified and aggregated economic measurements that do not necessarily show the whole picture.

The future of ICT could be a part of what would be one of the most important steps in mankind's history; a step away from a society focused on material needs, towards a society engaged in pursuing that which gives life a moral and ethical meaning. In this process. The economy must be viewed as a mere tool for the creation of welfare, material goods and services that simplify personal development.

In relation to the world's poorer countries, ICT faces important challenges. It must contribute to bringing together all parts of the world to reach a situation in which every individual can meet their basic needs. As the more economically disadvantaged parts of the world cannot take the same developmental path as those that are already industrially developed, ways must be found for these countries and regions to leapfrog economically and socially over the more wasteful and polluting societies. If this does not take place, the current loss of valuable nature and the extinction of species will not only accelerate, but increased tensions within and between countries, the haves and the have-nots, will be created, causing potential flash-points for conflict, and worse.

The biggest danger on the global level from a sustainability perspective is if ICT only will be used to make the existing economy more efficient. As influential groups might try to use ICT in order to reap short term benefits, globally targeted policies must be carefully developed so as not to create the wrong incentives, since this could worsen the current negative social, economic an ecological trends.

The complexity of the different societies in the world existing in parallel with different needs must not prevent action. As the world becomes more economically integrated, the need for specific and targeted solutions will most likely increase. In this situation, simple solutions such as "free trade "or "economic growth "must be used with caution. If history has one lesson to teach, it is to be careful with simple and "obvious "solutions.

As for global institutions, the challenge is significant, as they have to address different kind of needs. There are still large areas of the world that lack fundamental services, food, housing, medical care, etc, and those may still use parts of the old economic models in their development process, whilst incorporating environmental and social aspects. At the same time, other areas need to redirect their economy away from material production and consumption.

Many actors, new inventions, new values and unforeseen events are interacting with each other and, often with the help of ICT networks on different levels, cross-pollinating each other. What makes current developments even harder to direct is that there is not merely rapid development along several different paths, but also a situation in which the entire system, as well as parts of the system, are in the process of leaping from one level of importance to another. Different subjects, organisations and technologies that have existed on the margins are therefore all of a sudden becoming the centre of attention.

In a society where the economy has been designed to solve the problems of material scarcity, the focus revolves around maximising the material output. Most existing structures and institutions in the industrial society are therefore formed to maximise the production and distribution of basic material needs, such as food, housing and medicine.

Today, when large parts of society have their material needs satisfied, the situation is different, and the provision of services has come to the fore. Two issues must, however, be highlighted:

First, the existing focus on "more "has resulted in a wasteful economy that barely acknowledges Nature or social concerns. This system is not sustainable, and needs to be entirely rethought in order to lift the whole world to a sufficient level of material welfare, whilst remaining ecologically and socially sustainable, and providing the more intangible benefits of a society where more ethical concerns are the focus.

Second, and even more importantly, in the more affluent parts of the world, most people do not need more products in order to increase their welfare. They might need better products, but far more often what is required is better services, or that which has become the most precious commodity in our society: time. In order to change today's society and culture to one focusing on quality and service, a paradigm shift is required. This shift, would, however, be more linked to changing mores than to the external and superficial aspect of institutions.

Every product that exists or is planned should be examined to determine whether the service provided by the product is a necessary one, and the best manner in which to deliver that service. If this is the angle taken from the beginning, a more dynamic environment will be created where people, institutions and corporations do not feel tied to a certain way of delivering a service.

Investigating the substitution by services of today's products, a number of important improvements can clearly be achieved, however, they will remain marginal. In addressing most of today's important issues, the larger infra-structural systems also need to be examined. Two situations in which a change in focus could have dramatic repercussions for the environment are: the production of energy, and the provision of transport.

Almost all participants involved in today's energy systems focus on energy production, and not on sustainable energy services. With regard to the transport system, the responsible departments in governments and the corporations involved all have their focus on physical transport, and most specifically on transport by road.

By shifting focus, the emphasis could be changed: instead of coal, oil, fossil gas and nuclear power, energy services themselves would be the hub; instead of cars or even transportation, communication would be the focus. This change of focus can be relatively simple, as demonstrated by an increasing number of participants within these industries who see the possibilities in this change, but it is hard to change structures wherein "experts "have invested much of their time, energy, and pride.

With regard to the transport industry, an airline might transform itself into a meeting company and introduce videoconferences as a complement to the traditional business, while another might define itself as a transport company and look for sustainable ways to transport goods and people. In the same way, one manufacturer of fridges might shift to become a supplier of cool space, and another supply fresh nutritious ecological food.

As technological breakthroughs make new things possible, the need should be communicated and prioritised for solutions that could make the different systems truly sustainable. There is often a reluctance today to admit that current systems are far from sustainable, with the result that it is hard for other participants in society to see what kind of needs exist and how to contribute to sustainable development.

Today's economic system creates frustration, and much indicates that many would like to live in a culture where more room is left for reflection, participation and discussion. ICTs role in enhancing these elements will be a great opportunity for change, despite many traditional influential actors seeing this as a threat to their short term profit. On the other hand, many would probably enjoy the challenge of solving many of today's problems, and of being a part of a cultural change where "quantity "is left behind, and a new focus put on "quality ". If we are to shift from a product-focused society to a service-orientated one, we must look at what kind of culture is promoted by the ICT system.

As the ICT-system develops, there must be room for values beside consumerism. If those using ICT are treated only as consumers and never as citizens, a global ICT-network might turn out to be the biggest threat to sustainability ever encountered. A global culture based upon the frustrating feeling of not being able to consume as much as wanted, and with little or no time for reflection and discussion about other values or the future of society, leads a clear comparison with Aldous Huxley's "Brave New World ". When a new technology is introduced in a rapidly changing environment, unexpected problems should be expected; so-called rebound effects. These effects occur when an unforeseen consequence in one part of the system is the result of an attempt at problem solving in another part. As ICT, by its very nature, is a network technology, the rebound effects can be significant.

One key challenge from an environmental perspective is that the main driving force today behind the growing use of ICT is not sustainable development, but the urge for short term profit. Increased competitiveness, shorter time to market, increased profit margins and increased market shares; these are the principal reasons for investing in ICT technologies today.

Occasionally these goals may result in a better environment and improve the social situation, but this is relatively rare. By introducing environmental and social considerations from the beginning, many problems could be solved before they even occurred. As no one wants to destroy the environment, create social problems and exacerbate inequity, there should be good opportunities for addressing the existing and potential rebound effects as the new ICT infrastructure is built. The rebound effects that need to be addressed can be divided into three different categories: direct rebound effects, indirect rebound effects and systemic rebound effects.

With ICT penetrating through to new layers of society, many new products will be introduced, and some old products will be altered to include communications capacity.

The potential direct rebound effect of this development could result in a significant increase of new materials as well as increased energy use in different sectors. Two issues are important in this area. First, many of the direct rebound effects can easily be addressed by the introduction of environmental concerns early in the development process. In many cases today, corporate R&D divisions are not even aware of phase out scenarios for toxic substances, and the need for minimal use of energy in all modes and functions. Secondly, the final product must not be the only focus when analysing material use and energy consumption. Even if the product itself does not contain much toxic material or use a lot of energy, the production process might result in toxic waste or be energy intensive.

To solve this problem, all toxic substances should be avoided as far as possible, as should materials that generate toxic material when produced. Furthermore, all energy that is used over the product cycle should come from renewable energy sources. To reduce the material needed for production, products should be designed in modules that can be easily updated and recycled.

It should also be acknowledged that a negative rebound, with effect upon the public image of these products, could be the result if unintelligent solutions are introduced. A situation with higher energy use and more toxic substances released into the environment could create a situation where all ICT-actors would run the risk of being perceived as not taking sustainable development seriously. All serious ICT actors should therefore disclose phase-out strategies for toxic materials and their energy efficiency work.

Indirect rebound effects are not due to the products themselves creating a problem, but to the result of ICT use. These rebound effects are harder to address as they are often beyond the direct control of the ICT producer or user.

The most common example of an indirect rebound effect relates to E-shop-ping. Many times E-shopping "saves "a trip to the shop, with it's attendant pollution and waste of resources, but this environmental gain can easily get lost with an inefficient distribution system. This phenomenon is sometimes called the "Harry Potter rebound effect ",after the event when a new Harry Potter book was sold over the Internet after an intensive marketing campaign. All E-buyers were promised that they would have the book the same day it came out. The result was an extensive transport operation, including airplanes and lorries. Thus, this way of distributing the book was probably one of the worst possible ways from an environmental perspective.

Other indirect rebound effects relate to new cultural and behavioural patterns. A number of virtual contacts with people all over the world, no matter whether professional contacts or personal, could result in an increase in transportation when contacts wish to make the event "real ".On a local scale, specific issues arise when telecommuting becomes more popular. Even if travel to work did decrease, other travels might increase, as telecommuters still need to buy food, obtain child care and make social visits.

When looking at rebound effects, a distinction must be made between temporary transitional indirect rebound effects, and long term systemic rebound effects. In some situations, a higher environmental impact during a short transition period could be necessary to reach a long term sustainable development path. In the same way, a short term improvement can result in a long term systemic rebound effect.

Three of the most serious potential systemic rebounds effects include more transport, more land use and increased consumption. Increased transport is the most obvious systemic rebound effect. If ICT does nothing more than to accelerate the current trend, it will increase the need for the transportation of goods, even if this is done in a slightly more efficient way.

As transport, for the near future, will take place by vehicles using fossil fuel, this is a serious challenge in a situation in which countries that are more affluent must reduce their emissions of carbon dioxide by 60-90 percent. With more control over supplies, less space would be required for storage in warehouses, but on the other hand, it could result in a situation with more goods on the roads, on the way to different shops and factories.

ICT also makes geographical distances less visible, and when using ICT it can be difficult to find out where the product being bought is from, geographically. By using the technology without analysing the long term consequences, incentives for investment in the traditional transport sector can easily be created, resulting in more aeroplanes, lorries and cars, all increasingly polluting the environment and increasing land use.

By using ICT, geographical borders could become less important. This would create incentives for companies and individuals to move to new, still unspoilt areas -and these new settlements would interfere with the small spaces of nature left that humans do not yet dominate. Combined with increased traffic the result would be an even more fragmented environment.

As ICT gives opportunities to consume more and more, the risk of increasing the environmental pressure on our planet and increasing our ecological foot print also expands -along with the risk of creating a culture with no link to nature, and very little time to reflect upon what is important in life.

In order to direct ICT development in a sustainable direction, the different rebound effects must be analysed. This will require new networks, where groups that usually do not have much contact must discuss the challenges. Furthermore, tools must be developed to assess and share information on the different kinds of rebound effects, especially for the systemic rebound effects.

When encouraging the development of a sustainable ICT society, it is tempting to give examples of perfect solutions to today's ecological and environmental problems. Unfortunately, many of these solutions only work under perfect conditions, and their performance under other circumstances can turn out to be counterproductive. There are two main reasons for the exaggeration of ICTs performance.

Firstly, many of those working with ICT are used to talking about efficiency gains of hundreds to thousands of times, and about entirely new ways of solving problems, and understandably want to push the limits. Regrettably, unforeseen, or unlikely, events may be overlooked when the focus is on the highest possible number in a best-case scenario.

Secondly, in order to attract investors and customers, those involved in development and construction of new ICT-enabled products must be heard loudly and clearly in the market. The easiest way to attract attention is to communicate the simplest and most positively staggering numbers -even if these are only valid under certain circumstances.

To strengthen the robustness of the ICT system, three factors should be included in all discussions about new ICT systems and products: possible technological and human errors, feedback mechanisms, and a "cradle to grave " perspective. If all three factors are included, there will be an improved chance of obtaining solutions that resemble dynamic living systems. ICT systems would then be able to handle a vast range of disruptions - however, everything has limits, and when those are reached, the system breaks down.

One good example of where ICTs potential to solve important problems must be dealt with in a responsible manner is product tagging, i.e. providing products with their own identification card. This technology will probably revolutionise the way our economies work, as well as improving environmental protection, making a significant contribution in improving production efficiency and inventory.

At the same time, the introduction of new technologies should not be used as an excuse to delay or halt the phase out of the most toxic substances Keeping this precautionary principle in mind, even a robust ICT-system controlling toxic chemicals should not include chemicals that could be very harmful to the environment.

Another kind of problem relates to the problem when different parts must work together. Often the different parts of a larger system may function effectively, but when errors are encountered, problems such as the "Nimbus-7-blindness "might occur. This name refers to a satellite that was measuring the ozone layer effectively and correctly, but the low values that it was reporting had been covered up by a computer-program designed to discard sudden, large drops in ozone concentrations as "errors ".

It is not hard to design a system that works perfectly in a perfect world, but it is hard to design a system that works well in the context of technological and human error. In every important system, such as systems responsible for energy supply, or toxic measurements, there should therefore be fully redundant back-up systems, as well as planned-out alternative ways of solving the problem, including non-ICT solutions. Instead of trying to build a system that tries to be perfect, in most cases it is better to have a system that is slightly less efficient, but that is robust and can deal with a wide range of errors.

A robust system must be able to handle unforeseen inputs and treat them in a systematic way. As we can anticipate rapid and sudden changes in both ecological systems as well as in society over the coming years, there must be room for unexpected events in all large ICT systems.

In the ICT world, the speed of change is sometimes so rapid that many people forget that many structures will exist for a long time. Whenever sustainable ICT solutions are implemented, no matter their nature, whether application, single product, or the ICT system as a whole, their functions must be optimised instead of maximised. As an ICT response to the precautionary principle, all solutions should be built around the concept of robustness.

Corporations, organisations and political parties are all very enthusiastic about ICT and its possibilities, but judging from the actual results so far, these ideas and thoughts are seldom transformed into concrete action. This lack of results often seems to stem from a lack of focus. Backed only by vague ideas, the process leading up to actual implementation often seems to wind to a halt somewhere before a concrete result has been achieved.

In an attempt to focus attention, this chapter will explore seven strategic areas where action must be taken immediately. These areas cover a wide span of issues and are all important, but in different ways. The areas chosen are, of course, not all that need to be addressed, but are among those that require rapid progress in order to ensure that ICT development will not contribute to the acceleration of the current negative trends, but will instead contribute towards sustainable development. If they are addressed in a successful way, ICTs chances to be used as a positive and useful tool for the future will have been considerably improved.

Importance of ICT Products

The importance of ICT products is due to two basic causes. First, even if ICT products themselves have only a marginal environmental impact, there is a great risk that the political system and mass media will judge the whole sector as environmentally unfriendly if the sector as a whole does not have a clear environmental strategy. Thus, ICTs broader credibility is threatened. Second, the rapid increase and penetration of ICT products can, if no action is taken, result in increased energy demand and bigger quantities of toxic substances. Even if these problems never reach the same magnitude as they have in other sectors, they must not be ignored as they have been so far. This would be easier with clearer targets for energy efficiency and phase out strategies for toxic chemicals used in production.

In order to address the issue of sustainability, the sustainable approach must be integrated throughout the entire life cycle of every new product. Low energy use and the no use of toxic substances should be goals that are encouraged from R&D right through to the final act of recycling a product. In a networked society where hierarchies and responsibilities are often not so simple, combined with rapid technological development, central solutions cannot always be waited upon. Instead, each person involved in interaction with a product should be encouraged to improve sustainability performance.

Many ICT products themselves are very small, but they are numerous. In many cases they have significant ecological baggage, i.e. having created large amounts of waste from the creation of their basic materials through to their production. The cost of solving these problems are, however, small when compared to the overall cost for most ICT products. The ICT sector could therefore play an important leading role when it comes to, energy efficiency, sustainable production and the use of nontoxic materials.

One area where ICT can contribute significantly in the short to medium term relates to the transport of goods. It is clear that ICT can be used to find more optimal transport routes and keep track of large fleets of vehicles.

At first, this would appear to be positive contribution, but it could also result in further investment in a system that is inherently unsustainable. Due care must therefore be taken in order to avoid a situation where investments only result in marginal short term reductions and create an infrastructure that makes it hard to reach the necessary long term solutions.

Physical transport of a product always results in environmental degradation. The biggest environmental challenge today in the field of transport is probably the use of fossil fuel, but even with sustainable energy sources, transportation will come with an environmental cost in terms of energy use and resource consumption. A second inherent problem with physical transport is land use. As soon as goods are moved, there is a renewed demand for space, both for the vehicles to travel on and for the storage of the products. When considering a sustainable transportation system, it is important therefore to always think in terms of service.

This process, along with the encouragement of local production, could set in place a less ecologically damaging economy. Already some sectors have started a process towards a "smart cookie business ",i.e. a business built around the concept of trading and exchanging "recipes ",instead of actual "cookies " thus allowing the product to be made locally. As there will always be a need for the transportation of some goods, there is a clear need to improve the quality of transportation. There is today a rough correlation between the level of environmental impact, and the speed with which goods are transported. This is rarely shown in the price of the product, nor is the environmental impact of the chosen way of transport. By introducing systems where the customer could choose the mode of transportation according to its environmental impact, there would be greater incentives for a sustainable transport system.

One strategic area where more advanced technology already exists, and where there could be a rapid and important shift towards sustainability, is business travel. Not only would a reduction in business travel result in significant environmental gains; but done in the right way it could also contribute to a corporate culture where physical transport would be an option to be avoided if possible.

Increased use of ICT would most certainly be an improvement to today 's economy. Introducing ICT would make the economy more efficient in a number of ways; more accurate estimation of demand, the optimisation of production processes and facilitated updates of products. However, very little indicates that these improvements, sometimes called eco-efficiency, would be sufficient to reduce overall resource and energy use. Efficiency gains so far have been balanced, in most cases, by increased production and consumption by those already consuming a disproportionately large share of the planets resources. If the existing pattern where mankind 's ecological footprint is increasing and the differences in society are dramatically increasing is to change, perspectives must also change.

The first issue to be addressed is the very different economic and social situations on the planet. For the first time in history, a significant proportion of the world 's population is living a life without material scarcity. At the same time, a much larger proportion is still living in poverty. By using the same development model for both systems, many of the negative trends seem to be accelerating instead of reversing.

Solving this challenge requires elaborating solutions for the more affluent parts of the globe to shift their economies from growth economies to quality economies, keeping sustainable development in focus instead of the old economic indicators. This transformation should take into account that the poorer parts of the world need basic goods and services, such as food, transportation, communication, medicine and housing. By shifting the research and production patterns in the more developed economies, a situation would be created which would facilitate a jump forward for the poor countries, over the resource-intensive industrial society, and straight into a post-industrial society with low environmental impact.

The energy system is just one example where most rich countries today have a centralised large-scale system that is designed to deal with very large fluctuations. In a situation with a small-scale decentralised system, where it is possible to communicate between producer and consumer, there is no need to build the same kind of overcapacity, nor would it necessarily have to be based on fossil fuels.

From the customers' perspective, ICT could be used to find the product that is most environmentally friendly for the specific situation. This of course requires that companies make available information about the environmental performance of their products on the Internet. As the amount of information freely available continues to increase, there will be a need for tools that help to identify sustainable solutions, for example "intelligent agents ";programs that help to search for specific information on the Internet. By introducing environmental and social parameters, these agents could help users to find products and producers that supply sustainable solutions to different needs. If these agents could be tailor made to fit different needs, they could play an important part in increasing the level of sustainable development.

Although many new technical solutions will be created in the future, the most important development from a sustainable perceptive would be if ICT could contribute to a society that focused less on people as consumers, and more on their role as citizens. ICT-systems should therefore encourage the distribution of free information, whilst being developed to leave room for dreams and visions. Looking ahead, many of today 's trends show that the exploitation of natural areas will continue. Resources required for the poor of the world, growing urban sprawl, increased transport, and the larger ecological footprints of more affluent societies all contribute to a situation where a minimal part of Nature is beyond immediate danger of exploitation. In order to address this issue a multi-prong strategy is required, wherein ICT could play a significant role. Transportation and consumption have already been discussed, but there are many more gains that can be made in the field of sustainable land use.

First, ICT can help monitor land use in a more efficient manner than is currently the standard. Satellites and probes in remote areas can help to understand and identify different threats, such as illegal cutting of forests. Geographical Information Systems (GIS) may also be used to optimise land use in different areas.

Second, ICT can be used to communicate not only the threats to, but also the beauty of untouched areas. New technologies could be developed that would make it possible to follow life in remote areas from anywhere on the planet, which would improve personal identification with Nature and its values, such as those that exist in remote places like Antarctica, the coral reefs and the untouched rainforests.

ICT can also be used for more direct educational purposes, such as calculating and communicating the footprints left by various lifestyles in different parts of the world. This helps to determine different ways of reducing society 's ecological footprints, and aids the realisation that high quality life can be combined with a small footprint. With ICT, strategies to align local, regional, national and international conservation work could also be further developed, which would make all of these far more effective on a global scale.

With ICT and genetically modified organisms (GMOs) already available, difficult ethical, environmental and economic questions beg to be discussed. Much indicates that ethical questions regarding new technologies will be even more important in the years to come, as there will probably be new breakthroughs in areas such as biotechnology, nanotechnology, robotics and quantum computing.

If these technologies, and especially the combination of these technologies, are to be used in a responsible way, and if technological development is to contribute solving at least some of the challenges faced today, there is a clear need to approach the issue in a strategic way.

Today, whilst many products are developed only for the richest parts of society, this is partly due to the type of economic structures, including business models that have been created over time. These structures are often built around the idea of a large-scale production system, where the market consists only of a high or medium-income population. This system therefore tends to exclude many parts of the worlds population and ecology that really need the help of the newest technologies.

In order to direct ICT and broader technological development in a sustainable direction, independent agencies should be created on both the national and international level to evaluate emerging technologies. One way to address this issue would be to develop an International Convention on New Technologies, to assess the societal and political implications of emerging technologies before their commercial release.

Today a digital divide, both within and between countries, is growing. This divide is a serious issue, as it tends to increase already existing gaps, making the poor on this planet even more isolated than before. At the same time, most new ICT-technologies are built around new principles such as decentralisation and flexibility, all principles that make leapfrogging over stages of development easier.

Two things need to be taken into account when talking about the divide between those who have the technological resources, tools and the knowledge to generate and distribute information, and those who do not.

First, the digital divide must be addressed together with the wider, and more classical economical divides. Far too often, attempts to bridge the digital divide are presented either as being in opposition to other development goals, or as the single solution to all problems.

Neither of these approaches is particularly constructive. To address this challenge, there must be a change in the methodology for addressing basic needs, acknowledging that it will be impossible for a purely commercial perspective to be used to close the digital divide.

Secondly, the cultural gap must also be bridged where the commercial values from one kind of culture dominate the design and development of large parts of the ICT system. There is an urgent need to develop strategies for the creation of cultural space and education for groups, so that the ICT system becomes a system built around diversity, wherein all different groups have their needs fulfilled.

3

Development of E-Commerce

The measurement of people's access to the Internet and the use they make of it remains far from perfect. The problem is particularly acute when it comes to quantitative information about e-commerce in developing countries, where internationally comparable, freely accessible figures are especially scarce. Nevertheless, even if discrepancies in terms of absolute levels exist even among the most reliable sources, a trend towards a rapid increase in the relevant magnitudes is apparent. The Internet continues to grow rapidly

According to the International Telecommunication Union (ITU), the number of Internet users worldwide stood at 500 million people at the end of 2001. This represents 115 million more than at the end of 2000 (or about a 30 per cent increase). The ITU forecasts that at the end of 2002 the global number of Internet users will have grown to 655 million, which would represent a yearly rate of growth of around 31 per cent. In other words, more than 150 million people, roughly the equivalent of a country like the Russian Federation, or 2.5

per cent of the world's population, would be joining the numbers of Internet users every year.Owing to differences in definitions and methodologies, other sources provide slightly different figures; table 1 provides an overview of various estimates of Internet demographics at the end of 2001 and forecasts for 2002. A figure of 500 million current Internet users around the world would therefore seem to be a safe estimate.

Table 1
Estimates of Internet users worldwide (millions)

Source	2001	2002
ITU	500.07	655 (forecast)
Nielsen//NetRatings	498.20	
IDC	497.70	
Nua.com	527.57	580.78 (May)

Table 2 uses ITU figures for 2000 and 2001 to show the geographical distribution of the growth in the Internet population:

Table 2
Internet users (thousands), 2000 -2001, by region

Region	2001	2000	Increase	% change
Africa	6 738	4 601	2 137	46.4
South Africa	3 068	2 400	668	27.8
Egypt	600	450	150	33.3
Kenya	500	200	300	150.0
Morocco	400	200	200	100.0
Tunisia	400	250	150	60.0
Others	1 770	1 101	669	60.8
Latin America **& Caribbean**	26 320	19 331	6 989	36.2
Brazil	8 000	5 000	3 000	60.0
México	3 636	2 712	923	34.0
Chile	3 102	2 537	565	22.3
Argentina	3 000	2 500	500	20.0

Peru	3 000	2 500	500	20.0
Venezuela	1 300	950	350	36.8
Colombia	1 154	878	276	31.4
Others	3 128	2 253	875	38.8
North America	156 323	136 700	19 623	14.4
United States	142 823	124 000	18 823	15.2
Canada	13 500	12 700	800	6.3
Asia	157 779	108 231	49 547	45.8
Japan	57 900	37 200	20 700	55.6
China	33 700	22 500	11 200	49.8
Republic of Korea	24 380	19 040	5 340	28.0
Taiwan Province of China	7 820	6 260	1 560	24.9
India	7 000	5 500	1 500	27.3
Others	26 979	17 731	9 247	52.2
Europe	144 410	108 339	36 071	33.3
Germany	30 000	24 000	6 000	25.0
United Kingdom	24 000	18 000	6 000	33.3
Italy	16 000	13 200	2 800	21.2
France	15 653	8 500	7 153	84.2
Spain	7 388	5 387	2 000	37.1
Netherlands	5 300	3 900	1 400	35.9
Sweden	4 600	4 048	552	13.6
Russian Federation	4 300	3 100	1 200	38.7
Poland	3 800	2 800	1 000	35.7
Others	33 369	25 403	7 966	31.4
Oceania	8 505	7 635	870	11.4
Australia	7 200	6 600	600	9.1
New Zealand	1 092	830	262	31.6
Others	213	205	8	3.9
World	500 074	384 837	115 237	29.9

The data show that a growing share of new Internet users are in developing countries. Overall, developing countries accounted for almost one third of new Internet users worldwide in 2001. In the most developed markets penetration is nearing saturation levels as the numbers of those who do not plan to get Internet access in the near future seem to have stabilized.

Therefore, the growth in the share of developing countries will continue. Already Asia, excluding Japan and the Republic of Korea, added almost 21 million new users to the Internet in 2001, more than North America. Recent data from sources other than ITU would put the number of Internet users in China at 56.6 million, thus making China the second largest Internet population in the world in absolute numbers.

In spite of the encouraging increase in the number of users, penetration rates in most developing countries remain very low. On the basis of ITU estimates, the percentage of the world's population using the Internet at the end of 2001 should have been around 8 per cent, that is 30 per cent higher than the 6.4 per cent that the ITU calculated at the end of 2000, but still far below the 50 per cent and above penetration rates in the most advanced countries.

The fact that more and more people are using the Internet, which is a prerequisite for the expansion of e-commerce, is not necessarily an indication of the existence of such expansion or of its pace.

Some estimates of the numbers of Internet users count anyone (including, for instance, children) who has had access to the Internet in the previous 30 days. A much higher frequency of access is necessary in order to acquire the familiarity and generate the confidence that are needed in order to become an e-commerce practitioner. Particularly in the case of those engaged in business-to-business (B2B) e-commerce, the order of magnitude of their use of the Internet cannot be of some hours per month, but of hours per day.

Indeed, when asked about the use they make of the Internet, people rarely mention e-commerce as a frequent online activity. In a survey of 12 countries, e-mail was the only Internet activity in which more than 50 per cent of respondents in every country surveyed had been engaged in the previous six months. It is safe to assume that in developing countries the proportion of Internet users who are also e-commerce practitioners is lower than average, owing of course to lower per capita incomes but also to other well-known factors such as low credit card usage, lack of relevant products or services or poor logistics and fulfilment services.

It seems that the gap between developed and developing countries in terms of access to and use of the Internet is smaller than the one in terms of e-commerce volumes. The differences between forecasts are remarkable. However, while the estimates and forecasts of the absolute levels of e-commerce for a given year can vary by a maximum factor of 2.8 times, the expected rates of growth move in a narrower band, with the highest value 17 percentage points above the lowest. Compounded even over a relatively short span of time, such differences in growth rates yield massive differences in absolute figures, but all three of them represent extremely rapid increases in global e-commerce volumes.

Job opportunities for women

E-commerce offers some attractive possibilities for small business owners in the developing countries' business-to-consumer (B2C) or retail sector, many of the enterprises in which are owned by women. Numerous examples have been cited as digital opportunities for women entrepreneurs along the models of telecentres in Senegal and Morocco, phone shops in Ghana, Internet cafes or kiosks in Thailand and Malaysia, and the Grameen Phone in Bangladesh. The latter has been cited as a successful example of women entrepreneurship, where financing from the Grameen Bank allows women to buy cellphones and provide mobile pay phone services in their shops or local markets at a mutually agreed mark-up with Grameen Telecom.

Aside from telephony services, women's handicrafts could also be developed using B2C, although difficulties in terms of marketing and management skills, and supply and delivery logistics need to be addressed. A number of success stories concerning B2C endeavours are to be found in South Asia, Latin America, Africa and the Middle East.

In India, an e-marketplace called IndiaShop eliminated the middlemen in the selling of saris. One woman allegedly sold a silk sari she tailored for $ 1,100, a price that is way above an average Indian's annual income.

In Peru, a nationwide network of housewives called Tortasperu, which is involved in baking confectioneries sold over the Internet, showcased lucrative work for women at home taking care of children yet providing the country with much needed foreign exchange. Ethiopia has opened a gift shop that sells, using the Internet, traditional Ethiopian costumes, food items and spices produced by women.

Finally, handmade products made by women artisans in Egypt, Jordan, Lebanon, Morocco and Tunisia are sold through a virtual shop called Elsouk. These digital opportunities are particularly significant for women in Asia, considering that women head 35 per cent of small and medium-sized enterprises (SMEs). It has been reported that in China women initiate about 25 percent of new business start-ups and in Japan four out of five small business owners are women.

The main advantage of the Web for small home-based businesses is the information and networking opportunities that would make these endeavours profitable rather than marginal. Despite these success stories in e-retailing, it will be necessary to evaluate carefully in which segments of e-commerce women's opportunities lie. Women's prospects depend primarily on the trading strength of the countries concerned.

In many cases, the use of the Internet is confined to advertising, ordering and possibly collecting payments; hence women have to develop strategies to build consumers' confidence in the quality of their goods. The limited evidence available so far shows that some women have also found a market niche in the buying and selling of information rather than tangible goods. In addition to the example of the Grameen Phone cited earlier, women in India and Malaysia use online delivery of their services as freelance journalists to newspapers and other publishers.

More promising opportunities for women lie in the B2B segment of e-commerce. The advances in computer and communication technologies have made it possible to transfer digitized data online when there is an adequate supply of infrastructure and bandwidth. Through the use of networking technologies, large amounts of information can be transported at very low cost from the companies' core offices to satellite or subcontracting units. This possibility has led companies to externalize and decentralize non-core sections of business operations to distant and often cheaper locations. The targeted sites are usually the ones that offer the promises of a cheap, skilled computer-and English-literate workforce. This phenomenon explains why companies in OECD countries outsource service operations to countries such as India or Malaysia. The International Data Corporation (IDC) estimated that spending on IT outsourcing had reached $ 56 billion in 2000 and would exceed $ 100 billion by 2005. There has been some evidence of companies in developing countries outsourcing operations within the country as well as to other developing countries where wages are even cheaper. Some of the Indian companies, for example, look towards Nepal for the requisite workforce at times of peak demand, particularly from abroad.

In Malaysia, subcontracting or outsourcing takes place primarily within national boundaries. There is a relationship between the availability of a skilled, English-speaking female workforce and where outsourcing normally happens. From this, one can also propose the hypothesis of the existence of a relationship between the availability of a skilled female workforce and foreign direct investment in information processing work in the developing countries.

The software services sector in countries such as India and the Philippines could support this hypothesis. The salary differences between the United States and India, or the Philippines, for similar skills are considerable. Yet these differences cannot fully explain the absence of relocation of software services to countries such as Bangladesh or Uganda where salaries are even lower. In addition to the requisite skills, the success of replicating the experience of India or Philippines depends on creating the right policy framework. Software and IT-enabled services could be export-oriented as in the case of India and the Philippines; they could also be domestically oriented as is in the case of Malaysia, China and Brazil.

The global expansion of those services has broadened the job prospects of women in new areas. The limited statistics that we have so far indicate that women in some of the Asian and Latin American countries occupy more than 20 per cent of professional jobs in software services.

Recent research and projections have indicated that the prospects for women lie more in the IT-enabled services than in software services. The worldwide demand for IT-enabled services or business process outsourcing (BPO) is expected to grow at a dramatic rate in the coming decade, reaching $ 611.4 billion by the year 2005. India hopes to capture a large share of this newly created market. With revenues of $ 870 million from IT-enabled services in 2000-2001 and an annual growth rate of 66 per cent, it currently has the potential to address 38 per cent of that market.

Again, there are no gender-disagregated statistics on employment arising out of these outsourced IT-enabled services from the developing world. According to the Deputy Director of the Confederation of Indian Industries (CII), in India at least 40 per cent of these newly created jobs are given to, and taken by, women.

Remote services or IT-enabled services largely consist in the relocation of back-office operations. One has to be cautious about the future, however, given that there are various types of back-office services requiring different levels of skills from women and men.

The increasing trend towards outsourcing by major American and European corporations entails jobs ranging from those at the lower end of the skills level where women are mostly employed, such as data entry and data capture, to those at the higher end such as software programming, geographical information systems (GIS) and systems analysis. There is a discernible trend towards hiring women for operations that require less complex skills.

For the benefit of the women and for augmenting or retaining the competitive advantage of countries, policy makers need to ensure that women receive the same opportunities and encouragement to acquire skills that could equip them for more complex and specialized jobs.

The outsourcing or externalizing of business processes to distant units within or across the national boundary could range from satellite offices, such as call centres, to homes of employees or vendors or to offices of customers or clients.

With the computer and a modem, a woman can be connected to the head office and can perform her professional work from a distant site such as a neighbourhood centre or her own home. This is possible as long as her work involves storing, processing, retrieving and delivering digitized information. This new mode of working is known as teleworking and has received much attention, particularly in the context of women's career prospects. The use of ICT in itself can, in theory, offer a solution that is attractive both to women and to the corporate sector interested in retaining skilled women employees.

"Tele" implies distance and teleworking refers to ICT-mediated distant work. The term covers both home-based work or telecommuting and institution-based work as carried out in call centres, neighbourhood centres or satellite offices. Home-based teleworking could, in theory, enhance the participation of women in the digital economy as it allows a certain flexibility in both the timing and location of work. Women with caring responsibilities at home welcome this flexibility, but not without reservation. Whereas some women appreciate the opportunities that teleworking brings, the majority fear that the home-based work will deprive them of the status of working women and hinder their professional or business efficiency.

Surveys of home-based teleworking carried out in Mumbai and Kuala Lumpur revealed that women had a preference for institution-based teleworking as in call centres (home-based teleworking accounted for only 1.0 and 0.35 per cent respectively). According to Ng and Khoo, in Malaysia, "interviews with women's groups indicated that the (institution-based) centres, commercial and state sponsored, may be the ideal site for externalised work that will allow women (and men) to combine work with collective childcare facilities; enable women (and men) with peer groups and thus allow them to acquire and improve their tacit skills; and provide facilities for state and corporate sector supported vocational training in the field of computer literacy".

Managerial concerns may also explain the low prevalence of home-based teleworking in India and Malaysia. In a survey of management perception of teleworking in Malaysia, most respondents reported that in Malaysian culture face-to-face interaction was essential. In India too, research revealed a cautious attitude on the part of management towards home-based teleworking. In the financial sector, for example, companies find it prudent to outsource work to call centres rather than to teleworkers.

In institution-based teleworking it is easy to monitor and supervise employees in the traditional way, whereas widespread implementation of home-based teleworking will require a fundamental shift in the culture of management from direct supervision to a basis of trust. For self-employed and freelance workers, home-based teleworking will involve self-management and time management skills. It is important for women to acquire these skills in order to avoid being distracted by household chores or over working while teleworking from home.

There is no uniformity in the preference for types of telework among women in the developing countries. Age and stage of life are key factors in moulding women's choice regarding the type of telework. In Mumbai, while young women work in call centres or offices of foreign airline companies in the export processing zones, older women, with young children, opt for and receive home-based telework.

Companies such as Datamatics - a rapidly growing software house - receive assignments from their international clients. In turn, they pass these to women teleworkers who work from their homes, mostly online and with their own computers. These home-based teleworkers comprise a wide range of women: housewives, doctors, lawyers and chartered accountants.

All that they have in common is that they had to give up regular employment at some stage for the sake of their families. Teleworking gives them a welcome and much-needed opportunity to be in touch with the world of work. Yet it is difficult to ensure that these women can progress, with adequate access to training and childcare, to high value-added jobs. The experience of Malaysia is similar. "The case studies in software, as well as in printing and publishing, indicate that some women often opt for and find satisfaction in home-based work, either as freelancer or as employees. This happens in a particular phase of their life cycle, especially when there are inadequate child care facilities". The provision of childcare thus remains a key issue in recruiting, retaining and retraining women in the new economy, as it was in the old economy.

In some countries, such as India, Malaysia, the Philippines and Jamaica, call centres have already proved to be a success in allowing women to participate in the digital economy. The proportion of women employed by call centres varies from 40-70 per cent. They tend to be between 20 and 25 years of age and in most cases this is their first job. In view of the projected growth of these call centres, women are likely to benefit at least numerically from this segment of e-commerce.

There are risks of a reduction in demand for outsourcing call centre services to developing countries resulting from the improvement of voice recognition by computers. In addition, changes in technology may alter the volume and the nature of call centre service provision. Instead of providing a central base for teleworking, call centre services may be provided virtually, supported by fast data communication linkages among a network of home-based teleworkers. Again, the deployment of web-based technologies may reduce the market for call centre service provision.

In banking, for example, customers may conduct their own transactions. In this new environment, instead of focusing on a single task, institutions such as call centres or satellite offices will be engaged in multidimensional tasks. Women therefore need to have access to appropriate training and lifelong education in order to retain their share in this changing market. Second, there is a prospect of "burn out" syndrome.

One reason given was the highly competitive environment as incentives are given to top performers in call success rates (for example, in debt collection efforts), implying reprimands and threats of dismissals for low success rates. These employees have to deal most civilly with their recipients many of whom tend to be abusive or even hysterical.

While the call centre industry has the ability to provide young women with the means of entry into the banking sector, the danger lies with it being a dead-end job, with limited career promotion prospects." For women, call centres located on the outskirts of cities reduce the need to commute; for the management they offer the possibility of adequate supervision for ensuring quality control.

ICT and e-commerce can create a number of promising economic opportunities for women in developing countries. They have also pointed to the various obstacles that need to be addressed in order to enhance women's participation in the information economy. One of the most important impediments to women's engaging in ICT-enabled employment possibilities Why is there such an uneven distribution of male and female employees across ICT-related occupations and what could be done to address this? The training policies in developing countries are in theory gender-neutral.

In practice, however, they are often geared to the life cycle and aspirations of men. Women, particularly of child-bearing age, find it difficult to cope with the training given either by employers or by private sector institutions. The dropout rate for women even in the high-skilled software services sector has been alarming, even in areas where there is a need for trained personnel.

The major ICT markets are now faced with a serious shortage of IT skills. IDC estimated a total of 3.7 million IT jobs in 2000 (excluding people who used some IT expertise in their main functions). In relates to skills and training and will be considered in this section. Assessing the parity between women and men in the digital economy is a complex task.

In order to enhance women's participation in e-commerce at all levels, it is important to identify areas of expertise needed by the corporate sector for e-commerce in developing countries. This is particularly so as ICT-related trade in services has led to a dichotomy between ICT-focused and business-focused activities. For the purpose of monitoring and facilitating women's entry into key occupations, it could useful to consider the various core activities for conducting e-commerce.

IDC divides ICT services industries into two categories:

(a) IT activities primarily targeting information systems and technology-enabled processes; and

(b) Business activities primarily targeting business processes along the value chain (e.g. primary activities such as manufacturing, marketing and sales and services; and support activities such as procurement and logistics, human resource management, and research and development).

The potential implications for women of this distinction between information technology activities and business activities could be enormous. Many business activities and corporate functions, especially back-office support operations such as typing, scheduling, filing or communications, are now becoming ICT-based and it is women in many, if not all, corporate entities who carry out these functions. Thus, women should learn these required ICT skills to prevent bottlenecks from occurring in the corporate infrastructure. In addition, this framework could be used for benchmarking women's progress, or the lack of it, in key areas of activities related to e-commerce.

Given the scenario of a prevailing IT skills shortage and the increasing trend towards business activities and corporate functions becoming IT-based, another manifestation of the gender digital divide is the lack of adequate representation of women in the higher echelons of IT-related jobs. Few women are actual producers of information technology as Internet content providers, web designers, software programmers or computer troubleshooters.

In the United States, females comprise a minority in mid to upper-level IT-related jobs, notwithstanding the fact that 50 per cent of Internet users in the country are women. For instance, only 9 per cent of engineers, 28.5 per cent of computer programmers and 26.9 per cent of systems analysts in the United States are females. Women, however, reportedly constitute the majority (85 per cent) of data entry workers. Moreover, there are gender disparities in the salaries between men and women in IT in the United States. According to Taggart and O'Gara, women in IT career jobs earn 67 per cent of what their male counterparts earn. It is to be expected that this disparity would be much wider in developing countries.

In contrast, the networking or programming courses are predominantly attended by their male counterparts, who would thus obviously be equipped for higher-paying jobs and more remunerative IT career paths. The authors suggest therefore that trends in access to and use of IT are not sufficient indicators for the equitable participation of women in the information society. Instead, what should be looked at is how women use the Internet and what skills they are equipped with, as these would determine their role in and contribution to the digital economy. In order to meet the impending skill shortages in critical areas, women must therefore be prepared for careers at all levels of the ICT sector, from data entry to software design, network management and IT entrepreneurship. In considering how ICTs and the Internet could benefit women economically and socially, policy-makers should think beyond women selling their crafts via the web, to women selling their skills as website designers, network managers or IT services consultants.

Women in developing countries do not yet find it easy to obtain suitable jobs or income-generating work in the fields of network management, web design or software development, because they are not equipped with the necessary skills. The explanation does not necessarily lie in discrimination against women in centres of education and training in developing countries.

In developing as well as in developed countries, there are difficulties in attracting and retaining women in ICT training and education. An example used by Taggart and O'Gara from the experience of Cisco's international

Networking Academy Program (CNAP) provides some answers to why women's participation in IT training has been minimal . Cisco Networking Academy Program (CNAP) is an international training program that teaches students to design, build, and maintain computer networks. The CNAP curriculum is offered in over 70 countries and taught through web-based modules facilitated by on-site instructors in secondary schools, technical colleges, universities, and non-governmental organizations. Minimum education requirements are an eighth grade reading and math level.

Students and instructors in Cisco's program voice a common message that once women are in the programme, they excel, and in fact perform better than male students.

In the Philippines, where employment and career prospects are more limited than in the United Kingdom, opportunities for overseas work depict a higher proportion of women graduating in ICT. While women lag behind their male counterparts in ICT enrolment, they are ahead of males in terms of

Apart from skills and training, there are a number of other constraints that prevent women from fully engaging in the opportunities created by the digital economy. These obstructing factors, described below, are essentially access to Internet technologies, availability of credit or financing, the language of the Internet and other social and cultural barriers.

Many researchers and policy makers have expressed concern that inequality in access to Internet technology will increase the existing polarity between countries as well as between groups within a country. In such discussions on the digital divide, gender issues have received attention. The ITU gave a timely warning on impending cyber sex discrimination, since it viewed cyberspace as a predominantly male area where the technical and managerial roles are assumed by men.

Its World Telecommunication Development Report 2002 (WTDR) portrays a different and more optimistic future. The spread of very small aperture terminal (VSAT) technology and mobile telephony has considerably narrowed the teledensity gap between the developed and developing world. Also, the third-generation mobile telephone promises to bring networking technology in a cost-effective way to women who are not privileged, even in the rural areas. Access to infrastructure alone, in the absence of access to market and skills, will not enhance participation in e-commerce.

Human resource development issues that focus on technical and marketing skills should perhaps feature as prominently as infrastructure in a policy framework. The cost of infrastructure, however, is likely to remain a major issue for both women and men, particularly in the poorer countries. In Bangladesh, for example, the cost of a computer equals nearly two years' salary for a professional person, and a modem costs more than a cow.

The collective use of telephone and Internet facilities to some extent helps, or might help, traditionally disadvantaged groups, such as women, to overcome the challenges of infrastructure constraints. The use of cyberkiosks and Internet cafes are examples of collective use facilities that come from the market-oriented private sector. Telecentres present possibilities of collective use with subsidies and support from donor agencies and the public sector.

Concerns about bandwidth are often overlooked in the discussion of collective use. To conduct e-commerce in a sustainable and efficient way, it is not enough to have connectivity - the right amount of bandwidth is also needed. Developing countries generally lag behind the developed ones in a dramatic way in terms of access to bandwidth.

According to the ITU, there is an uneven distribution of bandwidths among countries - for example, the 400,000 citizens of Luxembourg between them have more international Internet bandwidth than Africa's 760 million citizens. Given their position in the economy and in society in poorer parts of the world, it is likely that women more than men will have problems in having access to adequate bandwidth necessary for conducting e-commerce. This is an issue that policy makers should be concerned with.

Disagregation of Internet usage by gender is difficult to obtain, especially from developing countries, and if available the data are not very reliable and comparable. However, even if the figures are not reliable, the numbers of women Internet users are very likely to be small in developing countries, considering that statistics that are not even disagregated by gender show already a very small or insignificant proportion of Internet access for the entire population.

Home access to the Internet in many developing countries is a rare phenomenon. Unlikely to have computers at home, most women in developing countries also cannot afford to use public access sites. User fees charged for Internet access at public venues may not be affordable for women, who are generally less able than men to pay fees (averaging $1 to $3 an hour).

When women do have access in developing countries, it is usually in the workplace. This creates a dichotomy between the use of ICT by women as tools of production (e.g. routine office work, data entry, programming) and tools of communication (e.g. creation and exchange of information). As to the latter, women working for non-governmental organizations have used the Internet mainly for political advocacy to protect women's rights and women's causes ranging from domestic violence issues to sexual slavery.

Apart from access to infrastructure and education (skills), lack of capital is the third key obstacle facing women (especially women entrepreneurs) wishing to engage in e-commerce and e-business. To start up ICT-enabled businesses or to employ ICT tools to enhance existing businesses, women will need capital from special financial institutions in developing countries that lend specifically to women entrepreneurs who have no collateral, and who work mostly in the informal sector. The most likely source of the necessary financial capital could be microcredit schemes that specifically target women because of high take-up and repayment experiences and social dividends reaped from lending to them. In this sense, ICT-enabled businesses are no different from other traditional microenterprises in which women in developing countries are engaged. They both involve light-based manufacturing, trade, or service activities; employ about five people or less, mostly family members; have low barriers to market entry; are home-based; and require less professional experience and knowledge than those of their male partners. The only differentiating factor is the use of new technologies.

The microfinance or microcredit programmes are aimed at empowering women beyond just the setting up or expansion of microenterprises. Specifically, microcredit schemes increase women's income levels and their economic independence, enhance their autonomy over household decisions about expenditures, promote positive attitudes to women's social and political roles in communities, and provide them with information and support networks to protect their individual and collective interests at the local and macro levels.

In the case of ICT-enabled businesses, the Grameen Phone Project in Bangladesh described in section B stands out as a best practice model combining lending to women's microenterprises with literacy training and skills development. As described by Hafkin and Taggart, among the two million borrowers of the Grameen Bank, who received wireless phones as an in-kind loan to village phone operators, 75 per cent are women. The operators resell the mobile phone service to fellow villagers, earning an average annual income of $300 as against the national average per capita income of $286. About 90 per cent of the women operators are married and have no formal education. The phone business can be managed simultaneously with another business or while doing household chores.

The major advantages of this type of ICT-enabled enterprise are the minimal educational requirements (just some basic mechanical aptitude), and the small capital needed, enough to be supported by microcredit schemes. There are positive externalities also in accelerating rural development where telecommunication density is sparse.

Another successful example of ICT-enabling business with a microfinancing component is the use of smart cards by Indian women milk collectors in Rajasthan. The smart cards were used to record the quality, fat content and sales of milk to distributors and served as their bankbook, thereby empowering them to make spending decisions and increasing their profits while eliminating the middlemen (called dhudhwala).

The dominance of English as the language of the Internet represents a serious problem for the majority of the world's population, which does not speak English. Women without access to formal schooling that allows them to learn foreign languages are again marginalized, but so are men in countries or regions where English is not "the" language, such as Latin America, the Middle East, French-speaking Africa and Eastern Europe.

Even where women do have equal access to formal schooling, they may need to receive additional training in foreign language skills, for which time and resources will be scarce. While the predominance of English is a threat to the social inclusion of non-English-speaking women in the digital economy, the increasing trend towards multilingual content provides a digital opportunity in terms of language translation in software development and in web design in native languages.

Many of the previously discussed factors affecting women's participation in the information economy are directly linked to the roles and positions of women in society and the family. In low-income families, parents tend to give priority to the education of boys rather than girls. Also, women often have less control over family income (in particular if men are the main income earners), which makes it more difficult for them to pursue (fee-based) training in IT-related fields or spend family income on ICT access and use. Prevailing gender stereotypes discourage girls from pursuing science, technology or engineering careers in many developing countries, especially in Africa, where the numbers of female students in these fields are particularly low.

In some cultures, women's presence in public is restricted. Women may not be able to travel to undergo training or attend courses by male teachers, while at the same time few female teachers in the IT and engineering fields may be available. Also, women may not be allowed to use public Internet access centres or telecentres and hence will depend more heavily on home-based access. Lack of interaction with the public also restricts women's opportunities to practise foreign language skills. Even in societies where women's presence in public is not restricted, the cur-remote services, this could work well for women wishing to combine household responsibilities with income-earning activities.

Since the top two outsourcing markets - the United States and the United Kingdom- are both English-speaking, those developing countries that would want to tap those markets would have to learn English. English proficiency has been mentioned by outsourcing companies as one of the key requirements. This gives rise to some policy implications for improving the schooling and literacy of women where a second language -English - should be learned.

Improving women's access to Internet technologies requires extensive infrastructure building of basic telecommunications (including wireless and satellite) in rural and peri-urban areas, which are currently underserved in many developing countries. This should involve common facilities such as telecentres and phone shops that offer public Internet services and are located in venues which women frequent, such as markets, churches, health clinics, schools and post offices.

Microcredit programmes should target the poorest, marginalized women, improving delivery mechanisms that involve men so as to increase their perception of the intervention as supplementing family income instead of being a threat to status. Women should be allowed greater control over their incomes and be given greater powers of decision about family expenditures. A perhaps more radical implication would be the empowerment of women by allowing them titles to conjugal assets so that they could eventually be able to qualify for financing from the formal financial sector.

In the area of job creation, policy makers need to promote IT-enabled employment such as teleworking. In developing countries institution-based teleworking generally appears to be a more attractive option than home-based teleworking, both for working mothers with young children and for management. For relatively highly skilled women, for example in software programming and the media, home-based teleworking, at certain stages of their lives, could provide a solution to problems of combining childcare responsibilities with those of ICT-related professions.

But even for these women, policy makers need to ensure better provision of childcare facilities so that they do not settle for home-based and/or less challenging occupations because there is little choice. In other words, a policy framework needs to take into account the complexities of women's aspirations and life cycles with regard to enhancing their participation in all segments of e-commerce.

Women in small-scale business face additional hurdles as regards making use of ICT either for marketing or for advertising because of their limited access to market information, finance, assets and infrastructure. This is where the real challenge lies for policy makers in their efforts to bridge the (gender) digital divide and include the poorest segments of the population.

E-business developments

The IT industry provides essential instruments that make e-business possible, including not only computer hardware and software but also fixed telephones, mobile telephones, telecommunication equipment and wireless transmission equipment. The availability of IT equipment goes hand in hand with Internet connectivity and is therefore clearly a prerequisite for e-business. Even though e-business impinges on IT goods, this does not necessarily imply that having a local IT producing industry would be an advantage for the local business sector when it moves into e-business.

However, when the business sector starts adopting new information and communications technologies in its operations, it relies heavily on local or locally available IT expertise in order to fully realize all the efficiency gains that the Internet makes possible at the level of a single firm as well as at the level of the industry and of the country's economy as a whole. In this connection, the existence of a local IT sector or of investment from IT multinationals might contribute to the takeoff of e-business in developing countries if it promotes IT awareness and culture in the local business sector, if it advances the IT competencies of the workforce and if it brings the technology closer to the local business community. Although reliable data on the IT industry are hard to find, it is safe to say that IT is one of the world's largest industries. According to one estimate, "worldwide IT spending has reached almost $988 billion and is expected to increase at a compound annual growth rate (CAGR) of 9.4 per cent from 2001 to 2006 to reach $1.5 trillion".

The IT industry, having suffered a setback in 2001 due to the economic recession and the effects of the tragic events of 11 September, might experience a modest recovery in 2002. Growth should then pick up again in 2003. The IT sector was the subject of intense negotiations during the Uruguay Round and remains so today. In December 1996, at the first WTO Ministerial Conference held in Singapore 54 WTO Member States signed the Information Technology Agreement Its two most important characteristics are that:

— It was signed as a separate document, and is therefore not a part of the "Single Undertaking': for this reason, participation in the Agreement is not compulsory for WTO member countries and for countries that are in the process of accession to the WTO;

— It is a tariff-cutting mechanism that obliges its members to cut tariffs of all products covered to zero.

Trade in IT products grew tremendously over the last decade and was worth over $ 900 billion in 2000. In particular, exports of IT products from developing countries grew at a compound annual growth rate (CAGR) of 23.5 per cent over the last decade, while exports from developed countries grew at a CAGR of 10.8 per cent. By comparison, total world exports grew by 6 per cent over the same period. As a consequence, the share of developing countries and economies in transition in IT exports grew from 15.6 per cent of exports in 1990 to 35.5 per cent in 2000.

It is also worth noting that IT exports represent a higher share in the exports of developing countries than in those of developed countries. In fact, IT exports grew from 12 per cent of total developing countries' exports in 1990 to 22 per cent of their total exports in 2000, while for developed countries the share was respectively 10 per cent in 1990 and 14 per cent in 2000. This phenomenon was a result of transnational corporations strategies for locating hardware production in emerging markets, as well as of developing countries' efforts to develop local IT production capacities which resulted in important outsourcing of IT production to those countries.

The main sub-sectors within the IT industry were semiconductors, electronic data processing (EDP), office equipment (OE), telecommunications equipment, components and miscellaneous goods. The two largest of these - accounting for almost 60 per cent of IT exports - were EDP and semiconductors.

EDP was the largest sub-sector, with 29 per cent of total IT exports in 2000. This segment includes personal computers, mainframe computers and peripherals such as keyboards, printers, monitors, cables and modems. Storage units, for example hard drives but also CDs and diskettes, are also included in this category. It is interesting to note that trade in EDP includes trade in packaged software, although this is not specifically mentioned. This happens for two sets of reasons: on the one hand, a large proportion of internationally traded software is installed in new computer devices, and users pay for it as part of the price of their new machine; this makes the distinction between hardware and software difficult to capture in import and export figures. This problem is compounded by the fact that, in the current trade nomenclature, there is no distinction between virgin disks and disks containing data, information or programs, so that even software that is sold separately from new computers is not adequately recorded in international trade figures.

The share of developing countries in EDP hardware was quite high, accounting for 40 per cent of exports in 2000. Developed countries - and in particular the United States and Japan - are the main producers of high-end computer products, but Asian countries, particularly Singapore, the Republic of Korea, Malaysia, Thailand and China, are also powerful competitors, especially in the PC sub-segment. Thus, the presence of developing countries is higher in the commoditized IT products, which are characterized by low value- added.

As regards software, the United States is the world's leading exporter, and it has been estimated that 'American off-the-shelf software accounts for 70 per cent of the world market". Among developed countries, Japan, Ireland, Singapore, the United Kingdom, France and the Netherlands are emerging as software industry hubs. Among the developing countries, a number of Asian countries are promoting production of software and software services, in particular India, Pakistan, Malaysia, the Philippines and Thailand among others.

The second largest sub-sector, with 25 per cent of exports, was semiconductors, and it was the one with the largest participation by developing countries, accounting for 43 per cent of exports. Again, the largest producers were the United States and Japan, together with a number of ASEAN countries, whose market share has been increasing steadily. Leading exporters from the ASEAN region are in particular the Republic of Korea, Thailand and Taiwan Province of China.

IT goods is currently low in developed countries and it is quite likely that since developed countries are the main markets for these products, this was one of the factors that enabled the rapid growth of developing countries' exports of IT goods. However, tariffs remain relatively high in the developing world and especially so in least developed countries.

The level of protection is highest in the office equipment and components sub-sectors. The reason for this, with regard to the components sub-sector, is in part that some products included in that sub-sector are difficult to separate from components of an electrical and even mechanical nature. Thus, these products were not subject to the sweeping tariff-cutting exercise that focused on the IT sector.

Even when this is taken into account, the rate applied by some of the least developed countries appears to represent one more obstacle for companies located in those countries in accessing technology at reasonable cost. In order to enable developing countries' manufacturers and service providers to engage in e-business and to take full advantage of the opportunities offered by the new technologies, the tariffs levied on these products need to be reassessed.

In the last three decades a number of countries have used the IT industry as a tool for their development, for a number of reasons. First, the sheer size of the industry now makes it an important investment opportunity. Second, since many segments of the industry do not require a large amount of upfront capital, entry in this sector is relatively easy for countries that have adequate human capital. Third, as mentioned in the previous section, the protection level for the IT industry is relatively low in the major importing markets, and this no doubt was among the factors that favoured the growth of the IT industry in some of the developing countries.

A number of developing countries have therefore undertaken strategies to attract investment in the field of IT and/or develop the IT industry. The IT industry has grown in waves, as regards both technological developments and market demand, so according to one interpretation, the countries that have succeeded in developing an IT local sector were those that recognized and consequently targeted an emerging trend, investing in the production of goods for which the technology was already established, but for which the market was not yet saturated. Some of the South-East Asian countries were, for example, successful in penetrating the PC industry in the early 1980's when PCs relied on a robust technological base and the industry was growing fast.

One clearly emerging new wave in the next few years concerns the development of open-source software. As explained, open-source not only offers promising opportunities to the software industry in developing countries but also is particularly well adapted to fitting in with developing countries' current pattern of hardware production.

Another emerging trend in developing countries is the customization of IT and especially software products for the use of their local or regional markets. In fact, a number of SMEs from developing countries are closely cooperating with transnational corporations in order to make their products or services suitable for the particular needs of a niche clientele or a foreign market.

IT makes to development in its widest possible sense. In fact, IT is among the factors that underpin the globalization taking place in virtually all business sectors. New ICT such as the Internet give companies the opportunity to develop new products, to access world markets at lower costs and to source the goods and services needed in the production process in wider and more competitive markets. This translates into increased efficiency not only at the level of the firm, but also at the level of the business sector and the economy as a whole.

While it is clear that many companies in developing and transition economies are using e-business in a variety of forms, to fully benefit from the new technologies and integrate them into everyday business requires a technological infrastructure and a level of workforce expertise that are beyond the reach of the majority of small and medium sized enterprises in developing countries. It is for this reason that business associations, local and national governments, and international organizations are developing a number of initiatives in order to create a nurturing environment into which the business community can successfully integrate e-business practices.

The present analysis is complementary to these efforts, in that its aim is to offer hindsight on the role of the IT industry in facilitating the adoption of e-business by the local business sector in developing countries. In this connection, the next paragraph presents the survey designed and conducted by the UNCTAD secretariat in order to highlight some of the basic facts of foreign investment in IT in developing countries and especially the relationship between IT transnational corporations and the local workforce and the local business sector.

UNCTAD survey

The UNCTAD secretariat undertook a survey of the determinants of IT companies' investment and use of e-commerce in developing and transition economies. It used several databases in order to identify all the IT companies of a size large enough to justify overseas investment. Information about the sample population, the rate of response and a copy of the questionnaire can be found in annex.

The questions included in the questionnaire were carefully selected and worded in such a way as to minimize the work required of the respondents and to facilitate the analysis of the results. This meant that - with only one exception - multiple-choice questions were preferred to open questions. As an example, many of the questions requested the respondents to choose among alternative strategic options or rank various factors that guide their investment decisions or desired government strategies. Of course, this implied a certain loss of spontaneity and of generality in the answers, which are typical and have to be accepted in these surveys. While a question on the magnitude of worldwide revenue from IT products was included, questions aimed at extracting quantitative information such as the magnitude of planned or existing investment, the revenues from sales at a specific location or the number of personnel working in any given site were deliberately excluded for a number of reasons. First, quantitative information would be difficult for the companies to disclose, and would prevent many from participating in the survey and providing a valuable insight into policies and strategic business options. Second, these questions would not necessarily have given indications about the magnitude of developing country operations. For example depending on the different ownership arrangements and on the business strategy adopted by the mother company or by the local management, a very small upfront investment could result in a larger or a smaller business venture. Including a question on the number of employees could have been equally misleading, depending on what part of the work was subcontracted and on the labour or capital intensity of the goods that were produced.

The answers, which are presented below, are intended to be of assistance in the design of policies and strategies that will not only attract the kind of IT investment that best matches a country's strengths but also allow developing countries and countries in transition to increase the IT competence of the workforce and to deepen the linkages between national firms and IT multinationals. Unless otherwise indicated, the source of all the data presented in the next paragraphs is the UNCTAD survey.

Results of the survey

Composition of the sample

As regards the composition of the sample of respondents, the 35 companies that replied to the questionnaire had a cumulative turnover from IT products of $ 413 billion, which represents around a half of IT worldwide production. The average turnover was $ 12 billion: it should be noted however that this is not the total turnover of the companies - which is even larger - but exclusively the revenue from IT sales.

The sample included companies of different sizes and revealed that even relatively small-scale companies in the field of IT invest in overseas markets. Twelve companies had a turnover of less than $ 1 billion, nine companies between $ 1 and 10 billion, five companies between $ 10 and 20 billion, five between $ 20 and 40 billion, and 3 with more than $ 40 billion.

The survey was not addressed to local IT-producing companies in developing countries for two sets of reasons. First, multinational companies make up an important share of production in the IT sector. For instance, the sum of the revenue of the top ten hardware and of the top ten software producers, according to Fortune magazine, is $ 311 billion, or roughly a third of worldwide IT spending. Secondly, it would have required two different questionnaires to inquire about the local operations of small IT companies and the overseas operations of IT multinationals, so that it was decided that this second line of analysis should be treated separately.

It is interesting to note that the companies which indicated that they invested primarily in hardware and components had an average turnover of $ 18.82 billion, while those that invested primarily in software had an average turnover of $ 4.28 billion. In other words, many of the "smaller" companies in our sample were mainly investing in software. This replicates the underlying structure of the industry: by way of comparison, the 12 largest companies in the field of computer hardware and office equipment had an average turnover of $ 21.3 billion, while the 13 largest software producers had an average turnover of $ 4.3 billion.

Type of ownership arrangements

Respondents were asked to rank the means that their company used in order to establish a presence in developing countries. Companies were given four choices.

The majority of respondents answered that investment was of the greenfield type (building or leasing a facility), while mergers and acquisitions were the least utilized among the available options. Interestingly, this is the reverse of the finding by the World Investment Report: "Over the past decade, most of the growth in international production has been via cross-border M&A rather than greenfield investment". The difference in conclusions may be explained by the fact that the corporate IT sector in developing countries has not yet presented advantageous acquisition targets or merger partners owing to the relative infancy of the entire IT sector.

Our finding could be related to the particular characteristics of the IT industry as opposed to other economic sectors. One should be careful, however, about potential definitional discrepancies. In particular, in our survey, greenfield investment was defined quite loosely to include building or leasing a facility. In other words, this answer could point to strikingly different patterns, such as building a new plant for the production of IT hardware or leasing an office for the distribution of a company's products.

Nevertheless, reading through the answers, and combining this answer with the one on the purpose of investment, led to the conclusion that quite a number of the respondents were indeed undertaking greenfield investment with the intention of starting local production. The prevalence of greenfield investment is a positive sign, because it results in a net increase in the developing countries' production facilities, and can contribute to the overall improvement in macroeconomic and export trade performance. Another important expansion tool, utilized extensively by the respondent companies, was the formation of joint ventures with local companies, whereby the multinational corporation is typically contributing its command of state-of-the-art technology and the local partner the knowledge of the market. In many cases, joint ventures are preferred to the alternative of directly acquiring local companies, because this strategy requires a lower upfront investment, and because continuity in the operations of local companies is preserved.

The relatively low number of companies that chose mergers and acquisitions as their preferred expansion tool could be due to a number of factors, including the fear that local companies may be burdened by debt or tied down by the composition of their workforce.

Utilization of e-commerce by IT multinationals

The respondents declared that - on average - 35 per cent of their purchases and 16 per cent of their sales were done over the net. Reliable statistics on enterprises' use of e-commerce are notoriously difficult to find, and so it was not possible to compare this finding against other figures collected at the worldwide level, as would have been desirable. As a tentative comparison, in the United States, a recent survey by the United States Department of Commerce found that: "E-shipments account for 18.4 per cent of the value of all shipments from US manufacturing plants in 2000". In account of the fact that our sample includes companies from countries that are less advanced in e-commerce than the United States, we can conclude that companies from the IT sector are as would have to be expected - comparatively heavy users of electronic commerce.

In this light, it is interesting to see whether developing countries' operations are able to seamlessly integrate into the multinationals' system of production, which relies on high technology for the execution of contracts with established suppliers.

The respondents were asked what proportion of their developing countries' operations used common information and telecommunication technologies. On a scale of 1 to 10, 10 would represent an answer such as "all developing countries' facilities utilize the technology" and a value of 1 "none of the developing countries' facilities utilize it". A large proportion of developing countries' facilities utilize e-mail and operate a website, but few of them are yet engaging in e-commerce operations such as managing online catalogues, receiving online orders and handling online payments, and more generally becoming integrated into the company's online production system.

It is perhaps for this reason that a rather high percentage of the respondents declared that the various aspects of e-commerce did not facilitate "at all" the setting up and operating of developing countries' facilities (9 per cent). An equal percentage of respondents held an opposite view - namely that e-commerce had greatly facilitated such operations - and the great majority of respondents thought that e-commerce had made things significantly (32 per cent) or somewhat (47 per cent) easier. More research would have to be done to qualify this perception, but it appears that in the operation of overseas facilities the "handshake" and personal contacts still retain their importance in spite of technological advances and that developing countries' facilities continue to be managed utilizing ordinary telecommunications tools rather than the new technologies, in view in particular of the still limited availability of ICT in developing countries.

Location of investment

The respondents were asked to provide details of the regions where they invested or where they intended to invest in the near future, indicating for what purpose they were investing or were intending to invest there. In order to keep the design of the questions simple, the companies were offered six choices: Africa, Eastern Europe, Latin America, Middle East, South-East Asia (ASEAN countries) and other developing countries in Asia (including India and China). The majority of the respondents (70 per cent) indicated that they invested in "other developing countries in Asia", while a slightly lower percentage (67 per cent) in South-East Asia. These regions were followed at a distance by Eastern Europe and the Middle East, and then by Africa and Latin America.

Next, in view of this strong concentration of IT investment, which appears to be even more important than that encountered in many other industries, it becomes interesting to see what are the factors that draw investment to specific countries and what are the consequences of alternative policy actions that countries can take in this regard.

In the first place, the location of the investment was influenced by the location of the mother company's headquarters. On the Asian and Latin American markets, the bulk of the investment was from United States' firms, while in Eastern Europe it was from

East markets the percentages of European and American companies were identical. A surprisingly high percentage of investment in Latin

As for the other factors that directed IT investment to specific markets, the most important was access to markets (market size and potential, proximity to larger markets, participation in regional/bilateral free trade areas), followed by general policy environment (political stability, trade policy, tax policy), cost of production, workforce IT competence, workforce education and investment incentives.

This ranking basically reflects the findings of other surveys - see, for instance, the Foreign Direct Investment Survey 30 - but shows that IT companies attach particular importance to the competences of the workforce. IT multinationals will select the location of their subsidiaries according to fundamental macroeconomic variables, which the country can alter only in the medium to long term. For instance, the most important factor in TNCs decisions appears to be "access to markets": while access is a geographical factor over which the policy maker has little control, partially, it can be enhanced by signing free trade area agreements at the regional level and marketing the country as the potential production hub to service the regional market. The case is similar for factors such as "general policy environment" and "cost of production": Governments can influence them by making the country an enabling environment for investment - both local and foreign- but clearly this can only be a long-term policy goal. Factors such as investment incentives, which can be altered in the short term, are instead likely to have less effect on companies' decisions on the location of investment.

Next, it is interesting to analyze the purpose for which the respondent companies invest in developing regions. The questionnaire gave the companies five choices: Customer Support Service (CSS), Distribution, Production for export on the world markets, Production for local or regional markets, Research and development (R&D) and Other. The most important reason for investment in developing countries was customer support service and distribution, followed by R&D, and production.

Since customer support service and distribution are critical factors that draw IT investment to the different markets, it is safe to assume that IT multinationals will invest more heavily in the very regions in which they are more intensively exporting. Thus, as e-commerce

and e-business lead the business sector in developing countries to make more intensive use of the new technologies more IT investment will flow to those regions. The relative importance of customer support service also points to the growing market which tends to the needs of corporate clients for the customization of hardware and software and which - as was discussed - also offers business opportunities for developing countries.

A cross-analysis of the reasons why multinationals invest in the different regions, accord-To summarize, the findings from the questionnaire point to an intensive concentration of IT investment in South and South-East

Asia and in particular to the concentration of investment for productive and research purposes in those regions. Furthermore, it appears that government policies can only alter investment decisions on location in the medium to long term.

We turn now to the last set of questions, which focused on what actions Governments could take in order to maximize the positive fallback of IT investment, in terms of use of local labour by TNCs and enhancement of workforce skills and in terms of deepening the linkages between TNCs and the local industry.

Labour

A key benefit of FDI - and especially so in the field of IT - is the potential for human resources development. TNCs may in fact act as a powerful pull factor, because they often offer better wages than domestic firms, but at the same time require a higher level of competence. As a result, they stimulate the development of a technically skilled workforce and encourage Governments and households to invest in education. In addition, the characteristics of jobs in TNCs are such that they often require on-the-job training so there TNC investment may have a direct impact on the qualifications of the workforce.

This brings us directly to the next question - how much of the employment generated by the multinationals is local. The respondent companies reported that - on average - local labour represented 79.7 per cent of the total workforce in their facilities in developing countries.

The variation among companies was quite high for this answer, and over half of the companies in the sample reported percentages of 90 per cent and higher. It is also interesting to observe that the multinationals mostly employ skilled 31 labour in their developing countries' facilities: in fact, it represented close to 69 per cent of the total workforceing to the purpose of investment.

It appears quite clearly that investment in production facilities and in research and development - which is the one that most facilitates the transfer of technology from multinationals to local companies - is still heavily concentrated in South and South-East Asia. In fact, while R&D represents 20 per cent of all investment in those two regions, the percentage is only 6 per cent in the Middle East and 7 per cent in Africa. Similarly, investment in production facilities represents 37 per cent of total investment in South-East Asia and only 23 per cent of total investment in Africa.

The respondents were then asked to specify which policy actions would be desirable in order to increase the number of high-skilled local personnel and improve their competencies. The companies were of the view that the most important policy action in this regard was developing and expanding local universities, followed by increasing the quality and reach of primary education.

Subcontractors

One last important dimension that deserves to be explored is that of the linkages between multinationals and local industry. The concept of "linkages" was the central theme in UNCTAD's World Investment Report 2001, which summarizes its benefits as follows:

> "A key factor determining the benefits host countries can derive from FDI are the linkages that foreign affiliates strike with domestically owned firms. Backward linkages from foreign affiliates to domestic firms are important channels through which intangible and tangible assets can be passed on ... They can contribute to the upgrading of domestic enterprises, provide opportunities for production and employment by domestic suppliers and embed foreign firms more firmly in the host economies".

For these reasons, our survey included a question on the linkages that TNCs made with local firms. The companies that responded to our survey maintain intense linkages with local companies in the host countries. In particular, 65 per cent of companies indicated that they were buying generic office supplies from local firms and 56 per cent that they sourced from them direct inputs into the production process. Only 9 per cent of the firms declared that they did not rely on local partners. Additionally, the respondents were asked to specify which policy actions would encourage them to make further use of local firms. The most important ones are the strengthening of enforcement of contracts either by reinforcing local courts or through international investment agreements, developing the competencies of local firms in the field of IT, improving telecommunication infrastructure and improving information on the stability and financial security of local firms.

4

M-Commerce Opportunities

The most common definition of 'm-commerce' is the buying and selling of goods and services using wireless handheld devices such as mobile telephones or personal data assistants (PDAs). A broader definition that extends m-commerce to "mobile business" may be more appropriate. This involves business-related communication among individuals and companies where financial transactions do not necessarily occur. In the last four years, the growth in the number of mobile telephone users worldwide has exceeded the growth in the number of fixed lines, expanding from 50 million to almost one billion in 2002.

Today, over 90 per cent of countries have a mobile network, and nearly one in every six of the world's inhabitants has a mobile telephone. Almost 100 countries have more mobile than fixed-line telephone subscribers and this will become a global phenomenon in the early part of 2002. The introduction of wireless communications has not only expanded telephony in many developing countries, but also introduced wireless data services which are essential for conducting m-commerce. For many people in developing countries, mobile handsets may be the first and main access route to information and communication technologies (ICT), the Internet and e-commerce technologies.

The challenge is to provide access to the global telecommunications system for a significant number of citizens in developing countries. Mobile communications may be the technology that overcomes the barriers constituted by the high cost of installing fixed-line infrastructure that developing countries continue to encounter.

Current m-commerce applications and trends, including banking and insurance, logistics, securities, and information services, are also reviewed. In addition, regulatory issues related to data security and privacy are assessed. Finally, the main findings and recommendations for developing country m-commerce readiness are presented.

Features of M-commerce

Wireless communications provide the long sought after platform that can make digital data transfer possible in many developing countries. This is due in part to the lower costs of mobile systems relative to fixed networks, the provision of short message services (SMS) and the enabling of wireless Internet connections. In developing countries most mobile services are prepaid using stored value cards. This mitigates post-paid subscription problems of creditworthiness and billing. By mid-2002 there were 300 million mobile telephone users in the Asia-Pacific region.

China has the largest number of mobile telephone users in the world: more than 170 million in mid-2002, with over 400 million forecast by 2005—2006. Europe is an important mobile market with over 300 million subscribers forecast for 2002. The number of wireless communication has already exceeded the number of fixed-line subscribers, and it is expected that in many countries, particularly developing countries, telecommunications operators will continue to rapidly increase the number of mobile subscribers thanks to low infrastructure and operating costs. Surveys in the United States indicate that wireless services are expected to be a major vehicle for customer relationship management (CRM) and that the amount of business management and marketing activities carried out using remote communications is continuously growing.

M-commerce represents the extension of e-commerce merce - B2B, B2C, B2G and P2P-remain. In developing countries mobile business applications, especially when used by small and medium-sized enterprises in remote areas, may become a key method for reaching potential customers, and are expected to be highly important features of m-commerce.

In 2002 worldwide m-commerce revenues are forecast to be just below $50 billion. The United States and Western Europe will dominate actual and forecast revenues through 2005. But by 2005 sales generated in the Asia-Pacific region and the rest of the world are expected to register a significant increase, approaching 40 per cent of the global $225 billion m-commerce revenues forecast. Given that global revenues in 2001 were about $20 billion and very small in regions outside North America and Europe, it is difficult to determine what the major m-commerce transactions have been.

Most m-commerce is B2C where micro-purchases are involved. Larger transactions continue to be conducted using the usual e-commerce methods. The surge in mobile handset use throughout the world, the dramatic growth of the Internet, and the proliferation of PDA (personal data assistants) are expanding the e-commerce market in which m-commerce is expected to flourish. A number of unique advantages of m-commerce have been identified:

— *Immediacy:* Consumers are constantly moving, working, commuting, travelling, socializing and shopping. M-commerce lets them buy goods and services as soon as the need arises.

— *Connectivity*: Users sharing a common location or interest can be instantly connected via text messaging and mobile chat capabilities. Advertisers can use such access to promote products and make special offers with the expectation that subscribers will answer and listen to their messages.

— *Localization*: With the deployment of positioning technologies, such as the global positioning system (GPS), companies can know users' where-abouts and will be able to offer goods and services specific to their location.

— *Data portability*: Users can store profiles of products, company addresses, information about restaurants and hotels, banking details, payment and credit card details, and security information, and access these when needed for purchases or for making contact, all from their mobile handsets.

Internet use has been dependent on personal computers (PCs) and a fixed-line network. And the growth of the

Internet drives e-commerce. Consequently, until the advent of mobile telephone, e-commerce has been dependent on expensive infrastructure and equipment. Today, however, there is a growing convergence of the Internet and mobile communication. Handsets are acquiring functionalities that were limited to desktop PCs only a few years ago.

Many are already running slimmed-down versions of PC operating systems and applications, and the difference between future handheld and desktop devices is likely to be related to the ergonomics of the physical user interface that will be designed to serve a particular purpose, rather than lack of processing power, memory or network accessibility. The ITU reports that 225 countries and territories have dial-up Internet connections - that is, a link to the Internet through a local telephone line.

In 2001 there were over 500 million Internet users, representing 8.2 per cent of the world's population. Global distribution of Internet access, however, remains dominated by developed countries, where over half of the adult population is online. Wireless access is likely to be the principal means of bringing more people in developing countries to the Internet. For that purpose, mobile networks and handsets need to be upgraded to carry data and messaging, as well as traditional voice services. The introduction of "third generation" (3G) and Internet-enabled handsets in North America and Europe is imminent. For the rest of the world, second generation (2G and 2.5G) mobile capabilities have opened-up opportunities for narrow-band Internet access and SMS.

The goal of 3G is to enable broadband mobile Internet and data services capability. After expensive 3G licences were auctioned, mostly in Europe, telecommunication companies accumulated large debts and as a result, mobile broadband infrastructure and 3G have yet to be introduced.

Many telecom operators are questioning whether customers will take-up 3G as rapidly as originally expected. The launch of 3G services has not been as successful as first forecast because potential early adopters are reasonably satisfied with pre-3G service offerings, thereby reducing the attractiveness of 3G's additional features. The situation is quite different for most developing countries.

The first objective of governments and telecommunications authorities is to expand the number of subscribers for mobile telephone voice and short message services. Upgrading to 2.5G or 3G is unlikely in the near future. The burning question for companies that have grown dependent on the Internet as a business vehicle is whether mobile telephony will result more in B2C applications than in B2B applications.

It is impossible on the basis of existing experience to extrapolate what will happen in the years ahead. As regards B2B, there is little evidence that companies will change their purchasing practices because of m-commerce. The short-term potential for e-commerce growth resides with the one billion mobile telephone users, who could supplement existing B2C e-commerce with m-commerce. There is rapid growth in micropayments for small items and information services. The key to increasing traditional B2C purchases such as banking transactions and to trading in securities through m-commerce is the implementation of payment systems that are low-cost and customer-friendly.

Mobile telephony is also helping to eliminate the seemingly endless waiting for a fixed-line subscription. With a mobile network, consumers can simply buy a handset together with a pre-paid card and start using it as soon as the first base stations are in place. As mobile networks are often set up by private sector companies, the investment burden can shift away from the State. The extent of developing countries' involvement in m-commerce is dependent on the access and connectivity of the population to wireless communications. Providing millions of citizens in developing countries with access to wireless voice communications coupled with text messaging, and with an eventual upgrade to the Internet, is crucial to building m-commerce markets in those countries.

Engaging in m-commerce, however, requires more than mobile empowerment. Initiating purchases and completing payments remains a bottleneck for m-commerce in many if not most developing countries. Unless selection, ordering, payment and delivery can be managed at costs that are lower than in traditional commerce, both e- and m-commerce may face serious problems. This may no longer be the case when m-commerce is fully utilized. Because PCs are not required, and fixed-line subscriber fees do not have to be paid, the cost of m-commerce can be relatively low.

A handset may cost less than $100 and prepaid cards have become dominant. An important mobile application that can be used for commercial activities is SMS, particularly because it can exploit the existing wireless infrastructure in many developing countries. However, if there is to be true m-commerce, mobile phones must be Internet-enabled.

Mobile telephony has been taken up to a considerable extent in Asia. There are currently more than 200 million handsets in use, of which more than 120 million are enabled to use data services. In Asia there is much more involvement in m-commerce. The most developed countries in the region - Japan and the Republic of Korea - have large mobile telephone populations with millions of Internet-enabled terminals. The leading developing country example of m-commerce deployment in the region is China. This is not only because the country now has 170 million mobile telephone subscribers, but also because SMS has become very popular and has created a vast potential for m-commerce applications.

Africa has more than 20 million mobile telephone users. By the end of 2001, 28 African nations had more mobile than fixed subscribers. The number of mobile subscribers in 30 sub-Saharan Africa countries, not including South Africa, rose from zero in 1996 to 1.7 million in late 2001. Because most new African mobile subscribers have no fixed line available and very few own or can access a PC, their handset becomes their only communication device. Consequently, there is likely to be a great interest in using mobile handsets for as many applications as possible.

In the least developed countries (LDCs), mobile technology is increasing telephone access in a surprisingly short space of time. Uganda is an example of how mobile telephony has radically transformed access to communications in an LDC over a short period. As a result of the liberalization of the telecommunication sector and the low cost of installing wireless networks, the number of subscribers rose eight times from 1995 to 2000. Uganda's mobile density ranking among LDCs rose from 28th in 1997 to 8th in 2001 and today it has the third largest mobile network in the LDCs.

In many countries, this transition took a little over a year: more mobile telephone users were added to the national network during that period than during the entire period of fixed-line operations. Another example is Afghanistan, where it is expected to take years to fully replace the infrastructures of electricity and fixed-line communications that have been destroyed.

However, this is not the case with wireless communications: inhabitants of Kabul have obtained handsets and began using mobile services with pre-paid cards in April 2002. By the end of May there were more than 2,000 handsets in use, a significant addition to the existing and inadequate 12,000 fixed lines.

Mobile telephone customers in many developed countries are starting to use handsets to make purchases from retail stores, conduct personal banking and make travel reservations, as well as to view sports and news programmes, and search the Web.

In Germany, for example, mobile users are said to "have a moderate attitude toward many new services", yet about 25 per cent are particularly interested in m-commerce possibilities. In the United States mobile phones are often kept in family cars and used as auxiliary communication devices, rather than being carried and used continually by family members.

In Europe, the greatest interest in m-commerce seems to be in Italy whose large population of mobile telephone customers have indicated an interest in paying bills and conducting banking transactions via wireless devices. Mobile service providers allow both prepaid and post-paid account subscribers to register and link their cash/debit cards with mobile phone subscription accounts.

This allows subscribers to conduct mobile transactions for services and goods offered through their particular mobile service provider, for example topping up of prepaid accounts and purchase of theatre tickets. Certain commercial activities using SMS, such as hotel and restaurant reservations, could eventually lead to a growth in m-com-merce applications. The following discussion takes a more detailed look at several promising applications.

Since 1992 SMS has allowed people to send and receive text messages using their mobile phones. Each message can contain up to 160 alphanumeric characters. SMS is the backbone of m-commerce, with the number of messages totalling billions in 2001. One of the greatest concentrations of SMS users is in Singapore, where 52 per cent of phone users utilize SMS more than once a day. SMS use in Australia, China and the Philippines is reported to be almost as high. The global average, however, is 23 per cent.

In December 2000, Filipinos were sending almost 50 million short messages a day, or around 9 per subscriber. The Philippines is the leader in per capita SMS usage, accounting for some 10 per cent of all short messages sent around the world. The Philippines had 8.5 million mobile telephone subscribers in June 2001.

The number of mobile telephones in use exceeded the number of fixed lines in 2000; it continues to grow rapidly and is expected to reach 15 to 20 million. SMS is said to offer a practical alternative for those who do not have a computer; mobile telephone subscribers outnumber PCs in the Philipinnes by 4 to 1. A mobile short message is actually much cheaper than a telephone call. SMS was initially free. A nominal 2 cents charge was introduced in 1999.

In Hong Kong, China, wireless data traffic was underdeveloped because local mobile telecommunications operators were not eager to expand this business while revenue from voice traffic alone was growing rapidly. In December 2001, six local mobile operators announced an agreement to make their SMS interoperable and forecast significant new revenue from SMS in the years ahead.

M-commerce offers vast opportunities to make micro-purchases easier. These can be as simple as buying from a vending machine, paying a parking meter or purchasing gasoline. Among the most widespread m-commerce applications using SMS, is making payments through post-paid accounts linked to debit cards. In the case of subscriptions to information services, the mobile service provider charges the customer through monthly bills. However, in many developing countries a shortage of consumer credit systems and the lack of automated payment systems that can be conveniently used for wireless electronic payments are hampering advancement of m-commerce.

Micro-payments and settlements via wireless are growing rapidly in a number of developed countries. Estimates for 2002 are typically around $1.5 billion. Forecasts for wireless micro-payments speak of $ 200 billion worldwide by 2005, with more than $ 40 billion in the United States.

In the Republic of Korea, mobile Internet customers prefer to integrate charges for purchases into their monthly telephone bills. Japanese often prefer to pay mobile Internet charges and usage fees in cash at convenience stores. Prepaid value cards are widely used in Japan. However, a growing number of services, such as specialized information services, can be charged to monthly telephone bills. A new system will be introduced before the end of 2002 that uses mobile handsets with an infrared interface that would automatically debit pre-paid cards.

The cost of equipping handsets with an infrared interface will be absorbed by savings resulting from operators and vendors not installing new vending equipment. In Japan there is great interest in this new mobile technique. Saving time, simplicity and speed of payments are the main advantages of mobile settlements. The following characteristics are listed in order of importance:

— Payments;

— Rapid payment;

— Record of payment provided;

— Less cash to carry around;

— Point-of-sale convenience;

— Signature not required.

A number of concerns still exist and demonstrate the novelty of mobile settlements and people's lack of awareness about how to take advantage of them. The main concerns are:

— Difficulty in making a payment or a financial transaction;

— Risk to the confidentiality of personal data;

— Difficulties in processing payments, including loss of payments;

Mobile banking is still hampered by the requirement for standardized payment cards and online systems. There has been more success with securities trading, however, where investors can buy and sell shares using their mobile handsets. Other areas are opening up -for example, insurance, where potential customers can receive offers and submit personal details for premium quotes by insurers, all with their mobile phones. Mobile communications provides insurers with yet another way to interact with, and obtain information from, potential customers.

The most immediate benefits are reducing administrative costs and bringing innovative and less expensive services to a wider market. An important facet of mobile technology will be to enable insurance agents and field representatives to provide better customer service. Buying habits are changing in that many customers want online access to product information and quotations and want to pay premiums, compare prices, access and update their policy information and claims status and receive customer service - all online. Regarding direct insurance sales, a vast market of potential buyers could be reached through the use of mobile-based insurance marketing methods. The present level of mobile media richness and the interface quality of commercial handsets may not satisfy regulatory requirements for selling insurance products, including policy delivery and payment, in most countries. Owing to government supervision and policy complexity, mobile insurance may have to wait for 3G before making real m-commerce headway.

Mobile services include all those products provided by securities brokerage firms. Wireless technology enables customers to bypass ordering in person or by telephone, thus opening the securities market to a large number of potential buyers. In addition, brokerages supply financial information and market data to investors through their mobile handsets. This provides individual clients who have online accounts with instant access to the buying and selling of securities. However, because of poor user interface of mobile telephones and PDAs, significant mobile trading is not expected before 2005 and the full roll-out of 3G and associated handsets.

The potential of mobile communications for generating greater efficiency in transport and logistics is widely acknowledged. The movement of goods within developing countries, as well as with regard to imports/ exports, has traditionally been slow and inefficient owing to a lack of modern logistics systems.

ICTs have become the key to achieving efficient logistics. Logistics costs in developed countries add about 12 per cent to the retail cost of a product, whereas in developing countries this may be as high as 20 per cent. Transport and logistics will clearly benefit from the introduction of wireless services and, in doing so, expand m-commerce. Wireless data access will make it possible to follow goods movements throughout the supply and value chain. With the growing use of information technologies in cargo booking, tracking, clearance and delivery by major shipping lines, as well as in customs clearance, ports, warehouses and stock points, external and internal trade will become more efficient. The challenge lies in the introduction of hardware, software and networking which are costly and require technical expertise to operate. Trackability and traceability need to be ensured through interfacing technologies such as ID chips and bar codes. Mobile communications devices will then help link-up the supply chain.

Transport is typically multimodal, ranging from rail-water-air-shipping to express delivery services. The introduction of intelligent transport services further increases the value of mobile communications in the logistics supply chain, in particular for support services such as pick-up and delivery of goods.

News, weather reports, and traffic and map information have increasingly become the services most sought after by mobile telephone subscribers. Since the launch of mobile services in Japan in 2000, as many as 30 per cent of all mobile customers indicate that they are users of those information services. This is three times the PC-based usage of paid information services. There is a charge by mobile service providers of about $2.50 (300 yen) per month for unlimited access to a menu of information services.

Value added text messaging is the use of SMS to provide a content service or product to the consumer at a premium price. The value added to the text message by the application or the content contained therein is assumed to be above and beyond that of a standard text message and the consumer knowingly consents to be billed for that added value. In Ireland, this is known as premium text messaging. It will involve the allocation of a 5-digit short code so that consumers will understand they are accessing premium services and will be prepared to pay for them.

An early entrant will be m-Perium, which will launch an m-payments solution using text messaging that will enable websites to charge their audience for time-metered access on their mobile telephones. Other services that could be available are: event-driven content - sports alerts for a favourite team, personal investment information and alerts, industry sector news alerts, travel information such as localized real-time traffic news, and other local information.

Customer relationship management (CRM) services usually consist of a set of methodologies, software and Internet capabilities that are coordinated and co-integrated and whose purpose is to help an enterprise manage its relationships with customers. Company activities can be very varied and may not always be managed in a coordinated way from a customer-centric point of view. The advantages for consumers of having better coordination between, say, research and development, manufacturing and after-sales services may translate for the company into marketable value-added or increased competitiveness.

Much of any commercial organization's activities, including business operations and customer servicing, falls within the scope of CRM. Therefore, its large size, is not unexpected. CRM can transform knowledge and data stored in companies by applying them, in real time, to existing and potential sales and service opportunities, in particular through access to an enterprise's data, message systems, remote sales force automation and order tracking. It has been forecast that in the United States between 35 per cent and 40 per cent of company sales and support personnel will be using mobile devices within the next two to three years.

Mobile technology is starting to emerge as the newest value-added feature for CRM. Extending CRM to wireless devices will enable enterprises to be more proactive in their marketing and sales by providing continuously updated information to field representatives, as well as by offering customers a broader array of contact and self-service options. Three levels of benefits are expected:

— Wireless CRM enables greater mobilization of the sales force, replacing periodic data synchronization with real-time information concerning products, client status, purchase history, inventory levels, product vendor information, order tracking and related data. The sales force will also have wireless financial transaction capabilities, shortening the sales cycle and increasing enterprise responsiveness.

— Wireless CRM facilitates a higher level of customer support by providing additional contact channels for clients seeking information or technical assistance. By extending customer data to mobile devices, the enterprise enables its support staff to better anticipate and respond to customer issues and enables customers to take advantage of self-service support and transactions via their mobile phones or PDAs.

— Location-based marketing will be an extension of current marketing automation and customer analysis systems. These emerging applications are expected to stimulate m-commerce by extrapolating location-specific buying behaviour to provide information to mobile device users.

M-commerce opens up a myriad of options for new electronic services. These include making appointments, voting, applications for membership or membership renewal and entitlement cards, and alarm systems. Norway provides an excellent example of this diversity of m-commerce.

A survey of frequently purchased items in the Republic of Korea found buying habits similar to those in Japan. About 12 per cent of mobile subscribers indicated that their main preferences are buying movie tickets, cosmetics, banking, audiovisual and electronics products.

The need to protect personally identifiable data has received the attention of national policy-makers and international organizations for more than 30 years. With the advances in wireless communications, concerns have again arisen about loss of control over personal information.

Some 40 countries have adopted national data protection laws, ranging from Canada and Argentina to Sweden and Greece, and Thailand and the Republic of Korea. Internationally, the Organisation for Economic Cooperation and Development and the Council of Europe, have adopted legal instruments for their member countries governing the collection and use of personal data.

Because mobile communications services are new and operators are being licensed to compete with incumbent carriers, a number of policy and regulatory issues must be resolved. Interconnection between fixed-line operators and competing mobile operators has been the major difficulty constraining mobile development.

The predominant conflicts over mobile interconnection have occurred in developed countries where several operators are seeking to gain market share. Developing countries have experienced fewer problems when national regulators have insisted on rapid deployment and fairly priced interconnection rates. Many developing countries, however, have limited geographical coverage for mobile telephone use, some operators charge both caller and receiver, and transmission standards still need to be harmonized.

A new European Community Directive that "adapts and updates existing provisions to new and foreseeable developments in electronic communications and technologies" is now replacing the existing telecommunication Directive. It is expected to be adopted before the end of 2002. The revised Directive stipulates that the location data, giving the geographical position of mobile users' terminal equipment, as in road transport services that provide traffic information and guidance for drivers, may not be used for surveillance purposes. Traffic data in general may be collected and used only with the consent of the subscriber.

It has been recognized that commercial users of wireless communications should be subject to codes of fair personal information practice, established by public law or self-regulation. The Wireless Advertising Association (WAA), an international trade group, has adopted a privacy policy that should be readily available to consumers. Under this policy WAA members should give users notice and choice regarding the use of personal information obtained. It may be used only for the purpose for which it was collected unless users explicitly consent to its being used for other purposes. Furthermore, WAA members are required to make every effort to ensure the security of personal information and, where reasonable, allow wireless subscribers to correct or delete such information.

The specific provisions of the WAA privacy policy require that a member company must make known to potential recipients:

(a) what information is being collected;

(b) its policy on data storage;

(c) the choices available to an individual regarding policy on collection of personal information;

(d) the use of personal information;

(e) any third-party collection of personal information, together with a statement of the organization's commitment to data security; and

(f) what steps the organization takes to ensure data security and access by the consumer to his/her records.

Concerns about e-commerce security are only heightened in the m-commerce domain. Fixed-line Internet and PC-based browser technology provides a media richness and interactivity that can be used to implement technological security and assure commercial partners that transactions are under way safely and surely. In contrast, the present-day mobile interface, be it SMS or WAP, is fairly poor and does not inspire confidence.

Furthermore, worries about data interception in the wireless medium are heightened, unlike in the case of fixed-line access, through an imperfect understanding of the technology. Finally, mobile handsets are more prone to theft and consequential misuse, particularly since they may contain passwords, keys and personal identification numbers (PINs) used to provide the authentication and data integrity required for verifying financial transactions. Security is vital if m-commerce is to become an electronic wallet for micropayments for customers worldwide.

In addition to digital signature laws and regulations, certification authorities are being created by governments, financial institutions and other bodies, or are licensed to private entities, so that parties to e-commerce transactions can know the identity of all entities or individuals involved.

To ensure m-commerce payment interoperability among devices and networks, the financial-services-backed Mobile Payment Forum was established in November 2001. Initial members were Master Card International, Visa International, American Express and the Japan Card Bureau.

The Forum now has 89 members. It is cooperating with the PayCircle consortium and the Mobile Electronic Transactions initiative, supported by wireless and Internet infrastructure vendors and handset manufacturers. The Forum's work should lead to secure m-commerce by migrating existing security mechanisms to the mobile environment, or by installing similar security levels for authentication, data integrity, privacy and non-repudiation. Its work covers both existing and emerging technologies, including symmetric keys and biometrics.

Another organization, Radicchio, is a global initiative of over 50 companies in m-commerce and security industries that promotes m-commerce solutions based on public key infrastructure technology for personal handheld devices and wireless network. This initiative is a cross-industry non-profit organization, representing the interests of mobile operators, system integrators, hardware manufacturers, certification service providers and financial service providers, as well as software houses.

The growth of wireless communications in less than five years has created new voice and data communications services that are essential for launching widespread business and consumer m-commerce applications. It is becoming clear that m-commerce will not parallel earlier expansion of e-commerce. B2C transactions will be far more extensive than B2B transactions. This may be in part the result of already well-established fixed-line channels of e-commerce activities among companies.

Individuals are finding it increasingly attractive to initiate B2C contacts with companies to order purchase products and services. The conduct of m-commerce is limited by difficulties in making electronic payments and concerns about security and privacy of transactions. Technology also plays an important role because mobile terminals must be Internet-enabled in order to provide full m-commerce possibilities.

There is a new dimension of m-commerce that involves introducing products and services that may not directly result in immediate transactions. In the United States, companies use mobile telephony to contact employees, conduct sales and marketing programmes and provide customer care. Enterprises in developing countries may find mobile communications very attractive for marketing in remote locations. Methods to maximize benefits from mobile business clearly require further examination.

Fundamental to a rapid expansion of m-commerce is improved access to mobile services by consumers in developing countries, for which a number of government actions are required. These involve liberalizing the telecommunications market, licensing new mobile operators, creating an independent regulatory body that will establish a fair and competitive market supporting compatible standards and facilitating the interconnection among operators. National Governments should exercise leadership in the adoption of authentication, security and data privacy policies and regulations. Improving connections to the Internet backbone remains vital.

5

E-Publishing: Challenges in the New Millennium

Electronic publishing (e-publishing) is the publishing of information in electronic format. It is implemented by creating, maintaining, archiving and distributing documents using computers and networks. Electronically published materials may be created initially only for electronic transfer, or they may have been converted from material originally published on paper. E-publishing represents an improvement over print publishing technology and is considered a major development that may revolutionize information-related activities in society.

Consequences of e-publishing can be compared to those resulting from Gutenberg's invention of the printing press. This invention is considered the origin of mass communication. For the first time, it became possible to disseminate information and knowledge to large numbers of people who could share it simultaneously. Before then, there were only handwritten books made by monks, scholars and scribes and read only by churchmen, government officials and academics. With the introduction of print, intellectual life was no longer restricted to the elite as publications became more widely available to the general population.

E-publishing can bring about major reductions in the cost of producing and distributing publications, thus making it easier for many individuals and enterprises to participate as authors and publishers and for more titles to be published. Because of increased access to publications by readers and the availability of technology that permits more enterprises to enter the industry, e-publishing can foster a higher degree of competition and increased price transparency.

The benefits of e-publishing may be significant for developing countries. These countries lag behind developed countries in access to published material, including educational publications. Furthermore, their imports of published materials are substantially larger than their exports of those materials. By enhancing the capacity of individuals and enterprises to produce and distribute publications, e-publishing provides great potential for promoting the growth of the publishing industry in developing countries and a reduction in this trade imbalance. A discussion of e-publishing may touch on issues such as technology, the costs of production and distribution, pricing models, industry structure, the quality of published materials and intellectual property.

With the advent of new technologies, the relationships between publishers, the media and consumers which were traditionally based on contractual licensing agreements with copyright protection, have completely changed in ways that make the situation difficult to control. There are many types of publications, including magazines, nonscholarly periodicals, newsletters, pamphlets, booklets, research reports, bulletin boards, catalogues, dictionaries, and encyclopedias. Also, each category may include many subcategories; for example, magazines include general-purpose and specialized ones. Furthermore, even the main categories overlap a great deal in content and format. In some cases, old journal articles by one or more authors are assembled into a book. There is therefore some degree of competition and interchangeability between different types of publications.

Despite this diversity, however, the issues raised in connection with the three selected types of publications are relevant to the other forms as well. The choice is partly based on the fact that newspapers and books have mass markets of a much larger scale than other individual publications. Scholarly journals differ in many ways from the other two types, and also their recent history highlights to a greater degree the economic aspects of publishing, such as cost, pricing models and industry structure.

In each of the selected cases, a general description of the publication is provided in order to give the context in which issues are examined. Also, while the main focus is on economic aspects of e-publishing, brief accounts of technical and other related issues are given in so far as they have economic implications. For example, while the formats in which publications are presented electronically and their functionality are technical matters, at the same time they determine the software and other requirements imposed on users, as well as the searchlights and quality of the published materials, and these are important economic dimensions.

Newspapers

Newspaper are serials usually issued daily or weekly. Their primary function is to report public news of general interest, although they may also include features, commentary and advertisements. Newspaper publishing enterprises range in size from small, locally based publishers to national and international ones owned by international conglomerates or industrial groups. All countries around the world publish newspapers, but the number of newspapers and the circulation of individual newspapers vary widely.

There is presently a great deal of interest in on-line newspapers, and numerous newspapers are now posted on the Internet. Some directories of online newspapers list over 10,000 newspapers covering practically every country around the world, including least developed countries (LDCs). While there is no evidence that all the listed online newspapers are fully functional, the sheer numbers involved demonstrate the overwhelming perception by newspaper publishers of the importance of an online presence and also the existence of demand for electronic newspapers.

The volume and quality of content and the level of sophistication of the browsing functionality vary considerably between newspapers. Most online newspaper publishers maintain print versions alongside the digital versions. The majority of the latter can be accessed through the World Wide Web (WWW) and use the hypertext mark-up language (HTML) format, making them readable with a standard Internet browser. This means that the reader has to be connected to the Internet in order to read the newspaper. An alternative means of distribution for e-newspapers is e-mail. For e-mail distribution, besides HTML, formats such as PDF (portable document format) and plain ASCII text are also used. E-mail distribution avoids the necessity of establishing an Internet connection at the time of reading the newspaper. Further, the PDF format may allow the publisher greater control of layout and content so that material cannot be quickly and easily copied, modified, and then distributed by third parties.

Some newspapers have automated search and archiving capabilities that enable readers to access back issues containing previous related articles and other background information for a given news item. In some cases, news items appearing in a current issue of the print version are reported in greater detail or with additional data in the online version. For example, the latter may contain more pictures, longer narratives, full interviews, and so on. In addition to text, online newspapers may offer other features, such as audio, video, graphics and charts, that enhance the news presentation. Links may give access to online libraries through which readers are connected to various reference sources. Another service is the provision of personalized newspapers, whereby a reader can receive an individualized selection of articles published in a given newspaper.

To achieve this, the reader identifies preferred subjects such as current events, sports or cultural and political issues and the newspaper automatically designs a personalized edition containing articles that match the reader's interests. Yet another useful feature of online newspapers is continuous updating of news, something that would be too costly to accomplish for print newspapers. However, in spite of the possible technical and economic viability of a continuous updating, apparently at the moment only a few newspapers are providing continuous updates perhaps because most newspapers are still closely linked to their print counterparts in their production systems.

The majority of online newspapers are free and provide unrestricted access to their ripostes. Some, while free of charge, impose access restrictions by requiring the reader to enter an ID and password, both of which are issued after the reader has provided a selection of personal information. Other papers employ differentiated pricing whereby parts of the paper are free while other parts that contain special information require a subscription.

Some papers even offer two separate online versions, one free and the other subscription-based. Where the entire online version is free, the funding comes from advertisements appearing in the print versions and, in some cases, in the online version as well. Some observers think that online versions are being offered for free merely on an experimental basis to allow publishers to gain information about readers and their Internet habits. In due course, more and more newspapers are expected to charge for access to their websites. While this change is already happening, it has not yet become widespread. In some cases the online version comprises only selected parts of the print newspaper, which obliges readers to obtain the print version if they wish to access all the articles. Unlike print journalism, where interaction with readers is largely limited to letters to the editor, online newspapers permit wide-ranging contacts between and among readers, editors and journalists that allow the newspapers to receive feedback from readers.

E-publishing has had an impact on newspaper journalists trained for or experienced in print publishing by obliging them to learn new methods of information collection and reporting. For example, it requires them to use skills needed for online presentation, including the use of video, animation and audio. Journalists are emerging who can combine information technology skills with elements of traditional news reporting.

Scholarly journals

Scholarly journals play a role as channels and sources of information important to society, in fields including scientific discovery, medicine, public policy, business, technology, industrial development, and so on. Articles in scholarly journals are based on original research and written by experts or scholars in specific academic or professional fields, as opposed to newspaper journalists. A published article is usually identified with the author who derives recognition from it. Journals typically have a review board consisting of peers or other scholars in the field that decide which submitted articles will be accepted for publishing. Unlike newspapers, scholarly journals have limited interest for the general public.

However, they have dedicated markets comprising authors and readers who depend on them as publishing outlets for career advancement and as sources of scholarly or professional knowledge. Therefore, individual journals tend to have a higher degree of continuity and less demand elasticity than, for example, newspapers. Furthermore, the major stakeholders for scholarly journals - journal publishers, scholars, public and private institutions and libraries - are different from those for newspapers, and thus some of the underlying issues in relation to e-publishing are different. On the consumer side, libraries play a pivotal role in the purchasing of scholarly journals, accounting for the bulk of subscription revenue.

Many scholarly journals have traditionally been published by nonprofit academic associations, although there is increased participation by commercial publishers. In recent years, scholarly journals have faced severe financial problems resulting mainly from escalating subscription prices and from budgetary constraints faced by libraries, which are the major subscribers.

Increases in the prices of journals appear to be the result of a combination of factors including rising production costs and the ability of publishers to charge as much as the market can bear. The latter ability is enhanced by the monopoly enjoyed by certain publishers and by the presence of inelastic demand. It has been suggested that the largest journal publishers may be playing the role of price leaders and influencing the prices of the other publishers.

Another possible explanation is that too many journals have entered the market in recent years, which has led to reduced circulation for individual journals and in turn to an increase in the average fixed costs. Interestingly, journals published by commercial publishers differ substantially from the prices of those published by nonprofit professional associations.

Like newspapers and other publications, journals are now embracing electronic publishing. Scholarly or academic electronic journals have shown a very high rate of growth. As of 2000 nearly 20,480 active serials or periodicals were available online. These included academic/scholarly journals, bibliographies, bulletins, consumer journals, directories, government publications, newsletters and newspapers. According to the database, online was the leading single format alternative to print, followed by microform/fiche/film for 13,580 periodicals. Equally significant, Ulrich's reports that as of October 2000 a total of 2,401 online-only serials had been launched, most of which were still active.

E-publishing of scholarly journals is likely to expand readership, especially in developing countries where learning institutions are usually undersupplied with journals for budgetary reasons, and where scholars have limited access to outlets for scholarly publication. It also makes possible the introduction or expansion of advertising, which traditionally has not been a major source of income for scholarly journals.

In many ways, the business models used for electronic journals resemble those for online newspapers. Many journal publishers offer both print and electronic versions of each issue, what is referred to as parallel or dual publishing. At present this model is useful in that it gives users a choice, particularly at a time when e-publishing is still at a formative stage. It seems that many publishers of scholarly journals are unwilling to make a complete shift to electronic only publishing because this new business model is still being tested.

It is too risky to abandon print publishing, which continues to be the mainstay of the publishers' cash flow. Similarly, some subscribers (e.g. libraries) prefer to have access to electronic journals without abandoning the print versions, for which they have well-established cataloguing and archiving systems. In some cases, the electronic versions are full-text versions of the print issues, while in others they present tables of contents only, or selected parts or articles of the print version. Presenting the table of contents alone does not constitute true e-publishing, and probably the real objective is to use the electronic version to advertise the print version.

On the other hand, presenting selected articles is an attempt to provide free access without jeopardizing the volume of subscriptions. In other cases the electronic journal contains additional information, including raw data used for research, thus allowing other researchers to test the same data in different ways.

Some e-journals provide hypertext links, which are particularly useful in scholarly publishing, given the large number of sources that researchers usually consult in a given research project. Interactivity and searching capability are also being extended to the creation of databases, which bring together texts, indexes and abstracts of articles published in different journals.

E-journals employ more or less the same formats for delivering content as those used by newspapers, that is, HTML and PDF. When journals make extensive use of symbols and graphics, these may be inserted into HTML or PDF in their original graphic file formats, of which the GIF and JPEG formats are the most common.

Like newspapers, scholarly journals adopt a variety of pricing and licensing methods. Some publishers bundle the electronic version with the print subscription by providing free access to the electronic version to those who subscribe to the print version, while others charge an additional fee for access to the electronic one. Still others supply the electronic version as the base price, and the price of the print version is added to the electronic one. Yet other publishers use separate pricing for print and electronic versions, as well as charging per article accessed by the reader. In most cases, institutions such as libraries pay a site license fee for electronic access and must then ensure that only entitled persons in the institution get access. The licenses are negotiated separately even in cases where an institution also subscribes to the print version.

The question of the cost of e-publishing is contentious. First-copy costs are high, although the marginal costs of printing additional copies and physical distribution costs are low. On the other hand, the processing of articles, marketing and administrative costs are costly. Some studies have suggested that costs are considerately lower for e-journals than for print journals. For example, a study commissioned by Industry Canada concluded that the production and distribution of a new e-journal could be 28 to 48 percent less expensive than the cost of the print counterpart.

However, some publishers contend that set-up costs for e-journals are high and that the largest share of publishing costs is fixed, including editing and marketing costs, which apply to both print and electronic publishing. Also, the additional capabilities that come with e-journals lead to cost increases. Some publishers enter e-publishing with no experience in the business and are obliged either to invest in developing in-house the skills and competencies required for e-publishing or to contract out the technical work of website development and maintenance and to support outside vendors in acquiring the necessary state-of-the-art technology.

Users of e-journals see an increase in other fixed costs, for example, involving site licenses, new cataloguing systems, the hiring of extra library staff members to manage journal access, the training of staff members and costumers in the use of the new system, and hardware costs including computers and printers. Some costs (e.g. printing) are actually passed on to end users.

Thus, overall, the comparison of costs between e-journals and print journals is inconclusive. This uncertainty clearly presents a dilemma for publishers as well as their main customers. For the publishers, it is not clear which model will prevail in the long run. In the short run, the parallel printing system is proving to be very costly.

As e-publishing expands, some readers move to e-journals, thus reducing the subscription base for print journals without the former fully compensating the latter in the form of increased revenue from e-journals. This tends to oblige publishers to increase subscription rates for print journals, which in turn encourages libraries and other institutions to cut back further on subscriptions.

The financial difficulties faced by scholarly journals that were referred to earlier have led to a number of initiatives with implications for e-publishing. Even though there is no general agreement regarding the relative costs of electronic and print versions of journals, some observers have encouraged self-publishing by scholars and the formation by scholars and libraries of network-based electronic publishing projects as a way of bringing down journal prices.

Self-publishing by scholars is becoming viable as new technology makes it feasible for authors to format their own papers. It is also significant to note that peer review and editing are usually offered for free by other scholars, and thus self-publishing would not involve prohibitive costs for authors. Partly to implement such a strategy, scholarly and professional associations have been urged to use electronic submission of manuscripts and to distribute journals to subscribers electronically. These initiatives may help account for a large increase in the number of e-journals launched by scholars in recent years.

However, the academic community has not fully accepted e-journals as a form of scholarly publishing. E-journals are considered by some to have lower quality and prestige than print ones, and usually authors of articles in e-journals are denied academic credit for these publications. It has been pointed out, for example, that some e-journals cut costs by eliminating professional copy editing and peer review. However, it appears that the lack of recognition of e-journals for academic credit is partly due to inertia and uncertainty vis-à-vis a new system.

Proponents of e-journals have pointed out that even scholarly print journals evolved over time, at a pace dictated largely by developments in scholarly culture rather than by technological developments. They note that scholars tend to be conservative in their intellectual pursuits. What matters most are the norms and standards being enforced rather than the technology used for publishing and delivery. Technically, manuscript submission and peer reviews can be managed through e-mail. Similarly, editing and correction can be performed electronically.

Furthermore, quality can be ensured if publishers and libraries establish codes of best practices for authors regarding such matters as peer review. There is nothing inherent in e-publishing that prevents scholars and publishers from maintaining high publishing standards. Some observers have suggested that electronically managed peer review could be rendered faster, more efficient and more transparent than the traditional process. For example, the use of the Internet could permit contact with a large population of possible peer reviewers and a much faster circulation of manuscripts. It could also allow open peer comments, thus providing a supplementary level of review. Also, available information shows that e-journals do care about quality; for example, a study on e-publishing acceptance rates revealed that rates for accepted and rejected manuscripts were not lower for e-publications than for print publications.

Authors of journal articles are able to circulate the initial drafts of their articles before they are eventually submitted for publishing. Electronic publishing facilitates this process as authors can carry out the distribution more cheaply and to a wider readership online. Authors can use pre-print servers to send manuscripts to central databases or post them on directories that are accessible to the general public. Preprints create opportunities for authors and help alleviate the problem of high journal prices, but at the same time they create difficulties for publishers: readers who can access preprints for free have little or no incentive to subscribe to the journal, and budget-constrained libraries, too, may tend to rely largely on free preprints.

Books

Books are the single most numerous type of publication outside the category of periodical publications. For statistical purposes "book" as a "non-periodical printed publication of at least 49 pages, excluding covers". Eelectronic books (e-books), have aroused great interest in the publishing industry, with some expecting that e-books would completely revolutionize book publishing. Particularly note worthy was the publication by a best-selling commercial author, Stephen King, of "Riding the Bullet" as an online-only book in 2000. The considerable demand for the book convinced the industry, including traditional bricks and-mortar publishers, that there was really a potential for e-books. At the time it was predicted, for example, that sales of digital books (e-books), digital downloads and print-on-demand books would grow from $9 million in 2000 to $414 million in 2004.

E-books are created as computer files that can be read by various mechanisms - computers, personal digital assistants (PDAs) or special hand-held book reading devices using proprietary software. They can be delivered to the reader either as downloads from the Internet or as e-mail file attachments. E-books can also be made available on diskette and CDROM. They use a variety of file formats and can be read using various operating systems or in files that are equipped with reading software. These various formats provide different functionalities, for example, an e-book created as an HTML file gives the capability to include multimedia features with audio, video and animation

Demand for E-books

There is an apparent lack of consensus regarding how well the market for e-books has performed. Some analysts point out that there have been very few commercial success stories between 2000 and 2002. It is pointed out that most established book authors continue to publish with traditional print publishers, and those in the industry who had forecast the rapid growth of e-books no longer support those expectations. On the other hand, some industry actors continue to support and invest in e-book-related activities contending that e-books have enjoyed high growth rates and will continue to do so.

Furthermore, a number of print publishers are preparing to distribute their existing titles electronically. Other interests such as the Open eBook Forum are promoting e-books by raising reader awareness of the benefits of e-books. Indeed, supporters of e-books suggest that the real issue is not that there is a poor market for e-books but that the initial growth forecasts were exaggerated. A quick look at promotional materials indicates that a large number of e-books are being advertised and points to the existence of an impressive array of e-book distributors, publishers as well as on-demand publishers. The problem in making an independent assessment is to determine the actual volume of e-book sales.

Another relatively new distribution format, print on demand (POD), is a sort of combination of e-publishing and print publishing. This technology allows a book to be stored as an electronic copy and be printed and bound only according to the number of copies actually demanded or paid for. For book publishers, printing on demand solves the perennial problem of having to print copies without being certain of the actual number required by the market, and then having to absorb the resulting unrecouped production and storage costs.

Benefits of e-books

Where the print publishing model prevails, many books that are written are never published. Because of the high cost of editing, formatting and printing, the publishers tend to select only the "best" books, largely on the basis of expected sales. As a result, publishers have tended to dominate the process of deciding which books get published and which do not.

E-books allow authors to publish online themselves at an affordable cost. This increase in outlets and opportunities has empowered authors to decide what materials actually get published. Further, as e-publishing increases competition between publishers, e-publishers are more willing to publish books that would have been rejected in print publishing.

Some e-publishers are willing to work more directly and closely with them than traditional publishers would be. Also, some e-book publishers assist authors with the editing and distribution of e-books. The books may be advertised on the publisher's website, and other services may also be offered - for example, copyright and ISBN registration and registration in the Books In Print database as well as with major online book distributors. This generosity may be explained by the fact that many e-publishers are new to the industry and are in the process of establishing business networks.

E-publishing can also provide improved customer service and can allow authors to receive quick feedback from readers about their publications. For example, authors can establish direct contact with readers by providing e-mail addresses and websites through which readers can express their views and suggestions concerning a book. Such information may help authors in preparing updates or new editions of their works. Also, e-publishing has been credited with increasing the royalties paid to authors. It is reported, for example, that on average e-publishers pay authors royalties in the range of 20 to 30 per cent of the net price received from sales of a book, compared to the royalties of 8 to 10 per cent typically paid by print publishers. Some e-publishers provide even higher royalties, such as a 50-50 split of royalties with authors.

As the cost of Internet access declines, e-publishing stands to benefit from an increase in the number of readers to whom publications are distributed without consequential cost increases. The cost of distributing an e-book remains the same regardless of the number of people reading the book, subject to the size of the bandwidth available. Authors who self-publish are able to eliminate intermediaries nd deal directly with readers, thus reducing transaction time and other transaction costs, although they must pay for marketing costs. Thus, overall, e-publishing lowers barriers for new entrants and offers the potential for a much greater number of individuals to publish their books which in turn creates the potential for a large increase in published titles.

Largely due to economies of scale, traditional print publishing requires books to be printed in large numbers in order to maximize opportunities for profitability, although the existing market may not ensure that the whole print run is sold. Printing numerous copies of a book has the disadvantage of tying up capital and also involves considerable costs for shipment, warehousing, inventory and distribution to retailers. The alternative, namely printing fewer copies, poses the risk of running out of stock, which can result lost sales opportunities.

Also, small print runs are less profitable than large ones, as unit printing costs tend to decrease with increasing numbers of printed copies.

The tendency towards large print runs is due largely to the difficulty of ascertaining demand. Available information shows that, while book publishers often distribute large numbers of copies of printed books to retailers, eventually many copies are returned unsold to the publishers.

The above problems can largely be eliminated with e-books. As e-publishing minimizes the amount of printing, the need to determine demand is also minimized. Physical transportation of books is significantly more costly than the distribution of e-books. Similarly, e-publishing reduces or eliminates warehousing and inventory costs.

E-publishing has still other benefits. New editions can be produced more frequently than in print publishing. Publishers can publish shorter titles, reprints and books that are out of print, with few or no overhead costs. E-publishing also makes it possible to sell parts of a book or other publication and thus provide new sales opportunities for a given publication. Length limitations are far less important than in print publication, and authors can include additional content such as annexes, additional data, and so on, which is not always feasible in print versions.

Unlike printed books, which eventually run out of print and tend to remain available in bookstores for relatively short periods of time, e-books can theoretically remain available for any length of time. Generally, e-publications have lower sale prices than their print counterparts. For example, the prices of e-books in a particular category might range from $1 to $6 whereas comparable paperbacks might sell for $6 to $10. Like e-newspapers and e-journals, e-books enable the use of features such as sound, video, automatic cross-referencing and interactivity. They also allow readers, through hyperlinks, to be linked to other texts, audio, video or other digital content outside a book that is accessible on the Internet. Further, they permit publishers to reach global markets more readily.

Disadvantages of e-books

E-books have the disadvantage of being less portable than printed books. An e-book has to be read on a computer screen or using an e-book reader. Generally, text is harder to read on a computer screen than in print form; characters are not as clear, and looking at a screen for extended periods of time can be tiring. As regards e-book readers, consumers have been concerned by their cost and by the fact that all devices are not compatible with all e-book formats. This obliges customers to keep track of which e-books can be read on their systems, and creates difficulties for publishers in deciding on which formats to use.

Cost comparison

The relative costs of online and print publishing are of major concern to publishers because they are a major factor in deciding whether to get involved in e-publishing. At first glance, e-publishing appears to be less expensive than print publishing, since in the former the marginal costs of printing and physical distribution, are low or nonexistent. However, a more meaningful comparison must consider both fixed and variable costs. Fixed costs include the cost of editors and other staff and the technology infrastructure needed for production. Some of these costs may be higher in e-publishing than print publishing. For example, staff costs may rise because of heavy dependence on skilled technology workers.

However, today most book "manuscripts" are prepared as computer files and are delivered to the printer in electronic format. Converting these files to the widely used HTML or PDF format should not require substantial additional resources. Also, increased competition may create greater demand not only for high-level customer services but also for high-quality publications with sophisticated functionality. As in the case of journals, therefore, there appears to be no clear consensus, at least in the current run transition atmosphere, as to whether, overall, e-books are less costly than printed books.

Since e-books are a relatively new form of publishing, publishers are still searching for the most appropriate pricing models. Because of this and other factors, including efforts by institutions such as libraries to overcome budgetary constraints, the pricing of e-publications has generally become fairly complex and in many ways contentious.

E-Publishing in Developing Countries

The preceding section outlined the state of the art in e-publishing and the potential benefits this model offers. As regards the actual growth of e-publishing, it was mentioned that some sectors, such as e-journals, have seen much progress in spite of uncertainty caused in part by the ongoing crisis of high journal prices in the face of limited library budgets. On the other hand, there are clearly opposing perceptions concerning e-books, with some observers feeling that e-books do not yet have a significant presence and are not likely to do so soon, while others think their market role is substantial and growing.

E-publishing is already having a significant impact, given, for example, the number of online newspapers and e-journals currently in existence. There is therefore justification for taking a positive view of this new technology and supporting e-publishing activities for the benefit of all stakeholders in the publishing chain. The slow growth of e-publishing should not be interpreted to mean that this form of publishing has no future. Historically, a number of other technologies, including press printing, have taken decades to have a major impact on society.

E-publishing uses technology and business models that make it easier for individuals and small enterprises to publish cost-effectively. It also allows their publications to reach a global readership at a minimal cost. The net effect is to enable enterprises in developing countries to compete with established publishers, although initially they may need to rely on niche markets at the national or regional level.

Publishers and users in developing countries have lagged behind their developed- country counterparts. This lag can be attributed to a variety of factors, including the low level of Internet connectivity, without which e-publishing is not possible. However, more fundamental problems exist that are directly linked to the publishing industry itself.

Some of the problems concerning publications in developing countries and their implications for the growth of e-publishing are summarized below. The publishing industry as a whole is generally less developed in developing countries than in developed ones.

Developing countries, with a much larger share of the world population, had more or less the same number of newspapers as developed countries. Even more significant, in developed countries the volume of circulation per 1000 inhabitants was more than twice than in developing countries. In this connection, other sources show that in developing countries with a sizable publishing industry the main publishers are branches of major publishing houses in developed countries. Other indicators, such as the number of book trade organizations, show the same uneven distribution across countries.

The following summary by the UNESCO Institute for Statistics provides a succinct picture of the uneven distribution of the production of published materials and access to such materials:

— Over 50 per cent of countries worldwide have an estimated daily newspaper circulation of 50 copies per 1,000 inhabitants.

— In more than half of the world's countries, there are fewer that 10 newspaper titles. Only 8 per cent of countries have over 100 newspapers.

— Around 50 per cent of countries worldwide produce, on average, less than one book per inhabitant per year; 30 per cent produce between one and three books per inhabitant; and 20 per cent produce four or more books per inhabitant annually.

— Around 60 per cent of countries have fewer than 50 copies of school textbooks per 1,000 inhabitants, while just 20 per cent of countries have more than one textbook for every inhabitant.

— Around 70 per cent of countries worldwide provide fewer than 200 public libraries per million inhabitants; 16 per cent provide between 200 and 500 libraries; and 15 per cent provide more than 500.

— In nearly 50 per cent of countries worldwide, all the libraries combined contain less than one book per inhabitant; 20 per cent contain between one and three books per inhabitant and 30 per cent contain four or more books per inhabitant.

The following observations further illustrate the poor state of publishing in developing countries:

— There is limited information on what publications are published in developing countries. For example, only a few articles published in developing countries are listed in the world's major journal indexes and book directories. This lack of information undermines readers' ability to access these publications and authors' ability to research opportunities for publishing in these countries.

— Partly because of the above and for reasons of quality and prestige, many scholars in developing countries tend to publish with publishers in developed countries, thus failing to contribute to the growth of the local publishing industry or those of other developing countries.

— While many scholars from developing countries strive to publish their work in developed countries, a number of factors such as competition for authorship and biased peer review, make it relatively difficult for developing-country authors to be published. In other words, authors in developing countries fail to realize their full publishing potential due to limited access to publishing outlets or lack of knowledge about the outlets.

— High journal costs have been exacerbated by a proliferation of scholarly journals on different subjects. This means that many journals available on the market are not being purchased and therefore, are not used by readers. Journals published in developing countries thus face particularly stiff competition from those of developed countries. The latter have a larger readership base, which generates a more substantial cash flow, ensuring regular publication and consistent quality.

— Some journals and textbooks produced in developing countries have relied on government and corporate sponsorship, but these sources have decreased with the countries' overall poor economic performance in recent years. Also, limited readership has meant limited advertising revenue.

The problems facing publishing in developing countries can be overcome or reduced by e-publishing. As was mentioned earlier, the technology and business models applied in e-publishing may provide business opportunities for enterprises, including small ones, in developing countries. In recognition of the potential social and economic impact of publications, a number of national and international initiatives have been launched to promote e-publishing and access to e-published materials in developing countries.

Such initiatives are new and there is little information regarding their current status and successes or failures. It is notable, however, that the provision of access to e-publications to institutions in developing countries for free or at reduced prices appears to be similar to pricing models that are used by a large number of publishers worldwide. It was pointed out that free access was at times used as a marketing strategy which could change in due course. On the other hand the initiatives involving the access to publications produced by developing country publishers, if successful, could result in genuine growth of e-publishing in the developing countries.

Copyright Issues

Intellectual property is an intangible form of property and includes four types of human works that are protected by copyright laws: inventions (patents); symbols, names and images (trademarks); designs used in commerce (industrial designs); and literary and artistic works (copyright). Copyright law grants the author of a work the exclusive right to reproduce the work, prepare derivative works and perform and display the work publicly. Copyright protects published and unpublished literary, scientific and artistic works in any form of expression. Protection automatically occurs when works are actually created and fixed in a tangible form. Registering copyright may be convenient for commercial or litigation purposes but is generally not necessary to obtain a valid, enforceable copyright.

Since the advent of new technologies in the 1990s, the development of adequate national and international copyright legislation has been of particular concern. Indeed making works accessible via the Internet or other digital channels, authors and publishers are losing control over the distribution of their works. The concern of copyright owners has thus taken on new and challenging dimensions.

New technologies enable anyone to make exact copies of a work and share them almost anonymously with others. The Internet allows people to steal contents freely and share them with others using tools such as peer-to-peer technology (P2P). P2P on the Internet is a network that allows computer users with the same type of networking software to access files from one another's hard drives. This was the technology that was employed by millions of Napster users.

While basic computer equipment is needed for carrying out piracy, copying and distribution process have been dramatically facilitated by advanced digital technology. Cases have been recently reported in which books were being illegally translated or copied, sometimes even before their official release.

This happened, for example, with J.K. Rowling's famous "Harry Potter" series. Before the advent of the Internet and related technologies, many countries were already facing copyright infringement on a large scale. The illegal copying of books presents a real danger to the survival of the legal publishing industry. For example, the UNESCO Courier in its March 2001 edition published figures showing that : while the legal publishing industry annual turnover in Latin America and Spain is $5 billion, the illegal business makes $8 billion.

The copyright issues related to the publishing industry are similar to those faced by the software and music industries, both of whose products are copyright protected. However, piracy of published works, including books, newspapers and journals, has not yet reached the same level in terms of volume, monetary value and popularity as that of music, for example.

Nevertheless, it is likely to become a serious problem as e-publishing takes off. It has been reported that digital piracy (involving software, music, films and books) is responsible for multi-billion-dollar loss annually. So far, thousands of books are said to have been illegally exchanged on the Web in 2001; figures or estimates are not available for journals and newspapers.

Developed countries, as major exporters of intellectual property, have made great efforts to ensure its protection. Since the 1990s, a worldwide trend toward the harmonization of national laws has been influenced by international negotiations that led, in particular, to the adoption of international agreements such as the WTO Agreement on Trade-Related Aspects of Intellectual Property (TRIPS), the 1996 WIPO Copyright Treaty and the WIPO Phonogram Treaty, known as "the WIPO Internet Treaties".

The increasing economic importance of intellectual property rights makes them a more and more prominent issue in trade relations between countries. The main argument advanced in international debate in support of the protection and enforcement of intellectual property rights is that they lead to greater international trade for the benefit of all.

Given that developed countries are the major exporters of intellectual property, the intention is clearly to protect their exports by keeping pirated products out of the destination markets. The main justification of copyright for developed countries has always been economic.

The largest exporter of intellectual property rights is the United States. In 1990, the United States formed the International Intellectual Property Alliance (IIPA), which divided copyright-based industries into four groups, and provided statistics on their contribution to gross domestic product (GDP), employment and trade in the United States. The IIPA 2002 Report confirms the important role of copyright-based industries which represent one of the fastest-growing sectors of the economy, making significant contributions to domestic employment and revenue growth as well as to international trade.The Report states that in both developed and developing countries, studies have generally reported contributions to GDP in the range of 3 to 6 per cent.

According to the Report, it is estimated that in 2001 the core copyright industries in the United States accounted for 5.24 percent of the country's GDP, or $535.1 billion - an increase of over $75 billion from 1999. Over the last 24 years (1977 - 2001), the copyright industries' share of GDP grew more than twice as fast as the remainder of the U.S. economy (7 per cent vs. 3 per cent). The IIPA's estimate of the revenues generated by foreign sales/exports of selected U.S. core copyright industries in 2001 was $88.97 billion, an increase of over $52.78 billion from 1991. To put these figures into perspective, it is necessary to look at the extent the importance of trade losses in the United States due to copyright piracy.

IIPA's estimate of total trade losses for 2001 was $9.4 billion, an increase of $898 million from 2000. Business software applications represented 29.3 per cent of the total trade losses in 2001, closely followed by record and music, losses related to this sector increased from $2.9 billion in 2000 to $3.2 billion in 2001.

Estimates related to book losses, which in 2001, represented 10.3 per cent of the total trade losses at $650.8 million, while their value was $671.8 million in 2000. IIPA's estimates that worldwide loses due to piracy of United States copyrighted materials are in the annual $20-22 billion range, and does not include estimates due to Internet piracy. The United States' trade losses from piracy are increasing and are expected to grow even more with the development and expansion of new technologies.

In most developing countries, copyright issues have not acquired the same urgency because copyright-based industries remain smaller. As was pointed out by the World Bank in 1999, from the viewpoint of developing countries, the relevance of copyright is usually limited to artistic and literary works and the motion picture and television industries. With the expansion of Internet use, it is expected that copyright- based industries will grow in locations offering adequate IT skills and lower production costs, as has happened in some Asian countries in recent years. Efforts made by developing countries to address issues concerning national and international copyright legislation will occur when the capacity of local industries to generate intellectual property increases.

Copyright laws have been technology-driven and have tended to follow the development of technologies pioneered by the developed world. In the publishing industry, the invention of the printing press, computers and new technologies has led to reform of copyright legislation. The Statute of Ann, enacted by the British Parliament in 1710, known as the corner stone of copyright, responded in particular to booksellers' fear of their books being counterfeited and illegally distributed. Further to the Statute of Ann, national legislation was enacted in several countries: in 1790 the United States promulgated its first federal copyright statute, and thereafter several Western European countries (France, Germany, Austria and Spain) enacted laws recognizing authors as the owners of rights in their works.

In some developing countries, the laws regarding the protection of intellectual property were modelled on existing laws of developed countries. As the number of copyright-based industries in developing countries is generally quite low, the development of national laws was not high in the development agenda. Even developing countries that have implemented and ratified national and international agreements still do not fully meet their obligations in enforcing these laws. However, with the growth of copyright-based industries facing competition from foreign products, many developing countries have now realized the impact of copyrights and more generally intellectual property rights on their economies following.

Copyright protection is provided in the Berne Union of the Protection of Literary and Artistic Property, known as the Berne Convention. The Convention establishes standards for protection of copyrights in literacy and artistic works. It envisages the principle of automatic treatment by providing protection to artistic works and national treatment that allows the courts of a country to apply national laws to offences occurring within that country. To date, 140 member countries have ratified the Berne Convention.

More recently, the concern over digital rights has forced national, regional and international authorities to adapt their legislation to face the new threats posed by virtual and global distribution of contents. The WTO Agreement on TRIPS, which came into effect on 1 January 1995, is the most comprehensive multi-lateral agreement on intellectual property.

The areas of intellectual property covered by TRIPS include copyright and related rights (i.e. the rights of performers, producers of sound recordings and broadcasting organizations), trademarks (including service marks), geographical indications (including appellations of origin), industrial designs, patents (including the protection of new varieties of plants), the layout designs of integrated circuits and undisclosed information (including trade secrets and test data).

The international debate on copyright issues in a digital era also led to the adoption in 1996 of the "WIPO Internet Treaties", which entered into force in 2002. The common objectives of these treaties are to protect copyright owners in the digital age, favour the development of human creativity and promote electronic commerce.

The adoption of the TRIPS and WIPO Internet treaties has influenced the adoption by developed and developing countries of national legislation in line with the principles set forth by the two treaties. For example, in adopting the Digital Millennium Copyright Act (DMCA), the United States updated its copyright law for the digital era and prepared itself for the ratification of the WIPO Internet treaties.

The DMCA included provisions concerning the circumvention of copyright protection systems, fair use in a digital environment, and online service provider (OSP) liability. Moreover, the IIPA is responsible for tracking developments in the area of copyright legislation and enforcement in over 80 countries. In doing so, it determines whether the acts, policies or practices of any foreign country infringe on intellectual property rights or fair and equitable market access for individuals in the United States entitled to intellectual property protection.

The European Union has prepared a European Copyright Directive which was adopted in April 2002 and allows the European Union and its member States to ratify the WIPO Internet Treaties. This is expected to happen by the end of 2002. By 2004, all European countries will need to have adapted their national legislations in order to extend copyright protection to the Internet and other new media in accordance with this Directive.

After many years of legal discussion, to balance the rights of creators and the privacy of users, the Directive offers the possibility for European Union member States to adopt all or part of copyright exceptions that it envisages would allow for copying for technical reasons, personal use and archival purposes. Modernizing the traditional legal instruments of multilateral copyright conventions and treaties is essential, but the costs and benefits of harmonization are not always equally shared. Indeed, developing countries lag behind in terms of producing intellectual property as a whole, including published materials. However, this should not draw attention from the benefits that developing countries stand to gain from ratifying and enforcing copyright legislation.

The adoption of the WIPO treaties in 1996 generated an international pressure on developed and developing countries to comply with international agreements and thus, enforce anti-piracy mechanisms with regard to imported products. Indeed, the recent flurry of implementation of copyright legislation at the national level responds to pressure exerted on Governments by international bodies and local industries to provide effective enforcement of these laws.

As part of WIPO's and WTO's joint efforts to help developing countries meet their commitments regarding intellectual property and conform with the WTO agreement on TRIPS, since 1998 technical assistance in preparing legislation, training, institution building, and modernizing intellectual property systems and enforcement has been extended to developing countries.

National legislation has been enacted by the majority of countries worldwide to ensure copyright protection in the digital age, but it is too early to assess the effectiveness of these actions. While software and music piracy remain the most important economic issues for all countries, other works, such as books, are also under threat as advances in digital technologies facilitate the expansion of piracy.

In one of its country reports, the IIPA indicates that piracy "is rapidly changing: it is becoming more predominantly digital, moving online, and migrating to dispersed production formats such as CD-Recordable (CDR). Piracy of analog formats - audiocassettes, videocassettes, and books and other printed materials - remains a serious, and in some instances a worsening, problem. But technological and market trends are clearly pushing piracy in a new direction. Simply put, technological advances are increasing the opportunities for piracy, and pirates are taking full advantage of them."

All countries, including developing ones, are urged to comply with international agreements to protect works from piracy for the benefit of exporters of intellectual property products. However, enforcement of intellectual property rights depends on the effective functioning of a country's judicial system.

Beyond legal solutions and actions carried out by the local police, prevention campaigns have recently been launched by developing countries to demonstrate their commitment to fighting copyright infringement. Creating awareness of intellectual property rights, including copyright issues, has for the past few years been the preoccupation of intellectual property and copyright offices both in developed and developing countries. The advent of new technologies has spurred a large number of countries to reform their national copyright law in order to ensure copyright protection for materials available over the Internet.

However, bringing copyright laws into line with the WTO Agreement's and WIPO treaties, and providing effective enforcement of these laws with regard to piracy, counterfeiting and other forms of intellectual property rights infringement has proved to be difficult.

Due to the complexity of intellectual property laws and their enforcement, developing countries still lag behind and have still not managed to comply with the TRIPS requirements and enforcement mechanisms. Priority must be given to the development of a policy framework that allows great flexibility while ensuring implementation of international agreements.

The following are some key questions relating to business models and strategies to be considered. They are outlined here to provide a guide and an indication of the scope of the work involved and the types of investments to be made.

Strategies for prospective publishers and authors:

(a) As e-publishing demands new skills, publishers would need to take measures to train staff members to use new technologies, especially in areas that do not exist in traditional print publishing, such as interactivity and multimedia capability etc. One option is to contract out the technical tasks to technology firms or established e-publishers. If the publishing is to be undertaken in-house, an analysis of the capital and operating costs associated with the required information technology and infrastructure needs to be undertaken.

(b) Where a publisher is a start-up firm with no existing investment in print publishing, there appears to be a widely held view that such a venture should commence on an electronic-only basis, although this is feasible only where the majority of readers have Internet access. The question is more complex for publishers that have invested in print publishing. The "parallel" model of print publishing combined with electronic publishing appears to be the most prevalent. The decision essentially involves weighing costs against marketing opportunities. The publisher needs to assess the expenditure costs of converting from print publishing to electronic-only publishing and compare them with the expected gains. On the marketing side, if most users can only access print publications (as would be the case in most developing countries), a move to electronic-only publishing may entail a total loss of market.

(c) Other questions that would need to be addressed include the following:.

   (i) Whether to establish on one's own website or be hosted by other sites;

   (ii) What kinds of materials are suitable for e-publishing;

   (iii) Whether to place online the full text, only the table of contents, or only selected chapters;

   (iv) Which distribution channels to use, including institutional buyers (libraries), wholesale and retail stores, specialist document delivery services, etc. A decision also has to be made whether a publication should be delivered online or through a portable device such as a CDROM. A CDROM may be the better option in developing countries where Internet connectivity is still poor, although the trend is now towards online publishing, and a CDROM cannot be updated or easily link readers to Internet sites. E-publishing on CDROM should therefore be considered a transitional stage. Online delivery can occur via optical disk systems through public network connections (ISDN) or directly over the Internet. The publisher has various options regarding the format or language to be used, including ASCII, HTML and PDF. There are also options with regard to the graphic and audiovisual tools to be used. These choices require a fair amount of knowledge about IT and should also take into account trends in languages used on the Internet in order to ensure compatibility.

(v) Whether to build own databases as a backup information source;

(vi) Whether to "bundle" books or journals -that is sell them as a package;

(vii) Which pricing models to use;

(viii) How many of the value-added features enabled by e-publishing (e.g. searching capability, multimedia) are to be provided, taking into account the costs involved and the market being targeted;

(ix) How the publication should be marketed;

(x) Undertaking copyright, ISBN and other registrations;

(xi) How to obtain editorial services;

(xii) Whether the publisher should cooperate with other publishers to gain economies of scale, a factor that has driven some major publishers into mergers and acquisitions; and

(xiii) Whether an author should engage in self-publishing and what external support is available for this purpose.

A number of guidelines for e-publishing dealing with these types of questions and more technical ones are available and may be consulted.

Strategies for users of e-publications

Users include individual buyers of publications and institutional buyers, essentially libraries of different types. Usually publishers negotiate deals when issuing licenses for publications such as journals to libraries. These arrangements specify prices for various print and electronic versions. A library has to weigh cost against the importance it attaches to print relative to electronic versions for reasons other than cost.

Given fixed budgets, when adopting e-publications users may have to choose not merely between print and electronic versions but also between different types of publications - for example, between e-books and e-journals to the extent that there is scope for substitution between them. In their purchasing and other operational activities, libraries may create or join library consortia in order to gain bargaining power vis-à- vis publishers. Such consortia are now being used widely at the national, regional and international levels. Their functions include selecting electronic publishing resources and entering into licensing arrangements with publishers in order to rationalize price negotiations.

Members monitor the market for publications, obtain offers and evaluate them for negotiating purposes. Collaboration between consortia members also extends to providing joint access to acquired e-publications, which is the equivalent of interlibrary loans for print publications. If a group of libraries wishes to establish a consortium, there are published guidelines that provide information on how to create such an institution. Libraries may also join existing consortia such as the International Coalition of Library Consortia (ICOLC), which has worldwide membership.

There are a number of other possible strategies for institutional users. For example, while not many titles may currently be available as e-books, such books provide a cost-effective solution to libraries' budgetary constraints in that a library owning an e-book may transfer the content into several readers' e-book devices and thus avoid purchasing several copies of the same book.

E-books may also help libraries reduce the delays typically involved in interlibrary loans of printed books - a library can obtain the contents of an e-book from another library in a matter of minutes. However, a decision to purchase e-books format has to take into consideration the present and projected availability of needed titles in e-books and the suitability of the available technology for reading books, as well as its cost.

Role of governments

Most developing countries have traditionally printed many types of official documents. Because of high printing and distribution costs, such documents are usually distributed only within government circles and to a few external outlets.

Most governments and government- related institutions in developing countries now have websites or at least make use of other web-sites and portals to publish various types of information. This means that there is scope for governments to provide their publications online.

An expansion of electronic publications by governments would not only widen the distribution of vital government information, it would also provide leadership by example to authors and publishers in the private sector.

To promote e-publishing, some governments in both developed and developing countries have encouraged all government institutions to progressively adopt e-publishing. Some governments have established minimum standards for government e-publications. These standards are intended to ensure the quality and accessibility of the published information. Developing countries should find these examples a useful guide in establishing their own protocols.

6

Digital Trends

Progress in new technology and its speedy development has resulted in many new applications such as multimedia products and services, and 'intelligent' interfaces. These new possibilities, which began in industrialized countries, have gradually spread around the world and offer new opportunities for distance learning, health and many other activities designed for development. Access to knowledge and information via new networks can be a positive contribution to the sustainable development of different sectors of society.

The question, however, is how to apply the new information and communication technologies effectively to development and how to use them in order to bridge the gap between the rich and the excluded, between nations and within those selfsame nations. The question stems from the heated debate between researchers and communication professionals about the conditions for transferring new information and communication technology to developing countries. A certain number, the advocates of the 'modernization paradigm', consider that the transfer of new information and communication technology is a major stimulant for the development process that, in the long run, will enable the developing countries to catch up with the industrialized countries. For others, the opponents of 'cultural dependence', any such transfer would merely be a step further not only towards inequality, but even towards the destruction of the cultural identity of societies in the Southern hemisphere. Finally, for others again, both the paradigms of transfer and dependence are outdated.

New information and communication technology and its applications provide developing countries with the ability to perform a kind of 'technological leapfrogging' that could enable them to reach the connection capacity required for the information networks far more rapidly. Similar forms of leapfrogging might also enable economies with a high level of skilled labour to switch to 'value-added' economies. An increasing number of states share the latter point of view and have opted for the most advanced forms of technology to implement or renew their communication infrastructures.

On the one hand they have adopted policies of adaptation and technological transfer by offering attractive subcontracting capabilities, thereby relocating communication multinationals; on the other hand, they are investing in communication programmes or setting up new communication infrastructures. Other countries, particularly in South-East Asia, have achieved something of a feat in telecommunications and the audiovisual field. Some of these nations even form the driving force for economic expansion that counterbalances the climate of recession elsewhere in the world. South-East Asia currently enjoys the highest rate of economic growth worldwide and operates as an accelerator for the whole continent: 11 per cent per year since 1983 compared with a global growth rate of 6 per cent. Its telecommunication equipment population is now close to that of the industrialized countries and in some areas is even a length ahead of European states.

China, India and several countries in South-East Asia have launched their own satellites. Nevertheless, it would probably be a mistake to think that all developing countries could automatically attain this level of development. The countries in this region of the world find themselves in widely differing economic situations as a result of a series of factors, the most important of which are the ability to attract investment, the educational level of the population, the economic policies adopted by their leaders and, finally, their cooperation with the industrialized countries and the impact of all these factors on new information and communication technology and its applications.

In fact, most of the developing countries are confronted with economic and political alternatives of a strategic nature, but also with constraints and obstacles that they will have to overcome or manage if in the future they wish to set up gateways with the networks and services promised by the information society. These obstacles are financial, technical and political in nature. First and foremost, the introduction of new information and communication technology requires extremely heavy investment, estimated at several hundred billion dollars, a sum that most developing countries can neither raise nor commit.

In addition, most of these states are currently confronted with obstacles to development and are subject to structural adjustment plans that force them to limit their expenditure. Second, the hypothetical presence of these countries on the future electronic networks presupposes the installation of terrestrial or satellite telecommunication networks, the management and control of which seem incompatible with the obsolete and under-equipped level of local telecommunication services.

Third, the future information society presupposes fair, universal access to the Web for the whole population of a country. The geographical dissimilarities within these countries, however, are alarming. They stem from the political options that have been adopted by governments which are generally centralizing in outlook, resulting in fairly top-heavy media concentration, with telecommunication services located in the capitals and major provincial capitals Together, those problems and obstacles clearly illustrate the challenges that the developing countries must face: implementing a new information and communication policy in order to modernize, democratize and diversify the services on offer. The first of these challenges entails favouring a worldwide strategy for the reform of communication services.

The need to modernize communication equipment presupposes the transfer of the new technology and intensive use of the services it provides. The funds required, however, are such that modernization inevitably entails monopoly deregulation, a fact which has now become the reference framework for any upgrade or modernization of communication policy. Most developing countries are fully aware of this need, and have already opted for deregulation or privatization by having their companies join the trend of internationalization and partnerships with the major operators in the industrialised countries. Without subscribing to some form of liberal economic determinism, privatization can probably solve a number of requirements, including that of providing the specific value-added services necessary for any connection with telecommunications networks.

On the other hand, privatization can be seen as a legitimate means of socioeconomic change only if every class of society gains some benefit from it. This is precisely the reason why privatization must be accompanied by a statutory framework guaranteeing that all sectors of the population, in particular those people living farthest from the major cities, have access to the basic information and communication services, just as, through partnerships or alliances, it should facilitate access to every form of information and communication flow, whether by telephone, audiovisual programmes, the written press, etc.

Finally, the success of privatization presupposes the existence of an open market, strong local enterprise, and fair market rules and regulations to counterbalance the risk, inherent to privatization, of the emergence of new monopolies. The second of the challenges mentioned above is linked to the conditions in which access is gained to technology and to its content. Most developing countries have modest, even outdated telephone services and audiovisual equipment, which cannot easily be adapted to the digital transmission used by electronic networks.

The experts take the view that this deficiency can be made up by satellite technology which will complement the existing terrestrial cellular telephony systems and transport large amounts of data at low cost. The system of transmission by satellite seems to offer several advantages, notably that of covering vast areas and reaching populations in regions with difficult terrain and hostile climates that cannot be covered. Satellites make it possible to broadcast educational and cultural programmes and distance learning courses throughout a country, and finally to connect up to electronic networks.

Since the technical capabilities and possibilities of planetary networks, the most well-known of which is the Internet, seem closest to the idea of open, limitless communication. It is also a practical, economical solution for developing countries if they wish to have access to a universal system of communication that can make good a number of deficiencies, notably in terms of point-to-point communication.

The capability of developing countries to adopt an overall strategy that links the transfer of information and communication technology to a training and research policy. Access to know-how and training in every country is a major priority. The acquisition of know-how and knowledge, which today fill the role played first by landownership and later by capital in transforming modern society, has become a priority in national development strategies.

New information and communication technology is seen as an important means of completing and consolidating the traditional techniques of teaching and learning. Virtually everywhere around the world, development programmes are making increasing use of satellite television, telematics, and even video-conferences in education, health, family planning and community development. The technology permits transmission throughout the national territory of adult training programmes and distance learning courses tailored to suit all kinds of publics.

The technology offers immense possibilities for reaching vast numbers of people, with more efficient and attractive teaching methods than those used in traditional education. In addition to these advantages, if the various costs of training, such as travel in developing countries between badly-serviced rural areas are taken into account, distance learning based on new technology seems particularly cost-effective, and will become even more so as its use develops. In the medical field, new technology such as picture phoning, video-conferences and medical encyclopedias on CD-ROM are responding increasingly to a demand which already exists at the experimental level.

In a few years, doctors, hospitals, laboratories and universities will be networked and capable of telemonitoring diagnoses, analyses and examinations transmitted from one end of the world to the other in record time, via computer and video systems. Examples of experimental applications are already on the increase, notably between hospitals in developed countries.

It is not enough to buy technology to gain access to the information society, however, nor should a straightforward purchase be seen as a miraculous solution. Access entails a considerable degree of effort, information, learning and popularization that developing countries will have to uphold if they wish to benefit from technological change and have the tools necessary for their autonomy, namely new information and communication technology. Nor should the latter be seen as some sort of magic wand far removed from the socioeconomic facts of life of the countries into which they are introduced.

The technology concerns every kind of user: researchers, academics, students, company executives, etc., who have to adapt to their new environment and learn to use their navigation system properly in order to optimize its potential. In addition and in parallel to this, technology transfer has to be supported by a research drive. This consists, first of all, in analysing the breakthroughs made in information technology, the conditions permitting its transfer, and its interaction with the local socioeconomic environment, and discovering the ways in which all these factors occur and interrelate.

The result will be a clearer understanding not only of the use of technology, its effects, and the economic and technical constraints, but also of its advantages and the room for manoeuvre in its application. Within this global framework, research can provide a genuine form of 'strategic surveillance' used to guide policy-making by developing countries with respect to technological options. Research is also a prerequisite for development which is often put to one side by countries that are consumers of new technology.

Many developing countries since their independence have built highly diversified industrial tools in the field of communication systems, while remaining technologically dependent on supplier countries. They often find themselves confronted with R&D issues designed, driven and developed in industrialized countries. The latter have taken the high ground in the field of new technology—or are seeking to do so - by developing scientific research, taking the view that the capability to appropriate and assimilate technology depends on the degree of mastery and development attained in the strategic sector of research and development, a branch of activity in which the most advanced countries have dominant positions.

The issue of international co-operation in the field of communication. The balance sheet, after several decades of international co-operation for development purposes, is disappointing. On the one hand, it shows that very few countries have entered the newly industrialized country category, and that the use of traditional methods of development aid to enhance economic growth must be re-examined. The efforts made by the international community must be upheld and widened to include other underprivileged regions around the world, through a different approach to co-operation.

In concerted fashion, this must include international organizations in order to facilitate partnership agreements with the private sector, include professional skills and ensure marketing and management know-how, and enhance understanding and knowledge with respect to the new legislation on the independent written press and the audiovisual field—in short, a different conception of co-operation altogether, leading to an authentic transfer of knowledge, in a spirit of balanced interests, solidarity and sharing.

ICTs and Digital Divide

ICT is not just another sector of economic development, nor can it simply be looked upon as a set of tools. Instead, ICT permeates every aspect of today's societal activity. Ironically, the very factors that have phenomenally improved productivity by intelligent use of the technology, also risk driving the poor to the periphery, thus creating barriers within and between societies, and could lead to social unrest and tension. Countries and people lacking capacity for ICT will be marginalized in the new economy. New trade barriers will be erected. Moreover, without access to ICT, countries will not be able to benefit from the many innovative ways of addressing poverty and basic needs that these technologies offer.

One reason why the information gap is widening is that the potential of ICT in social and economic development has not been fully understood. There are still too many people in key positions in governments and aid agencies who seem to believe that only when basic needs are met does technology have a role to play. If they were right most of the poor would have to wait forever. The debate must move beyond choosing between ICT and other development needs such as health and education. The issue is not about a trade-off between one or the other, but an understanding that these must go hand in hand. However, technology alone is not enough. Technology must be applied within its social context and that, in many countries, is providing a real challenge. One thing is clear. The new technologies, notably ICT, will bring about major transformations in society.

The structural logic of the information society will be vastly different from that of the industrial society. One eminent scholar, who has given a lot of thought to the implications of the ICT revolution, is Professor Harlan Cleveland. Here is how he perceives the future: "Information -symbols, not things -will be playing the lead role in world history that physical labour, stone, bronze, land, minerals, metals and energy once played. We will have to burn into our consciousness how very different information is from all its predecessors as civilization's dominant resource." In his speech to the American Association for History and Computing Cleveland continues: "Information expands as it's used-no "limits to growth "around here. It is ready transportable, at close to the speed of light.

Information leaks so easily that it is much harder to hide and to hoard than tangible resources were. The spread of knowledge empowers the many, by eroding the influence that once empowered the few who were "in the know". Information cannot be owned, only its delivery service can. And giving or selling information don't give rise to "exchange" transactions; they are acts of sharing." If Cleveland is right, we are at the doorstep of a democratic revolution. In the industrial era, poverty was explained and justified by shortages of things. In the coming years, physical resources will still be important, but their role in wealth creation will gradually be overtaken by information.

And since each baby is born with a brain, there ought to be radically different prerequisites for development and progress at the level of the individual, also in the poor regions of the world. But there is a catch: whether or not the information revolution is really going to lead to greater fairness depends to what extent the poor will have access, not only to the modern information technologies, but also to education. If such access is not provided, the expected fairness revolution will be turned into its opposite.

In February 2001, well above 400 million people worldwide were users of the Internet. This represents phenomenal growth, given that the Internet is less than three thousand days old. But the spread of Internet use is very uneven. The vast majority of Internet users are found in OECD countries. There are more hosts in Manhattan than in continental Africa; more hosts in Finland than in Latin America and the Caribbean; and notwithstanding the remarkable progress in the application of ICT in India, most of its villages still lack a working telephone. To bridge the digital divide is both a moral and a social imperative. If we do not succeed, entire regions and hundreds of millions of people will be left behind. The consequences in terms of poverty and deprivation will be devastating.

But there is another, equally compelling argument for developing countries to embrace the new technologies. By investing in cutting-edge technology, through leapfrogging, they will be able to bypass certain stages of development. The benefits can be financial, social, as well as environmental. As "late-comers", developing countries can be better placed to take advantage of the newest technology developments, not the least in ICT, since they are not hindered by the previous investments in obsolete technology. Since prices come down very quickly in the area of ICT, investments in a telecommunication infrastructure today may cost just a fourth or a fifth compared to what was the case a few years ago.

The environmental benefits would be significant, since leapfrogging would make it possible for developing countries to avoid repeating some of the mistakes of industrialized countries. Take energy. Worldwide total energy production-related investments for 2000 to 2030 are estimated at between 12 and 17 trillion dollars. The majority of these investments will be made in developing countries. Presently, most of them will favour fossil fuels, primarily coal. If this trend continues, the resulting emissions in terms of carbon will be disastrous. And these emissions will negatively affect people all over the world.

New systems of energy supply and consumption are badly needed. Less polluting and more efficient energy technologies are available, but normally at a higher investment cost than conventional fuels. The challenge is at least twofold:

i) to help build the necessary capacity in terms of institutions and skills in developing countries to enable them to adapt and expand on new discoveries and make them applicable to their specific needs, and

ii) to provide investors with the right kind of incentives to make investing in alternative energy solutions attractive.

Only if these preconditions are fulfilled will leapfrogging be possible. Investing in clean energy and transport are the most obvious examples of how the natural environment in developing countries could benefit from technology leapfrogging. But the opportunities do not stop there.

The ICT revolution by itself offers fascinating possibilities for enhancing energy and resource efficiency and reducing pollution. When society becomes more digital, the possibilities for major structural change and efficiency gains multiply. New avenues open up. Concepts such as dematerialisation, teleworking, teleconferencing, distance education, the flexible office, e-Commerce all promise great leaps forward in terms of enhanced resource efficiency. Environmentally sound technologies (ESTs) often depend on sophisticated measuring devices, data transmission networks and automatic data processing equipment. This can be provided by ICT, thus bringing about more efficient production processes as well as greatly enhanced product performance.

Moreover, with advanced communications many conventional products will be transformed into services. A newspaper becomes an on-line news service; an instruction manual becomes an interactive technical advice service; cinema film reproduction becomes a "video-on-demand "service in the home, etc.

It appears obvious to us that a high-tech economy based on knowledge, skills and innovation ought to be a cleaner, greener economy. But few attempts have been made to assess specifically to what extent the digital revolution and the sustainable development agenda complement each other.

In some areas developments so far have been disappointing. For instance, as long as e-Commerce is a marginal phenomenon in society, demand for transportation seems to increase, not the opposite. When more and more people will shop on the Net, things will change. The main reason is economics. When volumes increase it will be good business to organize transport and logistics in the most efficient way. As a result the environment will benefit.

The reader may find that most of what ICT can offer in terms of enhanced energy and resource efficiency are relevant examples only in the context of OECD countries. Activities such as telework, e-Commerce, on-line services were pioneered in the US, Japan and Europe. But there is no reason why such activities should not start penetrating countries of the South as well. In fact, they already have.

Many people do not realize that China is the single biggest market for mobile phones in the world today. As the volume of foreign direct investments in developing countries has multiplied in recent years, the result will be an increased transfer of high-tech from OECD countries to developing countries. True, private investments in the South are concentrated to a limited number of countries. The challenge is to include more countries in this process, and to focus specifically on applications that would promote sustainable development.

Traditionally it was accepted that economic growth, as measured by GDP, was inevitably linked to growing demand for raw materials and energy as well as the negative consequences of pollution. If such linkages were to last long into the future the overall consequences for mankind would be disastrous.

There are already clear signs that pollution levels are exceeding the absorption capacity of the global ecosystem. Climate change is the most obvious example but there are others. Parallel to excessive pollution levels, the pressures on forests, farmland, fresh water resources and fisheries are mounting. Efforts to try to de-link GDP growth and demand for energy and materials have therefore become a priority for policymakers in several OECD countries.

The achievements are still limited, but there are signs of progress. For instance, the energy intensity of OECD countries has been reduced in the recent past. This is the result of a shift towards more energy-efficient technologies and less energy-intensive materials. Scientists claim that this trend will continue, as a gradual saturation of traditional consumer goods will take place. One obvious reason is the move into the information economy. In such an economy an increasing part of transactions will be immaterial. Many products will be turned into services, which depend less on energy and material throughput.

Long-term studies of energy-intensity in several countries indicate that economies use more energy per unit of output during the early phases of development, reach a peak, and then start to decrease. Liberalization and information technologies should allow knowledge to be transferred more easily, enabling emerging economies to climb the so-called energy and technology ladders more quickly. This means that latecomers ought to be able to avoid the peak in energy demand by benefiting from more modern methods of manufacturing and more efficient energy technologies. However, there are many barriers to overcome for such change to happen. Studies do confirm that energy intensity is on the increase in most developing countries, not the opposite. The only exception is China, where deliberate efforts are being made to use both energy and materials more efficiently.

In order for the necessary transformation to more efficient and environmentally sound technologies to happen in developing countries, several barriers to change have to be tackled. Most important is to address the capacity needs. While much knowledge for improved problem-solving is now available in many scientific and engineering institutions around the world, very little of that know-how is geared specifically to addressing development and environment needs in developing countries. Most of these countries lack the scientific institutions and infrastructure to adapt and expand on new knowledge and discoveries in order to make them applicable to their local needs.

We are dealing with capital-intensive infrastructure, which is meant to provide a public service at an affordable price. In most countries energy distribution, public transport, waste management etc. are considered to be public services. Increasingly, public authorities are choosing to delegate the operation and management of public services to the private sector. If and when this happens, it is crucial that the necessary regulatory framework is in place to guarantee environmental quality.

To create an adequate legislative and regulatory framework for the protection of the environment is a difficult process in any country. This is particularly true for most developing countries, where government structures are weak. Governments need to implement fiscal and regulatory policies that encourage innovation and provide direct incentives to companies that develop or disseminate technologies that contribute to sustainable development.

Fiscal incentives should also be used to stimulate businesses and households to purchase such technologies. Parallel to that, subsidies in support of fossil fuels and other technologies that are harmful to the environment should be dismantled. The next step would be for governments to apply the Polluter Pays Principle, i.e. to make sure that environmental externalities are reflected in market prices. This represents a real challenge in OECD countries, and even more so in developing countries, but it has to happen.

As already stressed, the strengthening of institutional and human capacities is a primary prerequisite for ESTs to become a priority in the development process of developing countries. The same is true for most development co-operation agencies. In a recent study on "Technology co-operation in the field of environmentally sound technologies "to the European Parliament by IED the authors conclude that "a review of organisational structures and portfolios of bilateral and multilateral co-operation agencies and banks shows that there are grossly insufficient human capacities in the areas of energy co-operation. If ESTs are to become a priority of development co-operation, the institutions of international co-operation must first and foremost be given the means to understand the issues and to formulate and manage projects ".

Until recently, science and technology was more or less absent from the sustainable development debate. More recently a change can be discerned. The Human Development Report 2001 "Making New Technologies Work for Human Development "is one example. The report emphasizes the crucial relationship that exists between science, knowledge and human capacity in addressing issues of sustainable development. One important message from the Human Development Report is that technological progress and knowledge applications are key drivers of economic growth. The logical conclusion is that support to science and technology ought to become a top priority for development co-operation.

The little attention given by ODA, so far, to science and technology also means that support to ESTs have been largely neglected. The only mechanism at international level worth mentioning in this context is the Global Environment Facility (GEF). The GEF has given support to capacity building in the field of sustainable energy and to renewable energy pilot projects. But compared to the total investments in energy production in developing countries, the resources of the GEF have been woefully inadequate.

One possible source of finance, that ought to be utilised in support of investments in ESTs, is the export-credit agencies (ECAs) of OECD countries. However, until very recently these agencies were paying no attention at all to the environmental aspects of their lending. On the contrary, during the period of 1994-99, it is estimated that more than 100 billion of US dollars were being mobilised through the ECAs in support of investments in carbon-based technologies. Just imagine if the same attention had been given instead to investments in energy efficiency and renewables.

Efforts have been made within the climate convention to establish new sources of finance to assist developing countries both in climate adaptation and investments in clean technologies. It is too early today to judge to what extent the new mechanisms will make a difference.

Presently, we experience the technologies of the information and communication revolution at the cutting edge of progress. Their application also offers momentous opportunities for development. They present developing countries with real opportunities in helping to bridge the economic and prosperity gaps between them and developed countries.

Today, village computer centers in developing countries help farmers check the going prices for their produce in the city, thus avoiding arbitrary mark-ups by middlemen. The same centers provide distance education and learning and help improve health services. Today, rural artists and craftsmen in remote villages can reach a global market with their products, thanks to non-profit

Internet sites. Yet, at the same time, billions of people still live untouched by the digital revolution. Only about 7% of the world 's population can claim connectivity, and the greater majority of these are living in the developed countries. As a result, the income gap between the developed and developing countries is being further aggravated by the digital divide.

This holds ominous consequences for the developing countries in terms of increased poverty, unemployment and underdevelopment. This is not the result of some conspiracy against the poor. Rather it is the result of a development where access to information and knowledge are becoming the most important factors of production. Those with access to information and technology naturally benefit in this situation; those without access become further marginalized.

However, the situation should not be regarded as hopeless. Even if the information revolution so far is widening the gap between the rich and the poor, this need not become a pattern for the future. There are many tangible examples from around the world of how ICTs are being deployed to address important development goals. Evidence shows that ICT initiatives need not be confined to countries with high per capita incomes, well-developed infrastructures and high levels of venture capital in order to succeed. Indeed, remarkable progress is evident where some of these elements have been lacking. The experiences of a few countries, including both developing countries and transition economies, have demonstrated that bold actions in bringing their countries into the digital age have paid off and brought tangible results in economic, social and political terms. Prominent examples are Estonia, Mauritius and Costa Rica.

Costa Rica attributes much of its recent economic growth to the widespread adaptation of ICT. The focus has been on the educational sector. Computer laboratories were installed in all of the country's public high schools, thereby reaching 50 per cent of the children enrolled in public schools. "Smart cards" have been introduced nationwide in public administration, transportation, public telephones and health services. Parallel to that a variety of efforts have been made to use ICT to help integrate isolated rural populations, notably by introducing multipurpose/multimedia mobile units that can be taken to any rural community and provide a variety of functions (Internet access, ICT training, e-mail facilities etc.).

Today, the country has one of the highest degrees of connectivity in Europe. All schools have been connected to the Internet; more than 80 per cent of bank transfers are made over the Internet; "smart cards" were introduced for interaction with government services etc. The per capita income has risen from US 600 in 1991 to more than US 5000 in 2000, a development largely made possible by the very proactive ICT strategy pursued. Mauritius adopted a National Information Technology Strategy Plan early on. The primary objectives were to bring Government closer to the people through e-Government, to use ICT to enhance the education system and the service sector, and to improve the efficiency of the public sector. A special Ministry was created to promote ICT applications in different sectors of the Mauritian society. As a result of the dedicated efforts Mauritius has attracted a great number of small and medium-sized ICT-based companies.

The great majority of developing countries, however, have done little in terms of a coherent strategy to embrace the ICT revolution. This does not mean that nothing is happening in all these countries in terms of ICT for development. There are numerous initiatives, mainly among NGOs, that hopefully will help raise awareness and demonstrate, to governments as well as aid agencies, the great opportunities that the new technologies offer both for accelerating economic development and, more specifically, to help advance the human development agenda.

Among the many examples of initiatives at the grassroots level, the following may provide an illustration of the significance of ICT in addressing basic human needs:

The overall aim of the Technology Community Centres Access (TACC) pilot project -established with support of UNDP was to "provide rural and remote communities with public access to information technology, especially the Internet, and with the training to utilize it effectively." The project's ultimate goal was to demonstrate how information technologies could contribute to "the empowerment of community members" and how such technologies could be used "for a variety of applications benefiting sustainable human development." A pilot, consisting of several cyber cafes, was established in Sharkeya.

The pilot has succeeded beyond the most optimistic expectations. Some 6,000 persons have received IT training with a view to supporting various development activities at the community level. To date, TACC staff - national and international (mainly United Nations Volunteers)-have developed and posted over 1,000 web pages, most of them in Arabic. The websites provide information on ICT training, health, agriculture, e-commerce, the culture and history of Egypt, recreational activities, etc.

In light of the success in Sharkeya, the government of Egypt recently decided to establish similar centers in all of the country 's Governorates. The TACC concept is also being replicated in Jordan.

The experimental telecentre project in South India was initiated in 1998 by the M.S.Swaminathan Research Foundation. Four centers have become operational, located in villages with illiteracy rates above 50%. The project is based on the understanding that networked information requires "mediation "by professionals if it is to be accessible to poor rural villagers. The information compiled and collected for the project is primarily based on requests by the village end-users. This information - which includes items like commodity prices, weather forecasts, daily news, government information, methods of dealing with crop diseases, fishing methods etc.-is translated into Tamil, packaged into audio files and distributed via the Internet to the four Village Knowledge Centres. The local centers broadcast the audio files over loudspeakers to the illiterate villagers. Evidence suggests that the villagers benefit significantly from the information in regard to making decisions affecting their lives and well-being.

Women members of Grameen Bank are offered micro-credit loans to purchase cellular phones, which are subsequently rented out to village farmers and other community members. As of July 2001 phones had been placed in more than 1.000 villages. Phone services in rural areas are highly valued in Bangladesh and have rapidly increased incomes and savings among phone owners. The village phones allow family members to stay in touch and communicate with family members abroad about financial matters like remittances. Local farmers use the phones to have access to market information, weather reports and pest alerts. The phone services have also contributed to improvements in disaster response, crime rates and livestock mortality through better access to public services.

The association of Uganda Women Medical Doctors was started in 1987 with a mission of improving and facilitating the promotion and protection of health to women, young people and children in Uganda. They decided in the spring of 2000 to try to make use of Internet in their work. The aim of the project was to disseminate information on reproductive health electronically to other women NGOs. Medical doctors in Kampala download the necessary information, repackage it and send it online to the participating NGOs. Feedback from the NGOs is also received via the Internet, including specific questions asked by clients at health clinics. Already after a few months the project had demonstrated increased awareness among rural women of reproductive health issues.

A fascinating pilot project in the field of ICT for development is currently being developed by Development Alternatives, Delhi. The main objective of TARAhaat (Technology and Action for Rural Advancement)—the Internet Portal connecting rural India to the global village -is to use the power of ICT to bring knowledge, services and products to the villages in India. Starting in Punjab and Uttar Pradesh, the plan is to establish tens of thousands of Internet and computer enabled business centers all over the subcontinent in the years to come.

The portal offers email, eCommerce, education, entertainment, access to e-Government facilities, etc. Eventually TARAhaat plans to bring the village manufacturers in contact with buyers and designers the world over. Access to the portal is being provided by franchised cyber kiosks, which are operated by local village entrepreneurs. Satellite communication, wireless broadband and local power generation will be used where there is no electricity or phone. Overall few donor-funded ICT projects in developing countries have proven to be self-sustaining once external assistance has run out.

The encouraging thing about TARAhaat is that its pilots shows signs of being able to stand on their own feet only after six to twelve months of operation. This means that the revenues generated by these kiosks are sufficiently large to provide a surplus. What this demonstrates is that even in the poorest of villages there is significant demand for communication and ICT services.

In Tanzania, Masai pastoralists living in the Ngorongoro have used the Internet to voice their opposition to Government conservation management policy that threatened their land and their livelihood. A member of the Masai community came up with the idea of putting his people on the World Wide Web after he made a video about the critique of the pastoralists on the Governments management plan for their land. He put clips of "real people" from the video to the website and managed to mobilize support for the cause of the pastoralists around the world. In addition to obliging the Tanzanian Government to listen to the voices of the local communities, the Masai say that their web site makes them feel less isolated: they feel part of a "bigger world".

ICT has been extremely beneficial for those nations that have used it with determination and enthusiasm as part of their national development strategies. Many individual examples from developing countries also demonstrate how ICT, appropriately applied, can help address basic social needs. In spite of this, the international donor community has been slow in addressing the digital divide. There has been much talk but little action. At the receiving end, there has also been a lot of resistance. Quite a number of developing country governments have been slow to open up to ICT, either for political or cultural reasons, or simply because they do not believe that ICT can be of importance to the development of their countries.

If the general trend among donors can be characterized as passivity, a few institutions have understood the importance of ICT for development. Canadian IDRC has been a strong promoter of ICT capacity building for over a decade. Swedish SAREC also played a supporting role in the early years. The main focus for IDRC and SAREC has been to build capacity for ICT at universities and scientific institutions in the South. IDRC has also been a pioneer in other areas, using ICT in natural resources management, the provision of health care, etc.

ICT for development became a central issue for the World Bank in the mid 1990´s. Jim Wolfensohn had joined the bank as president and soon declared that he wanted to turn the bank into a "knowledge bank." The bank has since launched several good initiatives, like InfoDev and Gateway. Support to ICT capacity building, however, is still far from being among the Bank 's priorities in terms of funding.

The UN system has been a disappointment, mainly because of shrinking funding support for UN agencies in general. There are two exceptions, the ITU and UNDP. The ITU has done its part in terms of awareness-raising activities, but -true to its mandate -focusing mainly on the need for reform and liberalization of the telecommunication sector.

UNDP was a pioneer with its Sustainable Development Networks Programme and its ICT for development project. But the budgetary resources were limited, which meant that activities had to focus on information, awareness-raising activities and pilot projects.

The European Union commands significant resources for development co-operation, in fact significantly larger than the UN. But the European Commission has so far largely neglected the information revolution and its implications for development. This is in stark contrast to the efforts undertaken within the Union itself. The European Commission has taken on a very active role in the promotion of ICT through the launching of eEurope -a broad programme aiming at enhancing ICT skills in society with special efforts made towards public schools, universities, SME:s, people with different kinds of handicaps, etc. One of the main objectives is to make sure that no citizens of the Union are being excluded from the technology developments.

If developments have been slow in the past as regards donor support to ICT for development, however important changes took place during 2000. In this year, major international bodies launched potentially highly significant initiatives to apply ICT to the needs of the developing countries.

The United Nations Millennium Summit called on the UN "to play a leadership and catalytic role in helping to bridge the digital divide and accelerate development by harnessing the development potential of information and communication technologies (ICTs)". A Special Task Force has been established to provide overall leadership in helping "to formulate strategies for ICTs development and putting them at the service of development for all, to forge a strategic partnership between the United Nations system, private industry and financing trusts and foundations, donors, programme countries and other relevant stakeholders, and to mobilize new resources for ICT for development ".

Parallel to the discussions in the UN, the G8 meeting in Okinawa in July 2000 decided to establish two special task forces; one on the digital divide and one on renewable energy. The task forces included members from governments, the private sector, science and civil society. By initiating this work, the major economic powers of the world demonstrated their concern both for the issue of income poverty - access to modern energy services is a precondition for development -and information poverty. The two reports were presented at the G8 meeting in Genoa in July 2001. Both reports are of high quality and include a large number of very sensible recommendations. It is however not at all clear to what extent G8 countries will act upon the recommendations.

Comments in Genoa, notably from Mr.Bush, stressed unequivocally that there was nothing binding about the recommendations. Leaving aside implementation, the two task forces did serve an important function. Their analysis is cutting-edge and they will most certainly be used to advance the agenda in terms of bridging the digital divide as well as promoting environmentally sound technologies in the South.

Professor Jeffrey Sachs has pointed out that the greatest divide between rich and poor nations is the inequality in innovation and diffusion of technology. Even as we speak this divide is widening. Among the solutions, Sachs suggests to follow the example of the Rockefeller Foundation in creating and funding great research centres around the world. New partnerships are also needed to bring together academia, governments and industry, from both rich and poor countries.

Capacity building in the new technology areas at universities, government institutions, schools, among entrepreneurs, etc, is a major prerequisite for technology leapfrogging to become successful. Furthermore, developing countries need considerable help to develop the right political, fiscal and legal frameworks to stimulate investments in ICT as well as ESTs. One of the mistakes of the past was that development co-operation was primarily seen in the context of the governments involved.

But experience has taught us that governments seldom are good at handling and managing technology. This should be the responsibility of the private sector. Hence there is a strong need in developing countries for new types of partnerships between the public and private sectors. This is particularly true in areas like telecom and energy, where rigid state monopolies very often are the main stumbling block for improvements in customer services.

There is no doubt that the economic opportunities which ICT generates will create a lot of wealth for those who master them. However, left entirely to market forces, these technologies are likely to marginalize the poor and disenfranchise them even more.

A purely public sector approach will not work either. What is very much needed are partnerships between the private and public sectors, where the key role of the public sector will be to strengthen the capacity of all major sectors in society to have access to the Internet and to use it for their benefit. The private sector should be responsible for ensuring efficient and commercially viable dissemination of the technologies. Academia and civil society would help develop content so as to address important social, environmental and cultural needs in the process.

Many different kinds of technology can contribute to sustainable development. Some of these may be designed specifically to tackle environmental or poverty-related problems (e.g. solar photovoltaics). However, other technologies that have not been designed to directly address these kind of problems - like computers and mobile phones -will have an equally important role to play.

The technologies needed for sustainable development will differ from country to country. Those best placed to identify their technology needs are the different stakeholders themselves. However, they will only be able to do so if there is a supportive and enabling environment: if they have a well-developed skills base; strong, well-targeted programmes of research and development; an entrepreneurial private sector and if financing is available to the companies that are developing and utilising the technologies.

The private sector will need a lot of support in most developing countries in order to invest in the new technology areas. FDI flows are, as we know, concentrated in a few developing countries. For the great majority of countries the political as well as financial risks are perceived to be too high. Moreover, FDI will not take place in countries were the infrastructure in terms of roads, ports, telecom, energy, etc, is poor. A classic Catch 22 situation. Here the international donor community could play an important role by providing credits and risk guarantees.

Small-scale enterprises and service companies have a key role to play in developing and disseminating technology. Smaller companies in developing countries often experience difficulties to obtain financing. They are either too large for micro-credits, too small to qualify for project financing or perceived as too much of a risk for commercial loans. Strategies for providing funding to small private businesses need to be developed.

The international community should play a central role in assisting development country governments in pursuing the goal of Digital Opportunities for all and to support green technology leapfrogging.

The following priority actions ought to be considered:

— Support to national eStrategies, based on broad stakeholder dialogues. These strategies should include the development of regulatory and policy frameworks so as to improve competition in telecommunications and the provision of IT services to the public.

— Support for the establishment of community access points in all developing countries. The goal should be that all communities in the developing world should be connected before the end of 2004.

— Promotion of ICT dissemination among children in developing countries, notably by connecting schools and educational facilities.To be effective, such a program must be complemented by adequate teacher training.

— Support for university-based centres and research networks, focussing on research and learning at the intersection of ICT and development. Special attention should be given to content building within areas like tele-medicine, distance education, democracy and participation etc.

— Strengthen efforts to mobilize public and private support for improvements of basic ICT infrastructure in developing countries. Sufficient ODA funds -a combination of grants and soft loans -must be raised to cover political and financial risks and to guarantee connectivity in remote areas.

— Support to national strategies for sustainable energy, i.e. strategies based on energy efficiency and renewable.

— Support to capacity building within developing country governments for sustainable energy; the same capacity needs in donor agencies and development banks must also be addressed.

— Before 2010, reduce by half the number of people without access to modern energy services, notably through investments in renewable energy. This would require a crash programme in terms of donor assistance. Priority should be given to small-scale. projects that meet local needs, and on leveraging private finance.

— The development of renewables should be strengthened through focussed R&D efforts and public procurement, thereby driving down the costs of ESTs.

— Launching of a special programme to promote renewable energy systems in remote locations to which traditional grid-based infrastructure does not reach. In such locations solar-based systems can be the only cost-effective option. Through such solutions, vital energy needs like lighting, refrigeration, etc, as well as ICT connectivity can be met.

— Encourage the use of Export-Credit Agencies to promote investments in ICT infrastructure as well as in energy efficiency and renewables.

— Make sure that access to modern energy services becomes part of developing country poverty eradication strategies.

— Promoting debt swaps, by making money made available through the HIPC initiative to support the implementation of technology development programmes.

— Promoting new international centres of excellence in research in technologies for sustainable development.

7

Challenges of Online Environment

The Internet consists of a network of computer networks which span the world. The Internet was developed in the 1960's for military purposes, as a decentralised communications system which could survive damage to one part of the network. Decentralisation remains an important characteristic of the Internet. By the 1970s, academics began to use the Internet as the computer networks which had emerged in universities were first linked with networks in other academic institutions and later to the Internet. In recent years there has been a dramatic expansion in Internet usage around the globe with an equally dramatise increase in the amount and range of material available on-line.

Part of the reason for the growth in Internet usage flows from the relatively low costs of participation relative to other media. The necessary equipment comprises a computer, a modem and access to a telephone line, the cost of which is not insignificant but which is within the reach of many individuals and organisations. It is important to note that the Internet did not depend on commercial incentives for its growth. Rather it has developed essentially from a desire to share and obtain information, entertain, and communicate. Many Internet users view themselves as part of an 'Internet community'.

The on-line environment has now become a rapidly expanding international medium in which literally millions of users are providing and accessing content on a daily basis. For this reason the Internet offers unprecedented variety and quantity of content that is continuously changing as content is added, updated and moved around the world. As no single entity controls the operation of the Internet or the material available on it, it is impossible to form a picture at any point in time of what exactly the Internet looks like, its size or the quality or quantity of content available. Content accessible on the Internet is stored in thousands of linked computers and is equally available by and from governments, corporations, interest groups, institutions and individuals from anywhere around the world. At present most of this content is provided free of charge. Whilst material can be accessed from any computer connected to the network, it is important to note that the content may be actually stored on a number of different computers or 'servers', which need not be in the same jurisdiction as the person accessing or creating the material.

In order to understand the nature of the Internet it is useful to identify the functions which are being performed by those who are participating in the medium. These functions include providing content, accessing content, connecting others to the network and/or providing the telecommunications infrastructure. However, it is important to recognise that, unlike traditional broadcasting and publication models where the roles of content providers, publishers and viewers tend to be fairly fixed, the activities being performed by a participant on the Internet often encompass more than one function and many participants perform different functions at different times. Of all the functions being performed in the on-line environment the distinction between 'users' and 'content providers' may be the most blurred. This is because any person or organisation can access and/or add to content available at any time. For example, a person can read and send text to a newsgroup or mailing list, create a web site or browse and retrieve information, all of which may occur in the same Internet session.

Accordingly, drawing a distinction between accessing content and providing content is more a theoretical construct that usefully describes the two separate functions, which are often performed by the same participant in the on-line environment. The term 'user' is generally used to refer to a consumer of on-line services who accesses material available on-line, typically via a link with the network through a service provider. A 'content provider' is described as a person or organisation which provides content in the on-line environment. Content may comprise text, data, still graphics, audio, video, computer programs or a combination of all of these. Organisations and individuals who provide access to on-line services to other users and content providers are referred to as 'service providers'. This incorporates those who merely provide access to the computer network which makes up the Internet, sometimes called 'access providers', as well as those who provide access along with additional services to their clients, such as assisting clients to transform content into an attractive format display on the world wide web, facilitating easy access to new and/or interesting sites and help desk facilities. Service providers range in size from individuals to small businesses, universities, government corporations and multinational organisations with operations in several countries. Service providers usually provide their clients with 'space' to store content, such as web sites, on their computers, which are sometimes called 'servers'. This enables their clients to create and provide Internet content which can be accessed by other Internet users.

Different service providers have different policies regarding the material which their clients provide and store on their servers. Some service providers requiring content providers to meet certain standards, whilst others do not wish to concern themselves with the nature of content at all. Some service providers also temporarily store or 'cache' popular Internet content from remote computers onto their servers in order to facilitate faster and more efficient access to this material for their users. Service providers who provide access to the Internet operate as part of a network of computers. Accordingly, they enable users to access content contained on their own servers, as well as material held on the network of computers which make up the Internet, which may be stored on computers within the country in which the service providers operate, or on other computers around the world.

Due to the vast amounts of Internet content which can be accessed from computers all around the world, along with the fact that Internet content is constantly changing, service providers are often not aware of, and are not in a position to be aware of, most of the material which can be accessed by those who use their service.

Encryption transfers and the use of alternative routes and protocols further exacerbates this issue and renders the blocking of even those sites which have been identified extremely problematic. The network infrastructure necessary to support on-line services in any country is usually provided by telecommunication carriers.

On-line service providers usually lease telephone and data line capacity directly from the network infrastructure providers, or from 'resellers'. The potential uses and opportunities presented by the Internet for enhancing the way we communicate and access information, educational and entertainment resources appear to be unlimited. Some of the major modes of communication presently available on the Internet include e-mail, newsgroups, the World Wide Web, Internet Relay Chat, voice and teleconferencing facilities to name only a few. Each of these services can be used for a wide range of purposes and each uses its own set of technical protocols. Given the extremely dynamic nature of the Internet, it is highly likely that the range and nature of the services available throughout the medium will continue to develop at a rapid rate.

From the time the Internet was first developed it has been used for virtually all forms of communication, from one-to-one communications to one-to-many communications. Forums also exist for group discussions in real time, as well as over time. One of the main methods of communications is Electronic mail, or e-mail as it is widely known. E-mail allows users to send text messages and files to one another via personal computers. Its popularity stems from convenience, speed of delivery and low cost, as well as the capacity to reach millions of people throughout the world. In addition, the ability to transmit files of information in the form of documents, spreadsheets, graphics, sounds and computer programs as attachments to messages makes e-mail a powerful application.

E-mail is increasingly being used as a mainstream form of communication for individuals, governments, educational bodies and industry. E-mail messages are most often used for private communication, as they are addressed to an individual person or group of named individuals. In this respect, e-mail can perform a similar function to letters, faxes and telephone calls. E-mail messages can also be sent to groups of people who are members of mailing lists. These lists are usually maintained on specific computers to which individuals can subscribe by submitting their e-mail addresses. While some mailing lists are not controlled in any way, others are supervised in that each message sent to the list is reviewed by a moderator who then decides whether to allow the message to be sent on to members. Similarly, the acceptance of new members to a list may be controlled by a moderator. An e-mail can also serve as a form of identification when a person subscribes to additional services or seeks to access content from other computers. However, it is important to note that e-mail addresses need not reflect the actual name of any given person or organisation and a person may have several e-mail addresses and/or use pseudonyms or aliases in their on-line communications.

Usenet 'newsgroups' are another popular mode of communication. The term 'newsgroups' generally refers to a world wide distributed system of discussion fora. Fora have been set up on virtually every topic imaginable and users whose service provider subscribes to a particular 'newsgroup' can access and participate in these open group discussions. Messages are posted onto news servers which are distributed to other news servers around the world. Content providers may identify themselves or participate anonymously. Content providers can also communicate with a wide audience by establishing a web site on which they can display text, graphics, or provide video, audio services and software. The ability to use these modes of communication to reach a potentially international audience is one of the most important aspects of the Internet. It has the potential to enhance social and political participation of individuals and enable the exchange of ideas across geographic and political boundaries.

The Internet's capacity as an educational and cultural resource is enormous. Via the Internet users can access data bases, texts, journals, articles, reports, state documents, encyclopedias and legislation which are held by public and university libraries, government departments and organisations around the world. Many art galleries, museums and cultural institutions have also established web sites containing images and information about works in their collections, providing an enormous amount of musical, video and other audio material of educational value. The Internet also enables researchers and students to communicate directly with others with similar interests around the world. For this reason the Internet has been an extremely important resource for a large number of educational organisations for over a decade and the use of on-line services is well-established in the university and research environments. In recent years, other sectors of education including schools have begun to utilise on-line technologies to extend the reach and effectiveness of teachers' work in terms of curriculum development, delivery of material and provision of professional support and development services. The

Internet also offers new possibilities for 'open learning' and learning by distance education. This has enormous potential to increase access to educational facilities for those in rural or non-metropolitan communities. It also enables students to enrol in a course of study with educational institutions around the globe.

The Internet has the potential to become an important source of entertainment for users world wide. Already vast numbers of computer games, on-line magazines, newspapers, video and audio services are available on the Internet. Whilst many users can entertain themselves for hours 'surfing the net' for information, images and discussions regarding matters of interest to them, it is also important to note that in recent times many existing content industries are starting to use the Internet to deliver traditional audio and video products.

Although the bandwidth available in most countries currently precludes television broadcasts from easily being provided on-line, many predict that it is only a matter of time before full motion videos become widely available on the Internet. Over the next few years it is anticipated that the Internet will increasingly become a major source of the type of entertainment products which are currently available on television, radio, video and CD-ROM. As more secure methods of collecting payment for services over the Internet become available, it is expected that the Internet will also provide a common medium by which entertainment products are purchased.

The international, interactive and decentralised nature of the Internet and its potential for making available vast quantities of content to and from anywhere in the world give rise to a number of legal and ethical challenges. The following is not intended to be a complete discussion of all the issues which arise from the Internet, but an outline of some of those issues which create significant challenges, particularly in relation to content.

Any individual who has access to the Internet can participate in the many modes of communication which function in the on-line environment, expressing their views in the form of text, images, or sound and accessing the vast array of content provided by others. For this reason the Internet has enormous potential to create a dynamic international on-line community in which the relative parity amongst users enhances freedom of speech and cultural, social, political, religious and linguistic diversity.

However, it is important to recognise the critical role which access and active participation will play in this equation. Equitable access to the Internet remains a fundamental issue which will impact on the ability of individuals to participate in the benefits available through the Internet. This will be affected by the economic paradigms operating within both national and household frameworks.

The nature of the available telecommunications infrastructure and the costs of connecting to the network, typically via a service provider, will also impact on the opportunities presented to any given individual. Accordingly, ensuring equity of access to on-line services is emerging as a major challenge which is likely to have a concomitant impact on the issue of access to information, educational facilities and cultural resources and all of the opportunities which flow from these. It is also recognised that whilst the Internet provides the opportunity for immense diversity of content, at least at present, a significant proportion of Internet content appears to originate in Western liberal democracies, and particularly the United States. This material inevitably reflects some of the social, political and ethical values of those communities. A substantial proportion of Internet content is also only available in the English language. One of the challenges if the Internet is to reach its potential as a diverse medium will be to ensure that it does not become an increasingly homogenised environment which enhances the dominance of particular languages and cultural perspectives. In this regard it is noted that many countries have adopted strategies for television and radio to ensure local content and community participation in those mediums. These strategies are not easily adopted or even appropriate for Internet communications.

To maximise the diverse content and range of cultural and linguistic perspectives which can be accessed on-line it will be important to not only maximise access to the Internet but also to encourage all participants in the on-line environment to play an interactive role and contribute to the body of data which can be accessed by others through that medium. If content is provided from a wide variety of sources then the Internet may can maximise its enormous potential as a source of cultural, political, ethical and linguistic diversity which can increase understanding of cross-cultural issues and perceptions. As many new and existing entertainment services, including video services, are delivered on-line in a manner which requires a more passive response from Internet users, it will be increasingly important to ensure that the Internet remains an interactive and participatory experience rather than become a predominantly passive medium.

Most countries in the world place some restrictions on the type of material which may be possessed and/or disseminated within their borders. The extent and degree to which material in any given country is subject to restrictions reflects its particular political, cultural, religious and legal traditions. These traditions vary immensely around the world. For example, in many countries it is an offence to disseminate certain types of explicitly sexual or extremely violent material. Some countries also make it an offence to publish and/or transmit material which vilifies on the basis of gender, race or sexual orientation. In other countries it is an offence to publish material which criticises the government or may threaten national or racial harmony. In most countries certain dealings concerning child pornography are prohibited. However, the features of the on-line environment, including the vast amount of content which is available on the Internet, the international source of much of that content and the fact that the Internet is decentralised, make it extremely difficult to prevent material which contravenes the laws of any particular country from being provided or accessed across national boundaries. The inconsistency between the laws of different countries means that material which may be illegal in one country may be stored and subsequently accessed from countries where the material is legal. It may also be transmitted through a number of other countries, each of which has its own laws regarding the material.

Even where there is some consistency across jurisdictions relating to certain material, such as child pornography, the specific provisions of the various laws relating to the topic can differ significantly, making prosecution and international cooperation difficult. Even determining what is illegal in any particular country can be difficult due to the generality of the various national laws. For example, laws often set out broad categories of restricted material, such as 'obscene' material, and rely on the discretion of courts to give content to the prohibition. This makes it particularly difficult to identify what is prohibited in any given country at any given time. The ability to communicate anonymously in the on-line environment, which enables users to express themselves in a manner that may not be possible in the off-line world, also renders detection of those providing and accessing material which is prohibited extremely difficult. Anonymous re-mailing services can exacerbate this difficulty as Internet messages can be re-routed and copied in such a way that it is not possible to reliably ascertain their source. The encryption of content adds a further dimension to the difficulties of dealing with illegal material in the on-line environment.

Whilst certain kinds of content may be appropriate for adults to access, it may be unsuitable for children. Material which is sexually explicit or violent is often included in the type of content which is considered unsuitable or harmful for minors. Perceptions about the types of material which are suitable for children and young people vary immensely not only across national boundaries but also across cultures, religions and political systems. In some communities there is a high level of concern regarding sex and nudity, while in others material containing violent matter or drug abuse is considered to be the most offensive. Even within fairly homogeneous cultures there may be a wide range of differing views held about the appropriateness of certain material for minors, particularly where the material relates to sex, nudity, violence, language, and drug use. In existing media many mechanisms have been adopted to minimise children's access to unsuitable material.

These range from age restrictions on material which can be purchased or screened in cinemas to time zone classifications which restrict the type of programs which can be screened on television at times when children are likely to be watching. However, the availability of material which is considered unsuitable or harmful for minors presents particular challenges in the context of the Internet.

The Internet allows material to be accessed at any time in an interactive manner. Most material is not restricted in any way, the main exception being material which requires credit card details or some other form of payment is required. Accordingly, there is growing concern about the ability of minors to access material which is unsuitable for them but at the same time a recognition of the rights of adults to provide and access material which is legal in the off-line world. In response to this concern a number of technical options, including filter software products and the Platform for Internet Content Selection (PICS) have been developed. One of the important challenges in this area will be to ensure that these products are able to accommodate the diverse range of views and cultural perspectives which prevail around the world in relation to the protection of minors.

The international and decentralised nature of the Internet gives rise to a vast range of issues which challenge the mechanism previously used to deal with these matters on a domestic basis. The issues raised in the on-line environment include privacy, intellectual property, defamation, issues of electronic commerce and consumer protection, taxation and on-line gambling, along with illegal content and content which may be harmful to minors, to name a few. The role and responsibilities which service providers can and should have in relation to these matters is an area in respect of which there has been widespread debate and raises many technical, legal and philosophical issues. Part of the difficulty stems from the complex nature of the service providers role in relation to providing, disseminating and enabling access to content.

In some situations service providers seek to exercise some control over the content that is available through their service whilst in others they may have no knowledge or ability to control the content which is provided or accessed by users or content providers. In such an environment it is extremely difficult to allocate legal responsibility in same the manner that may have been possible in traditional broadcasting and publication models, creating many legal and ethical uncertainties.

The Internet presents immense legal and ethical challenges, particularly in relation to content. It must be accepted that by its very nature the Internet cannot be controlled by any central body and that its dynamic nature means that it is impossible to even assess the amount or nature of Internet content at any given time.

However, many argue that does not mean that nothing can or should be done about content on the Internet. There have been a number of regulatory responses adopted or proposed in several parts of the world which seek to address some of the issues relating to on-line content. These regulatory responses include:

1. the development of codes of practice for service providers with varying degrees of governmental input;
2. the application of existing legislation or the introduction of specific legislation penalising dealings

with certain on-line content, along with the establishing of e-mail hotlines for the reporting of 'illegal' content;

3. technical developments for controlling children's access to Internet content, including filter software and content labelling; and

4, the adoption of programs for community education.

A number of international bodies have also begun to consider the issues raised by the growth of the Internet, and the opportunities for international cooperation.

Codes of practice, or codes of conduct as they are sometimes called, are increasingly being used in various industries around the world to provide a regulatory framework which is more flexible than legislation and in respect of which the relevant industry plays an important role. Codes of practice may be developed entirely by industry, or they may be developed following a consultative process between industry and government. In some cases codes of practice operate within class licensing regimes. Codes of practice, mainly for service providers, are being developed in a number of different countries to try and address some of the issues arising in the on-line environment by setting out goals and best practices for participants in the on-line environment. The codes may deal with a wide range of issues, including but not limited to the rights and responsibilities of relevant parties in regard to providing and accessing content, the minimum age of subscribers, privacy and data protection, fair trading, advertising and promotional material, and the provision of information about the options available to parents to manage children's access to material which may be unsuitable to them.

In Australia a substantially self-regulatory regime for on-line services was recommended by the Australian Broadcasting Authority in its Investigation into the Content of On-Line Services: Report to the Minister for Communications and the Arts, delivered in June 1996 . The report recommended that industry codes of practice should be developed by on-line service providers. The main elements of the proposed regulatory framework are:

1. the identification of matters which should be included in codes of practice for service providers, which provide appropriate community safeguards, including complaints handling procedures;
2. the registration by the ABA of such codes of practice, developed by service providers after a process of public consultation; and
3. the monitoring of the codes of practice, and their effectiveness, by the ABA.

The matters identified for inclusion in the codes include age verification procedures which aim to limit the holding of open on-line accounts to persons over the age of 18 years; the adoption of procedures to deal with illegal material; the provision of information for users and content providers on legislation which may be relevant in an on-line environment; and the provision of information to users regarding filter products or on-line services which are available to those who wish to restrict access to material which may be unsuitable for children. It was also proposed that the codes should encourage content providers to label their content in accordance with PICS compatible labels. In the United Kingdom the on-line industry has developed a self-regulatory regime which has the support of the Department of Trade and Industry, the Metropolitan Police and the Home Office.

The central tenet of the scheme is the Safety-Net initiative which has the support of the Internet Service Providers Association (ISPA), along with the London Internet Exchange (LINX).

The scheme involves three key elements; rating content; reporting of content which may be illegal; and the exercise of responsibility by service providers in putting in place appropriate procedures to deal with illegal material once it has been identified. As part of the scheme ISPA has developed a draft code of practice as a starting point from which a more comprehensive code could be developed. The current draft code requires ISPA members to use their reasonable endeavours to ensure that services and promotional material does not contain content which is in breach of the law; encourages anything which is in any way illegal; contains material which incites violence, sadism, cruelty or racial hatred; or facilitates prostitution. The code also addresses matters of data protection, fair trading, pricing information and complaints procedures. The UK Government has stated that service providers who cooperate with the Safety-Net proposals will reduce their risk of prosecution by demonstrating that they have done all that can reasonably be expected to comply with the law.

A somewhat different regulatory scheme has emerged in Singapore. In that country a class licensing scheme for the Internet has been developed . Under the scheme Internet service providers must register with the Singapore Broadcasting Authority (SBA) and comply with the conditions of the class license. All licensed Internet service providers and relevant Internet Content providers are required to comply with the Internet Content Guidelines which have been developed as part of the scheme and satisfy the SBA that they have taken adequate steps to fulfil this requirement. Service providers must also develop Acceptable Use Policies for Internet account holders and comply with any codes of practice as the SBA issues from time to time. In Malaysia, a major source of regulation to date has been the conditions of service pertaining to the state owned Joint Advanced Research Integrated Networking (JARING) network. These set out the rules applying to Internet services and include the provisions that those using the network shall not use it for any activities not allowed under any law of Malaysia . Until recently the JARING was the only service provider in Malaysia but recently a second operator, Malaysia Telekom Berhad, is reported to have begun trading in Malaysia.

Most countries have some laws which makes it an offence to publish and/or distribute certain material. In some countries it is also an offence to possess certain material, such as child pornography. In some cases existing legislation regarding the publication, distribution and possession of certain types of content has been drafted in a manner which enables it to encompass material transmitted and accessed on-line. However, in other jurisdictions specific legislation to deal with illegal content in the on-line environment has been proposed or introduced.

In Singapore licensees are required to use their best efforts to ensure that their services does not include Internet content which is 'against the public interest, public order, national harmony or which offends against good taste or decency'. The scheme identifies particular Internet content which falls within this category. This includes, inter alia, content "which propagate permissiveness or promiscuity", "tends to bring the Government of Singapore into hatred or contempt, or which excites disaffection against the Government of Singapore." In contrast it seems that at least some content of this nature would not be illegal in the United Kingdom and Australia.

In the United Kingdom codes of practice are being utilised to place obligations on service providers to deal with, and where possible, remove illegal content from their servers once it has been identified. In exchange for complying with these procedures service providers may receive some protection from prosecution . In Australia the proposed regulatory regime also envisages that codes of practice for service providers will include appropriate procedures to deal with illegal content if and when it has been brought to a service providers attention. It has been suggested that compliance with codes of practice could be a defence in any prosecution against a service provider.

One of the recent responses to the issue of illegal content has been the setting up of reporting agencies, often referred to as 'e-mail hotlines'. These agencies enable Internet users who locate content which they believe is illegal to report their finding to a reporting agency which will investigate the content and may take action in relation to the material. To date e-mail hotline services have been identified in Singapore and the United Kingdom. In the United Kingdom an e-mail hotline has been set up under the Safety-Net Initiative. The Hotline service is operated by Internet Watch and "aims to enhance the enormous potential of the Internet to inform, educate, entertain and conduct business by ... hindering the use of the Internet to transmit material which is illegal in the UK". The first priority of the scheme is child pornography.

Internet Watch operates by encouraging Internet users to report content which they believe to be child pornography. Reports can be made by telephone, facsimile or e-mail and should contain a brief description of the material in question and the location of the site (i.e the world wide web address or the Usenet newsgroup details).

Upon receiving a report Internet Watch examines the material and if it considers it illegal will seek to trace its origins. Where the material has been identified as being sourced within the United Kingdom then Internet Watch will request that the relevant service provider contact the person who has placed the material on-line and seek to have the material removed. If material is not removed and/or if it involves child pornography, then Internet Watch will forward details to the Police. Under the scheme the police are to provide feedback to Internet Watch on the outcome of their report. Where the material is sourced from outside of the United Kingdom then Internet Watch will forward to the police the information about the site who will notify the relevant overseas law enforcement agency.

In Singapore, as part of its regulatory regime established in July 1996, the Singapore Broadcasting Authority has also set up a 'hotline' for identifying 'objectionable content'. The SBA has stated that the success of Internet content will depend very much on industry self-regulation and community action and has welcomed public assistance in the identification of material which is considered 'objectionable' under the laws of Singapore. Reports can be made by e-mail, telephone or post. In Australia the Australian Broadcasting Authority in its Report on the Content of On-Line Services supported in principle the establishment of e-mail hotlines for the reporting of child pornography. The ABA understands that the police bodies and law enforcement bodies are presently examining the viability of establishing such an agency in Australia.

Parental or teacher supervision is the most effective way of managing children's access to the Internet. However, it is widely recognised that this is not always possible and over the last decade, a range of software products have been developed for use on computers in the home and in schools in response to the perceived need for parents, teachers and supervisors to filter out or block Internet content which they do not consider suitable for minors in their care. Filter software can be provided to the user by the on-line service provider or purchased independently by the consumer for use at the individual computer level.

Some service providers also offer a filtering service which is specifically designed for use by minors. Filtering programs work in three main ways:

1. sites are blocked with reference to a list of known newsgroups, world wide web sites, File Transfer Protocol (FTP) and Gopher sites. Censoring decisions may be made centrally by the software producer with sites updated regularly, and/or by users instructing their system to block a particular site(s);
2. requests for, or receipt of, information which contains specified keywords or phrases are blocked. The keywords or phrases can be specified by the software manufacturer or by the end users who can manage the blocking of web sites by entering keywords and phrases in accordance with criteria they consider appropriate; and

3. all sites are blocked except those which are specified by the supervisor ('blanket blocking'). These programs usually provide an original unblocked list of known educational sites, and the supervisor is able to unblock new sites through a password secured interface.

Some products enable parents to combine some of these functions, while others offer additional features such as auditing of all on-line activity, including listing sites accessed, restricting the amount of time spent on-line and limiting access to some services such as bulletin boards. Whilst the first generation of filter products offer parents some tools to control their children's access to unsuitable material, some users have found that they have a number of limitations. For example, products which are based on recognition of keywords and phrases are not able to filter explicit graphic images or deal with encrypted data or transposed text. Conversely, sites of value to the user may also be blocked if they contain specified keywords or phrases. For example, press reports stated that at one time access to the White House web site was blocked by a filter responding to the word 'couple'. Where software producers are responsible for the blocking of material they may restrict content which is considered acceptable to the parent/supervisor. Where filter software operates by means of 'blanket' blocking, access to a considerable amount of potentially valuable material would be denied and parents and teachers would in many cases have to allocate considerable resources to enable access to appropriate material. However, there have been some recent international developments with content and selection software which have provided additional options for parents. This technology is called the Platform for Internet Content Selection (PICS). PICS was developed by the World Wide Web Consortium (W3C). W3C is a non-governmental cross-industry group which has offices in USA, France and Japan and comprises representatives of the computer, communications and content industries, as well as trade associations and public interest groups. PICS works by establishing a series of file formats that allows independent rating services to label Internet content in a form that can be recognised by PICS enabled software. The PICS labelling conventions do not dictate the use of any particular labelling scheme or determine who should pay attention to which labels.

The PICS technology allows any organisation or individual to develop a labelling system which reflects their tastes and standards and, if they wish, enable others to also use these labels. PICS compatible software can be set to block out all unrated content, or to only block content which has been rated in a certain manner. There are a number of scenarios in which PICS labels can be used. For example, labels may be developed to indicate whether Internet content contains sexual or violent material, enabling parents to select or block the material accordingly. A teacher might label a set of materials which are relevant to an astronomy lesson and block student access to everything else during that class. Those concerned about Nazi propaganda and other hate-speech available on-line, could label material that is historically inaccurate or that promotes hate, and businesses may wish to use labels to block their employees from visiting recreational sites during hours of office hours. Labelling can be applied directly by content providers at the time or after a site is posted on the Internet or it can be applied by a third party in accordance with an established labelling system. The creators of PICS envisaged that it could be used to support a large number of different labelling schemes which may have a multitude of different purposes. A number of organisations have already begun to establish labelling schemes which can interact with the PICS standards, most of which have been developed in North America and aim to assist parents in managing their children's access to Internet content. Examples are the Recreational Software Advisory Council labelling scheme for the Internet (RSACi), SafeSurf, Cyber Patrol and Net Shepherd.

One of the PICS compatible labelling schemes which has gained increasing prominence is the descriptive labelling scheme developed by the Recreational Software Advisory Council (RSAC) and is discussed below by way of example. The RSACi labelling system addresses four matters. These are the level of violence, sex, nudity, and language, including hate language, which a site contains. Internet content can be given a rating between 0 and 4 on each of these topics. The label aims to provide a description of the content in an Internet site rather than make a judgement about the appropriateness of content for any given audience or purpose. In some ways the descriptive RSAC labels can be seen as analogous to the labels applied to foodstuffs which merely provide information about ingredients of a product, rather than vouch for its suitability for consumption. One of the uses of a descriptive labelling schemes is that it enables parents to set their own standards about the material which they or their children access. For example, parents who are concerned about sexual content are able to set their PICS compatible software to block out material which has been given a high rating for sexual content. Other parents may be more concerned about language and/or violence and so can also can set their software to block out highly rated material of this nature. If the material has been rated then parents can use the labels to control Internet content, regardless of where they or the content is located. Importantly, those who are not concerned to block their own access to Internet materials need not activate those tools.

A proliferation of PICS compatible labelling schemes, perhaps being developed by a range of industry, community and governmental bodies around the world could serve many functions, including giving consumers a range of choices in relation to the values and perspectives which underpin the various labelling schemes and the purposes for which they can be used. This has the ability to reflect a diversity of different cultures and values and provide individuals with real choices about the filtering software and nature of Internet content which they access. However, for labels to be a truly effective tool for parents and supervisors many argue that a critical mass of content needs to be labelled. This raises the issue of whether it would be advantageous to develop a small number of international labelling schemes which can be widely recognised by content providers and users around the globe.

The Safety-Net initiative developed in the United Kingdom originally supported the use of the RSACi labeling scheme and proposed that service providers require their users to rate their web sites using RSACi labels. However, the ABA understands that there have been some recent developments in this regard and that Internet Watch Foundation has undertaken to work with the on-line industry in that country to develop a PICS compatible labeling scheme which meets the specific requirements of users in the United Kingdom. In

Australia labelling Internet content was given detailed consideration in the ABA's Report into the Content of On-Line Services. While recognising that labelling schemes might have many uses, the protection of children from unsuitable material was seen as one of the primary uses. The Report recommended that an On-Line Labelling Task Force be established to encourage development of an Australian labelling scheme for on-line content which was compatible with PICS or any superior standards which might be developed. The ABA is also conscious of the need to ensure that an Australian Labelling scheme is, as far as possible, consistent with international ratings developments. This is to ensure that Australian content providers and users of the labelling schemes are not disadvantaged in terms of both having Australian content accessed by users around the world, or accessing a wide variety of material when using utilising the labels.

Under the Singaporean regulatory regime for on-line services, localized service providers and parents are encouraged to use filter software products such as Net Nanny, SurfWatch, Cyber Patrol and Net Shepherd. The ABA notes that some of these filter products are compatible with the PICS standards. As an additional measure to protect young Internet users the SBA also requires schools, libraries and Internet service providers which provide access to children to institute tighter levels of controls. The SBA has announced that it is presently working with the Minister of Education and National Library Board to identify options for implementing an acceptable level of control.

The potential benefits of the on-line environment for enhancing the way we communicate, educate, inform and entertain ourselves has been widely recognised.

However, it is also recognised that community understanding of the nature of on-line services, including the opportunities which they present and the options available for managing children's access to those services will be critical if the Internet is to be used in the most productive manner. Many countries have adopted or proposed strategies for enhance community understanding of the Internet and the opportunities which it offers. A priority for many of these programs is parental education, as many parents feel that they do not have as much experience in relation to on-line services as their children and therefore are unable to effectively utilise some of the technical options available to them for limiting children's access to unsuitable Internet content. A number of programs have also been proposed or introduced to enhance the knowledge and technical ability of teachers who will play an important role in ensuring that children are able to maximise the benefits of on-line services.

In Australia the importance of community education in terms of promoting the most beneficial use of the Internet and ensuring that users, particularly parents, were aware of the options available for managing children's access was recognised in the ABA's Report on its Investigation into On-line Services. The report recommended, inter alia, that a community education strategy be developed to provide information about on-line services and that the strategy target parents and guardians. It was proposed that information might be distributed via school and parent networks, at the point of sale for computer hardware and software, as well as on relevant web sites. The report also recommended that research be undertaken by the ABA and other relevant bodies to assist in determining the requirements of parents and guardians in relation to managing children's access to Internet content.

There have also been a number of initiatives developed in the school environment. These include the Education Network Australia (EdNA) project which obtained in principle agreement form all Australian, State and Territory Governments at a meeting of the Ministerial Council on Education, Employment, Training and Youth Affairs in May 1995. The project aims to provide Australia wide access to educational products and services relevant to Australian educators. Another project which has been developed is oz-TeacherNet.This is a service which has been developed to meet the needs of teachers to make greater use of the resources, professional development and curriculum opportunities which the Internet offers. In terms of student usage, a number of different approaches have been adopted by schools to manage access to unsuitable material, including the development of acceptable use policies, student contracts, and restricting access to particular sites or Internet functions such as newsgroups at the school or service provider level.

In Malaysia, as part of the drive to ensure the success of the Multimedia Super Corridor (MSC), a number of major initiatives are being undertaken. One of these is the connection of all schools within the MSC to the Internet by 1998. In a speech for the opening of Multimedia Asia on 1 August 1996, the Prime Minister of Malaysia, Yab Dato Seri Dr Mahathir Bin Mohamad announced that the Malaysian Government is working to increase the role of multimedia in education: Teachers will need to change their role in the electronic classroom from being information providers to counsellors in order to help the students know how to select information sources, to make judgements about what they are downloading ... The measure of our success in 2020 will be the number and quality of our people who can add value to information. To that end, we will be creating a Multimedia University and technology schools within the MSC.

In Singapore the SBA has expressed an intention to complement its regulatory regime with public education initiatives which alert parents to the ways in which they may protect their children from 'objectionable material and cyberspace abuses'. As part of its strategy the SBA has also set up a web site called 'Tips for Parents' page. In the UK there have been a number of initiatives undertaken by various organisations which seek, amongst other things, to enhance community understanding of the Internet and provide some guidance for parents on how they might manage their children's use of the Internet. NCH Action for Children, Britain's largest child care charity, provides an example of a non-government organisation (NGO) on-line initiative aimed at educating parents about the Internet. The organisation's web site includes a 'Parent's Guide to the Internet' and advice on getting the best from the Internet. It also attempts to explain some commonly used Internet jargon, as well as provides some useful contacts. These contacts include the NETCOM parent's advice line, a 24 hour telephone advice line, and the parents information network. The network is a national information technology organisation offering help to parents who want to use computers with their children. The 'Useful Contacts' page also includes hyperlinks to the PICS and RSACi web sites. In July 1996 the House of Lords Select Committee on Science and Technology published a report titled Information Society: Agenda for Action in the UK on 23 July 1996. The report contained 40 recommendations for action to promote the development of the Information Society. A number dealt with information technology in schools and the Government has responded to the Report with a number of strategies to improve teacher competence in this area and increase the number of schools connected to the Internet.

There has been an increasingly amount of discussion regarding the importance of international cooperation in maximising the opportunities and meeting some of the challenges presented by the Internet. Two international bodies who have recently focussed on these issues are the European Commission (EC) and Organisation for Economic Cooperation and Development (OECD). The European Commission (EC), in its Green Paper on the Protection of Minors and Human Dignity in Audiovisual and Information Services, considered that the main tasks which the on-line industry should address are:

1. drawing up a code of conduct and concrete measures within a framework defined by cooperation between national government departments;
2. identifying areas where there may be a need for common standards on the labelling of material; and
3. promoting the PICS standard or equivalent systems with a view to reaching, as quickly as possible, a critical mass of labelled material, navigation systems and/or parental control devices which are mutually compatible.

The Report of the European Commission's Working Party on Illegal and Harmful Content on the Internet has also proposed, inter alia, that a self-regulatory scheme be developed for the on-line environment comprising:

1. a code of conduct for Internet service providers, including access providers, host service providers and anonymous re-mailers; ?a hot-line for complaints from the public, with appropriate safeguards against misuse; and
2. an independent self-regulatory body, including representatives of industry and users, to advise on whether or not a breach of the code of conduct has occurred (without prejudice to the due process of law).

The Organisation for Economic and Cultural Development (OECD) has recently been asked to consider two proposals concerning the regulation of the Internet. The first of these is a proposal of the French Government for a general agreement on international cooperation for regulation of the Internet with a view to enhancing the economic and cultural potential of the Internet and to combat illegal activities.

The proposal points to three priority areas for cooperation:

1. the definition of a typology of players and the methodological rules to be applied;
2. a list of guidelines aimed at guaranteeing the respect of basic ethical rules and improving consumer protection; and
3. principles for judicial and police cooperation.

Signatories to the agreement will promote the establishment by economic players of a voluntary code of conduct. The codes are to safeguard various principles, including the principle of respect for human dignity and of public order (in particular through use of filtering software), the principle of protection of privacy, and the principle of consumer protection. The Belgian government has also recently put forward a proposal to the OECD for a convention aimed at prohibiting the transmission on the Internet of content that encourages the exploitation of and sexual violence to children. The ABA understands that this matter is presently being considered by the Committee for Information, Computer and Communications Policy (ICCP).

The unique features of the Internet give rise to an environment which provides enormous opportunities for enhanced communication and civic participation, education and entertainment for individuals and organisations around the world. The Internet has the potential to reflect a diverse range of cultural, political, religious and linguistic perspectives and enhance our understanding of across different cultures. But along with these immense opportunities, the Internet also presents a number of particular challenges.

Privacy on Internet

The impacts of Globalization, Relativism, the New World Order, Materialism, Egocentricism, Hyper Consumerism, invasive technologies, the uncontrollable flood of information, the advent of genetic manipulation and perhaps genetic control, the corrosion of the notion of the sacred in modern post-industrial societies and many other factors have disturbed the ladder of values in each and every society. The insatiable greed for more instant pleasure has added a spinning potential to the tempo of change. Due to this uncontrollable hyper acceleration in all the venues of life including cyber crime, some would state that a rational utilitarian scale of values could govern human behaviour.

As mentioned in Sautter's report "To prevent the loss of hundreds of thousands of dollars in wasted man-hours and bandwidth more and more employers are using special software to monitor their employees' Web browsing and e-mail traffic". Marketers can spy on you by using cookies. A cookie is a unique text file that is placed on your hard drive the first time you access certain websites. It is like a personal serial number used to identify your computer on your next visit to the site but the cookie also enables the marketers to gather information about your browsing preferences.

According to the Washington based privacy research group EPIC, 86 out of 100 tested online companies work with cookies. The gathered information about the customers could be sold to other persons or entities".Hackers can spy on you by using Trojan horses coming in the guise of backdoor computer programs which once infiltrating into your computer allows hackers to access it and take control. Hackers can even spy on your E-mail as it passes through the several web servers. At any of these relay points your message is vulnerable to snooping.

Skillful hackers can also hijack a router and then read or mess around with the text messages stored in it. Sniffer programs may scan traffic for specified terms, cyber snoops can capture Internet account login IDS & passwords and use them to surf the web at owner's expense and web based E-mail services are particularly open to intruders. Some sovereign states run electronic surveillance systems around the world and scan the web for signs of criminal activity, monitoring E-mail communications eavesdropping on chat room conversations and generally tracking the traffic on the net. Echelon, a massive cold war-era surveillance network run by the intelligence services of the U.S., U.K., Canada New Zealand and Australia, is the world's most extensive spy system for nonmilitary targets and the one most likely to be watching as you roam the Web. Some 90% of Net traffic is said to be scanned by Echelon. Several countries also run their own national Web surveillance systems.

According to Duncan Campbell "the Echelon system can access and process all of the world's satellite communications automatically". A large part of Echelon is devoted to the INTELSAT network of Geo stationary communications satellites. Cable tapping is harder, however, as with cryptography itself Echelon is fighting a loosing battle.

As more and more phones become low power digital devices, the range over which they can be monitored and the effort needed to decode them increases, a brand new wireless technology called pulse wireless - already used by the security services - promises to make many transmission virtually undetectable. By autumn of this year, the Echelon interception system will be subject to a legal battle that threatens to blow the lid on this covert surveillance network Echelon when the issue reaches the courts.

David Nataf of the Jean Pierre Millet law firm in Paris is leading the assault on America's National Security Agency (NSA). The plaintiffs, several French corporations and individuals who cannot be identified, allege that the (NSA) has spied on them illegally. He says his team has enough evidence against the (NSA) to pursue damages for lost business and for illegal covert activity. At the center of the allegations is evidence implicating the (NSA's) involvement in spying on European nations' commercial dealings. Nataf's team will try to convince the American courts that stolen information was passed onto US companies, giving them an unfair advantage over their French competitors.

In March 2000, a former CIA director, James Woolsey, confirmed that the US monitors European communications to keep an eye on any economic bribery activities. "We have spied on that (bribery) in the past," said Woolsey responding to the (Interception Capabilities 2000) report presented to the parliament's Citizens Rights Committee. "I hope that the United States government continues to spy on bribery". The controversial impact of Echelon was also apparent on a broader platform, in July 2000 the European Parliament voted to set up a Temporary Committee of inquiry on the Echelon interception system.

It is suggested that multinational companies may have taken their cue from Echelon and are carrying out their own surveillance work. Some have suggested they may even cooperate with secret government snooping. Industrial espionage is not a new phenomenon, but as information becomes ever more vital to companies and integral to their practices it is easy to see that the incentives are greater than ever.

A Scientific and Technical Options Assessment (STOA) report called Development of Surveillance Technology and Risk of Abuse of Economic Information presented to the European Union December 1999 concludes that: "Although it is very difficult to quantify the losses caused by industrial espionage, the losses incurred by European firms can reasonably be put at several billion Euros per year". These are some of the issues affecting the Right of Privacy on the networks. The matrix of interceptors includes individuals, corporations, multinational companies and even sovereign states. Efforts are evolving to inquire into these interception activities and even to condone their acts pursuant to the right of privacy on the networks and global communication. As with any issue involving communities at large, a multitude of interception techniques have been described and elaborated on. Some even sound extremely credible and others are generally discarded as unimaginable at the current state of technology.

Legal Protection to Privacy

The law has a functional role by deterring any potential perpetrator from committing a criminal act and it also has a curative effect in devolving compensations for damages if an illicit act is committed. The legal texts covering this area are various as we have previously mentioned and they constitute two faces of one coin. One face is information protection laws and the other is telecommunications protection laws. Their symbiotic effect produces the legal deterrent and protection. To be criminalized and penalized by the law, the acts of violation of the right of privacy should constitute crimes in conformity with the old Latin rule. We should bear in mind that criminal law texts are interpreted very strictly.

In the modern world, we first find on the international level the international agreements and conventions such as:

I The Universal Declaration of Human Rights in which Article 12 states that: "No one shall be subjected to arbitrary interference with his privacy, or correspondence, Everyone has the right to the protection of the law against such interference". A key word in this Article is (arbitrary). Lawful interference is not excluded.

II The International Covenant on Civil and Political Rights. This UN Covenant builds on the Universal Declaration and is legally binding.

By Art. 2.1, the Contracting Parties are obliged to respect and ensure all of the rights recognized by the Covenant, and by Art. 2.2 they are required to take steps to meet their obligations within their own legal systems. Art. 4 allows Contracting Parties to derogate from some of the specific Articles (i.e. Rights) in a Public Emergency. Article 17 states that: "No one shall be subjected to arbitrary or unlawful interference with his privacy" and that: "Everyone has a right to the protection of the law against such interference". This appears to address only natural, not legal persons and reinforces the idea that lawful interference is permitted". The second layer of legal sources comprises the national legislations either enacted by parliament in the form of legislations and acts or in some countries by means of presidential decrees and in said context, we state the situation of the legislation in some developed countries.

In the U.S.A., privacy on the networks is protected by "the Federal Electronic Communications Act (ECPA), which protects all forms of electronic communications - telephone voice communications as well as computer digital communication. ECPA applies to the government as well as private persons and entities. It prohibits any person from intentionally, intercepting an electronic communication, or from disclosing the contents of any intercepted electronic communication unlawfully. It applies not only to hackers but also to those who own and operate such systems such as an internet access provider, a private network operator, the sys-op of a computer bulletin board and the like.

ECPA also prohibits any person or entity who provides an electronic communication service to the public from divulging the contents of any communication. The anonymity of communications emanates according to the U.S. Supreme Court from the right to speak anonymously and is protected by the first amendment to the US constitution. ECPA in the USA sets in place a procedure to authorize lawful interception. Network operators and service providers are required by CALEA (the Communication Assistance for Law Enforcement Act) to have the necessary technical facility and to render assistance to law enforcement agencies. The Foreign Intelligence Surveillance Act of 1978 (FISA) authorized electronic surveillance of foreign powers and agents of foreign powers is regulated to protect the US national security.

To target communications need not relate to any crime, FISA surveillance action are implemented operationally by FBI. Said surveillance is classified. In addition to said legal vehicles the Privacy Act of 1974 imposes limits on the collection and use of personal information by federal government agencies. The Privacy Protection Act of 1980 establishes safeguards relating to materials held by a person reasonably believed to have a purpose to publish a newspaper, book, broadcast, or similar public communication.

The Fair Credit Reporting Act of 1970 regulates information maintained by creditors. The Right to Financial Privacy Act restricts government access to the financial report of any financial institutional customer. The Telephone Consumer Protection Act of 1991 protects the consumer from advertising via e-mail. In addition to a plethora of state laws and regulations. However, the situation in the European Union is thoroughly exposed as can be seen in the comprehensive study prepared by Dr. Chris Elliot for the scientific and technological option assessment program of the European Parliament. According to the executive summary of said precious study "the EU countries are committed by international treaties, EU decisions and directives and each national country by its national laws. Most countries have legal recognition of the right of privacy of personal data and many require telecommunications network operators to protect the privacy of their users.

All EU countries permit the use of encryption for data transmitted via public telecommunications networks (except France where this will shortly be permitted). Electronic commerce requires secure and trusted communications and may not be able to benefit from privacy law designed only to protect natural persons. The legal regimes reflect a balance between three interests: privacy; law enforcement; electronic commerce. Legal processes are emerging to satisfy the second and third interests by granting more power to governments to authorize interception (under legal controls) and allowing strong encryption with secret keys. There do not appear to be adequate legal processes to protect privacy against unlawful interception, either by foreign governments or by non-governmental bodies. A course of action open to the EU is to require telecommunications operators to take greater precautions to protect their users against unlawful interception. This would appear to be possible without compromising law enforcement or electronic commerce"

In Egypt, the right of privacy is governed in by consecutive layers of legal texts both on the supranational and the national levels. On the international level, Article 12 of The Universal Declaration Of Human Rights together with The International Covenants On The Civil And Political Rights are enforced according to Article 151 Para 1 of the Egyptian Constitution which stipulates the following: "The President of the republic shall conclude treaties and communicate them to the People's Assembly, accompanied with a suitable clarification. They shall have the force of law after their conclusion, ratification, and publication according to the established procedure". On the constitutional level, article 45 of the Egyptian Constitution stipulates the following: "The law shall protect the inviolability of the private life of citizens. Correspondence, wires, telephone calls and other means of communication shall have their own sanctity and secrecy and may not be confiscated, divulged or monitored, except by a causal judicial warrant and for a definite period according to the provisions of the law".

In the same context, Article 57 of the Constitution stipulates: "Any assault on individual freedom or on the inviolability of private life of citizens and any other public rights and liberties guaranteed by the Constitution and the law shall be considered a crime, whose criminal and civil lawsuit is not liable to prescription. The State shall grant a fair compensation to the victim of such an assault". We would like to state also that before the prevailing Constitution of 1971 the previous

Constitutions including the Constitution of 1923 safeguarded the right of privacy by stipulating in Article 11 "It is prohibited to divulge the secrets contained in letters, telegrams, phone communication except in the cases provided for in the law".On the legislative level, secrecy and privacy are maintained in several legislations such as Tax Laws, Banking Secrecy Law, The Laws pertaining to Correspondence and mail the laws pertaining to the Civil Status, the laws governing Statistics and Census, the Code of Criminal Procedures, the Penal Code and the Civil Code.

From the analysis of the texts of the constitution and the several legislations previously mentioned, we can conclude the following:

a) The right of privacy pertaining to personal data and information is protected both by constitutional texts and by legislative texts.

b) Eavesdropping, hacking, and unlawful surveillance by using phone lines as a medium of communication are penalized by the texts of the penal code. In the opinion of the majority of the Egyptian jurisprudence.

c) Privacy on the networks is in general protected by the texts of the prevailing laws.

d) To ensure maximum protection, amendments should be made to the text of Article 309 of the Egyptian Penal Code. To penalize eavesdropping, unlawful intrusion, or penetration or unlawful surveillance of telecommunications since the prevailing law protects phone conversations and the penal law is interpreted in the strict sense.

e) A new law governing telecommunications is on its

way to being discussed by the new parliament to be elected, this law organizes telecommunication. In said draft of law an article governing the secrecy of telecommunication is appearing. We shall see the final product after its enactment by the competent constitutional authorities.

f) Contractual undertakings to safeguard privacy may be added to any contracts.

Further elaboration leads me to display that the current Egyptian Civil Law distinctly provides for the right to demand for compensation sustained independently from the right of the state to impose penalties. Egyptian Civil Law stipulates in Article 50 the following:

> "A person whose rights inherent in his personality have been unlawfully infringed, shall have the right to demand the cessation of the infringement and compensation for any damage sustained thereby". And it stipulates in Article 163 the following: "Every fault which causes injury to another, imposes an obligation to make reparation upon the person by whom it is committed".

The sanctity of the right of privacy is protected by the civil law. If the right of privacy has been unlawfully infringed, the victim of said infringement shall have the right to demand before a court of law the cessation of infringement and compensation for any damage sustained thereby. The right to receive the compensation for damages according to the civil law is an independent right from the right of the state to impose corporal or financial penalties on the perpetrator of a crime committed in violation to the Right of Privacy and as mentioned previously. The perpetrator is penalized if proven guilty by imprisonment and/or fine.

The modern world is composed of independent sovereign states. Each sovereign state has its own constitution, laws, and competent courts. As a result of said situation, each law in each sovereign state determines the material acts that constitute a crime. As state laws differ in general from country to country, we are sometimes faced with the quandary of conflicting laws. Some examples can be as follows:Networks intrusion could be considered as a criminal act in a state and not considered as such in another state.A sovereign state may have a law penalizing the hacking and interception of messages on the networks and another state may not have in its legislations any text penalizing said act.

An individual may act innocently on the networks with a party in another sovereign state without real knowledge of the laws of the country with whom he is accessing through the networks and most probably said country would have a criminal text penalizing his behaviour and most probably another legal text stating that.

Furthermore, some procedural laws in several sovereign states would give to the public prosecution the right to prosecute specific crimes such as attempts to disrupt the national security of a state even if the act is perpetrated outside of the borders of said sovereign country. Accordingly, the conflict of laws is a crucial topic pertaining to the governance of the legal conduct on the networks.

The conflict of jurisdictions is another issue triggered by the fact that different Courts in different countries may be considered by each and every sovereign state as the competent courts to see into a case. The law of one country may indicate that a criminal court is competent to try an eavesdropping crime on the networks perpetrated by a citizen of a foreign country against an individual or an entity in the first country. On the other hand, the foreign country and according to its procedural laws may consider its courts competent since its citizen committed the crime on the soil of said country. A third country may consider its courts competent to view the same case before a state security court and not before a traditional criminal court since the act is considered according to said third country laws a state security crime. In one federal state, you may find conflict of laws and conflict of jurisdictions between state laws and federal laws, state courts and federal courts.

International treaties and conventions are the tools used in international law to homogenize the legal principles in the different sovereign states and to harmonize the stipulations of the different national laws & to solve the conflicts.

Due to the international aspect of most of the crimes perpetrated via the Internet or the other networks, the reasonable and ideal solution according to some lawyers would be the governance of the international networks by an international treaty containing positive clauses governing the behaviour of the individuals and entities on the networks and penalizing any infringement of the clauses of said treaty through international prosecution, courts and law enforcement agencies. Said idealistic approach should give rise to an international judiciary able and capable to issue orders and verdicts enforceable against the perpetrators of any criminal act on the net in the various jurisdictions. Said solution is a farfetched solution. A compromise could be reached by having an international treaty stating minimum requirements in the different national laws to safeguard the right of privacy and other rights on the net. In many countries including Egypt treaties and conventions when signed, approved, promulgated, and enacted by the parliament have the force of the national laws. The European model in this context is one of the successful models the model of the United States of America pertaining to the relation between the different states of the union and the supremacy of the federal laws. The elaboration by jurists and professionals of a model law to be used as an example by sovereign states to legislate internal laws, is also another solution. However, enforcement of the Law is a crucial issue facing several problems. In an attempt to display the current inherent difficulties faced in enforcement of the law:

1. The anonymity of the perpetrator;
2. The quasi immateriality of the criminal act that should be proven before a court of law according to procedural laws which are not always modeled to tackle cyber crime issues and especially the immateriality of the conduct on the networks and the immateriality of the evidence;
3. The technical incapability of most police forces to track and apprehend the perpetrator on line;
4. The geographical and territorial barriers; and
5. The preoccupation of the police force with other types of conventional crimes which are called natural crimes or with other life threatening crimes or national security issues and not with cyber crimes against natural personsÿ and many more aspects.

This enumeration is not a complete list but a count of the more relevant aspects that should be taken into consideration regarding enforcement of the law against perpetrators.

UNESCO Virtual Forum on INFOethics

VF-INFOethics is an open worldwide electronic discussion forum carried out from October 1997 to April 1998. This forum was organized as a follow-up to a recommendation made by the participants at the first INFOethics Congress held in Monaco from 10 to 12 March 1997. The forum was designed and managed by the Information Science Department of the University of Konstanz.

VF-INFOethics is not a substitute for meetings in a real-life environment — the advantage of face-to-face communication is too obvious and knowledge and experience with electronic forums is not yet wide-spread enough, at least not among UNESCO experts, who are normally not the typical Internet users. But experimenting with electronic forums can provide UNESCO with knowledge about the potentials of the new medium and can contribute to a more extended word-wide awareness about the importance of information ethics in a globalizing information society. VF-INFOethics thus supports UNESCO's objective as a world-wide laboratory of ideas, in this case via a forum on information ethics, identifying ethical principles, guiding action, devising immaterial strategies and mobilizing political leaders in their resolve to implement them. As potentials or value-added effects of electronic communication forums the following deserve mention:

- Electronic communication forums allow exchange of information between people who are not likely to meet in real life.
- Electronic communication forums, organized according to hypertext principles, allow flexible navigation in heterogeneous information material and can thus develop into a platform of knowledge with respect to the topic of the forum.
- Electronic communication forums, in a Web-based technical environment are normally organized in an asynchronous mode (although synchronous chat techniques or tele-conferencing facilities are becoming more and more available for forum purposes as well). Asynchronous communication allows quasi real-time reactions to the forum's statements but also allows delayed reactions after a period of information gathering or, simply, of thinking.
- Electronic communication forums, compared with the high costs for real conferences with participants from all over the world, are a cheap technology once the technical equipment is available.
- Electronic communication forums, in particular when data-base supported, allow flexible adaptation to different users' needs/expectations, or to users' dialogue behaviour, and to different pre-established parameters such as access and editing rights.

The hopes for VF-INFOethics were only moderately high because we could not expect that knowledge and experience with new electronic communication devices would be very advanced among UNESCO experts. This was all the more likely, given the fact that we tried to avoid an Anglo-saxon and Western-Europe dominated expertise and insisted instead on selecting people from all over the world. The particants were chosen on the basis of UNESCO expertise and recommendations from active members. Only these experts, altogether about 60, had the right to write, but the forum, as a WWW application, was open to the public for reading purposes. The forum's main objective was to augment knowledge and public awareness on topics concerning information ethics and to provide UNESCO with recommendations for further action in the field of information ethics based on the world-wide electronic discussion among experts in the field. In addition to statements from experts, additional information, for example references to pertinent literature on information ethics, to other web sites, to data bases, and to other discussion groups with a similar scope was provided by the central Constance monitoring group of VF-INFOethics. Additional links could be provided by all members of VF-INFOethics. VF-INFOethics has thus developed into an open forum, a platform, or a market place with numerous links to the world's knowledge on information ethics.

The INFOethics forum was carried out in two rounds. The first round lasted from October 97 until the end of the year 1998. The second round was opened for discussion as of Februar 20th 1998. At the end of round 2, UNESCO can be provided with recommendations for further action. It is very likely that the forum will continue to be an electronic floor for UNESCO-related discussions on INFOethics and will then be opened to a broader UNESCO public or to the public in general. This, of course, will raise many new problems. In the near future, the forum will be used before, during and after the second UNESCO conference on INFOethics, which will take place in October 1998, again in Monte Carlo. The software, which was developed for VF-INFOethics and which is continously being improved, can be used for other UNESCO activities, in particular by national commissions for UNESCO or for educational purposes. At the moment, we are using the VF-INFOethics software for a virtually organized course on information ethics in the information science curriculum at the University of Konstanz, Germany.

The forum was opened with a brief general statement about the concept of information ethics:

Information ethics, in general, is the study of commonly held values related to the belief in equality of access, justice and mutual respect arising from the development and application of new information and telecommunications technologies (e.g. the Internet).

Information ethics concerns many fields such as philosophy (ethics), anthropology/ethnology, linguistics, economics, law, sociology, political science, education, religion/theology, artificial intelligence, information and computer science. Information ethics covers both the private/individual and the public/institutional aspects of ethical problems, more and more on a global basis.

For many people, information ethics is likely to be considered as a substitute for traditional civic behavior in the advancing global information society. For UNESCO, information ethics is particularly related to science, education, culture, and civil society in general, both in developed and in developing countries.

The following questions were formulated with respect to the role of UNESCO on the topic ‚Information rich and information poor':

What can UNESCO do to prevent modern societies from being divided into the information elite and the information underprivileged? Is there a need and a chance for UNESCO to fill the widening "abstraction gap" between the dominant information rich and the information poor? Is UNESCO an appropriate advocate to defend the rights of the information underprivileged? What is the role of organizations such as UNESCO in overcoming the information and communication gap both within countries and between them?

With education being considered a major means to overcome the barriers between information rich and information poor - what can UNESCO do to help topics in information ethics be included in curricula at all levels of education?

Can UNESCO play a major role in programs designed to overcome the language barriers between people and nations? How can UNESCO protect the language rights of the non-English-speaking-world against economic interests in one-world-one-language markets?

When information competence is both the ability to access/use globally available information and the ability to produce information services - what can UNESCO do both to allow easy access to the global information resources and to move more passive (reading) societies into active (writing) societies?

What can UNESCO do to protect the rights of developing countries to represent their own way of thinking, of culture, science and economy in regional and global information networks and services?

The discussion on this topic was rather intensive. As a result of the discussion on the topic ,Information rich and information poor' the following recommendations were formulated.

- Bring net access to poor countries by putting existing resources to sensible use in order to promote the development of global and local information cultures and economies.
- Support the development of a World Information Ethos.
- Support concrete projects in information poor countries in order to create country-specific information centres.
- Public awareness on these matters through virtual forums, publications, and conferences should be promoted.
- Provide permanent, specific, and detailed knowledge of existing information activities in information poor countries.
- UNESCO should promote the rights of non-English-speaking-countries and their economic interests.
- UNESCO should promote topics in information ethics to be included in curricula at all levels.
- Promotion activities through international organizations should be based on grassroots efforts as well as on a decentralized and well coordinated basis.

The following questions were formulated with respect to the role of UNESCO on the topic Information as a public and/or a private good:

What can UNESCO do to help the development of public/private structures as an appropriate balance between economic and social interests? What can UNESCO do to achieve and finance the provision of information falling in the public domain to all members of the societies in all countries? What can UNESCO do to provide open access to the world public knowledge heritage? What can UNESCO do to develop a world-wide awareness for the importance of information and communication technologies and systems for all societies and for the balance between them?

As the result of the discussion on the topic ,Information as a public and/or private good' the following summary was formulated.

"Information as a public and/or a private good" stimulated some discussion about the status of information in modern societies. Some concern was expressed about the negative effects of modern information structures (virtualization) on the job market. The participants did not see any realistic alternative economic model by which the shortcomings of the neo-liberalism approach could be overcome. It was suggested that cooperatives may play a major role in the usage of information as a common good. UNESCO should not get involved in general abstract discussions about a new world order. Instead UNESCO should concentrate on feasible projects such as supporting efforts for the digitization of public information (as the world people's heritage) as a counterweight to the power of the market, where information is considered a commodity only.

The role of copyright should be reconsidered as well in order to define a new generally accepted fair use of information. By encouraging free access to the world's public knowledge (the people's own heritage) UNESCO can contribute to establishing a counterweight to the power of the market, where information is considered a commodity to be paid for. UNESCO should use a set amount of funds to support the digitization of public material (e.g. to finance portable scanners). The role of copyright (so far mainly used to enforce market rights) should be reconsidered. Particularly, the rights of users to access public materials should be balanced against the predominantly private exploitation of information. Preservation and transmission of information was considered as among the ethical responsibilities of the present for future generations.

The following questions were formulated with respect to the role of UNESCO on the topic, Trust, ownership, and validity of information in cyberspace':

What can be done by UNESCO in order to establish an ethics instrument for information/content providers by which they may be obliged to care for trustworthy, approved, or true information? Which is the main role of UNESCO in the new property right debate, for example on digital objects? What can UNESCO do to establish a new "fair use" and/or "copyleft" of information which establishes a compromise between the rights of the holders and the interests of society to have free access to information?

Can UNESCO play an active role in establishing trust in information services and electronic markets, in particular when sensitive subjects are involved, such as medicine, law, or political information? Is UNESCO an appropriate and world-wide accepted institution to develop, maintain, and survey generally accepted quality criteria for the reliability and authenticity of information services? What is the role of UNESCO in establishing trust in machine intelligence and services such as intelligent agents or in keeping it under public control?

There was an innovative and provocative proposal to rethink the role of copyright: It doesn't make any sense for authors who already get paid by public institutions to receive additional copyright income. Giving up copyright income could break the circle of high prices and lack of access, at least in scientific environments. Access to the world's knowledge should have higher priority than supporting commercial interest in information commodities. A different answer may be required with respect to entertainment and literature.

On the other hand it was not considered realistic that authors would voluntarily give up commercial rights. Therefore it is not sufficient to change our attitude towards ownership and profit. A solution could be for publishing companies to pay a certain percentage of the author's income to the public, which is explicitly designed for supporting the construction of a powerful and royalty-free world wide public domain of information. This idea of sharing profits from knowledge products can be extended to all organizations which produce value-adding information/knowledge products originally based on publicly produced and financed primary/raw information for the market.

UNESCO is not either WIPO or WTO (although the protection of authors/publishers' rights cannot be ignored, it is not the main concern for UNESCO). Instead UNESCO must bring its own added value to the debate on intellectual property rights, and this means to promote the free flow of ideas by word and image, to give fresh impulse to popular education, and to support all means for the diffusion of knowledge. All scientific articles produced by public universities or public laboratories could be made freely available on the servers of these institutions.

UNESCO should take the lead in a world wide movement to promote this public domain information, and present innovative ideas to ensure distribution and free access to it. In particular with respect to developing countries, economic barriers created by a purely market oriented approach towards knowledge and information need to be overcome. UNESCO should use all its prestige to convince governments and institutions involved in the information/knowledge industry all over the world that they should share profits from knowledge products (especially those which are originally based on publicly produced and financed primary/raw information) with public institutions. These institutions then can produce value-added free-access information for those who cannot afford to pay for it.

The following questions were formulated with respect to the role of UNESCO on the topic ,Privacy, confidentiality, security, hate, violence in the Internet':

What are appropriate measures for UNESCO in order to diminish the amount of violence and hate in the Internet? Is UNESCO the appropriate organization for developing a world-wide code for information privacy? Is such a code desirable or possible? What are appropriate control structures if such a privacy/confidentiality code were ever to be agreed on? What can UNESCO do to encourage and establish the free flow of information in the traditional and new media

Although the concept of information ethics was a topic of discussion in itself and was permanently referredto, there was no formal agreement about this concept besides general remarks such as that information ethics deals with principles of equality, justice and mutual respect under the conditions of a global information society.

Global networks and electronic market places and information services (in the Internet and other prorietary networks) are the environment and the only means in which and through which information ethics develops.

One can doubt whether there is a need (or a possibility) for something like information ethics (or science ethics or market ethics) in addition to ethics in general. The principles of ethics in general — if any — would also be valid for information ethics in particular. The forum's participants were particularly careful in simply transferring western ideas to a global information world and were also very concerned that the unification influence of the global Internet can lead to an unwanted dominant general and ethical culture. This is clearly to be seen on (ethical) topics such as property right, violence in the media, information access and information equity, individual freedom of information, where Western philosophical, political, and economic traditions dominate.

Information ethics is not a matter of abstract academic (philosophical) discussion and cannot result in a new (single) world order of information behaviour, but can be a permanent world-wide process of exchange of positions between people who are involved in structuring the new information world. The global information society is thus a platform for information ethics and the result of the discussion cannot be a single world information ethics but the development of an ethos that makes the public aware and sensitive of the need to take a responsible and not only merely economically determined approach towards information, its production, distribution and usage.

This is the major information ethic topic in the information society. The topic is in its global character comparable to ecological questions and should thus be treated on the same level of political decision-making and public disussion. There is a real need for an international information agenda. What VF-INFOethics thus recommends is the development of a world-wide public responsibilty for information equity (an information ethos) by establishing an institutionalized dialog on information policy issues at a world level, 'some authors hold that a new UN/UNESCO information agency would be an approriate institutional means - and by supporting an open world forum (or many interlinked forums) on information ethics, using the electronic medium and other media as well.

Both an institutionalized and a communicative approach will create global (and local!) information policies and information cultures. This means that one should give up the ideal of a rational, clean and transparent ethical world information order, and see the multi-cultural reality not as a threat but as an opportunity.

The continuing globalization of all aspects of the production, distribution and usage of information is the central challenge for information ethics. The production of information is based on the need for information and refers to its content and quality. The distribution of information raises the question of information ownership and depends on the information resources in which information is represented and on the design and management of information market places where information can be accessed and exchanged.

The usage of information is mainly a question of competence and money — being informationally educated in order to profit from the information resources and being able to pay for the costs of information usage. This is a (political) question of information equity or inequity or how to overcome information gaps.

Considering the importance of the global information society, it has turned out that the participants were mainly concerned about the growing gap between those who are able and willing to take advantage of modern information and communication technology and those who are not. The problem of information gaps cannot be restricted to the difference between developed and developing countries but is a problem in all societies, whatever their technological status. If access to information and the possibility to actively take part in the exchange of knowledge (to have the right to read and write in open information environments) is the necessary basis for all activities in our public and private life, then it is UNESCO's responsibility to support all activities which aim at establishing an information balance in the information society.

A society is information-balanced when information gaps can be overcome. Therefore a consideration of information equity seems to be at the center of all ethical discussion. This is not a technological problem. It cannot be solved by providing everyone in the world with a computer and telecommunication equipment (although the importance of such a programme — to provide in principle everyone with the technological basis needed — should not be underestimated), but by solving the information problem.

The forum's participants agreed that only a free market can develop powerful information market places, information systems and information goods but that there is a need for international organizations such as UNESCO and for other nation-wide activities to solve the global problem of information inequity. Overcoming information inequity does not necessarily mean that global information can be accessed from everywhere by everyone (and at no cost). The creation of content in an appropriate environment and the exchange of information among those who need it (for instance, the south communicating with the south and not being restricted to access of information from the north, as is the case today) is increasingly important.

eEurope 2005: Information Society for All

The *e*Europe action plan focusing on: "the widespread availability and use of broadband networks throughout the Union by 2005 and the development of Internet protocol IPv6 and the security of networks and information, *e*Government, *e*Learning, *e*Health and *e*Business". The *e*Europe 2002 action plan endorsed by the Feira European Council in June 2000. *e*Europe 2002 is part of the Lisbon strategy to make the European Union the most competitive and dynamic knowledge-based economy with improved employment and social cohesion by 2010. It was complemented by the *e*Europe+ initiative launched by the candidate countries in reply to the invitation of the European Council to take on board the Lisbon strategy. Many of the objectives of *e*Europe 2002 have already been achieved and the remainder will largely be completed by the end of this year. To create a knowledge economy, *e*Europe 2002 focused on extending Internet connectivity in Europe. In order to generate growth, connectivity needs to be translated into economic activities.

Progress During eEurope 2002

— Internet penetration in homes has doubled

— Telecom framework in place

— Internet access prices have fallen

— Almost all companies and schools are connected

— Europe now has world's fastest research backbone network

— e-commerce legal framework largely in place

— More government services available online

— A smartcard infrastructure is emerging

— Web accessibility guidelines adopted and recommended in Member States.

This is the focus of *e*Europe 2005: stimulating services, applications and content that create new markets and reduce costs and eventually increase productivity throughout the economy. Developing content, services and applications and rolling out the underlying infrastructure is predominantly up to the market. Therefore, the action plan will concentrate on those areas where public policy can provide an added value and contribute to creating a positive environment for private investment. Fast progress in digital technologies and the decline in prices for information technology equipment provided business and consumers with more powerful devices. Investment in digital equipment grew throughout the 80s and 90s but when computers became interconnected as the World Wide Web took off in the mid 90s there was a particular boost to productivity. The contribution of the Internet to productivity and growth, particularly in Europe, is therefore relatively recent and much more can be expected. Two new developments will have a major impact on the further development of the Internet: multi-platform access/convergence and broadband.

New communication platforms beyond PC-based Internet access are now becoming available. In particular, interactive digital television and third generation (3G) mobile systems driven by common standards open up possibilities for multiple platform access to services. They can be both substitutes and complements. The same holds for the supporting networks. The Barcelona European Council stressed the importance of open platforms for convergence. Broadband connections significantly increase the speed of transmission between computers, mobile phones, TV set-top boxes and other digital devices. This will improve quality of Internet access, making it more user-friendly and convenient for consumers, and enable the full scope of multi-media applications to be applied.

The next generation of services will rely on these features. If fully exploited, broadband technologies will improve the effective use of networks, and thereby increase productivity and employment. Having any time, anywhere access to information will contribute to greater effectiveness. However, achieving productivity gains through effective use can only be realised by restructuring of economic behaviour to exploit the new technologies: adapting business processes, bringing public services online, enhancing skills.

Realising the potential of broadband requires that everyone is given the ability and opportunity to enjoy and exploit its richness and benefits (in terms of health care, education, and business for example). This means that the goal of the *e*Europe 2002 action plan of achieving an 'information society for all remains valid for *e*Europe 2005. By supporting the emergence of alternative access platforms, such as digital television or 3G mobile systems, the new action plan will further facilitate e-inclusion, also for people with special needs.

The more networks and computers become an essential part of business and daily life, the more security becomes a necessity. Because of the value of current and expected transactions carried out online, networks and information systems need to be secure. Security has therefore become a key enabler for *e*-businesses and a pre-requisite for privacy. The internationalisation of Internet management will also be a key parameter for the harmonious development of the Internet, and the EU will continue to work actively towards this aim.

Broadband enabled communication, in combination with convergence, will bring social as well as economic benefits. It will contribute to *e*-inclusion, cohesion and cultural diversity. It offers the potential to improve and simplify the life of all Europeans and to change the way people interact, not just at work, but also with friends, family, community, and institutions and the way companies operate. This is what users are interested in, and this is where *e*Europe 2005 starts from. The objective of this Action Plan is to stimulate secure services, applications and content based on a widely available broadband infrastructure. The *e*Europe 2002 action plan proved to be a successful format and the basis for similar actions not only in the candidate countries (*e*Europe+), but also in third countries. Its method of

i) speeding up the adoption of new legal measures,

ii) re-focusing existing support programmes, and

iii) defining clear targets to be achieved, combined with benchmarking, had a major impact.

The new action plan will build on these successes and maintain *e*Europe as the symbol of European Union policy to develop the information society. However it needs to be adapted with regard to three requirements.

1. Broadband technology is transforming the Internet and opening up new possibilities for interactive multimedia services only possible at very fast transmission speeds. Infrastructure investment is driven by availability of content and services and the development of new services and content depends on infrastructure deployment. The infrastructure evolves and upgrades when new services and applications emerge and vice versa. *e*Europe 2005 will try to stimulate a positive feedback between infrastructure upgrading, both broadband and multi-platform and service developments.

2. Many measures at European, national and regional level in support of the knowledge economy are already underway. Most Member States have national action plans for information society policy, many of which were inspired by *e*Europe 2002. The *e*Europe 2005 actions should therefore go beyond current policies and make a real difference. They must also be in line with the Barcelona conclusions and take account of the discussions at the Informal Telecom Council in Vitoria.

3. Before the end of this action plan, it is likely that a number of candidate countries for accession to the

EU will be members. It will be a challenge for them (and for the current Member States) to meet the targets and to implement the actions contained in *e*Europe 2005. *e*Europe 2005 therefore needs built-in flexibility and should provide for a midterm review of actions to ensure a smooth phasing in of the new members in the action plan.

The *e*Europe action plan is based on two groups of actions which reinforce each other and build a virtuous circle. The first one concerns services, applications and content, covering both online public services and e-business, and the second one concerns the underlying broadband infrastructure and security matters. The targets of *e*Europe 2005 can be summarised as follows:

By 2005, Europe should have:

— modern online public services

—e-government
—e-learning services
—e-health services

— a dynamic e-business environment and, as an enabler for these

— widespread availability of broadband access at competitive prices

— a secure information infrastructure The action plan is structured around four lines which are interlinked:

– Policy measures to review and adapt legislation at national and European level, to strengthen competition and interoperability, to create awareness, and to demonstrate political leadership.

— the implementation of policy measures is supported by the development, analysis and dissemination of good practices. Projects will be launched to accelerate the roll-out of leading edge applications and infrastructure.

— policy measures will be monitored and better focussed by benchmarking of the progress made in achieving the objectives and of the policies in support of the objectives.

— an overall co-ordination of existing policies will bring out synergies between proposed actions. A steering group will provide a better overview of policy developments and ensure a good information exchange between national and European policy makers and the private sector.

The Actions

Policy measures

Modern online public services

i) e-government

Under the *e*Europe 2002 Action Plan, Member States agreed to provide all basic services online by end 2002. Much has been achieved in this area but many services still have limited interactivity. The Commission and the Belgian Presidency held an e-government conference in November 2001 to identify and disseminate examples of good practice. The ministers participating in the conference adopted a declaration stressing the need to further develop the exchange of good practices and to ensure inclusion and security in online public service delivery.

The development of secure and seamless access to e-government services depends on deployment and the effective use of electronic authentication means. The action taken in support of smart card take-up will continue and could effectively serve this purpose by also providing a secure device to support electronic signature. Improved access to public web sites for disabled people is an objective of *e*Europe 2002. In October 2001, the Council adopted a resolution on e-inclusion and a further resolution in March 2002 stating that Member States should speed up their efforts in implementing the 'Web Accessibility Initiative' guidelines. Access to government services can be facilitated by providing multilingual content and making it available on various platforms. Initiatives regarding e-government exist at national, regional and local level.

These are complemented by actions carried out at European level: the IDA programme is supporting interoperability of back office processes, standardisation and the provision of pan-European services and the IST programme is financing research activities. In addition, the Commission is preparing an initiative to follow up the Communication on creating a EU framework for the exploitation of public sector information. At the Barcelona European Council, Heads of State and Government decided on the creation of a 'one stop European Job Mobility Information Web Site'. This and the portal of the EU administration developed in the framework of the IDA Programme will offer multi-lingual point of access for online information and services to citizens and enterprises supporting mobility across borders. The IDA portal will also serve as test bed for multi-platform technologies. In this context, the use and improvement of machine translation systems to fully cover the linguistic diversity of European users of such web sites will be of importance. The Barcelona European Council also invited the Commission to analyse the role that electronic authentication systems can play in removing obstacles to the development of e-government.

ii) e-learning

Member States responded positively to the ambitious *e*Europe 2002 targets. Most schools are now connected and work is underway to provide convenient access to the Internet and multimedia resources for schools, teachers and students. In Barcelona, the European Council set the target of ensuring by end 2003 a ratio of pupils per on-line computer for educational purposes in EU schools. Trans-European networks connecting national research and education networks have been upgraded substantially but, as yet, few schools are connected.

The Commission has contributed to financing some of these actions through the IST Programme, the eLearning initiative and other actions co-ordinated under the eLearning Action Plan. EU measures included support to the provision of equipment, co-operation and exchange of good practices, teacher training, pedagogical research, and the development of e-learning content and services.

iii) e-health

The work of medical practitioners at all levels is becoming more information intensive as sophisticated medical equipment and computer applications are more widely used. At the same time, demands on healthcare budgets are increasing in the face of medical and scientific advances, an ageing population and changing patient expectations. Digital technologies are becoming more important in health management both at individual practitioner level and at national and regional level. They offer the potential to reduce administrative costs, to deliver health care services at a distance, to avoid unnecessary duplicate examinations.

In addition, the Internet is increasingly used by citizens to obtain medical information. Against this background, it is critical that e-health content and services are developed efficiently, are available for all and health related web sites comply with established quality criteria. More than 10 years of research and development in health telematics and in the framework of the IST programme have been undertaken.

Examples of results are integrated regional health information networks, standardised electronic health records, reliable and effective telemedicine services (teleconsultation and home telemonitoring) as well as personal systems for citizens to support and manage their health status. Another important action already underway which will be contributing to *e*Europe 2005 is to improve the use of telematics in the community pharmaceutical regulatory system (e.g. Eudravigilance for safety of medicines, Europharm Database or e-submission for information exchange between regulatory authorities and industry) which is expected to deliver first results by end 2003.

*e*Europe offers the possibility to combine efforts into a strategy to deliver visible results at the end of the action plan. Health data is particularly sensitive, and all actions in this area must be accompanied by the development of the technical and organisational means to ensure the protection of individuals' health information from unauthorised access, disclosure, and manipulation.

e-business Environment

e-business comprises both e-commerce (buying and selling online) and restructuring of business processes to make best use of digital technologies. Since the publication of the ecommerce communication in 1997, the Commission has developed a comprehensive policy in this field. Among the achievements have been the rapid adoption by the EU of a series of directives, which are aimed at establishing an Internal Market for information society services, as well as a number of non-legislative initiatives aimed at promoting self-regulation, notably in the field of "e-confidence" and online dispute resolution (ODR), and the launch of the 'Go Digital' initiative to help small and medium-sized enterprises to better use e-business. In addition, the tax environment of e-commerce has been adapted and simplified, mainly through the adoption of a directive on electronic invoicing as well as a directive and a regulation on VAT on digital supplies.

The Commission has also launched a debate on the future of consumer policy, regulation and its enforcement. It highlights the need to eliminate regulatory distinctions between the on and off-line world and for future regulation to be created in such a way that it neither becomes redundant or stifles innovation and new technology.

Building on the European Competitiveness Report and on the Communication on the e-economy, the Commission is working in co-operation with Member States to support e-business in Europe. The goal is to promote take-up of e-business with the aim of increasing the competitiveness of European enterprises and raising productivity and growth through investment in information and communication technologies, human resources (notably e-skills) and new business models, whilst ensuring privacy. *e*Europe 2005 will be instrumental in making this policy work.

Information Infrastructure

The European Union has already launched a comprehensive strategy based on the Communications on network security, cyber crime, and the current and forthcoming data protection directive regarding electronic communications. The suggested approach was endorsed and further developed by the Council Resolution of 28 January 2002 and by the recent Commission proposal for a Council Framework Decision on attacks against information systems.

Based on the 28 January Resolution, a number of initiatives (e.g. the establishment of a cyber security task force, awareness campaigns, promotion of good practices, and improved exchange of information mechanisms) should be completed by the end of 2002. This will provide the basis for the work towards a secure information infrastructure. Work on the creation of a secure European smart card infrastructure should continue and the roll-out of applications be intensified. Community research activity on security will continue under the Sixth Framework Programme. Priorities will be: trustworthy network and information infrastructures with an emphasis on emerging technologies (e.g. broadband, wireless architectures, ambient intelligence); the identification of vulnerabilities and inter-dependencies in infrastructures. It also intends to support standardisation with a view to wider use of open standards and open source software. Research activities should also take into account the 'human factor' in security, e.g. basic security standards, user-friendliness of systems.

Broadband

Governments world-wide are increasingly realising that broadband access will be central to the economic development of their countries. Wide availability of broadband communication would have a significant impact on the economy, and several EU Member States have started reviewing broadband development on their territory. Their common objective is to accelerate its deployment. The importance of 'widespread availability and use of broadband networks throughout the Union by 2005' has been recognised by the Barcelona European Council. The actions proposed in this Action Plan correspond to this priority.

Investment in broadband will mainly come from the private sector. In its broad economic policy guidelines, the Commission recommended that "Member States should: ... ensure effective competition in local telecommunication networks (the 'local loop') in order to speed up the development of the European broadband network". Competition is expected to drive investment, generate innovation and lower prices. Therefore, public policy should focus on issues where competition is not effective or where political objectives, e.g. territorial coverage with a view to cohesion, need to be ensured. The new regulatory framework, which will be applied in all Member States from July 2003, takes full account of the convergent nature of broadband. Encouraging efficient investment in infrastructure (by new entrants and incumbent operators) and promoting innovation are explicit objectives for regulators.

This means taking account of the need for investors to obtain an adequate return on their investment, in the light of the risks taken. This also means that regulatory uncertainty for investors must be reduced as much as possible. In the wider context of the European Research Area project, the Commission is supporting the full exploitation of broadband networks by the research community. This will continue under the Sixth Framework Program using the new priority instruments of Networks of Excellence and Integrated Projects.

In specific terms, it will support the upgrade and efficiency of technology for optical fibre access networks, mobile broadband wireless services (beyond 3G), broadband access satellite systems (also taking into account the needs of the Galileo system), convergence of fixed and mobile networks, including the transition to the next generation Internet Protocol (IPv6) and take account of security and privacy issues (wireless, always-on) etc.

The Commission has already set out the steps needed to support the next generation Internet in its IPv6 Communication, "Next Generation Internet - priorities for action in migrating to the new Internet protocol IPv6" and those recommendations should be followed up. A broadband strategy will have a complex task as it is affected by many different policies: town and country planning, research policy, taxation and regulation. They are carried out at all levels: international, European, national, regional and local, and by a range of different actors, private sector as well as public sector.

The Commission will deepen the analysis of policy options and existing obstacles to broadband deployment, in particular with a view to widespread access to new services through open platforms in digital television and 3G, in line with the request from the Barcelona European Council.

Dissemination of Practices

In all areas of *e*Europe 2005, commercial and public applications are being developed, support programmes are running, and experimental applications are being tested. These activities are a rich source of knowledge and expertise. Progress is rapid but uneven, for example one administration or school may be trying to develop or use an application already working somewhere else or for which there is a viable private sector solution. *e*Europe 2005 aims to build upon these experiences. It will not only identify and exploit good practices, but further advance them to act as a showcase which will be instrumental to the achievement of the *e*Europe targets. Good practice activity will therefore be complementary to the policy actions. A three-step approach is proposed:

i. Examples of good practice will be identified, and selected.

The Commission, in close co-operation with Member States, candidate countries, and the private sector, will identify examples of good practice world-wide. This would include practical working examples from the public sector and commercial applications in the areas of the action plan.

ii. Where appropriate, selected good practices will be enhanced to broaden their applicability and an analysis will be carried out to produce a template or guidelines for good practices.

Relevant examples would be extended in scope (e.g. multi-platform instead of single platform or additional users) or complemented by additional developments (e.g. greater functionality or multi-lingual interaction). The demonstration and evaluation aspects of these projects will be reinforced, so that a thorough analysis of the results may be undertaken. The detailed analysis of good practice should result in templates or guidelines.

These provide proven, well-documented approaches to tried and tested applications for e-services. They would be modular and customisable for any particular user and would typically consist of a methodology, an associated set of tools and software in open-source form. This would result in a critical assessment of success factors and lessons of failure, which may lead to transfer and dissemination of good practice across Europe, particularly in the less favoured regions.

iii. The good practices and the results of the project analysis will be disseminated. For the dissemination of good practices, the Commission in co-operation with the Council Presidencies will organise promotional campaigns covering the EU and candidate countries.

This will be based on the following mechanisms:

— Conferences/workshops: The e-government conference with its exhibition of good practice examples is one successful model for an exchange of experience and lessons learnt. An e-health conference which will follow this model is planned for the first half of 2003, as is an e-learning conference and a second e-government conference is proposed for the Italian Presidency.

These conferences normally address policy-makers. They will be accompanied by special dedicated workshops which would bring together the actors for the respective strategies. These events will address in detail the good-practice showcases, templates and guidelines.

— Support networks: Results will be disseminated using existing business, academic, research and user networks - e.g. the e-business support networks to the SME's or the European School Net- and other such channels at the European, national or regional levels. Comparable networks will be sought for actors in all *e*Europe areas. The new Innovative Actions programmes within the framework of the European Regional Development Fund (ERDF) offer regions (in particular, less favoured regions and areas under reconversion) the possibility to test innovative tools and to exchange good practices in regional e-services. This will contribute positively to regional development strategies and thus play an important role within the *e*Europe 2005 action plan.

— A web site: Links to the good-practice templates and guidelines will be published on a specific web site which will provide tools supporting their use and feedback mechanisms.

Benchmarking

Benchmarking of *e*Europe is a 3-stage process.

Definition of indicators

For *e*Europe 2002, indicators were used. The rationale behind these indicators is to focus on output, i.e. the final objective of policy, not the policy itself (e.g. % household connected to the Internet rather than any measure of local loop unbundling). The objective of benchmarking is policy development and this means it is essential to obtain political endorsement of the indicators.

Indicators will need to be updated for *e*Europe 2005 to reflect the revised political objectives. From 2004 onwards, i.e. after the end of *e*Europe+, the new indicator list will also serve as a basis in the Candidate Countries. Where appropriate, regional indicators will be developed.

Measurement and analysis

Internet related statistics soon become outdated and, to retain policy relevance, indicator measurements must be available quickly. Inevitably there is a trade-off between speed and quality. To improve the quality, measurement of *e*Europe 2005 indicators should make greater use of official statistics from the National Statistical Institutes and Eurostat. To allow for regular and comparable data collection in Member States, a legal base is needed for information society statistics.

The Commission will propose this legal base before end 2002. Analysis of the factors underlying indicator values is a key element in exploiting the data for policy development. To enable Member States to undertake their own analysis the results are regularly updated on the *e*Europe web site.

The Commission and the Member States will encourage the development of regional benchmarking, especially with less developed regions in relation to the development of national and regional information society strategies.

Policy development

The value of benchmarking to policy development is evidenced by the Commission's Spring Report to the European Council and the Benchmarking report which provided impetus for the *e*Europe 2005 Action Plan. Benchmarking can be further exploited by exchanging policy good practices. To facilitate this, the Commission will analyse the benchmarking results to identify policy good practices, including regional policies of those Member States, or other countries, with best results in terms of the indicators.

A C-ordination Mechanism for E-policies

Over the recent years many policy initiatives have been launched either as a direct response to the e-economy or to build in an e-dimension into existing policies. Examples at European level are policies such as regional (e.g. support for *e*Europe in structural funds), development (e.g. dotforce - the G8 initiative), education (e.g. e-learning), employment and inclusion (e.g. employment guidelines), trade (e.g. e-commerce in WTO) and the *e*Europe+ action plan. At national level equally, many policy initiatives related to the e-economy have been taken. It is not always guaranteed that the various national measures are well communicated at European level. A better overview and an exchange of information between the various actors would enhance the efficiency of e-policies. For this reason, an *e*Europe steering group, chaired by the Commission (composed of Member States and candidate countries representatives, the European Parliament, and, where necessary, representatives of the private sector and of consumer groups, and funded by the follow-up to the PROMISE programme), should be established. This steering group would monitor progress of the *e*Europe action plan with the aim of improving the implementation of *e*Europe 2005. It would also provide a forum to exchange experiences. It would allow to bring in the private sector and make an early participation of candidate countries possible. The group would in general meet twice a year and with executive level participants to allow a strategic discussion.

Financing

The action plan sets ambitious objectives and proposes actions that will need significant resources. This will be met by using and, where necessary, re-focussing existing programmes. To finance projects and actions at European level, the Commission will make full use of the eTEN and the IDA programmes. Both programmes are currently being re-orientated to support *e*Europe objectives. In particular the financial regulation with respect to the eTEN programme would need to be adapted to make this programme an appropriate tool. The Commission will, where possible, also use available funds of the eContent programme, the follow-up programme of PROMISE , the multiannual programme for enterprise and entrepreneurship, as well as the standardisation, the Internal Market and the industrial competitiveness budget lines. The forthcoming eLearning Programme will also support *e*Europe related activities. The use of funds from these programmes will be in accordance with their legal base.

IST financed projects have been directly relevant to the *e*Europe 2002 action plan and the new IST priority in the Sixth Framework Programme intends to continue to finance research and demonstration projects covering these fields, thus contributing (mostly in an indirect way) to the *e*Europe objectives. This action plan is a proposal to Member States to take some far-reaching commitments. It is an invitation to the private sector to work with the Commission and Member States to realise the *e*Europe objectives. It sets out the initiatives the Commission will or is willing to take. Overall the action plan sets the scene for a co-ordinated European policy approach on information society issues.

The *e*Europe action plan has been confirmed as a key element in the Lisbon strategy. If successful, this plan will have a significant impact on growth and productivity, employment and social cohesion in Europe. One lesson learnt from *e*Europe 2002 is that it would be useful to review actions during the course of the action plan. Therefore a mid-term review, which would coincide with the proposed interim benchmarking report, presented in advance of the 2004 Spring European Council is suggested. The European Council in Sevilla is expected to endorse an Action Plan and invite Council and Parliament to adopt as quickly as possible the necessary legal and budgetary instruments to implement it.

Bibliography

Daniel, Evelyn, 'Information resources and organisational structure', *Journal of the American Society for Information Science,* 1983.

Davis Ruth M., "Computers and Electronics for Individual Services", *Science,* February 12, 1982.

Dray James and Joseph A. Menosky, "Computers and a New World Order", *Technology Review,* May-June 1983.

Franken, H., *et al., Information Technology and the Law,* Lelystad (Netherlands): Koninklijke Verrmande, 1991.

Lane, Elizabeth S. and Summerhill, Craig A., *An Internet primer for information professionals: a basic guide to networking technology,* Westport, Meckler, 1993.

Lloyd Andrew, "Europe Examines Electronic Democracy", New Scientist, June 2, 1983. On Council of Europe report, *New Possibilities for Democratic Participation Resulting From Information and Communication Technology,* Brussels, 1983.

Lynn, M.S., 'Digital Preservation and Access', *Collection Management* 22, nos. 3/4/1998.

Maciuszko, Kathleen, 'A quiet revolution: community online system', *Online,* Nov. 1990, 24-32.

Malamud, Carl, *Exploring the Internet: a technical travelogue,* London, Prentice-Hall, 1992.

Marks, Robert 'The Economic Challenges of Publishing Electronic Journals', *Serials Review* 21, Spring 1995.

McMillan, G., 'Technical Processing of Electronic Journals', *Library Resources and Technical Services* 36, October 1992.

Parag Diwan & Shammi Kapoor, 'Cyber & E-Commerce Laws, Bharat Publishing House, 2000.

Parsons, G. L. 'Information technology: a new competitive weapon', *Sloan Management Review*, Autumn 1983.

Simons G. L., *Privacy in the Computer Age* NCC, Manchester, England, 1982.

Rahul Mathan, 'The law relating to computers and Internet', Butterworths India, 2000.

The Spreading Danger of Computer Crime, *Business Week*, April 20, 1981.

Weizenbaum Joseph, *Computer Power and Human Reason: From Judgement to Calculation* W. H. Freeman, San Francisco, 1976 and Penguin, Harmondsworth, England, 1984.

Whisler, Thomas, *The Impact of Computer on Organisation*, Praeger, 1970.

Wood Michael, *Introducing Computer Insecurity* NCC, Manchester, England and John Wiley, New York, 1983.

Index

INFORMATION TECHNOLOGY
A Revolutionary Change

INFORMATION TECHNOLOGY
A Revolutionary Change
(In 9 Volumes)

Volume 2
(Disparities in ICT Access and Use)

Editor
RAMESH CHANDRA
Vice-Chancellor, Bundelkhand University, Jhansi (U.P.)

KALPAZ PUBLICATIONS
DELHI–110052

INFORMATION TECHNOLOGY: A REVOLUTIONARY CHANGE

(Information Technology)

Rs. 8000 (Set)
Rs. 900 (Each Volume)

ISBN: 81-7835-201-X (Set)
ISBN: 81-7835-221-4 (Vol. 2)

Published in 2003 in India by
Kalpaz Publications
C–30, Satyawati Nagar
Delhi–110052
E-mail: kalpaz@hotmail.com

Laser Typesetting at: Varsha Graphics, Delhi
Printed at: Mehra Offset Printers, New Delhi

Contents

Preface

Today, Information and Communication Technology (ICTs) disparities usually exacerbate existing disparities based on location such as urban-rural, gender, ethnicity, physical disability, age, and, especially, income level, and between 'rich' and 'poor' countries. The digital divide is not an isolated entity, but a complicated patchwork of varying levels of ICT access, basic ICT usage, and ICT applications among countries and peoples. The private sector has slowly spread technology to middle income groups, but on the whole they fail to see the developing world and underserved populations as viable markets that require targeted products. Governments often tend to the short-term demands of their constituencies, but do not provide a coherent, long-term plan for prosperity and effective ICT integration, and a legal and regulatory framework that foster ICT use.

Dealing with the digital divide is beyond the scope of any single initiative and technology is not a silver bullet for the world's problems. It is important for organizations doing community ICT projects to bring a global perspective and an entrepreneurial approach, and they must cooperate with like-minded efforts to tackle the range of problems collaboratively. There are some of the key elements necessary for integrating technology into society in an effective, sustainable way so that people can put technology to use to improve their lives. ICT disparities are usually exacerbate existing disparities based on location, gender, ethnicity, physical disability, age, and, especially, income level, and between 'rich' and 'poor' countries.

Measures of the digital divide exists in number and cost of PCs, phones, Internet hosts, Web sites, Internet users, residential/organizational/international Internet bandwidth, technical capacity, and advanced applications like e-commerce. The spread of Internet users among the world's population is much more unequal than that of the use of other ICT such as TV or telephones. The inequality of Internet usage is even bigger than the spread of GDP between the world's rich and poor countries.

National governments can play a fundamental role in creating an environment that will foster technology use and encourage national and international investment in ICT infrastructure, development, and a skilled work-force. These include telecommunications privatisation, standards setting, consumer protection, and government usage of ICT. Economic growth and social equity are both needed to bridge international and domestic digital divides. However, no consensus exists on exactly what policies are needed for either of these goals.

Editor

1

Impacts of Information and Communication Technologies (ICTs)

Information and Communication Technologies (ICTs) represent to today's world what industrial machines represented during the industrial revolution; they have revolutionized ways of working, transformed the economy, had an irreversible impact on the way people live, and have shaped a new information society. The fundamental role of ICTs in the information and knowledge society is widely recognized, as is the fact that there is unequal distribution and sharing of this technology and of access to information.

Universal access or universal service are a fundamental point of all declarations, in particular with reference to the needs of developing countries, where the information society both opens up great potential for development and poses new risks, widening disparities between and within countries. Universal service is the long-term objective of making communication facilities available to every member of society on an individual or household basis, and it is used in particular in the regulatory-legislative framework to indicate the obligation of telecommunication operators to provide their services to the entire population.

However, the objective of universal service is still far from turning into reality in developing countries, and the universal service concept has been complemented by the concept of universal access, i.e. the opportunity for everyone, at home or at work, to be within a reasonable distance of a telephone. In fact, to connect the majority of the poor, especially those living in rural and remote areas, requires innovative approaches, including a shift from individual connectivity, which has been prevalent in developed countries, to community connectivity.

Public access points are indeed the first step toward universal service, and also contribute to raising public awareness about the benefits of communication and information technology-possibly even providing opportunities to acquire computer skills and training. The necessity of universal access to information services is stated in several declarations, which stress the need to broaden access to and use of ICTs, declaring that everyone, everywhere should be enabled to participate in the global information society. The term "universal access", however, sometimes also assume social, economic and cultural connotations, encapsulating issues concerning equality of opportunities, literacy, diversity of content, and so on.

Universal access should therefore be interpreted as material and physical access to information infrastructure and services. Lack of infrastructure, according to a Statement from Developing Countries in the DOT Force, "[is] one of the major challenges developing countries have to face in their efforts to access ICTs as a tool for development". The principle of "universality" should therefore be limited to the need to develop this infrastructure. The need for universal service, several declarations mention the necessity of giving particular attention to the development of telecommunication infrastructures in rural and remote areas, where the telecommunication system is inadequate to sustain essential services-or where there is no service at all, but which are often home to a high percentage of the population.

The physical existence of infrastructures is essential but not sufficient for development of the information society: factors of gender, level of education and literacy, household income, language, race and ethnicity are all critical determinants of ICTs utilization and access within countries, whence the necessity to promote equality of opportunity to citizens, and in particular to encourage the participation of weaker categories in the use of ICTs.

Each country should also promote measures "to help people of every age, background and location and level of physical ability to access ICTs", and States should "actively involve the youth in national and regional ICT activities; ensure better gender balance in ICT use while instituting specific programmes that address the need of women particularly those aimed at rural and disenfranchised areas." The use of voice and touch screen applications that enable a greater number of people to access ICTs and the development of applications and content suited to local needs, harness the potential of information and communication technologies, enabling the population to participate in the information society.

The fundamental element for the utilization of ICTs content. Development of local content on the Internet is a means to ensure a culturally and linguistically diverse cyberspace, and this diversity is also an important part of the cultural heritage and has to be protected.

ICTs provide new channels for the expression of this diversity and for the worldwide dissemination of locally created content. Diversity of content on the Internet would enable the participation of all and ensure sustainable access, realizing the full potential of the Internet as a source of information and knowledge. Appropriate content would also benefit the utilization of ICTs for educational purposes, training and human resources development. The quality and variety of content is of "great importance to encourage more people to join online activities", and "special emphasis should be placed on the promotion of applications that are useful for various languages, such as translation, as well as development and distribution of contents that reflect local cultural or linguistic characteristics."

The Bamako Declaration acknowledged the continent's rich cultural diversity and urged that it should be reflected in cyberspace, affirming the need to "invest in African media content as well as new technologies and develop independent production." The production of local, national and regional content in native languages, and the location of that content on regional servers, can also help in rationalizing access for local and regional traffic and promoting its exchange via the most direct route. Creation of local content, with the help of the international community and the collaboration of the private sector, should therefore be given high priority.

Diversity of content, including cultural and linguistic diversity, should be promoted. The private sector should therefore develop and build information networks with abundant capacity to accommodate a wealth of information, both locally produced and that developed in other regions and nations. Communications can be a vehicle for the implementation of the principle of freedom of expression, as stated in Article 19 of the United Nations Universal Declaration of Human Rights: "Everyone has the right to freedom of opinion and expression; this right includes freedom to hold opinions without interference and to seek, receive and impart information and ideas through any media and regardless of frontiers."

Access to information and knowledge is essentially determined by connectivity, capabilities, and content. It is in these three areas that urgent action is required to ensure full access to ICTs for developing countries. Furthermore, unless connectivity and access are affordable, reliable and secure, prospects for development of the knowledge economy are dim. Where necessary, and particularly in developing countries, physically building up the infrastructure to access to the global information society is the first step. This is then followed by optimizing the use of the information and communication infrastructure through convergence of technologies, interconnection among different networks, standardization and management of scarce resources.

Lack of infrastructure and connectivity are still the biggest challenges to the development of the information society in most developing countries. Very often, infrastructures fail to meet local demand and cannot guarantee a reliable access to global communication networks, therefore, immediate steps have to be taken "for the development of the basic infrastructure necessary for connectivity including for most remote areas." The Tokyo Declaration affirms the urgent need "to develop the necessary infrastructure that will provide access to such resources as the Internet" with the encouragement and support of government and international community, where appropriate.

The promotion of the development of state-of-the-art national and regional communication infrastructures will lead to "upgrading the "capillarity" of information and communications networks within their various territorial units, substantially upgrading key functions such as applicability and interoperability, and facilitating a swifter diffusion of technological innovations". The utilization of the optimal mix of technologies is considered a key element for the deployment of the information society. Asia-Pacific countries affirm that, in order to effectively promote the balanced development of information and communication infrastructure, taking into consideration the geographic and economic diversities of Asia-Pacific countries, it is necessary to use "different technologies and equipment according to local conditions, as well as to take account of changes such as technological convergence."

Convergence is opening up new perspectives for the ICT sector, offering opportunities for e-learning, e-commerce, e-government, e-health, environmental protection, post-war reconstruction and many other applications which are highly beneficial for social cultural and economic development. Owing to the tremendous and multiple impacts on nations and individuals, there is growing attention to multimedia convergence, and more recent declarations are taking this into account in the definition of new telecommunication regulations and development strategies.

Technological convergence is also leading to greater optimization of costs, thus leaving scope for cost reduction and resulting in greater network access. The convergence of communication and computing technologies, especially through the Internet, is the most significant feature of this information technology revolution. The Internet is a widespread information infrastructure. It is at once a worldwide broadcasting system, a mechanism for information dissemination, a medium for interaction between individuals, and a marketplace for goods and services.

It is therefore rapidly becoming a global communications and information tool and a source of considerable economic potential for individuals, firms and countries. For the efficient development of the information and communication infrastructure, harmonization and cooperation is also necessary in such fields as interconnection, standardization or management of radio frequencies.

Interconnectivity is a fundamental tool for the achievement of universal access to services, and for the growth of the information society. "Optimum conditions" should be created for interconnectivity and interoperability. The G7 States, in the conclusion of the Brussels meeting in 1995, affirmed their commitment to pursue the interconnectivity of networks and the interoperability of services through the promotion of a consensual standardisation process which is market-led and which encourages open interfaces. Standardization is another essential ingredient in extending the global reach of telecommunications: accelerating the standardisation process conducted by international bodies will contribute to developing timely and market-responsive standards.

While the standardization process is 'international' in nature, the role of the private sector is always prominent: the G7 affirmed that [c]ooperation amongst all actors should be built on private sector-led dialogue aimed at identifying critical interfaces. Telecommunication services are also based on the utilization of radio frequencies, which are a scarce resource, the allocation of which is carried out by ITU Members at the international and regional levels and by national administrations, through a licensing procedure, at the national level. For a fair and effective allocation of these resources, transparent criteria must be applied.

International cooperation and harmonization, under the auspices of ITU, should be pursued, in particular for services such as international mobile services and the implementation of global mobile and personal systems. International co-operation is essential in such fields as standardization or management of radio frequencies that are needed for cost-effective and efficient development of Information and communication infrastructure.

To improve ICT infrastructure in African countries, the Bamako Declaration, also mentions the need to establish public access points and called for the creation of an African backbone using innovative communication infrastructures, to rationalize access to the Internet. Probably today the global community is ready for a further step in the definition of ICTs development principles and strategies.

Universal access is of course the basic issue, but afterward it will be necessary an effective development of networks, and an efficient use of resources and new technologies. Secure and clearly-established conditions for the use of these technologies must also be ensured for users and operators alike. An enabling regulatory environment, a favourable investment climate and cooperation and funding of the international community are fundamental elements for the overall development of the information society. However, some basic requirements for the development of ICTs have emerged. These include:

— appropriate policy adapted to the new demands of the information society, and transparent and non-discriminatory regulation, to favour investment in telecommunication technology, mobilization of new resources and participation of private enterprises in ICT development;

— cooperation, at international, regional and national levels, coordination of efforts, exchange of information, transfer of technology and knowledge and sharing of experiences and best practices.

In the ECOSOC Ministerial Declaration the need for "a conducive environment" at a national level is considered essential for the "rapid diffusion, development and use of information technology". Similarly, ESCAP points out the necessity of a "supportive policy environment, including telecommunications policy and cyber laws" as one of the fundamental parameters for e-readiness.

The private sector "should be the driving force behind the information society" and "has a vital role to play" in investment in the development of information and communication infrastructure. For this reason, governments should work to create an environment that allows and encourages private-sector participation, for instance by establishing transparent legal frameworks. The private sector plays a leading role in the development of information and communication networks in the information society. But it is up to governments to create a predictable, transparent and non-discriminatory policy and regulatory environment necessary for the information society. Sector reforms are among the major forces shaping the development of telecommunications, and lead to greater private sector participation and competition.

This new trade and regulatory environment places even greater pressure on policy-makers, regulators and operators to acquire the necessary skills and resources to manage the evolving ICT environment. The new model of telecommunication investment, and the entry of new players onto the scene, gives rise to the need for new and "creative models of partnerships between government, the private sector and NGOs.

While the private sector may be the driving force behind the growth of the information society, governments and organizations should not forget that private initiative is market driven, which does not necessarily cater for the needs of the whole population, particularly in developing and least developed countries. In such cases, it is essential for governments to take the lead in promoting equitable participation of the whole population in the information society. However, given the high cost of this participation, individual governments of developing countries find it difficult to carry this objective without international support.

In the establishment of an enabling environment for the development of the information society, the necessity of international cooperation and of "regional and global pooling of resources" is affirmed, in particular with reference to the growing digital divide between developed and less developed countries and to the necessity to foster universal access. Efforts to bridge the digital divide, as in our societies, crucially depend on effective collaboration among all stakeholders.

Bilateral and multilateral assistance will continue to play a significant role in building the framework conditions for IT development. International cooperation should focus on the major impediments to the participation in the ICT revolution, such as lack of infrastructure, education and connectivity. Concerted actions at the national, regional and international levels are imperative for bridging the digital divide and global regional and national financing and investment institutions are urged to attach high priority to the growth of telecommunications, particularly in developing countries.

International cooperation is mostly directed at supporting and financing the development of ICTs in less industrialized countries, but also at promoting "greater international dialogue to bring together the 'best practices in the field of ICTs. Cooperation mechanisms touch every aspect of the information society, and can be applied, where appropriate, to the dialogue, awareness campaigns, the definition of appropriate policies, the development and interconnection of information infrastructures, the provision of training, the distribution of applications and the development of their contents. Exchange of information and experience are among the main objectives of regional coordination, which is focused on tackling public policies on the information society and enabling the "sharing of experience among countries in the region on preparing for the digital era.

The international community is called upon to contribute to the development of the information society by providing "technical and financial cooperation. Cooperation in an era governed by technology must involve not only financing or exchange of information and best practices, but also the transfer of technology and knowledge, in particular in favour of developing countries. [Collaborative] efforts should include transfer of technology to developing countries on a concessional and preferential terms, as mutually agreed, especially technology related to knowledge-based sectors.

Technology transfer programmes and technical cooperation are defined by the ISAD as a key policy issue and are considered fundamental also at a regional level, to harness intraregional competencies to facilitate the transition of member countries into networked societies and economies. Cooperation is essential to develop a harmonious and equitable information society, the benefits of which are truly global. The utilization of ICTs to generate, process and transmit data and information is creating new legal dilemmas, resulting in the need to reform legal protection mechanisms for users and operators.

There is a different perception of intellectual property (IP) in the digital era and new technologies are challenging the traditional instruments of protection of IP. Therefore new approaches are needed to fight violations and guarantee the adequate reward to creativity. Protection of intellectual property rights for IT-related technology is vital to promoting IT-related innovations, competition and diffusion of new technology. With the advent of e-commerce, and of online transactions, the protection of privacy and the security of personal data, from credit card numbers to home addresses or reserved information, is at stake.

Protecting privacy and personal data alongside the safeguarding of plurality of opinion play an essential role in maintaining citizens' confidence in the information society and thereby encourage user participation and strengthen competition and market access. Misuse of personal data and the circulation of indecent information, are serious threats to the stability of ICT-based economies", therefore the definition of a new regulatory system "to minimize the risks and uncertainties of the new environment generated by the information and communication technologies" is sought, to "ensure and lead to the swift expansion of electronic commerce protecting the privacy and other interests of users, consumers and small-scale producers that engage in electronic commerce.

Information security is effectively guaranteed will individuals or organisations take full advantage of information infrastructure. Citizens and society should be protected against criminal abuse of the developing networks. To protect data, however, it is not always enough to ensure the correct functioning of communication networks: cyber crimes such as hacking or the spread of computer viruses could undermine public trust in network resources. Countries should therefore cooperate in sharing information and in coordinating their efforts to prevent these crimes and to ensure network security.

ICTs in Education

Investment in basic literacy and ICT education remains the fundamental way of increasing human capacity in developing countries and should be part of every national information technology strategy. Without the knowledge and skills required to use ICTs, the use of new communication technologies will be impossible, therefore information literacy, i.e. basic skills in acquiring, managing and communicating information is essential to familiarize people with new technologies, and their use. Human resources training, in particular for teachers and students, will also increase demand for the use and application of information and technology and promote content and infrastructure growth, thus facilitating the development of the ICT service industry, in particular in developing countries.

Investment in education, research and human capacity is seen by African countries as an essential element to reverse Africa's marginalization, and could enable the continent to address its scientific and public policy challenges. The Brussels Declaration affirms the need to pursue adequate information technology education and training, which should be integrated into the regular school system, and ISAD adds the necessity of lifelong learning. In addition to the need for training in their use, ICTs can also help in promoting learning: to participate in the knowledge based economy requires new skills, openness and creativity, acquired through life-long training.

Whence the necessity to provide citizens with the tools to learn in an information society, by means of advanced multimedia information services, which can meet such requirements whilst complementing and enriching traditional education and training systems. For the rapid development of the information society, ESCAP points to the necessity of training for trainers. Along the same lines, to promote awareness of ICT issues, many South American countries given a high priority to the necessity of ICT training for political and community leaders.

The use of ICTs can enhance a large number of applications: from electronic commerce and valorization of small and medium-sized enterprises to the empowerment of small communities and groups, they can help in the promotion of good governance and decentralization, the observance of human rights, allow long-distance education and telemedicine, and help in the environmental management and monitoring.

In other words it can help the creation of a balanced and efficient society, based on the free flow and free access to information. In order to allow ICT to provide the benefits of speedier and more efficient economic and social interaction, it is essential to develop various applications. There is general agreement on the potential of ICT applications to help reduce poverty, foster sustainable development, improve health, education and skills, facilitate new and transparent governance mechanisms and reinforce popular participation and informed decision-making. ICT represents a tremendous opportunity for emerging and developing economies.

Countries that succeed in harnessing its potential can look forward to leapfrogging conventional obstacles of infrastructural development, to meeting more effectively their vital development goals, such as poverty reduction, health, sanitation, and education, and to benefiting from the rapid growth of global e-commerce. Some developing countries have already made significant progress in these areas.

The international community recognizes the need to support the development of such applications in developing countries through the mobilization of the necessary resources, cooperation, exchange of information, transfer of technologies as well as new initiatives and projects. Public authorities have an important catalytic role to play in the promotion of research, applications and generic services. They can also further initiatives in the development of applications in areas of common public interest.

Development of E-commerce

ICTs have allowed the creation of a global marketplace, and in particular have enabled small and medium-sized enterprises (SME) to participate, giving rise to good prospects of economic growth and development through electronic trade, investment and commerce. ICTs are now offering SME new opportunities for investment "to compete in the global marketplace and to have access to new business opportunities. Financing and means of promoting SME innovation and modernization need to be sought, special programmes should be undertaken and measures aiming to offer support and incentive to small to medium enterprises to get online and to use the Internet effectively will also be pursued.

Europe needs to accelerate the growth of e-commerce, especially for SMEs, so that they can consider the whole European market as their market. This requires a reliable Internal Market legal framework, which provides legal security, removes barriers to cross-border services, encourages on-line innovation and consumer ttust. One of the main socially relevant areas to be largeted for the development of cost-effective and integrated solution based on ICTs is education.

Education and training are a prerequisite to the use of new information and communication technologies, but they can also help in the achievement and reinforcement of educational goals, thanks to their flexibility and their potential for interactivity.

The innovative approaches to education allowed by the advent of ICTs are highlighted in the Florianopolis Declaration, which sees distance learning, non-formal education and teacher training as an essential basis for enabling the population to play a positive role in new forms of knowledge-based production, while also promoting the access and use of information and communications technologies in methodologies designed to accelerate the educational processes of marginalized population groups and those living in extreme poverty. Human resource development is essential for sustainable social and economic prosperity, and activities that use ICT itself, such as distance learning, can be of great help in human resource development.

ICT in Health

The health sector has become one of the major users and promoters of the use of ICT tools to gather and disseminate knowledge. ICTs give professionals and researchers access to rapid exchange of information, distance learning, and access to diagnostic assistance, and in the view of many countries should be part of national health care reforms and strategies. African countries have underlined the capacity of ICTs to enhance regional approaches to major social issues, as the struggle against HIV/AIDS, and the G7 Heads of State consider "global health care applications" to be one of the main areas of concern, re-affirming the great potential of the application of telematics technologies in the field of telemedicine to fight against the major health scourges.

ICT and Administration

The use of ICTs as a tool for governance can help to foster democracy, efficiency and transparency, and may lead to an increased possibility for countries to attract foreign investment and financial assistance. As stated during the Palermo conference on e-Government for development, ICTs have the potential to dramatically broaden political participation, to increase access to information about the ways in which governments operate, and in facilitating knowledge acquisition and utilization. [...] they are as much about enhancing public administration as about improving the ways in which a society governs itself" The administrative use of ICT particularly through e-government and e-commerce to help improve the efficiency of business and public services including in rural areas.

E-government initiatives should be undertaken in the framework of broad government reform and of an enabling environment, in which connectivity and capacity constitute basic elements. The United Nation Millennium Declaration stressed the importance of ICTs to help achieving the much broader goals of the Millennium Declaration, and affirmed the need to ensure that the benefits of new technologies, especially information and communication technologies, are available to all. Digital technology is also a vital component for environmental information assessment and for early warning mechanisms.

As the World Meteorological Organization (WMO) recently commented, a universal and equitable access to meteorological, hydrological and related information is essential for the mitigation of dangerous weather' related phenomena. Access to climatological information also affects social and economic development, and is of crucial importance for the sustainable development of less industrialized countries. The diffusion and application of ICTs will also have a major impact on global employment. Telework (or e-Work) allows companies to source work independently of location, and offers to countries (industrialized or developing) that have adequate infrastructure and skills the benefits of participation in the new global economy.

It can also decrease the need for migration in urban areas. Telework, however, could have negative effects as it may contribute to the digital divide as well as to the establishment of new laws and regulations for the protection of online workers. In short, the information society is growing, and has to be open to new opportunities for the improvement of human life.

Global Information Society (GIS)

The world is in the throes of a new and highly potent revolution. This revolution will forever change the way we live, work, play, organise our societies and ultimately define ourselves. Unlike previous technological resolutions which were focused on energy and matter, this fundamental change involves our understanding of time, space, distance and knowledge. This revolution is leading to the creation of the Global Information Society (GIS).

In February 1995, Ministers from the Group of Seven Highly Industrialised Nations (G-7) and Members of the European Commission (EC) met in Brussels at the G-7 Ministerial Conference on the Information Society. This Conference re-emphasised the need for all countries, including developing countries and countries in transition. to be integrated in the GIS. However the challenges of integrating the less industrialised countries of the world into the GIS are tremendous.

As South African Executive President Thabo Mbeki argued in his keynote address to the G-7 Information Society, Conference, "there are more telephone lines in Manhattan than in all of sub-Saharan Africa" and that "half of humanity has never made a telephone call." Mbeki challenged the G-7 and the EC to convene a follow-up conference bringing together a cross-section of the developing world with the G-7 and the EU to exchange on such questions as strategy, finance and international coordination in confronting the global information and communication challenge. He offered South Africa as host for such an initiative. The Information Society and Development (ISAD) Conference is the result of that challenge.

The ISAD Conference, held in Midrand, South Africa under the auspices of South African Executive Deputy President Thabo Mbeki, included representatives from 40 countries and 18 international organisations. Delegations consisted of government ministers and senior officials, CEOs and other private sector participants, and civil society representatives. This historic conference accomplished its three primary objectives of:

— Launching, a dialogue between the developed and developing worlds and within the developing world on the emerging Global Information Society;

— Initiating the process to define a shared vision for the Global Information Society between the relevant societal sectors in the developed and developing countries.

— Working towards "Common Principles" and Collaborative Actions" to strengthen our shared vision and meet the challenges of the Global Information Society.

While we speak of a "global" information society, the Present reality is daunting. The technological gap between the less developed and industrialised countries of the world is widening. This situation must be addressed by the world community if we are to build a Global Information Society. In respect to the present reality, we acknowledge the following:

— Information and Communication Technologies and Services Have the potential to offer a significant contribution towards the promotion of sustainable growth in all countries.

— There currently exists a huge gap between the highly-industrialised countries and the less-industrialised countries in terms of information infrastructure;

— Through developing an information infrastructure and effectively utilising information and communications technologies and services, developing countries can narrow the current gap in economic and social development and prevent it from widening;

— There are tremendous and diverse needs in the developing world ,which often differ from the need of the more industrialised countries; and,

— Developing countries must assess their own requirements and strategies for entry into the Global Information Society based on their specific realities.

There is clearly an unsatisfactory level of investment in information infrastructure development in the less industrialised countries. Being able to mobilise the necessary investment, particularly from the private sector is of paramount importance to the developing countries. Of equal importance, is being able to develop networks which enable the whole of their populations to gain access to the global information infrastructure and participate in the GIS at affordable prices. In respect to mobilising the required investments for information infrastructure development, we acknowledge the following:

— There is currently an insufficient investment in developing information infrastructures in the less industrialised countries;

— There is an extensive demand for information and communications technologies and services in the developing world; and,

— To create a truly Global Information Society, we must mobilise appropriate investment.

The new techno-economic paradigm of the global economy is increasingly driven by knowledge-intensive sectors which utilise information and communications technologies. These economic sectors could form the basis of entirely new multi-media industries, products and services which could contribute to attracting investment and creating employment within national economies. In respect to employment, labour market and work in the GIS, we acknowledge the following:

— A new knowledge intensive global economy is emerging

— The new global economy can stimulate new industries and employment opportunities.

— We must attempt to minimize the risk and enhance the opportunities for Labour; and.

— Access to training and lifelong learning must be promoted.

Meeting basic needs, developing human resources, growing the economy, creating a culture of effective delivery of public services, promoting a participatory democracy and conveying different cultures and ideas are challenges jointly faced by all countries in the world. New information and communication technologies, affordable as their costs continue to fall, could help developing nations "leapfrog' entire stages of development in setting up their own information infrastructures and applications. In respect to using the potential of information technologies, we acknowledge the following:

— Information technologies have tremendous potential to: meet basic needs, develop human resources, grow economics facilitate

— new competitive advantages, improve the efficiency of government management and delivery of public services, promoting

— participatory democracy as well as cultural and linguistic diversity in each country;

— To achieve these benefits, the particular environment in each nation must be considered to promote the optimal mix of technologies in deploying the information Infrastructure; and,

— These new information and communication technologies will help developing nations "leapfrog" entire stages of development.

Key opportunities exist in the following areas:

— Enhanced capacity for the development of human resources skills and competencies;

— Improved debt management within each country;

— Improved effectiveness. efficiency and productivity in the workplace;

— Greater decision-making capability through timely access to information.

— Efficient delivery of public services through improved mechanisms and greater customer responsiveness;

— Increased access to public information;

— More efficient interface between the public and private sectors;

— Economic growth and development through electronic trade, investment and commerce, particularly for Small, Medium and

— Micro Enterprises (Smes);

— Decrease in the need for migration to urban areas.,

— Health care improvement;

— Better management of natural resources and the environment, and,

— Early warning systems for weather and other environmental phenomena.

The establishment of an advanced information and communications infrastructure requires a favorable investment climate. In many countries, achieving such an environment might necessitate changes in the regulatory framework and economic restructuring aimed at a more liberalised telecommunications sector, which could provide more choice, higher quality and better access. In attracting direct investment, national regulatory policy objectives need to be transparent and consistently applied. In respect to mobilising investment through appropriate regulatory conditions, we acknowledge the following:

— In order to mobilise and attract investment, developing countries must create a climate conductive to investment;

— This necessitates an adaptable regulatory framework based upon competition and aiming at the provision of more choice, higher quality and better access;

— The process should take into account the particular realities in each country and,

— Investment in indigenous content creation should be encouraged.

The information society has the potential to enhance the quality of life of all participants. However, the scale pace of improvements in social welfare and economic development will depend heavily on the universal enabling environment. The social and societal benefits of the information infrastructure will be optimised by an approach which aims at the highest possible levels of participation. The alternative would lead to the emergence of two "information-classes" of citizens. In the developing world, the risk of creating a two-tiered society, where only one group of the population has access to new network services, and equipment, is even greater than in the developed countries. In respect to social and societal aspect of the GIS, we acknowledge the following:

— The Information Society must enhance the quality of life for all participants and avoid developing a two-tiered society;

— Life-long Education is a major key to enable full and active participation by all citizens in the GIS; and,

— Indigenous content creation should address the cultural and linguistic requirements of each

The potential rewards of working together towards a GIS are enticing and include: a better balance in economic and social progress between nations, growth of the global economy; the capacity to solve common societal problems, enhancing the progress of democratic values, and sharing as well as augmenting cultural creativity, traditions and identities. On this shared vision of human enrichment, we acknowledge the following:

— A consensus is emerging about the importance of global information society;

— No single, model is universal; and,

— A globally cooperative approach is required.

Like all societies, the GIS needs to be built on a set of common norms, on tolerance, on respect of diversity and on habits of collaboration and combined efforts. Easing its birth like dealing with all major "shifts", means overcoming uncertainties and a break in continuity. While it is bringing our world closer together, existing differences in social and economic development are becoming more apparent and the difficulties they create are worsening. In respect to launching a dialogue between the developed and developing world we acknowledge the following:

— Building the GIS requires common guidelines, tolerance, respect for diversity and collaborating actions; and,

— Distinct national visions should converge into a shared global vision.

— Encourage further discussions towards identifying and implementing Global Information Society Projects in conjunction with non-governmental organisations and international organisations;

— Share information on best practices of development programmes and usage of information and communication technologies;

— Call upon international organisations to re-assess and refocus their development tools to give active follow-up to the principles and policies identified at this conference; and

— Fully utilise various policies and private and public financial instruments available for the development of the Global Information Society

Participants welcomed the contribution of representatives of civil society and business leaders in the proceedings of the Conference. They re-emphasised the need of public and private sector co-operation and partnership in achieving common goals. These ISAD conclusions are informed by a commitment to ensure that the development of the Global Information Society benefits all humanity

The developing and developed worlds should. agree on the principles for cooperation in the GIS. Close collaboration at the highest level will ensure the efficient introduction and development of a truly "Global" information society and prevent the marginalization of some countries from this inevitable revolution. Like all societies, the Global Information Society needs to be built on a set of principles, on respect of diversity and on collaboration.

Following the principles endorsed by the Brussels conference which are:

— promoting dynamic competition

— encouraging private investment

— defining an adaptable regulatory framework

— providing open access to networks while

— ensuring universal provision of and access to services

— promoting equality of opportunity to the citizen

— promoting diversity of content, including cultural and linguistic diversity

— recognising the necessity of worldwide co-operation with particular attention to less developed countries and taking into account the key policy issues identified at the ISAD conference, which are:

a) universal service

b) clear regulatory framework

c) sustainable socio-economic development

d) employment creation

e) global co-operation and competitiveness

f) diversity of applications and content

g) diversity of language and culture

h) co-operation in technology.

i) private investment and competition

j) protection of intellectual property rights

k) privacy and data security

l) narrowing the infrastructure gap

m) co-operation in research and technological development

n) the ISAD participants are therefore resolved to continuing the dialogue and taking appropriate action on these principles and policy issues.

Furthermore we are committed to:

— Fostering partnerships between the public and private sectors;

— Continue or begin a process of national information society planning in each of our countries which is ultimately in concert with the development of a Global Information Society;

— Encourage further discussion towards identifying and implementing Global Information Society Projects in conjunction With non-governmental organisation;

— Share information on best practices of development programmes and usage of information and communication technologies;

— Call upon international organisations to re-asses and refocus their development tools to give active follow-up to the principles and policies identified at this conference; and,

— Fully utilise various policies and private and public financial instruments available for the development of Global Information Society

Participants welcomed the contribution or representatives of civil society and business leaders in the proceedings of the Conference. They re-emphasised the need of public and private sector co-operation and partnership in achieving common goals. These ISAD conclusions are informed by a commitment to ensure that the development of the Global Information Society benefits all humanity.

Social and Ethical Impacts of ICT Applications

The social and ethical implications of ICTs warrant special attention and have resulted in the creation of a discrete area of research that has attracted people from sociology, philosophy, law, psychology as well as computer science and information systems.

In the information age, people are working in a location independent manner. This means we need to think about why direct interaction is advantageous. Interaction with others gives the possibilities and advantages of friendship. Yet, traditionally, friendship has needed face-to-face interaction.This 'virtual friendship' gives rise to problems for workers:

— *Creativity:* it is easier to explore apparently wild ideas face-to-face, in private and unmonitored. Many ideas eventually implemented start life as debates about 'wild' ideas

— *Isolation:* even the most advanced communications technologies cannot prevent feelings of isolation. Remote workers may also either be forgotten or fear they will be forgotten

— *Personal Development:* much personal development takes place informally at work. For many this can be one of the great benefits of working life. A high proportion of informal contact is lost if communication is down-the-wire.

The Location independent working (LIW) can affect:

— Capacity for the employer/manager/ supervisor to manage work: management by results moves to the forefront, when it might not have been considered for location dependent working

— Capacity for employees to negotiate conditions (partly because union organisation is more difficult among isolated workers)

— Trust and privacy, if electronic surveillance techniques are used.

— Location Independent: Working radically affects the relationship between work and the community. Much of our world is structured around there being set places of work: whole service industries survive on providing for workers in those workplaces.

Similarly, LIW can radically affect the home and the community around the home. Virtually all LIW involves either work at home or work much closer to home. Greater presence in the home community in daytime means more trade for local shops. Less time spent travelling means more time for involvement in community activities. Reductions in travel associated with work can also be expected to reduce pollution and road congestion where LIW is introduced. When some work is within the house, it takes up space that could be used for household activities.

The information age can be expected to have substantial effects on work. There is increasing globalisation of work. Some industries are 'geographically footloose'. These industries are increasingly using ICTs to redistribute work around the globe. This looks likely to involve the retention of the most sophisticated and high value roles in what are currently the most economically dominant regions of industrialised countries, while less economically rewarding roles are 'exported'. This might lead to increases in levels of incomes in the countries and regions that receive the 'exported' employment. At the same time, global inequality may still increase further. Work is increasingly becoming knowledge-and skills-based. Those without the knowledge and skills, and without the means of obtaining them, are increasingly being excluded from well-paid work.

This exclusion is amplified if they are also excluded from access to advanced information and communications technologies, whether in less industrialised countries or areas of deprivation in more industrialised countries. Increasing numbers of workers are suffering repetitive strain injuries (RSI) from over-intensive use of keyboards, and use of ergonomically poor workplaces. Technologies that might reduce the use of keyboards also appear to give rise to RSIs, so there is little cause for optimism Often this can be an intrusion. When the house is small the intrusion will be greater: meaning that this intrusion will be greater for less wealthy workers. Beyond this, there is the psychological intrusion of work on the home. A lack of physical distance can cause a lack of emotional distance: work in the home can make it impossible to get away from work. Equally, someone calling at the door of the house on personal business may interrupt work for someone working at home: whereas if they are at work in a traditional workplace, the caller is inevitably ignored. Where a traditional workplace has a culture of long hours, and the team also includes some working at home, those working at the traditional workplace have been known to call those working at home 'teleshirkers'. Colleagues working in a more traditional way can easily resent the flexibility offered to LIWorkers. Changing work patterns can also be expected to have effects on the design of offices and homes. More homes are likely to be built with one or two offices as part of the design. Meanwhile, if people are spending less time in traditional workplaces, it is to be expected that less space will be needed by these traditional workplaces. This can mean cost savings for employers. Perhaps some of the space no longer needed for offices will be taken over by housing, although the evidence seems to suggest that this will be largely by new employment using less offices while the more-or-less normal turnover of posts reduces the number intensively using offices in the traditional way.

ICTs bring ever more data to the desk of many workers. Information overload can be a severe problem, leading to excessive stress. Technology is enabling more employers to consider the use of surveillance. This 'threatens to undermine the autonomy and dignity of workers'. This can lead to a breakdown of trust between the employer and employee, to the detriment of both.

The advent of the digital age and the information society has increased the opportunities to collect and store information. Traditionally organisations kept information on personnel, products and payroll. Now information is collected on, for example, the buying habits of the supermarket shopper or the on-line behaviour of a bank's internet customers. There is often little clarity either within or outside the organisation about how the data will help the organisation's business, who should access it, or, indeed, whether the information becomes a commodity in its own right to be sold on.

As the Internet appears to have the effect of speeding up our world there is more concern about the products of endeavours rather than the manner in which these endeavours are undertaken. Product rather than process becomes all. An inclusive perspective on planning, designing and implementing information systems with a wider rather than a narrower horizon. Study of information system where the perception of what and whom should be considered was narrow. All the stakeholders were internal to the organisations and in close proximity to the projects.

There is a much wider range of potential stakeholders in any information system development that wishes to achieve a socially and ethically sensitive outcome. Included among such stakeholders would be owners, employees, unions, capital providers, government, customers, suppliers, community groups and competitors. If all the relevant stakeholders are taken on board at the outset of a project the process will embrace 'the views and concerns of all parties affected by the project.' Concerns over, for example, deskilling of jobs and redundancy effect the whole community relating to the enterprise.

The need to move away from the 'supplier-centric' model of information systems. A user-centric view with cultural, behavioural and social issues being addressed. A user-centric view recognises that information arises at the point of understanding rather than from the point of provision.

The use of information involves making judgements as to the relevance of the information, its value and its potential effect on the actions of the individual and the organisation. Thus information may be labelled as valuable or worthless, as company confidential or non-confidential, as private or public, by both the individual and the organisation. Such interpretations will determine what information is gathered, how it is searched for, how it is arranged and what use it is put to. The meaning placed on the information is influenced by the attitudes and values of the individual and the organisation. An individual's attitudes and values are informed by their cultural, religious, political and economic circumstances. These may, or may not, match the purpose of the organisation and the often unwritten culture of the organisation they work within.

Ethical use of information highlights issues of:

— privacy and confidentiality

— ownership and accessibility

— equity

— accuracy

— quality and reliability.

The issues above may equally be adequately addressed by an organisation running a website selling pornography as by a social services department dealing with sensitive personal information. A web business may well assure its customers of privacy and confidentiality, quality and reliability. The crucial issue of individual privacy and the need to manage the use of personal information in a way that balances the needs of all parties in an acceptable manner. The difficulties of identifying 'all parties' and the fact that their needs or interests may not be determined in a straightforward manner.

The concept of 'balance of interest' is flawed, both as an outcome and a process and that "ultimately it is a political process involving conflict as well as consensus involving data controlling organisations, individuals, regulatory organisations, judicial and political bodies, and others." This idea is supported by Whittington who sees problems balancing the needs of different stakeholders even within an organisation "where there are conflicting drivers and issues of security against availability".

Increasingly the balancing act has to take on the complexity of crossing national boundaries, including different legal entities, cultures and norms. Ethical codes are increasingly having an impact on information provision. Ever more professionals dealing with the information systems are members of bodies with codes.

For ethical outcomes there is a need for integrity, moral attitudes and judgements. Many in the criminal fraternity operate under a self-regulated and strictly enforced code of conduct. One would be unlikely to conclude that the mafia, for example, was an ethical organisation in consequence.

The challenge for socially responsible information provision is therefore multiplied. This is because what are addressing is:

— the need and means of educating information system developers who are able to integrate the ethical dimension into their work, and

— the need to develop a society where the norm is for organisations and businesses to behave ethically, morally and with integrity in all their transactions.

Occupations in information and communications technology may require detailed knowledge, and there may be internally defined codes of conduct for some; but they don't have closed memberships, or professional bodies with meaningful sanction powers. One of the factors that has long marked out the professions in the minds of the public is that members of the public accept that they do not themselves have specialist knowledge and they therefore trust the better judgement of professionals in these areas. True professionals are those that respect this trust, and earn and deserve it, by looking beyond their own narrow self-interest and the self-interest of their employers.

Professionalism and excellence require much more than delivering on time and within budget. There are occasions when to deliver what is requested on time and within budget would mean to deliver a dangerous and/ or malfunctioning system.

Ethical awareness should be part of the job specification for jobs in ICT; this could be tested at interview — however: there could well be practical difficulties finding candidates who would meet this criterion, at least in the short term. If cannot recruit ethically sensitive staff: in-house ethics education sessions should be run. These should not be just a one-off session at induction, but an approach that encourages continuous staff development and on-going discussion of ethical issues There are doubts about whether staff could be trained into an organisation's value system when they may already have developed a value system of their own; however there is evidence that ethical training can be effective. Impartiality is impossible: the aim should be to help staff recognise this and to become aware of their own biases.

In many organisations, the IS community is quite separate from the rest of the organisation; it would be themselves and publicise what they are doing. IS departments should be open to outside scrutiny and audit. The boundaries of responsibility for each job need to be clear. Nonetheless, it is important to avoid a narrow task focus. The aim should be towards a more holistic view of responsibilities: to all stakeholders.

— Responsibilities don't stop at the doors of the company: responsibilities are wider than to personnel within the company.

— Standards for ethical behaviour should be specified and evaluation of employees' performance against them should be included in their annual appraisal, with direct links to salary and/or promotion prospects.

— The Individual Professional and the Wider Profession Because there is a moral responsibility on professionals to look beyond their narrow self-interest, there are a range of obligations in the way they interrelate to the wider profession.

— New recruits to the profession will look around them to see what behaviour is expected of them. The professional has a responsibility to new recruits, to set high standards, and to lead by example. A professional has a duty to other professionals: eg to share new ideas or examples of good practice.

It is the duty of the IS/IT professional to provide leadership and guidance to the end-user community; a senior 'champion' for ethical issues is one idea worthy of further consideration.

The concept of an ethics advisor and/or advisory

The concept of an ethics advisor and/or advisory committee needs investigation. There is a real possibility that organisations can be persuaded that it is more profitable to correct a poor system than to release it onto the market. At the same time, though, there is a risk 'professionals' will stop thinking seriously about ethics, taking the view that it is the work of the advisors. Few would deny that professionalism is part of the answer to the ethical worries raised by ICT. However, the professionals are likely to be white, literate, middle aged or young, urban, not disabled, and men. The information age affects, and can be affected by very many more people than the professionals in the ICT sector.

The driving forces behind virtual education (VEd) were meeting with a number of practical constraints. The vision of VEd includes a 'global' education community introducing a variety of cultural approaches and attitudes to education. Issues such as mode of address, voice tone, attitude to assessment, language and understanding, and the type of pedagogical approach may have an impact on learning. The issues under discussion were wide ranging, but can be categorised under the headings of infrastructure, human factors in teaching and learning, and wider social implications. The infrastructure supporting virtual education is a combination of technological and human resources. The most pressing concerns are: technological capability; reliability; predictability; controllability; cost of access. It must be remembered that there is usually a considerable performance difference between institution-based resources and home-based resources.

There is a great deal of concern about the loss of face-to-face interaction. Education is characterised as "more than information or knowledge transfer". Even in established distance learning initiatives contact time is considered a vital ingredient. Face-to-face communication carries a wealth of subtle aids to mutual understanding, giving vital feedback to both tutors and students. Contact time between tutors and students is important to clarify misunderstandings, provide alternative explanations, correct incorrect assumptions, and to encourage and provide support to the student. Although text messages and/or video conferencing can be used in this way, these methods are not as efficient as face-to-face interaction: more time and effort may be needed on the part of both the student and the tutor to get the same results.

Face-to-face communication both between tutor and student, and students and their peers, is an important factor in the integration of students in a social world. Aside from the commonly voiced concerns with regard to isolation through extensive engagement with computers, learning is enhanced through informal and ad hoc discussion with others.

A predominant concern regarding technology-based learning is the question of equal access. It is obvious that economic factors and levels of literacy are constraints to equal access. Less obvious, in the UK at least, are cultural constraints and language barriers. Methods of teaching and approaches to learning vary between cultures. Learning can be inhibited in a cultural context that differs from that of the provider of the learning module. Most of the development of virtual education has been carried out from a western perspective, and uses the English language. Yet much VEd development aims to sell western education, through the English language, to other parts of the world. Combination of these factors are likely to widen the education gap, in contrast to the utopian picture of 'education for all' painted by the advocates of VEd.

The implementation of virtual education is still at an experimental stage. The three case studies summarised below consider different perspectives: operational; access; and questions of viability. There are a wide range of social and ethical implications inherent in the adoption of virtual education. The apparent emphasis on the problems and potential adverse consequences of education delivered via ICT is a reaction to the heady utopianism of advocates and initiators of virtual education. It arises from a desire to seek a balanced perspective. This is not to say that these concerns are in any way trivial—far from it. What is evident is that the vision of virtual education as the answer to education for all does not match the current reality, either in technical or human terms. A number of questions need to be answered, and myths exposed, before virtual education is taken up as the route to the promised land of education and lifelong learning.

Privacy Issues

A huge proportion of the information that drives the information age is derived from data that is about individuals, or can be linked to individuals. On top of this, it is easier than ever to store, duplicate, manipulate and communicate that data, which can take the form of text, images, and recordings of sound, video and at times even touch. It is also easier than ever to associate these data types with each other. It is technically easier than ever to quickly gather, and search, vast amounts of data about individuals.

The technologies that facilitate 'data mining' and matching large data sets are becoming ever more commonplace, with legally sanctioned crime and disorder partnerships and attempts to detect fraud resulting in new data matching programmes. One result of the increases in data collection and data mining is the practical possibility of data surveillance. This means that a human being can now be tracked across the globe by the data shadow they leave behind them.

As with so many other issues in life, the impacts of loss of privacy will not fall equally or equitably. Due to distinctive names, or less common skin colouring, or disability, some people are easier to identify than others - equally some people are easier to mistake for each other. Beyond simple identification, some people have more need for privacy than others. Not everybody is equally likely to be targeted as a potential victim by criminals. Similarly, well educated, articulate, native speakers of English are more able to pursue the legal remedies available to protect their privacy. Thus a key question is how to prevent abuse of data in the first place. The most worrying kinds of abuse seem to fall into two main categories:

— individuals seeking illegitimate personal gain, perhaps through criminal acts

— authoritarian governments seeking to control populations.

While there is legislation to protect privacy in very many jurisdictions, there is a mismatch between the size of these jurisdictions and the largely global nature of trade, especially in data for which the transport costs are so near zero. Thus global trade is threatened by data protection and privacy legislation formulated by one trading block if due regard is not paid to other trading blocks. Given the all-conquering power of global trade, it seems apposite to ask what degree of protection is feasible or acceptable in a technological age that demands greater data collection, provides for easier surveillance and provides increasingly limited scope for withholding information? Even if legislation remains of some practical use, it depends for its force in deterring breaches. Short of repressive enforcement, this will need those with access to data and influence over security measures to act responsibly.

Future technologies raise new issues about privacy. For example intelligent agents could be making decisions about highly sensitive personal data outside the human context that might be automatically implicit to any other human. Similarly, geographical information systems can have privacy implications when tied to systems monitoring physical mobility. There is a strong argument for an impact assessment whenever a new technology is developed that takes account of privacy effects, although it is not widely thought that it should be an absolute requirement in every case— research is needed on what form such assessments should take. Data protection laws, human rights and freedom of information legislation may have an impact, putting pressure on public bodies to release information about which there are privacy concerns.

2

Information Revolution and Digital Divide

Today, Information and Communication Technology (ICTs) disparities usually exacerbate existing disparities based on location such as urban-rural, gender, ethnicity, physical disability, age, and, especially, income level, and between "rich" and "poor" countries. The digital divide is not an isolated entity, but a complicated patchwork of varying levels of ICT access, basic ICT usage, and ICT applications among countries and peoples. The private sector has slowly spread technology to middle income groups, but on the whole they fail to see the developing world and underserved populations as viable markets that require targeted products.

Governments often tend to the short-term demands of their constituencies, but do not provide a coherent, long-term plan for prosperity and effective ICT integration, and a legal and regulatory framework that foster ICT use. Dealing with the digital divide is beyond the scope of any single initiative and technology is not a silver bullet for the world's problems. It is important for organizations doing community ICT projects to bring a global perspective and an entrepreneurial approach, and they must cooperate with like-minded efforts to tackle the range of problems collaboratively. There are some of the key elements necessary for integrating technology into society in an effective, sustainable way so that people can put technology to use to improve their lives.

ICT disparities are usually exacerbate existing disparities based on location, gender, ethnicity, physical disability, age, and, especially, income level, and between "rich" and "poor" countries. Measures of the digital divide exists in number and cost of PCs, phones, Internet hosts, Web sites, Internet users, residential/organizational/ international Internet bandwidth, technical capacity, and advanced applications like e-commerce. The spread of Internet users among the world's population is much more unequal than that of the use of other ICT such as TV or telephones. The inequality of Internet usage is even bigger than the spread of GDP between the world's rich and poor countries. The monthly connection cost for the Internet in much of Africa exceeds the monthly income of a significant portion of the population. In nearly all developing countries, phone calls are charged by the minute, and are often extremely expensive.

Additionally, Web pages are becoming increasing graphic-heavy and "large" in terms of file size. The dominance of English, and especially U.S. content, makes it less useful to other countries. Additionally, non-English countries produce less local content making the Internet less relevant to their lives, and less of a tool of self-expression and local communication. Advanced uses of ICT such as e-commerce applications show even greater disparities than in basic access to computers.

E-commerce is dominated by the U.S. and to a lesser extent some European countries. The U.S. has 64% of all secure servers in the world; the next highest is the U.K, with only 5.32%, and the vast majority of countries have less than 0.1%. There is a wealth of real and anecdotal evidence of the digital divide. Wealthy nations comprise some 16 per cent of the world's population, but command 90 per cent of Internet host computers.

Of all the Internet users worldwide, 60 per cent reside in North America, where a mere five per cent of the world's population reside. One in two Americans is online, compared with only one in 250 Africans. In Bangladesh a computer costs the equivalent of eight years average pay. Ethnic and racial divisions in ICT use have been studied in the U.S., but are much less studied outside. Gaps also exist in adoption by gender, and the sector of disabled individuals show especially low levels of Internet use.

Major cities are far more likely to have Internet, phone, and PC access than smaller cities and rural areas. These gaps are even more significant given the fact that more than 50 percent--and as many as 80 percent--of the population in poorest countries, live in rural areas. The "number of users" online statistic is only a small part of the "digital divide". For practical reasons, current statistics focus on the raw numbers of PCs or numbers of people using a technology. They do not measure well how well people are using the technology, and whether the impact is positive or negative for themselves and their communities for business, educational, governance and social uses. While the current set of statistics can only provide rough estimates of how technology is used between countries and socio-economic groups, more than enough information is known to show that these divisions exist to spur reasoned action.

E-readiness assessment, combined with conventional "digital divide" statistics could provide this action plan. A deeper understanding of ICT use can be gained from the wealth of "e-readiness" assessments around the world. The e-readiness assessments seek to gauge how ready a country is to participate in the information economy or information society. In the process, the assessments draw upon many of the statistics used above as well as many more, including use of computers in schools and in healthcare.

National governments can play a fundamental role in creating an environment that will foster technology use and encourage national and international investment in ICT infrastructure, development, and a skilled workforce. These include telecommunications privatisation, standards setting, consumer protection, and government usage of ICT. Economic growth and social equity are both needed to bridge international and domestic digital divides. However, no consensus exists on exactly what policies are needed for either of these goals.

Many African and Middle Eastern countries seem to be far behind in policies needed to bridge international and domestic digital divides. There are a number of African countries with no registrar for their top-level country codes. The majority of countries with laws on electronic authentication have not yet developed detailed standards, although a number are working on them. At the same time, a number of projects geared for the developing world offer promising new technologies and adaptations.

India's "Simputer" and Brazil's "Volkscomputer" are often cited examples of locally produced, locally appropriate technologies that fit the needs and budgets of the developing world. Two developed world projects are also seeking to produce new "developing market" technologies—the MIT Media Lab, and HP's 1 Billion dollar E-Inclusion project. On the software side, India is the prime example of a country that has succeeded in developing a globally competitive IT sector—though the replicability of their success may be doubtful for other countries. Digital divide programmes are operated by organizations ranging from the smallest NGO to the largest multinational corporation.

Private telecentres provide telephone access for a fee. Some are adding fax, email, and Internet services, such as Senegal's micro-enterprise Phone Shops and Africa Online's "E-Touch" centres in Kenya. Donor-funded telecentres include such projects as the Nakaseke Multipurpose Community Telecentre in Uganda.

Digital Divide: Definitions

The gender divide will steadily decrease, at least in terms of users of the Internet. In South Africa for example, the number of women online recently surpassed the number of men. It can be reasonably expected that the ratio of women online in these countries will reach levels similar to the country's overall gender and power balances—which is often quite unequal, but should be considered in that larger context. Some small-scale ground-level projects show that computers can level the playing field for everyone and especially help people out of poverty. But on a country-wide level, and around the world, the statistics indicate that computers simply have not played that role.

Most countries could simply be shut out of the global competition, without the existing resources and investment to develop local ICT sectors; only a few countries may be able to develop strong ICT-fuelled economies. While the international and domestic digital divides may shift—including a few new countries and a slightly larger segment of society—the gulf between the "haves" and "have-nots" will deepen without adequate pro-active measures.

The term 'digital divide' may be taken at the broadest level to refer to the gap between those individuals and communities who own, access, and effectively use information and communication technologies (ICT) and those who do not. However, the term is often employed in a generalised way that masks its complex and diverse nature. This detracts from more informed and coherent debates surrounding its existence and extent. The definition has become unclear, and it is recognised that there are now multiple 'digital divides'. As the range of ICT and its capabilities increase, what constitutes a 'digital divide' and how to measure it become unclear. It is possible to dispute the size, characteristics and reality of its existence, and hard to clearly measure any progress made in reducing disparities. Clearer definitions and measurement criteria are needed in order assess the effectiveness of policies and initiatives. The absence of such criteria can leave policy initiatives open to criticism and difficult to defend. Divides can be seen to exist in relation to:

— ownership of new technologies

— access to those technologies.

However, issues of ownership and access are not as straightforward as they are often presented. For example, ownership does not necessarily equate with use, and ownership of household ICT does not necessarily mean that all individuals within that household own or use the technology. Thus, statistical accounts about the extent of the divide may be insufficient and may mask the complexities and extent of divisions. Similarly, ICT and internet access are largely devoid of qualitative understandings about the type and size of disparities.

— Type of technologies

— Age, capacity and functionality of devices

— The availability of technological and human support and resources to which different people have access.

However, as people obtain different levels and types of access in a number of different locations, divides can also occur on individual, educational, community and even wider demographic bases. There are definable gaps between:

— those who own state-of-the-art computers and subscribe to an ISP

— those who have access to computers and the internet at work, libraries or other locations and know how to use them

— those who have minimal access to computing technologies and few reasons for use

— those who have no experience of computer and information technologies.

The speed with which new technologies develop, coupled with wider societal differences, mean that it remains highly unlikely that complete parity will be attained. A clear and agreed indication of the levels and type of access sought and why these would be effective in reducing the divide(s) would be beneficial. 'Digital divides' involve a complex web of interconnected social, economic and cultural factors that cannot be fully captured by a definition that focuses solely on access or ownership. Whilst access is a key factor to be addressed in bridging the 'digital divide', it is merely one aspect.

Universal access to computers and the Internet is considered necessary to avoid social divisions and offer opportunities for all by ensuring that future 'knowledge economies' include everyone. Failure to bridge the divide may result in powerful digital communication tools exacerbating and entrenching societal disparities. As ICT continues to proliferate, the development of 'digital divides' may require the whole concept of poverty itself to be re-examined. Digital divides have repercussions in the following areas:

1. *Education and standards*: The proliferation of ICT in education and the expansion of Internet-based information and services further amplify the chasm between the information 'haves' and 'have nots'. Those on the wrong side of the divide(s) may have less opportunity to participate and engage with both formal and informal education, training and information. Changes in education are likely to mean that ICT skills will become the 'indispensable grammar of modern life' and a 'tool for lifelong learning'. Social inclusion and economic development in the 'Information Age' are mutually reinforcing, and for people in low income neighbourhoods, gaining and exploiting ICT skills lead to opportunities to participate fully in local and national economies.

2. *Economic competitiveness and employment*: Ninety per cent of new jobs in the UK require some degree of computing ability. In the US, it is estimated that around 60% of new jobs require 'advanced' technological skills. It is feared that demand for ICT skills will not be met by the adult population if ability levels do not increase significantly, particularly as the UK is currently the biggest e-commerce market in Europe. Failure to tackle the 'digital divide' and increase ICT skills could reduce the nation's ability to compete effectively in an increasingly technological global economy. Employers are increasingly considering ICT skills when recruiting staff and locating new businesses. American research also shows that those currently using ICT in their occupations earn significantly more and have better health levels.

3. *Social inclusion*: ICT skills and the ability to access technology facilitate a range of benefits that can be gained as electronically based products and services become accessible on line. Equality of access, skills and aspirations are essential to ensure that the gap between information rich and poor does not extend to gaps in access to electronically based participatory mechanisms. The digital divide constitutes the most pressing civil rights issue of the millennium. Exclusion can be reduced by using ICT to build and extend communication links and enabling improved access to information sources and services. However, failure to tackle divides in the immediate future may entrench inequalities further with ICT being most effectively used by the most advantaged groups.

Disparities in terms of the following must also be considered:

— *Content*: Does computer-based content that has equal relevance and value for all groups in society exist, or does content tend to reflect wider inequalities and power differentials. A number of more recent reports have highlighted how content can be a barrier to ICT engagement for many disadvantaged individuals and groups.. For example, The Children's Partnership suggest that one in five Americans faces at least one of the following content-related barriers.

  — *lack of local information* - material that is relevant and useful for specific under-served communities

  — *language barriers* - for instance, it is estimated on the basis of this research that 87% of all documents on the Internet are in English, yet a great number of individuals do not have English as their primary language, thereby leaving them in an inferior position in relation to advantages gained through uses of the Internet

  — *lack of cultural diversity* - there is a dearth of internet content created by ethnic minorities or organised around specific cultural interests or practices

  — *literacy barriers* - the vast majority of information on the Internet is written for an audience with average or above literacy levels, yet it is argued that over one-fifth of Americans do not have the necessary reading and writing skills to function effectively in everyday life

— *Literacy:* Certain levels may need to be achieved to use and benefit from a range of new technologies. Yet literacy levels are often left out of debates surrounding the 'digital divide'. Moreover, it is argued that new technological tools may require a consideration of a range of literacies that enable individuals to utilise them effectively. For example, the Bertelmann Foundation argue that aspects such as contextual literacy, media creativity, social competence and responsibility should be included. To incorporate these aspects presents formidable challenges in three key areas, namely education, workplace skills and civic engagement. Similarly, Carvin suggests that in terms of digital equity we should also consider issues beyond 'basic literacy' to include: functional literacy; occupational literacy; technological literacy; information literacy; adaptive literacy.

— *Pedagogy:* From an educational and occupational perspective, ICT may be of little use without effective training, curriculum and teaching. With much informal learning with and about ICT being undertaken in the home, the human and educational resources that individuals can draw upon in the home and cultural background become significant in discussions about the 'digital divide'.

— *Community:* Does the technology enable the development and spread of effective and strong communities on and off line? Are there disparities in the relevance, desires and needs for different communities to use ICT?

Whilst there is significant evidence showing the existence of a 'digital divide', there is no consensus as to whether it is remaining constant, is a narrowing and transient phase, or is indeed growing. Research shows the number of people owning and accessing ICT has increased significantly over recent years. This is illustrated by the growth in the number of internet users.

In UK, according to a 2001 ICT survey, thirty per cent of all households can access the Internet via a home computer, more than double the number identified in 1999. The number of over-55-year-olds and socio-economic groups C2DE on line is increasing rapidly. There has also been a decrease in the relative wealth of the 'average' user in recent years. One in 14 Internet users have already used mobile phones or digital TV to access the Internet. Access via digital TV is becoming an increasing possibility for a growing number of people as uptake has risen to around a quarter of all homes. Twenty-eight per cent of the respondents in one study felt that delivery through their TV would make them use the Internet more. Some evidence suggests that divides will decrease in the future. Children's use of home computers is increasing, as is the number of households where the child is the main PC user. Two-parent households with one or more children are most likely to have internet access.

Despite the increasing numbers owning and accessing ICT, there are still significant gaps between the 'information rich and poor', and closer analysis of evidence casts doubts over claims that 'digital divides' are narrowing. In UK, over half of the individuals in social grades AB are connected to the Internet at home. This is true for little more than 1 in 10 over-55s or social grades DE. Existing home internet users are more likely to have access in other locations, to have more informal information sources, and also to have access and use of other ICT in the country. There are groups of young people who are uninterested in ICT, and these are often from backgrounds where inequalities already exist.

Dimensions of Digital Divide

Digital divide has been identified along a number of dimensions. For some individuals and groups these may be interconnected and present multiple barriers to the effective use of ICT. Let us consider the situatiuon in UK.

1. *Socio-economic status*: In UK, in socio-economic profile DE the number of those who do not own or have never used a PC is double that of those in profile AB. Home internet access ranges from 53% amongst social grades AB down to as little as 12% in groups DE. Subscription rates for digital TV are also greater in the highest income group (31%) than they are for those in the lowest (14%). There are differences in the type and quality of hardware and software in households that may exacerbate inequalities further. There are qualitative divides in ICT use, with children from higher income backgrounds using home computers for a much wider range of activities than those from lower income families. Technology impinges upon the lives of the less privileged in a number of ways, yet is less likely to be fully understood or as effectively used.

2. *Employment status*: Over twice as many employed people are 'on line' than there are unemployed. Seventy-one per cent of employed compared to 32% of those not working were found to have a computer at home. Sixty-one per cent in social groups ABC1 compared to 28% in C2DE thought ICT was essential to their work. Those in rented property are less likely to have internet access than owner-occupiers. Four per cent of council tenants, compared to 22% of residents in high income areas, were found to have internet access. Other groups with lower-than-

average take-up are described as 'independent elders', 'blue collar owners' and 'Victorian low status'. Households with two adults and one or more children have internet access rates of up to 35%, whilst single-parent families access rates range from 7% to 11%.

3. *Gender*: Women are 14% less likely to have ever used a computer. They are 10% less likely to use one at home and 6% less likely to use one for work. Fifty-two per cent of men, compared to only 39% women, have access to the Internet, and 7% more men than women state they have access in the home. Boys own and use ICT more in the home than girls, and have more positive perceptions of their own ICT use and ability. Research identified that educational computing is constructed as a 'male' activity during classroom interactions. This can diminish participation and enthusiasm amongst girls and affect educational and occupational choices. Women and girls are also often under-represented, or represented stereotypically, in ICT media and content. Female use of ICT is related to wider societal structural inequalities and barriers to power, and discrimination against women in traditional pathways such as education and employment can lead to resistance to learning with ICT.

4. *Geographical location*: London (34%) and the South East (30%) have the highest regional rates of internet access. The North East (22%), Wales (20%), Scotland (19%) and Northern Ireland (16%) have the lowest. The majority of ICT-related economic and job opportunities are concentrated in London, the South East and in the regional capitals. Charges for

telephone calls may contribute to the structuring of ICT use based upon geographical location. Fewer incentives exist for companies to offer competitive services to rural areas. Fewer community-based projects, initiatives or training opportunities are offered in rural locations, due to the lower numbers of immediate residents. Distance and travel create further barriers.

4. *Ethnicity*: Many deprived neighbourhoods have high proportions of ethnic minorities, who have less access and ownership of ICT due partly to economic factors. Barriers exist to those whose first language is not English, as the majority of training, content and operating systems are in English. Certain literacy levels are necessary to benefit from ICT. Factors relating to culture impact upon use. Large variations in attitudes, use and experiences with ICT could exist between groups from various cultural backgrounds, but there is little research in this area.

5. *Disability*: Both computer use and internet access were found to be markedly lower amongst disabled people. Designers often fail to recognise the rights and access requirements necessary for people with disabilities. There is a wide range of disabling conditions that require specific approaches to ICT design and provision. Nonetheless, some core issues and barriers relevant to a number of cases include the following:

   — Hardware and software is generally not specialised or adaptable.

   — Lack of awareness: negative and incorrect assumptions are made about the levels of disabled people's achievements.

- — There is a lack of resources, both real and perceived.
- — Efforts for inclusion are diluted through segmentation of services and incoherent initiatives.

6. *Age*: The over-65s represent almost 20% of the population but are the group least likely to be connected to the Internet, or to subscribe to digital television. Internet use drops from 14% amongst the 64-75 age group to 4% for those 75 or over. Retired households are least likely to have internet access, with only an estimated 1% of those living alone ever going on line. Those over 55 are significantly less likely to own or use a PC and have fewer current or desired computer skills. A large proportion of older 'non acceptors' report having no interest in using a computer.

Causes of Digital Divide

The major factors which are contributing to the digital divide are:

1. *Shortcomings of the markets*: There is an argument that commercial providers target the most profitable segments of society first and unconnected sections last. There are no guarantees that market provision will deliver affordable ICT for all groups in society. Market-led provision may reach 'natural' saturation levels and inequalities may be exacerbated following new technical waves and inventions.
2. *Cost*: The cost of purchasing equipment, telephone costs, tuition and perceptions of costs have also been reported as barriers for non-internet users. Cheaper

calls (26%), unmetered free access (17%), and cheaper subscriptions would encourage greater internet usage amongst existing home users. The cost of internet use by children is a central concern for many families, particularly low-income groups.

3. *Lack of relevance, interest and aspirations*: A significant number believe ICT is not relevant to their lives. Fifteen per cent of all people have no interest in using the Internet. Over half of those unconnected state they will never get on line. The perceived lack of relevance has a socio-economic dimension. Many people still largely associate ICTs with the 'economic domain'. Individuals in higher socio-economic occupational categories are more likely to use ICT at work.The number of outlets for use in the wider community, or in employment locally, are factors that impact upon the perceived relevance of ICT. Children also develop their use of ICT in relation to its perceived relevance to their current social position, gender role and peer group culture. Poverty of aspiration and opportunity are factors that lead to the development of self exclusion and further inequalities. Perceptions of the utility of computers is mediated by individual family discourses, wider learning communities, and particular software environments. Use tends to supplement rather than transcend existing social arrangements.

4. *Lack of access and support*: Forty-two per cent of all 'non regular users' stated that the biggest obstacle to internet usage was lack of access to suitable equipment. Twenty-one per cent of all non-users lack the confidence and skills necessary to use the Internet. Fifteen per cent felt there was a lack of people to help them learn about ICT both in formal

and informal settings. This may be particularly true in deprived neighbourhoods.

5. *Lack of literacy*: Many people do not have sufficient literacy levels to use ICT effectively. This poses a particular problem for groups whose first language is not English. Most keyboards are in English and do not include characters used in some other languages. Common computer programs tend to use English-only instruction, and the information on the Internet is in predominantly English. Higher levels of illiteracy in deprived areas may severely restrict the numbers using public access points. Lack of computer literacy can compound this problem and also present a barrier to effective mobilisation in other contexts.

6. *Lack of joined-up approaches*: The 'digital divide represents one aspect of wider inequalities. The 'joined up' nature of social problems is one of the key factors underlying the concept of social exclusion. There is often little collaboration or communication between local projects, or strategic thinking across organisations and few mechanisms for sharing good practice.Community groups still struggle to find funding from 'one time-limited initiative to another'. The private sector is still largely absent from debates surrounding ICT and social inclusion in deprived neighbourhoods.

7. *Barriers to community access*: Learning in mixed groups at community access points can make some groups feel uncomfortable. Barriers may exist relating to location, opening times, lack of adequate child care, security, facilities for the disabled, ethnic minorities and the elderly. Unsustainable,

inconsistent, unsuitable and partial funding are barriers to community-based initiatives. ICT access points may be poorly promoted or marketed, and their role and content may lack a local focus. Access based around community technology centres is not sufficient, and efforts should be focused toward access based in the home.

Policies to Bridging Digital Divide

In national as well as internation levels, a number of initiatives and policies aimed at bridging the 'digital divide' are in operation, but as yet few independent evaluations are available. In UK, as an overall concept, the *UK online* initiative encompasses a number of themed strands of activity, including providing access and learning at newly established centres, offering low-cost computers 'within reach', putting all public libraries and schools on line and supporting businesses. *The Computers Within Reach Scheme* is currently running a pilot phase covering up to 35,000 individuals from deprived areas and claiming benefits, and providing them with recycled computers and associated peripherals. Up to 100,000 recycled computers will eventually be issued. *The Wired Up Communities Project* aims to put many homes in disadvantaged areas on line and assess how individual access to the Internet can transform opportunities by enabling access to work, training and leisure services. School children in 'Wired Up Communities' will be involved in schemes that push computer ratios significantly higher than the National Grid for Learning targets. UK's *National e-Learning Foundation* has been established with the clear aim of providing affordable, individual access to laptops for children, particularly those in deprived areas. Local foundations are being established to deliver laptop learning locally. Typically, these will be innovative partnerships between local charities, businesses and parents. Digital divides have no single, identifiable cause or effect. Many government initiatives, therefore, are integrated alongside broader concepts and policies that aspire to tackle deprivation and exclusion. *The Social Exclusion Unit* has been tasked to identify and report on the problems facing those in the most deprived areas and tackle social exclusion in the poorest neighbourhoods, and findings are incorporated into the *National Strategy for Neighbourhood Renewal*. Improving IT in these areas is identified as one 'key' area.

A sample of recommendations and suggestions that propose methods for tackling the 'digital divide' drawn from a range of sources and are loosely matched to the factors contributing to the 'digital divide' identified above are presented below.

1. *Supplementing/enhancing provision from the markets*:
   - Raise awareness about the extent and dimensions of the divide to industry. This would help them to identify specific areas of product development and marketing as sales level out due to saturation.
   - Give recommendations to software producers to develop products with more non-textual representation in minority languages, and for teaching English as a second language. Create partnerships to identify areas for product development and incentives for companies to design products specifically for excluded groups.
   - Create further competition to provide cheaper services amongst telecommunications, software and resource companies.

— Promote the concept of corporate social responsibility within the IT industry to raise awareness and involvement.

— Further develop the market for resale and refurbishment of used IT hardware.

2. *Reducing costs*

— Further develop hardware lending and low-cost purchase schemes, particularly in disadvantaged communities and also for the benefit of other under-represented groups.

— Co-ordinate, develop and identify a range of low-cost technical solutions to access provision for all types of ICT. This would help to reduce the numbers who perceive ICT as unaffordable.

— Continue to develop a national infrastructure of low-cost or free access points in under-served communities, with future developments being informed by research findings pertaining to existing centres.

3. *Increasing relevance, interest and aspirations*

— There needs to be continued and active promotion that the 'digital divide' has to be overcome because it undermines the basic rights of every individual.

— Internet service and content providers to develop alternative perspectives to attract non-users and give clearer messages about how they can benefit from on-line activities.

— Develop a range of incentives to use the Internet, both financial and non-financial, and produce content and programmes that are of relevance to people's life and encourage skills acquisition.

— The provision offered should reflect the interests and make-up of the community it aims to serve. Attention and initiatives should focus upon helping and encouraging people to package the information they already have, present their own thoughts and knowledge, and find relevant outputs and uses.

— Opportunities to learn skills with people in similar situations and from similar backgrounds should be offered and promoted.

— Develop 'taster' courses that link ICT directly to other aspects of life relevant the communities involved.

— 'E-missionaries' such as teachers and students should be encouraged, or recruited, to train the 'unconnected'.

4. *Increasing access and support*

— Encourage businesses to pass on their technical and general commercial expertise to community groups during the development of initiatives, including the negotiation of better deals on hardware and software, help with marketing plans, and hands-on help and support.

— Home outreach, childcare provision and women-only groups should be provided to encourage greater numbers of women to participate, especially where cultural backgrounds restrain women's activities.

— The provision, extension and development of home-loan laptops should be considered and supported by other forms of support service.

— Develop the use of existing community resources and locations, including schools, in order to help offer further free or inexpensive access and training.

— Arrange 'drop in', and open access facilities geared to those with little or no prior ICT experience.

5. *Increasing literacy*

— Encourage and develop special language facilities in areas where there are relatively high instances of individuals whose first language is not English. Offer appropriate software and courses for those with limited literacy, and develop initiatives that combine support for beginners in the use of ICT alongside relevant language and literacy support, such as translation and interpretation.

— Meeting the information needs of non-English speakers should be promoted and content should be readily available in languages other than English. Developments in ICT and language fonts mean that it is reasonably inexpensive and easy to set up and provide information in many other languages.

6. *Increasing joined-up approaches*

— Councils and local authorities should have a duty to develop plans illustrating how the resources available in the local communities can be maximised through a joined-up approach. This would also require more comprehensive data gathering and collaboration with local community groups, which, if handled sensitively, could increase understanding about the needs of community groups and help to deliver provide communication and collaboration.

— Continue to tackle the 'digital divide' in tandem with wider aspects of inequality.

— Involve the private sector in community initiatives to build the social capital necessary for community groups to effectively mobilise ICT.

7. *Overcoming barriers to community-based access and use*

— Audit disadvantaged communities to establish their needs and requirements in terms of content, and promote initiatives that involve them in directly creating materials.

— Develop better policy and delivery design by identifying clear lines of responsibility for co-ordinating advice and help through a single communication channel to all those who wish to develop community focussed initiatives. A more 'joined up' approach would reduce the fragmentation that can create barriers to community participation.

— Allow plans and projects to evolve organically from the people they aim to help, but provide support mechanisms to scaffold the development of sustainable community projects.

— Identify and work with recognised information leaders within the communities. Undertake social mapping to find key individuals, community needs and interests.

— Attempt to lure existing ICT-related businesses into deprived communities, and support new community-based ones through a range of subsidies and tax incentives.

Asia-Pacific Meeting on Bridging the Digital Divide

The leading Inter-governmental regional telecommunications organisation, Asia-Pacific Telecommunity (APT), organised the Asia-Pacific Meeting on Bridging the Digital Divide & Preparation for WTDC-02 in New Delhi, India from 13 -16 February 2002. The meeting discussed the initiatives of APT member countries and other regional players from the Information and Communication Technology (ICT) sectors in bridging the digital divide and exchange of information in promoting partnerships, mobilization and sharing of resources.

ICT play an important role in achieving maximum synergy of efforts and added useful value to the users. These efforts in addition to other efforts at national, intra regional and inter regional levels will help in bridging the digital divide. The rapid improvement in technology such as Mobile SMS needs to be leveraged for bridging the digital divide in the rural and remote areas.

In this meeting, OECD presented a comprehensive paper of OECD Approaches to Policy for e-Commerce, ICTs and the Digital Divide. They outlined their work on electronic commerce, the DOT Force Action Plan, ICT for Development and OECD's The Way Ahead for cooperation. While emphasizing their work on the Digital Divide, they also presented some activities that engaged with measurement and indicators in promoting the Understanding of the Digital Divide. The presentation was concluded by stressing some ways ahead of OECD cooperation and by actively joining through its workshops and conferences initiatives like OECD Global Forum on the Knowledge-Based Economy, Asia, early 2003, OECD Centre for Co-operation with Non-Members,

Global Forum on the KBE, Emerging Asian Economy Programme, Latin America and China Programmes, Participation of OECD in work of other bodies and co-operation with other International Organisations and Contribution of OECD to international initiatives.

The advent of digital technology and Internet is overcoming the limits of space and time and at a lower cost. The extent of digital divide, in terms of lower Tele-density, as compared to other parts of the world while it accounts for almost 2/3rd of world population and highlighted the asymmetric distribution of Internet hosts, Internet bandwidth and TV distribution in the world. The need for building on the regional Internet bandwidth to route the traffic economically.

The big gap between the developed and developing countries and also within the region and expressed the need for an immediate action for development of ICT. A creative policy by having commitment, leveraging on the advantages to develop other sectors, prepare a national plan, have partnership between public and private sector, encourage infrastructure expansion and maintain focus of policy on market principle. The policy should focus on rural communication development taking into account scale of community, operability of facilities and the economic viability.

One participant in the meeting illustrated the status of women participation in the ICT sector and highlighted the existence of a gender divide. Only a small portion of the female population of Asian developing is digitally empowered and pointed out that women concentrated at lower skilled employment levels. While concluding he made the following recommendations that have been derived from an ESCAP group meeting:

— Access: Need to build Cybercafes, alternative sources of software that are cost competitive and there is also the need to have specific allocation in national budget;

— Encourage education and training using ICT;

— Creation of enabling environment by participation of gender equality advocates, resource allocation and gender accountability, monitoring and reporting requirement.

A participant from South East Asian Ministers of Education Organisation (SEAMEO) informed the participants about the activities of SEAMEO. He mentioned that 15 regional centres in various countries of Asia promoting education, health and other cultural activities. He illustrated the extent of divide that exists in the South East Asia region and mentioned the factors like economic development, available of infrastructure, availability of education and income level. Following are the SEAMEO recommendations:

a) SEAMEO infrastructure should be linked to Public Infrastructure;

b) Linkages with existing International and regional organisations should be established

c) Content and infrastructure should be increased simultaneously;

d) More focus should be given to improve the skill and Knowledge.

In the future, there will be a need to encourage ICT and informed that a task force has been setup to facilitate the development of SEAMEO program. The future course of action is to improve the Infrastructure, promote Cyber education and establish virtual library so that SEAMEO can act as an information hub. The challenges to the digital divide include the lack of national policies and strategies, lack of awareness and upscaling of the successful projects to national ones, use of different access models and non availability of low cost devices. The challenges relating to ethical use of ICT, standards setting, training needs and modules.

Developing countries can use ICT to bridge the social divide in much better way. Working with partners to access global trust fund for supporting ICT infrastructure, building human capacity and extending use. Market failure in this area is still pervasive and there is, therefore a need for public involvement. There is lack of legal and institutional framework. There is need to stimulate local entrepreneurship and set the national policies. She also highlighted the problems of brain drain. UNDP is proactively working on analysing the potential of ICT to address social inequities.

The main policy areas of ILO, which included ensuring information economy becoming a job economy, need for ICT to become tool for development and key challenges facing education and training. On the whole there was greater gains with the introduction of ICT. ILO mentioned that investment, improving aceessibility, quality, training, fostering enetrprise and entrepenuership are necessary. In the Indian context, ILO is trying to push the report forward through a tripartite effort and trying to analyse the impact of automation.

One participant explained that Grameen Telecom (GTC) program is making efforts to bridge the digital divide in Bangladesh through handheld simple IT devices. It provides micro credit for the purpose.

Grameen Telecom was established in 1995 and is now a success. He also introduced the Telecom Scenario in Bangladesh and explained the relationship of GrameenPhone and its relationship with Grameen Telecom.

The Village Phone Program started in 1997. At the beginning of February 2002, the number of Village Phones stood at 9754 covering 8,637 villages out of the 68,000 villages in Bangladesh. The monthly average earning amounts to US$ 100 per month, which has helped in changing the social and economic status of the Village Phone ladies and their villages. He explained the role that Grameen bank plays by acting as a first point of contact.

GTC's future plan to have 50,000 village phones connecting equal number of villages by 2004 and upgrading a number of those into Village E-Mail and Telecom Centres (VETC). These VETCs will act as the building blocks to extend other I-T enabled services such as Tele-Medicine, Tele-education, weather, business and market information.

Mr. S.R.Das, Department Of Information Technology, India, emphasised on the digital unity brought about by I-T between freedom and distance. He informed the observation of the Working group on I-T, which includes introducing new opportunities and briefed on the recommendations that include Infrastructure development, e-Governance, education, rural development, Indian languages for Internet & standardisation and improving mass awareness.

Some of the initiatives that have been taken by the government include promotion of Internet access, creation of content with multimedia techniques,

Telemedicine and health care, IT applications for disabilities, Mass IT campaigns, technology development of basic tools and preserving cultural heritage. The recent achievements have been the computerisation of land records, national program on Low Cost Multimedia Content Creation, computerisation of Braille system and Computer Aided Tools for Celebral Plasy affected people, initiation of Tele-Medicine Projects, opening of Community Information Centres in North Eastern India and adult literacy programs. Prof. Jhunjhunwala started his presentation by introducing briefly the status of Telecom in India. He emphasised on the need for making the services affordable.

Speaking about the affordability, he mentioned that only 3% of household could afford the present cost per line and emphasised that this percentage can be significantly increased by reducing the cost to around $200. He introduced the CorDECT technology developed by IIT, Chennai that supports voice and Internet at a price of $US 200 and covers around 25Kms in rural area. He informed that this technology is deployed in India and also in a number of countries.

Prof. Jhunjhunwala also introduced n-logue, which focussed on rural areas only. He highlighted the success story of STD PCOs which account for 25% revenue and around 800,000 entreprenuership and low cost Cable TV ($2 per month). He emphasized on the need for Local Service Provider and having public access. Introducing low cost kiosks, he mentioned that the total cost for the entreprenuer is only $1000. He also informed the participants about various pilot projects going on.

The SchoolNet Thailand project, which connects 4200 schools to the Internet. The project is a joint effort of

Ministry of Science, Communication Technology and Education and promotes awareness, promotion of content development, training of teachers, providing access and promotion of classroom activities. The access to Internet is free of Charge. For creating content the concept of digital library was introduced that covers seven academic subjects.

A digital library schoolkit was provided to teachers for developing library material. The contents developed for archieves were indexed and a suitable Search engine was also developed. The project evolved in the years 1995-97 and is currently under development stage. In the forthcoming years the project will be expanded to include more schools, more number of web sites and larger bandwidth.

Japan's initiative for bridging the digital divide mentioned that we are witnessing an era of ICT revolution. He introduced the current status of Internet user in Japan. The total number of users currently are 42 Million and the household penetration is about 37%. In Japan, the number of Mobiles (72 Million) has exceeded the number of fixed, which is about 61 Million. 68% of these mobile customers access the Internet. He informed the participants about the governments national plan of e-Japan to become world's most advanced ICT nation by 2005. The priority policy areas include Ultra high speed network infrastructure to 30 million households by 2005, e-Commerce Rules and Infrastructure, realisation of e-Governance by 2003 and Human resource Development.

There are many types of digital divide such as those based on geography and those based on age and physical disability. For the process of bridging the digital divide, Japan has identified five priority areas relating to formulation of most advanced infrastructure, education & HRD, e-Commerce, digitization of Administration and Security and Reliability uses. The Japan initiative also informed about government initiatives of fair competition & Pro-competitive policies and establishment of Broadband network. He also informed the participants about the support to operators in terms of finance, special loans, tax reliefs, construction of Base Station by local operator etc. to encourage roll out.

Ms. Suriah apprised the participants of the profile of Malaysia and the policy thrusts that included Infrastructure development, Infostructure development and Industry development. The direction of efforts is to achieve the 2020 vision that Malaysia beholds.

Malaysia has a Cyber law to facilitate e-Commerce and protection of consumers. The market has been open to competition and Universal Service supports are envisaged for funding some of the initiatives. In 2000 a new converged regime has been implemented. A set of targets has been developed for the year 2005 laying down the key indicators. Ms. Suriah described the Multimedia initiatives like Multimedia SuperCorridor and mentioned that plans are on to roll it out to other parts of the country.

A Universal service Provision (USP) policy has been approved by the government. The government's contribution for the 8th Plan is a total of US$ 250 Million for Universal Service as it considers that the targets would be difficult to achieve by market forces only. There are plans of infrastructure development to schools and provision of Telecentres. Besides the government contribution, there are also contributions from Service Providers. She informed the participants about MCMC, which is an effective regulator with the necessary flexible and autonomous authority. She identified the challenges of bridging the digital divide, building the critical mass and e-culturalisation.

Another partipant in Japan presented the various satellite based initiatives for communication and disaster management. Many disaster areas are still devoid of access to modern tools. He explained how this project will be able to manage, monitor and mitigate disasters through timely information communication from different mobile and airborne terminals.

Mr. Shafiee informed the participants of the initiatives taken by IRAN towards the TOKYO declaration plan. He emphasised on the need for larger private sector participation.

A national ICT plan was approved specifying specific targets of roll out of various services including Internet. The charges for Internet has been reduced. Pilot projects have been initiated to improve e-Commerce. Special efforts are being taken to promote distance learning, virtual library, e-Governance and education. Iran is co-operating with Regional development organisations to promote ICT. Mr. Ahmed started with a brief overview of demographic and technological scenario in Maldives. He informed about the plans to introduce competition in Maldives and enumerated the current subscriber trends.

Some of the challenges to the growth of ICT are closed markets, high prices, lack of high speed, small market and low teledensity. The policy initiatives to take up this challenge include opening up of ISP market, deployment of Multipurpose Telecentres, available of telephones at discounted rates for public access centres, holding of Internet fairs, Free Internet Account, reduction of import duty on computer and introduction of IT in educational Curriculum. Ms. Dugarmaa informed the participants about the level of Telecom development in Mongolia including the number of exchanges, telephone lines and PCOs.

The private participation in ISP was opened in 1994 and as on 2001 thre are 7 ISPs and 10000 subscribers. In the area of Mobile Services, 2 joint venture companies are operating. She also informed that a separate regulatory body has been established and a Universal Service Fund has been created. The Policy aims to provide a teledensity of 15 in Ulanbator and 10-12 in the provinces, provide reliable access and Internet access to 50% of population. Ms Dugarmaa also detailed various policy objectives and ICT projects going on in Mongolia.

A participant in Bangladesh, identified the impediments to the bridging the divide as Lack of Education, fear of technology use, economic conditions, lack of english education, pressure of family responsibility and prevalent social and cultural aspects. He mentioned about various problems pertaining to infrastructure. BTTB has plans to provide telephones in rural areas using VHF and Cellular Mobile, The long terms plans include a submarine optical linking nationwide OFC newtork, liberalising satcom policy in 2010, project to provide at least one telephone in a village and educating the youths. India enquired whether BTTB sees a co-operation in Bangladesh and West Bengal province in India.

The policy of the government to encourage local and foreign investors to compete and cooperate in the investment for construction, development and expansion of telecommunications network. He detailed the policy plans formulated for the development and various targets laid down in the development Plan.

Mr. Choudhary from IBM mentioned that digital information is fast changing the behavourial needs of the society. The digital divide has four drivers, viz., Technological, Social, political and economic drivers, the impact of which were illustrated by the speaker using statistical evidence. Mr. Choudhary discussed initiatives on how can the government compete in the global market place. He expressed the need for integrating the front-end to the legacy.

The focus has to be on customer centric applications and services. He called on the government to understand the business and take concrete steps thereon to move towards integration. Mr. Sawhney provided an example of health care using pervasive computing, which can be quite effectively used as a Tele-Medicine tool for real time integration.

In India, there are about 600,000 villages with 91% having population less than 2000. The rural areas lack in infrastructure, have agriculture based economy and call for heavy income without matching return. New Telecom Policy has now laid down specific targets of rural telecommunications that include teledensity targets, provision of village public telephones, provision of Internet to every district headquarters. The rapid development has taken place due to indigenous efforts and enquired whether the Cyber dhabas are managed by BSNL or individuals. The size of the digital divide in India adds new challenges.

A participant from Zurriyadi highlighted development of public access to government, HRD, development of content and application as the three elements of e-Government. He introduced the concept of Information System Solution for Autonomous Region which provides various e- Services from Community Access Centres and Community learning centres.

SIMTAP, a web based public system was introduced in Takalar in Indonesia, which has resulted in productivity increase. He also made a proposal to APT from Indonesia to contribute towards a pilot project for introducing e-Governance to improve quality of service, introduce e-learning and develop SMEs.

3

Access to ICTs and Electronic Economy

During the late 15th and 16th Century in Europe, the spread of knowledge triggered by Gutenberg's printing press both helped to drive, and was supported by, a continent-wide rivalry of religious ideas. Now, the Internet has become both the fuel and the vehicle for a dramatic spread in democracy, intensifying demand for and supporting the spread of genuinely transparent and participatory and more efficient systems of government at both the national and global levels.

The number of democracies worldwide has doubled in little more than a decade. But in too many countries, institutions remain fragile, services are weak, officials unaccountable. And the lack of a democratic dividend-in terms of jobs and better services-has been undermining public faith in these new systems, particularly among the poor. ICT offers real hope in all these areas, offering greater citizen input into decision-making and better social services for all. From the Philippines to Zimbabwe, we have seen over the past year how cell-phones and e-mail have been used to gather supporters and spread ideas and information across grassroots and global networks with dramatic effect.

ICT is also proving a vital tool in helping link new civil society networks around key issues, from global warming to women's empowerment to attempts to make globalization more responsive to the needs of developing countries and the poor. ICT can also make government services and institutions cheaper, more efficient and more accessible. Developing countries like Brazil and Chile already have successful experiments underway in these areas.

In parts of India, online government licensing is cutting through traditionally tortuous bureaucracies. There is little point talking about the impact of ICT on democracy and development in countries where ICT barely exists. Just 0.4 percent of Africans and South Asians have used the Internet, compared to over half of North Americans. So the first challenge in harnessing limited resources is to identify the strategic levers of change that best help countries to boost the spread and application of ICT.

Human Development Report 2001 argues, governments need to put in place an enabling environment that encourages investments in hard-ware and tertiary education. A Digital Opportunity Initiative study that UNDP recently undertook with Accenture and the Markle Foundation shows the need for developing countries to put in place comprehensive national e-strategies that address issues such as connectivity, regulatory environment, and human capacity.

Usually a well-educated technically-qualified pool of potential IT employees is a more critical advantage than the quality of a country's telecom infrastructure. This revolution really is about people. Helping countries to move forward in these ways will be a central feature of our Global Network Readiness initiative that we are rolling out first in Bolivia, Romania and Tanzania. Estonia is one of the world's best examples of how much can be achieved with the right enabling environment.

That country's Tiger Leap project, sup-ported by UNDP, wired the entire coun-try starting in the early 1990's and has ensured that the current generation of Estonian student is 100 percent computer literate. Tiger Leap has also been a catalyst for regional economic development and provides access points across the country, which citizens can use to conduct most of their transactions with the government. Almost all government documents-as well as Real Audio broadcasts of parliamentary sessions-are available online. Other countries should follow Estonia's lead. The global surge of democracy is real but fragile. And ICT can help consolidate the gains of the past several decades.

The new information and communication technologies (ICTs) are the outcome of technological development, and the digital divide is the inevitable consequence of income differences. Admittedly, today, the people of developed countries have a greater access to the benefits of technological progress as their incomes increase, but a number of techniques also represent tools for human development which enable the population to improve its income and its life expectancy, to enjoy better health and living standards, and to be more innovative.

Like education, technology represents a means for the poor to surmount their condition. It therefore represents a tool for growth and development and is not only an outcome of them. The United Nations

Millennium Declaration signatories' leitmotiv "[to undertake] among other things, to ensure that the advantages of the new technologies, and in particular ICT, should be granted to all", should be viewed in this context. Access to information, and to knowledge acquisition, is viewed as crucial for the development process. On one hand it involves the existence of adequate ICT networks and services, on the other hand, the capability to use these tools in order to design applications useful to the whole of society. However, both these tools and the capacity to use them are unequally distributed". The Millennium Declaration acknowledges the specific problems faced by the vulnerable communities such as least developing countries (LDCs), the small developing insular states and landlocked countries. It also acknowledges the necessity to enable these countries to fully participate in the world economy.

The vulnerable communities are, even to a larger extent than the others, dependent on ICTs because of their isolation. Indeed, in spite of considerable progress achieved in recent years, access to ICTs, namely to the fixed and mobile telephone, the Internet and to radio - broadcasting, remains unequally distributed. The double-speed development is particularly felt in Africa, the continent which contains 39 out of 49 least developed countries in the world. According to the International Telecommunications Union (ITU) 1991 estimates, total telephone penetration represented 49 per cent in the developed countries, against 3.3 per cent in the emerging countries, and only 0.3 per cent in the least developed countries.

The large-scale diffusion of the new ICTs in developing countries appears as an unavoidable challenge to be met. Should "the digital divide " which can currently be observed persist, developing countries could become even more isolated from economic circuits, and extremely marginalized, and their takeoff opportunity once more heavily at stake. This situation entails, once more, that the issue of the means to be implemented and the mechanisms to be promoted in order to help these countries to become less isolated and benefit from the progress in the new information technologies, and to integrate them in the global exchanges be addressed.

The necessity to bring in the relevant support so as to enable these countries to benefit from economic globalisation is largely recognised and established. According to this stance, the debate can take place at the level of the analysis of the fundamental constraints, the determination of the potential for the improvement of institutional and human capabilities, taking into account existing mechanisms, and finally the definition of an appropriate strategy based on specific national, regional and international needs.

The LDCs are defined as low income countries whose growth has been hampered for a long time, in particular by a low level of human resources development, and/or serious structural problems. These countries are included in a list established by the United Nations General Assembly, which is revised on a three-year basis. There are currently 49 LDCs in the world, of which 34 are to be found in Africa, with a population of 427 million, living, according to the United Nations, on less than one dollar a day. Most analysts consider that LDCs' situation has worsened, which has resulted in a limited growth of the telecommunication sector.

The problems are on one hand technical, linked to the telecommunications services obsolescence and under-equipment, on the other hand political, with geographical discrepancies resulting from political choices implemented in general by centralising States which promoted a more or less exclusive concentration of telecommunication services in the capital cities. However, the future information society assumes a universal and equal access to all the populations in a country. The main obstacles and bottlenecks should be looked for in the following fields: infrastructure status, the financial and institutional capabilities, and the level and qualification of human capital, cultural differences, etc.

The discrepancy between development levels in Africa, and more particularly in the least developed countries, and levels attained in the rest of the world has widened in the field of ICTs more than for more classical criteria used for measuring development. The fact is that African population in its large majority has never made a telephone call, or in terms of quality of communication, because of existing networks obsolescence or saturation. Irregular power supply, if any, a common feature to the whole of the landscape represents a major hindrance to an intensification in the use of ICTs, especially out of the large towns.

Many countries' power distribution networks are very limited and penetration in rural areas has just been initiated. Long power cuts are more or less the norm, even in such capital cities as Accra or Dar es Salam. Further, most tax regimes continue to consider ICT products, almost exclusively imported, as luxury goods, which makes their purchase price even more expensive, thus preventing most people from buying them. Under these conditions, it is not surprising that radio -

broadcasting still remains the most widely used mass communication means, and the ownership of a radio set is much more common than any other electronic device. It is also worth observing that many people listen to or watch the same TV set at the same time.

According to the 2001 UNESCO Report the existing radio transmission networks reach more than 60 per cent of the sub-Saharan African population, while television coverage is essentially limited to the larger towns. However, it can be said that most LDCs are experiencing an expansion and a modernisation of their telecommunication networks, which is reflected in an annual increase of the number of main lines of around 10 per cent. In addition, a large part of the telecommunication network is analogue and a large number of sectors operate to capacity saturation or they are not very reliable, especially during the rainy seasons.

Moreover, 50 per cent of the available lines are concentrated in the capital cities, where only 10 per cent of the population live. Compared to the rest of the world, it appears that the region avails of by far the least developed infrastructure. The existing telephone networks status varies greatly depending on the countries. Some, like Botswana and Rwanda, which have made telecommunications one of their priorities, are installing digital switches with optical fibre links between towns together with the most up to date cell and mobile telephone technology.

At the other extreme, countries such as Madagascar and Uganda have analogue telephone systems which, in general, are not very reliable and poor national links between urban centres. Thus, in terms of main lines capacity, the change which took place in the 90s shows considerable discrepancies from one country to another, since in some countries capacity decreased while in other countries it increased 300 per cent. The countries whose capacity stagnated are obviously those in which the political and economic situation have experienced serious problems in the past decade such as Liberia, Rwanda, Congo, Angola etc.

Conversely, neither are countries where the situation experienced the greater improvement characteristic of an average situation; in general, growth took place in small countries where networks development cost is much lower, such as in Cape Verde. At the sub-regional level, Sahel and Central African countries, such as Mali, Niger and the Democratic Republic of Congo, have less than two telephone lines per 100 inhabitants. With the advent of the mobile telephone, access to telecommunications increased considerably.

Uganda enshrines the example of the mobile telephone revolution in LDCs. This east African country granted in 1998 a licence to a second national operator (MTN Uganda), whose priority was access to prepaid mobile telephones. Microwave network installation is rapid and, in a country where the majority of the population cannot afford a subscription, prepayment makes telecommunications more easily affordable to many. The results were spectacular.

In slightly more than one year, MTN became the most important operator in the country. The company has since actively undertaken to expand the network to the rural areas. More than 50 per cent of the population and about 80 towns are currently covered by the cell phone. An increasing number of LDCs are now implementing the Uganda project.

The Internet is still a privilege in the least developed countries, where two out of a thousand inhabitants use it. This ratio, which is clearly less than the average of other developing countries is well below certain developed countries, where one out of four inhabitants has access to the Internet.

The Internet requires excellent quality and very fast connections, and the corresponding infrastructures. But, in the major part of these countries, especially landlocked territories and remote islands, there are very few national and international links.

These countries are not yet equipped with optical fibre links, and satellite links are limited and very expensive. Furthermore, internal telecommunication infrastructures are, generally speaking, concentrated in a few of the larger towns, while they are seriously insufficient in rural areas. As a remedy to this situation, certain countries have made the decision to supply access to the Internet via local call over the whole of their territory through the use of a determined zone code.

An additional characteristic of LDCs' situation is the difficulty in bearing the cost of the use of communication technologies. Indeed, the proportion of the population that can afford to pay the price of a telephone is much lower than in other countries.

Human poverty and institutional fragility deepen the gap between technologies adapted to the incomes and capabilities of rich and poor countries alike. Furthermore, revenue generated from international calls, especially incoming calls represents more than half the telecommunications revenue, while it also represents a source of foreign currency.

The main obstacles to the implementation of national information and communication services are listed below:

(1) lack of adequate standards for homologation of materials prototypes;

(2) difficulties in obtaining authorisations to have access to international telecommunication companies;

(3) lack of an appropriate legal framework for the creation of companies or value-added services suppliers' associations;

(4) lack of support services, computer training, information strategies planning;

(5) difficulties in obtaining the required funding;

(6) delay in the provisions relative to intellectual property rights;

(7) restrictions on freedom of speech;

(8) lack of satisfactory management and coordination mechanisms at the national, regional and subregional levels;

(9) lack of awareness of the importance of the implementation of the information and telecommunication infrastructure.

A study carried out UNCTAD, on electronic commerce development in ten LDCs, the most important obstacles mentioned by companies wishing to start electronic commerce in LDCs are of a regulatory character: foreign exchange control, telecommunications monopoly, restrictive commercial practices, miscellaneous prohibitions with respect to encryption, Internet telephony, and the possibility to use their own access portal, and so on.

While the use of a fixed telephone does not require any prior training, handling a mobile phone is already more complex; Furthermore, the poor level of technological knowledge in LDCs should also be taken into consideration. Certainly, the Internet provides access to the whole of global information, but one needs to be able to read and write in order to use a complex system and retrieve what one is looking for.

LDCs are not only the countries where per capita income is the lowest, but where the illiteracy rate is the highest, the enrolment rate in primary education is the lowest, and the educational divide between girls and boys the widest. Although an improvement of competence has been achieved in the last twenty years in certain deprived countries, some countries do not avail of the adequate capacities as yet. This shortcoming makes them incapable of adapting the technologies available in the world at large to their needs, and a fortiori to extend the use of ICTs and define their own programmes in order to meet their needs. Policies and instruments have been implemented in most countries in order to promote human resources development.

In the education and training sector varying levels were achieved in different countries. Indeed, in certain countries the efforts have resulted in human resources development in IT both in the formal academic system and in training institutions while in some other countries the performance levels remain poor. In addition, policy implementation faces difficulties, which are generally associated with hardware and software acquisition and shortage of a qualified workforce. The risk of cultural colonisation by nations producing most of the cultural goods on information highways is real, and exposes ICTs to being rejected by developing societies. The greatest handicap, which represents an inhibiting factor is the fact that, gradually, a certain "cyber-culture" is settling on the network with a specific behaviour, and with particular standards and languages.

Since the 1995 G7 Information Society Conference expressed its concern in respect of the digital divide dividing industrial countries from developing countries, and launched an appeal for "a shared vision of human empowerment", issues related to the digital divide have become an international priority. During the Okinawa Summit in July 2000, the G8 prepared the Okinawa Chart on the Global Information Society and created the Digital Opportunity Task Force (DOT Force).

The DOT Force designed a plan, "Digital Opportunities for all: Surmounting the Challenge ", presented during the G8 Summit in Genoa in July 2001. On the occasion of its Millennium Session, the United Nations General Assembly paid specific attention to ICTs, and a United Nations working group on ICTs was created, as a practical step, in order to reinforce the United Nations system role and leadership, and to develop effective partnership with the private sector, civil society and other relevant parties.

The ECOSOC session in July 2001 took up the theme of ICTs, with special emphasis on knowledge networks. The financing implemented by the international cooperation in ICTs clearly shows the importance given by the international community to this sector.

Among the United Nations agencies, the International Telecommunication Union (ITU), plays a key role in telecommunication development and the dissemination and exchange of information, in particular through its Telecommunication Development Bureau and the Strategy and Policy Unit. The World Bank, which offers assistance in the telecommunications field and ICT development. The United Nations Conference on Trade and Development (UNCTAD) has made Africa the priority region for the next two years. A financial commitment of 30 million Euros was obtained from the European Union for networks regional development for the improvement of local trade in Africa. UNESCO gives a high priority to initiatives in informatics and telematics in Africa through support to the Regional Informatics Network for Africa (RINAF).

In addition, UNESCO implemented the Creating Learning Networks for African Teachers .project designed to help teacher training familiarise themselves with ICTs and their application in teaching, and to connect them to the Internet. The project, already operational in Zimbabwe, has been initiated in Senegal, and will be, in principle, extended to other African countries. In recent years, UNDP has launched several initiative and partnership agreements with the private sector and some foundations.

The UNDP Sustainable Development Programme for the Creation of Networks (SNDP) includes ten operational nodes in Africa (Angola, Benin, Cameroon, Malawi, Morocco, Mozambique, Chad, Togo, and Tunisia. National projects implemented within SNDP are funded for a two or three year period, and should, in principle, provide starting capital to launch a sustainable operation, either through remunerated services or incorporation to the State budget. The United Nations Programme for the Environment (UNPE) Mercury Project which utilises the VSAT (Very Small Aperture Terminal) technology for the implementation of an information exchange network on the environment in Africa.

Catalysing Access to ICT's in Africa (CATIA), initiated by the U.K. Department for International Development. CATIA has several objectives including support for key organizations influencing regulatory policy in the telecommunications and Internet sectors and CATIA will also encourage private/public partnership activities that facilitate low cost Internet access opportunities across Africa. In addition, UNESCO implemented the Creating Learning Networks for Africa Teachers project designed to help teacher training familiarize with ICTs and their application in teaching, and to connect them to the Internet.

Since 1973, ITU has significantly assisted LDCs. Currently, the 49 LDCs receive a technical assistance in various fields in order to accelerate the pace of development in their telecommunications, which, in turn, will entail socio -economic development in these countries. In conformity with the Buenos Aires Action Plan, and subsequently the Valetta Action Plan, crucial priorities include the introduction of new technologies, the reform and restructuring of the telecommunications sector, rural telecommunications development, human resources development, and telecommunications networks extension funding through partnership.

The main objective of these special actions towards LDCs is closing the digital gap between the poorest 49 countries and the rest of the world. In practical terms, the programme aims to increase average teledensity up to five main lines per 100 inhabitants, and connections to the Internet to 10 users per 100 inhabitants by 2010. The strategy will consist in focusing on a small number of countries, starting with those with the least means, and gradually covering the others.

A special assistance is equally brought to LDCs, which have just emerged from war, internal troubles or natural disasters, such as Somalia, Rwanda, Burundi, Liberia and East Timor. The aim of the assistance is to consolidate their political and regulatory frameworks in the telecommunication sector and to improve access to rural areas to services by encouraging private investment. The World Economic Forum (FEM) which launched, in April 2000, a global digital initiative to make the digital divide an opportunity for growth and which adopted an action plan in October 2001.

Within a development strategy, the ICT objective consists in allowing LDCs to benefit from these technologies in order to achieve the objectives of their collectivity/community in social, economic, educational and health care development. Some priority problems delay LDCs development including health and education; ICTs represent some of the possibilities for their resolution.

UN General Assembly states that it is urgent to utilize knowledge and technology potential in order to implement the objectives of the Millenium Declaration and find efficient and novel means to put this potential in the service of development for all. The main challenge is linked to the danger of creating a two-speed society in which only one part of the population has access to the new technologies, and is able to use them with ease, and enjoy the advantages they procure.

There is then a risk of a rejection of the new information culture and its tools. Hence, the preparation of LDCs for the advent of the information society is a priority task. Teaching, training and awareness building will necessarily play a central part. The opportunities offered by the global information and communication revolution to developing countries are considerable if adequate policies are correctly implemented. Indeed, the advantages of the new ICTs are no longer limited to the communication and information sectors; they now represent general use technologies, penetrating all fields and sectors, for instance :

a) *In the field of education*: ICT use has potential promise for drastic cost reduction and for an improvement of training and education quality. Education and training should be considered as a priority for the promotion of equal opportunity for participation in and benefit from the information Society. ICT integration in the curriculum and in teachers' education and training should be reinforced as teachers are knowledge multipliers in ICT use. Technological skills acquisition in all levels of education, especially the broadening of knowledge in informatics, is essential for attracting investment, and sustains entrepreneurship, which are both crucial for economic development.

b) *In the field of health care*, ICTs will play an important part in the alleviation of certain problems, which can be achieved by improving access to health care services in rural areas, by extending public education campaigns in order to promote sanitary behaviour, through the transfer of diagnoses information to the specialized centres, by reinforcing information for decision making, promoting information exchange between researchers and students, and valorizing public health establishments.

c) *In business*, where exchanges are hindered by poor transport and communication networks and lack of information, ICTs will allow business companies to become more competitive thanks to updated and adequate commercial information. Indeed, ICTs boost the establishment of links between chambers of commerce, commercial companies, and commercial associations and firms, so as to help small and medium-sized firms and develop regional and international exchanges, and further reduce the cost of business transactions.

d) *Food security*: for example, ICTs are a way of receiving drought alarms on time, enabling the timing of the planting of crops to be modified, thereby reducing the risk of famine.

e) *Women and development*: ICTs provide access to information and indicators which help in identifying problems. They provide equitable information opportunities for women, together with access to technology and technical education.

f) *Culture*: the new opportunities are numerous, including saving the cultural heritage on electronic media, supporting it with documents and carrying out its diffusion, and the original production of local contents.

g) *Development of governmental services*, as well as electronic registration of marital status and tax forms, for example.

The African countries' ICT needs listed in the New Partnership for Development in Africa (NEPAD) represent a significant reference point. The various studies carried out agree on the notion that the building an information and communication sector requires the utilisation and development of the following elements as supporting factors prior to the implementation of an ICT policy:

(1) a legal and institutional framework,

(2) human resources,

(3) technological infrastructures, and

(4) information resources.

LDC social and economic development is, to a large extent, determined by the size and quality of the employed population - its human and intellectual capital - education, training, and the valorisation of human resources will represent milestones for the new information society.

Furthermore, on one hand human resources development requires novel attitudes from decision-makers and new skills among both the executives and the labour force, i.e. the capacity to adapt, adopt and utilise the new technologies and master change, and, on the other hand, the creation of new labour markets in which the technical competence and knowledge acquired could be used.

No information and communication system can operate efficiently without reliable inexpensive and abundant technological means, in the form of computers, software and all the elements of a telecommunications infrastructure allowing data and information processing. Not only will it be necessary to modernise and develop the infrastructure and the telecommunications material and logical network at the national level, especially in rural and remote areas, but also to improve interconnection at the regional level and include international transit centres for access to international telecommunications networks.

The poor are solely beneficiaries of information and knowledge technology. It is obvious that this is not the case. Deprived communities produce their own information and knowledge. Thus, ICTs may play a positive part by allowing the wider diffusion of indigenous information and knowledge. But information gathering is not an end in itself; it should also be processed and routed to the end-user without delay. The challenges of information highways are first and foremost technological.

The nations with the know-how and performing infrastructures for information processing and distribution are undeniably those well ahead of the others. Information highways represent an opportunity for LDCs, and can help compensate for lower levels of technological and economic development. The sectors in the best position to draw a maximum of benefit, and very rapidly, are education, scientific and technical research, medicine, tourism, the valorisation of the cultural heritage and trade and industry.

The rural world, which represents 85 per cent of the population in LDCs, should not be excluded from this process, hence the importance of developing community information systems allowing the codification of all of the information required for the rural sector development by:

— designing interfaces for information access by an illiterate population;

— making such information as civil status data, economic statistics linked to the agricultural sector, handicraft, fishing and cultivation available.

In Senegal, according to the telecentres managers union, the some 10,000 operational telecentres in the country generate an annual turnover of circa 50 million Euros, an activity which, in addition, contributes to the creation of a large number of jobs particularly for young people.

In the light of the analysis of ICTs in the least developed countries and of the identification of the potential needs, it clearly appears that the constraints hindering the development of information and communication of a society are closely linked to the economic and social context and to the different factors belonging to the transfer of technology. Thus, the actual issue to be addressed by a strategy for the promotion of ICTs is that of determining in what way such communication tools as the Internet or the telephone, radio and television can contribute to the local development of communities, thereby creating the conditions of a sustainable development in each of these countries and in the regions which surround them.

The government's role is, first and foremost, to present a vision for the future, a strategy and an environment favourable to the implementation of a national information and communication infrastructure, and to ensure that all sectors are benefiting from it. Its mission should consist in:

— Elaboration of national plans for the adoption of informatics and new communication technologies by government or public bodies, and follow-up on their implementation;

— Promotion of the use of the new information and communication technologies in the civil service in order to improve public services productivity and stimulate information and communication industries;

— Significant support to public establishments, such as higher education bodies and research institutions;

— Creating a framework and procedures for the participation of all sectors in the implementation of a national information and communication infrastructure, the coordination and harmonisation of different actors' efforts, including the private sector, non-governmental organisations and the media.

— Establishing relationships with other countries, international organisations and regional bodies, for coordinated and harmonious development at both the regional and the international levels;

— Designing the legal framework and the required regulations to resolve the problems related to costs of telecommunications and accessibility, universal service objectives, intellectual property, respect for privacy, free circulation of information and the convergence of radio and television broadcasting with telecommunications;

In this respect, governments' principal tasks are listed below:

— *Telecommunications*: the issue is to facilitate the liberalisation of national telecommunications and radio and TV broadcasting public services. In this respect, legislation should be defined and incentive measures for the private sector's collaboration in the implementation of this infrastructure should be offered, and an independent and strong regulatory body in charge of the regulation of partnerships between the public sector and the private sector and, particularly, international participation, should be established.

— *Intellectual Property*: LDCs require a legal framework which can take into balanced consideration intellectual property as an international obligation and the necessity to meet the basic intellectual needs of the poor. Governments should pass and implement copyright legislation and increase public awareness of intellectual property rights. They should also simultaneously forecast and design palliatives in respect of the negative impact of such laws on society.

— *Respect for privacy*: laws for the protection of private persons against any breach of their privacy that could be caused by the new technologies should be adopted.

— *Free circulation of information:* formulation and application of laws and regulations for the protection of the freedom of speech, which represents a guarantee for easy access to information and services.

— Facilitate equal access for women to the new information technologies.

This aims to develop in the private and public sector decision- makers informed decision-makers, allowing them to improve their knowledge of the value of the use of information, national and international information resources, research methods and direct information retrieval on the Internet network or on other international information networks, the electronic mail and "knowledge bases" networks, potential social, economic and cultural effects of the new information and communication systems and the necessity for training in order to adapt structures and work methods in order to benefit from electronic media and spaces. The objective is the introduction of the new ICT in schools and universities.

The government's role should be supported by development cooperation, resulting in the impleme-ntation of institutional and regulatory frameworks in order to stimulate a proper use of ICTs in the educational sector. The role of NGOs may range from the articulation of needs which may be increasingly marginalized by technological progress, to the assessment of the popul-ation's real information needs, including the supply of relevant data at local level. The private sector can both provide the technical infrastructure and promote the creation of content by means of innovative ideas.

Access to Eelectronic Economy

The digital economy is being shaped not only by the development and diffusion of computer hardware and software, but also by much cheaper and rapidly increasing electronic connectivity. The Internet in particular is helping to level the playing field among large and small firms in business-to-business e-commerce. In the past, larger companies had increasingly used private networks to carry out electronic commerce, but high costs kept the resulting efficiencies out of reach for most small businesses.

Citizens of developed countries have definitively crossed into a new era of economic and social experience bound up in digitally-based technological changes that are producing new ways of working, new means and manners of communicating, new goods and services, and new forms of community. It measures the economic performance of information technology (IT) industries and their substantial impact on growth and inflation, and sketches the emerging dimensions of e-commerce. For the first time, it can be reasonably claimed that the extraordinary dynamism of the IT sector and the new, proliferating forms of e-business and e-commerce are part of an enduring and broad economic pattern.

The rapid pace and proliferation of innovation associated with IT, and the substantial increases in U.S. productivity and growth associated with IT-related innovation, now appear to be persistent. At the core of the proposition that the digital economy can produce higher long-term productivity gains and national growth than we knew in the 1970s and 1980s are certain singular qualities associated with information technologies.

Most obviously, these technologies provide new ways of managing and using a resource that is common to every sector and aspect of economic life; namely information. Compared, for example, to the introduction of refrigeration or jet propulsion, IT innovations can be applied across the economy and throughout the economic process. As a result, economic gains directly associated with improving the capacity to obtain, process and transmit information mount up.

Further, many IT markets exhibit what economists call "network effects": The more the technology is deployed, the greater its value. Compare certain information technologies to automobiles. When you own a car, its value to you is basically the same whether 5,000 or 1 million other people own the same brand of automobile. When you buy a computer operating system or graphics program, its value to you increases as more people buy it, because their purchases of the same program increase your ability to digitally communicate and interact. The spread of IT innovations in the digital economy affect growth in other ways.

For example, IT innovations appear to raise business investment in equipment. The last seven years have seen the fastest growth of business investment in equipment on record, and IT investments have accounted for almost two-thirds of that growth.

The digital economy also can stimulate improvements in workers' skills, since many firms have to train their employees to use information technologies. This may be one reason why Americans across the work force are making real wage gains for the first time in two decades.

Further, IT markets with the network effects described above tend to be dominated by a handful of products and companies, and this tendency creates the possibility of beneficial economies of scale. Perhaps most important of all, a dynamic of cascading or continuous innovation has characterized the development and deployment of information technologies in this period.

Productivity gains come not just from deploying innovative technologies that enable workers to process information faster. In addition, firms intent on taking advantage of innovative new technologies often have to rethink the way they operate and reorganize their operations, which can produce a round of organizational innovation. Many firms also have discovered that the new technologies can be used to develop and produce new goods or services for themselves, producing yet another round of innovation.

Furthermore, as these areas of potential are widely recognized and the process spreads from firm to firm, this generates demand for faster information processing. This can lead to another round of innovation in IT itself—part of the basis for the doubling of chip capacity every 18 months, articulated as Moore's Law—and the cascade can begin again.

A leading example of this dynamic is the Internet itself. Regular and large increases in chip power provided a technological foundation for the Internet, which in turn generated myriad innovations first in software and then in how businesses organize themselves and operate, which in turn has led to more myriad innovations in the goods and services available to businesses and individuals. The complex of hardware and software innovations that encompass the IT sector have made information the most important basis for creating value in the economy. The process of creating value from information, throughout and across the economy, is the ultimate basis for the digital economy.

At the same time, the U.S. economy has enjoyed a remarkable resurgence. Productivity growth, one of the most important indicators of economic health, doubled its pace from a sluggish 1.4-percent average rate between 1973 and 1995, to a 2.8-percent rate from 1995 to 1999. Evidence is increasing that these two phenomena are not coincidental but derive substantially from the same phenomenon: the synergistic convergence of dramatic increases in computer power, an explosion in connectivity, and increasingly powerful new software.

These advances in technology have produced sharp declines in the prices of computer processing, data storage and retrieval, and communications, that are in turn driving both the surge in Internet activity and the increases in business investment in IT hardware and software. Such investment has been a major source of recent U.S. economic strength.

The advances in computer power overwhelm imagination. Technologies associated with computer use, such as data storage technologies, have also shown dramatic improvements in performance and even more dramatic cost reductions.

The capacity of today's hard- disk drives is doubling every nine months and the average price per megabyte for hard-disk drives has declined from $11.54 in 1988 to an estimated $.02 in 1999. As a consequence of technological advances in microprocessors, storage, and other components, already steep annual declines in computer costs from 1987 to 1994 accelerated sharply beginning in 1995. Similar improvements have occurred in communications technologies.For example, wavelength division multiplexing, digital subscriber lines, and cable modems have produced exponential increases in the speed of data communication and the carrying capacity of the communications infrastructure. The carrying capacity of fiber is currently doubling every 12 months.

Between 1994 and 1998, the price of telecommunications equipment declined by 2 percent per year. Price declines for computers and peripheral equipment and for communications equipment have spurred major increases in business IT investment and extraordinary growth in U.S. production of computers, communications equipment and semiconductors. In addition, the declining costs of computing and communications are helping to drive complementary investment in new software that harnesses and further enhances the productive capacity of IT hardware and infrastructure. The new economy is being shaped by developments not only in computer hardware and software, but also in electronic connectivity.

Larger businesses have been increasing efficiencies through standardizing and automating routine transactions electronically for some time. Until recently, however, most small and medium sized businesses found that the costs of necessary hardware, software, and communications service for these systems exceeded the benefits. The advent of the Internet as an instrument of commerce fundamentally altered this equation by cutting the costs of software and communications services needed to conduct electronic transactions.

Beginning in the mid-1990s, as a result of the convergence toward digital formats and the development of de facto standards for digital networks, such as the Internet's technical specifications, the expansion and commercialization of the Internet made connecting computers and communications devices easier and cheaper.

Commercial opportunities on the Internet and the falling costs of computer and communications hardware created an extraordinarily fertile environment for innovations that are creating new value and new efficiencies for businesses of all sizes. The Internet is both an effect and a cause of the new economy. It is, in part, a product of the powerful technological and economic changes that are shaping a new epoch of economic experience. Networks, like telephone networks or the Internet, are subject to a phenomenon called "network effects" or "network externalities." Establishing a network involves large, up-front fixed costs, but adding an additional user to an existing network costs very little.

Conversely, the value of a network to participants is low when the number of participants on the network is low, but rises rapidly as network participation expands.

For example, a network of a single telephone is of no use. Adding another telephone increases the value of the network because now calls can be made between the two phones. As phones are added, the number of possible connections rises almost as fast as the number of phones squared. Similarly, as the number of people online has grown, so has the value of being online to each Internet user.

Moreover, as the Internet gains popularity, its technological specifications have become a default standard, encouraging new hardware and software innovations that use Internet technology as a platform. Fundamental engineering breakthroughs alone do not have important economic effects until their costs and applications become favorable.

For example, by the mid-1970s, Xerox PARC had already made several breakthroughs underpinning today's IT revolution: a microcomputer with a mouse, graphical user interface, and Ethernet communications capabilities.

But there was no mass market for their machine, which at the time cost about $25,000 each to produce, especially given its slower processing speed and the absence of applications software that drives computer use today. In contrast, technological advances in recent years have brought IT costs down to a far more commercially attractive range, and new software applications for networked systems have been developed.

Nothing approaching the activities now conducted over the Internet was possible a few years ago. Push back the technology or cost declines in any one of the four elements--computer processing, data storage, software, or communications—just a few years and the Internet activities we now view as commonplace would be too frustrating or too costly for a mass market.

Likewise, roll back any one of those elements and business would have found IT investment to be far less productive. As applications software is developed to exploit the continuing plunge in hardware prices in coming years, businesses and consumers will find new ways to create value and increase efficiency.

Impact of E-Commerce

The U.S. economy coincides with the growing use of the Internet, including the rapid growth of electronic commerce. In ever greater numbers, people are shopping, looking for jobs, and researching medical problems online. Businesses are moving their supply networks online, participating in and developing online marketplaces, and expanding their use of networked systems to improve a host of business processes. And new products and services are being created and integrated into the networked world.

Over the past year, Internet access in the United States and Canada grew by more than 40 percent; over the same period, Internet access in all other parts of the world more than doubled. Consumers today--wherever they are in the world--go online to shop, learn about different products and providers, search for jobs, manage their finances, obtain health information and scan their hometown newspapers.

While many of these activities are not captured by official output and productivity measures, a growing body of anecdotal evidence suggests that the digital revolution is improving many people's lives. Individuals with Internet access increasingly approach the Web as a market space. People online do research before they buy, make purchase commitments, arrange financing, take delivery of digital products, and obtain followup service. The "commerce" in e-commerce encompasses all of these activities.

However, when measuring business-to-consumer (B2C) e-commerce in particular, it is the commitment to purchase--the transactional component--that both buyers and sellers can easily identify and quantify. This transactional component is the focus of most current e-commerce measurements. In March 2000, the U.S. Bureau of the Census released the first official measure of e-retail, an important subset of business-to-consumer e-commerce. By contrast, private estimates for consumer e-commerce in the fourth quarter of 1999 ranged from approximately $4 billion to $14 billion.

However, many private estimates of B2C e-commerce include the value of a wide range of consumer online purchases such as airline tickets, hotel rooms, and shares of stocks that are not captured in The Census Bureau's survey of retail establishments. When these private estimates are adjusted to cover only those purchases included in the retail measure, the Census Bureau estimate of $5.3 billion appears to fall in the midrange.

Private surveys conducted shortly after the holiday season indicated that such problems were minimal and that online customer satisfaction was high. Nonetheless, some analysts believe that delivering goods ordered by consumers from e-retailers will prove to be more costly and complex than currently appreciated. The ultimate size of online consumer sales will depend on resolving these fulfillment issues, along with other important matters such as taxation, consumer protection, privacy, intellectual property rights, security, and network reliability. In the consumer realm, the most significant impact of e-commerce may be on the pricing of goods and services.

Potential buyers can check the price and availability of products from a variety of sites in far less time than it would take to conduct store-to-store comparisons in the world of bricks and mortar. Furthermore, online digital shopping spaces can be perused for consumers by software specialized to operate as digital shoppers. Such digital agents, known as "bots," cruise through numbers of Internet sites almost instantaneously, searching for the most favorable price and feature combinations. One would expect that this ability to easily and cheaply gather information on prices and product characteristics would force Internet retailers to charge the same low price--one that would approach their cost--on the same or comparable products. One might also expect these online prices to influence prices charged in physical stores. Thus far, however, the data on these matters are mixed.

Live auctions have existed for a long time, but their practical uses have been limited by the expense and difficulty of getting prospective buyers to a single location at the same time. Sealed bid auctions are less expensive, but they often do not produce the highest possible return to the seller. By contrast, the Internet provides a relatively low-cost and convenient way of bringing buyers and sellers together, and the use of auction sites such as eBay has grown rapidly.

A "single price" model holds for most offline goods and services since most offline sellers do not have sufficient information to vary their prices from customer-to-customer and because changing the price of individually tagged items may involve considerable cost. Where providers do have sufficient customer information and price adjustments are relatively easy to make, however, variable pricing can produce benefits to both seller and consumer.

For example, airlines have long set lower fares for tickets issued 21 days in advance that include a Saturday night stay and much higher fares for next-day tickets. More recently, airlines have developed an e-mail strategy to attract "spur of the moment" travelers with last minute travel deals. As a result, while vacation travelers obtain fares at a lower cost than if the airline charged a single price for all seats on the plane, business travelers can be confident that they can secure seats with little advanced notice, and airlines operate with a higher proportion of their seats filled.

The Internet opens up this airline-type variable pricing to many other types of goods and services, creating the potential for greater specificity in variable pricing. By gauging the price sensitivity of particular consumers relative to the marginal cost of the good and its availability, online sellers can fine tune prices for individual customers to maximize profits. Manufacturers, retailers, and online magazines now offer detailed product, warranty, and repair information, along with comparisons of competitive products. Rather than comparison shopping at brick-and-mortar stores, consumers can now get reliable information conveniently on the Web.

Consumers cannot test drive an automobile on the Web, so auto buyers still want to visit car dealerships. However, consumers who do their homework online can approach dealers with a wealth of information that can strengthen their bargaining position and reduce some of the stress of car buying.

The Internet increases the ability of patients to participate more actively in matters related to their own health. A study by the California HealthCare Foundation cites estimates that the Internet offers at least 17,000 different health care sites and that some 24.8 million U.S. adults have searched for health information. This number is projected to grow to over 30 million during 2000. Jupiter Communications has estimated that 45 percent of online consumers access the Internet for health information. Today, some patients arrive at their doctors' offices carrying possible diagnoses downloaded from sites such as Healtheon/WebMD or America Online Health Channel.

In addition, people with Internet access can obtain information about their healthcare plans, find doctors, and in some cases submit claims for fee reimbursement. Doctors, too, are increasing their use of the Internet as a source of information on the latest news in medical research. Other aspects of health care delivery, including laboratory results reporting, prescriptions, office visit scheduling, and records transmittal may move online once issues such as privacy and authentication are resolved.

Many private companies now post job openings on their company's Web site, and in some cases these sites can accept online applications. Web site recruiting among the North American-based Global 500 was even more prevalent, with over 90 percent of such firms participating and 71 percent accepting applications online. In addition to firm-specific online recruiting, a growing number of Web sites offer online employment classifieds, grouping together requests from multiple employers.

Some of these sites are maintained by newspaper companies, traditional providers of employment classifieds. Others have been established to specialize in specific employment areas. Some observers believe that effective online recruiting faces substantial barriers. The Internet's original purpose was to disseminate research and information, and this use continues to be important today.

Educational research and technical materials are available online to students, researchers, scientists, and engineers anywhere in the world. Many universities make their research papers available on the Internet, and most academic and professional journals are available online. In addition, previously unpublished information is increasingly available on the Internet. For example, students can download lectures at their convenience, and live classroom presentations are broadcast on the Internet with students submitting questions via e-mail. The Internet also provides access to research of a more general or recreational nature.

News with frequent updates is available from local, national, and foreign sources, as are weather and traffic information. Numerous online services also provide information covering everything from the floor plans of museums and restaurant reviews, to local television and radio listings. During several recent foreign conflicts and natural disasters, the Internet played a role in providing news and information when traditional media outlets were closed.

Federal, state and local governments also are rapidly developing new ways of using the Internet to communicate with clients and to provide public services to businesses and individuals. Many state and local governments are also moving services online. Interested individuals and businesses can find information on a wide variety of topics such as registration, parks, and trash removal. The spread of Internet access is being accompanied by a proliferation of new community spaces online.

Some of these are commercial spaces such as online auctions that allow consumers to sell or trade goods and services. Others are meeting spaces where individuals interact around a particular interest or topic--from chat rooms for hobbyists, and online current events discussions, to support groups for people facing similar challenges. In the process of providing places for individuals to interact, these online spaces create virtual communities.

Digital Business

Business-to-consumer e-commerce is the most visible aspect of e-commerce, it is only a small part of what is now possible due to recent technological advances. Increasingly, business-to-business (B2B) e-commerce is emerging as an area of critical importance for businesses faced with rapidly changing markets and opportunities.

Transactions between businesses account for the lion's share of commercial activity, and e-commerce technologies appear to have an enormous potential to make these transactions more efficient. Companies are also using these technologies to increase the efficiency of their internal operations. One important difference is the degree to which non-Internet network transactions, such as those conducted over electronic data interchange (EDI) systems, are included in the estimates of B2B e-commerce.

Irrespective of the dollar amounts, the market researchers all expect strong growth as companies seek to cut costs and increase efficiency by streamlining their purchasing, sales, and other business processes. At present, many firms are at the beginning stages of implementing e-commerce technologies in their business processes. A recent National Association of Manufacturers survey found that 68 percent of manufacturers are not yet using electronic commerce to conduct business transactions.

A Purchasing Magazine survey shows that 38 percent of buyers currently use the Web to conduct at least some of their company's transactions. The survey also finds that of those who do not currently conduct transactions over the Internet, approximately 35 percent say they will begin to conduct transactions electronically within the next year and 54 percent say they will do so within the next three years. Only 11 percent of those not currently online have no expectation of using the Internet for procurement. The potential of e-commerce technologies to transform business practices is evident in the new marketplaces that are developing online.

These important intermediaries have emerged rapidly in virtually all industries, providing new places for buyers and sellers to meet, allowing a variety of pricing schemes to flourish, altering the roles of traditional intermediaries, enabling complex transactions, and, by making vast amounts of information available at very low costs, shifting the balance of power among market participants. E-Bay, for example, which started out providing a marketplace for consumers selling to other consumers (C2C) in online auctions, has expanded to include B2C and B2B transactions.

While the large buyers organizing these online marketplaces hope to achieve significant cost savings, it is difficult to gauge a priori the impact these new arrangements may have on their supply communities. Some suppliers and potential suppliers that had been unable to justify the cost of EDI connections may be much more willing to use the Internet to bid on work that they would otherwise have missed. Concerns have been raised, however, about the potential for these large players to use these markets to reduce competition.

The overall impact will depend on the extent to which actual efficiencies can be achieved as opposed to squeezing supplier margins. One probable side effect of moving these supply networks to the Internet will be to increase the level of investment in Internet technologies. E-commerce technologies also appear to be driving changes among traditional intermediaries—i.e., firms such as wholesalers, travel agents, or shippers, that add value between the production of a good or service and its sale to the final consumer.

Early predictions were that the Internet and e-commerce would create efficiencies by eliminating the need for intermediaries. Manufacturers and service providers would begin selling directly to the customer and "middlemen" would disappear. However, the early speculation failed to appreciate the important role that intermediaries play or the resourcefulness some intermediaries would exhibit in finding new ways to add value in an online world. Instead of vanishing, traditional intermediaries are adapting to exploit new possibilities as providers of logistical, financial, and information services. Internet-based market spaces also broaden market participation by decreasing the costs of participating in B2B markets.

For decades, large companies have used EDI to automate routine paperwork surrounding business transactions, to manage arrangements such as automatic inventory replenishment, and to make purchases according to pre-established terms. Until recently, the use of this e-business activity was limited to large volume supplier/customer relationships because EDI required a fairly sizable investment in dedicated hardware and proprietary software and use of expensive leased telecommunications lines.

As costs of computing power, memory, and storage declined throughout the 1990s, the size threshold at which EDI became cost-effective also declined, but still remained too high for many trading applications. Now, however, the Internet with its open nonproprietary protocols and global reach has emerged as a platform for spreading the efficiencies achievable through the automation of business processes to firms of all sizes. The bulk of B2B e-commerce remains EDI-based, although analysts are predicting that most of the future growth of B2B e-commerce will be Internet-based.

The National Association of Manufacturers estimates that among businesses that currently use the Web for business, 17 percent are using it in place of EDI. The Boston Consulting Group estimates that 86 percent of the

$671 billion in B2B e-commerce in 1998 was EDI conducted over private networks. However, they estimate that the EDI component will fall to 28 percent by 2003. In addition, businesses and even governments have discovered the potential of the Internet as an auction space.

Businesses are using auctions to sell off surplus goods, dispose of used equipment, and post requests for purchase. Business purchasers are also using online auctions to request bids. Owens Corning used an online reverse auction run by Freemarkets, an online auction company, to put bids out for corrugated packaging materials for its 21 U.S. plants. At the end of the day the company had 17 two-year contracts with corrugated packaging material suppliers and had saved an estimated 10 percent.

E-commerce transactions represent only one way in which innovations in computers and communications can add value and make business processes more productive. All business processes have some information component. Specifications for a design must be shared between architects and engineers. The latest maintenance information must be delivered to the mechanic working on the airplane.

The manufacturer of auto interiors needs to know how many blue interiors must be delivered for a manufacturing run at the auto plant. All of these processes benefit when information flows faster, more accurately, and in greater detail to the people who need it. Many companies are experimenting with processes that enable them to share information over a network or the Internet.

For example, BOC Gases replaced a slower, more costly certification procedure with a process that sends product certification results over the Internet for customers that need specialized gas products. Businesses are also using networking technologies to improve processes, such as design and engineering, reducing development time, simplifying manufacturing processes, and integrating design processes. Using Internet technologies to coordinate product design.

A semiconductor producer, has created Web-enabled tools for its new product development process. The company's 2,000 engineers use a standard Web browser to access the company's portfolio of projects and obtain information on phase of development, team composition, deliverables, and time frame. Using communications networks to improve human resource functions.

Using wireless networks to manage inventory more efficiently. Cablevision, a telecommunications and entertainment company, uses wireless mobile computer appliances over a local area network to process inventory transactions in real time, at the point of activity. Using the Internet to provide customer services and answer frequently asked questions.

Many companies are using their company Web site to offer customer services and product information. Ford offers product information and links to dealers, and their "Owner Connection" Web page provides Ford car owners with maintenance information, safety tips, service reminders, do-it-yourself pointers, and online manuals.

Using the Internet to reduce project administration and management costs. Not only are individuals, businesses, and other organizations going online in increasing numbers, but the products and services used in everyday life are becoming increasingly integrated into the networked economy.

The Internet provides a new way to have goods and services delivered. Music, legal advice, software, opera tickets, news reports, books, photographs, movies, and product designs—can all be downloaded directly into a computer. The most dramatic growth in direct, digital download sales will probably be in the music sector, where such sales could rise from 0.1 percent of online sales in 1999 to 25 percent in 2004, followed by software and books. Digitalization is also changing the design of products, so these products can be networked.

For example, home-electronics producers have joined together to develop Home Audio Video Interoperability (HAVi), an open, consumer-electronics-industry standard that will allow digital audio and video devices from different vendors to work together when connected to a network in the consumer's home. Appliances that can be networked are beginning to emerge in other areas as well. New home electronics and appliances will not only be networkable, many of them also will be "network appliances"--that is, appliances that can access the Internet. The television has long been viewed as a potential portal for Internet access.

More recently, simple, low cost dedicated Internet access devices have been introduced. In addition, connectivity is increasingly being viewed as an important feature to add to existing products. At recent trade shows, for example, home appliance manufacturers have unveiled prototype Internet-enabled refrigerators and ovens that offer features such as e-mail, calendar management, automated grocery ordering, and tracking of the service requirements of the appliance.

The development of new technology is still limited by slow connection and transmission speeds and the lack of standards to facilitate individual appliances communicating with one another. As these limitations are addressed, however, the developmental pace of digital products is likely to increase. New technologies that exploit the potential of wireless connections are already creating new ways of communicating and conducting business, reconfiguring many traditional industry and product definitions.

As Internet access migrates from the desktop computer to a range of products, the lines that now separate the transmission of voice, data, and pictures will disappear. New devices under development today will combine cellular telephone, geopositioning, and Internet access in a handheld or automobile device. The technologies that make the digital economy possible are still evolving, as is the environment in which these technologies are being used. Many businesses and individuals remain hesitant about e-commerce because the business environment online does not yet have the same predictability and reliability as it does offline. And the medium itself offers new challenges.

IT and Industries

Information Technology (IT) producing industries—the firms that supply the goods and services that support IT-enabled business practices across the economy, as well as the Internet and e-commerce. Over the past decade, and especially since the mid-1990s, these industries have been a powerful factor in the economy's rapid and sustained growth, a significant restraint on inflation, and a focal point of prolific technological innovation. Since the mid-1990s, IT-producing industries have shown extraordinary dynamism. Prepackaged software and computer services had the highest growth rate, increasing their output.

Over the same period, the computer hardware and communications equipment industries increased their output at a 9 percent annual rate, and output in the communications services sector rose at a 7 percent annual pace. The rapid increase in these industries' share of the economy after 1994 is particularly impressive in view of both the rapid growth of the economy as a whole and the accelerated decline in IT prices over the period.

A modest share of IT growth also reflected spending related to addressing Y2K-related computer problems. ESA analysts have estimated that Y2K-related spending accounted for roughly 7 percent of the output of IT-producing industries in 1998 and 1999. The declining prices of IT goods and services have worked, directly and indirectly, to reduce overall inflation in the U.S. economy. Over the same period, lower prices in the IT sector reduced overall U.S. inflation directly, on average, by about 0.5 percentage points a year--from 2.3 percent to 1.8 percent.

IT equipment, including software, plays in business investment activity. In current dollars, industry spending on IT equipment and software rose from $198 billion in 1992, or 44 percent of all equipment spending, to $407 billion in 1999, or 46 percent. Over the same period, "other capital equipment," including industrial equipment, fell from 38 percent of total equipment and software investment spending to 32 percent, and transportation equipment ranged between 18 percent and

21 percent. Because prices for IT equipment and software have been falling, investment spending shifts are even more pronounced when expressed in real dollars, rather than nominal amounts.

Since 1995, prices of IT capital equipment and software have dropped by an average 6.7 percent per year, while prices for transportation capital equipment have increased at a 0.6-percent average annual rate and prices for other types of capital equipment have increased at a 1.5-percent rate. As a result, real business investment spending on IT equipment and software more than doubled between 1995 and 1999, from $243 billion to $510 billion, while real spending on transportation equipment increased by about half and real spending on other capital equipment increased slightly.

Over the decade of the 1990s, growing industry spending on IT equipment and software was a significant factor in the high rate of growth of U.S. spending on all categories of equipment to 9-to-10 percent per year, compared to 5-to-6 percent a year in the 1980s. In 1999, business spending for IT equipment and software represented more than three-fourths of the 12 percent real growth in total equipment and software spending that year, compared to 65 percent of the real growth in equipment spending for 1995-1998 and less than 50 percent for 1993-1994.

Despite the rapid decline in computer prices, computers' share of IT equipment investment in nominal dollars remained relatively constant over the 1992-1999 period. Other IT equipment, including spending on communications equipment, remained the largest category of IT equipment purchases, although its share declined from 47 percent in 1992 to 41 percent in 1999.

Analysis of the composition of IT investment in real rather than nominal dollars yields a somewhat different picture because prices have declined far more rapidly for computer than for other kinds of IT equipment and software.

Measured in real dollars, beginning in 1994, investment in computers accelerated more rapidly than investment in the two other IT categories, surpassing investment in these categories by 1998. In 1999, price-adjusted spending for computers totaled $222 billion, compared with $149 billion for software and $170 billion for other IT equipment. The surge in IT investment since 1994 has been accompanied by sharp increases in R&D investment in the economy as a whole and in IT-producing industries in particular. Growth in IT industries' share of private R&D is largely the result of increased R&D investment by manufacturers of electronic components and software.

In the computer industry, annual R&D investment dropped from an average $11 billion during 1990-92, to $5 billion during 1993-95, then rose to $10 billion during 1996-98. One reason for this lack of overall growth may be that as computer demand has shifted toward micro-computers, more computer-related R&D has shifted to component manufacturers and software firms.

Impact of IT on Labour Productivity

Today, U.S. productivity pattern, in which productivity gains have strengthened as the expansion has matured, is unprecedented for the postwar period. In previous postwar expansions, productivity growth has slowed as the expansion enters its mature phase. One reason for the extraordinary pattern of productivity in the current expansion appears to be the rapid growth in the real net stock of IT capital per labor hour, especially computer hardware.

This rapid growth of real net IT capital created significant IT "capital deepening," beginning in 1991 and accelerating sharply after 1995. The ratio of the capital stock of computer hardware to hours worked increased, on average, by 16.3 percent per year over the period 1991-95, and 33.7 percent per year during 1996-99. Capital deepening in computer software also grew at double-digit rates during both periods, while the growth rate in communications equipment increased from 2.4 to 5.0 percent. A major factor behind IT capital deepening has been the falling prices of IT, especially computer hardware, reflecting rapid and continuous improvements in quality.

Multifactor productivity (MFP) growth reflects the impact of factors in addition to quality-adjusted capital and labor inputs--for example, technical changes not directly incorporated in capital and labor, organizational improvements, and economies of scale. All categories of IT capital contribute disproportionately to labor productivity growth, compared to their shares of the total private nonfarm business sector and their shares of the total net capital stock.

However, the contribution of computer hardware to productivity growth has been extraordinarily large. A research indicates that during the years 1996-99, computer hardware deepening accounted for 24 percent of all labor productivity growth. The size of this contribution is especially remarkable because computers constitute just 1.8 percent of the private nonfarm business sector and less than 1 percent of overall capital stock. The reason that IT, with such a small share of the economy and of the total capital stock, has contributed so powerfully to productivity growth is that the rapidly growing IT investments have been unusually productive.

Market conditions dictate that business investments in computer hardware must earn very high rates of return. For one thing, the rapid and continuous improvements in IT quality mean that existing computer hardware becomes obsolete and hence depreciates very quickly. In addition, sharply falling hardware prices mean that businesses investing in IT equipment face rapid capital losses as purchased equipment quickly loses market value. Economists who held until recently that the impact of computers on U.S. productivity could be a transitory effect of unusually favorable economic circumstances have begun to credit IT for dramatic increases in the trend growth rates of U.S. output and productivity since 1995.

One reason for this change in view has been the increasing attention paid by researchers to the productivity effects of software and communications equipment, in addition to computer hardware.

The Congressional Budget Office talks about "computers," distinguishing between computer "use" and computer "production", while the Economic Report of the President refers to "computers and software." Jorgenson and Stiroh include in IT "capital services" those from computer, software, and communications capital. There are factors contributing to labor productivity growth acceleration other than capital deepening and technical advance that are intended to highlight IT's contribution to the acceleration of labor productivity growth.

Since IT investments improve productivity, those industries making the most intensive use of IT should show higher productivity growth than industries that use IT less intensively. Evidence of such a pattern at the industry level, however, remains mixed.

IT-producing industries have recorded astonishingly high productivity gains and have been a dominant force in aggregate U.S. productivity growth. Furthermore, outside the IT-producing sector itself, goods-producing industries that are IT intensive have achieved higher productivity gains than their counterparts that have not invested heavily in IT.

However, official output measures for IT-intensive service industries do not indicate significant productivity gains. Indeed, between 1990 and 1997, despite heavy investments in IT and a three-decade buildup of the real net IT capital stock, IT-using service industries as a group recorded declining productivity. The significant multifactor productivity growth in IT-producing industries, improved labor productivity growth in both IT-producing and IT-using goods industries, and alternative views of IT's effect on productivity in service industries.

A study found strong labor productivity, as well as multifactor productivity gains in the computer-producing sector, implying that this sector positively contributes to overall productivity growth. IT-using service industries actually showed a negative growth rate of 0.3 percent a year, compared to 1.3 percent annual productivity gains by non-IT intensive service industries. These results largely reflect the difficult problems in conceptualizing and measuring output in many service industries. In view of these measurement problems, we compared growth in GPO/W of IT-using service industries with that of the non-IT intensive service industries, but excluding 10 hard-to-measureservice industries.

IT-using service industries show slightly greater GPO/W growth than non-IT intensive service industries, and the overall annual average GPO/W growth for 1990-97 rises from 1.38 percent to 2.34 percent. Because hard-to-measure service industries together account for 44 percent of the total GPO by IT-using service industries, the effect of IT on service industry productivity will remain clouded until development of better output measures.

Like the macroeconomic studies, recent firm-level analyses show that IT contributes substantially to productivity growth. This contribution is especially strong where businesses undertake organizational and other changes that complement the adoption of IT. In one study, analyzed firms in four groups based on their levels of IT investment and degree of decentralization. While they found that average productivity was highest among firms that were high in both IT investment and decentralized organization, they also found that productivity was lowest among those firms that were high in IT investment but low in decentralization.

IT Workers

Information technology workers produce and maintain the knowledge, ideas and information critical to the development of the digital economy. Demand for IT workers has increased with the spread of networked computers, the Internet, e-commerce, and the associated growing demand for high-quality digitized products and services. Moreover, the demand for IT workers is increasingly focused on more highly-skilled and highly paid people, as the rapid pace of innovation rewards high skills and technology reduces the number of less-skilled and lower paid IT jobs. In 1998, the IT workforce--covering workers in IT-producing industries and workers in IT occupations in other industries-- totaled roughly 7.4 million workers, or 6.1 percent of all workers.

While IT employment has grown faster than overall employment for many years, the growth in both IT-producing industries and IT occupations accelerated in the mid-1990s. IT industry employment grew almost 28 percent from 1994 to 1998, and employment in IT occupations increased by 22 percent over the same period. By contrast, over those same years, total U.S. nonfarm employment rose by about 11 percent.

Jobs in IT-producing firms, after growing more slowly than overall employment in 1993 and 1994, increased dramatically in 1995 and thereafter, growing at an average annual rate of 6.5 percent. The number of workers in IT-producing firms grew from 3.9 million in 1992 to 5.2 million workers in 1998. Even at this level, employment in IT-producing firms in 1998 accounted for less than 5 percent of total private employment. The overall growth in IT-producing industry employment masks a churning of IT jobs, with significant job increases in some areas and significant declines in others. Many information technologies have short life cycles, and employers intent on quickly getting a product or service to market often prefer to hire workers skilled in new technologies rather than retrain their current workers.

Computing and communications technologies have lowered barriers to entry, especially to markets that provide information technology and other services. These technologies provide small businesses with size and resource advantages usually available to larger, established companies. By using the Internet, they can compete outside of local markets, even in global markets. The same technologies allow foreign companies greater access to U.S. markets. More players in the market means more job churning as there will be winners and losers. Employment in IT-producing industries is also affected by the increasing use of outsourcing to other industries. Among workers in all IT-producing industries, those in software and computer services industries, including computer programming services and software development, earned the highest average wage of $65,300 in 1998. These industries paid wages that were higher than the total private industry average wage in 1998, and almost all of them had higher than average annual wage growth from 1992 to 1998.

The broadest definition would recognize that, as the economy becomes more digitized, most occupations will involve the manufacture or operation of equipment that includes forms of information technology, such as a computer chip. A more narrow definition might include only the "core" IT occupations of computer scientists, computer engineers, systems analysts and computer programmers; these are the IT positions that require the most education and skills, are the highest paid, and are in greatest demand.

There are number of highly-skilled IT workers, or IT workers in occupations that generally require at least an associate degree, increased from 2.2 million in 1992 to 3.2 million in 1998. The fastest growth occurred among those with the highest skills - core IT occupations - who increased their share of total IT employment from 28 percent to 41 percent. Between 1994 and 1998, total high-skilled IT employment increased 35 percent, more than three times as much as the national average, and core IT occupations grew more than five times faster than all other jobs.

By contrast, employment in lower-skilled IT occupations, such as computer operators, communications equipment operators and billing and posting clerks, declined from 926,000 to 852,000, or 9 percent. During the same period, employment among moderately-skilled IT workers, including telephone and electronic equipment installers, assemblers and repairers, grew somewhat more slowly than the national average. Private surveys and interviews with Chief Information Officers provide additional insight into the specific IT skills in greatest demand.

The growth in e-commerce, for example, has increased demand for workers with Internet-related technical skills, including network specialists, help desk/ end user support staff and Internet/intranet developers. E-commerce growth has also increased the demand for workers with a knowledge of sales, marketing and business planning.

Many IT workers that used to work in back offices are now required to learn how to deal with customers and convince them to make online purchases. In addition, as more firms outsource for IT services, demand has increased for project managers and people who can negotiate and manage vendor contracts. Earnings in IT occupations also vary by geographic location and company size, as they do for many other industries.

In America, Bureau of Labor Statistics examined the available national employment and wage data for core IT occupations over the period 1992 to 1997. They reasoned that an imbalance should produce above-average growth in both employment and wages, and below-average unemployment rates. BLS found that while the unemployment rates for core IT occupations were consistently lower than the national average for this period, employment and wage growth had not been consistently above average for all core IT occupations.

IT and Trade

US's IT companies are powerful competitors in markets around the world. Yet the United States ran a trade deficit in information technology goods of almost $66 billion in 1999. In 1997, a study shows that when the United States exported $121.4 billion of IT goods and services, foreign sales by overseas IT affiliates of American companies totaled $196 billion. In the same year, American-based IT affiliates of foreign companies reported U.S. sales totaling $110.5 billion. Over the same period, U.S. imports of IT goods increased at an average rate of 12.3 percent a year. In fact, the United States has run trade deficits since 1983 in many categories of IT hardware, including semiconductors, household audio and video equipment, and computer storage devices. The negative balance of payments on cross-border sales of telecommunications services is a reflection of calling patterns and differences in national telecommunications rates. More international calls originate here than in other countries because of the strong U.S. economy, relatively high U.S. income levels, and large immigrant populations in this country. In addition, because American markets are more open and competitive, foreign callers pay less to U.S. carriers to complete calls to the United States than Americans pay to foreign carriers to complete calls going the other way. Many U.S. IT firms, spurred by competition from low-cost foreign producers and the liberalization by a growing number of countries of controls on direct investment and capital flows, have moved lower value-added production overseas.

As a result, intra-firm trade, defined as cross-border sales between parents and affiliates of U.S. and foreign multinational companies, accounts for a significant portion of the trade in IT products. In 1997, for instance, U.S. exports to affiliated firms in core IT hardware industries--computer and office equipment; electronic components and accessories; and audio, video and communications equipment--amounted to roughly 60 percent of U.S. exports of goods in these classes of IT hardware. Trade between U.S. parent companies and their overseas affiliates has contributed to a reduction in the size of the U.S. trade deficit in information technology products.

The global competitiveness of the U.S. IT industry is apparent in the comparison of sales by U.S. IT affiliates abroad with sales by foreign-owned IT affiliates stationed in the United States. In 1997, for example, foreign sales by U.S.-owned overseas affiliates in the computer and office equipment industry exceeded sales in this country by foreign-owned U.S. affiliates in the same industry by $67 billion. Similarly, the balance of sales in 1997 favored American-owned foreign providers of computer processing and information retrieval services by $41 billion and U.S.-owned foreign producers in the electronic components and accessories industry by $20 billion.

The information technology sector has played a critical role in the economic success of recent years. Businesses across the economy have been investing heavily in IT hardware and software to harness the potential created by falling prices and by the increasing capacities of computer processing, storage media and communications links.

Business strategies and even the structures of companies and industries are being transformed as communication within companies and among the members of corporate alliances occurs more rapidly, with more customized information, and with greater security, interactivity, and timeliness than before. The same quality of communication that once was limited to a narrow group of close contacts can now be extended to a much wider "reach" of contacts. The IT revolution is affecting everyone's life.

The advances and spread of IT are part of the reason why we now have the lowest unemployment rate and fastest growth in real wages in three decades and the longest expansion on record. Consumers are making a small but increasing amount of their purchases online and using the Internet to make more informed purchases offline. IT is also transforming the way most firms operate. As employers substitute IT for labor, workers have to develop new skills.

The hallmark of the New Economy is higher sustainable growth due to faster improvement in labor productivity. IT can support higher rates of labor productivity gains and output growth, so long as IT innovation and price declines persist, and non-IT industries continue to invest heavily in IT products and services.

Both of these conditions are expected to persist into the future. Experts in the semiconductor, computer, storage, and communications industries have expressed confidence that rapid rates of product innovation and price decline can continue for at least another decade. Experts in non-IT industries also have expressed confidence in their capacity to benefit enormously from further substantial investments in IT. The prospect of healthier productivity gains over both a medium term and a longer run has significant implications for the future standard of living and a range of fiscal issues facing government at all levels.

For example, faster productivity growth translates into more tax revenue, which in turns creates larger budget surpluses and longer positive balances for trust funds such as those for Social Security and Medicare. Faster productivity growth also means lower inflation, reducing the additional costs of COLAs for most entitlement programs.

In most industries, IT investments do not expand capacity; rather, they provide general cost savings, reduce errors, provide the basis for more prompt and informed decisions, and increase customer satisfaction. For industries in which IT investments directly expand capacity to provide services a slowdown in demand should directly slow IT investment. Because IT investments are commonly driven by pressures to keep pace with competitors, in terms of costs and satisfying customer demand for more responsive products, IT investment should weather a slowdown in demand better than capacity expanding investments. The spread of IT could also moderate the sharp declines in manufacturing inventories that occur in recessions.

By improving communications with suppliers and customers, IT has facilitated manufacturers' efforts to limit their inventory exposure. If U.S. manufacturers of durable goods today held inventories at the 1988 inventory to sales ratio, they would be holding an additional $115 billion in inventory. The cost savings from reduced inventories takes several forms. First, there is the average savings of about $10 billion a year from not having to pay to accumulate as much new inventory in each of the eleven years. Second, the cumulative $115 billion in funds that would have been spent for inventory have been used to invest elsewhere or pay down debt. By this point, the financial benefit of the second effect exceeds the benefit from the first. Third, the companies are spared the expense of storing and securing one-third more inventory than they now hold. Fourth, they avoid the inevitable losses from holding inventories for products that lose favor in the marketplace.

Today's leaner inventories should, other things equal, cushion the depth of the next recession by narrowing the gap between declines in output and demand. The U.S. labor productivity boom of the last four years has outpaced not only its own performance from 1973 to 1995, but also the labor productivity gains of other major industrial countries in recent years. The U.S. macroeconomic environment since the early 1990s has stimulated an investment boom. Both fiscal and monetary policy have contributed. The 1990s began with very large budget deficits projected to grow even larger. However, prudent policies to curb spending and raise revenues were introduced, and the fiscal picture has reversed. Sound macroeconomic policies have helped lower unemployment and inflation, but they cannot account for the recent multi-year doubling of labor productivity growth. For that, look to more technologically based explanations. For example, there is the view that fundamental technological changes, from electricity to IT, take a very long time to generate labor productivity breakthroughs - and when they do, labor productivity rises very sharply.

Another important issue concerning the dynamics of the New Economy is their effect on jobs. In an aggregate or macroeconomic sense, the New Economy has been characterized by strong job and wage growth. With lower inflation and accommodating monetary policy, unemployment has fallen below 4 percent, the lowest rate since 1969.

The unemployment rate of those with less education and experience has fallen along with the rates of everyone else, although it remains higher than those of better educated and experienced workers. Similarly, with everyone else, workers near the bottom of the ladder in recent years have enjoyed strong real wage growth.

The number of well-paid jobs in the IT producing and IT-using sectors is growing rapidly, even as the number of lower-paid IT-related jobs is shrinking. It is reasonable to assume that IT, by raising labor productivity, must displace jobs somewhere in the economy. However, there is no clear evidence about what types of jobs are displaced most rapidly by IT. A significant percentage of jobs in modern America involve collecting and/or processing information, and/or making decisions based on information; but some sectors, such as education and financial services, have a higher proportion of information-intensive jobs than other sectors.

Measures of the IT-intensive banking industry now indicate significant annual labor productivity gains, in contrast to the negative labor productivity changes portrayed under the old method. Producing true output measures for all service industries presents a daunting task. The Bureau of the Census should do more complete surveys of service industries broken down into more detailed and current categories. Even with such data, BEA faces difficult conceptual challenges in developing satisfactory methods for measuring the output of health, legal, business, and other services.

However, BEA has pioneered the use of creative new methods for measuring the quality, price and output changes for computers, semiconductors, and certain telecommunications equipment, along with the development and use of sophisticated methods such as chain-weighted indexes to properly gauge real output changes in a world with some sharply falling prices. Without these statistical advances, it would not have been possible to assess the contribution of IT at the macroeconomic level. In the absence of more accurate measures of output for IT-intensive services industries, we cannot rule out the possibility that IT has made a very modest contribution to labor productivity outside the IT producing sector itself.

Students are assigned to do their research on the Web, at home and not just in the library. Increasingly, job-seekers find job openings on the Web. Sign-up lists passed around at the PTA or other local organizations include a column for e-mail addresses, along with name and telephone number. In each instance, the Internet provides the means for communicating information critical for students, job-seekers, and members of organizations, that could not occur as effectively in other ways. In 1998, 42 percent of all American households had computers at home, and 22 percent had Internet connections at home. Some groups, however, are better networked.

Among the 5.5 million White, Asian, and Pacific Islander families with incomes of at least $75,000, living in a metropolitan area, headed by someone with at least a college education and age 30 to 55, 87 percent had computers at home, and 68 percent had Internet connections. Among households with these levels of income, education, age and living in a metropolitan area, Black and Hispanic households were just as likely to have home computers - but roughly 14 percent less likely to have Internet access at home - as White, Asian, and Pacific Islander households in the same income, education and age group.

Since 1998, more households have obtained computers and Internet access and alternative points of access, such as state employment commission offices, public libraries, and community centers and clubs, have expanded. When the results from a new Census Bureau August survey of households become available this Fall, we will learn the extent to which different groups have improved their access to the Web and capacity to create networks on the Internet.

4

Multicultural Disparities

Despite the rapid increase in computer use and Internet access during the late 1990s, there is still a formidable gap that separates the haves from the have-nots. The term digital divide entered in the mid-1990s in response to the large gap in computer and Internet access separating haves and have-nots. Particularly in the early days, when computers were more expensive and the Web was still the domain of scientists and scholars, it was widely believed that low- and middle-income families would not benefit from these new tools.

Over the years, the costs of having a home computer and an Internet connection have become more affordable to the majority of families in devloped countries, but there are still a large number of low-income families who are left behind. It is important to recognize, however, that access is just the first step in bridging the gap. For example, in US, families with people are more likely than ever to own a computer and be connected to the Internet. All boats are rising, but poor and minority people are playing catch-up to their more affluent, white peers-both at home and in the classroom. Almost all upper-income households have computers, yet only one-third of households with children and a family income of less than $15,000 had a computer in 2001.

Over the past several years, the number of American children with access to information technology has improved. Between 1993 and 2001, the share of all children (ages 3-17) living in households with computers increased from 32 percent to 71 percent. In addition, access to school computers further reduces the number of school-age (5-17) children who have no access to information technology. Data from September 2001 show that about 25 percent of school-age children were able to access computers at school even though they did not have one at home. Nonetheless, 7 percent of teens ages 14 to 17 and 16 percent of kids ages 5 to 9 had no access to computers, either at home or at school. Access to the Internet is still relatively low-less than 60 percent of kids who have a computer at home also use the Internet at home-but home access to the Internet is expanding even more rapidly than computer availability.

Research showing that home access to technology can improve education outcomes for at-risk children makes it even more important that policymakers ensure that these children can take advantage of these powerful tools. As the data below demonstrate, a disproportionate number of the children who have no access to home computers are from low-income and minority families. Much of the disparity in home computer ownership is due to income: Ninety-five percent of children in households earning $75,000 or more a year had a computer at home in 2001, compared to 33 percent of children in households earning $15,000 or less a year. Children from homes with higher incomes also have a rate of home Internet access that is more than 4 times that for poor children.

Internet connections at home are available to almost 63 percent of children living in house-holds in the highest income category, but to only 14 percent of children in the lowest. Furthermore, research documents significant differences in the ways that children from various income groups use their home computers. Compared to their wealthier peers, low-income children are less likely to use their home computers for word processing, school assignments, and other standard software applications and more likely to use them for games.These results confirm that while access is the first barrier to overcome, training in 21st-century literacy skills as well as parental involvement are also necessary.

Geographic fault lines often have been used to characterize the digital divide. For example, in US when introducing the "E-Rate" program in 1998, national leaders pointed out that these new tools made it possible for a child in the most isolated inner-city neighbourhood or rural community to have access to the same world of knowledge at the same instant as a child in the most affluent suburb. While access improved for all children throughout the 1990s, conspicuous inequities and geographic disparities still persist.

Between 1997 and 2001, there were huge increases in the rate of home computer access for black and Hispanic children. The share of black children living in a home with a computer grew from 24 percent in 1997 to 46 percent in 2001, a 92 percent increase. For Hispanic children, home access to a computer more than doubled, from 23 percent in 1997 to 47 percent in 2001. During the same period, the rate for non-Hispanic white children increased by 34 percent. Despite a rapid increase in computer availability for minority children, a large racial gap remains. In 2001, 83 percent of non-Hispanic white children lived in households with computers, compared to only 46 percent of black children and 47 percent of Hispanic children. There are similar gaps in access to the Internet at home. Based on data collected in 2001, 50 percent of non-Hispanic white children were able to connect to the Internet at home, compared to only 25 percent of black children and 20 percent of Hispanic children. While high poverty and lower educational attainment among minority families contribute to their below-average access to home computers and the Internet, they still do not offer a full explanation.

The US Census Bureau data indicate that geography is an important factor affecting children's access. In 2000, only 53 percent of children who lived in central cities had access to a home computer, compared to 61 percent of rural children and 73 percent of children living in suburbs. Similarly, only 24 percent of children in central cities use the Internet at home, compared to 29 percent of rural kids and 35 percent of suburban kids. In its 2001, "A Nation Online," the US Commerce Department acknowledged that during the past few years, Internet access increased more rapidly in rural areas than in central cities. In rural areas, people over the age of 3 who used the Internet from any location jumped from 29 percent in 1998 to 53 percent in 2001. In contrast to this strong growth in rural areas, central-city residents have not kept pace with national-level increases between 1998 and 2001.

The rate of Internet use from any location for people in central cities was only 2 percentage points lower than the national rate in 1998-but by 2001, the divide had grown to 5 points, 49 percent versus 54 percent.States range from a high of 69 percent in New Hampshire to a low of 31 percent in Mississippi. There is a striking pattern of low Internet penetration across the South. The 10 states that have 45 percent or fewer households with children able to access the Internet from home are all in the South or Southwest. By contrast, all six states in the New England region have high rates of Internet access. Other states where more than 55 percent of households with children have home Internet access are more geographically diverse, including Alaska, with the second highest access rate (64 percent), followed by Washington (60 percent). The only other states outside the Northeast that have high Internet penetration are Minnesota and Colorado, each at 58 percent, and Utah at 56 percent.

A 2000 US Census Bureau details on computer and Internet access found that schools help close the technology gap for children who lack computers at home. The net result of the effects schools have in giving computer access across income, racial, and ethnic groups is a levelling of the computer access that children of different groups have compared to what they would have had if home were the only place available for them to use computers. Without school computer access, the gap between high-income children and low-income children is 60 percentage points, but schools reduce that gap by two-thirds to 20 percentage points. Data from the US Department of Education demonstrate that schools have experienced a tremendous increase in Internet access in recent years, growing from only 35 percent of public K-12 schools in 1994 to 98 percent in 2000.

While having Internet access at the school level is important, a better measure than school connectedness is how many instructional classrooms include wired computers. At that level, there has been a striking change from only 3 percent of instructional classrooms having an Internet-equipped computer in 1994, to 77 percent of classrooms having one in 2000. No doubt much of this increase is due to an infusion of federal and local funding throughout the 1990s.

While the federal government's 7 percent contribution to overall education spending is relatively small, its share of ed-tech funding is substantial, accounting for 25 percent to 35 percent of all annual K-12 technology funding, depending on the state. By fiscal year 2001, U.S. Department of Education funding for ed-tech programs had risen to $872 million, compared to the $23 million appropriated in 1993. These resources support an array of services, including purchasing computers and software, training teachers, and revamping curriculums. A change in the nation's telecommunications laws in 1996 also provided new resources for schools.

Universal service provisions, traditionally focused on ensuring nationwide phone service at a reasonable cost, were expanded to include discounts on telecommunications services for schools, libraries, and rural health clinics. Included are discounts on phone service, Internet access, internal networks, and related equipment. Local and long-distance telephone companies contribute funding with fees collected from consumers. In the first 4 years, this "E-Rate" program has provided more than $8 billion in discounts to needy schools.

Technical infrastructure is critical, but basic training is also necessary to remove barriers-such as low levels of literacy and lack of computer experience—that hinder effective use of technology by underserved youth. Teacher training is a critical element of effective classroom technology use and must be supported at all levels as a cornerstone of ed-tech policy. Additionally, the availability of high-quality, appropriate content is an essential ingredient, without might have high-speed pipes with little of value for consumers on the other end. Increasingly, states are trying to ensure that students and teachers are computer literate by mandating such proficiency. This is a sensible strategy to help maximize the benefits from the substantial investments in school technology that have been made over the past decade. In 1999, 35 states had passed technology standards for students, and 26 had introduced technology standards for certification and recertification of teachers.

Despite the clear correlation between state poverty rates and computer and Internet access, some states are bucking the odds with innovative programs. Although Florida has the 10th highest child poverty rate, it is ranked 16th in home Internet penetration, as a result of some innovative statewide technology programs, such as putting computers in community centers and providing extra technology investments to low-performing and low-income schools.

Achieving equitable access to technology, and all of the inherent opportunities that it gives young people, will require the highest level of commitment from decision-makers and the public. To reduce or eliminate the digital divide, develop and adopt a comprehensive national agenda that is fully funded and embraced by government, educators, business leaders, philanthropic organizations, and the public at large. That agenda should be considered as crucial as providing national roads and transportation, Social Security for all citizens, and mandatory childhood immunization.

Web Access Among Racial/ethnic Groups in US

Since the mid-1990s, the World Wide Web has been riding an exponential growth curve. Currently, over 43 million hosts are connected to the Internet worldwide. In terms of individual users, somewhere between 40 to 80 million adults in the United States alone have access to around 320 million unique pages of content, globally distributed on arguably one of the most important communication innovations in history. The Internet is expected to do no less than virtually transform society. Yet even as the Internet races ambitiously toward critical mass, some social scientists are beginning to examine carefully the policy implications of current demographic patterns of Internet access and usage. Key demographic variables like income and education drive the policy questions surrounding the Internet.

In US, almost 70 percent of the schools have at least one computer connected to the Internet, less than 15 percent of classrooms have Internet access. Not surprisingly, access is not distributed randomly, but correlated strongly with income and education. A recent study of Internet use among US college freshman found that nearly 83 percent of all new college students report using the Internet for school work, and almost two-thirds use email to communicate. Yet, closer examination suggests a disturbing disparity in access. While 90.2 percent of private college freshman use the Internet for research, only 77.6 percent of students entering public black colleges report doing so. Similarly, although 80.1 percent of private college freshman use email regularly, only 41.4 percent of students attending black public colleges do. Further, although numerous studies suggest that the gender gap in Internet use appears to be closing over time and that Internet users are increasingly coming from the ranks of those with lower education and income, the perception persists that the gap for race is not decreasing.

In another study Hoffman and Novak examined racial differences in Internet access and use at a single time point and found in 1997 that, overall, whites were significantly more likely than African Americans to have a home computer in their household and also slightly more likely to have PC access at work. Whites were also significantly more likely to have ever used the Web at home, whereas African Americans were slightly more likely to have ever used the Web at school. As one might expect, increasing levels of income corresponded to an increased likelihood of owning a home computer, regardless of race. Although income explained race differences in computer ownership and Web use, education did not. That is, they found that whites were still more likely to own a home computer than were African Americans and to have used the Web recently, despite controlling for differences in education. Their most striking findings, however, were for students. Hoffman and Novak found no differences among white and African American students when students had a home computer. However, among students without a computer in the home, white students were much more likely than African American students to have used the Web, and also more likely to have used the Web at locations other than home, work or school. They concluded that "access translates into usage," and that whites are more likely than African Americans to use the Web because they are more likely to have access.

In 1998, the Commerce Department's National Telecommunications and Information Administration analyzed data on computer penetration rates from the October 1997 Census Current Population Survey (CPS) as part of an ongoing examination of the digital divide. The survey concluded that the gap between the technology "haves" and "have-nots" had increased between 1994 and 1997, with African Americans and Hispanics actually farther behind whites in terms of home computer ownership and Internet access and with an even wider gap between individuals at upper and lower income levels. In an investigation of home computer ownership and Internet use among low-income individuals and minorities in US, Babb, Stephanie F., found that African Americans and Hispanics were less likely to own computers, even after adjusting for income and education and termed this finding, consistent across seven different data sets under examination, "the single most important finding" of her study. Interestingly, some have suggested that United States policy itself may be a contributing factor in the growing digital divide. Cooper and Kimmelman argue that the Telecommunications Act of 1996 has had the unintended and unfortunate consequence of increasing the division between the telecommunications "haves" and "have-nots."

A comparative analysis of web usage and access across racial/ethnic groups in the United States will help us to study the digital disparities in detail. The analysis is based on primary data from three population projectable, US representative surveys of Internet use among Americans, including the first survey on Internet use to collect data on race and ethnicity. The three surveys are Spring 1997 CommerceNet/Nielsen Internet Demographic Study (IDS) conducted in December 1996 and January 1997; Fall 1997 IDS, conducted in August and September 1997; and Spring 1998 IDS, conducted in May and June 1998. Hereafter, these studies will be referred to as the IDS 2, IDS 3, and IDS 4, respectively. The IDS 2, conducted in December 1996/January 1997, was the first nationally projectable survey of Internet usage to collect data on race and ethnicity. That permited us, for the first time, to obtain baseline estimates of differences in Internet and Web use among racial and ethnic groups in the United States. The IDS 3 and IDS 4 also included race and ethnicity, permitting changes to be tracked over time. Additionally, the survey instruments used in IDS 3 and 4 were identical, though slightly modified from IDS 2, thereby ensuring complete comparability across two of the three surveys, and reasonable comparability from IDS 2 to IDS 3 and IDS 4. Each CommerceNet/ Nielsen IDS is based upon an unrestricted random digit dial sampling frame, and used a computer assisted telephone interviewing system to obtain respondents. Eligible respondents were persons 16 years and older in the U.S. and Canada. When weighted, the respondents represent and allow projection to the total population of individuals in the United States aged 16 and over. Respondent weights in the IDS were adjusted by Nielsen so that marginal weighted distributions of Education, Gender, Race, Hispanic Origin, and Age were equivalent to Census estimates for the US and Canada. The particulars of each survey are summarized below.

	Spring 1997 IDS	Fall 1997 IDS	Spring 1998 IDS
Survey	IDS 2	IDS 3	IDS 4
Time Frame	December 1996 -January 1997	August 1997- September 1997	May 1998 June 1998
NO. of US respondents	5,813	7,157	4,042
Total weighted US population aged 16 and over	199.9 million	202.3 million	202.4 million

Table 1 compares the three CommerceNet/Nielsen Internet Demographic Studies, IDS 2, IDS 3, and IDS 4, conducted in December 1996/January 1997, August/September 1997, and May/June 1998, respectively, to March 1995 Census Current Population Survey (CPS) estimates for key demographic variables. The Nielsen IDS samples are representative of the US population.

By comparing the weighted percentages from each Nielsen IDS with corresponding weighted percentages from the Census CPS, it can be find that the distributions reported in Table 1 differ only slightly. One point of departure is race, specifically the percentages for white and other categories in IDS 2 and 3 and "other" in IDS 4. Note that the Census CPS reports more whites, while the Nielsen IDS 2 and 3 report more "other race.".

Table 2 presents the distributions of key demographic variables for each IDS by race and Hispanic origin, compared to the Census CPS and it can be found that:

— Distributions for whites are comparable and consistent over time.

— African-Americans, in the IDS 2, are both slightly overrepresented in the oldest and youngest age categories and in the lowest and highest education categories. There is a larger difference in IDS 2 and 4 for ages 25-45, with African Americans underrepresented in this age group. In the IDS 3, African Americans are overrepresented in the oldest age category and the highest education category, while high school graduates are underrepresented. In IDS 4, African Americans are older and less educated. In IDS 2, 3, and 4, there are more African American students and women than in the Census CPS.

Table 1:
Demographic Comparisons of the Three CommerceNet/Nielsen Internet Demographic Studies with the 1995 Census CPS (US Population Aged 16 and Older)

	CommerceNet/Nielsen Internet Demographic Survey						1995 CPS
	IDS2		IDS3		IDS4		
	Raw	Weighted	Raw	Weighted	Raw	Weighted	Weighted
	Count	%	Count	%	Count	%	%
Age:							
<25	909	15.37	1,024	15.30	608	15.29	16.3
25-45	2,780	43.39	3,295	42.95	1,738	42.32	43.9
46-64	1,402	25.35	1,743	25.90	1,034	26.55	24.0
>64	722	15.89	1,095	15.85	662	15.84	15.7
Total	5,813	100%	7,157	100%	4,042	100%	100%
Education:							
less than h.s.	659	21.89	830	21.88	478	21.88	21.9
high school grad	1,723	31.98	2,007	31.98	1,167	32.01	32.3
some college	1,641	25.44	2,330	25.39	1,303	25.40	25.6
college grad	1,790	20.69	1,990	20.75	1,094	20.71	20.2
Total	5,813	100%	7,157	100%	4,042	100%	100%
Gender:							
Male	2,444	48.01	2,954	48.03	1,624	48.02	48.1
Female	3,369	51.99	4,203	51.97	2,418	51.98	51.9
Total	5,813	100%	7,157	100%	4,042	100%	100%

Student status:							
Full time	469	8.51	523	8.06	296	8.55	7.7
None/part time	5,318	91.49	6,615	91.94	3,726	91.45	92.3
Total	5,787	100%	7,138	100%	4,022	100%	100%
Race:							
White	4,906	78.59	6,000	79.54	3,447	83.41	84.0
African American	493	11.75	691	11.75	441	11.76	11.7
Asian	127	2.09	130	1.99	97	3.03	2.6
American Indian	75	1.62	101	1.85	57	1.80	0.5
Other	212	5.95	235	4.87	0	0	1.2
Total	5,813	100%	7,157	100%	4,042	100%	100%
Ethnicity:							
Hispanic	319	9.51	448	9.50	164	9.51	9.3
Non-Hispanic	5,494	90.49	6,709	90.50	3,878	90.49	90.7
Total	5,813	100%	7,157	100%	4,042	100%	100%.7

Table 2

Demographic Distributions over Time Conditional on Race and Ethnicity of the Three CommerceNet/Nielsen Internet Demographic Studies Compared to the 1995 Census CPS (US Population Aged 16 and Older)

	White				African American				Hispanic			
	IDS2	IDS3	IDS4	CPS	IDS2	IDS3	IDS4	CPS	IDS2	IDS3	IDS4	CPS
N	4,906	6,000	3,447		493	691	441		319	448 1	64	
Age:												
<25	12.79	13.87	13.81	15.5	22.63	19.18	21.16	20.8	31.63	22.02	23.44	23.5
25-45	43.53	41.38	42.03	43.1	38.66	47.20	39.92	47.5	51.04	52.19	43.11	50.6
46-64	26.75	27.72	27.63	24.7	20.81	19.27	24.49	20.7	13.34	17.32	23.08	18.2
>64	16.94	17.03	16.53	16.8	17.84	14.35	14.44	11.0	3.98	8.47	10.36	7.7
Total	*100%*	*100%*	*100%*	*100%*	*100%*	*100%*	*100%*	*100%*	*100%*	*100%*	*100%*	*100%*
Education:												
less thanh.s.	18.56	18.69	19.11	20.4	35.93	31.65	38.18	30.2	36.67	49.47	44.22	48.9
high sc grad	33.45	33.38	32.64	32.5	27.27	27.58	28.66	34.1	24.68	25.47	23.73	25.4
some college	26.44	25.66	26.28	25.8	20.30	26.54	22.86	24.6	26.16	16.69	21.70	18.2
college grad	21.56	22.27	21.97	21.3	16.50	14.23	10.30	11.1	12.49	8.37	10.35	7.5
Total	*100%*	*100%*	*100%*	*100%*	*100%*	*100%*	*100%*	*100%*	*100%*	*100%*	*100%*	*100*
Gender:												
Male	47.87	48.09	49.07	48.5	42.32	43.86	40.41	45.1	46.09	49.09	45.54	50.2
Female	52.13	51.91	50.93	51.5	57.68	56.14	59.59	54.9	53.91	50.91	54.46	49.8
Total	100%	100%	100%	100%	100%	100%	100%	100%	100%	100%	100%	100%
Studentstatus:												
Full time	6.94	7.45	7.32	7.3	12.98	10.64	11.21	9.4	19.36	8.91	15.48	8.2
None/pttime	93.06	92.55	92.68	92.7	87.02	89.36	88.79	90.6	80.64	91.09	84.52	91.8
Total	*100%*	*100%*	*100%*	*100%*	*100%*	*100%*	*100%*	*100%*	*100%*	*100%*	*100%*	*100%.*

— Results for Hispanics, particularly in the IDS 4, and to a lesser extent in IDS 2, are based upon smaller numbers of respondents and in some cases exhibit substantial departures from Census CPS demographic distributions. IDS 2 Hispanic respondents were much more likely to be younger, more highly educated, and students. In IDS 4, Hispanics were more likely to be older and better educated, female, and full time students. Sample sizes permitting, comparisons of Hispanics with other groups will need to statistically adjust for these demographic variables, before final conclusions can be drawn.

— Due to the large samples sizes for whites and African-Americans, the majority of the analyses contrast whites and African-Americans.

The comparisons in Table 2 are important because they point out the challenges inherent in obtaining truly representative weighted samples. Additionally, these comparisons illustrate that readers must be careful when generalizing survey sample results to determine how the weighted sample compares to the population. Schement presents a detailed discussion of the overlap between Census race categories of white, African-American, Native American, and Asian-American and the ethnic categories of Hispanic/non-Hispanic.

Demographic Differences in Web Across

The major demographic differences between whites and African-Americans occur for age and income. The youngest (16-24) age segment differentiates usage segments more for African-Americans than for whites. African American Web users are more likely to be under 25, across all three surveys.

Overall, Web users are more likely to be under 46 years of age. Web users are more likely to have some college or a college degree, although African American Web users are more likely to have less than high school education than white Web users.

Tables 3a and 3b may provide evidence of an education-driven digital divide. However, it is larger for African Americans than for whites, though it appears to narrow in IDS 4. Of African Americans with no Internet access, 70.27% were high school graduates or had less than a high school education in IDS 2, compared with only 62.11% of whites in the same educational categories with no Internet access.

Of course, African Americans are more likely, in general, to have less education, so this result requires further study. Similarly, of African American Web users, 56.34% had some college or college degrees in IDS 2, compared with 70.89% of white Web users. This gap also does not appear to be diminishing over time. However, to the extent that African Americans are less likely to have some college or a college degree, this result is tentative.

The professional, homemaker, full-time student, and retired/not currently working categories were self-identified single-response. The white-collar category included those respondents who indicated their primary occupation was either technical, administrative/managerial, clerical, sales, or service worker. The blue collar included those respondents who indicated their primary occupation was laborer or craftsman/craftswoman.

Due to its extremely low representation in the sample, respondents indicating they were in the military were excluded from analyses including the occupation variable. For this reason, the Occupation column totals may not necessarily sum to 100 percent. Web users are most likely to be professional, white collar, and students, regardless of race. The percentage of African American Web users who are blue-collar workers has more than tripled over time.

The lowest incomes group (<$40K) differentiate usage segments much more for African-Americans than for whites. Of African-Americans with no Internet access, 80.72% had household incomes less than $40,000 in IDS 2, compared with only 60.9% of whites with no Internet access. Thus, within African-Americans, the income-driven "digital divide" appears larger than for whites. Further, it is not diminishing over time. Again, however, African Americans are more likely to have lower incomes than whites, so these results are tentative until further study. Similarly, of African American Web users, 59.73% had household incomes above $40,000 in IDS 2, compared with 71.01% of white Web users. This gap has also not diminished over time. This concern of an ever-widening gap within African-American income segments has been identified by sociologists as a serious concern.

Katz & Aspden reported evidence of what Lloyd Morrisett of the Markle Foundation has termed a "digital divide", with Internet users being generally wealthier and more highly educated. Sparrow and Vedantham summarize the broader information technology situation as follows: "Information technologies include basic telephone service, personal computing, and computer networking. Although these technologies are becoming everyday conveniences for many Americans, some communities are being left out. Disparities exist in levels of access between rich and poor and between suburban and inner-city residents."

Tables 3a, 3b, and 3c show evidence of a digital divide for both whites and African-Americans.Within both racial groups, "Web users" were most likely to be among the wealthiest individuals, while the "no Internet access segment" was the most likely to be composed of individuals with the lowest incomes. The same holds true for Education. The "Web user" segment was most likely to consist of individuals with some college or who had completed college, while the "no access" segment was most likely to be composed of those with a high school education or less. All these effects were more pronounced for African Americans than whites and these effects appear to persist over time.

There are differences among whites, African Americans and Hispanics in Web use. The statistics on recent Web use for each IDS are presented below.

Aggregate recent web use over time (in millions)

	IDS 2	IDS 3	IDS 4
Raw-count	1555	2305	1562
Recent web-users	45.02	56.23	69.55
% recent web users	22.5	27.8	34.4
Total no.of people	199.93	202.34	202.37

Recent web use over time by bace (in millions)

	White			African			Hispanic		
	IDS2	IDS3	IDS4	IDS2	IDS3	IDS4	IDS2	IDS3	IDS4
Raw-count	1304	2015	1368	104	151	117	91	96	56
Recent web-users	35.22	48.36	60.41	3.9	4.04	5.21	4.79	2.91	5.38
% recent web users	22.4	30.04	35.78	16.6	16.97	21.89	25.2	15.16	28.02
Total no.of people	157.12	160.95	168.81	23.5	23.8	23.8	19.01	19.2	19.2

In IDS 2, 16.6% of African-Americans had used the Web in the six months preceeding the survey. This translated into 3.9 million African-American Web users at the beginning of 1997.

Table 3a:
Demographic Differences Over Time in Web Access and Use for Whites

	IDS2			IDS3			IDS4		
	no-access	*access-only*	*web-user*	*no-access*	*access-only*	*web-user*	*no-access*	*access-only*	*web-user*
N	2,825	569	1,365	3,183	569	2,227	1,630	285	1,522
Age:									
<25	7.41	15.66	25.39	6.81	11.14	26.58	7.10	8.50	23.49
25-45	38.95	50.04	52.74	36.02	46.90	48.75	34.81	46.30	50.57
46-64	29.61	25.52	19.52	29.63	34.15	22.93	29.99	38.09	22.35
>64	24.02	8.78	2.35	27.54	7.81	1.74	28.10	7.11	3.59
Total	*100%*	*100%*	*100%*	*100%*	*100%*	*100%*	*100%*	*100%*	*100%*
Education:									
less than h.s.	21.93	13.38	11.64	21.99	12.33	14.66	25.04	9.62	13.22
high school grad	40.18	30.74	17.46	42.23	35.75	17.69	43.01	37.84	18.60
some college	23.68	30.79	31.58	22.37	30.18	30.13	21.39	38.78	29.77
college grad	14.20	25.09	39.31	13.41	21.74	37.51	10.56	13.76	38.41
Total	*100%*	*100%*	*100%*	*100%*	*100%*	*100%*	*100%*	*100%*	*100%*
Occupation:									
Professional	12.28	22.33	26.33	11.33	17.51	26.24	11.00	17.67	27.64
White collar	28.51	38.76	39.16	27.16	38.27	38.95	23.76	37.82	38.40
Blue collar	13.68	9.64	5.63	15.16	15.14	7.04	16.65	15.96	7.34
Homemaker	13.92	9.32	3.80	13.94	11.16	4.47	16.43	9.38	4.29
Student	2.13	9.59	18.28	1.64	7.46	17.78	1.42	5.78	15.27
Retired	29.10	9.63	4.85	30.77	10.45	5.52	30.40	12.74	5.78
Total	*100%*	*99.26%*	*98.06%*	*100%*	*100%*	*100%*	*99.67%*	*99.36%*	*98.72%*

Household Income									
<$10K	11.49	3.79	2.59	12.80	3.10	2.87	13.60	5.51	2.53
$10K - $19,9	14.12	6.73	5.34	15.87	8.65	5.01	15.91	9.11	4.47
$20K - $29,9	17.67	12.47	9.69	18.97	14.28	9.63	17.39	15.60	10.16
$30K - $39,9	17.62	16.20	11.36	17.35	14.37	13.48	18.31	12.37	11.65
$40K - $59,9	20.93	28.41	27.44	21.14	30.53	26.13	19.21	30.46	25.95
$60K +	18.17	32.39	43.57	13.87	29.07	42.88	15.58	26.95	45.24
Total	*100%*	*100%*	*100%*	*100%*	*100%*	*100%*	*100%*	*100%*	*100%*
Gender:									
Male	43.65	48.22	60.68	44.96	44.51	54.66	44.71	45.37	55.40
Female	56.35	51.78	39.32	55.04	55.49	45.34	55.29	54.63	44.60
Total	*100%*	*100%*	*100%*	*100%*	*100%*	*100%*	*100%*	*100%*	*100%*
% orcolumn who...									
Owns a PC?	26.52	63.43	81.86	23.61	54.51	77.57	21.63	51.28	77.57
PC access at work?	23.39	58.43	68.16	26.32	58.18	64.48	23.75	54.89	63.05

Table 3b:
Demographic Differences Over Time in Web Access and Use for African Americans

	IDS2			IDS3			IDS4		
	no-access	*access-only*	*web-user*	*no-access*	*access-only*	*web-user*	*no-access*	*access-only*	*web-user*
N	298	73	109	387	108	190	266	30	144
Age:									
<25	16.20	21.25	46.30	13.00	17.53	38.51	10.78	5.46	49.47
25-45	37.23	53.43	39.13	46.72	51.82	50.12	38.40	47.24	41.76
46-64	22.76	21.04	14.10	22.02	22.96	11.01	28.68	46.46	8.31
>64	23.80	4.28	0.47	18.27	7.70	0.35	22.15	0.84	0.47
Total	*100%*	*100%*	*100%*	*100%*	*100%*	*100%*	*100%*	*100%*	*100%*
Education:									
less than h.s.	40.52	16.09	29.45	36.57	25.39	16.37	41.57	38.27	30.63
high school grad	29.75	33.70	14.21	35.35	24.71	11.57	33.00	32.20	17.14
some college	17.71	27.45	26.04	20.70	36.96	37.51	18.75	22.90	32.50
college grad	12.03	25.58	30.30	7.37	12.94	34.54	6.67	6.63	19.74
Total	*100%*	*100%*	*100%*	*100%*	*100%*	*100%*	*100%*	*100%*	*100%*
Occupation:									
Professional	11.32	24.02	28.59	12.36	25.23	26.55	11.84	15.60	18.95
White collar	23.13	35.66	28.56	25.80	39.60	38.91	22.89	54.82	28.94
Blue collar	14.00	7.46	2.99	18.47	10.36	3.08	13.09	18.61	9.61
Homemaker	10.28	2.72	0.00	11.13	3.37	1.10	20.75	0.00	2.15
Student	7.10	17.33	30.46	5.39	9.01	28.36	4.42	3.18	29.60
Retired	33.56	9.87	8.09	26.85	12.43	1.99	25.68	5.29	4.66
Total	*99.39%*	*97.06%*	*98.70%*	*100%*	*100%*	*100%*	*98.67%*	*97.49%*	*93.91%*

Household Income									
<$10K	34.28	9.02	15.62	30.92	12.63	4.55	26.80	4.75	8.56
$10K - $19,9	19.87	11.31	2.90	28.80	12.23	4.24	21.50	22.54	6.98
$20K - $29,9	17.70	22.00	10.63	15.43	19.71	11.93	19.07	27.86	12.44
$30K - $39,9	8.87	8.32	11.23	6.00	16.33	19.36	12.00	14.33	14.48
$40K - $59,9	10.94	24.28	27.43	12.52	26.46	18.81	11.25	19.81	24.75
$60K +	8.34	25.07	32.30	6.33	12.64	41.11	9.38	10.71	32.79
Total	*100%*	*100%*	*100%*	*100%*	*100%*	*100%*	*100%*	*100%*	*100%*
Gender:									
Male	38.15	53.55	55.40	38.68	44.01	55.78	34.10	46.46	53.61
Female	61.85	44.65	44.60	61.32	55.99	44.22	65.90	53.54	46.39
Total	*100%*	*100%*	*100%*	*100%*	*100%*	*100%*	*100%*	*100%*	*100%*
% or column who...									
Owns a PC	16.70	44.18	65.05	14.82	34.53	65.62	12.09	29.30	68.24
PC-access at work	18.74	65.39	63.54	24.49	58.20	67.49	24.45	44.85	63.00.

Table 3c:
Demographic Differences Over Time in Web Access and Use for Hispanics

	IDS2			IDS3			IDS4		
	no-access	*access-only*	*web-user*	*no-access*	*access-only*	*web-user*	*no-access*	*access-only*	*web-user*
N	182	32	93	278	41	121	84	15	61
Age:									
<25	16.85	46.51	55.20	13.92	34.30	47.99	10.01	33.56	46.91
25-45	61.51	36.09	36.39	53.83	58.02	40.92	45.86	41.13	41.22
46-64	16.98	17.40	5.45	21.29	7.68	10.17	30.41	25.32	8.36
>64	4.67	0.00	2.96	10.96	0.00	0.92	13.72	0.00	3.51
Total	*100%*	*100%*	*100%*	*100%*	*100%*	*100%*	*100%*	*100%*	*100%*
Education:									
less than h.s.	35.00	29.67	41.20	55.55	36.21	28.85	52.01	14.60	34.38
high school grad	32.75	28.18	8.64	27.95	35.94	14.11	24.58	37.44	20.62
some college	22.58	29.98	30.62	12.12	21.39	32.49	18.26	43.94	22.37
college grad	9.67	25.78	19.55	4.37	6.46	24.55	5.15	4.02	22.63
Total	*100%*	*100%*	*100%*	*100%*	*100%*	*100%*	*100%*	*100%*	*100%*
Occupation:									
Professional	11.83	14.18	16.22	6.95	11.22	21.77	8.93	16.14	23.32
White collar	28.59	32.88	30.62	26.86	30.59	43.83	16.35	45.55	30.77
Blue collar	19.37	8.35	4.36	25.62	35.24	4.91	14.02	0.00	0.00
Homemaker	19.52	3.62	2.07	20.09	0.00	0.62	37.98	0.00	2.52
Student	5.60	40.97	38.14	3.75	17.51	26.32	3.20	33.56	35.50
Retired	14.50	0.00	7.37	16.73	5.44	2.54	18.05	4.76	2.37
Total	*99.42%*	*100%*	*98.77%*	*100%*	*100%*	*100%*	*98.53%*	*100%*	*94.48%*

Household Income									
<$10K	10.33	3.70	12.24	20.94	29.03	5.85	20.25	4.01	10.79
$10K - $19,9	30.70	2.54	13.11	32.70	16.75	3.50	27.38	0.00	6.10
$20K - $29,9	19.09	4.50	11.65	21.78	17.12	9.39	19.79	20.13	7.23
$30K - $39,9	14.34	27.27	10.29	11.20	10.67	16.03	10.34	9.06	8.05
$40K - $59,9	15.02	25.24	18.83	9.25	21.84	24.56	10.22	12.69	25.81
$60K + 10.52	36.77	33.87	4.14	4.59	40.67	12.02	54.11	42.02	
Total	*100%*	*100%*	*100%*	*100%*	*100%*	*100%*	*100%*	*100%*	*100%*
Gender:									
Male	42.93	38.91	56.35	45.42	63.21	55.60	31.99	40.72	70.86
Female	57.07	61.09	43.65	54.58	36.79	44.40	68.01	59.28	29.14
Total	*100%*	*100%*	*100%*	*100%*	*100%*	*100%*	*100%*	*100%*	*100%*
% or column who...									
Owns a PC	26.26	58.21	61.99	13.90	36.16	72.00	11.54	20.09	77.45
PC-accessatwork	24.23	50.92	49.58	21.85	61.62	59.52	19.02	54.52	50.00

Race Differences Over Time in Web Use

A series of comparisons among whites, African-Americans and Hispanics on key indicators of Web access and use are presented in Table 4. In IDS 2, overall, whites were more likely than African-Americans to have access to the Internet, and to have ever used the Web. Whites were also more likely to own a computer, have PC access at work, and have fax, cable, and a satellite dish at home. The percentages of access and use for both whites and African Americans has increased over time, but the gaps persist. In fact, the overall gap between whites and African Americans in Internet access and having ever used have actually increased over time.

In IDS 2, 35.8% of whites had Internet access, compared to 31.68% of African Americans. By IDS 4, although 49.33% of whites had access, the percentage of African Americans with Internet access had risen only a few percentage points, to 35.54%. Similarly, in IDS 2, 24.34% of whites had ever used the Internet, compared to 18.76% of African Americans. In IDS 4, eighteen months later 40.37% of whites had ever used the Internet, compared to 27.98% of African Americans. Although whites are still more likely to own a PC and to have PC access at work, these gaps have not increased over time. Further, the gaps in cable and satellite ownership have disappeared. In fact, satellite penetration has doubled among African Americans and the penetration rate in IDS 4 equals that for whites. The gap between whites and African-Americans in computer ownership has been cited as the key explanation for corresponding gaps in Web usage. A Yankelovich Monitor study "suggests that what bars entry to cyberspace among African Americans is owning a home PC, not lack of interest in the Internet."

However, a Forrester Research study cites "technology optimism" as an important predictor of technology adoption. Further research is required to understand these increasing gaps in access and usage. A number of reasons have been provided in the popular press for the gap between whites and African-Americans in computer ownership. Price and value are often cited as explanations.

The PC penetration rates are not increasing overall among African Americans. Although the percentage of whites owning a home computer has increased slightly over time, approaching fifty percent, the overall percentage of African Americans who own a home computer has remained at 29%. Overall, the gap in access and use is persistent and appears to be increasing. In IDS 2, whites were more frequent and more recent Web users than African Americans. White recent Web users in IDS 2 were also more likely to have ever used the Web from home and work, while recent African American Web users were more likely to have ever used the Web from school. African Americans in IDS 2 were much more likely to be newer users, and whites were much more likely to have been using the Web for two years or more. But over time, is apparent that African American Web users have made significant gains in Web use. Indeed, the gaps are diminishing rapidly.

The gap in Web use at home has decreased dramatically and African Americans now appear to be more likely than whites to have ever used the Web from work, school or other locations. Additionally, African American Web users are becoming more recent and more frequent Web users. In fact, differences between white and African American Web users in their recency and frequency of Web use have disappeared. African

Table 4: Race and ethnicity differences over time on key web usage variables

	White			African American			Hispanic		
	IDS2	IDS3	IDS4	IDS2	IDS3	IDS4	IDS2	IDS3	IDS4
Among all respondents									
N	4,906	6,000	3,447	493	691	441	319	448	164
Current Access	35.84	43.25	49.33	31.68	38.99	35.54	38.64	29.84	39.73
Ever used	24.34	33.56	40.37	18.76	23.22	27.98	28.06	19.73	31.77
Own a PC	44.24	44.62	46.66	28.92	29.05	29.07	39.86	26.86	32.33
PC access at work	38.23	42.07	42.35	32.97	38.96	36.70	33.56	32.31	31.52
Home fax	14.00	13.68	14.86	9.04	7.26	8.03	14.31	8.72	14.29
Cable	68.46	72.87	74.49	63.36	72.87	75.11	65.61	63.87	68.30
Satellite	10.55	11.96	13.52	5.06	7.49	12.69	7.74	7.27	11.23
Among Recent Web Users									
N	1,304	2,015	1,368	104	151	117	91	96	56
First Used									
...in past 2 years +	16.17	33.14	49.47	6.79	31.91	43.98	14.96	27.28	48.94
...in past 1-2 years	18.41	23.95	19.99	15.78	20.77	17.61	5.01	22.86	16.94
...in past year	22.40	23.77	15.69	15.42	26.09	19.46	22.10	31.27	18.13
...in past 6 months	18.65	9.39	8.81	18.39	9.23	6.10	21.35	11.88	5.59
...in past 3 months	24.36	9.74	6.05	43.62	12.00	12.85	36.58	6.71	10.10
Last Used									
...in past 6 months	8.40	7.68	5.37	10.50	4.70	2.32	8.70	4.67	6.58
...in past 3 months	12.09	11.67	6.57	30.94	21.19	11.46	10.18	15.35	0.56
...in past month	21.95	19.38	19.30	23.77	26.86	21.44	33.68	23.34	23.92
...in past week	27.89	26.81	30.19	18.90	25.62	35.62	32.18	23.62	39.01
...in past 24 hours	29.68	34.46	38.56	15.88	21.63	29.17	15.25	33.02	29.94

Frequency of Use									
...once a day +	18.49	22.20	26.79	15.33	15.67	25.33	10.31	25.94	30.97
...few times/week	28.59	29.30	31.54	25.92	27.97	32.26	36.44	29.34	31.30
...two-four times/month	26.67	24.77	25.03	28.25	26.10	23.28	28.05	30.76	30.42
...once a month or less	26.25	23.73	16.64	30.50	30.26	19.13	25.21	19.96	7.31
Ever Used									
...at home	61.36	64.94	68.85	46.44	55.02	60.83	35.98	65.74	73.34
...at work	44.15	51.77	50.55	36.73	63.37	61.06	32.07	44.83	44.69
...at school	28.31	29.26	28.79	44.39	40.18	57.07	48.58	32.58	51.84
...at other locations	26.22	39.40	35.06	24.39	48.36	53.69	30.28	50.29	46.87.2

Americans are still among the newest users, but are now also joining the ranks of the long-term users. By IDS 4, 43.98 percent of African American recent Web users, compared to 49.47 percent of white recent Web users, had been using the Web for two years or more.

Student Status

The differences on most indicators of Internet access and use, and also home computer ownership between whites and African-Americans is greater for student than non-students White non-students in IDS 2 were more likely to have access to the Web, to have ever used the Web, to own a PC, and have PC access at work. Additionally, white non-students were also more likely than African Americans to have a home fax, cable, and a satellite dish. Over time, and similar to the previous analysis, overall differences between white and African American non-students actually appear to be increasing. Note that the percentage of white non-students who own a home computer is increasing slightly, but that the percentage of African American non-students who own a home computer is actually decreasing over time. At the same time, the percentages of African American non-students who have cable or a satellite dish have increased and are now similar to the penetration rates for whites.

Since IDS 2, African Americans are increasingly likely to have been using the Web for two years or more, more likely to have ever used the Web at home, work, school, or other locations, and more likely to be more recent and frequent users of the Web. However, white non-student recent Web users are making similar gains, and in some cases, their use still outpaces that of African Americans. For example, whites are still more likely to be among the most recent Web users. In IDS 4, 39.96 percent of whites reported using the Web in the past 24 hours, compared to 30.55 percent of African Americans. On the other hand, differences in Web use frequency between white and African American non-student recent Web users have disappeared. Additionally, African American non-students are more likely to have used the Web from work, school or other locations.

African American non-students are significantly less likely to own a home computer than white non-students (and in fact, even less likely over time), and consequently exhibit lower overall rates of access and usage. Yet, among recent Web users, who by definition have access somewhere, recency and frequency usage rates for African American respondents has over time come to mirror that of whites.

Table 5b shows clearly that, overall, Web access, usage and PC penetration rates are considerably higher for students than non-students, regardless of race. Additionally, Web access, usage and PC penetration rates are all rising over time, for both white and African American students. In fact, 53.83 percent of African American students owned a home computer in IDS 4, compared with only 25.67 percent of African American non-students. Eighteen months earlier, in IDS 2, the PC penetration rate was considerably lower: only 31.88 percent of African American students, compared with 28.66 percent of African American non-students, owned a home PC. At the same time, Table 5b reveals clear disparities in Internet access and use between African American and white students. For example, though both groups have higher rates over time, white students are more likely to have Web access, and to have ever used the Web, and these differences persist over time.

White students are more likely to own home computers than African American students and this difference remains over time, despite the fact that home computer ownership over time among white students is flat and home computer ownership among African American students has been steadily and impressively rising. However, the gaps in access and usage are clearly decreasing over time and this may in part be due to increasing rates of PC ownership among African American students. Additionally, African American students were more likely to have access to a PC at work in IDS 4. Thus, one could hypothesize that as PC ownership and PC access rates continue to rise, so will overall Web access and usage rates. African American recent Web user students, like their white counterparts, are increasingly likely to be more recent and more frequent Web users. In fact, the differences between the two groups, as for non-students, have effectively disappeared. However, white students are still more likely to have ever used the Web from home, while African American students are more likely to have ever used the Web from work and school.

Home Computer Ownership

Table 6a compares Web access and usage patterns for white and African American non-students who do not own a home computer. Table 6b shows the same comparison for white and African American non-students who do own a home computer. The presence of a computer in the home has a dramatic impact overall on access and usage. Non-student respondents, regardless of race, are much more likely to have access to the Web and to have ever used the Web if they own a home computer.

Table 5a: Race and ethnicity differences over time on key web usage variables for non-students

	White			African American			Hispanic		
	IDS2	IDS3	IDS4	IDS2	IDS3	IDS4	IDS2	IDS3	IDS4
Among all non-student respondents									
N	4,554	5,581	3,212	423	619	388	264	405	138
Current access	32.59	39.60	46.05	27.31	35.29	30.34	29.05	25.59	30.65
Ever used	20.94	29.94	36.89	14.69	18.66	21.98	20.92	15.79	24.17
Own a PC	42.09	42.51	44.90	28.66	27.94	25.67	35.28	24.19	26.32
PC access at work	39.12	43.19	43.06	34.71	40.17	35.61	37.34	32.84	31.18
Home fax	13.70	13.28	14.40	9.27	7.78	8.20	13.25	8.81	13.04
Cable	68.29	72.54	74.49	64.23	73.06	74.91	66.27	64.85	68.92
Satellite	10.69	11.87	13.77	5.02	7.60	11.37	8.39	6.39	9.82
Among recent non-student web users									
N	1,089	1,722	1,194	83	123	88	63	81	41
First Used									
...in past 2 years +	16.74	32.90	49.54	6.99	29.15	37.85	22.65	30.20	56.23
...in past 1-2 years	19.02	22.59	19.37	20.91	20.38	19.96	6.19	20.13	4.41
...in past year	22.62	24.74	15.17	16.70	26.89	20.40	20.85	32.25	18.90
...in past 6 months	18.32	9.50	9.27	19.96	10.19	7.51	16.76	12.96	8.71
...in past 3 months	23.41	10.27	6.65	35.44	13.40	14.28	33.56	4.45	11.75
Last Used									
...in past 6 months	7.65	6.65	5.59	11.54	5.97	3.34	9.38	5.96	7.93
...in past 3 months	12.08	11.07	7.02	31.74	16.26	11.66	5.65	14.04	0.84

...in past month	21.82	19.07	18.81	21.42	28.65	19.48	30.43	21.10	24.93
...in past week	27.28	27.54	28.62	18.26	26.42	34.97	34.72	19.47	32.68
...in past 24 hours	31.17	35.68	39.96	17.04	22.70	30.55	19.82	39.43	33.92
Frequency of Use									
...once a day +	20.08	22.69	28.16	12.61	14.83	24.39	11.37	30.97	39.97
...few times/week	27.54	30.50	31.03	26.28	28.59	34.28	41.27	26.18	30.85
...two-four times/month	26.34	23.72	22.76	25.82	25.61	20.58	26.47	27.33	18.31
...once a month or less	25.73	23.09	18.05	35.59	30.97	20.75	20.88	15.53	10.88
Ever Used									
...at home	63.17	65.54	68.12	49.56	59.94	64.48	41.24	72.63	76.35
...at work	50.74	56.99	55.60	46.64	68.81	66.86	46.92	52.24	59.38
...at school	18.23	19.69	20.77	30.82	29.12	38.67	31.39	29.04	36.01
...at other locations	24.83	36.44	32.59	29.29	42.69	52.35	26.07	44.39	40.62.

Table 5b: Race and ethnicity differences over time on key web usage variables for students

	White			African American			Hispanic		
	IDS2	IDS3	IDS4	IDS2	IDS3	IDS4	IDS2	IDS3	IDS4
Among all student respondents									
N	336	405	218	64	68	50	55	41	26
Current Access	80.33	87.82	90.25	62.78	71.12	74.97	81.87	72.79	87.85
Ever used	62.72	78.15	83.26	43.20	58.16	72.82	55.38	54.66	71.03
Own a PC	72.98	69.24	69.50	31.88	39.77	53.83	58.86	55.16	65.12
PC access at work	26.62	27.97	32.95	22.04	30.67	47.60	17.58	27.98	33.40
Home fax	18.42	18.19	20.59	7.77	3.09	7.21	18.72	8.27	21.01
Cable	71.54	76.16	74.84	62.21	72.51	75.73	62.88	57.13	64.95
Satellite	9.17	13.50	10.60	4.85	6.95	23.93	5.00	16.66	18.90
Among recent student web users									
N	212	289	170	20	28	29	28	14	15
First Used									
...in past 2 years +	13.81	34.02	48.58	6.29	42.09	57.83	2.02		
...in past 1-2 years	15.85	31.20	23.31	0.00	22.21	12.32	3.03		
...in past year	21.04	19.23	18.66	11.73	23.14	17.35	24.20		
...in past 6 months	20.36	9.02	6.41	13.86	5.70	2.89	29.08		
...in past 3 months	28.94	6.53	2.84	68.12	6.86	9.62	41.68		
Last Used									
...in past 6 months	11.90	12.91	4.28	7.46	0.00	0.00	7.56		
...in past 3 months	11.80	14.87	4.23	29.10	39.42	0.00	17.82		
...in past month	22.09	20.34	22.37	31.66	20.23	5.34	39.16		

...in past week	30.91	22.89	38.63	19.19	22.67	73.28	27.90
...in past 24 hours	23.30	29.00	30.49	12.58	17.67	21.37	7.56
Frequency of Use							
...once a day +	11.60	20.22	18.80	24.09	18.72	27.47	8.52
...few times/week	32.27	23.00	34.32	25.37	25.70	27.66	28.29
...two-four times/month	27.55	29.69	37.66	37.31	27.91	29.42	30.70
...once a month or less	28.58	27.09	9.22	13.22	27.67	15.46	32.49
Ever Used							
...at home	52.80	62.24	70.42	37.63	36.86	52.55	27.11
...at work	15.01	26.65	23.81	6.40	43.26	48.02	7.06
...at school	73.50	76.75	73.69	80.47	98.93	94.79	77.54
...at other locations	32.35	53.92	49.37	9.49	70.35	56.76	37.37

Additionally, among non-students with a home computer, whites are more likely to have access and to have ever used, but the differences are small. Yet, there are striking gaps in access and usage among non-students without a home computer. In IDS 4, whites were more likely than African Americans to have access to and have ever used the Web. Gap in use among non-students without a home computer is increasing over time.

Whites and African Americans have similar rates of usage frequency and recency, suggesting once again, that given access, usage follows for both groups. African Americans without a home computer are more likely than whites to have ever used the Web at school or other locations. Among non-students recent Web users with a home computer, both recency and frequency of Web use increase over time for both whites and African Americans, and differences are diminishing rapidly. By IDS 4, 73.85 percent of white non-students with a home computer had last used the Web within the past week, compared to 67.58% of African Americans and 64.62% of whites had used the Web a few times a week or more, compared to 59.05% of African Americans. Both groups enjoy similarly high percentages of having ever used the Web at home; 80.55% of whites and 82.12% of African Americans in IDS 4 had ever used the Web at home. In IDS 4, African American non-students were more likely than their white counterparts to have ever used the Web at work, at school and at other locations. Tables 6c and 6d show the analysis for students with and without a computer in the home. Sample sizes are much smaller for African-American students when segmented by whether they have a computer at home, so the results must be interpreted with caution.

Compared to Tables 6a and 6b, Tables 6c and 6d show that students are more likely to have access to the Web and to use the Web, compared to non-students. Regardless of race, non-students with a home computer have access and usage rates that are similar to students without a home computer. Students with a home computer enjoy the highest levels of access and use, while non-students without a home computer have the lowest levels of access and use.

Additionally, having a computer in the home leads to much higher levels of Web access and use for students of both races, but the difference is clearly more dramatic for non-students than students.

The differences in access and usage for non-students with and without a home computer are larger than the differences for students with and without a home computer. Presumably this is because students have more opportunities for access at school, even if they do not own a computer at home. However, without a computer in the home, there is a much larger gap between African-American and white students in terms of Web access, and the corresponding percentages of having ever used the Web are also smaller.

In fact, the gap in access for students without a computer in the home appears to be increasing. The presence of a computer in the home is bringing African American and White students to parity in Internet access and Web use. Increasing the Internet access opportunities for students, especially African-American students without home computers, may help to reduce the gaps in access and usage.

Table 6a: Race and ethnicity differences in web access and use by student status and home computer ownership

Non-student respondents without a home computer

	White			African American			Hispanic		
	IDS2	IDS3	IDS4	IDS2	IDS3	IDS4	IDS2	IDS3	IDS4
Among all non-student respondents without a home computer									
N	3,258	3,134	1,733	282	421	271	158	274	94
Current access	13.91	19.35	22.87	14.23	22.77	16.91	17.65	14.39	14.35
Ever used	6.47	11.37	14.84	4.99	7.04	8.84	12.21	5.37	6.29
Among recent non-student web users without a home computer									
N	207	417	276	22	32	24	18	22	12
First Used									
...in past 2 years +	11.45	23.22	37.30	5.98	21.47	34.17			
...in past 1-2 years	8.53	19.76	21.35	8.26	13.04	12.30			
...in past year	21.02	28.09	22.81	21.37	32.34	15.02			
...in past 6 months	22.88	12.57	10.97	35.61	16.71	10.12			
...in past 3 months	36.13	16.36	7.57	28.77	16.44	28.40			
Last Used									
...in past 6 months	17.04	12.64	11.97	31.20	17.53	0.00			
...in past 3 months	15.75	20.00	12.36	25.36	14.95	9.83			
...in past month	30.26	25.54	26.27	12.96	26.36	30.44			
...in past week	21.96	24.35	27.40	22.08	30.43	30.97			
...in past 24 hours	14.99	17.46	22.01	8.40	10.73	27.75			
Frequency of Use									

...once a day +	16.34	13.73	14.13	15.29	7.74	19.77
...few times/week	18.56	20.21	25.20	44.08	38.12	37.84
...two-four times/month	24.22	23.14	28.14	7.65	13.22	22.83
...once a month or less	40.89	42.92	32.53	32.98	40.93	19.56
Ever Used						
...at home	7.54	19.63	24.80	10.83	12.36	14.59
...at work	58.22	56.10	64.99	41.88	69.29	64.27
...at school	21.56	21.11	22.17	35.75	26.52	53.38
...at other locations	33.18	50.40	45.89	31.05	53.94	60.47

Table 6b: Race and ethnicity differences in web access and use by student status and home computer ownership

Non-student respondents with a home computer

	White			African American			Hispanic		
	IDS2	IDS3	IDS4	IDS2	IDS3	IDS4	IDS2	IDS3	IDS4
Among all non-student respondents with a home computer									
N	2,025	2,442	1,479	140	197	116	105	130	44
Current access	58.36	66.87	74.31	59.76	66.56	69.35	50.80	59.76	74.42
Ever used	40.87	55.09	63.82	38.50	48.53	60.19	37.21 48.56	72.72	
Among recent non-student web users with a home computer									
N	882	1,304	918	61	91	64	45	59	29
First Used									
...in past 2 years +	17.88	35.75	52.88	7.31	31.46	39.12	34.10	35.27	59.33
...in past 1-2 years	21.29	23.43	18.83	24.87	22.59	22.59	6.23	22.44	5.85
...in past year	22.84	23.77	13.09	15.24	25.25	22.25	15.50	30.23	13.11
...in past 6 months	17.34	8.55	8.80	15.06	8.22	6.62	10.39	7.32	11.56
...in past 3 months	20.66	8.50	6.40	37.52	12.48	9.42	33.78	4.74	10.15
Last Used									
...in past 6 months	5.61	4.90	3.83	5.39	2.50	4.53	3.82	0.85	1.53
...in past 3 months	11.29	8.41	5.55	33.73	16.35	12.30	6.13	5.97	10.52
...in past month	19.98	17.19	16.76	24.06	29.34	15.59	16.33	37.13	19.04
...in past week	28.44	28.48	28.95	17.07	25.20	36.39	29.15	28.50	19.39
...in past 24 hours	34.68	41.01	44.90	19.74	26.31	31.19	44.57	27.54	49.53

Frequency of Use									
...once a day +	20.88	25.26	32.00	11.81	16.90	26.03	7.73	36.34	51.30
...few times/week	29.83	33.47	32.62	20.99	25.82	33.02	45.92	28.28	28.48
...two-four times/month	26.80	23.84	21.30	30.84	29.21	19.78	28.24	39.47	13.93
...once a month or less	22.49	17.43	14.08	36.36	28.07	21.17	18.11	5.91	6.30
Ever Used									
...at home	75.27	78.97	80.55	61.68	74.26	82.12	57.96	86.96	87.11
...at work	49.12	57.29	53.01	48.13	68.66	67.79	53.76	43.77	44.33
...at school	17.51	19.29	20.39	29.28	29.90	33.47	23.65	33.67	32.93
...at other locations	23.02	32.31	28.94	28.74	39.26	49.48	27.22	43.18	35.85

Table 6c: Race and ethnicity differences in web access and use by student status and home computer ownership

Students without a home computer

	White			African American			Hispanic		
	IDS2	IDS3	IDS4	IDS2	IDS3	IDS4	IDS2	IDS3	IDS4
Among all student respondents without a home computer									
N	89	125	59	42	41	24	22	17	9
Current access	65.14	73.13	78.76	59.65	60.22	61.90	82.49		
Ever used	45.21	65.99	65.78	38.47	51.98	60.02	51.93		

Table 6d: Race and ethnicity differences in web access and use by student status and home computer ownership

Students with a home computer

	White			African American			Hispanic		
	IDS2	IDS3	IDS4	IDS2	IDS3	IDS4	IDS2	IDS3	IDS4
Among all student respondents with a home computer									
N	247	280	159	22	27	26	33	23	17
Current access	85.59	94.40	95.30	69.06	87.61	86.19	81.49	87.63	
Ever used	69.19	83.55	90.93	53.13	67.53	83.80	57.79	64.73	

Education

Tables 7a-7d show the influence of education on Web access and usage between whites and African Americans. In general, increasing levels of education lead to higher levels of Web access, usage, PC ownership and PC access at work. However, these levels are higher for whites than for African Americans and these race differences persist even after adjusting for education. In fact, the gaps in access and usage are largest for those with a college degree.

At the lowest levels of education, whites are more likely than African Americans to have access to the Web, to have ever used the Web, and to own a computer. What is more, these differences persist over time. Among those with less than a high school education, African Americans are gaining ground faster than whites in Web access, use and PC ownership over time. Overall, the gaps are smaller here. Whites are more likely to have access to a PC at work, in IDS 2 and IDS 3. By IDS 4, there is no difference between whites and African Americans with less than a high school education on this variable. However, students are included in this group and that could account for some of these gains.

Among high school graduates, levels of computer ownership among both groups are stagnant, and whites are more likely than African Americans to own a PC. African American high school graduates are more likely to have access to a PC at work than are white high school graduates. Additionally, the gap in access and use between whites and African Americans is larger for high school graduates than for those without a high school degree.

The results for respondents with some college are shown in Table 7c.In IDS 4, whites were more likely to have Web access, to have ever used the Web, and to own a home computer. Except for access, the gaps are diminishing over time. African Americans are more likely to have PC access at work. Larger sample sizes permitted us to examine Web usage patterns among recent Web users with some college. In IDS 2, twice as many African Americans as whites with some college education reported using the Web for the first time (50.62 percent of African Americans compared to 25.25 percent of whites). More than twice as many whites as African Americans reported using the Web for two years or more. Thus, in IDS 2, whites were more likely to be long-term users and African Americans were more likely to be newer users. By IDS 4, similar percentages of African Americans and whites have been using the Web for two years or more; 43.81 percent of whites and 46.59 percent of African Americans had been using the Web for two years or more. In IDS 2, whites were more both recent and frequent users of the Web, compared to African Americans.

Over time, however, these differences have effectively vanished, with 65.82 percent of whites and 66.87 percent of African Americans in IDS 4 reporting using the Web within the past week. Similarly, 29.13 percent of whites and 26.30 percent of African Americans with some college used the Web once a day or more in IDS 4, and African Americans with some college are actually more likely than whites to have used the Web a few times a week. In IDS 2, whites with some college were more likely to have ever used the Web at home and work, and African Americans were more likely to have ever used the Web at school.

Table 7a: Race and ethnicity differences over time on key web usage variables for respondents with less than high school cducation

	White			African American			Hispanic		
	IDS2	IDS3	IDS4	IDS2	IDS3	IDS4	IDS2	IDS3	IDS4
Among all respondents with less than high school education									
N	492	609	360	93	125	98	73	130	41
Current access	23.46	32.89	32.83	21.41	25.92	29.96	40.55	19.35	27.83
Ever used	14.93	26.45	28.26	15.46	11.85	22.40	31.30	11.28	25.15
Own a PC	28.92	31.99	32.60	15.26	10.25	20.70	29.75	15.71	20.39
PC access at work	11.26	16.72	13.28	7.64	10.09	13.73	11.98	16.11	7.83
Home fax	8.29	9.48	9.55	2.40	0.97	6.93	9.60	4.90	7.35
Cable	61.41	69.63	68.88	42.19	62.78	64.48	62.51	54.41	58.62
Satellite	10.82	13.76	13.17	3.89	8.32	16.56	7.33	9.16	13.13

Table 7b: Race and ethnicity differences over time on key web usage variables for respondents with less than high school education

	White			African American			Hispanic		
	IDS2	IDS3	IDS4	IDS2	IDS3	IDS4	IDS2	IDS3	IDS4
Among all high school graduate respondents									
N	1,475	1,710	998	149	187	129	75	122	44
Current access	23.09	28.13	33.35	25.64	23.38	25.37	21.17	24.67	39.15
Ever used	12.42	17.77	22.87	9.39	9.52	16.69	9.46	10.60	26.91
Own a computer	32.31	31.18	35.30	20.26	22.23	21.34	27.33	20.66	32.71
PC access at work	30.01	32.20	31.67	26.98	35.18	36.20	32.21	39.44	34.55
Home fax	8.95	8.69	9.87	7.87	4.30	5.66	6.86	7.59	12.02
Cable	68.61	72.37	74.08	70.69	70.86	81.44	59.29	68.13	68.03
Satellite	12.34	13.72	15.20	3.09	8.20	9.34	9.34	4.98	10.62

Table 7c: Race and ethnicity differences over time on key web usage variables for respondents with some college

Students with a home computer

	White			African American			Hispanic		
	IDS2	IDS3	IDS4	IDS2	IDS3	IDS4	IDS2	IDS3	IDS4
Among All Respondents with Some College									
N	1,397	1,943	1,117	131	242	151	103	127	55
Currently	42.51	50.67	58.85	41.46	53.51	47.25	45.85	50.19	49.06
Have access									
Ever used	28.40	39.40	45.49	23.31	32.06	39.69	31.84	37.23	31.92
Own a computer	53.44	52.03	51.33	44.34	36.37	46.31	52.07	49.03	38.34
PC access at work	47.09	52.98	53.26	49.36	58.22	60.64	47.41	54.14	55.75
Home fax	16.65	15.79	16.60	10.62	10.19	9.99	17.01	12.09	17.98
Cable	70.09	73.24	77.22	75.10	80.42	80.03	69.84	76.92	82.21
Satellite	11.42	12.40	13.51	4.68	7.76	12.60	5.97	6.01	6.11
Among recent web users with some college									
N	388	700	451	32	53	48	29	37	18
First Used									
...in past 2 years +	14.23	31.18	43.81	5.97	20.58	46.59	15.48	12.75	
...in past 1-2 years	19.53	22.24	22.05	1.16	26.86	25.44	8.10	19.07	
...in past year	21.70	26.78	17.08	22.10	29.96	16.62	18.25	46.81	
...in past 6 months	19.28	10.90	9.53	20.14	10.90	3.55	24.04	13.37	
...in past 3 months	25.25	8.89	7.53	50.62	11.70	7.79	34.12	6.01	

Last Used								
...in past 6 months	10.59	6.79	4.89	4.19	5.78	0.00	9.49	7.05
...in past 3 months	12.97	12.04	9.65	27.72	22.24	9.14	13.97	17.62
...in past month	18.44	22.36	19.64	28.25	25.92	23.98	22.00	29.43
...in past week	28.03	28.77	26.13	20.23	27.08	37.02	37.94	27.88
...in past 24 hours	29.97	30.04	39.69	19.61	18.99	29.85	16.60	18.03
Frequency of Use								
...once a day +	18.44	20.27	29.13	16.58	18.23	26.30	0.00	20.13
...few times/week	27.49	30.30	28.33	21.57	35.74	39.73	38.74	24.81
...two-four times/month	24.55	26.66	24.15	29.50	24.12	18.28	32.02	42.49
...once a month or less	29.53	22.77	18.39	32.35	31.91	15.69	29.25	12.57
Ever Used								
...at home	60.06	61.31	68.99	47.33	50.05	76.52	35.51	65.08
...at work	38.76	48.20	47.87	27.99	61.16	67.30	45.72	39.90
...at school	26.26	29.78	24.51	40.02	44.12	44.19	36.56	27.25
...at other locations	24.24	38.77	32.74	22.73	48.52	54.01	25.10	36.48

Table 7d: Race and ethnicity differences over time on key web usage variables for college graduates

	White			African American			Hispanic		
	IDS2	IDS3	IDS4	IDS2	IDS3	IDS4	IDS2	IDS3	IDS4
Among all respondents with college degrees									
N	1,542	1,738	972	120	137	63	68	69	24
Current access	57.85	65.92	75.78	51.00	69.10	58.34	53.63	64.18	70.77
Ever used	43.37	56.50	70.18	33.09	55.09	53.49	42.69	56.12	67.75
Own a PC	64.65	66.81	70.21	54.09	70.43	43.60	69.01	67.23	69.66
PC access at work	63.21	65.52	70.86	76.40	74.16	70.09	70.02	62.77	75.04
Home fax	23.47	22.26	24.79	23.52	21.72	14.40	37.22	28.03	40.18
Cable	72.28	75.92	76.74	83.00	85.13	85.96	78.11	80.86	81.17
Satellite	6.49	7.29	11.34	6.40	3.76	7.83	9.47	5.59	15.22
Among Recent Web Users with College Degrees									
N	650	913	623	43	68	31	32	34	16
First Used									
...in past 2 years +	21.98	40.61	58.12	16.06	42.92	49.41	43.23	38.74	
...in past 1-2 years	21.30	24.39	20.29	41.77	23.83	19.43	0.00	22.25	
...in past year	22.80	20.85	12.13	11.68	22.19	21.69	13.65	23.90	
...in past 6 months	16.57	7.47	5.60	15.49	6.70	3.69	13.86	9.34	
...in past 3 months	17.36	6.68	3.85	15.00	4.36	5.78	29.26	5.77	
Last Used									
...in past 6 months	5.58	5.64	4.24	7.46	5.12	3.85	2.40	0.00	
...in past 3 months	12.12	10.10	5.55	26.93	12.77	5.11	7.21	6.03	
...in past month	22.68	15.29	16.27	17.19	34.77	12.56	22.16	12.58	
...in past week	24.86	28.01	28.01	24.82	23.83	41.29	33.62	21.63	
...in past 24 hours	34.76	40.96	45.93	23.60	23.51	37.19	34.61	59.76	

Frequency of Use								
...once a day +	23.67	25.78	31.32	17.92	17.92	17.92	21.51	41.94
...few times/week	27.76	31.51	31.51	21.49	25.88	35.34	45.96	25.24
...two-four times/month	24.62	23.28	21.87	23.68	32.18	29.82	5.66	26.87
...once a month or less	23.95	19.42	15.30	36.90	24.02	16.92	26.85	6.95
Ever Used								
...at home	66.47	69.01	67.52	60.75	56.83	67.92	50.22	81.26
...at work	62.69	68.00	68.51	70.15	72.38	71.52	62.34	68.28
...at school	23.53	19.86	22.23	28.39	24.05	23.20	43.67	22.02
...at other locations	24.34	31.56	28.55	33.17	35.27	37.02	36.03	24.51

By IDS 4, African Americans were more likely than whites to have ever used the Web at work, school or other locations. The percentage of African Americans who have ever used the Web at home has risen dramatically, going from 47.33 percent in IDS 2 to 76.52 percent by IDS 4. College Graduates.

Table 7d examines differences in access and use for college graduates. In IDS 2, whites had higher levels of access, usage, and home computer ownership than African Americans. In IDS 3, it appeared that these differences had disappeared. But then in IDS 4, African American rates dropped, leading to dramatic differences and larger gaps.

Thus, it appears that education does not account for the digital divide in access and usage and home PC ownership. Interestingly, both whites and African American college graduates have high levels of PC access at work and there is no gap on this variable. Outside of this finding, it is an interesting question to ask why there is such a large gap in access and usage between educated African Americans and whites. Further examination of college educated African Americans in IDS 4 is warranted.

Whites and African Americans report similar levels of recency and frequency of use, as with those with some college. Whites and African American college graduates are also equally likely to have ever used the Web from home, work, or school. However, there is a small tendency for African Americans college graduates to be more likely to have ever used the Web from other locations, and this difference has persisted over time.

Income Tables 8a and 8b show the relationship between income and Web access and usage for whites and African Americans. Not surprisingly, respondents whose household income is above the median income of $40,000 report higher levels of access, use, home computer ownership and PC access at work.

At household incomes below $40,000, whites are more likely than African Americans to have access to the Web, to have ever used the Web, and to own a home computer. The gaps in access and use may actually be increasing, although the gap in home PC ownership appears to be improving slightly. There is no difference between whites and African Americans in PC access at work at this income level.

Above the median household income of $40,000, differences between whites and African Americans in access, usage, PC ownership and PC access at work are greatly diminished compared to respondents with less household income. In IDS 2, there were significant differences in the length of time that whites and African Americans had been online. White 170.8 percent of whites had used the Internet for two years or more, only 9.08 percent of African Americans had. In contrast, African Americans were almost twice as likely as whites to be new users in IDS 2.

By IDS 4, these gaps had disappeared with over fifty percent of both African Americans and whites to have been Web users for two years or more. In IDS 2, 59.48 percent of whites, compared to 44.21 percent of African Americans were the most recent users. By IDS 4, this gap had largely disappeared, with 73.78 percent of whites and 75.22 percent of African Americans with incomes of $40,000 and over reporting they last used the Web within the past week.

Table 8a: Race and ethnicity differences over time on key web usage variables for respondents with household income below $40,000

	White			African American			Hispanic		
	IDS2	IDS3	IDS4	IDS2	IDS3	IDS4	IDS2	IDS3	IDS4
Among All Respondents with HH Income < $40,000									
N	1,967	2,472	1,315	244	381	223	164	247	69
Current access	24.67	28.69	32.92	21.68	28.13	24.98	24.98	18.73	19.45
Ever used	14.52	20.63	24.68	10.83	13.51	17.42	19.38	7.87	15.23
Own a PC	29.49	28.45	30.52	14.39	16.26	19.81	23.45	14.08	14.64
PC access at work	26.37	30.93	28.72	19.55	30.83	30.65	25.41	25.92	20.83
Home fax	6.31	6.23	7.27	3.54	2.91	6.36	5.49	4.90	6.90
Cable	63.16	66.67	68.43	60.29	67.64	75.95	60.17	62.18	57.18
Satellite	10.90	12.14	13.42	4.96	6.02	11.30	8.53	5.69	3.36

Table 8b: Race and ethnicity differences over time on key web usage variables for respondents with household income $40,000 and over

	White			African American			Hispanic		
	IDS2	IDS3	IDS4	IDS2	IDS3	IDS4	IDS2	IDS3	IDS4
Among All Respondents with Household Income $40,000+									
N	1,993	2,332	1,366	138	173	114	108	113	54
Current access	51.55	60.07	66.84	58.42	64.26	58.01	54.12	60.03	63.80
Ever used	35.66	47.78	56.51	35.60	44.92	50.36	37.66	47.77	49.68
Own a PC	62.31	61.24	63.60	64.95	63.61	61.26	55.35	62.96	54.67
PC access at work	57.78	61.28	63.02	75.32	72.40	60.48	54.38	60.89	62.11
Home fax	22.25	21.69	22.61	26.75	19.72	18.10	23.87	21.70	27.48
Cable	75.26	77.75	78.94	87.23	90.10	84.26	72.36	86.56	87.27
Satellite	11.05	12.22	14.33	9.27	9.80	12.96	8.86	11.68	16.74
Among Recent Web Users with Household Income $40,000 +									
N	753	1,063	750	57	71	56	44	49	28
First Used									
...in past 2 years +	17.08	33.70	52.00	9.08	33.13	56.29	23.26	33.47	69.24
...in past 1-2 years	20.32	25.45	19.20	26.93	21.92	21.27	8.50	17.71	7.68
...in past year	20.68	24.87	14.60	7.75	24.52	17.99	20.48	33.82	10.27
...in past 6 months	18.74	8.27	9.11	15.25	7.54	0.00	14.53	8.58	8.12
...in past 3 months	23.19	7.70	5.09	41.00	12.89	4.45	33.23	6.42	4.70

Last Used									
...in past 6 months	7.93	6.48	4.31	5.86	3.35	4.08	8.23	2.58	3.13
...in past 3 months	10.26	9.60	4.77	29.22	21.13	8.83	12.52	18.76	0.00
...in past month	22.31	17.06	17.14	20.70	31.69	11.87	24.27	15.27	18.46
...in past week	28.17	28.42	31.17	22.69	20.71	44.50	41.68	21.48	50.20
...in past 24 hours	31.31	38.43	42.61	21.52	23.13	30.72	13.30	41.91	28.21
Frequency of Use									
...once a day +	18.18	24.25	30.06	12.51	14.60	31.52	3.20	30.68	33.35
...few times/week	31.51	31.07	32.80	18.43	29.10	27.56	43.01	25.00	34.77
...two-four times/month	26.50	25.70	22.71	37.80	24.95	28.81	27.79	29.90	28.03
...once a month or less	23.81	18.98	14.43	31.26	31.36	12.11	26.01	14.42	3.86
Ever Used									
...at home	65.64	68.32	71.85	53.85	62.40	78.73	40.27	76.78	82.24
...at work	52.22	61.87	59.26	56.91	69.19	64.38	45.52	57.04	48.85
...at school	23.00	24.21	22.89	28.76	25.75	37.26	33.36	25.45	40.04
...at other locations	24.43	34.97	32.00	31.26	35.64	47.29	30.35	43.72	35.89

Gender

Tables 9a and 9b report the relationship between gender and Web access and use for whites and African Americans.Overall levels of Web access and use are lower for women than men. Among recent Web users, men are more likely to have been using the Web longer, and to have used the Web more recently. Women are more likely to be newer users. While white men are more frequent users than white women, African American men are not more frequent Web users than African American women.

White men are more likely to have access to the Web, to have ever used the Web, and to own a PC at home than African American men and these differences have persisted over time. Interestingly, the percentage of respondents who report owning a PC at home has grown for white men, but not African American men. There is a small tendency for white men to be more likely to have PC access at work.

Among recent Web users, African American men are much more likely than white men to be newer Web users and this finding persists over time. In IDS 2, white men were more than three times as likely as African American men to have been online for two years or more (20.31 percent versus 6.20 percent). By IDS 4, over fifty percent of white and African American men had been online that long. In IDS 2, white men were more likely than African American men to be the most recent Web users (65.46 percent compared to 37.04 percent). By IDS 4, both white and African American men were equally and highly likely to have used the Internet recently (75.03 percent compared to 71.37 percent, respectively).

Table 9a: Race and ethnicity differences over time on key web usage variables for men

	White			African American			Hispanic		
	IDS2	IDS3	IDS4	IDS2	IDS3	IDS4	IDS2	IDS3	IDS4
Among All Male Respondents									
N	2,045	2,465	1402	192	265	151	136	187	72
Currently	41.97	47.05	53.85	38.94	45.74	45.72	42.99	35.27	57.19
Have access									
Ever used	30.08	38.14	45.45	22.02	28.85	37.04	33.51	21.66	49.51
Own a PC	47.59	47.64	49.66	31.43	33.40	34.03	41.66	27.34	42.69
PC access at work	43.55	46.25	45.47	39.38	42.23	42.01	39.43	34.01	36.61
Home fax	16.89	15.77	16.78	12.42	9.81	10.19	17.27	10.87	21.17
Cable	68.01	73.12	74.15	64.41	77.42	78.24	69.92	67.10	76.70
Satellite	12.02	13.10	13.17	2.98	4.70	15.28	7.65	7.72	14.02
Among Male Recent Web Users									
N	714	1,042	662	55	81	53	49	55	35
First Used									
...in past 2 years +	20.31	36.90	57.44	6.20	29.56	55.37	14.51	36.69	53.65
...in past 1-2 years	20.55	24.91	18.66	17.27	19.93	19.12	4.73	21.25	16.92
...in past year	20.26	22.11	13.15	13.07	28.40	10.07	28.81	25.82	13.84
...in past 6 months	17.14	7.80	6.54	18.34	10.58	0.00	13.46	11.19	4.35
...in past 3 months	21.73	8.28	4.19	45.11	11.53	15.44	38.49	5.06	11.24

Last Used									
...in past 6 months	6.98	6.22	3.88	10.04	3.43	2.63	7.64	5.92	0.00
...in past 3 months	9.31	10.52	4.87	29.90	21.62	3.89	4.55	17.54	0.00
...in past month	18.25	16.57	16.21	23.03	22.49	22.12	32.96	18.24	27.27
...in past week	28.42	24.55	28.35	16.56	28.28	40.08	35.32	22.11	34.57
...in past 24 hours	37.04	42.14	46.68	20.48	24.18	31.29	19.53	36.20	38.18
Frequency of Use									
...once a day +	23.82	28.56	34.12	9.75	16.87	25.97	11.60	28.56	39.09
...few times/week	32.12	31.85	33.38	29.15	29.60	28.68	45.54	31.95	25.16
...two-four times/month	24.48	19.94	20.08	27.06	22.94	22.40	26.48	27.33	31.30
...once a month or less	19.58	19.65	12.42	34.04	30.59	12.95	16.37	12.16	4.46
Ever Used									
...at home	63.74	67.66	70.12	41.86	53.70	64.65	39.47	64.98	73.57
...at work	48.87	54.54	54.71	35.65	59.24	60.62	39.21	54.55	44.12
...at school	28.35	28.49	28.89	39.80	44.06	62.58	40.89	39.11	53.18
...at other locations	60.43	42.24	36.57	30.12	48.68	55.27	33.58	61.00	51.93

Table 9b: Race and ethnicity differences over time on key web usage variables for women

	White			African American			Hispanic		
	IDS2	IDS3	IDS4	IDS2	IDS3	IDS4	IDS2	IDS3	IDS4
Among All Female Respondents									
N	2,861	3,535	2,045	301	426	290	183	261	92
Currently	30.12	39.72	44.98	26.26	33.80	28.62	34.90	24.58	25.43
Have access									
Ever used	17.98	29.33	35.29	15.63	17.97	21.74	22.19	16.87	16.78
Own a PC	41.16	41.82	43.78	27.07	25.65	25.70	38.33	26.39	23.67
PC access at work	33.34	38.19	39.33	28.32	36.39	33.10	28.58	30.66	27.27
Home fax	11.35	11.74	13.02	6.56	5.28	6.57	11.79	6.65	8.63
Cable	68.87	72.65	74.82	62.58	69.31	72.98	61.92	60.77	61.28
Satellite	9.21	10.90	13.85	6.59	9.68	10.93	7.82	6.83	8.88
Among Recent Female Web Users									
N	590	973	706	49	70	64	42	41	21
First Used									
...in past 2 years +	9.74	28.03	39.31	7.58	35.41	30.29	15.57	10.11	
...in past 1-2 years	15.07	22.66	21.66	13.77	22.02	15.80	5.38	25.81	
...in past year	25.74	26.04	18.92	18.58	22.64	30.76	13.07	41.22	
...in past 6 months	21.01	11.55	11.70	18.46	7.22	13.42	31.96	13.15	
...in past 3 months	28.45	11.73	8.42	41.61	12.71	8.73	34.02	9.72	

Last Used								
...in past 6 months	10.62	9.64	7.27	11.12	6.60	1.95	10.13	2.47
...in past 3 months	16.39	13.23	8.74	32.35	20.54	20.65	17.77	11.48
...in past month	27.67	23.19	23.25	24.77	33.37	20.60	34.65	32
...in past week	27.06	29.88	32.54	22.07	21.65	30.20	27.95	26.28
...in past 24 hours	18.26	24.05	28.20	9368	17.83	26.59	9.50	27.42
Frequency of Use								
...once a day +	10.23	13.58	17.35	22.73	13.85	24.55	8.57	21.21
...few times/week	23.13	25.84	29.18	21.65	25.50	24.47	24.18	24.61
...two-four times/month	30.06	31.33	31.40	29.83	30.89	24.34	30.15	39.96
...once a month or less	36.59	29.25	22.06	25.80	29.76	26.64	37.10	17.22
Ever Used								
...at home	57.66	61.23	67.22	52.62	57.00	65.20	31.28	67.08
...at work	36.83	48.00	45.23	38.18	69.52	61.61	22.47	27.70
...at school	28.26	30.32	28.68	50.57	34.43	50.38	58.93	21.06
...at other locations	19.67	35.54	33.13	16.66	48.55	51.78	25.38	31.40

White men were also more frequent Web users than African American men in IDS 2. White men were still more likely to be more frequent Web users than African American men by IDS 4, though the difference had shrunk considerably. Over time, the percentage of African American men ever using the Web at home, work, school or other locations has increased considerably. In contrast, the percentage of white men who ever used the Web at school is flat, has grown only modestly for home and work, and has fallen for ever used at other locations. By IDS 4, African American men were more likely to have ever used the Web at school or at other locations, compared to white men.

White women are more likely than African American women to have access to the Web, to have ever used the Web, to own a PC and to have PC access at work and these differences have persisted over time. As for men, the percentage of women owning PCs at home has increased over time for white women, but not African American women. In IDS 2, African American women were much more likely than white women to be new users, but over time this difference has vanished. White women were more likely in IDS 2 than African American women to have used the Internet most recently. By IDS 4, 60.74 percent of white women, compared to 56.79 percent of African American women, had used the Internet within the past week. In contrast to previous results, African American women were more likely than white women to be the most frequent Internet users. By IDS 4, this gap had diminished with 49.02 percent of African American women, compared to 46.53 percent of white women having used the Web a few times a week or more. African American women were more likely to have ever used the Web at school or from other locations.

Tables 10a and 10b compare Web use in the presence of children in the home for whites and African Americans. Not surprisingly, overall levels of access and usage are higher for respondents who report having children under seventeen in the household. In IDS 4, whites without children at home were more likely than African Americans without children at home to have access to the Web, to have ever used the Web, to own a PC, and to have PC access at work. Some of these gaps were persistent. Among recent Web users, over fifty percent of both groups had been using the Web for two years or more by IDS 4, although African Americans without children at home were much more likely than whites to be newer users, especially in IDS 2 and IDS 4.

By IDS 4, there were few differences in recency and frequency of Web use between whites and African Americans. African Americans, were more likely to have ever used the Web at school and other locations. Children Under Seventeen.Whites were more likely to have access to the Web, to have ever used the Web, to own a PC, and slightly more likely to have PC access at work. The percentage of respondents owning a home PC, though higher for whites than African Americans, has remained constant over time.

Among recent Web users, whites with children at home were more likely to be long-term Web users and to be more recent users, but not more frequent users, compared to African Americans with children at home. Whites were also more likely to have ever used the Web at home, though this has diminished over time. African Americans were more likely to have ever used the Web at school and other locations.

Table 10a: Race and ethnicity differences over time on key web usage variables for respondents with no children under 17 in household

	White			African American			Hispanic		
	IDS2	IDS3	IDS4	IDS2	IDS3	IDS4	IDS2	IDS3	IDS4
Among All Respondents with No Kids < 17									
N	3,067	3,777	2,272	256	393	236	156	203	85
Current access	30.26	35.97	42.91	27.71	36.94	27.04	34.41	22.31	43.15
Ever used	20.47	28.32	35.39	16.18	20.56	23.67	27.12	16.59	33.60
Own a PC	36.36	36.82	40.59	19.18	25.49	24.37	33.20	22.55	33.83
PC access at work	34.15	37.54	39.69	25.56	34.67	33.29	27.44	27.76	35.18
Home fax	12.09	11.29	12.65	7.81	5.55	5.53	14.31	8.99	10.80
Cable	68.28	73.43	73.69	61.26	71.32	73.25	60.31	63.75	75.42
Satellite	9.56	11.27	12.62	2.71	5.39	12.80	7.53	5.16	6.82
Among Recent Web Users with No Kids < 17									
N	771	1,145	817	53	89	54	43	48	29
First Used									
...in past 2 years +	18.92	35.62	53.35	10.79	33.41	52.93	22.25	29.64	
...in past 1-2 years	18.17	23.51	19.05	15.04	14.11	16.10	0.00	19.33	
...in past year	23.73	24.11	14.70	15.97	33.55	13.62	25.81	41.75	
...in past 6 months	18.84	7.86	7.98	14.61	9.77	1.91	16.60	5.67	
...in past 3 months	20.34	8.90	4.93	43.59	9.16	15.44	35.54	3.61	

Last Used								
...in past 6 months	7.55	6.64	4.56	2.53	6.09	5.25	5.16	3.18
...in past 3 months	11.91	10.41	6.10	21.02	19.68	4.25	6.17	12.46
...in past month	18.41	19.77	18.30	27.68	27.37	13.62	25.76	27.06
...in past week	27.38	27.91	28.54	25.40	24.45	37.18	45.02	22.34
...in past 24 hours	34.74	35.27	42.50	23.37	22.42	39.70	17.88	34.97
Frequency of Use								
...once a day +	23.93	22.60	29.52	20.35	13.69	30.72	9.95	30.32
...few times/week	28.90	30.89	30.40	25.52	31.01	38.48	44.28	28.56
...two-four times/month	24.67	23.52	24.60	19.28	27.18	18.70	26.82	31.02
...once a month or less	22.50	22.98	15.47	34.85	28.13	12.10	18.95	10.11
Ever Used								
...at home	60.90	63.92	67.87	54.25	54.70	60.82	34.38	66.49
...at work	47.29	52.53	56.63	37.42	62.77	58.88	47.31	53.01
...at school	27.98	28.25	25.17	32.55	39.92	49.50	50.40	29.73
...at other locations	25.55	37.93	32.92	26.33	45.87	49.46	27.94	35.05

Table 10b: Race and ethnicity differences over time on key web usage variables for respondents with children under 17 in household

	White			African American			Hispanic		
	IDS2	IDS3	IDS4	IDS2	IDS3	IDS4	IDS2	IDS3	IDS4
Among All Respondents with Kids < 17									
N	1,838	2,220	1,172	237	297	205	163	245	79
Current access	44.59	54.20	59.46	36.24	41.48	45.45	42.17	35.59	36.80
Ever used	28.97 4	1.57	48.08	20.83	25.53	32.98	27.65	21.47	29.84
Own a PC	56.45	56.35	56.30	40.38	34.06	34.55	45.35	30.14	31.01
PC access at work	44.58	48.93	46.45	41.58	44.63	40.69	38.62	35.80	28.30
Home fax	16.93	17.25	18.32	10.49	9.64	10.96	14.32	8.51	17.26
Cable	68.76	72.00	75.73	65.81	74.90	77.29	70.03	63.97	62.03
Satellite	12.09	13.00	14.98	7.83	10.04	12.56	7.91	8.89	15.11
Among Recent Web Users with Kids < 17									
N	533	867	549	51	62	63	48	48	27
First Used									
…in past 2 years +	13.22	30.55	44.81	3.94	30.24	36.82	10.26	25.67	
…in past 1-2 years	18.66	24.30	21.16	16.30	28.11	18.63	8.24	25.26	
…in past year	20.98	23.48	16.82	15.03	17.86	24.14	19.70	24.15	
…in past 6 months 18.45	11.02	9.81	21.08	8.64	9.45	24.41	16.10		
…in past 3 months	28.69	10.65	7.40	43.65	15.15	10.77	37.38	8.81	

Last Used								
...in past 6 months	9.32	8.78	6.34	16.17	3.18	0.00	10.99	5.66
...in past 3 months	12.28	12.91	7.14	37.99	22.85	17.17	12.77	17.27
...in past month	25.73	19.04	20.54	20.99	26.29	27.63	38.79	20.87
...in past week	28.43	25.74	32.13	14.29	26.91	34.38	23.89	24.47
...in past 24 hours	24.24	33.54	33.85	10.56	20.77	20.82	13.56	31.73
Frequency of Use								
...once a day +	12.64	21.74	23.44	11.83	17.88	21.06	10.54	23.10
...few times/week	28.26	27.64	32.97	26.21	24.58	27.32	31.38	29.85
...two-four times/month	28.62	26.15	25.61	36.49	24.89	26.91	28.84	30.59
...once a month or less	30.28	24.46	17.97	27.48	32.65	24.71	29.25	16.47
Ever Used								
...at home	61.79	66.02	69.99	40.89	55.39	60.84	37.01	65.24
...at work	40.79	51.03	43.26	36.24	64.03	62.77	22.25	39.39
...at school	28.67	30.32	32.90	52.80	40.47	63.08	47.41	34.48
...at other locations	26.93	40.86	37.45	23.01	51.72	57.05	31.79	60.43

Web Shopping

The rate of searching for information on the Web and purchasing products on the Web is increasing over time. In IDS 2, whites were more likely to use the Web to purchase a product or service online. In IDS 3 and IDS 4, whites were also more likely to purchase online, but the gap is closing. However, in IDS 2, both whites and African Americans were equally likely to search for product information online. Yet in IDS 3 and IDS 4, whites are more likely than African Americans to have searched the Web for product information. Potential explanations of the differences in search behavior are that African-Americans are less interested in comparing products and services online, are obtaining this information from other sources, or are simply finding less of interest to search for online.

Internet users ranked business opportunities as a relatively unimportant reason for current Internet users, but a very important reason for non-users. This was phrased, however, in terms of "making money." Table 12 shows business uses of the Web among recent Web users with access to a PC at work.

As with Web shopping variables, items in IDS 2 are not comparable to items in IDS 3 and IDS 4, so no direct comparisons may be made from IDS 2 to IDS 3 or IDS 2 to IDS 4. In IDS 2, whites were more likely than African Americans to use the Web to research competitors, publish product information, sell products and services, for customer service and support and for vendor support and communication. In IDS 3, a number of these race differences in business uses of the Web have gone away and some new differences emerged.

For example, whites were more likely than African Americans to use the Web for internal communication, and still more likely to use the Web for customer service support and vendor support and communication. By IDS 4, African Americans were, for the first time, more likely than whites to have access to an Intranet at work, to use the Web for internal communication, and for customer service and support. However, whites were more likely to use the Web to buy products or services. It is likely that these differences may reflect different job functions.

The role of access to the Internet at home needs to be much more clearly understood. Whites are more likely to have access to the Internet and to have ever used the Web than African Americans and these gaps appear to be increasing over time. By IDS 4, in most cases there were no or only slight differences between whites and African Americans in how recently they had used the Web, how frequently, or in their length of time online. Gaps in general Web access and use between African-Americans and whites appear to be driven by whether or not there is a computer present in the home. Access to a personal computer, whether at home, work, school or somewhere else, is important because it is currently the dominant mechanism by which individuals can access the Internet. Formal coursework was the least often mentioned way people were introduced to the Internet. Long term Internet users were most likely to have learned at work; for recent Internet users, friends/family and self-taught were equally important. These results reinforce the importance of the presence of a computer at home, or the opportunity to access the Web from locations other than the home, in stimulating Web use.

Insight into the importance of reducing this gap in Web use between whites and African-Americans is provided by Anderson and Melchior's discussion of information redlining. Information redlining signifies the relegation of minorities into situations where satisfying their information needs is weighed against their economic and social worth. From the minority point of view, this is both an access issue and a form of discrimination.

The new technologies of information are not simply tools of private communication as a telephone is, or tools of entertainment as a television is. They provide direct access to information sources that are essential in making social choices and keeping track of developments not only in the world at large, but also within their immediate neighborhoods. Unless the neighborhoods are properly served, there is no way out of information redlining for most of these disadvantaged groups.

In addition to gaps in home computer ownership, the implications of differential Internet access at locations outside the home, including school, the workplace and other locations needs to be clearly understood. Additional access points stimulate usage. Research is necessary to understand the impact of multiple access points on Web use, particularly for individuals who have no access at home. Public-private initiatives such as Bell Atlantic's efforts in Union City and Bill Gates announcement of a $200 million gift to provide library access to the Internet are a step in the right direction. It has also been noted that "community networks and public access terminals offer great potential for African-American communities". Further, the recent roll-out of E-rate funds provides a significant opportunity for researchers to understand the factors important in stimulating Web usage among those least likely to have access.

The role of Web access in the schools, compared to other locations, needs to be clearly understood. Students enjoy the highest levels of Internet access and Web use, especially when there are computers in their households. However, white students are still more likely than African American students to have access and to use the Internet, and these gaps persist over time.

Access to technology does not make much sense unless people are properly educated in using the technologies. Understanding the differences in Internet access and use among all racial and ethnic groups in the United States is required for a comprehensive understanding of technology adoption and its impact on the digital economy. Subsequent studies need to oversample members of minority groups. This is required so that there will be sufficient numbers of all minority groups to perform post-stratification adjustments to create weights that yield population-projectable results for each minority group.

Reasons for the gap between African-Americans and whites in Web search behavior need to be clearly understood. Such differences could have important implications for the ultimate success of commercial efforts online. White Web users are more likely to report searching for product or service-related information than African Americans.

Whites are more likely to search for information online than are African Americans. More generally, consumer behavior in the commercial Web environment is complex and only weakly understood. Further research is needed to explore fully the differences in consumer behavior on the Web and their implications for commercialization.

Studies investigating the extent of multicultural content on the Web are needed. Another possibility for the gap between African-Americans and whites in Web search behavior is that there is insufficient content of interest to African-Americans. Interactive Marketing News claimed that "while there are about 10 million sites on the Web, there are fewer than 500 sites targeted" to African-Americans. However, others have commented on the multicultural diversity of the Web.

Household income explains race differences in Internet access, use, home computer ownership and PC access at work. In terms of overall access and use, higher household income positively affects access to a computer. But at lower incomes, gaps in access and use between whites and African Americans existed and were increasing. Research is necessary to determine the efforts most likely to be effective to ensure access for lower-income Americans, especially African Americans.

5

Educational Constraints

The speed with which the revolution in information and communication technology (ICT) has taken place is phenomenal. The changes the ICT revolution has wrought are not limited to one single sector of society, nor do they just add another column in the aggregate tables of macro-economists. The impact of the ICT revolutions provide modern illustrations of Says's law: Supply creates its own demand.

The way the hardware of ICT was produced and operated has itself become one of the foremost expressions of globalization; components come from all continents-chips from Asia, software from America, mobile phones from Europe. Brand names have instant recognition around the world: Acer, Sony, Intel, Microsoft, and Nokia. On the other hand, satellites orbiting the globe allow for instant communication on an unprecedented scale.

The development of new products and services was part of a vast distributed and yet integrated global division of labour, whether it was in the development of new for-profit products and services or the more altruistic open-source contributions from a diverse crowd of enthusiasts.

The new links-the Internet and the World Wide Web-became the first truly dynamic and interactive network that individuals could access from all over the world. Much of what is on the Web is not mass communication in the classical sense: one source, one way, many users. It is by and for interacting people. Indeed, in many respects individuals were ahead of institutions in realizing the Web's potential. For example, music was swapped via the Internet before it became commoditized.

The ICT revolution has been very much about spotting opportunities and inviting everybody to learn to make good use of them. Indeed, the ICT revolution is perhaps above all else a revolution in learning. Individuals have seen the potential of the new tools and introduced them into their homes on a vast scale. Firms have applied them to an ever-widening range of activities: bookkeeping, production control, management, communication, marketing, and drug development. Public authorities have incorporated them into all of their activities, from vaccination programs to tracking criminals.

The first revolution started during World War II, with the first large, automatic, general electromechanical calculator, Harvard Mark. It was 50 feet long, eight feet tall, and weighed five tons. A couple of years later, ENIAC was presented in Philadelphia, based on radio tubes and practically without any internal memory, yet using 18,000 vacuum tubes and weighing 30 tons. Each time a new task was to be performed, some 6,000 switches covering three walls had to be thrown. In 1947, the first transistor, and, on its basis, faster and more powerful computers were constructed. Computers became a new catchword, and input-output technology graduated from punch cards to magnetic tape, faster printers, and more languages for programming. Applications also were expanded, from use in academic research to weather forecasting, from airline ticketing to accounting. This development continues; the first ICT revolution is still under way.

The second ICT revolution has its roots in the 1970s, when the first "processors on a chip" and magnetic discs were constructed. But as late as 1977, Ken Olson, the legendary president of the computer company, Digital, stated: "There is no reason anyone would want a computer in their home." He was definitely wrong. In the same year, Steve Jobs and Steve Wosniak started to sell their Apple II, and Bill Gates and Paul Allen had already founded a firm called Microsoft. From being an esoteric toy, the personal computer gradually became a valuable tool for word processing, accounting, and, after a while, pictures. IBM, which at first grossly underestimated the markets for the personal computer (PC), launched its first machine under that name in 1981. Now the PC has become as widespread as the radio when grandparents were young-indeed, as widespread as bicycles are among today's youth. This second ICT revolution continues like the first: the capacities of the machines increase, their applications expand, and the number of people who use them multiplies.

The third ICT revolution is that microprocessors have become embedded in an ever-widening range of products: the steering systems of airplanes, the control panels of hydroelectric power stations, domestic air conditioning systems, the traffic lights in streets. Even when we do not recognize it, they have become part of everyday lives: in video players, credit cards, remote controllers, cameras, hotel room door locks, and smart buildings. There is a microprocessor embedded in digital scale in the bathroom. If you use an electric toothbrush, its functions are governed by some 3,000 lines of programming. Microprocessors translate bar codes into prices at the cash register, monitor electronic injection of fuel in cars, and determine where the elevator stops in building. An ordinary household now contains some 100 microprocessors, in everything from dishwashers to alarm systems. Microprocessors constantly expand their capacity, applications, and users.

The fourth ICT revolution stretches back to the late 1960s, when the US Department of Defense drew up guidelines for a communication network among computers (ARPANET). After a while, universities in and outside the United States were hooked up to it, and some started to use it to send messages. France developed its variant-its Minitel system-at the beginning of the 1980s, at the same time the U.S. National Science Foundation set up its own network among academic institutions that later became part of Internet. A dozen universities on the U.S. East Coast with IBM mainframes contributed with BITNET. In Europe, EARN became a network among academic institutions, while CERN in Geneva was crucial in the development of the World Wide Web, which got its name in 1990. A couple of years later, surfing on the 'net started, and more and more people hooked up. A PC needed a modem to use its potential fully. This fourth ICT revolution continues like the others as more and more computers are interlinked with an ever-growing number of "servers" and an expanding range of applications. Yet, the most important part of the fourth ICT revolution was this: on the computer networks engineers had constructed, users built social networks to make them useful and effective-in this case, the social superstructure built on the material basis became really super.

The fifth ICT revolution was linking without lines-the new possibilities opened by mobile phones. At first, they were big and bulky. Reduction in size and weight was accompanied by expansion of reach and functions, and miniaturization was accompanied by multifunctionality. Mobile phones could be used not just for talking, but also to exchange messages, receive news or stock exchange quotes, review restaurants, or order movie tickets. Phones are no longer only for transmitting phonemes; now they can transmit written messages, pictures, and music. Linking without lines now takes place not just intercontinentally via satellites, but also via high-frequency short-range radio transmitters covering a specific area or cell and inside buildings by "Bluetooth" and infrared light.

Educational Potential of ICTs

Since the ICT revolution is a revolution in learning, it also has transformed available technologies, the means and methods of studying, the modalities of school operations, the manner of investment and expenditure of resources, and the very way think about what education could be and should do. Even before the Internet became a new mode of communication, and the World Wide Web made it possible to access learning material anywhere, universities had started to use telecommunications and computers for teaching. But with the advent of the Internet and the Web, these opportunities have expanded vastly, and educational institutions have made more and more varied use of them. Course material is posted on the Web, assignments can be communicated through the 'net, and teachers can be accessed around the clock by the new modes of transmission. The new education programs have reached out to off-campus students, often from long distances, but they also have reached in to regular students in novel ways by providing learning materials in new forms. They include a wide spectrum, from French grammar to fractal geometry, from guides to trilobites to flash cards for physics. The Internet also changes the ways schools work by making possible closer cooperation and interaction among them, within the same country and across continents and oceans. One example is joint "virtual projects." Likewise, parents can be kept informed via the Websites of schools-virtual PTAs, so to speak.

Not only has ICT transformed the way learning institutions work, it also has changed the organized education. ICT has become a medium in the original sense of the word: something in the middle, between the substance to be learned and the student who is to master it. First, it liberates provision of education from the constraints of time and place: many courses can be accessed from more or less anywhere and at any time. Second, training can be customized, by allowing material to be adapted to individual levels and tasks to be paced according to personal progress. But tailored capacity and development does not mean that students cannot interact-individualized does not mean isolated.

To the contrary, the physical network allows students to work together, whether for mutual consultation and advice or support and encouragement.

Hence, the new education technologies alter the means and modes of studying. Students can link to other students, across boundaries and across continents. Children can take part in the development of learning materials for each other in other classrooms or countries. Teachers in the remotest places can be encouraged to take part in important professional development projects. Indeed, the whole education system can work like a neural network, where cells with synapses to other cells can fire them up. The Internet also can become a network for altruism. Institutionally, so much on the Web is there for free and for all. A large part of the available educational resources is created by groups outside of schools and academic institutions, yet is free for all and provides excellent inputs for learning. Sometimes, such worldwide community service is well organized, such as the scanning, typing, or proofreading of classical texts that are entered on Websites open to all, or when the classification of craters on Mars is set up as voluntary work among informed amateurs linked by the Internet. Individually, some communities have experimented with tutors mentoring students from home. Such acts of generosity allow those participating in them to engage their minds and help others; it sure beats the millions of clicks wasted on solitaire.

The ICT revolution offers new intrinsic opportunities; it dramatically changes what can be learned and by whom as well as what can be produced and provided by whom. These potential changes, however, pose many new challenges for educational planners. These challenges can be divided into two broad types: those that pertain to equity and those that pertain to quality. But unless educational planners respond to these changes and challenges with commensurate speed, they will become, so to speak, technologically challenged. Although in many Western countries, the majority of households have PCs linked to the Internet, considerable differences remain along regional and class lines. Several studies document that boys are more active than girls in using the new technical tools. And though schools also are increasingly well equipped and connected, standards vary within countries with educational level and type. The same applies to teacher training and skills. This raises the broader question of equity: within countries as well as between countries, particularly between the industrialized and developing world. It is true that millions of PCs are sold every year and millions gain access to the Internet.

Similarly, there are great differences between corporate actors, public as well as private, in their capacity to become-to use the current jargon-"net-based education providers." Many countries have adopted ICT policies for their education systems that cover not only hardware and infrastructure, but educational materials available for schools and students as well. Such materials, increasingly available on the Internet, range from mathematics resources in Norway to lists of recommended books for California's schools. They can be accessed freely by both domestic and foreign users. In addition, many teachers and professional associations make their best work available free for anyone to use. For example, a simple search for the "Pythagorean theorem" on the Web yields more than 10,000 sites, many of which make available all kinds of useful material-e.g., animated proofs that are much easier to follow than their textbook equivalents. In this sense, the Internet is the greatest venue for exchange of educational good deeds ever constructed.

Education equals finance-public funds to be spent and private demand to be targeted. Hence ICT, and particularly the Internet, is not only an arena for altruism and experiments, but also for business, entrepreneurship, and, sometimes, exploitation. In other words, education is increasingly becoming a market, and a global one at that. In a market, there are customers and producers. And access to the production side of this market is even less equitable than access to its usage side. Some nations also actively promote programs for foreigners by distance education via the Internet. Australia is a prominent example, where services from its educational institutions have grown into a whole export industry. This is a very interesting and, in many respects, auspicious development, but it also raises a whole range of questions for educational planners about quality, certification, and accreditation. It is notable that the World Trade Organization is considering proposals to add the import and export of higher education courses to its protocols on services marketed internationally; "education products" can then be traded as a commodity from one country to another. This development provides further opportunities for students. It releases education from national control, and it makes the market a stronger force in the globalization of education. On the other hand, planners and officials in developing or smaller countries may face an expanding international market with powerful actors and many new ventures about which they have imperfect knowledge, exercise scant control, and have few possibilities for participation.

Thus, the issue of equity pertaining to ICT has to be addressed along two dimensions: equitable access of students as consumers, where the poorer peoples and nations are put at a disadvantage; and equitable provision of content, where the poor are even worse off. Ideally, one wishes for equal opportunity to participate. But access for different actors-both as users and producers-is weighted by their resources. Hence, initial differences are often reproduced, reinforced, and even magnified. A formidable challenge, therefore, continues to face planners of international education: how to define the problem and provide assistance for development.

As ICT is rapidly becoming an integral part of the social environment and jobs are being transformed rapidly into tapping on keyboards and looking at screens, traditional literacy is no longer sufficient—what could be called, 'Iteracy,' becomes imperative. Learning to work a PC and surfing the Internet is becoming crucial for functioning in the workplace, for effective citizenship, for entertainment, and for personal growth. With the rapid change in technology, training cannot be a one-shot affair; we have to be updated continuously to stay abreast of developments. Planning and designing educational systems so that they familiarize students with a technology that is being modified and evolving continuously is not just an intellectual challenge, it is also an economic one.

This problem is exacerbated by the fact that many vendors of new technologies are sometimes more pushers than providers, promoting solutions that have a short useful life or little compatibility with what emerge as industry standards. The history of information technology is not just a history of innovation but also a history of misguided investments. This situation applies to hardware as well as to "learning packages" and software that promise more than is delivered. What is bought is often expensive and inappropriate, resulting in costly mistakes, not just in economic terms, but in terms of time stolen from students who would have been better off using more proven methods of learning. Sometimes new solutions are pushed by politicians and ministers as well: they feel they need to prove they are "modern" by going for gadgets, but they are out of office when the negative results are in. Moreover, it takes time to discover where the potential of ICT in education can best be tapped, and as technology itself is changing, final solutions will continue to evade us.

The learning process also may be skewed in unfortunate directions. Much is made of the fact that ICT has become increasingly "interactive." Learning programs can be tailored to each student, learning at his or her own pace, and being introduced to more challenging tasks as learning proceeds. However, interaction in learning cannot be restricted to per-son-machine relations; person-person relations will always remain crucial. In industrialized countries, no previous generation of children has had so little contact and communication with the world of adults. Learning has become more age-graded, as has all social interaction. TV, videogames, and Internet-provided pictures and music draw the young into a more virtual world. Hence, rather than formal education also placing students increasingly in front of a screen, planners must be concerned that students are engaged in more real than virtual interaction and connected to actual adults rather than just to their products. Children and youth need positive feedback from applets, but they also need to be seen and respected by peers and grownups as real people. What holds for the educational process also holds for educational content. Demand-driven education means, increasingly, education that is "just in time" and "just enough." Learning what is deemed not immediately relevant may be discarded as definitely wasted. But this concept of knowledge and skills is a perversion, even of a utilitarian justification of it. It is a perversion of the rationale for a broad liberal arts education where the goal is not just to enable one to solve a problem at hand but to develop abilities as a human being to perceive and to participate, to experience, to empathize, and to excel. But then the whole diversity of one's talents must be nurtured and developed. Education, after all, means to "lead out," within and beyond one's present confines, by bringing out latent abilities and talents.

There is another issue with demand-driven education as it is commonly practiced. The growth in knowledge does not just generate a steady stream of new facts, findings, and products—about viruses, proteins, or superconductors. It also means that older knowledge becomes superseded. For instance, it is no longer useful to know which electronic vacuum tubes could be used in a computer. But new facts and data do not only mean that knowledge may become obsolete. They also mean that certain types of established knowledge become more important.

Even from a purely utilitarian view, "just in time" and "just enough" knowledge is misguided. First, it takes knowledge to know what you need to know. Second, truly new insights are often the result of serendipity-the happy chance combination of seemingly unconnected ideas to a new conception. "Just in time" knowledge is, in practice, often too late, and "just enough" knowledge often makes you miss the critical piece to solve the big puzzle. Educational planners have to consider what a well-rounded education is. The whole point of education as a common human enterprise is that no student can bring out his or her potential if left to the student's own haphazard personal search. Students have to be led out, "educated" in the original sense of the word.

ICT does not suit all students, all subjects, or all phases of learning equally well. There are already considerable differences say, between the offerings in mathematics and history compared to those in music and physical education. Much depends on how ICT-assisted learning is done, and, as in traditional teaching, there are no fast formulas. Discovering and developing the potential of ICT will surely take time, and what we find may not be valid for all time because the context surely will change. Technology in itself is not a panacea; uploading Web content in different subjects does not in itself result in quality teaching or effective use. Teachers have to be trained and need to feel knowledgeable and skilled-not always easy in an environment where young students are often quicker than their teachers to learn new technologies.

On the other hand, the lack of willingness to mobilize the young to learn from one another—in the same way as they learn the tricks of new video games—is not only old-fashioned but even counterproductive. Educational planners can focus no longer just on how to secure implementation; they need to arrange for continuous experimentation and innovation to learn by doing in an ever-changing environment where even what is being learned and done is changing. There are optimistic theories about development-about a great technological leap forward or about latecomers' ability to leapfrog generations of already outdated technologies. Yet, the digital divide will be with us for years to come, and the poor will remain in the worst position for a long time, even under the most ambitious programs.

Social, economic, and technological changes of the past decades are making education and training for all more crucial than ever. Yet, educational systems, to different degrees worldwide, are struggling to afford educational opportunities for all, to provide their graduates with the necessary knowledge and skills for evolving marketplaces and sophisticated living environments, and to prepare citizens for lifelong learning. To meet these challenges, countries have to focus concurrently on expanding access, improving internal efficiency, promoting the quality of teaching and learning, and improving system management.

Some countries and institutions have turned to ICTs and are exploring ways by which ICTs may help them in pursuing their educational goals. As Table 1 illustrates, one technology may have different potentials depending on the purpose for using it. Many of the technologies have similar characteristics. Therefore assessments of the potential and appropriateness of particular technologies must be based on educational needs and objectives, rather than on the technologies themselves.

Table 1

ICTs and their Potential for Education

Technology	*Outreach*	*Flexibility*	*Sensorial Stimulation*	*Interactivity*
Radio	High	Limited	Audio only	Limited
Television	High	Limited	Audiovisual	Limited
Video	Low	High	Audiovisual	Limited
PC	Low	High	Audiovisual	High
Internet	Highest	High	Audiovisual	Highest

Expanding access to education is a matter of both economic development and social justice. It is true that worldwide illiteracy rates have declined in the past 30 years, but it is also true that the demands on knowledge are much higher now than 30 years ago. In the past, an agrarian society could thrive economically even when more than half of its population was barely literate, but this is no longer possible in modern societies in the Information Age. To remain economically competitive and prosper in this global. In many countries, whose budgets already are stretched thin, expanding access to education under traditional models is not an option.

Dramatic conflicts and the burgeoning HIV/AIDS crisis in many countries have disrupted social services, including education, and diverted resources that could be used to maintain, let alone, expand educational opportunity. Public expenditure on education already represents 25% of total government expenditures. The country's illiteracy rate for youth aged 15-24 is close to 30% for both genders (45% for girls). A program to eliminate illiteracy that relies on constructing more schools and hiring more teachers will require a level of public investment in Togo that may deplete the country's budget, leaving other essential services unattended.

For more than a century, education has used technology to expand beyond the physical limits of schools and university campuses and reach more and nontraditional groups of students. For instance, in the beginning of the last century, Australia and New Zealand used a system of itinerant teachers to educate children and youth living in sparsely inhabited territories. The teachers maintained contact with their students through postal correspondence.

Radio, television, and computer-related technologies have expanded outreach potential further, and higher education institutions have been at the forefront of this expansion. In 1992, 41% of higher education students in Thailand and 38% in Turkey studied at a distance. The China TV University System (Republic of China) and Anadolu University in Turkey each serves more than 500,000 students per year. The United Kingdom Open University has provided education to more than 2 million individuals since it was established about 30 years ago.

Distance learning institutions generally use a mix of technologies that may include printed material, videos, video-conferencing, CD-ROMs, e-mail, and the Internet. Many of them start with less expensive technologies, such as printed materials, and move to faster and more powerful resources as the need for expansion increases. The Open University of Hong Kong is an example of this movement.

Expanding access also means integrating populations that have been traditionally excluded from education for cultural and social reasons. In cultures with strict rules regarding interaction between genders, girls may be forced to leave school before puberty to avoid contact with male colleagues and teachers. For girls who remain in school, the rules regarding with whom they may or may not talk make it difficult to succeed. If a girl is having academic difficulties, she may rather fail than address the male teacher. Technology can promote alternatives for educating women that are more cost-effective than all-female schools without disrupting cultural traditions.

Television and radio broadcasts or Internet-based technologies enable girls to continue their studies from home or small learning centers. Technology functions as a neutral mediator, without gender or cultural allegiances, thereby facilitating communication. An essay exercise in a co-educational class at the African Nazarene University that required the use of computers illustrates the potential of ICTs to overcome barriers in communication. Faced with the challenge of learning a new technology, the students forgot tribal rivalries and gender differences to exchange information and work side by side. For persons with disabilities-who represent another significant and forgotten sector of the world population-technologies provide essential supports enabling them to participate in the educational system and the job market. VisualTek is a camera and monitor that enlarge print materials for people with visual disabilities. Voice synthesizers enable individuals with muscular dystrophies to communicate. Special computer software can be used to ameliorate learning disabilities or to enhance the memory of individuals with traumatic brain injury. Keyboard adaptations enable individuals with motor disabilities to write, and the Internet can connect homebound individuals to classrooms and workplaces. Lifelong learning and economic development for populations living outside mainstream cultures are two other venues for using ICTs.

A multilingual database catalogue offers the artisans' work to a worldwide customer base. The network receives and fills orders and is responsible for quality control. Currently, the Virtual Souk involves more than 700 artisans in Morocco, Tunisia, and Lebanon. Business organizations are investing heavily in distance learning technologies, particularly Internet-based applications, to train managers and employees while avoiding the costs and disruptions related to travel. The Ford Motor Company spent $100 million on a training network using interactive satellite technology that transmits up to eight live training sessions at a time to any of the 5,000 Ford dealerships across the United States.

The internal efficiency of an educational system is measured by its ability to deliver quality education in cost-effective ways. The traditional model for providing primary through tertiary education, adopted across the world, relies on three basic principles. There must be a predetermined path, divided into grades, that leads to a diploma, and students must follow this path, regardless of their interests, needs, or abilities. There must be a hierarchic structure where the instructor is the provider of knowledge and the students are the recipients.

The traditional school is, therefore, a physical entity organized into classrooms where learners congregate according to a grade structure and constrained by the limits of space and time. If a school serves students from grades 1 through 12, it must have at least 12 classrooms to accommodate each grade separately. Each classroom must have one teacher. A certain number of teachers require a principal and, often, administrative and teaching support. If the number of students or grades increases, so must the number of needed classrooms, teachers, and support personnel. Generally, beginning in the seventh grade, another dimension is added to the classroom/grade framework: specialization. From then on, the number of teachers is related to both the number of classrooms and the number of specialties offered. Each school must have at least one mathematics teacher, a science teacher, a social studies teacher, and so on.

As the educational level advances, classroom organizations will rely more on specialization than grades, but the framework is maintained. To be cost-effective within this structure, the learning place must have a critical number of students that justifies school construction and maintenance, particularly personnel costs. In areas of low population density, building and maintaining schools to serve the traditional paradigm is economically prohibitive. The requirement of one specialist per specialty makes secondary schools an even more expensive venture. Some countries sidestep the problem by leaving the solution to individual families, with catastrophic results. If the families choose to move to urban areas and ensure their children's education, they jeopardize their country's fragile economic balance and further deplete the economy of their native regions. If they decide to remain, they jeopardize their children's future. Areas of high population density but weak economy are not free of problems. In this case, the traditional model encourages administrators to accommodate as many students as possible in one classroom to control personnel costs, which leads to overcrowded and unsafe environments that are unfit for learning.

The capacity of ICTs to reach students in any place and at any time has the potential to promote revolutionary changes in the traditional educational paradigm. First, it eliminates the premise that learning time equals classroom time. To avoid overcrowded classrooms, a school may adopt a dual-shift system without reducing its students' actual study time. Students may attend school for half a day and spend the other half involved in educational activities at home, in a library, at work, or in another unconventional setting. They may be required to watch an educational radio/television program and complete related activities, or work on a computer-assisted lesson at the school technology lab or in a community learning center. For areas with low population density, multigrade schools become viable alternatives. While more advanced students listen to an educational program on the radio or watch a television broadcast, the teacher can attend to the students who are in less advanced levels or vice versa. Latin America began experimenting with television to bring education to rural, low-population areas as early as the 1960s.

In 1964, the Mexican government tried television as an alternative to provide secondary education (grades 7-9) for children in rural communities. Telesecundaria was created to respond to the needs of rural areas where a general secondary school (grades 7-9) was not feasible, because there were not enough students and it was difficult to attract teachers. A quarter-century later, Telesecundaria has become a success story about the power of television to expand access and improve education in cost-effective ways.

Traditional educational systems also tend to rely on curricula that were developed at the beginning of the Industrial Revolution and are now disconnected from the realities of the job market. For bright students, these systems offer little in the way of motivation. Eventually, a few extraordinary students will be able to skip a grade, but rushing through the system is not encouraged, and early graduates may find obstacles when they attempt to gain access to the next level. For low-income students, who have less academic support, the schools offer even less: the wealthier schools lure the best teachers, leaving the least prepared for schools in poor and remote areas. When the need to work conflicts with schools' requirements, the student sees no reason to stay in school. As a result, these systems perpetuate social inequalities, lose many excellent students to boredom, increase the costs of education through high dropout rates and grade retention, and pass on to employers or other systems the costs of retraining their graduates.

ICTs have the potential to bring the products of the best teachers to classrooms anywhere in the world. For self-motivated, disciplined students, ICTs can speed the path toward a degree and expand their learning options through self-study. Students can shop courses on the Internet and choose their own program of study and schedules. Students in virtual schools can take extra online courses to graduate earlier or fulfill specific interests and curiosity. For those who need to balance studies with work and family obligations-full- or part-time workers, parents of small children, homebound individuals-this flexibility may be most cost-effective for them. The management of distance learning is not without difficulty, and, in many cases, local regulations function as obstacles to innovations. However, the demand for more and specialized education is encouraging new arrangements that rely on ICTs to establish communication networks among partner institutions and facilitate student-centered, rather than program-centered organizations, such as the University of the Highlands and Islands. Research on brain physiology and cognitive psychology is challenging the traditional model of learning as mastery of facts and concepts. Thoughts, feelings, dreams, and imagination are equally involved in the complex phenomenon that is human nature. Perception, for instance, includes at least two basic components:

— an objective component mediated through the senses, which provide the brain with information about the objects surrounding us, their descriptions and location, and position in relation to them; and

— a subjective component that analyzes the perceived objects through the lens of personal experiences and idiosyncrasies, previous knowledge, and cultural biases.

Images are key components of the process of acquiring and using information because of their ability to condense large amounts of data. Research on working memory proposes that information is stored as images in visuospatial sketch-pads to be used later. The process involves both imageries-the mental reconstructions of objects no longer present to senses, and imagination-the mental construction of unknown objects. In addition to their role in retention and recall, images have the ability to decode unfamiliar symbols into known representations, a helpful function in language acquisition.

Textbook images traditionally have been used in foreign language classes with this decoding function. Images are equally important in the acquisition of science and mathematics, which, similar to a foreign language, have their own symbols, terminologies, and grammatical structures. Although definitions of quality learning may disagree on details, it is generally accepted that, for learning to occur, the learners must be motivated, basic concepts must be understood, and knowledge must be advanced through more complex, higher-order thinking skill tasks. As we move away from linear learning, we get closer to how the brain functions.

ICTs diversify the systems of representation through the use of various types of stimuli (images, sound, and movement) and address the needs of diverse types of learning (visual, psychomotor, and affective). In addition, ICTs have the potential to enhance educational quality by increasing motivation, facilitating acquisition of basic skills, promoting inquiry and exploration, and preparing individuals for the technology-driven world.

An effective teaching/learning process must stimulate intellectual curiosity and offer a sense of enjoyment that will move the students from the passive role of recipients of information to the active role of builders of knowledge. Yet, engaging the learner in this process can be the most challenging task for teachers. ICTs are effective instructional aides to engage students in the learning process. Videos, television, and computer multimedia software provide information that can be authentic and challenging in addition to stimulating students' sensorial apparatus through images, color, sound, and movement.

A training program for bank clerks in the United States was unable to offer on-the-job training because banks refused to accept trainees without some experience. The instructors decided to use videos of actual clerks working at a local bank and trainees role-playing clerk-customer situations. Trainees watched the movies and discussed the tasks involved, potential problems, preferred solutions, and their weaknesses/strengths. After the videos were introduced, the program placement rates increased from 70% to 93% over a two-year period. Although radio programs do not have the visual appeal of television or computer, Interactive Radio Instruction (IRI) uses songs, drama-like plots, and comic situations to attract and maintain the attention of students of all ages in rural and low-income areas of developing countries.

Transmission of accumulated knowledge to new generations is an essential component of the educational process. This includes basic skills and information that are at the foundation of more complex knowledge. It would be inefficient to use a time-consuming process, such as inquiry and exploration, to transmit basic information. In addition, nonstructured learning environments based solely on inquiry and exploration may be confusing and overwhelming for some children and youth. These students will do better in well-structured classrooms, where the information is broken into less complex units, thus making it easier to understand. Exposition and practice strategies help to structure the classroom, enhance retention and recall, and cut learning time.

Computers have three attributes that make them powerful aides for drill and practice strategies: large memory, speed, and the capacity to repeat the same task an infinite number of times without reducing performance. In addition, they provide students with the opportunity to learn on their own time and at their own pace. Computer-aided instruction (CAI) has been used successfully in different settings for basic skill instruction. CAI programs are divided into modules that maintain a hierarchy of concepts and skills. The students have to master each module before being allowed to move to the next, more complex level. An evaluation at the end of each module gives the students immediate feedback. If they respond correctly to a determined percentage of questions, they advance. Otherwise, they repeat the module or enter remedial units until the skills or concepts are mastered. The program can keep a history of the students' performance-lessons learned, topics with which the student had more difficulty, strategies that improved learning, and how many times the student had to repeat the module.

With this information, the teacher can develop an individualized plan that addresses each student's specific weaknesses and strengths. CAI was introduced as an aid in mathematics classes, but it is now used for different disciplines, grade levels, and objectives. The military has used CAI in training for a long time. Overall, research shows that when CAI is applied well, users learn faster, retain more, and tend to have a more positive attitude toward learning than students receiving traditional instruction. Computers also can be used as auxiliary tools in mathematics and science classes to free teachers' and students' time. While computers work on repetitive tasks (such as long calculations and statistical computations), teachers and students can concentrate on analytical activities that require higher-order thinking skills. Research indicates that elementary and secondary school students who use calculators have higher test scores and better attitudes toward mathematics than their peers who do not use calculators. Elementary school children who use computers and calculators in the classroom were found to understand mathematical concepts much earlier than expected.

Although basic skills and information are essential components of the teaching/learning process, learning is more than information transfer. Learning requires the ability to analyze and synthesize information, use it in diverse circumstances, and propose new lines of inquiry that foster knowledge. Inquiry and exploration are essential strategies to attain those abilities. ICTs have the potential to restore curiosity to education. ICTs can take students on exciting journeys through time and space. Movies, videos, audio technology, and computer animations bring sound and movement to static textbook lessons and enliven children's reading classes. They also provide social studies and foreign language students with vicarious experiences of distant societies and bygone times. Spreadsheets can store and analyze large amounts of data necessary for complex math and science studies.

Computer simulations transform risky and expensive experiments into safe and cost-effective procedures. The Internet offers virtual reality settings where students can manipulate parameters, contexts, and scenarios. Computer simulations are a good example of the power of technology to improve the learning process. The flight simulator has been used for decades as the initial step in training airplane pilots. A flight simulator offers trainees the opportunity to practice the proper skills to control the plane and deal with emergency situations without risking lives or property loss. Although flight simulators can be complex and expensive machines, no pilot training program would question their utility. Simulators also are becoming essential tools in medical training. Through their use, medical students and residents are introduced to risky and invasive procedures without endangering patients' lives or exposing them to unnecessary pain and discomfort. Simulations are particularly helpful in situations that are too risky, expensive, or time-consuming to allow real-life experiments.

For instance, welding simulators have proved to be a cost-effective method to train future welders. Without simulators, this training requires long hours of practice and burning expensive electrodes. Simulations also enable students to test explosive materials virtually without running the risk of real explosions, and to experiment on animals without the ethical implications of real-life procedures. For elementary and secondary school students-and sometimes even for adults-exploring the

Internet can be a fun and enriching experience, or a frustrating adventure in trivia. Teachers and instructors play an important role as guides and facilitators by providing background material and guidelines for the search. They also need to monitor the process, particularly for younger students, who tend to browse the Web, rather than follow structured search plans. Teachers and instructors also are instrumental in helping students to separate unreliable sources from reliable ones and make sense of the large amount of information that may overwhelm them.

Globalization, creativity, and collaboration are key words in the modern workplace, where employers and employees are expected to share knowledge and work together toward common goals. In traditional classrooms, students work in isolation, doing tasks that emphasize conformism and boost competition. Trained in such environments, students may leave the school ill prepared to share ideas, divide tasks, or accept different points of view. Since ICTs can overcome physical and geographical barriers and facilitate communication, they have the potential to eliminate the artificial boundaries between schools and the outside world, and promote an environment that emphasizes collaboration rather than competition. Videos and computer animations enable students to "witness" a volcano eruption to learn about pressure, rock formation, or psychological and sociological responses to crises.

A simple radio or tape recorder can allow students in a foreign language class to listen to native speech regardless of their teachers' origin. Better yet, with interactive technologies, such as two-way radios or video-conferencing, students can communicate with native speakers without leaving their classrooms. Videos,

DVDs, computer software, and the Internet bring to schools anywhere in the world information that can be obtained only through the use of powerful scientific instruments that no single school can afford. More than any other technology, the Internet opens new opportunities for collaborative work. From group discussions to full collaborative research, the Internet has the potential to connect classrooms to research centers and students to actual scientists, as does the Global Learning and Observations to Benefit the Environment (GLOBE). Research on the Apple Classrooms of Tomorrow (ACOT) indicates that technology-rich classrooms promote teamwork and encourage tolerance for alternative viewpoints, two essential skills for increasingly complex and diverse workplaces.

Learning is only one component of the educational process, and quality learning cannot be attained without good teaching. Yet, teachers in general, and good teachers in particular, are in short supply even in developed countries. In the United States, for instance, the National Commission on Teaching and America's Future anticipates the need to hire an additional two million teachers in all teaching fields over the next decade to replace an increasingly aging work-force. For developing countries, in rural areas and in some specialties such as math and science, the teacher shortage has become critical. Simply hiring a teacher does not ensure quality education. To be effective, teachers must keep abreast of new perspectives on learning theories and their area of specialization, a task that becomes impossible when teachers work in distant, isolated areas. The mentoring process that has been used traditionally to prepare new cadres is an extra burden on experienced teachers, particularly in places where they are already in short supply.

Some schools of education are using videotaped sessions to prepare new teachers to enter the classroom without relying solely on mentors. The process frequently involves videotaping experienced teachers during regular classroom time. Student teachers observe their experienced peers in action, analyzing in detail the strategies used to present the material and interact with the students. The trainees then practice mock lessons with a group of peers or volunteer students while being videotaped. Peers and instructors review the tapes, highlighting weaknesses and strengths and making suggestions for improvement. Only after completing this process is the student teacher sent into actual classrooms.

Videos can also be used to analyze teaching styles and idiosyncrasies and help educational systems to change their approaches. A research related to the Third International Mathematics and Science Study (TIMSS) videotaped mathematics and science teachers in Japan, Germany, and the United States. The study analyzed variations in teaching style and lesson content among the three countries, looking for correlations between those dimensions and students' performance.

ICTs can be used as tools for training and support of teachers, regardless of their geographical dispersion. Scripted lessons in conjunction with educational programs via radio and television, such as the IRI and Telesecundaria, ensure that all students receive quality, updated information, while imparting to inexperienced and generalist teachers the appropriate content knowledge and new pedagogical strategies. The use of technology for teacher training has at least three major advantages: it reduces travel costs, avoids disrupting classroom routines, and familiarizes the teachers with the technology.

The Internet has myriad Websites to help teachers develop or improve lesson plans, exchange ideas, obtain information, and find free animations and simulations to enliven their lessons. Most Internet-based collaborative learning include teacher support and training, and conference proceedings are published regularly on the Web. Chat rooms or forums may become a laboratory for new ideas. For instance, teachers in Soweto, South Africa, used their online connection with schools in Birmingham, U.K., to create a support network and promote discussions on curriculum reform and school management practices. Indeed, contrary to the notion that technology is replacing the teacher, ICTs have expanded the quantity and quality of resources available to making teaching a less lonely endeavour.

More important still, research indicates that the introduction of ICTs for educational purposes has the potential to bring positive changes to teaching practices. In a survey of more than 2,000 teachers and school principals across the United States, the teachers stated that the technology helped them to become more effective (92% of respondents) and creative (88%). Both teachers and administrators agreed that technology had reinforced instruction, and functioned as a motivator for the students, who were more prone to ask questions and participate in the lessons.

Despite this potential for training and support, ICTs have not been accepted easily among teachers. Some complain that scripted lessons take away their ability to address students' individual differences and improve their own teaching strategies. Others fear that technologies will reduce the role of teachers in defining curriculum and educational strategies, or totally replace them.

Education policy development is an intricate process that requires reliable, timely, user-friendly data. ICTs can be valuable for storing and analyzing data on education indicators; student assessments; educational, physical, and human infrastructure; and cost and finance. The use of computer-related technology is particularly helpful in this field. For instance, administrators and policy makers can construct virtual scenarios around different policy options to determine needs and analyze potential consequences. Each scenario can be analyzed and evaluated systematically, not only in terms of its educational desirability, but also in terms of financial affordability, feasibility, and sustainability over a sufficient period of time to show results. The same elements of computing and telecommunications equipment and service that have made businesses more efficient and cost-effective can be applied to schools and educational systems.

ICTs can help administrators and school principals to streamline operations, monitor performance, and improve use of physical and human resources. More than other technologies, computer-related technologies have the potential to support the management of complex, standards-related instructional processes in relatively simple ways. They also can promote communication among schools, parents, central decision makers, and businesses, thus fostering accountability, public support, and connectivity with the marketplace. For instance, the Union City School District, located in one of the most impoverished communities in the United States, accepted an offer from the local telephone company to install computers in a pilot middle school and the homes of its teachers and parents. All those involved received training. The communication significantly among parents, teachers, and school administrators and was expanded to include other schools. An example of the use of computer-related technologies to address increasing demands in a time of reduced resources is provided by the Joint Board of Teacher Education (JBTE) in the Western Caribbean.

The effectiveness of ICTs-the realization of their potential-depends to a large extent on the context and quality of application. Moreover, since ICTs are only tools for education, it is difficult to isolate the factors that may be contributing to a positive result-such as educational philosophy, quality of teaching, parent support, and students' characteristics.

With these caveats in mind, evidence from large studies and meta-analyses suggests that use of ICTs, particularly computer technologies, is correlated to positive academic outcomes, including higher test scores, better attitudes toward schools, and better understanding of abstract concepts. A longitudinal study of a statewide experiment with computers in the classroom found that those most in need of help-low-income, low-achieving students, and students with disabilities-made the most gains.

ICT for Education : Prerequisites and Constraints

This section focuses on prerequisites and constraints that influence the use of information and communication technologies as tools to expand and improve education, with an emphasis on current status and existing trends and on possible ways to overcome identified barriers. To facilitate the analysis, the factors identified are organized schematically into three broad areas: access, acceptance, and availability.

1. *Access*—includes the basic requisites for the installation and use of technologies:

   — Infrastructure-foundations for the technology

   — Costs and finance mechanisms

   — Legal frameworks-laws and regulations that facilitate or constrain the use of technologies for the proposed objectives.

2. *Acceptance*—cultural and political factors that create or promote barriers to technology:

   — Cultural perspectives-nationalism, traditions, attitude toward innovations

   — Political perspectives-priorities, interests, and negotiation power

   — Interest groups-influence of unions, businesses, parents, and other groups

   — Educational systems-objective, structure, and organization.

3. *Availability*—technology-related factors that facilitate or hinder implementation:

   — Contentware—what the technology can offer in terms of content, language, quality, and relevance of material

   — Experts—presence or absence of qualified staff who can implement a quality programmes.

   — Capacity building-interest in building or ability to build an expert workforce.

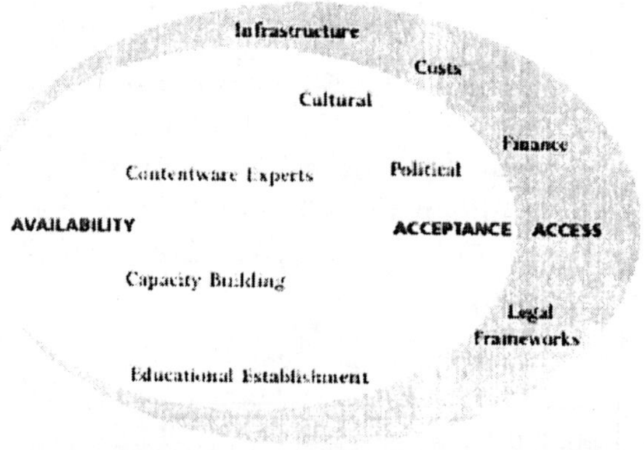

Figure 1: Prequisited Constraints ion the use of the technology for education

Five major trends have characterized the development of ICTs:

— *Complementarity*—ICTs complement, rather than replace each other. Videoconferencing and digital radio are two examples of how different technologies are associated to improve results.

— *Speed of growth*—ICTs have grown exponentially. In 1950, personal computers were little known or used, but within a generation, they became essential work and communication tools. The number of Internet hosts worldwide grew more than 1,100 times in eight years Figure 2. Reduced costs-Increased use of ICTs is associated with reduced costs and improved technology. This trend is particularly felt in the computer industry, where hardware prices have fallen, despite significant increases in memory and speed. Internet access is another area where growth has been accompanied by some cost reduction. From 1999 to 2004, the number of U.S. households online is estimated to increase by 66% (from 40.5 million to 67.1 million), but spending on access is estimated to rise only 9.2% CAGR (compound annual growth rate). Similarly, broadband Internet access is expected to increase 800%, from 2.1 million subscribers in 1999 to 18.9 million in 2004, while broadband spending will grow 527%, from US$1.1 billion to US$6.9 billion, respectively.

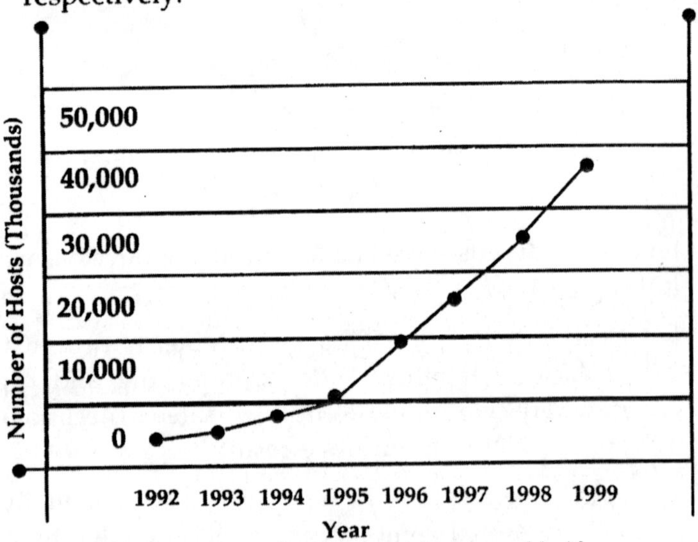

Figure 2: Growth of internet hosts worldwide

— *Simplification*—ICTs strive for simplicity of use, even when the technology becomes gradually more complex. The first disk operating system- (DOS-) operated personal computers (PCs) required some training for simple tasks; however, children have no problems dealing with modern PCs. This concern with the user may explain, at least partially, the rapid popularity of the medium.

— *Problem-solving focus*—Perhaps more than any other technology, ICTs strive for efficiency: they are faster, simpler, less costly, and more productive. This search for efficiency propels ICTs to continuous improvements. Auto industries have relied on one source of fuel for the past 100 years, despite warnings ranging from potential extinction of this sole source to environmental disasters. In less than 50 years, telecommunications have experimented with simple telephone lines, fiber optic cables, satellites, and wireless technologies, and research continues. These characteristics encourage and challenge a planning process that aims at introducing technology in education. The encouragement comes from the fact that educational agencies and countries can leapfrog from pretechnology stages (e.g., the absence of telephone lines) to state-of-the-art strategy (e.g., wireless technologies), thus bypassing less efficient and generally more expensive alternatives. The challenge is that technology planners must be creative and look toward the future to ensure they are not missing a better and less costly option.

— *Access to ICTs and the digital divide*—Access to modern information and communication technologies varies greatly around the world. Until now, ICTs have not corrected the divide between technology-rich and technology-poor countries initiated with the Industrial Revolution. In the United States, for instance, there is a correlation between race and computer ownership or Internet access. Whites are more likely to own a computer than blacks, even when controlling for differences in education, except for those at the highest income levels. Between December 1998 and August 2000, the gap in Internet access between black households and the national average grew from 15% to 18%; for Latino households, the gap grew from 14% to 18%. In China, significant differences exist in age and gender among Internet users-approximately 50% of Internet users are between 18 and 24 years of age and 75% are male. A similar trend is found in Brazil, where 61% of the Internet users are male, and 56% are aged 14-24. Access to ICTs depends on three basic prerequisites: infrastructure, costs and financing mechanisms, and legal frameworks.

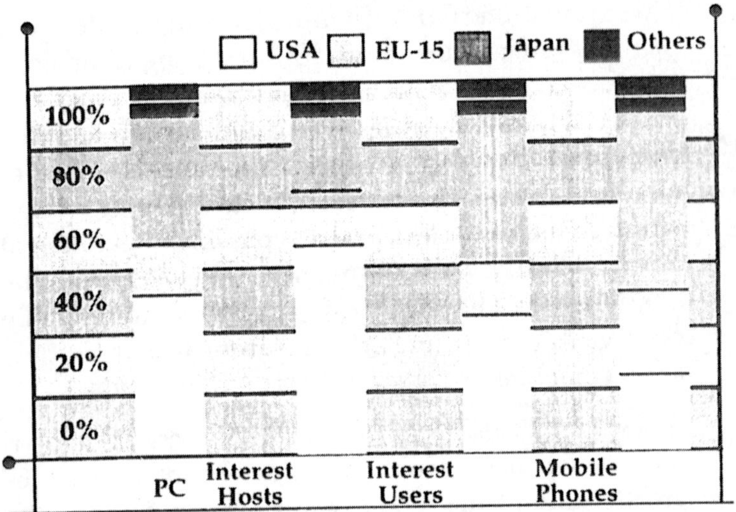

Figure 3: The Information society (per 100 inhabitants)

Until recently, most information and communication technologies depended on electric power and telephone lines. The production and consumption of energy varies broadly across countries in direct relationship with their economic development. Developing countries tend to have lower levels of energy production, less efficient systems that produce great loses during transmission and distribution, and lower consumption levels. On average, poor countries consume 5% of the energy consumed by wealthy countries. The consumption range is wide, varying from 21KWh in Ethiopia to approximately 24,000 KWh in Norway.

Availability of telephone mainlines follows similar distribution: wealthier countries-and wealthier regions within a country-have more phone lines per inhabitant than countries and regions with weaker economies. In South Asia, urban residents will be five times more likely to have telephone lines, in contrast with the European Union, where the ratio between urban and nonurban areas is approximately 1:1. Within the same world region, differences also can be significant. In Latin America and the Caribbean, for instance, Chile has 203 mainlines per 1,000 (281 in the largest city), while Haiti has eight (17 in the cities). In the Middle East, the United Arab Emirates have 389 mainlines per 1,000 (374 in the largest city), while Iraq has 31 and 75, respectively.

Costs strongly influence access. Despite reduction in costs in the past decades, indicators still show significant cost differences among countries and within countries in a single region. In 1999, average monthly rates for Internet access in Latin America ranged from US$81.71 in Trinidad & Tobago to US$12.75 in Peru, with a regional average at US$36.23. Business's rates are much higher. In Bermuda, for instance, businesses can pay more than US$850 a month for unlimited Internet access.

As a means of mass communication, radio has many advantages: it has broad outreach, is relatively inexpensive, is easy to use, and is present in almost all households around the world. In addition, radio programs are less expensive to produce than television, videos, or computer software. Although radio lacks the visual effects of television and computers, educational programs broadcast via radio have popular appeal. Most of all, radio does not require complex infrastructures. Battery, windup, or solar-powered radios ensure transmission even where electricity is not available or dependable. Walker describes a portable FM radio system operated entirely by solar power, part of the Commonwealth of Learning Media Empowerment (COLME) in Uganda.

To overcome the limited and unreliable electricity supply in the region, staff built a structure with eight solar panels and seven deep cycle batteries. This structure provides all the lighting and power needed to operate the station during the 18-hour broadcast day. In addition, the solar installations have a life span of more than 10 years and low maintenance costs.

If a 'catch-up' strategy seems doomed to fail, the technological search for faster, broader, and more efficient means of communication offers new hope to countries or regions with limited infrastructures. Trends in ICTs include:

— *Digital radio*—The association of streaming technology and the conversion from analog to digital radio broadcasting enabled radio stations to reach global audiences. Different from analog radio, where the power of transmitters is essential for broadcasting success, digital radio has low power requirements, which means lower operating costs. This capability enables smaller stations to offer power and quality similar to their wealthier competitors. In addition, digital audio broadcasting allows for transmission of text or graphic information that can be displayed on a small screen on a digital radio. This increases the usefulness of radio as an educational tool, particularly for disciplines where visualization is an essential decoder, such as foreign language, mathematics, or science.

— *Satellites*—Satellites have been used to transmit multimedia information, including television broadcast, for many decades. The large, geostationary satellites orbit Earth at high altitudes (36,000 Km), and data are sent to the satellites and back to large terrestrial transceivers through high-frequency beams. The technology is expensive and limited in quality, with a long propagation delay-about 0.25 sec.-which restricts its use for voice transmission. More recently, low earth-orbiting satellites (LEOs) are being launched. These are small, computerized devices that circle Earth at high speeds and low altitudes (780 Km). Their short propagation delay-about 12 msec. and virtually error-free connections to ground stations make them popular tools for wireless communication. In addition, LEOs' receivers can be very small, thus increasing their outreach mobility. To compensate for the expensive technology, particularly in the case of geostationary satellites, regional partnerships are multiplying. The Regional African Satellite Communications (RASCOM) is an organization of 44 African nations that aim at connecting all major African cities via satellite network. RedHUCyT is a satellite-based network of higher education and research institutions in the United States and Latin America, with support from the Organization of American States.

Cables, wireless, and others—As communication moves from e-mail to complex electronic transactions, capacity or bandwidth requirements increase. Traditional telephone lines are no longer sufficient to carry the amount and type of information that is being exchanged electronically. A simple 2400-baud connection can only transmit about 240 characters per second of an e-mail message. Audio and video applications through the Internet require a minimum of 14.4Kbps, and videoconferencing needs 128Kbps.

The expansion of the Internet and, more recently, e-commerce created a new demand for more bandwidth. The bandwidth demand between Europe and the United States is expected to grow by approximately 80% a year. In response, digital subscriber line (DSL) cable and alternative proposals are multiplying, mostly through private companies' efforts to ensure their share of a promising e-market. Between 1995 and 1997, the private circuit capacity between the United States and other OECD (Organisation for Economic Co-operation and Development) countries had a compound increase of 172% and surpassed the capacity allocated to international message services.

Education factors may profit from this market-driven growth. In the past 10 years, wireless technologies have gained increasing acceptance among residential and business users. However, they should not be seen as the solution for all the problems with infrastructure. Start-up costs are high, and requires highly trained technicians; some wavebands are highly sensitive to weather conditions, thus increasing the probability of errors, and they require a high level of coordination to avoid interfering with other radio spectrum users. In places with an already well-developed network, fiber optic cables offer more transmission capacity with smaller margins of errors and at lower cost. Where the infrastructure is missing, wireless technologies may be a solution, even if only a temporary one.

Considering the speed of change in the ICTs industry, discussions on the use of ICTs for educational purposes should focus not only on the technologies available, but also on those that are in the planning stage, and should evaluate how feasible and affordable they are for each specific case.

As stated earlier, decisions on the use of technology for education are, first of all, educational decisions. Yet, the immediate costs of a technology have greater impact on decision makers than its potential benefits. Discussions on costs of the educational uses of technology tend to compare traditional and technology-mediated approaches as if they had similar purposes. For instance, estimates of higher education costs compare campus universities with distance learning as if they served the same group of students. Similarly, research on the use of technology for elementary and secondary students uses traditional measures of outcomes, such as standardized test scores, to compare technology conventional approaches. Results may be disappointing, with many studies concluding that the two approaches have similar results, but the technology-assisted approach is more costly.

Missing in those studies is an approach whereby technology for education is not viewed as a replacement for face-to-face methodologies, but, rather, to attain objectives that have not been attained efficiently otherwise: expanding access, promoting equality, improving the internal efficiency of educational systems, enhancing the quality of education, and preparing new and old generations for a technology-driven marketplace. For each of these objectives, different technologies may prove more or less cost-effective depending on two aspects:

The characteristics of the technologies: Producing a television program, for example, is 10 times more expensive than producing a radio program. While radio may reach a broader audience, television has a visual impact that is missing in radio. Computer-related technologies are costlier than radio or television, but they have greater potential to promote higher-order thinking skills activities while familiarizing students with a technology that is becoming essential in the workplace.

Specific conditions where the technologies will be used: These include local infrastructures, availability of expertise, and appropriate contentware, as well as regulatory and cultural obstacles.

Educational factors frequently suffer from having only short-term objectives. Within this perspective, investing in technology may not seem reasonable. However, research shows that Interactive Radio Instruction (IRI) and television factors (such as Telesecundaria) can increase retention rates and improve academic performance. Likewise, appropriate use of computers in schools has been shown to improve academic outcomes.

By reducing the number of years a student spends in the system and producing better-prepared workers, technology-mediated, improve the efficiency and effectiveness of educational systems and promote savings in the long run. Cost comparisons based solely on short-term objectives will not reflect those savings.

Curran proposes a simple formula to estimate costs in technology factors: TC = FC+VC(N), where:

— TC (Total cost) is the sum of fixed costs plus the product of variable costs multiplied by the output, N;

— N is the output, generally measured as number of students served, number of graduates, or student. contact hours;

— FC (Fixed costs) are the costs incurred with the development and initial implementation of the include new buildings, or renovation of old ones, buying and installing hardware, and all expenses related to the development and production of courses, programs, and related material; and

— VC (variable costs), sometimes called recurrent costs, include expenses related to administration of the programme, training, distribution of material and supplies, and student support.

The problem is not so simple. Administrative cost (a variable cost) does not change linearly with variations in the number of students served (N). These costs will remain constant until N increases, or is reduced by 10%, after which, the administration will have to be adjusted, although by smaller proportions. He calculates that a 20% increase in the numbers of student increases administration costs by 7%.

Understanding this balance between fixed and variable costs is key to technology-mediated factors. As a rule of thumb, it can be said that:

— Technology-mediated with high fixed costs and low variable costs, such as those involving radio and television, have greater potential for economies of scale.

— Technologies that replace conventional teaching, rather than complement it, also have an immediate cost advantage, since personnel tends to be the largest component of the variable costs in education.

— Technologies with high variable costs and that work in conjunction with conventional teaching are unlikely to bring short-term cost advantages; in the long run, though, they may reduce costs by increasing the · quality and efficiency of the system.

For a lower-income country, the scale of the programmes is a key variable. A small-scale programmes (100,000 students) may represent as much as 84% of the potential discretionary public spending on primary education for the country, while a large-scale (1 million students) represents only 23%. For upper-middle-income countries, the relationship between scale of the potential discretionary spending is less significant: 7% for a small-scale programmes and 2% for a large-scale one.

For computer, infrastructure preparation and hardware are the largest part of the bill, but savings can be obtained if schools act in coordination. A school district has greater purchasing power to negotiate volume discounts than each school has separately. For instance, the U.S. state of North Carolina buys telecommunications equipment and services for all of its schools, saving up to 50% on some items. Partnering also allows schools to share resources, including software, Internet connections, training programs, and full-time support staff, thus reducing significantly the overall cost of the programmes.

Legal frameworks

In planning a technology-mediated programmes for education, attention must be paid to the laws and regulations that will affect the programmes, either facilitate it or create barriers to it. ICTs, with their ability to reach beyond political boundaries, defy many of the national and international legal frameworks that were created for a world with frontiers. Solutions, albeit necessary, are difficult to find and slow to implement. Proposals that have been advanced by experts include the following.

Telecommunication monopolies and restrictive regulations have been part of strategic defense programs in many countries; however, calls for deregulation and liberalization of this sector are now heard everywhere. Deregulation is expected to bring competition, thus promoting more supplies and lower prices. While protecting equal access to all must remain a central concern, there is evidence that government-controlled monopolies are not always the best answer in a fast-moving technological environment. In Europe, leased-line capacity expanded significantly in countries that liberalized their telecommunication frameworks. In Denmark, Finland, and Norway, for example, the direct leased-line capacity with the United States in 1995 was seven times that of Sweden. Sweden moved toward deregulation, and, two years later, its leased-line capacity was 11 times greater than the three countries' combined total. In many countries, local education authorities are profiting from liberalization of telecommunication services by entering into agreements with private providers, many of which see agreements with community-based programmes as a public relations investment that enhances the company's image and increases its local support.

Accreditation and certification must in the long run maintain confidence in educational offerings by guaranteeing their quality and the acquisition of qualifications both to individuals and to employers. Systems of accreditation developed for concrete institutions may not apply in the virtual environment. Regulations on building safety or student/ instructor ratios do not pertain to the virtual world. Credit hour is another concept that does not fit distance learning. Created to protect students in the traditional learning environment, accreditations might become a barrier against a global education market.

A student may be discouraged from taking online courses if the institution offering them is not accredited in his or her country, regardless of how prestigious the institution may be. Countries with centralized education may have an advantage in terms of recognizing credentials or facilitating transfer of credits. Decentralization, in this case, may be one more obstacle for students and institutions alike. Country, state, and local regulations can be mutually exclusive, making it cumbersome or potentially impossible to create distance-learning programmes that meet the diverse requirements. The members of the European Union began conversations on ways to simplify regulations and recognize qualifications and credentials across country borders, but such discussions are still rare.

Intellectual Property

Since 1886, with the Berne Convention, and later with the Universal Copyright Convention-administered by UNESCO-as revised at Paris on July 1971, countries have recognized the rights of an author over his or her intellectual property. Laws also have been enacted to ensure the financial remuneration of authors and protect the integrity of their work. Each new technology brings challenges to the existing laws, however. While users come to the Internet in search of more and free information, producers look for ways to expand copyright laws and ensure their rights. The Trade-Related Intellectual Property Rights (TRIPS), negotiated under the World Trade Organization (WTO) umbrella, establishes new arrangements for technology-related intellectual property that cover software code. Developing countries see TRIPS as a tool to give developed countries control over the benefits of the new economy. Developed countries, on the other hand, argue that strong intellectual property laws are necessary to promote economic growth and development that eventually will benefit all. For educators, these laws may appear cumbersome. Kerrey and Isakson cite the case of a music instructor who can use songs and pieces of music in her classroom, but has to draft numerous letters seeking permission from copyright holders to incorporate these works into an online version of the same class. Yet, educators and researchers are also rightly interested in preserving their property rights. These global discussions bring to the table problems of jurisdiction and the anachronism of legal systems developed for societies enclosed within political boundaries. The balance among national and global interests, rights of individuals, and freedom of information is a challenge that must be faced if the potential of ICTs is to be fulfilled. International organizations, such as UNESCO, can have a leadership role in bringing stakeholders together to face this challenge.

Ensuring access to technologies is just one step in the success of ICT-mediated educational programmes. Cultural and political factors may promote or create obstacles to the use of technology or limit its use to certain subgroups of society. Likewise, the structure and organization of local educational systems may favour integration of technology or create a technophobe atmosphere that hinders efforts to change. Overall, acceptance of technologies has not been a problem.

ICTs have been well received worldwide, and it appears that the older technologies opened the door for the more recent ones. In India, places that did not have a telephone now have Internet kiosks where families can e-mail their relatives abroad.

Radio and television are now part of the world culture. However, computer and Internet use is still dominated and controlled by a small group of predominantly wealthy, educated, urban males. Regardless of the country, the data are very similar. For instance, males constitute 61% of the Internet users in Europe, 71% in Argentina, and 67% in Korea.

Students and professionals make up 70% of Internet users in Russia and in China, 86% of whom have college degrees. Access is a key issue, but access alone does not explain the data. The elderly and women, even in urban areas, trail behind young and men in ICT use. Surveys on acceptance of computer-related technologies among these population subgroups were not found; yet, anecdotal information from the field suggests that males and females of all ages and cultural backgrounds are potentially open to technologies that improve their lives and put them in contact with the world.

The Telecenters or the Virtual Souks (markets), prove that rural populations are open to technologies that connect them with the world and improve their standard of living. The challenge to expanding ICTs to rural populations is more political than technological. Government employees and businesses tend to see rural areas as bad investments. Still, experiments with carefully planned rural programmes have been successful and even profitable.

The Village Phone program of the Grameen Bank in Bangladesh installs rural telephones in strategic points that can be accessed by hundreds of local villagers. Women staff the programmes to facilitate access by both men and women. One telecommunication operator say that 1,500 rural "public calling offices" generate as much revenue as 12,000 urban subscribers to cellular telephones. Likewise, by charging users' fees, telecenters in rural areas of Africa are becoming self-sustaining and are, in fact, expanding.

With few exceptions, generally related to religious beliefs, cultural factors seem to have little effect on the acceptance of technology. But, attention to cultural differences when implementing technological innovation is essential to avoid unintended consequences. Internet use among the elderly is growing. From 1999 to 2000, Internet use among North American women aged 55 and over grew by 110%, making it the subgroup with the second-largest growth in the country, just behind teenage girls. Educating the elderly is a measure of good economic and social policies. The median age of the world's population is rising, and among the elderly, the older subgroup is the fastest-growing group. Medical knowledge indicates that an active life is the best protection against emotional and physical illnesses, regardless of age. Moreover, in some countries, such as those devastated by the AIDS epidemic, the elderly already are assuming the unexpected roles of principal breadwinners and caretakers of orphaned children.

Preparing them for these responsibilities is essential to reduce the emotional and economic impact of changed roles. These are the strategies required to learn new technologies. China is catering to its elderly population through the Universities of the Third Age (UTA). UTAs use distance learning technologies—from postal correspondence to the Internet—to reach urban and rural elderly across the country. The rapid growth of the UTAs reflects not only the large demand, but also the ability of the elderly to adjust to alternative learning environments mediated through technology.

In many developing countries, women are caught in a circle of poverty, illiteracy, and cultural traditions that function as barriers to computer-related technologies, which are expensive, literacy dependent, and defined as a male realm. The stereotypical view of computers as male tools exists even in developed countries. Research in the United States shows that girls are not expected to excel in technology and are given less encouragement to use computers or pursue a career in the field. Parents buy computer-related gifts for boys more often than for girls, and teachers in technology classes tend to give more time and assistance to boys than girls. The fact that training generally is provided by men adds one more barrier, particularly in countries that impose limits on contact between genders. The scarcity of female role models in technology-related professions is another disincentive on a path already full of obstacles. Yet, research shows that, when girls are given the same opportunities and support provided to boys.

Since the reasons for the problem are varied, the solutions must be multiple. Suggestions include:

— At the elementary and secondary school level-train teachers and school administrators to understand their biases in relation to girls and technology and develop strategies to overcome this bias; train female teachers as technology instructors; work with parents to encourage or support their daughters' interest in technology; encourage and support girls to participate in computer clubs and other technology-related activities.

— At the tertiary level-implement public and/or private scholarships targeted to women pursuing technology careers, and provide encouragement and support for those who are in predominantly male schools, including offering opportunities for studies abroad.

— For adult education-include female instructors in telecenters to ease women's transition into technology; educate the public to understand that technology promotes economic growth for the whole family; promote programmes targeting women, since men can profit from them as well, while the reverse may not happen.

Acceptance of technology is also related to the level of political support or resistance at local and national levels. National governments have been key players in the expansion of educational programmes that depend on technology. Most mega-universities have privileged access to telecommunication systems that is controlled or regulated by the government in their base country. Countries such as Brazil and China have invested massively in infrastructures and financed educational programmes to spread computers into the schools. Mexico's Telesecundaria is a federally funded programme, and many IRI and telecenter programmes include partnerships between governments and international funding agencies. In 1994, Botswana developed a national strategy for the use of computer technology in secondary education and integrated a

Computer Awareness Program for the Junior Community Secondary Schools in its Nine-Year Basic Education Program. The South Korean government is promoting a nationwide strategy that uses computer technology to foster an open and lifelong learning society. Measures that government can take to support and expand technology-mediated programmes include:

— Invest in infrastructures.

— Review fiscal policy to favour educational and nonprofit use of technologies.

— Deregulate telecommunication monopolies while protecting educational use of telecommunications.

— Reorient funding policies to serve students, rather than institutions.

— Fund technology-mediated programmes directly or encourage these programmes through tax relief and other benefits.

— Access to technology for underrepresented populations.

— Promote teacher training that uses technology to familiarize teachers with these tools.

— Simplify regulations and accreditation requirements to facilitate transfer of credits across states or neighbouring countries.

— Implement standards of quality for distance education courses.

— Foster progressive policies on education that encourage activities related to higher-order thinking skills rather than memorization.

Interest groups outside the educational establishment may have powerful influence on promoting or creating obstacles to the use of technology for education. Digital corporations, such as Apple, funded pioneer computer experiments in schools. Many technology giants, such as Lucent Technologies, are directly involved in providing training. Policies to attracting more such groups to educational programmes at the elementary and secondary levels is a way to expand the support base for the programme, ensure expertise, and improve the programme's effectiveness.

Within the education establishment, acceptance of technologies is an issue, and the expansion of distance learning institutions has been met with its share of resistance. Teachers, from basic to higher education, are essential to the success or failure of educational programmes, but rarely are they involved in the planning stage of these programmes. Despite all the rhetoric about modernization, teacher education programs rarely include technology as content or strategy. Graduates of most teacher training institutions have little experience in using technology and no information about how to integrate ICTs into curricula and practice.

The technology is mostly seen as an add-on to traditional classroom teaching, and many times as an unfamiliar, and therefore, threatening imposition. An add-on approach inhibits the potential of the technology to improve the quality and effectiveness of education and decreases support from parents, students, and the public in general, who see technology as an expensive investment with no visible trade-off. Totally integrating use of technology into the teaching/learning process presents another challenge. Teachers may feel they are losing control over the content of the course and the students. The path from center of instruction to facilitator requires a new paradigm, and many teachers are not prepared to make the change.

Distance learning stretches the paradigm even further. The personal interaction that had been the basis of the teacher-learner society is no longer there. For students, the distance learning approach may be seen as depriving them from contact with the teacher-although many times, this contact in a campus university is a myth as a weekly class for 300 or more students jams into an auditorium. For instructors, distance education requires greater preparation for planning and production, extra training in technology, and less control over students' reactions to the material. It also brings concerns over job security.

For schools and universities, distance education requires greater investment, including preparation and delivery of materials ahead of class time, ensuring office hours for student queries related to academic content and to technology issues, access to library and other resources, and an efficient system of tutoring and support. Yet, changes in the student population and their interests, employee demand for training and retraining of the workforce, and market pressures will be the determining forces in the expansion of technology-mediated learning.

The movement toward distance education has the potential to bring cultural changes that have yet to be understood fully. The use of imported standardized packages will impose extraneous cultural values on developing nations. The result of a movement toward a learner-centered, more specialized education may be a fragmented education that will preclude the "civilizing function" that has historically been associated with universities. In other words, the boundary-less characteristic of distance education seems to equally threaten the existence of national cultures and of a universal culture shared by all educated human beings. These are epistemological concerns that raise a new perspective on the social role of education in the years to come. Few studies on cultural and political influences over the acceptance or rejection of technology-mediated educational details are available. More is known about teachers' reaction toward technology. In general, this reaction moves from resistance to acceptance as soon as the value of technology is understood. Ensuring access to the technology without promoting its acceptance may lead to an under used programme. Likewise, securing access and acceptance without availability of content, experts, and a potential for capacity building may result in a well-received but short-lived programme plagued by technological glitches.

Educational materials for ICTs are easy to find; the challenge is to find good materials that incorporate sound pedagogical strategies and use the potential of the adopted technology fully. Two basic criteria that must be taken into account when evaluating an education material are quality and viability. The quality of a product can be judged through direct examination, references, reviews, testimonials from users, or awards. Viability is related to the useful life of the product. A good product that maintains its usefulness for a long period will produce reasonable returns on the investment. This is easier when the potential number of users is large, posing particular challenges for groups limited in size by language, culture, or educational needs. Many organizations have developed criteria to evaluate contentware, particularly software, but each educational system should define its own standards to reflect the programmes objectives and curricular requirements and the specific needs of students and teachers. The use of commercially developed material saves time and avoids production costs, but also has disadvantages, such as:

— The material may not meet local curriculum standards or educational objectives;

— The content will reflect the ideologies and lifestyles of the producing country, generally the United States;

— For non-English-speaking countries, language is a barrier; and

— Most of all, product licensing and royalties can erase the savings realized at the production stage.

Sharing materials among countries is a better option when agreements on royalties can be reached. Sharing is easier for countries with the same language and similar customs, and for topics that have a more universal nature, such as mathematics and science. Translations, albeit expensive, may prove cost-effective, and software translators are becoming common, although the quality of their work is still questionable. Partnerships with universities, broadcasting, or software companies offer another prospect for obtaining educational materials that are customized to a country's reality and needs.

Open-source software is a response from the digital community to the increased control of technology-related property by large corporations. Not all open-source programmes are free, although most require only nominal fees or voluntary contributions.

The movement regulates itself through ethical norms that ensure recognition to the author and protect the integrity of the product, while encouraging new product development. Since the program codes are open to reviews and improvements from a number of experts, the quality of open-source software tends to be superior to that of commercial products. In addition, the programs can be customized to the user's specific needs. One disadvantage is that most programs are written for UNIX or Linux, two platforms that require technical expertise to use. For developing countries, the open-source movement makes it easier to obtain high-quality products, avoid the costs of commercial software, and develop an expert workforce. Rather than buying a package of commercial software for each of its computers, a school district in a developed country can hire a skilled programmer to configure an open-source material to the district's specific needs and duplicate it for as many computers as necessary. The district will have a quality product for less cost, without infringing on national or international laws. In addition, the process stimulates growth of local programmers, supported by an international network of experts.

In technology-mediated programmes, two different types of expertise are required: the technical expertise related to the hardware employed, and the content expertise in using the technology for educational purposes. Programmes fail when planners invest heavily in hardware and software, but minimally in hiring and training competent people, thus leaving the programme without expert support and guidance.

Equipment failures are common, particularly in the initial stages of programmes, when the lack of familiarity with the technology increases the numbers of errors. The more complex the equipment is, the greater the probability that technical problems will occur.

Continuous glitches will hamper the flow of information, reduce students' enthusiasm and motivation, and threaten the success of the programme. A teacher with a good working knowledge of the technology may be able to solve the most common problems. However, not all teachers are technology-savvy, nor are all technology problems easily solved. Rarely does an educational system have the luxury to pay for a technician to support the instructors and ensure that the hardware is functioning appropriately.

Technicians are difficult to find, and with the expansion of the digital industry, they are in great demand. Individuals with expertise in technology are finding jobs before graduation and offered salaries that educational systems can hardly afford. Training for educators generally is limited to use of specific programs or software packages; beyond that, educators are on their own. No institution will train educators to be technology experts, and few will provide them with a broad understanding of the requirements and potential of the technologies they will be using. Improvisation is currently the norm in this field. However, countries should look more carefully at technology for education.

The development of specialists in educational material reduces dependency on imported products, while increasing the probability that the language and content of the products are appropriate for the users. It also creates a workforce that brings a fresh perspective to a field controlled by a small group of producers-a competitive advantage in the global market of educational services. Over time, investments in this workforce will bring large returns. Education services constitute the fifth largest service export in the United States. In 1997 alone, the United States spent US$26 billion on education-related goods and services, including textbooks and supplementary materials (US$11.6 billion), technology (US$4.8 billion), and testing/test preparation (US$3 billion). The growth of educational expenditures is not limited to the United States. Worldwide sales of educational software to schools in 2000 were estimated to be US$4.1 billion, with another US$2.1 billion sold to consumer markets outside schools. By 2009, the education market is programmes to grow to US$200 million in India, US$580 million in South Africa, and US$1.7 billion in China.

Capturing this market is a tempting possibility for many commercial enterprises, particularly if developing countries choose to remain buyers rather than producers. Currently, few tertiary institutions and programmes seek to create this cadre of specialists. The Universidade de los Andes, in Colombia, has a programme focusing on the development of interactive games for education. The International Virtual Education Network (IVEN) for the Enhancement of Science and Mathematics Education in Latin America is forming teams of content experts, graphic designers, instructional designers, and programmers to develop educational material focused on mathematics and science for secondary eduction. A few universities in Latin America offer courses to train distance learning educators, such as the Universidade de Brasilia or the Universidad Abierta de Venezuela. This is a new frontier that merits careful attention and support from educators and decision makers.

In estimating an educational programmes's potential for success, decision makers should take into account four characteristics: desirability, feasibility, affordability, and sustainability. A desirable programme responds to identifiable needs and is more likely to garner support and funding. A feasible programme is one that may be accomplished within an established time frame, available personnel, and budget. Programmes that are badly planned and underfunded are less likely to fulfill their obligations within the proposed time. They also risk being discarded as failures, when, in truth, they were not given an opportunity to succeed.

Affordable is not synonymous with inexpensive. The concept of affordability is relative to the benefits expected from the programme in relation to its costs. Even if a large-scale IRI programme represents a high proportion of the potential discretionary public spending for primary education in lower-income countries, if it also reaches a substantial proportion of the country's young people who otherwise would be without schooling, it will surely be affordable over time. A programmes affordability must be estimated in comparison with the costs of building and maintaining traditional schools for all those children or maintaining the status quo.

Many parents and community members are willing to help a programme they consider helpful and one that gives them a feeling of ownership. Private enterprises may look at such programmes as a way to gain the support of potential clients. Successful programmes are careful to involve community members from the beginning.

Resolution Adopted by the General Assembly (without reference to Main Committee [A/55/L.2]) United Nations Millennium Declaration

The General Assembly Adopts the following Declaration:

United Nations Millennium Declaration

I. Values and principles

1. We, heads of State and Government, have gathered at United Nations Headquarters in New York from 6 to 8 September 2000, at the dawn of a new millennium, to reaffirm our faith in the Organization and its Charter as indispensable foundations of a more peaceful, prosperous and just world.

2. We recognize that, in addition to our separate responsibilities to our individual societies, we have a collective responsibility to uphold the principles of human dignity, equality and equity at the global level. As leaders we have a duty therefore to all the world's people, especially the most vulnerable and, in

particular, the children of the world, to whom the future belongs.

3. We reaffirm our commitment to the purposes and principles of the Charter of the United Nations, which have proved timeless and universal. Indeed, their relevance and capacity to inspire have increased, as nations and peoples have become increasingly interconnected and interdependent.

4. We are determined to establish a just and lasting peace all over the world in accordance with the purposes and principles of the Charter. We rededicate ourselves to support all efforts to uphold the sovereign equality of all States, respect for their territorial integrity and political independence, resolution of disputes by peaceful means and in conformity with the principles of justice and international law, the right to self-determination of peoples which remain under colonial domination and foreign occupation, non-interference in the internal affairs of States, respect for human rights and fundamental freedoms, respect for the equal rights of all without distinction as to race, sex, language or religion and international cooperation in solving international problems of an economic, social, cultural or humanitarian character.

5. We believe that the central challenge we face today is to ensure that globalization becomes a positive force for all the world's people. For while globalization offers great opportunities, at present its benefits are very unevenly shared, while its costs are unevenly distributed. We recognize that developing countries and countries with economies in transition face special difficulties in responding to this central

challenge. Thus, only through broad and sustained efforts to create a shared future, based upon our common humanity in all its diversity, can globalization be made fully inclusive and equitable. These efforts must include policies and measures, at the global level, which correspond to the needs of developing countries and economies in transition and are formulated and implemented with their effective participation.

6. We consider certain fundamental values to be essential to international relations in the twenty-first century. These include:

— *Freedom*: Men and women have the right to live their lives and raise their children in dignity, free from hunger and from the fear of violence, oppression or injustice. Democratic and participatory governance based on the will of the people best assures these rights.

— *Equality*: No individual and no nation must be denied the opportunity to benefit from development. The equal rights and opportunities of women and men must be assured.

— *Solidarity*: Global challenges must be managed in a way that distributes the costs and burdens fairly in accordance with basic principles of equity and social justice. Those who suffer or who benefit least deserve help from those who benefit most.

— *Tolerance*: Human beings must respect one other, in all their diversity of belief, culture and language. Differences within and between societies should be neither feared nor repressed, but cherished as a precious asset of humanity. A culture of peace and dialogue among all civilizations should be actively promoted.

— *Respect for nature*: Prudence must be shown in the management of all living species and natural resources, in accordance with the precepts of sustainable development. Only in this way can the immeasurable riches provided to us by nature be preserved and passed on to our descendants. The current unsustainable patterns of production and consumption must be changed in the interest of our future welfare and that of our descendants.

— *Shared responsibility*: Responsibility for managing worldwide economic and social development, as well as threats to international peace and security, must be shared among the nations of the world and should be exercised multilaterally. As the most universal and most representative organization in the world, the United Nations must play the central role.

7. In order to translate these shared values into actions, we have identified key objectives to which we assign special significance.

II. Peace, security and disarmament

8. We will spare no effort to free our peoples from the scourge of war, whether within or between States, which has claimed more than 5 million lives in the past decade. We will also seek to eliminate the dangers posed by weapons of mass destruction.

9. We resolve therefore:

— To strengthen respect for the rule of law in international as in national affairs and, in particular, to ensure compliance by Member States with the decisions of the International Court of Justice, in compliance with the Charter of the United Nations, in cases to which they are parties.

— To make the United Nations more effective in maintaining peace and security by giving it the resources and tools it needs for conflict prevention, peaceful resolution of disputes, peacekeeping, post-conflict peace-building and reconstruction. In this context, we take note of the report of the Panel on United Nations Peace Operations and request the General Assembly to consider its recommendations expeditiously.

— To strengthen cooperation between the United Nations and regional organizations, in accordance with the provisions of Chapter VIII of the Charter.

— To ensure the implementation, by States Parties, of treaties in areas such as arms control and disarmament and of international humanitarian law and human rights law, and call upon all States to consider signing and ratifying the Rome Statute of the International Criminal Court.

— To take concerted action against international terrorism, and to accede as soon as possible to all the relevant international conventions.

— To redouble our efforts to implement our commitment to counter the world drug problem.

— To intensify our efforts to fight transnational crime in all its dimensions, including trafficking as well as smuggling in human beings and money laundering.

— To minimize the adverse effects of United Nations economic sanctions on innocent populations, to subject such sanctions regimes to regular reviews and to eliminate the adverse effects of sanctions on third parties.

— To strive for the elimination of weapons of mass destruction, particularly nuclear weapons, and to keep all options open for achieving this aim, including the possibility of convening an international conference to identify ways of eliminating nuclear dangers.

— To take concerted action to end illicit traffic in small arms and light weapons, especially by making arms transfers more transparent and supporting regional disarmament measures, taking account of all the recommendations of the forthcoming United Nations Conference on Illicit Trade in Small Arms and Light Weapons.

— To call on all States to consider acceding to the Convention on the Prohibition of the Use, Stockpiling, Production and Transfer of Anti-personnel Mines and on Their Destruction, as well as the amended mines protocol to the Convention on conventional weapons.

10. We urge Member States to observe the Olympic Truce, individually and collectively, now and in the future, and to support the International Olympic Committee in its efforts to promote peace and human understanding through sport and the Olympic Ideal.

III. Development and poverty eradication

11. We will spare no effort to free our fellow men,

women and children from the abject and dehumanizing conditions of extreme poverty, to which more than a billion of them are currently subjected. We are committed to making the right to development a reality for everyone and to freeing the entire human race from want.

12. We resolve therefore to create an environment - at the national and global levels alike - which is conducive to development and to the elimination of poverty.

13. Success in meeting these objectives depends, inter alia, on good governance within each country. It also depends on good governance at the international level and on transparency in the financial, monetary and trading systems. We are committed to an open, equitable, rule-based, predictable and non-discriminatory multilateral trading and financial system.

14. We are concerned about the obstacles developing countries face in mobilizing the resources needed to finance their sustained development. We will therefore make every effort to ensure the success of the High-level International and Intergovernmental Event on Financing for Development, to be held in 2001.

15. We also undertake to address the special needs of the least developed countries. In this context, we welcome the Third United Nations Conference on the Least Developed Countries to be held in May 2001 and will endeavour to ensure its success. We call on the industrialized countries:

— To adopt, preferably by the time of that Conference, a policy of duty- and quota-free access for essentially all exports from the least developed countries;

— To implement the enhanced programme of debt relief for the heavily indebted poor countries without further delay and to agree to cancel all official bilateral debts of those countries in return for their making demonstrable commitments to poverty reduction; and

— To grant more generous development assistance, especially to countries that are genuinely making an effort to apply their resources to poverty reduction.

16. We are also determined to deal comprehensively and effectively with the debt problems of low- and middle-income developing countries, through various national and international measures designed to make their debt sustainable in the long term.

17. We also resolve to address the special needs of small island developing States, by implementing the Barbados Programme of Action and the outcome of the twenty-second special session of the General Assembly rapidly and in full. We urge the international community to ensure that, in the development of a vulnerability index, the special needs of small island developing States are taken into account.

18. We recognize the special needs and problems of the landlocked developing countries, and urge both bilateral and multilateral donors to increase financial and technical assistance to this group of countries :o

meet their special development needs and to help them overcome the impediments of geography by improving their transit transport systems.

19. We resolve further:

— To halve, by the year 2015, the proportion of the world's people whose income is less than one dollar a day and the proportion of people who suffer from hunger and, by the same date, to halve the proportion of people who are unable to reach or to afford safe drinking water.

— To ensure that, by the same date, children everywhere, boys and girls alike, will be able to complete a full course of primary schooling and that girls and boys will have equal access to all levels of education.

— By the same date, to have reduced maternal mortality by three quarters, and under-five child mortality by two thirds, of their current rates.

— To have, by then, halted, and begun to reverse, the spread of HIV/AIDS, the scourge of malaria and other major diseases that afflict humanity.

— To provide special assistance to children orphaned by HIV/AIDS.

— By 2020, to have achieved a significant improvement in the lives of at least 100 million slum dwellers as proposed in the "Cities Without Slums" initiative.

20. We also resolve:

— To promote gender equality and the empowerment of women as effective ways to combat poverty, hunger and disease and to stimulate development that is truly sustainable.

— To develop and implement strategies that give young people everywhere a real chance to find decent and productive work.

— To encourage the pharmaceutical industry to make essential drugs more widely available and affordable by all who need them in developing countries.

— To develop strong partnerships with the private sector and with civil society organizations in pursuit of development and poverty eradication.

— To ensure that the benefits of new technologies, especially information and communication technologies, in conformity with recommendations contained in the ECOSOC 2000 Ministerial Declaration, are available to all.

IV. Protecting our common environment

21. We must spare no effort to free all of humanity, and above all our children and grandchildren, from the threat of living on a planet irredeemably spoilt by human activities, and whose resources would no longer be sufficient for their needs.

22. We reaffirm our support for the principles of sustainable development, including those set out in Agenda 21, agreed upon at the United Nations Conference on Environment and Development.

23. We resolve therefore to adopt in all our environmental actions a new ethic of conservation and stewardship and, as first steps, we resolve:

— To make every effort to ensure the entry into force of the Kyoto Protocol, preferably by the tenth anniversary of the United Nations Conference on Environment and Development in 2002, and to embark on the required reduction in emissions of greenhouse gases.

— To intensify our collective efforts for the management, conservation and sustainable development of all types of forests.

— To press for the full implementation of the Convention on Biological Diversity and the Convention to Combat Desertification in those Countries Experiencing Serious Drought and/or Desertification, particularly in Africa.

— To stop the unsustainable exploitation of water resources by developing water management strategies at the regional, national and local levels, which promote both equitable access and adequate supplies.

— To intensify cooperation to reduce the number and effects of natural and man-made disasters.

— To ensure free access to information on the human genome sequence.

V. Human rights, democracy and good governance

24. We will spare no effort to promote democracy and strengthen the rule of law, as well as respect for all internationally recognized human rights and fundamental freedoms, including the right to development.

25. We resolve therefore:

— To respect fully and uphold the Universal Declaration of Human Rights.

— To strive for the full protection and promotion in all our countries of civil, political, economic, social and cultural rights for all.

— To strengthen the capacity of all our countries to implement the principles and practices of democracy and respect for human rights, including minority rights.

— To combat all forms of violence against women and to implement the Convention on the Elimination of All Forms of Discrimination against Women.

— To take measures to ensure respect for and protection of the human rights of migrants, migrant workers and their families, to eliminate the increasing acts of racism and xenophobia in many societies and to promote greater harmony and tolerance in all societies.

— To work collectively for more inclusive political processes, allowing genuine participation by all citizens in all our countries.

— To ensure the freedom of the media to perform their essential role and the right of the public to have access to information.

VI. Protecting the vulnerable

26. We will spare no effort to ensure that children and all civilian populations that suffer disproportionately the consequences of natural disasters, genocide, armed

conflicts and other humanitarian emergencies are given every assistance and protection so that they can resume normal life as soon as possible. We resolve therefore:

— To expand and strengthen the protection of civilians in complex emergencies, in conformity with international humanitarian law.

— To strengthen international cooperation, including burden sharing in, and the coordination of humanitarian assistance to, countries hosting refugees and to help all refugees and displaced persons to return voluntarily to their homes, in safety and dignity and to be smoothly reintegrated into their societies.

— To encourage the ratification and full implementation of the Convention on the Rights of the Child and its optional protocols on the involvement of children in armed conflict and on the sale of children, child prostitution and child pornography.

VII. Meeting the special needs of Africa

27. We will support the consolidation of democracy in Africa and assist Africans in their struggle for lasting peace, poverty eradication and sustainable development, thereby bringing Africa into the mainstream of the world economy.

28. We resolve therefore:

— To give full support to the political and institutional structures of emerging democracies in Africa.

— To encourage and sustain regional and subregional mechanisms for preventing conflict and promoting political stability, and to ensure a reliable flow of resources for peacekeeping operations on the continent.

— To take special measures to address the challenges of poverty eradication and sustainable development in Africa, including debt cancellation, improved market access, enhanced Official Development Assistance and increased flows of Foreign Direct Investment, as well as transfers of technology.

— To help Africa build up its capacity to tackle the spread of the HIV/AIDS pandemic and other infectious diseases.

VIII. Strengthening the United Nations

29. We will spare no effort to make the United Nations a more effective instrument for pursuing all of these priorities: the fight for development for all the peoples of the world, the fight against poverty, ignorance and disease; the fight against injustice; the fight against violence, terror and crime; and the fight against the degradation and destruction of our common home.

30. We resolve therefore:

— To reaffirm the central position of the General Assembly as the chief deliberative, policy-making and representative organ of the United Nations, and to enable it to play that role effectively.

— To intensify our efforts to achieve a comprehensive reform of the Security Council in all its aspects.

— To strengthen further the Economic and Social Council, building on its recent achievements, to help it fulfil the role ascribed to it in the Charter.

— To strengthen the International Court of Justice, in order to ensure justice and the rule of law in international affairs.

— To encourage regular consultations and coordination among the principal organs of the United Nations in pursuit of their functions.

— To ensure that the Organization is provided on a timely and predictable basis with the resources it needs to carry out its mandates.

— To urge the Secretariat to make the best use of those resources, in accordance with clear rules and procedures agreed by the General Assembly, in the interests of all Member States, by adopting the best management practices and technologies available and by concentrating on those tasks that reflect the agreed priorities of Member States.

— To promote adherence to the Convention on the Safety of United Nations and Associated Personnel.

— To ensure greater policy coherence and better cooperation between the United Nations, its agencies, the Bretton Woods Institutions and the World Trade Organization, as well as other multilateral bodies, with a view to achieving a fully coordinated approach to the problems of peace and development.

— To strengthen further cooperation between the United Nations and national parliaments through their world organization, the Inter-Parliamentary Union, in various fields, including peace and security, economic and social development, international law and human rights and democracy and gender issues.

— To give greater opportunities to the private sector, non-governmental organizations and civil society, in general, to contribute to the realization of the Organization's goals and programmes.

31. We request the General Assembly to review on a regular basis the progress made in implementing the provisions of this Declaration, and ask the Secretary-General to issue periodic reports for consideration by the General Assembly and as a basis for further action.

32. We solemnly reaffirm, on this historic occasion, that the United Nations is the indispensable common house of the entire human family, through which we will seek to realize our universal aspirations for peace, cooperation and development. We therefore pledge our unstinting support for these common objectives and our determination to achieve them.

Bibliography

Abrams, Alan (1997), *Diversity and the Internet, Journal of Commerce,* June 26.

Anderson, Teresa E. and Alan Melchior (1995), *Assessing Telecommunications Technology as a Tool for Urban Community Building,* Journal of Urban Technology, Vol. 3, No 1, 29-44.

Coley, Richard J., Cradler, John, and Engel, Penelope K. (1997), *Computers and Classrooms: The Status of Technology in U.S. Schools, ETS Policy Information Report*. ETS Policy Information Center.

Harmon, Amy (1997), *Net Day Volunteers Back to Wire Schools for Internet,* New York Times, October 25.

Hoffman, D.L. and T.P. Novak (1996), *Marketing in Hypermedia Computer-Mediated Environments: Conceptual Foundations,* Journal of Marketing, 60 (July), 50-68.

Hoffman, D.L., W.D. Kalsbeek and T.P. Novak (1996), *Internet and Web Use in the United States: Baselines for Commercial Development, Special Section on Internet in the Home, Communications of the ACM,* 39 (December).

Hoffman, Donna L., Thomas P. Novak and Alladi Venkatesh (1997), *Diversity on the Internet: The Relationship of Race to Access and Usage,* Paper presented at the Aspen Institute's Forum on Diversity and the Media , Queenstown, Maryland, November 5-7, 1997.

Holmes, Tamara E. (1997), *Seeing a Future With More Blacks Exploring the Internet,* USA Today, February 20.

Katz, James and Philip Aspden (1997), *Motivations for and Barriers to Internet Usage: Results of a National Public Opinion Survey,* Paper presented at the 24th Annual Telecommunications Policy Research Conference, Solomons, Maryland, October 6, 1996.

Keller, James (1996), *Public Access Issues: An Introduction.*

Kelly T: *IP connectivity in the Least Developed Countries;* ITU April 2002

Kirkman Geoffrey S.: *Out of the Labs and Into the Developing World: Using Appropriate Technologies to Promote Truly Global Internet Diffusion,* Center for International Development at Harvard University, March 2001.

Lawrence, Steve and C. Lee Giles, (1998), *Searching the World Wide Web, Science,* Volume 280, Number 5360, p. 98. Network Wizards (1998), Internet Domain Survey, July.

Nielsen Media Research (1997), *The Spring 1997 CommerceNet/ Nielsen Media Internet Demographic Survey,* Full Report, Volume I of II.

Princeton, NJ. CyberAtlas (1998), *Demographics: Who's on the Net in the US?*

Rutkowski, Anthony M. (1998), *Internet Trends,* February. Center for Next Generation Internet, Washington, D.C.

UNCTAD (2001) ; *Report on electronic trade and development ; United Nations publications,* Geneva

UNESCO (1999-2000) *World report on communication and information*

Index

INFORMATION TECHNOLOGY
A Revolutionary Change

INFORMATION TECHNOLOGY
A Revolutionary Change
(In 9 Volumes)

Volume 4
(Evolution of Information and Communication Technologies)

Editor
RAMESH CHANDRA
Vice-Chancellor, Bundelkhand University, Jhansi (U.P.)

KALPAZ PUBLICATIONS
DELHI–110052

INFORMATION TECHNOLOGY: A REVOLUTIONARY CHANGE

(Information Technology)

Rs. 8000 (Set)
Rs. 900 (Each Volume)

ISBN: 81-7835-201-X (Set)
ISBN: 81-7835-223-0 (Vol. 4)

Published in 2003 in India by
Kalpaz Publications
C–30, Satyawati Nagar
Delhi–110052
E-mail: kalpaz@hotmail.com

Laser Typesetting at: Varsha Graphics, Delhi
Printed at: Mehra Offset Printers, New Delhi

Contents

Preface

The second half of the twentieth century has witnessed the global phenomenon of an information explosion. The development of different electronic technologies has made it possible for millions of people to have fast access to huge information resources stored in different places on the planet, to communicate with each other and to handle information presented in various forms. The Information and communication technologies (ICTs) pursue two main goals: processing information and transmitting information from one geographical point to another, from one person to another, to a group of people or to the whole community.

The singular technological feature, which is a turning point for ICTs, is the pre-eminence of the Internet Protocol (IP) for communication, around which ICTs are re-orienting and growing. This versatile connection-less protocol is a method by which data is sent over the Internet as packets from one computer to another, each having a unique address. Different packets may be delivered through different routes to their destination, where they are re-sequenced by the Transmission Control Protocol (TCP) and put back in the right order. The Wide

Area Networks (WAN) which are identified as Internet (international networks), Intranets (corporate or intra-organizational networks) and Extranets (extra-organizational networks) are all IP-based. IP has left its imprint not only on Metropolitan Area Networks (MAN) and Local Area Networks (LAN), but also on equipment such as the network computer, workstation, work group server, media server, Web server, cable TV networks, wireless 'last mile link' to the customer premises, set-top-box and even a kiosk.

With the whirling pace of change in communication technologies as we move toward an increasingly converged media environment, it remains vital to keep abreast of these developments. The digital media create unique opportunities to harness the power of technology as a positive force in the lives of people. However, the full potential of the digital media will not be realized unless there are clear public and private policies to help guide their development. In order to achieve this goal, we need a new framework for thinking about the media and their relationship to society.

Editor

1

Information Resources

The singular technological feature, which is a turning point for ICTs, is the pre-eminence of the Internet Protocol (IP) for communication, around which ICTs are reorienting and growing. This versatile connectionless protocol is a method by which data is sent over the Internet as packets from one computer to another, each having a unique address. Different packets may be delivered through different routes to their destination, where they are resequenced by the Transmission Control Protocol (TCP) and put back in the right order. The Wide Area Networks (WAN) which are identified as Internet (international networks), Intranets (corporate or intra-organizational networks) and Extranets (extra-organizational networks) are all IP-based. IP has left its imprint not only on Metropolitan Area Networks (MAN) and Local Area Networks (LAN), but also on equipment such as the network computer, workstation, work group server, media server, Web server, cable TV networks, wireless 'last mile link' to the customer premises, set-top-box and even a kiosk.

Hardware and Software Developments

Early computers were huge, expensive, complicated machines that consumed a lot of electricity, generated a lot of heat, needed specialist operators and were used for processing data in specialist laboratories. Their size, complexity and cost meant that they were not used for any library or information work until the mid-1960s, when transistors replaced the original valves. By then codes (such as the American Standard Code for Information Interchange or ASCII) had been developed so that text could be input, stored and output on these computers with the individual characters being translated into strings of binary digits.

Very large scale integration of the electronic components that comprise any computer has resulted in a huge increase in the power available and a decrease in the cost of processing. The 1980s saw the development of the microcomputer, which enabled many libraries and information units to acquire their own computer systems.

By the mid-1990s Personal Computers (PCs) have become commonplace in libraries and information units worldwide, and many people also have PCs at home. These PCs may be used for what has become known as 'edutainment', where educational packages which parents hope will improve their children's education are used, as well as encyclopedias on CD-ROM (such as Microsoft Encarta) and games, of which a large number are available.

With the development of the information superhighway many of these domestic PCs can now link to the Internet to access information sources that previously were only available in a library or information centre. Many professionals, including doctors, pharmacists, veterinary surgeons and lawyers, now have PCs on their desks. The battery-powered 'lap top' computer is a portable device that can be used when travelling on trains and planes. The hardware of a current PC comprises:

Central processor: The speed with which the processor carries out basic instructions (measured in millions of instructions per second (mips) or given as a frequency and measured in megahertz (MHz)) and the amount of main store that can be accessed are factors used to describe a processor.

The earliest computers processed up to 10,000 instructions per second and there has been continuous increase in this speed so that current PCs have a processing speed of thousands of mips. Intel is a major manufacturer of processors and in mid-1996 it announced plans for a 200 MHz Pentium processor which means that it will operate at two to three times the speed of current Pentiums.

RISC or Reduced Instruction Set Computer chips have been designed with the aim of speeding up the time taken to process an instruction by limiting the number of instructions to include those most often used. Another approach to improve speed is to have parallel processors so that the processor is not, as in most situations, processing a set of instructions one after another (or serially), but instead several processors obey instructions in parallel. Although the speed of processing has increased dramatically the cost of processors has decreased equally dramatically.

The main memory: The main memory of any computer is used to store information that is currently being processed. The earliest computers were capable of storing only 1,000 to 8,000 characters of information. The amount of store has increased continuously over the years with a parallel decrease in costs.

The most common form of memory can be written to as well as read from, and is referred to as RAM (Random Access Memory). The standard PC of today has a RAM of about 8, 16 or 32 MB (the unit normally used to refer to storage of one character is a byte; 1,000 bytes are called a Kilobyte or KB, and 1 million bytes are called a Megabyte or MB).

Input: A variety of input devices may be attached to a computer to enable information in any form (for example, text, voice, image) to be converted into the appropriate binary codes. The keyboard (many of which follow the QWERTY layout developed for typewriters in the late nineteenth century) is often the primary device for entering information.

The original ASCII code was seven bits long and capable of recognizing 128 separate symbols. This is not adequate for representing the range of symbols used in languages throughout the world. There are various other standards used. For instance the Arab Organization for Standardization and Metrology (ASMO) developed the ASMO 449 for Arabic characters, and the East Asian Character Code is based on work undertaken by the Research Libraries Group (RLG) in the United States for the processing of Chinese, Japanese and Korean ideographic characters. Unicode is the general name used to refer to the International Standards Organization (ISO) 10646 standard 16-bit code which encompasses the world's principal scripts and has been developed by a consortium involving computer manufacturers such as

IBM and Apple, and software developers such as Microsoft, as well as RLG and ISO.

A major input device of the 1990s has been the mouse, and its use to 'point and click' at sections of the screen is a common feature of current computer systems. Scanners can also be attached to PCs to input images or graphics.

Laser scanners are used to input the information from barcodes on books and borrower cards in circulation systems or from journal issues for serials control systems. Video scanners can be used as input devices so that a videoconference can be set up over linked PCs with the participants able to see each other, or for medical diagnoses. Touch-sensitive screens allow the user to point directly at, for instance, a particular option from a menu of possibilities displayed.

Storage devices: The traditional medium for storing data is based on magnetic materials. Most PCs have a hard disk which is in a sealed cartridge that contains the read/write heads. The capacity of hard disks has increased greatly over the years from about 5 MB in 1980 to as high as 2.5 GB in 1996 (a Gigabyte, or GB, is equal to 1,000 MB). Data can also be input and output on to floppy disk and most workstations have a floppy disk drive capable of reading and writing 3.5 inch diameter disks. Optical storage media have become increasingly popular in recent years and many PCs now have an integral CD-ROM reader. The price of CD-ROM technology has dropped dramatically over recent years owing mainly to the popularity of CD-ROM as the medium for games and entertainment products.

Output: The most common output device is the screen or monitor. Many monitors now do not just display text information but can also display the complex graphics and video that have appeared for games in the home computer market, and are also used in multimedia CD-ROMs. Speakers can be attached to deliver sound linked to images on the screen so that, for instance, Nelson Mandela's voice or the national anthem of Estonia can easily be heard when using Encarta.

Lap top computers use flat screens based on liquid-crystal display technology as this consumes little power. Hard copy printout is still required and there are now many high-quality laser printers available. Again the technology of printers has developed greatly and prices have decreased over the years.

The July 1996 issue of Personal Computer World published a comparison of what £1,500 would buy at various dates, showing the incredible developments in this area: 1979 Research Machines 380Z microcomputer with 16 KB RAM, tape interface and a second-hand teletype printer. 1983 BBC Microcomputer with disk filing and 800 KB store on two 5.25-inch floppy disks, a colour monitor and a dot-matrix printer. 1989 PC with 10 MHz processor, 640 KB RAM, graphics capability and a dot-matrix printer. 1992 386SX PC with 1 MB RAM, printer and Microsoft Works. 1993 486SX PC, 10 MHz processor, 8 MB RAM, 120 MB hard disk, Works for Windows. 1994 486DX PC, 33 MHz processor, 8 MB RAM, 424 MB hard disk, Works for Windows. 1995 486DX PC, 66 MHz processor, 8 MB RAM, 528 MB hard disk, multimedia capabilities with double-speed CD-ROM and sound card. 1996 Pentium PC, 75 MHz processor, 16 MB RAM, 1 GB hard disk, quad-speed CD-ROM drive, 17-inch monitor and modem (for Internet connection). Probably the major recent software development for library, information and archive work has been the use of the Windows interface.

In the mid-1980s an operating system known as PC-DOS (PC-Disk Operating System) was produced by the American firm Microsoft for IBM to use with its PC. At about the same time a completely different interface and operating system was developed for the Apple Macintosh computer; this made use of the point and click features of a mouse with different options displayed on the screen in the form of small pictures or icons. This type of interface became very popular with users and by 1990 Microsoft had developed a similar type of interface, known as the Windows 3 interface, for the IBM PC.

Microsoft has also developed a wide range of office support software that is used in many libraries, information units and archives. Examples include Word (for word processing), Access (for basic database management) and Excel.

Many archive and records offices use industry-standard software for their work. Simonson describes the use of general word processing and database management software (that is easily and cheaply available) for archive purposes at the Surrey Record Office in the United Kingdom. He notes that the advent of multimedia computing, networks and the information superhighway places the onus on archivists to find ways of making the information in their custody available electronically. There is also an urgent need for archivists to understand and get involved in the information revolution that is currently taking place, so that a coherent strategy can be developed for managing the electronic archives of the future. During 1995 Microsoft launched Windows 95, a 32-bit multi-tasking operating system, and this is now beginning to be used in libraries and information units worldwide.

Network Developments

This portion will provide a small flavour of how these developments impact on libraries and information units. When computers were first used in libraries it was often necessary to link terminals or workstations from remote branch libraries to the main computer system, or to link together various PCs so that they could, for instance, share a CD-ROM drive or a printer. These activities involved the implementation of some form of data communications network.

A network used to link equipment over a limited area is known as a local area network or LAN. In many universities around the world there are campus-wide LANs that enable students and staff from all over the campus to link to, amongst other things, the library's Online Public Access Catalogue (OPAC). Many libraries and information units have also become involved in providing access to a range of CD-ROMs via a LAN. There are many advantages to this approach:

> Several users may have concurrent access to the same CD-ROM. Library users may connect to a number of CD-ROMs from their own desktop PCs without having to handle the actual disc. Expenditure on CD-ROM licences may be reduced. CD-ROM discs and drives are protected from vandalism and theft.

—CD-ROM titles can be centrally updated.

There are various approaches to providing a CD-ROM network. The CD-ROMs can be attached to a network file server such as SCSI Express. Another approach is to use an optical server which is dedicated to running a group of CD-ROM drives. Products which provide this facility include CD-Net, CD-Manager and CD-Connection. A final approach, which is beginning to be popular, is to copy the CD-ROM data to magnetic disks. A major recent advancement in this area has been the development of products such as SilverPlatter's Electronic Reference Library (ERL), which provide the user with a seamless way of accessing CD-ROM databases, local databases and remote databases. CD-ROM has proved to be very useful in many countries. However, bibliographic databases on CD-ROM do provide users with information on items that may not be accessible locally and so the number of interlibrary loans rises significantly.

National or regional networks that link LANs or other computing facilities are known as wide area networks, the major one being the Internet. Often national libraries act as focal points in helping others in a particular country with this activity. The Conference of European National Libraries (CENL) is involved in the development of Gabriel -a World Wide Web server—which provides links to sources of information about the services and collections of members of CENL. It developed from work on Web servers carried out at the British Library (with its Portico server which, inter alia, provides access to images of treasures including the Magna Carta and the Beowulf Manuscript) and the Koninklijke Bibliotheek (KB) in the Netherlands (with its Alexicon service and the Hundred Highlights of the KB, recognized as a model virtual exhibition of a national library's treasures). The National Library of Malaysia is coordinating a project known as JARINGAN ILMU (or knowledge network) which involves many libraries in the country providing information for access on the

Internet. The Network of Networks project in Latin America, which is supported by the International Development Research Centre (IDRC), aims to improve the flow of information between eighteen networks in the region by the use of electronic mail, computer conferencing and the distribution of databases on CD-ROM.

The project started in 1993 and, as it developed, the possibilities of regional communication increased owing to the establishment of Internet nodes in places such as the University of Costa Rica and the University of Chile. Development of library housekeeping systems Library housekeeping (or management) systems typically are integrated packages which include modules for various cataloguing, OPAC, acquisitions, circulation, serials control and interlibrary lending. A detailed description of almost forty such library systems available in Europe is given by Leeves.

These systems include those that originate in one of the European countries and are available in others (for example, BIBDIA (Germany), LIBER (France), Pica (Netherlands), SuperMax (Denmark) and VUBIS (Belgium)), as well as those that are non-European in origin, mainly coming from North America (for example, ADVANCE from Canada and Dynix, Unicorn and VTLS from the United States). An overview of some twenty-seven companies involved in library housekeeping systems for North America, minicomputer based systems were sold by nineteen vendors, and sales in 1995 totalled 1,605 (as compared to 1,364 in 1994); the corresponding figures for microcomputer-based systems were ten vendors with sales in 1995 of 25,364 compared to 24,064 in 1994. The vendors selling most systems to academic libraries were Innovative Interfaces (INNOPAC), IME

(TINLIB), Ameritech (Dynix and Horizon) and Data Research Associates (DRA).

Great political changes have taken place in Eastern Europe during the 1990s and this has, amongst other things, opened the market for library systems. Developments related to library automation in Croatia, the Czech Republic, Hungary, Poland, Slovakia and Slovenia.

The Regional Library Programme of the Open Society Institute in Budapest, Hungary, was established in 1994 to support, promote and advance the information sciences in Central and Eastern Europe and the Commonwealth of Independent States, and has recommended long-term goals for automated access to library information. In order to support these goals a series of library automation workshops has been held in various countries of the region.

Some of the library housekeeping systems hold records in the Machine-Readable Records (MARC) format whilst others allow for the import and export of MARC-based records. There are a variety of MARC formats available and Campos et al. (1995) provide an overview of some of the national MARC formats (for example, CATMARC (Catalonia, Spain) and IndoMARC (Indonesia)) as well as the increasing use of the UNIMARC format. Countries that have adopted UNIMARC as a national standard include Croatia, Greece, India, Italy, Portugal and Slovenia.

The OPACs of many libraries worldwide can now be searched using the Internet. Some of these OPACs have been designed to be searched over the Web whereas others can be accessed using a Telnet connection. A special facility known as Hytelnet was developed in Saskatoon, Canada, and is designed to help users in searching OPACs at all Internet-accessible libraries via Telnet. Facilities are available to search by country and by system type, and to look at help files for searching the different OPAC types. Recent additions to the list of OPACs looked at during the writing of this chapter included those of: the National Library of Turkey (ALEPH), Shanghai (China) Jiao Tong University (in-house system), Universitat de Girona (Spain) (VTLS) and Universidad de Mexico (TINLIB).

The concept of an integrated library housekeeping package with the various modules accessing the same bibliographic record is beginning to be replaced by the concept of de-integration, with libraries buying different packages from different suppliers, and mixing and matching to best suit their particular needs. This has become possible because of various recent developments:

> The move away from the proprietary operating systems used by the integrated systems of the 1980s to open systems based on UNIX; examples include Geac's ADVANCE, Innovative Interfaces' INNOPAC, Fretwell Downing's OLIB, Sirsi's UNICORN and IME's TINLIB.

The move away from the proprietary database management systems to industry-standard relational database management systems. Examples include Geac PLUS's use of Informix, Dynix HORIZON's use of Sybase and OLIB's use of ORACLE. The use of client-server architecture in the design of systems. In the client-server model of computing a division is made between the applications software (which runs on a computer known as the client) and the database software (which runs on a computer known as the server). The two communicate with each other over a network using a communications protocol. Processing which involves data manipulation or screen display can be carried out on the client computer (thus reducing traffic on the network) and only database queries from the client and responses from the server need be communicated across the network.

The use of Z39.50: As defined by Dempsey et al. Z39.50 is a 'retrieval protocol which allows client programs to query databases on remote servers, to retrieve results and to carry out some other retrieval-related functions'. Its main impact on libraries is to enable users to search, say, the OPAC of a neighbouring library using the same OPAC interface as in their local library. For this to happen the local system must have a Z39.50 client and the remote system must have a Z39.50 server. Dempsey et al. list some of the library systems which incorporate Z39.50 client-servers; these include Geac ADVANCE, Dynix, INNOPAC, LIBERTAS, OLIB, Talis and UNICORN. Some of these clients are integrated with the standard OPAC (for example, LIBERTAS) while others are available as stand-alone products (for example, Dynix's WinPAC).

Networking developments: Library housekeeping systems no longer operate in a stand-alone fashion. Libraries which use a system to manage local processing of stock also need to provide their users with access to a range of information services as part of the electronic library; this could include access to networked CD-ROMs, locally loaded databases, the Internet and so on. Several suppliers now make information about their products and their company available on the World Wide Web.

The process of choosing an automated information system for libraries, museums and archives in the county of Suffolk in the United Kingdom. The chosen system provides traditional library management functions as well as access to networked CD-ROMs, local databases, the Internet and (for a trial period) access to OCLC FirstSearch databases. The factors influencing the choice of library software in sub-Saharan Africa. There, as in many other regions, good vendor support is an important factor as there is a marked absence of staff in libraries with relevant computer skills. Some software producers organize for local agents to supply the necessary training and maintenance functions of support. If local support for Western software is poor and/or very expensive there is an argument for the development of local software; examples include the SISPUKOM library management software developed within Malaysia and the INGRID system, based on Informix, developed at Tartu University Library in Estonia.

Library systems of the future will be very dependent on adhering to international standards. Work on standards forms part of the Open Interchange Initiative being carried out for the European Commission, and current information on a wide range of relevant standards for library and information work can be found on the Commission's web server. Developments in information retrieval systems A general overview of the developments in both local and remotely accessible information retrieval systems. Particular developments will be highlighted in this section.

Text retrieval software

For many years a range of software has been available

specifically aimed at information storage and retrieval of text-based information. Examples of such software include BRS/Search, CAIRS, CDS/ ISIS, Cardbox Plus, HeadFast, IdeaList and InMagic. CDS/ISIS is very widely used all over the world as it is available free of charge to non-profit organizations in UNESCO Member States and exists in a number of language versions. A regular feature on CDS/ISIS is included in Information Development. One recent example given of the use of CDS/ISIS is the DRAiN (Drainage Information System) project which aims to co-ordinate information from various relevant research organizations in Egypt, France, India, Mexico, Pakistan and Uzbekistan involved in irrigation and drainage research.

For many years text-retrieval software was used to process bibliographic data, but recent developments in storage technologies have meant that this software can now be used also for full-text retrieval purposes. The producers of this software have continued to develop their products and many now run under Windows, can deal with graphical data as well as text data and can be used when creating local CD-ROMs. A special category of text-retrieval software is personal bibliographic software (such as Pro-Cite, Reference Manager and EndNote Plus) which may be used by academic researchers and which offers pre-defined data structures and pre-defined output structures (to comply with bibliographic styles adopted by organizations such as the American National Standards Institute (ANSI)) as well as standard facilities such as Boolean searching and batch importing of records.

An introductory essay by David Bearman (1994) in a directory of about eighty software packages for use in archives and museums notes that the 'problem with archives software has historically been that the market is too small and diffuse to support a range of products'. However, he points out that the Internet provides an exciting domain for archivists with the possibility of setting up World Wide Web servers of archives holdings which might include images and sound information as well as document delivery services (for example, British Columbia Archives and Record service. Geographic information systems (GIS) GIS software comprises tools for the collection, analysis, retrieval and display of spatial information.

Technologies that integrate the management and analysis of this type of data (from maps, weather satellites and so on) are being used in a variety of ways for environmental studies, global change research, transportation planning, urban planning, marine studies, and so on. As with bibliographic data, there is a need to share resources worldwide and the MARC format is being investigated as one possible solution. One of the projects - Project Alexandria (not to be confused with the plan for the new library of the same name at Alexandria in Egypt) - being funded in the United States as part of the National Science Foundation (NSF) digital libraries programme, is developing a system to access spatial data in distributed databases. A number of papers on GIS is included in Information Technology and Libraries, June 1995.

Traditionally the information that can be stored and retrieved in computer systems used for library and information work has been structured into databases. The growth of databases has been rapid. A database as a collection of data or a body of information that is organized for retrieval via a computer in any storage medium', and they cover databases that may be online directly from the producer, through a third-party online service or in CD-ROM format. The types of information covered in these databases include:

> Bibliographic data relating to articles published in the primary journals: MEDLINE (medical), Compendex (engineering), LISA (librarianship), Inspec (electrical engineering and computer science).

Details from the book trade (BookBank, BNB, BookFind, Books in Print). Full-text information such as newspapers (The Times, the Guardian, the Independent), articles from specialist journals (ADONIS - Biomedical, BPO (Business Periodicals Online), New Scientist), literature (English Poetry) and patents (US Patents FullText).

Multimedia products (McGraw Hill's Encyclopaedia of Mammalian Biology, Hulton Deutsch CD Collection, Encarta, Cinemania). There is a wide range of organizations involved in publishing databases; these include traditional academic publishers (Oxford University Press, Elsevier), learned societies (Institute of Physics, Institute of Electrical Engineers), commercial companies (Institute for Scientific Information, Derwent), the computer industry (Microsoft) and the entertainment industry (Sega, Disney, Nintendo). Work on quality issues of publicly available databases has been undertaken by various online user groups, and Armstrong describes the concept of 'database labelling', which would provide the potential user with basic information about the database and the extent to which the information contained could be trusted.

As well as the traditional online search services (such as Dialog, DataStar, STN and ESA-IRS) there are now many others ways in which libraries and information centres provide access to publicly available databases for their users. Examples include stand-alone and networked CD-ROMs, locally mounted databases and Internet access. The online search services provide access to a range of databases. Many of the early databases were bibliographic and dealt with scientific and technical information.

During the 1980s more specialist services appeared and the existing services broadened their scope. FT Profile, for instance, specializes in the provision of full-text online information tailored for the business community. OCLC entered the online search service field in late 1991 with FirstSearch, a service designed particularly for end-users. In the United Kingdom the Joint Information Systems Committee (JISC) of the funding bodies for higher education has organized the establishment of centralized databases for the academic community. By charging a university a fixed annual fee, searching becomes 'free at point of use' for researchers, teaching staff and students.

The rise in the use of the Internet has been accompanied by the development of commercial, consumer-oriented online services. Examples include America Online, Prodigy, Compuserve, Genie and Delphi which are popular with end-users as they cover a range of information such as news, general health matters, encyclopedias, business information and magazines.

CAS-IAS provide access to the table of contents of several thousand current journals and also provide means of transmitting requested articles. By making use of CAS-IAS services some libraries are moving from a just-in-case mode of operation with respect to serials holdings to a just-in-time mode. Examples of CAS-IAS include OCLC FirstSearch (with the Article 1st and Contents 1st databases), UnCover (now owned by Knight-Ridder, which also owns Dialog and DataStar) and Inside Information (from the British Library).

Interface Developments

The early online search systems such as Dialog, DataStar and ESA-IRS relied heavily on command languages for carrying out online searches, and this helps to explain why these systems were mainly searched by specially trained intermediaries. With the developments of OPACs and CD-ROMs in the 1980s, an interface was needed which could be fairly intuitive with searchers and needed no special training. The technique adopted was to provide the searcher with a menu of options on the screen so that an appropriate option could be selected which would then lead to another set of options or to the data. On the positive side, menus can be self-explanatory, easy for the novice searcher and give a structure to the search. However, they may be slow to work through and irritating for frequent searchers.

With the major move to a Windows environment, many producers of search systems are developing their software to work in Graphical User Interface (GUI) mode. When a screen of potentially clickable items is presented it is not always obvious to the novice searcher where to go next in this two-dimensional environment and so there are many aspects of screen design that need to be borne in mind by the interface developer. Eight golden rules for any designer of a search interface. Paraphrased these are: strive for consistency, enable frequent users to take shortcuts, offer informative feedback, give action sequences a logical structure, offer simple error handling, permit easy reversal of actions taken, make the user feel in control and reduce short-term memory load.

Retrieval techniques

Most retrieval software is based on the user combining chosen terms or phrases using the standard Boolean operators AND, OR, NOT in the search statement. Over the years various alternative techniques have been developed by researchers; these are referred to in the literature as best match, nearest neighbour, probabilistic retrieval, fuzzy sets, relevance ranking or ranked output. Some of these ideas are now appearing in commercial services such as Personal Library Software's Personal Librarian, Dialog's TARGET, and FREESTYLE developed for the LEXIS legal service and the NEXIS news service. Evaluating the performance of various information retrieval systems has been a topic of interest for many researchers over the years. A major initiative, known as the Text Retrieval Conference (TREC), involves a number of research groups from around the world testing their information retrieval techniques on the same databases of full-text items.

Human aspects of automation

There are many potential problems related to the use of information technology in archive, library and information work, and these can result in useless, expensive and inappropriate systems. There have been examples of libraries where much time, effort and money is spent on the latest software and hardware but little time has been spent on revising work practices or ensuring that workstations are ergonomically designed for the people who use them.

Only about 10% of the literature on library automation covers human aspects, whereas about 80% of the problems that arise in automation projects are thought to be caused by human or organizational matters. It is most important to consider people at all levels when setting up any form of computer system in a library. The real needs of the users must be taken into account in the design; library staff and computer staff need to know enough about each others' areas of expertise so that they can communicate properly; systems librarians and network managers need to have suitable job descriptions so that they do not become too 'techno-stressed'; workstations need to be suitably designed for their likely users; users need to have realistic expectations of the new system; and library staff need to be kept informed in an appropriate way.

Traditional organization structures may need to be adapted with the introduction of new systems. In many countries where legislation is in place to cover the health and safety aspects of, say, working with VDU (Visual Display Unit) screens, managers are being forced to think about the human aspects of automation. There is much to be done in making sure that human factors are considered at all stages in the design of a computer system for use in libraries or information units. The impact on people of electronic libraries (IMPEL) is one of the supporting studies to the e-Lib project.

All librarians and information workers must be able to cope with the vast quantity of electronic information now available as well as to advise their users how to cope with it.

The use of information technology in libraries in the Philippines, and notes that problems are due to lack of know-how, lack of direction, lack of funds and a weak telecommunication infrastructure. The first three reasons could be applied to many libraries all over the world.

Some manufacturers make their products available on the world market and have invested efforts in translating the interface dialogue of their systems into various languages. TINLIB, for instance, is available in about twenty-five different languages and is used in libraries on five continents.

ALEPH, from Israel, can handle several different scripts (including Arabic and Hebrew) within a single record and has been used in many East European countries, including the Czech Republic, Hungary, Slovakia and Romania.

There are, though, few examples of truly multilingual systems for information retrieval; the Institut Textile de France developed a system (TITUS) which enabled searchers to search, in say German, for a document which might have been input in Spanish; the Swiss Federal Institute of Technology in Zurich has developed ETHICS; and in Malaysia, SISDOM is a retrieval system which deals with documents in Malay and English. The madness of technolust and describe how 'effective users of electronic resources must learn to surf the networks, and on occasion, to swim in information without drowning in data'.

Multi-media Technologies

During the last decade, there have been endless and dramatic technological changes in all three major areas of information technology computing, communications and content. We have witnessed the advent of personal computers, worldwide packet networks, optical disk and other mass storage media, interactive video technology, image technology, digitizing and scanning technology, computer graphic technology, and the growth in both size and number of massive public and private databases - bibliographic first, then numeric, and now multimedia. These three major areas were rather disparate in earlier years. Now, they are becoming integrated and quite international in scope and impact. There is every reason to believe that this situation will continue at an even faster pace. Now, the world is going digital, and there is no turning back.

The concept of mixed media or multimedia has been around for some time, the form and its impact having been registered well before the advent of the computer, personal or otherwise. Though many people even today think of the computer mainly as a number-cruncher, early visionaries like Vannevar Bush already saw its future role as an information and media processing powerhouse in the 1940s. In his famous 'As We May Think', published in the July 1945 issue of Atlantic Monthly, Bush advocated mechanizing scientific literature by association with a device called 'memex'.

Bush's idea endured and inspired two people about twenty years later—Douglas C. Englebart of the Stanford Research Institute and Ted Nelson of Xanadu. Englebart, influenced by Bush's vision, developed a system for knowledge workers, called NLS (oNLine System) in 1963, which embodied many original ideas and concepts of hypertext, including windows, the mouse, electronic mail, and a hypertext-like ability to link and annotate documents. Nelson coined the word 'hypertext' in the 1960s, which he described as non-sequential reading and writing that links different nodes of the text.

Hypertext and hypermedia/multimedia

Hypertext mimics the brain's ability to access information quickly and intuitively by reference. At the basic level, a hypertext system is a database management system which permits one to connect screens of information using associative links, and by allowing users to link information together, thereby creating trails through associated materials.

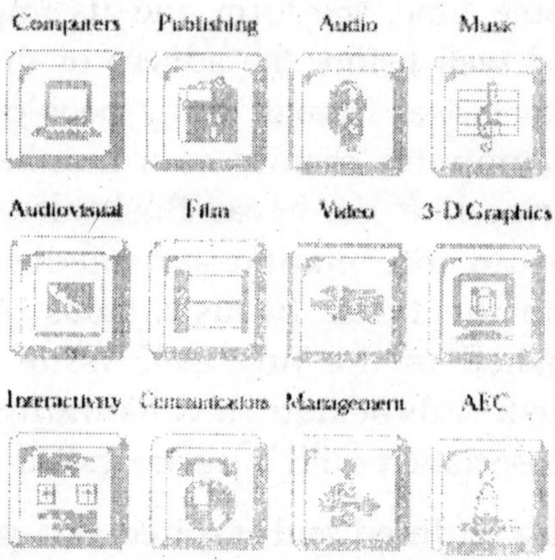

Figure 1: Hypermedia Map

At the more sophisticated level, a hypertext system has a software environment which supports collaborative work, communication and knowledge acquisition. When the system's database structure is complex, it is common to supply a special node called a graphical browser which displays the structure of the database and serves to re-orient users who are dislocated. Hypertext is the forerunner of multimedia/ hypermedia. Although the concept of hypertext has been with us since the 1940s, it was brought down to the 'household' level only after the introduction of Apple's HyperCard in late 1987. Using HyperCard, one can create links in a given work—an electronic book, multimedia presentation or anything that might best be explored in a non-linear way. Then, when users are reading or exploring, they can click on icons to zoom to related topics which may be in the same file or in another one.

Hypermedia extend the hypertext concept to link textual material to all forms of material—graphics, image, video, animation and sound—that may bedigitally encoded for storage and retrieval through computer-based systems. As early as 1988, Casa-Bianca, in his attempt to publish a hypertext-like journal, Hyper-Media, graphically presents a typological framework of hypermedia in what he calls HyperMedia Map. He uses graphic icons, as shown in Figure 1, to illustrate how the world's communications media - audio, audiovisual, film, music, video - have been incorporated with computers, communication networks, publishing and information resources, 3-D graphics, design and system management to enable us to provide multimedia/ hypermedia information in a new, global, 'wired society'.

Clearly, multimedia technologies are not one single technology, and there is no single product, or definable market. The term 'multimedia technologies' epitomizes technology integration through the use of multimedia tools. In order to summarize the above and facilitate our discussion on multimedia, a simple working definition of multimedia is proposed as follows.

Multimedia extends the hypertext concept of non-linear and non-sequential links of textual material to all forms of material that may be digitally encoded for storage and retrieval through computer-based systems, including images, sound, graphics and animation . . . Thus, multimedia refers to a synthesis of text, data, graphics, animation, optical storage, image processing and sound. Clearly, multimedia technology is not a single technology, and there is no single product, or definable market. It epitomizes technology integration.

Multimedia tools and technology Input and output technologies: hardware and software for digital data, sound, image, video and films As librarians and libraries everywhere are still handling largely printed materials, it is important to understand that the information seekers are no longer satisfied with only printed materials. They will want to supplement the printed information with more dynamic sound, music, graphics, animation, photography and video, all of which can now be fed into an ordinary computer where they can be cut, changed, shaped, combined, manipulated, enhanced and reconstructed into all kinds of exciting information products. In order to benefit from the current multimedia environment, one needs to know the multimedia tools available in the marketplace so that they can be used to bring multimedia to the desktop.

Hardware and software for users of multimedia

Currently the marketplace is full of multimedia products, as shown by the thousands of titles included in any directory of multimedia titles, many of which are multimedia CD-ROM titles. For libraries' interest, multimedia products of every reference type, as well as subject topics, are available. Because more and more products have incorporated rather large numbers of images, sound and digital videos, much more powerful hardware than the bare minimum requirement for a PC system will be required:

— 80386 CPU.

— EGA/VGA or VGA A Plus Graphics.

— 2 MB RAM.

— Double-speed CD-ROM Drive.

— Microsoft Windows 3.1.

The general rule is that whenever possible, try to acquire a system with as much speed, hard disk space and RAM as possible. For example, some products will run properly only with a 486 or Pentium processor with at least 16 MB of RAM and a four-speed CD-ROM drive. The unfortunate fact is that most multimedia application products are developed for users with the higher-end systems, and few have kept the low-end systems users in mind.

Multimedia production tools

Only a couple of years ago, producing multimedia applications was generally difficult, since most multimedia production tools were either not readily available or simply too expensive for general use. But fast technological development has made it possible for many to consider producing their own multimedia applications now. To facilitate librarians' use of these tools for production purposes, those for both Macintosh and PC systems are included below. Although Macintosh tools are often preferred for the development of multimedia applications, they might not be readily available to libraries in developing and less developed countries.

There are simply too many multimedia production tools to cover all adequately. For example, for the Macintosh platform alone, the Macintosh Multimedia & Product Registry lists on forty-five pages over 700 tools in every possible category of production work.

A similar publication including tools for the PC platform is IBM's yearly issue, Multimedia Today: The Sourcebook for Multimedia. The issue for 1995 lists over 600 production tools. For illustrative purposes, the following discussion covers only a very small number of selective tools in some distinctive categories.

Animation

The best known animation tool is Macromedia's Director 4.0 (H) which is available for both Mac and Windows. Macromedia's Director is a powerful animation and authoring tool. Users can create, combine and synchronize graphics, text and animation with audio and video; add full interactively with buttons and scripts; export and import QuickTime movies, etc.

Conversion software is also available to convert Mac Director applications to PC and vice versa. Other notable software includes Adobe's Premier 4.1 (H), Avid's VideoShop 3.0 (M) for Mac, and Gold Disk's Animation Works Interactive 2.0 (L) for PC.

Clip art and photography

In this category, Photo-CD technology has been utilized fully by most producers to store about 100 images of clip art and photographs on almost every subject for both Mac and PC platforms (some store 600 when the top two levels of higher-resolution images are sacrificed). Of international interest, Educorp's International Graphics Library is a CD with 32-bit QuickDraw images (L). These clip art images can be copied and pasted on multimedia applications. More clip art CDs can be found in various software catalogues from Image Club in Milwaukee.

Development tools

The marketplaces has over fifty development tools for multimedia authoring and digital publishing. For Macintosh, the most noteworthy is HyperCard (L) (current version is 2.3). It features an intuitive interface designed to guide users through the construction of hypermedia programs and presentations of various media elements such as pictures, paint graphics, QuickTime movies, audio, videodisk sequences and text, where users want them simply and quickly. Other popular ones include Macromedia's Author-ware 3.0 (H) for both Mac and Windows, the Voyager Co.'s Expanded Book Toolkit (L) and SuperCard 3.0 (M). Other PC systems include Aim Tech's Icon Author (H) and Motion Works' Media-Shop (M) and ToolBook (M).

Most noteworthy in the drawing and painting category are Adobe Illustrator 5.5 (M), Canvas 3.5 (M), Macromedia's Freehand 5.0 (M), Claris' MacPaint 2.0 (M), and Adobe's SuperPaint 3.5 (M). All are powerful illustration and design tools that simplify the creation, manipulation and refinement of artwork with advanced features for editing, text handling, colour support and more.

Image processing

(Photoshop 3.0.3 for Mac) is the most recognized and most powerful image processing tool. It lets users design artwork with a wealth of powerful painting and selection tools, or retouch and correct true colour or black and white scanned images with image editing tools and filters. It also has a wide range of third-party plug-ins for enhanced image manipulation, most notably Kai's Power Tools 2.1 (L), which provides a set of three dozen powerful extension and filter plug-ins that expand the ability to create computer-generated artwork and manipulate scanned images. Aldus PhotoStyler 2.0 (M) for Windows is also a popular tool for PCs.

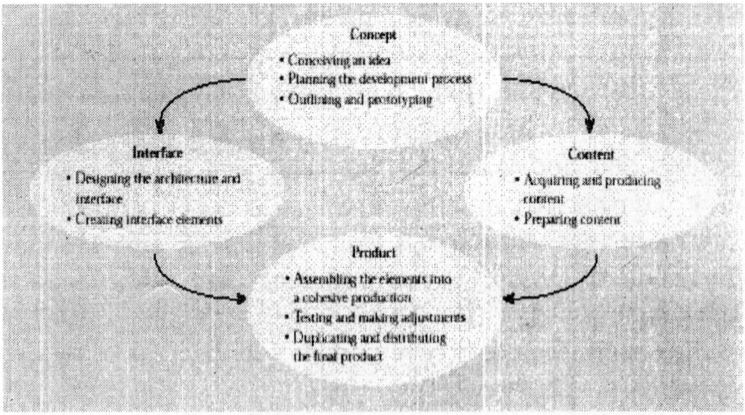

Figure 2: Basic Steps in Developing multimedia applications

Media catalogues

A number of tools are available for organizing and quickly retrieving digital photos in categories. Adobe's Fetch 1.2 (L), In space System's Kudo ImageBrowser (L) and Kodak's Showbox (L) fall into this category for Mac, while Electronic Imagery's Image-Manager (L) and Lenel Systems' Media Organizer (L) are for PC users.

Modelling and rendering

Numerous powerful tools are available in the marketplace for creating photo-realistic computer images and animation at an affordable price (under US$1,000) for the type of sophisticated work that was possible only with mainframe and minicomputers a few years ago. Some powerful tools are Specular International's Infini-D 3.0 (M), Strata Inc's Strata Virtual (L) for real-time renderer, Macro-media's Swivel 3D Professional 2.0.4 (M) and Virtus Corp.'s Virtus VR (L). Tools from Strata and Virtus are for both Mac and PC systems.

Music software

Music is an important element of a multimedia production. Various tools are available as a MIDI (Musical Interface for Digital Instruments) sequencer, editor and performance tool that provides multitrack recording, precise editing of all musical events, etc. These include Unicorn's Performer 5.02(M) and Opcode Systems' Vision 2.0 (M) for Mac, Midisoft's Studio (M) for Windows and Turtle Beach System's Wave for Windows (M) for PCs. Digi-Design's SoundTool (M) consists of a sound accelerator card and Sound Designer II (software) which allow hours of CD-quality sound to be recorded on to a hard drive and edited with unparalleled precision.

Optical character recognition

For multimedia applications, there is a great need for text materials as well. Thus, it is important to have effective tools to be able to turn hard-copy printed texts into digital word-processing files. Optical character recognition (OCR) software is very useful for this process. An outstanding example is Caere's OmniPage Professional (M), which is an advanced OCR solution to turn printed texts into word processing files. It is available for both Mac and PC. Another competitive OCR software for Windows is Xerox's TextBridge Pro 96 (M).

Presentation and video-editing software. Many high-powered software tools are available foron-screen animation presentations with motion, sound and QuickTime, and flexible non-linear editing systems for Mac. For presentation purposes, Gold Disk's Astound and Adobe's Persuasion 3.0(M) are powerful graphic and digital video software that will produce or deliver data-intensive multimedia presentations. Macromedia's Director 4.0 (H), Adobe's Premier 4.1 (H), and Avid's VideoShop 3.0(M) are powerful tools providing an economic means of professional video editing. Director and Premier are available for both Mac and PC systems. Other PC desktop presentations include Motion Works CameraMan (L), Eduquest's Linkway 2.01 (L) and Linkway Live! (L), Lenel Systems' MultiMedia Works (L), and IBM's Storyboard Live! 2.0 (L).

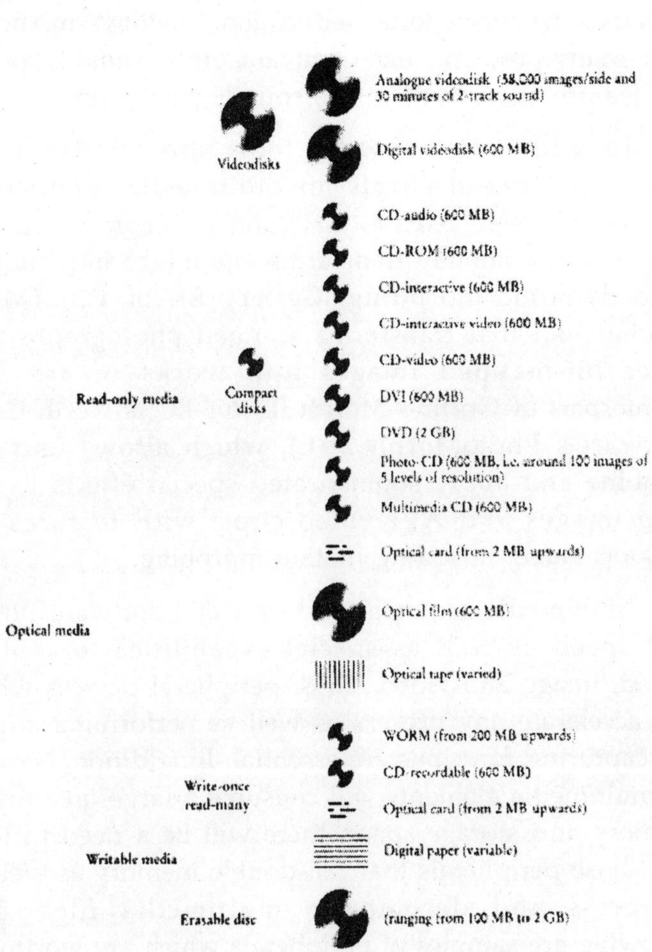

Figure 3: Types of optical media

Special effects

Like clip art and photographs for fast and easy use of still images, there are many clip media products available for immediate use of ready digital videos, such as Macromedia's ClipMedia˙ (M) with professional animation, sounds and videos arranged on CD-ROMs in various subject categories (education, business, medicine, etc.). Many products, like Olduvai Corp's Sound Clips 1.0 (L), feature an average of 100 sounds per volume.

In addition, software tools are available for producing special effects for multimedia production. One of the most used is Gryphon's Morph 2.5 (L) for Mac, which smoothly transforms one image into another with dynamic morphing. Gallery Effect 1.51 (M) is another tool that transforms scanned photographs and other bit-mapped images into works of art. The counterpart of Griffin's Morph (L) for PC is North Coast Software's PhotoMorph 2 (L), which allows users to combine and apply sophisticated special effects to bit-map images and AVI video clips, with features for desktop video, including motion morphing.

Multimedia requires hardware and software power and speed as well as special capabilities to capture sound, image and video. Thus, peripheral devices which can accelerate any process as well as performing any of the capturing functions are essential. In addition, because all multimedia elements will consume a large quantity of memory and storage space, there will be a need to look into those peripherals that can double memory as well as compress and decompress multimedia files. The following are samples of peripherals which are worthy of serious consideration.

Accelerators

Many accelerators and chargers, such as DayStarDigital's Image 040 (H), can accelerate imaging functionsup to 600%. Unfortunately these boards are generally quite expensive (over US$1,000) and are intended for high-end operations.

Audio/video controllers

IBM's M-Motion Video Adapter/A (H) for PS/2 can receive and process analogue signals from multiple external video and audio sources, and then send them to a monitor and external speakers for immediate viewing/listening in multimedia application settings. In this way, a PC can be connected directly to an analogue videodisk device and grab the analogue videos directly to integrate into multimedia applications. The Creative Labs' Sound Blaster 16 boards for PCs provide rich CD-quality stereo sound for multimedia, education, business, home and entertainment applications at affordable prices.

Digital cameras

In the last two years, several reasonably priced high-performance digital cameras have been introduced. Apple, Canon, Kodak and others have produced such digital image capture devices at a cost ranging from $350 to over $1,000. Users should acquire cameras only after studying carefully their need for digital images. These digital cameras can be connected to hardware systems using any platform. Most digital cameras function like regular cameras and therefore are mainly for capturing individual images. Another type of digital camera which can capture both colour pictures and videos is becoming quite popular. Examples include VideoLab's FlexCam (L) and Connectix's QuickCam (L). These are compatible with all leading video digitizing boards. Each is an integrated colour camera and microphone and can produce video output in both NTSC and PAL.

In addition to software, built-in hardware capabilities or addition digitizers and frame grabbers (generally these are additional peripheral boards) are required for real-time digitizing of sound, images and video. For example, Macromedia's MacRecorder Sound System (previously marketed by Farallon) includes both the digital sound recorder hardware and SoundEdit software for users to record, edit and play back live or prerecorded sounds on a Macintosh. Digital frame and video grabbers are abundant in the marketplace. For example, Radius' SpigotPower AV (M) provides full-screen, full-motion capture and playback of interlaced and non-interlaced JPEG video. It is able to capture and save full 24-bit colour data. Creative Labs' Video Blaster boards of different models can bring full-motion video sequences to a PC. Users can capture analogue video sequences at up to thirty frames per second. Generally one connects the television video recorder, and/or video camera to these boards.

Scanners

Scanners are essential for turning hard-copy texts, pictures in both positive and negative forms and films into digital files. Because of these different original formats, there are also different types of scanners. These include:

> Flat-bed scanners, such as Microtek's ScanMaker II (M) and III (H) models, that convert printed and artwork to digital files. For example, the ScanMaker III (H) is a 36-bit colour high-resolution flat-bed scanner up to 1,200 dpi. Generally, a scanner with at least 300 dpi can be quite effective for multimedia application development. Although more expensive and higher resolution drum scanners are also available, they are generally too expensive (some are over $35,000) for general-purpose use.

Slide scanners that will do the same with photographs, such as Microtek's ScanMaker 1850S (M). Film scanners, such as Microtek's ScanMaker 35t (H), that can scan any 35 mm slide in 24-bit colour mode in up to 16.7 million colours or in 8-bit grey-scale mode to capture up to 256 shades of grey.

Hand-held scanners (L) that generally provide a low-cost alternative for producing digital images for multimedia applications. However, the resolution of these scanned images is low and the images can easily be distorted. Need for mass storage in information work (archives, library and information services)

Library, information and archival work generally deals with very large quantities of information. Regardless of whether information sources are in printed or electronic formats, space is always a key issue. Mass storage is required to meet:

— The need for a large-volume digital storage system for archival management.

— The need to provide users with immediate access to the rapidly growing volume of data and information that is stored in digital information systems and is likely to be distributed on optical media in the future.

— The need to provide users with access to multimedia information quickly and interactively through the integration of technologies.

— The need to transfer a large volume of data and/or files from one system to another.

The following will discuss briefly the technologies available for mass storage and the types of storage media as well as the drives available for using these media.

Various technologies available for mass storage Traditionally libraries have used conventional media like film, microfilm and microfiche to store information materials, but they are bulky and rather expensive.

With the advent of computer and optical technologies, mass storage has shifted mostly to electronic media. There are several different technologies available for mass storage on magnetic tapes, high-density floppy disks, portable hard disks with a capacity of over 2 GB, and optical disks. But it is optical media that are the primary ones for mass storage.

Because of this, the following section will explore further the different types of optical media. Storage media: optical disks, CD-ROM, etc. The various types of optical media offer different storage densities, media formats, transfer rates, capabilities and compatibility among commercial vendors' products.

In the last decade alone, a flood of new media and applications—CD-ROM, laser videodisks, write-once and read-many devices, erasable disks, to name just a few—have been introduced, promoted and utilized. There is a wide range of optical alternatives available to provide the highest application flexibility to end-users. Optical media can be grouped into three major categories:

— Read-only media.

— Write-once and read-many.

— Erasable.

Under each of these major categories, a multitude of optical storage media can be found. For more detailed information on each of these optical media. All of them are essential for multimedia application developments.

Drive and interface

Each different kind of optical media requires an appropriate drive to be connected to a microcomputer system. Multimedia CD-ROMs have become popular products in recent years. Earlier, interactive videodisks were the popular means of presenting multimedia applications. Even today, some applications still choose videodisks as end products if quantities of still and moving images are large. For example, one side of a videodisk can store 58,000 still images and thirty minutes of video in dual sound tracks. These are huge in comparison to what can be stored digitally on a multimedia CD-ROM even with high-ratio compression. For the latter, we are talking about a few hundred digital images and less than twenty minutes of digital video in small windows. Thus, videodisk disk applications are still substantial. The major manufacturers of videodisk players are Philips, Pioneer and Sony. Each has produced several different models—industrial or general models with different playing speeds, and some with the capability of playing both NTSC (National Television System Committee) and PAL (Phase Alternation Line) disks.

CD-ROM drives

The CD-ROM drive is currently the most popular device; it can be used to play regular CD-ROMs (mostly text-based) and Photo-CDs as well as multimedia CD-ROMs. Speed is one of the most significant considerations when acquiring such a drive. In order to run a multimedia CD-ROM, the minimum requirement is a double-speed (2X) drive. However, 4-speed and even 6-speed are available in the marketplace. The 4-speed drive is very affordable and can be purchased for less then US$200 per unit in the United States.

CD recorders

WORM and erasable drives are essential for mass storage, publishing and back-up of multimedia development materials. Earlier WORM drives played discs generally holding 100 MB to 200 MB of data. The latest WORM CD medium is CD-R (CD-Recordable) which can store 600 MB of data and requires a CD recorder with appropriate software to record information on the disc according to the appropriate CD standard. For example, JVC's Personal RomMaker, Kodak's PCD Writer and Philips' CDD 522 Compact Disc Recorder are only a few samples of such CD recording devices with hardware and software solutions that allow users to premaster and master their own CD-ROMs in-house on the desktop for both PC and Mac platforms. Optical Media's TOPiX is a CD publishing system used to record information on CD. Once the information is recorded, the disc will be used in the same manner as any other CD-ROM by using a regular CD-ROM drive. It goes without saying that for multimedia application development, such CD recording devices are most useful!

Erasable drives

For multimedia work, no matter how big the size of the hard drive, one will quickly run out of storage space. Thus every multimedia product developer has some kind of device that can expand the hard drive's capacity substantially. Such devices are also used to back up the materials on the hard drive. An erasable medium is very attractive for this purpose as it can be modified and/or re-used. However, erasable optical disk technology is still not very stable, and both the medium and the drive are quite expensive. An erasable drive can cost over US$2,000. Thus, one of the more popular products has been the SyQuest drive; each SyQuest cartridge can store from 44 MB to about 200 MB of data/information. Two of the hottest products in this line now are Iomega's Zip and Zap drives, which are both easy to use and affordable. The Zip drive, which runs with its Zip disk (100 MB per disk) costs only a meagre $199 per drive and the disk is less than $20, depending on the quantity purchased (over ten will cost only $14.99 per disk). The Zap drive, with a disk capacity as big as 1 GB, costs only around $599. Because of this incredible offer, many personal computer manufacturers have decided to include a Zip drive as part of the regular system configuration.

Multimedia operating and file system Multimedia hardware and peripherals. To enter the interactive multimedia world, a minimum equipment configuration should be more than the bare minimum described earlier. It should consist of the following components:

— A computer system with a minimum of 4 MB of RAM.

— A 350 MB hard disk drive.

— A 14.4 kbps modem (fax modem would be preferable).

— A double-speed CD-ROM drive.

— A portable videotape recorder.

A fixed videotape recorder capable of being connected to a computer output either directly or through an appropriate AV card inserted into one of the bus slots in the computer. A television monitor for use during taping and playback.

— A scanner.

Additional hardware in the form of an LCD display panel or LCD projection system is highly recommended.

The minimum software configuration for using multimedia products is rather low, since most products have plug-and-play capabilities with very few requirements other than the installation processes. However, the following are varying levels of software requirements for producing simple multimedia applications:

— A basic editing software package, such as those available from Adobe, Avid, Radius and others.

— An intermediate-level software system that would include all of the above plus a freestanding audio editing software package, a two-dimensional modelling or rendering software package and a graphic/titling package such as Adobe Photoshop.

— An advanced-level software system that would include all the above plus an advanced-level three-dimensional modelling or rendering software package, and an authorware package for output to hard, floppy disk or to read/write compact disc.

The equipment cost varies greatly from one model to another, and from one configuration to another. Thus it is best to check with the vendors for current price information. However, it is safe to estimate that a PC

Pentium multimedia system can be acquired from US$1,500 to $4,000, and a Macintosh Power Mac from US$2,000 to $5,500, depending on the system model, RAM size, hard disk size, and connected peripherals. Whenever possible, efforts should be made to acquire a system with as large a RAM and hard disk storage capacity as possible. The cost of software also varies greatly, ranging from less than $100 to over $1,000. However, powerful software like Adobe Photoshop costs about $600 and Macromedia's Director about $900.

The abundant multimedia tools are to be used for creating multimedia applications. Yet how one goes about developing multimedia depends on the nature of the application and how it will be viewed and used. Although there is no multimedia development formula, the process does follow a series of basic steps. These steps include:

— Concept.

— Content and interface.

— Product.

It is impossible in a short paper like this to cover every aspect of the process, but each major step, and the subsets within each step.

Planning and design is always the most important component of any development, regardless of whether it is technology-related or not. Usually at least half to two-thirds of project effort is devoted to this phase. In other words, the better a project is planned and designed, the more likely it is that it will be successful, effective, efficient and useful. For a multimedia application, after the idea is conceived and a conceptual framework developed, the planning process will have to go into the more minute details of plans and design, so that these will lead to the successful implementation of the application development. Many questions will have to be addressed:

— What are the goals and objectives of the application?

— Who is it intended for?

— What is it going to deliver which is either not available or not sufficiently available now?

— What is the delivery platform?

— What multimedia elements will the application include?

— What are the existing information sources and which and how will these be used for the application?

— Where can help and/or contributions be found?

— What is the budget for the application, and how will it be budgeted?

— What are the environmental limitations?

— What existing multimedia tools - both hardware and software - are required?

— Who is going to do what?

— How will it be published?

— What is the target completion date?

Once these questions have been addressed, the multimedia developer can deal with all the problems and issues surfacing during both the pre-production and production periods. It is important to stress the importance of project design. This includes both the application design and interface design. Remember that an application can deal with 'gold-mine' source materials which are rich, relevant and essential, but if the presentation is not well thought out and the interactive feature of multimedia technology is not fully utilized, then the richness of the available knowledge base will not be fully exploited. On the other hand, even if the presentation of the multimedia application is well designed conceptually, it can still fail if the interface design is either poor or uninviting/confusing to the user. Few would be willing or able to visit the 'gold-mine'.

Design criteria for effective integration of different media In designing multimedia applications, it is essential to realize that the process of linking multimedia information in a hyperweb environment can be both confusing and disorienting. The following multimedia functionalities under three categories - essential, expected and desirable:

Essential	*Expected*	*Desirable*
Integration	Diversity	Programmability
Freedom	Extensibility	Orientability
Flexibility	Sociality	Guidability
Usability	Spatiality	Recreatability
Attributability	Communicability	

One needs to remember that beyond the many demanding technical elements that allow multimedia to come together, there is a sense of transcendentalness that occurs during the production process. While combining massive amounts of information, one commonly observes coincidences and encounters baffling developments. Great care must be taken to separate the intelligent realities from the illusions. Integrating the complex threads of interactive electronic communication requires an emphasis on the relationship between the designer/ producers and their reader/listener/user/viewer. New access paths to source material and new procedures for protection and licensing must be developed. Industry standards must emerge to facilitate diversity and universal connectivity.

Preparation of Multimedia Documents

After the planning, one has to determine what kind of information is to be included and published, and then prepare and process this information. Information sources can include all formats - textual, still images and motion videos, sounds and animation. This step involves information-gathering and preparation, and electronic management. The former determines the format to be chosen for inclusion, and the latter considers how to turn all the desired information to electronic forms and also how to manage them.

Data preparation and processing

Text: The existing text information can be available in both printed and electronic forms. For the printed information, all three popular ways of conversion to an electronic format - keyboarding, imaging (scanning), and optical character recognition - will be used. For the electronic files, once the delivery platform is decided, electronic text files will have to be converted for the chosen platform.

Images: Hard-copy images will have to be scanned and stored in acceptable format for multimedia applications. The most popular format is JPEG (Joint

Photographic Experts Group), but PICT (a Macintosh graphics file format, closely related to PCT and commonly supported in Macintosh format) and TIFF (Tag Image FileFormats) are also popular with multimedia application software. When multimedia is moving closely with Internet and World Wide Web applications, GIF and JPEG with a very high rate of compression are preferred. Scanned images often need to be processed and enhanced by the use of software like Adobe Photoshop.

Video: Using the video-capturing software via a video-capturing board, one can convert video sources from television, video recorder and video camera to digital video and save them in popular formats such as QuickTime movies (in both platforms), or AVI (Audio-Video Interleaved) for PC applications. The standard for digital video is MPEG (Moving Pictures Experts Group). Again, liked the scanned images, captured digital videos will have to be edited by the use of software tools like Macro-media's Director, Adobe's Premier or Avid's VideoShop.

Sound: Through the use of sound recording software and a sound recorder, sound sources from tapes, cassettes and video can be converted to digital sound files, which can also be manipulated and enhanced by means of existing tools, some of them described earlier in this paper. Data compression for digitized data, sound and fixed and moving images Non-text files consume a large amount of storage space (for example, one colour image at screen resolution can easily take up about 1 MB of disk space or more); thus the issue of size becomes very significant, and hence compression and decompression. Compression is a widely employed technique to reduce the size of large files without appreciably changing the way a viewer sees the images or digital videos or hears the sounds. Once compressed, the file must be decompressed before it can be used. Compression and decompression can be accomplished by software alone or through the use of a combination of software and hardware. Take image as an example: compression software analyses an image and finds ways to store the same amount of information using less storage space. Compression hardware usually consists of a ROM chip with built-in compression routines for faster operation, or a co-processor chip that shares the computing load with the computer's main processor. There are different levels of software compression:

— *Lossless compression:* no information lost through the compression process. In this way, the file size is generally not reduced much.

— *Lossy compression:* through the compression, some information is lost. This will reduce the file size more dramatically than the lossless one.

The most common method for compressing image is called JPEG, which is a standard way of reducing image file size that discards information which could not be detected easily by the human eye. In compressing the digital video, the standard is MPEG. MPEG is an industry standard for moving images that uses interframe compression (or frame differencing) as well as compression within frames. There are different MPEG standards, such as MPEG I, which optimizes for data rates in the 1 to 1.5 MB/sec range (the common transfer rate of CD-ROM drives and T-1 communications links), and MPEG II, which optimizes for data rates above the 5 MB/sec rate (specifically for broadcast video applications).

There are many compelling reasons for using multimedia for education, training, information delivery, business, entertainment, etc. First of all, the power of pictures is enormous. Only recently, with the advent of multimedia technologies, have we been able to tap the undeniable power of visual images and other non-textual information sources. But equally appealing for multimedia technology is the power of interactivity - a concept extended from hypertext as discussed in the introductory section. Through the ages, information has been presented and absorbed in a linear fashion. Interactive multimedia brings the incredible freedom to explore a subject area with fast links to related topics.

Storage and use of digital data and documents

Mass storage and storage media were discussed above. Currently, most digital data have been stored on optical media such as CD-ROMs, CD-Rs, and Photo-CDs, and most interactive multimedia products are produced and distributed as multimedia CD-ROMs, or interactive laser disks. The portability of these products, specifically those on CD-ROMs,is great.

When multimedia applications are stored or published on an optical medium such as CD-ROM, they can be distributed easily for intra-organization-aluse. For a few copies, in-house CD-R technology can be used to produce the CD-ROMs. When published formally, whether commercially or not, the CD-ROMs or laser disks will be mastered by companies like 3M, DMI, Philips, etc. The cost of production generally is around US$1,000 to $1,500, with an additional cost for each unit ranging from $1.50 to over $10 depending on the quantity of the order.

Commercially produced CD-ROMs are generally published and distributed much like books, and they will be properly packaged with an attractive graphically designed cover, and publicized for sale either directly from the publisher or via distributors, or both. Currently over 10,000 multimedia products have been published.

Use and reuse of stored documents. When information source materials are in digital form and stored electronically on a digital medium, they can be used and reused for any suitable purpose. They can be retrieved easily to answer an information inquiry, used to create multimedia applications, or used for resource-sharing in either a network environment or for electronic publishing on the Internet or the World Wide Web. The important thing is being digital!

We are very much aware of the need to back up electronic data with additional copies of floppy disks, backup tapes, Zip or Zap disks, or CD-Rs. It is important to add that optical media, specifically something like CD-ROM, tend to give an impression that they are the ultimate conservation medium with no possibility of data loss. Actually this is not the case.

The lifetime of optical media such as CD-ROM, suggesting thirty years or more. However, it is difficult to verify the accuracy of these predictions at this time. All electronic media have the possibility of wearing out, and thus it is important to make duplicate copies in order to avoid data loss due to wear and tear. Optical media such as CD-ROMs and laser disks should be used carefully to prevent possible scratches on the surface. Non-optical electronic media, such as magnetic tape and floppy disks, should be stored under proper temperature and humidity control.

As for the storage of the source materials, it is important to continue finding the best ways to preserve and conserve them regardless of whether they are electronic or not. Most images and videos originally came from film or microfilm sources. These should be kept using the best conservation methods, since electronic image-capturing - still or moving -cannot currently produce images of as high a resolution as those on films and microfilms. Thus, as tech-nologiesadvance, there will be need still to reuse the source materials in order to produce new images of higher resolution.

Emerging Technologies and Fure Trends

As the use of multimedia will continue to expand, it is fair to expect that more tools in every category outlined earlier will be introduced with more functionalities and at lower cost. Thus, creating multimedia applications will be easier as time goes on.

With the explosive development and use of the Internet and the World Wide Web, and the exponential growth in use of Web browsers like Netscape, we are witnessing the exciting marriage of multimedia and the Internet/World Wide Web in a way never possible before.

Instead of Web publishing with mainly still images, graphics and text, now virtual reality and Web publishing with avitars are being introduced by all major companies like Netscape and Microsoft. The forthcoming versions of Web browsers, like the 3.0 version of Netscape, are filled with all kinds of features and capabilities to present digital videos, sound, animations, etc.

In addition to the increasing capability to include all types of multimedia publishing on the Web, emerging technologies will enable exciting live multimedia Internet publishing as well as real-time fast delivery of multimedia broadcasting onto the desktop.

A good example of live multimedia Internet publishing is the '24 Hours in Cyberspace' event on 8 February 1996. On that day, Rick Smolan, producer of award-winning multimedia products such as From Alice to Ocean and Passage to Vietnam, pulled off the most ambitious Internet event ever undertaken by deploying hundreds of speed global network so that texts, images and even voices can be transmitted from one part of the world to another.

At the same time, however, nationalism becomes a stronger theme: building national collections, serving as an information source for national government, and collecting national history or culture are of concern now more than ever.

The use of multimedia and Knowledge Navigator permit the delivery of this information, as well as information from other countries, to citizens' homes, schools and offices. In this kind of environment, printed information sources, such as books, journals and archival materials, meet a highly competitive technology.

Digital information sources become essential. The enormous possibilities for combining multimedia and the Internet/World Wide Web together have also been demonstrated. At the click of an icon, to jump to any national library or other major library in a given country instantly. Access can also be gained to information on the award-winning multimedia product, The First Emperor of China.

As long as the resources are in digital format - regardless of whether they are still images, video or sound - and are on a Web server, one can obtain this information almost instantly from anywhere in the world. A graphic directory of over thirty national library homepages around the world can be found in Chen. This is an exciting time!

Telecommunication Technologies

Telecommunication technologies have been changing the nature of personal and business transactions since the commercialization of the telegraph in the 1840s. The synergy between information service providers and telecommunication carriers was recognized in the United States as early as 1867, when an exclusive contract between Associated Press and Western Union was signed. The impact of telecommunication control on information dissemination has been researched by many authors since then. But telecommunication is more than a means of information dissemination; it also provides information users with a means of searching out and interacting with information. With the emergence of digital computers, information became represented more frequently in digital format, so that it became possible to search databases and transfer information from remote locations. This trend began with large corporations and their centralized databases and has since permeated many aspects of life in industrialized countries, especially with the emergence of the World Wide Web on the Internet.

Since the 1980s the use of computer-based information retrieval systems has become popular with many libraries and information service providers. In many public libraries, computer-based catalogues have replaced their traditional card counterparts, offering capabilities such as simultaneous access by multiple users, keyword searching and remote access. With the emergence of the CD-ROM, much original information has become accessible over computer networks. This paper addresses many of the key questions surrounding the basic technology and its application to the information industry.

This section defines and describes the requirements for the most common forms of services in use by information service providers. Many of these require telecommunication technologies, although analogous services are often available without this technological infrastructure. In subsequent sections, the commonly used implementations and infrastructure requirements will be described.

Remote access is a user's ability to make use of an information provider's services at a distance. This is desirable because it enables information service providers to economize their operations (through appropriate centralization) without eliminating access for distant users. Thus, a large population of users can be served without extensive need to travel.

Traditionally, remote access has involved the use of postal or telephone inquiries. This method has a number of both advantages and disadvantages over electronic information technology solutions. These can be summarized under three main headings: cost, training and speed. Traditional remote-access technology is more labour-intensive but less capital-intensive; electronic technologies are more capital-intensive and require skilled 'backroom' personnel, but fewer information specialists. Traditional remote-access technology requires virtually no user training but considerable information-specialist training; electronic remote access requires user training as well as computer professionals. Finally, traditional remote access is very slow by comparison to electronic access.

Electronic remote access generally requires users' data terminals to connect to an information service provider's serving computer. This connection may be handled via a modem and telephone lines or a public or private packet data network. When connected to the service provider's computer, users are able to interact with the system as though they were local to the service provider's computer. In the Internet, the Telnet service is an example of this service type; in Open Systems Interconnection (OSI) systems, this service would be the Virtual Terminal (VT) service. Electronic remote access also implies a reliable, high-quality telecommunication infrastructure.

Remote access implies that the information being sought remains at the server when the session is over. If any information is retained by the user, such as notes or printouts, it is generally a small fraction of the information and is not kept in digital form. If the user wishes to acquire pieces of information of a larger size, then a file transfer operation is usually preferred. Traditionally, this might involve the acquisition, either in person or via the postal system, of books, journals, articles, etc. This analogy is not perfect because electronic file transfer allows pieces of information to be transferred that may not exist in print or other traditional media.

While file transfers can be accomplished using remote-access services (if the user's device has sufficient capabilities), this operation is limited and not efficient. Using file transfer mechanisms instead enables the efficient transfer of both text and non-text characters without the insertion of special characters. Furthermore, most file transfer protocols have additional error-checking functionality built into them. Thus, information transfers can take place completely and efficiently. Commonly used file transfer protocols are ftp for the Internet, and File Transfer, Access and Management (FTAM) for OSI-based information systems. Electronic messaging

The most common form of this technology is electronic mail, although it need not be limited to this. The objective in electronic messaging technologies is to allow the efficient transfer of messages of all kinds between the users of a network (humans as well as machines). Recent research has taken a broader view of this question and considers the use of still, animated and video images, as well as audio, graphics and text, to pass messages. In this broader context, then, 'voice mail' is also a form of electronic messaging.

Numerous standards exist for electronic mail. By far the most widely implemented standard is Internet mail. Designed to support the transfer of text files only, this standard has been modified to support non-text information, such as images and binary files, through the Multimedia Internet Mail Extensions (MIME) system.

As with most Internet standards, these represent relatively limited, although highly functional, solutions to specific problems. In response to the more comprehensive needs of the user community, the International

Telecommunications Union (ITU) developed the X.400 series of standards. These standards represent a systematic and comprehensive approach to meeting the needs of electronic mail users. The implementation is much more complex, hence costly, than Internet mail; as a result, it has yet to be adopted as widely.

Database searching is an application that is increasingly network-based. The databases that are searched were organized historically as a single database on a single machine. This is gradually changing with the introduction of distributed databases, in which the database is logically a single database but is physically distributed over several computers. Many of the CD-ROM-based databases seem to exhibit this characteristic, although they are frequently a collection of independent databases that must be queried separately.

Traditionally, database searches have been performed by attaching to the computer that houses the database a remote-access protocol (such as Telnet) and executing queries on the database. In recent years, searches based on the American National Standards Institution/National Information Standards Organization (ANSI/NISO) standard Z39.50 and Z39.59 have begun eliminating the need for users to connect directly with, and therefore have accounts on, remote database machines. These standards allow for the delivery of query results to an end-user using a standardized remote-access protocol. This mode of database searching is more efficient and flexible for both the network and the database machines, so it can be expected to be implemented more widely in the future.

On the World Wide Web, search engines (such as Lycos and Yahoo) have emerged to facilitate information searching in this decentralized environment. These systems create an index of Web pages that can be searched. The results of these searches are brief descriptions of a page and the links to those pages. These are different from traditional database-searching systems in that the search engines must actively compile and update information, since the World Wide Web is perhaps the ultimate example of a distributed and decentralized database in which no attempt at consistency is made.

Electronic Data Interchange (EDI) is the direct computer-to-computer exchange of information. While this is a very general definition, EDI is really focused on the exchange of information normally provided in business documents such as bills of lading, purchase orders and invoices. With the emergence of EDI standards, such as EDIFACT and ANSI X.12,EDI has gained significant popularity. When both partners in a transaction use compatible EDI systems, the benefits of using this approach over traditional mechanisms include cost savings, speed, error reduction and security. EDI standards define specific transaction sets that in turn define the way in which information is to be communicated; a transaction set is the equivalent of a form in a paper-based communication system. A transaction set must have certain content and format specifications to ensure that both parties can interpret the information correctly. Just as a form has 'boxes' for information, a transaction set has segments that contain defined data elements.

computer systems that are interconnected by telecommunication technology. This section will present an overview of the telecommunication technologies that are relevant to the user needs defined above.

Physical infrastructure

In broad terms, the physical infrastructure consists of three components: cables, switching systems and signalling systems. Cables are used to interconnect devices, switches are used to route calls through the network (over cables), and signalling systems allow network devices (such as telephones and switches) to exchange information. This section will summarize each of these components.

Cables

The physical infrastructure consists of a combination of cables and their associated outside plant. The primary types of cables in use are twisted pair, optical fibre and coaxial. Twisted-pair cables consist of two insulated wires twisted together; these types of cable are most often used to connect the subscriber's equipment with the telephone network. Optical fibre is used most often for high-capacity transmission within the network, that is, to connect large subscribers. Finally, coaxial cables are used both within the telephone network and for high-bandwidth transmission to subscribers' premises, as in cable television applications. The former use is being replaced by fibre optics, while the latter use is fairly well developed and embedded.

Wireless infrastructures have been important since the 1940s, but the locus of their use has changed. Early non-broadcast uses of wireless were focused on interconnecting telephone company facilities using point-to-point microwave systems or satellite-based systems. The emergence of fibre optics as a technically and economically viable technology in the 1980s has stimulated the replacement of existing wireless facilities of this kind and limited the new installations to situations where cable is not feasible. Today, the use of wireless is focused more on connecting 'nomadic' or 'untethered' subscribers. Cellular, General System for Mobile (GSM) and Personal Communications System (PCS) systems are examples of this use.

Switching

While many other elements do exist, the other key element of the infrastructure is switches. Switches serve to interconnect subscribers with each other, either directly (if they are local) or via other switches and interoffice transmission facilities (if they are not local). In order to function properly, the devices on the network must pass certain information to each other, such as 'off-hook' and 'on-hook' (which corresponds to 'busy' and 'idle') and the dialled number. The mechanism by which this information is passed is the signalling system.

Switching technology has undergone a radical evolution since the early days of telephony. The simplest (and also the earliest) switches consisted of a panel of electrical jacks, one for each subscriber and trunk (as an inter office transmission channel is called). A human operator connected subscribers with each other (or to trunks) using patch cords with plugs on both ends. In the

United States, these manual systems were gradually replaced with electromechanical switches during the early part of the twentieth century. In the 1960s, these electromechanical switches began to be replaced by digital electronic switches. In other countries, this investment/ replacement cycle may not be consistent with the experience of the United States.

Signalling technology also has changed. The earliest signalling consisted of sharply rapping the transmitter to get the attention of the operator or called party. This was soon replaced by a combination of magneto and bell. The destination number was originally spoken into the telephone by the caller to the operator, who would complete the call. As automated switches and digit dialling came into service, these signalling functions were replaced by in-band techniques. As the network grew in size, and as electronic switches were introduced, it became possible to introduce out-of-band signalling systems, such as Signalling System 7, that allow faster call setup and the implementation of new services.

Out-of-band signalling systems, like Signalling System 7, are implemented by creating a packet-switched data communications network, and treating the voice switches and service providers as users of the network. The messages and protocols are standardized and optimized for the rapid exchange of short messages between these devices. Many ISDN (Integrated Services Digital Network) systems require a Signalling System 7 infrastructure.

speech is converted to electrical energy by a microphone. Microphones create an electrical signal that is modulated in proportion to the strength and characteristics of the speech energy. Commercially available microphones always generate an electrical signal that is continuous in time; such a signal is called an analogue signal. Voice telecommunications were transmitted in analogue format throughout the telephone network until the 1960s.

As an electrical signal is transmitted over distance, it is subject to certain deleterious effects, most notably noise and distortion. Noise consists of all unwanted electrical signals that are added to the signal in the transmission channel. Distortion is generally due to imperfections in the design of transmission equipment. Neither noise nor distortion can be avoided. Many types of noise are additive; that is, they are added to the signal in the transmission channel. As the distance increases, more noise and distortion is added, so that, as a rule, the signal deteriorates as distance increases. In an analogue system, the noise and distortion cannot be removed from the signal at the receiver because of the continuous nature of both the signal, noise and distortion.

In the 1940s researchers at Bell Laboratories developed methods by which an analogue signal could be sampled in such a way that the samples could be used to reconstruct an accurate facsimile of the original signal. When a signal is sampled in this way, it becomes possible to represent these samples by a number that is proportional to the strength of the analogue electrical signal at the time it was sampled. Since this number can be represented in any number system, the engineers chose the binary number system. In the binary system, the number takes the form of multiple digits (eight, in the case of telephony) comprising only ones and zeros.

The primary advantage of representing a signal and transmitting it in this way is that the essential information contained in the signal is in discrete levels rather than in continuous levels. Thus, when the signal with the added noise and distortion arrives at the receiver, the receiver can remove much of the noise because it can reconstruct the signal that was transmitted based on the discrete levels (if the system was properly engineered). It is possible to engineer a digital transmission system with very low noise levels. Since binary numbers are in the format that is natural for computational devices, it is also possible to engineer a reliable transmission system through long and noisy channels using sophisticated signal processing and error detection and correction techniques. The spacecraft that send pictures to Earth from distant planets provide an example of such a demanding environment.

Data and voice communications

When speech is rendered as a digital signal, the distinction between voice signals and data signals begins to become arbitrary, since neither the switches nor the network equipment can distinguish between them. None the less, the services that are constructed on the network infrastructure to support voice applications and data applications are different. These different applications place different demands on the network infrastructure. Voice communications, whether analogue or digital, historically have been implemented by dedicating a portion of the network capacity to a call for the duration of that call.

No other call can use the bandwidth dedicated to that call. For data applications, this arrangement was wasteful, since the line was idle for a large fraction of the time. Communications between computers are frequently 'bursty', that is, communication between devices occurs infrequently but when it does the devices need a fast connection for modest quantities of data. As a result, engineers developed mechanisms for sharing a line's bandwidth among several simultaneous but different calls so that the line would be utilized more efficiently.

The most widely adopted technique for this uses a set of technologies referred to collectively as packet switching. In packet switching, several data streams are bundled and transmitted together by sending a small portion of each data stream at a time in the form of a 'packet'. Each packet contains the address of the destination computer as well as other necessary control information, so that the packet switches (special purpose computers in the data communications network) have the information to handle each packet. The packet switches collect traffic from many computers and determine how to direct each packet so that it reaches its destination (a function called routing).

While packet-switched networks clearly provided a more economical solution for data communications applications, packets can arrive with a variable delay because all facilities in the network are shared by all packets in the network. Although this is not troublesome for most data applications, it can pose difficulties when traffic, such as voice traffic, is routed through packet networks. New network technologies, such as those based on the Asynchronous Transfer Mode (ATM), are seeking to solve these difficulties so that a single network infrastructure can be constructed for all major telecommunications applications.

Integrated services digital network (ISDN) ISDN is an approach to extend the digitization of the telephone network to the user's telephone. It is defined by a set of ITU standards that were developed in large part during the 1980s. Today, these original services are known as Narrowband ISDN, or N-ISDN. In recent years, the ISDN concept has been extended to highspeed services under the auspices of Broadband ISDN (or B-ISDN). This section will focus on N-ISDN, since those services today are defined and supported by commercially available equipment and services.

ISDN goes beyond a simple definition of a digital signalling and transmission standard for the local loop (which connects the user's telephone with the telephone switch). It defines an architecture for the delivery of a comprehensive set of integrated services over an end-to-end digital architecture. This architecture includes the standards for the necessary hardware, communications protocols and software functionality.

From a user's point of view, the most common N-ISDN services that can be purchased are the Basic Rate Interface (BRI) and Primary Rate Interface (PRI) services. Residential subscribers are most likely to purchase the BRI service, since it consists of the digital equivalent of two voice lines and a data line. In digital terms, each of the two voice lines is a channel with a bit rate of 64,000 bits per second (a 64 kbps channel, in telecommunications jargon). In ISDN terminology, channels that carry information at 64 kbps are called 'bearer' channels (or B-channels). The BRI signalling channel (data or D-channel) has a 16 kbps bit rate. The D-channel is used to provide services to the subscriber, including basic services such as call setup. Because of its configuration, BRI ISDN is often referred to as a '2B + D' configuration because it consists of two B-channels and a D-channel.

For large users, such as businesses, a collection of BRI channels may not be ideal as they would lack flexibility. Such organizations would normally opt to purchase a Primary Rate Interface or PRI service. Unlike BRI, users under PRI can choose several channel configurations. Thus, PRI users (in the United States) might choose a 23 B + D service, a H0 + 17B + D service, or others. Users must negotiate the specifics of the interface with their service provider. Much more could be said about ISDN in terms of its functionality and its role in organizations. In brief, ISDN provides users with the capability of true end-to-end digitial connectivity with other users and service providers. Furthermore, ISDN provides much higher data rates than can be achieved using modems, with the possibility of having value-enhancing services integrated with the transport.

ISDN's bearer and highspeed channels provide basic transport for a user's voice and data. Functionally, this is similar to the traditional analogue channel provided by telecommunication service providers (although the equipment varies). When computers are communicating, new demands are placed on both the network and on the end-user devices—demands that do not exist in voice communications.

As computer networks evolved, many more problems had to be addressed in addition to that of 'bursty' traffic. These include error control, synchronization, security and information representation. It also became apparent that standards were important in computer networks. Two major groups of standards have emerged for computer networks - the standards consistent with the OSI Reference Model and developed by the ITU and the International Standards Organization (ISO), and the standards that emerged out of the ARPANET project in the United States, which are referred to as the Internet Standards.

Open systems interconnection (OSI)

The OSI Reference Model and its associated standards (generally referred to as OSI standards) emerged in the late 1970s. The origins of this movement are complex, but include user frustration with incompatibility between large system vendors and concern among the smaller of the large system vendors about the dominance of one company, IBM.

The OSI Reference Model is a systematic approach to the generic data communications problem. It organizes communication in seven layers, each of which is assigned specific functionality. The bottom three layers (1-3) are network-related layers in that they explicitly involve network components. The upper layers (4-7) are end-to-end, and do not involve network components. Specifically, the data communications function is organized as follows:

Physical layer (1): Standards that relate to the physical and electrical interconnection of computing or networking devices, and standards related to the encoding and physical transmission of bits over a communications medium.

Link layer (2): Standards that relate to the transmission of information on a single medium. This includes error control, framing, synchronization and local addressing.

Network layer (3): Standards related to the transmission of information across several links and nodes. This includes global addressing and routing.

Transport layer (4): Standards related to the transport of information from end to end over a network. This may include multiplexing of a connection between several user processes and end-to-end error control.

Session layer (5): Standards that define naming and control for multiple connections associated with a single user process.

Presentation layer (6): Standards that are concerned with the representation of information.

Application layer (7): Standards that define protocols to support higher-level user functions.

Internationally, one of the most important data communications standards is the X.25 developed by the ITU. The X.25 standard defines the interface between a user's equipment (Data Terminal Equipment, or DTE) and the network (Data Communications Equipment, or DCE) at the network, link and physical layers of the OSI Reference Model. The X.25 standard is formally limited to speeds of 64 kbps and lower, although higher-speed implementations can sometimes be found. X.25 uses the High speed Data Link Control (HDLC) protocol at the link layer and the X.21 physical layer connection.

Since the X.25 Packet Layer Protocol (PLP) operates at Layer 3 of the OSI Reference Model, it must use globally unique addresses: X.25 uses the X.121 global addressing scheme developed by the ITU. Since X.25 only defines the interface between DTE and DCE, it does not define the manner in which data are handled within a packet network. In fact, different commercial networks use various protocols and network control techniques internally. X.25 does not make specific statements about the operation of a packet network; it merely addresses the interfaces to the network.

X.25 is a connection-oriented network protocol because the protocol requires that a virtual circuit be established in the network before information can be transferred. A virtual circuit is a route through the network that all packets between the users will follow. It is a virtual circuit because it is not dedicated to the two parties, as it would be in a telephone connection; it merely behaves as though it were, even though the physical bandwidth is shared among many users.

X.25 assumes a relatively unreliable network infrastructure from the point of view of bit errors. Thus, error checking and correcting is done on each link as it passes through the network. This process turns out to be very time-consuming, limiting the effective throughput of X.25 networks. As networks have improved over the last twenty-five years with the introduction of optical fibre and digital transmission, this performance penalty has become increasingly apparent, resulting in technologies such as frame relay, which forgo link-by-link error checking in favour of end-to-end error checking.

X.400 and X.500 standards

ITU's X.400 series of standards provides for a comprehensive approach to electronic mail services. It gives service providers a broad range of services that can be offered to their customers. This richness comes at the expense of ease of implementation and product cost, factors that have delayed the implementation and adoption of products based on the X.400 series of standards. X.400 is a series of standards because it consists of a number of distinct, albeit interrelated, elements. These elements include User Agents (UAs), Message Transfer Agents (MTAs) and several service elements, as well as the protocols by which these elements communicate with one another. The message body can contain information in text, facsimile, video, image, telex, videotex and other formats. The X.500 series of standards is designed to support the development of directory services. A directory service is a system-level capability that allows users to find the 'symbolic name' (or address) of a user or a service. Broadly speaking, a directory service supports not only the binding of a symbolic name with an entity (such as a user or a resource), but also allows for the management of that information in a systematic and structured way.

The developers of the Transmission Control Protocol/Internet Protocol (TCP/IP) suite originally solved this problem in a decentralized way by using the Domain Name System (DNS). X.500 considered the directory problem from a global and commercial perspective, and in the light of experience with X.25. Thus, they developed a hierarchical system that allows a system of locally maintained Directory Service Agents (DSAs) to be tied together into a logical tree structure. A DSA communicates with as many other DSAs as necessary, using the standard protocols defined by X.500, to resolve requests from an attached Directory User Agent (DUA).

TCP/IP protocols

The TCP/IP protocols, referred to above, are an

important suite of protocols for data communications, developed under the auspices of the United States Department of Defense. These protocols have gained considerable commercial popularity and are the foundation of the Internet. Unlike the ITU and ISO standards, the TCP/IP-based protocols evolved through a collegial, informal process that emphasized working implementations. As a result, these protocols are often focused on a 'simple' solution to a specific problem without considering (and sometimes explicitly ignoring) broader functionality and systematic design. Despite these shortcomings, these protocols always produce working prototypes that may be (and often are) adapted for use in commercial products.

The TCP/IP protocol suite consists of a set of lower-layer protocols (often Local Area Network standards such as Ethernet and Token Ring), a net-work-layer protocol (Internet Protocol, or IP), a transport-layer protocol (such as Transmission Control Protocol, or TCP), and application protocols (for example, Simple Mail Transfer Protocol, smtp; File Transfer Protocol, ftp; and a virtual terminal protocol, Telnet). This approach completely omits the session and presentation layers. Unlike the X.25 packet-layer protocol (which is connection-oriented), IP is connectionless.

In a connectionless protocol, no virtual circuit is established at the outset; instead, each packet contains the source and destination addresses of the end-users, and each packet is routed through the network independently. As a result, packets may take different paths through the network and arrive out of order. The network provides no guarantees to the end-users, leaving error control to them. IP provides global addressing (but not via X.121). The number of available IP addresses has become limited owing to the structure of IP addressing and the explosive growth of the Internet.

A new version of IP (IP version 6) is due to be released in the near future to tackle that problem. The most commonly used transport layer, TCP, is connection-oriented and provides end-to-end error control as well as flow control. Given the military environment that was assumed when TCP and IP were developed, the combinations of protocols make sense. IP is very resistant to node and line failures, since the connectionless packets automatically find an available path to the destination. TCP ensures that messages arrive error-free at the destination in a way that does not excessively congest the network.

The TCP/IP set of protocols has been a favourite of many academic researchers because it is extraordinarily flexible and amenable to experimentation. As a result, new concepts and services, such as the gopher information retrieval protocol and the World Wide Web concept (with its associated protocols and standards) are able to emerge quickly and easily.

Governments and international organizations have been intimately involved in telecommunication from its inception. The United States Government financed Samuel F. B. Morse's experimental telegraph line between Baltimore (Maryland) and Washington, D.C., in 1837. In most countries the government soon entered the business by building networks and providing telegraph (and later telephone) services. As telegraph (and later telephone) systems expanded in Europe, it soon became necessary to interconnect separate national systems.

This interconnection imperative motivated the development of technical standards as well as guidelines for negotiating the terms and conditions of interconnection. Out of this need, the predecessor of the ITU was born. It did not take long for this need for interconnection to expand beyond Europe. With the arrival of the telephone, the charter of the ITU expanded beyond telegraphy, just as its charter would later be expanded to include radio transmission.

Governmental roles

Government plays several important roles in telecommunication, depending in large measure on whether the service provider is public or private. If it is public (that is, either a government agency or owned by the government), then government provides financing for the infrastructure. If it is private, the role of government falls more into motivating infrastructure development and regulation of private firms. Note that the term 'public carrier' refers to a carrier whose services are generally available to all, whether publicly or privately owned. One of the important roles of governmental and international organizations has been to finance the development of telecommunication infrastructures. This has ranged from special projects (as in the Morse example cited above) to complete infrastructure development, as with governmental Post, Telegraph and Telephone (PTT) organizations. Internationally, the World Bank and the International Monetary Fund (IMF) have become involved in the financial support of telecommunication infrastructure building in developing countries.

Regulation

In countries where the telecommunication service provider is private (an increasingly common occurrence), regulation is often necessary. Regulation is particularly important in situations where no viable competitor exists to prevent monopolistic pricing by the service provider. Governments must usually establish a credible regulatory capability as they look to privatize their telecommunication operators. The regulatory body must be independent of the service providers and serves the functions of preventing 'abusive' pricing, ensuring the economic viability of the service provider, and providing a stable legal and economic framework for telecommunication to enable the service providers to engage in long-term planning.

Regulation frequently takes the form of tariffs: A tariff defines a service as well as establishing the price of the service. As common carriers, many telecommunication service providers are obliged to apply the tariffs uniformly to all persons or parties requesting the service. Since the underlying cost of the service varies by customer, this averaging implies an implicit subsidy from the low cost-of-service customers to high cost-of-service customers.

As competition is introduced into telecommunication markets, these implicit subsidies (and hence the averaging strategy implicit in tariffs) become harder to sustain. This occurs because the relatively high-tariffed prices for low cost-of-service customers presents a market opportunity for new entrants. Regulation may also take the form of rules and standards. Unlike tariffs, which have explicitly economic subject-matter, rules and standards seek to restrict the behaviour of firms. Rules and standards can govern technical matters (radio broadcast, for example, and the ways in which different carriers must interconnect) or structural matters (for example, how firms must separate regulated business from non-regulated business, and which markets are open to competitive entry). Although these rules are often not explicitly economic, they can frequently have profound economic implications.

International regulations have been set forth by the ITU and tend to focus on technical standards and mechanisms for co-operation between interconnecting carriers. The ITU has not engaged in price regulation of service providers, although it has established a set of structures to facilitate the creation of international tariffs and periodic settlements between carriers.

The establishment and operation of transnational communication links poses some special problems. While the ITU provides useful frameworks to facilitate this, many of the details must be worked out through bilateral negotiations between the countries involved. While there is a significant precedent for most negotiations, special problems can sometimes arise. These include landing rights for cable or satellite systems; accounting and settlements rates and procedures; facilities ownership; and telecommunication market structure issues, such as public versus private and competitive versus monopoly. Governments have taken active roles in defining these issues, although there is a clear worldwide trend toward private ownership and competitive markets (and away from public ownership and monopoly service provision).

When telecommunication is provided by the government or by a government-owned firm, representation on international bodies and the status of the carriers is straightforward. With a privately owned carrier, or a multitude of privately owned carriers, this becomes more difficult. While the representation on international bodies, particularly the ITU, remains the same, the way in which international regulations are enforced and the way in which national policy vis-à-vis international telecommunication is made become more difficult. While each country with competitive, private carriers has developed different strategies for this, the general approach is relatively constant: private carriers with international links must agree to abide by ITU regulations by registering as a Registered Private Operating Agency (RPOA) and by collaborative development of public policies through national advisory councils of the foreign ministry.

Multinational corporations

Multinational corporations are often advanced users of a country's telecommunication infrastructure. These corporations normally do not have the goal of enhancing a country's infrastructure; rather, they are interested in the efficient operation of their global enterprise. Multinational corporations were most frequently the first users of technologies such as X.25, Frame Relay and EDI, for example. But multinational firms can have a bigger impact.

As a large and advanced user, a multinational can command significant investment by the public network service provider because the multinational offers a future stream of revenues to justify that investment, and also because it has the means and technology to bypass the public carrier, if necessary, to ensure that its communication needs are met. While the bypass threat can be mitigated to some extent by the use of 'landing rights' and licensing, the use of these measures may be detrimental to further investments by multinationals. Once the infrastructure investments are made, many users can take advantage of the advanced services, since it is unlikely that the multinational will consume the entire capacity of the carrier. The multinational, then, can provide a stimulus for infrastructure development that can assist a country in further economic development. From a public policy perspective, then, a multinational can pose significant challenges to the status quo and to public policy goals. The needs of multinationals have stimulated the move to privatization and the entry of competition as mechanisms to meet their needs.

The focused infrastructure investments needed to support a multinational's needs can lead to conflicts with social equity concerns inherent in universal service policy goals. This conflict is particularly acute if annual investments are fixed, requiring the carrier to defer other investments to meet the needs of the multinational user.

Telecommunication is a 'standards-intensive' industry by its very nature: Thus, an important role of governments and international organizations is to foster the establishment of standards. There are many ways in which standards may be set and many organizational structures within which standards may be developed. Originally the ITU, as a treaty organization, was created very much to serve the needs of public telecommunication networks, while ISO was more focused on meeting the needs of equipment, system and software manufacturers and vendors. The Internet Engineering Task Force (IETF), the body within which standards for the Internet are developed, is loosely organized and informal. The traditional distinctions between these organizations are blurring and a good deal of cooperation takes place among them.

The two most visible standard-setting organizations in the telecommunication business are the ITU and ISO; hence, only those will be profiled below. These profiles are very brief; more detailed information can be found on the World Wide Web.

International Telecommunications Union (ITU)

The ITU, a Specialized Agency of the UnitedNations, is the primary focus for international cooperation in telecommunication. As a treaty organization, the recommendations and regulations of the ITU carry considerable weight. It dates back to 1865, and became a Specialized Agency of the United Nations in 1947. In 1992, the ITU was reorganized, and has been aggressively pursuing procedural reforms to accelerate the development of technical standards. In general terms, the mission of the ITU is to facilitate international telecommunication, and its standards development activities are concentrated on fostering that mission. As a result, the ITU has been active in developing standards for radio transmission (and coordinating frequency usage), digital and analogue telephone systems, telegraph and telex, and selected data communications standards. In the domain of data communications, the focus has been on those standards of interest to public network operators, including X.25, Frame Relay and X.400.

Telecommunication standards are developed within the ITU-T. The actual work of standards development is not funded by the ITU; rather, the 'volunteers' who prepare the documents that define the standards are supported by telephone carriers, industrial organizations and other interested parties. The ITU provides a framework and organizational support for these activities.

International Standards Organization (ISO). Unlike the ITU, ISO is not a treaty organization. Its purpose is to achieve worldwide agreement on international standards - a purpose with a much larger scope than just telecommunication or information systems standards. For example, ISO sets standardsin areas such as Fire Safety, Plastics, and Information and Documentation. Unlike the ITU, ISO is a federation of national standards bodies, governmental or non-governmental. As a result, industry has a strong voice and the right to vote.

The Internet

In a remarkably short time, the Internet has evolved from an academic curiosity to a mass medium. It has been heralded as the basis of economic salvation for developing nations, as a new scholarly communications system and even as an entertainment alternative to television. However, the Internet has also thrown into relief controversial issues relating to censorship and freedom of expression, pornography and intellectual property rights that have profound ramifications for both individuals and nation-states. This chapter describes and seeks to explain the phenomenon that is the Internet.

The earliest experiments in what later became the Internet began in 1966 with the United States Department of Defense Advanced Research Projects Agency

(DARPA). The first nodes in the resultant ARPANET were created in 1969. In 1977, the TCP/IP (Transmission Control Protocol/Internet Protocol) protocols that underlay the Internet were demonstrated for the first time. In 1986, the National Science Foundation (NSF) created the first NSFNET backbone and allowed regional networks, mostly supporting universities, to feed into this backbone.

By 1990, the Internet was supporting commercial activities. Even after all this growth and development, the same basic TCP/IP protocols remain in use and still serve to unify the Internet. In March 1989, the first World Wide Web (WWW) proposal was elaborated and circulated at the European Laboratory for Particle Physics (CERN) in Geneva, Switzerland, and in November 1990 the first prototype Web browser was created.

Growth

The most comprehensive and regularly administered survey of Internet-connected computers, or hosts, is the Internet Domain Survey. The number of Internet hosts from 1981 to 1995, is based on this survey. From the data, it can be seen that the number of host computers on the Internet doubles approximately annually. Additional statistics on Internet growth are provided by the Internet Society, and Matrix Information and Directory Services. The number of computers on the World Wide Web, currently the most popular portion of the Internet, is doubling every four or five months. The number of electronic mail messages sent over the Internet is doubling approximately every year. As of January 1996, there were an estimated 9,472,000 host computers on the

Internet. International growth is highly variable. There is also considerable variation in Internet presence for different industry sectors.

A defining feature of the Internet is that no one person, company, government or organization has ultimate control. The Internet Society (ISOC), an international, non-governmental organization whose members consist of governments, corporations, individuals and not-for-profit organizations, co-ordinates many activities related to technical standards, globalization, administrative procedures, education and training, and scaling. The ISOC Board of Trustees is the governing body of the ISOC. The Internet Activities Board (IAB), a technical advisory group to ISOC, is responsible for oversight of Internet technical standards, for the standards-making process and for all protocols and architectures used on the Internet.

In addition, the IAB acts as a liaison with other national and international standards-making organizations, such as the International standards Organization (ISO) and the American National Standards Institute (ANSI), and publishes the Request for Comments (RFC) document series that effectively defines Internet standards and conventions.

The IAB and the Federal Networking Council (FNC) have delegated responsibility for coordinating the management and dissemination of unique Internet host computer numbers, domain names and other parameters to the Internet Assigned Numbers Authority (IANA) at the University of Southern California. The Internet Network Information Center (InterNIC), maintained by AT&T and Network Solutions, provides site, host, domain and personal directory services to the Internet.

Protocols and standards are researched and developed by the Internet Engineering Task Force (IETF), which also administers the overall Internet standards-making process. An open organization of network designers, vendors and researchers, the IETF, manages Internet standards through the RFC document series. The chair of the IETF, along with the area directors of the IETF, form the IESG (Internet Engineering Steering Group) that handles policy issues related to protocol research and development. RFCs, the official and published documents of the IETF (and thus the Internet), are divided into four different types: Standards Track, Informational, Experimental and Historic. Standards Track RFCs go through three phases: Proposed, Draft Standard and Standard.

Access

Access to the Internet is often divided into three classes, a trichotomy first proposed by Matrix Information and Directory Services: the Core Internet, consisting of those who can provide or distribute information over the Internet, the Consumer Internet, consisting of people who can receive information over the Internet, and the Matrix, consisting of users with access to electronic mail systems who can exchange mail with Internet users, including most proprietary, corporate e-mail systems. Until recently, the most common way to access the Internet was through a university or government agency. However, in the course of 1995, the number of hosts in the commercial domain exceeded the number of hosts in the educational domain for the first time.

Users with personal accounts generally access the Internet by dialling in with a modem, either through a commercial online service such as America Online, CompuServe or Prodigy, or directly to the Internet through a local Internet Service Provider (ISP), otherwise known as a Point of Presence (POP). These commercial services provide additional proprietary information not available on the Internet as well as Internet access. ISPs can range in size from a couple of simultaneous connections operating from an individual's home to large, national providers such as PSI in the United States or I-Way, Pipex, U-Net and Demon Internet in the United Kingdom. In developed nations, the telephone call to the ISP is most often a local call.

Almost all the United Kingdom and much of the United States are covered locally by ISPs. Recently, ISPs have also begun to appear in other countries. In the United States, the Telecommunications Act of 1996 makes it likely that telephone companies, both local Regional Bell Operating Companies (RBOCs) and long-distance carriers, will begin offering Internet connectivity as a standard service. France Telecom has also announced intentions to provide a consumer internet service, one that will include (for an extra fee) access to its existing Minitel service. If this happens, it is unlikely that local ISPs will be able to survive without offering significant added value.

In addition, some users have access to limited parts of the Internet (often just electronic mail) through local computer bulletin board systems (BBS) or community networks ('freenets'). An alternative means of connection is through what is called a 'shell account', in which a user dials into a remote computer connected to the Internet. Users in this case may have limited access to certain Internet services (e-mail, Usenet newsgroups, and even the World Wide Web), although they generally do not have access to graphics or many of the more advanced services. The advantage of this type of account, however, is that it requires only a low-end computer and a slow modem, and it is particularly popular in developing countries, where higher-end equipment is often unavailable.

Pricing models for Internet access are varied, and have been the subject of much study. The economics of the Internet in terms of the characteristics of its primary underlying technologies, leased lines and routers (computers used to direct data traffic), both of which are subject to large economies of scale. Additional factors to be taken into account are the continually declining costs of the computer hardware and the statistical multiplexing techniques used to combine the traffic from different sources into a steady average traffic stream, both of which serve to drive down marginal costs.

Internet economics from the perspective of congestion control. They compare fixed-rate access to the Internet with the 'tragedy of the commons', wherein there is no penalty for increased use, resulting in 'over grazing' of the resource (for example, excessive cross-posting of messages). They posit an Internet costing model based on: incremental packet cost, social cost of delay to others, network infrastructure fixed costs, incremental cost of connecting an additional user, and cost to expand network capacity.

Most authors, even those in favour of a more use-based Internet pricing model, agree that some subsidies for civic, educational and not-for-profit use are required. The provision of subsidies to schools and public libraries for Internet access. Subsidies are not peculiar to the United States, however. For example, in Tarragona, Spain, TINET (Tarragona Internet) has begun offering users free basic Internet service (electronic mail and Usenet news), and below-market rate full Internet service, and the Peruvian Scientific Network (RCP), seeded with monies from the United Nations Development Programme (UNDP), is providing subsidized Internet access and training to the public.

A Web site or page can also be the level of economic analysis. Thus far, relatively few sites charge for the content they provide, with the information either being funded through advertising or provided as a loss-leader to entice the user to purchase a more complete version of the product. The Fourth World Wide Web Survey revealed that the number of people unwilling to pay anything for access to Web sites had increased to 31.8% from 22.6% in the previous survey.

Internet services

Internet services are combinations of protocols and software programs that allow people to use the Internet in different ways. A number of genres have emerged over the lifetime of the Internet, and most are still being used today, albeit in various incarnations. Usenet is a distributed network of computers, predating the Internet but now running almost entirely on the Internet infrastructure, that exchanges messages via a set of agreed-upon protocols in collections of messages called newsgroups. These newsgroups can be thought of as electronic discussion groups, and are arranged in hierarchies. There are seven top-level international hierarchies of newsgroups, called comp (for computer-related discussions and information), sci (for the sciences), soc (for sociocultural issues), rec (for hobbies and recreational activities), news (for activities related to

Usenet itself), talk (for debate-oriented activities) and misc (for activities not fitting into one of the existing categories or spanning categories). In addition to the global hierarchies, there also exist local, regional and national hierarchies (de for Germany, in for Indiana, etc.). Finally, there are alternative hierarchies that are carried by some news servers, including the anarchic alt hierarchy, which has been the subject of controversy owing in part to the sexually explicit nature of some of its newsgroups. While there is no central Usenet authority, a number of accepted rules and procedures have evolved that users and news server administrators abide by in the maintenance of Usenet newsgroups for the seven major global hierarchies. These procedures include calls for discussion about the creation of new newsgropus, calls for voting on the creation of such newsgropus, and protocols for the collection and counting of votes and subsequent action.

Gopher, developed at the University of Minnesota in the United States, was the first multi-media-oriented network navigation tool. Designed to simplify network navigation for the user by allowing providers to present their information in the form of navigable hierarchical menus, Gopher, and its companion Internet search index, VERONICA, played a major role in increasing the accessibility of the Internet to the nontechnical user. Although many Gopher-based servers still exist, Gopher has been largely superseded by the World Wide Web, which duplicates and significantly enhances its functionality.

Undoubtedly, the most significant Internet service is the World Wide Web - often referred to as the multimedia portion of the Internet. The World Wide Web is based on the concepts of hypertext and hypermedia.

Information available via the World Wide Web is provided in the form of hypermedia pages, which look like pages from a magazine, combining graphics and text, but with the added feature that the user can follow links provided by the author to other documents. Users view these hypermedia pages with the aid of software programs known as Web browsers. While the first widely available Web browser was Mosaic, more recently Netscape Navigator has become the browser of choice for most people. Browsers on the World Wide Web access Web servers via HTTP, or HyperText Transport Protocol. Information on the Web is generally marked up with HyperText Markup Language (HTML), a subset of the Standard Generalized Markup Language (SGML). HTML provides facilities for the incorporation of text, graphics, sound, video and hypertext links into Web-based documents, as well as document formatting. To provide documents over the Web, information providers mark up these documents using HTML codes (or tags) and make them available via an HTTP server.

HTML is a continuously evolving standard, and HTML 2.0 is the currently accepted version, supported by almost every browser. HTML 3.0 is currently under discussion, though many Web browsers have already implemented some of its features. Some browser developers, notably Netscape and Microsoft, have implemented nonstandard features, and a major discussion item among Web service developers is the degree to which these features should be utilized.

Most recent developments in Internet service are intended to fit within the World Wide Web and HTML framework, which has proven remarkably extensible and flexible. Virtual Reality Modeling Language (VRML) is a technology used to represent three-dimensional interactive objects and scenes.

2

Information and Communication Technologies: A Social Development Approach

Beyond economic growth, which is an engine and not an end in itself, development is first and foremost social; it is also intimately linked to peace, human rights, democratic governance, environment, and last but not least, the culture and life styles of the people. The United Nations Development Programme (UNDP), on its side, launched in 1990, together with its Human Development Report, the concept of human development, which has become the 'leading alternative to the view of development equated exclusively with economic growth. Human development focuses on people. One result of this change in focus is that the eradication of poverty has become a multidimensional activity.

Poverty is considered to be more than a lack of material well-being. It also reflects poor health and education, deprivation in knowledge and communication, inability to exercise human and political rights and the absence of dignity, confidence and self-respect. ICTs play a prominent role in this broader conception of poverty. They provide important tools for the improvement of health and education, offer new channels for the diffusion of knowledge and create physical and virtual spaces for social communication. This human approach does not ignore the importance of economic growth and productivity, but addresses the question of how economic performance relates to human empowerment and thus asks whether such growth is equitable and sustainable.

Human development implies that people's capabilities are enhanced and their lives enriched. In the annual reports of the UNDP, human development is defined as the 'process of enlarging people's choices'. This is achieved 'by expanding human capabilities and functionings. At all levels of development the three essential capabilities for human development are for people to lead long and healthy lives, to be knowledgeable and to have access to the resources needed for a decent standard of living'.

The essential features of human development are:

— equity in access to vital resources and capabilities

— sustainability of resources and institutions

— acquisition and distribution of knowledge for human empowerment

— people's participation

Attempts to measure the impact of ICTs on the economies of industrialized and developing countries encounter severe problems of statistical classification and data availability Data are not always reliable . They may be unclear or use different definitions, classification schemes are contested and some data are protected as company property. An important reason for the difficulty in measuring productivity is that ICTs are used to produce an intermediate good or product, information. The value of information in use varies dramatically depending upon the context.

A further complication for a full global assessment is that most of the developing countries still have to begin the process of harnessing ICTs to their development goals . Another problem is that ICT deployment and economic growth have a dialectical relationship so that there are no unilateral causal links. Economic growth may be partly the result of the growth in the use of ICTs, but then the proliferation of ICTs is itself dependent upon the availability of economic resources. If the definition of development is extended beyond mere economic growth, the assessment is complicated even further.

Across all industries, there has been a strong growth of investments in ICT applications. Spending on ICT equipment as part of overall spending on business equipment has grown dramatically in most industrial countries. In the United States, for example, such spending rose from less than 5% in 1960 to over 45% by 1996 and if the current trend continues the figure could be over 50% in 2000.

According to an estimate of the United States Department of Commerce (the United States Bureau of the Census and Bureau of Economic Analysis for 1990-1995) in 1998, the American ICT-industry generated $683,000 million. In some industrial countries ICT-related activities produce a growing share of the Gross Domestic Product (GDP).

In the United States, the ICT-industry accounted for almost 8% of the GDP in 1997 and was responsible for over 12% of GDP growth. In the Organisation for Economic Development and Co-operation (OECD) countries, the ICT market sector generally accounts for 15% to 25% of current real economic growth. Investments in the telecommunications sector are an important indicator of the economic significance of ICTs. Worldwide investments in telecommunication rose from $115,000 million in 1990 to $152,000 million in 1995. These investments have often been linked to the privatization of public telecommunication operators (PTOs). The privatization schemes introduced in a number of countries have raised considerable funds.

The ICT industry encompasses the manufacturing of telecommunications equipment, computers, semiconductors and other electronic equipment, the provision of telecommunications services, computer services and software. It is the world's most important and fastest-growing industry. Of the fifty largest companies in the world, ten are ICT companies. They account for 17.5% of the total revenue of the fifty largest companies, for 23% of the total profits and for 26% of the total number of employees. In 1997, four ICT companies, General Electric, Microsoft, NTT and Intel, were among the ten largest companies in the world in terms of market value. In the same year three ICT companies, General Electric, Intel, and International Business Machines (IBM), were among the ten most profitable companies in the world.

Telecommunications, semiconductors and computers are among the high growth industries in the emerging-market economies. Among the 200 top companies in these economies, twenty-two are telecommunications market operators and ten are electronics products manufacturers.

ICTs are affected by a great deal of merger activity. The largest transactions of 1998 include the SBC Communications merger with Ameritech for $272,400 million, AT&T with Telecommunications Inc. (TCI) for $48,000 million, Worldcom with MCI Comm for $37,000 million, Northern Telecom with Bay Networks for $9,000 million, and Alcatel with Digital Service Corporation (DSC) for $4,400 million. There is high degree of concentration in this industry. In the telecommunications equipment market, for example, 50% of all sales are controlled by only five companies. In the market for public telephone switching equipment, five firms (Alcatel, Siemens, Lucent, Ericsson and Nortel) control 76% of all activity. The major companies that carry the bulk of international telephone traffic have formed global alliances. These are:

— Leading companies in the ICT industry, 1997;

— Concert Communications Company (of which 75% is owned by British Telecom and 25% by WorldCom-MCI) with revenues in 1995 of $37,300 million;

— Global One (Deutsche Telekom, 10% + France Telecom, 10% + Sprint USA) with 1995 revenues of $88,500 million;

— Unisource (Telia of Sweden, Royal KPN of the Netherlands, the Swiss PTT and Telefonica in Spain) with 1995 revenues of $37,400 million;

— Cable & Wireless (a United Kingdom based company with interests in over 25 public telephone operators

(PTOs) throughout the world) with revenues in 1995 of $8,500 million.

These four alliances are responsible for some 30% of worldwide telecommunication services revenues. Another example of concentration is provided by Internet traffic. The world's largest Internet Service provider (ISP) is UUNET, which is the subsidiary of the company WorldCom (that merged with MCI), responsible for over 50% of the Internet backbone traffic. One company, Netscape, controls 74% of the market for World Wide Web navigators, with 8% for America Online and 4% for Microsoft (Forrester Research).

The ICT market is growing rapidly and expanding globally. The top ten companies in the manufacturing of telecommunication equipment derive an average 61% of their revenues from sales abroad. These are Motorola (United States), Alcatel (France), Lucent (United States), Siemens (Germany), Ericsson (Sweden), NEC (Japan), Nortel (Canada), Nokia (Finland), Fujitsu (Japan), and Bosch (Germany). Most analysts expect a further growth of global sales since the domestic markets in many countries are either too small or already saturated. From various trade figures, it can be estimated that the share of the ICT industry in the world economy ranges from between 10% to 15% of total world trade.

In several ICT sectors the world market shows rapid growth rates. The market for computer hardware and software, for example, grew at about 15% annually in the 1990-1995 period. In the same period, the average growth rate for total world trade was 8%. In 1997, worldwide revenues in the telecommunications industry were nearly $600,000 million. Some analysts expect this figure to grow to $1,400,000 million by the year 2000.

The value of total imports in the world trade of computer equipment grew by 67% from $87,500 million in 1992 to $145,500 million in 1996. The value of total exports grew by 75% from $73,000 million in 1992 to $127,000 million in 1996 (Comtrade, United Nations Statistics Division). The market for personal computers (PCs) is still growing and may reach a sales figure of over $250,000 million in 2000. There is also rapid growth in the world market for computer software, which in 1996 generated $109 , 3 00 million in revenues.

In the world trade of telecommunication equipment the value of total exports grew by 68% from $65,000 million in 1992 to $108,000 million in 1996. The value of total imports grew by 58% from $66,000 million in 1992 to $104,000 million in 1996. Growth rates in this sector are linked to the worldwide increase in the number of telephone lines. The growth from 519 million lines in 1990 to 693 million lines in 1995 represents an average growth rate of 6.8% per year.

In 1995, 45 million new fixed telephone lines were added and 33 million people became new subscribers to mobile communications. In fact, the strongest growth rates are in the mobile communication market, particularly in the United States and Japan. In the OECD countries in 1996-67, the contribution of mobile communications to overall telecommunication services revenues amounted to some 12% and the number of subscribers doubled. In 1990, the worldwide trading of telecommunications services generated some $377,000 million. This figure increased in 1996 to over $600,000 million.

Largely as a result of the further internationalization of transnational corporations and increases in the volume of travel, this sector of the market continues to show very high growth rates. There is an ever-growing demand for telecommunication services around the world and thus for the building and renovation of networks.

The total value of exports in the world trade of audio and video recording equipment grew by 23% from \$18,000 million in 1992 to \$21,000 million in 1996. The total value of imports grew by 6% from \$17,000 million in 1992 to \$18,000 million in 1996.

Trade balance

According to data from the International Telecomunications Union (ITU), the developed countries represent some 70% of overall telecommunication equipment exports, showing a \$9 billion trade surplus. Particularly striking is the shift from a trade deficit for the USA in 1990 to a trade surplus of \$3.2 billion in 1995. Over 100 developing countries produce no exports at all. They are obliged to import and thus show trade deficits that in 1995 exceeded \$10,000 million.

For most developing countries, the obvious problem is lack of capital for imports, since low overall income means that local telecommunications generate minimal revenues. The profits in national telecommunications operation are, without exception, found in international traffic, but the financial gains from overseas services do not benefit the national telecommunications carrier. For political and other reasons, many countries decide not to reinvest a sufficient share of this income in the expansion and upgrading of telecommunication facilities.

Moreover, there is growing competition in the provision of international telecommunications services and strong pressures to lower rates on busy routes. Foreign investments in telecommunications have been stimulated by the privatization of former national public telecommunication operators as part of the worldwide trend toward deregulation that emerged during the 1980s. In the 1984-96 period the 44 PTOs that were privatized raised in total a sum of $159,000 million. Almost one third of the financing came from foreign investments.

Electronic Commerce

The increasing economic importance of ICTs is also linked to the growth of electronic commerce. Although for the moment electronic commerce is still a factor of limited economic significance, with revenues of approximately $26,000 million in 1998, this figure is expected to exceed the trillion dollar mark in the early 21st century.

Since it is difficult to measure precisely the economic significance of electronic commerce. Several of its important features, such as easy access to data, cannot be quantified, and reliable and comprehensive statistics are not yet available; this uncertainty leads to widely varying estimates. The OECD definition of electronic commerce refers to commercial transactions that take place through open networks, like the Internet. These transactions are both business to business and business to consumers. The growing number of people around the world connected to the Internet have begun to develop a digital economy.

In cyberspace, consumers can purchase flowers, shirts, jeans, books, compact disks (CDs), tickets, hotel reservations, skin care products, pornography, kitchen equipment and household consumer goods. World Wide Web sales grew approximately from $8,000 million in 1994 to over $45,000 million in 1998. According to various analysts in Business Week, digital trade could grow from $1,200 million in 1998 to $65,000 million over the next three years. Other forecasters propose even higher figures, for instance in the travel industry, book and music sales and financial services. Electronic sales of software also hold enormous growth potential.

Whatever the precise significance and validity of the forecasts, the general expectation predicts formidable growth in this sector of the global economy. Most analysts observe that this will be mainly business-to-business trading. Expectations of growth in the business-to-consumer trade are based on the assumption that on-line trading will lower production, and thus distribution, costs by up to 10% of total sales. Some 50% of this reduction of costs may be used to lower consumer prices thus stimulating further purchases by consumers.

Electronic trading via the Internet is in fact the successor to the Electronic Data Interchange (EDI) that is already used by many companies. EDI is the exchange of electronic documents in goods trading and financial services and usually operates within closed Value Added Networks (VANs).

EDI is expensive because complicated software applications have to be installed for each new trading partner and flexibility is limited because invoices and orders must be exchanged in fixed standard formats. The Internet facilitates the exchange of electronic data by accepting many different formats. However, many of the big EDI users see EDI as more reliable than current Internet traffic. In the United States at present, the volume of EDI-traffic is some fourteen times greater than that of Internet traffic.

Many analysts expect that in the years ahead this ratio will change, first to a more equal distribution between EDI and Internet transactions and later to a definite advance for the Internet. This situation will be reinforced by the rate at which companies begin to share their 'intranets' with more trading partners and thus create 'extranets'.

Controlling Access to Cyberspace

An increasingly important part of all commercial activity on the digital market is geared toward the control over access to cyberspace. The gates that provide access to the World Wide Web - the so-called web-portals - have become crucial targets in the struggle for dominance in this market. In 1998 a veritable 'portal-fever' emerged as more and more companies sought to secure a piece of the expected profits.

In June 1998 the media giant Walt Disney announced it would spend $70 million for the purchase of 43% of the stock in the search engine Infoseek. In 1998, the American National Broadcasting Company (NBC) invested $165 million for the purchase of the online service Snap! from van Cnet Inc. Time-Warner and News Corp. began to develop their own web portals.

Manufacturers of personal computers, vendors of operating systems, producers of browsers, telecommunications operators, Internet Service Providers, search engines, the big producers of information and entertainment are among the many contenders in this field. Recent acquisitions or investments among the various companies involved in cyberspace illustrate the high level of competition in this area. In 1997, Microsoft bought a 5% participation in Apple Computer for $150 million. As part of the deal, Microsoft insisted that Apple Macintosh computers be delivered with the Microsoft 'browser', Explorer. In 1998 Compaq Computer acquired Digital Equipment in a deal valued at $9,600 million. The combined revenues are estimated at around $38,000 million. WorldCom controls 60% of worldwide Internet traffic and can be seen as a major gatekeeper of access to lines and networks.

In September 1997, America Online (AOL) acquired Compuserve through a complicated deal that made WorldCom the owner of Compuserve's infrastructure. WorldCom paid $1,200 million to H&R Block (Columbus, Ohio) for the purchase of Compuserve. The subscribers to Compuserve were sold to AOL. Through this deal AOL became the largest ISP on the European market with 1.5 million subscribers. On the world market, AOL has some 12 million subscribers.

The ISPs provide access to the services on the Internet and exercise considerable control over access to cyberspace. Some of them conclude agreements with the search engines. Provider MCI, for example, concluded a deal with Yahoo! in order to guide clients to the Web page of this particular search engine. The world market of ISPs is concentrated. If interest in the Web continues to grow, ISPs are likely to allow certain websites to purchase a right of 'priority'. This would mean that if too many clients browse the Web at one time, customers of the privileged sites will have priority and have to wait less time than others. There is also market concentration in this area and many linkages among the players.

ICTs and Employment

In 1996 in the United States, over 7 million people were employed in ICT firms and in ICT-related jobs. This means that ICT-related employment represented over 6% of overall employment. The indications are that this growth will continue. The picture is, however, very different when different economies and market sectors are considered. In several state economies, there has been an increase of employment in such ICT-related professions as technicians, programmers, operators, assemblers and analysts.

Growth of employment opportunities is particularly strong in the software sector. In California's Silicon valley, over 50,000 new jobs were created during 1996 with higher incomes than the national industry averages. However, in the sector that manufactures the technologies themselves, jobs decreased.

The creation of new employment is often related to various uses of ICT, for example in new service applications in banking, shopping, education, health and business services. The development of networks combined with the lowering of communication costs has stimulated the growth of 'teleworking'. This means that people work from home and use telecommunication services. The fastest growth is generally expected in 'telecommuting' where people work alternately at home and at the office.

The Internet could play a major role in creating employment for the design, maintenance and management of sites on the World Wide Web. The growth of electronic commerce initially raised concerns about implications for the labour market, but there is also the expectation that few jobs will really be lost since companies will continue to use traditional forms of commerce along with digital trading. When digital trading finally predominates, some jobs will be lost, but new ones requiring new skills will also have been created. The overall picture is characterized by contradictions. Information-related service jobs are associated with the dislocation of family and community life and threats to the health of workers, especially of women. On the other, new types of employment and modes of work organization can be highly beneficial leading to improved quality of life and greater economic resources.

There is some empirical evidence that automation eliminates jobs, but there is also evidence that automation creates new jobs. What remains uncertain is the eventual balance. The notion of a single standard impact is very inadequate and it is preferable to look at plural impacts. The skills implications of ICTs are varied and are related to differences in socio-economic, cultural and political environments. Different countries will choose different ICT-applications in order to reap different benefits from technological development. It is too early to foresee how all these factors will operate. The observation that in the affluent economies more and more employees use ICT applications in their daily work is generally uncontested. By and large, ICTs are used by some 50% of the workforce in the industrial nations.

ICTs and Economic Productivity

The processing capacity of ICTs doubles every two years, but this is not matched by growth in economic productivity. There are indications of a real ICT contribution to overall economic growth, although no definite assessment is possible. In his testimony to Congress, US Federal Reserve Board Chairman Alan Greenspan pointed to increasing growth rates in productivity for the American economy and stated that: 'The dramatic improvements in computing power and communication and information technology appear to have been a major force behind this beneficial trend'. Other analysts raise serious doubts about such a causal link between ICT power and productivity.

Of the world's total investment in capital goods, 50% concerns computers and peripherals. Yet expected growth in productivity has not materialized. During the period 1970-90 white collar productivity remained stagnant at around 0.9% per year and improved in the early 1990s to 1.3% - a low figure despite the announcement by Fortune magazine that 'the productivity payoff arrives'. It is not clear at present what factors cause this ICT-paradox. One possible explanation refers to the criteria that are used for the measurement of economic productivity. Another factor may also be the inadequate way in which organizations adapt to the use of ICTs. It could also be that what looks like an unexplainable delay is in fact the normal time lag needed before new technologies can lead to higher levels of productivity.

ICTs are 'synergetic' technologies and their growth therefore leads to growth in other sectors of the economy. They create an infrastructure around their products and services, similar to that of car technology earlier in the century. As with the transition from manual power to mechanization techniques and later to electromechanical innovations, today's shift towards the pervasive application of ICTs has given rise to a range of new industries such as software production, processing services, time-sharing facilities, semiconductor manufacturing, database management or electronic publishing.

This potential for new economic productivity requires an educational infrastructure that teaches the knowledge and skills required for ICT-related occupations. Although there has been a considerable increase in ICT teaching in many schools and universities around the world, new multimedia tools are still widely underused or used only to supplement conventional teaching methods. There is also a lack of solid and creative training materials that cater for the specific needs of the developing countries.

The economic benefits that may accrue from the development and the deployment of ICTs are unequally distributed throughout the world. There seems to be general agreement in scientific literature and in public policy statements that the ICT gap between the developed and developing countries is widening and will be a major obstacle to the integration of all countries into the so-called Global Information Society.

The seriousness of the ICT gap is clearly demonstrated by figures on the world distribution of telephones. In 1996 there were 743.66 million main telephone lines in the world. Europe (274.23 million), the United States (170 . 5 7 million) and Japan (61.53 million) represent 68% of this total, compared with 1.8% in Africa. The density of telephone lines per 100 inhabitants is also very unequally distributed. Whereas the world average is 12.88 lines per 100 inhabitants, Europe provides 34.6, the United States 63.9, Japan 48.9 and Africa 1.85. In early 1997, some 62% of the world's main telephone lines were installed in 23 affluent countries, which account for only 15% of the world's population. Over 950 million households in the world (65% of the total) were equipped with a telephone. Another indicator of this gap is the revenue from telecommunication services, which reached a world total of $620,000 million in 1996. Europe, the United States and Japan benefited from 77% of these revenues, while Africa received a mere 1.5%. Investments in the telecommunication sector show a similar distribution. In 1996 the world total was worth $166,000 million. Europe, the United States and Japan are responsible for 67% of these investments and Africa for 1.7%.

Total ICT equipment installation reveals highly uneven geographical distribution. The estimated number of PCs in the world in 1996 stood at 234,200,000. The share for Europe (72,864,000), the United States (96,600,000) and Japan (16,100,000) was 79%, while for Africa it was only 1.3%, representing 0.64 computers per 100 inhabitants. The world average for that year was 4.6 computers per 100 inhabitants. Far above this average are the figures for Europe, 9.6, the United States, 36.2, and Japan, 12.8. Of all the 47,972,000 fax machines operating in the world in 1996, Europe was using 10,942,500, the United States 17,000,000, and Japan 14,300,000. These figures combined represent 88%, in contrast with the 0.5% in use in Africa. Of the total number of television sets in the world in 1996, Europe, the United States and Japan possessed 47% while Africa possessed only 3%.

At the present time the worldwide distribution of ICT resources is enormously unequal. In terms of availability, accessibility, and affordability of equipment and services as well as the mastery of technical and managerial skills, there are great disparities not only between affluent and developing countries, but also among different social groups within all countries. A very problematic factor is that these disparities, rather than diminishing, are growing throughout the world.

Gender inequity

A particularly skewed worldwide distribution of ICT resources and use concerns women. An immediate problem is the fact that ICT skills are linked almost completely to literacy and 'it seems likely that the vast majority of the illiterate population will be excluded from the emerging knowledge societies'. This situation particularly affects women, since around the world illiteracy rates for women are higher than for men. In the developed world, a large majority of the population is literate, and most devices ensuring user-machine communication hardware and software - therefore reflect reading or writing capabilities.

ICTs could have developed devices based on sound, touch, images or symbols which do not require literacy, but markets are the driving force for technological developments, and the needs of illiterates in the developing world were, and still are, completely ignored. In terms of sharing ICT knowledge, women are also disadvantaged, since their numbers in enrolment for science and technology education lag far behind the figures for male enrolment. In 1990, the percentages of women enrolled in science and technology at the university level in Africa were 10%, in Latin America 40%, in Western Europe 32%, in Eastern Europe less than 30% and in the Asia/Pacific region 34%.

ICTs offer new forms of communication that may enable women to break through their often isolated social situation. They also create new opportunities of employment for women in jobs that require new skills. However, the technologies themselves will not achieve this. The full use of opportunities that are in principle created by the deployment of ICTs will depend upon social variables such as cultural factors, class and age. Robust policies are needed for the ICTs to have a beneficial impact on women's lives.

In the emerging 'knowledge societies' access to communication is becoming the key tool for social inclusion'. In most developing countries women are disadvantaged in terms of scientific and technological literacy, in terms of opportunities for education and training for the acquisition of technical skills, and in terms of real access to information and knowledge.

The ICT rush

In the 1980s, the expectation that innovations in telecommunications and computer technologies would improve industrial performance and increase economic productivity in the industrialized nations became firmly established among the leader of the developing countries. The common position that emerged was that ICTs would allow them to leapfrog over the industrialization of their economies into a post-industrial society. Countries began to launch policies and programmes to acquire a share in international satellite communications and transborder data flow networks. In many countries, however, concern arose that ICTs might entail serious social risks, such as a potential for cultural colonialism, the replacement of jobs by machines, and the erosion of individual privacy and national sovereignty.

Towards the end of the 1980s these fears seemed to have abated. A new phase began in the 1990s, characterized by a very strong fear of being left behind and cut off from the emerging global digital highway system. The general belief seems to be that without adequate access to the system, countries cannot hope to be economically competitive in world trade.

In many developing countries, the 'digital rush' is on to ensure connections with the electronic networks for trade, finance, transport and science. This phenomenon has been inspired by the obvious benefits that digital information and communication technologies - at least in principle - seem to offer. Educational facilities can be improved by providing distance learning and on-line library access.

Electronic networking has also been used to improve the quality of health services by providing remote access to the best diagnostic and healing practices and cutting costs in the process. Digital technologies for remote resource sensing can provide early warning to areas vulnerable to seismic disturbances or identify land suitable for crop cultivation.

Computer technology can contribute to the development of flexible, decentralized and small-scale industrial production. Thus the competitive position of local manufacturing and service industries can be improved. In Singapore, Brazil and Hong Kong the introduction of computer-aided manufacturing (CAM) technologies has been very successful in small-scale industries.

The World Commission on Environment and Development, in its report Our Common Future suggests that 'new technologies in communication, information, and process control allow the establishment of small-scale, decentralized, widely dispersed industries, thus reducing the levels of pollution and other impacts on the local environment'.

The currently available computer-communication technologies make it fairly easy for PC users around the world to create a public sphere in 'cyberspace'. Personal computers, modems and telephone lines are being used to establish new global communities. Organizations in developing countries find it increasingly possible to join these forms of horizontal, non-hierarchical exchange that have already demonstrated their ability to counter censorship and misinformation.

Groups of all types, from ecological movements, human rights activists, farmers, senior citizens, to the Zapatistas and the groups attending the Women's summit in Beijing, have made impressive use of the new, fast, reliable and effective networks of communication. The combination of telecommunication technologies with desktop publishing software has created new opportunities for even the smallest action group to disseminate its messages across the globe with relative ease and at minimal expense.

In the late 1980s and early 1990s, various aid projects introduced electronic information systems into rural health services (India), agricultural extension projects (Peru), infrastructural development (Pakistan), or energy management (Malaysia). In some developing countries, special computer training courses have been developed in schools and colleges (Sri Lanka).

The growing ICT-demand in developing countries can be seen in the long waiting lists for telephone connections, the increase in cellular systems and the rapidly expanding numbers of Internet users. To meet this demand, more and more developing countries have placed the ICTs at the centre of national agendas for social and economic development.

There are plans in many developing nations to enhance telecommunications infrastructures in order to facilitate participation in world markets. The planned increase in telephone lines over the next five years in developing countries represents a need for $200,000 million in investments, which it is expected will be provided largely through a massive inflow of foreign capital.

Human development challenges

Human development is forcing policy makers to face the complex challenges of equity of access with respect to vital resources and capabilities, the sustainability of resources and institutions, the acquisition and distribution of knowledge for human empowerment and people's participation. The reality of the widening gap in digital capacity raises the serious concern that the poorer countries may not be able to overcome the financial and technical obstacles now limiting their access to the digital technologies.

In early 1995 the concern about the ICT-gap inspired many public and private donor institutions to propose plans for the elimination of digital disparity. For example, the World Bank established the Information for Development Program to assist developing countries with their integration into the global information economy. In the same year, the ITU established World Tel, an ambitious project to generate private investments for bridging the telecommunications gap in the world by developing basic infrastructures. WorldTel aims to establish 40 million telephone connections in developing countries over the next ten years, which will require a minimal investment of $1,000 million.

The equitable sharing of communication infrastructures (the electronic highways systems created by carriers such as satellites, cables, fixed lines and mobile transmissions), computing capacity (computers, peripherals, networks), information resources (databases, libraries), and ICT-literacy (intellectual and social capabilities to deploy ICT in beneficial ways) will require an enormous effort from the international community.

Massive investments are required for the renovation, upgrading and expansion of networks in developing countries, for programmes to transfer knowledge and for ICT skill training, in particular for women. In 1985, the Maitland Commission estimated that an annual investment of $12,000 million would be needed to achieve the goal of simple, universal access to a telephone early in the 21st century.

To attract private funding, countries will have to liberalize their ICT markets and adopt measures in favour of competition. In this context the World Bank has recommended the creation of investor-friendly business environments, the protection of investments and security for repatriating revenues. When public companies are privatized there may be losses in revenues as a result of the change in service charges or severance payments. The World Bank is therefore proposing to finance the adjustment costs of the adoption of liberalization schemes in individual countries.

The World Bank's policies are characterized by a strong emphasis on economic growth and a key role for the private sector. The expectation is that, in a sufficiently free market, economic growth will also benefit the poorer sector of society. In this context the contribution of the ICTs is to provide the essential infrastructure for economic development. This position bypasses the question raised earlier, as to whether the deployment of ICTs does indeed lead to growth in economic productivity and, if so, whether such growth will be equitably distributed.

The governance of ICTs is in fact left to freely operating private entrepreneurs. The basic assumption is that a country's telecommunication infrastructure can be managed by private companies and that, whenever parts of the network are unprofitable, the state will provide the public means to ensure that no citizen is disenfranchised. There is some debate about the expectation that private funding will create worldwide equity in the access to and use of ICT resources. It appears in any case that the international community and national governments of affluent countries need to bear in mind that problems stem not only from a lack of financial resources but also from a lack of political will.

Creating adequate access to ICT resources worldwide should not be a problem in a world economy with income amounting to roughly $22 trillion. The core issue is that expenditures for development assistance represent only $55,000 million and thus a mere 0.25% of this income. The annual costs for all developing countries for adding one thousand million telephone lines, subsidizing over 600 million households that cannot afford basic telephone charges, providing PCs and access to the Internet for schools over a period of ten years could represent from $80,000 to $100,000 million. This is not a prohibitive level of funding.

It represents about 11% of the world's annual military expenditure, about 22% of total annual spending on narcotic drugs, and is comparable with the annual expenditure on alcoholic drinks in Europe alone. For a variety of political and economic reasons, many donor governments are presently reducing budgets for financing ICT-development. Between 1990 and 1995, multilateral lending for telecommunications decreased from $1,253 million to $967 million. Bilateral aid for telecommunications decreased from $1,259 million in 1990 to $800 million in 1995. Financial obstacles are, however, not the only concern. The transfer of ICTs also raises questions about their appropriateness and about the capacity of the recipient countries to make the best use of them.

Over the past few decades the prevailing international policies on technology transfer have placed formidable obstacles in the process of reducing North-South technology gaps; the present discussion on the ICT-gap provides no convincing evidence that the technology owners will change their attitudes and policies towards the international transfer of technology. There is no indication that current restrictive business practices, constraints on the ownership of knowledge, and rules on intellectual property rights that are adverse to developing country interests are radically changing, and there are no realistic prospects that the relations between ICT-rich and ICT-poor countries will change in the near future.

The question must be raised as to whether there can be any serious reduction of the ICT disparity, given the realities of the present international economic order. It may well be an illusion to think that the ICT-poor countries could catch up or keep pace with progress among countries in the Northern hemisphere, where the rate of technological development is very high and is supported by considerable resources. This is not to say that poor countries should not try to upgrade their ICT-systems. They should, however, not act with the unrealistic expectation that those who are ahead are planning to wait for them. The situation may improve for the poorer countries, but the disparity will not go away.

In most countries, the problems concerning access to ICTs are handled through public policies based on an already defined technological environment. Developing countries thus find it difficult to assess what digital technologies would be appropriate for their specific development strategies. A problem compounding this situation is that in many cases 'peripheral states seem to have no disinterested non-governmental organizations to advise them on telecommunication technology and the social objectives of regulation that would safeguard those interests that private profit will not meet. Without adequate regulatory intervention to ensure accountability to the general public, market forces that respond to those groups with purchasing power are bound to generate unequal development'.

Most developing countries lack the capacity to identify appropriate digital technologies, and, to make matters worse, there is also a critical absence of co-ordination of 'digital' policies among the developing countries themselves. It is essential to recognize that planning for the adoption and deployment of digital technologies can no longer be a local affair. Global negotiations, such as the recent General Agreement on Tariffs and Trade (GATT) Uruguay Round of Multilateral Trade Negotiations, heavily affect national technology plans, while the processes of globalization.

Information and communication technologies and social processes (in trade, finance, culture, etc.) determine the playing field for local actors. As a result, local planning has to take into account the effects of global forces, possible only when planners in the periphery pool resources and mobilize a constituency that counteracts the Northern dominance in global planning. Since today's globalization process is largely determined by Northern forces, 'many developing countries do not obtain a fair share of the benefits of globalization, and some actually suffer net losses'.

The North is in control not only due to strength but also because of lack of co-ordination in the South. National technology policies are largely determined by the work of global institutions and their rules and standards. It is vital that developing countries participate more forcefully and effectively in these institutions. This requires policy co-ordination among developing countries: 'Without policy co-ordination, Southern countries will stand to lose out in the formulation of international policy frameworks that will have important impact on their national policies'.

UNESCO's Communication Strategies

UNESCO's constitution requires the Organization to facilitate universal access to information through international co-operation, 'for the purpose of advancing .

the objectives of international peace and of the common welfare of mankind'. UNESCO pursues this mission by defending freedom of expression and its corollary freedom of the press, encouraging the development of pluralistic and independent media, promoting the free flow of information, ensuring that the new electronic media are of benefit to the greatest possible number of people and taking measures to avert the risks of uniformization and exclusion.

At the end of the cold war, the General Conference of UNESCO adopted a new communication strategy which, inter alia, solemnly reaffirmed the principle of the 'free flow of information' and reiterated that freedom of expression must be exercised 'without any obstacle'. With this return to constitutional basics, UNESCO regained its moral authority in this area. UNESCO is playing a leading role within the United Nations system for the defence and promotion of freedom of expression and its corollary, press freedom, which, in the words of the General Conference, is an 'essential component of any democratic society'.

Together with the United Nations, UNESCO organized five regional seminars on the promotion of independent and pluralistic media. Their conclusions and recommendations contained in the Declarations of Windhoek, Almaty, Santiago, Sana'a and Sofia were endorsed by the General Conference, as was the decision by the United Nations General Assembly taken at the initiative of UNESCO, to proclaim 3 May, the anniversary of the adoption of the Windhoek Declaration, 'World Press Freedom Day'. These activities and events have done much to promote freedom of expression worldwide. The launching in 1997 of the 'UNESCO-Guillermo Cano

World Press Freedom Prize', the Director-General's systematic public condemnation of crimes committed against journalists, and UNESCO's discreet diplomatic action on behalf of journalists and other intellectuals in prison or missing, are all examples of initiatives in keeping with this fundamental role of the Organization.

In several conflict zones, UNESCO is playing a pioneering role by helping to promote a culture of peace with and by the media. For more than five years now, in the countries of former Yugoslavia, the Organization has been offering assistance to independent media in order to preserve their freedom of expression. UNESCO has taken a number of initiatives to provide opportunities for exchange and co-operation among media professionals belonging to antagonistic national, ethnic or religious groups. This allows them to analyze together their attitudes towards each other and to create, through dialogue, a climate of mutual understanding to ease tension and foster reconciliation. The establishment of press houses in Rwanda and Burundi, open to both Tutsi and Hutu journalists, the setting up in Latin America of the REDIPAZ network and the launching in Jerusalem of the Israeli-Palestinian Media Forum, are examples of UNESCO's contribution to a culture of peace with and by the media.

UNESCO also makes a special effort to strengthen communication and information capacities in developing countries so that they can participate more actively in the communication process. This is done through the programmes and projects responding to the needs of these countries and of society in general. There is no doubt about the growing impact of communication media in today's society, both the conventional media (press, radio and television) and the information technologies such as the Internet, and the rapidly developing digital media. In this context, UNESCO has become a principal world forum for the discussion on such issues as Public Service Broadcasting and Editorial Independence; strengthening democratic voices; The Young and the Media - Tomorrow; and Sexual Abuse of Children, Child Pornography and Paedophilia on the Internet.

The Organization also issued a Global Study on Media Violence, based on a survey administered by leaders of the World Movement of Scout Organizations and computer-analyzed by Utrecht University. The UNESCO International Clearing House on Children and Violence on the Screen, established in February 1997 at the University of Gothenburg, regularly issues information on this subject, and published a yearbook entitled Children and Media Violence in 1998 and 1999.

Women and the media have also figured prominently in UNESCO's programme. Thousands of women media practitioners, people's movements, news and features services and information resources on women's issues participate in the WOMMED world network. A practical handbook, Women on the Net, has been issued in English and French and under a special project, Women Speaking to Women, community radio stations are run by women in six countries in Africa and Asia.

UNESCO's regional and national training programmes are an important part of communication development, particularly for independent local newspapers and community media. This work is further reinforced through the Global Network of Journalism Training Centres and Institutes organized in 1997 and launched with support from the International Programme for the Development of Communication (IPDC) in 1999. This complements the work done in universities by the UNESCO Chairs in Communication, including the most recent one created for communication technology for women at the Sook Myung University, Seoul.

International Programme for the Development of Communication

Freedom of expression is meaningful only when there is a wide range of media in existence, such as newspapers, radio stations and television channels. That is the basic philosophy on which the IPDC was founded. Established by a resolution of UNESCO's General Conference, it is a specialized programme focusing exclusively on building up the means of mass communication in developing countries. Since its establishment in 1980, IPDC has mobilized some $41 million in voluntary contributions for its special account and nearly $45 million for projects financed under funds-in-trust. Fellowships sponsored by individual countries have provided retraining for 1,500 communication professionals.

The projects carried out with IPDC funding cover a wide range of activities which seek to promote the concept of media pluralism and independence. They include the launching of community radio networks, newspapers for women and rural communities, the training of journalists for all types of media and the computerization of the editorial offices of news agencies, television channels, radio stations and newspapers. In addition, IPDC finances and supports the setting up of networks to denounce violations of press freedom.

In the area of information and informatics, UNESCO is promoting international development of both 'content' and 'infostructure'. UNESCO is fostering access to diversified content in cyberspace by promoting the concept of the electronic 'public domain', accessible on-line and off-line. The 'Publica' CD-ROM series of electronic documentary heritage, produced in co-operation with institutions in developing and developed countries and made available free of charge, covers, for example, electronic anthologies of development literature, free software and classical literature. The Memory of the World programme helps to inventory, preserve and disseminate the worlds documentary heritage including manuscripts of unique cultural significance.

UNESCO itself aims at providing a portal to the global 'cyber commons' of public domain information and applications through its own Web site, and regularly organizes activities to promote creativity and diversity on the Internet, such as through the annual UNESCO Web Prize awarded for outstanding achievements in creating Web sites in the areas of education, science, culture, and communication.

Another content-related focus concerns the use of electronic information to improve governance and facilitate democratization, which was the subject of a global UNESCO survey in 1998/99 to identify promising technologies, applications and approaches in this area of particular relevance for developing countries. Within its Infoyouth programme, UNESCO supports the establishment of Info-centres, info-skills and info-bulletins for young people.

In the 'infostructure' area, UNESCO provides assistance in the establishment of regional computer communication networks for public service applications and for new approaches to virtual communities for learning, for scientific exchange and for cultural development. Examples are a pilot project for the use of the Internet in priority development sectors in the Eastern Caribbean, extending the European Union's Trans-European Tele-Education Network (TEN) to four East European countries, the HeritageNet project linking libraries, archives, museums, art galleries and universities in Central Asia, and, in Africa, 'Learning Networks' enabling teachers to use the Internet for the improvement of education and multi-purpose community telecentres in rural or disadvantaged locations.

Since its beginnings, UNESCO has been promoting library and archive development through the preparation of guidelines and methodologies, advisory services, training of specialists and technical support to selected institutions. More recently, over 300 libraries have been linked through the UNESCO Network of Associated Libraries (UNAL) which was launched in 1990, and within the MEDLIB project major libraries in the Mediterranean region are focusing together on improving the management of and access to electronic information.

Given the critical importance of skills for the development of an information society, UNESCO pays particular attention to the training of information professionals (librarians, archivists, documentalists, computer specialists), as well as of users at all levels. For example, a complete modular framework for training in informatics, covering undergraduate, and postgraduate and continuing education programmes, has been developed in collaboration with the International Federation for Information Processing (IFIP) to serve as a framework for development, testing and international exchange of training materials in these areas.

Sustainability

An important concern has arisen in connection with the possible proliferation of digital technologies in the developing countries, namely, whether ICTs can be used in environmentally sustainable ways. The global use of ICTs would drastically increase the emission of carbon dioxide (from printers, copiers, computers, and so on) to environmentally untenable levels. More ICTs would also imply more production of computers. The production of a single PC requires approximately as much energy as the average electricity consumption of a European household per year. One PC needs twenty tons of natural resources and after three to four years when the equipment is obsolete, the PC will be dumped on the growing heap of electronic scrap, along with toxic waste such as cadmium (in the batteries) and lead (in the screens). The situation has to be seen in the light of a rapidly growing world population which could by the mid-21st century amount to some 12,000 million people.

Knowledge

One essential dimension of human development is knowledge, crucial in enabling people to broaden their choices. ICTs are the basic tools of emerging knowledge-based societies. They represent an important shift from the utilization of natural and material resources to the deployment of data and information and related analytical and processing skills. This development is, however, accompanied by national information and informatics policies through guidelines, workshops and technical assistance. Special consideration is given to 'info-ethical' questions, to achieving a balance between the common good and economic imperatives, and to facilitating the use of information and communication technologies for development purposes by the public sector and the civil society.

A strong commitment by the international community is necessary to ensure that commercial interest do not dominate the development of ICTs in the world, more particularly in developing countries. Governments, public and private institutions have to assume their responsibilities if the gap between information-rich and information-poor is not to continue to widen a strong trend toward the privatization and commercialization of knowledge sources and the concurrent enforcement of legal measures to protect private intellectual property. The emerging global regime for Intellectual Property Rights (IPR) tends to give more emphasis to the economic aspects of IPR protection than to public interest considerations. There is a dominant economic angle in this regime which gives priority to the interests of large producers over those of small creators and consumers.

The central focus is on the misappropriation of corporate property rather than on artistic and literary creativity. The move to give IPR protection to material in the public domain when it has been entered in an electronic database could render access to knowledge more costly - and thus prohibitive - for large numbers of people. In addition, the initiative to extend copyright protection to all forms of digital copying could make the Internet a pay-per-view medium creating obstacles to the access to knowledge for those who cannot pay. Developments in the international regime for intellectual property protection are an attempt to create and maintain a balance between a set of rival claims to the control over knowledge and its dissemination.

The protection of intellectual property rights must provide the incentives, rewards and recognition for individual producers of knowledge in order to stimulate progress. Benefits for the creator, and public access to artistic, literary and scientific works must both be secured. Whereas IPR protection seeks to promote the progress of science, it also restricts access to knowledge, since it defines knowledge as private property and has a tendency to facilitate monopolistic tendencies.

It may well be that the current trends in the trade-oriented IPR regime lead to more restricted access rather than better public distribution. Although an absence of legal protection could have adverse effects on intellectual production, the move toward overprotection is 'not conducive to access to the networks by research workers and academics of developing countries'.

ICT developments are more technology driven than user oriented. If the ICT potential for human development is to be successfully exploited, the needs and aspirations of users must be central to the whole process of design, construction and application. Present experience is concisely summed up by Mansell and Wehn:

> 'There is substantial evidence that if applications do not reflect user needs or involve them in the process of development, they simply will not bring the expected benefits. They are likely to create new problems that will be costly to address. If the specific

> social, cultural, and economic conditions, the expertise and commitment of users, and components of the infrastructure are not assembled together, ICT applications will fail to yield benefits'.

The essential requirement of user orientation is hampered by the strong tendency to delegate social responsibility for the governance of the ICT-sector to a global trade regime. In fact, the politics of world communication represent a historical shift from a public service orientation to private competition with a predominantly commercial focus.

ICTs and Cultural Production

The information and communication technologies (ICTs) are advancing with unprecedented speed, particularly in the most economically developed countries, it would be a mistake to regard them as solely responsible for the current changes. This long-heralded momentum, which seemed slow at the beginning but is now well under way, seems likely to continue at a rapid pace and, if some authors are to be believed, will usher in a new information society or information age. It is, however, one thing to note the dynamic development of telecommunications, information technology and the audiovisual media, and quite another to credit them with changes in culture and in other areas of social life.

Technical innovation is a by-product - only rarely a driving force - of transformations whose origin lies elsewhere. Technology provides such changes with new areas of opportunity, encouraging activities which would otherwise have been blocked by the dominant organizations in the sector and weakening the barriers set up to defend vested interests or to safeguard specific practices. It is important to look beyond the usual thought patterns, which see the issue as one of adaptation to technological changes, and turn our attention instead to changing trends in cultural production.

ICTs may strengthen cultural production and help it to gain widespread recognition, or conversely, they may cause it to be confined to a restricted area or even to decline. Throughout the world, cultural production tends to be community based. Anthropologists, historians and cultural sociologists rightly emphasize this recurring feature which explains the persistence of locally-rooted and even non-commercial forms of culture, as well as the different ways in which viewers interpret television series, according to their own culture. In other words, despite more than two centuries of industrialized cultural production and despite the aggressive strategies of the increasingly-powerful communications groups, independent forms of entertainment still thrive all over the world. Folk productions are not declining - far from it: books and newspapers are published, films and television series are produced and music is recorded independently of the major companies.

The pessimistic forecasts of the imminent globalization of cultural production heard over the last two decades have been proved wrong - or at least exaggerated. Culture remains an area of social activity in which industrialization meets with resistance and constraints, even though increasingly governed by markets, and despite a growing trend towards the internationalization of production and the transnationalization of subjects, styles and standards. The fact that predictions have not so far been fulfilled is, however, no guarantee for the future.

ICTs and the momentum they undoubtedly generate will eventually provide the means to move decisively ahead towards the industrialization and internationalization of cultural production. What in the past was only partly successful is now allegedly resulting directly from ICTs. In other words, what the mass audiovisual media merely launched in the past has now become firmly established and universal through ICTs, which have proven to be more successful at sidestepping the cultural structures of countries and peoples, and certainly more favourable to the worldwide circulation of transnational flows. Individual tools of communi-cation and/or access to data and ready-made programmes are ushering in sweeping transformations in cultural production.

The history of the cultural industries is by no means linear. Until recently, it has progressed unevenly, whenever production techniques were adopted and made widely available, so that works of literature became accessible as books, musical works as records, and films and audiovisual works as screenings in cinemas or as video cassettes. The industrialization of culture has, however, encountered difficulties and setbacks. For producers and publishers, the values attached to culture usually act as 'restrictions', or at any rate as contingencies, for which marketing techniques have yet to be found.

It has been more convenient to market the equipment used to deliver cultural works than to introduce successfully on to the market works available either in a physical medium or accessible through projection or broadcasting by the audiovisual media. So the picture of the relationship between culture and industry today presents sharp contrasts.

There are striking divergences between:

— developed and developing countries;

— countries which give more or less free rein to market forces, and those in which the public authorities provide impetus and co-ordination;

— countries where the market and industry are the major controlling factors in the cultural sphere, and those where small-scale productions, live entertainment with a popular appeal and non-commercial productions predominate;

— the various art forms: it is very difficult to create added value in dance, poetry and narrative performances, as opposed to filmed enter-tainment, which should be considered an activity straddling art and industry;

— individual access to works and live entertainment;

— cultural productions broadcast through the mass audiovisual media and those which, once published, are bought by consumers.

Nevertheless, ICTs are capable of strongly reinforcing trends begun at least two decades ago, thereby giving a decisive boost to the expansion of cultural industries. The areas in which ICTs can make an impact need to be carefully evaluated, however. Contrary to what professionals often claim, it would be wrong to expect multimedia production to create innovative products - apart from games -and important markets in the short term. Innovative products of a truly multimedia type are still too rare and production costs remain too high for rapid progress to be expected.

If there is not a rapid change in product design and production methods during the next decade, ICTs will probably not be instrumental in extending the scope of commercial and even industrialized culture, since with the products which are currently available they are increasingly marginalizing certain cultures, standardizing universally accessible products and excluding those who lack the purchasing power to be ICT consumers. The solution to this problem would appear relatively easy and involves speeding up product flow, which is the second major feature of the development of the cultural industries.

Distance-shopping for products hitherto almost e xclusively supplied by specialized end-product distributors or by mass distribution outlets, and downloading products accessible from a distance are two activities that have been made possible by the efficiency of communications networks and the growing sophistication of access terminals. The scope of this new electronic commerce is still difficult to gauge, but there is no doubt that in 1997-98 its growth was such that the major distribution groups all rushed headlong in that direction, preceded by small pioneering firms. This strategic choice was made despite the fact that monetary transactions on the Internet are still not totally safe and that arrangements for remunerating artists and publishers are still under negotiation.

Most specialists consider that cultural products are particularly well-suited to this new form of distribution. There are substantial advantages for consumers: real-time access; the opportunity to browse through all available catalogues and products; access to catalogues of foreign firms which used to be accessible only, if at all, with long delays involved. In other words, these new ways of accessing cultural products are of special interest both to the consumers least concerned by mass products, and to specialist publishers and producers.

Paradoxically, the people who are apparently the most critical of this rapid change in the distribution of cultural products ('cultivated' members of society, let us say, who prefer the existing methods of accessing art forms, and also scientists) are those who, for the moment, find it most advantageous to purchase directly via the networks.

There is an additional paradoxical aspect to these immediate advantages for the most selective and demanding users. Producers and artists who offer the most distinctive products and who frequently encounter great difficulty in distributing the works they create and publish will obviously be tempted to bypass the large broadcasters and distributors (who demand a high percentage of the selling price) in order to contact consumers directly. This is all the more likely to happen because, throughout the history of the cultural industries, artists and their publishers have tried to eliminate intermediaries with little success. They themselves then joined that enviable group, thus only reinforcing the existing oligopolies.

The current trend consists mainly of users purchasing products after browsing through catalogues on publishers' sites and on the sites of artists acting as producers of their own works. Soon it will be possible to download actual works, meaning that publishers of books and recorded music will no longer need to reproduce and record the work in a physical medium. This is not a utopian prospect; it is already possible to access literary and musical works in this way, or even extracts from them. This phenomenon raises two essential questions about cultural products. Is a work on offer a finished product just because it has been stabilized in a medium? Next, have the forms of monetary payment by consumers, here encouraged to buy works piecemeal, and 'paying-as-they-go', been fully considered? These are not merely technical innovations which, by encouraging a commercial shift, coincide with changes in systems of accessing works. Here technical innovations are changing the very substance of cultural products in various ways, especially by calling into question their finished appearance, an aspect considered fundamental up until now.

In modern societies, the values and images associated with the concepts of leisure, information and culture are still sharply differentiated. Although these concepts are evolving and now sometimes overlap, it would nonetheless hardly be possible to confuse them taken in a strict sense. They have relatively stable definitions: infor-mation is more ephemeral than culture, and this idea orients the functioning of those who produce news and information; leisure time is primarily for entertainment, but leisure pursuits encouraging the development of cultural activities are judged as positive. Although the trend began earlier, ICTs are causing these distinctions to grow more and more blurred, and in some cases it is becoming difficult to distinguish between information products and cultural products.

Methods of creation (by journalists or artists, with an increasing use of streamlined methods), production structures (more and more often controlled by the same multimedia groups), distribution procedures (via networks or in the form of products accessible on- or off-line), consumption time and conditions of consumer use (use is often individual and involves interactivity with the hardware acting as intermediary in programme communication) are now closely related, not to say identical. These similarities cannot be considered as either secondary or insignificant.

Behind all the confusions and convergences, the question that arises is more than ever that of mass culture, although in forms different from those observed in the 1960s when the phenomenon became evident. As the transmission of standardized and increasingly transnational mass culture boosted by ICTs develops, cultural distinc-tiveness tends to be maintained within an elitist, or at any rate a niche, context.

Although distinctive cultural production is not declining, and examples of it which successfully express popular and national identities continue to receive considerable attention, they enter into competition with mass products that are easily distributed on communication networks. The struggle is to some extent unequal, not because of inadequacy of supply but because the major communications groups are strengthening their hold on the circulation of products. Insofar as future developments can be inferred from the situation today, culture seems to be going the same way as leisure and information. For most people, ICTs have not yet become part of a familiar landscape. They have already led, however, to some fairly radical changes in the functioning and regulation of public services, resulting in considerable hesitation on the part of those responsible for cultural policy.

An increase in the supply of commercial products almost inevitably leads to the reduction, if not the disappearance, of non-commercial products (heavily subsidized by public funds) and of semi-commercial products (e.g. small-scale productions and those enjoying tax and customs protection). A movement of this type has recently become apparent in television production. In response to competition from powerful new commercial channels and in order to increase their output of programmes to compete with the commercial channels, with approximately the same resources, the managers of public channels have been obliged to subcontract production, placing it in the hands of new private producers for whom the origin of the orders they handle is of no importance.

As a result, production variety in public television programmes has declined sharply, and some types of programme are less available or have actually disappeared since they are not commercially viable in a situation where audience ratings are all-important. Poetry and other literary programmes have disap-peared or been banished from prime-time slots. Even once-popular variety shows have been downsized or incorporated into shows with a wider appeal, since the popularity of a group or singer is no longer sufficient in itself to attract a mass audience. Over the past ten or fifteen years, some national cultural industries have continued to function and have even grown as a result of certain trends in public policy.

In the European Union, community-wide or domestic measures have undoubtedly been beneficial to certain industries in Member States, such as book publishing (the French system of retail price maintenance for books has allowed a network of specialized bookshops to survive), recorded music publishing (radio stations are obliged to play a quota of nationally-produced songs and music), cinema and audiovisual production (a system incorporating various forms of aid to production) and television production.

There is, however, no guarantee that these hitherto undeniably advantageous effects will continue in the future. Not only do quota systems run into operational difficulties attracting regular criticism because of their singularity in world commercial transactions, but the fact that programmes can now circulate on the networks and largely escape control from public authorities will tend to reduce the effectiveness of support measures for small- and medium-sized industries operating mainly within a specific cultural or linguistic framework. This does not mean that such measures are unnecessary, but that their effectiveness may become more uncertain, simply because con-sumers will tend to diversify demand, including demand for products from the sphere of high culture.

A number of authors representing different schools of thought have long been predicting a trend towards the individualization of social behaviour, and the emergence of this trend does seem to be reinforced by ICTs, particularly in the developed countries. ICTs, unlike the media that developed earlier, usually require user-consumers to take active steps not only to access a specific programme but also to interact with it in order to obtain responses tailored to their personal requirements. To this extent, ICTs, more than any other earlier technology, promote a one-to-one correspondence between the content on offer and the user's demands, which are apparently unlike those of anyone else.

Where ICTs are involved, cultural consumption is not simply a question of narcissistic contact with works. Likewise, collective forms of consumption are not doomed to disappear, because individualization does not necessarily spell a decline in public performances and other forms of collective entertainment. Despite predictions to the contrary, the proliferation of individual delivery systems for recorded music has not led to a decline in concerts of all types of music. Complex interactions and processes of mutual i n fluence are observably taking place between different types of music, but it is not to be expected that this will have any practical outcome, although new linkages can be foreseen.

ICTs encourage a fragmented, episodic pace of consumption which has little in common with the heyday of collective cultural consumption and this tendency may lead to a number of fundamental cultural changes. One consequence may be for increased cultural consumption to go hand in hand with a decline in discussion and debate focused on cultural productions. It is also possible that performances may become almost exclusively opportunities for the 'promotion' of cultural merchandise, something that would be inevitable if public aid earmarked for live performances were reduced or even abolished, with those responsible taking as their pretext the variety and quantity of commercial products available. This would mark the culmination of the process by which culture becomes a commercial product and, as noted above, is absorbed into the leisure and information sectors.

ICTs have promted American English to the status of an international language. According to a 1998 Euromarketing study, more than one of every two

Internet surfers (58%) uses English. Other languages - Spanish (8.7%), German (8.6%), Japanese (7.9%) and French (3.7%) - are much less commonly used. These data, which are obviously difficult to establish, have nevertheless been confirmed by other studies. However, they are difficult to assess because change is so rapid in both hardware and habits.

Furthermore, it is not possible, on the basis of data on the preferred language of communication (used for electronic mail and forums), to draw similar conclusions regarding trade in cultural products. For example, after an initial phase when English.. predominated, the satellite channels are now beginning to diversify into other languages. Will automatic translation systems contain applications that will help to reduce misunderstandings between languages and promote genuine multilingualism?

In the past, research has proved disappointing, and researchers are at present cautious, pinning their hopes on the development of computer-assisted translation systems. This indicates recognition of the fact that, in this field, approximations and simplifications are not sufficient, because they undermine languages as vehicles of specific cultural features. Only strong support for translation from producers and from authorities responsible for public policy can help to bring about a more balanced flow of cultural works. If this is not forthcoming, English and probably a few more of the most widely spoken languages will eventually dominate the cultural marketplace.

Support for translation and for the development of translation aid systems will not, however, be enough in the absence of systematic efforts to support productions suitable for distribution outside their country or region of origin, and support in distributing them. Recent experience has shown that the successful exportation of films, works for television and sound broadcasting or even literary works, depends as much on international standards being met as on the availability of an appropriate distribution system. It is also important for production costs on national broadcasting networks to have been absorbed in advance, which explains the recent success of Brazilian and Mexican series outside the areas where they were produced. The same factors are likely to be important in the future.

Although in theory the new communications networks guarantee wider distribution, and even distribution that crosses borders and cuts out intermediaries, which may be helpful for niche products that may even be boycotted in their place of origin, it would be illusory to think that world markets will develop on this basis. Direct transactions will leave room for a few new actors, but free flow will probably lead to a rapid jump in production costs and a concentration of distributors. The major communi-cation groups are preparing for this eventuality. Their uncertainties about the future focus on the plans of their direct competitors rather than on the emergence of newcomers or the development of direct commerce that would be beyond their control.

ICTs undeniably complicate a number of issues facing the production of culture in all its diversity. However, the more or less rapid spread of hardware and networks is not the only factor involved in sustaining artistic pluralism within countries and regions and keeping a variety of production methods in place. Blithe and often exaggerated statements to the effect that we are now living in an information society which will impose its ground rules on culture should be viewed sceptically. It should also be remembered that, for complex reasons that research into technical innovation has already begun to elucidate, technical developments seldom fulfil expert predictions. In other words, ICTs do not contain a blueprint for the future. They will not be the sole factors shaping the future. If, however, those responsible for cultural production worldwide adopt a wait-and-see attitude and fail to grasp the importance of what is at stake, then culture will be increasingly subservient to the norms of mediatized communication and information flows.

In conclusion, it must be emphasized that public cultural policies are important and should be reinstated in areas where the field has been left free for the commercial audiovisual media and transborder flows of information. Public action will have little effect, however, if it is confined to protective and defensive measures which are in any case liable to be inefficient, if not impossible, to implement. This issue is likely to give rise to considerable debate and to social movements and even 'resistance' instigated by artists, producers, users and political leaders. During the 1993 General Agreement on Tariffs and Trade (GATT) negotiations, France strongly supported the idea of 'making an exception of culture' and provisionally won its case, arguing that with the opening of world markets, cultural products should not be treated like other commercial commodities.

Since then, the question has been asked worldwide, some counting on a de facto abolition of the 'cultural exception' by technological development, while others are waiting for international organizations and regional bodies to come out in support of cultural pluralism.

Another crucial issue being debated is the future of copyright and authors' continuing control over their works in an environment complicated by the emergence of multimedia products. Many developing countries have not yet stated that they are directly concerned by these discussions, which nevertheless do affect them.

In order to maintain cultural pluralism, it is pointless to avoid or side-step negotiations on these basic issues. An attempt was made to do this in the case of the Multilateral Agreement on Investment (MAI) by seeking to negotiate behind closed doors within the OECD. What are needed are balanced agreements that acknowledge the distinctive nature of cultural products and do not treat them simply as industrial goods.

Impact on the Media

The increasingly interconnected nature of the mass media industry has encouraged integration in a complex variety of reciprocal connections. The first set of logical mergers were between different types of media, such as television with radio and the press to create multimedia conglomerates. Mergers of media entities across countries and regions also occurred in order to attain the critical business strength needed to reach global markets.

A few hardware manufacturers made strategic moves to purchase media houses producing films, music and other media products. The strategy has paid off in recent years through co-ordinated releases of new generations of hardware, such as Digital Versatile Disk (DVD) players, digital television receivers, and digital music recording devices, together with media products and software to be played back on these new devices.

The synergy is mutually beneficial. There would have been no demand for the hardware had there been a lack of attractive media products to play on the devices.

Without the devices, the media companies would not have been able to launch a new generation of both old and new releases which help to produce a new stream of revenue for the existing libraries of intellectual properties owned by these media companies. In an interesting new twist to integration and convergence, a major television sports broadcaster has mounted a takeover of one of the most famous soccer teams in the world.

The business strategy is to acquire full control of broadcast and merchandising rights through the outright purchase of the team. If this proves to be a profitable move, it is not impossible that media companies may begin to purchase properties as diverse as universities and restaurants in order to secure publication copyright for scholarly titles and courses, and broadcast licences for cookery programmes.

There are two sides to integration and convergence. The case against concentration of ownership can be seen within the printing sector in the United States, where extensive research shows that the twelve largest newspaper conglomerates control almost 50% of all circulation in the largest market for news in the world. In book publishing, nearly every one of the major commercial publishing companies has also been bought and assimilated into larger businesses, while independent bookstores are being forced out of business by a handful of powerful national chains. On the positive side, the sale of some cable television companies, again in the United tates, helped raise much-needed financial investment to upgrade distribution systems. The merger of Cable News Network (CNN) with the Time Warner group led to the pooling of extensive complementary intellectual properties, particularly in politics, which has resulted in service on the Internet which offers more depth and data than either company alone could have provided in the print and television media.

The expansionary trends of the media conglomerates, coupled with media technologies which ignore political borders, have forced government-owned media organizations in newly developed and developing countries to respond. Within Asia, the response has generally been to privatize state-owned media in an effort to make them more competitive and attractive to domestic audiences. However, the privatization has been structured in such a way as to protect, preserve and empower traditional cultural values and maintain key government controls at the same time. The Association of South-East Asian Nations (ASEAN) plans to launch a regional direct satellite television broadcast channel, but these plans have been delayed by the financial problems affecting the region.

When several large media organizations merge, they create media giants with huge audiences. This is an invaluable asset which helps in maximizing advertising revenue, the lifeblood of media. The merger also pools strategic market information, such as subscriber and advertiser databases which are used to cross-sell media products and advertising across the organizations within the merged group.

Direct selling is probably the showcase innovation of the private sector on the Internet, and Amazon.com is the current undisputed star in this area. Amazon began by selling books over its Internet site and subsequently added music CDs to its virtual bookstore. A strictly e-commerce company, it has captured the imagination of media organizations because it has so far dealt exclusively with media products. Indications are that it will diversify rapidly to include a large variety of consumer products.

Every media company with tangible products must at some time have reviewed Amazon's methods for possible emulation. The arithmetic of direct selling to consumers worldwide without having to incur high distribution and sales discounts is an irresistible idea, and an increasing number of media organizations with such product offerings have launched websites to test the feasibility of an Amazon-like sales outlet. Attracting less public attention, but perhaps more exciting in its technological concept, are the direct sales facilities of newspapers, journals, bulletins, and electronic book publishers. Amazon uses the Internet only to promote and process payment for a product before resorting to fairly conventional means for delivering a traditional tangible media product to the consumer. In contrast to this, specialized publishers are offering articles and information from databases for instantaneous downloading over the Internet immediately after a payment has been made at the site. Book publishers will be interested in the mass consumer response to several electronic book devices introduced recently into the market and which approximate the size and feel of a book. They lend themselves to the direct sales of books bought and delivered over e-commerce systems.

The North American book distributor Barnes & Noble has negotiated with various publishers to offer more than 1,000 titles of books for downloading into the devices which have a capacity to store anything from about 1,000 to 500,000 pages at any one time. The e-book is an extremely attractive proposition to book publishers because they do not have to commit expensive print-runs and warehousing expenses up front; the risks are therefore minimum. This may encourage publishers to accept a larger number of manuscripts for publication. It is likely to facilitate the release of traditionally short-run titles, which have been rejected in the past because they were not viable as expensive paper editions.

The e-book is a viable alternative to currently available publish-on-demand technology, which deploys high-speed photocopying machines linked to collating and binding machinery. The music industry may be on the verge of making similar direct sales. A new device which downloads and stores audio digital recordings from the Internet for repeated playback by consumers was cleared for public sale, following a court hearing in California (USA) to determine if such a device threatened the preservation of intellectual property rights. The legal endorsement for the device has set the stage for music to be sold directly to consumers, a song or 'cut' at a time, rather than as a compilation on longer-playing discs.

New Business Models

The evolution of a new generation of media technologies has presented the industry with many possibilities for developing new products and services. One of the key factors, which will help in identifying the final list of possibilities for sustained development, is the parallel evolution of business models applicable to these possibilities. The successful candidates must operate with a business model acceptable to the consumers, and attractive enough to engage media operators.

The private sector has long been the primary source for funding of media operations in North America, Europe, Latin America and parts of Asia. With the trend towards the privatization of state-owned media in developing countries, the importance of feasible business models has become critical in the determination of how technologies will be deployed, and what content and software will be offered.

Large audience base models

This type of business model dominate for traditional mass media such as radio, print and television. It has also become one of the most important models for Internet-related operations where 'portal' sites offering search and directory services to the vast World Wide Web have drawn the largest number of users and attracted the keenest interest of investors and entrepreneurs. As with most broadcast organizations, portal sites do not charge for their services but instead derive revenues by selling advertising.

In this model, the number of people served by a particular Web site or broadcasting station is crucial in determining the pricing of its advertisements, and eventually its revenue. The same applies to the print media products, which are often priced for the recovery of production and distribution costs only, while profits and creative costs derive from the sale of advertising space. These numbers will take on added importance when members of the audience become customers and shoppers on interactive television and electronic commerce Web sites.

New audience-tracking technologies and sophisticated audience research methodologies enable these numbers to be desegregated into groups with a high propensity to purchase certain goods and services. These advances are a boon to advertisers and will pose a challenge to media operators, who, in the past, were required simply to broadcast advertisements for large groups. The tougher requirements are already apparent in advertising at Web sites where operators are required to broadcast advertisements in the style of banners at the top or bottom of specified Web pages, and the cost of advertising was determined by the number of people accessing the page and seeing the advertisements. This simple formula became a little more complicated when the cost was computed on the basis of the number of people who clicked on the banners and visited the Web site linked to the advertisements. The third formula which is evolving will very likely be based on a sales commission on the actual business transacted as a result of exposure, click-throughs and other services rendered at a particular Web site or page.

Electronic commerce model

This model has captured the imagination of the industry as the most appropriate for the Internet with Amazon.com as the premier prototype company. Amazon has demonstrated both the potential and the problems of this model. Although it is popularly cited as the most successful electronic commerce company, it has not shown a profit since it started. On the contrary, Amazon consistently incurred losses until the end of 1998. Researchers who have tracked the company's exponential growth blame the losses on high operating costs. Its economics also reveal a staggering scale of business. One study estimated that Amazon must generate $1 billion in annual sales just to break even.

The electronic publishing model has been given a boost with the introduction of secure electronic transaction software and systems which permit payments for purchases made over the Internet to be securely debited from credit card accounts. Further progress is expected in the near future when 'smart cards', which enable payment purchases using secure computer codes, are launched worldwide.

Subscription access model

Subscription access was widely thought to be a promising model for the electronic publishing of newspapers, magazines, journals, and newsletters. The typical electronic subscription begins when a person makes a lump sum payment to the publisher, who then provides the subscriber with a unique password, which then permits access to each new edition at a Web site.

Although the model was based on very sound logic, it was not well received by people on the Internet. For the present, it appears that the founding principle of the Internet for the free sharing of information still persists. Major content providers have indefinitely postponed plans to charge for access to their sites. To replace this, some providers require visitors to their Web sites to register themselves, or encourage them to click on the advertisement of a corporate sponsor, as a kind of surrogate payment. This has caused extensive revisions in the business plans of media companies started for the exclusive purpose of publishing and selling information over the Internet.

Conventional media, such as television news networks, newspapers, and magazines, which extended their dissemination by recycling selections from their products on the Internet, have enjoyed more prosperity. Their sites regularly clock up millions of visitors each month who in turn each read several Web pages and help to generate a total of many millions more 'page views' for the sites.

While people visiting the sites do not pay for their visits, the media organizations running the sites benefit in several ways: firstly, by promoting or cross-selling their flagship on printed or broadcast products via free access to excerpts at the Web site; secondly, by offering archival information such as previously published articles or transcripts of old broadcasts for sale through an automated system of database searches and electronic commerce; and lastly, by exposing people to this new outlet for their products and developing a global audience for future sales of a new generation of products and services.

The Economist and The Wall Street Journal now publish simultaneously on paper and on the Internet. There are many sites on the Internet that provide news. One type are the special Internet news sites, often provided by the Internet Service Providers (ISPs). Others are sites maintained by already-existing newspapers as a complement to the printed product. One can find daily newspapers and news-oriented periodicals from almost every country in the world, representing a mixture of national and regional/local press, as well as news targeting specific groups in terms of language and/or ethnic belonging. One significant result of this development is that, whereas the possibilities of access to traditionally disseminated press were limited, especially concerning regional and local press, news via the Internet means worldwide dissemination.

The former provides subscribers to the printed product and free access to the Internet edition. The latter sells subscription access to both versions. Some newspapers have used their Internet editions to enhance the attractiveness of their classified advertisements by offering package deals, which place such advertisements simultaneously on both printed and Internet editions.

As a result of the financial crisis of 1997/98, media organizations throughout Asia, Latin America and Russia are struggling to stay solvent. The media in these regions have been hit by high increases in repayments of bank loans and other forms of business financing, increases in the price of newsprint, and significant drops in advertising revenue, as companies have trimmed their advertising budgets as part of cost-cutting measures.

Internet services providers have suffered from the crisis as well, because the values of local currencies have fallen in relation to the US dollar in which the cost of telecommunications connections are calculated. At the same time and for the same reason, the cost of imported networking hardware and soft-ware has also increased. Many media companies will therefore consider the new technologies with an eye on costs and their potential contribution to cost cutting.

Communication Development

The tendency to use new technologies to meet commercial objectives is problematic for people and regions without the necessary financial resources to attract companies to fulfil their needs. The challenge is made harder by the need for stable telecommunication links and electricity to power nearly all the new technologies. Both are in short supply in the poorest regions.

The case of developing countries illustrates the way in which technology evolves and is diffused at different speeds across the world. Whereas new technologies are represented by state-of-the-art digital innovations in the developed world, for parts of the developing world telephones, television or even radio may be the latest technologies. It is in this context that two recent innovations in radio broadcasting represent important advances in the medium. The clockwork (or wind-up) radio is the first.

Communication specialists in development have been aware of the problem faced by isolated communities in obtaining dry-cell batteries to power radio receivers for several decades. Crystal-sets and solar-powered receivers have not proved to be entirely successful. The clockwork radio is powered by a patented power source, which with a few minutes of winding-up will keep a receiver playing for about an hour. It is an exciting invention which has been adapted to work on lap-top computers and other devices, which previously depended on batteries for electrical power. For the present, the relatively high-costs of these radio sets prevent their extensive diffusion across the developing world.

The other innovation is at the broadcaster's end. UNESCO has taken the lead in helping to develop affordable low-power radio transmitters for operating community broadcasting services. These transmitters are assembled from generic components by local technicians, who also assist with maintenance. Such services facilite the decentralization of media control to the community. They help promote participatory communication, which empowers communities, and support the planning and implementation of sustainable development programmes. The main hindrance to the spread of this technology is legislative.

Most developing - and even developed - countries discourage community broadcasting by limiting access to radio frequencies and to a broadcasting licence. A classic example of a new technology converging to support an old predecessor is the technology to stream sound over the Internet. This is the developed world's version of the developing world's evolution towards community broadcasting. The technology is very affordable at both ends. People can receive such Internet radio broadcasts with a relatively low investment while broadcasters can be 'on the air' broadcasting literally to the whole world at very minimal cost. These technologies represent an extremely small fraction of the total number of innovations introduced into the media industry.

The developing world with its highly limited purchasing power has sustained minimal research and development efforts to increase their access to relevant content and channels of mass communication. A study in the Philippines found that where privatization of media has been the norm, programming is not meeting the needs of local populations. This sentiment may extend quite widely across the developing world.

Transmission frequencies are a very valuable resource in some areas of the world where finding a frequency for broadcasting to minority groups is a daunting uphill battle, since regulatory authorities and established media companies have vested interests to protect. The introduction of digital television broadcasting technology with the capacity to place four channels in the same space that one analogue channel used to occupy, will soon make plenty of new broadcasting space available. A significant amount of this newly freed-up space should be reserved for minority interest broadcasting, which is now limited.

Developing countries will probably have to wait for several years before the cost of digital technologies reaches an affordable level. The early users, namely the developed countries, should therefore establish a precedent for safeguarding minority interests and those of disadvantaged groups by reserving such open digital spaces for them. Spaces must be held in trust, not only for minorities, but also for the common good in areas such as education, science and culture, which are not very profitable, but are socially vital.

The ICT technologies, with their capacities to move multimedia content anywhere in the world in a matter of seconds, provide the perfect tool for gathering and disseminating news. They have become available at a time when the demand for news is rising rapidly, fuelled by the globalization of trade and national economies. The increasing demand is not only for a greater quantity of news, but also for higher speeds in reporting. This in turn presents developers of technology with demands to increase further the capabilities and speed of technologies creating a powerful iterative spiral, which will lead to even more, exciting technologies.

The demand for news worldwide is obviously not uniform. Television ratings are a good yardstick by which to gauge demand. News dominated the top ten television shows in the United States; soap operas of different origins seem to be the most popular in many other countries such as Brazil, China and South Africa. The demand for news over the Internet appears to be more consistent, with nearly all news sites registering the most number of visitors and Web pages downloaded. Sites operated by newspapers around the world commonly serve millions of page views per month.

While most newspapers continue to provide only text and static images on their Web sites, radio, television and other integrated media conglomerates now offer multimedia content which includes text, and sound and video clips of headline news items. Several financial publications operate Web sites with access to constantly updated databases and expert systems software to work out investment computations and projections.

The exponential growth of the Internet as a channel for distributing news can be seen in the meteoric growth of Microsoft National Broadcasting Company (MSNBC), a joint venture between Microsoft and the National Broadcasting Company (NBC) in the United States.

By the first quarter of 1998, the news site served an average of 300,000 users a day with the occasional peak of 900,000 users. Together, they read 200 million pages a month. Measured by reach, it is the fifth largest daily newspaper in the United States. The top four Internet news sites in the country, MSNBC, USA Today, CNN and the American Broadcasting Company, collectively serve up 700 million pages of news every month.

Direct satellite broadcast television news channels and the Internet benefit people around the world who want and need to have constantly updated access to news at all times of the day and night. This has caused an insatiable demand for the latest news, which has in turn created the twenty-four-hour news cycle. News operations in the past were governed by deadlines fixed by printing schedules, in the case of newspapers and magazines, and airtimes for conventional radio and television news. Now that the audience is global, every moment of the day and night is the deadline.

All news programming is by definition perpetually incomplete and in a state of being constantly updated. The concept of 'the edition' has been replaced by devices such as 'breaking news' when regular programming is interrupted in television broadcasts, to show raw, unedited, live coverage about a still-evolving news item. On the Internet, a similar device is the 'latest' button, which provides a link to a usually brief write-up of a news event in the making.

The race to be the first on the air or the Internet with the latest news has created an approach to news reporting which concentrates on the immediate, the gathering of eye-witness accounts, and a follow-up of the event as it unfurls and draws to a conclusion. Attention to analytical writing is on the decline. The twenty-four-hour news cycle, and the quickly changing news agenda discourages reflection, research and analysis which take up time, and time is what the editorial departments no longer have to spare. The result is sometimes news reporting which is disconnected from history and the broader geo-political context. Merrill Brown, editor-in-chief of MSNBC, is mindful of the shortcomings of journalism on the Internet: 'Those of us producing for the Internet haven't always been as thoughtful as we might about putting today's incremental developments into perspective'. Andrew Heyward, the News President of Columbia Broadcasting System (CBS), one of the dominant North American television networks, is equally conscious of television's short-falls. He identified 'the seven daily sins of television news' as imitation, predictability, artificiality, laziness, oversimplification, hype and cynicism.

Although not as profitable as the owners would like, the media is now big business. During the con-centration of ownership, large financial investments were made; owners are now eager to recover them. At the same time, profits at many media organizations have shrunk. Together, these considerations have driven media organizations to cut costs and this has harmed the quality and diversity of news services. Among the elements which have been slashed are foreign news bureaus and the amount of original reporting undertaken.

News editors are also less inclined to dispatch their own reporters, photographers and camera crews to cover an event, preferring instead to rewrite wire service stories and tap into news footages from large television news agencies. The impact of this trend is a significantly reduced plurality of perspectives, especially where international news items are concerned. The same television news clips are broadcast by stations around the world, while the same wire service dispatches are carried in the newspapers. This provides the handful of international news agencies which feed the media. organizations around the world with an oligarchic grip on the flow of news and views. This phenomenon is called 'consonance'. Research has shown that the further the geographic origin of a news story from the editorial headquarters of a media organization, the higher the level of consonance. Accuracy of information has also suffered as a result of cost-cutting. Reduced resources to research and confirm facts often lead to the release of not completely accurate news and content. Because of the concentration of media organizations, the effects of these errors are sometimes multiplied across several types of media.

The internet has helped to inject a level of participation in news commentary that did not exist in the past. This has taken the form of on-line polls of audiences and readership using customized software which operate at media Web sites. Although the samples reached in such polls are obviously not always representative, they are nevertheless a good beginning in getting the audience involved in developing opinions about issues. Current methods of polling offer audiences a limited number of choices, identified by the media, which may not always reflect the full spectrum of opinion. Perhaps more useful are facilities at certain Web sites for visitors to post their comments.

The Internet version of a phone-in comment is tremendously popular with interactive radio stations. A few international radio and television broadcasters have also started to use audience postings of comments at Web sites and e-mail, as a channel for the audience to participate in live panel discussions. The low cost of using the Internet by the audience permits this form of live participation at the global level on a sustained basis and, if facilitated effectively, will contribute towards enriching the diversity of perspectives in all types of media. In participation of a different sort, newsmakers now use the Internet to reach out directly to the audience, bypassing the media. Court judgements have been posted directly on to the Internet, as have copious copies of original reports of powerful government-appointed investigating authorities. Such events are being multiplied in a myriad of other events, ranging from the birth of a child to an expedition on Mount Everest.

Quick-thinking editors and their lawyers have found an interesting innovative use of the new technologies in the defence of the freedom of the media. United States media organizations subpoenaed for information in their possession, and faced with prospects of losing the legal challenge when no important information is involved, have been known to publish photographs or broadcast footages so that they can honestly claim that they have not surrendered any unpublished material to the prosecutors. The new technologies allow news stories and pictures to be rushed out into the public domain over the Internet. Television companies, faced with the need to place uninteresting and insignificant footage in the public domain, have been known to broadcast this material in the middle of the night using an idle satellite.

3

Universal Information Infrastructure

Universal access to the new information services and media is in many minds the most important of these principles, and is implicitly embodied in the Universal Declaration of Human Rights, particularly Article 19 bearing on freedom of expression and Article 27 relating to freedom of access to information and protection of users' security and privacy.

Governments, industry and the civil society are seeking to apply these long accepted principles to the electronic information environment, but these efforts are hampered by major difficulties and challenges, including the critical issue of how to ensure fair conditions for the developing countries which are entering the digital age at a major disadvantage.

At the same time, however, most of the national and international debates seem to be concentrating on the technological and economic aspects of information and communication technologies (ICTs), because of their more immediate perceived impact, perhaps to the detriment of the others which will ultimately have a deeper, more fundamental significance in achieving an Information Society for All. We therefore feel that this panel is a particularly timely forum to explore the "right of access to information" and national and international strategies by which information and knowledge resources can be developed as a global public good, stressing important "infoethical" issues.

At the most basic level, universal access means ensuring all citizens access to telecommunication services and other ICT facilities. Disparities and inequalities in Internet access - now commonly referred to as the "digital divide" - are considerable, particularly in developing countries where the Internet is most often far too expensive to be accessible to ordinary citizens and most public service institutions and is often available only in major population centres.

The case of Internet service connections, for which there is no regulation at the international level, and that of access to the underlying telecommunication channels which falls within the regulatory framework developed by the International Telecommunication Union (ITU).

In the telecom area, with the mounting pressure to abolish bilaterally negotiated cost sharing arrangements (the so-called "accounting rate" system of the ITU), developing countries will face an unprecedented burden to maintain their telecommunication systems.

The net result of this "rate re-balancing" is that the telecommunication operators in developing countries will be forced to offset the costs by increasing their national call charges which are often already very high relative to local means, particularly in rural areas, thus placing further constraints on access to knowledge resources for disadvantaged populations.

Solutions require balanced consideration by national and international regulators since the telecom privatisation and deregulation movement which is at the root of the these tendencies is also enabling many consumers in developing countries to access the Internet by leased line and dial-up access at reasonable prices, especially where monopoly public telecommunication operators had been inefficient or did not reinvest their high profits in infrastructure to improve access.

In another, but related, development, advanced technology, high speed Internet backbones and powerful network nodes, built up over a period of time, have led to an overwhelming concentration of Internet backbone business in one country, the USA.

Currently, even for intra-European networks, local Internet service providers (ISPs) often use Virginia as their international Internet hub, and the majority of ISPs in developing countries are linked to the US-based operators for intra-regional and sometimes even national, traffic. ISPs outside the USA must in most cases pay the entire costs of these two-way links, and ironically, under these circumstances, even the poorest countries are obliged to subsidize the Internet providers and users in the United States.

The issue of strengthening intra-regional networks, combining commercial and public service traffic, has to be brought forward high on the agendas of regional forums. Serious thought should be given to the possibility of establishing high capacity regional backbones to connect each country within a multi-hub global network in which nobody dominates connectivity - as is already under consideration, for example, within the Asia Pacific Economic Cooperation (APEC) forum.

Public service institutions in many developing countries - universities, research centres, libraries, museums, NGOs and government agencies - are facing special difficulties in participating in the information revolution because of economic and associated obstacles to access, particularly where the Internet has been developed mainly on a commercial basis as opposed to the situation in the industrialized countries where its origin was as a service to the academic and research communities.

The general idea of a "public service sector ICT consortium" can be useful in ensuring the access of public service institutions to networks and services. Such a consortium relies on the principle of self-help, drawing on the strengths of the different institutions to consolidate demand for services, to promote appropriate public policies, and to provide cost-effective support for training, infrastructure and content development. This approach is not about duplicating facilities of the private sector, but rather about complementarity and co-operation between the public and private sectors to ensure improvements in public services through ICTs.

Public service sector consortia can take many forms. One model which has been promoted by UNESCO and other UN agencies is the multipurpose community telecentre (MCT) - a shared, sustainable facility empowering local communities to service their information and ICT requirements to improve literacy campaigns, basic and non-formal education, government programmes and participatory development action, all within the framework of a viable business plan. The basic justification and strategies for public service sector consortia were developed some years ago in a joint study of the ITU and UNESCO1, but need to be reviewed and updated in view of new developments in technologies and networks.

National authorities, telecommunication operators and ISPs could promote development and future markets by establishing concessionary rates for Internet access in public service institutions such as schools, academic organizations and public libraries. Such schemes, sometimes known as "e-rates" have been successfully promoted by governments and regulatory agencies in several countries, most notably the USA. The idea of an "Internet tax" has been proposed in various forms and forums to the cross-subsidization necessary to ensure universal access to the Internet.

Perhaps even more important than physical access to telematics facilities is universal access to knowledge content, which is at the root of building a "Knowledge Society" based upon lifelong learning and basic human values and rights. Education and knowledge must be considered in this context as not simply advantages for personal and professional fulfilment, but also as social capital - "global public goods" which are the natural concern of public authorities as developed in a very interesting recent publication of UNDP.

The knowledge base for the future knowledge economy is being developed largely through publicly funded instruments such as universities and research grants, while the exploitation of knowledge to produce products has become mainly a concern of private industry. While it is true that industries increasingly do their own product research, it is also true that the publicly funded institutions produce the researchers, and publicly funded academic institutes continue to be the fountain of knowledge.

The challenge is to define new concepts and frameworks to promote the common public welfare while encouraging private initiative and protecting rightful economic interests. A key concept in this strategy is that of the electronic public domain - information free of copyright including classical literature, fundamental and indigenous knowledge, and the information and data of governments or produced with public funds at the national and international levels - which represents a vast world documentary heritage accessible to all, a window on national cultures and an invaluable support for education and cultural industries in developing countries.

Paradoxically, public domain information, which is free of copyright and belongs to everybody, is often not well enough known to potential contributors and users because of lack of interest in promoting it, no direct profit being expected due its very "public" nature. In order to ensure effective management of and access to this knowledge, the principles of free access to information in the public domain will have to be defined and promoted through appropriate public policies and international agreements, and the necessary public service infrastructures such as virtual libraries and archives appropriately developed.

Another important consideration is that of "fair use" of protected information and knowledge.Current law and practice generally allow free use of published information for research, study, reviewing and reporting, and fair access to electronic knowledge resources can be seen as a corollary to this fair use principle. The most forceful counter-arguments to extending the concept of fair use to the electronic domain come from publishers who note that electronic texts available on the Internet are not only storable but also can be duplicated and re-distributed at will, while the analogous printed materials are browsed either in a library or a bookshop and hence are less vulnerable to copyright infringements.

Therefore, pressure is mounting from publishers to tighten copyright laws and to make browsing protected works on screen, and sharing them through networks without permission, illegal. An example is the "sui generis" right which can accorded under European law to databases irrespective of their original content or literary value, but which has not been questioned by many developing countries and not generally extended into international practice.

Policing of such tightened laws will be problematic with the difficulties of proving how and where the material is obtained and with ample opportunities to make changes to electronic text. In extreme cases some preventive technological solutions such as disabling of printing can be applied. However, it would seem more fruitful to expand the definitions of "fair use" and to work to inculcate in the world's citizens "infoethics" principles of respect for intellectual property.

Protecting human dignity in the digital age

The Internet is indeed a new mass medium, but also differs qualitatively from the "traditional" media in the degree to which it permits individual as well as mass interaction, providing new possibilities for creativity, expression and provision of personal services while raising new dangers of exploitation of citizens.

The creation of an international rating and filtering system for Internet content has been proposed as an alternative to national legislation regulating online speech. But contrary to their original intent, such systems may actually facilitate governmental restrictions on Internet expression.

Additionally, rating and filtering schemes may prevent individuals from discussing controversial or unpopular topics, impose burdensome compliance costs on speakers, distort the fundamental cultural diversity of the Internet, enable invisible "upstream" filtering which can infringe on the rights to information of citizens worldwide, and eventually create a homogenized Internet dominated by large commercial interests. In order to avoid the undesirable effects of legal and technical solutions that seek to block the free flow of information, alternative educational approaches could be emphasized as less restrictive means of ensuring beneficial uses of the Internet.

National education systems and publicly funded projects will have major responsibilities in producing skilled and knowledgeable people who will become both producers and users of ICT based content. The increase in the use of technologies in business, government organizations, and communities of all kinds are also posing serious threats to our fundamental right privacy.

In addition to the risks associated with new economic activities (e.g. on-line banking or data mining for the personal information market), the anonymous nature of the Internet may facilitate personnel harassment or "cyberstalking" which is becoming an increasing concern in some countries, as well as impersonation by unauthorized use of someone else's email address.

The focus of the global information society, with its intelligent networks, micro processors and ability to access massive reservoirs of knowledge has for the most part been on commerce and trade related issues. It is essential to consider the significance of information technology for human development and the "social capital" of knowledge.

Although the social, educational, ethical and cultural needs of our communities are intimately linked with economic welfare, it is essential to see the digital technology and the advent of global networks as offering much more than the means of doing e-business. This same technology can address many other vital human needs and support initiatives to improve education, research and knowledge levels and to deliver community services and an enormous range of public benefits.

A practical measure to achieve these goals is to expand the amount of, and improve access to, what is known as "public domain" information or "public content". Another way of thinking about public domain is to think in terms of rights to access information. Funding is a separate matter.

The link between access to information and economic welfare will in the near future become so significant that if the gap between the information rich and the information poor widens too far (whether as between communities or countries), there could be increased risk of global instability and negative impacts which reach well beyond local or national boundaries.

All countries have a vital interest in the development of a global information society and in the benefits that flow from a better informed and more knowledgeable population.

A government which promotes public content is an open government and therefore more likely to encourage greater participation by its citizens and to believe in greater transparency and accountability for decision-making. This is one way of encouraging citizens to participate in an information society. An informed population can contribute to debate, make their views known on issues and influence outcomes. These forces are a very powerful incentive for citizens; the various FOI (freedom of information) models can both encourage and empower citizens to participate in accessing and generating information.

The people's welfare will be better served through access to or disclosure of information, rather than a paternalistic approach where decisions are made on behalf of the people without informing or consulting them. One of the critical challenges is the tension between social objectives and the other economic interests in controlling or restricting the availability of certain types of information. This economic interest manifests as the intellectual property ("IP") rights of the content provider, author, inventor or other "owner" of the information.

However, the expansion of IP rights needs to be kept in check while the economics and impacts of other stakeholder interests are considered. There are specific ways to improve the balance of interests; for example, ensuring a limited duration of IP monopoly rights. In some jurisdictions, it is not possible to have copyright in a fact, only in an expression of an idea or in the particular compilation of the facts or a format.

There have always been a number of categories of exemptions from IP protections. For example: for human rights (eg freedom of the press); for public interest reasons; for library or archive deposits; for education and under special rules for non-profit institutions; under competition law; to adapt the law to new circumstances, as technology develops; and, for perceived market failure.

Many legal systems then apply various tests or factors as a guide to whether or not a proposed use will fall within these statutory categories of fair use. The scope of the fair use exception is unclear and so it has been left to the courts in many jurisdictions to define the boundaries of what amounts to fair use and is therefore non-infringing.

The origin of the fair use exception is directly relevant to the concepts underlying the public domain. Copyright is intended to advance learning and knowledge by creating an incentive system to induce authors to create and disseminate their works. However, the fair use exception is a more direct intervention or redistribution of rights to ensure access and equity for some socially beneficial purposes.

One of the most significant IP developments in the digital era is the automated rights management technology (ARM) or digital copyright management systems (CMS). These include technologies to monitor and track the exchange of digital information, such as payment per use for encrypted documents and software applications embedded in the information being accessed over the Net to ensure that the user pays for accessing protected information.

ARM technology will have a radical impact on the enforcement of IP rights in digital media and on the scope of fair use doctrine. Instead of seeking protection through very cumbersome and expensive copyright actions, the author (or content provider) can resort to the technology to ensure protection and rely on standardised one-to-one or bilateral licence contracts to ensure payment for use. This enables the content provider to bypass the public law of copyright and to impose restrictions on the re-use of the information, irrespective of the application of the fair use doctrine.

The use of ARM technology could reduce transaction costs for copyrighted material. The result may be net economic benefits in the efficiencies of ARM because of the long term effect of pushing access prices down. It can be argued that the effects of ARM increase the value of copyrighted works and encourages greater production and improved distribution.

While this trend may benefit consumers by improving both the quality of and access to this information, there is still an issue for those that are concerned with the need for direct and immediate access to certain categories of information through the public domain; it is unknown how much of this licensed information will fall into the public domain. It is therefore very important to resist any further erosion of the fair use exception.

The new IP rights management technology is making it relatively inexpensive to control the boundaries of digital IP rights. Current policing methods, through registration and court action, are so costly and cumbersome that asserting private ownership (through the use of licensing contracts) may become a more efficient method of managing our society's creative and cultural resources.

The economic effects of these efficiencies need to be analysed in terms of their social and long term impacts on the availability of information in the public domain. There is also a trend by the courts to narrow the fair use doctrine as it applies to online information where it can be argued that a new ARM licensing regime establishes a market for that information. This judicial trend undermines the original social benefit bargain implicit in the fair use exception and in the other constraints on copyright protection.

There are numerous instances where information rights are not exclusive; for example, where personal information is held about an individual. This may give rise to a privacy right to access that information or constrain its subsequent re-use, even though another may regard that same information as intellectual property. There are many precedents where the law recognises shared interests and allows modified or limited entitlements. It is essential to retain the mechanisms of fair use and to address the public benefit of having relatively unrestrained access to certain categories of information.

The widespread use of digital ARM technology, will pre-empt fair use and abrogate the balance which most copyright laws seek to achieve. This is why the fair use doctrine needs to be developed in a way that could equally be applied to private contract or licensing regimes.

The fair use doctrine, adapted, clarified and modified from public copyright law, could be another such example of public good or benefit or welfare, requiring articulation in our IP treaties and laws at both international and national level. By commodifying information and promoting a private law (contract) regime for digital content, we narrow our vision to assessing value purely in individual preference and neo-classical market terms.

This fails to appreciate the impact of knowledge development and progress, and ignores other means of valuation, such as whether overall value can be realised for society. There is much work being done on developing other economic models for valuing information, which challenge current presumptions, and are worthy of exploration.

The protection and enforcement of intellectual property rights should contribute to the promotion of technological innovation and to the transfer and dissemination of technology, to the mutual advantage of producers and users of technological knowledge and in a manner conducive to social and economic welfare, and to the balance of rights and obligations. This means that the recognition and enforcement of intellectual property rights can be subject to higher social values and, in particular, that a balance needs to be found with other users of technological knowledge.

New technologies developed by the defence industry are spreading into law enforcement, civilian agencies, and private companies. At the same time, outdated laws and regulations are failing to check an expanding pattern of abuses. It is now common wisdom that the power, capacity and speed of information technology are accelerating rapidly. The extent of privacy invasion - or certainly the potential to invade privacy increases correspondingly. .But it is not merely the increased capacity and decreasing cost of information technology that creates threats to privacy.

Globalisation of systems such as the internet removes geographical limitations to the flow of data. Convergence is leading to the elimination of technological barriers between systems. Modern information systems are increasingly interoperable with other systems, and can mutually exchange and process different forms of data. Meanwhile, the phenomenon of multi-media, which fuses many forms of transmission and expression of data and images, creates vast difficulties for legislators wishing to protect personal privacy.

Governments and private sector organisations have moved in recent years to incorporate surveillance into almost every aspect of our finances, communication and lifestyle. While paying lip service to privacy, they argue that surveillance is necessary to maintain law and order and to create economic efficiency. The rationale is often self serving, and somewhat bogus, but a substantial number of people have nevertheless been persuaded that the surrender of privacy is the price we must pay for a better and safer society.

Throughout the past quarter century, no other fundamental right in the arena of public policy has generated such turbulence and controversy. And yet, as one writer has observed "privacy is the right from which all other rights derive". It is central to the freedom and autonomy of people, and it is perhaps the key factor that limits the power of the State. Torture, discrimination, racial hatred: these issues have achieved baseline consensus within the international community. Privacy, however, is viewed by many governments and corporations as the bogeyman of human rights. It is conventional wisdom amongst many organisations that privacy of the individual and the protection of personal information impedes economic performance and law enforcement.

Access to Networks and Services

Access to information is a critical input for rural areas, in addition to its long-term implications in human development. This is not just a problem for rural inhabitants, but rather a public concern of the whole society. In any service, Universal Access roots on three multi-layered regulatory principia:

1) Geographical coverage, to bring it to every community.
2) Affordability -reasonable prices respect to the income of the users.
3) Equitability -same opportunities to all regions and social groups.

The objective of Integrated Development implies maximum values for all such dimensions, and the regulatory framework acts as an intermediate layer between commercial and group interests, and the moral obligation to promote it.

The coverage depends on the size and the capillarity of the network, but experience in developing countries has shown that even a huge investment effort to expand the system is not enough per se: moreover, a strong growth in the overall teledensity may mask increasing regional inequalities and rural-urban teledensity gaps.

Therefore, equitability is also a goal for Universal Access, since public telecommunications systems are supposed to perform balancing roles in the development of the economy. A particular access policy can drive rural-urban gaps either to exacerbation, to statu-quo or to regression phases. The effectiveness of Universal Access regulation depends on how close to the needs put by the Integrated Development layer can it drive the natural action of market forces and interest groups.

Typical complaints from Internet users in South America are low speed, scarcity of local content, low security and high prices. It is important to keep track of income disparities among regions and social groups, even in the same country.

Usually, expenditures in telecommunications services should be limited to about 1 to 3% of the total income, in order to yield a net increment in the social welfare of individuals, so a typical household in Santiago will find difficult to afford even a PSTN lifeline subscription. In communities without local ISPs, dial-up sessions require expensive long distance calls, almost impossible to afford. Others with just a small provider often do not benefit from discounts or special rates. Conversely, Internet users in large cities obtain better prices and higher quality of service, due to strong competition and more connectivity options.

In 1994, during the First World Telecommunications Development Conference in Argentina, UNESCO and the ITU submitted the joint document: "The right to communicate: at what price?" It´s worth reading it again, as a start point in successive policy proposals submitted by international organizations to foster Universal Access. The 1999 Report on the Internet from the ITU has specific recommendations to promote the industry, to build infrastructure, to expand access, to stimulate usage and creation of local content, and to promote competition in the access market.

Many countries are actively working in these issues. For example, there are several programs to facilitate public access to information through public libraries, schools and community telecenters.

In another policy toolkit, drawn from the Informatics Initiative 2000 Conference for the Americas -promoted two years ago by the Inter-American Development Bank- again there are recommendations to extend access via community telecenters, as well as special e-rates for schools, libraries and healthcare.

Universal Access to Information is largely more than a matter of regulation. It requires a strong involvement of the private sector and local institutions of the communities. There are a number of large projects with government funding, like in Canada, Australia and the USA, but also good experiences born in communities, like in Hungary, Estonia, Western Australia and the United Kingdom, while Internet access projects in Ghana and Peru are rather based on entrepreneurship and franchising.

The largest potentially suitable access networks in every country include the schools, the post offices, the public libraries, the FM radios, the cable TV providers and lately, the community telecenters. Government support is often necessary, but is not a guarantee for a smart allocation of resources.

The marginal impact of public access to information is inversely depending on the size and the resources already available in the community. Provided that every facility will require a minimum number of users and a sort of balance between affordability and sustainability, the usefulness of public access points tends to increase for small, distant and low-income communities, with little exposure to technology and to alternative information sources.

Encryption and information infrastructure

A variety of "key recovery," "key escrow," and "trusted third-party" encryption requirements have been suggested in recent years by government agencies seeking to conduct covert surveillance within the changing environments brought about by new technologies. This report examines the fundamental properties of these requirements and attempts to outline the technical risks, costs, and implications of deploying systems that provide government access to encryption keys.

The deployment of key-recovery-based encryption infrastructures to meet law enforcement's stated specifications will result in substantial sacrifices in security and greatly increased costs to the end-user. Building the secure computer-communication infrastructures necessary to provide adequate technological underpinnings demanded by these requirements would be enormously complex and is far beyond the experience and current competency of the field. Even if such infrastructures could be built, the risks and costs of such an operating environment may ultimately prove unacceptable. In addition, these infrastructures would generally require extraordinary levels of human trustworthiness.

These difficulties are a function of the basic government access requirements proposed for key-recovery encryption systems. They exist regardless of the design of the recovery systems -whether the systems use private-key cryptography or public-key cryptography; whether the databases are split with secret-sharing techniques or maintained in a single hardened secure facility; whether the recovery services provide private keys, session keys, or merely decrypt specific data as needed; and whether there is a single centralized infrastructure, many decentralized infrastructures, or a collection of different approaches.

All key-recovery systems require the existence of a highly sensitive and highly-available secret key or collection of keys that must be maintained in a secure manner over an extended time period. These systems must make decryption information quickly accessible to law enforcement agencies without notice to the key owners. These basic requirements make the problem of general key recovery difficult and expensive - and potentially too insecure and too costly for many applications and many users.

Attempts to force the widespread adoption of key-recovery encryption through export controls, import or domestic use regulations, or international standards should be considered in light of these factors. The public must carefully consider the costs and benefits of embracing government-access key recovery before imposing the new security risks and spending the huge investment required (potentially many billions of dollars, in direct and indirect costs) to deploy a global key recovery infrastructure.

A collaborative effort to study the technical implications of controversial proposals by the United States and other national governments to deploy large-scale "key recovery" systems that provide third-party access to decryption keys. Insofar as is possible, we have considered the impact of these policies without regard to individual encryption schemes or particular government proposals. Rather, we have attempted to look broadly at the essential elements of key recovery needed to fulfill the expressed requirements of governments (as distinct from the features that encryption users might desire). This report considers the general impact of meeting the government's requirements rather than the merits of any particular key recovery system or proposal that meets them. Our analysis is independent of whether the key-recovery infrastructure is centralized or widely distributed.

We have specifically chosen not to endorse, condemn, or draw conclusions about any particular regulatory or legislative proposal or commercial product. Rather, it is our hope that our findings will shed further light on the debate over key recovery and provide a long-needed baseline analysis of the costs of key recovery as policymakers consider embracing one of the most ambitious and far-reaching technical deployments of the information age.

Although there are many aspects to the debate on the proper role of encryption and key recovery in a free society, we have chosen to focus entirely on the technical issues associated with this problem rather than on more general political or social questions. Indeed, many have suggested that the very notion of a pervasive government key recovery infrastructure runs counter to the basic principles of freedom and privacy in a democracy and that alone is reason enough to avoid deploying such systems. This reasoning is independent of whether the key-recovery infrastructure is centralized or widely distributed. The technical nature of our analysis should not be interpreted as an endorsement of the social merits of government key recovery; in fact, we encourage vigorous public debate on this question.

Encryption and the Global Information Infrastructure

The Global Information Infrastructure promises to revolutionize electronic commerce, reinvigorate government, and provide new and open access to the information society. Yet this promise cannot be achieved without information security and privacy. Without a secure and trusted infrastructure, companies and individuals will become increasingly reluctant to move their private business or personal information online.

The need for information security is widespread and touches all of us, whether users of information technology or not. Sensitive information of all kinds is increasingly finding its way into electronic form. Examples include:

— Private personal and business communications, including telephone conversations, FAX messages, and electronic mail;

— Electronic funds transfers and other financial transactions;

— Sensitive business information and trade secrets;

Data used in the operation of critical infrastructure systems such as air traffic control, the telephone network, or the power grid; and Health records, personnel files, and other personal information.

Electronically managed information touches almost every aspect of daily life in modern society. This rising tide of important yet unsecured electronic data leaves our society increasingly vulnerable to curious neighbours, industrial spies, rogue nations, organized crime, and terrorist organizations.

Paradoxically, although the technology for managing and communicating electronic information is improving at a remarkable rate, this progress generally comes at the expense of intrinsic security. In general, as information technology improves and becomes faster, cheaper, and easier to use, it becomes less possible to control (or even identify) where sensitive data flows, where documents originated, or who is at the other end of the telephone. The basic communication infrastructure of our society is becoming less secure, even as we use it for increasingly vital purposes. Cryptographic techniques more and more frequently will become the only viable approach to assuring the privacy and safety of sensitive information as these trends continue.

Encryption is an essential tool in providing security in the information age. Encryption is based on the use of mathematical procedures to scramble data so that it is extremely difficult -if not virtually impossible -for anyone other than authorized recipients to recover the original "plaintext." Properly implemented encryption allows sensitive information to be stored on insecure computers or transmitted across insecure networks. Only parties with the correct decryption "key" (or keys) are able to recover the plaintext information.

Highly secure encryption can be deployed relatively cheaply, and it is widely believed that encryption will be broadly adopted and embedded in most electronic communications products and applications for handling potentially valuable data. Applications of cryptography include protecting files from theft or unauthorized access, securing communications from interception, and enabling secure business transactions. Other cryptographic techniques can be used to guarantee that the contents of a file or message have not been altered (integrity), to establish the identity of a party (authentication), or to make legal commitments (non-repudiation).

In making information secure from unwanted eavesdropping, interception, and theft, strong encryption has an ancillary effect: it becomes more difficult for law enforcement to conduct certain kinds of surreptitious electronic surveillance (particularly wiretapping) against suspected criminals without the knowledge and assistance of the target. This difficulty is at the core of the debate over key recovery.

Key Recovery

Requirements and proposals

The United States and other national governments have sought to prevent widespread use of cryptography unless "key recovery" mechanisms guaranteeing law enforcement access to plaintext are built into these systems. The requirements imposed by such government-driven key recovery systems are different from the features sought by encryption users, and ultimately impose substantial new risks and costs. Key recovery encryption systems provide some form of access to plaintext outside of the normal channel of encryption and decryption. Key recovery is sometimes also called "key escrow."

The term "escrow" became popular in connection with the U.S. government's Clipper Chip initiative, in which a master key to each encryption device was held "in escrow" for release to law enforcement. Today the term "key recovery" is used as generic term for these systems, encompassing the various "key escrow," "trusted third-party," "exceptional access," "data recovery," and "key recovery" encryption systems introduced in recent years. Although there are differences between these systems, the distinctions are not critical for our purposes. In this report, the general term "key recovery" is used in a broad sense, to refer to any system for assuring third-party (government) access to encrypted data. Key recovery encryption systems work in a variety of ways.

Early "key escrow" proposals relied on the storage of private keys by the U.S. government, and more recently by designated private entities. Other systems have "escrow agents" or "key recovery agents" that maintain the ability to recover the keys for a particular encrypted communication session or stored file; these systems require that such "session keys" be encrypted with a key known by a recovery agent and included with the data. Some systems split the ability to recover keys among several agents. Many interested parties have sought to draw sharp distinctions among the various key recovery proposals. It is certainly true that several new key recovery systems have emerged that can be distinguished from the original "Clipper" proposal by their methods of storing and recovering keys. However, our discussion takes a higher-level view of the basic requirements of the problem rather than the details of any particular scheme; it does not require a distinction between "key escrow," "trusted third-party," and "key recovery." All these systems share the essential elements that concern us for the purposes of this study:

— A mechanism, external to the primary means of encryption and decryption, by which a third party can obtain covert access to the plaintext of encrypted data.

— The existence of a highly sensitive secret key (or collection of keys) that must be secured for an extended period of time.

Taken together, these elements encompass a system of "ubiquitous key recovery" designed to meet law enforcement specifications. While some specific details may change, the basic requirements most likely will not: they are the essential requirements for any system that meets the stated objective of guaranteeing law enforcement agencies timely access, without user notice, to the plaintext of encrypted communications traffic.

Key recoverability

Key recovery systems have gained currency due to the desire of government intelligence and law enforcement agencies to guarantee that they have access to encrypted information without the knowledge or consent of encryption users. A properly designed cryptosystem makes it essentially impossible to recover encrypted data without knowledge of the correct key. In some cases this creates a potential problem for the users of encryption themselves; the cost of keeping unauthorized parties out is that if keys are lost or unavailable at the time they are needed, the owners of the encrypted data will be unable to make use of their own information. It has been suggested, therefore, that industry needs and wants key recovery, and that the kind of key recovery infrastructure promoted by the government would serve the commercial world's needs for assuring availability of its own encrypted data.

Several recent government proposals (along with commercial products and services designed to meet the government's requirements) have been promoted as serving the dual role of assuring government access as well as "owner" access to encrypted data. However, the requirements of a government and the requirements of the commercial world and individual users are very different in this regard, so different that, in fact, there is little overlap between systems that address these two problems.

The ultimate goal of government-driven key recovery encryption, as stated in the U.S. Department of Commerce's recent encryption regulations, "envisions a worldwide key management infrastructure with the use of key escrow and key recovery encryption items." The requirements put forward to meet law enforcement demands for such global key recovery systems include:

Third-party/government access without notice to or consent of the user. Even so-called "self-escrow" systems, where companies might hold their own keys, are required to provide sufficient insulation between the recovery agents and the key owners to avoid revealing when decryption information has been released.

Key recovery helps law enforcement only if it is so widespread that it is used for the bulk of encrypted stored information and communications, whether or not there is end-user demand for a recovery feature. High-availability, around-the-clock access to plain-text under a variety of operational conditions. Law enforcement seeks the ability to obtain decryption keys quickly - within two hours under current U.S. and other proposed regulations. Few commercial encryption users need the ability to recover lost keys around the clock, or on such short notice.

Access to encrypted communications traffic as well as to encrypted stored data. To the extent that there is commercial demand for key recovery, it is limited to stored data rather than communications traffic.

In fact, the requirements of government key recovery are almost completely incompatible with those of commercial encryption users. The differences are especially acute in four areas: the kinds of data for which recovery is required, the kinds of keys for which recovery is required, the manner in which recoverable keys are managed, and the relationship between key certification and key recovery. Government key recovery does not serve private and business users especially well; similarly, the key management and key recoverability systems naturally arising in the commercial world do not adapt well to serve a government.

Communication Traffic vs. Stored Data

While key "recoverability" is a potentially important added-value feature in certain stored data systems, in other applications of cryptography there is little or no user demand for this feature. In particular, there is hardly ever a reason for an encryption user to want to recover the key used to protect a communication.

4

Educational Approach in ICTs

Information and communications technologies (ICT) are a diverse set of technological tools and resources used to communicate, and to create, disseminate, store, and manage information. Communication and information are at the very heart of the educational process, consequently ICT-use in education has a long history. ICT has played an educational role in formal and non-formal settings, in programs provided by governmental agencies, public and private educational institutions, for-profit corporations and non-profit groups, and secular and religious communities. Much has been written about the use of film, radio, telephones, and television in education. Because access to digital tools, applications, and networks continues to grow worldwide and media are increasingly available in digital form, ICT-use in education can be expected to increase dramatically.

Education worldwide is facing a significant challenge in preparing students and teachers for "our future 'knowledge-based' society" during a time when most teachers are not prepared to use ICT and "the majority of existing school buildings, even in the most developed countries, are not equipped to integrate the new information and communication technologies." In this chapter, we focus on "new" digital ICTs with special emphasis on educational uses of the Internet and the World Wide Web. Several important issues in respect to the use of ICTs in educational settings including how newer ICTs differ from older technologies, why these differences are thought to be educationally important, what research shows about the effectiveness of ICTs in education, what measures are being taken to create ICT-enabled learning environments, and some of the significant issues facing educators and policy-makers when considering implementing ICT.

Although our focus will be on formal education, we will also refer to the use of ICT in non-formal and informal education. Along the way, we will provide a few of the innumerable possible examples of current educational ICT applications. To illuminate trends that will help readers to understand current directions and promising practices in the application of these systems in educational settings. However, although digital ICTs are quickly becoming more accessible, it is important to note that earlier ICTs continue to play a critical role in education worldwide. Access to films, videotapes, telephones, television or radio is still far more commonplace than access to a computer or the Internet and World Wide Web. For example, the Telesecundaria in Mexico, which began in 1965 as a closed-circuit pilot, today delivers classes designed for lower secondary school level to over 12,000 rural communities enrolling more than 800,000 students. The Mexican government plans to open an additional 4,500 Telesecundaria schools enrolling

250,000 more students between 1998 and 2002. The China TV University system enrolls over half a million students in degree programs and graduates over 100,000 per year.

The new digital ICTs are not single technologies but combinations of hardware, software, media, and delivery systems. Today, ICT in education encompasses a great range of rapidly evolving technologies such as desktop, notebook, and handheld computers; digital cameras; local area networking; the Internet and the World Wide Web; CD-ROMs and DVDs; and applications such as word processors, spreadsheets, tutorials, simulations, electronic mail (email), digital libraries, computer-mediated conferencing, videoconferencing, and virtual reality. It should also be noted that use of newer ICTs is being integrated with use of older technologies. For example, it is not uncommon to find textbooks sold with CD-ROMs containing multimedia materials or links to related websites. An exhaustive review of all of these technologies, combinations of technologies, and applications is not possible here. We also acknowledge the difficulties in implementing such innovations, and we are sensitive to the fact that whatever is said now about ICTs in education will quickly become outdated as the technologies and educational applications continue to rapidly evolve.

Changes in Communications and Information Industries

Our emphasis on digital ICT tools and applications in education mirrors profound structural changes occurring worldwide in communications and information industries. The ability to digitize analog signals and transmit them over telecommunications networks is resulting in the restructuring of the radio, telephone, television, publishing, entertainment, and computer industries into new multimedia industries that create digital products combining voice, video, text, graphics, images, and animations, and deliver these signals electronically. An example of this trend can be found in Hong Kong where New World Telephone is installing "PowerPhones" from which users may read or send electronic mail, send a fax, search online multimedia directories about hotels and tourist spots, and make a telephone call. Another example is Internet 'telephony' software that now makes it possible to place domestic and international calls from a computer to any telephone anywhere in the world.

ICT Access Worldwide

Our emphasis also mirrors the increasing access to digital tools and resources worldwide. Although estimating the number of people with Internet access is difficult at best, one current estimate places the total number at around 150 million in late 1998, an increase of over 60% since early 1997. Internet access is at present strongly concentrated in a small number of countries, providing services to a fraction of the world's population: over 90% of Internet hosts are located in the world's richest 29 counties.

However, this may be expected to change over time as telecommunications costs continue to drop precipitously and governments deregulate access. For example, the number of Internet users in India is expected to climb from half a million in 1998 to 1.5 million by the year 2000. In Africa, it is estimated that there currently are between 800,000 and 1 million Internet users. The current ratio of Internet users to people in Africa is estimated to be one for every 5,000 compared to a world average of about one Internet user to every 40 people. But here, too, the situation is rapidly changing. In 1996, only 16 countries in Africa had Internet access. Now, 53 (three-fourths) of the capital cities are online and the rest will soon follow.

A number of international infrastructure building initiatives are underway on the continent including the United Nations Secretary General's programme Harnessing Information Technology for Development that will substantially improve the Internet infrastructure by the year 2000. The Russian Non-Profit Center for Internet Technologies estimates that there are now about one million Russians online and that this number is doubling every year. And, in the next two years, the number of Internet users in Latin America is expected to grow from 8.5 million to about 34 million. The number of Latin American websites, most of which are operated by businesses, could triple in the next year to over 500,000. In Asia, estimates place the total number of Chinese online in Hong Kong, Taiwan, and Singapore at 2.6 million. The number of users in China almost doubled (620,000 - 1.175 million) from late 1997 to mid-June, 1998. Some estimates predict there will be 20 million Internet users in China by the year 2000. As these few examples help illustrate, although ICT access is still chiefly available to citizens of developed countries; such access is fast becoming possible in developing countries worldwide.

Although no comprehensive data on ICT in schools worldwide apparently exists, it is clear from many national examples that schools are also increasingly being equipped with ICT. It is also apparent that ICT equipment and Internet connectivity is still much more abundant in North American schools than elsewhere. In the United States, the ratio of students per computer dropped from 63:1 to 6:1 from 1985 to 1997 while the number of schools with internet access has grown from 35% in 1994 to 72% in 1997. In Africa, the Creating Learning Networks for African Teachers, part of the UN's Harnessing Information Technology for Development initiative mentioned above, will equip a maximum of four teacher training colleges (TTCs) in each of 20 African countries with a computer and full access to the Internet. The teacher training curriculum development and the creation of 20 national educational WWW sites. In Europe, more than 80% of schools in Solvenia have access to the Internet - 93% of secondary schools and 80% of primary schools—which is similar to the percentages of developed countries. Nearly two-thirds of secondary schools have a website.

In the United Kingdom, the pupil to computer ratio is 16:1 in primary schools and 9:1 in secondary schools, while 43% of schools in the United Kingdom are connected to the Internet. The British Government plans to connect all schools, colleges, universities, libraries, and as many community centers as possible to the Internet by 2002. In Germany, the Schulen ans Netz initiative begun in 1996, will connect 10,000 schools to the Internet by mid-1999. As of late 1997, of approximately 6,500 were connected and 1,700 had their own website. And in Italy, a national program in 1995 resulted in 120 schools being supplied with multimedia equipment. Last year, plans were announced for the installation of computer and multimedia facilities in 15,000 Italian schools to be carried out by the year 2000. At the end of the programme, approximately 25% of all Italian state schools will have access to on-line facilities and the Internet and will be equipped with advanced hardware and multimedia educational software.

In Asia, similar developments are taking place. In Japan, as of 1997, over 94% of pubic schools were computer-equipped and 10% were connected to the Internet. The Government plans to provide a pupil to computer ratio of 2:1 in middle schools and 1:1 in high schools by 1999. All of the public schools in Japan will be connected to the Internet by 2003. In the People's Republic of China, the central government will increase funding for basic, vocational and higher education over the next two years. These plans include strategies to make increasing use of Internet-based educational programs. In South America, in 1993, the Chilean government established the Enlaces (Links) to connect schools and related institutions to Chile's national computer network. By 1996, over180 primary schools and 62 secondary schools had been connected and, by the year 2000, the Chilean government plans to have 50% of the 8,250 primary schools and 100% of the 1,700 secondary schools connected. The Enlaces initiative also includes equipping schools with computers and a combination of locally produced educational software and commercial products that are available in Spanish language versions.

These few examples serve to illustrate that efforts to provide ICT and Internet access to teachers and students in developed and developing countries around the world can be expected to continue and accelerate until most, if not all, schools are equipped and connected in the next century.

ICT access in informal and non-formal education

Informal and non-formal education refers to educational activities and programs that are offered outside of formal educational institutions, including those offered by libraries, museums, community schools and centers, zoos, planetariums, commercial companies, and many other organizations. Informal and non-formal education institutions, too, are increasingly being equipped with ICT and connected to the Internet. At present, about 20% of libraries in the United Kingdom are connected to the Internet. The British government's National Grid for Learning initiative will connect all British libraries and museums to the Internet. In the United States, a 1998 survey sponsored by the American Library Association found 73% of the nation's public libraries offered basic Internet access to the public.

Many public and privately funded museums are offering ICT-based learning opportunities. For example, the Computer Museum's website offers activities designed to help individuals learn about computers. The British Natural History Museum, as part of a European Union funded to enable multimedia applications such as virtual museums and galleries to be accessed from remote locations, has constructed a virtual model of the Endeavour, Captain Cook's (an English explorer) ship. The ship, as well as virtual reality objects of seabirds and other animals encountered by Cooke on his voyages, are available on the Web. And, in a joint with the Fraunhofer Institute for Software and Systems Engineering, the German Historical Museum in Berlin and the Haus der Geschichte of the Federal Republic of Germany in Bonn are developing a virtual exhibition of German history for the Internet. Community school efforts, too, are increasingly making use of ICTs. The Lighthouse in Thailand is offering non-formal educational programs at five locations in Thailand as well as an online 'community magazine'. The community school-based initiates a challenge against the existing educational system ... The new environments and new technologies will be the main mechanism to help learners generate their own ideas, expand them, and share them with others".

ICTs are rapidly becoming available for use in every setting. This trend is true for formal, informal, and non-formal teaching and learning programs. However, such access is much more common among the rich, and in the developed countries, than for the poor, or in developing countries.

In part, efforts to connect educational organizations to the Internet are being driven by societal pressure. But such efforts are also being driven from within education by powerful differences between older and new ICTs, differences that greatly enhance the usefulness of such technologies to teaching and learning. New ICTs differ in several important dimensions from older technologies, including the integration of multiple media, interactivity, flexibility of use, and connectivity. Understanding these differences will?6 provide a clearer picture of why the use of ICT in education can be expected to continue to grow.

Integration of multiple media

Because of advances in digital technologies, it is now possible to integrate multiple media into single educational applications. Multimedia applications on CD-ROMs and websites may incorporate text, pictures, audio, graphics, animations, simulations, full-motion video, and links to other software or websites greatly enriching the learning experience. For example, Astronomy Village: Investigating the Universe is a CDROM-based multimedia program developed at the NASA Classroom of the Future that contains ten complete four-week-long investigations for secondary students. Multimedia tools available on the CD-ROM include an image-processing program, an image browser, a telecommunications program for accessing the World Wide Web, a star life cycle simulator, an orbital simulator, and a 3-D star simulator. Multimedia resources include 85 minutes of digitized video clips; more than 300 images from the Hubble Space Telescope and other instruments; 12 illustrated audio lectures by astronomers discussing their work; over 100 computer animations and graphics; and 180 full text documents such as book chapters, NASA publications, and articles from astronomy journals and magazines.

Interactivity

Earlier technologies used for instruction were passive in nature. That is, the delivery of instruction required no action on the part of students beyond listening, watching, and perhaps taking notes. Such ICTs were one-way channels of instructional delivery. New ICTs give the student and teacher the ability to control, manipulation, and contribute to the information environment. On the lowest and least valuable level, this may simply mean the student controls the pace and order of a presentation. But much more is possible. Using ICT students may not only make choices about the pace and order of a presentation, but may choose topics; take notes; answer questions; explore virtual landscapes; enter, draw or chart data; run simulated experiments; create and manipulate images; make their own multimedia presentations, communicate with others, and more. Previously, ICT-use required students to be grouped together in a controlled environment at a specific time and location. With some technologies, for example radio and television, use was rigidly tied to schedules developed by people far removed from the day-to-day functioning of the classroom.

New ICT applications have given rise to the term 'anytime-anyplace,' a reflection of the flexibility possible in using ICT to support teaching and learning. The outgrowth of this flexibility has been the development of 'virtual' educational experiences. A virtual experience refers to educational situations in which distance and time separate the teacher and students, who use ICT to interactively to share resources, communicate, and learn. Virtual education allows students to study at their own time, place and pace. In essence, a virtual education means having educational transactions accessible?7 from the home, workplace, or anywhere that the student chooses to be. Virtual classrooms, schools, colleges, and universities offering classes by email, computer-mediated conferencing (CMC), videoconferencing, or websites, or combinations of these technologies, are proliferating.

Perhaps the most powerful feature of new ICTs is connectivity. Prior to the 1990s, computers in educational settings were seldom connected to local area networks (LANs) or the Internet. With the widespread adoption of LANs, decreasing telecommunications costs, increasing bandwidth, and the invention of the World Wide Web, educational access to the Internet is becoming commonplace. If equipped with a computer, appropriate software, and Internet access, students and teachers have access to every other person on the planet who has an Internet account, hundreds of thousands of information archives, and millions of webpages of educationally relevant content. These four dimensions - integration of multiple media, interactivity, flexibility of use, and connectivity - distinguish digital ICT from previous technologies. Because of these differences, educators are finding powerful new ways to integrate digital ICTs into the curricula.

Effectiveness

Perhaps the most important question about ICT is how effective is its use in education? To answer this question one must consider three aspects. How effective is ICT-mediated instruction when compared to traditional face-to-face instruction? What does ICT enable that would not otherwise be possible? And third, are ICT worth their costs?

ICT-mediated instruction

The effectiveness of ICT in education is what, if any, impact ICT-mediated instruction has on student performance. ICT-mediated instruction refers to instruction delivered via a technological channel such as television, radio, or a computer and network. ICT-mediated instruction can be synchronous, with both the instructor and the student participating simultaneously. For example, instruction may be delivered via desktop videoconferencing by a teacher located at a university to employees at widely separated companies. ICT-mediated instruction may also be delivered asynchronously, with the instructor and student participating at different times.

Instruction based on teaching materials placed on a website does not requiring simultaneous participation. Or synchronicity may not matter, as when self-contained instructional materials are packaged on a CD-ROM. In this case, the instructional designer may have developed the materials months or even years before the student uses them and communication between the two is impossible. Early studies of ICT-mediated instruction's effect on student learning have been characterized as the "no significant difference" phenomena. That is to say, whatever medium of instructional delivery - film, radio, television, telephone, or computer—was used, no significant difference on performance measures was found between students receiving ICT-mediated instruction and those receiving traditional face-to-face instruction in a classroom. Both groups perform equally well. Studies focusing on the use of computer-mediated instruction conducted in the 1980s found more positive results. In a meta-analysis of over 500 individual studies.

Sudies of computer use prior to the 1990s. Such use was often limited to drill and practice and tutorial software programs. In the 1990s, use of ICT in schools is moving toward engaging students in "authentic" learning tasks in which students use computers, software, and network access to simulate events, communicate, collaborate, analyze data and access information resources. For these applications of ICT in schools, the research data are less extensive. However, some individual studies have been conducted that demonstrate positive learning and affective outcomes. A recent study by ETS of student achievement in mathematics and the use of ICT -the first such study to document relationships between student use of technology across the United States and higher scores on a national standardized test - concluded that "technology does matter to academic achievement, with the important caveat that whether it matters depends upon how it is used".

In another recent study undertaken by the Bertelsmann Foundation of students in a German school and a school in the United States concluded "that the use of media and technology improves learning outcomes, instills key qualifications for the information age, and increases motivation". And finally, one concern often expressed about ICT is that its use will isolate students from each other and from their teachers. In a 10-year longitudinal study undertaken by Apple Computer, "Dispelling widespread myths, the researchers found that instead of isolating students, access to technology actually encouraged them to collaborate more than in traditional classrooms. And instead of becoming boring with use, technology was even more interesting to students as they began using it for creating and communicating". It appears, therefore, that ICT, properly used, may enhance and increase communications between people.

In conclusion, evidence has consistently shown ICT-mediated instruction using conventional teaching methods is as good as traditional face-to-face instruction and, in the case of computer-based instruction, may in select instances improve student learning and attitudes towards learning. However, the picture is less clear - but promising - for more sophisticated uses of ICT in the classroom, especially for the host of applications and methods that support "constructivist" learning, in which students are encouraged to work in rich environments of information and experience to build their own understandings about them. Worldwide, research into the effectiveness of ICT-mediated instruction is continuing and should provide a clearer picture of the effectiveness of ICT in supporting constructivist pedagogy.

ICT-enabled education

A second way to assess the merit of ITC-use in education

is to consider what, if anything, such use enables students and teachers to do that they would not otherwise be able to do. To explore this question, we consider five aspects of the educational use of ICT -supporting new pedagogical methods, accessing remote resources, enabling collaboration, extending educational programs, and developing skills for the workplace.

Modern constructivist educational theory emphasizes critical thinking, problem solving, 'authentic' learning experiences, social negotiation of knowledge, and collaboration -pedagogical methods that change the role of the teacher from disseminator of information to learning facilitator, helping students as they actively engage with information and materials to construct their own understandings. That is, students learn how to learn, not just what to learn. ICT has the potential to be used in support of these new educational methods, as tools enabling students' learning by doing. ICT can make it possible for teachers to engage students in self-paced, self-directed problem-based or constructivist learning experiences; and also test student learning in new, interactive, and engaging ways that may better assess deep understanding of content and processes. Two examples may help illustrate how ICT can support constructivist teaching methods. Computer Supported Intentional Learning Environments (CSILE), developed at the Ontario Institute for Studies in Education, is a network system that provides support for collaborative learning and inquiry within a school. CSILE promotes student interaction through referencing, connecting ideas, sharing authorship, and "building-on" the work of others to advance knowledge.

The central feature of CSILE is a 'communal' database into which students can enter text and graphics, and can read, add to, and comment on other's work. The commercial version of CSILE, Knowledge Base, is being used in both work and educational settings in Canada, Japan, the United States, Finland, and the Netherlands. The Physics Teaching Studio, pioneered at the Rensselaer Polytechnic Institute in the United States, incorporates the systematic use of ICT in a cooperative learning environment for instruction in undergraduate physics. Laboratory data acquisition and analysis tools are embedded into a hypermedia text that introduces scientific topics, links the students to related materials, and poses questions for the students to answer with the ICT tools. Studio courses emphasize a hands-on, learning by doing approach engaging students in various problem solving and active learning sessions. This approach has been applied to mathematics courses and the concept has spread to other universities including City University of Hong Kong and Curtin University of Technology in Australia.

Improved assessment tools can also be developed using ICT. Such assessments can engage students in tasks that require data manipulation, simulation or other interactive acts of knowledge construction. VizQuiz is a multimedia program that allows students to take a chemistry quiz at a computer, but with the added advantage that color graphics, animations, and video clips can be included in the questions. In addition to multimedia capability, such programs can provide hints, remedial feedback, worked out solutions or explanations, and instantaneous grading. However, although ICT offers the opportunity to construct powerful learning experiences, it is pedagogically neutral. That is, instead of being used in the ways described above, ICT can be used in support of traditional teaching methodologies like the large group lecture, student note taking, and examinations. Teachers can use a computer and projector to show slides to illustrate a lecture, students can use laptop computers to take notes during the lecture, and multiple choice quizzes about the content of the lecture can be put on a website. How these new ICT tools and resources will be used is a human decision, not inherent in the technologies themselves.

As previously mentioned, connectivity is one of the main differences between older and new ICTs. Below, we discuss two aspects of connectivity—access to material and to human resources. Historically, information resources at libraries, schools, and universities have only been available within the walls of these institutions, in a wide variety of physical media, at certain times of the day, and in limited quantities. Because of advances in ICT, it is no longer necessary for students and teachers to be at a certain location at a specific time to acquire a physical object. The Internet represents the greatest collection of human knowledge ever assembled, and it is available to every student and teacher properly equipped with ICT. An unlimited number of digital representations of physical objects can now be made available to students at any time and from any place. Digital library initiatives are being undertaken in countries around the world that will provide collections that are electronically accessible of the Internet including printed works (e.g., textbooks, journals, illustrations, maps, charts and graphs), photographs, films and videotapes, paintings, 3D models, graphics, animations, software, reference materials, audio files, and so forth. A joint effort between the European Union and the National Science Foundation in the United States is exploring international collaboration on research to develop such libraries. Specialized collections of digital information are also being created. For example, the entire works of William Shakespeare may be accessed, searched, and downloaded from a website at the Massachusetts Institute of Technology (MIT).

Web-based language dictionaries, such as the LEO English/German Dictionary, provide a means to translate words and phrases from one language to another. A virtual tour and access to digitized images of major works from its collection. The NASA Image eXchange offers access to hundreds of thousands of images taken by US spacecraft of the Earth, the planets, moons, asteroids, and other extra-terrestrial bodies. Thousands of websites now exist that contain collections of high quality curriculum guides, lesson plans, and instructional activities. For example, the United Nations CyberSchoolBus website contains teaching units on urbanization, disease, the environment, and women and politics, as well as interactive games, maps, databases, and quizzes. Specialized websites designed to provide information and assistance in specific subject areas are also proliferating. Lingu@NET is a website developed by the British government to provide "quality-assured resources for language teachers and learners worldwide".

And finally, remote access to expensive scientific instrumentation is also possible. In the United Kingdom, the Virtual Microscope of the Open University can be used by students to view slides over the Internet (or from a CD-ROM version). The Hands-On Universe, at the Lawrence Berkeley National Laboratory, co-funded by several U.S. government agencies, has developed and piloted an educational program that enables high school students to request their own observations from telescopes at professional observatories. Students download digital images to their classroom computers and use powerful image processing software to visualize and analyze their data. This ability to access remote resources and use them locally, although not without negative aspects, fundamentally changes the quantity, nature, and potential uses of information resources available for educational purposes. In addition to efforts to digitize existing physical resources, many new information resources (e.g., websites, digital images, electronic journals and newsletters) are being created which can only be accessed electronically. As digital representations of physical resources are created, and as more information resources are distributed only in digital format, it will be critical that students and teachers have ICT access.

ICT enables educational collaborations between individuals and groups of people. Such collaborations may take place locally or between people in widely separated geographical locations. They may be temporary or long-term. Students?12 may collaborate with peers in other schools, teachers may collaborate with university professors, members of the local business community may serve as mentors to students, scientists in government agencies may work with school children, and so forth. Only educational usefulness and access to ICT limit the possibilities. Email, computer-mediated conferencing, and desktop videoconferencing are all being used to support collaboration between individuals and groups. Collaborations are also taking place by means of real-time chat systems; whiteboards; newsgroups; computer-mediated conferencing (CMC); and specialized software like CaMILE: Collaborative and Multimedia Interactive Learning Environment and The Knowledge Integration Environment. Other applications include MUDs (Multi-User Domains) MOOs (Multi-user domain, Object Oriented), and MUSHs (Multi-User Shared

Hallucinations). Such applications are Internet-accessible, text-mediated virtual environments in which participants can both interact with others as well as help construct the common virtual space. At the University of California, Berkeley, classes in language, literature, linguistics, law, and communications are making use of such applications. Combinations of these ICT applications are also frequently used in educational programs.

Online experts

Many organizations offer 'ask an expert' services. For example, students may send inquiries about scientific topics to working scientists at the Canadian Centre for Marine Geology of Dalhousie University and the US Argonne National Laboratory. In other examples, online experts offer advice in health, weather topics, and construction engineering. In an extreme example of how ICT can bridge distance to enable students to access remote expertise, last spring students from four universities in the US and Canada and discussed physiology experiments with astronauts orbiting the Earth aboard the space shuttle Columbia.

ICT can also enable mentoring programs to provide one-on-one guidance to individuals by well-established members of a particular community. Such virtual collaborations between individuals are an effective ways for senior members of a community to teach, inspire, and support newcomers. Mentor High School in the United States offers an electronic Quest Forum in which freshmen students may discuss course options with students in the senior class.

Virtual learning communities

ICT makes it possible to engage people in widely dispersed locations in 'virtual learning communities.' Virtual learning communities are learning groups based on shared purpose, not artificial distinctions of location or age. Through ICT, learners can be drawn together from almost anywhere, and they can construct their own formal or informal learning groups. Such communities may transverse barriers of time, geography, age, ability, culture, and social status. ICT that supports such efforts can be as simple as email or as sophisticated as desktop videoconferencing systems. In an example of how email is being used to enable virtual learning communities, a course titled International E-Mail Debate is being offered by professors at universities in Turkey, the United States, Germany, and the Czech Republic to promote writing skills across cultures and enhance intercultural awareness. Students enrolled in the course debate position papers on timely and relevant topics using E-mail.

Virtual Design Studios, begun in 1993, are collaborations between teams of Architecture students in universities worldwide. Teachers and students, on different continents and in different time zones, work on a common design, using computer-aided design systems, email, a central database, and video-conferencing. Participants use the World Wide Web to display their designs and a virtual international jury of architects and teachers judges the relative merit of the work. Past student included re-designing housing in Shanghai and designing a Center for Cultural and Religious Studies in Japan. A similar effort took place in 1996 between students and teachers at Union College (USA), METU (Turkey), and Queen's University (Canada). Virtual Design Studio techniques are being utilized by other disciplines, such as Engineering. The Global Learning and Observations to Benefit the Environment (Globe) program, sponsored by the U.S. Government, links students, teachers, and the scientific research community worldwide in a virtual learning community to study the global environment. Internationally, GLOBE is being implemented through bilateral agreements between the U.S. government and governments of partner nations. As of December 1998, thousands of schools in 74 countries have registered as participants. In the GLOBE program, scientists design protocols for specific measurements they need for Earth Science research that can be performed by K-12 students. Teachers are trained in the GLOBE protocols and teach them to their students. Students make the measurements, enter data via the Internet to a central data archive, and the data becomes available to scientists and the general community. Scientific visualizations of the data are provided over the Internet. Students benefit by having a 'hands-on' experience in science, math, and technology, using their own local environment as a learning laboratory. Students also benefit from the opportunity to communicate with their peers around the world, thus increasing not only their environmental understanding but also their understanding of other cultures and their sense of global community.

Beginning in 1995, a series of online 'Quest' have brought together students and teachers together around the world into a virtual community to learn about specific topics framed in an interactive learning expedition. For example, during MayaQuest, a 1995-96, over one million students, teachers, and others from around the globe followed the progress of a five-rider scientific bike expedition among Mayan ruins in Mexico and Central

America, learning about the ancient Mayan civilization and learning from on-site archaeologists. The bicyclists carried laptop computers and a satellite dish to connect to the Internet. Students voted on team decisions, explored 21 Maya sites and were virtually on hand for several major archaeological discoveries. The original MayaQuest website (no longer available) received over a 1.2 million hits in 90 days. It offered team updates, photographs, teachers' guides, and direct interaction with eight of the world's top archaeologists. The company has since offered educational scientific expeditions to Africa and the Galapagos Islands. Other organizations are offering online learning adventures for teachers and students.

Using specialized software, teachers can create Internet-based simulations for role-playing activities in language learning. The simulations, incorporating email, chat, and online creation and editing of documents, are thought to motivate oral and written communication amongst the participating groups, while students are guided through scenarios relevant to the country of their chosen language. The UNICEF Voices of Youth website offers opportunities for teachers and students to participate in discussions on current global issues, such as the effects of war on children; take part in interactive global learning, and exchange experiences about the use ICT in education.

Home/school communications

Although such virtual learning communities can span the globe, they can also be formed locally. For example, in the U.S., students, parents, teachers, and administrators in the Los Angeles Unified School District's, REBUILD have joined together into a virtual learning community with the objective of improving the performance of Limited English Proficient (LEP) students. Staff at 11 schools are using interactive videoconferencing over computer networks to jointly plan lessons and team-teach from different sites. All students in REBUILD schools, mostly minority children, are provided with access to the Internet and electronic mail in their classrooms and from their homes. Homework assignments are placed on the web and informal parent-teacher conferences take place electronically whenever necessary. Staff members at the school sites receive continuing professional development instruction and consultation via videoconferencing from staff at the Center for Language Minority Education and Research at California State University Long Beach.

Students in the program have made substantial gains in English reading proficiency. In the United Kingdom, Microsoft, Comtel and International Computers Limited (ICL) have funded the Highdown Information Hub which connects homes and schools via the Internet. Parents are able to send email to their children at school during the working day, view that their children are working on, and electronically converse with teachers, opening up new learning opportunities by enabling close collaboration between parents, students, and teachers.

ICT makes it possible to extend the reach of educational programs in two important ways. First, ICT makes it possible to deliver educational programs anywhere in the world. Second, ICT also can help individuals learn throughout their lifetime.

Distance (distributed) education

Distance education programs, also known as 'distributed'

education programs, are those in which the teacher and students are physically separated, and teaching and learning takes place by means of single technologies or combinations of ICTs. In the past, such programs made use of print, radio, and television. Now, new ICTs are driving changes in these traditional 'open' or distance education programs. Such programs are increasing using the Internet and the World Wide Web for the delivery of courses. For example, the International Francophone Consortium of Distance and Open Learning Institutions (CIFFAD), a consortium of open and distance learning institutions spread over 49 countries, of which 80% are in developing nations, has recently entered into a phase of reengineering to make use of new ICTs. The group aims to provide at least one hundred access points to the Internet per year in member establishments with the major part of the consortium having access to the network by the end of 1998. In an initiative making use of a combination of virtual and traditional educational programs, Singapore's two leading research universities - the National University of Singapore and Nanyang Technological University - and The Massachusetts Institute of Technology in the U.S. recently signed an agreement to "create a new global model for long-distance engineering education and research".

The jointly developed degree programs will enroll their first students in July 1999, and will be created and delivered by instructors from the three institutions, using a combination of faculty and student exchanges and state-of-the-art communications technology. Typically, distance education courses have been offered as supplementary programs by campus-based educational institutions. Now, however, digital ICTs have stimulated the creation of "virtual" non-profit and for-profit educational institutions that exist partially or only in "cyberspace" and whose programs are offered entirely by means of ICT. Such efforts are making it possible for ICT-equipped individuals located anywhere to participate in educational programs. The Western Governors University is an example of a "virtual university," a university that has no physical campus. WGU, initiated in 1996 by the governors of 18 of the Western United States, is a competency-based, degree-granting, virtual university: "a 'cyber' university that is not bound by its location because it doesn't have a campus in the physical sense. The Open University in the United Kingdom and the Virtual University of the Monterrey Institute of Technology in Mexico to collaborate on the development and delivery of distance learning programs.

In Germany, the four Baden universities Freiburg, Karlsruhe, Mannheim and Heidelberg recently announced the establishment of that country's first virtual university. The initiative's objective is to establish individual distance learning via e-mail, ISDN or digital television. In Africa, the World Bank is funding the development of the African Virtual University (AVU). This effort holds great promise for improving educational access for people on a continent where relatively few enjoy the benefits of education, let alone a tertiary education:

> Very few African countries have attained primary education for all, despite the fact that many have been independent for some thirty years. At secondary level, the record is even worse, with many African countries able to provide secondary education to only 4 or 5 per cent of the age-group. Most African countries can boast of less than one per cent of the relevant age-group attaining any form of tertiary education, compared to between 25 per cent

> and 75 per cent in industrialized countries. And those who do attain tertiary education are unlikely to specialize in science or technology.

AVU completed a pilot phase in 1996-98 and is now moving into an operational phase when it will begin delivering full-fledged undergraduate degree programs in Science and Engineering in January1999. The AVU's programs will be delivered by a combination of ICT including interactive television and the Internet. The program is developing a digital library of scientific engineering as a resource to students and teachers. Virtual educational programs are not limited to postsecondary education. The U.S. Department of Education has funded the Virtual High School (VHS), a collaborative of U.S. high schools that develops and shares web-based courses.

During the 1997-98 school year, VHS offered 29 Internet-based, credit-bearing courses to about 500 students in 27 schools located in 10 states. This approach is thought to be particularly useful as many of the participating schools either have no qualified teacher or insufficient enrollment to justify individually offering some of the courses available through the collaborative. In addition to traditional institutions using ICT to enhance or create distance learning programs, commercial companies like Sylvan Learning Systems, Inc, in the United States and the Wall Street Institute School of English in Europe are starting ICT-based for-profit distance education programs. Although alternate and distance education providers currently make up less than 2% of the postsecondary education market, almost $2 billion dollars has been raised on Wall Street since 1996 to finance such new ventures.

Unlike in the past when a person's education took place for a specific period of time during their youth, education is now widely seen as a continuing activity taking place throughout the lifespan. Establishing lifelong learning habits among citizens and providing lifelong learning opportunities has become a major goal of government initiatives worldwide. Lifelong learning is thought to be important for at least two reasons. First, it is no longer possible to master an entire discipline in a few short years. The amount of information available and the speed at which new information is being created makes this impossible. Consider, for example, that printed scientific information doubles approximately every 10 years. Half of all available scientific information has been published in the last 10 years. Second, career changes are becoming more frequent as are changing requirements within individual professions. For example, the People's Republic of China is facing changes of unprecedented magnitude in its traditional industries, and a large number of workers are being forced to change careers or take early retirement.

In order for these industries to survive and to take advantage of market opportunities, the workforce will need to be upgraded to work at higher knowledge levels with new technology. Because ICT can enable teaching and learning from anywhere at anytime, it is seen as an effective means to provide lifelong educational opportunities. The World Bank's Consultative Group on International Agricultural Research (CGIAR) noted:

> In industrialized nations, it is widely recognized that lifelong learning has become essential in a world driven by new science and technologies, with frequent retraining being needed for many

> professions. Fortunately, we now have a new tool that makes this type of education much more readily possible. The Worldwide Web is being used as a direct teaching tool that allows virtual classrooms of interacting students and faculty to be created through "asynchronous learning networks."

Many examples of how ICT is being used to foster and encourage lifelong learning can be found. In Africa, LWF is supporting the implementation of "Multipurpose Community Telecenters" in five countries at which locals may have affordable access to ICT. By enabling users to share the costs of facilities and support, the Telecentres will offer low-cost means of Internet access as well as information support for literacy campaigns, basic and non-formal education, and information on government programs. The Telecenters will also provide facilities for the generation and exchange of community-based information. In Great Britain, the Department for Education and Employment has established a 'UK Lifelong Learning' website that provides news and lists of lifelong learning opportunities. Earlier this year, the Dutch government launched a national program for lifelong learning "to ensure that better use is made of the country's intellectual resources." As part of the program, teacher-training colleges will receive extra funding to experiment with ICT. The European Lifelong Learning Initiative makes use of ICT, "to initiate the dissemination of information, the co-ordination of projects and studies, the mobilisation of actions, people and organisations to bring Europe into the Lifelong Learning Age. It covers all sectors and all countries".

The Asia Pacific Economic Cooperation (APEC) Forum has established three mechanisms to assist countries across the area to establish lifelong learning: the creation of a database of Asian scholars, researchers and practitioners involved with lifelong learning issues and programming across the region; the development and publication of a book of papers on lifelong learning policies, practices and programs across the Asia Pacific region; and a lifelong learning conference for APEC members to discuss issues identified in the book.

After leaving school to embark on a career, young people can expect the day-to-day practice of every discipline to be affected by the use of ICT. In the future, economic competitiveness, employment, and personal fulfillment may no longer be based on the production of physical goods. Personal and national wealth creation may be linked to the production and dissemination of knowledge and depend on research, education and training, and on the capacity to innovate. Having advanced ICT skills and knowing how to use discipline-specific applications may help students secure suitable employment and enhance their productivity once employed. Furthermore, as has been noted above, the ability to engage in life-long learning opportunities offered by educational institutions around the world is increasingly dependent upon access to, and use of, ICT. In light of changing perceptions about what constitutes appropriate skills for the modern era, some organizations are promulgating educational standards, attempting to codify what all students should learn about ICT. For example, the National Educational Technology Standards (NETS) in the United States has released an initial set of national educational technology standards for pre-college students (cnets.iste.org). The NET standards are divided into six categories including "Basic Operations and Concepts," "Social, Ethical, and Human Issues," "Technology Productivity Tools," "Technology

Communications Tools," "Technology Research Tools," and "Technology Problem-Solving and Decision-Making Tools".

However, although it can be anticipated that the increasing use of ICT in education and society will change the nature of the knowledge and skills students must acquire in order to compete and contribute in an increasingly ICT-dominated global economy, what skills will be necessary is not clear:

> What do students need to know and do with technology? Unlike the more stable content and goals we have for other areas of school study, technology continues to change and evolve; with these changes come ever-new goals for how technology should serve learning, and what students should know about technology. A review of the "prevailing wisdom" about appropriate technology use since the early 1980s takes one down an ever-turning road that includes programming in BASIC, then with LOGO; and on to drill and practice applications on integrated systems; word-processing and curriculum-specific tools like history databases, simulations, and microcomputer-based labs; then multimedia; the Internet; and now Web page design. While there may be some logic to this progression, the reality is that, just as educators get their arms around one approach, with the attendant investments in software, training and possible curricular readjustments, the messages about appropriate technology use change.

There does seem to be a growing consensus that all students must achieve "Information literacy": "It is the task of general education to provide every girl and boy with the versatile basic skills in acquiring, managing and communicating information which are necessary in the information society and essential for successful further study". The American Library Association has outlined seven steps representing the basic elements in an information literacy curriculum: Defining the need for information, initiating the search strategy, locating the resources, assessing and comprehending the information, interpreting the information, communication the information, and evaluating the product and process. Genric skills that "information society literate" citizens should have, suggest three categories into which such skills might be categorized: Connectivity, Logic, and the Structuring of Data and Information. It is clear that new skills and knowledge will be necessary to compete and contribute in a global "knowledge society." However, because of the rapid pace of change of ICTs, it is less clear what skills can be taught to today's students that will still be relevant by the time they graduate and enter the workforce. Focusing on concepts like "information literacy," rather than on specific technologies or applications, may be essential in planning and developing new curricula.

The third issue we consider when assessing the effectiveness of ICT in education is the question of cost-effectiveness - information is of critical importance, especially to developing countries with fewer resources to invest. However, assessing the cost-effectiveness of ICT in education is difficult, if not impossible, for at least four reasons -lack of meaningful data, variability in the implementation of ICTs, difficulty of generalizing from specific programs, and difficulty of assessing the value of qualitative educational differences. In addition, cost-analyses do not consider the societal and economic consequences of not investing in ICT for education. First, direct comparisons between traditional and ICT-based educational programs are hard to make because meaningful data are lacking. When considering the costs associated with ICT use, what variables are included in such studies vary widely. For example, in addition to hardware and software costs such an analysis may or may not take into account factors such as teacher training, support personnel, facilities renovation, security systems, insurance, and so forth. Furthermore, many institutions making use of ICT in their programs simply do not collect such data. Problems in conducting a cost-analysis in developing countries because of the lack of local effective efforts to do real world cost analysis and the difficulty to obtain the kind of information we would have liked to include in our cost analyses.

Second, there is the question of which technologies and applications to compare. The costs associated with any ICT-based educational program may merely indicate the choices that have been made, not the choices that are possible. Evaluating the cost-effectiveness of email-based courses will return a different result than comparing courses using videoconferencing technologies, although the educational goals may be similar. Making judgments as to the cost-effectiveness of ICT-use in general from the analysis of particular programs is difficult. Third, as has been noted earlier, ICTs are not single technologies or applications, but an array of possibilities. Many ICT-based educational programs use a combination of technologies and applications, making the analysis of costs and comparisons with other programs even more difficult. This is further complicated because of the rapid evolution of ICT and changes in its uses in education. Studies typically take a long time to complete and longitudinal studies take years. Such efforts may be doomed to failure because the subject under study is a moving target.

And finally, there is the question of what metrics are useful in measuring "effectiveness." Is "effectiveness" determined by units of instructional time, by student retention rates, by performance on assessments? Quantitative measures are easier to construct but may not ultimately tell us much. Qualitative differences may ultimately be more important in assessing the cost-effectiveness of ICT, but may not be measurable. For example, approaches to incorporating ICT into education can be roughly grouped into three categories - learning about (computer literacy and programming), learning by (drill and practice and tutorial software), and learning with computers (collaborating with remote groups, conducting research over the Internet).

None-the-less, even in the face of such obstacles, attempts to establish the relative costs of ICTs in education. In general, these studies find that the use of new ICTs is more expensive that instruction delivered by older technologies like print and radio, but less expensive than instruction delivered by television.

Education and ICT in Latin America and the Caribbean, the costs of using a computer with an Internet connection in a school was much less expensive per pupil than broadcast television, but substantially more expensive than radio. It should be noted that even these findings may be misleading because of the variability across regions and individual countries in the cost of Internet access and what such costs mean in the real income of individuals in various countries. As should be clear from the information below, although Internet access is absolutely less expensive in Africa than Europe, the "real" cost to individual users in Africa is much higher. Currently, the average cost of using the Internet for 5 hours a month in Africa is about $60/month. This contrasts with figures of the Organization for Economic Cooperation and Development (OECD) which estimated recently that 20 hours of Internet access in the U.S. costs $29, including phone and provider fees. Although European charges are more all of these countries have per capita incomes which are 10 - 100 times greater than the African average. Despite the general lack of cost data that can be used to estimate the cost of information technology in developing countries, compare the per pupil costs of setting up a computer laboratory in a school for computer-assisted instruction. A similar analysis of the costs of equipping a classroom, not a laboratory.

ICT in developing countries, assessed the annual per-student cost of providing computers for instruction in developing countries at $84 USD. This finding is in close agreement with the study by Potashnik and Adkins. By extrapolating the expenses if 30 computers were used 300 days per year, 10 hours per day, as a resource to raise the skills and education levels of all members of the community, not just students, Osin estimates the cost drops to 34 cents per hour of interaction. He concludes, "There is no alternative system known that may provide the benefits possible by integrating computers in the education system, while at the same time serving the whole community."

Another factor that must be considered when calculating the cost-effectiveness of ICT use is the question of alternatives. The costs of building sufficient campuses to handle the rising demand for education may be prohibitive. Virtual educational institutions do not require the same campus infrastructure and related costs traditional campus-based institutions must support.

The number of places in conventional colleges and universities and school systems will always be limited, reflecting in part the fixed capacities of the campus and the faculty. Developmental and operational costs associated with conventional colleges and universities are high. By comparison, distance education has lower start-up costs, and much lower operational costs. With 'campus-free" distance education, variable costs, once the system is operational, tend to be flat. That is, beyond a relatively small number of students, the costs per student are the same or slightly less. The increasing use of technology to broaden the scope of distance education has great potential for further reducing costs per student. In Chinese Taipei, the distance education-based National Open University, with its budget of NT$800,000,000, accommodates approximately 30,000 adult students each year. By comparison, the National Taiwan University, one of the larger universities in Chinese Taipei, has an annual budget of $NT3,500,000,000 for its 21,000 students. Though gross numbers of this sort beg some level of refinement, the differential costs remain substantial and manifest.

The above analysis does not consider that other costs, such as curriculum development and library resources, can be shared across virtual collaborations of institutions thereby lowering the costs to individual institutions. For example, the Pennsylvania Online World of Electronic Resources (Library POWER) initiative, will make thousands of periodicals and documents accessible over the Internet to state residents.

And finally, when discussing cost-effectiveness, one must consider the societal costs to developing countries of not preparing their citizens to participate in an information-based global society. The World Development

Bank warns that the global explosion of knowledge may either lift hundreds of millions of the world's poor out of poverty or it may create a widening knowledge gap, in which poor countries lag further and further behind:

> If knowledge gaps widen, the world will be split further, not just by disparities in capital and other resources, but by the disparity of knowledge. Increasingly, capital and other resources will flow to those countries with the stronger knowledge bases, reinforcing inequality.

The ICT can play a major role to play in reducing information inequities:

> This new technology greatly facilitates the acquisition and absorption of knowledge, offering developing countries unprecedented opportunities to enhance educational systems, improve policy formation and execution, and widen the range of opportunities for business and the poor. One of the greatest hardships endured by the poor, and by many others who live in the poorest countries, is their sense of isolation. The new communications technologies promise to reduce that sense of isolation, and to open access to knowledge in ways unimaginable not long ago. And, as Potashnik and Adkins have pointed out, "even in countries which do not believe in the cost-effectiveness of information technology as a tool for mass education, it is important that they begin acquiring experience using this technology for educational purposes. Otherwise, educators in developing countries will be marginalized in the international dialogue on education".

In conclusion, assessing the effectiveness of ICT in education is a difficulty, multidimensional endeavor. When comparing ICT-mediated instruction with face-to-face instruction, it seems clear that ICT-mediated instruction is at least as effective. When considering what ICT-use enables educationally, it seems equally clear that ICT-enabled education has a distinct advantage over traditional methods in its ability to support new pedagogical methods, provide access to remote resources, enable collaboration, reach more people less expensively, and reach them throughout their lifespan. When considering whether ICT is "cost-effective" in educational settings, a definitive conclusion may not be possible for a variety of reasons. However, when considering the alternative of building more physical infrastructure, the cost savings to be realized from sharing resources, and the societal price of not providing access, ICT as a means of enabling teaching and learning appears to be an attractive and necessary alternative.

Creating an ICT-Enabled Learning Environment

In this section, we will concentrate on the development of ICT-enabled learning environments, specifically on infrastructure, content, teacher education and training, and technical support.

In order to make use of digital ICTs schools must be equipped with computers. In order to access the Internet from a computer, schools, homes, libraries, and other educational venues must be equipped with an Internet connection, either by means of the telephone or cable network and a modem or a direct connection. Many creative means to providing computers and building the necessary Internet infrastructure are being explored in countries throughout the world.

Collaboration, including cost sharing, between education and industry to build ICT infrastructure is becoming commonplace.

One promising approach to equipping schools with computers inexpensively is to transfer the technology from government organizations and businesses to schools. In the U.S., the Government's Computers for Learning program donates surplus federal computer equipment to schools and non-profit educational organizations. Established by Executive Order, the program aims to provide hundreds of thousands of computers for teaching and learning. Other non-governmental programs, such as the non-profit Detwiler Foundation's Computers for Schools and the charitable organization Computers for Children in the United States and the industry supported Computers for Schools program in Canada, are soliciting donations of "obsolete" or redundant computers from business, industry, and individuals, and refurbishing them before donating them to schools. The goal of the Computers for Schools program in Canada is to place 250,000 computers in schools and public libraries by 2001. To date, the program has donated over 70,000 refurbished computers to Canadian schools and libraries.

Although not primarily intended as infrastructure, partnerships between schools and universities often result in new infrastructure development. These typically target university/school connectivity for research, teacher education, and Internet access.

'Netday' initiatives, characterized as 'high-tech barn-raising,' are grass-roots efforts by community volunteers to wire classrooms, libraries, and computer labs so that they may connect to the Internet. Organizers of such efforts typically help schools to develop a technical plan that includes instructional goals, network and wiring architecture, network management and technical support, training, and an operating budget. On a specific day, volunteers from the local community do the physical labor necessary to run network wiring; greatly reducing the costs of providing Internet access within the schools.

Netdays began in 1995 as a local initiative in California, but have since become an annual national initiative endorsed by the President of the United States, and have spread to countries throughout the world. For example, Netdays now take place Australia, many European countries.

Although not strictly intended for educational purposes, many Community Networking initiatives have educational components and are worthy of mention. Community networks bring together entire villages, towns or cities into virtual communities to strengthening social ties, promote social participation, promote economic development, and build a sense of civic responsibility. Such initiatives establish affordable, community operated ICT systems that involve local individuals and organizations in learning about electronic communications, and help construct these systems to meet unique local needs.

In an interesting example of how community networking can benefit educational institutions, the International Telecomputing Consortium is working with schools and universities in China to create school-based community networks. In these participating schools establish computer centers with Internet access for use by students and teachers in class. After hours, the center is open to parents and other members of the community who may not have Internet access.. Teachers and students in these schools provide ICT training for members of the community. The school thus becomes the Internet access point for the entire community with some revenue going back to the school. Another useful method of providing support for ICT in education is the provision of specialized grants to individuals and educational institutions. Such grants programs serve a dual purpose of stimulating innovation in the educational community and targeting scarce resources on particularly promising applications.

Many for-profit and non-profit organizations offer such grants to teachers and schools. For example, the Hewlett-Packard, Compaq, IBM, and Microsoft companies all offer equipment grants to educators. In the United States, the Department of Education's Technology Innovation Challenge Grants annually funds large-scale educational innovations with ICT.

Beyond equipment and software, appropriate content is necessary to make use of ICT for educational purposes. In this section, we consider a few of the many initiatives related to educational content creation and standards.

Content is being created by many organizations including governmental agencies, commercial and non-profit organizations, mainstream and extremist political and religious groups, social clubs, universities, colleges, trade unions, public and private schools, libraries; collaborations between such groups; and individuals. Although some online content is specifically designed for educational purposes, most is not. Indeed, the sheer amount of information available on the Internet, the ease with which it may be accessed, and the lack of standards for cataloging such information have created problems of information overload and quality control for parents, students, and educators worldwide. These problems, coupled with the preponderance of Internet-accessible content having been produced by a few developed countries - particularly the United States have led many to believe the Internet is a mixed blessing for education. The speed of the development of information overload may be illustrated by the fact that in June 1993 there were only 130 websites worldwide. By January 1997 this number had grown to a staggering 650,000. The number of websites has been more than doubling, sometimes trebling, every year since 1993 and is expected to do so for the foreseeable future. As each website usually contains multiple webpages, it is literally impossible for one person to view every webpage on the Internet. In another example, it is estimated that there were fewer than 100 Chinese webpages in 1994. Today, estimates place the number at over a quarter million offering everything from book reviews to travel guides, and the numbers continue to increase dramatically.

Countries with similar languages, cultures, or that have migrant populations may be able to economize in the creation of ICT-based content and tools by collaboration. For example, in Europe, the TOPILOT telematics involved a management team and 15 school-based partners in the UK, the Netherlands, Belgium, and Germany in the development of a multimedia educational program for fairground, circus, and bargee families within the European Community, all living a traveling life-style. The developed interactive CD-ROMs students could use while on the road as well as tools to be used for Internet-based interaction between tutors and students.

One approach to facilitating access to appropriate educational content is the creation of a 'Schoolnet.' Schoolnets, also known as 'national education grids,' are regional, national or local projects that may include efforts to physically wire schools to information services, but that are fundamentally developed to provide access to appropriate educational content. Schoolnets may contain curriculum guides; collaborative online projects; email directories; links to other teachers, schools, and governmental organizations; online classes; tutorials; and news about conferences. For example, the United Kingdom's National Grid for Learning (NGfL) "is both an architecture (or structure) of educationally valuable content on the Internet, and a programme for developing the means to access that content in schools, libraries, colleges, universities, workplaces, homes and elsewhere". Schoolnet are being developed worldwide. European Schoolnet, of the European Union, offers teachers access to a wealth of information about ICT use in education. Schoolnets now exist in Canada, France, Ireland, Japan, South Africa, Thailand, and other countries.

The Canadian government has recently signed an agreement with the China State Education Commission and a Sino-Canadian joint business venture to establish a Sino-Canada SchoolNet that will develop online Chinese-Canadian educational programs and resources. This will deliver services to students and teachers in both countries through a virtual campus. One of the advantages of new ICTs is that it empowers users to not only consume information, but also produce it. With a computer, printer, and desktop publishing software, any local educational group can produce high quality printed materials. With an Internet connection and website, any educational organization can "publish" content derived from local knowledge and experiences. For example, eighth grade students in the United States at Dakota Meadows Middle School in North Mankato, Minnesota, have written short, two-minute mysteries posting them on the World Wide Web and challenging other students to "Use your wits and detective skills to solve these cases." Over 20,000 people have visited the students' website. These same students have collected oral histories from members of the Mankato community about their experiences during World War II and made them available on the web. In another example, the Summer Institute of Linguistics (SIL) has helped set-up Literacy and Awareness Publication (LAMP) centers in each of the 20 provinces of Papua New Guinea to promote literacy in approximately 850 local languages. Few, if any, literacy materials exist in the majority of these languages, and over 55 per cent of the population aged over 10 is functionally illiterate. At these centers, literacy texts are produced covering a wide variety of subjects including healthcare, hygiene and preservation of the environment that can be shared between the centers. The computers, scanners, digital duplicators might be new technology, but the materials produced on this equipment are in local languages based on local customs and culture for local audiences.

At the moment, finding specific educational materials on the World Wide Web can be likened to a difficult and cumbersome scavenger hunt, often resulting in wasted time and unexpected results. For example, a teacher searching the Web using a popular search engine, Alta Vista, for educational materials on "Southeast Asia" would find over 77,000 related webpages including information about books, travel agencies, journals, music, colleges, personal travelogues, pictures, satellite images, maps, newspaper articles, and so forth. On the other hand, if the teacher had entered "Asia, Southeast", the search would return over 800,000 webpages! Faced with such a hodgepodge of information, a teacher or student is hard-pressed to locate specific information or materials of use within the curriculum at a particular grade level. The results of such indiscriminate searches also raise the issue of the validity and reliability of the information.

Once found, because of varying technical standards, materials created with one ICT-based learning system may not be usable in a different environment. Several efforts to bring order to the chaos of the Internet and World Wide Web are underway.

By the creation of technical standards, like the Dublin Core Metadata Initiative and the Instructional Management Systems (IMS) may 'help transform the end-user experience of the Web from the unstructured tangle it is today into something more like a digital library or virtual learning centre'. If international agreement can be reached on an acceptable set of technical standards, educational materials developers will be able to embed in electronic materials information such as subject matter, grade level, educational objectives, and pedagogical approach. Teachers and students will then be able to search for educational materials with common descriptors and be assured that the materials, once found, will be compatible with local ICT applications.

Teacher education and training

To create ICT-enabled teaching and learning environments, it is also necessary to provide ICT training for teachers. The changes being asked of faculty members in restructuring their work lives will be extraordinary and will require them to function in ways they never conceived of and for which they were not trained." In some countries, for example Great Britain, it is now required to have training in ICT-use to earn a teaching credential. Beyond preparative training, as educational applications of ICT continue to evolve, refresher training for experienced teachers will be necessary. In one possible framework for organizing ICT training for teachers, McDougall and Squires identify five foci: (1) skills with particular applications, (2) integration into existing curricula, (3) IT related changes in curricula, (4) changes in teacher role, and (5) underpinning theories of education.

But, even more vital than ICT training for teachers and administrators, there is a continuing need to educate qualified teachers to staff schools. ICT is being used in a wide variety of ways to support teacher education as well and teacher training in ICT use. Email, websites, desktop videoconferencing, and other technologies and applications are all playing a role in such efforts.

Teacher education

Preservice teacher education refers to the formal preparation of individuals to enter the classroom as qualified teachers. Inservice teacher education refers to on-going professional development programs offered to teachers once they have entered the profession. In a review of ICT use in teacher education, note that while most teachers working in schools worldwide have received some preparation, not all have received adequate preparation. In fact, many have received none at all. In India in 1996, for example, there were about 240,000 teachers who were not fully qualified. There also are severe teacher shortages in many countries, the problem being especially severe in South Asia and Africa. Even in developed countries where there are sufficient numbers of teachers, as in the U.S.A., many are unqualified or underqualified to teach specialized subjects like mathematics and science. ICT is being used in a wide variety of ways to support both preservice and inservice teacher education. In Africa, UNESCO is developing a large distance education to help eight countries train teachers and principals unreached by traditional training.

Also in Africa, education ministers from six Southern African Commonwealth countries have signed an accord to co-develop distance education programs with a priority given to the in-service training or teachers in science, mathematics, and technology. In Australia, the Faculty of Education at the University of Wollongong is linking teachers and postgraduate students directly to lecturers through email networks and provides online support to teachers in schools. TeacherNet UK, an independent organization, offers teachers the opportunity to develop an online profile of their interests, needs, and prior achievements, and then matches the individual participants accredited professional development programs. TeacherNet UK also enables peer support and mentoring through email and web-based discussion groups. In Iceland, the University College of Education offers a Bachelor of Education (BEd) degree via the Icelandic Education Network. In Denmark, teacher education is being conducted using ICT including computer-mediated conferencing (CMC) supplemented by satellite-based teleconferencing, multimedia and standard computer-based training. And, in a final example of how ICT is being used to support teacher education, the TRENDS, a collaborative effort of the seven European Union countries, is developing an in-service, school-based teachers training system based on multimedia and network technologies.

Teacher training

How computers are used in education depends on the pedagogical competence and technical skills of the teaching staff who must know how to exploit these modern technologies in pedagogically meaningful ways. Regional, national, and local plans for ICT in education typically include provisions for teacher training. ICT training for teachers has at least two aspects—technical training and preparation to integrate ICT use into the curricula. First, teachers need technical training to learn how to use and maintain ICT equipment and software. Such technical training is being offered to teachers in a wide variety of ways. Preservice university-based courses, inservice workshops, commercial training programs, and other opportunities abound, many of which make use of ICT to deliver instruction. Second, as "integration of technologies into curricula requires changes of huge magnitude", training in how to integrate ICT-use into the curriculum is necessary. Such instruction should including effective teaching methods with ICT and the use of discipline specific applications:

Most faculty members say they don't have the time or skills to experiment with the World Wide Web, let alone try complicated courseware, streaming video, or on-line message boards. They need sophisticated guidance, which most computer-help desks and student assistants can't provide. And they need more than a computing center's basic training in how to use Windows or word-processing software. Many promising approaches are being developed to provide such support for faculty. In an expensive but effective approach, several universities have established "expert partners" programs. People who fill the jobs have one thing in common: a hybrid expertise that blends academic computing with college teaching". Staff who are both qualified academics within a discipline, and who have expertise using ICT for instruction, are hired "to provide faculty on-site, intradepartmental consulting and support in information and instructional technology for academic purposes to foster their awareness and use of technological resources, both within and without the University".

Training methodologies vary, but "training of trainers" models are common and, in most instances, may be more cost-effective than on-site, small group or individual ICT training. In such programs, "teacher-leaders" are selected by a variety of criteria, usually including prior experience with ICT in education, staff development expertise, and commitment to the program by school and district administration. These individuals receive intensive training courses to master technical details and approaches to integrating ICT into the curricula. Once trained, they return to their educational institutions and provide ICT training and support for their peers. Such programs may also include on-going, long-term support for the trainers including site visits, computer-based conferences, and email mentoring. In large geographical areas, the responsibility for such training and on-going support may be delegated to regional ICT consortia, coordinated by a central administrative body. For example, the U.S. Department of Education has funded six Regional Technology in Education Consortia "to help states, local educational agencies, teachers, school library and media personnel, administrators, and other education entities successfully integrate technologies into kindergarten through 12th grade (K-12) classrooms, library media centers, and other educational settings, including adult literacy centers".

In an innovative and less inexpensive approach, students are being enlisted to provide ICT support and training for teachers. At Wake Forest University in the United States, incoming freshmen are hired and trained to work as Student Technology AdvisoRS (STARS). STARS are assigned faculty members to help implement ICT-based matters. Also in the U.S., a consortium of educational associations has launched a national grassroots to train public school teachers to use computers and the Internet. The 21st Century Teachers hopes to recruit 100,000 educators this year to train their peers.

In the United Kingdom, the ICT Training Initiative of the Teacher Training Agency (TTA) offers a combination of technical and discipline-specific applications training. The TTA, working with other educational organizations and a commercial company, will produce a package—including CD-ROM, video and paper-based materials—to help teachers identify their specific training and development needs in the use of ICT in teaching their subjects. Starting in April 1999, training - some of it Internet-based - will be offered to enable existing teachers to acquire the ICT knowledge, understanding, and skills which will be expected of all newly qualified teachers entering the profession from 1999. In Australia, the Connecting Teachers to the Future, is providing teachers with training and a laptop computer, modem, and an Internet account "to empower teachers with personal skills in the use of information and communications technologies and to help them enhance the curriculum they develop for their students". Technical Support Although standard service agreements, purchased separately or included in the purchase of ICT equipment and software, typically cover regular maintenance and repair costs, and may even include email or telephone support, such arrangements may fall short of what is necessary in educational settings. Without adequate technical support, schools have experienced "large workloads for existing staff, maintenance backlogs, and reduced computer use because computers were out of service". The provision of on-site, timely technical support may be critical to the success of an ICT-based educational program:

> There appears to be general agreement among observers that, at least in the foreseeable future, schools that are attempting to implement technology on a wide scale need to have on-site technical assistance. Although some sites have attempted to make do with help from a knowledgeable teacher volunteer or with part-time services from a district technology coordinator, such arrangements are often unsatisfactory. Like all of us, teachers trying to use technology in their classrooms want technical help on demand. Controlling a classroom full of students in the midst of some activity that requires technology when the system goes down requires flexibility and skill. If technical problems arise frequently and teachers have to wait hours, days, or weeks to get them resolved, they will abandon their efforts to incorporate technology.

In universities, such support may take the form of technical staff assigned to a computer center, "media center," or "distance learning center." In schools, knowledgeable peers, students, volunteers, specialized computer lab teachers are providing such support, and, less frequently, trained technical staff located either within the school or district office. In an example of students' expertise being utilized, members of the American Technology Honor Society (ATHS) provide ICT support and training for faculty members at their schools. In an example of how volunteers may provide such support, tech corp, a U.S. based, non-profit organization, draws volunteers from the local communities who conduct teacher training seminars, serve as technology mentors to students and teachers, repair and install computers, participate in technology planning, and assist with the integration of technology into the curriculum.

ICT implementation in education is a difficult, expensive, and complex undertaking that must consider a host of issues including infrastructure, curricula changes, teacher training, technical support, and so on. Such an undertaking, especially on a national level, requires careful planning. Numerous developed and developing countries have implemented national strategies and plans for education that include ICT.

Osin, summarizing the experiences ofmeant to introduce computers into the educational systems of developing countries, offers prudent advice. He warns against beginning purchasing computers, which often results in "a waste of money that could be put to better use". Instead, he advocates an eight step planning process beginning with gathering together the necessary expertise in an Advisory Committee that will define and implement a plan beginning with the careful execution of pilot. Osin also recommends training a cadre of instructors for teacher training, introducing computers into teachers colleges, and conducting both formative and summative evaluations of the pilot before attempting a large-scale ICT implementation. Beyond planning, national governments have a role to play helping remove political and economic roadblocks that prevent sharing educational resources between countries. Distance education, advocate: "Courses offered globally should encourage broad international participation and have sliding scale tuition policies. Sharing in developing educational materials and courses saves the duplication of time and effort and conserves valuable national resources".

Employers and universities are now drawing both staff members and students from all corners of the globe. Consequently, they face new challenges in evaluating course work done at, and degrees earned from, unknown institutions in other countries. While accreditation has typically been controlled by individual countries, the globalization of distance education has created a whole new challenge in accreditation and certification of learning. The Global Alliance for Transnational Education (GATE), an international alliance of higher education, government, and business, as one effort to carry out the formidable task of creating a global certification and review process for education delivered across borders. Government intervention may also help assure affordable ICT access for education. For example, telecommunications rates may be regulated to assure economical ICT access to educational institutions. In late 1996, the U.S. Congress enacted the Telecommunications Act of 1996.

The universal service section of the law, Section 254, will help US schools and libraries obtain access to telecommunications services and technologies at discounted rates. And tax incentives, such as the 21st Century Classrooms Act for Private Technology Investment, enacted by the U.S. Congress in 1997, are a potent means to encourage corporate ICT equipment donations to educational institutions. The Act allows companies to deduct the full price of a computer donated to a school within two years of purchase. However, because ICTs are rapidly evolving, national educational policies on ICT, once put in place, "have to be regularly updated if they are to respond adequately to the challenge of effectively exploiting these constant changes to the technologies and their applications".

Intellectual property refers to original or novel creations of the human mind. Intellectual property rights give the creator exclusive right to use such creations for a specified period of time. These creations may include literary works, industrial designs, musical compositions and arrangements, paintings, trade secrets, sculptures, computer programs, performances, inventions, and so forth. Copyright, trademarks, and patents are legal methods to protect such rights. The creation, maintenance, protection and transfer of intellectual property assets are increasingly important in today's global economy. The availability of ICT and the ease with which the fruits of human creativity may be duplicated, incorporated into multimedia products, and transmitted worldwide has led to increasing efforts to govern such use. In an era when every student and teacher is a potential publisher of multimedia materials that incorporate the works of others, information and training about the ethical use of intellectual property should be an important component of efforts to bring ICT use into the classroom. Without international laws protecting intellectual property, and mechanisms by which to "meter" charges for its use, efforts to share resources globally will be inhibited.

The web-based system enables researchers to request articles from more than 10,000 Chinese academic journals housed in libraries throughout China, Hong Kong, and Taiwan while scholars from those countries have direct access to articles from most American journals. However, once requested electronically, the articles must still be printed and mailed because of publishers fears that copies will be distributed illegally over the Internet. In universities, copyright concerns may be inhibiting the creation and use of ICT-based instructional materials. For example, increasing use of ICT has led to a re-examination of the question of ownership of materials produced by faculty:

> The ownership of intellectual property is among the most widely debated issues on university campuses today, and those debates go far beyond the distance learning issue itself. Typically, in settings other than universities, it is well settled that the material created by employees within the scope of their employment is owned by the employer. However, the unique mission of the university, academic tradition, and the essential principles of academic freedom have led faculty to claim that they own the material they create. Historically, many university administrations have asserted institutional ownership, but then allowed, or not challenged, the faculty position with regard to copyrights, at least in part because both the financial "cost" and the value of most copyrightable creations were usually insignificant when compared with the cost and value of patentable inventions. But as the potential value of copyrighted material escalates, particularly with the advent of multimedia software, and as financial resources diminish, many universities are revisiting who owns the intellectual property created by faculty.

International efforts are underway to develop global standards and agreements that will protect intellectual property rights while developing methods to allow access to, and sharing of, intellectual property. For example, The United Nations' World Intellectual Property Organization (WIPO), an intergovernmental organization with 171 participating countries.

ICT itself is being used to provide assistance and information to educators and others interested in intellectual property laws. WIPO has just begun work on a global information network using the Internet that will facilitate the storage and rapid exchange of intellectual property information between all interested parties in governments and the private sector in member States. A global association of 152 independent law firms, offers a website directory with links to hundreds of legal guides about countries around the world, most of which contain information concerning intellectual property laws. Other organizations, such as the U.S. Franklin Pierce Law Center, Ruslaw in Russia, and the Australian Copyright Council, offer websites with information about national laws governing intellectual property rights.

Equity of access, put simply, means that all people, whether rich or poor, living in a developed or developing country, male or female, have access to the benefits of ICT-use. While this ideal is widely supported, it is a long way from realized.

Access to and use of ICT is still predominately a phenomenon in developed, wealthier countries. This disparity leads to concerns that ICT will broaden and deepen the economic, educational, social, and political gaps that divide the developing from the developed nations.

Poor countries - and poor people - differ from rich ones not only because they have less capital, but because they have less knowledge. This inequity has been recognized by international agencies such as the United Nations and World Bank, and governments of the developed countries. As was noted earlier, UNESCO, through the Learning Without Frontiers (LWF) and other programs, is helping organize and finance pilot ICT in education in developing countries. National governments in developed countries, too, are taking measures to assist in the creation of ICT infrastructure in developing countries. For example, the Clinton administration in the United States is pushing for funding to help developing countries link to the Internet for commercial and educational purposes. But huge inequities exist that will be difficult to overcome. If inequities in access to ICTs in developing countries can be overcome, it may enable their citizens to leapfrog over economic and educational barriers developing countries need not reinvent the wheel - or the computer, or treatment for malaria. Rather than re-create existing knowledge, poor countries have the option of acquiring and adapting much knowledge already available in the richer countries.

With communications costs plummeting, transferring knowledge is cheaper than ever. ... Expanding telecommunications holds the promise to improve every developing country's capacity to absorb knowledge, for example by providing opportunities high-quality, low-cost adult learning. Expanding telecommunications capability also provides an avenue to reach distant markets with locally produced products while at the same time educating others about local cultures. The Catdang Village Project in Vietnam is using ICT to reach a worldwide audience with information about local cultures while exploiting economic opportunities. The web-based, selling locally produced lacquered bamboo baskets, is aimed at "providing sustainable regenerative income for village artisans and their families". While economically oriented, the website contains cultural information and images of Catdang; a small village located over a hundred miles south of Hanoi. Other inequities in ICT access exist. The poor are less likely to have access to ICT, in or out of school. Even in the developed world, access to the benefits of these technologies has by no means been equally available throughout all sectors of the population, with certain sections of society remaining deprived of many of the advantages offered by ICTs".

Schools in high-income areas were much more likely to have lower pupil-computer ratios and Internet access. Throughout the developing world, the situation is much worse. Access to even basic communications technologies is limited to a few. In South Asia and Sub-Saharan Africa, there are about 1.5 telephone lines per 100 people compared to 64 per hundred in the United States. In conclusion, when considering ICT, "threat and opportunity are opposite sides of the same coin". ICT has the potential to greatly enhance the information-base, knowledge, and educational opportunities of the poor and of developing countries. However, such benefits will depend upon whether there is equitable access to ICT. If not, ICT may increase the gap between the haves and have-nots of the world.

Gender According to UNICEF, over 130 million children of school age in the developing world are growing up without access to basic education, of whom nearly two of every three are female. If lucky or privileged enough to attend school, a number of studies have shown females are far less likely to enroll in science, mathematics, computer science and engineering courses.

In the winter 1997-98 surveys, 44% of the Web users were women, up from 21% in September 1995. As a portion of the overall US population, 3% of adult women in the September1995 survey said they logged onto the Web compared to 12% of men. Research now shows that

26% of all American women use the Web, as do 35% of men. However, U.S. women, too, choose ICT-related careers less frequently, and are more likely to change career fields: "Women are leaving or avoiding computer careers in droves, citing discrimination by male co-workers, few role models, family-unfriendly work environments and a general sense that the field is irrelevant to their interests ... The most immediate effect is to worsen the nation's shortage of high-tech workers"

ICT is also being used both to provide information about gender issues to teachers, and to encourage women's use of information and communications technologies. For example, the Women'sNet in South Africa offers a variety of information on women's issues and is planning to offer an Internet training program for women in the near future. The Ada Project (TAP) and its TAP Junior offshoot at Yale University in the United States, serves as a clearinghouse for information and resources relating to women in computing. The Center for Women and Information Technology at the University of Maryland Baltimore County (UMBC) is dedicated to addressing the technology gender gap. Its website includes curricular resources, news articles on gender and technology, and links to sites focusing on women, girls, and information technology.

Whether the changing language demographics on the Internet will result in English becoming a common language for ICT-enabled discourse, or will result in a "tower of ICT-enabled babble" is an open question. Language translation software may offer some solutions to this problem, but such technologies are far from mature. We should not lose sight of the potential of these applications for enhancing global understanding. ... Dance, music, collected memories, and shared imaginings can provide a common global language." Paradoxically, despite fears of cultural imperialism on the Internet, use of ICT is also seen as a means to protect and project cultural, religious, and other differences: There is an important counter-effect or internal contradiction in our global, Net-based information society: simultaneously with the rise of global networked society there is an increase in national, ethnic, and religious identity politics and the resistances to globalization inherent in these movements. Many of the identity groups represent themselves as explicit points of resistance to a global system of any kind while simultaneously using the tools of globalization.

ICT is also enhancing the ability of people from different cultures to interact with and create cultural materials. Whether the Internet will create a "Global Village" in which all participants' cultures and languages are equally valued, or foster an "invasion" by which diverse cultures and languages will be electronically subjugated, is an open question.

Although connectivity, including access to remote resources, is a major beneficial feature distinguishing newer ICTs from old, such access has negative aspects. Whether - and to what extent - the free exchange of information will take place using ICT is being widely debated, with the transborder nature of ICT adding new, complex dimensions to such discussions. Concerns about pornography, violence, and crime on the Internet are widespread, and Internet political activism is also raising alarm in some countries. Anti-censorship and pro-censorship organizations are carrying the debate to a worldwide audience through ICT.

ICT manufacturers are introducing ways of overcoming the problem of school children being able to access content deemed inappropriate by local schools and parents. Such tools include "proxy servers" and "filtering" software. A proxy server is a computer on the school network on which educators can store pre-screened and approved information. Use of a proxy server limits student access to only those resources placed on the local server. "Filtering" software scans incoming information for specific words, phrases, or websites and blocks access to banned content.

Beyond the questions raised by pornographic, violent, politically unsuitable, or criminal information on the Internet, another issue facing educators is the validity of the information available on the Internet. "While a wide realm of information is available on the Internet, it must be remembered that there is no monitoring agency and no restriction on posting false information for all to see". Students searching the Internet for information about the question of life in outer space are just as likely to find arguments based on religious believes, paranormal cults, as on scientific evidence. It appears unlikely that this situation can be resolved. As Peace recommends, "Care must be taken by the instructor that students are made well aware of this situation, and that policies are developed to deal with the inevitable dilemma raised by a student citing incorrect information, found legitimately on the Internet, in support of a flawed argument".

As we trust has been demonstrated in this chapter, the use of newer, digital ICTs - because of the ability to integrate multiple media, interactivity, flexibility of use, and connectivity -are inspiring remarkable transformations in education around the world. These transformations hold promise for the improvement of the lives of the rich and of the poor, whether living in developed and developing countries. We have chosen to focus on existing, widespread uses of ICTs in education, but advances in wireless telecommunications, virtual reality, pervasive computing, artificial intelligence, speech recognition, and "next generation" networking technologies promise to remodel today's educational applications as comprehensively as the computer revolutionized yesterday's. If we can claim to have detected any "theme" in our overview of ICT in education worldwide, it is this - ICT is neutral, human choices will determine how ICT will be used and whether the revolution in information and communications technologies will benefit all humanity.

This is true at the micro-level, in the choices teachers make when deciding whether and how to use ICT in the classroom, to the macro-level, by the choices international, regional, and national governmental and non-governmental organizations (NGOs) make to support, or not, ICT access in formal and informal educational settings. Of course, we hope the information contained within this chapter (which will no doubt be out-of-date shortly after publication) can help individual decision-makers reach informed choices about ICT in education. But more than that, we hope the remarkable developments in this chapter have touched the imagination and helped inspire a sense of urgency to act to so that all children may benefit.

5

Governing ICTs

In most countries, the electronic media and telecommunications were directly owned by governments or subject to interventionist government regulatory regimes well into the 1980s. As a result, national cultural and economic policies shaped the development of the world's communications for over a century. Some theorists of the digital revolution suggest that nation states will lose their relevance in a borderless future cyberspace, where transactions and communications will occur beyond the reach of government regulation or control.

There are two common versions of this particular view of the future. Some see the decline of national regulation as a positive step towards the exercise of greater individual freedom in communications and more direct democratic participation. A variant of this view is that a digital enfeeblement of government will only strengthen the powerful transnational commercial interests that are already dominant. The latter view serves as a reminder that it is national governments which constitutionally represent the individual citizen. An alternative approach is to see the new technologies as 'embedded in the real world', as the Internet was once described by one of its pioneers.

Without ignoring the potential of new communications systems, this approach emphasizes both the economic, legal and policy factors that influence the emergence and adoption of these services. Innovation in communications occurs within a longer historical pattern of evolution. Recognizing the fact that few, if any, governments will have the capacity or inclination to control every aspect of increasingly sophisticated communications systems does not mean the end of long-standing responsibilities. Governments will need to balance the potential benefits of new information and communication technologies with the threats that they pose. Questions of preserving privacy, protecting children, and enforcing the rights of authors are more complex in the new media, but they have not disappeared.

The transition to digital broadcasting transmission systems in developed societies, and the proliferation of subscription television, is likely to lead to much greater diversity in media services, including interactive data transmission, high definition television, more targeted special interest programming, pay-per-view programming and electronic commerce facilities. The technical key here is the expansion of bandwidth, the capacity of a communications channel to convey information. The shortage of frequencies is much less a factor in limiting services than in the past. This factor has important ramifications for policy: in the context of a generally more liberal, market-oriented approach to media and telecommunications, spectrum scarcity can no longer function as a primary rationale for close government regulation of electronic media. At the same time, the diversification of electronic media appears to challenge the traditional unifying, 'nation-building' missions of public sector broadcasting services.

Global computer networks have only recently become mass communication systems in their own right, with the worldwide spread of small, cheap and easy-to-use desktop computers, which are now in use in almost all areas of human activity. New telecommunications technology made it possible to adapt the telephone system for data transmission. New kinds of software expanded enormously both the variety and the purpose of networked information: beyond their traditional messaging and database functions, computer networks became systems for publishing and distributing information of all kinds.

As their sophistication increased, networks ceased to be strictly text-based. High-resolution colour images, video, and sound documents have become commonplace network resources. Applications in the form of browser plug-ins, Java 'applets' and proprietary components are also becoming commonplace.

At the same time, the world's computer networks have become more interconnected, and therefore more readily accessible. The network of networks that has evolved into the Internet uses a decentralized, packet-switched architecture to link computers in over two hundred countries. Proprietary online services - the self-contained, subscription-based, market-oriented systems of the early 1990s - were by the mid-1990s forced to connect to the Internet since many were failing to compete with the larger, freer, public system.

But while these technologies have developed quickly, and the ultimate objective of an accessible, low-cost global information infrastructure has become available, the consequences of their diffusion will take much longer to recognize and respond to. Actual applications and benefits remain hazy. It is not yet clear that greater diversity in services will deliver greater diversity in content. Critical issues which are yet to be resolved include the scope of the public domain in the digital environment, and the ability of governments to adapt existing systems of regulation.

Policy Responses

Since the beginning of this decade at least, governments and international organizations around the world have devoted substantial resources to understanding the implications of 'the digital revolution' in communications. Indeed such is the volume of this material, and the enthusiasm with which it embraces technologically-driven change, that we can scarcely doubt that the very concept of an 'information revolution' must be in part the product of official policy discourse, despite the advocates of a cyberspace without rulers.

The phenomenon of governments embracing new communications technologies has several facets. In highly industrialized societies, the early and middle years of the 1990s were characterized by a 'visionary' fascination with the promise of future interactive broadband delivery systems. National government documents such as Denmark's Info-Society 2000, the United States' National Information Infrastructure and Global Information Infrastructure reports, and Singapore's IT2000 fell into this category; at the international level, the European Union's Bangemann Report and the G-7 summit's Information Society conference were comparable.

These visionary information policies 'tend[ed] to be more statements of aspiration than realistic policies aimed at achievable goals'. Yet these grand if somewhat unfocused visions still shape information policies around the world. New technologies were seen as the key to improved delivery of essential government services, especially in health and education. They were also seen as major driving forces for economic growth, offering improved productivity and new demand for skilled labour.

In general terms, governments accepted without critical scrutiny the potential benefits of information technology, focusing on the perceived need for a broadband infrastructure. At the same time, the absence of this infrastructure was uniformly seen as a significant disadvantage from which other problems flowed: deficiencies in technological skills, uncompetitive industries, low growth rates. The analysis was circular.

A broadband infrastructure was not, in fact, necessary for many practical improvements in communications, either in the West or elsewhere. The success of the narrowband Internet, for example, rests on its accessibility through standard twisted-pair telephone lines and comparatively inexpensive modems. The rise of the Internet has made possible the proliferation of network computing earlier than the most ambitious prophets of the information revolution imagined; but it has done so without the expensive broadband infrastructure which was so widely considered a prerequisite for information societies. Nevertheless, the best of these broad policy statements have had a number of important effects.

First, they gave information policies greater political priority. What was once an obscure dimension of Teledemocracy is the adaptation of Internet-based information tools by government, business, and civil society to create an advanced participatory form of democracy. In its purely theoretical form, teledemocracy is the use of the Internet to produce an informed and publicly active citizenship. But in its current form, teledemocracy is a misused and misconstrued term: while the prefix tele explicitly means 'distance' or 'way of', adding the conception of the Internet gives teledemocracy a more technical characteristic.

Empowerment is the foundation of teledemocracy. In order to fulfill the ultimate goal of empowering citizens, two measures must be put in place:

— All citizens must have access to information tools. This highlights the importance of universal access to knowledge and participation in the Information Society.

— Government, business, and civil society must have a strong and committed Web presence. Teledemocracy cannot advance properly without the necessary balance between these three groups.

In existing democracies, the process starts locally with a virtual administrative body which consists of Web sites sponsored by local governments to facilitate exchange between elected officials and local citizens. Experiments of this kind are being carried out all over the United States, in parts of Europe, and other democratic countries. The Web sites are a dedicated forum for public policy debate, government outreach program, and in some cases, replace conventional mail with e-mail. Teledemocracy is further promoted through cyber-neighbourhoods, which are connected communities with access for each individual family, and cyberparties, which are representative groups that encourage online public participation. Both serve the function of increasing citizen partnership, through direct, active lobbying by citizens.

Online lobbying is no longer restricted to government and business; informed and empowered individuals may take an active role in voicing their opinions. In non-democratic countries and governments in transition, teledemocracy is practiced differently: through teledemocratization, which is the use of Internet-based information tools to promote knowledge-sharing among citizens and to organize citizen opposition groups. In turn, it may be used to circumvent oppressive regulatory efforts and facilitate discussion among civil societies, government and business.

The effect of teledemocratization cannot be underestimated: the technical aspects of the network allow for technical solutions to offset government propaganda, censorship, and other repressive measures. Such is the case with Radio B92 in Belgrade. When shut down for its anti-government broadcasts, the station moved onto the Internet, and was rebroadcast into Yugoslavia by Radio Free Europe and Voice of America. It has become the sole source of independent reporting in Yugoslavia and a rallying point for democratic opposition.

Teledemocracy is only beginning to gain recognition for what it is: a valuable tool to produce an empowered and active society. While the theoretical evolution is still in its infancy, functional teledemocracy is already spreading to many parts of the world. Virtual local administrations are being envisaged and constructed, citizens are becoming more active in communities through cyber-neighbourhoods, and government regulations are circumvented by the technical solutions offered by the Internet. In step with the advancement of information and communication technologies, teledemocracy may well be a fast-developing, governing characteristic of the Information Society.

Governments have begun to make strategic connections between issues that were hitherto fragmented across traditional administrative boundaries - issues such as data protection, intellectual property, electronic commerce, and computers in school education.

Some of these early government responses did adopt a wider social perspective on the possibilities and consequences of the new communications environment. Denmark's Info-Society 2000 policy, for example, looked beyond the provision of infrastructure. It was concerned with how a future 'info-society' might retain the distinctive Danish characteristics of equity, democratic participation, and openness. It was much more concerned with applications than the supply of technology, and addressed the ways in which the public sector could cooperate with business. It emphasized the need to consider questions of access to government information. These issues were developed alongside an agenda for micro-economic reform, which concentrated on the need to liberalize Danish telecommunications.

The wide-ranging information policies developed in the mid-1990s have led to more concrete, if somewhat scaled-down, programmes for change. The aspirational thinking of the mid-1990s may have diverted attention from such practical policy questions as access to the Internet, improvements in basic telecommunications, and the development of real services and industries. But these issues have recently become the focus of policy attention, especially since the emergence of the Internet as the most important and fastest-growing global computer network. Singapore's IT2000 plan provides an example.

Like so many other visions of the information age, IT2000 was aimed squarely at a universally accessible broadband network. The rise of the Internet changed this priority, forcing Singapore's National Computer Board to concentrate on the emergence of markets for interactive services rather than the development of the enabling technologies. This in turn meant an analysis of Singapore's particular strengths in fields such as logistics, transport and government information provision. The increasing pervasiveness of information and communication technologies in the everyday activities of citizens has spurred governments to develop policies aimed at ensuring maximum community participation.

In *A Strategic Framework for the Information Economy*, the Australian government states its commitment to provide all Australians with open and equitable access to information available online as a way of securing 'a strong democratic, informed and inclusive society', and to avoid 'a social polarization between the so-called "information rich" and "information poor"'.

The challenge highlighted by the Secretary-General of the United Nations is to use the technologies to make information available to all and harness its democratizing power. However, as discussed later on, citizens in many countries do not have the opportunity to share in the benefits of the new technologies. Participation of developing countries, in particular, is being impeded by a lack of adequate communication infrastructure and relatively high computing costs. These issues were highlighted at a seminar sponsored by the United Nations Population Fund and the Government of Turkey in December 1998. The seminar also discussed the need for policies to address social and gender inequality to prevent information and communication technologies from further marginalizing disadvantaged groups. Even so, available information and communication technologies are being used in developing countries as tools in advocacy and to promote social change. For example, in the area of reproductive health services, new media are being used to build political commitment and community support. In Senegal, youth leaders have organized cyber-cafes where young people can discuss life-planning skills and connect with the world's youth. Ecuador has a service using the Internet to provide news to community radio stations. There is a website linking a network of Turkish NGOs against gender-based violence. In South America, distance learning programmes are offered on population and reproductive health.

Framework for Governance

ICTs provide comparatively decentralized and open environments which appear to promote these rights. Networked environments like the Internet allow individuals to create their own content and interact with a large audience worldwide at relatively low cost. This in turn increases the diversity of information and views that are expressed by and accessible to users around the world.

The new technologies can assist the democratic process by facilitating greater accountability and transparency of governments: official documents are increasingly being made available on line and opportunities for direct communication with elected representatives are being created. A concomitant of this situation is that the medium may be used to generate and disseminate content, which may itself be seen to be anti-democratic and offensive to many that receive it.

The characteristics of the new media mean that, unlike traditional broadcast media, there are higher expectations of individual freedom and autonomy. However, as more parts of the networked world and the real world overlap, the need for governance increases. Numerous commentators have highlighted the difficulties of governance in a computer-generated public domain that has no territorial boundaries or physical attributes and is in perpetual use.

Democratic governance requires public interests and values to be reflected within the rule-making processes. In attempting to meet these challenges and retain the democratic characteristics of networked environments, there has been a tendency toward a governance model that is decentralized or self-regulatory in nature, especially in Australia, Canada, Japan, the United Kingdom, the United States and many European countries, particularly under the influence of the European Commission.

A number of international organizations are also influencing the emerging framework for governance of new information and communications mediums, including the United Nations (UN), the Organization for Economic Cooperation and Development (OECD), the

World Trade Organization, the International Standards Organization, and the World Intellectual Property Organization.

The OECD is actively contributing to a global framework for electronic commerce. A Ministerial Conference on electronic commerce held in October 1998 in Ottawa proposed an action plan to bring notions of physical world governance into the networked world. The action plan is organized along the following lines:

— building trust for users and consumers, so that the safeguards which provide confidence in the physical marketplace are adjusted to instill equivalent confidence in the digital marketplace;

— establishing ground rules for the digital marketplace, including providing protection that is as effective as that provided by legal and commercial frameworks in the physical world;

— enhancing the information infrastructure for electronic commerce, including creating effective competition in telecommunications markets;

— maximizing the benefits of electronic commerce.

The emergence of an information society, with new systems and modes of expression, representation and action, is a major challenge for UNESCO and its Member States. As part of its response to this phenomenon, the Organization is striving to 'help its Member States frame integrated policies and strategies, taking account of the convergence of telecommunications, information technology and the electronic media, which will enable them to adapt themselves to this new technological environment and take advantage of the opportunities it offers'.

The most striking aspect of this new environment is cyberspace, which is also known as 'information highways'. This new electronic space, open to all forms of expression, information exchange and transactions, is becoming progressively accessible to an increasing number of people, whatever their age, geocultural origins or occupation. The ICTs which form the infrastructure of cyberspace, more particularly the Internet, are used for many different purposes, for the best and the worst. This new environment transcends state borders and largely escapes national juridictions.

UNESCO's governing bodies, the General conference and the Executive board, have urged the Organization to take a leading role to ensure that education, science and culture are given adequate intellectual space on the information highways. UNESCO's strategy is being developed around two complementary main lines of action. The first is to encourage international interdisciplinary reflection on the ethical, cultural, legal and social issues which characterize the emerging information society and, second, to promote the use of information technologies for the development of education, science, culture and communication.

In collaboration with producers and users of the ICTs and providers of cyberspace information and services, the Organization promotes the ethical values and legal principles essential for a democratic and participatory information society. In particular, UNESCO's efforts are directed towards promoting universal access to information and creating the conditions under which the information society can guarantee respect for privacy and personal data, enrich all lives, include the excluded and disadvantaged, ensure cultural pluralism and be free from violence, pornography, paedophilia, racism, alienating ideologies and criminality. These are the objectives of the Project on ethical and sociocultural challenges of the new information society.

The Organization is also working to ensure that ICTs are used more effectively to foster freedom of expression, the free flow of information, access to knowledge for all throughout life, scientific research, artistic creativity, the protection and enhancement of the heritage and the common good. The programmes being implemented contribute to these ends in different ways and include: the diversification of educational services, especially through distance education; the establishment of networks and discussion forums on the Internet for educational, scientific and cultural communities; the digitization and online presentation of the cultural heritage, the organization of virtual curricula, libraries and laboratories; 'online governance'; the provision of computer hardware and software and means of access to networks; and the training of electronic network managers and trainers in informatics, telematics and multimedia.

Together with its international, regional and national partners, UNESCO has taken several initiatives in organizing a series of conferences and expert meetings worldwide. These include the African Regional Symposium on Telematics for Development, the Conference on Electronic Publishing in Science, organized with the International Council for Science, the International UNESCO Symposium on Copyright and Communication in the Information Society, the second International Congress on Education and Informatics, the regional symposium on The Arab World and the Information Society, the Asia-Pacific regional meeting of experts on A Legal Framework for Cyberspace, the Expert Meeting on Cyberspace Law and the two infoethics congresses held in Monaco in 1997 and 1998. To fulfil its role as a platform for international debate, UNESCO has initiated an Observatory on the Information Society on the World Wide Web with a focus on ethical, legal, social and cultural aspects.

Education and IT

Technology has a major impact in the field of education. It demonstrates more clearly than any other the influence of information policy, and the efforts of governments to address the problems identified by information policy. The recent OECD Information Technology Outlook made an explicit link between increased government emphasis on information technologies and the transition of OECD economies to 'knowledge-based' economies. According to the report, it was imperative for nations that their people have the knowledge and skills needed for participation in a knowledge-based society.

In the United States, which is often to assumed to be far advanced in the introduction of information technology into the classroom, a recent Federal Report noted that 'few schools have adequate numbers of modern computers or access to the Internet, and relatively few teachers are prepared to use technology effectively. Further, access to computers and other technologies is not enough; integration of technology into the curriculum is also needed'.

A recent Irish government report describes what it calls the 'down side' of new technologies. A host of potentially illegal uses of the Internet have emerged as major issues for national policy and international coordination. These include:

- *Piracy of intellectual property*: the infringement of copyright in cultural property; the infringement of moral rights of authors; and the illegal distribution of copyright works such as books or videotapes.
- *Gambling*: the emergence of unlicensed and unregulated Internet casinos.
- *Invasion of privacy*: unsolicited electronic communications; misuse of personal information in databases; theft of personal information; unauthorized interception of personal communications.
- *Commercial crimes*: fraud, including credit card piracy.
- *Harmful communications*: illegal material, including child pornography, violent material, and racial or religious vilification; defamatory publications.
- *Hacking or cracking*: illegal entry into private or government computers; theft of data or malicious damage to data.

One of the great attractions of the Internet remains its capacity for comparatively free global communication, including communication to and from countries where open discourse may be suppressed. It can collapse geographical space, apparently transcending boundaries.

Information services in the field of illegal or harmful material

Another most significant area of need for regulating new information services is in the field of illegal or harmful material. A recent UNESCO Expert Meeting on Paedophilia on the Internet is one example in this area. We know that whether information is considered harmful or not depends on the cultural, religious and social context in which it is circulated. Within and between nations, these standards vary enormously.

At local, regional and national levels, governments have long sought to control the distribution of material deemed harmful. Clearly the task has become much more complicated in the age of global digital networks. It is no longer possible for government censors to mandate the classification of all the material that may be available in any jurisdiction.

It is no longer possible to physically police the information that crosses jurisdictional borders; and while screening technologies may be effective in some circumstances, data has the capacity to slip across a frontier in many forms and from many sources including international phone lines, Internet services, satellite transmissions and broadcasting.

Many countries have constructed classification or censorship systems which work by making distinctions between different kinds of analogue media, based on assumptions about the different patterns of circulation of, for example, books and broadcast, free to air television. How are these graduated systems of classification or censorship to be applied to digital media? The question which arises is whether it is too simplistic to merely insist that 'what is illegal off line is illegal on line'. There are dilemmas in balancing the principle of freedom of expression against citizens' rights to be protected from illegal or harmful material.

A recent Human Rights Watch report demonstrates the range of methods employed to control content on the Internet. Some countries, such as Ireland and Australia, are moving towards the adoption of co-regulatory structures, sharing responsibility between national agencies and industry for raising public awareness, responding appropriately to illegal material when necessary, and providing effective complaints procedures.

Co-regulation is being facilitated by technologies that make the development of tools such as content labelling and complaint hotlines possible. Other national authorities, such as those in Saudi Arabia, Bahrain and Malaysia, seek to control the Internet more tightly, often by restricting access to the global network through a limited number of gateways which may then be monitored and configured to block access to sites considered harmful or undesirable.

The report notes the widespread international endorsement of technical tools to assist in the regulation of content on the World Wide Web. In particular, the labelling technology known as Platform for Internet Content Selection (PICS), first developed by the World Wide Web Consortium, has attracted great interest in Europe, Australia, Asia and North America.

PICS provides a means for the labelling, and subsequent filtering, of Web content which may be both more standardized and more powerful than simple site-blocking software. One of its features is that such labels may be generated, published and used by anyone: it brings an effective classificatory apparatus within the reach of schools, libraries, community groups, parents, or any interested party.

The PICS protocol can support a variety of ratings and labelling systems so they can be tailored to the needs of each user, and allows content rating to reflect the vast range of cultural perspectives on appropriate access to certain material. In this way it belongs to that tendency of thought about the Internet which stands in opposition to the notion of a distinct and remote digital space, separated from the daily circumstances and places of its use.

Instead PICS works from the assumption that 'the Internet is embedded in the real world'. Supporters of PICS have pointed to its feature of enabling, and in fact encouraging, a multiplicity of classification standards as the means to retain local control and responsibility over content. PICS is therefore seen, in the European Union and elsewhere, as a means of preserving cultural and social diversity within a global system.

Organizations in several countries have established labelling schemes designed for use by parents. Violence and pornography have invaded the Internet. Photos and videos of children and young teenagers engaged in sexual acts and various forms of paedophilia are readily available. Reports of children being kidnapped, beaten, raped and murdered abound.

The information and communication technologies have not only changed the rules of the game, they have also moved the playing field. Save our Children, a California based child protection organization, has identified over 8,000 Internet sites dealing with paedophilia. A Japanese wire service reported 500,000 pornographic sites, based in Japan, of which a considerable percentage contain paedophliac images. The danger is not that children will accidentally happen on to theses sites.

Most of the blatantly illegal sites are well hidden to escape detection by the police. The real danger is that other public sites continue to increase in number and to perpetuate paedophilia and the production of pornography all over the world. One such site addressed to 'boy lovers' has links to over 800 other sites - all of them with 'legally acceptable' images of children.

The Internet has in many cases replaced the media of such paedophiliac magazines, films and videos. It is a practical, cheap, convenient and untraceable means for conducting business as well as for trafficking in paedophilia and child pornography. The Internet has also become the principal medium for dialogue about paedophilia and its perpetuation. Fully aware of the need to safeguard freedom of expression, UNESCO nonetheless seeks to make the Internet a safe place for children. It is in this context that the Director-General of UNESCO convened a meeting of experts at UNESCO Headquarters on 18-19 January 1999. More than 400 specialists and institutions, from over 40 countries attended. The participants adopted a Declaration and a Plan of action. UNESCO, as the UN agency with a primary role of catalyzer, was asked to take the lead in 'breaking the silence'. In accordance with its mandate, UNESCO proposed to use its educational, cultural, social and communication expertise to contribute to providing safety nets for children online. This means:

—setting up an electronic clearing house for NGOs, researchers, media, judiciary services and other actors to inform and be informed, to seek advice and resources in total transparency. As there are already several networks in operation, this should be rather an electronic interactive index of child care organizations and networks.

—the creation of two electronic watchtowers. One will act as an online helpline for young children to obtain advice and help. The other is for reporting illegal contents or sites, and will enable quick links to appropriate police forces regardless of the country where the sites are hosted, or the country reporting the crime.

— a polyglot glossary of terms covering all the themes of this meeting.

— generating funds and using this first circle of donor partners from the private sector to create what the Director General has referred to as a strategic group of personalities and leading citizens to lend resonance to the work, to marshal resources, and to state the case of children to the world.

— promoting and supporting the design of handbooks and safety brochures for children, teachers and parents.

Copyright and Neighbouring Rights

Transmission through electronic networks raises problems in the field of copyright and neighbouring rights and it is widely recognized that international co-operation and coordination is necessary to solve them. To explore these problems and be able to advise Member States accordingly, UNESCO organized an International Symposium and three regional Committees of Experts on Communication and Copyright in the Information Society and published a number of articles on these problems in UNESCO's Copyright Bulletin. A crucial role has also been played by the World Intellectual Property Organization (WIPO).

Having organized four international forums and eight Committees of Experts to draw up a draft of two new international instruments to govern the digital transmissions, this organization also convened a Diplomatic Conference of States in December 1996 which adopted a new WIPO Copyright Treaty (WCT) and WIPO Performances and Phonograms Treaty (WPPT). The solution proposed by these treaties was to extend the existing right of 'communication to the public' (the term 'public' was initially interpreted as referring to an undetermined number of people) to digital networks transmission (which may be considered as communication to private persons/subscribers) since the latter make the protected subject matters available to the public 'in such a way that members of the public may access from a place and at a time individually chosen by them'. The treaties also aim to provide additional protection for copyright owners in the digital environment by sanctioning the abuse of technological copyright protection measures, such as hardware or software locks or other encryption mechanisms. Sanctions are also provided against any deliberate tampering with 'rights management information', the ownership data which may accompany digital works.

Largely as a result of argument from African countries at the 1996 Diplomatic Conference, these measures do not restrict the existing cases of 'fair use' or of limitation of and exception from this protection. The new treaties, and their policy background, were discussed in UNESCO's 1997 World Communications Report and in UNESCO's 1998 World Culture Report. It remains to be seen whether adequate legislation is enacted in member countries in the near future. The challenge for policy makers in this field has been the preservation of an appropriate balance between the rights of owners, and the public interest in the free circulation of information. There has been criticism, particularly from developing countries, that enhanced copyright protection inhibits equitable participation in the information society because it further increases the cost of accessing content and applications.

International copyright agreements do not conflict with the more general principle of freedom of expression, which is guaranteed in the Universal Declaration of Human Rights, by article 8 of the European Convention on Human Rights and Fundamental Freedoms and in relevant conventions. A major achievement of the 1996 WIPO Diplomatic Conference in Geneva was the recognition in the preamble to the treaties of the importance of this balance. Copyright law is not merely a legal means to protect the rights of copyright owners: it is directly concerned with the wider goals of enhancing education, science and culture.

Ownership data

Copyright laws around the world have been designed to protect original intellectual works, although the definition of what constitutes originality in this context varies considerably across jurisdictions. Beyond the problem of protecting creative works, however, there are also major policy issues concerning the ownership of factual information or data, such as environmental information, which in itself is usually unprotected by copyright. The new information economy means that what was once a recondite legal question is now a pressing policy issue at an international level.

Information once freely exchanged between countries and organizations is now increasingly seen in a commercial light, with serious consequences for those smaller countries dependent on information - such as meteorological data - which has been gathered by others. This is particularly the case where countries have privatized the public sector organizations that used to collect and distribute information in the past.

Governments around the world are grappling with the question of who should own data and what rules should govern public access and use. The new global networks have made data more valuable than ever before. The market for information has increased enormously as expensive proprietary databases have been replaced by ubiquitous public standards. But these same public networks are also seen as a threat to the data that they carry. In Europe and the United States, database publishers claim that they are now at greater risk of data piracy and attacks from hackers.

Tough new laws are required to protect existing databases, and provide sufficient incentives for the industry to grow. They highlight the vulnerability of data, pointing to the ease with which large quantities of digital information can be copied and redistributed internationally. A database worth millions of dollars, they say, can now be pirated and resold at minimal cost over the Internet. After various discussions held at the international level, agreement has been reached that the provisions of the Berne Convention dealing with copyright protection of compilations of various materials, originally relating to compilations in printed form, should also cover the compilations in electronic form, i.e. databases. The criteria for the protection should be the same as for the compilations in printed form: they are protected by copyright only if by reason of selection or arrangement of their contents they constitute intellectual creations. This was further expressly confirmed under the Agreement on Trade Related Aspects of Intellectual Property Rights (TRIP) adopted in 1995 under the aegis of the former GATT and at present annexed to the World Trade Organization Treaty, and the above mentioned WIPO Copyright Treaty and WIPO Performances and Phonograms Treaty adopted in 1996.

According to these two new international instruments, the exploitation of compilations/databases in digital environment is subject to the copyright owner's authorization in virtue of his/her right of communication to the public. Before the adoption of the treaties the notion 'public' related only to an undetermined number of people.

Although in the digital environment exploitation of the contents is made by individual subscribers, i.e. private persons, digital transmissions were considered to be the equivalent of communication to the public, since the contents are made available to members of the public who may access to the protected subject matter 'from a place and at a time individually chosen by them'.

As in the case of original intellectual works, not only the entire compilations/databases, but also their substantial parts cannot be used without the authorization of the copyright owner. The latter will be determined under national copyrightlaws. However, the treaties failed to resolve the extremely important question of whether the traditional 'fair use' cases or limitations of copyright protection should apply in the digital context. The above solution only partially resolved the problem.

Producers of unstructured databases, those relating to remote sensing for example, which do not correspond to the copyright criteria of 'compilations' also insist on their protection under intellectual property laws to better protect their investment and ensure development of the market. In this respect there were three closely-related proposals to deal with this problem, from the European Union, the United States, and the World Intellectual Property Organization (WIPO).

Europe has progressed the furthest, with a Directive that was largely implemented in member countries by the beginning of 1998. Apart from the provision dealing with the copyright protection of structured compilations/ databases it also provides for *sui generis* protection for those databases which do not correspond to copyright criteria of compilations, but where 'there has been qualitatively and/or quantitatively a substantial investment in their obtaining, verification or presentation of their content'. Owners of such databases are granted the right 'to prevent extraction and/or reutilization of the whole or of a substantial part' of the contents of the database.

In the United States, the initial proposal was strongly opposed by the scientific communities which considered it as limiting the access to and dissemination of scientific information. Compromise legislation on the matter providing for minimal, simpler and more transparent protection is currently being debated in Congress. The problem remains on the agenda of WIPO and has been discussed in a number of their meetings.

The prevailing opinion of the participants in these meetings, including a representative of UNESCO, was that some kind of protection should be granted to the 'non-original' databases to protect the economic interests of their developers. However, the protection should not hamper the specific interests of scientific and educational circles working for the benefit of the society at large and interested in free access, exchange and dissemination of information. In this respect, UNESCO also suggested that a clear distinction be made between the databases produced with public funds and those produced by private enterprises.

The former must be freely accessible to all users, excluding only their exploitation for commercial purposes, and therefore the rules for their protection should not be derived from the logic of competitive exploitation relevant only to databases financed from private funds. At the last meeting held in November 1998, the Permanent Committee asked the International Bureau of WIPO to organize, before it meets in May 1999, regional consultations on the problems, update its documents on national solutions and approaches and prepare a study on the economic and scientific import of the protection of databases for the developing and least developed countries.

Therefore, the problem is likely to be discussed for some time, and no new international treaty on this subject should be expected in the near future. Much will depend on the solution to be adopted in the United States which tends towards the creation of a new kind of intellectual property right, specifically tailored for developers and publishers of databases founded on the notion of 'substantial investment' in the production of a data-base.

It remains to be seen whether this solution is sufficiently flexible with regard to the public interest and 'fair use' cases to strike a balance between the private interests of producers of databases and the interests of the scientific and educational communities in the free circulation of ideas and information.

The new database rules should not have the potential to restrict the scope of fair use or free use. The 1996 European Directive provides for sui generis protection similar to that established under the Berne Convention. Librarians, scientists and educators have expressed concern at both national and international levels that any proposed new database rules should not significantly inhibit researchers seeking to reuse and combine data for publication or for research, or educators wishing to use portions of data sets for instructional purposes.

The new rules are being prepared at a time of increasing fiscal pressure on educational and research institutions in many countries. Governments around the world increasingly look to these bodies to adopt a more commercial approach. The new information technologies provide them with an infrastructure for commercialized data services.

Bibliography

Bjorn-Anderson, N. and Numford, E. (eds)., *Information Society*, North-Holland, 1982.

Brindley, L.J. (ed.), 'The electronic campus: an information strategy', *Library and information research report 73*, London, British Library, 1989.

Coates Joseph F., "The Future of Computer Data Security", *Vital Speeches of the Day*, February 15, 1982.

Computer-Based National Information Systems: Technology and Public Policy Issues Office of Technology Assessment, US Congress, Washington, DC, 1981.

Davis Ruth M., "Computers and Electronics for Individual Services", *Science*, February 12, 1982.

Earl, Michael. *Management Strategies for Information Technology*, Prentice Hall, 1989.

Frieden, R. 1996. *International Telecommunications Handbook*. Northwood, Mass., Artech House. 419 pp.

Gorea. 1995. "Infrastructure for the Global Village". *Scientific American*, pp. 156–9.

Hawkridge David, *New Information Technology in Education*, Croom Helm, London, 1983.

Hogan, M. 1998. "The PC of Tomorrow". *PC World*, January, pp. 132–42.

Kahin B., Nesson , C. (eds.). 1997. *Borders in Cyberspace*. MIT Press, Cambridge, Massachusetts.

Kobayashi, K. 1986. *Computers and Communications. (A vision of C&C)*. Cambridge, Mass., MIT Press. 190 pp.

Rabb, C. D. 1997. Privacy, Democracy, Information. In: B. D. Loader (ed.), *The Governance of Cyberspace*. London, Routledge.

Simons G. L., *Privacy in the Computer Age* NCC, Manchester, England, 1982.

Smith, Christine H. (ed.), *Open Systems Interconnection: the Communications Technology of the 1990s*, London, KG Saur, 1988.

Weizenbaum, Joseph, *Computer Power and Human Reason*, W. H. Freeman, 1976.

Whisler, Thomas, *The Impact of Computer on Organisation*, Praeger, 1970.

Wood Michael, *Introducing Computer Insecurity* NCC, Manchester, England and John Wiley, New York, 1983.

UNESCO. 1997. The World Information Report. Paris, UNESCO.

Index

INFORMATION TECHNOLOGY
A Revolutionary Change

INFORMATION TECHNOLOGY
A Revolutionary Change
(In 9 Volumes)

Volume 5
(Net Based Guidance and Councelling)

Editor
RAMESH CHANDRA
Vice-Chancellor, Bundelkhand University, Jhansi (U.P.)

KALPAZ PUBLICATIONS
DELHI–110052

INFORMATION TECHNOLOGY: A REVOLUTIONARY CHANGE

(Information Technology)

Rs. 8000 (Set)
Rs. 900 (Each Volume)

ISBN: 81-7835-201-X (Set)
ISBN: 81-7835-224-9 (Vol. 5)

Published in 2003 in India by
Kalpaz Publications
C–30, Satyawati Nagar
Delhi–110052
E-mail: kalpaz@hotmail.com

Laser Typesetting at: Varsha Graphics, Delhi
Printed at: Mehra Offset Printers, New Delhi

Contents

Preface

We are living in an information age and advanced technology continues to influence the lives in the world of work and at home. Computers, the World Wide Web, the Internet, and e-mail are discussed on a regular basis. The Internet is quickly becoming a revolutionary force in everyday private and business life. Many of the interest assessment devices and occupational data bases available via computer based systems are now available online via the Internet. Thus, the benefits and possible drawbacks of providing this information via computer apply to the provision of this information via the Internet.

Net-based guidance and counselling programmes involve synchronous distance interaction among counsellors and clients using what is seen and heard via video to communicate. The standards which govern the practice of Internet counselling are intended for use by counsellors, clients, the public, counsellor educators, and organizations that examine and deliver Internet counselling. These standards are intended to address practices that are unique to Internet counselling and Internet counsellors and do not duplicate principles found in traditional codes of ethics.

Within the limits of readily available technology, Internet counsellors have an obligation to make their

Web site a barrier-free environment to clients with disabilities. Internet counsellors are aware that some clients may communicate in different languages, live in different time zones, and have unique cultural perspectives. Internet counsellors are also aware that local conditions and events may impact the client. The rapid development and use of the Internet to deliver information and foster communication has resulted in the creation of new forms of counselling. Developments have occurred so rapidly that it is difficult to communicate a common understanding of these new forms of counselling practice.

Counsellors need to become electronically and technologically competent to appreciate career development, job hunting, and employment difficulties in the twenty-first century. However, it is warned that technology cannot replace basic career counselling skills for a number of reasons. Acknowledging the impact of technology on guidance and counselling, internet resources are provided for use by counselling professionals and clients in conjunction with professionals.

The main controversies regarding the use of technology in counselling involves the use of computers to provide career guidance counselling and the use of the Internet in career counselling. Underlying these controversies, however, is a more fundamental issue, the purpose of guidance and counselling The counselling and guidance profession has seemingly indicated its acceptance of this use of computer technology within career counselling, as many colleges and universities and government centers now use career information delivery systems.

Editor

1

Internet-based Counselling

Counseling is the application of mental health, psychological, or human development principles, through cognitive, affective, behavioral or systemic intervention strategies, that address wellness, personal growth, or career development, as well as pathology. Depending on the needs of the client and the availability of services, counseling may range from a few brief interactions in a short period of time, to numerous interactions over an extended period of time. Brief interventions, such as classroom discussions, workshop presentations, or assistance in using assessment, information, or instructional resources, may be sufficient to meet individual needs. Or, these brief interventions may lead to longer-term counseling interventions for individuals with more substantial needs. Counseling may be delivered by a single counselor, two counselors working collaboratively, or a single counselor with brief assistance from another counselor who has specialized expertise that is needed by the client.

Forms of counseling differ with respect to participants, delivery location, communication medium, and interaction process. Counseling participants can be individuals, couples, or groups. The location for counseling delivery can be face-to-face or at a distance with the assistance of technology. The communication medium for counseling can be what is read from text, what is heard from audio, or what is seen and heard in person or from video. The interaction process for counseling can be synchronous or asynchronous. Synchronous interaction occurs with little or no gap in time between the responses of the counselor and the client. Asynchronous interaction occurs with a gap in time between the responses of the counselor and the client.

The selection of a specific form of counseling is based on the needs and preferences of the client within the range of services available. Distance counseling supplements face-to-face counseling by providing increased access to counseling on the basis of necessity or convenience. Barriers, such as being a long distance from counseling services, geographic separation of a couple, or limited physical mobility as a result of having a disability, can make it necessary to provide counseling at a distance. Options, such as scheduling counseling sessions outside of traditional service delivery hours or delivering counseling services at a place of residence or employment, can make it more convenient to provide counseling at a distance.

A taxonomy of currently available forms of counseling practice are given below:

— Face-To-Face Counseling

— Individual Counseling

— Couple Counseling

— Group Counseling

— Technology-Assisted Distance Counseling

— Telecounseling

— Telephone-Based Individual Counseling

— Telephone-Based Couple Counseling

— Telephone-Based Group Counseling

— Internet Counseling

— E-Mail-Based Individual Counseling

— Chat-Based Individual Counseling —

— Chat-Based Couple Counseling

— Chat-Based Group Counseling

— Video-Based Individual Counseling

— Video-Based Couple Counseling

— Video-Based Group Counseling

Face-to-face counseling for individuals, couples, and groups involves synchronous interaction between and among counselors and clients using what is seen and heard in person to communicate.

Technology-assisted distance counseling for individuals, couples, and groups involves the use of the telephone or the computer to enable counselors and clients to communicate at a distance when circumstances make this approach necessary or convenient.

Telecounseling involves synchronous distance interaction among counselors and clients using one-to-one or conferencing features of the telephone to communicate.

Telephone-based individual counseling involves synchronous distance interaction between a counselor and a client using what is heard via audio to communicate.

Telephone-based couple counseling involves synchronous distance interaction among a counselor or counselors and a couple using what is heard via audio to communicate.

Telephone-based group counseling involves synchronous distance interaction among counselors and clients using what is heard via audio to communicate. Internet counseling involves asynchronous and synchronous distance interaction among counselors and clients using e-mail, chat, and videoconferencing features of the Internet to communicate.

E-mail-based individual Internet counseling involves asynchronous distance interaction between counselor and client using what is read via text to communicate.

Chat-based individual Internet counseling involves synchronous distance interaction between counselor and client using what is read via text to communicate.

Chat-based couple Internet counseling involves synchronous distance interaction among a counselor or counselors and a couple using what is read via text to communicate.

Chat-based group Internet counseling involves synchronous distance interaction among counselors and clients using what is read via text to communicate.

Video-based individual Internet counseling involves synchronous distance interaction between counselor and client using what is seen and heard via video to communicate.

Video-based couple Internet counseling involves synchronous distance interaction among a counselor or counselors and a couple using what is seen and heard via video to communicate.

Video-based group Internet counseling involves synchronous distance interaction among counselors and clients using what is seen and heard via video to communicate.

The standards which govern the practice of Internet counseling are intended for use by counselors, clients, the public, counselor educators, and organizations that examine and deliver Internet counseling. These standards are intended to address practices that are unique to Internet counseling and Internet counselors and do not duplicate principles found in traditional codes of ethics.

Internet counseling standards of practice are based upon the principles of ethical practice embodied in the NBCC Code of Ethics. Therefore, these standards should be used in conjunction with the most recent version of the NBCC ethical code. Related content in the NBCC Code are indicated in parentheses after each standard. Recognizing that significant new technology emerges continuously, these standards should be reviewed frequently. It is also recognized that Internet counseling ethics cases should be reviewed in light of delivery systems existing at the moment rather than at the time the standards were adopted.

In situations where it is difficult to verify the identity of the Internet client, steps are taken to address impostor concerns, such as by using code words or numbers. Internet counselors determine if a client is a minor and therefore in need of parental/guardian consent. When parent/guardian consent is required to provide Internet counseling to minors, the identity of the consenting person is verified.

As part of the counseling orientation process, the Internet counselor explains to clients the procedures for contacting the Internet counselor when he or she is off-line and, in the case of asynchronous counseling, how often e-mail messages will be checked by the Internet counselor.

As part of the counseling orientation process, the Internet counselor explains to clients the possibility of technology failure and discusses alternative modes of communication, if that failure occurs.

As part of the counseling orientation process, the Internet counselor explains to clients how to cope with potential misunderstandings when visual cues do not exist.

As a part of the counseling orientation process, the Internet counselor collaborates with the Internet client to identify an appropriately trained professional who can provide local assistance, including crisis intervention, if needed.

The Internet counselor and Internet client should also collaborate to determine the local crisis hotline telephone number and the local emergency telephone number. The Internet counselor has an obligation, when appropriate, to make clients aware of free public access points to the Internet within the community for accessing Internet counseling or Web-based assessment, information, and instructional resources.

Within the limits of readily available technology, Internet counselors have an obligation to make their Web site a barrier-free environment to clients with disabilities. Internet counselors are aware that some clients may communicate in different languages, live in different time zones, and have unique cultural perspectives. Internet counselors are also aware that local conditions and events may impact the client.

The rapid development and use of the Internet to deliver information and foster communication has resulted in the creation of new forms of counseling. Developments have occurred so rapidly that it is difficult to communicate a common understanding of these new forms of counseling practice.

The Internet counselor informs Internet clients of encryption methods being used to help insure the security of client/counselor/supervisor communications.

Encryption methods should be used whenever possible. If encryption is not made available to clients, clients must be informed of the potential hazards of unsecured communication on the Internet. Hazards may include unauthorized monitoring of transmissions and/or records of Internet counseling sessions.

The Internet counselor informs Internet clients if, how, and how long session data are being preserved.

Session data may include Internet counselor/Internet client e-mail, test results, audio/video session recordings, session notes, and counselor/supervisor communications. The likelihood of electronic sessions being preserved is greater because of the ease and decreased costs involved in recording. Thus, its potential use in supervision, research, and legal proceedings increases.

Internet counselors follow appropriate procedures regarding the release of information for sharing Internet client information with other electronic sources. Because of the relative ease with which e-mail messages can be forwarded to formal and casual referral sources, Internet counselors must work to insure the confidentiality of the Internet counseling relationship.

Internet counselors review pertinent legal and ethical codes for guidance on the practice of Internet counseling and supervision. Local, state, provincial, and national statutes as well as codes of professional membership organizations, professional certifying bodies, and state or provincial licensing boards need to be reviewed. Also, as varying state rules and opinions exist on questions pertaining to whether Internet counseling takes place in the Internet counselor's location or the Internet client's location, it is important to review codes in the counselor's home jurisdiction as well as the client's. Internet counselors also consider carefully local customs regarding age of consent and child abuse reporting, and liability insurance policies need to be reviewed to determine if the practice of Internet counseling is a covered activity.

Computer-related Technology in Counseling

During the past 30 years, counseling professionals have shifted their focus on the application of computer-related technology (CRT) to counseling tasks that center on therapeutic intervention and counselor supervision. Particular attention has been given to positive and negative aspects of using the Internet as a medium for service delivery. Although counseling via the Internet, typically referred to as "cybercounseling" or "webtherapy", has received so much attention lately, there has been scant exploration of

(1) the extent to which counselors are using various other types of CRT in their work, and

(2) other work-related tasks performed by counselors that could be aided by CRT.

Cybercounseling is not the only way counselors can use the Internet in their practice. Likewise, although therapeutic intervention may be the focal task that counselors perform in their work, CRT can help counselors perform many other work-related tasks included in marketing, record-keeping, and professional development. The potential uses for Internet-based CRT tools by counselors to accomplish specific work-related tasks include:

Internet-based CRT Tools	*Potential Uses by Counselors*
1. electronic mail (e-mail)	therapy; marketing; screening; client/therapistcorrespondences for scheduling, inter-session monitoring and posttherapeutic follow-up; client record trans-fer; referrals; intake; homework and professional collegiality
2. websites/homepages	marketing/advertising; information dissemination; and publications
3. videoconferencing	therapy; homework; referrals; and consultation
4. bulletin board systems	consultation; referrals; resou-rces for information; and professional collegiality
5. computerized simulation	supervision and skills training
6. databases/FTP sites	research; information resources for therapists; self-help librar-ies; client record transfers; and assessment and analyses
7. chats/electronic discussion	group therapy; self-help; and support
8. software	skills training; self-help; and homework.

There are other, non-Internet-based CRT tools that counseling professionals may find valuable in their work:

Non-Internetbased CRT Tools	*Potential Uses by Counselors*
1. spreadsheets	record keeping; data organization; client information; and research
2. word processors	record keeping; correspondence; marketing; and research publication
3. software	skills training for the professional and clients; self-help information; marketing; office management; reference sources; and case-notes

Use of computer applications by counseling professionals has continued to steadily increase with a particularly rapid expansion of computer use in the early 1980's. In these pioneering years of CRT use, counseling professionals concentrated primarily on the development of software programs designed to simulate therapists, computer-assisted career guidance systems, and computer-assisted testing and assessment

A great deal of technology is available for use by mental health professionals in a variety of work-related tasks. To date, no trend assessment has been made concerning the variety of ways CRT might be used by mental health counselors and counselor educators to perform all aspects of their work, including therapeutic intervention and supervision, in the near future. Without these assessments, educators and policy makers lack important information that could enable them to better design training programs for preparing professionals to upgrade their skills in order to remain competitive in a field struggling for independent identity. These assessments would also help establish long overdue computer competency requirements and training standards for the next generation of counselors to meet the demands of a technologically sophisticated clientele. Information concerning the extent and types of CRT use by counselors both now and in the next 10 years could also provide a foundation to help guide research into many of the issues raised by an ever-increasing use of the Internet as a vehicle for counseling service delivery.

In order to ensure competent and standardized acquisition of the technological skills important to the work of counseling professionals, both now and in the future, counselor training programs must adopt mandatory evaluation of continuously updated minimal computer skills. By so doing, professional counselors and counselor educators will be in a better position to take advantage of the opportunities offered by new technologies, to remain professionally competitive in an increasingly technological world, and begin meaningful research to proactively guide technology's development and use by mental health professionals.

Delphi method

Delphi is a method of acquiring the opinions of a group of geographically dispersed individuals, considered experts in their occupational fields, who remain anonymous to each other throughout the data-gathering process. The group of experts is referred to as the Delphi panel. Panel members are sent a series of questionnaires, called rounds, which list a number of statements pertinent to the topic of investigation. Statements are to be rated by the experts, and returned to the investigator for summarization. After each round of questions, summary data, in the form of a median or mean response for each statement, are computed by the investigator, and relayed to the panel of experts in the subsequent round of questions. Panelists are then asked to consider the summary responses of other members, give a new response to each statement, and provide reasons for non-compliance with the group rating. This process continues until group consensus is reached or as dictated by the researcher. After the last round of questions are returned and analyzed, panelists are provided the final summary results of their ratings.

There are many variations on the traditional Delphi first developed in the 1950's for the RAND Corporation by Olaf Helmer and Norman Dalkey. In a standard Delphi, the initial round of questions sent to the panel of experts are open-ended, allowing panel members the freedom to provide information that the investigator will use to create the Delphi questionnaire. In a modified Delphi, this phase of the Delphi process may be completed by a committee of individuals representative of the Delphi panel prior to the beginning of the rounds of questioning. A futures Delphi asks panelists for their opinions on matters that may occur in a future time frame.

Nominations for the Delphi experts were acquired through a search of major publications in the fields of counseling and computer technology, posting formal requests to professional listservs on the Internet, requests made to departmental chairpersons at major U.S. universities, and by personal referrals. Correspondences with Delphi panel members were conducted via e-mail.

In a study counselor and technologist nominees were asked to have achieved the following description of expert status:

An expert may be defined as someone with special skills or knowledge evidenced by leadership in professional organizations, holding office in professional organizations, presenter at national conventions, published in recognized journals, etc.

Additionally, counselor nominees were asked to meet the requirements for and hold the title of National Certified Counselor and/or Licensed Professional Counselor in their state of practice or to have held such titles, and to have counseled individuals on issues of mental health for a period of at least five years. Counselor nominees were required to possess expertise in at least one of the following four counselor categories:

— Counselor educators defined as persons currently employed by an accredited college or university to instruct master's and/or doctoral-level students in counseling.

— Counselors who work in agency settings such as state mental hospitals, community mental health agencies, or large, corporate-owned mental health agencies.

— Counselors who work in private practice, either as an individual or with other individuals.

— Counselors who work in college or university counseling centers that help students with a variety of mental health issues.

In addition to having achieved the above description of expert status, technologist nominees were asked to possess demonstrated skills and/or titles in computer-related technology including, but not limited to:

designing and/or developing web pages; computer programming; software development; knowledge of operating systems; network administrator; hold a computer science degree; background in engineering; instructional technologist; information systems manager; and/or database administrator.

Delphi panel of the study was consisted of 5 counselor educators, 7 private practitioners, 3 agency counselors, 8 counselors who work in university counseling centers, and 7 computer-related technologists, for a total of 30 panelists completing the Delphi Round 1 questionnaire.

Questionnaires were developed for the Delphi study by committee members representative of the Delphi panelists, and posted in a web-accessible database by the study's computer programmer. In an effort to achieve a more accurate understanding of the opinions expressed by the Delphi panelists, the research questions for the study were posed from several perspectives.

The Round 1 questionnaire asked panelists to rate 46 generic counselor tasks in 7 task categories for current and future use of CRT, and to provide specific examples of current and future CRT use in counseling.

The Round 2 questionnaire asked panelists to rate 7 new counselor tasks, including 1 new category of tasks, provided by them during Round 1, and to indicate frequency of use for 10 specific CRT tools.

The Round 3 questionnaire listed all 53 counselor tasks in 8 categories of tasks. Panel members were asked to review their previous ratings of each task in consideration of group median ratings and make final ratings for how much counselors and counselor educators use CRT to accomplish the work-related tasks, both now and for the year 2008. Finally, panelists were requested to select reasons for their final ratings of CRT use and non-use. It was during Round 3 that individual members of the Delphi panel of experts, after consideration of the median responses of other panel members, gave their final ratings of the completed list of 53 counselor tasks in 8 categories for use of CRT to complete those tasks, both now and in 2008. Each task was rated twice-once for current and once for future use of CRT-using the following scale:

— 5 = Essential if it allows counselors to do things they never could do before

— 4 = Very Helpful if it significantly decreases effort, make things much more efficient, or improves the quality of the product or service

— 3 = Helpful if it makes the job easier to perform, but is not essential

— 2 = Not used, but would like to if CRT and/or the skills to use it are not currently available, but would be used if they were available

— 1 = Not used, and no need for if there is no interest in using CRT for the task, its use would be inappropriate for the task, or no desire to use.

Panel responses to the final Delphi Round 3 questionnaire task ratings were summarized using eight steps. Results indicating counselor tasks accomplished with the help of CRT, both currently and for the year 2008. Tasks panel members rated as "2" for both time frames. In Round 2, Part B, counselor panelists were asked to indicate how often they, personally, used the following 10 specific CRT tools for each of 7 counselor task categories by choosing "NA" for Not Applicable, "D" for Daily use, "W" for Weekly use, "O" for Occasional use, or "N" for Never use: e-mail, word processor, web, spread sheet, project management, graphics, animation, simulation, statistics software, or other.

Technologist panel members were asked to indicate how often they felt counseling professionals were using each of the 10 CRT tools. Panel responses to the Delphi Round 2 questionnaire CRT tool usage ratings were summarized using four steps. Results of Round 2 CRT tool usage ratings, grouped by CRT tool item. Round 2 CRT tool usage ratings, grouped by counselor task category. After Delphi panelists had given their Round 3 final rating of each counselor task for both current and future use of CRT, they were asked to indicate the following reasons for their final choices: E = Efficiency means able to produce more with less effort, Q = Quality means able to produce a superior product or service; can do the job, and O = Opportunity means able to do things that may not have been previously possible, as reasons for using CRT. For tasks for which CRT was not used, panelists were asked to indicated the following reasons: T = lack of Training to use, C = Costs of soft/hardware, S = no available Software, I = CRT is Inappropriate to task, or O = Other, please write in and reasons for not using CRT.

The Delphi study addressed four research questions. Major findings are summarized below:

Research question 1: How much do counselors and counselor educators rely on computer-related technology to complete job-related tasks today?

Answer: It has been proposed that CRT can be used to assist counseling professionals in numerous ways. The data from the study suggest counselors and counselor educators are using CRT to assist them in over half (59%) of job-related tasks today. The experts in this Delphi inquiry indicated that counselors currently find CRT helpful in making 40% of generic work-related tasks (31 of 53 tasks) easier to accomplish, e.g., professional writing, preparation and delivery of advertising, and test administration and scoring. In addition, the experts believe CRT to be very helpful in significantly decreasing effort, increasing efficiency, or improving the quality or services of another 19% (10 of 53) of work-related activities. In all, the experts indicated that counselors and counselor educators currently rely on CRT to complete 59% of job-related tasks. In addition, counselor experts who participated in the study reported at least weekly use of a variety of CRT tools in their work.

Research question 2: Which counselor-related tasks are counseling professionals currently accomplishing with the help of CRT?

Answer: All categories of work-related tasks are represented in current CRT use assessment with the exception of tasks concerning professional accountability. The experts in the Delphi study rated CRT use as helpful for: all counselor tasks listed related to marketing/client recruitment, report and record-keeping (paperwork), clinical assessment/testing, and consultation and referral; all but one task in supervision/training; and all but two tasks in professional development. Half (50-57%) of the counselor experts expressed the opinion that CRT is not currently being utilized by professional counselors for most therapeutic intervention tasks, such as establishing rapport with clients, confidentiality discussions, evaluating presenting problems, and utilizing affective interventions, because CRT is inappropriate for these tasks. In addition, these experts indicated therapeutic tasks involving the determination of treatment length and interventions using cognitive, behavioral, or a combination of therapeutic techniques were not currently being accomplished with the help of CRT due to a lack of available software.

In all, only 3 of 18 in-session intervention/therapy/counseling tasks and no tasks in professional accountability were thought to be currently accomplished with use of CRT. However, the panel of experts suggested counselors would like to use CRT for these tasks if the technology or skills were available.

Research question 3: What are specific ways in which counselors and counselor educators are currently using CRT in performing job-related tasks?

Answer: Various CRT tools have been explored in the literature as potentially useful to mental health professionals in their work. Results of the Delphi study indicate counselors and counselor educators are utilizing a large variety of CRT tools in their work. Delphi panelists gave 73 specific examples of current CRT use by counselors and counselor educators for work-related activities. These examples fell into three main categories. The first category included the use of software for word processing, spreadsheets, statistical analysis, and publishing for tasks in marketing/client-recruitment, report and record-keeping, insession intervention/therapy/counseling, clinical assessment/testing, and professional development. The second category of examples included use of e-mail, both private and on professional listservs, for activities in therapy, consultation and referral, super-vision/training, and professional development. The third category of CRT examples involved use of the WWW, including websites, chat-rooms, and teleconferencing, for tasks in marketing, therapy, consultation and referral, super-vision/training, and professional development. Panelists expressed caution about current CRT security issues where client data is concerned.

Research question 4: How much and in what ways will CRT be used by counselors and counselor educators to do their work in the next ten years?

Answer: The experts in the study forecast a significant increase in use of CRT by professional counselors in the near future. It is expected that counselors will be utilizing CRT for at least 90% of their work, in all categorical aspects, including professional accountability. The Delphi experts indicated they believe counselors will find CRT very helpful in significantly decreasing effort, increasing efficiency, or improving the quality of services for 72% (38 of 53) of counselor tasks by the year 2008. CRT will be helpful in making the job easier to perform for another 21% (11 of 53) of work-related tasks. In all, counselor and technologist panel members agreed that 92% of the work counselors do in 2008, including all task categories, i.e., marketing/client recruitment, report and record-keeping (paperwork), in-session intervention/therapy/counseling, clinical assessment/testing, consultation and referral, supervision/training, professional development, and professional accountability, and all but 4 individual generic tasks, will be accomplished with the help of CRT. Three of the tasks for which panelists believe CRT will not be used were therapeutic activities, while the fourth concerned professional accountability. However, experts in the study suggested that if the technology or skills were available in 2008, counselors would use CRT to accomplish these tasks as well. The only reason given by half of the counselor experts for not using CRT in 2008 was that CRT is inappropriate for the specific task of confidentiality discussions with clients.

Finally, panelists gave 79 specific examples of how they believe counselors will use CRT in the near future. Panelists forecast increased software development and use of the WWW for the following: marketing of counseling services; demographic databases for research and statistics; electronic test administration, scoring, and diagnosis, as well as development of more self-assessment software; activities related to consultation and referral, supervision/training, and professional development; and therapy, both professionally and through psychoeducation/self-help. In addition, panelists indicated their beliefs that:

(1) audio/visual equipment will become more commonplace in web communications, and

(2) expressed more optimism toward security issues related to future CRT use. Although not explicitly stated by panelists, the occurrence of these two forecasts would alleviate most of the current objections to web use in therapy, and may explain the significant increase in future ratings of CRT use for therapeutic interventions/counseling/therapy work-related activities.

Experts of the study expressed their beliefs that the following conditions exist in professional counseling concerning current and future use of CRT:

CRT is currently an important and highly utilized part of professional counseling. The results of the study suggest counselors are using a wide variety of CRT tools to accomplish tasks in many different aspects of the work they perform in helping others.

The use of CRT by professional counselors will continue to increase to the extent that by 2008, almost all aspects of the work counselors do will be accomplished with the help of CRT. Counselor education programs need to recognize the importance of CRT use by professional counselors in the work they do. There has been a plea for more CRT skills training of student and professional counselors. Counselor education programs are not currently incorporating minimal computer literacy standards or providing coursework to optimally train counselors in technological skills. Counselors will need these skills in order to be proactive in developing the professional roles they play in the future.

Counselors are not currently receiving the training they need to utilize the technology available to them in ways that could result in making counselor tasks easier to perform and able to be more efficiently accomplished, and result in the production of qualitatively better service delivery. Programs that are not providing adequate CRT skills evaluation are producing graduates who begin their work as professional counselors at a distinct disadvantage to other health care providers endowed with appropriate technological skills. Those graduates must be burdened with the task of acquiring the technological skills they need on their own, in whatever haphazard manner they can, depending on available time and resources.

Although counselors are currently using CRT in limited ways to accomplish tasks involving therapeutic intervention, it is realistic to expect more extensive use of CRT in therapeutic tasks in the near future. This presents counseling professionals with the need to conduct research investigating potential effects CRT use may have on the therapeutic process. The literature is replete with calls for research to investigate potential important differences between therapeutic work accomplished with the help of CRT, as well as therapy conducted in more traditional ways in which technology is not utilized.

Increasing use of CRT offers both challenges and opportunities for us to expand the understanding of the therapeutic process by requiring us to closely examine which aspects of effective therapeutic intervention are uniquely "human" and why. This understanding can help us develop objective criteria for training mental health professionals to help others, as well as provide us with valuable information concerning which techniques clients can learn to help themselves. In addition, by more precisely defining the processes of therapeutic intervention, counselors can more objectively measure outcome effectiveness associated with a given technique.

Information literacy of counselors

Information literacy requires knowing how to access information effectively and efficiently. In this Information Age, to provide the best service to their clients and to promote their own lifelong learning, counselors need to develop information literacy. The American Library Association (ALA) has defined information literacy as having abilities to "recognize when information is needed and to locate, evaluate, and use effectively the needed information." Being able to access information effectively and efficiently is one of ALA's standards for an information literate individual.

Psychologists, whose work settings are often similar to those of counselors, have reported that to carry out their job responsibilities they often needed information, and that they had to find it themselves. The Association for Counselor Education and Supervision (ACES) Guidelines for Technical Competencies for Counselor Education Students recommend counseling students should be able

(a) to help clients search for various types of counseling-related information via the Internet...

(b) to access and use counseling related... data bases,

(c) to use the Internet for finding and using continuing education opportunities in counseling, and

(d) to evaluate the quality of Internet information.

The US Council for Accreditation of Counseling and Related Educational Programs standards indicate counselors should be familiar with the counseling research and literature by specifying that counseling programs must demonstrate application of research data and include instruction in technological competence and computer literacy. Sexton called for more emphasis on research training in counselor education, having noted earlier that counseling practitioners must be aware of what research is available. There can be no doubt that counselors need to become information literate to provide the best services to their clients and to promote their own lifelong learning. The Internet has created an increased number of sources from which counselors can access and learn about counseling research and obtain information to help their clients. However, counselors may not feel sufficiently prepared to identify and utilize them.

Graduate students reported that they feel unprepared to fully utilize library resources and insufficient attention had been given to bibliographic instruction. Various authors have addressed bibliographic instruction for psychology students, but none have addressed what counseling students need to know about bibliographic resources to be able to access information for themselves and their clients.

The Internet has expanded the nature of bibliographic resources by offering information on web sites and by increasing the accessibility and the number of databases that provide either indexing or full-text of the counseling literature. So much information in various formats is available on the Internet, that it can be a challenge to find the most relevant information quickly.

As an information environment the Internet is subject to rapid change and a lack of uniformity. Specific sites may alter their addresses, contents, or even availability, while others may fail to load needed updates. The creators of web sites, their sources, and their credibility, can be difficult to determine. Internet resources may include web sites of professional or government organizations, educational or scientific institutions, or privately maintained sites, both commercial and non-commercial.

Counselors should be aware of the types of information providers associated with the common Internet address endings—.gov., edu,.org, or.com-and the new addresses—.info,.biz,.pro,.name,.coop,.museum, and.aero recently authorized by the Internet Corporation for Assigned Names and Numbers. Although these addresses are not quality indicators, sites sponsored by governmental, educational, or scientific institutions are generally more credible than commercial or private sites. Many Internet sites sponsored by these institutions provide an abundance of information at no cost.

The rapid proliferation and mutability of Internet sites quickly dates printed directories that identify them. Most Internet researchers employ commercial Internet search engines to identify web sites of interest. Reviews and critiques of Internet search engines are available in print and on web sites. Meta search engines like ProFusion combine the functions of other search engines. Users of search engines should be aware of the criteria by which the engine selects web sites and the best strategies for searching. Some search engines provide excellent online help for users to develop search strategies. For those with subscription access, a useful database for identifying web sites is the On-line Computer Library Center's (OCLC) NetFirst, which catalogs over 100,000 Internet sites and provides up-to-date concise descriptions and links to the sites.

The delivery of electronic journals in full text, and sometimes, even multi-media, is one of the Internet's most exciting possibilities. The Association of Research Libraries' New Jour web site lists journals and newsletters as they become deliverable via the Internet. While some journals are available on the Internet for both education and psychology, Shroyer and Row found the Internet provided free full-text counterparts of only 2% of psychology journals. Many sites associated with journals were promotional or existed to encourage either membership, subscription, and purchase of products. They may offer a limited sample of full-text articles. For example, the American Counseling Association's (ACA) web site requires membership in order to access the text of the Journal of Counseling and Development.

Similarly, the American Psychological Association's (APA) web site offers information searches, but it is difficult to determine the extent of the database being searched or how to search effectively. An experienced researcher will quickly recognize that the results of APA's site search are hardly comprehensive, but a new graduate student may not. A sample of current journal articles can be downloaded in full text at the site, but subscription is necessary to access APA's PsycINFO database and full text journals.

Counselors are often delighted by the massive amount of information they can access via the Internet, but they may not access much of the full-text of peer reviewed, scholarly sources of counseling research unless they have access to some of the major commercial databases.

There are two useful databases for counselors, ERIC and Ingenta, available free on the Internet. Another major free database is PubMed that, although it provides less coverage of the counseling literature, may be useful to counselors concerned with client's medical conditions. However, with some exceptions, these databases are not full text, they are abstracting and indexing sources. There are numerous commercial producers of databases that cover counseling literature and that can be delivered via the Internet through subscription. Vendors typically sell databases delivered via the Internet by licensing agreements that limit access. Student researchers may not realize that they are able to access some journals in full text on their home computers because their university library has paid the subscription price or licensing fee for them. They are using their university's computer as the host, and the site is recognizing them as a subscriber by reading the IP number.

Students may set up a proxy server through their university's computers to access these databases through their commercial Internet providers. But graduates who no longer have the privileges of students are often confused and disappointed when they find they cannot access commercial databases via their own commercial Internet providers. Various vendors have begun marketing to individuals. This is another reason for counselors to be aware of what databases they need to best locate counseling research and literature. Databases vary in (a) years and content covered, (b) indexing policies, (c) search software employed, and (d) frequency of updates.

Information literacy must be integrated into the counselor training curriculum as "information literacy is recognized as making an important contribution to decision making, problem solving, independent learning, continuing professional development, and research. Information literate people are those who have learned how to learn and that learning should (a) be interactive and integrated, (b) be based on information resources of the real word, (c) be collaborative, and (d) utilize current media technology. Counselor educators' collaborators in infusing information literacy into the counseling curriculum include librarians, who are trained in collecting and organizing the numerous information formats, in recommending appropriate sources, and in teaching library and information research skills. Librarians may also help by teaching research classes, by advising counselors in their information research, and by creating web-based reference pages with bibliographies and Internet links to sources of counseling information.

Important points for information literate students and counselors include:

— The Internet is not entirely a free source of unlimited information. Various search engines are comparable to print directories in which those listed pay for that advertising. Many information sources on the Internet require access privileges via subscription.

— Delivery of full-text scholarly journals tends to be limited to recent publications of some, not all, journals. The majority of counseling research is published in scholarly books and journals that are still sometimes only available in traditional print format.

— Search engines and databases are powerful tools to identify relevant counseling research and literature. Databases vary in their coverage of the counseling literature and need to be selected purposefully. Effective researchers use multiple databases.

— Internet delivery of information is a rapidly changing environment. There is continual development that requires a proactive attitude toward lifelong learning to keep current with resources such as search engines and databases.

Many sources of information about counseling can be accessed on the Internet but to do so effectively and efficiently requires knowledge of search engines, web sites, and databases. The counseling curriculum typically requires students to find counseling research and literature. Students appreciate this knowledge when it is infused into the counseling curriculum.

2

Technology in Career Counselling

We are living in an information age and advanced technology continues to influence the lives in the world of work and at home. Computers, the World Wide Web, the Internet, and e-mail are discussed on a regular basis. Discussions often revolve around how computers and information networks are going to make the lives easier, or replace us as productive workers in society. Some people know how to utilize current technology and promote its use unabashedly. Other people are scared of the technology for it means change. Consequently, differing views on how this technology and information focused society will effect the world of work, and thus career counseling, have been expressed. Whereas some people may be strongly in favor of anything technological and promote technological change, others show fear regarding technology.

However, this is not the first major change in the world of work, we have survived other major changes. For example, we have moved from a society based on agriculture to industry and manufacturing to the current technological and information based society. Consequently, with planning, the society can survive and thrive while we experience technological change. We are in what is now called the Third Frontier or the Technological Revolution. Planning is needed to place technology in a context for proper use or the possible benefits of using the newfound technology will be lost, or at least minimized. This is especially so within the field of career counseling. Counselors need to become electronically and technologically competent to appreciate career development, job hunting, and employment difficulties in the twenty-first century. However, it is warned that technology cannot replace basic career counseling skills for a number of reasons. Acknowledging the impact of technology on career counseling, Internet resources are provided for use by counseling professionals and clients in conjunction with professionals.

The proper use of technology is a topic for debate especially within the counseling field. Indeed, since the introduction of technology into the counseling arena there have been supporters and detractors. For instance, one of the first to highlight some of the advantages of recording and replaying therapy sessions for supervision purposes was Carl Rogers. At the time, tape recorders were new technology and the use of audiotapes was met with some controversy. Similarly, the use of computers in therapy for client scheduling, intake interviewing, testing, and biofeedback was considered very controversial over a decade ago.

The main controversies regarding the use of technology in counseling, and specifically career counseling involves the use of computers to provide career guidance counseling and the use of the Internet in career counseling. Underlying these controversies, however, is a more fundamental issue, the purpose of career counseling. Thus, the purpose of career counseling will be discussed as the use of computers and the Internet in career counseling is explored.

The use of technology in career counseling will depend on the focus of career counseling. If we focus most on assisting individuals to make educational and vocational decisions, the greatest need may be for good data or information to make good decisions. This may include self-assessment of one's interests and values along with information regarding the current world of work. Computers can definitely help provide the information needed to make decisions. Complete and accurate as well as easily accessible data files on occupations can be found via computers.

Computers could provide the information needed to make what Parsons labeled as true reasoning. Indeed, information regarding the changing career market and resources for training may be better provided by computers due to the overwhelming amount of career information a career counselor would have to obtain to be helpful. The career counseling and guidance profession has seemingly indicated its acceptance of this use of computer technology within career counseling, as many colleges and universities and government centers now use career information delivery systems.

The use of computers to store and provide easy access to a multitude of occupational information could be said to have revolutionized the provision of career counseling. The computer guidance programs most often cited in use are the System for Assessment and Group Evaluation (SAGE), Computerized Career Assessment and Planning Program (CCAPP), Inquiry, Discover, SIGI, and SIGI Plus programs. These programs often include a large data bank of information on educational, leisure, and occupational opportunities. They often will also include a self-assessment component and are viewed as cost efficient.

It is important to have decision making skills and not just access to information. Consequently, some computer guidance programs also involve modules designed to help someone become a better decision maker and problem solver. Computers have been said to be able to help train clients to be more proficient decision makers via providing instruction with the decision making process. It is with the decision making process that controversy can enter into the use of computers within career counseling.

Interaction and feedback are important when one is making decisions and that one could use simulation games to aid in the development of decision making skills. However, one could argue that computers cannot provide appropriate interpersonal learning and that people could also easily ignore computer prompts regarding deeper thinking about a career decision. Similarly, the context in which a decision is made can have important implications for the decision-maker.

Can a computer be aware of context issues and the different complexities that context can bring to a career decision? As career counselors do not simply provide information to clients, in a 'test-and-tell' fashion, but they also guide and support and motivate people during their career transitions and decision making process.

If one conceptualizes career counseling, as also involving more personal counseling aspects, in addition to making career decisions, then the use of computers within career counseling is even more limited. For instance, career counseling may also involve discussions of balancing work and family obligations, reactions to sexual harassment, stress due to work, discrimination in the work force, bias, and pay inequities. Issues involving grief over the loss of a job and unemployment may also be addressed in career counseling. Similarly, many career counselors see career guidance as a lifelong process that involves effective general counseling skills. A computer is not currently able to adequately discuss a multitude of complex issues in a caring and interactive manner with clients in differing contexts with different personal backgrounds.

If computers are used for career decision making and advancing one's decision-making skills without the aid of a career counselor, problems can occur. Computers are often seen as faultless and accurate. Thus, those who use computers for career decision making may mistakenly believe that the computer test is telling one what to do unequivocally. This could promote decision making without attention to within-occupational variance and thus ignore personal variables effecting the career decision making process and/or career difficulty.

Few career centers require or recommend placement officer interviews for those using computer guidance systems. This is despite the fact that students have indicated preferring structured interventions when using computers versus independent computer use. Thus, the need to utilize computers as tools within career counseling in a structured and comprehensive manner is highlighted. Computers can not replace counselors but can be used as tools within career counseling.

Computers can be very helpful in career counseling in the area of providing up to date occupational data.

Assessments may also be expediently conducted via computers. However, the assessment of personal interests and abilities via computer can be tricky as the interpretation of low scores needs to be nonjudgmental and appropriate interpretation often requires clinical skill. Computers can be programmed with information but as of yet are not readily capable of highly applicable and flexible clinical skills.

The Internet and the availability of career counseling resources on the World Wide Web (WWW) and via e-mail is the second main current controversy regarding the use of technology in career counseling. The Internet is quickly becoming a revolutionary force in everyday private and business life. As reported by Mangelsdorf "call it a revolution. For better or worse, 1994 marked the year the on-line world, after quietly building momentum for years, finally hit the popular consciousness."

The Internet has the ability to quickly revolutionize the provision of career counseling. the Internet one can send and receive e-mail from individuals and subscription lists devoted to various topics were people e-mail each other as a group. In addition, one can view images and read text on individual World Wide Web (WWW) sites. The WWW is defined as a "global system of computer networks linked together by hypertext links that allow a user to jump from any place on the Web to another place on the Web." Many of the interest assessment devices and occupational data bases available via computer based systems, such as those previously discussed, are now available on-line via the Internet. Thus, the benefits and possible drawbacks of providing this information via computer apply to the provision of this information via the Internet. For instance, whereas one can have access to timely employment data on-line one could also miss the interpersonal aspects of counselor-client interaction.

The Internet can be used as a tool in career counseling to help clients investigate their interests, career options, employment statistics, and educational as well as occupational opportunities.

The need for career counselor involvement with clients as they use the Internet as a resource exists for many of the reasons career counselors advocate their involvement with clients using the previously described computer systems. The need for career counselor involvement may also be increased due to the fear some people have of computers and the lack of access some may have to computers. There is also a danger of information overload as so much information can be available on-line. One may additionally require assistance in evaluating Internet material as all Internet resources are not necessarily of high quality. Moreover, certain clients could also unwittingly become behaviorally addicted to Internet use. Internet addiction is currently a topic being researched. In addition, as feelings of isolation have been shown to increase with Internet use, the interpersonal relationship a client has with a career counselor could be doubly important.

The Internet can aid in career development and employment hunting in some additional ways.

First, as many employers are interested in hiring workers who are technologically literate, counseling clients using the Internet as a tool not only helps with the presenting career problems clients bring to session but also teaches clients a new and marketable skill: technological literacy.

Second, many people have made connections and thus network well on-line. However, one must remember that this does not diminish the importance of real life networking.

Third, many jobs are posted on-line and consequently one could have access to a larger job market if they are able to investigate Internet resources. However, once again one must be warned that not all jobs will be advertised on-line.

Fourth, clients can computerize their resume and candidate data and post this information on the Internet for employers to seek out.

Finally, clients can investigate possible employers for company stability and policies that may effect their satisfaction with a position within the agency.

Large amounts of employment information and career connections can be obtained and cultivated on the Internet if one knows where to look and has the support needed to evaluate and use this information. Internet fluency provides the career counselor with a highly interactive mode of communication and potentially up-to-date sources of information. Career counselors are in a perfect position to utilize these resources for their client's benefit. However, to do this effectively counselors must be technologically literate themselves.

Technology is listed as one of the 11 categories of minimum competence for the professional practice of career counseling. The need for students to use electronic communication technologies effectively exists. The question is not whether to use technology, but how to use it to best advantage given the setting in which one works" and the settings now include computers and the Internet.

Internet applications and careers guidance

The Internet could have massive implications for careers guidance. It has the potential to make careers information more accessible than ever before. It could also lead to new careers education and guidance practices. Technically, information can be sent via any available route across the Internet and users can follow their own pathways. In a careers context, this can increase the scope of their ideas about opportunities, encourage lateral thinking about what might be of interest, and appeal to those who see serendipity as an important part of career learning and development. At the same time, quality information providers can structure their sites to make it easy to focus on what is of value and to give access to more traditionally structured databases.

Access to Information

The Internet offers an unmediated link between user and information provider. Information can be stored as close to its source as possible, facilitating regular updating. However, the sheer quantity of unfiltered information can make it difficult for users to find and evaluate the information they need. There is a role for guidance services in providing a filter, a quality assurance process, as the number of apparently relevant sites delivered with each trawl of the Web becomes ever larger.

Direct access to computer-assisted guidance

Through file transfer or direct access to remote databases, the Internet could make it possible to access the full range of computer-assisted guidance systems `on-line', not just what happens to be available in the local school/ college or careers centre. Such systems might then be used without mediation or support from a guidance worker. The Web Site of CSU (Software Support) Ltd gives on-line access from anywhere in the world to occupational profiles from the AGCAS (Association of Graduate Careers Advisory Services) database, plus an extensive postgraduate study database. Users can also search the database of employers of graduates - SCAN on-line for information on employment relevant to their degree, desired location and choice of work etc. Information can be down-loaded or printed out.

Individual guidance at a distance

Counselling via e-mail is already being used: Chat mode allows two E-mail users to view the text sent and received simultaneously (a whole conversation on screen). For those who are shy of talking to new people about their concerns, distance contact provides a 'warm-up': a safe way to sample the relationship with the counsellor before embarking on personal contact.

Especially if coupled with (video) conferencing techniques, the Internet can provide a powerful medium for delivering distance guidance. It is even possible to see and talk with someone while viewing or using the programs on their computer. The Department for Education and Employment in UK, sponsored two programmes in 1996 involving videoconferencing to deliver guidance at a distance. One involves the adviser and client sharing the experience of doing a computer-assisted guidance program via the video-conferencing link. The adviser can discuss the results with the client and alter items in the result as needed. The other offers a video-conferencing link to the careers adviser for advice to support the use of computer-assisted guidance. Either of these activities could easily be carried on via the Internet, though video-conferencing may require a more expensive ISDN phoneline than normal internet usage.

New forms of group work

E-mail and newsgroups make possible new forms of group guidance. Anyone who registers with a newsgroup can read all letters and information posted by others, and respond or comment themselves. This offers a forum for group discussion of an issue. Extending a guidance service on to the Internet enables it to reach people in new ways and new places (including their own homes and workplaces) 24 hours a day. Conferencing facilities and the use of E-mail and newsgroups to spread information, ideas and skills, all contribute to this. At present many of the people guidance services target, when they engage in outreach, do not have access to the hardware and software needed. If this can be overcome (e.g. by providing workstations in public access points, community centres or 'telecottages') there may be particular potential for guidance via the Internet in rural, scattered communities, and for disabled or disaffected clients.

The Internet offers a speeding up and streamlining of the process of application and recruitment for jobs and courses. Current examples include:

— Electronic posting of vacancy information
— Electronic application forms

— Electronic submission of CVs and resumes

— Sites that teach job-seeking skills.

The ability to update on-line on Internet is an advantage of the clearing vacancy service offered by Hobsons on their Web site. Users can browse the data, and register an interest with an institution, giving more information about results, level of course required and so on. Alternatively, they can go from there to the institution's own home page on the World Wide Web for information. If more and more employers take to handling their recruitment via electronic media this will have considerable implications for guidance and employment services. The ability of job seekers to handle electronic applications and write effective electronic CVs and resumes will need to be supported by guidance and placement services requiring new techniques and skills. Employment services on the Internet mean the jobseeker can directly search a database of jobs for relevant vacancies, and may add his/herr own details to a central database of CVs and resumes. Employers then search the database for suitable applicants, sometimes using a computerised search of CVs to shortlist candidates. Some major employment services also offer links to other employment agencies.

Careers education programmes can offer opportunities for students to learn how to use the Internet critically and analytically to meet their own careers guidance needs. This includes teaching students to develop their own sense of quality, enabling them to make sound critical judgements about what information is offered and how to use imperfect information. These are key skills in career learning, increasing students' ability to use this medium for careers purposes will also add to their competence in other areas.

informal atmosphere and leisure facilities are offered alongside Internet workstations open to all.

— Linking to other guidance access points such as the national guidance helpline or local TEC/LEC training databases, or to phone in programmes on local radio or TV.

— Linking use of the Internet with use of other resources. Thus printed media or CD-ROM can be distributed which can either be used alone or enhanced by support from a World Wide Web site or via E-mail / newsgroup.

A major issue for the future is whether the Internet is to remain largely free-access or will become more commercialised. Business use is likely to increase with charges for access to some information. At present the main costs are:

— the cost of hardware—typically a modem for connecting the computer to the telephone line. If ISDN is used this will be a large additional expense;

— initial registration with, and monthly subscription to, a local service provider;

— the additional cost of renting Web space if a home page is to be set up for the school, college or guidance service, along with any programming costs involved;

— running and maintenance costs, including on-line telephone charges, usually at local rates;

— possibly some software costs, though software can often be downloaded free from the Internet or comes as part of the package from the service provider;

— staff time and training to use the system;

— the provision or hire of physical locations where the system can be used.

The number of people using the Internet is growing exponentially; because of the increased use of pictures and sound, the volume of traffic per user is growing even faster. This means a choice between expensive upgrading to ISDN lines and ever faster modems, or increasingly slow access times. Surfing' the Net is typically a slow and leisurely process because of the mass of uncoordinated, unstructured material that confronts the new user in particular.

Bookmarking of relevant and regularly used sites so that the user can return to them later. Collecting such sites, and material from them, might form the basis of a careers lesson in school. Similar signposting of useful material could be provided from a careers service homepage. Downloading of data/software from the Internet and World Wide Web. Information downloaded can be regularly 'refreshed' from the original site to ensure it is up-to-date, but used 'off-line' on one's own computer without further call charges (copyright issues may need attention).

Use of Intranet: Creating a local network linked to the wider Net, but fenced off from it, offers further possibilities for economy

Integration with other resources: E-mail and Web sites may be used sparingly, as part of a package of guidance or careers education. This ensures that the Net is used only when it is clearly the best way to deliver a learning opportunity, not because of the 'gee-whizz' factor. Training, to highlight effective and efficient ways of using the new resources.

The quality of information on the Internet is, by definition, difficult to guarantee. How important is it to do so? Those involved in education-based careers work may be less concerned about this: developing a critical approach towards imperfect information has been a traditional part of careers education. At the same time there is a natural desire to protect younger people until they have acquired such skills. But this tension is present in almost all teaching through whatever medium. For individual guidance purposes, however, information needs to be accurate, comprehensive, up-to-date, and comparable. Guidance services need to play a role in providing structure, coherence, quality assurance and 'kite-marking'. Web pages should:

— display the date of last update and the name of the provider;

— declare any vested interests or possible bias;

— offer relevant links to other sites which enhance the value of the original;

— be quick to download and easy to use;

— offer supporting resources via other media such as workbooks, video, CD-ROM, etc.

Security and Confidentiality

The security and confidentiality of personal information obviously needs additional safeguards on a system accessible from anywhere in the world. Again, the development of Intranet networks may provide some protection for guidance users. Password protected sites on the network may also help. However, the medium is clearly not best suited to the transfer of highly sensitive information.

The Internet has implications for the training needs of guidance workers. Attention to such needs will enhance the capacity of the guidance community to take a proactive part in the development of the Internet as a tool in guidance. Training needs include:

— technical awareness and understanding of the Internet and its facilities;
— ability to access the Net;
— use of E-mail;
— group facilitation skills of moderating newsgroups;
— conferencing skills;
— understanding electronic application and recruitment;
— research and information management skills;
— knowledge of sources;

There are few 'facts' in the area of career development and probably no laws. It is doubtful if many will argue with the general statement that guidance professionals try to help clients manage more efficiently the obstacles that life puts in their paths. In the case of those of us working in schools, our concern is to help young people cope with educational, vocational, and personal issues, and ultimately prepare for the adult world. For those of us working in the labour market, our focus is young adults and older people. Here our task is directed to helping the person obtain employment, or to cope with unemployment. Engaged in running self development courses or courses that help to re-skill individuals. Most guidance programmes try to encompass two fundamental tasks:

i) the task of enabling the individual to make appropriate educational or occupational choices

ii) the task of assisting the individual to manage the personal and emotional issues that attend most of the significant decisions that people make, not least the issue of career choice.

Traditionally, guidance programmes have tried, since the 1960s, to accommodate these two functions. Inevitably, theoretical differences will influence where the emphases are placed in the various programmes. Psychologists tend to place the emphasis on inner development in the belief that career choice is determined by one's self-concept. They attach much importance to personal evaluation, and they use psychometric tests to identify the aptitudes, vocational interests, and personality traits that the individual can bring to the job. Sociologists, on the other hand, attribute more weight to external factors, such as the opportunities provided by the environment. Vocational theory could be described as an inexact science in many ways and at the risk of sacrificing theoretical purity, one could say there is truth in both the psychological and sociological positions. Certainly change, mainly in the form of the microcomputer, has had the greatest impact of all. The definition of work has changed radically; traditional guidance is giving way to guidance which emphasises life-span, life space and role salience. There is no certainty that we will ever again have an abundance of the old fashioned jobs which guaranteed security for life. All of this is presently receiving intense scrutiny in Europe, no doubt inspired to a considerable extent by the high level of unemployment within the Union.

A number of characteristics have been identified by Watts and others in relation to the evolving practice of guidance. 'Guidance is now being perceived as continuous; as stretching across the life span. It is no longer seen as something limited to adolescents' For instance, guidance is now being perceived as continuous; as stretching across the life span. It is no longer seen as something limited to adolescents. An overarching trend is a concern for quality standards and evaluation. Some Member States have developed national councils to bring together the variety of interests in the delivery of guidance. They have also begun to evolve a strategy which recognises the importance of guidance within the context of educational provision, and recommends the value of access to a neutral base from which the individual can receive neutral guidance.

Facilitating educational and occupational mobility throughout the EU will increasingly become a major task of guidance counsellors as young people seek admission to educational courses or try to avail themselves of occupational opportunities in other Member States. Guidance counsellors must therefore become familiar with the European institutions that promote guidance, the support services in the various Member States, and the variety of guidance initiatives taking place, e.g. PETRA. Most of all, they must know how to access databases that contain transnational information and be able to obtain details of educational and vocational opportunities. It goes without saying that they must have a reasonable understanding of the type of guidance practised by their EU colleagues.

As the various agencies involved in guidance draw closer, training will begin to reflect their needs and perceptions. At present the guidance philosophies of education and the labour market have little in common and this gap, which is experienced by many guidance personnel throughout Europe, needs bridging. The goal of guidance is to promote the welfare of the individual client. It should never become the servant of economic or political policy Modules which have been identified by the PETRA participants as important elements in any future European guidance model include: education and training, labour market information, knowledge of social and economic conditions in the EU, intercultural competence, knowledge of Union policies and initiatives, the theory and practice of guidance and counselling, and an understanding of factors affecting educational and occupational mobility across the Union.

In practical terms this means that guidance personnel should emerge from their training with an understanding of the political, economic and social context which underpins guidance within the Union; they should be familiar with the guidance practices which operate in other States; they should be aware of good guidance practices in other countries and attempt to incorporate these in their guidance practice; they should participate in transnational networks in order to exchange experience, knowledge and information with other guidance personnel; and lastly, they should engage in the process of reviewing their own understanding of guidance and share their conclusions with other guidance practitioners.

In brief then, the shape of future guidance training programmes is likely to include modules which deal with guidance theory and practice, counselling theory and practice, national and EU education structures, national and labour market structures, the European dimension, computer assisted guidance, information management and knowledge of cultural patterns across the Union. Most important of all, it seems to me, is the need to remind ourselves that the goal of guidance is to promote the welfare of the individual client. It should never become the servant of economic or political policy. This is not to suggest that guidance and economic/political expediency may seek to override the best interests of the individual. And we should not lose sight of this in our concern to build quality control criteria into our guidance systems. Ultimately, guidance is about enabling people to reach self-fulfilment, and matters of the human heart have never been amenable to the logic of quality control.

Career planning services are differentiated from "career counseling" services. Career planning services include an active provision of information designed to help a client with a specific need, such as review of a resume; assistance in networking strategies; identification of occupations based on interests, skills, or prior work experience; support in the job-seeking process; and assessment by means of online inventories of interest, abilities, and/or work-related values. Although 'Career Counseling' may include the provision of the above services, the use of the term implies a deeper level of involvement with the client, based on the establishment of a professional counseling relationship and the potential for dealing with career development concerns well beyond those included in career planning.

Multiple means of online provision of career planning or career counseling services currently exist, the most common of which are e-mail, newsgroups, bulletin boards, chat rooms, and websites offering a wide variety of services. Telephone or audiovisual linkages supported by the Internet exist in their infancy, and will likely grow in potential as the technology improves and the costs decline.

— *Qualifications of developer or provider :* Websites and other services designed to assist clients with career planning should be developed with content input from professional career counselors. The service should clearly state the qualifications and credentials of the developers not only in the content area of professional career counseling, but also in the development of interactive online services.

— *Access and understanding of environment* —The counselor has an obligation to be aware of free public access points to the Internet within the member's community, so that a lack of financial resources does not create a significant barrier to clients accessing counseling services or information, assessment or instructional resources over the Internet. The counselor has an obligation to be as aware as possible of local conditions, cultures, and events that may impact the client.

— *Content of career counseling and planning services on the internet :* The content of a website or other service offering career information or planning services should be reviewed for the appropriateness of content offered in this medium. Some kinds of content have been extensively tested for online delivery due to the long existence of computer-based career information and guidance systems. This includes searching of databases by relevant search variables; display of occupational information; development of a resume; assessment of interests, abilities, and work-related values and linkage of these to occupational titles; instruction about occupational classification systems; relationship of school majors to occupational choices; and the completion of forms such as a financial needs assessment questionnaire or a job application. When a website offers a service which has not previously been extensively tested, this service should be carefully scrutinized to determine whether it lends itself to the Internet. The website should clearly state the kinds of client concerns that the counselor judges to be inappropriate for counseling over the Internet, or beyond the skills of the counselor.

— *Appropriateness of client for receipt of services via the internet :* The counselor has an ethical and professional responsibility to assure that the client who is requesting service can profit from it in this mode. Appropriate screening includes the following:

a) A clear statement by clients of their career planning or career counseling needs.

b) An analysis by the counselor of whether meeting those needs via Internet exchange is appropriate and of whether this particular client can benefit from counseling services provided in this mode. A judgment about the latter should be made by means of a telephone or videophone teleconference designed to specify the client's expectations, how the client has sought to meet these through other modes, and whether or not the client appears to be able to process information through an Internet medium.

— *Appropriate support to the client*—The counselor who is providing services to a client via the Internet has ethical responsibility for the following:

a) Periodic monitoring of the client's progress via telephone or videophone teleconference.

b) Identification by the counselor of a qualified career counselor in the client's geographic area should referral become necessary. If this is not possible, the web counselor using traditional referral sources to identify an appropriate practitioner, should assist the client in the selection of a counselor.

c) Appropriate discussion with the client about referral to face-to-face service should the counselor determine that little or no progress is being made toward the client's goals.

— *Clarity of contract with the client* —The counselor should define several items in writing to the client in a document that can be downloaded from the Internet or faxed to the client. This document should include at least the following items:

a) The counselor's credentials in the field.

b) The agreed-upon goals of the career counseling or career planning Internet interchange.

c) The agreed-upon cost of the services and how this will be billed.

d) Where and how clients can programmes any counselor behavior which they consider to be unethical.

e) Statement about the degree of security of the Internet and confidentiality of data transmitted on the Internet and about any special conditions related to the client's personal information.

f) A statement of the nature of client information electronically stored by the counselor, including the length of time that data will be maintained before being destroyed.

g) A statement about the need for privacy when the client is communicating with the counselor, e.g., that client communication with the counselor is not limited by having others observe or hear interactions between the counselor and client.

h) If the service includes career, educational, or employment information, the counselor is responsible for making the client aware of the typical circumstances where individuals need counseling support in order to effectively use the information.

— *Inclusion of linkages to other websites:* If a career information or counseling website includes links to other websites, the professional who creates this linkage is responsible for assuring that the services to which his or hers are linked also meet these guidelines.

— *Use of assessment*—If the career planning or career counseling service is to include online inventories or tests and their interpretation, the following conditions should apply:

a) The assessments must have been tested in computer delivery mode to assure that their psychometric properties are the same in this mode of delivery as in print form; or the client must be informed that they have not yet been tested in this same mode of delivery.

b) The counselor must abide by the same ethical guidelines as if he or she were administering and interpreting these same inventories or tests in face-to-face mode and/or in print form.

c) Every effort must be exerted to protect the confidentiality of the user's results.

d) If there is any evidence that the client does not understand the results, as evidenced by e-mail or telephone interchanges, the counselor must refer the client to a qualified career counselor in his or her geographic area.

e) The assessments must have been validated for self-help use if no counseling support is provided, or that appropriate counseling intervention is provided before and after completion of the assessment resource if the resource has not been validated for self-help use.

Professional and ethical guidelines related to the use of the internet for job posting and searching:

— The posting must represent a valid job opening for which those searching on the Internet have an opportunity to apply.

— Job postings must be removed from the Internet database within 48 hours of the time that the announced position is filled.

— Names, addresses, resumes, and other information that may be gained about individuals should not be used for any purposes other than provision of further information about job openings.

Use of a false e-mail identity when interacting with clients and/or other professionals. When acting in a professional capacity on the Internet, a counselor has a duty to identify him/herself honestly.

Accepting a client who will not identify him/herself and be willing to arrange for phone conversation as well as online interchange.

Sharking or monitoring .chat rooms and bulletin board services, and offering career planning and related services when no request has been made for services. This includes sending out mass unsolicited e-mails. Counselors may advertise their services but must do so observing proper "netiquette" and standards of professional conduct.

Since the use of the Internet is new for the delivery of career planning and counseling services, it is mandatory that the career counseling profession gain experience with this medium and evaluate its effectiveness through targeted research. The capabilities of Internet delivery of services will expand rapidly as the use of sound and video becomes more feasible. These early guidelines will need constant monitoring and revision as research data become available and additional capabilities become cost-feasible.

Web-oriented Career Guidance Services

Information and communication technologies are transforming career information and guidance services, just as they are transforming service delivery in other sectors. The evolution of the application of ICT in the field of career information and guidance can be divided into four phases.

1. The mainframe phase, from the mid-1960s to the late 1970s. A number of computer-aided guidance systems were developed which demonstrated the potential of ICT. But the costs of direct interaction with the computer meant that the only systems which proved widely practicable in cost terms were based on batch processing. The static nature of this process and the feedback delays limited the implementation of such systems.

2. The microcomputer phase, from the early 1980s to the mid-1990s. The advent of the microcomputer made interactive usage much more economical, and also made it easier to develop and market limited software packages; its attractiveness grew as more powerful versions of the personal computer were developed. The result was a substantial growth in the number of computer-aided guidance systems, and in the extent of their usage. By the 1990s it was difficult to find a guidance service in any developed country which did not make use of such systems.

3. The web phase, in the late 1990s. The advent of the Internet meant that instead of freestanding systems located in career guidance centres, websites could be developed which individuals could access instantly from a wide variety of sites, including their homes. The ease of developing such websites produced a massive increase in their number; the ease of interconnecting them meant that they no longer needed to be viewed as discrete entities. Rather than perceiving ICT solely as a service from external suppliers, guidance services began to develop their own websites.

4. The digital phase, which we are now entering. The hitherto separate 'analogue streams' of the computer, the television and the telephone are merging into an integrated 'digital river'. Individuals are now able to access the Internet not only through their personal computers but also through their televisions and mobile phones. Greatly enhanced bandwidth will shortly enhance its speed and its capacity for transmitting video and audio as well as text.

Across these four phases, three key trends can be discerned.

1. *Increased accessibility*— Whereas initially ICT-based career guidance and information services were available only at a select number of technically-equipped service locations, they are now available not only in most guidance services but also in a vast range of other locations—homes, workplaces, community locations.

2. *Increased interactivity*—In the early stages, resources were developed as separate systems, offering only limited interactivity with users. Now, they are highly interactive not only with users but also with each other and across inter-media boundaries.

3. *Much more diffused origination*—Whereas the initial computer-aided guidance systems were developed by large organisations with substantial resources at their disposal, anyone can now develop their own website.

Resources concerned with opportunity awareness include databases of learning and/or work opportunities, with a menu of search criteria which enable users to find data relevant to their needs. The databases may cover: education/training institutions or courses; occupations, employers, or job vacancies; voluntary-work opportunities; and information on how to become self-employed. Some include relevant labour-market information on supply and demand.

There are also some examples of work simulations which enable users to explore particular occupational areas in an experiential way. Resources concerned with decision learning include matching systems which enable users to relate their personal profiles to relevant learning or work opportunities. The outcome is a list of the opportunities which match the profile most closely.

Also included here are content-free decision-making resources designed to help users to explore options in a systematic way, balancing the desirability of particular options against the perceived probability of achieving them. Resources concerned with transition learning are concerned with helping users to implement their decisions. These may include support in developing action plans, preparing curricula vitae, completing application forms, and preparing for selection interviews; it may also include help in securing funding for learning opportunities or for becoming self-employed. From a policy perspective, it is important to recognise the range of these applications. Policy interventions are often confined to a limited sub-set of this range— databases, for example. Many separate packages and websites cover only one or two of these features; some, however, cover more.

In the days of computer-aided guidance systems on mainframes and microcomputers, there was a debate about the relative merits of mini systems, each addressing particular guidance functions, and of maxi systems which attempted to cover as many as possible of these functions and to facilitate 'cross-pathing' between them. Some argued that a plurality of "mini" systems encouraged diversity and choice, enabling users to select the mix of such systems which met their needs; others that maxi systems enabled users to move seamlessly between different functions, avoiding semantic discrepancies and conceptual discontinuities, and modelling the full scope and complexity of the career decision-making process.

The advent of the Internet reframed this argument, by making it possible for websites to build quasi-maxi systems on what Offer termed a 'Lego' model —piece by piece, sometimes through links to other sites. The feasibility of developing ICT-based systems which cover the whole of the guidance process poses the issue of how such resources relate to the role of the counsellor.

Traditionally, most guidance services have been built around one-to-one counselling interviews. The models used in such interviews have varied: from diagnostic approaches in which the counsellor has analysed the individual's attributes and made appropriate recommendations, to person-centred approaches in which the counsellor helps clients to explore their perceptions of themselves and of the opportunities open to them, and to reach their own decisions. In more recent years, however, there has been a move in many countries towards a more open professional model, in which the concept of the counsellor working with individual clients in a psychological vacuum is replaced or supplemented by a more diffuse approach, utilising a more varied range of interventions, with a greater emphasis on the individual as an active agent rather than a passive recipient within the guidance process. As part of this, some guidance services have moved away from a service centred on long interviews to an open-access model, with information rooms containing ICT and other resources supported by brief informal interviews, and with long interviews being available as a residual resource to those who need them.

Individuals who are initially judged to have a high level of readiness for decision-making are referred to self-help services: career resource rooms and websites designed to assist them in selecting, locating, sequencing and using needed resources with little or no staff assistance. Those judged to have a moderate level of readiness are referred to brief staff-assisted services: practitioner-guided use of resources, supplemented by group sessions. Those with a low level of readiness are referred to individual case-managed services: individual counselling and longer-term group counselling. Estimates of those requiring case-managed services tend to fall between 10% and 50%, depending on the population, with the remainder being divided between those requiring self-help and brief staff-assisted services.

A range of readiness assessment measures, using a variety of constructs, exist to help in the screening process; dimensions such as age, socio-economic status, gender and educational level represent administratively convenient but conceptually inadequate proxies for such measures. The choice of these constructs/dimensions is crucial in planning services.

A further important policy issue is whether decisions about the extent of staff assistance are to be made by policy-makers or counselling staff on a 'rationing' basis, by counselling staff in negotiation with clients, or by the clients themselves. Such screening models were initially devised to apply to clients who visit career guidance centres. In addition, however, ICT now has the capacity to take services to individuals who find it difficult to visit such centres—because they live in geographically remote areas, for example, or because they have disabilities or are home-based for other reasons, or because they are occupied during the centre's opening hours. The concept of 'distance guidance', by telephone or through the Internet, makes it possible to deliver guidance services to remote locations, with or without direct staff assistance.

In addition, some clients may prefer to access services at a distance. Increasingly, in all fields, consumers want a service to be available when they identify a need for it, with minimum delay and minimum effort: they want it here, and they want it now. They may be willing to undertake visits to dedicated physical centres where this is feasible and is perceived as offering added value, but their decision rules in this respect are becoming more and more discriminating. These decision rules may be influenced by their preferred learning style. In these various respects, ICT has the potential to significantly increase access to guidance services, freeing it from constraints of time and space. At the same time, however, there may be restrictions on access to the ICT resources themselves. There is widespread concern that the growth of the Internet is exacerbating inequalities between the information rich and the information poor: between industrialised and developing countries; between the rich and poor within each nation; and between those who are technically literate and those who are technically inept.

In the USA, for example, households with incomes of $75,000 and higher are twenty times more likely to have access to the Internet than those at the lowest income levels, and more than nine times as likely to have a computer at home. Growing access to the Internet through the television and telephone is likely to reduce these gaps; libraries and other public information points can also have an important role to play. For the present, though, the gaps remain substantial.

Most computer-aided guidance systems have been designed so that they are capable of being used on a stand-alone basis, without counsellor support. In general, however, most commentators on the use of such systems advocate the benefits of integrating them into more broadly-based guidance services. There are three models for such integration. The first is the supported model, in which the user is seen usually for a brief period before and/or after using the system. The second is the incorporated model, in which the system is used within another guidance intervention—within a classroom session, for example, or within a counselling interview, enabling counsellor and client to work with the system side-by-side. While this latter example can be very fruitful, it also means that, far from reducing the counsellor time required by the client, the system may increase it. The third model is the progressive one, in which the use of the system is preceded and/or followed by other guidance interventions—interviews, group sessions, experience-based approaches like work experience and work shadowing—in a developmental sequence. These models can also be applied to websites, but here levels of integration are potentially much stronger.

The distinguishes between independent websites which are freestanding and may be developed by a wide variety of commercial, governmental and other agencies, and integrated websites which are developed by career centres themselves. The integrated websites are of particular strategic significance for career centres because they sit at the interface between, on the one hand, their local face-to-face services and other resources within their centres, and on the other, the independent web-based services, which provide a rich range of additional resources but can also be seen as competition. Through their websites, career centres can identify the 'global' resources they wish to utilise, and then intertwine them with their own 'local' provision.

A career centre's websites can have at least five different purposes.

— As a funnel into their own existing off-line services, aiming to maximise take-up of these services.

— Act as a diversion, seeking to take the pressure away from these off-line services by diverting users to other, usually web-based resources where their needs can be met. An enhancement of such diversion, seeking to deliver on-line guidance within the site itself.

— Further enhancements: providing a forum for putting users in contact with others facing similar issues to their own, or with people who may offer help in relation to these issues; and providing a source of distance learning programmes in career management skills and related areas. Most of these purposes are not, of course, mutually exclusive, but the choice and balance between them require strategic decisions to be made, as do the choice of partners for any partnership arrangements. Not only this, but the process of making such decisions can be a valuable opportunity to review the strategic development of the centre as a whole. Many career centres clearly start by simply establishing a presence on the Internet: as puts it, 'were here, because were here, because were here'. Thereafter, it seems likely that they go through four developmental stages. The first is promotional: promoting what the service offers off-line. The second is adaptive: delivering some of these services in on-line form. The third is innovative: delivering new services on-line which are not possible, or less feasible, off-line—which is where any partnership arrangements may come into play.

> The fourth is synergistic: to intertwine on-line and off-line services in new ways. The further a career centre moves through these stages, the more it is using its website as an agent of change in relation to its service provision as a whole.

Alongside websites, there has been growing interest in the use of telephone helplines in delivering career information and guidance services. The largest telephone helpline service in this field is the Learn direct service in the UK, which was launched in February 1998 and by the end of 2000 had responded to 2.4 million calls. Other more limited helplines have been launched in other countries, including Canada and New Zealand. A comparative analysis of these helplines indicates that some have been promoted essentially as information services; others as career counselling services. Some are focused primarily on learning or on work; others on career, embracing the two. Some are aimed at young people or adults; others are all-age. Some are separate services based on call centres; others are integrated in various ways into more broadly-based services.

The decisions made about the framing of helplines in these various respects are critical. Included in this is the extent to which the service should be offered at national or at local level. With Learn direct, the original idea was that calls should be routed to helplines based as locally as possible. This is the model used, for example, by the UK National Health Service helpline NHS Direct: calls are routed to local call centres, and are only passed elsewhere when lines are busy; the notion being that, in time, it might become the 'gateway' to all local health services. In the case of Learn direct, by contrast, the helpline is offered largely at a national level. This can result in some loss of quality, in terms of access to local knowledge. Against this needs to be set the consistency of service and of helpline adviser training offered by relatively large-scale operation. Such decisions have a significant influence on the balance between 'global' and 'local' dimensions in guidance provision. This in turn is critical in determining the level of integration that is possible with face-to-face services.

A further important issue here is technological synergy. Whereas the Learn direct helpline was originally conceived as a separate service, a Learn direct website has now also been introduced, and increasing attention is being focused on integration between the two. The website includes not only courses and occupations databases, but also a diagnostic package which provides an assessment of skills, interests and values, and connects the results to occupational families. Each page of the website includes a 'call me' button which generates a telephone call from a Learn direct adviser. In principle, it should be possible in future for the adviser to bring up on their screen the caller's work to date—a draft curriculum vitae, for example—and work on it on-line with them. Conversely, more callers could be encouraged to access the website and be supported in doing so. Again, greater use of e-mail should make it possible to sustain contact over a period of time through a mixture of synchronous and asynchronous communications. The concept of flexible usage of the telephone, website and e-mail, linked with face-to-face facilities, opens up new opportunities for the delivery of career information and guidance. It means that individuals can initially access help in the form which is convenient to them and with which they feel comfortable.

Some feel comfortable visiting a careers centre; some do not. Some are more comfortable on the telephone, or on e-mail; some are not. A further dimension will be added to this by the likely move towards ready domestic access to videophones or interactive digital television. All of these could be regarded not as alternative services but as portals into a wide, flexible and well-harmonised network of services which can enrich the learning pathways available to the individual. Public policy sometimes seems to impede such harmonisation; it could, however, proactively promote it.

A key issue in relation to such models is the significance attached to the relationship between the individual and the counsellor. The model could be based on a co-ordinated range of resources, of which the counsellor is seen as one. Or it could place the relationship with the counsellor at the centre, viewing other resources as supports to this relationship. In the latter case, it needs to be recognised that the relationship can now be sustained in a variety of ways: not only face-to-face but also at a distance; and in the latter terms, both through synchronised communications like the videophone, the telephone and Internet "chat", and also through asynchronous communications like e-mail and voice-mail. The rationale for the relationship model is that career decisions have an important cognitive component, but that they are bound up very closely with people's feelings about themselves, their sense of identity, and their dreams and aspirations.

Accordingly, the individual can best be helped by working in a relationship with another individual who has the skills to enable them to address their distinctive identity. This is a strong tradition within the career guidance field, but has come under attack on two linked grounds: that by placing the relationship at the centre, it cedes too much power to the counsellor; and that because it is so labour-intensive and counsellors are costly, it is not practicable or sustainable as an extensively delivered model. This leaves the alternative view that guidance professionals should see themselves primarily not as counsellors but as managers of guidance resources: managing diverse resources in ways which enable individuals to find the means through which their personal needs can best be met. In relation to these two models, ICT tends to be viewed as leaning towards the resource-based model. But this is not necessarily the case: certainly ICT does not of itself demand a jettisoning of the relationship model.

Indeed, there is a risk that contrasting the two models too starkly may implicitly hold frozen the familiar and established practice of the face-to-face one-to-one interview. It is important to understand how technology is now transforming the ways in which human relationships are pursued and managed. Instead of assuming that crucial elements are lost when relationships are mediated by technologies, more attention needs to be paid to how technology is enabling such relationships to be developed and sustained in ways which are released from the constraints of space, time and physical presence. Constantly lurking beneath professional anxieties about the use of ICT in guidance has been the fear of reductionism: that the use of technology will lead to simplistic, 'quick-fix', information-based approaches, in which the human element is marginalised or eliminated. Increasingly, however, it can be used within an integrated approach not only to supplement but also to extend the range of this human element.

The key distinctions now are not simply between human interventions and ICT-based interventions, but between a more complex range of interventions: direct face-to-face counsellor-client interactions, on either a one-to-one or group basis; technically mediated counsellor-client interactions, on either a synchronous or asynchronous basis; and stand-alone ICT-based services in which standardised services can be repeatedly used by different users without additional human resource cost. An important issue is how these different interventions can be optimally blended in effective service delivery, attending to clients' varied needs and preferred learning styles. This has implications both for the training of counsellors, and for wider public policy.

The potential roles of public policy in relation to career information and guidance services are four-fold: legislation, remuneration, exhortation and regulation. Legislation is important in some countries in providing the essential base for such services, but is likely to apply to the services as a whole rather than to ICT in particular. The other three roles, however, can apply specifically to the use of ICT in career information and guidance services.

Many governments have seemed prepared to offer funding for initiatives involving the use of ICT in this field. Indeed, they have not infrequently seemed more willing to provide funding for such initiatives than for extensions of other forms of service delivery, and also less demanding in seeking evidence of effectiveness. In part this is because such funding is often linked to wider policy agendas: in particular, the interest of many governments in promoting e-learning and in improving the ICT capability of their citizens, as a way of seeking to ensure their nation's future economic competitiveness. It therefore has a kind of 'face validity' which sometimes seems to protect it from close critical scrutiny. Also, it is commonly justified in terms of promising future cost savings in expenditure on face-to-face career guidance services, or a somewhat different argument - extending access to such services without commensurate increases in costs.

Systematic evidence of such effects, and whether they involve any reductions in quality of outcomes, is however currently lacking. Indeed, there is some anecdotal evidence that ICT-based services may increase rather than reduce the demand for face-to-face services—and therefore lead to greater frustration if these services are not available. It may also be that the notion of evaluating the relative merits of different models of service delivery face-to-face, by computer, by telephone and so on as discrete alternatives is now outdated. In the past, these have tended to be viewed as alternative means to the same ends, which should accordingly be evaluated in comparative cost-effectiveness terms. If however as argued earlier in this chapter effective models of delivery are interweaving human and technical resources in ever denser ways, this may be an inappropriate approach. Instead, it may be that the important question now is how these models can be most effectively combined in a synergistic way, so that they add value to one another, and provide new service-delivery options for clients.

The role of government in funding ICT-based services is though open to question on more basic grounds: that the development of such services can be safely left to the market, and that public intervention is accordingly unnecessary. Certainly the Internet has fostered the growth of an open market in the field of career information and guidance: anyone anywhere can launch such services. For example, Web-based recruitment agencies are increasingly offering 'guidance' or 'careers advice' as a 'loss leader'.

The role of the market in relation to ICT in particular is closely linked to its role in relation to career information and guidance in general. The core of the case for public investment in such services is that they represent not only a private good but also a public good, in terms of their contribution both to economic efficiency and to social equity.

Traditionally, such services have often been perceived as part of social-welfare provision. In recent years, efforts have been made in a number of countries to apply market principles to social and economic activities wherever this is feasible. Under this view, public intervention in relation to public goods should be confined to areas where there is market failure.

In relation to career information and guidance, the market would seem to be potentially inadequate in three important respects. The first is impartiality. The market tends to respond to the needs of those with most resources at their disposal. In the field of career information and guidance, therefore, it tends to be drawn to the recruitment interface, and to the needs of employers at that interface. This can both constrain and distort the services that are offered, focusing them around the need to fill the vacancies on offer rather than to meet the individual's needs. This may not be sufficient to fulfil the public interest. Secondly, there may be market failure in terms of investment. This is particularly true in relation to career information, which is not 'excludable': individuals are not willing to pay for the collection and provision of information which will subsequently be available to others free of charge. This suggests that career information services should be provided by the state.

On the other hand, it is argued by some that guidance services should not be funded in this way, because they are specific to the individual and therefore are 'excludable'. It is significant, however, that in practice the only area where a significant market has developed for career guidance services is outplacement counselling, where the employer pays but has no interest in the nature of the outcome; elsewhere it seems to be difficult to commodify guidance in the way that a market with growth potential would require. In relation to ICT, the argument for the public interest in investment in career information is evident in the number of countries where governments have supported the development and maintenance of databases on educational and occupational opportunities. Such databases can either be made directly accessible to clients, or can be made available for private-sector organisations to package and distribute, whether on a fee basis or not, as a means of assuring the quality of non-government information provision.

In the USA, for example, federal and state funding have for many years supported a network of career information delivery systems, co-ordinated by the National Occupational Information Co-ordinating Committee. It is also significant, however, that all of the major 'maxi' computer-aided guidance systems were developed initially with funding from government or from private foundations. Similarly, publicly-supported Internet-based systems allow centralised planning of the resource and service design, increasing the likelihood that different functions will be effectively integrated (e.g. using the output of a transferable skills analysis as input for the creation of a curriculum vitae). Governments and foundations prefer to provide pump-priming funding for innovations which the private sector will then maintain, reinvesting a proportion of the profits into ongoing development. This is linked to the third potential source of market failure, which relates to ownership. If the aim is to integrate ICT as closely as possible into more broadly-based guidance services, and if these services are publicly-funded, then marketisation of the ICT-based services may impede the extent of the integration that is feasible.

It is also evident in, for example, current concerns in university career centres in the USA about the extent to which many of their 'mission-critical' activities are now dependent on commercial vendors. These vendors are perceived to be using their position to remove the career centres from the graduate recruitment process and establish a direct customer relationship with the student and employer —an argument that arguably would severely weaken the wider guidance role of these centres. Such arguments may provide a case for some level of continued public investment in ICT in career information and guidance services. Nonetheless, there is clearly an important role for the market too, harnessing additional resources and encouraging competition that will foster innovation. The balance is likely to vary across countries, depending on their structures and traditions and on the political philosophies of their governments.

Where the role of the market is extensive, there remain issues about whether governments should retain a residual responsibility for ensuring quality—either by exhortation, through guidelines and the like, or by regulation. These issues are particularly pressing in relation to the Internet. The quality of websites varies massively. Some are well-designed and user-friendly; some are not.

Many give no information about the sources of data and when they were last updated. A study of websites offering no-cost career assessment found that almost none included any reference to how instruments had been developed or to underpinning psychometric data on reliability and validity.

There often appears to be no security regarding the confidentiality of client data. Little account is commonly taken of clients with visual disabilities or low vocabulary levels. A variety of strategies can be adopted in response to such issues. One is to offer guidelines; another is to produce detailed quality standards. These can be linked to a self-assessed kitemarking system based on websites' affirmations that they meet these standards; or to an accredited kitemarking system based on verification by an external body. All these systems can be voluntaristic, or can be made compulsory—for example, for any services used by, or referred to by, guidance services in receipt of public funding.

Internet-Based Career Information Delivery Systems (CIDS)

An Internet-based career information delivery system (CIDS) is defined as including the following three components: assessment, search capability, and information delivery (educational and occupational data), and these components must be integrated to assist the individual in using the information from one element of the web site to complete another element of the site. Examples of integration include using assessment results to search for occupations, or looking up educational programs for an occupation being researched. This definition is congruent with the definition of CIDS adopted in the standards of the Association of Computer-Based Systems for Career Information, "A computer-based career information system delivers integrated assessment and search functions linked to career and educational information in an environment that provides user support."

An essential element in evaluating the appropriateness of potential sites for various users and populations involves an analysis of data on the effectiveness of CIDS with different populations. The process of completing research and evaluation studies is, however, a time-consuming process. Furthermore, CIDS are extremely dynamic, in that they are continuously being revised and updated as the nature of the Internet allows for immediate modifications. The rapidity of site change complicates the evaluation of Internet-based CIDS. These two problems, the time lag in publishing research and evaluation studies and the rapid evolution of CIDS on the Internet, necessitate a multidimensional approach to the evaluation process.

The use of a differential feature-cost analysis offers a potential solution to the above problems. A differential feature analysis allows the comparison of two or more CIDS in terms of the features available. In regards to previous feature-costs analyses of computer-assisted career guidance systems (CACGS), Literature relevant to CACG systems is also relevant for this analysis of Internet-based CIDS. Examining the features of an Internet-based CIDS allows practitioners to understand the most optimal ways to integrate the site into their existing service delivery.

Let us look into a study of Internet-based CIDS, conducted in US, to uderstantand it properly. The primary purposes of the study was to identify what Internet-based CIDS exist and to highlight similarities and differences among Internet-based CIDS, so that practitioners may make more informed decisions concerning the integration of sites into service delivery, Internet-based CIDS developers may more systematically present information about their site, policy makers may monitor the developing scope and direction of site features and costs, and researchers may more fully describe Internet-based CIDS in their studies.

The specific Internet-based CIDS included the study were:

1) e-Choices,
2) Career Information System - National site,
3) Embark.com - Education and Career Opportunities System (ECOS),
4) Georgia Career Information System,
5) Illinois Career Information System (Horizons),
6) Indiana Career and Postsecondary Advancement Center (ICPAC), and
7) Washington Occupational Information System (WOIS).

The US Career Information System (CIS) delivered sites for the states of Alaska, Idaho, Massachusetts, Nebraska, Nevada, Ohio, and Oregon that contain state-specific information. While these sites were reviewed, they were not listed individually due to substantial similarities to the Career Information System.

The following criteria were used in selecting Internet-based CIDS for inclusion in the study:

1) the state provider is included in the Association of Computer-Based Systems for Career Information (ACSCI) directory and the state has an Internet version of their system,

2) the site includes components that address self-assessment, the generation of alternatives through search, and the delivery of occupational and educational information, as well as integration among these components.

Features were established by beginning with the features utilized by Sampson, et al. in the cost-feature analysis of computer-assisted career guidance systems (CACGS). As the CIDS were reviewed, features were added or removed to best reflect the existing features of sites. Some features were included based on the emerging national standards for Internet delivery of CIDS, such as the NCDA Guidelines for the Use of the Internet for Provision of Career Information and Planning Services.

A four member research team was assembled to conduct the analysis. The research team met to review the purposes of the present research and then met as a group several times to discuss common criteria for features and to suggest the addition of new features or the deletion of previous features. Developers were contacted to ask if they were willing to participate in the study. All developers agreed to participate and supplied information (e.g., passwords) required to access their Internet-based CIDS. Each developer's Web site was then reviewed using the checklist by two members of the research team. Disagreements between team members over the presence or absence of specific features were resolved through group discussion and a second review of the site for the feature in question.

While every attempt has been made to be accurate, there are inherent limitations in any methodology. First, the analysis did not examine the effectiveness or desirability of the features identified for the sites. Although a site was be granted a "yes" for a particular feature, this feature was not be particularly effective or desirable for the goals of one's clientele. It is important not to confuse effectiveness with quantity of features. A second limitation involved was the use of a "checklist" approach in presenting the data. In an effort to present feature data in a succinct manner, a dichotomous yes - no "checklist" comparison of sites was used. This approach effectively simplified a massive amount of data. However, potential problems occur when this methodology oversimplifies and obscures reality. Certain features cannot be adequately explained by this "yes" - "no" analysis. This type of analysis does not capture some of the true differences.

Related to the limitation of using a "checklist" approach, the awarding of a "no" for any given site feature is not necessarily "bad" and the awarding of a "yes" for any given site feature is not necessarily "good." In some cases a "no" may not indicate the lack of a relevant site feature. For example, if the site administers an assessment on-line that a professional views as inappropriate for her client, then a "yes" for this site feature is irrelevant. The checklist approach was a tool to be used in evaluating a system for a specific population. A third limitation of the study involved the dynamic nature of the Internet. A strength of Internet-based CIDS is the ability to constantly update and add features and content.

The growth and development of the sites appears to have been supported by four funding mechanisms:

1) separate fees charged to organizations (e.g., schools) that in turn provide access to their members (e.g., students),
2) access is bundled with fees paid for PC-based systems,
3) access is free and granted to members of a certain group (e.g., an entire state) due to underwriting by a government agency, and
4) access is universal due to underwriting by a government agency.

There is currently no evidence of an Internet CIDS that derives direct support from an individual, fee per service basis. While these Internet-based CIDS are not directly supported by individual users, it is the individual who ultimately benefits from these sites. However, not all of these individuals have the capability to initiate or sustain the career exploration and decision-making process. Varying degrees of professional support for CIDS use may be necessary depending upon user needs. None of the sites include a description of circumstances where users may need help applying the information to their specific needs. It would benefit these users if sites included contact information for local referral sources based upon user needs.

Basing the design of Web sites for career information delivery on a needs-based model, helps individuals to more quickly find information that meets their needs while understanding how to use the information they receive. Traditionally, the user has been required to learn the navigation metaphors and "rules" of a particular Web site in order to find the information which they seek. In a needs-based design, CIDS features are categorized by commonly occurring user needs. For example, college graduates often need to conduct a job search and high school students often desire to explore their occupational interests. This approach requires user reflection and provides a framework with which users can match their needs to features available on the site.

A great deal of the information about site developers and site content is contained in separate Web sites about the developer or sponsoring organization. This information is not well integrated into the Internet CIDS themselves.

Users may begin their search for career information at the Web site address for the Internet CIDS, thus missing the opportunity to find this valuable information. For example, while developers often identify themselves on their CIDS site, this identification may not be linked to the qualifications of the developer, which is posted on a different Web site.

Therefore, consumers have less information with which to make informed choices about the quality of available sites. Although a qualified developer does not ensure the existence of a valid CIDS, it is one useful piece of information individuals may use in selecting quality sites. Similarly, none of the sites provide information on validity of assessments. This information is necessary to allow practitioners to ethically discharge their responsibilities and users to determine if the assessment will meet their needs.

Likewise, while original sources were cited in much of the information content, none of the sites provided a general statement about information gathering and authoring procedures or quality control methods. Practitioners and users must have confidence that the information delivered is accurate and relevant to their needs.

Users may potentially benefit from exposure to "original source content" via links to other sites. While there is a natural desire to keep users on one's own Web site, experience with real world content may be a valuable aspect of the exploration process. For example, links to union or employer web pages offering apprenticeships would provide the learner with

1) evidence to validate information in the CIDS,
2) a chance to build a schema by comparing and contrasting options; and
3) information on which to take further action (e.g., information interview, job shadow, or application).

The downside to providing users direct access to such content is that they can easily become lost and they may not be able to judge the variable quality of information presented.

The Internet offers a wide variety of media creation and integration tools to developers, however sites currently rely on text-based strategies for information presentation. This is most likely due to delivery issues that are associated with multimedia and the Internet.

However, the user experience could be enhanced by presenting complex information in the form of simple charts delivered as graphics. One form of information delivery offering rich possibility to developers is audio. None of the sites appear to use this presentation method, even though audio is a relatively bandwidth friendly form of multimedia. It can also be a relatively easy to produce and cost effective method of integrating "real world" content.

Audio offers additional benefits to those with visual disabilities or limited reading skills. It is also important for developers to consider other accessibility issues when designing and delivering their products. For example, all developers may wish to provide alternative means of navigation or text only versions of their Web sites for individuals with visual disabilities, who may depend on text-to-speech tools for navigating the World Wide Web.

Internet-based CIDS appear to be in an early stage of development in comparison with their older, PC-based siblings. While the core information contents of Internet-based and PC-based CIDS are almost identical, tools that users can use to integrate this information in the decision-making process appear less developed. For example, none of the sites offer the capability to compare two education providers or two occupations, a common feature of standalone CIDS. This situation will probably improve over time, as developers are more able to apply their past experience with CACG systems to an Internet environment that is more responsive and fully featured. Similarly, only two CIDS currently offer an online portfolio and keep a user record through an individualized access strategy.

While group access strategies are easier to deliver and manage, they may possibly provide a less powerful experience for the user. By users having their own unique records, tools for portfolio development (e.g., resumes, assessment records, and education) and information management become possible. One possible disadvantage the individual access strategy presents is a potential learning barrier or concern about confidentiality that users may choose to avoid. Such barriers and concerns may decrease site utilization. Currently, there is no reference to ACSCI standards on any of the Internet-based CIDS. These standards represent a powerful tool for educating users and practitioners about what they should expect from providers in terms of quality and use of career information. Rather than failing to meet standards, it may be that in the rush to make sites available, time was not allocated for showing adherence to standards.

3

Technology in School Counselling

Traditionally, the guidance programes werew considered an ancillary student service isolated from the instructional program and designed primarily to encourage students to attend college. Much of the counselor's work was reactive and crisis-oriented. Today, there is an unwritten agreement among counsellors that a guidance and counseling program should refers to a comprehensive, developmental program designed to benefit all students in their journey through school and in preparation for the future.

The US National Occupational Information Coordinating Committee's (NOICC) National Career Development Guidelines, which have been adapted by forty states across the nation, list the following processes of the career guidance and counseling program:

— outreach

— instruction

— consultation

— counseling

— career information

— referral

— assessment

— work experience

— placement and follow-up

Counseling is one process of the guidance program and refers to the interaction between a professional counselor and an individual or a small group. The school counselor's counseling skills are well-defined techniques learned through professional education programs. As certified and/or licensed professionals, most school counselors hold an advanced degree in guidance and counseling or a related field.

Ethically, school counselors only counsel students concerning normal development situations and refer students with psychological disorders to professionals with appropriate clinical training. Other facets of the guidance program, such as classroom instruction or providing information, are key components of the guidance programs. Adding to the school counselors' dilemma are perceptions that they place students in classes based on their personal biases.

Professional school counselors examine their own biases and stereotypes and understand they are ethically bound to avoid restricting choices of students. They are cognizant that students must be made responsible for all their decisions—including course selection, program selection, career goals, and future plans. Obviously, students must be aware of and understand all their options if they are to make informed decisions.

Today's school counselors are required to work with all students regardless of cultural or ethnic background, sex, age, affectional orientation, special needs, class, and so forth, making it imperative that counselors understand their students' needs.

One study found student-counselees rated discussions with the counselor as more important than objective tests, interests inventories, or vocational information. Thus, it is critical that counselors understand and respond to the needs of the nation's increasingly diverse student population. According to the NOICC's National Career Development Guidelines, students need assistance in:

(1) increasing self-knowledge,

(2) educational and occupational exploration, and

(3) lifelong career planning

These elements identifying exemplary career guidance and counseling programs by expanding the first group to include "self-advocacy" and the third group to include career preparation and transition.

Many students are disadvantaged when it comes to opportunities for career development. They have inadequate sampling of work world models on which to base their emerging career identity. It is not that they don't have any, but those they have generally are inadequate.

A lack of such opportunity, however, does not result in an occupational knowledge and value vacuum. Opinions are formed, judgments are made, and many times these result in premature educational and occupational foreclosure. An opportunity unknown is not an opportunity at all.

Students need a chance to explore and test out some of their notions about the work world. Possible career options require continuous testing to help them evaluate what such options may mean to them. They need help in translating their emerging career identities into reality. Students need the opportunity to continuously and systematically explore and test out from an internal frame of reference their personal attributes in relation to the wide range of educational and career opportunities that may be available to them.

It should be clearly understood that the primary goal is not to have students choose careers to fit jobs, but rather to enlarge students' capacities and vision to make decisions about themselves and their career development in the context of the society in which they live, go to school, and work. Furthermore, the STWO Act of 1994 explicitly states the strong need for career education and career development programs for all students. For this to take place, they will need information sharing, communication, career education, labor market information, job placement, work experience programs, counseling and assessment, and public relations.

School counselors have traditionally been expected to fulfill diverse—and often conflicting—roles. They have been called to act in the capacity of confidant, disciplinarian, consultant, scheduler, politician, administrator, and psychological helper. The ambiguity regarding counselors' roles and expectations has created confusion among teachers, support staff, parents, and students.

Some schools, counselors are told to focus much of their time on record keeping, administrative responsibilities, or crisis interventions with students.

There is little time for comprehensive career exploration and planning for life after graduation. In addition, facilities and resources for planning and implementing career guidance and counseling programs are sadly lacking. The student-counselor ratios in most schools limit the services that school counselors can deliver. The following list of tasks is limited, yet, typical:

— Counselors register and schedule all new students.

— Counselors are responsible for giving ability and achievement tests.

— Counselors teach classes when teachers are absent.

— Counselors send students home who are not appropriately dressed.

— Counselors assist with duties in the principal's office.

— Counselors compute grade-point averages and are in charge of student records.

— Counselors are assigned lunchroom duty and supervise study halls.

Few studies have explored what school counselors actually do or should do at the elementary level and at the secondary level, but counselor educators and researchers are in agreement—auxiliary or administrative support functions must be eliminated from counselors' day-to-day activities if they are to be effective in fulfilling their roles.

Many believe school counselors can be a key force in preparing the nation's diverse student population for the future. With the passage of the STWO Act of 1994, school counselors are being entrusted to take the lead in assisting our nation's young people to smoothly transition from school to work. As they comply with the

STWO Act's mandates, they must also meet the challenges of accommodating the needs of an increasingly diverse student population, including girls and women as well as the college-bound and the noncollege-bound.

They are called upon to provide leadership and facilitate schools' efforts to assist the career developmental needs of all their students. To enable them to meet the expectations of the student-counselees they serve and to have an impact in educational reform, it is important they not be burdened with any non-career guidance duties.

Career Guidance Programs

Guidance and counseling is only one component of the educational effort required to better assist students with diverse needs, it is a very important one. Because of this, a major activity of the National Center for Research in Vocational Education's Office of Student Services (OSS) is to identify exemplary career guidance and counseling programs serving diverse student populations and disseminate information about them to the field. For 1995, a major activity of OSS is to conduct a national search of career guidance programs that assist all students--secondary and postsecondary--to successfully transition from school to work or to further education.

Career development is a lifelong process which incorporates general education, occupational training, and work, as well as one's social and leisure life. Career education is the process designed to assist individuals in their career development. Career guidance is one component of a career education program. According to the National Career Development Guidelines (NOICC), a career guidance program has the following characteristics:

— Is identifiable but integrated with other programs within the institution.

— Enhances the career development knowledge, skills, and abilities of all students by establishing program standards.

— Uses coordinated activities designed to support student achievement of the standards.

— Supports the delivery of the program through qualified leadership; diversified staffing; adequate facilities, materials and financial resources; and effective management.

— Is accountable, with evaluation that is based on program effectiveness in supporting student achievement of the career guidance and counseling standards.

Guidance programs consists basically of three clusters of components:

(1) the delivery of career guidance programs;

(2) the collaboration and articulation efforts; and

(3) the leadership and support given the career guidance and counseling program by the institution.

According to a Department of Labor publication, there is widespread agreement that career guidance, properly implemented, addresses three broad competency areas involved in the career development process. Ideally, career guidance programs will enhance:

- *Self-knowledge and self-awareness*: Conscious examination of personal values, interests, and goals;
- *Educational and occupational exploration*: Presentation and integration of information and experience; and
- *Decision-making and career planning*: Understanding the interrelations between the self and the world and developing skills to make realistic choices and rational decisions.

For example, Springdale High School (SHS) in America, Arkansas is a public secondary school serving diverse groups of students in grades 10-12. Its mission is to *provide challenging opportunities for EVERY student in a positive environment*. To achieve this end, Springdale High School is heavily involved in the Tech Prep movement, School-to-Work Transition, and is one of the 19 Southern Regional Educational Board (SREB) work-based learning grant sites. It has also been selected as a *High Schools That Work* site.

The *High Schools That Work* initiative is based on the belief that students in general and vocational programs of studies can master complex academic and technical concepts and skills if schools create an environment that encourages students to make the effort to succeed. The two major goals of the program are to (1) increase mathematics, science, and communication achievement of students in general and vocational studies to the national average of all students by the year 2000; and (2) combine the basic content of traditional college preparatory English, mathematics, and science courses with vocational studies in grades 9-12.

The SHS's strong comprehensive guidance program is the key to the success of these initiatives. In order to achieve their goal "to prepare all students for the choices and challenges of the 21st century," the SHS guidance program has successfully moved from the traditional "available upon demand" model to a competency-based model. Through the latter model, the desired competencies for graduating students are identified and matched with programs and activities implemented through the guidance program. Counseling personnel collaborate with the administration and faculty to plan and implement the program.

Both the vocational program and the guidance program are recognized as exemplary programs in Arkansas. Career guidance professionals and educators come often to observe this unique career guidance program in action. SHS school counselors and personnel face the challenge of responding to the needs of a diverse student population. Springdale, Arkansas is located in a rural area with a very low unemployment rate (3%). While there is an abundance of jobs, many are entry-level and/or low paying. The majority of these jobs are in the poultry industry.

A large segment of the SHS student population are from rural, economically disadvantaged families. Many are children of migrant farm workers and have limited-English proficiency. Too often, their parents do not have the information or skills to help them make informed career, occupational, or educational decisions. The components of the SHS guidance program were compared to the three clusters of components described in the framework for identifying exemplary career guidance and counseling programs. The strengths of the guidance program at Springdale High School were validated by the presence of program components that research shows successful programs possess.

The career guidance and counseling program of Springdale High School is part of a total team effort within the school to help their 1,600 students prepare for the world of work or further education. A teacher advisor system, based on a "Career Action Plan" (CAP), makes it possible to respond to the career guidance needs of this large number of students. The CAP serves as a guide to assist students and their parents to explore educational and occupational possibilities by using extensive information about the students. Teacher advisors, trained by the counselors, meet monthly with approximately 20 students. The junior high school teachers work with students during their eighth and ninth grade, while senior high school teachers advise them during their tenth through twelfth grades.

Teacher advisors meet with students for a minimum of one hour each month. The advisor also meets annually with each student and her/his parent to plan for the following year. Counselors assist advisors throughout this program by providing inservice, offering information and strategies for the meetings, and providing materials. Curriculum units on video with accompanying handouts help the advisors give consistent information to students. The videos were prepared by counselors and are tailored to the educational/employment needs of Northwest Arkansas.

Springdale students receive intensive career guidance beginning in grade eight, when they take a one-semester course called Career Orientation (CO). During the course, their learning styles, career interests, and aptitudes are assessed. Information gathered from these assessments is used during the initial CAP conferences, and reviewed and updated in succeeding CAP conferences in grades 9-12.

During the CO classes, eighth graders begin building their career portfolio which includes scores on standardized tests, learning styles, career interests, as well as previous grades. At this stage, students get a better grasp of their career aspirations by understanding and analyzing their individual strengths and weaknesses.

In the ninth grade, students participate in guidance activities that stress teamwork, use of leisure time, and conflict resolution. The Economic Education Program—the district's K-12 career education program which emphasizes K-7 career exploration—gives students the opportunity for job shadowing that increases their understanding of the relationship between work and learning. The second annual student/parent/advisor CAP conference takes place in the spring.

When students come to the high school campus in the tenth grade, they are assigned peer helpers who—under the guidance of the high school counselors—help facilitate their transition from junior to senior high school. Students are also assigned their CAP teacher/advisor who meets with them each month for career review and planning.

Teacher advisors use curriculum units designed by area counselors to provide accurate planning information. Students begin choosing a "major" and developing a program of study, which includes the selection of courses for grades 11-16. The *Choices* computerized interest inventory, with follow-up and education information, is administered to all tenth graders.

Juniors continue to meet monthly with teacher advisors and receive career planning information. They are given opportunities for work-based learning, community service, and job shadowing. The ASSET by

ACT, a college placement test used by community colleges and technical institutes, is administered to all juniors in the spring. Those who show deficiencies which require remedial courses in college are encouraged to take an acceleration course during their senior years.

Students may then retake the ASSET and use the improved score for placement. Business representatives and counselors collaborate in developing a school-to-work conference where students attend a general session and then choose "break-out" sessions led by teams of teachers and business partners. Junior students also have the option to take the Armed Services Vocational Aptitude Battery (ASVAB).

Community service is encouraged by giving elective credit options. In addition, students learn the importance of volunteerism in the community. Students use sophisticated software in the Media Center and the Career Center to explore career opportunities and colleges. Representatives from the military, postsecondary institutions, and the community are available to meet with seniors in the Career Center on a regular basis. Students are given maximum assistance in applying for work, college, financial aid, and scholarships. The College View program located in the Career Center allows students to electronically apply to many colleges and universities. An annual event that juniors and seniors look forward to attending is the College Fair at SHS where they meet admission personnel from the military and over 60 colleges.

The SHS students who are at-risk of failing (those with multiple Ds and Fs) take part in the grade improvement program (GIP). Through the GIP, students participate in workshops focusing on goal setting, study skills, assertiveness, time management, self-advocacy, and "school survival." The GIP is conducted by school counselors who meet weekly with students in groups of 6-8 to teach them study skills and provide them with the needed support for behavior change. The program is an excellent means of providing group counseling as 150 to 200 students meet weekly with counselors in small group settings. The students frequently take advantage of the Career Center housed in the SHS Guidance Department. This state-of-the art facility, which is open to students and parents any time of the day, contains the most current technology in educational and occupational exploration.

Counselors and trained student aides are on hand to help students and/or parents maximize the information available at the Career Center. At the beginning of each year, students receive orientation on the wide range of information and technology available in the Center. In addition, teachers often bring classes to the Center to conduct career research. Over the years, SHS personnel have learned that by working together they can "do a whole lot more a whole lot better."

Counselors, teachers, and the administrators are committed to assisting their students in achieving a successful life. The career guidance and counseling program works because of the solid working relationship that exists among the school staff. Counselors work closely with Northwest Arkansas Community College and Northwest Technical Institute to facilitate the movement of students to postsecondary education. Parental support is essential in making a student's program of study relevant to his or her career goals.

Parents participate in each step of their student's career planning and attend CAP conferences each spring. This program has completed its third year with extremely positive feedback from parents. It is clear that parents who would have otherwise opted to be uninvolved participate in these annual career conferences.

Administrative support for the career guidance and counseling program at SHS is visible. Increased professional development activities and improved facilities exemplify the administrative leadership that career guidance and counselors at SHS receive. The guidance program is housed in an impressive facility that includes a large reception area, a full-time registrar's office, five large counselor offices, a centrally located Career Center, a classroom that seats 40, a room for small group activities, a large conference room, and men's and women's restrooms.

The Career Center is equipped with the latest technology including twelve computers, e-mail capability, and a sophisticated phone system. The involvement of SHS in the *High Schools That Work* initiative has helped administrators of Springdale Public Schools realize the importance of an effective guidance program. To strengthen the different components of the career guidance and counseling program at SHS, professional development activities have been planned.

Counselors regularly attend various workshops to improve their skills on career counseling, group counseling, individual counseling, and assessment. Counselors have initiated model programs for student improvement including the Grade Improvement Program and Renaissance Program. As a result, student performance has improved significantly.

Other student-oriented programs initiated by this innovative team of counselors include Peer Helpers, Elementary Tutors, and opportunities for students to receive school credit for community service. Additionally, school counselors assist students in the school's Learning Center/Night School, an alternative education program designed to prevent and reclaim dropouts of all ages.

Technology and School Counselling

Technology has the potential to enhance and change forever the way school counselors support teachers, foster student development, and interact with families. Today, we are witnessing a barrage of reports on the use of educational technology in the schools and classrooms; and once again, no mention in any of these reports is made of the unique and important use of technology by the school counselors. All policymakers should expect their school counselors to have in the area of technology:

— Possess basic computer-literacy skills. School counselors must know how to use a computer, computer peripherals, and computer-application software, including word processing, spreadsheets, and presentation software. They also must be proficient in either a PC/Windows or a Macintosh platform, knowing how to access files, install software, and use on-line help menus.

— Understand and be conversant in the current and emerging state of technology in education. Guidance professionals must have a general framework of knowledge on how technology is and is not affecting students, teachers, families, and their communities. Specifically, we should expect school counselors to be familiar with state and national technology initiatives, quantitative and qualitative research on the use of technology in and out of schools, pedagogical issues and concerns raised by the use of computers, instructional-intervention methods made possible by computers, social and cultural inequities in access and use, and the current literature on issues affecting educational technology.

— Comprehend and employ all major Internet components in guidance activities. The Internet will soon become the major communication tool available to schools and families. School counselors, then, must know how to incorporate such Internet tools in their work, from the World Wide Web, e-mail, mailing lists, chat rooms, and newsgroups and bulletin boards, to file transfer protocol (FTP), gophers, Telnet, and video-conferencing. They should know how to use the Internet to access professional and academic information, exhibit proper "netiquette" while on-line, and be able to locate and communicate with other school counselors worldwide. Counselors also should possess the skills and knowledge needed to create or participate in Internet forums, Internet projects, and distance-learning activities. They must learn how to contribute to the design, construction, and maintenance of their department's Internet Web page, as well as a personal home page.

— Articulate the implications and opportunities of technology. Counselors will have to examine and discuss how technology will change various aspects of their current duties and responsibilities, as well as the ways they have traditionally worked with students, parents, and colleagues. The paradigm shift occurring in the society at large will increasingly result in counselors' becoming more of the navigator, as opposed to the pilot, in the student-counselor relationship. As the navigator, counselors will have to know when and when not to use technology with their constituents, and how to help those constituents properly interpret and apply information gained through this new medium.

— Act as an educated and objective consumer of technology. Technology is constantly changing. Newer and faster computers are being sold each year. Thousands of new software programs are being developed and marketed to schools as the "best" product to meet their students' needs. So school counselors must learn how to objectively and systematically analyze the features, functions, and benefits of new products before they are purchased with departmental funds. They need, also, to be aware of software that will lessen the time spent on administrative tasks and permit them to spend more time working with students and families.

— Grasp the ethical and legal implications of technology. Although we don't yet know with certainty their full dimensions in the field, the ethical and legal implications of technology represent an area in which school counselors should be well versed. Current ethical standards for counseling must be examined and discussed to determine their applicability within the emerging technological environment. Legal experts should be consulted to ascertain what new guidelines might be needed when working within this emerging environment.

— Construct group and "virtual" guidance activities using technology. Synchronous and asynchronous on-line activities that help students exercise judgment, develop values, and analyze and evaluate information and opinions should be implemented by school counselors. Likewise, they should design and place on their schools' guidance Web pages Web-based activities for families, with a focus on how parents and other family members can assist a child's academic, career, and social and personal development.

— Use relational databases to monitor and articulate student progress. The use of data in planning and evaluating the effectiveness of an entire school and of its guidance department is critical. Collecting and analyzing the data should be a team effort, with input from the instructional staff, administrators, and parents.

— Counselors need to be knowledgeable and proficient in software that collects the aggregated and disaggregated data needed to review, monitor, and improve performance, specifically in the areas of student achievement, attendance, enrollment, discipline, socioeconomic status, mobility rate, language, dropout rate, graduation rate, college scholarships, postsecondary options, and standardized-test participation and results. Moreover, counselors should help make the data more available and understandable for parents, perhaps by including access to personal information on the Web.

— Contribute to the development of their schools' or districts' technology plans. As schools develop and revise their written technology plans, counselors must have the technical know-how to present clearly the rationale behind various equipment and training requests. They must understand the language and the various components of a technology plan, be able to review and critique sample school-based technology plans, and know how to develop an effective technology component for their guidance departments.

— Identify national, state, and private funding for technology. An estimated $5.2 billion or more will be spent on educational technology in fiscal 1999-2000, with 45 percent of the funding coming from the federal and state governments on a competitive basis. Districts pay for about 20 percent, and private sources account for approximately 15 percent of technology spending. All told, there is an unprecedented amount of money available to school counselors, if they are taught how to identify sources and submit effective proposals.

— Infusing technology into the guidance suite, like infusing technology into the classroom, will require a concerted district, state, and national effort. Policymakers at all levels must first recognize that technology has the potential to enhance and change forever the way school counselors support teachers, foster student development, and interact with families. While their use of technology may be different, it is no less important than that of the classroom teacher.

At the district level, administrators must re-examine the role and responsibilities of their counselors. Should they spend their time, for instance, on clerical tasks or on creating virtual guidance activities and forums for students and families? Imagine having the guidance department arrange and host a "Virtual Financial Aid

Night," for example. Hundreds of parents could participate—at home—in a live chat-room discussion with the directors of financial aid from major universities. Better yet, imagine a counselor creating and moderating an Internet listserv/mailing list for parents, thereby enabling the guidance department to e-mail its weekly newsletter to parents, and giving parents the chance to easily e-mail each other about colleges they have visited with their children or suggested ways to support a child with a learning disability.

District administrators must provide school counselors with the necessary resources--in-service training, modern equipment, technical support--and, most important, the time needed to incorporate technology into their professional activities. It would be advisable, as well, to include at least one counselor on all technology planning committees. Schools and colleges must re-examine their requirements for technology courses for school counselors and such courses' specificity, recognizing that a generic or a teacher-oriented course will not help counselors address the needs of today's students and families. These targeted technology courses should center around the national standards for school counselors established this year by the American School Counselors Association. Moreover, the as college faculty members must practice what they preach, actively using technology in all courses. No school counselor should be permitted to graduate without first demonstrating his or her proficiency with and use of technology in a counseling setting.

State departments of education can help ensure that technology is being used by school counselors by requiring districts to include counseling and guidance activities in their state-approved technology plans.

Technology funds should be carefully allocated to foster and create model high-tech guidance departments throughout the state, rewarding those schools that use technology and the Internet to partner or link with other organizations. The government can assist by instituting policies requiring that states and districts appropriate a portion of federal technology funds to support guidance- and counseling-related initiatives. At the same time, a national forum should be arranged, perhaps under the auspices of the Department of Education, allowing educators, scholars, government officials, and private-sector executives to discuss methods, products, and resources needed to bring school counseling into the 21st century.

4

Designing Career Services

As career development becomes an increasingly important component of educational systems, the issues of measurement and accountability are raised. In today's workplace, employment security is becoming "employability security"—the knowledge that one has the competencies demanded in a global economy and the ability to expand and adjust those competencies as requirements change. The challenge of preparing the young people for this new workplace has generated legislative efforts to stimulate educational reform directed at creating "world class" education and a comprehensive system for helping youth make a smooth transition from high school to productive, skilled employment and further learning.

In US, the "Goals 2000: Educate America Act" establishes eight national education goals and two national councils—one to stimulate the development of voluntary academic standards and the other to identify essential occupational skills. The "School to Work Opportunities Act of 1994" is a strategy to implement the purpose of the "Goals 2000: Educate America Act," that is, helping all Americans to reach internationally competitive standards through educational reform. Career development is a major component of the "School to Work Opportunities Act (STWOA)." Career guidance and counseling, which are interventions in the career development process, are recognized as essential in helping students to choose their career (educational) pathway. Section 102 of the STWOA states that

> "The school-based component of a School-to-Work Opportunities program shall include... career awareness and career exploration and counseling (beginning at the earliest possible age, but not later than the 7th grade) in order to help students who may be interested to identify, and select or reconsider, their interests, goals, and career majors, including those options that may not be traditional for their gender, race or ethnicity."

The Act also provides grants to states to plan for and implement school-to-work opportunities systems. Renewed interest in career development has led to an equal demand for accountability. In US there afe two major endeavors are helping schools to meet the double need of accountability and assessment. First, state and professional associations, as well as national leaders, practitioners, and career development experts, collaborated to develop the National Career Development Guidelines (NOICC). The National Career Development Guidelines offer a comprehensive, competency-based approach to career development that states, educational institutions and other organizations can use in developing effective career guidance programs. The Guidelines offer the processes, content and structure for such programs. More importantly, they provide the standards or competencies for career development at four different levels--elementary, middle/junior high, high school, and postsecondary/adult. The competencies fall within three areas of career development--self-knowledge, educational and occupational exploration, and career planning. The Guidelines, already being used in over 40 states as standards or as the basis for establishing career development standards, provide nationally validated competencies that can be used in assessment. The second significant effort has been the work of the Secretary's Commission on Achieving Necessary Skills (SCANS). In the Commission report, "What Work Requires of Schools", five areas of competencies based on a three-part foundation are delineated. Of the 36 specific skills or quaiities noted, over half are commonly included in a career guidance program.

Since self-assessment and reflection are important to developing personal responsibility in career decision-making, a portfolio that sets standards and also allows for reflection emerges as the instrument of choice. Until now, most efforts to document career development have been through career planners. Career planners are usually the end product of a career development process and, as such, are appropriate for secondary education or higher but not for the student at the awareness or exploratory stages. They also do not typically provide for the self-reflection essential to an individual's ownership of the process.

American School Counselor Association and the National Occupational Information Coordinating Committee designed a programme "Get A Life: Your Personal Planning Portfolio", through collaboration. It is one instrument that sets standards and allows for self-reflection. The portfolio is divided into four sections--self-knowledge, life roles, educational development, and career exploration and planning.

In US the National Career Development Guidelines for the middle and high school levels are used as competencies for both program and individual assessment. Program planners can analyze the comprehensiveness of their programs by evaluating their activities in relation to the expected student outcomes contained in the Guidelines. Individuals can determine if they have met the career development competencies through the programs offered. Within the competency file, a sign-off ascertains the strategies and the date on which each competency was addressed. In some schools, students make the decision whether, in fact, the activity or strategy presented did help them to master the competency. The personal files are a set of guiding questions that help students to reflect on their learning. The portfolio is an organizational tool that allows the owners to collect information about themselves to use in making personal, educational and career decisions. At the same time, the students are introduced to the idea that the process is lifelong, and that they must become "career negotiators", taking responsibility for their own development.

Cognitive Information Processing (CIP) approach

Within the framework of the Cognitive Information Processing (CIP) approach, readiness is defined as the capability of an individual to make appropriate career choices, taking into account the complexity of family, social, economic, and organizational factors that influence an individual's career development. Another way of viewing these two dimensions is that capability represents internal factors and complexity represents external factors that influence an individual's ability to make appropriate career choices.

Capability

Capability refers to the cognitive and affective capacity of an individual to engage in effective career problem solving and decision making. The following conditions influence individuals' capability to successfully engage in career problem solving and career decision making:

— Individuals are willing to honestly explore their knowledge of self (e.g., interests, skills, and values) so as to attain a clearer sense of identity (Self-knowledge).

— Individuals are motivated to learn about the world of work so as to enhance the development of occupational knowledge (Occupational knowledge).

— Individuals are willing to learn about and engage in career problem solving and decision making (Career decision-making skills). Important components of the ability to think through a career problem and to arrive at a career decision include:

(a) the capacity for thinking clearly about one's career problem, its causes, and alternative courses of action to solve it (absence of problematic decision-making confusion);

(b) confidence in selecting a best alternative course of action to solve the problem and the commitment to carry out a plan of action to implement a solution (absence of problematic commitment anxiety); and

(c) an acceptance of personal responsibility for making a career decision (absence of problematic external conflict).

— Individuals are aware of how negative thoughts and feelings potentially limit their ability to think clearly and remain motivated to solve problems and make decisions. Individuals are willing to seek assistance when they perceive that personal or external barriers are limiting their ability to choose. Individuals also possess the capacity to monitor and regulate lower-order problem solving decision-making processes (Executive processing).

Complexity

Complexity refers to contextual factors, originating in the family, society, employing organizations, or the economy, that make it more difficult to process information necessary to solve career problems and make career decisions. Family factors can contribute to or detract from readiness for career decision making. Individuals with few family responsibilities or stressors have fewer constraints to cope with, which can contribute to reduced complexity in career decision making.

Individuals with supportive family members typically have more resources for understanding and coping with problems that exist. Family factors that can contribute to complexity include deferral, e.g., compromise career development to meet needs of spouse or children or parents, role overload, e.g., roles of worker, parent, son/daughter, homemaker, student, and dysfunctional family input, e.g., over-functioning parents.

Social factors can also contribute to or detract from career decision-making readiness. While social support in the form of modeling, networking, and caring can greatly facilitate career development, other factors make individuals' career decision-making process more complicated. Discrimination on the basis of group membership, e.g., gender, race, ethnicity, age, religion, sexual orientation, disability status, obesity, poverty, and immigration status, may limit opportunity in education, training, and employment. The above groups may also be negatively impacted by stereotyping, lack of role models, bias in education, and harassment in education and employment.

Economic factors can support or inhibit readiness for career decision making. The influence of economic factors on readiness can be experienced on a general and a personal level. General economic factors include economic trends that influence the rate of change in the labor market. A greater rate of change results in greater complexity. On a personal level, poverty and the related difficulty in obtaining housing, health care, and childcare makes it more difficult to think clearly and solve career problems, and may also make it more difficult to fund education and training once an occupational choice is made.

Organizational factors can help or hinder the readiness of employed adults to make career decisions. The size of the organization influences complexity. The larger number of employment options in a large organization make the decision more complex than decisions made in small organizations with limited opportunities. Organizational culture influences complexity in relation to the amount of support provided for employee career development. In an organizational culture that supports effective mentoring, supervision, and performance appraisal, employees are more likely to have higher readiness to make career decisions. Organizations with a culture that does not support employee career development may result in employees being less well prepared to make career decisions. The stability of the organization can also influence complexity. Stable organizations with predictable opportunity structures tend to be less complex to negotiate in comparison with organizations that are rapidly expanding or are being downsized.

Generic Sequence for Career Counseling

A seven-step sequence can be used to guide clients through the problem-solving and decision-making process. Individuals referred for self-help services complete only step 1, while clients receiving brief staff-assisted and individual case-managed services complete all seven steps in the sequence. In group counseling, prescreening occurs in steps 1 and 2, while input from group members is included in steps 3 through 7.

1. *Initial interview*: An interview in which a professional or paraprofessional gains qualitative information about the context of the client's career problem.
2. *Preliminary assessment*: A screening instrument is completed by the client, to give the professional or paraprofessional quantitative information about the client's problem.
3. *Define problem and analyze causes*: Counselor and client come to a mutual preliminary understanding of the problem, defined in terms of a gap between real state and ideal state.

4. *Formulate goals*: Counselor and client together develop a set of attainable counseling goals to remove the gap.
5. *Develop individual learning plan (ILP):* The professional or paraprofessional assists the client to develop an individual learning plan (ILP) that will help in identifying a sequence of resources and activities necessary to help the client attain his or her counseling goals.
6. *Execute individual learning plan*: The client carries out the ILP with the professional or paraprofessional providing encouragement, information, clarification, reinforcement, and planning for future experiences.
7. *Summative review and generalization*: When the client has completed the ILP, the client discusses with the counselor his or her progress toward reaching the counseling goals established in Step 4. Plans for the continued use of career services are formulated. A discussion is held about applying the career problem-solving approach used in this instance to the solving of career problems in the future.

Career Service Interventions

Each individual has unique career problems and is best served by using unique combinations of career resources and services in making career decisions. A career service intervention combines assessment, information, and instructional resources with varying types and amounts of assistance to help individuals in making occupational and employment choices.

Career resources include assessment, information, and instruction.. The cost-effectiveness of career service delivery depends upon the level of staff support meeting, but not exceeding, the needs of the individual. Individuals with high readiness for occupational and employment decision making have the potential to be most cost-effectively served by self-help services. Individuals with moderate readiness for occupational and employment decision making have the potential to be most cost-effectively served by brief staff-assisted services, while low readiness individuals are potentially best served by individual case-managed services.

The readiness of an individual for occupational and employment decision making can be determined by simple screening questions (brief screening), and if needed, practitioner interpretation of quickly administered, hand scorable screening instruments (comprehensive screening).

A career center in an educational, agency, or organizational setting is being used to deliver resources and services to individuals seeking assistance with career, educational, training, and employment decision making. Individuals have the option to seek career resources on a self-help basis via the Internet or other self-help resources without being physically present in a career center.

If either clients or practitioners identify a lack of progress in the successful use of self-help resources, readiness assessment may be subsequently used to better match client needs with service delivery options. Readiness assessment occurs in one step for some clients and two steps for others.

Clients and practitioners may collaboratively decide to move from one level of assistance to another level to more appropriately meet clients' needs. For example, a client initially receiving individual case-managed services may improve in career decision-making readiness to where they move to brief staff-assisted services, or a client initially receiving brief staff-assisted services may be more cost-effectively served with a self-help or an individualized intervention as his or her level of readiness changes or is more accurately assessed.

If the request for information is vague or if a career problem is apparent that involves uncertainty when a decision needs to be made, disabling emotions, confusion, or a complex array of circumstances, more comprehensive screening step occurs involving the completion and interpretation of a readiness assessment measure. The use of a readiness assessment measure provides clients and practitioners with a common frame of reference for discussing individual needs.

Staff members' judgments about individuals' readiness for career decision making should be based on test results and interaction with the individual, as opposed to a relying on a simple score on an assessment instrument. The comprehensive screening function requires a professional or paraprofessional who has demonstrated knowledge of career development, assessment, and career service delivery along with supervised experience in the use of readiness assessment measures.

Self-help services

Self-help services are more likely to be cost-effective for individuals with a high readiness for occupational and employment decision making. This level of service does not include the maintenance of individual counseling records and places no emphasis on regular systematic monitoring of individual progress. Successful use of career service interventions in a self-help mode depends on:

— Accurately assessing user needs during brief screening to ensure that there is a reasonable likelihood that the use of career resources will meet the individual's needs;

— The availability of an effective "safety net" that provides reasonable opportunities for identifying individuals who are not making successful use of career resources, e.g., brief periodic checking with users;

— The availability of staff to respond to basic questions about career resource use, e.g., clarifying interpretation of self-assessment instruments and solving problems related to the use of a specific resource;

— The availability of easy-to-understand text and multimedia support materials and signage to direct users to specific career resources, as well as supplemental services, that relate to individuals' needs; and

— The availability of text and multimedia career resources that are self-instructional and easy to use, including appropriate readability for various populations.

Self-help career services involve self-guided use of self-assessment, information, and instructional resources in a library-like or remote setting, where resources have been designed for independent use by individuals with a high readiness for occupational and employment decision making who need little or no assistance to effectively use career resources.

Guiding and monitoring the selection and use of resources by individuals is the responsibility of the practitioner in brief staff-assisted and individual case-managed service delivery. In self-help career services the guiding and monitoring function is the responsibility of the individual with support provided within the resources being used.

Effective self-help resources are designed to help users understand when and how the resource should be used. Well designed self-help resources also help individuals identify when problems are occurring in the use of the resource and understand the further resource use or additional assistance that maybe need to resolve the problem. Text and multimedia support materials and signage can be used to guide individuals in appropriately sequencing various resources among the specific options available to meet their needs.

Brief staff-assisted services

Brief staff-assisted services are more likely to be cost-effective for individuals with moderate readiness for occupational and employment decision making. This level of service typically places less emphasis on the maintenance of individual counseling records and regular systematic monitoring of individual progress. Successful use of career service interventions in a brief staff-assisted mode depends on:

— Accurately assessing user needs during comprehensive screening to ensure that there is a reasonable likelihood that the use of career service interventions will meet the individual's needs;

— The availability of an effective "safety net" that provides reasonable opportunities for identifying individuals who are not making successful use of a career service intervention, e.g., brief periodic checking with users; and

— The availability of staff to respond to basic questions about career resource use, e.g., clarifying interpretation of self-assessment instruments and solving problems related to the use of a specific resource.

— The four options for brief staff-assisted services include self-directed career decision making, career course (with large group interaction), group counseling (short term), and workshops.

Self-directed career decision making involves practitioner-guided use of self-assessment, information, and instructional resources in a library-like setting by individuals with a moderate readiness for occupational and employment decision making who need minimal assistance to effectively use career resources.

Self-directed career decision making can be used to cost-effectively deliver career service interventions. The availability of practitioners in a library-like setting allows modeling of information seeking behavior and the provision of timely encouragement and reinforcement of client exploratory behavior. Practitioner availability also provides users with opportunities for relatively immediate follow-up of resource use while the experience is still recent. Experience has also shown that career service interventions in the self-directed career decision-making mode tend to be more successful when practitioners make specific recommendations about resource use that relate to identified user needs.

Career course (with large group interaction) involves instructor-guided use of assessment, information, and instructional resources in a classroom setting with minimal opportunity for interpersonal interaction among individuals with a moderate readiness for occupational and employment decision making who need minimal assistance to effectively use career resources.

The use of specific career resources can become student assignments in a career course. Screening is accomplished by students self-selecting to register for the course or by having an advisor or instructor recommend the course. Faculty grading of student assignments (e.g., use of career resources) provides the "safety net" to identify students who may have low readiness for occupational and employment decision making and who therefore may need more individual assistance. Orientation to resource use can be provided in class or by assigned orientation videos. Follow-up of career resource use can be provided via class discussion. The use of career resources can be individualized through student learning contracts or the same career resources can be assigned for all students in a predetermined order.

Group counseling (short term) involves practitioner-guided use of assessment, information, and instructional resources in a group setting with minimal opportunity for sharing information or for developing group cohesion among individuals with a moderate readiness for occupational and employment decision making who need minimal assistance to effectively use career resources.

Screening for career service intervention use can occur at the same time screening for group membership occurs. The use of video resources for career resource orientation (such as a computer-assisted career guidance system) minimizes using valuable group processing time for didactic presentations of orientation information. Group sessions can be used as a follow-up activity to process the insights and barriers group members experience in the use of career resources. It is important that group leaders be competent to respond to member questions from the use of various career resources. The use of career resources can be linked to specific needs via an individual learning plan (ILP) for each group member. Or, if a more structured group approach is followed where all members use a common set of career resources, group sessions can be used for follow-up by processing members' experience in using specific resources.

Individual case-managed services

Individual case-managed services are more likely to be cost-effective for individuals with low readiness for occupational and employment decision making. This level of service typically places more emphasis on the maintenance of individual counseling records and regular systematic monitoring of individual progress. Successful use of career service interventions in an individual case-managed mode depends on:

— Accurately assessing user needs during comprehensive screening to ensure that there is a reasonable likelihood that the use of career service interventions will meet the individual's needs;

— The availability of staff to respond to basic questions about career resource use, e.g., clarifying interpretation of self-assessment instruments and solving problems related to the use of a specific resource; and

— The availability of practitioners who are competent to integrate career and mental health counseling in dealing with individual's low readiness for occupational and employment decision making.

The three options for individual case-managed services include individual counseling, career course with small group interaction, and group counseling (long term).

Individual counseling

Individual counseling involves practitioner-guided use of assessment, information, and instructional resources in an individual office setting with individuals who have a low readiness for occupational and employment decision making who need substantial assistance to effectively use career resources. Individual counseling offers maximum flexibility in relating counseling interventions to the needs of the individual. The timing and content of orientations and follow-up to resource use can vary considerably among clients. The nature of individuals' use of career resources provides practitioners with information about factors that may be contributing to low readiness for occupational and employment decision making. For example, individuals' comments about potential occupations resulting from the completion of an interest inventory may indicate specific negative self-talk that can be identified, challenged, and altered. The nature of the supportive relationship established between the practitioner and the client over time may be a key element in client willingness to risk the inevitable change associated with decision making.

Career course

Career course (with small group interaction) involves instructor-guided use of assessment, information, and instructional resources in a classroom setting with considerable opportunity for interpersonal interaction among individuals with a low readiness for occupational and employment decision making who need substantial assistance to effectively use career resources. The previously described counseling interventions for a career course (with large group interaction) apply here as well. The difference is that by meeting with small groups of students, instructors have the opportunity to gain more information about the nature of student decision-making difficulties and can provide more assistance to students in improving their readiness for occupational and employment choice. Dividing the class into small groups of students can improve the capability of students to learn from each other via modeling and encouragement.

Group counseling

Group counseling (long term) involves practitioner-guided use of assessment, information, and instructional resources in a group setting with considerable opportunity for sharing information and the development of group cohesion among individuals with a low readiness for occupational and employment decision making who need substantial assistance to effectively use career resources.

The previously described counseling interventions for group counseling (short term) apply here as well. The difference is that the longer duration of the group allows the development of group cohesion necessary to confront and change typically long established problematic patterns of thinking, feeling, and behaving. The longer duration of the group also provides potential support over a larger proportion of the decision-making process, e.g., supporting members in following through on an action plan to implement their goals.

Career decision-making status

The career decision-making status of individuals can be conceptualized as decided, undecided, or indecisive:

Decided Individuals

1) *Decided-Confirmation*: Individuals who are able to specify a choice, but wish to confirm or clarify the appropriateness of their choice by contrasting it with other possible choices. For example, some individuals have a tendency to be careful and systematic in their approach to making any important decision. These individuals wish to ensure that the valuing phase of the CASVE cycle has been completed to the best of their ability.
2) *Decided-Implementation*: Individuals who are able to specify a choice but who need help in implementing their choice. For example, individuals may need assistance in getting a job or selecting training options related to an occupation chosen in the valuing phase of the CASVE cycle. These individuals

either realize they need assistance before they begin the execution phase of the CASVE cycle or they have attempted execution previously and experienced difficulty.

3) *Decided-Conflict Avoidance*: Individuals who present themselves as decided as a strategy for reducing conflict and stress, when in fact they have the characteristics of the undecided or indecisive individuals described below.

Undecided Individuals

1) *Undecided-Deferred Choice*: Individuals who are unable to specify a choice, but have no need to make a choice at the present time. For example, a college freshman taking general education courses and participating in various campus activities to obtain knowledge and life experience prior to committing to a college major, can appropriately defer a choice until a later date.

2) *Undecided-Developmental*: Individuals who need to choose, are unable to commit to a choice, and who lack self, occupational, and/or decision-making knowledge. These individuals should not be considered dysfunctional, rather they have not gained the knowledge or experience necessary to make a choice. In terms of the pyramid, these individuals need clarification or addition of self, occupational, and/or decision-making knowledge. Their self-talk about career choice is less negative in comparison with indecisive individuals.

3) *Undecided-Multipotential*: Individuals who have the characteristics of someone who is undecided, with

the addition of having an overabundance of talents, interests, and opportunities. These individuals are often overwhelmed with the diversity of available options and may experience pressure from significant others, including family members, for high levels of achievement.

Indecisive Individuals

Individuals who have not made a commitment to a specific occupational choice due to gaps in the knowledge necessary for choosing, while having a maladaptive approach to problem solving in general that is accompanied by a dysfunctional level of anxiety. Indecisive individuals are similar to undecided individuals in terms of knowledge gaps, but differ in terms of executive processing. Executive processing deficiencies present in indecisive individuals may include excessive negative self-talk, attentional deficits, or confused thought processes. These executive processing deficiencies limit the acquisition of decision-making skills and occupational knowledge, as well as limit the clarity and consistency of self-knowledge. Subsequent awareness of these limitations only serves to reinforce perceived inadequacy in decision making.

Decided and undecided individuals are often best served by self-help and brief staff-assisted interventions. In general, practitioners would rarely sit with a decided or undecided individual while he or she uses career resources. Indecisive individuals are often best served by individual case-managed interventions. Practitioners may occasionally sit with an indecisive client to help him or her to monitor negative self-talk that may be limiting the individual's ability to effectively use a career resource.

Career Problem Solving and Decision Making

Screening instruments can be used, along with a brief interview, to determine client readiness for career problem solving and decision making. A low identity score and high information need and barriers scores, plus concurring interview data, would indicate more need for staff support.

Assumptions Related to Selecting Career Service Interventions

The criteria for selecting career service interventions in the Cognitive Information Processing (CIP) approach are based on the following assumptions.

1. The type and frequency of career assistance should vary to take into account the readiness of the individual for career decision making and individual differences in information-processing capabilities.
2. The choice of career service interventions should take into account their costs so as to maximize the number of individuals who may receive appropriate assistance.
3. Group-based interventions, such as group counseling, courses, and workshops, offer reasonable effectiveness at the lowest cost to clients who
    (a) possess adequate readiness to benefit from the interventions that are offered;
    (b) are not under short-term time pressures or in a state of crisis that would make it inappropriate to wait for the next scheduled group, course, or workshop; and

(c) are willing to spend the time necessary to complete the intervention.

4. Individual counseling offers the greatest effectiveness at an acceptable cost for clients who

   (a) have low readiness for career decision making, short-term time pressure, or a crisis, that cannot be effectively addressed in a group; and

   (b) have access to counselors with the training and experience necessary to deal with the career, personal, and family dynamics associated with the indecisive client.

In some cases, legislation requires that individuals meeting specific eligibility requirements receive individual case-managed services.

Career Thoughts Inventory

The Career Thoughts Inventory is a theory-based assessment and intervention resource intended to improve the quality of career decisions made by adults, college students, and high school students and the quality of career services delivered to these individuals. The CTI is a self-administered, objectively scored measure of dysfunctional thinking in career problem solving and decision making.

The CTI was developed to integrate the functions of assessment and intervention within a career service delivery context. The goal was to link the measure and the accompanying workbook in such a way that clients might make more efficient use of their time and their human service practitioner's time, while more effectively incorporating the assessment concepts into intervention strategies for change. As a result, the CTI is comprised of traditional assessment components plus a learning resource.

Cognitive Information Processing theory postulates that effective career problem solving and decision making requires the effective processing of information in the following four domains:

1) *Self-Knowledge* includes individuals' perceptions of their values, interests, skills, etc.

2) *Occupational Knowledge* includes knowledge of individual occupations and having a schema for how the world of work is organized.

3) *Decision Making Skills* are the generic information processing skills that individuals use to solve problems and make decisions, including the subcomponents of communication, analysis, synthesis, valuing, and execution.

   — *Communication*: Individuals become aware that a gap exists between an existing and a desired state of affairs as a result of one or more external cues (positive or negative events or input from one or more significant others) or internal cues (client perceptions of negative emotions, avoidance behavior, or physiological changes).

   — *Analysis*: Individuals form a mental model of the problem and perceive relationships among the components, e.g., relating self-knowledge with occupational knowledge to better understand the necessary characteristics of the occupation or other option they seek.

- *Synthesis*: Individuals expand (elaborate) and then narrow (crystallize) the alternatives that they are considering.
- *Valuing*: Individuals evaluate the costs and benefits of each of the remaining alternatives to themselves, significant others, their cultural group, and their community or society in general, ultimately leading to a first choice.
- *Execution*: Individuals formulate and commit to a plan for implementing their tentative choice, including a preparation program, reality testing, and employment seeking.

4) *Executive Processing* includes metacognitions which control the selection and sequencing of cognitive strategies used to solve a career problem through self-talk, self-awareness, and control and monitoring.

In order to simplify the process of instrument development, the above domains and subcomponents were organized into eight cognitive information processing (CIP) content dimensions that include:

1) Self-Knowledge
2) Occupational Knowledge
3) Communication
4) Analysis
5) Synthesis
6) Valuing
7) Execution
8) Executive Processing

Dysfunctional thinking in any of the above CIP eight content dimensions could impair an individual's ability to solve career problems and to make career decisions. For the purposes of this instrument, the terms thinking and information processing are used synonymously.

Cognitive therapy theoretical concepts specify that dysfunctional cognitions have a detrimental impact on behavior and emotions. Through cognitive restructuring, collaborative empiricism, attention to emotions, and the development of an effective helping relationship, clients learn to replace dysfunctional cognitions with functional cognitions, resulting in positive changes in behavior and emotions.

In developing the CTI, the following assumption was made:

— While dysfunctional thinking in career problem solving and decision making cannot be measured directly, it can be inferred from an individual's endorsement of statements (test items) reflecting a variety of dysfunctional career thoughts.

— For the purposes of this instrument, career thoughts are defined as outcomes of one's thinking about assumptions, attitudes, behaviors, beliefs, feelings, plans, and/or strategies related to career problem solving and decision making.

— Regardless of whether CTI items refer to assumptions, attitudes, behaviors, beliefs, feelings, plans, and/or strategies, all items reflect dysfunctional thinking that inhibits effective career problem solving and decision making.

The CTI is designed for the following individuals:

(a) eleventh- and twelfth grade high school students who may be choosing a postsecondary field of study, choosing an occupation, or seeking employment;

(b) college students who may be choosing a major field of study, choosing an occupation, or seeking employment; and

(c) adults who are considering an occupational or employment change, seeking employment due to unemployment or underemployment, or reentering the labor market after a substantial period of nonpaid work.

In order to facilitate quick completion, scoring, and profiling of the instrument and avoid unnecessary delays or disruptions in the service delivery process, the CTI combines the inventory, answer sheet, and profile form into one booklet. The Test Booklet can be quickly scored by clients, human service practitioners, or clerical support staff. The CTI Profile is printed on the back page of the booklet.

In service delivery, the CTI can be used by practitioners to help adults, college students, and high school students identify, challenge, and subsequently alter dysfunctional thinking that impairs their ability to effectively solve career problems and make career decisions. Specifically, the CTI can be used as an instrument for screening and needs assessment, as well as a learning resource in delivering career services. The CTI Professional Manual provides additional details on the use of the CTI and CTI Workbook, including specific strategies for individual counseling, group counseling, self-directed career decision making, workshops and curricular interventions.

The CTI can be used to identify individuals who are likely to experience problems in making career choices as a result of their dysfunctional thinking. Individuals identified as having more dysfunctional thoughts will likely require more assistance in making effective use of career services, whereas individuals identified with fewer dysfunctional thoughts will require less assistance. The CTI Workbook can be used to facilitate an individual's understanding of how much help he or she will likely need to make effective use of career services. The CTI Total score is a single global indicator of dysfunctional thinking in career problem solving and decision making.

The CTI can be used to identify the specific nature of dysfunctional thinking noted in the screening process. In problem-solving terms, the CTI is used to help define the problem space. Career interventions to reduce career choice problems can then be recommended. The CTI Workbook can be used to facilitate an individual's understanding of the nature of his or her dysfunctional thoughts. Construct scores include: Decision-Making Confusion, Commitment Anxiety, and External Conflict.

— *Decision-Making Confusion (DMC)* refers to the inability to initiate or sustain the decision making process as a result of disabling emotions and/or a lack of understanding about the decision making process itself.

— *The Commitment Anxiety (CA)* scale reflects the inability to make a commitment to a specific career choice, accompanied by generalized anxiety about the outcome of the decision making process. This anxiety perpetuates indecision.

— *The External Conflict (EC)* scale reflects the inability to balance the importance of one's own self-perceptions with the importance of input from significant others, resulting in a reluctance to assume responsibility for decision making.

As a learning resource, the CTI and the CTI Workbook can be used with various counseling interventions in assisting individuals to challenge and alter the specific dysfunctional thoughts identified as problematic in the prior needs assessment process. The primary cognitive restructuring schema used throughout the workbook encourages individuals to identify, challenge, and alter any negative career thoughts and then follow up with action. This schema is repeated at several key points in the workbook to reinforce client understanding of the cognitive restructuring process.

By reducing dysfunctional career thinking, clients are more likely to effectively process information needed for exploration, problem solving, and decision making. By becoming more aware of the negative impact of dysfunctional thinking and by learning the process of cognitive restructuring, clients can become "freed up" to think in more creative, reality-based ways about their career choices. A theory-based decision-making checklist, included in the CTI Workbook, can indicate potentially useful areas for specific instruction in career decision making. The CTI and the CTI Workbook are designed to help clients make current career decisions as well as learn how to be better problem solvers in the future. The Workbook includes the following five sections:

— *Section 1.* Identifying Your Total Amount of Negative Career Thoughts: The CTI Total Score. The first section is designed to help clients understand that as dysfunctional career thinking increases, the level of practitioner assistance likely needed to benefit from career services increases as well. The intended outcome of using this section is that clients will be more motivated to seek a level of service appropriate for their needs.

— *Section* 2. Identifying the Nature of Your Negative Career Thoughts. The second section is designed to help clients gain insight into the development and maintenance of their dysfunctional thinking. The intended outcome of using this section is that clients will be more self-aware, more capable of monitoring and controlling cognitions, and more motivated to cognitively restructure negative career thoughts and take action to make career decisions.

— *Section* 3. Challenging and Altering Your Negative Career Thoughts and Taking Action. The third section is designed to improve self-awareness of the detrimental impact of dysfunctional thinking on career problem solving and decision making, to improve client capacity to monitor and control negative self-talk, to facilitate the cognitive restructuring of negative career thoughts through completion of an exercise, and to facilitate the development of an Individual Action Plan (IAP) for using career resources and services. The intended outcome of using this section is that clients will reduce their dysfunctional career thinking and more effectively use career resources and services, ultimately leading to a more consisfent reduction of dysfunctional thoughts and more appropriate career decisions.

— *Section* 4. Improving Your Ability to Make Good Decisions. The fourth section is designed to enhance the present and future decision-making skills of clients through decision-making instruction. The intended outcome of using this section is that clients will be better able to assess and apply their skills in career problem solving and decision making.

— *Section 5.* Making Good Use of Support from Other People. The fifth section is designed to help clients better understand how support resources can be used to their benefit in cognitive restructuring, career exploration, and decision making. The intended outcome of using this section is that clients will be more proactive, knowledgeable consumers in making effective use of available practitioners and significant others.

Diversity Issues

The influence of group membership relating to age, disability, ethnicity, gender, race, sexual orientation, and socio-economic status on career thoughts can be an important environmental factor in career choice. Group membership may enhance career choice via networking and mentoring or it may constrain career choice via stereotyping and prejudice. The specific nature and consequences of these environmental factors on career choice will likely vary with group membership. As a result, the specific career thoughts of an individual are a product of individual experience, mediated by personal characteristics and by group membership in a cultural context.

It is difficult to develop an instrument that reflects differences in life experience between group cultures, and within subcultures of specific groups, that is brief enough to be hand scored for use as a screening tool in service delivery. The CTI was designed to measure career thoughts that tend to be common across groups. In developing the CTI, potential items that were significantly associated with gender or ethnicity were eliminated from the item pool. It is possible, however, to collaboratively use the CTI with the client to identify, challenge, and alter career thoughts of an individual from a specific group. The Professional Manual includes specific suggestions for dealing with diversity issues in interpreting the CTI and using the CTI Workbook.

A variety of practitioners may make effective use of the CTI. In addition to general training in human behavior, helping skills, and assessment, practitioners need training in career development, career service delivery, and cognitive-behavior therapy. In addition to general experience in the delivery of human services, practitioners need experience in the delivery of career services with appropriate supervision. In particular, practitioners using the CTI with clients should be familiar with the professional manual, personally complete all components of the CTI, and make use of appropriate supervision.

A rational-empirical approach was used in developing the CTI. After reviewing the theoretical foundations of the CTI and the literature on dysfunctional thinking in career choice, criteria were developed for each of the eight CIP content dimensions. An initial pool of 248 items was then created based on actual client statements from the career counseling experience of the authors. After review by experienced career counselors for item clarity and realism, the pool was revised to 195 items and then reviewed by a six-member bias panel to identify and correct any bias related to ethnicity, gender, disability, and age. The 195 item pool plus 13 randomly inserted items from the short form of the Marlowe-Crowne Social Desirability Scale was administered to 320 volunteer undergraduate students. Eighty items were retained on the basis of their general psychometric quality, freedom from gender, ethnic, or social desirability bias, item-scale reliability, and content domain coverage.

A principal components analysis with Varimax rotation from an administration of these 80 items with a new sample of 196 volunteer undergraduate students revealed three interpretable constructs that were associated with dysfunctional career thinking: decision-making confusion, commitment anxiety, and external conflict. Items could then be identified as relating to one of these three constructs as well as contributing to one of the eight CIP content dimensions. The 80 items were also administered to clients seeking services, allowing an analysis of the capacity of individual items to distinguish clients (n=68) from non-clients (n=196).

A shortened 48-item version of the CTI was then derived on the basis of factor loadings, contribution to scale separation, capacity to discriminate clients from non-clients, and content domain coverage. The 48 items were then administered to a new sample of 145 volunteer undergraduate students. A second principal components analysis with Varimax rotation revealed the same three interpretable constructs as above.

In order to assist clients in challenging and altering their thoughts, reframing stimulus statements were written for each CTI item to show clients how negative thoughts interfere with their ability to make career decisions, and to provide information on making the best use of time spent on career decision making. Reframing stimulus statements include varying combinations of the following themes:

(a) the difficulty often encountered by individuals making career choices;

(b) the often inherent ambiguities in making career choices;

(c) the importance of assuming personal responsibility for decision making while also considering input from significant others;

(d) the importance of linking career choices with other life choices;

(e) the identification of factors that make it more difficult to think clearly about career options;

(f) the identification of absolute dichotomous thinking that interferes with career choice;

(g) the assumption that improved decision-making and information-seeking skills can be learned;

(h) the value of broad career exploration prior to final choice;

(i) the value of using a variety of sources of information in career exploration; and

(j) the value of obtaining assistance from a helping professional when individuals experience difficulty in career choice.

The reframing stimulus statements were then examined for potential bias regarding ethnicity, gender, disability, and age. The exercise was pilot tested and subsequently revised for clarity. Interpretive and decision-making instruction sections were then added to the workbook.

Standardisation

CTI normative data were collected for adults (n=571), college students (n=595), and eleventh- and twelfth grade high school students (n=396). Combined data on college student and adult clients (n=376) were also collected. In general, all groups were representative in terms of geographic distribution, gender, and ethnicity, with the exception that female adults were overrepresented, Hispanic American adults were underrepresented, and female clients were overrepresented.

Organizations and individuals are strongly encouraged to develop local CTI norms to allow more specific population comparisons. Analysis of normative data revealed that gender and ethnicity accounted for.2% and.1% of the variance, respectively, in CTI Total scores for all groups combined. Therefore, it was concluded that there is little relationship between gender or ethnicity with respect to CTI Total scores, and that there was no need to provide separate norms for either of these factors.

Reliability

Internal consistency. The internal consistency of the CTI Total score and construct scales was determined by calculating coefficient alphas for each of the respective norm groups. The internal consistency (alpha) coefficients for the CTI Total score ranged from.97 to.93. Alpha coefficients for the construct scales ranged from.94 to.74.

Stability. Stability concerns the extent to which individuals achieve the same CTI scores on two different occasions. The stability of the CTI Total score and construct scales was determined by having 73 volunteer college students and 48 volunteer eleventh- and twelfth grade high school students complete the CTI twice over a four week interval. Four-week test-retest stability coefficients for the CTI Total score was high (r =.86) for the college student sample, indicating little change in responses to the entire 48 items over the 4-week period. The stability coefficients for the construct scales ranged from.82 to.74, following a similar pattern as the data for internal consistency, with lower correlations for scales with fewer items. This pattern was also observed for the high school student sample, with the CTI Total at r =.69 and the construct scales ranging from.72 to.52, showing that adequate stability exists for the use of the instrument.

Validity

Content validity. Content validity concerns the congruence of CTI items, CIP content dimensions, and construct scales with the theoretical basis of the instrument. This congruence was built into the development strategy for the CTI items and scales. Individual items and construct scales are directly linked to CIP theory through content dimensions. CIP content dimensions (self-knowledge, occupational knowledge, communication, analysis, synthesis, valuing, execution, and executive processing) provided specific criteria for developing items. The CTI Professional Manual groups all 48 CTI items by content dimension and includes the corresponding criterion number or numbers for each.

Construct validity. Construct validity is concerned with the extent to which clusters of empirically associated items that are conceptually consistent with the theory can be identified and reproduced across populations. Evidence of construct validity was established through a series of factor analyses. The constructs of decision-making confusion, commitment anxiety, and external conflict, that were identified in two different samples during CTI development, were replicated for adults, college students, and eleventh- and twelfth-grade high school students based on normative data. The CTI Total score is highly correlated (r =.89 to.94) with DMC for all groups. These correlations, along with the large percentage of the variance accounted for by DMC (factor 1), suggests that a general predisposition toward dysfunctional thinking strongly influences subsequent specific aspects of dysfunctional career thinking, such as commitment anxiety. External conflict (EC) appears somewhat less related to general dysfunctional thinking, as represented by the lower correlation of EC with the CTI Total score and DMC. Correlations among construct scales, especially CA and EC, are distinctly lower for the client population than for non-client adults, college students, and high school students. CA and EC appear to be more distinct from DMC for clients than nonclients.

Given the magnitude of correlations among CTI factors observed above for adults, college students, and high school students, a Principal Components Analysis with oblique rotation was used to extract the factor structure of the instrument. A three-factor model was confirmed for the college population, the combined normative sample, and the client comparison group. A two-factor solution (decision-making confusion and external conflict) was the most interpretable solution for the adult sample, whereas a different two-factor solution (decision-making confusion and commitment anxiety) was most interpretable for high school students. The interpretation of these findings is that for adult non-client populations who are almost all employed or not seeking employment, commitment anxiety is not an operative construct when a career problem does not exist, whereas confusion about decision making and external conflict with significant others (such as spouses) are operative. For high school non-client populations, external conflict with significant others (such as parents and caretakers) concerning career problems is not yet an issue, whereas confusion about decision making and anxiety about post-high school commitments yet to be made are operative. The three-factor solution, including decision-making confusion, commitment anxiety, and external conflict, was again reproduced for the client population, for which the CTI was designed.

What these analyses reveal about the construct validity of the CTI is that there is a single powerful confusion entity that is pervasive in career problem solving and decision making. Beyond this, there are more specific issues related to one's anxiety about committing to a career choice and to potential conflict with significant others. Therefore, all three constructs may be viewed as indicators of the presence of dysfunctional thinking that constrains the cognitive system that undergirds career problem solving and decision making.

Convergent validity. Convergent validity is concerned with the extent to which the CTI Total score and construct scale scores correlate with other measures of similar constructs in a theoretically consistent direction.

Evidence of convergent validity was established by administering the above measures to 50 adults, 152 college students, and 151 eleventh- and twelfth-grade high school students. All samples were representative in terms of geographic distribution, gender, and ethnicity, with the exception that females slightly outnumbered males (56% to 44%) across all three groups and Hispanic American adults were underrepresented.

Across all three groups (adults, college students, and high school students), CTI scales were consistently inversely correlated with positive constructs such as vocational identity, certainty, and knowledge about occupations and training, and directly correlated with indecision. The CTI Total score was consistently directly correlated with neuroticism and vulnerability. Only career choice importance exhibited inconsistency in relationships across groups as was expected. Although CTI construct scales covaried directly with angry hostility, self-consciousness, and impulsiveness, the relatively low magnitude of the correlations have limited practical importance.

CTI scales for adults were consistently inversely correlated with comfort with choice, decidedness, and lack of information needs and positively correlated with anxiety. CTI scales for college students were consistently inversely correlated with comfort with choice and decisiveness, and correlated positively with depression for the CTI Total score. CTI scales for high school students were consistently inversely correlated with self-clarity.

Relationships between the CTI Total score and convergent variables were very similar to the relationships observed between DMC and the convergent variables. This is to be expected given the high correlation between the CTI Total score and the DMC scale. The number of correlations having practical significance (.50 to.75) were 32 for adults, 21 for college students, and 17 for high school students. This is also to be expected given the slightly lower alpha reliabilities for high school students and college students in comparison with adults. These lower reliability coefficients, combined with the lower alpha reliabilities from some CDP scales and small numbers of items in NEO facet scales, could explain the lower number of correlations between convergent variables and either CA or EC.

Criterion validity. Criterion validity is concerned with the extent to which the CTI accurately discriminates between persons seeking career services (clients) and persons not seeking career services (nonclients). Evidence of predictive validity was established by administering the CTI to 199 clients and 149 nonclients at two different universities. Both samples were representative in terms of geographic distribution and ethnicity, with the exception that females slightly outnumbered males and a greater proportion of clients were sophomores while a greater proportion of nonclients were seniors. Analysis of the data revealed significant differences in CTI Total and construct scales for each group, with clients having higher scores as predicted. Post-hoc CTI item-level comparisons revealed significant differences between clients and nonclients on 26 items, with clients scoring higher than nonclients on all 48 items.

Utility

The utility of a test concerns how well the test achieves its intended purpose within the constraints of "typical" practice. Many career service delivery organizations serve numerous clients. In this type of environment, an instrument used for screening, needs assessment, and learning is most cost-effective when it can be:

1) quickly administered,
2) rapidly scored,
3) easily interpreted,
4) easily integrated into counseling homework, and
5) inexpensively used.

The CTI was designed to meet the above criteria. Quick administration - most clients complete the 48 CTI items in 7 to 15 minutes. Rapid scoring - the CTI can be hand scored in 5 to 8 minutes. As a result, the CTI can be used as part of a brief intake procedure or during an initial session. Easy interpretation - the CTI includes a limited number of scales (the CTI Total score and three construct scales), which simplifies interpretation. The CTI Workbook presents interpretive information for all four scales with text, metaphors, and illustrations that practitioners can use to facilitate interpretation of CTI results. Easy integration - the CTI workbook has several components that can be assigned as homework, such as cognitive restructuring of negative thoughts, developing an individual action plan for using career resources and services, and learning about the decision-making process.

Career Guidance: Chaning Needs

The economic as well as technological revolutions has transfomrd the traditionsal needs of the labour markets. The initial effect of the reforms was largely to destroy economically inefficient jobs, without generating the means to replace them. It has now become evident that in many places there is a need for active labour-market policies, linked to economic development. Governments have to intervene in order to make the markets work. But this requires different kinds of intervention than those of the old command-economy model: interventions designed to support markets rather than replace them. In particular, it requires measures to be taken to build new markets, to regulate existing markets, and—where necessary—to compensate for market failure. Career guidance is a classic intervention of this kind. It is a means of helping individuals to maximise their choices within their environment. It cannot of itself act as a significant instrument of economic regeneration but, linked to a range of structural measures, it can provide a means of lubricating these measures and reconciling them with the individual empowerment which ultimately is the engine that will determine their effectiveness.

The subtlety of its modus operandi means that its importance can easily be overlooked by impatient policy-makers and belies its potential significance. Until fairly recently most political leaders saw school guidance and vocational guidance as a way of improving the match-up between the aspirations of the young people and adults and the jobs offered by the market. However, many people are now fully aware that what lies ahead of them is not a once-and-for-all transition from training to working life. People cannot hope to go through the whole of their working lives on the basis of what they learned during initial training.

Alongside the massive transformations in the countries of central and eastern Europe, all advanced industrial societies are currently experiencing the transition to a post-industrial era, in which the structures of work and of careers are being reshaped thoroughly. The pace of change stems from two linked forces: the impact of new technology and the globalisation of the economy. Today, all work organisations have to be prepared to change much more regularly and rapidly than ever before. As a result, they are less prepared to make long-term commitments to individuals. The psychological contract between the individual and the employer is being restructured: the old long-term relational contract, based on security and reciprocal loyalty, is in many cases being replaced by a short-term 27 transactional contract based on a narrower and more purely economic exchange; where the relational contract survives, it commonly involves exchanging job security for task flexibility. Individuals now have to take more responsibility for their own career development, including learning new skills and knowledge. Increasingly, security lies not in employment, but in employability, accumulating skills and reputation that can be invested in new opportunities as they arise.

The idea of life-long learning, which has come to the fore, has deep-seated implications for guidance. It implies a series of phases during which people seek to update their knowledge and skills—an almost permanent interchange between training and employment. These changes represent what has been called a 'careerquake'. The old concept of career was based on orderly progression up a hierarchy within an organisation or profession.

The foundations of this concept are being shaken and in many cases destroyed. In its place, a new concept of career is being built, redefined as the individual's lifelong progression in learning and in work. This new concept is in principle accessible to all, not just to the few. But it requires policy supports. One of these supports is life-long access to career guidance. This reframes our approach to career guidance. Instead of thinking of how to help individuals choose traditional careers, it focuses attention on how to help them construct their own careers through a series of decisions made throughout their lives. It shifts the focus of career counsellors to helping people to be authors of their career narratives: to tell the story so far; to shape the themes and the story-line; and to start drafting the next chapter. This implies helping individuals to develop the skills and attitudes which will enable them to construct their careers. Such learning needs to be adapted to the new concept of career.

Perhaps, instead of emphasising decision-making, emphasise the wisdom of open-mindedness. Perhaps unplanned events should be seen not just as an inevitable but also as a desirable aspect of everyone's career. Arguably, guidance services now need to encourage a clear but flexible sense of direction, which people are ready to adapt when unexpected events occur, but which will help them to spot these events and take advantage of them.

The relevance of all this to the countries of central and eastern Europe is evident. There are signs of regeneration of career guidance services in central and eastern Europe. The aid programmes provided by the World Bank and other international organisations have played an important role in supporting these developments. Underlying them has been a major shift in the philosophy of career guidance. In line with developments in Western Europe and North America, the paternalistic care-taking that once prevailed is being replaced by a form of counselling that offers help so that people will be able to plan and guide their own lives more independently and with more competence. But the harshness of the socio-economic reality have hampered the move towards modern counselling.

Many of the initiatives to date have, understandably, been linked to the need to respond to high unemployment levels. This has dangers attached to it, particularly if the guidance is largely placement-oriented and based on a narrow matching model. In this situation, the scarcity of vacancies can easily cast guidance into disrepute. While, also in central and eastern Europe, the theory may have penetrated into the core of the profession, its translation into practice has only just begun.

The deepest roots of career guidance and counselling in central Europe are closely entwined with those of western Europe. In Hungary, for example, the first professional publications on the subject appeared towards the end of the 19th century. A government initiative launched in the early 1920s resulted in the establishment of the first Careers Guidance and Counselling Institute in Budapest in 1927. Contemporary initiatives in north-eastern and south-eastern Europe were less advanced.

In central and eastern Europe further development of career guidance and counselling services came to a grinding halt and remained in hibernation for almost half a century. Full employment under the command economy invalidated the need for guidance to be more than a referral service. In Hungary though, the development of guidance and counselling institutions was already started again in the early seventies and flourished during the eighties. Other countries had to wait until the early nineties for this to happen. In Romania for instance, a nation-wide initiative to revive counselling services was not started until 1995. In general, the period of transition to a market economy, and the resulting turmoil in the labour market pushed the issue of career guidance into focus again. In Hungary, since 1991 career guidance and counselling services are gradually being moved to the labour centres, the new basic institutions of the organisation of the labour market. Other countries chose other institutions. During the 1990s, the institutions of vocational training and of the labour markets throughout the region underwent fundamental changes but, despite extensive legal regulation being applied everywhere, the development of institutionalised career guidance services in this area remained a weak element in most countries.

Putting Policy into Practice in the United States In the US, different federal and state agencies—like the US Bureau of Labour Statistics, the Census Bureau, and the National Center for Education Statistics—have long been collecting large amounts of relevant data but they did this for different purposes, over different time periods, using different classifications. This made them hard to locate, to understand, and to use in relation to each other. The challenge was to integrate data from already existing sources into comprehensive and coherent occupational and career information systems for educators, counsellors, employment personnel, and vocational rehabilitation staff. To this end, in 1976 the US Congress created the National Occupational Information Coordinating Committee (called NOICC). To guarantee extension of the problem beyond the boundaries of politics, it created counterpart State Occupational Information Coordinating Committees (called SOICCs) in all the states and territories. Members of the National Committee represented no less than 10 different agencies in 5 federal departments. It signalled the start of an exemplary inter-agency, inter-state, and inter-departmental collaboration programme.

Public agencies, professional associations, and private vendors collaborated in developing systems and products. Federal seed money was matched by state and local funds to support and sustain information resources, delivery systems, and training. Information systems and products were tailored to the needs of a wide array of user groups. As a result of the collaboration and teamwork, most States are now delivering useful occupational and career information to their constituents.

More than 40 states offer access to computer-based career information delivery systems (CIDS) to millions of users annually. CIDS have become a major tool for career counsellors in many different settings across the United States and Canada. Training for information users. Occupational and career information may be essential but the NOICC/SOICC Network quickly learned that counsellors needed training if they were to use it effectively in their work. Therefore, as new information systems and products were introduced, their sponsors developed training programs in their use. SOICCs prepared guides to help teachers use career information newspapers in their classrooms. CIDS operators offered special training for counsellors using their systems.

Policies, partnerships, and strategies are needed to support career development. In the United States, the delivery of career information and counselling varies widely from state to state. Much depends on a particular state's policy, priorities and needs. On the whole, however, the public has greater access to career information and assistance because of the efforts of NOICC. The impetus for these improvements came from federal and state policies, expressed in legislation or funding. To implement these policies, the NOICC/SOICC Network employed six basic strategies:

— it focused on identifying and addressing its user needs;

— it used federal funds as seed money to leverage state and private funds. This supported the development of information systems, products, and training programs;

— It encouraged states to share innovative models and best practices—at national and regional conferences, in newsletters, and, more recently, via the Internet. Its online Library now offers a global repository for best practices in career development;

— It provided technical assistance and training. This enabled states to adapt and enhance successful models from other states;

— It built partnerships—first among federal and state agencies and later among public and private organisations. It tried to engage all stakeholders in its initiatives. This allowed it to draw on the expertise of professional leaders in designing and disseminating materials and training in their use;

— It emphasised training. Its strategy of training trainers gave its small network a much larger outreach to state and local constituents.

The way in which the EU is adapting information provision and training to the changed needs of the providers and users of career guidance and counselling is not unlike that of the US. However, the time-path is inevitably different, given the fact that close international collaboration in Europe is a more recent phenomenon than inter-state co-operation in the US. In fact, many of the integrating and facilitating processes described above are taking place at this very moment in time in the EU or are planned for the very near future. EU action in the area of guidance dates back to April 1963, when a Council Decision laid down the general principles for the implementation of a common vocational training policy. In it, career guidance was recognised as an important part of the learning process.

The Council recommended, among other things, the implementation of ongoing arrangements for vocational information, guidance and counselling for young people and adults, and ensuring that people would be able to use this system in good time before selecting a profession, whether during vocational training or at any other time in their lives. From there, a leap in time moves us on to 1990, when a Joint Opinion by the European Social Partners on the transition from school to adult and working life pulled guidance into the spotlights again by stressing its preventive role in heading off failure at school and dropping out, in balancing supply and demand for training, and in creating and strengthening links between training institutes and the world of business and industry. The vocational guidance strand of PETRA, an EU youth programme, aimed at promoting Community co-operation on guidance and at exchanging national facts and figures, good practice and effective methods for vocational guidance. Its objectives were to ensure that all young people receive appropriate information, practical guidance and interviews, as well as personal assistance to help them discover the occupational channels open to them, to assess their capacities and to encourage them to go for a vocational qualification and get into training.

As a result, today all young people and their families can get access to up-to-date information on the training opportunities and guidance services available in the other Member States, and they are encouraged and supported to use such information. The first phase of the Leonardo programme brought about the most recent innovations in systems, arrangements and actions. It covered a wide range of activities and tasks in connection with training and with the development of human resources in general.

Guidance and counselling have thus taken on a new and increasingly important role. Professional guidance services have a crucial role to play in the development of human resources. However, availability and quality of guidance services vary considerably. In none of them are all vulnerable sectors sufficiently covered yet. The offer of guidance is less developed for adults than for young people. It is therefore important for most countries to improve their guidance systems. In particular, increased efforts should be put into widening the recognition of guidance as an ongoing process which should start at school and continue ever thereafter. As guidance lies at the cross-roads between training, employment and personal development, it can provide a meeting place for the three types of professional currently operating separately in guidance: those linked to education and training systems, those linked to labour offices, and those providing guidance within companies.

5

Online Training for Counsellors

Despite the exponential advances in technology and the use of the World Wide Web in the field of education, finding ways to demonstrate and deliver services to students at all levels continues to be a challenge for counselor educators. Technological skills needed by human services professionals include a common core of skills needed by all educators and some skills unique to each discipline. School counselors in particular need technology skills to include knowledge of internet resources as well as knowing how to help students access them, guidance and counseling software, use of distance learning, use of listservs, and the interest to keep up to date on the ever changing scene of computer technology. Further, they need to learn to use technology for monitoring student progress and educational/career planning as well as to apply data to their professional decision making.

The use of online assignments in counselor education courses has been one way to teach and model the use of such technology for counselors in training.

Results and comments from students who have completed and applied such assignments to their work have been very positive. School counselors and counselor educators are increasingly recognizing the benefits of using technology in many areas of their jobs and of increasing their resources to help their students. Such technology can significantly alter the work of counselors in the areas of information retrieval and dissemination, college and career exploration, actual counseling interventions as well as in establishing networks of communication and support systems for clients. However, school counselors need to be more actively involved in actually implementing such technology into their jobs on a daily basis.

Recent studies have shown that many school counselors believe they have had inadequate training in using computers in their work. Therefore, it is essential to infuse such information, training, and knowledge of resources into their graduate education. To help students develop such competencies, a major emphasis needs to be placed on effective teaching and modeling by university faculty. Such technology and training can include the use of electronic mail and newsletters as a means of communication with students, parents and the community, learning about relevant websites, networking and implementing counseling strategies. Specific examples of applying such technology to counselor education can include accessing online legislative information relating to schools in general and counseling services specifically, using the internet to help students obtain information about higher education, sources of financial aid, career opportunities, and learning about mental health resources. Helping students develop websites to post their own work as well as list resources and activities for their students is another valuable skill to be learned.

Counselor educators are viewing applied technology as both a teaching tool and a necessary skill for their counselors in training. Acquiring technological skills is a developmental approach for counseling students who must be supported by counselor educators to move from "word processing to web pages to data analysis...". Counselor educators are in a position to have access to many resources to share with their students yet they realize that it is imperative to "shape" assignments or point students in specific directions to maximize the effectiveness of the assignments.

There is an ever increasing amount of information available on the internet and an essential skill for students to develop is not only to learn about the resources, but to learn how to apply the information gathered to their work in schools. There are growing numbers of counseling courses and programs offered online. And, there appears to be increasing external pressure from working students as well as internal pressure relating to budget issues within universities to provide on-line coursework. But there is also plenty of room for the use of "online" assignments within a more traditional graduate program. Giving such assignments within their classes has been a very effective way of helping their students learn about the content of specific websites and make significant applications of the information gleaned from the sites.

There are a variety of ways in which counselor educators can organize online instruction. Assignments may be done by individual course such as Career Development, Organization and Administration of the

Guidance and Counseling Program, Multicultural Counseling, or Counseling Theories. Another means of organization could be by topics that may be included within a particular course or may be infused throughout a number of courses. Examples of such topics could include, Legal and Ethical Issues in Counseling, Professional Organizations and Publications (such as ACA, ASCA, and ACES), and Resources for Counseling Children and Adolescents. A third example of organizing online assignments could be integrating them into counseling supervision. In a practicum or internship seminar students could be given assignments via electronic mail and could be organized into cyberspace forums where they could respond to each other's contributions. The weekly seminar would be an excellent opportunity for students and the university supervisor to share resources that have proved successful in their work and to collaborate on the development of a website that could be used with their students. Further, if internships are being conducted at a long distance from the university, online assignments and e-mail would be the primary way that professors and students communicate with one another.

There are a number of considerations to facilitate the smooth delivery of and maximize the opportunities for students in using online assignments. Counselor educators may decide to set up their own websites with resources organized and electronic addresses called universal resource locators (URL) listed for students. In this scenario, students can go to the instructor's website and click on the specific resources required for the assignment. An example of this format is used in the "Career Development" assignment given earlier. Another option is to spell out the URL for each task on the assignment and the student is responsible for typing them into the computer. A third option is for the instructor to give more general assignments in which the student is required to search and discover sites by topic or subject. In this last case, there is more room for variety and variability in the tasks given and responses made. Instructors who feel confident and are prepared to guide students through the process help students feel more comfortable in using the technology as part of their repertoire of skills. Such guidance is offered during the first part of the semester so that students can complete the assignment at their own pace and can use the resources offered as they need them.

It is essential that students understand the purpose of the assignment as well as how to use the computer in accessing the resources. Demonstrating the use of the Internet in general as well as specific websites is necessary. Including the online assignment as part of the course syllabus is another option for introducing the requirement early in the semester. Although the assignments may include some local as well as state and national resources, each instructor can adapt these assignments to the needs of their local student population. It is important for students to have a "product" as a result of the assignment. Simply asking students to go to a website does not ensure that they check it out or apply what they might find there. Having them answer questions about the site, or make comments/recommendations about the site, which are turned in to the instructor, is essential to the intent of the assignment. After all, once instructors have led students to the website, they want to be certain that students have not only "clicked" but have learned something from the experience. After the assignment is due, it can be useful to have students take turns coming to the front of the class and typing in their favorite URL to share with their classmates.

Computer-oriented Training Programs

Computers have been more widely used in counseling for record keeping, data analysis, cybercounseling and cyberlearning. In addition, counselor educators are beginning to use computer applications in the training of counselors. In US National Board for Certified Counselors (NBCC) and the Council for the Accreditation of Counseling and Related Educational Programs (CACREP) have adopted guidelines on the use of technology in training counselors. These progressive movements provide the impetus for incorporation of technology training in counselor preparation programs. The Association for Counselor Education and Supervision (ACES) Technology Interest Network recommended technical competencies necessary for counselor training. It recommend that at the completion of a counselor education program, students should:

— Be able to use productivity software to develop web pages, group presentations, letters, and reports.

— Be able to use such audiovisual equipment as video recorders, audio recorders, projection equipment, video conferencing equipment, and playback units.

— Be able to use computerized statistical packages.

— Be able to use computerized testing, diagnostic, and career decision-making programs with clients.

— Be able to use email.

— Be able to help clients search for various types of counseling-related information via the Internet, including information about careers, employment opportunities, educational & training opportunities, financial assistance/scholarships, treatment procedures, and social and personal information.

— Be able to subscribe, participate in, and sign off counseling related listservs.

— Be able to access and use counseling related CD-ROM databases.

These competencies are directly related to training counseling students and establish the first level of technology skills a counselor may need to be technologically competent. While computer competencies may be absolutes for counselors, many have not considered computer competencies involve a developmental process and require technical skills. Since 1984, the University of Iowa has incorporated an introductory computer course into the counselor education curriculum to expose masters' level students to computer technology. This course is designed to advance the use of technology for guidance and counseling professionals. The course emerged from a response from the school guidance and counseling professionals. The first course provided training in computer fundamentals on AppleIIw computers, using interactive video skills and CD-I, word processing, spreadsheet and database with AppleWorks, and graphics with MacPaint. The course has now expanded into teaching internet searching related to counseling, cybercounseling ethical responsibilities, development of web pages, presentation software and statistical packages. A distance hybrid learning approach is utilized by facilitating learning through web-based instruction called WebCT.

In US a study was designed to examine the lack of uniformity among counseling students. An investigation of the effectiveness of a required technology course on student computer competency appeared necessary. Research questions were as follows:

1. Do students with or without computer instruction differ significantly in computer competencies?
2. Do students with or without computer instruction differ significantly on their motivation towards computer usage?

The researchers hypothesized that students with computer instruction would differ from students without computer instruction on their level of computer competency and motivation towards computer usage.

The empirical study utilized a quasi-experimental cohort research design. This quasi-experimental design assumed quasi-comparability between successive cohorts. Therefore, the successive cohort groups were the summer and fall semester classes of 7C: 281 course at the University of Iowa. Comparisons were made between an experimental group and a control group. Pre and posttest scores were reported for the experimental group and compared to the pre-test scores of the control group. The statistical comparison was made between the summer (experimental group) posttest scores and the fall (control group) pre-test scores.

Twenty-six (experimental group N=16, control group N=10) masters level counseling students in the Division of Counseling, Rehabilitation, and Student Development were involved in the study. All students were enrolled in the 7C: 281 Introduction to Computers for Counselors course during the summer and fall semesters of 2001. The master's level students were in four counseling programs within the division: rehabilitation counseling, school counseling, student development, and substance abuse. Students voluntarily participated in the study.

The study participants consisted of 26 students with 84.2 % females and 15.8 % males. The respondents ranged in age from 22-57 years with 50% between 22-27 years old. Sixty-seven percent had a status of being a full-time student. Thirty-seven percent of the respondents were in the school counseling program, 32 % rehabilitation counseling program, 13 % substance abuse program, and 18% student development program. The mean number of courses completed toward a counseling degree was 6.1 with an average of 19.0 semester hours accumulated. Sixty-five percent indicated they had taken a technology course.

The experimental group consisted of 16 students with 89.3% females and 10.7% males. Forty-two percent of the respondents were in the school counseling program, 33% were in the rehabilitation counseling program, 18% were in the substance abuse counseling program, and 7% were in the student development program. These respondents ranged in age from 22-57 years.

The majority (43%) of the respondents were in the 22-27 age range with 36% aligning in the 28-33 years age range. The pretest surveys revealed 57% of experimental group respondents were full-time students and 68% had taken a computer course prior to this course. The mean number of courses completed toward a counseling degree was 5.3 with an average of 17.6 semester hours accumulated. Only one experimental group member reported that they had taken a course within the counselor education curriculum that utilized technology in the course.

The respondents were asked to identify the types of technology they currently used or have used previous to this course. Responses indicated 100% had used word processing software, 81% had used electronic mail, 50% had utilized audiovisual equipment, 44% had a course using web-based or web-assisted instruction, 18% acknowledged use of statistical programs, 18% cited usage of a listserv, 6% had used a cd-rom, and 6% indicated other technology. The posttest survey was completed by only 12 of the 16 original respondents. Two respondents specified they had taken a course within counselor education curriculum that utilized technology. Respondents were asked to identify the types of technology they currently used or had used before the technology course. These responses yielded the following frequency information on usage was provided: 96% word processing software, 89% electronic mail, 53% audiovisual equipment, 54% web-based or web-assisted instruction, 32% statistical software, 25% listserv, 14% cd-roms, and 7% other technology.

The control group consisted of 10 masters students enrolled in the 7C: 281 Introduction to Computers For Counselors course. The control group consisted of 60.0% females and 40.0% males. Fifty percent of the respondents were in the student development program, 30% were in rehabilitation counseling program, and 20% were in the school counseling program. These respondents ranged in age from 21-33 years.

The majority (70%) of the respondents were in the 22-27 age range. Eighty percent were full-time students and 70% had taken a computer course prior to this class.

The average number of courses taken toward completion of a counseling degree was 5.6 with a mean cumulative semester hours score of 15.8. Two respondents from the control group reported they had taken a counseling course, which required the use of technology. Respondents were asked to identify the types of technology experience they held prior to the technology course. Their responses indicated usage in the following areas: 100% word processing software, 100% electronic mail, 60% audiovisual equipment, 60% web-based or web-assisted instruction, 10% statistical software, 60% listservs, 3% cd-roms, and 1% other technology.

Prospective participants were master's level counselor education students at The University of Iowa in the College of Education enrolled in the 7C: 281 Introduction to Computers in Counseling one-hour semester course. The students were given a cover letter introducing the research study, a survey and an informed consent document for voluntary participation in the study during the first class session. Students could choose not to participate by checking no on the informed consent document and returning the uncompleted surveys. Completed surveys to be given to the researchers were placed in an envelope. The informed consent documents were placed in a separate envelope to maintain the anonymity of the participants. Students were given the same survey again at the end of the semester as a posttest survey.

Demographic information. Students were asked to provide the following demographic information: gender, age, degree program, computer courses taken, degree of computer skills, types of courses completed, courses taken that integrated web-based or web-assisted instruction, types of technologies used, number of courses completed toward degree, and number of semester hours completed. Surveys were coded based on whether they were pre or post-test instruments.

Computer Technology Competencies Scale (CTCS). The CTCS was created using 12 competency areas recommended by the ACES Technology Interest Network and developed 15 items to measure an individual's competence level on the technology competency. A 5-point Likert scale was developed, ranging from 1 (not familiar) to 5 (very confident). Participants were instructed to indicate their competence level on each of 15 computer technology items. The initial reliability data revealed good internal consistency, with a with Cronbach's alpha of a =. 93. Validity data for CTCS are not available.

Situational Motivation Scale (*SIMS*). This 20-item Situational Motivation scale consists of five subscales with four questions designed to assess situational variables that affect the experience of intrinsic motivation, extrinsic motivation, and amotivation. Extrinsic motivation was identified through two extrinsic motivational subscales of identified regulation and external regulation. Intrinsic motivation was identified through one intrinsic motivational subscale. Amotivation was identified through one amotivation subscale. The measure of introjected regulation was developed by borrowing from a previously validated questionnaire. The items from the RTWS were adapted specifically for the study. The adapted items used precise experiences in distance education obtained from a literature review of self-determination.

The SIMS scale uses the response stem (e.g., "Why are you currently participating in distance education?" or

"Why are you currently not participating in distance education?"), with a 1 to 7 Likert response scale (strongly disagree, disagree, somewhat disagree, neutral, somewhat agree, agree, strongly agree) for each of the 20 items. Totals for each subscale were computed by averaging the relevant four items. Guay et al. reported the construct validity and assessed it by two correlation analyses. Their results found an overall pattern of interrelations among the subscales is formed from an ordered pattern of those subscales adjacent along the continuum. For example, intrinsic motivation correlated positively with identified regulation (r =. 36) but negatively with amotivation (r = -.41). The second correlation analysis was performed between the SIMS subscales and perceived competence and concentration/behavioral intentions. There was a strong positive correlation (SIMS subscales with motivational determinant and consequences) observed with intrinsic motivation and identified regulation but a strong negative correlation with amotivation and external regulation. These correlations were consistent with those predicted by self-determination theory. The subscales' internal consistency values or Cronbach Alphas were: intrinsic motivation a =.92, identified regulation a =.80, external regulation a =.86, and amotivation a =.77.

Prior to analysis, variables were examined for accuracy of data entry, missing values, and fit between their distributions. During data entry, precautions were taken to ensure there was no human error in the data entry process. The precaution procedures were to pull out every third questionnaire and check to see if the data entered into SPSS were correct. All analyses were performed using SPSS 9.0 to provide descriptive statistics. Internal consistency for the two scales used in the study was explored by calculating alpha coefficients of reliability for the total score of each scale as well as SIMS subscales. Frequencies and means were calculated for all demographic characteristics of the sample. In keeping with the cohort design, the statistical hypotheses were that the mean scores of the experimental group pretest did differ from those of the experimental group posttest scores on the CTCS. A one-way analysis of variance was performed to test this hypothesis. The CTCS scale items were computed by averaging items.

The dependent variables were CTCS averaged score. The independent variable in the research was time when the test was taken (pretest or posttest). The results revealed that computer competency was increased after taking the introductory computer course. The results of the analysis of variance revealed that the experimental group differed significantly from the control group on the Computer Technology Competency Scale ($F(1, 20) = 7.519$, $p = .013$). Examination of the group means revealed a significant difference in mean scores between the experimental group ($M = 3.60$) and control group ($M = 2.71$) on computer competencies. This result demonstrates an increase in computer competency after completing the required introduction to computers in counseling course. The results of the t-test revealed that several items on the CTCS scale yielded a significant difference between the experimental and control groups: ethics ($t[19] = 4.254$, $p=.000$), assisting client with internet searches ($t[19] = 2.199$, $p=.040$), statistical package ($t[20] = 5.520$, $p=.000$), listserv ($t[19] = 2.705$, $p=.014$), cd-rom ($t[19] = 2.827$, $p=.011$), presentation software ($t[20] = 2.237$, $p=.037$), and evaluating information from the internet ($t[20] = 2.359$, $p=.029$).

The group means indicate that the experimental group increased computer competency after completing the course under the following competency items: ethics (M=4.00), assisting clients with Internet searches (M=3.00), statistical software (M=2.92), listserv (M=2.91), cd-rom (M=3.00), presentation software (M=4.17), and evaluating information from the internet (M=3.92). The group means from the control group indicated computer competency were low before the computer course was taken under the following competency items: ethics (M=2.00), assisting clients with Internet searches (M=1.70), statistical software (M=1.10), listserv (M=1.60), cd-rom (M=1.60), presentation software (M=3.00), and evaluating information from the internet (M=2.70). The results of the analysis of variance revealed that the experimental group pretest and posttest results differed significantly on the Computer Technology Competency Scale (F (1, 26) = 38.007, p =.000). Examination of the group means revealed a significant difference in mean scores between the post-test scores (M =3.60) and pre-test scores (M = 1.97) on computer competencies. This result demonstrates an increase in computer competency after completing .the required introduction to computers in counseling course.

The results of the analysis of variance revealed that all the items with the exception of word processing on the CTCS scale yielded a significant difference between the posttest and pretest: word processing (F (1, 26) = 1.438, p =.241, email (F (1, 26) = 4.508, p =.043), bulletin board (F (1, 26) = 12.118, p =.002), knowledge of ethics Internet (F (1, 26) = 29.630, p =.000), computerized testing (F (1, 26) = 12.306, p =.000), assisting clients with Internet (F (1, 26) = 11.045, p =.003), statistical packages (F (1, 26) = 39.918, p =.000), Internet for research (F (1, 25) = 9.580, p =.005), counseling listservs (F (1, 25) = 7.080, p =.013), Internet for continuing education (F (1, 25) = 15.558, p

=.001), counseling CD-Rom (F (1, 25) = 14.103, p =.001), database (F (1, 26) = 13.180, p =.001), presentation software (F (1, 26) = 36.322, p =.000), developing web pages (F (1, 26) = 59.313, p =.000), and evaluate the quality of information provided via Internet (F (1, 26) = 30.128, p =.000).

Group means indicate the experimental group posttest results significant increase in their computer competency after completing the course in under the following competency items: ethics posttest (M=4.00), ethics pretest (M=2.0), computerized testing pretest M=1.56), computerized testing posttest (M=3.0), assisting clients with Internet searches pretest (M=1.50), assisting clients with Internet searches posttest (M=2.82), statistical software pretest (M=1.19), statistical software posttest (M=2.92), listserv posttest (M=1.50), listserv pretest (M=2.91), cd-rom pretest (M=1.50), cd-rom posttest (M=3.00), presentation software pretest (M=1.75), presentation software posttest (M=4.17), evaluating information from the internet posttest (M=1.88), and evaluating information from the internet posttest (M=3.92). Results that measure motivation towards computers revealed no group differences existed on motivation factors of participants in the study on external regulation, identified regulation (value toward computers), introjected regulation (participating because of guilt), amotivation (indifferent), intrinsic. Thus, indicating motivation toward computer usage may not be a factor in training.

Findings from the study support the research hypothesis that students will increase their computer competency based on completing a computer course. Both the experimental group (EG) and the control group (CG) yielded lower mean scores on some of the competency areas indicating the need for further research and instruction. These competency areas included: assisting clients with Internet searches (EG, M=2.82; CG, M=1.70), statistical packages (EG, M=2.92; CG, M=1.10), listserv (EG, M=2.91; CG, M=1.60), and cd-rom (EG, M=3.00; CG, M=1.60). The experimental group pretest and posttest results showed significant difference among all the items on CTCS with the exception of word processing. Therefore, student competency areas were low on all the items In the study both the experimental and control groups demonstrated similar levels of motivation to participate in computer technology as indicated by scores on the SIMS motivational scale. Thus, they were not hindered in participating in computer technology. However, the course appears to help students improve skills on some of the computer competencies. Areas such as, being familiar with statistical packages, assisting clients in internet searches, and knowledge of listservs need an increase in competency level.

Implications for counselors are tempered by considerations of threats to validity.

First, external validity is threatened by the restricted nature of the sample and the purposive sampling strategy.

Second, the multiple t-tests increase the probability of Type 1 error.

Third, the institutional cohort design, by its nature, is relatively a weak quasi-experimental design and leaves open some threat to internal validity, especially history.

Fourth, the pretest of the experimental group added an additional threat to internal validity. Although these threats to validity do limit the applicability of these results, they are partially allayed by the consistency of the previous studies using this design.

Computer competency increases with exposure to computer technology in a required introductory course. Application of computer technology to practice cannot be assumed, it must be taught. The application of computer technology is normally taught through performance assessment. Students are taught how to operate and demonstrate different software and equipment by producing several assignments for the course. These assignments can be graded as pass/fail. This may benefit the student by allowing them to learn programs without feeling pressure to receive letter grades. This also allows the instructor to discuss possible problem-solving techniques to help the student make connections between computer technology principles and professional practice decisions.

Finally, an introductory course, which discusses technology integration into counseling courses in the program, aids with future instruction for faculty because instructional time for technology is not used in the regular courses.

Development of Standards

The tremendous growth of technology led to standards being developed to impact the university training programs of both counselors and educators. School counseling programs are thus being impacted by technology developments and standards in both the fields of counseling and education and faced with the challenge of creating competencies that meet the technology issues and needs in both arenas. While the roots of computer assisted counselor training can be traced back to Wizenbaum's ELIZA in the mid 1960's, it was not until the 1990's that technology was truly recognized as a force impacting both the education and practice of counselors. Since the mid 1990's, technology in counseling has been the focus of numerous articles, chapters, and books.

Technology itself has become a medium through which information and scholarly publication on the use of technology in counseling is disseminated. Online libraries and CD-ROM databases carry full text journal articles. Electronic journals listed by the State Library of Colorado which specifically deal with technology in counseling, education, or psychology currently numbers 37. Listservs, email-based discussion groups, like the International Counseling Network (ICN) and the Counselor Education and Supervision Network-List (CESNET-L), while not specifically devoted to technology in counseling, often contain information related to its use in both training and practice. Along with the tremendous growth of technology in the field of counseling, professional organizations have seen the need for standards around its use.

The US National Board for Certified Counselors (1997) saw the impact that on-line technology was beginning to have upon the field of counseling and developed "The Practice of Internet Counseling". The National Career Development Association created "Guidelines for the Use of the Internet for Provision of Career Information and Planning Services" and, while the International Association of Educational and Vocational Guidance does not have ethical guidelines specific to the use of technology, their General Assembly, in the

"Declaration of Counsellor Qualification Standards", declared "an urgent need for internationally recognised qualification standards for counsellors, and ... [established] a committee consisting of members from different regions in the world to elaborate a draft of such standards."

Additionally, the Association for Counselor Education and Supervision (ACES), believing that the effective use of technology was a crucial skill for counselors, created a Technology Interest Network. The members of this network developed "Technical Competencies for Counselor Education Students: Recommended Guidelines For Program Development" which was endorsed by the ACES Executive Council. Even with these ethical and skill guidelines, the concern regarding the use of technology is so great that some continue to call for an expansion of the ethical guidelines and the creation of comprehensive standards for counseling related web sites.

While technology was coming into its own in the counseling field, it was virtually exploding into the field of education. In US throughout their eight years in office, the Clinton-Gore Administration made an unprecedented commitment to bring technology into the Pre-K-12 classroom. The Congress approved billions of dollars to provide teachers with training and support, develop effective software and online learning resources, provide access to computers, and connect every school to the Internet. The FY01 budget for the Education Office of Educational Technology alone provides $958 million for education technology and research. Additionally, private industry, such as Microsoft, Intel, Hewlett Packard; and foundations, such as the Bill and Linda Gates Foundation, and Verizon Foundation, have given billions of dollars to help schools and teachers obtain equipment and the professional development necessary to effectively integrate technology into the curriculum. National professional education organizations have developed technology standards. The International Society for Technology in Education, through the National Educational Technology Standards Project (NETS), created Standards for Students, NETS for Teachers, and is currently working on NETS for School Administrators. In US as the national scene was becoming filled with technology stakeholders, state legislatures and departments of education began to see the importance of technology in education as well.

In response to the demand for technology proficient educators, the National Council for the Accreditation of Teacher Education (NCATE) formed a Task Force on Technology and Teacher Education in 1996. This group studied the impact of technology upon education and the ensuing need for teacher education programs to integrate technology education into their pre-service training programs. Their report, "Technology and the New Professional Teacher: Preparing for the 21st Century Classroom", described the skills needed by educators to help students.

In US, the field of school counseling has been affected by the impact technology has had in both counseling and Pre-K-12 education. The Elementary School Guidance & Counseling journal published a special issue devoted to technology in school counseling in October 1995. In early 1999, as part of its Transforming School Counseling Implementation Grant, Indiana State University's (ISU) School Counselor Program began to seriously look at the specific technology skills that school counseling students should be able to perform by the time they have completed their two year masters degree program. In addition to studying the skill sets developed by ACES and Hartman, focus groups were conducted with area school counselors.

A careful review of the current and emerging trends in technology in both education and counseling was carried out in order to ascertain their possible impact upon the field of school counseling. Finally, ISU's own School Counselor Student Competencies were examined to see what technology skills would help students in the acquisition and performance of these proficiencies. The resulting 10 competencies became the School Counseling Program Technology Proficiencies, which are as follows:

— Be a knowledgeable consumer and skilled, effective, and efficient user of computers, technology, and the Internet. Understanding and being skilled in technology does not necessarily mean knowing how to effectively and efficiently use it. For example, unless school counselors know how to efficiently search the World Wide Web, a search for information on Attention Deficit Hyperactive Disorder will yield tens of thousands of "hits" and take hours of time searching for helpful and reliable information geared to a particular user, be it a student, teacher, parent, or the counselor. Additionally, once resources are found, school counselors must know how to evaluate the validity and applicability of its content.

— Be a knowledgeable and effective teacher and facilitator for teachers, students and parents concerning educational and career technology resources. School counselors must not only be proficient users of technology-related educational and career development resources, they must also be able to show students, parents, and educators how to effectively use these resources.

— Be familiar with trends in the use of technology in education and their impact upon student academic achievement levels and social, educational, and career development; and, intelligently contribute to the development of a school wide technology plan. Technology can positively or negatively affect not only a student's academic development, but their personal, educational, and/or career development as well. School counselors have the responsibility to understand the possible impact of technology upon student development and to advocate on behalf of their best interests.

— Be able to use a wide variety of technology resources, including Internet tools, appropriate software, and digit cameras, in the development, implementation, and evaluation of counseling and guidance activities. Based upon a sound understanding of the impact of technology upon development and academic achievement, school counselors must be able to effectively incorporate technology into their developmental guidance programs. This would include the development of student competencies that would include the use of technology in areas like study skills and career exploration.

— Be able to develop short and long-term technology plans for the counseling department that provide students and families access to guidance and counseling services, and, articulate the opportunities, as well as the ethical and legal implications of technology as a counseling and guidance delivery tool. When designing a comprehensive developmental guidance program, school counselors must think not only about staffing and facility needs, but also realize that the purposeful acquisition and intentional deployment of technology is an integral component of the plan. Technology should not be just a program add on. It should be seamlessly, yet deliberately, infused within the program's infrastructure.

— Be able to design, create, and evaluate an effective, interactive Internet site for a counseling and guidance program. A school's counseling program Internet site becomes a virtual office where students, families, teachers, area employers, etc. can gain information, submit forms, have discussions and participate in activities and projects. School counselors need to know how to design, create and evaluate effective sites, being mindful of the ethical issues and standards.

— Objectively evaluate counseling and guidance software and articulate software needs and plans to school technology professionals and commercial vendors. Schools will look to their counselors for direction in purchasing counseling and guidance related software. Therefore, school counselors must be able to objectively and competently evaluate the match between the objectives of the software purchase and the features of the reviewed software.

— Understand the ethical and legal implications of technology, including issues of equity and access and the implications of the digital divide upon students, families, and communities. While skill in the use of technology is important, school counselors have the responsibility to understand the ethical and legal issues which surround the use of technology. Additionally, they must understand ramifications inherent in the digital divide. All decisions concerning technology use must be predicated upon these considerations.

— Effectively use technology, including relational databases, spreadsheets and the Internet, that allows the analysis of student achievement and related data; and, how to use technology to support the change needed to raise student achievement levels. It is important for school counselors to know how to effectively and efficiently uses technology to monitor student achievement, from the individual student and classroom levels to the whole grade and school levels. Being able to effectively use technology in data analysis, to spur change in classrooms, and to facilitate whole school reform is especially important with education's current focus upon high standards and accountability.

— Effectively use technology as a tool in advocacy efforts and the procurement of funds and resources. Finally, technology can be an extremely effective tool in the advocacy efforts of school counselors. Whether it is used in the creation of a school board presentation with charts and graphs from presentation software, or in finding grant opportunities on the World Wide Web, technology is an important means to the furtherance of advocacy endeavors.

6

Psychological Problems of Netizens

The virtual world is quite different than the in-person world. Digitizing people, relationships, and groups has stretched the boundaries of how and when humans can interact. In different online environments we see different combinations of these features, thus resulting in a distinct psychological quality to each environment which determines how people experience themselves and others. These features as the fundamenal elements of a conceptual model for a psychology of cyberspace. In fact, the effect of these elements on individuals, groups, and communities is an important theme throughout this book.

Whether an environment in cyberspace involves visual and/or auditory communication will greatly affect how people behave and the relationships that develop among people. The multimedia chat environments, audio-video conferencing, and internet-phoning surely are signs of things to come. However, the sensory experience of encountering others in cyberspace - seeing, hearing, and combining seeing and hearing - is still limited. For the most part people communicate through typed language. Even when audio-video conferencing becomes efficient and easy to use, people will probably never be able to physically interact with each other - no handshakes, pats on the back, hugs, or kisses.

The limited sensory experiences of cyberspace has some significant disadvantages - as well as some unique advantages - as compared to in-person encounters. E-mail, chat, and instant messaging continue to be the most common forms of online interaction for reasons beyond their ease of use and inexpense compared to multimedia tools.

Drawing on different cognitive abilities than talking and listening, typing one's thoughts and reading those of another is a unique way to present one's identity, perceive the identity of one's online companion, and establish a relationship. E-mail relationships in particular have evolved into a very complex, text-based process - with chat or IM relationships approaching that complexity.

The lack of face-to-face cues has a curious impact on how people present their identity in cyberspace. Communicating only with typed text, you have the option of being yourself, expressing only parts of your identity, assuming imaginative identities, or remaining completely anonymous - in some cases, being almost invisible, as with the "lurker." The multimedia worlds also offer the opportunity to express yourself through the visual costumes known as "avatars." Anonymity has a disinhibiting effect that cuts two ways. Sometimes people use it to act out some unpleasant need or emotion, often by abusing other people. Or it allows them to be honest and open about some personal issue that they could not discuss in a face-to-face encounter.

While reading e-mail or text talk in chat rooms, some people experience a blending of their mind with that of the other person. In the imaginary multimedia worlds - where people shape-shift, speak via ESP, walk through walls, and spontaneously generate objects out of thin air - the experience becomes surrealistic. It mimics a state of consciousness that resembles dreams. These altered and dream-like states of consciousness in cyberspace may account for why it is so attractive for some people. It might help explain some forms of computer and cyberspace addiction.

In most cases, everyone on the internet has an equal opportunity to voice him or herself. Everyone - regardless of status, wealth, race, gender, etc. - starts off on a level playing field. Some people call this the "net democracy." Although one's status in the outside world ultimately will have some impact on one's life in cyberspace, there is some truth to this net democracy ideal.

Geographical distance makes little difference in who can communicate with whom. An engineer in Germany converses with a business woman from California on a server in Australia. It's a small world after all. The irrelevance of geography has important implications for people with unique interests or needs.

In their outside life, they may not be able to find anyone near them who shares that unique interest or need. But in cyberspace, birds of a feather - even those with highly unusual feathers - easily can flock together. For support groups devoted to helping people with their problems, that can be a very beneficial feature of cyberspace. For people with antisocial motivations, that's a very negative feature of cyberspace.

"Synchronous communication" involves people sitting at their computer at the same time (i.e., in "real time") communicating with each other via the internet. Chat rooms are one example. On the other hand, e-mail and newsgroups involve "asynchronous communication" that does not require people to interact with each other in the moment.

In both asynchronous and synchronous communication (with the exception of video conferencing and internet phoning), there is a stretching of time. During chat you have from several seconds to a minute or more to reply to the other person - a significantly longer delay than in face-to-face meetings. In e-mail or newsgroups, you have hours, days, or even weeks to respond.

Cyberspace creates a unique temporal space where the ongoing, interactive time together stretches out. This provides a convenient "zone for reflection." Compared to face-to-face encounters, you have significantly more time to mull things over and compose a reply. Some new internet users go through a period of adaptation to this novel temporal experience.

For example, they may expect a reply to their e-mail immediately. Enthused about e-mail relating, they assume (perhaps unconsciously) that their partner's reply will approximate the rate of an in-person conversation. Experienced e-mail users appreciate the advantages of time stretching, and even come to understand that different e-mail users have their own e-mail pace. In other ways, cyberspace time is condensed. If you are a member of an online community for several months, you may be considered an "old-timer."

Internet environments change rapidly because it's a lot easier to write and rewrite software infrastructure than it is to build with bricks, wood, and iron. Because it's easy to move around cyberspace, who we meet and the membership of online groups also changes rapidly. By posting a message on bulletin boards read by countless numbers of users, people can draw to themselves others who match even their most esoteric interests. Using a web search engine, they can scan through millions of pages in order to zoom their attention onto particular people and groups. The internet will get more powerful as tools for searching, filtering, and contacting specific people and groups become more effective.

The ability to sift through so many online possibilities for developing relationships amplifies an interesting interpersonal phenomenon well-known to psychologists. A user will act on unconscious motivations - as well as conscious preferences and choices - in selecting friends, lovers, and enemies. This "transference" guides towards specific types of people who address our underlying emotions and needs. Pressed by hidden expectations, wishes, and fears, this unconscious filtering mechanism has at its disposal an almost infinite candy store of online alternatives to choose from.

Most online activities, including e-mail correspondence and chat sessions, can be recorded and saved to a computer file. Unlike real world interactions, the user in cyberspace can keep a permanent record of what was said, to whom, and when. Because these interactions are purely document-based, we may even go so far as to say that the relationship between people are the documents, and that the relationship can be permanently recorded in its entirety.

These records may come in very handy to the user. You can reexperience and reevaluate any portion of the relationship you wish. You can use quoted text as feedback to the partner. One sign of a flame war is the blossoming of the infamous arrows >> that highlight the ammunition of quoted text. Although it's tempting to think of the saved text as an objective record of some piece of the relationship, it's fascinating to see how different your emotional reactions to the same exact record can be when you reread it at different times.

The beauty of computer simulated environments is their ability to transform reality as we know it. They do not have to recreate the actual world. Instead, they can construct imaginary environments, fantasy realms where the usual laws of reality are stretched, altered, or negated.

You walk through walls, communicate telepathically, live out a scene from a movie or book, do anything your imagination can conjure up in any surrounding of your choice. It can be a dream-like experience, if that's what you want. Perhaps the term "virtual reality" applies to these environments in the sense that the imaginary experience could feel AS IF it was real. Fantasy becomes reality. It's important to note that the magnitude of these imaginary features could be controlled.

Some scenarios might involve only a sprinkling of fantasy - like a walk to the top of the Eiffel Tower, where you eat lunch at your favorite cafe that has been transported intact from New York City. Other scenes could be intensely imaginative. Like being a flock of birds that dissolves into wispy clouds above the Grand Canyon.

A problem with imaginary environments will be disorientation and sensory overstimulation. Nature shaped the human perceptual system to work efficiently within specific parameters. Designing fantasy environments for a person must take into consideration that person's biologically predetermined limits for sensory stimulation.

Other problematic reactions to imaginary scenarios will involve more complex psychological factors. Alterations in one's virtual body could trigger dissociation, identity diffusion and disruption, or disintegration anxiety. It will be important to assess the appropriate fantasy scene for any given person. From a research perspective, experimenting with imaginative environments can help psychology better understand the parameters of human sensation, perception, and identity construction.

Using current multimedia chat software, some people prefer the third person view of their avatars interacting in a visual scene (e.g., Palace), rather than the more claustrophobic, "head-in-a-box" feeling of first person scenes. Once technology gives users more peripheral vision, that closed-in feeling may be less of a problem. Yet some people may still prefer the feeling of objectivity and even transcendence that third person views offer.

A powerful virtual reality will offer both options - to immerse and to step out and view the scenario from a distance. In "real" life, wouldn't it be very helpful to step out of a situation you're in so you can examine it from a safer, more objective distance? In virtual reality - especially scenarios that are especially arousing or disorienting - the ability to process the scene from a third person view might be very useful. Psychologists call it an "observing ego."

Ultimately, all dichotomies are more a conceptual convenience than an absolute truth. It's probably more accurate to think of true-to-life and imaginary VRs as opposite poles on a continuum. In between, there are varying mixtures of reality and fantasy - some more reality-rich, others more fantasy-rich. There is at least one other way that the two paths of VR weave in and out of each other. Any fantasy has its roots in the unconscious - in hidden wishes, fears, and needs.

Psychological Issues of Cyberworld

The new technology comes in the form of an international computing/telecommunications network known as the internet, and it may potentially have as significant an impact upon human culture as did the invention of the printing press. The precursor to the internet was created in 1969 by an arm of the Defense Department called the Defense Advanced Research Program Agency (DARPA).

This computer network, which eventually came to be known as Arpanet, was primarily designed as a means for Defense-sponsered researchers to operate different computers at a distance; the computer conferencing capabilities and subsequent social aspects of the network emerged as a byproduct of its operation. The network was purposefully intended to be decentralized so that, in the event of a nuclear attack, it would be practically impossible to shut down. Initially there were only four sites connected via the network. By 1971 there were about 24, and by 1981 there were more than 200 sites online. Today it is estimated that there are over 30 million people connected to the internet, with usage increasing approximately 10% per month, and the number of new applications and services growing almost as quickly. Along with this explosion there is emerging a new set of subcultural phenomena which is loosely referred to as cyberculture. Though some research has been conducted concerning the nature of this emergent culture, the main stream of social scientists has paid it little attention, or failed to notice its arrival altogether.

Most of the existing literature centers on issues pertaining to computer conferencing. However, computer conferencing is merely one aspect of computer mediated communication (CMC). One such neglected domain of CMC, though argued by some to be the most indicative of cyberculture is that known as the Multi-User Dimension (MUD). A MUD is a network-accessable, multi-participant, user-extensible virtual reality which is primarily text-based.

Typically, the term "virtual reality" refers to computer simulated environments which possess varying degrees of audio/visual interface, and although some experimental MUDs do offer AV components, this form of virtual reality is essentially text-based. The name "MUD" first appeared in 1978 when a student named Roy Trubshaw at the University of Essex, England, created a program that he called a "Multi-User Dungeon".

It was a multi-user adventure game loosely based upon the popular game known as "Dungeons and Dragons". In this fantasy adventure, players were encouraged to compete with each other for points by going on quests to slay monsters or find treasure.

All players started out on an equal footing, but after having accumulated a certain number of points a player could advance his rank, thus granting him access to new and greater powers. This eventually lead to a sort of social hierarchy which spanned from "Newbies" though various intermediate levels, and culminating in attainment of the title "Wizard", with all the special powers and privileges of such rank.

From this fantasy-adventure based beginning, MUDs have since proliferated and diversified so that at present one can find hundreds of MUDs throughout the internet, many of which have been put to uses other than merely recreation. To reflect this evolution, the acronym MUD has come to stand for Multi-User Dimension or Multi-User Domain as well as the original Multi-User Dungeon.

Additionally, the term MUD has recently differentiated into various sub-types such as MOO, MUSH, MUSE, MUCK, DUM, etc. Each of these acronyms is intended to indicate, though with quite a degree of overlap, the multiple environmental conditions and purposes of each community. One virtual space, created by Amy Bruckman of the Massachusetts Institute of Technology Media Lab, is called the MediaMOO (MOO designating MUD-Object Oriented). This environment provides a virtual meeting place for students and academics working in the area of media and communications.

Community members are encouraged to build onto this virtual world by creating new objects, rooms, and features via a MOO programming language.

It is generally speculated that computers and computer networks will transform (are transforming) the ways in which society functions. These changes are occurring on multiple levels, effecting our modes of production, our modes of learning, and even the ways in which we socialize. There is even evidence to suggest that use of interactive multimedia actually alters ones neurological configuration, and a preliminary draft of the DSM-V includes a section delineating newly emerging "Cyber Disorders".

MUD characters have no actuality, only virtuality. They are never immutable. MUD characters are not fixed, and they are always in the process of redefinition. They are cyborgs - entities made up of ones and zeroes and imagination, without bodies and without physical restrictions in the virtuality they inhabit.

The objects in MUD universes are treated as if they had the properties of the everyday counterparts. Houses are lived in, roses are smelt, food can be eaten and other players can be kissed. Such technology is a device which mediates between the physical and the imagined. It is an interface between the imagined world and the world of the body. It is in the spaces between the body and the self that cyborgs exists.

In the real-world one does have to contend with different types of social and environmental conditions to an extent, but at least one can be fairly certain of a multitude of constants (for instance, there are no dragons in the real-world and the laws of gravity are always in effect). In a MUD it is literally true that "reality" is created through language both by the actions of the players and through the code used by the programmers.

One study demonstrated that both the types and frequency of graphic accents correlated with player gender, with men being less prone to utilize such devices than women. However, it did not appear that there was a significant difference in the rate or degree of flaming. This tendency for women to be more challenging in CMC groups as compared to face-to-face interactions may be due to women feeling more at ease in CMC because of the relative anonymity, or that it may be that the women engaged in CMC might already be involved in male-dominated endeavors such as high tech. organizations or academia.

Since MU* interaction is essentially synchronous, these findings have to be considered with this distinction in mind. One factor that complicates gender related research in such environments is that, due to the anonymity of the medium, one can never be certain of the sex of a respondent. Gender switching has been documented by other researchers as well.

An interesting finding is that the vast majority of those adopting opposite genders seem to be men; women rarely report such behavior. Of the women that did admit to interacting as opposite gender characters, many of them expressed shock at what was perceived as an abrupt drop in the degree and frequency of helpful gestures and general civility offered by other "male" characters.

Conversely, men consistently reported that their female characters received more assistance and generally prospered better than did their alternate male characters. It should be noted however, that information gathered through on-line interviews may not be wholly reliable due to the very fact that one can never be absolutely certain of the true gender of the respondent. Indeed, any self-reports stemming from such an inherently fantasy laden construct must be accepted with a degree of skepticism.

There have even been reports of Internet related deaths, such as cardiac arrests resulting from sleep deprivation and lack of personal maintenance or suicides due to Net related stress. Such obsessive behavior has become quite a problem on some college campuses where computer facility administrators have had to literally "pull the plug" on some addicted students.

In fact, MUDing has been outlawed on the continent of Australia because of the excessive satellite link-up costs associated with such activities. Little is known about this new form of addiction, but as mentioned previously a preliminary draft of the DSM-V includes a section delineating some of these types of "Cyber Disorders". People may be friendlier towards one another in cyberspace.

A recent survey of public school teachers who utilize the Internet as a classroom resource revealed that, except for its function as an information archive, "the rewarding social atmosphere" was viewed as the most outstanding feature of Net access.

Likewise, studies conducted in educational settings where internet access is available have revealed that children are less critical of differences via CMC than in face to face groups. Additionally, a study by Masinter & Ostram on the effectiveness of multi-user information retrieval systems revealed that peer collaboration is higher in on-line information access than it is in "physical" libraries.

Yet a study of electronic bulletin boards conducted at Temple University revealed that Internet groups seem to form, interact and go through distinct stages just as do "real-life" groups, implying that virtual groups may only seem to be more cooperative, friendly, etc.. Likewise,

Kiesler et al, in one of the first studies ever conducted on Net related psychological phenomena, concluded that not only did computer mediated communication impede a group's ability to reach a consensus, but that it was practically devoid of the types of nonverbal social cues necessary to sustain the type of social climate Resnick claims is inherent in the medium.

The perception of friendliness may also be confounded by the temperament of the individuals under study as it relates to computer environments in general. For example, it seems plausible that those who are somewhat technophobic might find any form of CMC to be unfriendly, whereas individuals that embrace technology might perceive the same environment as warm and inviting.

Psychological dynamics of Online Conversations

The word "chat" surely connotes a superficial mode of relating. Indeed, conversation in a chat room often is less than "deep." But as we've seen in the log excerpts so far, the conversation sometimes is very meaningful. Despite the staccato style and the potential for buzzing confusion, discussions can be very fluid, sophisticated, and personal. In the beginning, there was TextTalk. And only TextTalk. But even with the advent of video and audio streaming, typed text continues to reign supreme as the primary mode of conversing on the internet.

This is especially true of "synchronous" modes of communication, as in the ever-popular IRC channels and chat rooms of AOL. Even in the multimedia chat communities, like Palace, where users communicate with avatars and sounds within a visual backdrop, typed text remains the front line method of "talking." TextTalk in online chat environments has evolved into a fascinating style of communication. In some ways, it is strikingly similar to face-to-face (ftf) dialogue.

In other ways, it is quite unique. Many of its unique qualities revolve around the fact that it is an austere mode of communication. There are no changes in voice, no facial expressions, no body language, no (or very little) visual/spatial environment as a context of meaning. There's just typed words. Some people find that experience too sparse. They feel disoriented, disembodied, adrift in that screen of silently scrolling dialogue.

Other people love the minimalist style of TextTalk. They love to see how people creatively express themselves despite the limitations. They love to immerse themselves in the quiet flow of words that feels like a more direct, intimate connection between one's mind and the minds of others. Almost as if the other is inside one's head. Almost as if you are talking with a part of yourself. Without the distracting sights and sounds of the ftf world, TextTalk feels like a more pure communication of ideas and experiences.

For some users, the bare quality of typed text allows for a greater flight of imagination and fantasy. Chat room banter can seem quite chaotic, especially when there are many people talking, or you have just entered a room and immediately dive into the ongoing flow of overlapping conversations.

There are no visual cues indicating what pairs or groups of people are huddled together in conversation, so the lines of scrolling dialogue seem disjointed (visual chat environments, where users can move their avatars close to each other, have an advantage in this respect). You have to sit back and follow the flow of the text to decipher the themes of conversation and who is talking with whom.

In almost all types of chat environments, you consciously and unconsciously set up mental filters and points of focus that help you screen out "noise" and zoom in your concentration on particular people or topics of discussion. Often, you become immersed in one or two strings of dialogue and filter out the others. With experience, you develop an eye for efficiently reading TextTalk. Some people may be better at this specific cognitive-perceptual task than others. Let's pop you into an excerpt from an ongoing chat room conversation and see if you can figure out what's happening in this "buzzing confusion."

In part, this is due to the fact that during a post-hoc reading of a log, you read at the pace you usually read any written material - which is QUICKLY, but much too quickly to absorb TextTalk. While online, the lag created by people typing and by thousands of miles of busy internet wires forces the conversation into a slower pace. And so you sit back, read, wait, scan backwards and forwards in the dialogue, and think about what to say next. There's more time for those perceptual/cognitive filters and lens to operate. There's also more time for a psychological/emotional context to evolve in your mind - a context that helps you follow and shape the nuances of meaning that are developing in the TextTalk.

You would think that the lack of ftf cues and the buzzing confusion of TextTalk would result in many misunderstandings. If five different conversations are scrolling before your eyes, it would seem easy to lose track of what was said. Situations involving humor and sarcasm usually were the culprits, because that smile, chuckle, or wry tone of voice were missing. But these misunderstandings were always cleared up quickly. A quick explanation accompanied by a simple smiley :) or winky ;) efficiently resolves the confusion. What's fascinating about TextTalk is that people mostly DO understand what others mean, despite the lack of visual and auditory cues. Of course, some chat users may like to play games with the potential ambiguity of TextTalk.

The excerpt that follows is an interesting example of how the lack of ftf cues can make it difficult to tell whether someone is intending humor or irony, and when they are being honest or sly. The use of the winky ;) and smiley :) are sometimes used to indicate irony or sarcasm, but in this excerpt the situation is perfectly ambiguous. The excerpt also illustrates how people play with the ambiguity of identity in chat environments.

Due to lag in network connections, messages do not appear on your screen at a steady pace, which causes temporal "hiccups" in the pacing of the conversation. People also may be fumbling with their typing, typing a long message, pausing to think... but you can't see that. A conversation may accidentally become crisscrossed until both partners get "in sync." Users skilled in online chat - and who have a talent for writing - will create incomplete sentences or ideas that lead the companion into the next message. To allow the other user to express a complex idea, you may need to sit back into a "listener" mode.

Text communication in a chat room or channel often assumes a staccato style. Most of the time people express what they have to say in a brief sentence or two, or in sentence fragments. This style works well when people are joking around and ribbing each other, often in what turns out to be a playful game of "can you top this."

In these kinds of exchanges, it usually doesn't matter too much if the other users' messages arrive on your screen out of the order in which the users may have intended them, since there is no specific logical sequence that is needed for the ideas. It is more of a group "free for all."

Because none of the visual cues of face-to-face encounters are available, people feel the need to quickly test the waters to determine the qualities of the users around them and whom they want to engage. Questions that would be considered less than tactful in face-to-face encounters are a bit more socially acceptable here. Terse inquiries tossed out to a fellow user, or the entire room, might include "Age?", "M/F?", "Married?"

The terse style of talking in chat environments can result in either superficial chat, or a very honest and "to-the-point" discussion of personal issues. One doesn't have the verbose luxury of gradually leading the conversation to a serious topic, so self-disclosures sometimes are sudden and very revealing. The safe anonymity resulting from the lack of ftf contact - as well as people not knowing who you "really" are - also contributes to this honest and open attitude. When a whole room is focused on discussing a single topic, the conversation often takes the form of group free-association.

Unlike face-to-face discussions, it's not clear who is reacting to whom because there is no eye contact. Any given user may be addressing a comment to one other particular user, or to the whole room. If people don't preface their message with the other user's name, it's not easy to tell who is reacting to whom, or if someone is indeed speaking to the whole group.

Messages also appear on your monitor in an intermixed, slightly non-sequential order, unlike face-face-discussions where people typically respond to the idea that was just previously mentioned. The logical flow and transitions of face-to-face encounters are much less apparent. The net result is a group "free association" where ideas bounce off each other and the "owner" and "recipient" of the ideas become secondary. Quite unlike face-to-face encounters, people can send private messages to another user in the room - a message that no one else in the room can see.

There may be very few or no messages appearing on YOUR screen, but the room may not be quiet at all. There may be numerous private exchanges among the other people. In face-to-face encounters, the equivalent would be a silent room filled with telepaths! If you are engaged in one of those private discussions, as well as conversing with people out loud, you are placed in the peculiar situation of carrying on dual social roles - an intimate you and a public you, simultaneously. Even more complex is when you attempt to conduct two (or more) private conversations, perhaps in addition to public ones.

You may be joking privately with user A, conducting a serious personal discussion with user B, and engaging in simple chit-chat out loud with the rest of the room. This highly complex social maneuver requires a psychological mechanism called "dissociation" - the ability to separate out and direct the components of your mind in more than one direction at the same time (the same mechanism that becomes pathologically exaggerated in multiple personality disorders).

It takes a great deal of online experience, mental concentration, and keyboarding skill (eye/hand coordination) to pull it off. There is no equivalent for this in face-to-face encounters, except perhaps having two or more people on different phone lines. But in that situation, your phone partners know you are dividing your efforts to other people, while the chat room users may have no idea of your social juggling.

Humans are funny. Present them with a limit, and they find ways around it. Give them a seemingly simple and straightforward medium, and they find all sorts of ways to creatively fiddle with it. For example, in TextTalk, all you have are some letters to represent your identity. Because there are no visuals in TextTalk, body language is impossible... Or is it? "Parenthetical action" can convey any almost physical expression, some that even may be impossible in the ftf world. Video and audio streaming will make it much easier for people to chat with voices, and facial expressions, and body language - almost like "really" being there. When that happens, will text-only chat environments die out? Will TextTalk become an amusing bit of history in the fast-paced world of internet technology? Perhaps not. Some people strongly prefer the minimalist style of TextTalk. They enjoy the anonymity, as well as the challenge of creatively expressing themselves given the barest bones possible. They see beauty in the clean, simple, quiet flow of scrolling words. Sights and sounds are but extraneous noise that clogs the pure expression of mind and soul.

In the "real" world of five senses, people freely can experiment with language, voice modulation, dress, hand gestures, facial expressions, body language, even perfume - all as ways to communicate nuances in meaning.

In cyberspace, the sensory options are not nearly as numerous or versatile. But that doesn't mean that subtlety is absent. When immersed in a medium that places some restrictions on paths to communicate, humans get downright clever and creative in overcoming the barriers. In the traditional text-only chat environments, users have developed a wide variety of symbols, phrases, and acronyms - a whole new vernacular - to get their ideas and feelings across to their cyberpeers.

In the newer graphical/auditory chat environments, the addition of even relatively simple sight and sound options has provided considerably more elbow room for subtlety in communication and creative self-expression.

Most chat environments have the option of sending a message to someone that other users cannot see. At the Palace, NO ONE can see it, not even a wizard or a god. This is something that is NOT possible in the real world, which makes it feel very special, even powerful as a unique feature of cyberspace. It's almost as if you are telepathically connecting your mind to the recipient of your whisper.

Whispering "Hi Lucy" is a sign of intimacy, something shared just between friends. It's a bit secretive, as if you don't particularly want anyone else to know that you're saying hello. If the recipient of your whisper is someone you don't know well, they may experience your hello as a bit intrusive on their psychic space, or as an "advance" of some sort - perhaps a gesture of friendship, or a hint at desired intimacy. All of this holds true for any chat environment where private messaging is possible. But at the Palace, there's an added visual dimension.

When you whisper, everyone else's avatar fades into grey while just you and the recipient of your message remain in bold, living color - as if the whole world has dropped away, leaving just the two of you. It's a very powerful visual effect. And at the Palace you also are located within the visual space of a room, which is absent in text-only chat. This can significantly affect how whispering is perceived. For example, there's a subtle difference between whispering to someone from the other side of the room (especially a crowded one), as opposed to being right next to them.

Visual chat is a simple way to describe them, although they have gone by a variety of other names, such as multimedia chat, GMUKS (graphical multi-user konversations), and "habitats," a term coined by Randy Farmer, the first to invent them. They are something of a cross between a MOO and a traditional chat room.

As social environments, they are unique in that they are graphical. Rather than limiting users to text-only communications, as in most chat rooms, multimedia programs add a visual dimension that creates the illusion of movement, space, and physicality. It allows people to express their identity VISUALLY, rather than just through written words. The result is a whole new realm for self-expression and social interaction with subtleties and complexities not seen in text-only chat rooms. One excellent example of a multimedia environment is the client/server program called the "Palace." There are basically two visual components to this environment. The first is the backdrop or "room" in which people interact with each other. There are hundreds of Palace sites located across the internet, many with their own unique graphical themes for the collection of rooms that make up the site.

The oldest and one of the most populated sites is the "Main Mansion" which has consisted of approximately 30 rooms, including a bar, a game room, bedrooms, a study, a beach, a moor, and several surrealistic scenes, such as the orbit of an alien planet and an underground cave that looks like Hades. Users can move freely within and between the rooms. Like characters in comic strips, you communicate with others via typed text that appears in balloons that pop out from your head or body. Head? Body? This is the second visual feature of Palace: "avatars" or "props." Although these words often are used interchangeably, there is a slight distinction in the minds' of some users.

Avatars refer to pictures, drawings, or icons that users choose to represent themselves. Props are objects that users may add to their avatars or place into the Palace room or give to another person. No doubt, the avatar-driven lifestyle at the Palace sets up a self-selection process that determines which users decide to stay, and in some cases almost LIVE there.

People who love graphics - and especially those who love costumes and masks - often make Palace their home away from home. This anonymity is very different than that found in text-only chat environments, where only the name you have chosen publicizes your online identity. At the Palace, you also have a costume. Wearing a costume at a real-life party does indeed filter out many of the physical features of your identity. You are somewhat "anonymous." But the costume also symbolically highlights aspects of who you are. It amplifies one of your interests, some facet of your personality or lifestyle, or something you wish for. As we will see, the same is true of avatars in a multimedia community.

There are two types of Avatars. The first are the standard set of "smileys" that come with the Palace program . Inspired by ASCII smileys, these faces are available to all users. They come in a set that displays basic human emotions and behavioral signals - happy, sad, angry, winking, sleeping/bored, blushing, head-nodding, head-shaking. The user also can change the color of the face or add to it one or more props, such as hats, wigs, scarfs, devil horns, a halo, a glass of beer, a bicycle, etc. Because the faces and props can be mixed and matched, users have at their disposal an almost infinite array of combinations to express themselves. As such, the standard set of avs are designed very cleverly and offer a wide range of behavioral and emotional expression.

On one level, his perception is inaccurate because the standard smileys and props are quite clever and artistic. On another level, though, he quite accurately touches on a pervasive attitude among many Palace members. The standard avs are associated with newbies, whom some consider a lower class in the Palace population. They are fresh arrivals who do not understand the Palace culture and have not yet established their identity and status in it.

In the early days of Palace, new users who had not registered their software (i.e., paid for it) were restricted to using only the standard avs and props. They did not have the power create their OWN customized avatars, which is tantamount to establishing your own unique identity among a horde of avatars.

Even for users who have that power, failing to create and display your own personal avs is taken as a sign that you don't know how to. The bottom line: to wear a standard smiley is to look like a newbie. This leads to the second major category of avatars - those created by the members themselves. This is the key to what is perhaps the most fascinating aspect of the Palace. Visually, you can be anything you want. Only your graphics skills and imagination limit you. Early in the development of Palace, Bumgardner noticed that people highly preferred the custom faces over the more anonymous smileys.

In cyberspace, most people don't want to be totally anonymous. But they DO like control over how their identity is expressed. They like it a lot. Hang out at the Palace for any length of time and a seemingly endless parade of avs of all shapes, colors, and styles pass before your eyes. Visit the Palace everyday, and within a few weeks your prop file can blossom to 10, 20, 30 megs. What kinds of avatars do members create for themselves? Some are pictures or icons borrowed from internet archives, scanned from hardcopy, or taken from other digital sources.

Users might edit or combine these pictures according to their particular tastes. Some artistic members create props from scratch, although this is a fairly rare - and envious - skill. The technical and artistic ability one demonstrates through personal avs is an important source of self-esteem and social status.

Animal avatars are some of the most popular at the Palace. Some people come as their pets. Because animals symbolize certain traits or attributes in myth as well as popular culture (e.g., strength, loyalty, grace, independence, cunning, transcendence), the animal chosen for an avatar probably bears psychological significance to the person - perhaps representing some real aspect of his or her identity, or some characteristic admired by the person.

While younger users (adolescents) may be more inclined to don cartoon costumes, older members frequently use them as well. The psychological significance of the cartoon character probably affects the choice made by the user. People select characters with whom they identify or admire.

Some cartoon characters have very specific cultural significance and may even represent archetypal personality types (e.g., Bugs Bunny as the confident trickster; Aladdin's genie as the powerful but benevolent friend).

Celebrity avatars tend to follow trends in popular culture. And like items in popular culture, they may quickly become epidemic and then disappear. There may be a variety of motives behind the use of these avs. People may use them to express personality traits or social issues that are associated with the celebrity's image (sensuality, intelligence, power, corruption, rebellion, etc.).

The user may identify with, desire, or be poking fun at these attributes. They may hope to bolster their self-esteem and identity by establishing their connection to the celebrity. They may simply wish to display a knowledge of current events in pop culture. Everyone has a dark or "evil" side to his or her personality. The definition of "evil" varies from person to person, although usually it has something to do with malicious, aggressive fantasies and/or feelings of guilt.

While some members may wear an evil av as their facade for the evening (which may reflect their mood at the time), others may "flash" it as a momentary cue to others. Mess with wizards, for example, and they may flash their evil av as a warning that they're getting annoyed and may pin, gag, or kill you. Some people may use evil or aggressive avatars as a way (consciously or unconsciously) to alienate or "put off" other people. This might indicate their anxiety about intimacy and being vulnerable.

Most users do not use pictures of themselves as their primary avatars. People prefer the partial anonymity of expressing only limited aspects of their personality through imaginative props. Or they simply enjoy the creative fun of experimenting with new identities through their avs.

In more rare cases, members find the use of real face avs to be an uncomfortable, dissociative experience. "I have a picture of myself in the prop file but I really don't like to use it any longer than it takes for me to show it to a new friend," said River, a wizard. "It is a little disturbing to sit here at home and see myself speaking in cartoon balloons in a non-reality. Whew!!!!" When users do present pictures of their real faces, it may be a gesture of honesty and/or intimacy - a sign of friendship, or even romance. Showing one's real face av can be a very poignant experience.

Several members have described to me encounters when an intimate conversation culminated in their companion showing a picture of themselves. "That moment will stay with me for a long time to come," one member stated, "The value I placed on that particular moment was, friendship, trust, a sense of oneness." This same member described how there seems to be a pattern when an entire group feels compelled to use their real faces - what he called "face nite."

For that period of time, the intimacy and friendship level reaches a point where people wish to step out of their masks and out of their anonymity. They want be as "real" as possible. Some members develop an entire set of real face avatars. Idiosyncratic Avatars become strongly associated with a specific member - almost as if it is that person's trademark. In some cases the avatar may be highly unusual or creative. Sometimes it is quite simple. Yet its association to the particular user is so strong that others experience it uniquely as that person. While trading props is a common practice, the owner of an idiosyncratic av rarely gives it away. It would be like giving one's identity to someone else to use.

Conscientious members also don't "steal"an idiosyncratic av and use it as their own. They respect its integrity. If someone does steal and attempts to wear an idio av, they must be willing to put up with criticism by the friends of the owner. Positional Avatars are designed by the member to be placed into specific positions within the Palace rooms. The avatar may be created for a certain type of environment, or may be designed specifically for a single room or even a very specific spot within a room.

These avatars illustrate how the graphics of the Palace rooms are NOT simply "background" that have little impact on behavior. Some members are exquisitely sensitive to the graphical environment. Creating props to match and interact with the features of the room is a highly creative activity. Such avatars also are a sign of status. By displaying them, the member is demonstrating a sophisticated awareness of the Palace environment as well as technical know-how in prop editing.

Many, if not all, people have conscious or unconscious fantasies of omnipotence. These types of avs seem to be most common among male adolescent users. In some cases the power theme is benign. Sometimes not, which may be a variation of the "evil" avatar. Because competition invariably accompanies displays of power, members seem to vie with each other in creating the most "awesome" power av. This competition is probably more common among the adolescent users. Members who persistantly display power avs may be troubled by underlying feelings of helplessness and insecurity.

Offenders first are warned by wizards, prop-gagged (forced into the standard smiley), and, if necessary, disconnected from the server. Adapting to these house rules, some users create avatars of partially naked or scantily clothed figures. Mischievious members sometimes push the envelope by wearing avs that test the limits and ambiguities of the rules.

Supreme court justices have had a hard time defining what is pornographic, so the task has been no easier for the officials who run the EC sites. Even though the rules have become very specific about what body parts can and cannot be visible in an av, borderline cases always pop up. Female seductive avatars tend to be more common than male - although these female avs sometimes are "manned" by male users.

In fact, the general impression among members is that males are more likely to prop up as females, especially seductive females, than women dressing up as males. Members usually wear seductive avs to draw attention to themselves. This works very well. Male users, especially guests, quickly flock to a sexy female form. The owner may be interested in harmless flirting, or (less frequently) be advertising his or her availability for cybersex. Some people wearing seductive avs wish to be admired as an attractive, sexy individual, without necessarily being interested in flirting or cybersex. "I have some very sexy stuff given to me by friends (all men!)," said one female member. The competition in creating and displaying props is especially visible for seductive avatars. "It's interesting how some of the women at the Palace are getting into more and more elaborate sexy props.

Almost as if it's a contest," noted one member. "But then, some of the guys too are into 'comparing' props!" For men, the competition usually involves power props, rather than seductive ones. As one member stated, "the stag with the biggest rack thing, ey?" A seductive, sexy, or simply "attractive" avatar can have a powerful impact on other members. One member described how his prop of a cartoon animal didn't seem to be getting him much attention from females. Most of them wouldn't talk to him. Curious about whether he could alter this situation, he searched the net and found a picture of Brad Pitt which he turned into a prop.

If he happened to be wearing his cartoon prop and found that he was being ignored by a woman, he would move to another room, switch to Brad Pitt, and then return. Or he would switch to Pitt right in front of her. Nine times out of ten, he said, the woman would strike up a conversation with him even if he hadn't said a word. He even established a relationship with someone who eventually wanted to meet him face-to-face. "The pic got her attention," he concluded, "but in the end it was me that won her over."

The curious thing about this phenomenon is that members KNOW that people are not their avatars. Just because a prop is pretty to look at doesn't mean that the user is. Nevertheless, that seductive av has tremendous drawing power. Perhaps some people enjoy the illusion of interacting with (and hopefully winning over) an attractive person.

Perhaps, as many critics of contemporary culture claim, some people can't resist the temptation of superficial appearances, despite knowing better. Or perhaps some people are just curious, "Who *IS* that person using that sexy av?" Other members may display seductive avs simply to be admired for their skill in knowing how to create a seductive av.

Because the Palace often feels like an ongoing party where people are going to flirt, playfully compete, vie for attention, and strut their stuff, it is almost a prerequisite that every experienced member owns a seductive av of some type. "Getting away with something" is an intrinsic component of the Palace culture, as Bumgardner intended. Having at least one seductive av is a cultural must. Of course, there are exceptions to every rule. There is such a wide variety of avatars that it's impossible to neatly classify them all. The same is true of personality styles (which is the origin of the prop).

Odd/shocking avatars are unusual, strange, and sometimes downright bizarre pictures - perhaps revealing people who like to surprise, goof on, or even startle and outrage others. Truly bizarre pictures might make you wonder about the person's grasp of social appropriateness, or even their mental health. Such very unusual avs are most popular among adolescents - for whom extreme behavior is a way to express independence and individuality, and to test the limits.

Abstract avatars may be used by people who enjoy enjoy symmetry, are good (non-verbal) conceptual thinkers, and/or are inclined towards visual artistic endeavors.

Billboard avatars are announcements of some sort - political, philosophical, personal. They are used by those who have something to say and are not reluctant to display their thoughts in a commercialized type format.

Lifestyle avatars, which are quite common and varied, depict some significant aspect of a person's life - usually something to do with occupation, hobby, or personal habit. It may be a way to attract like-minded individuals.

Matching avatars are designed to accompany each other and indicate the connection or bonding between the pair of members. Considerable imaginative and technical skills may go into creating such avatars.

Clan avatars are worn by members of the same social group, some might even say "gang." These avs tend to be similar in basic design with slight variations to differentiate each one from the others. As such, each user announces his/her allegiance to the clan by adopting its collective visual appearance, while also maintaining some measure of individuality. It reminds me of the songs in some bird species.

The species identifies itself and its members by a basic template that serves as the collective song. Yet each individual bird adds a small unique variation to that template in order to signify its individuality. Clan avs are found almost exclusively among adolescents for whom belonging to a peer group - and conforming to its standards - is a developmental hallmark.

Animated avatars contain motion, such as an eye tearing, a bird flying, or a flag waving. By visually diplaying "behavior" they can express a wide and subtle range of psychological meaning. Tapping a finger, blinking one's eyes, banging one's head against the wall - there are infinite expressive possibilties. The motion usually is cyclical and repetitious, which - depending on the type of avatar - may convey a feeling of persistance, determination, mindlessness, or rhythmic peacefulness.

The default size for an avatar is about 40x40 pixels. That's about as big as your average computer icon. When members create their first avatar, it's usually this size. They're pretty happy with their accomplishment, until they realize that other people have much BIGGER props. It takes a bit more know-how to master the technique of building large avs.

Some members quickly get into a competitive feeling about whose is biggest - although the contest quickly ends at about 130x130 pixels, which is the technical limit. People may rely on prop size to gain attention and admiration. I've heard some members state that younger users, especially male adolescents, like large props, while women tend to wear smaller props in general than men. These hypotheses certainly are amenable to quantitative research. The general consensus among Palatians is that "bigger is not better." Big avs sometimes are considered impolite.

They take up a lot of precious space in a crowded room. They're a bit ostentatious. What matters more than size is the quality and style of your avatar. What matters is how you apply it to express yourself. "It's not the size of the prop, but how you use it." Like masks of any kind, avatars hide and reveal at the same time. Behind it, people can conceal some personal things about themselves, but the av also selectively amplifies other aspects of their personalities. It may reveal something about the member that otherwise is not immediately obvious - maybe not even obvious if you met that person in real life. Maybe not even obvious to the owners themselves. What users express in their props is not always a conscious choice. Sometimes it's unconscious.

Psychoanalysts would describe them as the constellation of "introjects," "internalizations," and "identifications" that comprises our intrapsychic world. On a daily basis, we juggle and shift between several rather distinct selves, sometimes without being fully aware that we are doing it. How, when, and why these different facets of our identity manifest themselves is the story of our lives.

In the multimedia communities of cyberspace, you can tell a lot about people by examining their collection of avatars and how they use them. Each avatar reflects a distinct aspect of the individual's personality and lifestyle - whether it is a mood, an interest pattern, a social role, one's attitudes and values, or a wished-for state of being.

Many people have persona that are seductive, powerful, formal/sophisticated, silly/playful, and artistic/poetic. These may represent universal or archetypal sectors of personality. Most people cherish at least one original avatar because it represents their birth identity in the Palace community. It's like an old, reliable friend. Almost everyone has a primary, all-purpose av that they use most of the time. It's the familiar home base, the image they feel most identified with and most comfortable wearing.

Active members are always creating new avs. One's collection is a balance of new and old persona, which reflects the balance between experimenting with new identities and holding onto the familiar, stable aspects of self. The size and variations in one's collection probably reflects the extent to which the person explores and experiments with personal identity.

Many people have a secret avatar that they use when they don't want others to know who they are, as well as an avatar they wear when they're with friends - an appearance that readily identifies them to their friends, often that birth or primary avatar. Curiously, many people have an av which they really like, but aren't sure why they like it. It is a conscious reminder of an unconscious aspect of identity.

On the simplest level, they act as conversation pieces. If you can think of nothing else to say, express an interest in someone's prop. Talking about props is one of the most common topics of discussion at the Palace. It greases the social interaction, especially with people whom you are meeting for the first time. It's like discussing the weather - except people are more personally invested in their props than they are in whether it's rainy or sunny. On a more complex level, changes in avatars convey changes in mood and intention, without the person necessarily having to speak.

Many members have told me that what they are wearing affects how they behave, as well as influences how others will react to them. Wear a female seductive prop, or even just a pleasant looking female prop, and you will draw attention, whether you want it or not. If you're annoyed with someone and want to drive them away, put on that skull prop.

Using the brush for painting on the background room image, some users adorn the walls with graffiti, obscene drawings or words. Other mischievous members smear black over an entire room, or they fill the entire room with props, leaving newbies totally confused as to where they are or what's happening. Freud would want to label them "anal expulsive personalities." By "spoofing" someone with the "msay" command, you can throw your voice to make the cartoon text balloon pop out of someone else's head. Or you can make the words hang in mid-air with no body attached. Sometimes, it's hard even for sympathetic people to resist the antics and game-playing.

Users who make rapid, multiple changes of their avatars - especially large avatars - may flood the server, resulting in lag that makes it difficult for people to talk. Usually the person is not aware that he is causing a problem. But sometimes people do it on purpose. It may be a hostile attempt to gain attention, or a jealous ploy to disrupt the socializing in the room. Wizards will warn, pin, or, if necessary, kill for this offense.

Members consider it a social faux pas to place your avatar on top of or too close to another person's prop. Unless the person is a friend who's in the mood to be close, it's an invasion of personal space. "Please get off me!" and You're sitting on me!" are two common complaints. Again, some naive users do this without knowing it is inappropriate, or the person may be lagging and unable to move. But some hostile people deliberately accost others by blocking them. Wizards will warn, pin, or, if necessary, kill for this offense.

Sleepers usually are users who have walked away from their computer. They are completely unresponsive when you talk to them. The social norm is to put up a "BRB" (be right back) sign to indicate your unavailability. Sleepers fail to do this. Although sleepers may be found in text-only chat environments, the experience of them is a bit different in multimedia chat. It feels much more eerie to SEE a person (avatar) in front of you, yet the person fails to react.

By reducing their avatars to a single pixel and their usernames to only one character, members may try to become "invisible" and secretly listen in on conversations. As a type of "lurker," they are acting on voyeuristic tendencies to avoid intimacy and gain a sense of advantage and power over others.

People enjoy so much the ability to express themselves visually through their avatars that it seems self-defeating to avoid this opportunity by hiding. Maybe that says something about eavesdropping.

There are very specific rules about what avatars are acceptable and what ones are not. Unacceptable avs fall into four general categories: overly sexual; overly violent and aggressive; hate avatars (evidence of prejudice concerning gender, homosexuality, religion, ethnicity, and nationality); avatars that promote illegal activities.

Although nudity in avatars is not permitted at the Palace, some people nevertheless flash their naughty pictures. They may be goofing around with their friends, advertising their availability for cybersex, attempting to shock other people (like the typical exhibitionist), or defiantly and perhaps masochistically begging to be killed by a wizard.

In private rooms, behind locked doors, people engaged in cybersex will display pornographic props to one another. Because this is not public behavior, it is not punished. The exhibitionist and rebellious psychology of the prop-dropper is probably similar to the flasher, with the exception that they attempt to dissociate themselves from their "dropping." In the mind of a Freudian, the scatological implications of this behavior are very signficant. Stealing someone's avatar and wearing it is a no-no. Stealing someone's avatar, wearing it, and also using that person's name (or a variation of it) is a real no-no. You are abducting their entire identity. Palace users are not limited to the standard background graphics. The creators of Palace intentionally designed it as a virtual world where users could express themselves by shaping the environment. At the Member's Only Palace site, people could create their own room using any background image of their choice.

Cooperative "set-dressing" in these rooms developed into a complex art form. These custom rooms became the focal points of friendship subgrouping and cliques. If you are ambitious, you can create your own Palace site on your own server, which gives you total control over the look of all the rooms.

Each new space -whether it is a single customized room or a whole new site - will reflect the personality of its creator and will draw people of similar temperament. In order to attract people to a site, attempts are made to make the new environments as psychologically appealing to as many users as possible. Some multimedia worlds are 3D. Usually the view also is first person, so you live "inside" your avatar, looking out into the world much as you do in real life, without seeing your own avatar (body). You have to move through the graphical space in order to see other avatars and objects that may be hidden from view.

3D advocates like the feeling of "immersion" that such worlds create. You feel like you are really there, in the environment. Some advocates claim that this 3D living creates heightened emotional reactions because it mimics the sensory experience of the real world. Things come towards you, or withdraw. You don't know what's around the next corner. There is an element not only of realism, but even suspense. The problem with a 3D graphical experience is that it requires a lot of computing power and speed that cannot (yet) be handled too well by internet band width.

The result may be a slow, jerky experience that feels disjointed, unreal, and that jars the brain. Even under ideal conditions, some people don't feel comfortable with the "head in a box" or "tunnel vision" view of 3D, first-person worlds. Lacking peripheral vision, some people feel closed in, claustrophobic. The Palace is a 2D, third person experience. You look down onto the scene that includes your avatar and everyone else's avatar. Some people like this transcendent and somewhat paradoxical experience of being above but also in the scene. You get to see yourself, the way other people do.

You move yourself about in the environment and then sit back to see what happens. Your perspective of the scene and what people are saying may seem more "objective." You may feel more free. There may even be a magical, mystical sensation to witnessing oneself within the world.

Many mystical traditions emphasize the transcendent awareness that is the "observing self." The 2D worlds may address an archetypic need for such transcendence. This observing awareness is paradoxical. It simultaneously exists within the world and transcends it - a paradox that is manifested in the 2D virtual setting. Some Palace members take delight in the objective/

subjective fluidity of being in the scene and above it, at the same time. The avatar appears as an independent entity that actually is a manifestation of your personality and will. Separate but connected. It can be like an artistic creation, a self portrait. It's an "out there" expression of what's inside. It's possible that when first person, 3D worlds becomes more sophisticated with the advance of technology, people will prefer them. On the other hand, some people may always favor third person, 2D environments. These differences in preference may reflect differences in cognitive and personality style.

Avatar psychotherapy

In cyberspace, the term "avatar" is used to describe one's personal manifestation in a virtual world. It may be the visual image you create for yourself, as well as the psychological character or persona you present to others. The term comes from the Hindu religion in which it refers to the various forms that gods chose to manifest themselves in the human realm. Using computer-generated virtual environments, "avatar psychotherapy" could be the exploration of the client's healthy and problematic identities by exploring the manifestation of those identities within imaginary scenarios.

Using psychoanalytic terms, we would say that the client teases out, amplifies, explores, and therapeutically develops the various "representations," "identifications," and "internalizations" that make up their intrapsychic world, that are the nuts and bolts of their overall sense of self. The techniques of avatar psychotherapy could draw on a variety of psychotherapeutic approaches:

— exploring childhood memories in order to shape a more healthy life narrative

— the interpretation, reworking, and mastery of dreams, daydreams, and fantasy by reenacting them

— realistic and imaginary role playing of current life situations involving family, friends, and peers, including the reversal of roles

— creating dramatic "plays" to explore clients' identities as reflected in the mythology of their favorite literature and movies

— working with transference and countertransference reactions via imaginary scenarios

— developing and "installing" new, more adaptive facets of self

Therapists can participate in, direct, or simply observe these virtual enactments. When they participate, the may work with transference/countertransference dynamics as manifested in the avatars they chose or that are chosen for them by their clients. It's even possible that the client and therapist could create automated software characters to participate in the scenes. The basic assumption of avatar psychotherapy is that all of the personae created in the virtual scenario are the various manifestations of the client's psyche.

Those avatars concretize the complex constellations of memories, fears, wishes, idealizations, and expectations that comprise the client's sense of self. Those avatars give clients the opportunity to amplify, explore, modify, and develop those sectors of self. However, giving life to those avatars is not the ultimate goal of the therapy. Immersion in the virtual field could become a game with no conclusion, a distraction from or even an active avoidance of the final goal that is assimilation of the personae into a unified, cohesive self where the various facets of self are joined together seamlessly. The ultimate goal is carrying the newly integrated self forward from the virtual world into the in-person world.

Identity Management

The "asynchronous" communication of e-mail allows members to participate in the ongoing virtual meeting at their own convenience and at their own pace. Some of the unique features of asynchronous, typed-text communication also may alter the interpersonal dynamics of the group, which offers the opportunity to better understand and improve how the group functions. A group as well may use "message board" formats to meet online. When creating an e-mail list, obviously it's important to make sure that everyone has an e-mail account. Extending the group into cyberspace when some people don't use e-mail is a bad idea. It will encourage subgrouping, miscommunication, and perhaps conflict.

Doing so may even be a symptom of preexisting conflict and an acting out of hostility against subgroups or individual scapegoats. It's equally important to assess how much people know about using e-mail in general and an e-mail list in particular. Some study says that they use e-mail "a lot" (since it's fashionable) when in reality they may only be casual users who barely understand the basics. As a result, setting up the list may be a slow, sometimes frustrating process.

On the positive side, that process can serve as an opportunity for people to familiarize themselves with e-mail lists before the actual online meeting begins. It's a good idea to have a facilitator or "host" for the list - someone who can set up the list and has some technical understanding of how lists work, as well as some experience in the customs and social dynamics of a list.

E-mail can be a fascinating, subtle tool for communicating - different, in many respects, from talking. Some even consider it an art form. It might be a good idea to recommend some reading about e-mail to the group.

There are many practical uses for the list. On the most basic level, it can be used for announcements, scheduling in-person meetings, and generally serve as a substitute for hardcopy memos. However, limiting the list to this function alone - a kind of "memo mentality" - falls short of utilizing its full potential.

Memo mentality ignores how the list can be a group MEETING with many other possible applications. It can be used in a collaborative effort to edit, revise, and approve a document. The group can prepare for and afterwards discuss an in-person meeting. Under ideal conditions, the list can be an effective alternative for in-person meetings by encouraging open discussions of issues and decision-making.

Extending the group into cyberspace can have a double-edged effect. On the one hand, the exchange of messages via the list may draw out or highlight the preexisting interpersonal dynamics of the group.

Typed text has a way of making things stand out in bold relief, sometimes "demonstrating the obvious" in a very eye-catching, rubbing-one's-nose-in-it fashion. On the other hand, an online meeting also may alter the dynamics of the group because it entails a change in the boundaries of time, place, and communication style. For example:

— *Pacing*: Because e-mail involves asynchronous communication, people can speak to the group whenever they want and as frequently as they want. Avid e-mail users may have more input into the discussion than casual or inexperienced users, possibly altering in a dramatic way the usual in-person pattern of participation.

— *Writing, not talking*: Typed-text usually forces people to be more concise and to-the-point, resulting in a filtering out of extraneous conversation that typically pads a face-to-face meeting. The e-mail discussion may feel more efficient to some people, or blunt to others. Some members may be frustrated by the tedium of having to type everything they want to say, feeling a f2f dialogue is easier and more thorough. Because e-mail involves writing and not speaking, those with superior writing skills will have a communicative advantage. They may not be the same people who have the verbal advantage in an in-person meeting. Those who are ignored, interrupted, or talked-over during a f2f meeting may have a stronger voice in cyberspace. Those who dominate an in-person meeting may lose some of their influence online.

— *Disinhibition:* People can' t see you or hear your voice in an e-mail discussion, which results in a "masking" effect and psychological disinhibition. People may be more willing to express thoughts and feelings that they otherwise would keep to themselves during an in-person meeting. As a result, new ideas may pop up. Surprising opinions are expressed. Conflicts that were previously warded off now rise to the surface. In an ideal situation, this disinhibiting effect can jostle a group into new and productive lines of discussion. In unfortunate circumstances, the uncovering of hidden problems may destabilize the group, reducing it's ability to communicate and work effectively. In-person meetings will be needed to remedy that situation.

— *Permanent Record:* Any member easily can save all the group's message to an archive. Everything that was said online can be preserved indefinitely. This permanent record can come in handy in reviewing who said what and when, how decisions were made, and for attaining a bird' s eye view of the course of a discussion. Without visual and verbal cues, it's sometimes easy to misread the meaning or emotion within someone's message - particularly if you happen to be having a bad day. Going back to read a message at a later date can help you see it in a fresh light, with a new mental set and a bit more objectivity.

Because e-mail meetings are very different than being in-person, some people may show resistance to participating. That resistance may manifest itself in several ways: infrequent messages sent to the list; brief or unsubstantial discussions; frequent pleas for in-person meetings; habitual private (backchannel) e-mail or private in-person discussions (rather than bringing issues to the list); critical comments about using a list; and other assorted direct and indirect expressions of hostility.

In rare circumstances some people may staunchly refuse to participate, which can create considerable uneasiness and distrust in the group. There are a variety of possible reasons for resistance:

— Being unfamiliar or uncomfortable with using computers, e-mail, or e-mail lists. Some people may need time and experience to adapt; a little bit of training could be helpful.

— A fear of displaying one's writing abilities. It's very helpful to establish a norm where all writing styles are accepted - including being casual and making errors in spelling and grammar.

— A fear of "going public." People may worry that someone might save their messages and later use them as "ammunition" against them. This anxiety may coincide with the worry that people outside the group may have access to the list or may be given e-mail by a group member. Such concerns may be a low-level symptom of preexisting distrust within the group. From the get-go, emphasizing the importance of list confidentiality can help alleviate some of these worries.

— Angry withdrawal, indifference. These barriers are most likely a symptom of preexisting interpersonal dynamics within the group. The disinhibiting effect of e-mail communication may help people discuss and resolve these issues, but don't count on it.

In particular, the disinhibiting effect of e-mail could lead people to state things that they refrain from bringing to the in-person meeting. Sometimes the list discussions may even evolve into a kind of "subconscious" voicing of issues that are actively avoided in-person. It is possible to work through these issues on the list, allowing the beneficial effects to seep into the f2f meetings without openly discussing them in those meetings. However, the best approach is to head off the dissociation before it becomes too deeply embedded.

Under ideal conditions, in-person and e-mail discussions will complement and enrich each other. The group will come to recognize the pros and cons of each realm. It will learn to maximize the advantages and minimize the disadvantages of each. The degree of success is the degree to which the group can effectively integrate the two.

When the group moves fluidly from one realm to the other, when both realms give expression to all important group functions - brainstorming, decision-making, problem-solving, socializing, conflict resolution - then the group has fully succeeded in extending itself into cyberspace.

The username you choose, the details you do or don't indicate about yourself, the information presented on your personal web page, the persona or avatar you assume in an online community - all are important aspects of how people manage their identity in cyberspace. Identity is a very complex aspect of human nature. Here are five interlocking factors that are useful in navigating that maze of how people manage who they are in cyberspace:

Cyberspace offers a niche for each of these specific facets of selfhood. Some people even talk about how we can "deconstruct" ourselves online. Online communication tools even give you the choice about whether you want people to see how you look or hear your voice. The desire to remain anonymous reflects the need to eliminate those critical features of your identity that you do NOT want to display in that particular environment or group. The desire to lurk - to hide completely - indicates the person's need to split off his entire personal identity from his observing of those around him: he wants to look, but not be seen. Compartmentalizing or dissociating one's various online identities like this can be an efficient, focused way to manage the multiplicities of selfhood.

Cyberspace living is yet another manifestation of this shifting, juggling maneuver. It gives people the opportunity to focus on and develop a particular aspect of who they are. It may even give people the chance to express and explore facets of their identity that they do not express in their face-to-face world. Everyone in Jim's in-person world may not know that he is a romantic medieval knight in an online role-playing game. However, the importance of integrating the assorted components of selfhood should not be ignored.

Most of the time we will criticize a person's need to hurt other people and applaud compassion. But it's not necessary to present universal truisms about good and bad. Subjectively, a person can feel shame, guilt, fear, anxiety, or hatred about some aspect of their identity, while accepting and appreciating other aspects. People also strive to attain new, idealized ways of being. Those who act out in cyberspace - who are in some way hurting or violating the rights of others, or hurting themselves - are usually discharging some negatively charged aspect of their psyche. This purely cathartic act often goes no where. An insecure, passive-aggressive person gets stuck in an endless stream of online arguments. Others may use cyberspace as a opportunity to exercise their positive characteristics, or to develop new ones in a process of "self-actualization."

Online romances, even those involving a clearly recognized element of fantasy, can be growth-promoting. In some cases people may express a negative trait in an attempt to work through it. They are trying to transform the negative feature of their identity into a positive one, or perhaps change their attitude about that feature. A gay person who learns to accept his homosexuality as a result of participation in an online support group has changed the valence from negative to positive.

The various environments and styles of communication on the internet serve as a flexible testing ground for exploring those intertwining pluses and minuses. In back-channel e-mail, a fellow lurker in a listserv for professionals may help the quiet person learn the value of being silent in some situations. In a chat room, that same quiet person comes to realize the freedom and delight of spontaneously opening up, and how that leads to friendships.

In some online groups - for example, professional e-mail lists - you are expected to present yourself as you truly are. You don't pretend to be someone other than your true identity. Other groups in cyberspace encourage or even require that you assume an imaginary persona, as in the fantasy worlds of MOOs, MUDs, and other game environments. In multimedia chat communities, you have no choice but to wear an imaginative looking avatar to represent yourself.

Many other environments fall somewhere in between reality and fantasy. You could get away with pretending to be someone very different than who you are, or you could alter just a few features - like your name, occupation, or physical appearance - while retaining your other true characteristics. No one will know, especially in text-only environments. In fact, you don't know for sure if other people are altering their identities, or how many people are altering their identities. This power to alter oneself often interlocks with dissociation and valence. Hidden positive and negative parts of oneself may seek expression in an imaginary identity that comes to life online.

Similarly, in cyberspace, people choose a specific communication channel to express themselves. There are a variety of possibilities and combinations of possibilities, each choice giving rise to specific attributes of identity. People who rely on text communication prefer the semantics of language and perhaps also the linear, composed, rational, analytic dimensions of self that surface via written discourse. They may be the "verbalizers" that have been described in the cognitive psychology literature - as opposed to "visualizers" who may enjoy the more symbolic, imagistic, and holistic reasoning that is expressed via the creation of avatars and web graphics. Some people prefer synchronous communication - like chat - which reflects the spontaneous, free-form, witty, and temporally "present" self. Others are drawn to the more thoughtful, reflective, and measured style of asynchronous communication, as in message boards and e-mail.

There are personalities that want to show and not receive too much by using web cams or creating web pages; to receive and not show too much by lurking or web browsing; and still others who want to dive into highly interactive social environments where both showing and receiving thrive. The media chosen can intimately interlock with the degree of identity integration and dissociation, and with the extent to which a person presents a real or imaginary self.

7

Counselling: Theory and Practice

Every living being in existence, be it a plant, an animal or a human being, is born with a potential, and has the longing, the urge, the drive to fulfill its potential, to live itself. The longing and the urge of every living being is, to discover these intrinsic qualities that want to be lived and shared in existence. The plant kingdom and the animal kingdom are living their essence already. The program is inbuilt. A dog is born a dog, lives as a dog, and dies as a dog. He is spontaneous in that expression of life. He does not think whether he should be anything else than a dog. The same is happening with a rose, or a lotus or any other kind of flower or plant. It grows and becomes that which it is meant to become. And in that growing it continues to live in oneness. No animal or plant ever experiences separation. The human being seems to be different. The human being is born with a potential, and then it is up to him or her to nourish that potential, to develop it, to realize the essence, or to forget it. The whole focus aligns itself with the demands of surroundings. Very seldom somebody tells us: "Be!" Through the conditioning of becoming suffer many experiences of separation, and alienate ourselves more and more from who are already. This alienation is the main cause of suffering in the world. Counselling can initiate a healing process for this suffering.

What it call healing in this time is not just healing of the physical body, it is also healing of many misunderstandings of the mind, of the past, that has created wounds. These wounds are carried in the aura, the energy field surrounding and pervading each person. These wounds can have their origin in this life, or in past lives. It seems that suffering pattern repeat themselves. A family, the suffering pattern gets inherited, gets transferred from grandparents to parents to children to grand children and so on. The habits, the behavior patterns, difficulties in life, the mindsets seem to be very similar. This is what could call Karma. Underneath that conditioning is waiting to be discovered the true nature of each human being.

Counselling is using the psychological insights of this time to help the client to move from the personality to the individuality. It is using the expressions of this body—mind to move beyond the body—mind. It is using language, communication, emotions, sentiments, physical sensations, sensory experiences, be they visual, auditory, kinesthetic, olfactory or gustatory, as a key to unlock the door of the inner treasures. A great discovery is possible to find what is actually behind all these sensory experiences. As the counsellor is in contact with his/her own potential, he/she creates an energy field in which the client can resonate and uncover his/her own potential. From that essence the client can discover the very specific elements and traits of their individuality. He/she can discover the flower that is there already, the flower that he/she is meant to be in this life. The client can understand and stop trying to be someone else. Just like a rose does not try to become a lotus, but enjoys being a rose, the client can uncover and rejoice in what he/she is already. As the essence is not in any way affected by personality and by the change of personality, counselling can help the client to accept, embrace, enjoy anything that this lifestream in this body-mind is expressing.

Most of the suffering in life happens, because feel split, separate and disconnected from source. Suffering happened because it feel pushed or pulled, feel under pressure of some outside forces, where it become slaves and victims of outer circumstances, rather than masters. This victimization and suffering is a misunderstanding. It is due to energy moving out trying to identify with objects outside.

Counselling helps the client to turn the energy around and discover who is there already. The strange phenomenon is, that whatever is being experienced in the moment, be it sadness, anger, desperateness, hopelessness or joy, happiness and love, all become a door to discover ones individuality. As any emotion or state is experienced totally without rejection, without trying to make it different, without hope of any change, the very experience becomes pleasant. In the willingness to fully experience that which is in this moment, the negative or painful happening transforms into joy. Now why is that? It is because the pain of any negative experience lies in the interpretation that things should be different.

The moment one becomes one with the experience, the byproduct is joy, love, relaxation into who one is. The astonishing phenomenon is that in becoming one with any emotion, sentiment, or experience, the negative aspect simply disappears. The mysterious discovery is, that anything that was always desired outside, like happiness, bliss, peace, love and freedom, can be rediscovered as being already present inside. Everything that a human being is looking for, is running after, like running after money, a bigger house, a bigger car, a more interesting love partner, is basically an attempt to fulfill this need for happiness, bliss, peace, love and freedom. Every desire tries to fulfill a basic need of returning back to oneness. But once, willing to turn in and look what is there, never moved from this oneness. In that recognition a relaxation can happen, and the energy that is represented in the color and may have been rejected, can be welcomed home. In that very welcome, a healing happens, because oneness happens. The byproduct of that oneness is joy, love and bliss and peace.

In counselling, when a facilitator supports the client to simply see and recognize what is, without any hope of being different, the same phenomenon of becoming one is evoked. As the counsellor supports the client to fully experience what is, the energy that was trapped in fighting what is, becomes available. Since everything that fighting in ourselves is also reflected in the outer world, fight the same things outside of ourselves also. The moment, stop fighting ourselves and experience that which is in its totality, discover the love and acceptance inside. The whole gestalt changes, the whole way of seeing the world changes.

While schools of therapy have argued that different theories produce differing and nonequivalent outcomes, this position has been challenged on numerous occasions. Fiedler first observed that therapists of differing orientations were very similar in their views of the "ideal therapy." Sundland and Barker reported that more experienced therapists tended to be more similar, regardless of their theoretical orientation. In their extensive review of the subject, Gelso and Carter stated that "most clients will profit about equally from the different therapies". They go on to suggest that the effect of process and relationship do differ among therapies and that some clients may do better with one approach than with another, based upon these two factors. Stiles, Shapiro and Elliott argued that

a) common features shared by all psychotherapies underlie or override differences in therapists' verbal techniques and

b) these common features are responsible for the general equivalence in effectiveness.

Process and relationship, then, may be as relevant as theoretical conceptualization of the problem. How do counselors choose a particular counseling theory? Among the alternatives are:

a) the orientation of one's initial training program;

b) one's own philosophy or life view; and/or

c) one's therapeutic experience and evolving therapeutic patterns.

Counselors use theory to explain or conceptualize client problems. In addition, they may use theory to dictate what they do in the counseling process. Theory, whether in pure form or adapted by the individual counselor, can be used to define the nature of the relationship between the counselor and client, to conceptualize the nature of the presenting problem(s), and to define the resulting counseling goals or desired outcomes. While some counselors would also say that theory dictates the types of interventions used in counseling, increasingly the argument is being made that interventions are related more to goals and outcomes than to theoretical conceptualization.

If one examines theoretical integrity today, based upon what counselors faithful to that theory do with clients, a convergence of theories appears to be occurring. Humanistic theories have been infiltrated by some classical behavioral interventions. Behavioral approaches acknowledge the legitimacy of feelings and the appropriateness of affect change.

Cognitive approaches are frequently referred to as "cognitive- behavioral." Systemic approaches utilize many interventions that one can only describe as cognitive in nature. Thus, distinctions between theories are not as clearly defined as one might think, and intervention selection may be only indirectly related, and certainly not dictated by theoretical orientation.

How does the counselor who is working within a consistent theory, be it a textbook theory or a personal theory, choose the interventions to use with a particular client? Logic would hold that the counselor's choice of therapeutic interventions would derive from the conceptualization of the problem(s), thus from the counselor's theory. But the theoretical world of counseling and change isn't quite that neat. From an integrative perspective, that choice is made by relating the intervention directly to the nature or character of the problem being addressed. On the other hand, most client problems are typically multi-dimensional. A problem with negative self-talk ("I'm constantly telling myself I'm no good") is not only cognitive, but would also reflect an affective dimension ("I feel lousy about myself"), a behavioral dimension ("I choose to stay home and watch a lot of TV"), and a systemic dimension ("When I do go out, I avoid contact with others because they find me strange, or I behave strangely and others react to me accordingly").

Even though most problems are multi-dimensional, intervention at any of those dimensions affects the other dimensions, i.e., systemic change may influence affective and/or behavioral dimensions. How, then, does one plan a strategy for counseling interventions if multiple choices exist and "all roads lead to Rome?" A general guideline is that clients are most receptive when the choice of strategy matches their experiencing of the problem. If one examines the variety of counseling interventions that have been described in the professional literature, they tend to fall into four broad categories:

— interventions that produce affective change;

— interventions that produce cognitive change;

— interventions that produce behavioral change; and

— interventions that produce social system change.

In addition, within each of these four categories, one can further differentiate among theories in terms of the counselor skill required to implement the intervention and the level of change produced by the intervention.

Affective interventions: The primary goals of affective interventions are:

(a) to help clients express feelings or feeling states;

(b) to identify or discriminate between feelings or feeling states; or

(c) to alter or accept feelings or feeling states.

Some clients have never learned to identify and/or express their feelings. At a somewhat more complicated level, some clients come to counseling flooded with emotional reactions, overloaded by their awareness of and sensitivity to feelings. Their protective response may be to tune out the emotions, to be confused or disoriented. Interventions that may be used to unblock, bridge resistance, or develop expressive skills include teaching the client what a feeling is, affect focusing techniques, role reversal, the alter ego exercise, the empty chair, and so forth.

Cognitive interventions: The primary goal of cognitive interventions is to "reduce emotional distress and corresponding maladaptive behavior patterns by altering or correcting errors in thoughts, perceptions and beliefs. Cognitive interventions stress the importance of self-control. Clients are viewed as the direct agents of their own changes, rather than as helpless victims of external events and forces. Illustrations of cognitive interventions include Ellis's A-B-C-D-E analysis, thought suppression, thought postponement, therapeutic paradox, and cognitive restructuring

Behavioral interventions: The overall goal of behavioral interventions is to help clients develop adaptive and supportive behaviors to multifaceted situations. Developing adaptive behavior often means helping the client weaken or eliminate behaviors that work against the desired outcome, e.g. eating snacks when you wish to lose weight. A significant part of this process involves teaching the client. Illustrative interventions include live modeling, symbolic modeling, covert modeling, role play and rehearsal, relaxation training, systematic desensitization, self-contracting and self-monitoring.

Systemic interventions: Systemic interventions are premised upon the assumption that one's environment elicits and supports the individual's dysfunctional cognitive, behavioral and affective responses. The go goal of systemic interventions is to change the individual's social environment or system, thus changing the patterns of interrelationship that elicited or supported these responses. Examples of systemic interventions (in addition to those in the preceding categories that also produce system change) include: altering communication patterns through role play and renegotiation, altering family (or system) structure by reconstructing boundaries, the family genogram, family sculpture, and providing directives for change. Children pose special issues in the selection of counseling interventions for several reasons. They have little power or control over their environment, or may lack the cognitive or affective development to respond to some interventions. For this reason, a systemic view which involves significant adults in their world often is the most effective approach to intervention selection.

Client-Centered Therapy

Client-Centered Therapy (CCT) was developed by Carl Rogers in the 40's and 50's. It is a non-directive approach to therapy, "directive" meaning any therapist behavior that deliberately steers the client in some way. The client-centered therapy, did not intend to found a school of psychotherapy with a set practice.

This theory could be used as a basis for further research on psychotherapy, and also this theory was an approximation to the truth about therapy. He did not want client-centered therapy to be "frozen" but, rather, to be a working hypothesis, a stimulus to further inquiry about the therapy process. Rogers always has been committed to promoting openness, growth and change in the pursuit of truth about therapeutic process. He has always encouraged and supported research projects and theorizing by others.

The theory in terms of attitudinal conditions, not techniques, fostered openness to different ideas about therapeutic practice. This theory left it up to the practitioner to choose which behaviors or techniques could be used to communicate the therapeutic attitudinal conditions to the client. This development in client-centered theory opened the way for practitioners from many different therapeutic schools to incorporate the basic premise and thypothesesees of attitudinal conditions into their own therapy without abandoning their original orientations. It also set the stage for the creation of a variety of new therapeutic methods based on the fundamental principles of client-centered theory.

There are many different therapy practices, and more therapies continually developing, which share the basic theory of client-centered therapy. This situation, of many evolving therapies which are often referred to as client-centered therapies, is confusing to students and confusing when one wishes to discuss differences in therapy practice with colleagues. It would clarify this situation to classify a therapy practice as a person-centered therapy whenever a therapist is trying to work from the basic hypotheses: the inherent growth principle and the major attitudinal conditions for constructive change.

There are many evolving person-centered therapies and the practice of client-centered therapy is one of those.

Client-centered therapy can be described in terms of the theory it shares with the other person-centered therapies and by its distinctive features.

The client-centered therapy is a distinctive and important practice and that it can be defined as a practice and its parameters clarified. Its evolution would be conceived within certain limits. Functioning therapeutically outside those limits would be considered, perhaps, a new and other person-centered therapy. Or someone might, also, be developing a practice outside the defined limits of the person-centered therapies. Certainly many of those already exist. The point is, this system of classification gets around the problem of freezing client-centered therapy but also permits distinctions in respect to the practices of therapy that are out there in the reality of therapeutic work.

The differences distinguishable among person-centered therapies probably make substantial differences in the experience of therapy by both client and therapist and make differences in what is observable on tapes and films and, probably, make differences in the effects of the therapy on the lives of its clients. We can study and understand these different effects much better if we distinguish practices.

The clarification and definition of client-centered therapy as distinguishable from other person-centered therapy practices can contribute to the presentation and evolution of this unique and extremely effective way of working with clients. For some time, that client-centered therapy has been misunderstood, underestimated and underused, in part, because of its ambiguities as a practice and because of its confusion with other person-centered therapeutic practices.

The central hypothesis of this approach can be briefly stated. It is that the individual has within him or her self vast resources for selfunderstanding, for altering her or his selfconcept, attitudes, and self-directed behavior--and that these resources can be tapped if only a definable climate of facilitative psychological attitudes can be provided. There are three conditions which constitute this growth-promoting climate, whether we are speaking of the relationship between therapist and client, parent and child, leader and group, teacher and student, or administrator and staff.

The conditions apply, in fact, in any situation in which the development of the person is a goal. The beliefs and hypotheses that are central to the person-centered approach are the following:

— Belief that human nature is basically constructive.

— Belief that human nature is basically social.

— Belief that self-regard is a basic human need and that self-regard, autonomy and individual sensitivity are to be protected in helping relationships.

— Belief that persons are basically motivated to perceive realistically and to pursue the truth of situations.

— Belief that perceptions are a major determinant of personal experience and behavior and, thus, to understand a person one must attempt to understand them empathically.

— Belief that the individual person is the basic unit and that the individual should be addressed, in situations intended to foster growth.

— Belief in the concept of the whole person.

— Belief that persons are realizing and protecting themselves as best they can at any given time and under the internal and external circumstances that exist at that time.

— Belief in abdication of the pursuit of control or authority over other persons and, instead, a commitment to strive to share power and control.

The basic hypothesis, the theory of therapy and the additional beliefs stated above describe the person-centered approach. These beliefs are usually shared by the people practicing the various person-centered therapies including client-centered therapy. These shared elements do not, however, distinguish client-centered therapy from the other person-centered therapies.

The salient form of client-centered therapy is the empathic understanding response process. The empathic understanding response process involves the therapist maintaining, with consistency and constancy the therapeutic attitudes in his/her experience and expressing him/herself to the client through empathic understanding responses. Empathic understanding responses are the observable responses which communicate empathic understanding to the client. They are responses intended to express and check the therapist's empathic understanding experience of the client.

In a given empathic understanding response process between therapist and client many different types of empathic understanding responses may be involved. Examples of common types oempathic understandingng responses are the following: literal responses; restatements; summaries; statements which point toward the felt experience of the client but do not name or describe the experience; interpretive or inferential guesses concerning what the client is attempting to express; metaphors; questions that strive to express understandings of ambiguious experience of the client; gestures of the therapist's face, hands, body; vocal gestures, etc.

The empathic understanding response process can appear to be very different from therapist to therapist, and between therapies with different clients by the same therapist, depending upon the types of responses which are used by the therapist.

The particular way the therapist expresses empathic understanding to the particular client does not matter, from the point of view of remaining within the client-centered framework, however, as long as the way communicates to the client the therapist's intention to understand and as long as the client feels understood by the therapist. Client-centered therapy is also distinguishable by the extreme emphasis the practice places on the non-directiveness of the therapist.

In client-centered therapy the therapist is intensely mindful to respect and protect the autonomy and self-direction of the client. The client is viewed as the expert about himself and the therapist views himself as expert only in maintaining the attitudinal conditions in the relationship with the client, not as an expert on the client. The therapeutic relationship is inherently an unequal relation in which the client is self-defined as vulnerable and in need of help and the therapist is self-defined as one who can help.

An element in the person/client-centered perspective is the belief that unequal relationships are naturally, to some extent, hurtful or harmful to the persons involved in them. Unequal relationships are sometimes necessary, for example the physician and patient or the teacher and student, because they offer desired benefits.

But the person/client-centered perspective fosters the abdication of the pursuit of power and would argue for minimizing the hurt or harm by sharing the authority as much as possible. The client-centered therapist is particularly mindful of the harmful potential side-effect of the unequal therapeutic relation and tries to share his authority as much as possible.

This awareness and effort influences all of his actions in relations to the client. Basically, the client centered therapist's view on this matter is - the authority for the client's experience is the client and the way the client uses the relationship is always left up to the client. This non-directive attitude has a significant influence on the way therapy is conducted, influencing what is done and what is not done. For example, the client-centered therapist answers client's questions.

Obviously, if the therapist decides what questions it is appropriate to answer, or takes the view that certain questions are expression of a client's avoidance of something and the therapist interprets this to help the client get on the right track, or if the therapist takes the view that the client's question is an aspect of seeking dependence on the therapist and the therapist raises this interpretation, then the therapist is acting in ways that direct the client's process.

From a client-centered viewpoint, the idea that the therapist should evaluate the desirability for the client of having his questions answered is paternalistic and an exercise of authority over the client. A client-centered therapist remains free to not answer a question asked by the client. But the reason for not answering would be explained to be a personal one - the therapist feels he does not know enough, or he feels uncomfortable in divulging the particular information, etc. - not as something that is good for the client.

There are many, many implications for the way therapy is practiced when the client-centered therapist is acting from this strongly felt attitude that the client is his own best expert and that the therapist maintain non-directiveness. The non-directive character of client-centered therapy is not only for the purpose of protecting the client's autonomy and to enhance the client's self-direction. Client-centered therapy is a fundamentally non-directive therapy because being so contributes to the distinctive therapeutic quality of the relationship between therapist and client.

This quality involves the fostering in the client of a combination of feelings - of freedom, of a positive sense of self, and of empowerment The therapist provides the basic therapeutic attitudes of congruence, acceptance and empathy. This whole way of being produces a unique experience of an authority consistently behaving in a non-authoritative manner. This abdication of the usual forms of authority carries meaning to most clients. It conveys that they are not being evaluated, not being supervised and not being controlled.

That they are not being treated in these usual ways by an authority also carries the meaning that they are being treated with respect, are being trusted, and are free, to a great extent, in the relationship. As a consequence the relationship takes on the qualities referred to above, of freedom, of enhancement of the client's sense of self and sense of personal power. Client-centered therapy is a practice in which the hypothesis of the inherent growth principle is put into action. It is also a therapy wherein the theory of therapeutic attitudes as conditions for growth is taken as the basis for functioning with the client.

It is also a therapy practice that is distinguishable by the form that it usually takes- the empathic understanding response process. It is also a therapy which emphasizes non-directiveness and wherein this principle is maximized in the relation with the client. All together, these features distinguish client-centered therapy from other extant and possible person-centered therapies.

Client-centered therapy is not the technique of "reflection of feeling" or making "empathic understanding responses". It may be useful to look at the reflection or empathic understanding responses from the point of view of technique but this should be understood as an abstraction and contrary to the spirit of their actual production. Only if empathic understanding responses, are used as expression of the therapist's genuine attitudes of congruence, acceptance and empathic understanding are they an expression of client-centered therapy. Client-centered therapy is not identical with the empathic understanding response process. This is so even though the process is the salient form of interaction in relationship of client and therapist and even though this form is one of the identifying features of client-centered therapy.

Empathic understanding response process (EURP) is not identical with the total therapy for three main reasons. First, the functions of the therapist are more than the EURP. The therapist's adaptation to the individual client as a person in a concrete relationship situation requires the application of the hypothesis and the therapeutic conditions in many ways, including the set up of the therapy, the adjustments in language for the sake of mutual understanding, and the social aspects of the therapy situation. Second, the EURP is an optimal process, as a means to express empathic understanding and express the other therapeutic attitudes to the client, for most clients who choose to engage in therapy and wish to talk about themselves and their problems.

But client-centered therapy is not limited to this population of clients. The realization of the theory of therapy with clients who do not choose therapy, or clients who are unable to talk about themselves, or clients whose illness or defects distort their relation to reality or to a relationship, may require forms of interaction which appear quite different from empathic understanding response process. Third, there are, in the usual therapy situation when EURP is the salient form, often other forms of interaction which occur in the practice. These forms, such as answering questions, giving explanations, shaping experiments for the client to try, etc., occur in and may be an integral part of a particular therapy relationship.

These forms occur in client-centered therapy, however, only when they are requested by the client or when they become the way to be with the client that gets clarified out of expressed needs or desires of the client. If forms of interaction other than EURP occur in a particular client-centered relation, the way they are expressed or done is shaped by the belief in the growth principle, the presence of the therapeutic attitudes in the therapist and the non-directiveness of the therapist.

Client-centered therapy is not based on a belief in any particular therapeutic process occurring in the client. Even if it were to be shown that the most therapeutic process in clients is a particular way of expressing the self, or a particular way of relating expression to inner experience, or particular feelings developing-toward the therapist, or a particular pattern of insights, or any other idea about how the client should act or feel or express - as the maximally therapeutic way, client-centered therapy would remain non-directive and open to the process that emerged in the client and would not involve trying to influence that process.

Client-centered therapy does not excessively restrict the therapist's resourcefulness as a helper. This is the case in two different ways. First, within the framework of client-centered therapy as defined above, it is possible for therapists, depending upon their talents and the psychotechnologies they have learned, and if they are so inclined, to utilize techniques identified with other types of therapy.

Techniques of, for example, behavioral therapy, cognitive therapy, gestalt therapy, hypnosis, focusing, relaxation, meditation, etc., may be brought into the context of ongoing client-centered therapy. But - and this is a restriction the client-centered therapy would bring these in only at the request of the client or when the interaction brings out in the client an awareness of needs that might be met by such techniques.

The client- entered therapist does not, as said before, have any convictions prior to the therapy about what process in the client, or what ways of helping, a client may need. These techniques and psychotechnologies may, then, be incorporated into a specific course of client centered therapy, as long as the therapist is not imposing them and the client is given control of the occasions and limits on their use. The second way the therapist is not restricted in the forms of help that may be given to the client is that the client-centered therapist may serve as a source of information about other therapies or treatments and as the person who helps the client utilize the therapies or treatments provided by others.

Sometimes helping the client utilize other therapies means minimizing their damage to the client that takes place as they are benefiting him. Until other helpers - physicians, psychological and behavioral therapists, psychopharmacologists, etc., are, themselves, person-centered it remains the case that many of these experts violate the self-regard or the autonomy of their patients and clients. The client-centered therapist performs a crucial service in maintaining the basic client-centered therapeutic relation while his client goes through various treatments and therapies.

These treatments may, in their specifics, be helpful to the client - even necessary - for his well-being. But without the grounding in the client-centered relation the client may be totally unable to use the services of these experts, or may be hurt or damaged in the process. In the same way that the nature of client-centered therapy, in providing optimal conditions for growth and change, facilitates the client's constructive experience of, and way of relating to, his world, it also facilitates the client's strength, confidence and good judgement in utilizing the resources of the world, including its myriad therapies, treatments and educational and remedial resources. Client-centered therapy is not inhibiting or restrictive to the natural personality of the therapist.

The therapeutic attitudinal condition of congruence the realness of the therapist, the avoidance of a role fosters the development of individuality in the therapist's presence with the client. There is a marked similarity among client-centered therapists in their shared values and in the salient form of the therapeutic relation - the empathic understanding response process. Within that form, however, the unique mind and experience of a therapist shapes his empathic grasp of the client's presented experience and shapes the specific responses that are expressed to the client.

Individuality is also expressed in the extent of personal openness and the qualities brought out in self-disclosures when they are in answer to personal questions by the client or when they are an expression of congruence. The natural personality of the therapist is generally enhanced and developed by the practice of client-centered therapy itself. The practice requires the development of the attitudinal conditions in relation to clients.

In this development, for that context, the client-centered therapist tends to develop those qualities towards himself and is, thereby self-therapeutic and self-fostering of his own individuality. Client-centered therapy is not based simply on what works. It is based on what works within the parameters of what expresses and maintains the client's experience of the attitudinal conditions and of the therapist's non-directiveness and does not contradict the presence of these conditions. The achievement of insights, or the reduction of specific symptoms, in client-centered therapy, is only considered therapeutic if it is in the context of the larger perspective of preserving the therapeutic attitudinal qualities of the relationship perceived by the client.

Client-centered therapy stems from ethical values and beliefs, even though they are held with the reservation that they are hypotheses. These values assert respect for the individual person and the belief that unconditional caring for the person is constructive for the person and also for the social milieu of the person. Whatever scientific support there may be for the client-centered theory of therapy - and there is considerable support for it, the science is not the start of the practice for the practitioner.

The foundational belief of Client Centered Therapy (CCT) is that people tend to move toward growth and healing, and have the capacity to find their own answers. This tendency is helped along by an accepting and understanding climate, which the CC therapist seeks to provide above all else. So, this is what CC therapists do:

— Listen and try to understand how things are from the client's point of view.

— Check that understanding with the client if unsure.

— Treat the client with the utmost respect and regard.

— There is also a mandate for the therapist to be "congruent", or "transparent" - which means being self-aware, self-accepting, and having no mask between oneself and the client. The therapist knows themselves and is willing to be known.

Developmental Counseling and Therapy (DCT)

Developmental counseling and therapy (DCT) is an effective strategy for conceptualizing systems theory. The counseling field has seen an increase of family counseling theories over the past 20 years. Family counseling does not refer to one specific theory, rather, it is a broad term that encompasses many theories that share similar concepts such as circular causality, cybernetic epistemology, and the importance of family interactions.

Traditional approaches to counseling, such as, psychodynamic theory, cognitive-behavioral theory, and humanistic theory, have focused on the individual. Family counseling theories do not discount the individual, but recognize that individuals live within a family, and that family has an important impact on the development of the individual. The goal of family counseling like other counseling theories is to facilitate development.

The Developmental Counseling and Therapy (DCT) theory, which is an extension or reinterpretation that addresses the sequence and process of development. DCT can be used in assessment, treatment planning, and therapy.

The general concepts of family counseling theories and DCT to form Systemic Cognitive-Developmental Therapy (SCDT). SCDT is an integrative family theory that provides an environment for facilitating family growth. It is a theoretical integration of the various family counseling theories, as well as a systemic framework for assessing the cognitive, behavioral, and emotional style of the family. SCDT does not provide any techniques; rather it relies on the counselor to integrate his/her preexisting knowledge of family counseling theories and techniques within the SCDT framework. Family Counseling and DCT Therapy theory, discuss the general concepts of family counseling theories, and provide classifications of cognitive-developmental orientations and family counseling interventions.

According to Ivey's neo-Piagetian framework, the basic principles of childhood development repeat themselves again and again in the daily lives of children, adolescents, and adults. Development is continuous, and thus developmental concepts are directly relevant to effective counseling and therapy Developmental Counseling and Therapy (DCT) is not a new form of theory, rather, it is an attempt to integrate basic developmental theory into clinical practice.

DCT focuses on the client and the holistic development of both client and counselor. Developmental Counseling and Therapy integrates counseling theory and practice in both individual and family work. DCT provides a framework that aids the counselor to assess the client's development, to help expand and change the client's view of the world, to help the counselor understand both normal and severe psychological difficulties, and to generate treatment plans.

DCT can be used as an assessment technique, a therapeutic technique, and a treatment planning tool. There are four major tenets of DCT:

(1) it is possible to assess the cognitive developmental level of a client 'on-the-spot';

(2) it then becomes possible to expand horizontal and vertical development through matching or mismatching counseling theories and methods;

(3) cognitive developmental levels facilitate different types of client

(4) a combination of the first three concepts enables the generation of a comprehensive treatment plan.

DCT maintains that counselors must enter the world of the client and understand how the client constructs their knowledge and way of being in the world. In order for the counselor to enter the world of the client, the counselor must first assess the cognitive-developmental level of the client.

Children, adolescents, and adults construct their view of the world based on four major cognitive-developmental levels, which are anchored in the Piagetian concepts of sensori-motor, concrete operations, and formal operations. In addition to the three, DCT adds the dialectic/systemic level. Each of the four levels involves varying degrees of complexity of language and meaning; however the levels are not hierarchical.

Clients operating in the sensorimotor level present themselves in a random, disorganized, confused manner, frequently jumping from topic to topic and from emotion to emotion. In the sensorimotor level, clients are able to experience their hurt and confusion fully at the body level. Clients operating from the concrete level will give concrete, linear descriptions of events, thoughts, and behaviors.

The concrete client may lack self-reflection and the ability to see multiple perspectives as well as lack the ability to generalize from situation to situation. The formal level is characterized by self-reflection and analysis of patterns of thoughts, feelings, and behaviors. The dialectic/systemic level is characterized by the integration of patterns of thoughts and emotions into a system.

After assessing the cognitive-developmental level of the client, the counselor can choose appropriate interventions and theories either to match or to mismatch the cognitive-developmental level of the client. Horizontal development occurs when the counselor helps the client expand their understanding at their current cognitive-developmental level, thus helping the client develop all of the resources of the stage at which he or she is operating.

For example, if a sensorimotor functioning client enters counseling, it is important to match the client at the sensorimotor level and expand sensorimotor functioning before moving the client to concrete and formal understanding. Vertical development involves the counselor shifting styles to move the client to the other levels of development, thus helping the client expand developmental potential.

For example, after the counselor has helped the sensorimotor functioning client expand sensorimotor functioning, the counselor mismatches the client and helps the client move towards concrete understanding. Regardless of where the counselor begins with the client, the objective of counseling is to help the client move through the different developmental levels.

Effective counseling produces both horizontal and vertical development, thus helping the client explore and develop resources in each of the developmental levels.

The counselor's cognitive-developmental level greatly influences the manner in which the client replies. Clients will talk about what the counselor attends to and clients will talk and act at the cognitive-developmental level at which the counselor listens, asks questions, and conducts the session.

Using specific questions focusing on one of the cognitive levels, the counselor can help the client explore their issue at each cognitive-developmental level. Whether the counselor chooses to use the DCT model in assessment, treatment planning, and/or therapy, it is important to remember that central to DCT is the idea of co-construction.

The counselor and the client are co-constructing the nature of the relationship and the goals of counseling throughout the counseling process. DCT provides an integrative approach to understanding individual development; however, it does not consider the individual within the family context. It is apparent that individuals live in a family. One cannot discuss the development of the individual without discussing the family.

General Family Counseling

Family counseling is not one specific form of theory but a broad term that encompasses many theories. The counseling field has seen an explosion of family counseling theories and interventions making it impossible to cover each in detail. In 1982, Grunebaum and Chasin present a classification system, which assumes that families can be seen from three different perspectives, historical, interactional, and existential. The various family theories may differ in some aspects; however, all of them share a systemic worldview. In other words, general systems theory serves as the foundation of all family counseling theories.

General systems theory concludes the following:

1) elements of a system are organized and predictable,

2) families behave in a stable and predictable manner,

3) families are able to change as situations dictate

4) the family forms a single entity with its own characteristics,
5) family members are bounded by time and space,
6) hierarchies exist within families,
7) families seek homeostasis, and
8) families function according to feedback loops, by which individual family members influence the family and the family influences the individuals

In short, the following general concepts appear to be a part of most family theories:

1) the family is the primary unit,
2) the family influences the individual,
3) the individual influences the family,
4) the family consists of subsystems,
5) every event within the family is determined by multiple forces operating within the system/subsystem,
6) families form repetitive patterns over time,
7) family members have family roles,
8) family is viewed in terms of interactions and relationships, and
9) the focus of family counseling is on the family system

Because family systems are made up of individuals, it makes sense to integrate the concepts of DCT discussed earlier with the general concepts of family counseling theories in discussing the development and functioning of families.

Systemic Cognitive-Developmental Therapy (SCDT) combines the general concepts of DCT and family counseling theories to form an integrative theory that emphasizes the importance of providing a therapeutic environment that promotes family growth. SCDT proposes that families collectively move through cognitive-developmental orientations similar to the DCT levels. The cognitive-developmental orientations within SCDT include the sensorimotor family, the concrete-operational family, the formal-operational family, and the dialectic/systemic family. Families repeatedly progress through the four cognitive-developmental orientations over the life-time and families can become stuck and immobilized in one orientation.

Families tend to frame a specific issue in one orientation. Although families can operate on all four levels, they tend to have a preferred orientation. Families develop a collective worldview that organizes predictable ways of thinking, feeling, and acting that are anchored in one of the four orientations. The family uses its primary mode of operating to filter the way in which it views the world. A counselor can assess the cognitive-developmental orientation of the family through listening and utilizing a questioning sequence.

Families must be able to either integrate new situations and emotions into their existing worldview or modify their existing worldview to fit the new situation or emotion. Thus, a functional family can cope with new situations and emotions from their preferred orientation and also from each of the other orientations.

Dysfunctional families tend to choose extreme methods of integrating new situations and emotions. They hold strongly to their preferred orientation and are unable to move and operate under the other orientations. The role of the counselor in SCDT is very similar to the role of the counselor in DCT.

The counselor must first assess the cognitive-developmental orientation of the family, including any blocks, and then co-construct with the family the therapeutic relationship and goals. Ultimately, the goal of SCDT is to assist family to functioning within and among the four cognitive-developmental orientations, to empower the family to view their issues from multiple perspectives, and to generate solutions that are appropriate for the developmental needs of the family.

Similarly to DCT, SCDT begins the counseling process with a structured interview that identifies the family's cognitive-developmental orientation. Once the family's orientation has been identified, the counselor creates an environment helping the family use multiply orientations to explore different perspectives of the presenting issue. As in DCT, SCDT encourages change through horizontal movement, where the counselor helps the family elaborate and explore resources at their current orientation of functioning, and/or vertical movement, where the counselor helps the family move to and function at the other cognitive-developmental orientations.

SCDT does not offer new techniques beyond the specific questioning sequence, family counselors must use the techniques of other family counseling theories within the SCDT framework. Many interventions fit into multiple orientations. It is the intentional use by the counselor that determines the influence of the intervention on the family. For example, the genogram activity can be used to help the family identify interpersonal closeness, to organize family information (concrete-operational), to analyze repeating patterns, and to bring to awareness cultural and intergenerational influences.

Sensorimotor orientation Interventions that either match or help the client family move to the sensorimotor orientation include: genogram, family photos, family sculpture, unbalancing techniques, art therapy, and dance and movement therapy. A genogram provides a graphic picture of the family history over at least three generations.

The genogram can be used to reveal the family's basic structure, demographics, functioning, and relationships. A SCDT counselor can use the genogram activity to expand or move the family into the sensorimotor orientation by focusing on feelings the family is experiencing while creating the genogram and discussing family interactions. The family photo technique involves having family members bring in family albums, photos, slides, or videos and having family members discuss the emotional significance of the events or what feeling each family member is experiencing as they reflect on the picture.

Family sculpture is a re-creation of the family system that represents relationships to one another at a specific period in time. The family is asked to sculpt their family by physically arranging the family, paying attention to distancing and body positions. The counselor can use family sculpture to elicit powerful feelings from the family during the sculpting and afterwards as they discuss the final product.

The counselor purposefully chooses to side with one family member, creating a disequilibrium with the hopes that the other family members will emotionally respond to the disequilibrium. Counselors can use art therapy techniques to have family members draw images of their family or have family members jointly draw their family.

The counselor can help the family explore their feelings about their drawing as well as their feelings about the drawings of other family members. Art therapy can be used to encourage relatedness among family members as well as to stimulate expression of emotions. Concrete-operational orientation Interventions that either match or help the client family move to the concrete-operational orientation include: genogram, family sculpture, homework assignments, "going home" technique, miracle question, fast forwarding questioning, communication skills training, and exceptions to the problem.

The process of constructing a family genogram can help expand either the concrete-operational family or it can help move a family to the concrete-operational orientation. Organizing family information such as, putting names and dates on the symbols, and delineating family relationships can be a very concrete activity. Family sculpting, like the genogram, can be very concrete-operational. The task of creating the family sculpture, arranging the body position of various family members, and distancing the family members can be a very concrete task.

Homework assignments, the "going home technique" which involves having the client return to his/her family of origin and record interactions between family members, the use of the miracle question, and fast forwarding questions, and communication skills training, all help the client family explore or move into the concrete-operational orientation. These interventions help the client family organize family information, form concrete, tangible responses to specific questions and assignments, and provide straightforward directives for the family members to carry out.

Formal-operational orientation Interventions that either match or help the client family move to the formal-operational orientation include: genogram, family sculpture, reframing, relabeling, and "going home" technique. The genogram can be used to help explore family patterns. Throughout the genogram activity, the counselor can ask questions that will direct the family to look for and analyze family patterns. Like the genogram, the family sculpture can also help analyze family patterns. The counselor can help the family discuss the different relationships that are evident in the family sculpture.

Each family member and the counselor may view situations and behaviors differently. Although the family members share a common background, there are other outside influences on the individual family member that contribute to the individual's unique development. The combination of family and outside influences results in the development of an individual with his/her own way of thinking, behaving, and feeling. There are many other family counseling interventions that can be adapted into the SCDT framework. The specific intervention is not as important as the manner in which the counselor intentionally chooses to use the interventions. Many interventions can be used in multiple orientations. It is up to the skilled, intentional counselor to decide what intervention to use when, and how to use the intervention that would be the most beneficial for the family.

Therapy model and family counseling theories naturally fit together to form Systemic Cognitive-Developmental Therapy, a family counseling theory that places the general concepts of family/systems theory within the DCT framework. SCDT provides an alternative paradigm for the assessment, treatment, and conception of family issues that builds on preexisting family counseling theories and techniques. Although SCDT does not offer any new interventions, it does provide a framework for using the existing interventions in a new context.

When the counselor asks the family to construct a genogram, the counselor is not merely asking for a family tree. Within the SCDT model, the counselor can use the genogram to understand the preferred orientation of functioning for each of the family member and the family as a whole. Additionally, the counselor can have the family members think about the preferred orientation of functioning for other family members on the genogram to facilitate communication and understanding among the various family members.

The SCDT model provides an innovative and integrative theory of family counseling that does not discount other family counseling theories but provides a framework that recognizes the importance of the various perspectives within each of the four orientations. Although many interventions can be used in multiple orientations, there are some interventions associated with certain family counseling theories that appear to fit better with one particular orientation.

For example, mediation, body work, and gestalt approaches to family counseling appear to fit nicely within the sensorimotor orientation. Behavioral, reality therapy, problem-solving, strategic, solution-focused, and structural approaches to family counseling can be most helpful within the concrete-operational orientation.

Cognitive, client-centered, structural, psychodynamic, and constructivism approaches to family counseling align nicely with the formal-operational orientation.

Feminist theory, cultural identity theory, and most family counseling theories will help the counselor in the dialectic/systemic orientation. The SCDT model of family counseling is an advanced theory, which may intimidate beginning counselors. SCDT provides no clear direction but a framework for the counselor to build on.

Although SCDT provides an excellent framework that will easily aid the counselor in assessing the family's preferred orientation and blocked orientations, it provides no additional information to assist the counselor in choosing the appropriate intervention other than suggesting either horizontal or vertical movement. A counselor-in-training or novice counselor may know that the best intervention for the client family is to match the client family at the sensorimotor orientation; however, within the sensorimotor orientation, the counselor may not know enough about the various interventions to choose a genogram, movement therapy, or a gestalt approach.

The SCDT's reliance on counselors to use the techniques of other family counseling theories within the SCDT framework assumes that counselors already have knowledge of other counseling theories and techniques which may not be true for counselors-in-training or novice counselors. The SCDT model can be very helpful for advanced family counseling counselors who already have many intervention skills in their repertoire. However, for counselors-in-training and novice counselors who are just beginning to learn family counseling interventions, the idea of coming up with a number of interventions to help the family move along the orientations can be somewhat overwhelming. Overall, the SCDT model is a theory of family counseling, which provides a theoretical framework for counselors to understand their client family within a developmental perspective.

Multifamily Group Psychotherapy

Family therapists have long understood the complications in assessing and influencing a single family system. To assess several families and manage process between and among families simultaneously presents a considerable task. Yet, multifamily group therapy, combining group psychotherapy and theory and technique from family therapy, has the potential for significant treatment efficacy. Multifamily groups are a valuable treatment modality and provide a powerful medium for change. The curative factors within the group process and the reenactment of family issues in family therapy are only a few of the important reasons that make multifamily groups effective. For family therapists, a general systems model of treatment encourages this therapeutic approach. Combining techniques from both therapy models provide a wealth of interventions and resources from which the therapist can use to help their clients. MFG also allows the advantages of family therapy --seeing the family together, access to the dysfunctional patterns, and the therapeutic material from the family to be seen in the context of a group situation involving similar difficulties across families.

Multifamily groups (MFG) began as a adjunct to planned hospital treatment and has historically been linked with the education of family members concerning various presenting problems related to the patient who was hospitalized. Yet, most definitions now include a wider view of the multifamily group that can be adopted to outpatient and other treatment settings. O'Shea and Phelps provide the following definition of MFG:

> "...a deliberate, planful, psychosocial intervention with two or more families present in the same room with a trained therapist for all or most of the sessions. Each participating family should have two or more members that represent at least two generations in the family and are present for all or most of the sessions. Sessions should have an explicit focus on problems or concerns shared by all families in attendance"

They report that the focal problems of the group should pertain directly or indirectly to cross-generational family interaction. The sessions should reflect interfamilial and intergenerational interaction. Also, actual or potential alliances among members of different families based on similarities can be utilized to achieve group goals. Lacqueur is generally quoted by writers in this area as the first to attempt to combine family and group treatment. Lacqueur writes that only in this modality was society present in the form of several, unrelated family units. The larger, external influencing system was seen as having stronger, richer and more varied resources for change than group or family therapy alone. Thus, MFG has been described in the literature as a distinct hybrid that grew out of needs within institutions and their pragmatic concerns for providing efficient therapeutic treatment and a combination of group and family work.

MFG can be found in a wide variety of institutions, private agencies and among individuals providing therapy. A review of the literature reveals use with a large range of client populations including: schizophrenics, bulimics, learning disabilities, behavioral problems, mentally challenged, severely disturbed psychiatric populations, and adolescent substance abuse. However, it would appear that many family and interpersonal issues, yet to be addressed, could utilize multifamily group therapy. The multifamily group leader(s) must possess clinical expertise and have training in assessment, treatment, and evaluation in order to be effective.

While many disciplines are represented in the literature on MFG, the proficient leader, regardless of training program, must have a thorough knowledge of group therapy including group dynamics and development and competencies in family psychotherapy. Knowledge in the various schools of family therapy including: structural/strategic; inter generational; Bowenian, solution-focused, and psychodynamic is helpful. For the most part, the structure of the MFG varies with the setting in which the group leader works. In general, MFGs are composed of three or more families gathering to discuss common concerns. Lacqueur originally recommended that groups be heterogeneous in SES, and other characteristics, so that the group would focus on relationship issues.

The structure of the group refers to the process of establishing the type of group, planning, per-group interviews, beginning, middle and termination, and follow-up stages. First, a rationale for establishing a multifamily group must take into account several factors: the issues and the common concern for the group;

whether it be an open or closed group; how often and for how long will it meet; what type of family will benefit from the group; and group leadership. Pre-group interviews are important to facilitate orientation to the therapy model and to set expectations for membership. It also provides an opportunity for pretesting family functioning and allows for a subjective test of compatibility between families.

There are at least three distinctive phases or stages that structure the multifamily group process. The first stage is characterized by education of the members about the group intent. As with most groups, this phase involves settling in and establishing group norms and purpose. During this stage, the therapist is active and provides a good deal of structure emphasizing similarities between family goals and circumstances. Family members are encouraged to interact with each other within their own family and the therapist intervenes to model and promote constructive interactions. This gives the families time to adapt to their surroundings before demands are placed on them. Discussion may also lead to the group's relationship to other environmental systems, i.e., school system, courts, etc. as the group becomes an entity.

In the middle stage, the therapist interaction and direction decreases. Interventions become more selective. Intra-family interaction occurs spontaneously. The interfamily process increases and the therapist's linking of intra-family peers may decrease. Families may report that contact outside the group is occurring. For the multifamily group, this networking can be positive. Group rules set prior to this may help to prevent splitting or the type of subgrouping that is detrimental to group process.

Therapists continue to assess family relationships: what triangles are occurring, what distorted perceptions are there, sequential behavior patterns, family myths, and a measure of family flexibility and resolve to change. During this middle phase, spotlighting one family to work can be beneficial. This assessment will allow the therapist to intervene appropriately as intra- and interfamily problems arise. The processing of a particular issue may involve participation from all group members.

The ending stage allows for the gains and understandings from past sessions to be discussed, so that the group begins to end on a positive note and gains may be reinforced. Here, the therapist begins to take on a more directive role again. The intra-family process consists of review for each family and the discussion of expectations for the future.

In general, the family therapy techniques, fit well in the Multifamily Group model. Techniques associated with imagery and fantasy, structural exercises, family problem-solving, psychodrama, role-play, genogram drawings, behavioral contracting, and intergenerational homework are well adapted for MFG. Imagery work including guided visual imagery and relaxation techniques are also suited to MFG. Other techniques such as: early recollections, recall of early years, and empty chair techniques are extremely valuable. Roles such as fathers, mothers, teenagers, children, the targeted or symptom group, oldest, youngest, etc., that naturally occur in families can be included in structured exercises during the MFG. Structural family therapy techniques provide an opportunity for changes in perspectives. For example, family sculpting and family portraits are interesting and fun exercises for the participants. Strategic interventions, while well-suited for individual families, may be inadvisable due to compatibility issues across families in the group. Importantly, the processing of the results of these techniques becomes an most important component of the group work.

Impact Therapy and Group Counseling

Impact Therapy is a concrete approach to group leading with much emphasis on the leader leading the group. A number of different models of group counseling exist that tend to put much of the responsibility for the outcome of the group on the members rather than the leader. The emphasis of these models has been on the interpersonal dynamics or group process rather than on the intrapersonal experience of each individual.

The Impact Therapy approach to group leading puts more emphasis on the individual's needs and how the leader can make the group experience valuable for each member. Impact Therapy is an active, multi-sensory approach to counseling that encourages the leader to be creative by using props, chairs, movement, writing and drawing to tap into members' different learning styles.

Impact Therapy integrates creative counseling techniques and ideas from RET, TA, Gestalt Therapy, Reality Therapy, Adlerian Therapy. It stresses listening, thinking, action, and impact, whereas many other approaches primarily emphasize listening and facilitating. Impact Therapy group leaders are guided by the following four core beliefs:

1. People don't mind being led when they are led well.
2. Group counseling should be clear and concrete.
3. Group counseling should never be boring.

4. The leader is primarily responsible for what happens in a group session.

The impact therapist uses the initials PPFF (purpose, plan, focus, funnel) as the primary organizing "map" for setting up and conducting a group session.

— *Purpose.* The leader is very clear as to the kind of group (educational, support, counseling, or therapy) and why the group is meeting.

— *Plan.* The impact therapist always plans the session. Good planning of the warm-up, middle, and closing phases is essential and yet many leaders do not plan or plan superficially. In-depth planning helps greatly in making group sessions productive.

— *Focus.* The Impact Therapy group leader consciously focuses the session; that is, sees to it that relevant topics or issues are discussed. One of the biggest problems in groups is that the session never focuses long enough for there to be impact. Without focus, members go from topic to topic, causing the interaction to be superficial or disjointed. Unfortunately many leaders have been trained to wait for the members to focus the session.

— *Funnel.* The impact therapist is always thinking of how to funnel the session; that is, how to take the session to a deeper, more meaningful level. Impact Therapy leaders feel that it is their responsibility to funnel the session. Funneling is accomplished by asking good thought-provoking questions, by using deepening exercises, or by working with an individual using theory and the other members. Sessions have much more impact when they are funneled and often sessions will not funnel unless the leader actively intervenes and directs the group.

The impact therapist believes that funneling is the key to a successful group.

The Impact Therapy group leader has the courage and permission to do what it takes to make a session productive. The leader is willing to take the session to a meaningful level by using counseling theory, psychodrama, the other members, or him or herself in whatever way that may have impact on the members. The leader is willing to draw out and cut off members when it is appropriate to do so. In order to focus and funnel a session, the leader often will need to interrupt and redirect the flow of conversation. Cutting off is an essential skill for group leading. Leaders whc allow members to be inappropriate, ramble, distract the group, or tell long, detailed stories are not being as effective as they can be.

Creative techniques

Using creative activities is an integral part of being an Impact Therapy group leader. Creative techniques help make the group session more engaging, interesting, and meaningful. There are a number of creative techniques that have been useful in groups.

— *Large Newsprint Pad or Wipeboard.* Many people are visual learners. The benefit of having something large to write on cannot be over emphasized. It is helpful to visually represent concepts or ideas to the group such as irrational and rational self-talk, lists generated by the members, time lines, TA drawings, or drawings of enmeshment.

— *Use of Movement.* The Impact Therapy group leader often has members stand up and move around to make points more concrete or to generate energy in the group. Group exercises that involve movement are valuable. Having members "sculpt" how they feel about the group or move along a "progress" line as to how much they have progressed, or move along value continuums are excellent movement exercises. Having members move between chairs that represent different people, ego states, or goals can serve as a valuable visual and experiential learning activity. Physical movement can be very beneficial in groups.

— *Small Child's Chair*. Another essential tool for Impact Therapy group leaders is a small child's chair which can be used in a variety of ways. The chair can be used to represent the Child ego state or the little boy or girl in each of the members. So often, when a member is struggling with an issue, part of the problem has to do with the child part of themselves. The small chair makes the struggle more concrete for members. Having members sit in the chair or even look at the chair can be quite impactful.

— *Shield*. The impact therapist often will use a prop (some tangible item such as a shield, cup, filter, rubber band, or blocks) for an exercise or when working with an individual member. Frequently members talk about needing to shield themselves from verbal abuse from someone in their lives such as a parent, spouse, or boss. By having them hold a shield as they discuss how they need to protect themselves, the members get the point about how they can make themselves safe.

— *Other Props*. Styrofoam cups are used to represent one's self-worth. Punching holes in the cup to indicate "leaks in self-esteem" or smashing the cup to represent how members allow themselves to be psychologically smashed are two ways that cups can be used. A furnace filter is a good prop for getting members to discuss how they may need to filter input from certain people in their lives. Rubber bands can be used regarding stress--each person can stretch the rubber band to the level of stress they are feeling and then discuss either adding to the stress or reducing the stress. Wooden blocks with holes in them and pegs that either fit in the holes or nearly fit, or definitely do not fit can be used to symbolize the "fit" of relationships in members' lives.

Group Counseling for older personalities

Declining birth and infant mortality rates have combined with increased longevity to create an expanding population of older persons. Individually and collectively, the developmental task is to continue realizing the full potential, self-actualizing, and being fully functional. The counseling profession is challenged to help older persons and their caregivers influence society to create and maintain an environment in which ego integrity, empowerment, and meaning are not only possible, but probable. Group counselors can contribute in seemingly small but significant ways by offering groups which are small models of a larger world. They can teach older persons how to cope with a new and often difficult stage of development.

For older persons a major challenge is to traverse their graying years with a sense of ego integrity, empowerment, and meaning. The ultimate developmental task of ego integrity is marked by satisfaction with a life well spent, and the absence of despair or discouragement. Empowerment is the ability to develop positive, satisfying lifestyles and maximize developmental potential and life satisfaction. Meaning may be found in core values and themes, or a sense of continuity. Although many individuals spend most of their older years in good mental and physical health, sound financial status, and with a solid family and social support system, aging is inevitably accompanied by loss.

Increased vulnerability to health problems may create financial difficulties and unwelcomed lifestyle changes, resulting in loss of autonomy. The illness or death of a spouse and cohorts may render the healthiest older person fearful, alienated and lonely. Feelings of worthlessness may develop as older individuals internalize their devalued social position and lose control over their lives. The normal losses of aging are intensified for homebound or institutionalized older adults suffering serious mental and physical impairment.

Resisting discouragement and despair may become difficult for older persons coping with multiple losses. Feeling empowered and finding meaning may seem impossible in the face of alienation and isolation. If the challenge for aging persons is to transcend these obstacles to ego integrity, empowerment and meaning, the challenge for society is to create an environment where the effects of such obstacles are minimized. Groups for older persons and their caregivers can provide small but developmentally healthy environments where the losses associated with aging may be translated into gains.

Several types of groups for older people are described in the literature, each having benefits common to most groups, and benefits specific to the particular type of group. Developmental benefits common to most groups include

(a) increased feelings of community and belonging,

(b) strengthened social support and interaction,

(c) decreased isolation and loneliness,

(d) acquired coping skills,

(e) rediscovered uniqueness,

(f) resolved issues, and

(g) restored sense of control, self-worth and integrity.

Reminiscing groups are appropriate for older persons living independently in the community and functional older persons in long-term care facilities. These life review groups are especially helpful for finding order and affirmation in the patterns of one's life and in discovering central meanings in seemingly disconnected parts of life. Resolving past hurts and conflicts, discovering core values, and identifying personal themes help members find meaning from their past. Training groups may provide a safe environment in any setting for learning new coping skills to deal with losses. Participants can also learn interpersonal skills to develop new friendships, repair relationships, and rebuild a needed but weakened support network.

Psychotherapy groups in community or institutional settings help members with diminished coping skills adjust to life stresses and personal problems. Reality orientation groups are usually conducted in inpatient settings and are more appropriate for older persons disoriented in time and place. Preventing and slowing progressive deterioration are goals of this group type.

Additional benefits from a variety of groups are apparent in the group titles, such as remotivation, exercise, bereavement, assertiveness, family therapy, sexuality, self-esteem, or art, music and psychodrama groups. Groups for caregivers of older persons can help make the older person's environment developmentally healthy and conducive to empowerment. Caregivers experience problems with confinement, infringement on lifestyle, restricted social life, work and family conflicts, and emotional and physical stress. Groups can help caregivers reduce conflict and stress, deal with special parental needs, increase understanding of illnesses, and use available resources. When caregivers find information, resources, and support, they are able to significantly improve the environment of older family members. A group growing in popularity is the peer group. Seniors counseling seniors may be empathic, respectful and without the negative attitudes toward working with older persons reported of many professionals. Peer group counselors may also provide empowered role models for successful aging.

Counselors offering groups for older persons need the basic knowledge and competency skills recommended by the Association for Specialists in Group Work (ASGW). Counselors should also have specific training in developmental issues of aging, effects of various physical or mental limitations, intergenerational issues, common aging concerns, and resources available for older persons. Specific counseling skills needed for psychotherapy or reality orientation groups differ from those skills needed for reminiscing or training groups. Family therapy, art; music and drama, sexuality or other specialized groups would each require specific competencies in addition to general group and gerontological competencies. An ideal training format might be a combination of the Council for Accreditation of Counseling and Related Educational Programs (CACREP) gerontology speciality program and a formal counselor education program adhering to both CACREP standards and the ASGW standards for training group counselors. A counselor graduating from a program not approved by CACREP or a program not following the ASGW professional standards could plan an individualized training supplement to acquire the equivalent of the ideal training format. Caution is encouraged when advocating peer group counseling with older persons. Waters and Goodman emphasized the necessity of carefully selecting peer group counselors, and providing training that is skill oriented. Paraprofessional skills are rarely as developed as those of professional counselors.

Philosophical counselling

Philosophical counselling, following Achenbach, is essentially a method "beyond-method". It is not doctrinally committed, but rather is a philosophically informed dialogical practice, which enables individuals to explore their hopes, fears and anxieties within a setting which is likely to promote deeper self-understanding. What unites philosophical counsellors is their rejection of the excesses of the medical-model and their insistence that it is normal for a person to have psychological issues that need to be addressed. And herein lies a problem. There are no criteria generally accepted by philosophical counsellors which determine whether a psychological problem is susceptible to philosophical practice or not. Lets take schizophrenia as an example.

In its more severe manifestations, schizophrenia is characterised by: delusions (paranoia or grandeur); hallucinations; incoherent thought; disassociation from reality; flat emotions; and so on. It is normally treated by means of anti-psychotic drugs, which function to inhibit dopamine (a neurotransmitter) activity in the brain. But is there a role for philosophical counselling in the treatment of schizophrenia? Philosophical counsellors should not treat severe personality disorders, and presumably schizophrenia is included amongst their number. However, things are not quite this straightforward.

— It is not clear what kind of therapy a philosophical counsellor can recommend to a client who presents the symptoms of schizophrenia. Many philosophical counsellors reject the medical model completely, but anti-psychotic drugs, which have a direct and measurable somatic effect, have transformed the lives of many schizophrenics over the last 30 years.

— Perhaps more disturbingly,

Philosophical counsellors who endeavour to treat everything by philosophical means. They are deconstructed enough themselves to have taken what evidence the undermining of absolutism and to have applied it to the other extreme. Of course, many of them are scientifically semi-literate and they suppose, for example, that the theory of relativity proves that everything is relative (they say as much in their literature). They will then attempt to solve all sorts of problems by philosophical means that might not be philosophical problems. Of course, every therapeutic and mental health discipline will have its fair share of practitioners who perhaps should not be practising. But there is specific problem for philosophical counselling—and it is the problem of relativism. Because philosophical counselling lacks a delimited method and conceptual framework, the boundaries of acceptable practice are likely to remain fluid.

Consequently, it is unlikely that there will ever be a formal set of guidelines that specify which kinds of problems are philosophical in nature and which are not. If these guidelines do not exist, then there will always be philosophical counsellors who are willing to deal with disorders such as schizophrenia, which would be better handled by the medical profession. Moreover, this relativism extends also to the content of philosophical counselling. It is difficult to see, for example, why a philosophical counsellor could not encourage a religiously informed discourse to address the problems of schizophrenia. Or perhaps a discourse informed by Jungian concepts or Eastern philosophy.

It might be thought that this is not really a problem. Different people will have different preferences, in terms of what they want from a counsellor. However, this is to fail to recognise that many psychological problems can be very effectively handled by specific and established therapeutic programmes. For instance, embark on a programme of systematic desensitisation, because it works. In the first instance, visit a philosopher. The "horses for courses" view also suggests the relativism that Roger Scruton finds so repugnant. To be cavalier about the content of philosophical counselling seems to deny that philosophy has a privileged role to play in the pursuit of truth.

So the problem of relativism is not, that individual philosophical counsellors articulate their philosophies to the needs of their clients. It is rather that philosophical counselling as an institution is ambivalent about method and content. Consequently, it fails to specify either the kinds of issues that can be addressed by philosophical practice or the sorts concepts and methods that should be employed in the endeavour. In this "anything-goes" sense, philosophical counselling is suggestive of a post-modern phenomenon.

The open-ended character of philosophical counselling methodology confers enormous responsibility on counsellors for the well-being of their clients. Consequently, their credibility and integrity is absolutely essential. Indeed, more so than is the case in psychotherapy and psychiatry, where practitioners can follow clearly established methods, arguably regardless of their own personal qualities. The confident about the credibility and integrity of philosophical counsellors? In some ways, it is easy to see why a philosopher might make a good personal counsellor. For example, the ability to listen and to respond rationally is clearly essential to the task of counselling a couple with marital difficulties. And similarly, a background in ethics will be useful in aiding a woman to come to a decision with regard to her unwanted pregnancy. But one must not be carried away by such examples, for it is just as easy to construct instances which demonstrate the absurdity of philosophers as counsellors. For example, it is hard to imagine why a background in formal logic or the philosophy of science will help a philosopher deal with obsessive-compulsive disorder. And similarly, it seems unlikely that the poker waving Wittgenstein would have been particularly successful in aiding a man to control his violent temper. Of course, these kinds of examples will be dismissed as "straw-men" by the advocates of philosophical counselling. They will respond that it is a certain kind of philosophical training that lends credibility to the idea that philosophers will make good counsellors. And further that it is possible to ensure the high-standard of philosophical counselling by instituting programmes of official certification. But these responses are not adequate. The other standard response to the charge that philosophers lack credibility as counsellors is to point to the short-comings of psychology and psychiatry. It is the 'psychotherapy in crisis' response. But again it is not satisfactory.

In the first place, it is flawed logically. The alleged shortcomings of established therapies are no justification for instituting another kind of flawed therapy. If anything the opposite is the case. But perhaps more importantly, the "psychotherapy in crisis" response is disingenuous about the successes of the mental-health disciplines. Consider that prior to the 1950s, schizophrenia was thought untreatable, patients were confined to mental institutions and their wards were termed "snake pits". But with phenothiazine drugs many sufferers are now able to live relatively normal lives in the community. And successes are not restricted to the somatic treatments: behavioural therapies are very effective in dealing with specific anxieties and addictions; and cognitive-behavioural therapies are fruitful in treating depression, anxiety disorders and sexual dysfunction. Indeed, if philosophical counsellors are able to duplicate the successes of the established disciplines, they will be doing well.

8

Ethical and Legal Aspects of Guidance Counselling

The field of counselling has been moving towards a more self-confident professional status, in the past few years. There are many aspects of this process which are to be welcomed - not least because it helps to enhance the credibility of counsellors working in a variety of settings. The counselling and psychotherapy more and more pushed towards a purely surface-oriented, symptom-focused and cost-driven approach. The psychotherapy that has adopted the market approach par excellence is behaviour therapy. The practice of graded exposure to phobic stimuli incorporates the routine measurement of symptoms during treatment and the recording of hours of therapy.

Recent issues of counselling have contained strongly expressed arguments in favour of the growth of research, audit and evaluation in the field of counselling has also argued for counsellors taking an increasing interest in evaluation and audit. Potential employers will want harder evidence and it is likely that counsellors will be required to provide such evidence in the not too distant future. counsellor training courses will need to put evaluation and audit on the curricula. There can be a seductive fascination and excitement with the world of seemingly 'objective' statistical techniques. One of the greatest dangers of predominantly or exclusively quantitative research is that we end up knowing the price (or numerical value) of everything, and the value (or essential quality) of nothing.

The desire to quantify, irrespective of the appropriateness of such an approach to the subject matter under consideration, is one which has to be self-consciously and tirelessly guarded against - for the seductive power of quantification, and the appeal that it makes to the scientistic, technocratic mind at this point in the evolution of human consciousness, is such that we can so easily be seduced into entirely inappropriate research procedures without even realising it. Anyone of humanistic persuasion who is familiar with the empirical research literature in any of the social sciences (including many branches of the psychology discipline) can only surely wince at the aridity and disembodied irrelevance of a significant proportion of the conventional literature in the academic journals.

The dynamics of the global social system are driven by shared, species-wide developmental traumata which are normally repressed from awareness, and the effects of which only tend overtly to manifest themselves dysfunctionally under conditions of high stress and anxiety, and diminishing resources. Some study describes that the objectivist epistemology of empiricist methodology, and its associated zeal for quantification, can be understood in this light; and that it is only through the experiential task of working through and integrating the repressed and unintegrated material of early developmental experience that we will be in a position individually and collectively to heal our individual and collective psychic dis-integration and move towards a wholeness from which it is far more likely that an epistempology and methodology which is truly humanistic in nature will organically emerge.

There are inherent difficulties in any attempt to fashion a meaningful understanding of existence in terms of the moral and epistemological categories provided by scientific culture. The increasing attention being given to qualitative research will... help to introduce reluctant counsellors to the world of research as it is... more in keeping with the spirit of counselling than quantitative research. There is, further, a substantial literature on qualitative research philosophy and methodology; and the pioneering volume edited by John Rowan and Peter Reason on 'new paradigm research' provides an excellent base from which to develop the kinds of sensitive, person-centred research on which a humanistic evaluation practice should surely be based.

The quantifying methodology is the appropriate approach for evaluating the efficacy of humanistic-dynamic counselling; yet the kinds of factors that a humanistic perspective holds to be decisive in facilitating therapeutic change represent human qualities that are quite beyond the ambit of controlled and 'objective' scientific measurement and mechanistic modes of understanding. The positivist scientific practices, which place such emphasis on the principles of falsifiability, replicability, predictability and substitutability, are quite inappropriate for studying the human psyche and the therapeutic change process. There has been an almost 'intentional blindness' within the psychology discipline to the conditions of production of psychological knowledge. Any counselling training or degree course which is advocating or insisting upon its trainees or students carrying out research into counselling would do well to leave considerable space for reflection upon the dynamics of the research process itself - focusing on both the researcher's own particular personality dynamics in so far as they resonate with and determine the choice of research methodology, and also the wider cultural dynamics and ideology of modernity which underlie orthodox and received research practice.

Academic departments in counselling, counselling psychology and psychotherapy should surely pay close and attentive heed to the 'conditions of production' of research knowledge, if the kind of sterile and disembodied empiricism described earlier is to be avoided. There is also a steadily growing body of literature in the psychology field which offers a potentially devastating critique of empirical social-scientific research from the post-modernist standpoint. Anyone who is concerned to promulgate and advocate research-mindedness in the counselling field should at the very least be fully aware of the post-modernist challenge to empiricism, and be prepared and able to offer a coherent and sustainable response to the formidable post-modernist critique.

Some commentators are rightly concerned that a full embracing of the 'anti-epistemology' of post-modernist thinking might lead to a sort of formless relativism in which we end up in a solipsistic position where it is impossible to say anything about the world beyond the subjective and purely private. Perhaps post-modernism is a kind of 'reaction-formation' against the excesses of the soul-less scientism of modernity; and it seems to me that the fields of counselling and psychotherapy are in a unique position to develop an embodied, humanistic approach to research that transcends the ideology of objectivism, and which honours both our need for communicable inter-subjective knowledge about the world and our core humanistic principles, which elevate the values of holism and human meaning above those of mechanism and quantifiability.

Ethical and Legal Aspetcs of Counselling

The process of determining which ethical principles are involved and then prioritizing them based on the professional requirements and beliefs. Following are the five types of ethical dilemmas:

— Confidentiality

— Role Conflict

— Counselor competence

— Conflicts with employer or institution

— Degree of dangerousness

American Counseling Association (ACA) based its first standards on the original American Psychological Associate code of ethics. ACA code of ethics was initiated by Donald Super and approved in 1961. Ethical Standards exist for many reasons. Without a code of established ethics, a group of people with similar interests can not be considered a professional organization. Helps professionalize an association on a general level but also provide some guidelines for the professional behaving of members.

Ethical standards protect the profession from government. Allow the profession to regulate itself and to function autonomously instead of being controlled by legislation and also help control internal disagreements and bickering. Ethical standards protect practitioners from the public especially malpractice suits.

Following are the Professional Codes of Ethics:

— Set of standards of conduct based upon as agreed on set of values.

— Code of ethics designed to offer formal statements for ensuring protection of clients.

— ACA standards are arranged under 8 major sectional headings:

1. Nature of Counseling Relationship
2. Confidentiality in counseling
3. Professional Competence
4. Relationships with other professionals
5. Evaluation assessment and interpretation
6. Teaching training and supervision
7. Research and publications
8. E thical considerations.

Ethically counselors must be aware of ethical codes and be able to differentiate an ethical dilemma from other types of dilemmas. Different ethical principles in a code that offer conflicting guidelines about what to do in a given situation. Conflicts may occur when counselors belong to 2 or more professional organizations where codes of ethics differ.

Treating individuals together as a system to overcome problems can use six values that affect counselors clients and the counseling process.

— Responsibility

— Integrity

— Commitment

— Freedom of Choice

— Empowerment

— Right to grieve

As recently as the 1960, counseling didn't have a strong enough identity as a profession to be recognized legally. Counselors legally recognized as professionals who provided personal, vocational and educational counseling. Counseling is the process through which a trained counselors assists an individual or group to make satisfactory and responsible decisions concerning personal, educational and career development.

Following are the four basic types of professional credentials

— *Inspection* - A state agency periodically examines the activities of a profession's practitioners to ascertain whether they are practicing the profession in a fashion consistent with public safety health and welfare.

— *Registration* - Requires submission of information to the state concerning the nature of their practice

— *Certification* - Person meets the minimum skills necessary to engage in that practice state board or department issues certificate to an individual in a specialty

— *Licensure* - Highest form of credentialing is licensure . Counselors experience trouble when laws are not clear and when conflict between the law and professional counseling ethics.

— *Confidentiality* - Ethical duty to fulfill a contract or promise clients that the information revealed during treatment will be protected from unauthorized disclosures.

— *Privacy* - Evolving legal concept that recognizes individuals rights to choose the time, circumstances and extent to which they wish to share or withhold personal information.

— *Privileged Communication* – Protects clients from having their confidential communication disclosed in court without permission.

Today, there are a number of apparent reasons that the counseling profession has failed to adequately address social and political issues. The first reason is that counseling theory and practice have continuously and steadfastly championed a model consistent with the socioeconomic and class distinctions of its practitioners and researchers. Second, counseling and psychology, particularly in the past two decades, have come to be part of the media marketplace of ideas.

Such counseling "ideas" are more likely to be presented in the form of fleeting images and 15-second sound bites than by a penetrating critical analysis of issues. Cliched and shallow pop psychology seems to best fit the media ideal of "therapeutic" solutions to devastating problems such as family violence. Third, it seems that counseling and psychology would rather analyze complex problems free of their historical and geographic contexts so as to maintain a "universal" claim for their strategies. But whatever the reason, the unwillingness to confront the many devastating contemporary social and political issues has occurred at a critical time when numerous community, school and social agencies in which counselors are employed are under attack from radical right-wing political and religious groups.

The ideology espoused by these groups indicts many counseling clients, who are victims of racial, sexual, political, and economic oppression, as entirely responsible for their own predicaments. The counseling profession's culpability and complicity in these attacks on clients has been its collective silence. Although some efforts have been made to raise gender, multicultural, and sexual issues, the debate has been severely curtailed by the profession's desire for increased legitimacy.

In America, the guidance and counseling movement was one of many humanitarian efforts that grew in response to the upheaval caused by the industrial revolution. The early guidance practitioners were public school teachers and administrators who used the disciplines of child study, psychometrics, and education to actuate laws. In fact, counseling was not even mentioned in the literature until 1931 and even after that there were still only a few full-time counselors before the 1950s. In the years after World War II, guidance and counseling underwent dramatic changes influenced by third-force psychology and humanism, which moved counseling away from the deterministic approaches of psychoanalysis and behaviorism toward theories that emphasized self-determination.

The formation of the American Personnel and Guidance Association in 1952 and the National Defense Education Act of 1958 had a significant impact on increasing the number of counseling professionals. Equally influential to the emerging counseling profession was the ongoing search for professional credibility. Guidance and counseling did not develop from a largely theoretical or philosophical base; rather, it borrowed its "frames of reference" from education, psychology, philosophy, and the physical sciences.

The responsiveness of counseling to political ends is severely curtailed. The exclusive adherence to a model of individual growth and change has resulted in the development of a professional organization and a role for the counselor that makes it extremely difficult for counselors to effectively address larger societal issues.

Counselors are mostly unaware of how their role has come to inhibit change. School counselors attempt to make intolerable schools tolerable for students; career counselors help clients make "realistic" career choices without examining underlying societal inequities or the nature of a market-driven economy that in many regions largely creates low-paying, temporary jobs.

Finally, many other counselors help the alienated client "adjust" to society without examining the source of that alienation in the culture. As mentioned, inherent in both the professional organization and the counselor's role are structural limitations that hinder both the organization's and the counselor's ability to work or advocate for societal change.

Several of the structural limitations built into the counselor's role have been articulated by many others over the years. There are several barriers to the rediscovery of counseling as a profession that can transform lives and society. First, the preoccupation of counseling and psychology with individualism and individual analysis of problems has served to depoliticize all social and interpersonal concerns. Second, as these professions struggle for public acceptance and credibility, they exhibit a growing tendency to support the dominant paradigm, rather than to advance change. Third, historically, counseling has adopted scientism as a model and made a claim of value neutrality.

This claim has created a barrier to the taking of a strong moral or principled stance. Fourth, as the profession continues to compete with similar professions for a share of resources and jobs, credentialing and accreditation have become a prominent issue among counselors.

The implementation of most counseling theory and practice continues to focus almost exclusively on the domain of the individual . Such a strategy for counseling seems to be aimed at changing the client's perception of reality rather than acknowledging that societal factors may be responsible for the client's plight. Cushman called this idea the "empty self." This concept of the empty self in modern counseling suggests that the self has come to stand apart from history and culture and is therefore apart from formative social and historical forces. The result has been a fragmented view of human development.

The concept of the autonomous self has been encapsulated and set apart from the outside. This inner world of changing moods, thoughts, and emotions has gained the helping professionals' stamp of reality. In the current language of counseling and human development theory, the individual is typically offered a "lifestyle solution". Instead of a dialogue anchored by a critical social analysis, the client is frequently told new coping skills, new insights based on awareness of internal subjective states, or corrective thinking strategies. Referring to family therapy, Imber-Black strongly suggested that unexamined, family therapy can easily contribute to the homeostatis of larger systems .... Understanding the ways that models emerge out of a given social and historical context, and how work... may be coopted by a broader and often hidden sociopolitical agenda can sensitize family therapists not only to the family but to themselves and their own context.

Power issues are seldom acknowledged-perhaps because counselors lack their own power base from "which to confront the basic values of institutions or the larger society". Power comes from the institutions in which counselors work and from the agencies that license them. It is granted contingent on one's working within prescribed boundaries that serve the larger system, and it can be taken away or certification denied if individuals attempt to use that power against those same institutions. Therefore, through training, preparation, and licensure practices, counselors frequently have come to adopt a core set of values that often stand in glaring contrast and contradiction to those held by many clients. Adoption of these values can constitute a form of cultural oppression when applied to minority group members, even if done unwittingly. They contended that such basic counseling values can "lend support to the belief that counseling is an egocentric part of the Establishment that interprets behavior exclusively from its own reference point". The socialization of counselors has been largely framed in the spirit of ethical neutrality.

The example of career counselors whose belief in pluralism, meritocracy, individualism, and pragmatism have provided the foundation of a belief system that upholds the notions of equal opportunity and free choice for everyone while "ignoring the way those choices are delimited by gender, race, and class socialization". It is this assumed position of value neutrality that has allowed counselors to portray themselves as professionally outside of the political ideologies that shape their current social thinking.

From this presumption of value neutrality counselors have made the claim of objectivity. Through such a claim of an objective science of helping, counselors have donned blinders, preventing themselves from viewing the social, political, and institutional nature of counseling theories and practices. It is this pretense to a position-free ideology that has provided the basic conceit of modern counseling practice and presented a formidable barrier to effective change in the discipline. Psychology has been a primary model from which the emphasis on individual assessment and diagnosis was borrowed.

In turn, psychology has imitated the medical-scientific model as the overarching paradigm by which to establish its own credibility. This reductionistic approach has underscored the intrapsychic focus and fostered increased specialization. Such specialization has debilitated the medical profession to the point at which a team of doctors are more likely now to address a client's symptomatology from the standpoint that the sum of a patient's symptoms equals the whole of a person.

This counseling-medical paradigm has been expressed in its many variations through community psychology, school counseling, college counseling, mental health counseling, and other social services and often amounts to little more than helping professionals serve as guardians or defenders of the status quo.

The outdated notion that the American Counseling Association (ACA) must be based on an objective and neutral scientific approach belies the fact that counselors make value judgments and choices every day that have political and social consequences for their clients. The guidance and counseling are sociopolitical processes in which neither theories nor techniques are value free.

Pressing political conditions that dramatically alter lives and affect the mental and emotional well-being of individuals has seldom been addressed. The short-term discussion and critical examination of salient political issues is blunted. Consequently, the search for the sociohistorical and political values inherent in research and practice has been put aside in favor of a discredited value-neutral approach. The dominant prescribed ideology, masquerading as apolitical and therefore "scientific," can continue to frame what are or are not acceptable and appropriate research and practice concerns.

In more recent years, the quest for legitimacy through imitation has led the counseling profession into the domain of other health professionals, with the result that organizations of those professions have made efforts to restrict that movement. The damaging nature of this polarization among helping professionals has divided all of the power and set one against the other. These turf wars are many; witness the frequency with which the following tend to occur: counselors' fight with the marriage and family therapists for territory, social workers pitted against elementary school counselors for jobs, and psychologists battling against psychiatrists for the ability to prescribe medication.

Counselors have created their own system of credentialing and now seek to license counselors in every state and accredit counselor training programs. Aubrey's prophetic words have heralded the final regression to the mean during the summer of 1992 as the acronym for the organization was reduced to three letters (ACA), placing it symbolically beside the AMA (American Medical Association), and both APAs (American Psychological Association, and American Psychiatric Association).

Yet, it will do little to change the stepchild status of counseling vis-a-vis these other three organizations unless insurance companies replace the National Registry with the Yellow Pages as a hierarchical guide to mental health services.

Evidence of a major paradigmatic shift has been presented to the profession in the form of social constructionism and narrative-based approaches to the social sciences. Constructivists' relationships and their narrative description have served as a central and vital means by which meaning is determined for individuals and communities of individuals. Such a postmodern approach to identity and reality emerges from meaningful, horizontal relationships free of constraining preestablished "standards."

The participants in the narrative dialogue need to be free to construct new meanings for identity and fruitful action. At this point, taking action is the result of relational self-favoring interdependence, context specificity, and ongoing dialogue over the traditional values placed on detached rationality and the self-contained, autonomous self. Participants in the dialogue, whether they be counselor and client, teacher and parent, or counselor and administrator, are free to "construct" a dialogue in which the relational aspects of environments are emphasized.

As counselors become more socially and politically aware, environmental causes of human problems come to take center stage. We can now no longer draw artificial distinctions between the outside world of events and inner, subjective perceptions. Taken a step further, political awareness makes it difficult to distinguish individual well-being from collective well-being. The counselors can educate themselves regarding macro issues. This requires interdisciplinary academic perspectives in which students encounter coursework and experience in such disciplines as political science, economics, history, and anthropology.

The counseling professionals need to expand the context through an understanding that all human thought and action is context dependent. When counselors have begun these steps, they need to deal with the resistance that they will encounter in their academic discipline and professional organizations. In addition, counselors ought to have the courage to publicly confront elected officials who pander to the baser instincts of the citizens by using race, sex, and class to pit one segment of society against others for their personal political gain.

Bibliography

Holland, J.L. (1973), *Making Vocational Choices: a Theory of Careers*, Prentice-Hall, Englewood Cliffs, NJ.

Jackson, C. (1993), *The case for diversity in computer-aided careers guidance systems: a response to Watts*, British Journal of Guidance and Counselling, Vol.21 No.2, pp.189-195.

Lee, C. (2000), *Cybercounseling and empowerment: bridging the digital divide*, in Bloom, J.W. & Walz, G.R. (eds.)

McKinlay, B. (1989), *Information systems in career development: history and prospects.*

Offer, M. & Sampson, J.P. (1999), *Quality in the content and use of information and communications technology in guidance*, British Journal of Guidance and Counselling, Vol.27 No.4, pp.501-516.

Offer, M. (1998), *Guidance' websites: we're here, because we're here, because we're here?*, Newscheck, Vol.9 No.4, pp.13-14.

Offer, M., Sampson, J.P. & Watts, A.G. (2001), *Technology and the Future: Strategic Implications for Higher Education Careers Services of Technically Mediated Service Delivery*, Higher Education Careers Services Unit, Manchester (in press).

Oliver, L.W. & Zack, J.S. (1999), *Career assessment on the Internet: an exploratory study*, Journal of Career Assessment, Vol.7 No.4, pp.323-356.

Organisation for Economic Co-operation and Development (2000), *Learning to Bridge the Digital Divide*, OECD, Paris.

Sampson, J.P. (1999a), *Integrating Internet-based distance guidance with services provided in career centers,* Career Development Quarterly, Vol.47 No.3, pp.243-254.

Sampson, J.P. (1999b), *Effective design and use of Internet-based career resources and services: a North American perspective,* paper to International Association for Educational and Vocational Guidance conference, Wellington, New Zealand (mimeo).

Sampson, J.P., Palmer, M. & Watts, A.G. (1999b), *Who Needs Guidance?, Centre for Guidance Studies,* University of Derby.

Sampson, J.P., Peterson, G.W., Reardon, R.C. & Lenz, J.G. (1999a), *Improving Career Services through Readiness Assessment: a Cognitive Information Processing Approach,* Center for the Study of Technology in Counseling and Career Development, Florida State University, Tallahassee, FL (mimeo).

Tait, A. (1999), *Face-to-face and at a distance: the mediation of guidance and counselling through the new technologies,* British Journal of Guidance and Counselling, Vol. 27 No.1, pp.113-122.

Watts, A.G. & Dent, G. (2002), *Let your fingers do the walking': the use of telephone helplines in career information and guidance,* British Journal of Guidance and Counselling, Vol.30 No.1 (in press).

Watts, A.G. (1986), *The role of the computer in careers guidance,* International Journal for the Advancement of Counselling, Vol.9 No.2, pp.145-158.

Watts, A.G. (1993), *The politics and economics of computer-aided careers guidance systems,* British Journal of Guidance and Counselling, Vol.21 No.2, pp.175-188.

Watts, A.G. (1996a), *Computers in guidance,* in Watts, A.G., Law, B., Killeen, J., Kidd, J.M. & Hawthorn, R., Rethinking Careers Education and Guidance: Theory, Policy and Practice, pp. 269- 283, Routledge, London.

Watts, A.G. (1996b), *Careers guidance and public policy,* in Watts, A.G., Law, B., Killeen, J., Kidd, J.M. & Hawthorn, R., Rethinking Careers Education and Guidance: Theory, Policy and Practice, pp. 380-391, Routledge, London.

Watts, A.G. (2001), *Second International Symposium on Career Development and Public Policy: rapporteur's report,* Canadian Career Development Foundation, Ottawa (mimeo).

Index

INFORMATION TECHNOLOGY
A Revolutionary Change

INFORMATION TECHNOLOGY
A Revolutionary Change
(In 9 Volumes)

Volume 6
(Network Revolution: Challenges and Opportunities)

Editor
RAMESH CHANDRA
Vice-Chancellor, Bundelkhand University, Jhansi (U.P.)

KALPAZ PUBLICATIONS
DELHI–110052

INFORMATION TECHNOLOGY: A REVOLUTIONARY CHANGE

(Information Technology)

Rs. 8000 (Set)
Rs. 900 (Each Volume)

ISBN: 81-7835-201-X (Set)
ISBN: 81-7835-225-7 (Vol. 6)

Published in 2003 in India by
Kalpaz Publications
C–30, Satyawati Nagar
Delhi–110052
E-mail: kalpaz@hotmail.com

Laser Typesetting at: Varsha Graphics, Delhi
Printed at: Mehra Offset Printers, New Delhi

Contents

Preface

The network technologies allow remote, virtual collaboration in ways that were not possible just a few years ago. They offer unique opportunity to streamline the delivery of government services, enhance communication with its citizenry, and serve as a catalyst for empowering citizens to interact with government. Internet, the network of networks, is uniquely decentralized, global, abundant, inexpensive, interactive and user-controlled. It provides immediate access to information from around the world. With simple e-mail, it is as easy and inexpensive to send a message to another continent as to the building across the street. Search engines on the World Wide Web list local and foreign sites without distinction.

The networks provide individuals and informal organizations the ability to communicate inexpensively. From their virtual platforms, individuals and organizations are publishing newsletters, advertisements, voters guides and other election-related materials; creating dynamic forums that support issue-based organizing, interactive discussions, and political advocacy; and registering voters. A connection to the net can increase access to information in less-developed countries by putting within easy reach one of the world's great repositories of information, much of it free and continuously updated, and by making that information more easily manageable and transferable. Such benefits do not depend on a large number of persons having the means to purchase their own equipment and Internet accounts.

In light of the networks vast potential for empowering people to exercise the right to free expression, some have argued that governments have an affirmative obligation to facilitate Internet access for all segments of the population on terms of nondiscrimination. On-line communications are particularly susceptible to unauthorized scrutiny. Encryption technology is needed to ensure that individuals and groups may communicate without fear of eavesdropping.

The net has the potential to be a tremendous force for development by providing quick and inexpensive information, by encouraging discussion rather than violence, and by empowering citizens, to cite but a few examples. But this potential can be realized only if it becomes a truly global effort. Policy makers must make every effort to ensure that internationally guaranteed rights to free expression are extended to on-line communication and call for the repeal of censorship legislation. Without such commitments, individuals face the danger of seeing their rights eroded by the very technologies they are embracing.

Editor

Chapter 1

Global Information Development Strategies

The first phase of an emerging country's economic growth is typically based on providing low-cost labour to developed countries. Asian Less Developed Countries (LDCs) have in this way provided international companies with the opportunity to cut the costs of labour-intensive products, which has particularly appealed to the highly competitive electronics industry. Many electronics companies from the United States, Europe, and Japan relocated their labour-intensive electronics assembly operations to the LDCs of Asia starting in the late 1960s. Korea, Taiwan, Hong Kong, Singapore, and Malaysia were early beneficiaries of such labour strategies. For example, in the late 1960s, Sylvania moved low-end stereo production to Hong Kong and Singapore; in the 1970s, Intel and Motorola set up low-cost semiconductor assembly facilities in Malaysia; in the 1980s, Philips began production of colour TVs in Taiwan, and Apple began producing its computers in Singapore. Most major electronics companies have multiple operations in Asia, and most of them already have operations in China.

On the basis of the success and rapid expansion of their labour-intensive industries, in the past 20 to 30 years Korea, Taiwan, Hong Kong, Singapore, and Malaysia have all experienced significant increases in wages, living standards, and numbers of citizens who can be termed "middle class." Their successes in turn have made them less competitive in the low-cost labour market. Today, many of the companies formerly involved in labour-intensive activities in these countries are moving these operations to LDCs such as Indonesia, Thailand, Vietnam, and the Philippines to keep labour costs competitive and to gain access to new markets and revenues.

China has been the biggest beneficiary of this migration of lower-wage jobs within Asia. By June 1996, China had registered some 280,000 foreign firms with paid-in capital of approximately $155 billion that provided 17 million jobs. In 1997, some factory wages for computer assembly in China were as low as $65 a month for 72-hour work weeks.

Korea and Taiwan have located business subsidiaries in China or the countries of Southeast Asia; Hong Kong and Singapore have made a business of assisting foreign enterprises to set up new low-cost labour arrangements in neighbouring LDCs. Thus, while their own abilities to offer low-cost labour have declined, Asian NIEs are still involved in the low-cost labour market in ways that are attractive to Western companies. Summarized below are some of the means by which Asian NIEs have taken and are continuing to take advantage of low-cost labour to improve their economic status.

Korea: Building the Strength of the Chaebols

Korea is unique among the countries discussed in this report in that early on, several of its own industrial companies were the biggest corporate beneficiaries of the country's plentiful, inexpensive labour. Taking advantage of government-subsidized loans and tax breaks, Korea's chaebols (vertically integrated, family-owned industrial conglomerates) capitalized on the country's low wages (and licensing of foreign technologies, etc.) to mass-produce competitively priced light industrial and consumer exports; as a result, both the chaebols and the Korean economy grew very rapidly. Within the past decade or so, Korea's main chaebols have moved beyond their own labour markets to establish electronics and other assembly facilities in Hong Kong and China, Malaysia, Vietnam, and other parts of the world-not only to take advantage of cheaper labour and new market access, but also to establish a global presence.

Taiwan: Importing Labour and Investing Overseas

Following extraordinary successes in manufacturing and assembly endeavours, rising wages in Taiwan began to threaten the competitiveness of its electronics and other products. The government passed a law allowing firms to bring in workers from outside the country for up to two years, and by 1996, nearly 25 percent of Taiwan's manufacturing workforce was foreign. The majority of foreign labourers came from the Philippines, which offered a well-educated, hard-working, English-speaking workforce. In addition, Taiwanese firms began transferring labour-intensive production to such countries as the Philippines and China. Since so many of Taiwan's foreign workers came from the Philippines, building facilities in that country was ideal; the facilities could then hire repatriated workers who had already worked two years in Taiwanese factories.

Even though many Taiwanese firms have been eager to locate operations in China, government authorities have encouraged firms to balance political risks by investing elsewhere as well. The uncertainty created by the transfer of Hong Kong to China on July 1, 1997, caused the Taiwanese government to prohibit large-scale infrastructure investments in mainland China for dams, power plants, airports, roads, and ports. Such projects are typically capital-intensive and subject to political intervention. Electronics and related investments are less problematic; however, the government limits investments in any mainland Chinese project to a maximum of $50 million. With its proposed free-trade area, Okinawa may soon become a beneficiary of Taiwanese investment.

Hong Kong: Partnering with China

Although its economy was once synonymous with low-cost assembly, Hong Kong began responding in the late 1980s to the pressures of escalating wages, limited resources, and global competition by establishing manufacturing partnerships with Chinese companies. Both the real and the nominal growth of Hong Kong's industrial base declined 8 to 10 percent annually between 1988 and 1991 as operations moved across the border to take advantage of cheaper labour and land costs in China's Guangdong province. The Shenzhen special economic zone there allowed Hong Kong-based companies to supply parts and materials duty-free to Chinese companies, use their factories and workers to make products, then ship finished products duty-free back to Hong Kong for re-export to world markets. Between 1982 and 1994, Hong Kong's manufacturing workforce nearly halved its contribution to the GDP, from 20 percent to under 12 percent. In spite of Hong Kong's decline in manufacturing, total employment increased during this period from 2.4 to 2.9 million, and per capita GDP increased 21 percent as displaced workers continued to provide highly valued services such as product design, parts procurement, production coordination, and product marketing and shipping.

Singapore: Promoting Regional Cooperation

In 1960, Singapore's GDP was S$2.1 billion; in 1995, it was S$34.5 billion. In the same period, manufacturing's share of GDP rose from 18 percent to 27 percent, while the contribution of electronics to manufacturing output rose from under 10 percent to over 50 percent. Greater economic prosperity and full employment led to rising wages; in response to this situation as well as to its limited labour, land, and natural resources, Singapore has been aggressive in moving labour-intensive operations offshore. The government encourages both domestic and foreign companies to shift production and marketing operations to neighbouring countries where costs are lower while maintaining high-level management and administrative functions in Singapore.

Singapore's experience with Japanese audio equipment maker Aiwa exemplifies the country's movement away from simple, low-cost assembly work to higher-value-added phases of production. Aiwa, which by March 1997 had moved 90 percent of its production outside Japan, relocated its largest Asian production facility from Singapore to Indonesia, but at the same time established its regional centre for planning and research in Singapore.

Singapore links its domestic economy to regional outreach activity primarily in the form of trade "triangles" and industrial parks. Goh Chok Tong, Singapore's first deputy prime minister, created the first economic triangle for regional development in Southeast Asia in 1989. Under the original "SIJORI" triangle plan, the Malaysian State of Johor (next to Singapore) and the Indonesian province of Riau were to provide the land and low-cost labour for industry while Singapore provided technology and capital. Results have been mixed. While Singapore did expand its low-cost labour pool, Riau has become a tourist resort, and the State of Johor is now trying to improve its economic base by attracting technology, capital, and labour-intensive business away from Singapore. To facilitate exporting labour-intensive operations while keeping the administrative functions of multinational companies (MNCs), Singapore has built Southeast Asia's most complex and advanced infrastructure (airports, ports, transportation, power, telecommunications, human resources, finance, living conditions, tax system, etc.). Despite this effort, ongoing cost pressures have continued to erode Singapore's image as an attractive business centre. Singapore is now helping firms develop overall low-cost strategies by building high-tech industrial parks in China, Vietnam, and India, with varying degrees of success. Increasing the number of low-wage jobs provided the initial stimulus for Asian economic growth, but expansion in manufacturing output tended to occur primarily as a result of increasing capital input or numbers of workers. As capital inputs became less cost-effective and employment levels topped out (despite labour imports to fill shortfalls in unskilled workers), productivity rates began to level off and even decline. To ensure their continued economic competitiveness, the Asian NIEs have committed to further improving their civil and transportation infrastructures, legislative and tax structures, and educational institutions, and especially their advanced technology and research capabilities as part of long-range plans to achieve first-world economic status.

Upgrading Technology and Related Capabilities and Infrastructures Most of the emerging economies of Asia have based the second phase of their economic development strategies on upgrading their technology capabilities and related infrastructures. The addition of technology allows industries to increase the value added to products and services and increase their contribution to society. While Asian NIEs are moving away from low-skill, low-cost jobs, they are simultaneously working intently to develop domestic technology capabilities, building on their earlier successes in contract labour businesses. Three common aspects of Asia's technology-building strategy are building research and education infrastructures focused on science and technology; targeting critical advanced technologies and products for development; and attracting (and keeping) foreign technology leaders and state-of-the-art technologies. One approach practiced by all the countries covered in this study combines all three of the above: building advanced science and technology (S&T) parks.

Another common approach in this stage is modernizing and improving national education levels, especially in science and technology. Education has a historically high social value in many Asian cultures, but it is also a developmental imperative. The goals are clearly to prepare the workforces of tomorrow and to support continued economic development, although the particulars vary greatly from country to country. Korea's literacy rate is now one of the world's highest, about 95 percent, and the country is building impressive advanced research capabilities within its public and private universities (many are industry-funded), with a new emphasis on improving critical thinking and interdisciplinary cooperation to better support innovative capabilities.

China's literacy rate, narrowly defined as only 4.5 years of education, still is only about 80 percent. The country is struggling with resource allocation trade-offs between educating the masses broadly or educating a more elite group to meet the country's advanced economic requirements. Malaysia is building up both basic and advanced literacy levels and also has a unique program within its "Vision 2020" plan to instill in workers a work ethic that supports greater productivity as well as to train personnel in specific high-tech skills industry requires.

Building National Research Infrastructures Korea Government-supported research institutes (GRIs) have been set up throughout Asia. Korea has used GRIs effectively to prime the pump for its technological developments. The Korea Institute of Science and Technology (KIST), organized in 1966, was that country's first multidisciplinary industrial research organization. It has focused on basic problems relating to technology transfer. In 1971, the Korea Advanced Institute for Science was established to provide postgraduate education in science and engineering. The Electronics and Telecommunication Research Institute, one of Korea's leading GRIs, has evolved since 1976 out of a series of research organizations associated with different government ministries and is now affiliated with the Ministry of Information and Communications. It is recognized as the top information technology research institute in Korea and is a world leader in such technologies.

Through the 1970s, various GRIs carried out high-risk research in low-profit areas and in areas where Korean universities lacked capabilities. Before Korea's fiscal crisis, the Ministry of Science and Technology, just one of the ministries supporting S&T, gave GRIs roughly $10 million of support annually. Since the mid-1990s, GRIs have struggled to respond appropriately to industry's rapidly changing needs. The rapid pace of technological change has given a competitive edge to researchers with close industry and market ties.

Meanwhile, between 1982 and 1989, the number of private industrial research institutes in Korea increased from 46 to 749 because of the government's cooperative R&D program. By 1992, the number had increased to 1,435 thanks to government support and tax incentives. During the 1970s, much of the private research focused on imitating foreign products and licensing foreign technology. In the 1980s and 1990s, the focus of private research has continued to be on products, but increasingly, these products are based on proprietary technologies, not imported ones. This shift was dramatically demonstrated when Samsung announced in December 1995 its 1Gbit DRAM (dynamic random access memory) breakthrough, ahead of all competition.

Information services, multimedia, computer systems, satellite communication systems, and new display technologies are among the subjects of Korea's current private R&D efforts.

In Taiwan, the Ministry of Economic Affairs (MOEA) and the National Science Council direct most strategic technology investments and programs. One of MOEA's best-known technology centers is the Industrial Technology Research Institute (ITRI), which has played a primary role in providing advanced technological support for a wide range of industries, about half of which are electronics related. These electronics technologies are addressed through the Electronics Research and Services Organization (ERSO) within ITRI.

ERSO focuses on semiconductor integrated circuit (IC) devices, display devices, microwave components, and electronic technologies packaging. It also provides technical services to industry. ITRI's R&D function is critical in Taiwan, since many Taiwanese companies are too small to afford R&D; for this reason ITRI has concentrated its efforts on applied research and product development, particularly for key components that are medium (three to five years) and long-term projects (over five years). After product development and initiation of pilot production, ITRI terminates its direct participation. Its $260 million annual budget is about 80 percent government-funded. Indirect Taiwanese government sponsorship of favoured product development and commercialization includes initial tax holidays, 10 to 20 percent tax credits, 50 percent partial funding or loans, and up to 60 percent matching grants for training programs.

Extensive public involvement in high-tech R&D is relatively recent in Singapore. The National Science and Technology Board (NSTB) was established in 1991 to promote R&D activities required to enhance the electronics industry's core capabilities and to fund and coordinate R&D in universities, polytechnics, and industry, in accordance with Singapore's "E-2000" development plan. NSTB's mission is to make the city-state a centre of excellence in selected fields of science and technology to enhance its competitiveness in industrial and service sectors. NSTB's five programs are:

(1) partnering with industry,

(2) recruiting and training on R&D workforce,

(3) establishing and maintaining national research institutes and centers,

(4) providing an R&D infrastructure, and

(5) building international alliances and cooperative agreements.

NSTB undertakes precompetitive collaborative research with industry partners and has established the following national research institutes and technology competency centers:

1. The Institute of Microelectronics supports VLSI (very large scale integration) design, failure and reliability analysis, and advanced packaging and silicon processing.

2. The Center for Wireless Communications focuses on spectrum, wireless multimedia, modulation, and transmission.

3. The Data Storage Institute concentrates on magnetic computer-assisted design, magnetic recording, mechatronics, servo controls, laser processing, and optical technologies.
4. The GINTIC Institute of Manufacturing Technology provides computer-integrated manufacturing, automation, and process development support.
5. The Center for Signal Processing supports the computer, multimedia, consumer, and communications industries.
6. The Institute of System Science emphasizes applied research in natural language processing, neural networks, fuzzy logic, and broadband networks.
7. The Information Technology Institute emphasizes information management, multimedia, and artificial intelligence. NSTB's partnering programs include assessment of technology trends and industry needs, support of company-based research, and funding of consortia-type research.

Although Singapore's public research institutions are providing crucial support to the country's electronics and other modern industries, by far the largest amount of research expenditure in Singapore has been private. Since at least 1978, private sector R&D investment has generally equalled or exceeded the combined investment by the government, universities, and public research institutes. The overall R&D investment rate in Singapore has about tripled in the past decade.

Malaysia's GRIs include the Standards and Industrial Research Institute of Malaysia and the Malaysian Institute for Microelectronic Systems (MIMOS). MIMOS, started in 1985 within the prime minister's office and now a department of the Ministry of Science, Technology, and the Environment, is Malaysia's national center of excellence in microelectronics and information technology. MIMOS projects are product oriented and focused on boosting the competitive and innovative levels of the domestic electronics industry. Six research departments indicate the fields of interest: semiconductor technology, design methodology, computer technology, product development, industrial technology, and telecommunications technology. Large-scale MIMOS projects include a microelectronics center in the Kulim Hi-Tech Industrial Park and an operational microchip plant.

Targeting Technologies and Products

As Korea's private R&D activities have grown, the government has shifted its R&D activities to large-scale projects. By 1989, KIST had participated in 5,600 research projects valued at over $260 million and employing a staff of 592, including 459 in research. In 1992, the Korean government launched 11 Highly Advanced National (HAN) projects to address the development of next-generation products and technologies. These projects included development of the following:

— highly integrated semiconductors

— an integrated services digital network (ISDN)

— high-definition television (HDTV)

— new medicine and new agricultural medicines

— advanced production systems

— new advanced materials

— next-generation vehicles
— new functional biomaterials
— technology in environmental engineering
— new energy resources
— next-generation atomic reactors and verification

Product-oriented projects target future market opportunities. "Fundamental" projects develop technologies that focus on core technologies that will advance economic, social, and personal life. The HAN projects combine joint investment by the government and Korea's largest chaebols with interministerial cooperation and coordination. Universities, industries, and GRIs coordinate on each project. The results have been considered only moderately successful, since global competition intensifies the speed required for technology development. Aside from such government activities, Korean chaebols also have targeted certain technologies and markets-such as DRAMs-with great success.

Taiwan has targeted critical components and products to maximize the benefits of its research programs. MOEA has developed a systematic "program for the development of critical components and products." The program focuses resources of the government and the private sector on developing critical components and products, replacing imports with local suppliers, improving local capabilities, and supporting the development of emerging industries. Critical products included HDTV, digital audio tape recorders, electronic still cameras, a variety of computer peripherals, and automated manufacturing equipment.

Each item was classified into one of three groups: A, B, and C. In the A group, a GRI such as ITRI is entrusted to obtain licenses or to develop the technology, or both. In the B group, MOEA provides government financial assistance to develop prototypes of the targeted component or product. In the C group, the government supports production capacity by providing such incentives as tax credits, acquisition of industrial land, government participation in the investment, favourable loans, training of professional personnel, and special duties and import regulations.

In 1995, critical components in group A included fuzzy logic ICs, liquid crystal displays (LCDs), high-density static and dynamic RAM, a variety of radio frequency ICs for telecommunications, light-emitting diodes (LEDs) for displays, and charge-coupled devices for video. Most A components were also classified B and C. As A projects were completed, they moved into categories B or C: silicon wafer fabrication had only a C priority to ramp up output.

Display components. Taiwan is working hard to end its reliance on imported visual displays and related materials for high-end products, mostly from Japan. In 1995, Japanese firms provided all of the 10-inch LCD panels used in Taiwan-produced notebook personal computers (PCs); local vendors provided 90 percent of the LCD displays used in electronic dictionaries, although 90 percent of the materials used to produce them were imported, mostly from Japan. Japanese firms supplied 87 percent of the high-resolution cathode ray tube (CRT) monitors for computers and 30 percent of the mid-resolution monitors. To overcome this deficit, the government has designated displays as a critical component and has supported development of next-generation display products. In 1995, two firms produced high-technology active-matrix LCDs in Taiwan, and 13 firms produced lower-quality passive matrix displays. 10-inch colour passive-matrix and active-matrix LCDs have begun pilot production, and high-end active matrix LCDs over 10 inches are being developed. ICs for colour filter drivers are still imported.

Taiwan has become a close follower of the United States in high-luminance LEDs, and ITRI has developed blue LEDs, which allow full-colour displays to be developed with LED technology. In 1995, Taiwan firms produced 20 percent of the mid-resolution and 80 percent of the low-resolution CRT monitors for Taiwan-made computers, although 40 percent of the monitor materials had to be imported. Taiwan had already begun to mass-produce CRTs up to 21 inches, had pilot production of CRTs over 28 inches, and was developing a wide 16:9 ratio CRT for use in HD TVs.

Semiconductor components. Among the key components it has targeted, Taiwan has been successful in entering the semiconductor industry. In 1995, Taiwan had 12 firms producing ICs with total revenues of $4 billion. These firms supplied 19.1 percent of the domestic IC requirements and planned to provide 37.8 percent of domestic demand by 2000. By then, they planned to invest $16.5 billion in 20 semiconductor wafer fabrication facilities ("fabs") with a capacity of 4.8 million ICs per month. Taiwan's goal is to increase its global share of the semiconductor market from 2.5 percent in 1995 to 7.5 percent by 2000.

Taiwan's 12 IC firms are the result of strategic alliances and technology agreements with the world's leading semiconductor firms. United Microelectronics Corp. (UMC) was spun off from ITRI/ERSO in 1979. It has strategic alliances and technology agreements with SGS-Thomson, Thesys, Meridian, and Microstar (MSI). The Taiwan Semiconductor Manufacturing Company (TSMC), spun-off from ITRI/ERSO in 1982, has technical and strategic alliances with Advanced Micro Devices (AMD), Cirrus Logic, Amadent (AMAD), and Integrated Silicon Solution, Inc. (ISSI). TSMC, now the second largest foundry in Asia, supplies Fujitsu, Ltd., of Japan with 16-megabit DRAMs under Fujitsu's brand name.

TSMC planned to begin producing 64M DRAM chips for Fujitsu in 1997 using Fujitsu's technology. Acer has an IC joint venture with Texas Instruments. Taiwan's largest conglomerate, Nan Ya Plastics, has licensed the technology of Oki (Japan) for its new DRAM fab. In 1994, Vanguard International Semiconductor was spun off from ITRI/ERSO to produce submicron memory ICs in Taiwan. Most of the capital came from government and local banking sources. To further strengthen the IC industry's infrastructure, ERSO established the Electronics Testing Center in 1982. The first domestic mask manufacturer, Taiwan Mask Corporation, and EMMT System Corporation were spun off in 1988. In 1995, 26 companies in Taiwan were involved in IC design with total revenues of $593 million.

Attracting Foreign Technology Leaders

The example of Taiwan's targeted investment in ICs illustrates another ingredient of successful economic development in Asia: in order to enter and compete in markets for technologically advanced components and products, Asian NIEs have relied heavily on cooperation with foreign technology leaders, often by expanding on relationships begun in contract labour arrangements. For a newly industrializing economy, overcoming the financial and technical challenges of expanding into advanced fields may be feasible only with such cooperation. For this reason, Taiwan, Singapore, and Malaysia have been strongly committed to attracting and keeping the involvement of leading companies, especially in the 1990s. Once foreign corporations have a stake in local markets, they typically continue to upgrade technologies.

U.S., Japanese, and European firms are rapidly transferring technologies into Southeast Asia, reducing the time it takes to produce next-generation products locally. For example, because Intel's customers must be able to install new microprocessors in the latest products, it produces motherboards to facilitate the introduction of its latest microprocessors. It also transfers next-generation assembly technologies to Asian customers as quickly as possible to ensure market penetration. Orient Semiconductor Company in Taiwan licensed tape carrier production technology for making daughter boards for notebook computers. Singapore provides a full range of programs, while Malaysia and Taiwan offer much simpler and more focused incentives. Hong Kong has taken a more passive approach.

While many Asian NIEs are working hard to attract foreign firms, there is some hesitation about inviting too much foreign involvement. Most of them have used various import controls or regulations to place some restrictions on local operations of foreign firms. China, for example, is caught between its need to protect its weak state-owned enterprises (SOEs) from foreign competition and its need to increase their access to foreign technologies. To upgrade and modernize its SOEs, China is working to provide internal support while encouraging limited partnerships with foreign firms. The majority of PC exports from China are made by joint ventures of SOEs with foreign companies.

Malaysia has historically had a strong emphasis on national self-reliance—a theme that echoes throughout Asia-but in the past 10 years has decided that in the interest of accelerating its economic growth, it is willing to postpone this goal in the short term in order to achieve world-class economic status more quickly. Therefore, Malaysia has become more open to foreign direct investments since 1990, and has offered significant incentives to foreign companies willing to invest in enterprises that facilitate technology transfer. These incentives include generous "pioneer status" investment tax exemptions and allowances, financing of up to 100 percent of some costs if technology transfer is involved, infrastructure construction, relaxation of regulations governing employment of skilled expatriates and foreign workers, and specialized training of workers.

More than most other Asian countries, Singapore sees attracting MNCs as the centerpiece of its development strategy. Half the 4,000 MNCs located in Singapore have established regional headquarters there. Over 80 MNC offices, including Hewlett-Packard, Compaq, Motorola, Hitachi, Matsushita, Philips, Seagate, National Semiconductor, SGS-Thomson, Siemens, Murata, SCI, Sony, Thomson, Toshiba, IBM, and Texas Instruments each spend over $25 million per year in local expenses. Since MNCs are the driving force behind Singapore's industrial development, the Economic Development Board (EDB) plans to provide special incentives to attract another 120 regional headquarters, each spending over $25 million per year, by 2000. Companies awarded status as operational or business headquarters benefit from incentives that include tax concessions on offshore income. Responding to liberal incentives and excellent supporting infrastructures, MNCs continue to establish advanced technology centers in Singapore.

Motorola set up 120 engineers at its Asian Motorola Manufacturing Systems facility in Singapore to carry out manufacturing R&D and to transfer developments to other sites in the region. SGS-Thomson Microelectronics conducts semiconductor research on digital signal processing, BICMOS (bipolar complementary metal oxide semiconductor) silicon wafer processing, and advanced packaging technologies. Siemens Components has established an R&D IC design center, including testing, packaging, and manufacturing technologies for use in the region. In July 1997, Germany's Wacker Siltronic AG announced its plans to spend S$478.5 million (US$337 million) to build Singapore's first silicon wafer manufacturing plant, which will supply silicon wafers to wafer fabs in the Asia-Pacific region. With 400 companies from northern Europe, Singapore opened the North European center of trade and industry in 1998. It will house up to 100 midsize companies from Denmark, Finland, Norway, Sweden, and Iceland. The North European center will be 90 percent financed by Singaporean companies at a cost of $69.8 million. A German center opened in 1995.

Building Advanced Technology Parks

High-profile advanced S&T parks, like special economic

zones, are popular in Asia as a means of upgrading technology. They are designed to combine and concentrate the advantages of many of the kinds of strategies summarized above:

(1) support R&D, commercialization, and education activities;

(2) focus on key technical fields and products; and

(3) promote and facilitate international financial and technical participation.

They have the added advantages of bolstering national pride, fostering interdisciplinary synergies, and enhancing concentration and control of limited resources. Countries usually offer special incentives for both foreign and domestic investment in projects within the parks that further specific national development goals. For example, China offers foreign firms reduced tax rates of 15 percent and greater incentives at start-up time for qualifying projects in its industrial parks. Firms are exempt from taxes for two years once they begin to make profits; then they are exempt from 50 percent of their taxes between years three and five. Firms that export at least 70 percent of their output are taxed at a 10 percent rate.

Singapore, having successfully established science parks of its own, is making a business of helping other countries establish and run focused high-technology parks. The China-Singapore Suzhou Industrial Park, initiated in 1995, has attracted investment commitments of $2 billion from 62 international companies. About 20 companies are already in production, among them Selectron Corp., the world's second-largest producer of motherboards, which has established a $45 million facility. The Vietnam-Singapore Industrial Park was launched in May 1996 near Ho Chi Minh City. India and Singapore established the Information Technology (IT) Park in Bangalore in September 1995 specifically to take advantage of India's 140,000 low-cost computer programmers. With stiff competition from other IT parks in India and the region, such as Malaysia's Multimedia Super Corridor (MSC), the focus of the Bangalore park was expanded in early 1997, and it was renamed the International Technology Park.

In 1980, Taiwan established its Hsinchu industrial park, now home to a large share of the island's high-tech manufacturers, including, in 1995, 51 semiconductor firms, 39 PC/peripheral firms, 30 telecommunications firms, 25 optoelectronic firms, 16 precision machinery firms, and biotechnology firms; of these, 25 percent were foreign owned. The park provides one-stop permitting, five-year corporate income tax exemptions, low-interest loans, and tax credits for R&D investments, factory automation, and human resource development. Annual sales in 1994 were $6.4 billion. On the basis of the successes of the Hsinchu park, in 1997 the government opened a new science park at T'ai-nan in the south of Taiwan.

Thirty-eight wafer, computer, and other factories are being built there, including plants for United Microelectronics Corp., Texas Instruments-Acer, several Japanese electronics firms, IBM, Motorola, and new 8-inch- and 12-inch-wafer plants for TSMC, Taiwan's oldest electronics company. Mosel Vitelic is spending about $3.6 billion to build a 12-inch-wafer plant there. The new park fits into Taiwan's blueprint to become a "high-tech island" and its expectation that, by 2000, 40 percent of the island's manufacturing output will be in technology-intensive industries.

Malaysia operates several industrial parks under the premise that a group of industries working in a common environment can accomplish much more than in isolation. The government strategy is to include both public and private research institutions, promote hybrid technologies, upgrade local university laboratories, establish technology centers, and fund both joint and individual R&D projects. Two well-established Malaysian industrial parks are the Technology Park of Malaysia (TPM) near Kuala Lumpur and Kulim Hi-Tech Industrial Park near Penang.

TPM was started in 1988 "to be the best in providing the infrastructure, facilities, and services related to the development of knowledge-based industries." TPM's main thrust is support of industrial high-tech entrepreneurship. Over the next five years, TPM plans to focus on three broad technology fields: manufacturing and industrial engineering, information technology and multimedia, and biotechnology, emphasizing R&D, commercialization, and human resource development. As is common, general and customized financial and other incentives support foreign participation in the parks.

Developing Globally Competitive Businesses

With increasingly sophisticated technology capabilities, the third phase of an emerging country's successful economic development tends to be based on transforming local firms into first-class high-tech competitors in the global marketplace. While foreign-owned MNCs may aid in developing an economy, sustained development now requires establishing domestic industries' strength in emerging industries and technologies. Being able to upgrade imported basic technologies and develop higher value-added components and products is just the beginning. Domestic firms tend to contribute more to the local economy and are less likely to move out when costs of doing business rise. The success of local firms requires that they achieve economies of scale and size adequate to support state-of-the-art research and development of products for emerging industries. To reach adequate size, firms must expand into markets beyond their home bases, thereby competing with leading multinational firms. Like Japan, Korea has been especially successful in developing world-class competitors. Today, Singapore has the most dynamic strategy for building its own global players.

Korea's chaebols, large conglomerates, have been the major beneficiaries of government development policies and research support. Samsung, Daewoo, and LG have become leaders in the global electronics industry over the past 25 years. Despite current restructuring, these family-dominated companies established after World War II continue to rank among the largest companies in the world. Korean chaebols accounted for 8 of the 12 largest East Asian firms and 43 of the largest 100 East Asian firms in 1995 sales, excluding Japan and China. Korea's largest 8 chaebols are Samsung Electronics Co., Hyundai Motor Co., Korea Electric Power Corp., Pohang Iron & Steel Co., Yukong, Ltd., LG Electronics Co., Kia Motors Co., and Daewoo Heavy Industries Co. Chaebols produce almost 50 percent of Korea's gross national product (GNP) and account for 70 percent of the country's exports. The top 30 chaebols control 821 firms. In 1995, the Samsung Group, Korea's largest chaebol, had sales of $87 billion, 233,000 employees, and 340 facilities in 66 countries. The group's goal is to be ranked among the world's top 10 companies by 2000. Samsung has focused on four core industries: electronics, machinery, chemicals, and finance. Samsung's strategy of "globalization and localization" includes operations worldwide to access local markets. In 1995, Samsung had regional headquarters in Europe, North America, Japan, China, and Singapore. To compete globally, Samsung's strategy has been to produce the world's best products. The group invests more than 7 percent ($2 billion) of its total revenue in R&D in order to build technological leadership.

Daewoo Group revenues were $65 billion in 1996, with $13 billion in exports. Daewoo has 25 domestic companies, 277 overseas subsidiaries, and over 191,000 employees worldwide. In 1996, Daewoo ranked 34 in the Fortune Global 500. "Daewoo Globalization Through Daewoo Technology" is the theme of the company's Vision 2000. Daewoo had 12,000 R&D personnel in 1996 and invested $1 billion in R&D. It challenges member companies to become industry leaders by the year 2000. Goals include total group sales of $177 billion with a worldwide network of 650 facilities in over 150 nations. This network will include 430 sales subsidiaries, 130 manufacturing subsidiaries, 20 technical and design R&D centers, and 70 local branch offices engaged in trading and related activities.

The LG Group launched Leap 2005 in March 1996 with the goal of reaching annual revenues of $385 billion by 2005. LG intends to set the global standard for quality and service in emerging business sectors such as communications, multimedia, environmental technologies, bioengineering, broadcasting media, heavy industry, energy, and infrastructure development. LG's core industries include chemicals and energy, electronics, machinery and metals, trade and services, and finance businesses.

To help meet the ambitious goals mentioned above, Korean chaebols make significant investments overseas as they build global competitiveness. In 1995, foreign direct investment in Korea totalled $1.9 billion. In contrast, overseas direct investment by Korean firms reached $3.1 billion as the government reduced foreign investment restrictions and simplified procedures. The top five chaebols plan $70 billion in overseas direct investment in the coming decade. LG Group plans to build a home electronics and semiconductor plant in the United Kingdom at a cost of $2.6 billion. Hyundai Electronics Industries Company plans to set up a $1.4 billion semiconductor plant in Britain.

Korean chaebols are also buying foreign firms to gain instant access to foreign markets and to add brand names and new technologies. Daewoo purchased France's Thomson Multimedia and acquired a majority share of Zenith to become the world's biggest producer of televisions. Samsung bought a large stake in AST Research, a California PC maker. Hyundai acquired 40 percent of Maxtor in 1993 to build a position in the disk drive business.

Although for the most part the success of the chaebols has until recently impeded the growth of new, smaller companies in Korea's computer market, TriGem has become one of Korea's new success stories. This midsize firm held a 22 percent share of Korea's PC market in 1996. In 1995, TriGem manufactured over 600,000 PCs and recorded revenues of over $850 million. Foreign companies had only a 7 percent share of the

Korean PC market. Hewlett-Packard and IBM, the leading U.S. players in Korea, could garner only 2 percent and 1 percent of the market, respectively. The Korean government has been seeking ways to promote the growth of new businesses; TriGem's success indicates some progress on this front.

Taiwan's Global Market Position

Taiwan is concentrating on electronics, its top export; already it has become the world's fifth largest supplier of PCs. Taiwanese firms moved from assembling products such as transistor radios, TVs, and tape recorders in the 1960s, to manufacturing CRTs in the 1970s, to producing colour monitors, semiconductors, electronic watches, and IBM-compatible PCs in the 1980s, becoming larger and more successful in each stage. In the 1990s, Taiwan's strategy moved it into production of the microelectronic components needed for its leading suppliers of motherboards, monitors, scanners, and computer mouse devices. Taiwan's global market share in key electronics components. In 1995, computer monitors were a $7.2 billion business for Taiwan, which had a world market share of 57 percent. Taiwanese companies held 65 percent of the world motherboard and keyboard markets, 64 percent of the scanner market, 38 percent of network cards, 35 percent of power supplies, 32 percent of graphic cards, 27 percent of portable PCs, and 11 percent of CD-ROMs. Taiwan also held 72 percent of the worldwide computer mouse market in 1995.

Taiwan's computer-related output was valued at $19.7 billion in 1995. Information products rose from 22.8 percent to 33.8 percent of Taiwan's electronics output between 1986 and 1995. The shift into computers and related components has been highly successful. In 1995, Taiwan held 27 percent of the global notebook PC market and 10 percent of the desktop PC market. Taiwan supplies all computer components except hard disk drives. While Taiwan's share of notebook PCs was projected to exceed 38 percent in 1997, the production of desktop PCs was being moved to low-cost labour countries such as China and the Philippines. Taiwanese firms have excelled in introducing computers with the latest components.

Taiwanese vendors have become original design manufacturers that sell "ready to go" products to original equipment manufacturers. While it took three years for Taiwan to introduce the first IBM-compatible 286 computer in 1985, Taiwanese firms were only two months behind in introducing the first Pentium-based systems in 1993. By 1997, Taiwan was first to introduce the latest components and most advanced computer designs. With growing strength in product design and new product development, Taiwanese companies continue to strengthen their global market position.

The Taiwanese firms Inventec, GVC, Tatung, First International, Elite, Quanta, and Twin Head are the major suppliers to the world's top 10 PC companies, including Compaq, IBM, Apple, Packard Bell-NEC, AST, Toshiba, and Hewlett-Packard. They all aspire to stand-alone status like that of Acer, Inc., Taiwan's leading global player, which ranks as one of the five largest component makers in the world and has one of the top 10 PC brands in the world.

Singapore's Strategy for Local Enterprises

Singapore's EDB is working with over 250 local firms to help them become Asian MNCs with operations in at least three countries, with sales over $400 million, and with established brand names such as Creative Technology. EDB has identified promising local enterprises with strong core capabilities, clear vision, and high growth potential. Aztech Technology, which accounts for almost 90 percent of the world's sound card market, is one such company. Singapore's largest semiconductor foundry, Chartered Semiconductor Manufacturing (CSM), is 84 percent owned by the government and produces application-specific integrated circuits. Within the world's $6 billion semiconductor foundry market, CSM ranks second, with 5.3 percent of the market. (Taiwan Semiconductor Manufacturer Company is the leader, with about 20 percent.) Of CSM's $1 billion in revenues, about 60 percent comes from the United States, and another 30 percent comes from Taiwan. Toshiba Corporation and CSM have announced a five-year partnership to produce embedded DRAMs for multimedia applications. This leading-edge systems-on-silicon technology was to enter the market at the end of 1998. CSM plans two additional wafer fabs, including a joint venture with Hewlett-Packard and Singapore's EDB.

Singapore's strategy is to develop 100 promising local enterprises with revenues greater than $100 million each within 10 years. These firms are growing at an average of about 30 percent annually. By 2000, EDB expects that between 50 and 70 will exceed the $100 million goal and be capable of competing in the global marketplace. EDB manages a $1 billion fund for strengthening partnerships between MNCs and local enterprises, helping the local firms go regional. EDB shares start-up costs and business risks with key investor companies by co-investing in strategic projects both in and outside Singapore. It makes equity investments in projects that support its programs and fill critical gaps in industry technologies.

Future Developments

The rapid progress of the Asian NIEs through the three stages of development is due in large measure to careful planning, continuous re-evaluation, and long-range goals for product and component developments. With resources still limited, hard decisions must be made about what industries to support in order to continue planned development into the future. All the countries discussed here have detailed central plans for their development into the twenty-first century, and all of those plans include a renewed emphasis on targeting high-end electronics and information technologies, attracting multinational investment, providing a first-rate technology infrastructure, and fostering the growth of indigenous high-tech global players. The plans noted below offer a glimpse into the mind-set of Asian leaders.

Korea: Advanced Telecom and IT

Korea's national commitment to key technologies and products prominently features information technologies, including telecommunications, information systems and software. This country plans for this sector-6.9 percent of the national economy in 1996-to grow 19.6 percent a year to 2001 (double the average world growth) and to contribute a 10 percent share of the domestic economy by 2001. To achieve this goal, annual public and private sector investment-8.7 trillion won in 1996 (about $10.3 billion at 845 won/US$1)-is expected to almost triple by 2001. As an indication of the dedication to and progress in developing this sector, Korea's number of phone subscribers increased from 3 million in 1980 to 10 million in 1988 and to 20 million as of May 1997, in a country with a population of 46 million. In 1980, 10 percent of the switching systems were electronic (TDX); in 1988, 70 percent were electronic; and in 1997, 100 percent were electronic, 65 percent digital. The government's forecast is that by 2001, subscribers to wireless telecom services (cellular and PCS) will number 13 million; the wireless market will amount to 92 percent of the wired market; and online communications services will be worth 2.8 trillion won.

Taiwan: Information Technology

In 1995, Taiwan's ITRI ranked Taiwan among the world leaders in electronics products. It ranked fourth in information technologies, seventh in communications products, and fifth in consumer electronics products and in electronic components such as semiconductors, optoelectronics, displays, and IC packaging. As the fourth-largest producer of ICs, Taiwan had wafer fabrication factories producing $4 billion in semiconductors in 1995, was mass producing 16M DRAMs, and planned to have 20 8-inch wafer fabs operating by 2000. Although it plans to continue to be a world leader in electronics, Taiwan is beginning to move into other areas, including information technologies. Other critical products identified for support include medical diagnostic equipment, aircraft, robots, cogeneration equipment, and breathable fabric.

Of Taiwan's electronics output, information-related electronic components increased from a 38 percent to a 53.4 percent share between 1986 and 1995, and this share is expected to grow further. Although communication electronics has so far been a small proportion of the total electronics market, Taiwan is now targeting it as a future growth business. Between 1986 and 1995, consumer electronics fell from 30.9 percent to 7.3 percent of Taiwan's electronics output, after the government decided that electronic games and toys were intellectually unhealthy for its children. To sustain its economic development, Taiwan targeted 10 emerging industries in 1992: information, communications, consumer electronics, semiconductors, precision machinery and automation equipment, aerospace, advanced materials, speciality chemicals and pharmaceuticals, medical and health care, and pollution control and treatment industries. Of these, information, precision machinery, and speciality chemical industries are expected to become Taiwan's leading industries by 2002.

Malaysia: Multimedia and IT

Malaysia plans to invest more than $2 billion over the next decade to become the multimedia hub of Southeast Asia. In August 1995, Prime Minister Mahathir proposed the Multimedia Super Corridor (MSC) project to foster IT industries. MSC stretches south of the capital of Kuala Lumpur to where a new international airport and new federal capital are under construction-a 9-mile by 30-mile zone about the size of Singapore. This corridor will attract a workforce of 150,000. The Cyberjaya ("Cybercity") development company, Cyberview Sdn. Bhd., is a joint venture of five Malaysian parties and Japan's Nippon Telegraph and Telephone Corp. On May 17, 1997, phase one was initiated with a $1.6 billion investment in construction of the 6,900-acre Malaysian Multimedia University.

The electronic backbone of MSC will be a 2.5-10 gigabyte digital fiberoptic network that will link the corridor to Japan, Europe, and the United States. Multimedia experiments planned for Cyberjaya include the use of multipurpose integrated chip cards to serve as passports, identity cards, credit cards, and electronic money for such electronic administrative needs as the provision of driver's licenses. Some delays in the Cyberjaya project are expected as a result of Southeast Asia's current fiscal difficulties.

By creating an advanced information network, Malaysia's government hopes to lure leading R&D companies and software developers from abroad. More than 900 companies have applied to participate in the MSC program. Qualifying firms must be suppliers of multimedia and other information technology products or services and be willing to transfer technology to Malaysia. Nonmanual workers such as engineers should account for at least 15 percent of the workforce. Companies that joined the project by the end of 1997 will be exempted from corporate taxes for up to 10 years.

Forty-two foreign and local companies have met MSC qualifications to locate operations in Cyberjaya, including AT&T, Sun Microsystems, and NCR from the United States; Germany's Siemens; British Telecommunications; and Japan's NTT, Fujitsu, NEC,

Mitsubishi, Sumitomo, and Sharp corporations. NTT has already set up a subsidiary in Malaysia to benefit from the preferential treatment, including exemption from corporate tax and from mandatory rules on hiring local employees.

Singapore: Cluster Industries/Electronics

Singapore's 1991 Strategic Plan initially targeted 12 industries for development and support (aerospace has since been added):

— Commodity trading and shipping to strengthen Singapore's position as a leading international trading hub and regional headquarters for shipping and ship management activities.

— Precision engineering, electronics, and information technology to establish Singapore as the premier designer, marketer, and manufacturer of high-end precision components and systems, and high-value-added electronic products/components and as an R&D and product development center, and to support the export of software products and services.

— Petroleum and petrochemicals, construction, and heavy engineering to develop Singapore into a world-scale integrated petroleum and petrochemical hub, center for construction services for the Asia-Pacific region, and center for ship repair, oil rig construction, and manufacturing and servicing of oil and gas field equipment.

— Finance, insurance, and general supporting industries to establish Singapore as a major international financial center, regional insurance and reinsurance center, and a one-stop regional center for products and supporting services.

— Tourism to establish Singapore as a premier visitor destination with convention/exhibition and travel/ tourism-related services. Singapore's Economic 2000 plan stresses working relationships among government, industry, and academia to support its strategy. Singapore's infrastructure goals include maintaining the employment and GDP contributions from manufacturing at 20 percent and 25 percent, respectively.

The key to this goal is its electronics industry cluster, including semiconductors, communications, display, and data storage businesses. Singapore's successful electronics development strategy produced revenues of over $45 billion in 1995. The electronics industry accounted for 51.4 percent of the manufacturing sector's output and employed 34.2 percent of the manufacturing workforce. In 1995, data storage devices were the electronic industry's most successful business, accounting for 23.3 percent of its total electronic industry output, followed by semiconductors with 21 percent. Final systems fabrication of computers and multimedia products accounted for 19.7 percent; consumer electronics, 12.4 percent; communications products, 6.3 percent; and office automation products, 5.8 percent. These successes pave the way for continued development in these areas.

Singapore is using a semiconductor strategy similar to Taiwan's, with balanced development of design, fabrication, assembly, and test processes. Singapore's semiconductor industry cluster includes 23 IC design companies, 5 wafer fabs, and 19 assemble and test companies. EDB plans for 20 wafer fabs to be operating by 2005 and intends to attract 2 or 3 more companies as joint venture partners. It has also targeted microprocessors and flat panel displays as key components. To support Singapore's continuing economic growth, the government is offering tax incentives for pioneering investments, incentives for skills training and R&D training, and special reduced taxation for specific industries and technologies.

Singapore also has introduced a value-added tax system to reduce overall taxation on individuals as well as on corporations. Singapore does not tax capital gains or Singaporeans living overseas. Singapore's 1991-1996 five-year plan budgeted over $3 billion to support new initiatives and projects. One EDB initiative seeks to upgrade Singapore from a manufacturing center to an innovation hub capable of creating new and better products and services for the region and the world.

A $500 million innovation scheme grants up to 70 percent of project costs to promote innovation within companies. A second initiative ensures that worker skills are available and land requirements are met and that first-rate infrastructures will be attractive to international investors.

China: A Determined Example of Asia's

National Planning for Economic Modernization Under its ninth five-year plan (FYP) for 1996-2000, China has established supporting technological modernization as a major goal. Scientific and technological objectives include the development of rural industries, improvement of traditional industries and basic infrastructures, strengthening of export competitiveness, development of advanced technologies, support for new industries, product development, and development of technical and support services.

The top three priorities are to encourage technology advancement in agricultural industries, develop a national information infrastructure, and improve factory automation processes. China's national expenditure on S&T investments amounted to $10.6 billion in 1995, a third of which came from the government. In its new national economic plan, China's goal is to increase the percentage of GDP invested in research and development from 0.5 percent to 1.5 percent by 2000. In today's China, spreading scientific knowledge is considered a "social systems engineering project" of profound and far-reaching significance.

Science, technology, and education are considered the primary forces that will make the country prosperous. Part of the State's role will be to strengthen the training of high-caliber industrial workers in scientific knowledge. S&T advances combined with improved worker quality are considered essential for social development via raising national competitiveness and improving citizens' living standards.

Technology Advancement Programs

Carefully husbanding its resources, China has borrowed program elements from around the globe to help it achieve its economic development goals. Seven national R&D programs have been established to more effectively transform research into industrial production through various stages of innovation and development. The

Ministry of Science and Technology coordinates implementation of these programs.

1. The Key Technologies Research and Development Program targets R&D in the areas of information technology, manufacturing automation, advanced materials, space technology, laser technology, energy technology, and biotechnology. Twenty-four key technologies and one hundred twenty-four specific technology items have been selected for development within national laboratories and engineering research centers, to be integrated with other ninth FYP projects to address identified problem areas in the national economy.

2. The National Basic Research Priorities Program promotes development of education, laboratories, and equipment to support math, physics, chemistry, mechanics, astronomy, geology, and biology. The program includes a component of international cooperation and technology exchange.

3. The 863 Program or Advanced Research Program was enacted in 1987 to benchmark world technology developments and identify and pursue indigenous innovation capabilities in the seven priority development areas mentioned in point 1 above, specifically to serve the country's economic development goals.

4. The Torch Program, initiated in 1988, provides incentives for renovating traditional industries, training scientists, commercializing key technologies developed in the 863 Program projects, and promoting international partnerships to commercialize Chinese research. A core concept in

this program is the establishment of high-technology industrial zones (HTDZs), so-called "Torch Zones."

5. The Spark Program was established in 1986 to facilitate rural industrialization, including raising the technical skills and management level of village and township enterprises, helping rural industries to develop by relying on advances in science and technology, and raising the educational level of workers. The Spark Program diffuses agricultural technologies to farmers through loans, information dissemination, and training programs.

6. The National Science and Technology Diffusion Program targets agriculture and related economic development. The Technology Diffusion Program was initiated in 1990 to ensure that advanced, appropriate, and mature S&T achievements are used throughout the nation's economy, especially in rural areas.

7. The Trial Production and Appraisal Program links science and technology with the economy through new product development and production. Trial production of new products and the appraisal of advanced technologies are typically located in HTDZs. New products are classified as state level or regional level. New products developed and produced nationwide for the first time are state-level products. New products developed and produced for the first time within a province, an autonomous region, or a municipality are regional-level products. The National Tax Bureau identifies a list of new state-level products whose taxes are reduced or remitted.

In October 1996, the "Law on Promoting the Transformation of Science and Technology

Achievements" was enacted to facilitate technology activities. The law creates a system for the government to manage domestic technology commercialization, protect foreign and domestic intellectual property rights, provide royalties to researchers for inventions, protect trade secrets, and support technology-based transactions.

Economic and Technology Development Zones

China's first HTDZ was developed in 1988, the year the Torch Program was instituted, to integrate research institutions with start-up incubator facilities and local and international firms that are committed to commercialising China's high-tech R&D achievements. There are now 53 Torch Zones. According to information from the Torch Program as of November 1997, some 13,000 tenant companies were located within the HTDZs, which had conducted over 10,000 Torch projects since 1991, about one-third funded by the central government, more than two-thirds funded by local governments. Revenue derived from the HTDZs from 1991 to 1997 was $10.7 billion (89 billion yuan), including $1.2 billion in exports.

In addition, China has a number of special economic zones and free trade zones spanning China's coastal cities and industrial centers that allow for duty-free imports of materials and components used to produce goods for export. China uses its various types of development zones to deliver state incentives for commercialization of high-technology projects, whether by domestic or foreign companies (although foreign ones must generally have domestic partners). The zones encourage research institutes, colleges, universities, and start-up firms, among others, to set up new high-tech enterprises and industries. Over 40 high-tech pioneering service centers have been established in the zones to generate new projects. As an example, Shanghai's Caohejing Hi-Tech Park specializes in microelectronics, bioengineering, new materials, automation meters, aviation, and space technology. It has more than 500 companies, of which 150 are funded by such major multinationals as AT&T, GE, 3M, ICI, Philips, Toshiba, and DuPont.

The government plans to encourage enterprises from the Shandong, Guangdong, and Jiangsu provinces to invest in new industrial zones to be built inland over the next five years. Township enterprises from coastal provinces have already invested about $3.6 billion in land. The plan is expected to create five million new jobs.

Developing State Enterprises into Global Players

Growing foreign competition is putting pressure on China's state-owned enterprises (SOEs), which employ between 20 and 40 million workers. In 1996, SOE sales grew only about 3 percent. World Bank statistics report that 50 percent of SOEs lost money in 1996 and that debt ratios have reached 80 percent to 90 percent of assets. Only 5 percent of China's SOEs had been made into stockholding corporations. The Chinese government wants SOEs to go public to raise capital for expansion, but the SOEs must be reformed before they are desirable investments for public investors. SOEs must improve management practices, acquire advanced technologies where appropriate, train employees in information technologies, and commercialize research. The government is attempting to reform the largest 1,000 SOEs, representing 2.8 percent of SOE employees, 63 percent of SOE assets, and 70 percent of SOE sales. Chinese officials estimate it will cost 500 billion yuan (about $60 billion) to reform the SOEs during the next five years. In 1996, 300 Chinese firms were targeted to go global, becoming joint-stock companies with improved technological capabilities.

Upgrading Infrastructures

Besides these various approaches to upgrading technology levels throughout its economy, China's leadership is also working hard to improve the country's infrastructure. Though it has some ambitious and far-reaching goals, even the basic improvements will be costly. The World Bank has estimated that China will need $500 billion for infrastructure developments between 1995 and 2000. The World Bank's 1997 loan figures showed that China was once again its top recipient of loans in fiscal year 1997, receiving $2.8 billion to carry out its development strategy targeting poverty reduction, environmental protection, and job-creating growth. Since China joined the World Bank in 1981, it has received a total of $28.12 billion in loans.

The Chinese government has identified 44 infrastructure and basic material industry projects. Loans for major infrastructure projects such as those involving electricity and transportation usually come from international sources. In the first half of 1996, China raised $8.8 billion in foreign loans. Between June and October, it raised nearly $5 billion more in foreign-currency loans and bond offerings. The China

International Trust and Investment Corporation, a quasi-government investment arm of the State Council, raised another $100 million in two syndicated loans and $360 million in yen-denominated bonds from Japan. The Ministry of Finance issued a global bond to raise $1 billion.

The Japan Export-Import Bank has approved billions in loans to China for infrastructure projects. Japan's Overseas Economic Cooperation Fund proposed its fourth three-year, yen-denominated loan package of $5.1 billion in 1996. The loans will finance projects implemented in the second and third years of China's ninth FYP. Japan's Export-Import Bank has provided a $1.925 billion economic development loan for construction of a thermoelectric power plant in Zhuhai. One $200 million fixed-rate bond issue by Morgan Stanley of the United States, for a highway in Guangdong Province, will be redeemed through toll payments. All of this is still a long way from the infrastructure outlays that the World China's "Golden" Projects for IT One of China's most far-reaching infrastructure development goals is building a state-of-the-art telecommunications and information system. The core of this program consists of three so-called "Golden" Projects established in the early 1990s for completion by 2003:

1. The Golden Bridge project is designed to modernize the information infrastructure by developing an economic information and data communications network spanning 500 cities and 12,000 large enterprises. The project will include satellite and optical fiber cable networks for these sectors: finance, customs, foreign trade, tourism, interorganizational

communications, transportation, state security, and S & T. The goal is to transmit data, documents, human voice, and pictures across the network.

2. The Golden Customs project will track quota permits, foreign currency transactions, and import and export statistics. It will link all foreign trade departments and support paperless trading.
3. The Golden Card project will replace cash transactions with an electronic service system for savings, withdrawals, and payment through credit and debit cards. By 1997, the China Electronic Information Industry Group had tested operations in 12 cities, had issued 30 million cards, and was testing advanced smart cards.

The development of China's information superhighway requires co-ordination among more than 20 government ministries and countless other organizations. The production and marketing information system is expected to link 360,000 state-owned enterprises and 8.6 million other firms with government offices via networks that will improve utilization of personnel, capital, and natural resources. In 1995, a smart card was developed that combined the functions of a credit card, automated teller machine bank card, and telephone credit card. It was issued jointly by Visa International, the People's Construction Bank of China, and the Nanjing Posts and Telecommunications Bureau. GPT Company of Britain won a contract in May 1996 to install 500 smart card telephones in Zhejiang Province, and has signed contracts for 2,000 more smart card pay phones each for the Beijing and Guangdong telephone authorities.

Authorities forecast that 200 million smart cards will be issued over the next seven years. Card production systems are already in place. Meinen, Zeigel & Company of Germany installed 15 manufacturing systems in China and Asia in 1995 with the capacity to produce 100 million cards annually. Gemphlus Card International of France is setting up plants in China, and France's Schlumberger Smart Systems is developing applications for China in cooperation with the China Hua Xu Golden Card Company, a subsidiary of the Ministry of the Electronics Industry (MEI).

IBM has established a joint venture with MEI's China Great Wall Computer Group and Kaifa Technology (Hong Kong), Ltd., to develop, assemble, and test smart cards in Shenzhen Science and Industry Park. Tandem Computer, Inc., of the United States was chosen in 1995 to provide hardware platforms for the Golden Card project. An optical memory smart card is to contain personal health care data by 2002. These Golden Projects are expected to overcome many compatibility problems as the information infrastructure is modernized.

Other Chinese ministries have begun additional Golden Projects. The Ministry of Health and Jitong Corporation are creating a network to connect large hospitals and research institutions, facilitating transmission of critical medical information and images. The Ministry of Construction will develop a network to track real estate transactions. The Ministry of Finance, the People's Bank of China, the State Tax Administration, and MEI will spend over $1.2 billion to computerize the tax collection system with the installation of 85,000 computers in 30,000 tax agencies across the nation. Companies participating in the project include AT&T, Compaq Computer Corp., Hewlett-Packard Co., Hitachi Ltd., IBM Corporation, Intel Corporation, MasterCard

International, Motorola Inc., Corporation, and Visa International.

Australia: Getting the Most from ICTs

A growth accounting framework to compare the contribution of ICTs to productivity accelerations in Australia and the USA. Using the USA as a benchmark, it attributes up to 0.3 of a percentage point of Australia's 1 percentage point acceleration in labour productivity growth to ICTs. ICTs have had no net effect on capital deepening, as increased use of ICTs has substituted for other forms of capital.

The contribution of ICTs is attributed to gains from business restructuring and innovations in product and process that they enable. The gains to date have been concentrated in distribution (especially wholesaling) and financial services. The evidence of spillovers and network economies is not (yet) strong or widespread.

The Australian experience suggests that the central tenets of policy reform - competition, openness and flexibility - have been important in driving the uptake of ICTs and assisting firms to use them in productivity-enhancing ways.

In the USA, ICT production gains have been on such a scale as to show up in increases in aggregate productivity growth. The productivity gains have also led to rapidly declining ICT prices, which has stimulated increased investment in them.

Australia's productivity growth also surged in the 1990s. However, Australia's takeoff predated that of the USA and the magnitude of Australia's acceleration has been greater than that of the USA suggesting that some different factors are at work in the two countries. Microeconomic policy reforms are widely considered to have played the major role in raising Australia's productivity performance. Some credit should be given to deft macroeconomic policy settings, especially in the face of the Asian financial crisis. Education levels in the workforce have also risen markedly over the past two decades and are likely to have played some role.

The tendency to link Australia's 1990s productivity surge primarily to policy reforms and not to an ICT boom has reinforced a view in some quarters that Australia has not accessed 'new economy' gains. Furthermore, the US evidence has been read to suggest that ICT production is needed to tap 'new economy' productivity gains. According to this view, the lack of a sizeable ICT production industry in Australia has been seen as a preventive barrier to ongoing higher productivity growth.

Some have advocated that governments encourage and develop Australia's ability to produce ICTs, in order to take Australia into the 'new economy' era (irrespective of the tech stock boom and bust). Australia has moved toward the international forefront in use of ICTs. 'Smart' ICT use can enable productivity gains through business restructuring and by providing a platform for further product and process innovations. As a user, Australia has benefited from the rapidly declining prices of ICTs and has generated productivity gains from the 'smart' use of ICTs.

Computers, telecommunication systems and the Internet have brought revolutionary changes to businesses, consumers, education, health, entertainment and many other aspects of life. A defining characteristic is that the costs of storing, accessing and exchanging information have been greatly reduced. In so doing, ICTs have reduced the costs of coordination, communications and information processing. But, increasingly, they have also facilitated changes in what businesses do and how they do it.

A particular analytical interest has centred on the links between ICTs and productivity growth. Many studies of these links have employed a growth accounting framework, based on national accounts approaches to productivity estimation. In these studies, ICTs cover equipment (hardware and software), but exclude the delivery of ICT-related services, such as telephony. The framework provides three avenues for ICTs to influence labour productivity:

- *Increases in capital deepening*: Labour productivity can rise as a result of higher capital use per unit of labour. Stronger investment in ICTs can raise capital deepening. However, many analysts have noted that this mechanism accords ICTs with no 'new' or special production qualities. As they have become cheaper, firms have substituted ICTs for labour and other forms of capital - as could happen for many other inputs.
- *Productivity gains in ICT production*: Producers' ability to manufacture much more powerful ICT equipment, with little increase in inputs, generates substantial MFP gains. If the gains are of sufficient magnitude and production is on sufficient scale, they can show up as contributions to aggregate MFP growth.
- *Productivity gains in ICT-using industries*: This is the most controversial source of ICT-related productivity

gains. It requires that use of ICTs generates MFP gains. The 'new economy' concept has always been vague; and whilst assessments have come to focus on ICT-productivity links, the debate on the nature and extent of those links continues.

On the one hand, 'new economy' enthusiasts believe there are MFP gains from such sources as increasing returns from ICT use and spillovers from network economies. On the other hand, sceptics have either denied or found little evidence to support the existence of MFP gains from use. Dale Jorgensen accepts that there is a new economy, but without MFP gains from use. He believes the new economy lies in the productivity gains in ICT production and associated ICT capital deepening as firms substitute cheaper ICTs for other inputs. There is, perhaps, some middle ground on the possibility of MFP gains.

For example, US Federal Reserve Board Chairman, Alan Greenspan, pointed to gains that he believes come from greater and cheaper access to information - greater certainty, through the availability of real-time information about customers' demands and the location of inventories and materials flowing through complex production systems, which leads to less wastage from extra production, inventories and staff; more efficient and compressed distribution processes; the development of financial instruments to manage risks; and lower search and transactions costs in business-to-business transactions.

The measurement of ICTs has important bearing on the source and extent of estimated productivity gains associated with ICTs. The measurement of the volume of ICTs produced affects estimates of output and productivity growth in ICT production. The measurement of the volume of ICT investment affects estimates of growth in capital inputs and therefore the productivity residual in ICT-using industries. In keeping with modern practice, the Australian Bureau of Statistics (ABS) uses hedonic (or constant-quality) price deflators to estimate real volumes of ICTs produced and purchased. Hedonic prices take into account changes in a number of characteristics of ICTs -processing speed, memory capacity and so on.

The quality-constant prices of ICT characteristics have declined markedly. This stems from the fact that, whilst there have been rapid technological advances (especially in the capacity of microprocessors), there has been relatively little movement in the nominal prices of equipment.

Hedonic prices have not been specifically generated for ICTs in Australia. The ABS uses the US price deflator for hardware, adjusted for exchange rate movements and a time lag, and an assumed 6 per cent a year reduction in prices of software.

Investment in ICTs became a sizeable proportion of total investment in Australia from the mid-1980s. Since then, the growth of investment has been very strong, especially in the 1990s, when investment in hardware grew by 35 per cent a year and software investment grew by 20 per cent a year in real terms. Australia became a high user by international standards in the 1990s. It ranked 3 in 1999 among OECD countries in terms of proportion of business investment devoted to ICTs. Australia imports most of its ICT equipment requirements. Australia ranks at the very low end of OECD countries in terms of size of its ICT equipment production industries.

The contributions of ICTs to Australia's productivity growth are now assessed and compared with the US experience. With some assumptions, the US case provides a benchmark that indicates the extent to which Australia's productivity gains can be associated with ICTs. There have been a number of US studies of ICT contributions to productivity growth.

A capital services measure of capital input is used and labour input is measured by hours worked. US studies also include a labour composition or 'quality' component, which captures changes in the hours worked by groups with different marginal products. A comparable component cannot be estimated for Australia. Since allowance for compositional effects (as in the USA) effectively 'factors out' this component from MFP growth, this component is added back in to US MFP growth estimates, to assist comparability with Australian estimates.

Australian data cover IT, without communications equipment, whereas US data cover ICTs. The US estimates used here cover the private business sector, whereas Australian estimates cover the market sector. The main difference between the two is that the ABS-defined market sector excludes Property & business services.

With similar uptake of ICTs in the two countries, the USA can then be used as a benchmark to assess the extent to which Australia's productivity gains can be associated with ICTs. Furthermore, it seems reasonable to assume, consistent with the US leadership in productivity and ICTs, that US estimates establish the upper limit on productivity accelerations that can be associated specifically with ICT production and use. First, however, there are some timing issues to sort out.

Most studies have used 1995 as the dividing year between periods of comparison of productivity growth and for assessing the ICT contributions to productivity acceleration -for example, accounting for productivity growth in the second half of the 1990s compared with the first half. The 1995 year corresponds to the takeoff point in advances in ICT technology, declines in ICT prices, growth in investment in ICTs and, as just seen, growth in ICT capital deepening. The 1995 year also corresponds to the takeoff in US labour productivity growth. But 1995 was a trough year in US labour productivity, at a point below trend. Estimates from 1995 to the end of the 1990s are from a trough to a peak and therefore overstate the underlying rate of labour productivity growth.

Issues with the boundary point and sensitivity can be set aside by analysing contributions to trend rates of productivity growth. The ABS method of estimating productivity growth over productivity cycles - from productivity peak to productivity peak - is one way of measuring underlying rates of growth.

Adopting this method puts the prime focus on accelerations in underlying rates of productivity growth, rather than on the ICT takeoff and its effects. The productivity-cycle method introduces a difference between countries in time periods compared, but it ensures that changes in underlying rates of productivity growth are compared.

There are several similarities in the US and Australian results:

— The estimated labour productivity acceleration is lower according to the productivity cycle method, compared with the pre- and post-1995 method.

— ICTs have made strong capital deepening contributions. The ICT capital deepening contribution has increased steadily from the 1960s in both countries.

— ICT capital deepening accounted for around a third of labour productivity growth in both countries in their respective 1990s cycles. ICT capital deepening made a contribution of a similar order of magnitude to the 1990s labour productivity accelerations in both countries.

— However, much or all of the increased use of ICTs in the 1990s has been offset by slower growth in the use of other forms of capital. There has been little or no increase in the overall rate of capital deepening in either country, especially in Australia. This contrasts with most other studies of the USA which have found that ICTs have contributed to a marked increase in the rate of substitution of capital for labour.

— MFP growth accounted for over half of labour productivity growth in the 1990s cycle in both countries. Faster MFP growth accounts for most of the 1990s labour productivity accelerations in both countries, and entirely so in Australia.

The main difference between the US and Australian results lies in the strength of the productivity accelerations. The acceleration in underlying labour productivity growth in Australia, at 1 percentage point, is twice that in the USA. With similar capital deepening contributions, the chief explanation for the difference lies in the much stronger MFP acceleration in Australia than in the USA.

It seems reasonable to assume, consistent with the US leadership in productivity and ICTs, that the US estimates establish the upper limit on productivity gains that can be associated specifically with ICT production and use. Assuming that no other factor has generated a productivity acceleration, the US estimates set the upper limit on ICT-related gains. Some of the 0.3 of a percentage point MFP acceleration must be attributed to production of ICTs.

The benchmark assessment does not in itself establish that ICTs have been at work in both countries. However, some supporting - though still circumstantial - evidence comes from an industry perspective, which shows an overlap in the USA and Australia in the industries that are both high ICT users and relatively strong productivity accelerators.

Whilst the evidence suggests that the aggregate MFP gains to date from ICT use are significant, albeit not spectacular, there is evidence of strong links in certain industries. . Several studies of the USA have found evidence of productivity acceleration in the 1990s in Wholesale trade, Retail trade, Finance, insurance & real estate (especially in financial intermediation) and Business services. These industries have also been characterised as intensive users of ICTs.

A similar set of industries emerged in the 1990s as major contributors to Australia's productivity surge. In the first cycle, the relatively strong productivity growth in the 'traditional' contributors to aggregate productivity growth -Agriculture, Mining, and Manufacturing - is evident. These traditional sectors were joined in the 1980s and early 1990s by two other strong performers - Communication services and Electricity, gas & water.

Whilst productivity growth remained relatively strong in all these industry sectors in the 1990s cycle (except for Manufacturing), they all experienced a deceleration compared with the previous cycle. On these estimates, none made a contribution to the productivity surge from 1993-94. A new set of service industries made the positive contribution. The stand-out performer was Wholesale trade. Other service industries - for example, Construction and Finance & insurance - also increased their rate of productivity growth.

Whilst there is increased scope for measurement error at the industry level - of both ICT use and productivity growth - it appears that there is no strong, positive relationship between ICT use and MFP across all industries. There is a strong positive relationship between increased ICT use and MFP acceleration in Finance & insurance and a weaker relationship in Wholesale trade.

The lack of systematic relationship undoubtedly reflects the fact that ICT use is not the only factor affecting industry MFP growth. It also signals that the productivity gains from ICT use appear - for the moment at least - concentrated in distribution and financial intermediation. The lack of a relationship across all industries also tends to support the view that the gains to date cannot be attributed to network economies, which could be expected to be more widespread.

The relationships between ICT use and productivity growth are complex. ICTs are often viewed as general-purpose technologies that require time to bring to their full potential and that provide a platform for other innovations in products and processes.

The Australian evidence supports the view that it is the changes in products and processes that generate the productivity gains. The Finance & insurance industry has been restructured to operate much more through ICTs (for example, ATMs, Internet and phone banking) than through traditional face-to-face contacts. Many new products (for example, financial derivatives) are now on offer.

An earlier study by Productivity Commission staff also found that ICTs played a part in the restructuring of wholesaling activities. Wholesalers were able to use bar-code and scanning technology and inventory management systems as part of the process of transforming wholesaling from a storage-based to a fast flow-through operation.

But, importantly, reforms were acting as the underlying drivers and facilitators of productivity gains and ICTs were just one component of change. It was not so much that wholesaling became much more ICT intensive or that new 'breakthrough' technologies became available. It was more that the competitive incentives to be productive became stronger and that new flexibilities became open to businesses to use ICTs as part of a more general process of restructuring and transformation.

For example, the motor vehicle industry was looking for efficiencies all along the 'value chain', including in distribution, to meet the increased competition from cheaper imports entering under lower trade barriers.

Another contributor in some areas was the reform of industrial relations processes that allowed greater labour flexibility through the introduction of split shifts and reduced the rigidity of job demarcations. At the general level, policy reforms have fostered productivity growth through three main avenues:

- sharpening incentives to be more productive, chiefly by strengthening competition;
- opening the economy to trade, investment and technologies developed overseas; and
- providing greater flexibility (for example, less regulatory restriction, more flexible labour markets) to adjust production processes and firm organisation to improve productivity.

These conditions have also provided the incentives for businesses to take up ICTs, as well as ready access to the latest ICTs developed overseas, and the flexibility to use ICTs to productive advantage.

A major implication of the evidence in this and other Productivity Commission papers is that, from a productivity and policy perspective, a prime focus on ICTs and the 'new economy' is somewhat misplaced. There are three potential pitfalls:

— too much attention on ICT production as a source of productivity growth;

— insufficient attention on the factors that drive ICT use;

— insufficient attention on other factors that are potentially the source of greater productivity gains.

On the first point, and in light of calls for policy action to foster the development of ICT production, the Australian (and the US) experience is now providing clearer evidence that there are also (MFP) productivity gains associated with ICT use. ICT production is not necessary to access productivity gains. The US estimates suggest that there have been roughly equal productivity gains at the aggregate level from ICT production and use in that country.

But the scope for productivity gains in production in the USA does not translate as readily to other countries as does the scope for productivity gains from use. The US production gains come from a very large scale of operations and a degree of technological leadership that cannot be readily established in other countries. Aside from some niche areas (particularly in software), ICT production requires not only large scale operation but also sales in highly competitive international markets. This makes it tough going for a relatively small economy like Australia's.

By being open to imports of ICTs, Australia has been able to gain quickly from advances in ICT manufacture and has been able to capture a sizeable terms of trade gain from the rapidly declining international prices in ICTs. Taking the benefits of productivity gains generated by foreign producers through lower prices is a real income gain to Australians. An international comparison by Bayoumi and Haacker found that Australia is among the world's main beneficiaries from ICTs, even though it is not a significant producer. Welfare gains from lower ICT prices, accumulated over 1985 to 2001, amounted to 5 per cent of GDP not far short of the highest beneficiary, the USA, at 5.6 per cent of GDP. Australia benefits as a high-using importer with rapidly declining prices. But the estimated welfare gains in some major producer countries.

Finland, Ireland, Japan, and Korea have been lower than in Australia. And some major producers (such as Malaysia, Thailand and the Philippines) have not experienced major welfare gains. The second point is that a direct focus on ICTs (and in particular on production) masks the importance of the preconditions required to drive the uptake and smart use of ICTs (where 'smart' implies business restructuring and complementary product and process innovations, based on ICT use).

Sharper competitive incentives to be productive help to explain why Australia has moved from being a technology laggard in previous decades to being at the forefront of new technology uptake in the 1990s. Taking full advantage of declining prices and advances in technologies and not restricting them through trade or other barriers is also conducive to ICT uptake. And the development of skills in the workforce can also be important in identifying and developing applications for ICTs. Strong competition also affects the distribution of productivity gains.

A competitive environment means that more of the gains are likely to be passed on in lower prices and thereby assist in dampening inflationary pressures. ICT-related or other productivity gains do not in themselves dampen inflation, as some new economy advocates claim. Healthy competition is a necessary precondition.

Flexibility is also important in enabling the productivity-enhancing reorganisation of firms (outsourcing, better management of supplier and customer linkages) and work arrangements (team work, multiskilling, performance-based remuneration, shift arrangements) and so on. The third and related point is that it is important not to lose sight of factors unrelated to ICTs that are the source of substantial productivity gains.

The Treasury stated that ICT prices have fallen in domestic currency terms by 9.5 per cent a year and raised the terms of trade by 0.3 per cent a year between 1985 and 2001. Since 1995, ICT prices have fallen by nearly 15 per cent a year and raised the terms of trade by 0.75 per cent a year.

Australia has enjoyed an MFP acceleration of around 1.1 percentage points associated primarily with non-ICT factors, but with some contribution from ICT use not production. To state the obvious, it would be not make sense to focus on chasing a gain of (at most) 0.3 of a percentage point associated with ICTs - especially by concentrating on encouraging ICT production - if that came at the cost of realising a 1.1 percentage point gain from catch-up and 'smart use' of ICTs.

But there is a big policy overlap between developing the conditions for catch-up productivity gains associated with restructuring and modernisation, on the one hand, and developing the conditions conducive to uptake and smart use of ICTs, on the other. Promoting effective competition, openness and flexibility is at the heart of both.

The Australian economy became more focused on productivity and more flexible at just the right time to take advantage of the advances in ICTs that came on stream in the second half of the 1990s. It was not so much that policymakers deliberately set out with an ICT strategy. Without many predicting or perhaps even realising it, Australia became 'ICT-ready' (and ready for any other technological development that could be usefully employed). Given a history of lagging in the uptake of technology and of relatively poor productivity performance, it is unlikely that Australia would have been as quick on the uptake of ICTs, or as able to use them in productivity-enhancing ways, had it not been for the sea-change that reforms brought.

Even though fostering the right business conditions should remain the policy priority, there are nevertheless ICT-specific policy issues to consider as well. These also cover the provision of ICT-related services and include:

— the optimal development of complementary innovations, based on ICTs;

— the optimal development of communications infrastructure;

— the implications of use of ICT networks for the strength of competition in markets;

— the development of appropriate ICT-related skills;

— adjustment issues concerning job flexibility for those with specific skills displaced by ICTs;

— appropriate protection of intellectual property rights in distribution via the Internet;

— access to networks, including the issue of the 'digital divide';

— regulation of network content; and

— security of tax bases through use of Internet and other networks.

In short, Australia has entered the 'new economy' era in the sense that some of its productivity gains are associated with ICTs. Australia's link with the 'new economy' has come, firstly, from high investment in ICTs. However, the substitution of ICT growth for growth in other forms of capital has meant that there has been no overall capital deepening effect on underlying, labour productivity growth. Secondly, there is evidence that there have also been MFP gains associated with ICT use.

The production of ICTs is not necessary to access MFP gains. And so Australia's lack of significant manufacture of ICT equipment has not been a barrier to entry into the 'new economy'. Australia experienced a strong productivity acceleration in the 1990s. Labour productivity accelerated by 1 percentage point and MFP by 1.1 percentage points. Most of the MFP gains (0.8 of a percentage point or more) are attributable to international catch up.

Microeconomic reforms have assisted this process by releasing the shackles on the economy that were holding back growth in productivity. A relatively modest part of the MFP gains (up to 0.3 of a percentage point) can be more specifically attributed to ICT use. These gains have been focused in the distribution and financial services sectors of the economy. There is not strong evidence of widespread productivity gains from use of networks, such as the Internet (at least as yet). Aside from the fact that production of ICTs is not necessary, government encouragement of local ICT production could be questioned on a number of grounds. Australia's cost structures, the competitiveness of the market and the need for large scale production and technological leadership would make it a tall task to establish significant and viable Australian production.

As an importer, Australia has also been benefiting from terms of trade gains from the declining prices of ICTs. Taking the benefits of productivity gains generated by foreigners through lower prices has been a source of real income gain to Australians. The welfare gains from ICTs have been greater to Australia than to most other countries, including many major ICT producing countries. This also raises the question of where the welfare gains would go if Australia were to foster local production.

If Australia became an exporter, at least some of the gains would go to foreigners. And it is by no means clear that Australian businesses would have the same access to the latest technological developments at the same declining price. This in turn could affect the rate of uptake of technologies and/or the rate of complementary investments in productivity-enhancing innovation. The Australian experience suggests that the policy priority should be to enhance competition, openness and flexibility in the business environment, rather than focus too strongly or directly on ICTs and the 'new economy'.

Policy reforms in Australia have provided competitive incentives for firms to take up ICTs, enabled ready access to the latest advances in ICTs and have ensured that firms have the flexibility to use ICTs in ways that help to transform their businesses and raise productivity. A focus on the right business conditions means that the 'smart' and productive use of ICTs and substantial gains unrelated to ICTs can then follow.

This approach focusing on the conditions in which business operates has taken Australia toward the international forefront of uptake and smart use of ICTs. It has generated large welfare gains by allowing maximum benefit from falling ICT prices and promoting associated productivity gains. There are always ways to improve further. But Australia has been on the right path to get the most welfare gains it can from ICTs.

Brazilian E-commerce Strategy

Brazil understood that develop local e-commerce ought

to be a strategy specifically designed for Brazilian environment. The most important fact was the launching of the Information Society Program as a framework for all activities regarding information technology in the country.

The Program assured both focus and economical feasibility for all actions the Country should perform to ensure our participation in the knowledge era. Thus, under this framework, many strategies related to market, production, human resources, e-government, Internet content, cultural and social aspects etc. were designed and implemented to reach the same goal – a more equal and dynamic social and economic development for Brazil.

Under the Information Society framework the actions taken to reach one target was mostly the same to reach the other, so development was amazingly quick in Brazil, surprising even those involved with the strategy.

Regarding e-commerce a strategy based on three main points was designed:

—Infrastructure

—Legal framework

—Implementation

At the very first moment became clear for Brazilians that two different lines of action regarding e-commerce implementation should be designed : one for B2B and another for B2C, although both depend on the same infrastructure and legal framework.

Infrastructure – certainly universalization of telecommunication was the most important way to provide a basic internet access for everyone in the

Country. The telecommunications privatization process, started in 95, established targets for the new owners that they have to accomplish, in the early years after the privatization.

It became a great success considering the growing rates in the period – end of 1994 to end of 2001 – from 13.25 million to 44.5 million) in fixed lines and from 755 thousands to 33.4 million wireless lines, with a total investment of US$ 10.9 billion.

Nevertheless, the most important decision taken by the Government and approved by the Congress was the FUST – a special fund to promote universalization of access not only for phone lines but also for Internet access. It was strategic because, due the huge social gap among classes in Brazil, certainly there would be non profit areas where the conventional attraction efforts for private investment will not work.

The fund itself is formed by a deposit from the incumbent operator companies, and will be rebated to them in a competition bid for the best projects to reach those non profit areas. The estimated annual investment is US$ 500.0 million.

Another important strategy was to ensure local capacity for developing software and manufacturing IT goods, focused on keeping our local trade balance under control.

For software solution development, Softex, a huge new design program, was settled around the Country to improve local human resources in software development, either considering the Portuguese language and local cultural peculiarities (specially regarding accounts and taxes) as well as to promote the start up of new software companies.

To face the huge investment necessary to reach the predefined goals in telecommunication privatization contracts, another important strategy was to attract foreign investments in manufacturing facilities as well as strengths the local manufacturing companies.

Certainly Internet facilities were another main issue. Brazil started with Internet, back to the end of the eighties, through the academic network program approach, Brazilian RNP, which was similar to USA and European programs in order to guarantee academic internet connection.

The Government used this knowledge to open competition, establish a well developed use of dot br, and have invested in constant renewal of IP network development. That led us to a very interesting position in the World Wide Web ranking especially considering our condition of developing country.

Nowadays Brazil is the 11 th in number of host, the 5 th in ccTLD registrar, as well as capable to run IPv6 in the academic network.

Legal framework - With infrastructure running and with adequate funding instruments, it was time to take care of the legal instruments that should be constructed – and how to deal with them – to improve our e-commerce and e-government. It was clear that overcoming the brick world concept regarding contracts, documents, financial transactions, credit bonds, signatures and certificates would be a must.

To help technically both the Government and the Congress, a special Internet Security Committee was settled, dedicated to establish a safety environment regarding contracts and signatures. This Committee produced a reference document -the "ICP Termo de Referencia" -with all technical and financial alternatives issues that have been used to support the formal Government proposal to the Congress.

With this step completed, during 2000 and 2001 the Government established the discussions and got approvals for the PKI,-the root structure, the certificate entity regarding government formal signatures and the alternatives for private relationship. The Government itself started using electronic signature at Jan, 1 st , 2001.

With the same approach the acceptability of electronic document and digital signature was submitted to Congress analysis and was approved. To guarantee a complete safety environment for government transactions, an agency – the AGP Brazil- was created, in order to accomplish a formal mission : "to establish and manage the policies and acts related to the permanent operation of PKI-Gov in Brazil".

Under this agency, the following activities took place:

— Establish formal criteria for Certifying Authorities [AC] and Registrar Authorities [AR]

— Establish the periodicity for AC and AR audit;

— Definition about charges and fines to be imposed for breaking rules

— Operational rules related to: ACs, ARs, digital signature, secure cryptography, certificate storage, certificate revoke, security copies and key recovering, key automatic update, key traceability, cross certification, validity for certificates, unretractability guarantee for electronic transactions and operations.

The concepts defined for electronic document followed the basic 1966 UNCITRAL model and was formalized by Federal measurement MP 2200-1 and MP 2002-2. A resume of the main rules can be described as:

"the cryptographic key pair shall always be generated by the owner, and his private key will be under his exclusive use, control and knowledge."

- all public and private electronic documents are legal;
- Document contents are presumed truthful, regarding the signature owner, if certified by ICP Brasil structure and will be valid as defined in art 131 Law 3.071 1/1/ 1916 of the Civil Code
- Document exchanged among private persons are free to use any certification if agreed among those persons"

Some other important decisions related to electronic transactions are in process and will define the best practices about the agency interaction with the market, advertising and public offers by electronic means and legal charges regarding systems invasion, electronic piracy, modification, destruction and unauthorized use of data.

New electronic procurement rules for government acquisition are also to be sent for Congress approval and will be a great incentive for the use of electronic auction, thus being one of the most important instruments to improve e-commerce among small and micro companies.

A new banking payment structure [SBP] regarding electronic money transference, currency use and related issues are already in use since June 7th, 2002 and was launched without any problem. This was not a surprise because Brazil was the first country to use banking automation back in the early 80`s. This was due to the high inflation rate at those days and the peculiar process Brazilians used to deal with the problem which demanded a unique solution that was not available around the world at that time.

The AC root structure is running and since January,2001 all documents transferred from or to the Brazilian President by the Ministers must be done by electronic means and with an electronic signature. After January, 2002 this procedure was extended for authorities in the next level of the Federal Government hierarchy regarding their transactions with their Ministers. The next levels will follow.

Nowadays is running a special effort regarding technology development for e-commerce which includes cryptography.

Implementation – With the first two legs of its strategy running, Brazil started the Implementation As stated before, two different lines of action regarding e-commerce implementation should be designed: one for B2B and another for B2C.

To deal with this scenario the Government established another committee the e-commerce committee. This is a private and public committee with a tripartite coordination with members chosen by the Government and by the representative associations of society.

The committee was launched in July, 2001 and is running under the following bylaws:

Six Sub-Committees

I - Payment means for e-commerce—Government Coordination

II – Logistics & National Integration—Government Coordination

III –Economic Aspects —Brazilian Industry Association Coordination

IV– Applications and Projects (social approach)—IP Association Coordination

V - Technology and Products for e-commerce —Software Association Coordination

VI –e-commerce for Small Business—National Commerce Association Coordination

With these responsibilities respectively :

- I -Payment means for e-commerce - Government Coordination Full acceptance of electronic offers inside and outside national border;
  - — On line currency and credit markets;
  - — Electronic stock and future/options market;
  - — Full offers of goods, information and services;
  - — Third part safety regarding electronic documents;
  - — Full legal guarantee
- II- Logistics and National Integration - Government Coordination
  - — Logistics,
  - — local and national transport network and services,

— distribustion, regional access, cost, investments, new rules and statistics related to e-commerce logistic and transport aspects;

— competition.

- III – Economic Aspects

— Brazilian Industry Association Coordination International aspects related to e-commerce;

— investments;

— financing and credit;

— costs, international legislation, statistics, international agreements intellectual property rights;

— arbitration (new law)

- IV – Applications & Projects (social approach) – IP Association Coordination

— e-procurement ;

— local IP access, training and local capacity for Internet use and trade – focus on shorten the social and economic gap using e-commerce for local development in the community commerce

- V - Technology and Products for e-commerce – Software Association Coordination

— New technologies development ;

— local software solutions;

— experimental joint development;

— R&D promotion;

— innovation promotion;

— venture capital promotion;

— focus on new products and new services

- VI – e-commerce for Small Business – National Csommerce Association Coordination

— e-procurement promotion for small business;

— low cost hardware ;

— training and promotion of local capacity (SEBRAE);

— joint work with V and IV sub committees for local solutions.

The committee is running and influencing many decisions related to Government and private entities, and like all other projects under the Information Society framework, is using all the facilities achieved around the Country to reach its goals.

B2B - It is important to understand that B2B in Brazil started shyly before the launching of e-procurement for the e-government program which increased the use of electronic auction and acquisition using previously existing electronic supplier database.

Initially the new activity was broadcasted among potential suppliers. Once e-procurement succeeded, it was a boom in the specialized media and even in the regular media, thus encouraging the use of e-commerce among more and more companies.

The 2002 forecast for annual average amount per customer is US$ 1,882. (IDC scenario) The investments in this area have been very important and some known brands are also operating in the country.

IT infrastructure, space and bandwidth supply Over 100,000 square meters and over US$ 600 billions investment The e-procurement is playing an important role in this matter, but it is still necessary facilitate the effective entrance of SME into this market to have a real increase of B2B e-commerce in Brazil.

A new program to be launched probably during July, 2002 shall be an important step ahead. It intends to establish a general website and e-procurement address for all municipalities in the Country at the same time, based on a local software platform.

After that, and with a simultaneous training program and the Fust fund to interconnect all municipalities, the opportunities for SME will be tremendously increased, forcing them to join to this new e-commerce technology.

B2C – B2C is a complete different world. First of all Brazilians, unlike Americans, due a cultural peculiarity are not used to buy by catalog, even by phone. Brazilians like to be among others, discuss their options and, depending on social class level, to be oriented by someone they trust, before their buying decision. Added to this peculiarity, the general low income and the yet not completed universiliation of telecom or internet access had contributed to reduce the growth rate of B2C.

However, comparing with other countries, Brazil is not following a peculiar path, since most countries, including USA, have been facing similar growing rates between B2B and B2C regardless their level of development.

The B2C in Brazil is responsible for a small amount of 15% on e-commerce income, but, considering the annual average income/customer, the numbers (IDC scenario) are not so bad:

— 2000 – US$ 619

— 2001 – US$ 725

— 2002 – US$ 873

Another important decision about to be taken by the Government is related to Digital TV standard definition.

In Brazil, due the "tight relationship" that Brazilian population has with the TV –92% of homes have TV (even in the poorest areas) – depending on the chosen standard, digital TV might be the most important instrument for B2C development. An old trust relationship among television media and people have been constructed during years, so the new digital facilities, if well defined, could be easily used as an alternative for e-commerce B2C, keeping the communication and orientation bond demanded by people and offered in Television approach.

In short, Brazilian e-commerce seems to be an important consequence of e-government growth. This statement can be explained first considering Brazilian people is already very familiar with banking automation and, because with the daily personal demanding of e-gov services, the population is learning quickly how to use IT facilities.

At the same time the e-government success is spreading a base of confidence in such technologies, encouraging small business' to invest in e-commerce facilities as well as to reduce the common personal fear simple people used to have against incomprehensive new technologies.

Brazilian e-government success is well known also outside the country due two unique successful programs

: our long time running Income Tax Internet, and the 2000 complete electronic major election – 108 million voting at same day in all 5,561 municipalities around the country, electing mayors and local chamber representatives, and getting the complete and non questionable results at the end of the very same day.

To better show the link between e-gov and e-commerce, programs like those implemented by the Brazilian Post Office are good examples: they are taking advantage and establishing new ways for improving e-commerce.

The basic one is the Open Door program which motto is "Everyone must have an e-address" even the homeless. An e-address. The idea is prepare the population to use internet, get electronic messages, government services and goods through the post office, as they are used to do in the traditional way. The Post Office is installing public internet kiosks with experimental local programs using local/regional students.

CHAPTER 2

E-Commerce and Economic Growth

The new economic paradigm, according to which new information and communication technologies (ICT) would deliver ever-higher rates of inflation-free growth, seemed to be among the first victims of the dotcom crash. But even after the crash, e-commerce has continued to grow.

While e-commerce clearly has a positive impact on the business sector, doubts have been raised about its impact on macroeconomic growth, and productivity growth in particular.

In previous technological revolutions, productivity gains have in the long run helped to improve living standards - one of the main goals of development. The US, which leads the world in IT and e-commerce, has had an impressive economic performance, particularly in terms of productivity growth, since 1995.

Much of the acceleration in productivity growth is structural and attributable to changes induced by ICT and the Internet, through improvements in all aspects of corporate organization, production, finance, marketing and logistics. According UNCTAD, ICT will continue to support rapid productivity growth, citing several reasons: the cost of computing power is expected to keep falling steeply for several years; most enterprises are still learning how to reorganize themselves in order to benefit fully from the Internet; and even if productivity growth does not maintain its recent phenomenal pace in the United States, the rest of the world has a lot of catching up to do in the application of ICT to business.

But there will be no productivity growth for many developing countries if they fail to catch up technologically with the industrialized world, as the Report shows. To assess the broader economic impact of e-commerce and the ramifications of developing countries' catching up or not, UNCTAD has conducted a quantitative analysis based on two scenarios: one in which developing countries fall behind technologically, and one in which they catch up with developed countries. The analysis is centred on cost savings and assumes that e-commerce can reduce costs of services, particularly in retail and wholesale trade, transport, and financial and business services.

Cost savings in services are simulated through a productivity growth scenario, which allows for the analysis of such macroeconomic variables as GDP, welfare, wages and terms of trade. The analysis is a unique application of a computable general equilibrium (CGE) model to e-commerce at the global level.

Under the first scenario developed countries would have welfare gains of $117 billion, while the developing world would lose welfare of $726 million. The Asian region, on the other hand, would gain $802 million, largely attributable to the transport services sector. Besides welfare and GDP losses, developing countries would also experience a reduction in wages and deteriorating.

The value of ICT for development lies not so much in the share of the global economy that this sector may come to represent, but in the changes that ICT will introduce in the functioning of enterprises across the economies that assimilate them. If developing countries were to catch up with developed countries in productivity, they would increase output, wages and welfare. A 1% productivity growth in the services sector in Asia, for example, would result in welfare gains of $12 billion, GDP growth of 0.4%, a wage increase of 0.4% and a 2- to-3% growth in services exports. By reducing costs, increasing efficiency, reducing time and distances, e-commerce could thus become an important tool for development.

If the Internet is only a 'space' - cyberspace - it is a space without borders in which private international law has no meaning, since the rules of private international law are made in order to deal with different legal systems and borders. Among the thorny issues raised by the advent of the Internet and e-commerce. Privacy and consumer protection are also problematic, given the lack of international agreements and of transborder or dispute settlement mechanisms designed specifically for electronic transactions.E-commerce currently operates in a tax- and duty-free environment, in an unclear legal and regulatory framework - a situation calling for urgent intergovernmental cooperation to clarify the situation. Income taxation largely depends on whether a business has permanent establishment (PE) in a country or not.

OECD countries have agreed that a website by itself cannot constitute PE, while a web server can, if it is owned by a business that carries on business through the server. However, "proposals by OECD countries have given scant consideration to developing countries' concerns in the field of e-commerce taxation", according to the Report, which also notes the "major differences" between EU and US approaches to international taxation rules on e-commerce.

As to consumption taxes, such as VAT or sales tax, there is a growing tendency to apply taxation in the place of consumption. This would actually work in favour of developing countries, as most of them rely heavily on such taxes for their government budgets and will be net importers of e-commerce in the medium term.

Although no customs duties are currently imposed on electronic transmissions, this is much discussed at the WTO, with a number of countries advocating a tariff-free environment for e-commerce and others expressing concern about possible revenue losses if products previously subject to customs duties are imported duty-free.

Potential fiscal losses on border tariffs and other duties imposed on digital imports could total $8 billion worldwide. While on average this is less than 1% of total government revenue, tariff losses would be much greater in developing countries.

B2B e-markets, e-finance flourishing

Business-to-business (B2B) e-markets, which have already outstripped business-to-consumer (B2C) e-commerce in volume, are expected to play an even more pivotal role in future, becoming the single largest component of B2B by 2004. Online B2B sales in the US are forecast to reach $3 trillion by 2004, of which an estimated $1.5 trillion will be via B2B e-markets.

The highest growth in B2B e-markets will likely be in such sectors as computing and electronics, utilities, motor vehicles, petrochemicals and paper, office products and food and agriculture. These markets will also undergo consolidation, the formation of strategic alliances and greater focus on the provision of differentiated and specialized products and services.

Online financial operations - which make it possible to handle huge financial operations and related payments traffic both nationally and cross-border at a fraction of the former costs and time - are also experiencing explosive growth, according to the Report. Current forecasts suggest double-digit growth rates for e-finance over the next few years.

The Internet banking segment is slated to expand 25% annually, as compared to 3% for the overall banking industry. In developed countries, half of all banking and 80% of all brokerage activities are expected to go online.

For emerging economies, the figures range from 30% for e-banking to 40% for e-brokerage. But financial service providers, especially from developing and transition economies, will have to address the high initial costs and technological complexity of establishing online payments before they can hope for "e-finance preparedness", warns the UNCTAD e-commerce report. The technology still cannot cope with the needs of high-value and micro-payments in B2B and B2C alike.

Online payments and e-financing technologies are at an early stage of standardization, with the industry still choosing between competing models and solutions. Promises of "Net-only" banking and payment solutions becoming a "killer application" are proving highly exaggerated, but banks and other traditional financial services providers are under pressure to adopt aggressive Internet strategies and rapidly increase their online services.

No economic sector has been subject to more far-fetched growth forecasts or sweeping statements about a bright future than e-commerce. Venture capitalists, financial analysts and the public in general have blindly used these inflated numbers to take decisions on investments in start-up companies and the stock market - often with disastrous results.

E-commerce data are largely provided by private sector companies, which regularly publish reports on the latest developments in e-commerce, including short- to medium-term growth estimates. Unfortunately, the numbers differ considerably, depending on which methodologies, definitions and indicators are used. Estimates of global B2B e-commerce last year, for example, range from $200 billion to $604 billion.

Ecommerce Strategies in Malaysia

Electronic commerce or e-commerce is recognised as an important agenda for Malaysia to start moving into the new Economy. Malaysia sees e-commerce as the new way to do business through the digital network. E-commerce will enable. Malaysian businesses to create new value, raise the level of productivity, increase competitiveness in export markets and facilitate new type of business process for reaching customers in the world.

In the 7th Malaysia Plan, ICT was recognized as a strategic tool to support the growth of the economy. The Plan targeted the development process of ICT and promoted extensive application to the public. In the 8th Malaysia Plan, e-commerce was specifically mentioned for the first time. Like any other technology, ICT can have positive or negative effects. ICT can aggravate the rich-poor gap but it also presents possible solutions to many problems. If properly harnessed, ICT can improve standard of living more quickly and more dramatically than any other time in history. It has therefore become compelling for a managed process in using ICT for positive development.

To better understand the fundamental technological changes and how it can improve the quality of life, the National IT Council (NITC) was established in 1994. The NITC acts as a think tank and an advisor to the government and is the key initiator of programmes and strategies aimed at creating an information rich society.

The work of the NITC is guided by the National IT Agenda (NITA), a strategic framework for IT programme development at the federal, state and local government levels involving the participation with the private, non-government and voluntary sectors.

The Government of Malaysia has already initiated efforts to lay the foundation for e-commerce in the country. The government in consultation with the private sector has initiated a legal and regulatory framework of cyber laws and intellectual property laws to create a predictable environment for the implementation of e-commerce. Six cyber laws have been enacted. They are the Digital Signature Act 1997, the Copyright (amendment) Act 1997, the Computer Crimes Act 1997, the

Telemedicine Act 1997, the Communications and Multimedia Act 1998 and the Communications and Multimedia Commission Act 1998. A bill on personal data protection is pending and efforts to harmonise existing laws and regulations with cyber laws are on going.

Malaysia has established a clear set of policy objectives that takes into account the ramifications of the convergence of telecommunications, computing and broadcasting. Reforms were undertaken by putting in place an enabling legislation, that is, the Communications and Multimedia Act 1998 and establishing a new independent regulatory agency for the convergent industry, which is the Malaysian Communications and Multimedia Commission.

The Communications and Multimedia Act 1998 provides the necessary policies to regulate, facilitate and nurture the development of the communications and multimedia industry, the growth of which is needed to support e-commerce.

The "Growth with Equity" development strategy has been successful in maintaining balanced development for over 30 years in the country. However, socio-economic inequities still exist and may be magnified if the development of ICT is not constructively managed. The government has set aside allocations to fund special programmes to address the digital divide such as community internet centres for rural folks and computing infrastructure to rural schools. In addition, the government has set up a Universal Service Fund to finance the cost of building basic infrastructure and internet access to rural and other underserved areas.

The adoption of ICT by the government in providing services to the public is a catalyst for greater use of ICT in the country. The public is encouraged to use ICT to access government information, transact services and make payments through various electronic delivery channels provided by the government. For the business community, an e-enabled government helps reduce their cost of doing business.

To accelerate uptake of e-commerce, the government is also making efforts to convince the non-ICT sectors, especially the small medium sized enterprises, which made up more than 84% of all enterprises to use more ICT products and services in their business. Besides increasing productivity and competitiveness in the non-ICT sectors, greater ICT use by non-ICT sectors will increase output in the ICT sector itself.

Malaysia participates at regional and international fora to discuss e-commerce and e-commerce related matters such as the WTO, APEC and ASEAN. Participation gives the country the opportunity to influence the development of international guidelines and new practices. The country also participates in cross border e-commerce projects such as the pilot projects for the exchange of customs EDI messages among customs authorities in Asia.

Chapter 3

Transformation in Information Society

The meaning of the 'Knowledge Society' is derived from geopolitical analyses, which often pick up the globalisation theme. The next meaning is rooted in deeper social and cultural analyses. These range from optimistic – and, perhaps, rather mechanistic – accounts of social change such as Manuel Castells' trilogy on the Network Societys; to much more sombre accounts, such as that offered by Ulrich Beck in his Risk Society, which emphasise the fragmentation of social meaning and atomisation of individual experience.

Closely allied are the gloomy scenarios offered by environmentalists – and even the violent protests against globalisation. Also linked, although indirectly, are notions of intellectual volatility, verging at times on the excesses of postmodernism – because grand narratives, over-arching conceptualisations, meta-theories have been made redundant by the 'acceleration' of knowledge and the ability to manipulate massive data-sets.

The university is implicated in all these different meanings of the Knowledge Society – for example, of the source of the basic science from which highly sophisticated information and communication technologies are derived; as a 'national' institution (because, despite their internationalist rhetoric, universities are creatures of the nation state) threatened by the decay of the welfare states that have nourished their development and challenged by market-led globalisation; as critical institutions from which alternative, even oppositional, ideologies emerge. So the university itself may have become a problematic and contested institution.

The idea of the Knowledge Society, accounts of changes in scientific production do not provide with the firm foundations on which we can build secure scenarios about the future development of higher education. Also, as with the Knowledge Society, the university is complexly embroiled – as the producer of (most) basic science; but also as an increasingly aggressive exploiter of intellectual property and as the mediator (or broker) of research results.

The new players in the Knowledge Society are not as easy to identify as is commonly supposed; and that the path the University should follow is far from clear.

There are three major rivals are identified by the ever-increasing number of 'observatories' that have been established:

i) *The first is the development of so-called 'borderless education' institutions.* Some of these are based on global consortia of traditional universities, or by mixed consortia of world-class universities (world-class – because the 'brand' is all important in this arena) and global corporations, either mass media or IT. Others, of course, are more directly rivals to the traditional universities – and may take the form of on-line 'universities' established by such corporations.

The fundamental analysis underlying all these efforts is that the problem is not the development of intellectual concepts and content – which can either be brought off-the-peg or provided by academic entrepreneurs / sub-contractors as part of a supply-chain – but the customisation, delivery and marketing of these intellectual 'products' – the potential of which is now massively enhanced by the power of information and communication technologies.

It is rooted in a one-dimensional technology-deterministic account of the Knowledge Society; it ignores the complexities of cultural transfer and of 'local' takes on 'global' knowledge (and consequently is restricted in its operation to a narrow range of disciplines – overwhelmingly business and management, IT and computer science and some fields of science and engineering); and it fails to understand the synergies and complementarities between traditional face-to-face and 'virtual' forms of learning

ii) *The second group of rival institutsions are private for-profit 'universities'*. The University of Phoenix is the inevitable totemic example, but there are several other examples. First, these institutions, because they are in the private sector, are – apparently – unencumbered by the burden of state, and public, regulation and, therefore, free to operate more entrepreneurially.

Secondly, private for-profit 'universities' like Phoenix, because they are not universities at all in a traditional sense, are also unencumbered by the burden of intellectual, professional and cultural norms which 'proper' universities, public or (not-for-profit) private, have to carry. This may be a genuine advantage – or, better, difference. Such institutions are free to unbundle activities such as research and teaching, course design and course delivery; nor do they need to worry about disciplines as communities of intellect, because they are able to concentrate simply on knowledge 'products.

But many of the constraints which apply to 'borderless education' enterprises also apply to private for-profit universities. In addition the analysis that animates their existence is again rooted in a one-dimensional account of the Knowledge Society, the geopolitical triumph of the market states;

iii) *The third 'threat' to the traditional university is seen as coming from the proliferation of 'corporate universities'.* Sometimes these take the form of re-badged company training departments, perhaps with some R and D elements thrown in. This kind of development has been encouraged, and legitimised, by the growth of a powerful 'human resources' discourse.

At other times the establishment of corporate universities reflect a more concerted approach to workforce development. A good example is the recent formation in Britain of the 'National Health Service University'. However, although both are important developments.

First, many 'corporate universities' are engaged in lower-level training and/or short-course based continuing professional development; they often contract with universities for the provision of more sophisticated courses.

Secondly, their activities are largely complementary to those of existing universities. For example, the NHS University in Britain is not going to set up in competition with University Medical Schools, or even Schools of Nursing.

These new functions – technology transfer and knowledge management – are familiar to all. The nature of teaching and learning, of academic courses, of research programmes has also been transformed. There are now open frontiers between the academy and society, the economy, culture. Work-based learning, the accreditation of prior experience and similar practices and phenomena are evidence of cross-frontiers flows. So, if we ask who are the new players, the answer is – in part – ourselves; we are the new players;

The second form taken by the hybridisation of higher education is an extension of the first. It is the emergence of new organisational forms within the University that parallel traditional patterns of academic organisation such as Faculties and Departments. Of course, that traditional taxonomy has complex origins – some parts are based on academic affinities and are 'policed' by (fairly) endogenous scientific communities; other parts reflect the division of professional labour in wider society (although this division of labour has not been imposed on the University from the outside; law schools and medical schools play a key role in not only the reproduction but also the definition of professions). It is difficult to claim that research institutes or graduate schools are novel forms (especially, of course, in North America). However, the balance is now changing.

More and more organisational units within universities are based on neither principle –academic affinities or the division of professional (or expert) labour. Instead they have more in common with project teams, think-tanks, task-forces – and, of course, market entities designed to exploit the intellectual property that is generated within the University. These old and new organisational forms coexist, sometimes as rivals but at other times as allies. Again, if we ask where are the new organisations in the Knowledge Society, the answer – in part – is in the University; we are creating many of these new organisations.

The second phenomenon is the potential for growing 'activist' knowledge organisations which are in opposition to both traditional universities and to the new 'market' universities. They are opposed to traditional universities because they associate them with social elitism (or the reproduction of social hierarchies according to the division of labour in a capitalist society) and with restrictive definitions of knowledge that again are elitist, frequently gendered still (despite the impact of feminism) and generally dismissive of alternative and popular knowledge traditions.

As a result these 'activist' knowledge organisations challenge notions of evidence, objectivity, balance, debate which have typically been regarded as fundamental to the University (even if these high ideals have not always been met). However, these organisations are equally opposed to the 'market' universities which we take to be the principal rivals of the public university. They reject many of the 'givens' which most have been bullied into accepting in this (apparent) twilight of social democracy and the welfare state – the materiality of motivation, the efficacy of incentives, the drive to efficiency, the calculus of cost and benefits (on which, of course, the case for developing 'market' universities is based). And, paradoxically, they reject these 'givens' taking full advantage of the technologies of mass communication which we take to be typical of the market economy.

These 'activist' knowledge organisations take many forms – from local community groups, now with access to global data-bases and communication networks, through fundamentalists of all kinds perhaps even to global terrorist networks (However much we recoil from the notion that they are knowledge organisations, they employ sophisticated technologies and develop their own ideologies).

These organisations also range from fundamentalists, which fundamentally reject the culture of liberality associated with elite universities and the parallel culture of rationality associated with university science and scholarship, to organisations such as Green Peace which believe with some justice that their rational use of scientific evidence is equal or superior to that of the World Bank or the IMF.

At their best these 'activist' knowledge organisations, in their enthusiasm for a more democratic distribution of knowledge resources and their opposition to the more baleful aspects of globalisation, may be assuming some of the ethical responsibilities which universities willingly accepted a generation ago but from which they have more recently distanced themselves.

In short, a naive and one-dimensional interpretation of the Knowledge Society – which, in fact, is a problematical category with multiple, and contested, interpretations. Furthermore these accounts attach too little weight to the fundamental – but, again, complex and ambiguous – changes that are taking place in knowledge production.

2002 E-Readiness Ranking

Today the e-rankings have become an established benchmark for countries seeking to harness the Internet 's potential to spur business efficiency, improve the provision of public services and encourage integration with the global economy. "E-readiness " is shorthand for the extent to which a country 's business environment is conducive to Internet-based opportunities.

It is a concept that spans a wide range of factors, from telephone penetration to online security to intellectual property protection. It is an idea that has outlasted the Internet "bubble " that sparked such exuberance -and delivered such disappointment -in the late 1990s. "Despite the dotcom bust, the Internet is still reshaping the way companies do business, and countries ' e-readiness will be a vital feature of the global competitive landscape," notes Daniel Franklin, Editorial Director of the Economist Intelligence Unit. Covering the world 's 60 largest markets, the rankings provide a useful guide for companies seeking to invest in technology-savvy countries, as well as governments looking to reap the benefits of the digital age.

Both the Economist Intelligence Unit and IBM have engaged in e-business research for many years, so collaborative work on the rankings was a natural fit.The rankings model is a joint undertaking. The Economist Intelligence Unit, however, has sole responsibility for scoring and ranking the 60 countries covered by the e-readiness rankings.

E-business is taking root just about everywhere -but some countries are pioneers, others laggards. In the latest edition of the Economist Intelligence Unit e-readiness rankings, which cover the world 's 60 largest markets, North America, northern Europe and Australia take the top ten spots. The new edition of the rankings -the third since their launch in 2000 -shows steady improvement and increasing convergence among the top-tier countries, where heavy investment in Internet technologies is bearing fruit.

Many less-developed countries lag behind, however, their e-readiness hindered by a range of factors, including poor infrastructure, inadequate protection for intellectual property, lack of finance and unfavourable business environments.

The new round of rankings affirms two conclusions suggested by previous editions. First, neither size nor location is destiny. Although the US comes first in the rankings, the rankings place a premium on agility rather than sheer economic might. Many nimble smaller economies in Scandinavia and Europe thus score highly, whereas less innovative giants like Japan rank relatively low.

And although geographic regions tend to fall into one category or another, there are always exceptions: standout countries such as Singapore or Chile, which outshine their neighbours in e-readiness. Second, government policy makes a difference.

Many less-developed countries, such as the Czech Republic and Mexico, are making good progress in e-business thanks in large part to proactive government policies. Indeed, for countries near the bottom of our rankings, improvement in the e-business environment owes much to public policy. Where governments have drawn up clear plans for IT investment and computer literacy, enhanced competition among infrastructure providers and enacted laws to deal with the grey areas created by the Internet, e-business fares better.

The white paper, published by the Economist Intelligence Unit in co-operation with IBM, presents the rankings of the world 's largest 60 economies (which account for 95% of global GDP), explains the methodology used and provides detailed findings for the top ten countries in each ranking category. The next edition of the Economist Intelligence Unit e-readiness rankings is scheduled to appear in January 2003.

The US leads the pack, as it did in the 2000 and 2001 Economist Intelligence Unit e-readiness rankings. However, due partially to changes in our methodology, and mostly to developments in countries ' infrastructure, regulatory environment and economy, there have been significant shifts further down in the rankings.

The Netherlands has moved into second place from tenth in 2001, for example, and northern Europe now claims most of the other top spots, thanks not only to sophisticated IT infrastructure and high mobile-phone penetration, but also to smart government policy and a good overall business environment. Asia, Latin America and Africa trail further behind, but a few standouts in each region have made significant gains.

North America and Western Europe dominate the top ten places in our rankings, with Australia the lonely outsider. These countries score highest both because consumers and businesses have embraced the Internet, and because their economic and political stability and openness to foreign investment make them good bets for all kinds of business, particularly e-business.

Singapore and Hong Kong lead the pack in Asia, taking 11th and 13th place, respectively, while Vietnam and Pakistan languish at the bottom of the heap, in 56th and 57th place. The same is true of Latin America, where advanced Chile ranks 28th, while Ecuador stumbles into 50th place. In the Middle East and Africa, Israel alone ranks among the top 30 countries.

The US may rule the roost, but many of the world 's largest economies, including Japan, Germany and France, are outpaced by smaller, more agile, competitors, such as the Netherlands, Switzerland and Sweden. What sets these countries apart is the broad accessibility and affordability of the Internet, thanks to state-of-the-art IT infrastructure and high per capita income.

The US tops the rankings because of the degree to which the Internet has become embedded in commercial culture. Nowhere is so much business conducted over the Internet so routinely. This explains why the US scored highest in the category for e-business supporting services (the consulting and IT services and back- office solutions used to facilitate online business) as well as in the social and cultural category (which considers, among other things, the degree of innovation and entrepreneurship in business).

Singapore and Hong Kong rank as the most competitive telecom markets in the world, and among the best equipped, yet don't figure among the top ten countries. While high-grade infrastructure is important, more important is how people use it. Infrastructure is still evolving.

Even top-ranked countries have not yet satisfied consumer demand for fast, cheap, secure and reliable Internet connectivity. High-speed broadband services are not universally available and Internet-ready mobile phones are still in their infancy -even in mobile- crazed Scandinavia. In emerging markets, meanwhile, monopolistic telecom providers still inhibit the competition that can speed innovation and drive down prices, and tight budgets thwart ambitious development plans.

Internet business thrives when governments are committed to a clear, consistent strategy to develop IT infrastructure. Adequate funding is crucial, but so too is firm political leadership that builds public support.

Successful e-business depends on a strong legal framework that protects private property and encourages entrepreneurship. Increasingly, it also requires Internet-specific legislation. In the crucial category of legal and policy environment, Australia comes first, followed by Sweden, Switzerland, Finland and the UK. Other countries - even those without a strong e-business culture, such as Mexico and Chile -are enacting smart Internet legislation, recognising that good laws promote industry growth.

Methodology With every year the model for the Economist Intelligence Unit 's e-readiness rankings has grown in sophistication. This year, working in association with IBM 's Institute for Business Value, the Economist Intelligence Unit adjusted the rankings framework to shift away from the dotcom era 's emphasis on websites and e-commerce to the new imperatives of corporate efficiency, security and global connectivity.

Some countries demonstrate strength in all categories, while others stand out in a few categories but lag behind in others. What follows is a category-by-category assessment of country performance, along with an explanation of the Economist Intelligence Unit 's e-readiness criteria. Pointers are given, as well, to indicate how countries could do more to seize the advantages that the Internet offers.

Connectivity measures the access that individuals and businesses have to basic fixed and mobile telephony services, personal computers and the Internet. The affordability, quality and reliability of service -all functions of the level of competition in the telecom market -also figure as determinants, as does the security of content delivered and transactions conducted via the Internet.

For e-business to take root, countries at a minimum need to ensure secure access to the Internet. Where phone lines are inadequate, computer ownership extremely low and Internet connections prohibitively expensive, e-business has failed to take off. But even in wealthy countries where the infrastructure is reliable and secure, there is tremendous room for improvement. High-speed broadband services are not universally available, and Internet-ready mobile phones are still in their infancy -even in mobile-crazed Scandinavia. No country entirely meets consumer demand for fast, cheap, secure and reliable Internet connectivity.

Deregulation promotes Internet access. Singapore and Hong Kong have the most deregulated telecom markets in the world, followed by northern European countries and the US. At the other end of the spectrum are countries where the state maintains a stranglehold on telecom providers. Turkey 's government, for example, is dragging its feet on selling Turk Telekom, which controls not only the country 's fixed lines but also mobile telephony and Internet service provision. Such fixed-line monopolies hinder e-business in much of the developing world, as they are most often the largest Internet service providers as well.

The two faces of mobile usage. Three out of four Swedes carry a mobile phone. The reasons are clear: the country is tech savvy and gadget loving, and its liberalised telecom market offers lots of choice at low prices. All this bodes well for e-business.

Mobile phone penetration in the Czech Republic is not far behind, at 68%. Yet here the reason for mobile usage is altogether different: the incumbent fixed-line monopoly provides poor service at high prices. In the Czech Republic, as in many developing countries, mobile-phone penetration is high simply because the fixed-line alternative is so unattractive. Mobile usage on its own is not a good indicator of a country 's e-business environment. Uniform standards are important in encouraging mobile usage -and here the US falls far short of Scandinavia.

In evaluating the general business climate, the Economist Intelligence Unit screens 70 indicators covering criteria such as the strength of the economy, political stability, the regulatory environment, taxation, competition policy, the labour market, the quality of infrastructure, and openness to trade and investment. The resulting business environment rankings measure the expected attractiveness of the general business environment over the next five years. Calculated regularly as part of the Economist Intelligence Unit

Country Forecasts, these rankings have long offered investors an invaluable comparative index for 60 major economies.

Good for business, good for e-business. Not long ago, the Internet was seen as the engine of a new world of business that would leave "old economy " companies in the dust. The consensus now is that the Internet makes sense only when applied within the framework of traditional business rules. That said, it is clear that all types of companies and every industry can apply e-business solutions to improve efficiency and streamline operations.

Today, business is e-business, and vice versa. For this reason, countries that score highly in the Economist Intelligence Unit 's business environment rankings -those with stable governments, strong economies, developed legal and regulatory systems, and flexible labour markets -are generally also the best places to do e-business. Countries where competition is restricted and legislation is cumbersome are less e-ready.

The Netherlands scores highly in all the categories that the Economist Intelligence Unit considers crucial for doing business. It has a stable political framework. Its economy is characterised by low inflation, steady growth and openness to foreign trade. Competition policy is well developed. Taxes are low by European standards and financing is readily available. Infrastructure, especially telecom infrastructure, is excellent.

The Netherlands is well ahead of its neighbours in labour market deregulation. Thus the Netherlands takes first place in the business environment rankings. Not surprisingly, it is also near the top in the e-readiness rankings. The Netherlands has perhaps the strongest B2B infrastructure in Europe, and Dutch multinationals are using cutting-edge technology to improve everyday business practices. ING Bank, for example, equips its insurance salesforce with wireless Internet access.

Shell, a Dutch oil giant, has developed innovative ways of combining real-world and web-based training. Compare the Netherlands with one of Western Europe 's e-business slowpokes, Italy. Italy places 22nd in both the business environment and e-readiness rankings. It suffers from political instability, huge public debt and an over-regulated labour market. In this environment, e-business takes longer to develop. Only 6% of Italians shop online, and B2B e-commerce accounts for less than 1% of total commerce.

Many of the countries that score highly in the e-readiness rankings also allocate a large portion of public spending to information technology, or enact incentives that encourage private-sector infrastructure investment.

Relatively small economies, such as Austria and the Netherlands, must dedicate a larger share of total spending to IT infrastructure than massive economies, such as the US and Germany, in order to maintain similar levels of infrastructure; their ability to commit these funds indicates a strong commitment to e-business. Even countries further down on the list -including Korea, Portugal and Brazil -are also devoting tremendous resources to IT development, signalling their determination to become e-business leaders.

Logistics and delivery systems play a role. E-business relies on more than phone lines and PCs. It requires electronic payment systems and populations that habitually use credit cards. It also mandates efficient and secure postal, courier and other logistics systems involved in the delivery of goods purchased online or shipped as part of just-in-time manufacturing systems. Those ranking highly in this category have efficient, expansive, reliable and cost-effective delivery systems. Innovative start-ups need financing.

To move business online, companies need the help of other companies, from website designers, to payment facilitators, to hosting providers. These small, innovative firms depend on start-up capital. In Western Europe, North America and Australia, financing is readily available from a variety of sources and on generally good terms. In many emerging markets, however, banks function poorly, stock markets are embryonic and venture capital is practically unknown. Lack of financing is hampering e-business development throughout much of the world.

E-business development depends both on a country 's overall legal framework and specific laws governing Internet use. Governments that support the creation of an Internet-conducive legal environment -both through policy and enforcement -get high scores. Those more concerned with censoring content and controlling the web score lower. There 's a role for government. It 's easy for governments to declare ambitious Internet-development plans, but such declarations need to be followed by deeds. Even where funds are in short supply, action can be taken to ensure that the legal system supports e-business.

Developing a consistent and predictable legal and regulatory framework to address emerging e-business legal concerns is a good start. This can include ensuring a level playing field in the telecommunications industry, where old monopolists often retain effective control of the market, or passing legislation that extends to the Internet proper measures to protect intellectual property rights, or directing law-enforcement agencies to protect online security.

Putting public services online can help demonstrate the benefits of e-business while saving taxpayers time and money. The UK and Singapore are standouts in shifting paperwork-intensive processes to more streamlined web-based procedures. A good place for governments to start is to simplify the registration of a new business so that it can be accomplished in a single step via the Internet. This frees local entrepreneurs from red tape and makes the country a more attractive investment destination for foreign capital.

Literacy and basic education are preconditions to being able to navigate the web. In addition, the rankings consider a population 's "e-literacy "-its experience using the Internet and its receptivity to it -and the technical skills of the workforce. And because Internet business involves risk-taking, the rankings assess the national proclivity to business innovation and entrepreneurship.

Basic education is not enough. Internet users must have some degree of education. However, basic literacy is not enough. In poor countries where literacy rates are relatively high, such as China, Sri Lanka and Kazakhstan, e-business is often hampered by a shortage of both technically skilled workers and an "e-literate " population that has had exposure to the Internet.

In countries where both literacy and e-literacy rates are high, e-business is thriving. Scandinavians, and northern Europeans in general, are highly educated, tech savvy and multilingual. These factors bring the region nearly even with the US in our rankings. Many countries could do better. France, for example, receives high scores for education and literacy yet earns only an 8.25 in this category. There are several explanations. The French tend to start using the Internet at an older age than the typical American or Scandinavian, and many French cling to Minitel, the country 's long-established proprietary service. Less than one-third of the population speaks English, the lingual franca of international e-business.

No business or industry can function efficiently without intermediaries and ancillary services to support it. For e-business, these include consulting and IT services, and back-office solutions. The rankings also take into account whether there are consistent, industry-wide technology standards for platforms and programming languages.

Israel, a major exporter of software and high-tech products, is one of the few non-Western countries at the forefront of e-services development. The country is tech savvy, with an exceptionally high share of scientists, and entrepreneurial. Moreover, Israel boasts one of the most vibrant venture-capital sectors outside Silicon Valley. The result has been an ever-growing number of e-consultants, e-marketers and technical-support providers to underpin Israel 's high-tech sector.

Governments help set tech standards. An absence of global technology standards is emerging as an inhibitor of e-business growth and efficiency. Although the legend of the Internet is one of self-government, international mediation will be increasingly necessary to reap the benefits of global connectivity.

The US General Accounting Office recently joined the debate over the future of XML, the most widely used mark-up language. The GAO 's brief was to establish whether XML should be used to standardise government data and promote interoperability. But the agency expressed doubts not only about XML, but also about a plethora of competing standards. The report appears to have shaken up the notoriously slow-moving standard-setting bodies, which have promised to address the shortcomings.

In short, the Economist Intelligence Unit 's e-readiness rankings lend themselves naturally to an action plan for governments seeking to capture the benefits of the Internet and the changes it has wrought. Connectivity is a necessary first step.

Although it is consumers who ultimately drive adoption of the Internet, governments can help ensure that the proper infrastructure is in place, and that its reliability and security are protected. Protecting competition in the communications industry helps speed e-business.

E-business cannot thrive where other forms of business fail. So governments aiming to promote Internet usage need to adopt policies that facilitate growth, promote investment and reduce red tape. Measures that encourage entrepreneurship, including the availability of financing for innovative firms, are helpful.

Creating a conducive legal and regulatory environment is crucial as well. This means not only ensuring that traditional legal safeguards, such as protection of intellectual property rights, are extended into the digital world, but also training and funding the police and judicial personnel needed to enforce them. Adopting a coherent and far- reaching government "e-strategy "- particularly one oriented to universal Internet access -provides a vision of the digital future that can inspire both business and civic enthusiasm.

Making public services available online, in a citizen-friendly format, helps sustain that enthusiasm and gives governments an opportunity to lead by example -as well as to save time and money. Adding computer literacy to the basic education curriculum, and technological specialisation to the range of training options, promotes needed skills. Supporting countrywide industry standards helps promote data sharing without stifling competition, as does joining the international dialogue on global standards.

Yet, as the Economist Intelligence Unit e-readiness rankings suggest, savvy policy and creativity can often trump sheer size and power. Wealth is an obvious advantage, but lack of funds is no excuse for ignoring the potential of the Internet.

Estonian Transition in to Information Society

Societal inclination towards a fast acquisition of modern technologies, willingness to experiment with new solutions and internationally successful promotional campaigns have introduced Estonia on the international arena as a rapidly evolving information society. For example, the issue of technological developments and their impact on society has been analysed by different international analytical reports and Estonia has been ranked highly:

— McConnell International (2001), for example, indicates that in the fields of e-leadership, human capital and overall e-business climate the majority of conditions in Estonia are suitable to the conduct of e-business and e-government.

— The latest (2001) Human Development Report issued by the United Nations Development Programme (UNDP) also ranks countries next to human development index (where Estonia holds 44 th position and belongs to the group of high human development countries) also according to the technology achievement index.

Although Estonia was not ranked by the UNDP, according to the provided formula Estonia would be on the 30 th position belonging to the group of potential leaders. Indeed, the broad picture seems to confirm this concept, as figures and early growth rates are in some cases remarkable (particularly in the category of consumer goods and exports), and several initiatives that have been undertaken by either government or corporate agents are remarkable, inspiring other countries to imitate Estonian practices.

The early launch of the Estonian information society developments is frequently used as best practice for other countries. Without hesitation, the rapid development of the telecommunications market is a clear success story:

— A reasonable state policy has generated rapid catching-up both in the fields of fixed lines and mobile communications;

— Estonia has been one of the first countries amongst the CEE countries to open the telecommunications market for liberalisation, giving a good basis for further development;

— Public initiatives in the fields of eLearning (e.g. Estonian Tiger Leap) and eGovernment are also good examples that other (especially Central and Eastern European) countries attempt to imitate. Like other transition economies, Estonia is experiencing very rapid developments in the technical sphere with a number of problems arising at the same time on the social scale, such as the digital divide. Recent developments in the Estonian telecommunication market are characterised by the fast development of both telecommunications market and Estonian information society as a whole:

— Rapid increase in the number of telephone lines;

— Accessibility to modern telecommunication services (GSM, ISDN, DSL) and reduction of the prices;

— Total liberalisation of the telecommunications market (expiration of the exclusive rights granted to Estonian Telephone Company) since January 1, 2001;

— Promotion of technological development by the State through legislation (Cable Distribution Act, Telecommunications Act, Digital Signature Act). In general, the proximity of advanced Scandinavian technology forerunners is a significant driver. The rapid uptake of novel technologies, enhanced wireless communication infrastructure, a high number of conventional telephone lines and Internet hosts has created a moderately favourable platform for building up appropriate forms of applications.

As a well functioning telecommunications sector is considered important for enhancing the competitiveness of an economy and the quality of life, Estonia has paid much attention to the information society developments and directing these after regaining its independence.

Main issue in the beginning of 1990s was insufficient technological infrastructure and in order to support its development a Concession Agreement was signed. This helped to attract significant investments into extension and digitisation of the public telephone network.

During the 1990s the state has adopted also several important legislative acts and established the necessary state structures and has in this way organised the telecommunications The most influential enterprise in the Estonian telecommunications market AS Eesti Telekom was restructured already in 1991-93; in 1997 the state enterprise Eesti Telekom was re-established as AS Eesti Telekom and the decision was adopted to organise an initial public offering (IPO) to sell up to 49% of the shares.

The IPO took place at the beginning of 1999, and institutional and private investors purchased 49% of the shares owned previously by the Republic of Estonia. At the moment AS Eesti Telekom has 100% ownerships in AS Eesti Telefon (Estonian Telephone Company) and in AS Eesti Mobiiltelefon (Estonian Mobile Telephone Company).

Since the beginning of 2001 the number of telecommunications companies increased remarkably and currently the most important companies in the market are AS Eesti Telefon, Levicom BroadBand OÜ (TELE2) and Uninet AS. Estonian mobile telephone communications market has been liberalised from the very beginning and currently there are three operators on the market.

As for year 2000 there are 522 000 conventional main lines in Estonia and 557 000 mobile communication subscribers with the market turnover for carrier services being 259 million Euros. Since its early days telecom sector has shown a constant growth, though conditions for further expansion are somewhat more restrictive nowadays.

On the one hand, the market is reaching saturation point, though it might be just a temporary situation in light of the launch of the next generation mobile services; on the other hand intensive competition in the sector pushes down the prices. The predicted growth rate of the total telecom market was about 10% for 2001.

Access to the Internet is mainly realised through the use of dial-up services in Estonia, although DSL services are available in major cities. There are 8 major Internet Service Providers (ISP) in Estonia. Technology uptake and applications When looking at the ICT manufacturing in Estonia, it follows, that foreign orders are very important for the Estonian ICT sector - 73% of the subcontracting activity originates from abroad.

Typically, subcontracting involves assembly of various communication equipment and software outsourcing. As a result, subcontracting revenues constituted 60–100% of the Estonian turnover of telecommunications equipment production, industrial automation, consumer electronics and components, and about 15% of the computers and office machinery sub-sector in 2000. Due to high foreign demand, the export of the Estonian ICT industry has increased rapidly.

On the downside, most of the rise can be assigned to a single company's activity – Elcoteq Ltd provides 83% of the total Estonian ICT exports and 96% of telecommunications equipment exports as the statistics for the year 2000 indicates. Of domestic industries, manufacturing, the telecommunications sector, banking, wholesale and retail trade, and governmental structures are the important drivers of the emerging Estonian ICT cluster, as they demand most of the production generated by the ICT sector.

On the services side, the most popular application areas of Internet are banking services, but public administration's efforts in IT sphere have also generated new web-based services in public domain. As 41% of Estonians aged 15 to 74 are identified as Internet users, there seems to be challenge for both public and private sector organisations in introducing innovations in services fields, namely through the use of ICT.

The most popular electronic service in Estonia is Internet banking. Hansapank has indicated 365,000 Internet banking clients and Ühispank 150,000. To some extent the clientele basis is overlapping, but is still reasonable to believe that total number of Internet banking users exceeds 250,000, covering more than 18% of total Estonian population.

Factors that have put Estonia to the position of the leader concerning Internet banking among former Eastern block Countries and outdoes a lot of Western European countries, are simple-to-use software, free of charge transactions during the services' introducing time to the market and the impact of Nordic countries' IT culture on Estonia.

Other popular services offered via digital channels are digital taxation board portal and insurance payment systems. Digital taxation board is represented both in the system of Hansapanks Internet banking interface Hanza.net, Ühisbank's U-net as well as separately, via Tax Board's own portal. In the former case personal identification of Hansapank's and Ühispank's clients is used for electronic tax-related transactions, in the latter case special security codes are issued to clients upon request.

The number of income tax declarations submitted through Internet banking portals exceeded 36,000 for the declaration period of year 2000. There are other interesting services provided by the private sector, e.g. Mobile parking is another recent innovative initiative launched by the Estonian Mobile Telephone (EMT) and parking surveillance authorities.

In order to use the system, after parking a vehicle a SMS has to be sent to the parking centre, and finished upon further notification, also via SMS. The parking fee is subsequently added to telephone bill or deducted automatically from client's mobile bank-account.

LocateGSM is a service offered in cooperation with EMT and GIS developer Regio Ltd. This is a web-based mobile positioning system (MPS) enabling to display the location of EMT mobile subscriber on a map. This way the system is offering good bases for further development of different location-based services.

In addition there are also other remarkable initiatives carried out in the public sector. These are mainly dealing with the modernisation of the communication within the government, or provision of services to companies and individuals on digital bases (e.g. e-Citizen project under planning, electronic ID card initiative).

In 2000 the first phase of the project of "Information Systems for Government Sessions" was developed and implemented, forming thus a solid basis for Government's work digitalisation, as well as making available Government protocols and information concerned to general public.

The project aims at engaging citizens more actively into policy decision processes, as well as motivating public debates concerning nationwide and important initiatives. The citizen portal encourages submitting ideas, visions, directions etc. as well as comment on bills released by ministries already during the process of bill drafting. Steps towards modernising the governmental information exchange system were taken starting year 2000, at the initiative of the pilot project X-road (cross-road).

The objectives of X-road pilot project are to interconnect state databases, to enable requesting information to authorised user via Internet from any of the databases after authorised accession. This project is especially important as elements of the state information system were founded technologically independently, but also at different points in time, thus calling for operative modernisation and co-operation.

Parallel to X-road project incentives on bringing several main registries (Business Registry, Real Estate Registry etc) on full-electronic Internet basis are being implemented. The access is guaranteed to all users, and the information obtained has full legal power.

For projects like these governmental structures are important users of telecommunications equipment and services, office machinery, computers and software, whereas the government's affection for novel technological solutions has had a positive effect on a number of public sector initiatives.

Despite of the rapid spread of Internet connections, relatively high level of users and extensive investments into Internet stores, the turnover of electronic commerce is insignificant. According to Global eCommerce Survey e-commerce penetration is 6% in Estonia. For the USA the relevant figure is 33% and for Finland 17%. Factors impeding the development of e-commerce are sustainability of buying habits, limited product range in Internet stores, inconveniences in paying for goods and deliveries and security risks when using bankcards.

Forming a new electronic commerce culture is a world-wide problem and in this light Estonian developments are comparable to the most successful European countries. One of the strongest Estonian advantages in these developments is the widespread Internet banking (favours the rise of positive attitude towards e-commerce); the most important discouraging factors are the smallness of the potential market and conventional shopping habits.

Consequently, bringing more services onto digital basis is substantially dependent on the potential demand for these services. Presently the demand is derived mainly by the clients of Internet banking, who have their personal banking accounts for conducting electronic-transactions via Internet based web portal.

Evidently, the fast development of the Estonian banking sector and the high-tech solutions elaborated by the banks' own product development departments have reinforced the need for quality software, and trustworthy and secure products, thus having also positive effects on generating innovative solutions.

Also, collaborative actions undertaken by the banks and telecommunications operators have established strong links between these two sectors, paving the way for future m-commerce related activities. However, in this context the relations with content providers are insufficient, meaning that these relations have to develop towards a more active involvement of external content service providers in order for a large-scale functioning m-business or m-leisure to appear.

CHAPTER 4

Information Development in India

For most developing countries, the internet has been of relatively little significance for the large majority of businesses, except possibly for some larger countries. The reasons are not hard to find. For most countries, the primitive state of communications infrastructure is a difficult barrier to internet development. In most, business operations involve mostly small firms, often the last to benefit from improved means of communications even in richer countries. And, not least, poor countries generally lack the pool of technically trained people necessary to fuel change.

With the possible exception of China, India has been affected more by changes in IT than any other developing country, yet the country remains very poor by any standard. The country's businesses have until early in the 1990s been heavily influenced in their growth by the government's licensing regime, several companies having become very large firms operating nationally mainly through their ability to garner licenses.

The structure of many of these firms, therefore, has been dictated not by market demands, but rather by the availability of government licenses. In addition, many companies have benefited from the government's past policy of protection from international competition, a program that together with licensing has yielded gross inefficiencies and bloated enterprises. All of this is changing. The licensing regime is largely gone, and protection is beginning to be pared away. Foreign direct investment, while still not exactly encouraged in some sectors, is far more welcome than it was. The results have been dramatic. Large conglomerates have had to give attention to their competitive viability in a much tougher economic environment. Reorganization and restructuring to achieve more competitive focus is becoming the rule.

In IT more specifically, India has in some ways become a world leader, yet the degree of penetration of such new phenomena as the internet is still quite modest. Even so, at least the larger manufacturing companies and, perhaps more importantly, financial institutions have begun to use new technologies to improve efficiency and better serve customers. There seems little question that the gradual opening of the Indian market has been forcing businesses to pay more attention to competitiveness.

In some ways India is not representative of the larger developing world. Although illiteracy is still widespread, India has a long history of support for technical education and, as a consequence, has produced large numbers of technically qualified personnel. The country is, in fact, a not inconsequential exporter of engineers and scientists; Silicon Valley alone boasts around 150 Indian millionaires, for example, and American immigration rules allowing thousands of visas for technical people have benefited disproportionately Indians. At home, the large group of technically-qualified persons in India, to some degree utilizing their Indian-American contacts, has formed the backbone of a rapid growth in IT investment in India, a growth that is continuing today.

India possesses a substantial middle class, variously estimated at between 150 and 200 million people, depending on criteria. This group is concentrated in perhaps 150 towns and cities scattered around this very large country, and it forms the major source of customers for a variety of businesses, either directly or indirectly. In an increasingly competitive environment, this group appears to have provided strong economic incentives for businesses to find ways to improve efficiency.

IT provides an important vehicle to accomplish this goal and IT providers are being pushed incessantly to improve access and broaden services. Finally, the IT industry has expanded relatively free of the kind of government regulation that has affected other industries. As a result, the industry has been the source of considerable entrepreneurialism and has fostered development of the growing venture capital industry described above.

Moreover, as in the United States, the IT industry itself has been the source of productivity gains for the economy as a whole as manufacturers emulate production techniques in the West and output increases rapidly. The importance of the IT sector in India also is a feature not replicated in most other developing countries.

Because the internet provides the greatest possibility for overall economic gain among IT sectors, we begin with a description of the internet and how it is currently being utilized. Not surprisingly, India has lagged far behind many other Asian countries in the adoption of the internet. In a population of one billion people, there are fewer than two million internet subscribers, a figure that contrasts with India's closest comparator in size, China, which has more than three times as many telephone lines and four times as many internet users.

In fact, by the year 2000 India had only around 26 million fixed-line telephone connections and fewer than five million personal computers in place. Clearly, if the internet is to become a major vehicle in transforming the Indian economy, there is little question that rapid further development of India's communications and data transmission network is essential. Just as obviously, there is still a long way to go in this development.

Of major importance is the state of economic development in the country; India on average is still a very poor country, with a monthly per capita GNP of only 180 US dollars on a purchasing power parity basis. Despite the existence of a sizable "middle class," most people in India worry about obtaining the essentials of life, not in gaining access to telephones, much less internet service. Even so, given the availability of an adequate telecommunications network, India's internet audience could increase substantially.

But, that network, too, historically has been a major constraint. As noted, there exist relatively few telephone connections, and it is well known that the value of the internet increases geometrically with added connections. More importantly, however, the reliability of the system nationally has certainly not been adequate to support internet use, even if more connections were to become available.

The country has lacked a high-speed data communications backbone to speed transmission and interconnectivity. In some ways, these constraints are a "chicken and egg" proposition: without a better national telecommunications network, there is little incentive to connect; without more connections, the incentive to build a more adequate high-speed network diminishes. Breaking this deadlock promises to be an important determinant to internet growth and, more broadly, to the attractiveness of the country as a destination for high-technology foreign investment.

Another constraint to Indian internet development has been the structure of telephone tariff schedules. As in many other countries, tariffs have been based on time charges which can make internet usage a very expensive proposition. These tariffs have been changing and are now based on larger units of time. But, even now, the cost of internet service from the telephone monopoly is not cheap. Five hundred hours annually of dial- up service can cost $200 for a slow-speed connection, a figure that compares with a U.S. standard of perhaps $180 for unlimited time. Beyond the 500 hour yearly base, time is billed at about 35 cents an hour, also not an insignificant charge for users.

Internet expansion suffers from the generally poor condition of other parts of India's infrastructure. Internet use for commercial purposes is based importantly on increasing the speed of transactions, eliminating steps in the distribution chain and delivering products faster and more reliably. It is the last step of this process that is at risk in an India-like environment, because the physical infrastructure to deliver products from supplier to customer speedily is largely absent.

Even if high-speed telecommunications were in place, which as yet it is not, much of the transactional advantages of the internet in commercial practice would be lost owing to poor roads and inefficient rail facilities. To be sure, internet use provides opportunities for both consumers and businesses to compare easily large numbers of products and prices. But, without the ability to deliver products expeditiously, this advantage can be largely negated.

Widespread internet use within India is not necessarily a barrier to increasing and potentially benefiting from use of the internet by Indian companies. For example, with the much improved access to international gateways now becoming available businesses can easily expand their potential customer base globally through the internet, even if their local clientele is not yet connected.

In fact, buyers and, particularly, industrial purchasers in many industrial countries today are routinely posting detailed product and component specifications on specialized websites open to all with access to the internet. The purpose of such sites is to widen the net of possible suppliers, thus reducing costs. For Indian companies, therefore, opportunities to expand business relationships with foreign firms could be enormously enhanced through the internet, even though internet use in India remained relatively constrained.

Company utilization of the internet in India thus far is limited, but corporate interest in future use is intense. Firms are establishing special groups internally to investigate how the internet might be used both for internal control and for developing more efficient means for dealing with customers and suppliers. Generally, little will actually be done until the current efforts to upgrade India's telecommunications infrastructure are further advanced.

One exception, a company that has gone further than most, is Reliance Industries, a firm mostly engaged in chemical production and distribution, and a company actively involved in building a fiberoptic network linking Indian major cities. This company, in addition, expects that the internet will become a primary mechanism to improve operations, and it already has in place an internet-ready communications and control system. But, much of the system today uses leased telephone lines, not yet the internet.

For example, of the company's 20,000-odd customers around India, 3-4 thousand are major buyers, accounting for perhaps 75 percent or more of total sales. These major customers for chemicals are now linked electronically to an internet-based market exchange introduced by Reliance, one of several now existing in the country. In addition, through leased- line facilities, customers can process orders, and Reliance can deliver dispatching details, better manage inventory, carry out invoicing, and provide technical service, all done electronically. This customer network will be transferred to the internet at the earliest possible moment, since the internet should provide substantially lower operational costs.

To provide some measure of the benefits already apparent from this system, Reliance has been able to reduce receivables from 310 days to 90 days, only one area of savings. Cost improvements come primarily from a general tightening and acceleration of processing within the company and between the firm and its customers. Savings do not occur as a result of reducing manpower.

In addition, the speed of order delivery has been improved greatly and inventories reduced in a system that is now integrated into the firm's overall management control function that links not only important customers but also over 50 of the company's own operations. These results for Reliance are similar in nature to cost reductions experienced by companies in industrial parts of the world, even though thus far the internet has not been much utilized.

One might anticipate even greater savings in India, as compared with more industrialized countries, since operational efficiency prior to the introduction of electronic controls is likely to have been far lower than comparable figures for companies in the developed world.

Although the introduction of Reliance- like systems lags in India among larger manufacturers, there are other areas of the economy where considerable progress has been made, despite the as yet primitive nature of the country's telecommunications network.

A few Indian private banks and financial institutions represent a sector that has become a leader in using electronics to offer new customer services. Though still early in the process, banks see the internet as a vehicle not only to improve current services but, in addition, to bring into the banks new types of businesses. For example, some banks look forward to the time when client companies will choose to delegate most "back office" functions directly to their banks. Moreover, banks are attempting to link with Indian commercial web-sites to offer clearing services to clients of these sites.

One interesting example of bank activity is HDFC Bank, started as an off-shoot of India's Housing

Development Finance Corporation six years ago. The bank now has 125 branches and is adding new ones rapidly, including 60 last year.

Branches have been connected to the home office from the outset through a private data network operated for the bank by Wipro Infotech Software and Services Company, a large Indian software developer. HDFC Bank targets high-worth individuals and larger corporate clients but is also developing a sizable retail banking business. Telephone transactions of the type familiar in more developed countries (automatic payments, transfers, deposits, account balances, etc.) were introduced two years ago, but these functions are now also available through the internet.

Although precise cost estimates for serving customers via the internet are not available, banks have studied savings that are possible through telephone transactions, as compared with other means. For example, if a teller-based transaction costs, say, 150 rupees, the same transaction done via an automatic teller machine runs only about 15 rupees and via electronic connection 10 rupees, less than 7 percent of the teller cost. One other interviewed bank offering similar electronic services confirms these cost figures.

Internet-based services are a more recent introduction, but already demands for the services are expanding quickly. Today, HDFC Bank claims over 100,000 retail internet customers, almost half of whom utilize the service more than once monthly. Another aggressive bank, ICICI Bank, also is active both in telephone and internet service for its customers. Its internet customer base grew from 6,000 to 250,000 in a single year. As more customers are added in these banks, unit costs of transactions promise to fall rapidly, because the expense of adding more server capacity is minimal. In other words, the marginal cost of serving an internet customer is still falling.

In another aspect of its business, HDFC Bank is working closely with the Bombay Stock Exchange, which itself is in the process of automating transactions. Before automation was introduced, weekly reporting to the exchange was accomplished by brokers submitting floppy disks two days before each week's end.

Today, through clearing accounts maintained at HDFC Bank and elsewhere, clearing is instantaneous, and 400 brokers maintain accounts at the bank for this purpose. While such developments in the financial sector are encouraging, they should be kept in perspective. Private banks in India account for barely one- fifth of total deposits.

Although this proportion has been increasing, the vast preponderance of Indian banking is still done in state-owned facilities, which, thus far, have shown only modest interest in increasing efficiency. There has been talk of increasing the proportion of private ownership in state banks in order to increase productivity, but resistance to such moves by still powerful unions and others has stalled much action. Website Development Despite the lack yet of extensive broadband facilities in India, growth in the number of new websites has been explosive.

There are today hundreds of Indian commercial websites. Although financial figures are unavailable, it is likely that most of these sites are not yet profitable and are based on the joint expectation of much improved internet infrastructure and perceived first mover advantages. As in the United States, some of these sites will succeed, but most in all likelihood will never reach financial viability for a variety of reasons. Some will fail because they were formed too early to take advantage of newer infrastructure advancements to reach potential users. Advancements, in general, are not yet in place. Some will fail owing to their inability to change long-established commercial customs of their hoped- for clients quickly enough. And, still others will fall by the wayside because their creative motivations were not matched by realistic means to gain revenues from their clients, another cause familiar from the American experience.

Still, as in more developed parts of the world, enough of the new websites could survive to at least begin to change how business is being conducted in India. In the process, these websites may be a harbinger of widespread efficiency gains in an economy plagued by slow transactions, sluggish order processing and unnecessarily high inventory levels. A brief review of some of these websites follows.

Business-to-consumer websites (B2C) Although there has been extensive development of websites intended to attract household consumers, their future viability can be seriously questioned. Part of the reason lies in the extremely limited penetration of personal computers among Indian households.

Although the numbers are rising rapidly, there are fewer than 4 million personal computers in all of India and, of these, perhaps only 20 percent are used by households, including those used for home offices. Telephone access, the only means, has been expensive and unreliable, and methods of product delivery to customers are as yet underdeveloped. Even though a substantial middle class may exist among India's impoverished millions, a group who might eventually be attracted to electronic transactions, these handicaps present a formidable barrier to rapid development of B2C growth.

All of these problems, of course, are in the process of easing, but the transition will require substantial time. Meanwhile, B2C websites hope to make sufficient inroads among urban dwellers to at least survive until better times are possible. It will decidedly be an uphill fight. Some observers note that while the population of personal computers is relatively small and the technological means to connect them is still rather primitive, there are 37 million cable television subscribers.

As the fiberoptic network now being laid out is completed, it is thought, these subscribers might furnish the foundation for successful B2C expansion. But, even if cable viewers could be connected to the fiber-optic grid, the paucity of personal computers would still provide a difficult environment for B2C transactions to expand.

One can conclude, therefore, that extensive development of B2C websites probably is premature at this stage of India's development. This conclusion is supported by results from a recent study by the Gartner Group, as reported in India News. Of the few internet subscribers in India, only 2.2 percent had engaged in B2C commerce or paid for services online. Only 3.6 percent had ever placed orders over the net, usually for such services as movie booking or for products like books, audio cassettes and CDs, and software. Customers were largely well-to-do families Business-to-business websites

(B2B) Use of the internet between businesses, on the other hand, offers greater promise, and a profusion of Indian websites is one result.

As in the case of B2C sites, many of the B2B sites are likely to end up as casualties for many of the same reasons. But already there are indications that acceptance of the internet as a way of revising business practices to gain efficiencies is quite widespread. Many businesses are fully aware of the trade-related commitments the Indian government has made as a condition of joining the World Trade Organization and of the falling trade protection that will be one consequence.

The internet is seen by many of these firms as one possible vehicle among many others for gaining increased competitiveness. Even so, present use of the internet, either for direct inter-company communications or through business websites, is still early in its development.

A few examples of websites now in existence provide background. Typical of cross-sector sites, ones involving a number of quite different sectors, is Indiamarkets. com, started by IMO Communications. Development of Indiamarkets began in March, 1999, with venture funding from the Warburg Pincus Fund among other sources.

As the company's own literature puts it, Indiamarkets is "India's first comprehensive business-to-business infomediary, an aggregation of vertical supplier communities representing over a hundred diverse product categories. The site, launched only in January, 2000, offers a gateway to promote business between potential trading partners and provides transaction-enabling content that facilitates judicious business decisions." To accomplish its objectives, the site offers a variety of on- line services: sector-specific news, reviews of state policies affecting the sector, a buyer posting facility, a supplier posting allowing one to compare offerings from across India, and an auction facility to sell machinery or excess inventories.

By late 2000, the site claimed to have 30,000 subscribers, $600 million in inventory up for sale, over 2,000 "hits" and 150 transactions arranged daily. IMO also is opening 70 business centers around the country to provide services to businesses without access to computer networking. Indiamarkets.com faces a number of problems common to such sites.

Of primary importance are the site's planned sources of revenue, mainly to come from a combination of advertising on the site, an "enhanced" listing for companies who pay an annual fee and, most importantly, planned fees for transactions completed using the website. Transactions fees had not been put in place by October, 2000, but arrangements had been made with Citibank for a payment gateway on the site for easy clearing. This will be facilitated by credit checks through Dun and Bradstreet.

Whether or not users of the site will be willing to pay fees remains to be seen. However, IMO studies show that, aside from user savings from lower prices, transactions costs are reduced by 6 to 7 percent through use of the site, a not insignificant figure. Such sites also are likely to lower prices by bringing added competition to markets from better and more complete information.

The website, of course, also will be subject to its own competitive environment, as more B2B sites offering services to the same clients open up. Thus, while the availability of various savings might make customers more receptive to fees, the size of those fees could be constrained by competitive considerations. Much depends on the degree to which the more generalized website, exemplified by Indiamarkets.com, succeeds in competition with sites that are more focused on particular sectors.

One such portal is Kagaz.com, constructed by Ecomedia Infosystems to service only the pulp and paper industry. Kagaz.com is a subscriber site, with a subscriber base now numbering about 10,000 (half of whom are foreigners), each of whom pays a small monthly fee for access. The site offers news, data, and bulletin board-type notices on paper availability.

India has relatively few paper manufacturers, but there are about 80,000 paper traders who act as middlemen between manufacturers and converters, cutters and printers. Traders exist because of their local knowledge of customers, taxes and regulations.

The ultimate objective of sites like Kagaz.com, of which there are now an abundance in India, is to offer a full e-commerce portal where transactions can be facilitated for a fee. For example, when new deals are arranged between sellers and buyers, Kagaz guarantees the deal and accepts payment, which is released when delivery has occurred. The problems faced by Kagaz.com are typical of many other such sites.

The very low overall penetration of personal computers and internet connections in India is matched by the spotty existence of PCs among potential customers of the site. Most traders, for example, have no access presently to a PC. Yet, these traders ultimately are the foundation of the site's hoped-for business, because they, not manufacturers, are the ones who maintain inventories in the system and understand intimately their customers needs and peculiarities. The intention for now is to work through these traders, not to work around them. Therefore, one major marketing task of Kagaz.com and like sites obviously will be to broaden the base of internet-connected and conversant traders and dealers.

Such a task will not be a simple one, even if the expansion of high-speed data links across India in the next two years proceeds as anticipated. The trader community is likely to be tradition-bound, accustomed to carrying out business successfully in time-honored fashion.

Breaking old habits doubtlessly will prove much more difficult than has been the case in more industrialized societies, where PC use was common long before the advent of internet possibilities. Even so, if portals can demonstrate significant cost savings through internet use, a substantial marketing effort, competition should force change over time.

Business-to-government websites (B2G) The Indian government and some state governments have made a commitment to increased transparency and simplified procedures through their adoption of internet-based access to government functions.

Today, for example, governments account for over 28 percent of IT spending in India. In much of this effort, regional units have been in the forefront, computerizing operations to streamline services and, hopefully, reduce bureaucracy. Among the functions being made available through the internet are government procurement bidding and various application procedures, both familiar from more economically advanced countries. Whether or not such efforts do, in fact, reduce bureaucracy and lower government costs remains to be seen.

With burgeoning fiscal deficits at both national and regional levels, saving are obviously needed badly. In India, however, government service has often been seen as a sinecure, where employment is a continuing obligation. Transferring internal operations and some public functions to electronic forms may not have much in the way of employment effects, at least not in the short run.

Still, to the extent that the internet makes dealings with government at all levels easier and more transparent for non-governmental entities, and particularly for businesses, gains in efficiency could be substantial as internet use expands throughout the country. Moreover, to the extent that increased transparency and efficiency are accompanied by lower government employment and fewer opportunities for corruption, one might also anticipate that such advances will be fiercely opposed.

One rapidly expanding business for Indian companies is the provision of back-office services to international clients. The basic business has a long history globally; Ireland, the Caribbean and the Philippines, for example, have provided such services to companies in the United States for many years.

The typical task involves the transcription of raw data into electronic databases, where paper records are shipped in by air, local residents transform the data into electronic form, which is then transferred back to the developed country company via the internet. The business today involves a wide number of industries including, to name just a few, airlines, banks, insurance companies and medical establishments.

Currently, India employs between 50,000 and 100,000 people in what are termed "internet-enabled services," producing $500 million in export earnings. Growth has been so rapid that some observers anticipate employment of well over one million within ten years generating income of $10 billion.

Although such expectations may be overly optimistic, India does have some competitive advantages: like the Philippines, India has an abundance of English-speaking people, many with university educations, who are willing to work for a fraction of the cost similar workers earn in the client's home country.

Internet-enabled services have changed in recent years to involve other areas. For example, the transcribing of voice dictation by medical practitioners and others in the United States has become a big business.

A more sophisticated trend recently has been the transfer to India of some research and development operations, made possible by the instantaneous transfer of data and information through the internet. All of these services also rely not only on English language capability but also the availability of a reservoir of well-educated, yet under-employed, people. For example, typical employees in the Indian industry include graduates of university programs in science, liberal arts and even such professions as medicine or law.

Because the internet is only now just beginning to make its impacts felt across India, any discussion of development impacts is, at best, premature. Unlike in software development,now well established as an internationally competitive industry, use of the internet either by individuals or most businesses is still at a primitive stage. This picture almost certainly will change rapidly, however, as high-speed data networks are completed linking at least the larger cities. How rapidly, of course, will depend on the speed of finishing not only the underlying network but also "last mile" connections to individual homes and businesses. For larger businesses, this process is likely to proceed quickly, as the gains are clearest there. For others, one can anticipate that existing cable networks will provide the most likely vehicle, but the process will take longer.

The extent of gains from wider internet penetration is, at this stage, a matter of conjecture. Even in the United States, estimates of productivity gains as a consequence of information technology generally and the internet more specifically vary widely.

The range of opinion runs from Nobelist Robert Solow's well-known remark 13 years ago, "We see the computer age everywhere except in the productivity statistics," to much more optimistic statements from a variety of other economists more recently. Clearly, productivity has jumped in the United States in the past five years from some set of causes, but the sources continue to be elusive. It suffices here to note that the U.S.

Congressional Budget Office and the Office of Management and Budget both project productivity gains in the next ten years to be about 0.5 percentage point higher than the average for the years 1973 to 1995. 6 In the developing world, estimates are even more perilous, but it does seem clear that one cannot simply extrapolate the industrial country experience to developing countries. Some observers believe that efficiency gains are likely to be smaller in poorer countries. They point out that developing countries depend more on production in small and medium-sized enterprises, and these are less likely to experience substantial gains from internet use, at least not in uses internal to the organization, as compared with larger organizations.

Moreover, poorer countries typically rely more on commodity production and exports, which, in comparison with the manufactured goods produced and marketed by industrial countries, are less likely to find material productivity improvements from use of the internet.

Finally, the point has been made that introducing technologies from industrialized countries, possibly including the internet, can result in smaller productivity gains in developing regions, as compared with gains in the technology- innovating area. These technologies tend to be biased toward skill- intensiveness, which produce fewer gains in productivity when transferred to a developing country.

These observations are, of course, entirely speculative at this stage, since the internet is in its infancy in most poor regions. But, there seems little doubt that gains from the internet could be substantial and, despite more skeptical conclusions, could affect developing economies in even more profound ways than is the case for industrialized regions.

The case of intracorporate use of the internet is illustrative. In industrial countries, use of the internet for coordination between geographically widespread units represents only an incremental change from the way in which business had been done. For larger companies, management control typically had been exercised through dedicated networks long before the internet came into existence. Companies like Texas Instruments have operated sophisticated global networks linking their subsidiaries for decades. For such firms to move from these networks to the internet was really only a small, if less costly, step. In fact, many of these firms thus far have continued to use older networks in preference to the internet.

For a developing country like India, on the other hand, even dedicated networks are a relatively new phenomenon and are far less pervasive than in more industrialized parts of the world. Delivery of reliable telephony, the backbone of any dedicated system, has occurred only recently.

As a consequence, use of the telephone system as a vehicle for internal management controls has not been widespread, as the earlier Reliance Industries example illustrates. Assuming the internet, utilizing still- to-be-provided broadband facilities operated privately, becomes widely available in coming years, reliable opportunities for better management controls should become more popular.

Even smaller companies may be well placed to take advantage of it. The result might well be a much more productive industrial system made possible through better managerial controls. Again, however, at this stage much is conjectural.

The gains from improving transaction capabilities between firms should be even more striking in a developing country environment, particularly in a large country like India. Part of these gains will come through the B2B portals noted above and are similar to gains found already in industrial countries. Part will be the result of company-specific uses of the internet to increase awareness of procurement needs among a larger audience of potential suppliers. Again, tightening relationships between buyers and suppliers has been under way for many years in developed countries, starting with Japan and later being transferred to firms in other industrialized countries.

It antedates internet development in these parts of the world. In India, on the other hand, the distribution system at all levels remains antiquated and inefficient. The gains to be made from tightening this system, even apart from fixing the abundant remaining problems in physical distribution, are likely to be substantial.

In addition, although services in India are far less important as a proportion of GDP compared, say, with the United States, the internet still promises to yield efficiencies in the service sector. The examples of banks given above provide concrete evidence.

Clearly, financial clearings, among other financial services, can be enormously accelerated through the introduction of electronic banking, with commensurate savings in working capital requirements throughout the economy. To be sure, the larger benefits are not likely to be in consumer banking for some time to come, since internet penetration is so limited, even among the well-off, and overall income levels so low.

For businesses, on the other hand, the much greater ease of accomplishing financial transactions through the internet promises important gains. Similar benefits could be available in other services, including insurance processing, government licensing and permits, health care and transportation, among others.

Adding more competition to existing markets promises to be another development contribution, especially in the Indian context. Aside from a few large firms, markets in India tend to be regional and even local, isolated from one another by poor communications and inadequate roads.

The internet can at least partially alleviate these problems, in the process widening sources of information and, in all likelihood, lowering prices. The active interest in several B2B portals, as evidenced by the number of "hits" and associates transactions, provides some evidence that these benefits already are being found.

To be sure, much remains to be achieved in physical infrastructure improvement to assure that gains are truly widespread, but even in the short-run the evidence seems to be that through better information markets are broadened and prices reduced.

Finally, India's efforts vastly to improve connectivity internationally by allowing private parties to offer their own gateway facilities can be seen as belated recognition that the future of global commerce will more and more be intimately dependent on high-speed access to the internet.

The need for improved international connectivity goes well beyond the requirements of internet-enabled services, although for India these are likely to be rapidly expanding areas of business.

The wider reality is that if Indian manufacturing companies are to become more internationally competitive, as they hope to be, ready access to wideband internet services will be of paramount importance. Buyers in the industrialized countries that

Indian companies hope to service cxpect to be in instantaneous and continuous contact with suppliers through the internet, and firms that have inadequate electronic connections already find their possibilities compromised.

The Indian government has recognized this requirement and is moving quickly to improve both international gateways and the country's fiberoptic infrastructure, both largely through incentives directed to private sector providers.

As in most countries, computers and IT have been around for a long time in India. But, considered as an industry gaining global recognition and as having an internationally competitive future, IT's much-publicized growth in India has been a much more recent phenomenon.

Software exports, the earliest harbinger of a more widespread IT expansion, began only in 1985, when Texas Instruments established its subsidiary in Bangalore. This move was followed not only by other foreign software companies setting up operations in that city and elsewhere but also by a number of domestically-established software companies.

In more recent years, as the internet has expanded globally, these earlier investments have been followed by an explosion of start- up internet companies and by early efforts of a few well-established manufacturing companies at using the internet and other forms of communication to improve efficiency in their operations.

IT manufacturing also has occurred in India for many years and has included investment by multinational companies, as IBM's early involvement in

India suggests. Today, many foreign producers of computers and peripherals (HP, IBM, Compaq, Canon, etc.) have manufacturing operations in the country, often in joint ventures with Indian companies.

There are in addition a number of wholly Indian companies, exemplified by HCL, a company that formerly had a joint venture with HP but has now taken over the enterprise. A variety of other manufacturers exist, including producers of peripherals, electronic supplies and fiberoptic equipment, among others, including Modi Xerox, Tata Liebert and Wipro as examples.

Manufacturing growth in computers and peripherals has been less than spectacular in India. This is a reflection partly of the thus far limited growth in the domestic end user market and partly of the inability of the volume-limited manufacturers to be competitive. In addition, in recent years unit sales of equipment have grown faster than the dollar figures would indicate, as unit prices have fallen in response to more competitive moves by both domestic manufacturers and multinationals.

Historically, IT manufacturing has been a protected industry in India but, as in other technically-based industries, this policy has been changing. By and large, manufacturing in India has not been internationally competitive. As one consequence, India has been unsuccessful in following the lead of other Asian nations in developing robust export markets for IT equipment or components.

However, as a signatory to the IT Agreement of the World Trade Organization, the government has committed to a zero duty regime by 2003. This, together with a simplification of procedures for transacting business in the sector, could have positive competitive outcomes for the Indian industry, but it remains to be seen who will be the major beneficiaries: local businesses, foreign investors, or some combination of the two.

One possible vehicle for bringing IT manufacturing to the fore, through direct foreign investment as in Singapore or Taiwan (China), has not been successful for a variety of reasons. Foreign investors might have taken the lead in introducing leading edge technologies and manufacturing methods. But, when such investors did attempt to break into the Indian market, their hopes often were dashed.

Disagreements over intellectual property protection was one cause of difficulty, as IBM's early departure illustrates. This development, a result of India's sensitivity to foreign influence, alone discouraged other investors for many years afterwards.

More recently, attempts at joint ventures between Indian firms and outside technology investors, such as that between HP and HCL, often have failed, owing in part to inconsistent objectives among the participants. Foreign investors were interested mostly in producing for local markets, whereas Indian companies wanted eventually to develop export markets as well.

Unlike software development, which can begin small and technically simple, efficient hardware output in IT depends on a minimal scale of operation and continuous access to technological innovations largely derived in industrialized countries. Protection doubtlessly was conceived as a way eventually to develop adequate scale but, as in most other cases, has resulted only in inefficient producers without easy access to technology.

Moreover, manufacturing is more susceptible to India's familiar inadequacies in high-ways and port facilities which, particularly if exports are a goal, can add materially to delivery costs for goods shipped by methods other than air transportation. The reality in any case is that IT hardware production is as yet an insignificant industry in India. This situation, of course, could change rapidly if the internet and associated computer technology use expands as some anticipate will occur in India.

After all, the same technological talent that produced international competitiveness in some software areas, could be brought to bear on hardware design and production. But, success in hardware will come with considerably more difficulty than in software, where government influence has been minimal and where production has relied almost entirely on highly skilled engineers and technicians working in relatively small groups.

Software Development For now, India's major comparative advantages in the IT sector is software development. Software had its modest beginnings, at least as an internationally competitive sector, with the Texas Instruments investment in Bangalore noted earlier (See also the accompanying box). Today, the business is both large and expanding rapidly, directed almost entirely to overseas clients, and involves both domestic and foreign firms.

Most companies, multinationals and domestic firms alike, today use dedicated satellite links in their contacts with either their home offices or customers. Eventually, however, the speed and cheapness of internet connections may substitute for dedicated means, as international internet connections become better established and security issues are overcome.

Texas Instruments (TI), the first of several multinationals to establish operations in India, began as a wholly-owned operation intended to enable the company to continue software development 24 hours a day and to do so with decreased costs. At the time, engineering salaries in India were only 10 percent of those prevailing in the United States, which translated into software development costs of fifty percent less than in the US.

Today, owing to its early positive experiences, TI assigns not only much more sophisticated applications of software but also has expanded to include the design of integrated circuits. Although still dedicated entirely to TI's internal needs, the much-expanded facility in Bangalore now employs 350 people in a world-class computing and communications environment equal to any in the company's global operations.

Infosys Technologies, Limited, began in 1981 as essentially a two-man applications software shop for large companies. By 1985, sales had already reached $18.1 million. In the 1990s the company added satellite transmission capabilities to ensure reliable and fast connections with clients in the industrialized world. Rapid growth has continued, with fiscal year 2000 sales at $203.4 million, over 90 percent North America and Europe.

Today the company employs around 5,000 software professionals in seventeen development centers located throughout the world, up from just 585 professionals in 1985. In fosys is not the largest of India's dedicated software firms, as both Tata Consultancy and Wipro have greater sales, but in terms of its growth rate, employment expansion and customer base, it is a prototypical Indian applied software company.

The sector's growth has exceeded 50 percent annually in the period shown. Today, software shipments count for over 10 percent of India's total exports and two-thirds of sales for the entire IT sector, including equipment, training and maintenance.

The software market in the United States and Europe is simply orders of magnitude larger than in India. Moreover, potential customers in developed countries have dealt with software consultants for a long time. They tend to have a clear picture of software development costs and are, commensurately, receptive to the cost-saving opportunities Indian companies potentially make available. Professionals in India earn perhaps $12,000 annually, high by Indian standards but one-quarter or less of western salaries for like work. And, according to sources in the United States, the quality level of major Indian software producers can exceed typical standards in the U.S. for the types of programming undertaken.

Fast growth has been paralleled by a rapid expansion in the need for technically trained personnel in the sector. Professional employment for software production, according NASSCOM, reached 280,000 in 1999, up from only 6,800 when Texas Instruments formed its subsidiary. Companies have projected a need for another 140,000 professionals in the next year, far more than the 85,000 becoming available from various Indian educational institutions under the most optimistic projections. McKinsey consultants, who have done a major industry study for NASSCOM, estimate that India could absorb 2 million software engineers in various capacities by 2008. Clearly, the rapid expansion of both private and public institutions for technical education now going on in India is badly needed.

Development Contributions of Software Operations Taken in a narrow context, the software sector cannot be said to have had a major development impact on a country as large and as poor as India. Direct employment in the industry is minuscule in relation to the country's population and is concentrated in only a few metropolitan centers. Most of the sector's output is directed abroad, applications software presumably intended to improve operational efficiencies in US and European, not Indian, companies.

Few ordinary Indians can be said to have been affected one way or another by the software sector's astronomical growth and increasing international prominence. And yet, a case can be made for taking a somewhat broader view of the sector in terms of its potential effects on the larger economy. Some of these impacts are apparent already; others may take somewhat longer to come to fruition.

Aside from India's very large informal sector, software development is probably the only sector to have grown up largely free of inhibiting governmental regulation or interference. In fact, central and state governments have provided such incentives as tax exemptions, investment concessions and setting aside areas for technology parks, among other steps, to encourage the sector's growth.

Nurtured by these incentives, the sector has provided the primary example in India of the growth potentialities that can occur by allowing relatively unfettered entrepreneurialism to flourish. One consequence has been a commensurate growth in venture capital availability, as investors see the chance of multiplying their investments by a hopefully propitious selection of opportunities. The example set by the software sector has not been lost in government circles, where a similar growth pattern in a number of other high technology areas is a fervent hope, if not quite yet an expectation.

Plans that are afoot include the creation through private companies of a fiberoptic "backbone" linking the nation's cities and towns, a rapid expansion in the availability of fast internet connections, the building of a system of "info-kiosks" to bring internet availability even to rural areas, and an overall improvement in telephone service nationwide.

The hope is for India to become an international leader not only in software development, by now an accomplished fact, but to leapfrog many other developing countries by establishing a world-class telecommunications infrastructure and associated technology capabilities.

Matching these plans to reality, however, will require enormous efforts, including close coordination among and between central and state government units, and very large amounts of private investment capital. To attract the capital, private investors will need to be assured that they can move ahead without inordinate interference from various governmental units. It is not entirely clear, even in high technology sectors, that this freedom will be forthcoming, despite a new telecommunications policy. This is particularly true in areas where, in the past, government has maintained a monopoly, as in local telephone provision. Still, the point to be made here is that the success of the software sector has provided a useful role model for developing further high technology sectors and the message has not been lost even among the entrenched bureaucracies in the various capitals. Long distance voice and data communications, for example, have been opened up to private competitors, following the earlier lead of wireless communications.

The software sector also has been a source of additional export earnings for India, and one not dependent on the country's grossly inadequate rail, road and port network. Software now contributes ten percent of total export earnings, and it is a percentage that is growing rapidly as the industry expands at rates exceeding 50 or 60 percent annually, far higher than other, more traditional export industries.

Yet, although export growth by India's companies has been rapid, the Indian share of software production in global markets is still minuscule. In the year 2000, for example, Indian exports of software to developed country markets represented less than 2 percent of total production in those countries. Clearly, there remains ample opportunity for rapid growth to continue for some time to come.

Although direct employment in the software sector is both small in relative terms and specialized, there are a number of indirect employment effects that can be mentioned. Most obvious are the opportunities in other areas that have opened up as the sector has expanded, including jobs in construction, infrastructure improvements and suppliers. No estimates of such "trickle down" effects exist, but the impacts cannot be trivial if one judges by the large construction projects supporting the sector's expansion that can be seen around such cities as Bangalore, Mumbai, Hyderabad or New Delhi.

The fact that India is demonstrably competitive internationally in the production of sophisticated software brings other advantages to the country. Indian technological sophistication, though still narrowly defined, has begun to alter international perceptions of the country. Instead of viewing India as a country burdened by decades of heavy-handed government regulation of the economy, foreigners now view the country somewhat more favourably, though not yet as a country where future growth will approximate that of China and several of the Southeast Asian countries.

Whether or not much enhanced foreign direct investment and technological transfer will follow such changes in perception is, of course, decidedly problematical in today's political and economic environment in India. A weak set of national and state governments is plagued by high fiscal deficits and seems unwilling or politically unable to rein in the subsidies that are largely the cause. This weakness, together with a long-standing suspicion that foreign investment represents a continuation of imperialism under a different guise, continues to make life difficult for those investors who have shown recent interest in establishing a greater Indian presence.

Even domestic investors have had difficulty with the crowding out effects of Indian deficits. Add to all of these concerns the paucity of Indian public investment to improve physical infrastructure or general educational standards, and it should come as no surprise that investors still see India as one of the world's more difficult economic environments. The positive example of software obviously has much to overcome. Even so, the software sector's success has at least given greater voice to demands for educational improvements to support not only this sector but also other related sectors.

The immediate impact has been in the expansion of technical colleges and universities as well as more attention to lower- level training institutes. While not helping directly with the more basic problems of illiteracy and inadequate primary and secondary education, such moves certainly do support not only software producers but also other technology- based sectors that have been receiving attention as sources of more general economic growth in India.

Internet use has been relatively slow to evolve in India. This slowness has been characteristic not only of personal use of the internet but includes business use as well. Although there are abundant internet sites devoted to business-to-business (B2B) and business-to-consumer (B2C) transactions (reviewed earlier), few are yet successful in a financial sense.

Moreover, employing the internet for internal corporate transactions is still in its infancy in India, mostly because the underlying communications facilities are as yet not fast enough or sufficiently reliable for most corporate uses. It is fair to say that most data links used within large companies in India are not internet-based, but rather are dedicated leased telephone facilities.

Awareness of internet potentialities as a valuable tool for future business communications is now widespread. In fact, planning for internet use by corporations is advancing rapidly. On a more general scale, the internet is being seen as a necessary vehicle for improving the country's global prospects and, therefore, essential for contributing to further economic development, a view involving not only business interests but, as importantly, government ministries. As a consequence, several initiatives have been advanced to accelerate India's development of required infrastructure to support wider internet use, particularly by business interests. Several of these initiatives are reviewed briefly below.

Fiberoptic backbone: As noted, one of the major impediments to more advanced uses of the internet, particularly for business use, is the primitive nature of the country's communications system. While telephone quality has been much improved, India has lacked the necessary infrastructure for high-speed data transmission. It has been clear for some time that if such a system is to be built, it will not be done by governmental interests, national or local. In the face of large fiscal deficits in both national and state budgets, public investment has remained low. Nor has there been any expectation that the national telephone monopoly would find the enormous amount of funds to support the creation of country-wide, high-speed data networks.

To break this obvious logjam, permission has been given for private companies to lay optical fiber cable along road and highway rights-of-way at no charge and to allow private right-of-way arrangements with such other entities as power distributors and Indian railways. Moreover, permission has been granted to private parties to enter the long-distance telephone business. One result of such changes has been a number of privately funded efforts to build an interconnected system of fiberoptic cables to link at least the major cities in the country in relatively short order. Problems still remain on so-called "last mile" connections, but the apparent hope is that, for larger businesses, these problems will not be insurmountable and, for residences and small-businesses, ways can be found to link through existing cable television lines or through information kiosks. One example of a company that has entered the fiberoptic cable business is Reliance Industries, a company cited earlier regarding its present and future use of the internet. This firm is committed to developing a national fiberoptic network linking 115 cities which, together, represent about 50 percent of India's GDP. This $3-4 billion set of projects in a short time will permit Reliance to offer long-distance and local telephone service, internet service and high-speed data transmission. Eventually, the company expects to enter the already competitive business of selling back-office services. Reliance is only one of several private companies in India determined to profit from the provision of internet infrastructure.

Wireless services: By 2005, it is estimated that 1.2 billion people worldwide will be able to access the internet using mobile communications. And, for many, mobile connections may well be cheaper and more convenient than fixed lines. For relative latecomers to the cellular telephone explosion, like India, who can initiate digital systems from the start, wireless services may be one method for avoiding some of the disadvantages stemming from inadequate and often expensive dependence on landlines.

Wireless services in India, which have been digital from the beginning, are furnished largely by several large, private providers. The state-owned operator, MSNL, is only now beginning its own services Although growth in the market for mobile communications has been disappointing, mostly owing to high costs of both equipment and service, this picture is changing. Costs have been coming down, and the response thus far has been encouraging for providers. Today, there are perhaps 2-3 million subscribers in India, a very low number compared even with other developing countries. Growth, however, has approximated 85 percent over the past year, a figure that obviously is based on the low user base noted above. To provide a comparison, China has 54 million subscribers.. Whether or not mobile communication becomes at all important as a vehicle to access the internet remains to be seen in India. Thus far at least, mobile internet service is yet to be offered.

Fixed telephone service: In a recent enumeration of internet readiness, the Economist Intelligence Unit ranked India fiftieth of the sixty countries ranked. A major reason for the low rating was India's connectivity ranking, a measure taking into account not only the state of the existing telephone network but also other factors affecting access, such as dial- up costs and literacy rates. In this ranking, India was rated 3 on a scale of 10 in connectivity, along with such other countries as Egypt, China and Pakistan, among others. There are about 2.0 main telephone lines in India per 1,000 inhabitants, a strikingly low number but one that has increased by 60 percent in the past four years. One corollary of low telephone density is that service has not yet reached thousands of villages. And, while major cities are largely serviced, the quality of many lines is poor, largely owing to low quality last-mile connections. While telephone access and quality of service have both been improving rapidly, the system is still often subject to dropped connections, obviously a bane for reliable internet services.

Provision of telephone communications in India has until quite recently been a province exclusively of government as was the provision of internet services. Although local land- line service remains in the public domain, both long distance and internet services have been opened up to other providers. One consequence has been an explosion of internet service providers (ISPs); in 1999 alone new ISPs established over fifty sites. Interestingly, the potential presence of this new competition apparently motivated Videsh Sanchar Nigam, Limited (VSNL) dramatically to expand its own presence by adding thirty cities to its ISP network and to lower fees. One can anticipate a similar reaction as private long-distance providers gear up to enter aggressively into that market.

As to local services, the market is still reserved to the Department of Telecommunications, except in Mumbai and New Delhi, where Mahangar Telephone Nigam, Limited (MTNL), is sole provider. MTNL also is a public sector company under the Ministry of Communications. Both the DOT and MTNL have been under great pressure from within the government to expand telephone access, and the result has been a quite rapid expansion of services. Still, insofar as the internet is concerned, competition for the public companies to increase the quality of services and lower prices is likely to come not from within but rather from cable television providers linking with some of the private companies laying down fiberoptic cable across the country. Here a number of constraints unfortunately apply.

International Linkages: Until recently, all telecommunications gateways in India were the province only of the government through VSNL. Needless to say, with internet and other users seeking high-speed connections, the demand for international band width already far exceeds the supply. And, demands are increasing rapidly, even with only limited use of the internet thus far. Most Indian websites, particularly those being designed to service non-resident Indians, have attempted to evade this bottleneck by establishing their sites in the United States. But, in the longer run, if the internet is to become the vital communications means hoped for, the gateway constraint must be breeched. Recent changes in Indian telecommunications policy have opened up international gateways anywhere in the country to private internet service providers (ISPs).

These new carriers hope to team with foreign providers of undersea cable to rapidly expand international services. Although limited only to internet providers, not voice traffic, and burdened by somewhat excessive security requirements, the new licensing provisions promise to reduce the supply-demand gap in the near future.

There is, of course, much more to business success than access to the internet. Firms exist in an environment that is either supportive of their competitive efforts, not supportive, or something in between. Even with a completed high-speed fiberoptic network connecting most cities and with much- improved international gateways, both expected within the next two years, India's economic environment could, at best, be ranked as "something in between." For purposes here, it is unnecessary to run through the litany of well-known difficulties businesses face (continued government interference at both national and state levels, remaining protection, even in the IT sector, inadequate public investment owing to high fiscal deficits, the associated 'crowding out' effects in capital markets, government subsidies, sectors reserved to very small firms, labor laws, etc.).

The fact is that today few firms in India outside the software, textile and chemical industries are truly competitive internationally, especially among locally controlled companies. Even within the IT sector, domestic manufacturers of personal computers, peripherals and other equipment are concerned that opening markets in response to India's joining the WTO could be devastating if and when lessened levels of effective protection are introduced. Adjusting to increased international competition, in other words, could present difficult problems for many Indian companies.

Two negative factors affecting the growth and success of the internet in affecting productivity improvement seem particularly important. The first has been mentioned earlier, poor physical infrastructure for moving products within the country and, for export and imports, through ports.

The inability to ship goods easily and cheaply is a major constraint in building a true national marketplace in India and a constraint that will not easily be overcome. Some efforts have been made to improve ports through private sector initiatives, but much remains to be done both here and, particularly, in highway construction. Given low public investment and the apparent discomfort in relying on private methods of financing infrastructure projects, this constraint is likely to persist for some time to come.

The other factor that ultimately promises to compromise success, certainly as compared with several other Asian nations, is educational achievement. Fewer than 60 percent of Indian children complete the fifth grade, and 45 percent are illiterate. These percentages compare poorly with such competitive countries as Thailand, Indonesia or, especially, the Philippines.

Although lack of literacy has not thus far been a major problem for those parts of the IT sector that have been successful, particularly the software industry, the much wider impacts from the internet that are anticipated across the economy will depend increasingly on availability of trained or trainable workers. In some ways, India appears bifurcated between an educated middle-class, from which the technical schools draw, and the vast majority of the population with little, if any, formal education.

Appendix

Strengths and weaknesses of Asia's developing economics

Some of Asia's strategies to rapidly modernize and industrialize its economics, with some of their successes and difficulties. Despite the variations in the development schemes of the individual nations, there are several common themes. In general, industrial development in Asia seems to have been most rapid and most successful when conceived as a long-term effort that requires active governmental involvement to define goals and optimize limited resources, attract industry, encourage continuous technological progress through its various stages, and develop global competitiveness. Despite the stunning economic and technological gains achieved in the past quarter-century by the Asian countries described above, the recent downturn in 1997-

98 exposed serious weaknesses in infrastructures and financial systems, as well as overcapacity in industries such as electronics and petrochemicals. Table 1 lists some of the general obstacles to continued development. Table 11 summarizes specific strengths and weaknesses of the NIEs as they relate to continued growth potential.

Table 1. Asia's Obstacles to Continuing Growth

Overcapacity	:	The region is overbuilding in such manufacturing areas as autos, semiconductors, consumer electronics, and chemical processing.
Weak Capital Markets	:	Capital is channelled too often to state-owned companies or private conglomerates. Small businesses are starved for funds.
Rising Costs	:	Tight labour markets are pushing up wages, while rising affluence is increasing demand for goods and housing.
Poor Infrastructure	:	Asia needs better highways, pollution control, port facilities, and power plants.
Widespread Corruption	:	It hampers small businesses and scares off some foreign investors.
Inadequate Training	:	Some countries have poor elementary schools, while others cannot teach workers to act innovatively.

Mature and Newly Industrializing Asian Economies

A number of uncertainties face the countries of Asia as their economies mature. Japan, the dominant player in Asia and the most advanced, is struggling to solve problems in its real estate markets, financial institutions, and social security and health care systems for its aging population. Japan's ongoing economic woes despite its hard-won business and technical strengths caution Western and Asian observers to seek a balanced view of Asian economic growth policies.

The major strengths and weaknesses of Asia's NIEs can be summarized as follows.

Korea

Korea's chaebols are the strongest global players among Asia's NIEs. They have benefited from 25 years of government support and protected markets and are now recognized as major global players. Samsung leads in computer memory products and will expand its semiconductor capabilities. Other chaebols also are performing well in international markets, despite the country's fiscal woes. Korean industry is becoming increasingly autonomous as it moves abroad. Nurturing the growth of smaller companies has had some limited success. An outstanding educational infrastructure and hard-working citizens figure prominently among Korea's competitive advantages.

On the other hand, Korea faced declining exports and increased labour problems during the downturn. At the same time, it is paying the political price for its heavily regulated, highly politicized, and, by Western standards, corrupt banking system. Korea's currency and financial crisis resulted in loans worth $55 billion, including $21 billion from the International Monetary Fund (IMF), $10 billion from Japan, and $5 billion from the United States. Many financial companies closed operations. In addition, both security and economic threats from North Korea figure into the equation.

Korea's chaebols need to restructure and become more focused to meet the growing strength of global competition. Korea's 12th-ranked chaebol, the Halla group, filed for bankruptcy on December 6, 1997, with $5.3 billion in debt, 20 times the group's equity. Hyundai had guaranteed as much as $1 billion of Halla's debts. Daewoo faces financial problems in 1999. By law, the 30 largest chaebols are now required to lower their debt-payment guarantees to 100 percent of their equity.

Taiwan

Taiwan has successfully established a global position in electronics products and key components and has a significant number of firms capable of taking their operations into the global market. Taiwanese firms' original development strategy has made them leaders in new product introductions. The country's key component and product strategy ensures that adequate resources will be available for continued development of technological and product capabilities. Taiwan's economic successes are tempered somewhat by its ambivalent political status vis à vis mainland China, both in terms of its relations with other countries (few countries want to alienate China) and in terms of the political and economic aspirations of its people. Solution of this political problem does not appear to be imminent; meanwhile, however, Taiwan continues to engineer its rapid economic growth, based in no small measure on tapping business opportunities in China. In the long term, China hopes for Taiwan to provide a key technology base for its continued development.

Singapore

Singapore appears to have developed the most comprehensive approach to attracting MNCs and keeping them involved in its economy. The government provides incentives to establish management and operational headquarters in Singapore, actively aids companies in moving factory and marketing operations across the region, and provides incentives for firms to conduct their research activities in Singapore. Singapore is making major investments to establish the most advanced telecommunications system in Asia, while continuing to promote technology-based, value-added manufacturing. Singapore aspires to become the primary financial center for the Asia-Pacific region. Its goal is to become the "intelligent island" in the age of information technology. Some say its "economic miracle" has come from a totally managed society that critics argue is overregulated.

Malaysia

Malaysia achieved very high growth rates until the financial crisis that resulted from heavy foreign investment in high-tech manufacturing. Malaysia's vision still is to be totally developed by 2020. It plans to build the most advanced information technology infrastructure in the world. In spite of its recovering growth rate, the earlier rapid development has caused structural economic issues such as a huge current account deficit.

Malaysia is aggressively pushing to build an independent technological lead in multimedia. This follows a similar approach taken earlier in the automobile industry. By making a strong financial commitment, providing 10-year tax holidays to technological leaders, and developing next-generation infrastructure and products, Malaysia will continue to be an aggressive player in Southeast Asia.

China and Hong Kong

China's strong commitment to upgrading its technology base and infrastructure encourages foreign firms to locate operations close to its 1.2 billion-consumer market. In China today, fewer than 5 percent of the people own a dishwasher, clothes washer, vacuum cleaner, micro-wave oven, or car. There is one telephone for every 25 people, one fax for every 200 people, and one PC for every 400 people. High-tech industrial parks, such as the China-Singapore Suzhou Industrial Park near Shanghai, and special economic zones, such as Shenzhen, are central to China's strategy.

Hong Kong provides direct access to China. China fever abated somewhat in 1997, 1998, and 1999. For example, the total value of new pledged foreign investment contracts dropped 20 to 30 percent in 1996 and 1997. Few people can predict the long-term impact of Hong Kong's return to China. There are many questions about Hong Kong's ability to continue to provide world-class service under Chinese rule. It has become increasingly expensive to operate in Hong Kong, and the education base there has its own shortcomings. However, Hong Kong is expected to aid China's ability to upgrade its business skills and provide a key channel for raising capital.

Contrasts Between the Asian NIEs

There are sharp contrasts among the United States, Japan, and some of Asia's newly developed economies. Singapore stands out as the country with the highest percentage of population in the workforce. While Japan has the second highest percentage of workers, its aging population is likely to cause a decline in workforce percentage. In education, Korea has the highest percentage of university graduates in the work force, but still struggles to improve the indigenous innovative capability required to develop advanced technologies. This difficulty has a negative impact on GDP growth.

The countries in Asia are rivals in pursuit of Western business, which has resulted in overcapacity of operating facilities. This situation has provided an opportunity for Western firms to exploit low-cost sources of supplies in Asia, especially in electronics components. Continued development by the United States of close relations with Asian countries provides continuing economic opportunities. As Henry Kissinger has noted, "We are, or could be, closer to each of the contenders in Asia than they are to one another."

Less Developed Asian Economics

Less developed Asian countries such as the Philippines, Thailand, and Indonesia have benefited from the successes and rising wages of their more developed neighbours. They, too, are taking on the challenges of managing rapid industrialization. Those countries that are able to overcome political problems and build effective development strategies will also participate in Asia's future economic expansion. Growth in regional and global demand require continued expansion of Asia's industrial base. Rising wages and full employment in the NIEs provide continued opportunities for the LDCs of Asia. For example:

— The Philippines has benefited from the regional expansion of firms from more developed countries. However, political unrest and official corruption continue to be problems. Corrective actions seem limited as long as the powerful landed gentry resist moves toward economic reform and discourage foreign investment. While the closing of the Subic Bay and Clark military bases chilled relations with the United States for a time, the infrastructure that remained has served the Philippines well in attracting industry and jump-starting its economic growth. However, the thriving industrial complexes now located at the bases are in serious need of expanded infrastructure.

— Thailand had its financial crisis because of a banking system burdened by a host of bad loans. Pressures on its currency affected the fiscal stability of such neighbouring countries as Malaysia, the Philippines, and Indonesia. At the present, rising wages are making manufacturing in Thailand less competitive, and it is struggling in its effort to move up the ladder to higher-value products. It is further being constrained by an educational system in need of serious improvement.

— Indonesia still is in a state of political as well as economic crisis, although signs offer hope. As the people's economic and political aspirations continue to rise, Indonesia's leaders are addressing the difficult structural changes demanded by the IMF in return for a $43 billion rescue package to stabilize Indonesia's currency. The country also seriously needs an improved communication system because of its geographical structure. Its 13,500 islands stretch 3,200 miles east to west and 1,100 miles north to south.

— *Vietnam*: The addition of Vietnam to the Association of Southeast Asian Nations (ASEAN) appears to have been the most successful of the ASEAN expansion efforts to date. Vietnam is at the center of the most dynamic economic region in Asia. It is fast developing a market economy driven primarily by foreign investments exploiting its low wage rates. Vietnam is a country still debilitated by the ravages of war, with an almost nonexistent communications and transportation infrastructure. Its GDP per capita is about one-quarter that of Indonesia or the Philippines. The situation should, however, quickly improve because of major investments from Hong Kong, Taiwan, and Australia.

— *Cambodia, Laos, and Myanmar:* Although ASEAN has been a stabilizing and supportive force for areawide economic development, it has yet to have much impact on the least developed countries of the region. The concern for human rights in both Cambodia and Myanmar is politically distracting. At this time, prospects for development in these countries are limited. Myanmar may have some advantage because of its location and the completion of the China highway that will link South China to Thailand through the northeast corner of Myanmar. Indonesia and Thailand are expected to see shrinking economies in 1998 because of serious financial problems and the collapse of regional markets. However, 1999 forecasts put most Asian economies back on the road toward rapid growth. Even if the forecasts are too optimistic in the short term, many observers already see signs of recovery and restructuring in most countries that bode well for Asia's long-term economic recovery.

Table 2. Real GDP Growth in Asia (percent)

	1997 actual	*1998 actual*	*1999 forecast*	*2000 forecast*
China	8.8	7.8	6.6	7.0
Hong Kong	5.3	–5.1	–1.3	3.1
Taiwan	6.8	4.9	3.9	4.8
Indonesia	4.6	–13.7	–4.0	2.5
Malaysia	7.7	–6.8	0.9	2.0
Philippines	5.2	–0.5	2.0	3.0
Singapore	8.0	1.5	0.5	4.2
Thailand	–0.4	–8.0	1.0	3.0
Japan	1.4	–2.8	–1.4	0.3
Republic of Korea	5.5	–5.5	2.0	4.6
India	5.5	5.6	5.2	5.1
Australia	3.6	5.1	3.1	3.2
New Zealand	2.1	–0.3	2.7	3.3

Asian Model for Development

The Asian experience shows that there is no perfect set of actions that guarantees economic development without risks and setbacks. Governments must be flexible in dealing with the ever-changing competitive terrain by adjusting development strategies as conditions change and the relative strengths of competing countries grow. The lessons that can be learned from the Asian experience are worth noting. These lessons revolve around the strategies and trends in low-cost labour, infrastructure investment, worker skills, support for technology, and the business climate. They also reflect the growing impact of globalization and regional cooperation.

Competitive Strategies and Trends

Low-cost labour

The search for low-cost labour continues to be the primary driver of economic development across Asia and other developing areas of the world. It dictates constant changes and updates in strategies to attract and retain investment and increase standards of living. As development occurs and labour costs increase, there is a corresponding growth in the purchasing power of consumers for products and services that in turn creates a significant market opportunity. The growth in the purchasing power of Asia's population of 3 billion, especially its growing middle class, during the early and mid-1990s created a significant market opportunity. Domestic and foreign corporations invested in Asia in hopes of capturing an early market position.

Asian countries with rising labour costs turned to technology-led economic growth strategies as a way to continue to increase their standards of living as some types of investment inevitably began to move to lower-cost producers. Singapore has developed its own strategy to build and manage "world-class" industrial parks in Vietnam, China, Indonesia, and India to benefit from the move by helping firms expand low-cost operations across Asia. The impact of the economic slowdown on this scenario is mixed. Labour costs in some Asian countries have fallen, increasing their attraction for some types of investment. On the other hand, the purchasing power of much of Asia's middle class is stagnant or in some cases declining, negatively affecting market opportunity.

Infrastructure investment

Demand for all forms of infrastructure investments drives corporate and country strategies and is an important part of the Asian development model. Basic industrial infrastructure is a competitive advantage in attracting business to a country. Before the economic slowdown, infrastructure investment began to allow Asian economic growth to expand from a limited number of urban areas to broader geographical areas.

As Andrew Tranzer noted in 1996, "East Asia is now capturing over 60 percent of the world's private capital flows to developing countries, an inflow worth $100 billion in fresh capital every year-not to mention managerial and technical expertise (East Asia central banks collectively hold more than $600 billion of foreign reserves)." Despite the setbacks of 1997-98, Asian countries still are investing in building the infrastructures needed by tomorrow's information societies. It is expected that the Asia-Pacific region (excluding Japan) will spend a trillion dollars on infrastructure in the next 10 years. Singapore's IT 2000 strategy calls for the creation of a national information network with all homes, schools, businesses and government agencies interconnected in an electronic grid. China plans to spend more than $40 billion installing the equivalent of a Bell Canada-size network each year until 2000. China's government also has established its "Golden" projects to boost its communications systems, record-keeping, commercial transactions, and so on into the information age. And the Philippines is taking advantage of military bases vacated by the United States.

Where extending advanced infrastructures across an entire economy is too costly and complex to accomplish in the short term, science and technology "parks" have allowed countries to rapidly build state-of-the-art mini-economies within a geographically restricted area. Reduced tax rates, advanced infrastructure, and policies such as one-stop regulatory permitting give Asia's high-tech industrial parks an advantage in attracting or keeping global competitors.

Worker Skills

Ability to compete globally is not a function of national size, as Malaysia, Korea, Singapore, Taiwan, and Hong Kong demonstrate. There are many reasons for the success of their companies, but it is becoming increasingly obvious as their labour costs have risen that their primary competitive advantage is their growing knowledge base and number of skilled workers.

Today every country can easily tap into global technology, acquire advanced manufacturing practices, adopt the best financial techniques, acquire investment money from international venture capitalists, and employ knowledgeable workers from around the world. In today's globally competitive environment, the best jobs go where the most qualified workers are available. Conversely, advanced education in science and technology results in the highest-paying jobs and the most benefit to the economy. Countries with inadequately trained workers tend to find themselves locked into low-paying, low-value-added assembly-type jobs and industries. Lester Thurow expressed it well when he said, "The skills of the workforce are going to be the key competitive weapon in the 21st century" in Head to Head: The Coming Economic Battle Among Japan, Europe, and America.

Support for Technology

Asia's success in applying advanced technology resulted in part from substantial investment and commitment to specific emerging industries and critical supporting technologies. In the early stages of development, Korean government-funded research institutes provided an important mechanism in building the research strength of its chaebols. ITRI in Taiwan has been responsible for supporting the electronics industry and entering the semiconductor industry. In Singapore, government research institutes target industries and subsidize R&D for foreign firms willing to conduct local research and build a local technology base. In addition, Singapore's EDB directly subsidizes high-tech development programs. Malaysia's "multimedia corridor" called "Cyberjaya" provides various types of support for companies locating in it, including a new multimedia university.

Development of multitechnology/multimedia products often also requires strategic alliances for more rapid and efficient development, since internal development may be too slow in getting to market in a timely fashion. Taiwan's entry into the semiconductor business has included every major player in the world. Asian NIEs have effectively targeted growth industries and related technologies for development. Many of the targeted areas are in electronics, multimedia, and information fields. Taiwan is only one example of the practice of targeting. Its Critical Components strategy targeted 48 critical components and 24 critical products to provide global leadership in 10 emerging industries. The Taiwanese government has provided R&D, prototyping, and ramp-up incentives and support to semiconductor and LCD technologies.

As a result of this kind of targeting, Taiwan, as well as the other NIEs addressed in this study, is achieving first-rate competitiveness in global electronics, multimedia, telecommunications, and information markets, successfully challenging traditional leaders. Hong Kong's Vtech has over 50 percent of the world's electronic learning aids market. Taiwan's Acer ranks among the top 10 PC companies in the world, competing directly with U.S. and Japanese leaders. In key computer components, Singapore's Aztech Technology controls nearly 90 percent of the world's sound card market. Korea's Samsung is the world leader in DRAM technology.

Business Climate

The growing ease of doing business in Asia has facilitated economic growth. Singapore's "one-stop shopping" strategy has been very attractive to MNCs. Hong Kong's high-quality services and management infrastructures provide a critical bridge for companies seeking to do business in China's industrial parks and special economic zones. Similar strategies are being used across Asia to allow efficient local administration of industrial development policies. Offering attractive investment incentives is an important component of Asian industrial development strategies. Investment incentives offered by Asian NIEs include tax holidays, exemptions, and reductions; another factor that draws investors is improved access to new markets. In terms of sheer size of investments, China, despite large declines in the past three years, has been the Asian country most successful recently at attracting foreign investment, about a third of all manufacturing-related investments in developing nations.

Environment

Sustained and sustainable economic growth is also linked to the ability to integrate environmental and productivity decisions. A clean environment, particularly as it affects production of high-technology products, is increasingly a competitive issue in Asia. In Beijing, NEC had to isolate and air condition its entire factory to keep pollution from affecting the quality of its IC production.

Globalization and Cooperation

The Asian experience suggests that to improve competitiveness, local high-technology companies can and must rapidly begin to expand operations beyond the national economy, since economies of size and scale demand their involvement in as many markets as possible. Localization of business activities must then focus on marketing and distribution. The Korean experience also indicates that as companies go global, they must intensify efforts to develop next-generation technologies. Research centers must be established not only at home but also in major technical centers abroad, as Japan and Korea have done in the United States and elsewhere.

Regional cooperation is an increasingly important element in competitive Asian development practices. With eight cooperative growth triangles, superior technologies and development practices are moving rapidly throughout the Asian region. For example, the Southern China Growth Triangle unites Taiwanese technology and management skills with Hong Kong's distribution and service skills and Southern China's low-cost production expertise.

Singapore and Malaysia provide capital and leadership in the development of the Southeast Asian region through ASEAN. ASEAN is now sponsoring the Association of Indian Ocean Rim Countries and the South Asia Association for Regional Cooperation, which involves India, Bangladesh, Nepal, Sri Lanka, and Pakistan.

Project-based cooperation also exists. For example, in February 1997, a submarine optical fiber network was completed that links nine Asian nations (Japan, Korea, Taiwan, Hong Kong, the Philippines, Thailand, Malaysia, Singapore, and Indonesia)-a length of over 12,000 kilometers. The $650 million project, built by a consortium of companies from the United States, Japan,

France, and Great Britain, began in 1994 as part of an effort to build an Asia-Pacific Information Infrastructure. Another area in which cooperation is evident is the financial support extended by the healthier Asian economies to those experiencing fiscal difficulties at this time.

Obstacles to Continued Growth

Despite aggressive strategies to upgrade technologies and attain global competitiveness, Asian countries face various obstacles to sustaining their economic growth:

— Overcapacity and strong price competition have resulted from heavy investment in a small range of industries including automobiles, semiconductors, consumer electronics, and chemical processing. In addition, the Asian economic slowdown has cut recent forecasts of automobile sales in 2000 by nearly half for Thailand, Indonesia, Malaysia and the Philippines.

— Many local firms are ill prepared as they restructure to meet World Trade Organization membership requirements for local market access by global competitors. The IMF also is committed to opening the Asian financial system to global competition, with Japanese deregulation that began in 1998.

— The scarcity of local capital makes it difficult for developing nations to build infrastructures or properly capitalize their own local firms. Short-term foreign loans placed countries like Thailand in serious financial jeopardy, since signs of economic slowdown cause foreign capital to exit rapidly and generate pressures for currency devaluation. Small entrepreneurial firms cannot grow without access to such funds.

— There is a shortage of talent needed for advanced stages of development. Weak school systems and a lack of creative thinking are exposed as labour costs rise and higher-level skills are needed. Simple lack of experience operating in an international milieu increases risks.

— As some of the experiences of Japan and Korea have demonstrated, heavy regulation and administrative guidance directed at protecting local markets can prove to be dysfunctional to industry restructuring in the face of increased global competition and rapid technological and market change. Protective government regulations are difficult to dismantle, but if not dismantled can ultimately impede growth by slowing market responsiveness. As product life cycles fall from years to months, bureaucratic interventions or management delays can rapidly cause local firms to lose competitive advantage.

— Many Asian business relationships and activities (1) are illegal under the 1977 U.S. Foreign Corrupt Practices Act, (2) inhibit competition, restructuring, and rationalization of growing Asian economies, or (3) impede working relationships with potentially helpful multinational corporations and organizations such as the IMF. While seeking to stabilize the Asian economies, the IMF has a longer-term objective to reduce the incidence of political corruption. On December 17, 1997, 34 OECD nations signed an antibribery treaty that will make payments to government officials a criminal act following the U.S. Foreign Corrupt Practices Act. Such pressures to change traditional or accepted business practices can greatly stress rapidly developing economies. Despite these obstacles, overall, Asian countries are rapidly adopting proven strategies for economic development. As more and more nations commit to developing high-tech industries, national and corporate competition is increasing in both emerging and established industries. The focus in India, China, and the Philippines on software, challenging U.S. domination of this industry, is an example of the constantly changing competitive landscape.

While the aftermath of the financial and monetary crisis is expected to continue to slow Asia's growth rate in the next two to three years, economic expansion is not expected to stop; in fact, most Asian countries are counting on technology development to help them grow out of their present difficulties.

Considerations for U.S. Policymakers

The recent stability in the U.S. economy has generated steady growth and provides full employment. The breadth and depth of the U.S. technology base continues to be second to none. Long-term competitiveness, however, relies on education, infrastructure, innovation, and initiatives that encourage both domestic operations and global leadership. As the U.S. market diminishes in relative global importance, it must sustain its innovative and technical capabilities in order to support continued economic stability and growth. Asian (and other) nations are challenging U.S. leadership in emerging high-technology industries: as Japan has successfully targeted steel, automobiles, and semiconductors, Taiwan has successfully targeted computer-related technologies, and Malaysia is targeting multimedia technologies. Such challenges cannot be overlooked. As nations compete for leadership in advanced technologies, the United States must ensure that its "crown jewels" are not lost to foreign competition. Therefore, it is essential for the United States as well as less developed countries aspiring to higher standards of living to be mindful of the lessons of the Asian model of development. Asian global strategies are addressing five fields that all countries should consider crucial to success in high-technology industries:

1. Educating and effectively utilizing knowledge workers, creating new knowledge, and protecting related intellectual property.

2. Increasing their access to global markets to ensure competitive economies of scale and recognition of evolving product and market standards.

3. Developing advanced infrastructures to attract and support global technology leaders and to facilitate development of local firms that can compete in the global marketplace.

4. Attracting and investing the capital needed to build essential infrastructures and to develop technologies and capacity for emerging growth industries.

5. Using legislative and fiscal incentives to induce high-technology companies to locate and participate in local R&D and value-added operations.

There also are market opportunities to consider. Since many countries lack the technology base needed to enter emerging businesses by themselves, strategic alliances offer U.S. firms opportunities to participate in the establishment of future industries in many locales.

Careful management of international market alliances will be imperative to future U.S. economic success, as will open markets, rapid responses to market and technological change, and continued cost competitiveness. Like Japan, the Asian newly industrializing economies' growing technological base offers a source of a new and unique R&D. While the United States finds itself in a comfortable economic position today, it can expect growth in global competition supported by aggressive industrial development strategies from newly industrializing countries in Asia and elsewhere. The new competitive paradigm will demand continued infrastructure and technology development, global market access, and creative new responses to both competitive and cooperative challenges from the Asian countries of the Pacific Rim.

CHAPTER 5

Policy Issues and Legal Framework of E-Business

On 28 May, the European Commission adopted the eEurope 2005 Action Plan. At the Seville Council (21 June 2002) the Council endorsed the objectives of the Commission's Action Plan for eEurope 2005 as "an important contribution to the EU's efforts towards a competitive, knowledge-based economy, calling upon all institutions to ensure that it will be fully implemented by the end of 2005 and invites the Commission to present in good time for the spring European Council in 2004 a midterm review to evaluate progress and, if necessary, make proposals to adapt the Action Plan".

The eEurope 2005 action plan states that by 2005 Europe should have modern online public services, e-government services, e-learning services, e-health services, a dynamic e-business environment and, as an enabler for these, widespread availability of broadband access at competitive prices and a secure information infrastructure.

To achieve these objectives, the 2005 Action Plan comprises four separate but interlinked sets of action:

1) *A dynamic e-business environment:*

- The Commission in cooperation with Member States will review and adapt legislation at EU and national level, starting in 2003 with an e-business Summit By the end of 2003:
- The private sector is called upon to develop interoperable solutions for transactions, security, signatures, procurement and payments;
- The Commission will examine the possibilities of setting up a European on-line dispute resolution system and further work with stakeholders on creating consumer confidence;
- The Commission will examine how European companies could be provided with additional functionality relating to the .eu domain name (e.g. trusted cyber identity, trust marks and an authentication scheme).

(2) *On-line public services*

- Member States are to ensure that by 2005 all public services (administrations, schools, universities, museums and libraries etc.) have broadband Internet access;
- By end 2003, the Commission will issue an interoperability framework based on open standards to support the delivery of e-government services to citizens and enterprises.

(3) *A secure information structure*

- A 'Cyber security task force', constituted by Member states and the private sector, should be operational by mid 2003. This task force will work as a centre of competence on security issues and develop a concept for a European computer attack alert system and facilitate transborder co-operation in the field of information and network security;

- Development of a 'culture of security' though good practices and standards by end 2005;
- The Commission and Member states will examine the possibilities to establish a secure communications environment for the exchange of government information by end 2003.

(4) *Broadband*

- Analysis and support for development of broadband deployment and Ipv6;
- The Commission will ensure spectrum availability and efficient spectrum use for by wireless broadband services ad cooperate with Member States with the regard to the introduction of such services.

The Copenhagen Summit in December 2002 should adopt the eEurope Benchmarking Report. The vast majority of the actions in the eEurope 2002 Action Plan should be realised by the end of 2005.

On July 12, 2000 the European Commission adopted a proposal for a Directive on 'processing of personal data and protection of privacy in the electronic communication sector'.

The proposal is part of a package of proposals for initiatives which will form the future regulatory framework for electronic communications networks and services. It aims to adapt and update the existing Data Protection Telecommunications Directive to take account of technological developments.

Unlike the Telecommunications Directive the scope of the future Directive would not be restricted to telephony and data networks, but will also cover satellite, terrestrial and cable TV broadcasting networks, irrespective of the type of information concerned.

The key provisions of the proposal relate to the following:

- Location Data
- Processing of traffic data
- Security and confidentiality
- Ex-directory default
- Unsolicited commercial communications and spamming
- Privacy-compliant software and hardware

The vote in European Parliament (plenary) took place on May 30, 2002. There will be no conciliation procedure. Formal approval by the Council is likely to take place within six weeks. The main controversially discussed issues can be summarised as follows:

- *Unsolicited Commercial Communications:* Parliament accepted the Council's common position, thus approving an opt-in system for e-mail, faxes and automated calling systems, which means that users should give prior permission for receiving unsolicited electronic communications for marketing purposes.
- *Directories*: Consent of the subscriber to be listed in a public directory would be needed under the new proposal replacing the existing opt-out regulation. The Common Position follows the Commission's proposal. Parliament accepted the Council's common

position, saying that users should give prior permission. The EP has maintained the possibility for Member States to allow reverse search functions.

- *Cookies*: Use of cookies would only be allowed provided the user is given, in advance, clear and comprehensive information and is offered the right to refuse the processing. Parliament accepted the Council's common position that users should have the right to refuse them, specifying that users should be provided with clear and comprehensive information on their purposes.
- *Data retention*: In line with the EP's amendment, electronic communications service providers would be allowed to process traffic data in order to market any electronic communications service (also other then their own) or to provide value-added services, provided that the subscriber or the user (depending on the data to be processed, the type of service etc.) has given his consent. Under the common Position Member States may provide for retention of data for a limited time to safeguard national security, to solve criminal cases etc. On the contentious issue of data retention, it was agreed by Parliament that Member States may only lift the protection of data privacy in order to conduct criminal investigations or safeguard national or public security, when this is a necessary, appropriate and proportionate measure within a democratic society. In a recital, Parliament added that lawful interceptions of electronic communications should be subject to adequate safeguards in accordance with the European Convention on Human Rights and Fundamental Freedoms and with the rulings of the European Court of Human Rights.

- *Security*: Electronic communications service providers would be required to inform their subscribers of any security risk where they do not intend to take a measure to remedy it. This does not discharge them from remedying any new and unforeseen security risks. The European Parliament asked for a review of the Directive within three years of its application.

Distance Marketing

In October 1998 the Commission proposed a directive on the distance marketing of consumer financial services, modifying Directive 90/619/EEC, 97/7/EC and 98/27/EC. Aim of the proposal is to come to a harmonised framework for distance contracts on financial services in order to avoid the adoption by Member States of different consumer protection regulations for this new form of trade and guarantee the functioning of the Internal Market.

The aim of the proposal is to ensure a high level of protection for consumers of retail financial services (e.g. insurance, banking and investment services) marketed by telephone, by electronic means such as the Internet or by mail. This is to encourage consumer confidence in such services and provide financial service suppliers with a clearly defined legal framework valid for distance selling throughout the Single Market without hindrance.

The proposal should facilitate the development of innovative forms of trade in financial services within the EU and make it easier for consumers to buy financial services in other Member States.

The scope of the proposal covers the provisions of financial services at a distance. The key provisions related to the following:

- Prior information
- Right of reflection
- Right of withdrawal
- Settlement of disputes.

On May 14, 2002 the European Parliament approved in the second reading the Council's Common Position without any major amendments. The Council met to a high degree Parliament's demands from the first reading.

The European Parliament adopted only two amendments to the Council's common position, one of which states that the performance of the contract may only begin after the consumer has given his approval. The agreed solution is essentially based on the principle of maximum harmonisation, providing only a small scope for Member States to be able to introduce or maintain national rules.

The end result is that the text allows for:

- A high level of harmonisation of information requirements related to Article 3 of the Directive.
- The abandonment of the principle of minimum harmonisation, as initially called for by many Member States during the Luxembourg Council in April 1999.
- Far reaching harmonisation of the right of withdrawal payment of the service, unsolicited services, unsolicited communication, redress etc.

- Providing for the possibility of amending or further harmonising the provisions of the Directive in light of experience gained.
- Clarifying the relation of this Directive to the e-commerce Directive. Other changes included a clarification the text and layout of the Directive.

On 25 March 2002, the EU Telecommunications Council adopted the .eu regulation. Now the European Commission has to set up the infrastructure needed for the domain. A call for private, non-profit organisations to run the .eu registry can be expected soon. The .eu Top Level Domain will provide Europe's companies the possibility of identifying themselves as European or pan-European companies on the Internet.

The creation of .eu will also open up for the possibility of registering more names on the Internet and will thus boost internet use and e-commerce in Europe in line with the objectives of the eEurope Action Plan, endorsed by the European Council in Lisbon on 23 and 24 March 2000. The .eu regulation creates the legal framework for a Registry which will be the body that will run the domain in practice.

The Commission is in regular contact with the Internet Corporation for Assigned Names and Numbers (ICANN) so that the creation of the ".eu" code on the Internet can become a reality once the registry is in place. ICANN will be responsible for the organisation and management of Internet naming and addressing systems, known as Internet Governance.

Cross-border alternative dispute resolution

On request of the Council, the Commission is currently

working on the development of practical, efficient and inexpensive procedures for out-of-court settlement of consumer disputes should be promoted to strengthen consumers' confidence in e-commerce.

EEJ-NET

The European Commission officially launched a European Extra-Judicial Network for settling consumer disputes out-of-court (EEJ-NET). The European Network will cover any consumer dispute over goods or services. It is expected to reduce costs, formalities, time and obstacles in cross-border disputes, thereby boosting consumer confidence in electronic commerce. Rather than to harmonise and create general standards for out-of-court dispute resolution schemes the main provision of the EEJ-NET is to use the existing national out-of-court dispute resolution schemes and link them to national bodies to provide a EU-wide complaints network. The system is basically built on mutual recognition between the national redress bodies and exchange of information.

FIN-NET

On February 1, 2001 the Commission announced the launch of an out-of-court complaints network for financial services. The network will bring a number of national existing out-of-court dispute resolutions systems on the basis of a voluntary MoU.

Commission Recommendation on the resolution of consumer disputes On April 4, 2001 the European Commission adopted a non binding Recommendation on the resolution of consumer disputes. It applies to bodies which attempt to resolve disputes by bringing consumers and suppliers together to convince them to find a solution by common consent.

European Commission Green Paper of April 19, 2002 on alternative dispute resolution in civil and commercial matters. The Green paper is part of the Commission's policy of facilitating access to justice within the creation of an European area of freedom, security and justice. The paper covers ADR methods in civil and commercial matters, including employment and consumer law.

DG INFSO will be proposing a Communication on the promotion of Online Dispute Resolution (ODR) which is expected in July 2002. DG INFSO is particularly concerned with the promotion of Online Dispute Resolution in the context of eEurope and the desire to provide effective alternatives to the court system for settling disputes that arise across jurisdictional borders. These cross-border disputes will be more prevalent in the Information Society and in particular through electronic commerce.

The Communication will focus on the importance of developing awareness and trust in ODR services and will emphasise the need for a balance between flexibility and respect for basic quality criteria.

Taxation (VAT)

At the ECOFIN Council on May 7, 2002 Ministers adopted the long debated directive and regulation to modify the rules for applying value added tax (VAT) to certain electronically supplied services, including subscription-based and pay-per-view radio and TV broadcasting.

Aim of the new rule is to subject non-EU suppliers to the same VAT rules as EU suppliers, in accordance with the principles on the taxation of e-commerce agreed at the 1998 OECD Ottawa Ministerial Conference. The new rules thus modernise the existing VAT rules to provide a clear regulatory environment for all suppliers. They also contain a number of simplification measures aimed at easing the compliance burden for business. Member States have to implement the new measures by 1 July 2003.

The new VAT rules will apply to 'all electronically supplied services' such as software and computer services generally, plus information and cultural, artistic, sporting, scientific, educational, entertainment or similar services as well as to broadcasting services.

According to the new rules:

- EU suppliers do not have to charge VAT when supplying electronic services or broadcasting services to non EU-customers;
- Non EU suppliers will have to charge VAT on services electronically supplied to EU customers at the VAT rate of the Member State where their customer usually resides. They can register in the Member State of their choice (so called Member State of identification) and pay all VAT due on a quarterly base. The State concerned will then reallocate the VAT revenues to the Member States where the consumer is located.

In 2006 the Commission will either have to adopt measures on mechanism for charging, declaring, collecting and allocating VAT revenues on electronically supplied services which will ensure taxation at the place of consumption for all transactions, or it will have to extend the period of time during which the recently agreed rules will apply.

The Commission proposal for a Council Framework Decision of 27 April 2002 on "Attacks against information systems" is meant to provide basic framework for police and judicial co-operation on attacks against information systems linked to terrorism. It addresses the three most common threats: unauthorised access, disruptive attacks and malicious software. Other security threats, like accidental and environmental threats, misrepresentation and illegal interception are however not addressed in this Framework Decision.

The proposal seeks to approximate criminal law across the EU so that Europe's law enforcement and judicial authorities can take action against this new form of crime to protect users. It also aims to encourage and promote the security of information infrastructures, while trying to find the right balance between the need to curb cybercrime on the one hand, and protecting civil liberties and other societal interests on the other (privacy protection, users rights, development of new technologies).

The main provisions include:

- *Interference with information systems*: the offence of interference with information systems is divided into two aspects: attacks aimed at the serious hindering or interruption of the functioning of an information system (such as "denial of service attacks" where there is a deliberate attempt to overwhelm an information system or viruses directed at blocking an information system), and attacks aimed at the deletion or alteration of computer data.

- *Penalties*: Member States are required to take the necessary measures to ensure effective, proportionate and dissuasive penalties. Some offences might justify a maximum term of imprisonment of more than four years, such as offences that are committed in a group; cause substantial economic loss, physical harm to a natural person or substantial damage to critical infrastructure.
- *Jurisdiction*: the proposal intends to ensure that each Member State has jurisdiction for cases where a person physically present in the EU attacks an information system in a third country; or a person physically present in a third country attacks an information system in the EU.
- *Operational points of contact for high tech crime*: it provides for a legal obligation on Member States to establish 24 hour / 7 days week operational points of contact to facilitate the exchange of information on attacks against information systems. What is illegal "off-line" should also be illegal "on-line". The current proposal thus follows in its approach the latest Commission proposals for framework Decisions on the approximation of criminal law related to child pornography and racism and xenophobia.

The proposed Framework Decision on Cybercrime is the result of an extensive public consultation within the EU Forum on Cybercrime, involving all major players. It also takes into account other international activities such as the work of the G8 and the Council of Europe's Convention on Cybercrime which aims to harmonise national legislation on cybercriminal activities, promote international police co-operation and share electronic evidence across borders.

The Green Paper of October 2, 2001 on Consumer Protection puts forward a number of options for future action to increase consumer protection and hence increase consumer confidence in the internal market. It covers B2C transactions.

Digital Rights Management

Digital technologies have transformed the copyright environment and have given rise to a potentially huge market for content. The advent of broadband networks and their capacity to transmit large volumes of multimedia content at high speeds emphasises the importance of ensuring that digital content is available under the appropriate conditions, which meet the interests of both rightholders and users.

The Copyright Directive supports the use of DRMS by protecting technical measures, and by requiring Member States to take into account the application and non-application of technological measures when providing for fair compensation in the context of the private use exception for which fair compensation is required. The Directive also calls for voluntary measures by industry to protect copyrighted material while ensuring interoperability and compatibility of different systems in the protection of copyrighted material.

Against this background, the European Commission is open to playing a facilitating role aimed at encouraging the different stakeholders to tackle outstanding DRM issues together and find common ground.

The promotion of open, flexible and interoperable Digital Rights Management Systems (DRMS) was the subject of a workshop organised by the European Commission in Brussels on 28 February 2002.

Representatives of the content, information technology, and consumer electronics industries, as well as several user and consumer associations, participated and set out their views on how to make DRMS acceptable to all market players and how to bring about co-operation between them.

Software patents

The proposal for a Directive to lay down rules relating to the patentability computer-implemented inventions would harmonise the way in which national patent laws deal with inventions using software. Such inventions can already be patented by applying to either the European Patent Office (EPO) or the national patent offices of the Member States, but the detailed conditions for patentability may vary.

Under current EU law, computer software can only be protected by copyright but the legal protection of computer-implemented inventions is unclear (some Member States allow protection by patent and others do not). The proposed Directive is expected to clarify the legal protection of this kind of inventions.

The main provisions of the proposal relate to the following:

- To benefit from patent protection, inventions would have to be new, involve an 'inventive step' and be capable of industrial application. It implies that a computer-implemented invention which makes a "technical contribution" to the state of the art, which would not be obvious to a person of normal skill in the field concerned, is more than just a computer program "as such" and can therefore be patented.

- The mere computer implementation of a technique or business model already known would not be patentable.
- Patents would not be granted to computer programs on their own, i.e. an isolation from a machine on which they may be run. This marks a different approach to the direction taken until now by the EPO and some case law in Member States. The proposal therefore reflects concerns that if 'isolated' computer programs could be patented, this would blur the distinction between the scope of copyright and patent protection, and that if enforced, patents including such claims could be used to prevent "reverse engineering" and other activities considered legitimate in respect of computer programs already protected under copyright law.
- A patent would normally be granted to specific innovative components of a software and not to the entire software itself.

This is an important distinction with copyright law. While copyright protects the entire code of an operating system, game or piece of business software against unauthorised copying, distribution and use, a patent would cover only the specifically-patented components.

The proposal would require the Commission to monitor the impact of computer-implemented inventions and to report to the Parliament and the Council on the operation of the Directive within three years of its implementation by Member States. This provides an important safeguard which would allow any necessary adjustments to be made.

The Directive would have no direct legal effect on the European Patent Office. However, once the Directive was implemented, the Commission would consider taking action to resolve any inconsistencies in the context of the European Patent Convention. This has already been done on a previous occasion, with no particular difficulty. In any case, European Patents, once granted, become subject to national laws, so any patents granted after the Directive took effect and which were inconsistent with its provisions would need to be amended to bring them into conformity.

Public sector information

Increased access to, and exploitation of, information by the public sector is an essential basis for many digital information products and could become an important 'raw material' for new services and in particular for the wireless Internet.

A European approach to the conditions under which public sector information can be accessed is necessary because of the current national fragmented rules and practices. In October 2001 the Commission issued its Communication "eEurope 2002: Creating a EU Framework for the Exploitation of Public Sector Information" aimed at improving access to, and re-use of, public sector information.

The Communication focuses on economic and internal market aspects of public sector information and proposes a set of actions to overcome the market barriers that exist at European level caused by differences in national regulations and practices. Improved use of public sector information will held the European information industries to create added-value information products.

On 5 June 2002 the Commission issued a first provisional version of a proposal for a directive on improving access to, and re-use of, public sector information. This proposal aims at establishing a minimum set of rules governing the commercial and non commercial exploitation by any EU citizen or legal person.

Key provisions of the proposal are the following:

- Public sector bodies and bodies governed by public law would have to make available their documents in any pre-existing format or language, through electronic means where this is possible and appropriate. This does however not imply an obligation to create or adapt documents.
- The directive shall apply to all documents that are generally accessible. Excluded shall be documents that do not fall in the scope of the public tasks of the public sector bodies concerned, documents containing personal data and documents held by public service broadcasters, educational and research establishments and cultural establishments.
- Any applicable conditions for the commercial re-use or exploitation shall be nondiscriminatory.

Legal Framework for E-commerce and Internet

Much of the experience in creating such an enabling legal and regulatory framework on a national level is found in and derives from the industrialized, developed countries, the issues explored here raise particular challenges for policy makers in the developing world. Much of the international experience described points to certain advantages in harmonizing legislation, or at least moving towards an environment of interoperability. Yet there is also strong demonstration that in certain areas, particular national requirements must also be taken into account.

The variety of issues and requirements for the elaboration of the legal and regulatory infrastructure for e-commerce and the Internet highlight the necessity of a comprehensive approach to legal reform issues.

As de Tocqueville observed, law matters. Law gives effect to policy. As such, laws affecting e-commerce are in important and integral part of the enabling environment for e-commerce. And, the policies undertaken and the manner in which they are reflected in law will affect how e-commerce develops, how it is used, etc.

But laws alone are not enough. There are other attributes that make the legal and consequent institutional structures work in their respective environments. Among these are a history of market development (culminating in mature markets), and known outlets and predictable results for resolving disputes including respected, independent, credible judiciary and other mechanisms for resolving disputes that have the confidence of the general public. It cannot be said with certainty that all of the other, exogenous factors that support the legal, regulatory and institutional precedents in developed countries (mature markets, credible outlets for resolving disputes, etc.) exist to the same extent in all developing countries – and care should therefore be taken that while creating the essential legal infrastructure, other aspects of the market reform enabling environment not be ignored. The process of legal reform that is an integral part of developing an enabling environment for e-commerce.

The report by UNDP regarding ICTs and development, e-commerce is and should be viewed as a tool of development, not a reward. Efficient provision of ICT infrastructure and services will enhance production, which will contribute to growth and even help in alleviating poverty – a primary goal of the World Bank.

In this sense, the Internet, and e-commerce, are transformational. No longer are "old economy" concepts of capital formation and capital flows necessarily applicable. Now, productive assets do not need to be equated with natural resources, nor does value-added processing necessarily need to take place after export. But, for the equation to work, ICT infrastructure and services need to be provided on an efficient basis (which depends in part on removing barriers to entry), reducing users' costs.

Finally, in the context of the reform agenda, it is instructive to take account of the types of e-commerce activity likely to be undertaken. The following table 1describes the types of e-commerce activity that should be incorporated into an e-commerce legal and regulatory enabling environment.

Consideration should be given to the types of e-commerce that are to be encouraged. Additionally, as will be argued later, it is important that the legal framework not be designed for just one type of activity. Rather, a commercially neutral approach should be taken.

Difficult policy decisions need to be made and communicated to constituents. If the precepts of the ICT reform process are accepted (that efficient provision of ICT infrastructure and services aids in production and growth), this will undoubtedly lead to a the identification of a number issues that will need to be addressed in the reform process. Regardless of whether it is e-commerce, there are common elements of the reform process.

Table 1

Types of E-commerce and Related Internet Activities

	Government("G")	Business ("B")	Consumer ("C")
Government	G2G – coordination	G2B – information	G2C– information
Business	B2G – government procurement	B2B-e-commerce between business	B2C – e-commerce in consumer markets
Consumer	C2G – e.g., tax compliance	C2B – price & other comparisons	C2C – auction market

In the fist stage of reform, a change to the status quo is introduced through new policies. How to give effect to these policies results in reform issues that need to be dealt with. How these issues are dealt with is the strategy of introducing the reforms.

Finally to give effect to reforms, they need to be implemented. Because law is the embodiment of policy, the process of legal reform needs to start right at the beginning, during the shaping of the new policies. And while clearly some of the reform issues that will arise at the beginning of stage two, those engaging in law reform need to take part in developing the strategies and in their implementation being in part, the passage of new laws.

The importance to successful reform, especially legal reform, of broad public consultation, stakeholder "buy-in" and "local ownership" can not be overemphasized. To have a law, or series of laws, on the books, that stakeholders (government, regulators, owner/operators and users) do not understand or agree with will impair the success of the reform program.

In addition to the elements of the process of reform is the sequencing of reform. There are many variations on reform sequencing, taking into account urgency, parallel processes, local circumstances and the like.

Practical considerations may dictate modifications. Whatever the circumstances, however, where there is a legal element to the reform process, it is logical that in order to effect the shift from the market supported by the "old" legal framework to the market supported by the new legal framework, certain things have to happen. First, the policies giving rise to change need to be elaborated. These will, in turn, give rise to new legislation that reflect, embody and give effect to those policies.

To the extent that the laws provide for or anticipate regulation, a regulatory framework can be elaborated to implement the law. Finally, it is assumed that new entry will come into the market based on the certainty provided by the legal and regulatory framework.

The basic theme in legal reform is to create an enabling environment of predictability and certainty through good governance and respect for the Rule of Law that encourages use and confidence in the e-commerce market place. A non exhaustive list of underlying principles behind legal reform in the area of e-commerce follows:

— Preference for market-based approaches (regulate only what is necessary and when it is necessary; incentives should derive from the market)

— Make use and entry easy (infrastructure and services liberalization play a key role)

— Promote Certainty/Confidence (transparency)

— Enhance transactional enforceability

— Harmonize/Standardize (reference to international best practice, model laws, etc., interoperability of laws (not necessarily carbon copying) will facilitate use and growth of commerce beyond national borders)

— Neutrality as to commerce (the legal regime established should apply equally to and facilitate B2B, G2G, G2C, etc., this also allows "future-proofing" of legislation to facilitate the introduction of new forms of commerce that can be conducted electronically)

— Neutrality as to technology (the legal regime should also be "future-proofed" in terms of the introduction of new technologies deployed to conduct e-commerce – laws drafted today, based on today's technology may prove inadequate for new technological innovations)

— Protect Intellectual Property

— Protect Consumer Rights

A number of legal issues typically arise in developing a legal framework to enable e-commerce. First, there is both a national and an international dimension to the reform agenda. At the international level, a number of international, regional, and even private organizations affecting the content of national law.

Attention should also be paid to mandatory requirements (conventions, treaties, directives) that emanate form these bodies, as opposed to syntheses of good practice (e.g., model laws). These international elements point to the important considerations of harmonization, standardization and interoperability in facilitating entry into the global marketplace.

Clearly the UNCITRAL model laws and the EU directives (described below and in more detail by others) are in part aimed at accomplishing this. As successful reforms in e-commerce are out of necessity comprehensive, cutting across traditional technology and commercial boundaries, the role of regulators and regulation will need to be critically examined.

To name but a few areas where this will be important are regulation of communications services and infrastructure (telecommunications), public key infrastructure, domain name registration, and general principles of competition – and where appropriate the exercise of regulatory forbearance where market forces are operating.

A specific issue common to any e-commerce framework is how personal data privacy is protected. There are varying approaches, for example the "opt-in" vs. the "opt-out" approach. Experience has demonstrated a divergence of treatment regarding privacy, for example between the EU approach and the approach in the United States. It is therefore evident that different policy approaches lead to different legal approaches.

However, this particular issue also demonstrates problems of "interoperability" (the basic incompatibility between opt-in and opt-out systems) resulting from different legal approaches. Other issues include, protection of intellectual property rights, alternative dispute resolution, liability for content, taxation, jurisdiction and distribution of goods are all other important issue that will need to be addressed in framing a legal enabling environment.

Because of the borderless nature of e-commerce and trade facilitated through e-commerce, the value of minimum or common international standards has long been recognized as contributing to the interoperability of national legal regimes in developing truly global commerce.

Model laws, conventions and regional laws from a variety of sources contribute to the emerging body of international best practice that developing countries can look to for examples in framing their e-commerce legislative environments. Too often, however, there is a tendency to adopt international precedent (whether model law, directive or other precedent law) wholesale, without adapting it to local dynamics.

Certainly there is value in learning from the experience of others, but as argued above, the reform process should be a critical, thoughtful, deliberative and iterative process, balancing bespoke needs with underlying principles such as harmonization and interoperability. The result of adopting model laws verbatim, without a holistic approach, can be as ineffective to the growth of e-commerce as a framework that does not take account at all of the international dimension.

In addition, there is a large body of intellectual work regarding e-commerce and development, including legal issues of e-commerce development. They are too numerous to mention here, although the annual E-Commerce Reports of UNCTAD stand out as being well written and presented, comprehensive in scope, sufficiently detailed and addressing cutting edge issues.

The WTO played a major role in opening markets for telecommunications services. The role that liberalized provision of services plays in increasing access, lowering prices and facilitating new entry is well recognized.

Now the WTO and its members are debating new challenges brought by the online world. Whereas the various GATT agreements covered trade in goods, and the GATS covers trade in services, how should downloadable software be treated, for example? It is also an area which developing countries have an opportunity to make their voice heard in the debate.

UNCITRAL is probably best known in the e-commerce area for the two model laws it has promulgated: (1) UNCITRAL Model Law on Electronic Commerce with Guide to Enactment 1996 , with additional article 5 bis as adopted in 1998; and (2) UNCITRAL Model Law on Electronic Signatures with Guide to Enactment 2001.

The E-Commerce model law covers, inter alia, legal recognition of data messages and digital signatures, and certain elements of encryption. The Electronic Signature Model law covers, inter alia, PKI certification and certain elements of data privacy protection.

The Guide to enactment of the Electronic Signatures Model Law is particularly instructive about the issues surrounding PKI certification, for example. It should be emphasized that these are "model" laws, and while a synthetic project taking account of many legal systems and a broad range of experience, they can, bearing in mind minimum requirements of interoperability, be tailored to meet specific local needs ITU.

At the ITU's recent World Telecommunication Development Conference in Istanbul, ITU-D (Bureau of Telecommunication Development) was mandated, inter alia, with examining how to promote a favourable legal environment for e-services and applications in cooperation with other international organizations and financial institutions.

Hague Conference on Private International Law. A new draft Convention on Jurisdiction and Foreign Judgments in Civil and Commercial Matters is under consideration by the Hague Conference on International Law which, if promulgated in its current form, could have far reaching effects in the on-line world.

Provisions of the draft Convention could, in effect, lead to the intellectual property rights protection of one country being applied in another country where the rights protected might be different.

ICANN, though not an "international" organization like UNCITRAL, nonetheless plays an undeniably central role in global e-commerce through its domain name processes, especially in domain name registration and regulation of ".com", ".edu", ".org", etc. It's affiliated organization, IANA, is responsible for top-level county domain names ("ccTLD").

The following issues to be dealt with on a national level that are of particular importance to developing countries. These are not exhaustive, but representative. The four issues are

(i) convergence implications and competition law,

(ii) fundamental features of regulatory reform,

(iii) the role of intellectual property rights in development and

(iv) the use of alternate dispute resolution mechanisms.

Other legal issues of significance in the e-commerce enabling environment at the national level, but not discussed here in any length, include recognition of electronic contracts and issues of contract formation (e.g., recognition of "click through" and "browse through" concepts); recognition of digital signatures; protection of personal privacy; consumer protection; taxation; customs, import and distribution; limits on foreign direct investment; and content liability.

The list of laws that would need to be considered in building the national legal enabling infrastructure for e-commerce will naturally be dictated by local requirements and circumstances. It should be borne in mind that there may already be laws affecting commerce in the "off-line" world (contract formation, consumer protection, tax and dispute resolution, for example).

However, there are certain issues that are peculiar to the "on-line" environment, such as "click through" contract formation, P/PKI certification, digital signature recognition and domain name registration.

Convergence/Competition. It is now axiomatic that there is a phenomenon known as convergence among technologies and services brought about by digitalization. Where sector-specific, or technology-specific regulation may have been appropriate before, the converged nature of technology and services implies a greater reliance on competition policy, law and regulation to guard against abuses of dominance or other anticompetitive behaviour in the market place. It is important to note, however, that the object of competition law is not to protect certain actors but to ensure a competitive market by enhancing efficiency to stimulate development.

For example, a yet-to-be-privatized state-owned telecommunications service provider (or a private monopoly, for that matter) may through its dominant position exert control over the provision of leased line access to ISPs. If this results in discriminatory treatment among ISPs, or, the price of leased line access is not cost-based, or is otherwise slowing market entry of ISPs, the issue could be viewed as a matter of telecommunications regulation or as a competition law issue (abuse of dominance or anticompetitive behaviour).

Accordingly, to ensure fairness, resort could be made to the competition law of general application. If there is not a competition law of general application, consideration should be given to putting on in place. Comprehensive Regulatory Reform. The areas of regulation that touch upon e-commerce are many. These include, to name a few,

— regulation of the telecommunications infrastructure and services over which e-commerce is conducted; domain name registration; public/private key infrastructure certification regulation; data privacy protection regulation;
— competition regulation

— banking and financial sector regulation (including credit, payments systems, exchange controls, anti-money laundering; and

— import restrictions and intellectual property rights.

In designing regulatory functions and institutions, international best practice demonstrates that certainty and confidence in the regulator is enhanced through transparency and where there is functional, financial, legal and institutional separation of the policy setting, regulatory and ownership functions. This is to ensure against political and industry capture.

Intellectual Property Rights

From a developmental standpoint, it is recognized on the one hand that where intellectual property rights, such as copyright, are not protected by national law, holders of copyrighted software (or hardware with imbedded software) will be reluctant to export to that jurisdiction. Accordingly, developing countries wishing to expand economic growth through e-commerce, but where the protection of intellectual property rights is unclear, will face challenges of encouraging vendors to invest in those countries.

On the other hand, it is also recognized that there is a view held by some in the development community that continued protection of rights held by those in the developed world actually depresses local growth and development in developing countries –developing countries merely effect transfer payments to rights holders in the developed world while providing disincentives at home for innovation and growth of local high-tech industries.

Even in a market place dominated by "open source" and open systems, copyright and commercial concerns are still valid. In other words, open source systems still rely on copyright law to enforce the openness of open source systems.

The TRIPS Agreement provides national treatment, minimum standards and dispute resolution procedures. This international system, part of the WTO, protects rights to encourage foreign direct investment of hardware and software necessary for conducting e-commerce, preserves international standards, but would generally leave innovation and incentives with existing rights holders.

The new role of intellectual property rights advocated more and more within the development community still protects rights holders. However the reliance on open systems (including open source software) can reduce unit costs, allows for projects to be scaled to meet particular needs, allows development of local content and encourages innovation and entrepreneurship locally. A by-product of developing more content in local languages and more use locally is to slow "brain drain".

In the area of ADR, the focus is not on whether mediation is preferred to arbitration or whether ADR should be used as a matter of course as an alternative to the courts. Rather the focus is on whether the use of ADR to engage in non-adversarial resolution can create incentives for or encourage use of e-commerce.

Certain characteristics about ADR would indicate that it is susceptible to creating an incentive environment for resolving disputes. Among these attributes are that ADR can be non-adversarial; it can be flexible and scalable (smaller problems can be addressed through smaller, quicker procedures); it can be oriented towards a specific type of commonly recurring issue or to a particular industry issue; because it is more flexible, it permits the rapid introduction of best practices and related, relevant experiences into the dispute resolution process; and it can address situations not necessarily specifically dealt with in existing law (especially in civil law jurisdictions).

But in order for ADR to be a useful tool for creating incentives to use e-commerce. The procedures and institutions must be credible and transparent, and the results must be enforceable. Accordingly, national law should encourage ADR and provide for adequate enforcement measures.

6

Faces of Cyberspace

Information presentation in visual images, sound and natural language either as text or speech is gradually becoming the norm. The Internet is creating a global platform where a worldwide forum is evolving that is becoming vital to economic, social and political success. However, all these developments create problems. Examples of such problems are: access to much of the information may be available only to the computer literate and those who understand English. Also, due to the vast amount of information available, it is becoming hard to identify and select what is relevant that may satisfy a certain degree of credibility.

The development of interfaces and components that help users to identify relevant information and then present it to them in the most appropriate manner according to the information content and their cultural and linguistic backgrounds is still lagging behind the rate of information growth. Language engineering is an endeavor in which language technologies are integrated and embedded into language-enabled services and products to support business in a global context and to facilitate interpersonal communication across languages. The Role of Language Engineering Efforts now are concentrating in developing tools and standards that enable the creation of websites in several languages or in at least one non-Western language. Now an Internet standard (RFC 2070) based on Unicode supports HTML documents in practically every language.

In particular, some of the features dealt with are: Markup of bi-directional text, i.e. test where left-to-right and right-to-left scripts are mixed and control of cursive joining behavior in contexts where the default behavior is not appropriate. Also, the HTTP which is the hypertext transfer protocol in use since 1990 is being internationalized. The relevant aspects are character set labeling which ensures correct document interpretation and language negotiation which is used at a site to provide documents in the user's language of preference.Language technology will help in designing and implementing the systems needed to effectively deal with information and knowledge in a number of ways.

Speech recognition will help in interacting with a number of devices in our own native language. Also, information could be presented by generating speech. Understanding requests and browsing the vast amount of knowledge available is an essential component that can alleviate the problem of information overload and ensures that the relevant knowledge is accessed. It will also be possible to generate and present information in different languages through automated machine translation. Language engineering will be essential for supporting global business in general and electronic commerce in particular. The success of any business will depend on the quality of information about its customers, its competitors and the market in general. The needed information has to be identified, extracted and presented in natural language either as text or speech. In general, language engineering will deliver the right information at the right time and in the language of the recipient. Automated translation together with document management will improve the quality of service in a global marketplace. In general, success in globalization requires putting emphasis on localization.

Some companies interested in international markets organize their effort in a number of activities that could be summarized as follows:

1. Developers organize a product so that linguistic components can be modified easily (internationalization).
2. Translators make the product available in different target languages.
3. Editors review each version to ensure that culture-specific items are not missed.
4. Marketing division takes care of localization to adapt the product to the local market.

The Internet is dominated now by the English language. However, due to the near future possibilities of widespread use, it is becoming essential to consider its multilingual nature. Some efforts are being conducted in that respect - e.g. the Babel project which is a joint initiative between Alis Technologies and the Internet Society. They are considering the world's 20 main languages and are trying to study the actual distribution of languages on the Internet. Although the Internet penetration is not high at the moment in some regions, this is expected to change radically in the future. As an example, results of the Internet Domain Survey for Arab Countries is shown in Table 1 for January 1998. Efforts now are concentrating in developing tools and standards that enable the creation of websites in several languages or in at least one non-Western language. Now an Internet standard (RFC 2070) based on Unicode supports HTML documents in practically every language. In particular, some of the features dealt with are: Markup of bi-directional text, i.e. test where left-to-right and right-to-left scripts are mixed and control of cursive joining behavior in contexts where the default behavior is not appropriate. Also, the HTTP which is the hypertext transfer protocol in use since 1990 is being internationalized.

The relevant aspects are character set labeling which ensures correct document interpretation and language negotiation which is used at a site to provide documents in the user's language of preference.

Multilingual Machine Translation Issues

There are many situations in which multilingual translation is needed. Translation from many languages into a single language will be required by large information gathering and processing organizations. Translation from a single language into many languages will be required in the context of foreign trade when operation and other manuals for industrial equipment need to be translated into the language of the countries where the equipment is to be marketed.

Table 1 Internet Domain Survey Arab Countries, January 1998

Domain	*Hosts*	*All Hosts*	*DuplicateNames*	*Level 2 Domain*	*Level 3 Domain*
ku	4057	4749	692	9	2925
eg	2013	16930	14917	7	191
ae	1940	1955	15	8	56
lb	1134	1377	243	7	59
om	670	671	1	16	20
ma	431	463	32	5	339
bh	338	339	1	2	4
jo	249	249	0	5	13
qa	189	191	2	5	9
tn	69	69	0	10	68
sa	37	37	0	4	6
dz	16	17	1	1	16
ye	10	10	0	7	6
ly	1	2	1	1	1
sy, sd, iq	0				
	11154	27059			

Multilingual interlingual machine translation systems translate between a number of languages. In this approach, a universal language independent representation of text known as interlingua is developed. Therefore, the translation process is reduced to two phases: the analysis phase between the source language and the interlingua, and the generation phase from the interlingua to the target language. For successful machine translation, detailed knowledge of the languages is required at many levels: lexicon syntax, semantics and discourse. It is very difficult to provide such linguistic knowledge for an entire language. However, if we consider only language in a particular domain much of this knowledge could be obtained. The variety of language used in a given science or technology is not only much smaller than the whole language, but is also more clearly systematic in structure and meaning. Therefore linguists and computer scientists co-operate to study the properties of such specialized languages which are called sublanguages or controlled language. Each sublanguage has a distinctive grammar even though it is related to the grammar of the full standard language. Also, the theoretical problem of relating linguistic form to communicative function comes into sharper focus when individual sublanguages are examined.

Sometimes it is essential to distinguish between two translation activities. The first one is called localization (e.g. that used for computer manuals for end users) where it is important to adapt certain parts of the content and perhaps the style of presentation to a certain cultural and linguistic environment.

The second one is called diffusion translation where the objective content must be strictly rendered in another language without addition and omission. A brief outline will now be given for efforts related to Arabic/English translation. AppTek started an English-Arabic translator named TranSphere that uses Lexical Functional Grammar together with a general dictionary having 100,000 words. A number of domain-specific dictionaries have also been developed. This system could be either standalone or part of an integrated system.

Sakhr within Al-Alamiah Group [Sakhr, 1998] is also developing a translation scheme for Arabic-English and English-Arabic. It makes use of the available tools that have been developed before for morphological and syntactical analyzers, electronic dictionaries, semantic support together with a number of other development tools. It is also developing a general platform for dealing with Arabic computations. IBM Egypt is also developing Machine Aided Human Translation schemes. ALIS, Inc. offers a solution that integrates core language-handling technology and translation products. Electronics Research Institute in Egypt, in co-operation with the European Community is developing an English-Arabic and Arabic to English and German medical text translation.

This is done in the framework of CAT2 (Computer Assisted Translation) which uses an interlingua approach. Also, some work related to ambiguity in Arabic language processing is being studied. PRINCITRAN: In this system a large-scale lexicon is to be constructed for an interlingual machine translation system for Arabic, English, Korean and Spanish. For Arabic, the starting point was the use of the Alpnet bilingual Arabic-English online dictionary. Then automatic mappings between English glosses from Alpnet into LDOCE (Longman's Dictionary of Contemporary English) codes were performed. The codes were then converted into thematic grids which were then exhaustively hand-verified.

Electronic Commerce and Multilinguality

Global market opportunities are now increasing rapidly and is going to use heavily the facilities introduced by the Internet. Thus, the advent of global electronic commerce will add an economic dimension to cultural and linguistic issues. In international trade, companies that adopt a multilingual, multicultural approach are expected to gain a competitive advantage over their monolingual, monocultural competitors.

Regarding business-consumer relations, the following language issues could be stated: The seller of goods or services must be able to publish information in the language and cultural convention of the customers (multilingual electronic publishing). The buyer of goods or services must be able to find, understand and compare information in his own language (multilingual information retrieval). Both buyer and seller must be able to interact naturally and effectively in a common language or across different languages. There is a possibility that from the number of 5,000 to 6,000 languages spoken in the world today, only a few hundred will survive a century later.

The pressure on languages can take different forms: economic, social, cultural, etc.. Usually, people directly affected are minorities, but their languages represent the linguistic diversity that has developed over the course of human history. Some linguists argue that language endangerment is serious with great humanistic and scientific consequences. Can new developments in the information age help in preserving some of these languages and thus save language diversity. Information revolution is the global phenomenon that has an impact on all nations.

Nobody can stay out of the Information Society. That is why nowadays problems of ethical, cultural and social type has an increasing value. Only in resolving these problems the Information Society can achieve the declared goal of globalization: to promote quality of life and sustain a cohesive development. Due to the advent of the Information Society UNESCO faces new problems demanding to define its role in new world communication processes. That is why the UNESCO strategy should embrace the wide range of activities:

- concentration on key structures of the Information Society;
- ethic problems of the Information Society and the Cyberspace;
- elaboration of information policy;
- the impact of the globalization processes;
- specific education ;
- forming networks;
- fulfilling projects for the Information Society

These problems demand thorough considerations and constant attention. Textual information remains the main form of demanded information for majority of interstate or global international networks such as INTERNET. Due to the rapid success of communication technologies active use of spoken and visual information is foreseen in the nearest future.

Nowadays there are near 3000 spoken languages in the world and only 100 of them are written. Such a variety of languages under increased value of international contacts, high intensity of information flows of economic, political, scientific, technological and social types put forward as a priority task the development of human language technologies. Multilingualism is an inevitable historical attribute of the international communication process. The notion "multilingual information society " solidly occupies the place in the range of problems discussed by computer science specialists and predefined strategic directions of many international organizations and companies dealing with information distribution and processing.

Human language technologies obtained the valid political understanding and support. At the third UNESCO Congress on Informatics and Education held in Moscow, July 1996, more than 40 countries representatives confirmed their willingness to participate in the establishing multilingual telematics support for educational needs. The relevance of linguistic and cultural aspects of the Information Society in Europe has been stressed by the European Council meetings in Corfu, 24-25 June 1994, in Cannes, 26-27 June 1995 and on the G7 Conference of Ministers in Brussels, 25-26 February 1995. In May 1995 the European Commission has adopted the upcoming Fifth RTD Framework Programme which includes points devoted to developing human language technologies.

Technological Multilingualism

In the multilingualism problem there exists one important factor which usually slips out in discussions of this issue. The high level of technology of the modern civilization broadens the notion of multilingualism in information society including in it artificial intellectual electronic devices. This newly arisen complex communication structure forms the Cyberspace that is marked by extremely complex processes of control and self-development. In the Cyberspace the humanitarian multilingualism interacts with the technological multilingualism of communication protocols, computer interfaces, programming languages and data protection methods. Communication multilingualism of computing devices is to some extent being solved by introducing conventional technological standards regulating data exchange and transformation processes. Different computers in networks can transmit information using standard popular protocols TCP/IP (Transmission Control Protocol / Internet Protocol), IPX/SPX (Internetwork Packet Exchange / Sequenced Packet Exchange) or SNA (System Network Architecture). Such protocols as FTP (File Transfer Protocol), HTTP (Hyper Text Transfer Protocol), address standard URL (Uniform Resource Locator), standard sluice interface CGI are in active use in the INTERNET. High expressive possibilities of Web pages rely on implementations of HTML and Java languages.

For protecting information from different forms of eavesdropping cryptographic protocols SET (Secure Electronic Transfer) , SSL (Secure Sockets Layer) and some others have been elaborated. The "hardware multilingualism" aggravates the problem of the humanitarian multilingualism in the Cyberspace. It is interesting to note some resemblance in humanitarian and technical multilingualism. Communication multilingualism is stormy developing and to some extent repeats the dramatic way of human multilingualism. Here also numerous languages and dialects currently appear and die, conflicts of standards, programming languages and interfaces is an usual event.

Any technological innovation can lead to the chain, or may be it will be better to say "domino", reaction of expressive and communication means. The Cyberspace evolution is marked by constant attempts to resolve problems of humanitarian and technological multilingualism. The general common base for advances in these areas are backed by developing theory of semiotic systems, artificial intelligence, translation methods, algorithmic analyses, evolution of discourse, technologies sustaining lingual engineering.

Multilingualism Challenge

Historically formed present situation presupposes two general approaches for partial resolving the multinational communication problem. The first approach relies on the idea to adopt some universal unique well understanding language for invariant multilingual communication. The second approach lays on elaborating powerful technique for simulating expressive means of one language by expressive forms of another one. There are known three main variants in implementation of the first mentioned above approach.

- For some definite restricted knowledge areas to use specialized formalized languages such as Latin for medicine, language of formulas for mathematics, etc. This approach can be applied successfully only to very restricted object areas and cannot embrace cultural or social aspect of communication.
- To create one general artificial universal language which is neutral to national peculiarities of language communication. The most known language of this class is Esperanto. The less known is Sanskrit. The main drawback of this approach as in the previous case above is its impossibility to fill the communication gap in expressing national cultural potential.
- To conveniently adopt the use of one of national language. There is one well-known very strong candidate to play this role. Domination in the world processes (trade, science, technology, culture, etc.) of English speaking countries led to the huge spread of the English as a communication language. There are 1 billion and 400 millions of English speaking people

in the world. Only for 400 million of them this language is native. This means that for more than 1 billion of world population this language is the second or even the third one. And we are all witnesses that domination of the English as the communication tool in the Cyberspace is spreading with more and more increasing feedback link. The positive aspect of this event is extending for other nations the rich world of English speaking countries in all its appearances. The negative aspect is that such a global language invasion contradicts to natural eagerness of other nations to preserve local cultural achievements and adequate lingual means of their presentation. Even in the field of technological documentation complete relying on not native language information can affect the reliability of elaborating systems. Moreover, due to its internal evolution and rapid changing the fixed international English language can never be framed.

The second approach, which is simulating expressive means of one language by expressive forms of the other one, is traditionally reduced to the translation process. Before the computer era a bilingual or a multilingual interpreter was a man. Under computer expansion the language translation problem has obtained a new content - an automated language translation. In its full context this problem relates to the very complex problems of formalizing natural language understanding and cognitive context which are very far from the final decision. Nevertheless there are some recent evident successes in this area. The number of commercial systems for machine translation, as well as other types such as spell-checkers, multilingual mailers, dictionaries, etc. is rapidly growing.

During the last two years a few multilingual services available within Internet appeared. Multilingual Communication Corporation (USA) is offering its powerful WEB.TRANS service for global business. The two main browsers providers for WWW, companies Alis and Globalink, include the multilingual support in their products. The Tango, multilingual browser, using the Alis technologies, is a high performance Web tool that allows users to display Web pages authored in any of over 90 languages, select the languages of its interface, automatically retrieve these pages in the language version user prefers and input a text in a wide variety of languages. Alice Technologies has brought together several leading companies in the language industry to create Columbus - a suite of communication and translation tools and services designed to offer corporations the most comprehensive, convenient and cost-effective solutions on the market. There are other well-known companies offering a variety of multilingual solutions among them: ACCENT (Israel), Ajax Software Corp. (Russia), IBM, Intersol Brea, SYSTRAN (USA).

We can also concentrate on activity of BIT Software, Inc. (Russia), as well as ABBYY Company, formerly BIT Ukraine. These software companies are famous by their multi-lingual products like Stylus Gigant (powerul heuristic translator from five European languages to Russian and visa versa), Lingvo (large hyper-text interactive dictionary), WebTranSite (online "transparent" Internet translator), etc. There is one interesting frequently met feature of the multilingualism paradigm. Due to different historical reasons in one country (nation, popularity) there are two or several internal natural languages sharing the same information space. Such a situation exists in many NIS countries, Ireland, Canada,

India, Benelux countries and in many others. Ukraine is the bilingual country where the Ukrainian language has the state status. In this case specific domestic features could complicate the international multilingualism problem. Furthermore, problems become really global, e.g., after 7 years of official independence, Ukraine doesn't even have fully defined symbol code page (380), because four or five existing standards are already widespread and it's difficult to change any of them right now. Sometimes (as in Ireland) politics can influence the multilingualism decisions. Much attention is paid to the processes of creating computer supported information infrastructure in Ukraine.

The State program of informatization in Ukraine has been approved by the government. This program is backed by some legislative basis. There are three juridical laws concerning the informatization program. The first law defines the concept of the informatization in Ukraine. The second one defines objectives of the program. And the third law determines the content of the program. We would like to stress that the our Center is the leading organization in forming the concept and the governmental program of informatization in Ukraine.

International Research and Training Center of Information Technologies and Systems. In the organization we present here intensive research and technological works in language engineering are carried out. Let us mention briefly some of them.

- *Multilingual speech technology:* The technology of natural speech recognition and synthesis in a few foreign languages is developing by the specialists of our center for more than twenty years. In 1986 -1991 in frames of UNESCO contracts the multilingual (7 languages) speech dialogue system RECH-121 for CDS-ISIS Micro has been created. The works in the direction to create oral vocabularies-translators, dictating machines, machines simulating a human voice, individual speech passports, systems of multilingual speech interpreters are continued at present.

All these elaborations are based on the modeling of human intellectual activity and on the constructive analysis of digital information by means of its synthesis. The method that is used is recognized around the world.

- *Algorithmic analysis of the deep language structures:* Attempts to create systems of artificial intelligence demand the deep analyses of historical roots and evolution of language structures and human cognition processes. Such analysis has been done using new algorithmic methods. The kernel recursive structure of language sentences and literature constructions have been revealed. The algorithmic model of language constructions invariant to the natural languages has been suggested. The practical results of this research include applications to the authorship problem, psycholinguistics, associative expert systems, analyzes of myths, multilingual translators and some others.
- Automatic forming and translation of keywords in querying systems. In the navigating the multilingual Internet the problem of adequate translation of keywords is of great importance. The direct translation of keywords from a language A to a language B is connected with high ambiguity and can complicate the search of necessary documents. More correct idea to the keywords translation is based on

the comparison of texts in the language A, which correspond to the given set of keywords, with texts in the language B which could be found by means of all variants of translations of the given key-word set. In the process of looking for similarity of keywords an neural network model could be used.

The neural network methodology for implementation of this method has been elaborated. The methodology was checked in the automatic detection of user's interests.

These principles formed the base for creating neural networks supporting processes of making decisions and pattern recognition. Particularly, works in handwritten symbols neural recognition have been started with the Japanese company WACOM and at present gives good results. The same results could be used in the multilingual Internet.

- *Multilingual Internet and Educational Problems:* Multilingual Internet is thus becoming a real need for the nearest future, and important and urgent efforts should be made to solve the global problem of bi-directional communication barriers on different levels, addressing different user groups, etc. At the same time, due to low experience of the new users in the language and telematics, additional measures should be undertaken to provide training and educational facilities for these users.

Ukraine (and some CIS countries) can be considered as a typical "country in transition" concerning production, dissemination and use of multilingual information on the global information highways. There is an urgent need to develop an effective infrastructure in the field and to adjust to international standards. On the other hand, it is ready for international co-operative projects, having know-how and qualified specialists in many fields, including computer science, linguistics, programming, education, etc. Currently the following directions are considered as a first priorities in the National Informatization Programme: Basics in Telematics (Internet), networking of information and educational resources and multilingual computer-based support in science, education and communication, creation of the distance education centre.

Our preliminary analysis shows that the CIS countries have serious needs in the field of multilingual telematics support. Russian and French-speaking users are very conscious that they waste too much time and loose essential context information when they read/write texts in another language, even if they are competent in it. To keep one language such as English as unique language of communication is not cost-effective. There is a strong desire to stay within own native languages, which does not of course except trying to learn a few others for personal communicational and cultural purposes. The following specific multilingual user's needs are:

- support of communication at the basic level (reading and writing) via e-mail;
- opprtunities to use the adequate e-mail packages to remove essential obstacles in the way of communication both in countries, and in international communication;
- analysis of the multilingual products and services in Internet;

- analysis of the machine translators (on-line and off-line), dictionaries (on-line, off-line), thesauruses, multilingual mailers, tools for multilingual WWW-pages design, etc,
- training in multilingual Internet services (free distant courses via e-mail, WWW-courses etc.);
- updated information about new tendencies and products in multilingual telematics support;
- resolve the problems of standardization for multilingual software for every site in CIS countries;
- organization of the multilingual support of users' sites and consultation services.

The problems related to supporting user and/or suppliers groups and standardization becoming more and more actual both for East users and West suppliers. To make all relevant information available to its potential users and to provide an information exchange between Internet-users from various professional fields and from different countries, relevant national sites must be equipped by tools which form friendly and comfortable environment, making communication attractive for users world-wide, developing their information needs, widening their horizons and motivating their creativity. To facilitate a world-wide exchange via Internet specific needs of the users from wide range of cultural settings should be analyzed and generalized to find an effective solution. The general goals of the multilingual telematic support for education and training are the following:

1. to provide basic language tools for effective information exchange between Internet users from all possible professional fields and different English/ French and Russian speaking countries;

2. to improve accessibility of the Internet-based information for non-English speaking users;
3. to facilitate utilization of educational and training materials available in English for the French- and Russian-speaking users as well as to ensure share of such materials available on the net of the French and Russian-speaking countries;
4. to ensure exchange of educational and training information within Russian- speaking users groups directly, without necessity to pass through English.

To achieve these goals, the interested in multilingual applications sites must be equipped with tools which form user-friendly and comfortable multilingual environment. Communication within Network must be made attractive for users world-wide, developing their information needs, widening their horizons and motivating their creativity and inter- communications. The necessity of linguistic support for multilingual communication, information search and acquisition requires the use of modern linguistic tools such as spelling and grammar checkers, dictionaries, thesauri, vocabularies, elements of automatic translation and, eventually, multimedia voice encoders and decoders. To achieve the main goals for CIS countries, the translation tools for English into Russian and Ukrainian will be used.

- Virtual University as the examples of the multilingual telematics support for education and training. The life-long education of the 21st century will be global from two perspectives: from a horizontal perspective, cultures are meeting each other on the surface of the globe, entering into creative encounters that will produce a international collective virtual educational environment; from a vertical perspective, they must maximise using the world knowledge's for organisation of international virtual educational environment in order to provide a stable and secure base for future development. on the national and international levels .

The general goals of the multilingual telematic support for education and training are the following:

1. to provide basic language tools for effective information exchange between Internet users from all possible professional fields and different English/ French and Russian speaking countries;
2. to improve accessibility of the Internet-based information for non-English speaking users;
3. to facilitate utilization of educational and training materials available in English for the French- and Russian-speaking users as well as to ensure share of such materials available on the net of the French and Russian-speaking countries;
4. to ensure exchange of educational and training information within Russian- speaking users groups directly, without necessity to pass through English.

These problems must be solved at local, regional, national and international levels. The global aims of the IVU "Ukraine" are the following:

1. to provide inter-cultural courses, accessible to students all over the world through distance learning methods.
2. to create multilingual learning environment for telematic-based education and training

3. to stimulate learning to creative candidates in order to form complete human beings with erudition.

The multilingual telematics support for education and training should be based on innovative ways for flexible integration of modern technologies into the new solutions directed to the development of multimedia learning environment, which in its turn will contribute to the introduction of innovative solutions and skills for telematics-based training in world society, promoting new opportunities for life-long distance education. To facilitate a world-wide exchange within the Network its local/national sites should analyse specific needs of its users to find an effective solution within the Network.

One of this specific needs is the necessity of language support for multi-lingual communication and exchange of materials. To facilitate the use of samples and examples from different sources the Network should support a communication between teachers, as well as material translation into native language. This language service within local sites would not only promote the use of English-based materials outside English-speaking countries but also open the gates to teachers experience in other cultures and languages. The use of current machine translation tools, spell- and grammar-checkers, vocabularies would help to improve them making a necessary office tool, as text editor or word processor. Multilingual Internet support development. Main research direction is methods development for multilingual Internet technologies teaching to insure intencive use of the modern infornation resourses by the different groups of people.

Working in Internet multilingual environment create a large amount of the problems for non-English speakers.

Such users cannot to solve these problems allways self-sufficiently. Activity in this direction was initiated at Second International Congress UNESCO and was supported by the 42 counries round the world. Such developments are absent in Ukraine.

However, there is strong need to overcome language barriers and ensure certain translation or explanation of terms are selected by the user. Besides that, there isn't any materials about language barriers overcoming, in spite of existing such experience for English, Dutch and French languages. For Russian and Ukrainian languages we have only American translation off-line centers. So this problem is actual for Ukraine, that only tries to occupy certain place among leading countries in telecommunication issues. Object of investigation is ways of access to modern information Internet resourses with on-line and off-line electronic dictionaries and translators, and insuring flexible distance learning and providing measures, that will facilitate active use of the multilingual Internet environment.

Multilingualism: A Canadian Experience

Since its birth a generation ago, the Internet has been dominated by the English language and North American culture. In a 1998 survey conducted by the Internet research group, eMarketer, two-thirds (68 percent) of a little over 60 million Internet users worldwide reside in just two countries, the United States, with 37 million users, and Canada, which has just over 4 million. About 60 percent of the Internet host computers are located in the United States. Nine out of 10 Internet users today are English-speaking. No fewer than 82 percent of home pages (web sites) are in English, according to the Internet Society's survey of 60,000 computers with Internet addresses. Yet some foresee an end to this electronic hegemony.

The number of non-U.S. Internet users is about to outnumber those inside the country soon and increase by nine-fold over the next five years, from 16.4 million in 1997 to 143 million by the year 2002, representing an annual growth rate of 70 percent. In that case, the present practice of conducting business, presenting news and information, and performing discussion on the Internet will have to be drastically changed. The widespread use of English will eventually be contested and the Internet itself will become multicultural. This is already happening. A consortium of American computer companies has developed a universal digital code known as Unicode to allow computers to represent the letters and characters of virtually all the world's languages. Major search engines like Yahoo and Excite offer their services in multiple languages.

Netscape Communications in partnership with the leading Latin American Internet service, Star Media Network, provides a free Internet guide in Spanish and Portuguese. Internet services in languages other than English, like Star Media, are starting to provide world and regional news, weather, stock listings, e-mail, chat rooms, Internet access and more, all in the users' native language. Given such developments, optimists argue that far from ending diversity, the Internet will promote it by allowing even small groups of people to disseminate their messages worldwide. By overtaking the "middle range" languages, it may actually protect minority languages threatened with extinction. A wider range of languages on the Internet means at least in theory that a wider range of ideas will be exchanged in a cyberspace, the long-promised global village. Despite a tremendous influx of non-English languages in recent years, however, the Internet has a long way to go before it becomes a truly multilingual medium.

As long as English can be understood by the largest number of Internet users, the cyberspace will continue to be dominated by English as the primary language for international discourse and commerce, European languages as a tool for regional and specialized communication, and many other minor languages for local communication. At a glance there is an advantage to having one language dominant in the cyberspace. In a world of five to eight thousand different ethnic groups who reside in approximately 160 nation states speaking 5,000 distinct languages, some language must be the common language of the Internet.

Many people believe that English must be by default the standard language on the Internet, much as it is the international language of aviation. At present there are clear indications of English becoming a lingua franca in the cyberspace. The Internet, the network of networks, is most likely to be governed by the logic of the "Metcalfe's Law," the so-called magic of interconnections. Connect any number of machines, 'n', whether computers, phones or even cars, and you get 'n' squared in exponential value.

Simply put, the values of the interconnected entities increase exponentially. To expand this logic further, as English-speaking countries have happened to take the central role in world politics and economy in modern period (namely, Pax Britannica and Pax Americana), the

English language will deepen its hold on the world as more people go on line. As a recent British Council report shows, the evolution of the English language accelerates as it spreads beyond Anglo-Saxonism.

The critical mass of English amongst providers and users is likely to drive the usage inexorably towards monoglot English. Even the French, famously fastidious about guarding their language against dilution by foreign words and phrases, has been forced to surrender to American vernacular on Internet matters. As English continues to dominate the cyberspace with greater intensity and speed, global resistance to it accelerates with equal strength. Some countries already disgruntled by the encroachment of the American culture—from pop music, blue jeans, to videos—are worried that their cultures will be further eroded by an American dominance in the cyberspace. In their minds, English, by association, immediately evokes a negative image of colonial imperialism. They feel that it may threaten their cultures, their languages, even identities.

For this ideological reason, many people in the Third World countries are opposed to having English as the lingua franca for commerce and trade, crisis management, and scholarly and intellectual discourse on the Internet. While the Internet is awash in information, almost all of it flows in one direction, i.e., from the United Sates to the rest of the increasingly wired world. It brings home the age-old controversy regarding unbalanced and unidirectional flow of information from the world's richest countries to the Third World, an on-going controversy that prompted UNESCO to declare a New World Information Order (NWIO) on several occasions.

For the ideological as well as practical purposes, many countries have taken steps to protect the Internet from excessive American influence. The French government once filed a lawsuit against a Georgia Tech campus in Metz, France, whose web page did not translate its contents into French. Arab countries proposed creation of an Arab Intranet, a closed network in which indiscriminate access to pornography and political discussion could be blocked. Canadian content requirements are to be extended to the Internet to keep out the American "cultural vulture."

Multilingualism: A Korean Experience

American culture has continued to exert its influence in Korea, first through Christian missions, trade and Hollywood productions, and more recently via the Internet. Thanks to the Korean government's aggressive drive, an estimated 2.5 million Koreans are linked to the global medium. An equally large share of the credit for the phenomenal growth of the Internet goes to the media organizations in Korea, which have in recent years vigorously campaigned for introducing the "Net" to the school community through such programs as the KidNet (Chosun Ilbo) and Internet in Education (Joongang Ilbo).

In the vicissitudes of hopes and fears about the Internet, two isolated but interrelated events recently took place in Korea, all with a nationalistic overtone. One is the Microsoft's abortive attempt to buy out a local Korean software company in exchange for a multi-million dollar investment. The other has to do with a somewhat radical proposal by a Korean writer to adopt English as a common language on the Internet.

In the midst of currency crisis in Korea these days came the shocking announcement that the Hangul and Computer (H&C) Company, a Korean software company, had agreed with Microsoft to stop development of its popular Arae A Hangul word processor program in exchange for a $20 million capital investment. Apparently, what Microsoft hoped for in the deal was to secure a monopolistic right of its Korean language version of Windows and Word in the Korean market. When it first appeared in 1990, Arae A Hangul-- named after the Korean alphabet invented by King Sejong more than five centuries ago--was the only word processor based on hangul instead of Roman letters with the hangul mapping.

Arae A Hangul, "insanely great" in the words of Apple Computer's founder Steven Jobs, was multilingual at a time when DOS versions of Word and WordPerfect barely went beyond ASCII. This made it easy to develop a number of attractive fonts frequently used in displaying old Korean characters.

Media reports of the deal aroused anger and frustration among Korean computer users and non-users alike. Defenders of Hangul, who were opposed to the Microsoft's planned equity participation in H&C, quickly invoked the issue of Korean national pride to rally the public support for the program. A massive nationwide campaign saved Hangul at the eleventh hour from the threat of extinction as its developer, H&C, reversed its earlier decision to sell off the software, bowing to a nationwide campaign spearheaded by Korean scholarly community and venture capitalists. As hindsight, invoking Korean pride as a defense against predatory foreign companies appears to be too far-fetched and even xenophobic. On the other hand, Microsoft's aggressive marketing strategy to effectively terminate H&C's further development of Hangul can be viewed as too selfish and insensitive to the Korean nationalistic sentiment. Now that 2.5 millions of Koreans are linked up to form a global community, how will they communicate- Majority of Korean Internet users was found to use the global medium mainly for communication within the national boundary, according to an Internet user survey. To most of them the Internet remains largely an unexplored reservoir of knowledge and information due to language barrier.

Their grasp of English is quite rudimentary, sufficient only for processing basic information such as the weather, sports, and erotic visuals. Only a fraction of the Internet users can, to whatever degree, comprehend and produce written or spoken utterances in English. As a result, they are denied of the tremendous opportunities that the Internet has to offer, namely, in-depth information and more serious discussions with the netizens all around the world. To be an effective Internet user one has to be equipped with both receptive and productive abilities in English. Such an expectation, however, appears to be neither practical nor realistic as far as Korea is concerned.

Bok Koh-Ill, a professional Korean writer, thinks otherwise. He came up with a radical idea to make English as an official language of Korea along with Korean. Touching on the sensitive theme of Korean nationalism, Bok argued that "putting 'emotional' nationalism under control is not enough." "As the world is rapidly moving toward a Terrestrial Empire," he further asserted, "not only the political supranational organizations such as the WTO and IMF but also the communication tools like the Internet are increasingly integrated into one unity." Now comes his argument concerning English, the dominant language on the Internet. Bok observed that "the emergence of the universal language is interlocked with the enlargement of network." He predicted that "the Korean language will soon be little more than a museum piece as more nations will adopt a bilingual system in which their own languages coexist with English." His underlying perspective about language is that "language is a tool, and worshipping it as an idol is irrational."

Sensationalism notwithstanding, Bok's audacious proposal immediately touched off a flurry of verbal battle between the conservatives and liberals in Korea. In a wild exchange of high-pitched diatribes, Bok's opponents argued that English was not panacea and accepting his idea would wither Korea's unique traditions and hamstring the very cultural foundation.

Bok's supporters applauded accuracy of his observation that Koreans possess an excessive national pride, which Bok sees as the obstacle to the advancement of the Korean society. Bok even dared all his critics by asking, "If you had to choose between English and Korean for your child's native language, which one would you select? If you choose English, your child is sure to have faster access to cutting-edge technology and information. If the Korean language is your choice, your child is doomed to lag behind in competition with others." Whether he will succeed in his effort is far from certain. Bok says, "In our society, nationalism and national language are far too sensitive issues to be discussed with composure." Yet his other key point—that

Koreans are too sensitive to these kinds of issues—seems not that far from reality. A non-random online survey taken immediately after the verbal battle showed 58 percent of those polled were against Bok. Even more noteworthy is the fact that as high as 42 percent sided with Bok and his idea. The deepening dispute seems here to stay, at least for a while.

Multilingual Translation

For a truly multilingual Internet, the long-promised global village, to come of age, there are a host of difficult hurdles to overcome, including, among the many, technical difficulties of communicating in the majority of the world's languages and development of hardware and software for machine-aided translations. Some progress has been made, and more in sight, in the development of hardware and software for processing texts, from seven-bit ASCII to ISO-Latin, and more recently, to Unicode (ISO 10646), a coding scheme for characters of most of the world's scripts. Widely hailed as a significant breakthrough in electronic communication worldwide, Unicode character encoding, however, may not be the best one to use in our environment. For example, the Software Laboratory of Nippon Telegraph and Telephone Corporation (NTT) found that Chinese, Japanese, and Korean (CJK) ideographs share the same code space, when Unicode is used in a global search-engine context. Thus, if a Japanese searcher inputs a string for searching, it can equally match against Chinese and Korean counterparts.

Another major problem with Unicode for CJK users is that it doesn't contain enough code space to capture all ideographs. For the development of a perfect multilingual architecture, incorporating languages that build compound characters or right-to-left ordering needs further tests. Transmitting a message in a language of reader's preference is one thing; one's ability to comprehend it is quite another.

In order to send and receive a message, most readers will have to rely on human translators/interpreters. The Internet is home to many language translation sites that offer everything from simple online dictionaries to e-mailed translation services. From the desktop, one can request a translation by selecting to pay for human translation. The global nature of the Internet has proved a boon to translation services, such as TAR Communication in New York, which translated Web-based press releases into 28 languages during the Atlanta Olympic Games in 1996. Translation business via the Internet within the next five years is expected to account for 30 percent of their work.

Given the volume and variety of messages on the Internet, however, exclusive reliance on human translation appears to be an unrealistic proposition. It is too slow and costly to make it a sensible choice for maintaining multilingual websites. A viable alternative is machine-aided translation, which has been vigorously pursued mostly in Japan, Canada and Europe with somewhat mixed results. Systran, available on the French Minitel network since 1983 and Canada's Meteo system, which translates meteorological bulletins between French and English, are considered to be success stories.

In Korea there are several translation softwares capable of machine-translating foreign language texts into Korean. In an attempt to assess the quality of these softwares, the author had a wide variety of texts in Japanese and English translated into Korean by means of King Sejong, one of the most popular translation softwares in the market. To begin with a conclusion, the Japanese-Korean translation effort proved to be a resounding success, whereas the translated version of the English texts was dismally unsatisfactory.

In terms of the syntax and grammar both Korean and Japanese share a lot of things in common, whereas there is a mile of difference between Korean and English. It seemed as if the intercultural difference involved in the English-Korean translation were an insurmountable wall indeed. The English texts included Abraham Lincoln's Gettysburg address, a *USA Today* article headlined "White House Loses Round in Lindsey Case," a passage in Jean Baudrillard's La Pensee Radicale, excerpts from the novel Little Prince, and a paragraph in Nico Randeraad's article "Authority in Search of Liberty." This mini exercise yielded disconcertingly unsatisfactory results. The translated versions were totally unintelligible, and not good enough to be revisable even with the intervention of human editors. It appeared that the texts replete with sophisticated literary expressions—the Lincoln's address and Baudrillard's work in particular—simply defied machine-aided translation.

Of the five different kinds of the English texts, only the *USA Today* article—concerning a U. S. court's refusal of the White House appeal to block prosecutors from questioning a presidential aide about Monica Lewinsky--showed some sign of hope. Compared with the other texts, the news article revealed a relatively high level of fidelity in translation. Why did the newspaper article alone fare reasonably well, while other texts simply failed to be translated into Korean? The translator's familiarity with the subject matter, i.e. President Clinton's sex scandal, could be an important factor. A more plausible explanation lies in the journalistic style in which the article is written. Journalists are required to adhere to the journalistic principle of brevity and precision when they write about an issue or event.

All the important elements are to be clearly spelled without excessive literary ornamentation. Such a finding could have a practical implication for the information producers on the Internet. For the benefit of a large number of population worldwide they are strongly encouraged to provide a brief and concise abstract of the full text in a machine-friendly manner, so that the abstract can be translated into many languages without losing fidelity. Also useful in multilingual translation will be a two-step process now being implemented by several groups including the United Nations University in Tokyo. In the two-step process, a text is first thoroughly analyzed into component parts (title, paragraph, sentence), clarified when necessary and possible by a dialogue with the author, then translated into an intermediate, abstract representation—which is used to generate translations in different languages. In this way, readers who have no receptive ability in a foreign language could at least get the gist of the material in hand with the help of translation softwares.

Human-assisted Machine Translation

Given the low quality of machine translation and the expensive nature of human translation, the only logical option available to Korea--and for that matter to many countries in the world--appears to be human-assisted/ validated machine translation. Experts at numerous regional and international conferences have already addressed to the crucial importance of human-assisted translation. To briefly summarize their recommendations and suggestions:

1) it is vital that a human validator is used to correct automatic translation;

2) it is important to take cultural-specific notions into account when undertaking translations between culturally different linguistic areas;

3) human translations can benefit from processing of files against terminology databases to ensure that technical phrases are translated in a domain-specific way;

4) as keyword matching does not work across domains or across languages, searchable concept-based terminology resources and thesauri are needed;

5) it is important to integrate machine translation and domain-specific terminology sets with authoring tools to speed up translation services.

Technological solution to machine translation is one thing, financial difficulty associated with making machine translation services available through the Internet is another. Because these services take up too many CPU cycles, Information Service Providers would rather offer these services via specialist servers, not as a part of their mainstream operations. The question then arises as to who pays for such servers, and how. Also, the preponderance of English on the Web, with some estimates ranging as high as 95%, appears at odds with the huge investments in translation to be made by the software industry. Investments are likely to be made in the cost-effective European languages, but not in minor languages. Preparing for the multilingual Internet calls for a concerted effort by both public institutions and industry players that produce and utilize language services, tools, and systems.

Regional cooperation among nations that share cultural and linguistic similarities, such as Korea, Japan, and China, must be strongly encouraged not only by the governments concerned but also by regional and international organizations such as UNESCO. Through collaborative R&D arrangements, they can jointly develop multilingual translation tools and services in a much more cost-effective way. As personal computers become less expensive and user-friendlier, people outside North America and European countries are becoming increasingly linked.

In this atmosphere diversity of languages will further enrich the on-line environment by making it possible for people of different cultures and languages to engage themselves in more serious in-depth discussions with other people. There are many advantages of a multilingual Internet: it would allow much more effective and wide diffusion of information and knowledge than would otherwise be possible; common mistakes and misunderstandings resulting from language barrier will be curtailed; and it could be a crack in Americana hegemony over Internet culture.

Chapter 7

Emerging Challenges of E-governance

Mexico has taken the first step towards e-governance by facilitating the migration of certain governmental functions and services—namely, citizen participation, civil servant declarations, tramites (official solicitations and registrations), procurement, the registros publicos ("public registries"), and tax filings - to an expanding network of government operated websites. Reflecting the nascent state of e-government in Mexico, some of these websites have the look, feel, and functionality of static electronic brochures. Those sites that are not already interactive will undoubtedly become so, going forward, as the Mexican government comes under pressure to meet the demands of increasingly service- and performance-oriented citizens and investors. The ways in which the aforementioned governmental functions and services are amenable to the transformative influences of the Internet are discussed below.

Citizen Participation

Notwithstanding the fact that it has a governmental structure organically similar to that of the United States (i.e., a tripartite division premised on the notion of a separation of powers), Mexico has never had a strong tradition of citizen participation in government. Testifying before the House Committee on Small Business, noted Mexican scholar John Bailey characterized Mexico's political system as one "obsessed with central control, lacking a tradition of democracy and participation, and deeply skeptical about the uncertainties of risk taking inherent in democratic competition." Continuing, he noted: "Its basic instinct in confronting opposition is to co-opt, negotiate, and persuade; if these fail, its methods include divide, debilitate, denounce, and - as a last resort -repress."

The historic losses recently suffered by the PRI have profoundly impacted the legislative process in Mexico. Where the PRI's long-standing control of the congress facilitated a top-down, "metaconstitutional" approach to law making, the presently divided nature of Congress requires Mexican legislators to develop and deploy consensus and/or coalition building skills. As one trade publication relates, "Mexico is shaking off the authoritarian one-party state that has governed for most of this century and a more plural and democratic country is emerging. With it, too, a new culture is slowly forming, characterized for the first time by negotiation and persuasion and democratic give and take." The novel situation of shifting party alliances and legislative uncertainty produced by this change, coupled with the contemporaneous explosion of political awareness made possible by the rapid spread of information and communications technologies ("ICTs"), has opened up unprecedented opportunities for citizen participation in Mexico. In this context of real political competition, Mexico's elected officials are learning that legislative success comes to those who are most responsive to the input of an expanding range of increasingly organized constituents and interest groups. In recognition of the evolving political significance of the Mexican citizen, the Fox Administration has established a digital channel whereby individual citizens and civic groups can participate in the articulation of Mexico's National Development Plan (the "Consult a Ciudadana").

Based on the "E-Advocacy" and "Interactive Service" (G2C2G) models, the Consult a Ciudadana facilitates both the expression of opinion (Foro de Consult a) and the proactive presentation of legislative proposals (Buzon deConsultas). The creation of this channel is positive insofar as it enables more individuals and groups to gain admission to the law-making arena by removing the barriers of distance and political access. This is noteworthy given the fact that Mexico's laws have traditionally been made by Mexico City based elites with little first-hand knowledge of the social, economic, legal, and political interests and/or concerns of the people they govern. Going forward, the Consult a Ciudadana has the potential to serve as (1) an important conduit for the expression of fresh political thoughts, practices, and values, and (2) a mechanism for assuring that laws promulgated in the capital pragmatically relate to the reality of the subject matter they intend to regulate.

The emergence of digital spaces such as the Consult a Ciudadana, together with the promulgation of legislation designed to strengthen the participation of civil society, is additionally significant in that it opens the door to the disintermediation of politics in Mexico and the rise of a more "direct" form of democracy. Assuming the rectification of Mexico's substantial Internet access problem, and (2) the existence of the genuine political will to expand the substantive scope of the channel, the Consult a Ciudadana could help bring about a fundamental redefinition of the social contract underlying the citizen-government relationship. These ICT related developments could, in turn, contribute to the transformation of Mexican authority structures and facilitate the growth of self-regulatory practices.

Transparency

Mexico has a deeply entrenched history of non-transparency. The PRI's seven decade stranglehold on power, coupled with its careful control of information and self-serving manipulation of the canard of "national sovereignty," insulated Mexico from adverse scrutiny and, to a lesser degree, accountability. Considered in the context of Mexico's traditionally paternalistic and corporatist socio-political organization, this lack of transparency fostered rampant corruption and eroded economic, political, and legal certainty. Drawing on the successful experience of other Latin nations in using the Internet as a tool for overcoming the developmental impediments posed by non-transparency and corruption, the Fox administration has begun to use the E-Mexico program as a platform for capturing and recording the patrimonial information of public servants associated with the entities and dependencies of the federal public administration ("Declaranet"). Premised on the "Broadcasting/Wider Dissemination" model, this type of digital resource "opens up an alternate channel for people to access information as well as to validate information available form other sources." While Declaranet constitutes an important step in the direction of transparency, it may ultimately be of limited value in that the practices followed in valuing and accounting for the patrimony of a public servant are left to the absolute discretion of the government.

A further limitation entails the fact that article 40 of the LFRASP (not surprisingly) makes the subsequent publication of captured patrimonial information expressly contingent on the prior authorization of the individual public servant. The inescapable implication of this provision is that the ultimate utility of the Declaranet site as a publicly available anti-opacity/corruption tool will be a function of public servants' good will and, perhaps more accurately, confidence in the "cleanliness" of their personal affairs. Transparency in Mexico will likely be enhanced by the recent passage of landmark legislation involving the reporting of and access to information.

Conceptually and functionally a kin to the Freedom of Information Act ("FOIA") in the United States, Mexico's new Ley Federal de Transparenciay Acceso a la Informacion Publica Gubernamental promises to remedy information failure by (1) requiring the obligated subjects of the federal public administration to make structural and operating information (for example, regarding budgets, procurement contracts, licenses, concessions, etc.) available to the public via Internet and (2) creating an administrative mechanism by which citizens can proactively request and obtain information of a non-reserved character from all branches, entities, and dependencies of the federal government. Assuming the effective operation of the law's civilian oversight feature (i.e., the operationally autonomous Instituto Federal de Acceso a la Informacion Publica), Mexico's L.F.T.A .could function as a powerful tool for influencing governmental action and deterring corruption, facilitating the clarification and/or settlement of past controversies, strengthening the rights of Mexican citizens set forth in the Constitution and other international treaties to which it is a party, and assuring compliance with supreme court decisions. As was the case with the issue of Declaranet-related information disclosure, supra, the introduction of a mechanism for discovering information pertaining to government departments and personnel, coupled with an increased commitment to securing accountability, could result in the establishment of more stable developmental conditions in Mexico.

Electronic Tramites

One of the greatest obstacles to economic development faced by Mexico and Latin America involves the inefficient, formalistic, and corruption ridden process of soliciting and/or obtaining government permits, licenses, and or concessions (for example, in connection with incorporations, the registration of intellectual property, the issuance of powers of attorney, dissolutions, etc.). Faced with slow response times, high costs, complicated procedures, and uncertain results, citizens and foreign businesses frequently attempt to structure their affairs around the government. This practical hinders economic development to the extent that (1) informally operated small- and medium- sized companies are unable to title, insure, and leverage assets and/or avail themselves of potentially lucrative government programs and benefits (involving, for example, the obtainment of micro-credit, health care, export assistance, etc.) and (2) the government is unable to collect the tax revenue it needs to create and support infrastructure and industrial development projects, education and training programs, regulatory enforcement regimes, and social security services.

Cognizant of the obstacle posed to development by excessive and complicated registration and permit filing procedures, the Zedillo administration introduced a deregulation program designed to reduce "the bureaucratic red tape that stifles competitive markets and limits economic growth." Most recently, the Fox administration has sought to achieve further administrative and regulatory efficiency by making it possible for citizens and investors to realize certain filings online (Tramitanet). Borne of the Interactive Service (G2C2G) model, Tramitanet provides information pertaining to substantive and procedural filing requirements (for example, content, form, authentication, costs, etc.) and enables the electronic submission of a limited range of routine tramites and denouncements.

The legal viability of electronic filings made through the Tramitanet system is assured by the fact that Mexico's civil, commercial, and procedural codes, as reformed, expressly recognize the validity of electronically generated data messages and assure non-discrimination with respect to data messages as a form of proof Properly managed, this site could enhance economic growth and development in Mexico by (1) encouraging informally operated small- and medium-sized business entities to register with the government, (2) reducing opportunities for fraud and error, (3) saving citizens, investors and the government time and money, and (4) contributing to the formation of a robust and reliable database regarding economic and civic activity.

Electronic Government Procurement

Government procurement has traditionally been one of the most important drivers of economic activity in Latin America. In Mexico, it is estimated that 25% to 30% of the federal budget regularly goes to the purchase or lease of goods and/or services. Notwithstanding the substantial economic upside associated with this activity, government procurement in Mexico has long been a fertile breeding ground for inefficiency and corruption. Responding to the absence of clearly defined (and/or enforced) guidelines and the over-abundance of poorly paid intermediaries, private sector suppliers commonly assess up to a 20% surcharge on government sales so as to cover losses caused by bureaucratic inefficiency and bribes demanded by government purchasing officers. The net effect of this overcharging is to diminish the governmental resources available for the realization of development related projects such as schools, hospitals, and infrastructure.

As part of Mexico's attempt to promote development by reducing inefficiency and corruption, the Secretaria de Controloriay Desarollo Administrativo (SECODAM) has automated and disintermediated government procurement by launching the Compranet site. Representing a fully Interactive Service (G2C2G) model, Compranet is intended to simplify and modernize the procurement process by (1) making it easier for suppliers to discover government needs, (2) standardizing the procedures and documentation involved in procurement,

(3) minimizing the involvement of civil servants, (4) and providing for the electronic submission of bids. Each bid submitted must be authenticated by means of a digital signature.

As of October 1999, the Compranet site was accommodating more that 6,000 public sector tenders on a daily basis and had registered more than 20,000 service providing firms as regular users. The standardization, automation, and disintermediation of government procurement practices, considered in conjunction with the reduced cost of accessing the government's electronic procurement network, has improved economic transparency, increased citizen participation in the bidding process for public contracts, and enabled the government to curtail supplier surcharges.

More importantly, the expanded monitoring and auditing opportunities presented by Compranet's searchable archive of procurement records will make it easier to detect and punish civil servant fraud. In this regard, Mexico's recent experience with the "Towelgate" scandal clearly demonstrates the system's capacity to expose fraudulent violations of the public trust. Finally, by reducing opportunities for corruption, Compranet permits Mexico to more fully comply with its obligations under the OECD's Convention on Combating Bribery of Foreign Public Officials and the OAS' Inter-American Convention Against Corruption.

Electronic Public Registries of Commerce and Property

The unavailability of commercial credit that Mexico has experienced since 1993 has created a significant drag on the country's economic growth and development. While many factors account for this reality, one of the most important involves the non-existence of a functional and reliable system of secured financing. Referring to the "defective" form in which property is documented and held in many Latin nations (including Mexico), Hernando De Soto notes: "assets cannot readily be turned into capital, cannot be traced outside of narrow local circles where people know and trust each other, cannot be used as collateral for a loan, and cannot be used as a share against an investment." The underproductive nature of the majority of Latin America's capital constitutes a fundamental obstacle to the region's sustained development.

Consistent with its efforts to transform the country's moribund financial system into an engine of economic productivity, the Mexican government recently announced its intent to join forces with the states in integrating and automating Mexico's antiquated network of public registries of commerce and property (the SIGER network). Conforming to the Interactive Service (G2C2G) model, the completed system will respond to the requirements of art. 20 of the Codigo de Comercio, as reformed, by providing an Internet based means of interfacing with Mexico's registries. Considered from the perspective of secured financing, the SIGER will facilitate the conduction of registry searches and the registration of liens (and/or related mercantile acts). As was the case with the Tramitanet system, the juridical security of electronic filings in the public registries of commerce and property is assured by the recent reforms to Mexico's Codigo de Comercio, Codigo Civil, and Codigo Federal de Procedimientos Civiles.

The launching of the SIGER will improve Mexico's registry systems by reducing the likelihood of fraud and error, expediting the process for ascertaining the existence of specific filings (for example, a lien), and enabling the establishment of an integrated database of encumbered property. Assuming the establishment of meaningful degree of Internet access, these improvements will facilitate economic growth and development by providing merchants with the transactional certainty necessary for entering into an increased number of deals with an expanded range of business partners.

Electronic tax filings

The massive privatization program carried out in the 1990s, combined with the implementation of economic policies designed to reduce Mexico's dependence on revenues generated by the sale of oil, the continued loss of human capital in the form of the temporary or permanent migration to the United States, and generally weakened levels of in bound tourism has resulted in the elimination and/or circumscription of traditionally lucrative sources of budget revenue and underscored the need for diversifying government income. Lacking the funds to simultaneously service its foreign debt and operate the government in a way that adequately meets the needs of its citizens, Mexico has undertaken a program of fiscal reform designed to shut down loopholes, expand the tax base, and increase the federal budget.

Noting the success that other Latin nations have encountered in using the Internet to maximize tax revenue, Mexico recently expanded its e-government program to provide for the electronic presentation of declarations and payment of taxes (through the Servicio de Administracion Tributaria, or "SAT"). Constituting an Interactive Service (G2C2G) model, the SAT site (either independently or in conjunction with private sector financial institutions) permits inscribed users to file tax statements, make payments (realized via an electronic transfer of funds from the tax payer's bank to the Tesoreria de la Federacion), confirm receipt of payment, and review prior tax transactions.

Security for this system is accomplished through the use of a "security key" (i.e., a private key) bound by the "Modulo de Atencion Fiscal de la Adminsitracion Local de Recaudacion" corresponding to the tax payer's domicile (the corresponding digital certificate required to use the system is subsequently sent by e-mail). Similar online tax filing and payment systems have been set up by different state governments in Mexico. Again assuming adequate Internet access, the SAT system can help the Mexican government maximize tax revenue by (1) contributing to the preservation of scarce government resources (via the dissemination of tax filing information and instructions in a more cost effective manner); (2) removing distance as a barrier to tax filing; (3) minimizing the opportunity for fraud and error; (4) expediting processing time; (5) enabling the establishment of a reliable taxpayer database; and (6) facilitating the prosecution of tax evaders. These developments could, to the extent they expand the base of government resources, help avert a reduction in foreign investment occasioned by the perception that the weakened state of Mexico's public finances effectively precludes the realization of large scale infrastructure projects. The expansion of Mexico's tax base, on the other hand, could be accomplished by making the SAT's online tax filing and payment services available to all Mexican citizens.

Recognizing the power of the Internet to fundamentally improve traditional political and economic systems, Mexico has aggressively initiated the process of moving official functions and services online. As a result of these efforts, Mexico's citizens are better able to claim a stake in a more transparent and potentially less corrupt government. The communications and operational efficiencies associated with the Internet have, moreover, resulted in both increased revenues and substantial savings in terms of time and resources.

These developments, in aggregate, have justifiably improved the confidence of citizens and investors in exico. More can and must be done, however, if Mexico is to fully realize the developmental opportunities associated with the Internet. The adoption of the following policy recommendations will further strengthen democratic governance, economic development, and the rule of law in Mexico:

> Expand the E-mexico Programme to include electronic Voting and the administration of Justice While significant advances have been made in bringing the Mexican government into the digital age, the issues of voting and the administration of justice have remained largely outside the scope of the E-Mexico program. The subsequent sections identify and explore the benefits that would flow from the digitalization of these historically inefficient areas of public administration.

Electronic voting

Elections have long been problematic in Mexico.

Notwithstanding the creation of an independent Federal Electoral Institute, the presence of international observers, the dramatic rise to power of non-PRI candidates and parties, reports of missing and/or overstuffed ballot boxes (the latter tactic is known as the "taco"), unclear voting station procedures (a tactic known as the "raton loco," or crazy rat), identification fraud (tactics involving the fraudulent manipulation of voter lists are locally known as the "cambio de panal," or diaper change), vote buying, intimidation tactics, and questionable tabulation techniques persist.

The degree to which Mexican elections accurately reflect the will of the people is further reduced by the large number of voters who, for reasons of age, health, or distance, do not vote. Particularly significant in this regard is the increasing number of Mexicans that live, either permanently or temporarily, outside the country. The experience of other Latin nations indicates that the conduction of electronic elections can save scarce government resources (by minimizing the need for the deployment of large numbers of election personnel and reducing the volume of paperwork involved in the process), improve voter turn out (by eliminating the obstacles posed to rural inhabitants and expatriates by poor travel infrastructure and/or distance), counter the effects of illiteracy (by using photographic images in a touch screen format), and produce more objective, error-free, and timely tabulations.

Assuming the existence of the political will and the implementation of the appropriate authentication and/or security procedures, the introduction of an IFE managed interactive system of electronic voting could reduce the frequency with which the legitimacy of elected officials becomes controverted and mitigate lingering notions of disenfranchisement (i.e., on the part of those individuals and/or groups which claim to have been victimized by electoral fraud). These results could, in turn, help free up the Amparo dockets and enhance the overall perception of Mexico's stability in the eyes of both citizens and investors.

The Administration of justice

Latin America's political and economic development has been increasingly linked to the rule of law. As military dictatorships have given way to civilian rule and free trade in competitive markets has displaced trade protectionism (for example, import substitution), nations throughout the region have discovered that cosmetic changes in the law, unaccompanied by changes in the underlying culture and values of legal and political institutions, will not produce the certainty necessary for the growth and development of free markets and societies. Speaking to the economic aspect of this equation, noted constitutional scholar Lawrence Lessig states "if anything makes an economy work, it is a stable political environment governed by the rule of law." Focusing, in turn, on the political component of this equation, the President of Mexico's Supreme Court asserts "there can be no solid democracy [in Mexico] without a strong and independent federal judicial power."

Having determined that a greater level of legal certainty is critical to both the country's internal development and participation in the global economy, Mexico has, over the course of the last decade, undertaken the reform of its notoriously slow, corrupt, and costly system of judicial administration. In this connection, Mexico has identified - though not yet coherently developed - a central role for the Internet (premised on both the Broadcast/Wider Dissemination and Interactive Service models) in the process of strengthening the country's legal system. For example, Federal and state judicial authorities have recently begun to use the Internet for the dissemination of legal content, (laws, initiatives, jurisprudencia, teses, boletines, and other official publications) and the delivery of ADR services. While these developments undoubtedly make the administration of justice more efficient, there is significant room for improvement.

The federal and state legal databases available online are frequently uneven in terms of coverage depth and quality. Reglamentos—the critical regulations which accompany and flesh out primary Mexican legislation - are often not presented. In a related vein, the online version of the Diario Official is of limited value in that its coverage extends back only as far as 2000. The utility of the Mexican Supreme Court's database of jurisprudencia is, on the other hand, diminished by the sub-par functionality of the site's search feature. Finally, online notification systems (i.e., electronic boletines oficiales) - where the service is even available - tend to be primitive in terms of scope and execution.

Going forward, Mexico should consider bringing the administrative infrastructures of the federal and state judicial systems under the technical umbrella of the E-Mexico program. In networking these systems, Mexico would be able to (1) centralize and standardize legal content; thereby improving the functionality of the government's law-oriented websites; (2) improve the quality and timeliness of legal information disseminated online; (3) facilitate the use of online ADR services; and (4) expand the ability of parties to file certain pleadings and documents online (assuming the use of security measures to protect the content of filings), send and receive notifications electronically, and use information technology in the conduction of hearings (offering, for example, testimony by means of video-conference or video-deposition).

These developments could, in turn, strengthen the penetration of laws and jurisprudencia, expedite legal proceedings, clear dockets, improve judicial record keeping practices, eliminate sources of corruption, and decrease the cost of litigation. The ultimate beneficiary of a more efficient and equitable judicial system would, of course, be citizens and investors. Having increased faith in the ability of Mexican courts to resolve disputes in a swift, impartial, and cost effective manner, individuals and entities - national and foreign alike - would be less inclined to structure their affairs outside the court system and/or restrict their dealings to parties with whom they have established relationships. This certainty driven rise in the number of market participants would, to the extent it translated into enhanced levels of deal flow, promote economic growth and development.

Improve internet access

If Mexico's fledgling E-government program is to develop in accordance with its potential, Internet access must be improved. It is estimated that Mexico currently has 2.2 computers for every 100 people. Stated in terms of population, this signifies that only 1.5 million of Mexico's 96 million citizens (i.e., between 1-2% of the population) have access to the Internet. While these numbers are slowly increasing, the developmental benefits to be derived from moving governmental functions and services online will remain illusory pending the rectification of the access issue and the establishment of a functional "critical mass" of users.

The Internet may be growing exponentially, but it is only very slowly representing a more democratic cross-section of our society." Mindful of the obstacles posed to Internet access by relatively low PC penetration rates, high service and connection costs (i.e., telephone, ISP), and the poor quality of transmission signals caused by the country's weak telecommunications infrastructure, the government and private sector are working to raise the number of Internet users in Mexico. To this end, secretariats, institutions, and corporations such as the SCT, COFETEL, SEDESOL, SEP, the ITESM, and TELMEX, inter alia, have undertaken projects to boost teledensity (for example, by integrating the countries fixed and wireless communications networks) and increase Internet connectivity (by enhancing access to the necessary equipment and connections).

In the same vein, private sector entities are pursuing large-scale projects designed to bring Internet access, e-mail content, and multimedia capabilities to public places (for example, airports, bus terminals, hospitals, shopping centers, etc.).These endeavors have been supplemented by the introduction of alternative, less costly means of accessing the Internet (for example, via PDA, web phone, smart phone, cable set top box equipped with bidirectional modem, etc.).

The success of Mexico's e-government program will ultimately depend on its ability to create and assure infrastructure, investment, and regulatory conditions conducive to the realization of projects geared toward increasing Internet connectivity. In this connection, Mexico must take steps to enhance competition in the telecommunications and IT sectors by curtailing the monopoly power of TELMEX and vesting COFETEL with meaningful regulatory authority. Presuming such optimal developmental conditions, it is reasonable to think that Mexico will accomplish its goal of connecting approximately 2,500 municipalities to the Internet by the end of 2001 and 10,000 by the end of the Fox administration (2006).

Increase Information Technology Training and Support for Government Officials and Citizens

Another impediment to the successful development of the E-Mexico program involves the relatively limited technological skills and knowledge of Mexico's government officials and citizenry. Facing what one Mexican government official describes as "profound computer illiteracy," it is crucial that Mexico take steps to increase training and support with regard to new technology (for example, the use of electronic signatures, digital certificates, database management, etc.). Failure in this regard would undermine the communications and operational benefits of the E-Mexico program insofar as technologically unsophisticated government officials and citizens would be required to continue interacting pursuant to traditional paper based methods.

One way of avoiding this outcome would be for the Mexican government to establish "in house" training programs tailored to the specific needs and functions of each branch of government (as well as their assorted dependencies). Alternatively, the Mexican government could require key officials to attend the OAS-IACD sponsored "E-Government Academy." On another level, the provision of more detailed (yet nonetheless "user friendly") online instructions and expanded telephonic assistance could help Mexico's citizens master applications and programs with respect to which they have had no prior experience.

A good example in this connection involves the way Declaranet provides civil servants electing to file electronic declarations with training courses, technical assistance (via e-mail or telephone consultation), and comprehensive download instructions. An important corollary to the aforementioned endeavors involves the strengthening of information technology training programs at academic institutions and private sector corporations. While universities such as the ITESM and ITAM have recently launched graduate level IT programs for the benefit of citizens in major population centers, there are significantly fewer training opportunities available to citizens in other areas.

As virtual universities and other online training and learning centers become better established, however, it will be possible for a larger, more geographically diverse groups of citizens to obtain IT training. Corporations (particularly medium- to large-sized entities), on the other hand, are increasingly training employees to operate basic hardware and applications. In some cases, employee training has even extended to programming and software development. By acting to provide basic training for today's population - 40% of which is under age 15 - Mexico will assure the technological proficiency of the E-Mexico program's future users.

Ensure Citizen Privacy and Transactional Security

The final policy recommendation this paper makes focuses on the necessity of ensuring the privacy and security of electronically realized citizen-government transactions. Mexicans have in the past been unwilling to express their true thoughts and beliefs for fear of political and/or economic retaliation by local and/or regional political leaders. Despite the fact that the citizenry's susceptibility to this sort of pressure is gradually dissipating with the emergence of real competition amongst the country's political parties, many Mexicans - especially the rural poor - continue to keep their political views and actions closely guarded. As noted Mexican historian Enrique Krauze notes in this regard, the political process in Mexico is marked by a "culture of secrecy and private decision." If Mexico's citizens are to embrace the enhanced participation opportunities made possible by the E-Mexico program, it is imperative that their rights of privacy and anonymity be assured and strictly upheld.

An analogous issue exists with respect to the citizenry's willingness to entrust personal or commercial data in digitalized form to public officials and/or third party intermediaries (for example, banks or ISPs). Absent the introduction of adequate security measures, many Mexicans may be inclined to reject Internet based methods of filing tax returns, procuring government contracts, and registering assets. Consistent with the recommendation of the AMITI and other groups, Mexico has, over the course of the last two years, taken legislative steps to strengthen citizen privacy and transactional security on the Internet. Mexico's Federal

Consumer Protection Law, as reformed, sanctions the failure of a "provider" (for example, an ISP or other intermediary) to keep consumer-citizen information confidential.

Citizen privacy and security stand to be further strengthened by the terms of the March 22, 2000 initiative regarding information crimes. In its current form, the bill criminalizes (1) the interruption of communications on public networks, (2) the opening or accessing of written electronic communications directed to others, (3) the use of electronic data to fraudulently obtain, transfer, or acquire the property of another, (4) the unauthorized alteration, use, and/or modification of personal, financial, or commercial data registered in programs or codes, and (5) the unauthorized disclosure of the data mentioned in item "4," supra. Supplementing these steps, in turn, are the terms of the currently pending Ley Federal de Proteccion de Datos Personales.

Modeled largely after the Habeas Data action otherwise available in Latin America, the terms of this bill are intended to assure the integrity and privacy of personal information and data. Last, recently enacted NOM 151-SCFI-2002 bolsters transactional certainty in the online environment by elaborating the procedures to be followed in connection with the archiving of data messages. While these legislative endeavors appear to bode well for the E-Mexico program, it is too early to determine either the degree to which they will be enforced (assuming, in the case of the bills, that they are ultimately enacted) or the impact they will have on citizen confidence. Mexico could re-enforce online privacy and security by formally adopting the OECD Guidelines on the Protection of Privacy and Transborder

Flows of Personal Data and/or expanding the scope of art. 16 of the Constitution (regarding the inviolability of private communications) to expressly include data messages generated by electronic media. The fall of communism in 1989, coupled with the rapid evolution of global communications capabilities, resulted in the rejection of the state-oriented CEPAL agenda and the validation of developmental strategies premised on neoliberal economic policy and democratic governance.

In the case of Mexico, it was specifically hoped that liberalization would help overcome the economic setbacks of the 1980s (i.e., the "lost" decade Mexico experienced as a consequence of the enactment of high-risk and short-sighted policies) and plant the seeds of meaningful political and social transformation. While some positive economic and political outcomes have flowed from the implementation of these strategies, a review of Mexico's developmental record over the course of the last decade indicates that the hoped for recuperation and transformation have, on balance, yet to occur.

Ten years of neoliberal reform—as embodied by extensive privatizations, the NAFTA, and Mexico's insertion into the global economy - have yet to improve the living and economic conditions experienced by the majority of Mexicans. Pointing to decreased levels of government social spending, the diminished salaries and purchasing power of citizens, elevated rates of loan default and bankruptcy (particularly amongst small- to medium-sized entities), the disappearance of domestically controlled commercial entities (inciting, in turn, a nationalism-tinged resentment amongst Mexicans that they are no longer the masters of their own destiny), rising unemployment figures, unbridled child labour abuses, declining health, sanitation, and education standards, heavy flows of out-migration (commonly to the U.S.), and an increasingly unstable social situation (characterized by heightened levels of crime and drug cartel activity), many citizens now claim that Mexico's adherence to the neoliberal concept of withstanding economic "pain" before the "gain" has been excessive.

Mexico's experience with neoliberal economic policy appears, moreover, to have perpetuated the gulf between the nation's wealthy and poor. According to the recent "Human Development Study" conducted by the United Nations Development Fund, the "richest 20% of [Mexico's] population gets 57% of the country's income, which is 14 times what the poorest 20% get." These findings are corroborated by Nobel Prize winning economist Joseph Stiglitz's observation that, in the case of Mexico, the primary beneficiaries of the liberal economic policies encompassed by the so-called "Washington Consensus" have been the upper thirty percent of the population (with an even more marked concentration of benefits occurring within the top ten percent). Conversely,

Stiglitz goes on to note, "those at the bottom have gained little; many are even worse off." Given such negative results, it should come as no surprise that a Reforma poll found that (1) almost 60% of respondents thought Mexico had not benefited from NAFTA, and (2) approximately 90% of respondents thought NAFTA had produced increased levels of unemployment in Mexico. The current reduction in the level of U.S. FDI, coupled with the recent drop in industrial output occasioned by a weakening U.S.demand for Mexican exports, will only exacerbate Mexico's precarious economic situation. It is unlikely that Mexico will be able to pick up this economic slack by relying on its web of FTAs given the global nature of the present downturn.

Compounding the negative record of neoliberalism is the fact that the values and practices of the country's political and legal classes have failed, for the most part, to evolve in a way that engender greater citizen confidence in the operation and integrity of government and the rule of law. Notwithstanding the dramatic electoral accomplishments of the past four years, political and legal processes in Mexico continue to be characterized by corruption, inefficiency, and impunity. In the words of one high-ranking former Mexican official, the country's politicians are still "faced with the temptation to disregard their mandate and to govern in their own interests, or on behalf of the interest groups with whom they are allied." Because of this propensity on the part of Mexico's political leadership, "it is imperative to establish control mechanisms to ensure that elected officials, especially those in the executive branch, will perform their duties honestly and efficiently."

Focusing on the present administration, another Mexican commentator underscores the fundamental lack of real change by noting: "A year after his formal assumption of power, Fox appears more and more like the representatives of the regime he criticized so much during his presidential campaign. The crimes of the PRI regime - ranging from an abusive exercise of discretion with respect to public resources to violations of human, political, and labour rights - continue unpunished."

The cynicism and disillusionment which this situation incites within Mexico's citizens directly undermines the development of democratic and pluralistic institutions. Against this backdrop of discontent has emerged a growing rejection of U.S. inspired economic policies and political practices. Addressing the global manifestations of this backlash, Michael J. Mazaar of the Center for Strategic and International Studies (CSIS) observes: "Economic and social reform and democracy have swept the region, sparking alienation and exacerbated economic inequalities. Cultural and ideological reactions to capitalism are gaining strength.

The great expectations that accompanied reforms in Argentina, Brazil, Mexico, and Chile have given way to widespread disaffection with reform." While governments throughout the hemisphere have adopted the Inter-American Democratic Charter, the annual Latinobarometro survey reveals that the number of Mexicans which believe democracy to be preferable to any other kind of government is dropping. Even more alarming, however, is the survey's finding of a growing tolerance on the part of Mexicans for "dictatorship." Consistent with this finding, one Mexican publication recently stated: "the miseries of our democracy incite within many citizens a longing for the return of dictatorship."

Another Mexican commentator echoes this sentiment when he observes that democracy in Mexico - which has yet to be consolidated - "could still fail, creating a vacuum that could engender conflict and violence." Reflecting the dissatisfaction of the times, Mexico has, since 1994, witnessed increased levels of civil disobedience and guerilla activity - as well as the corresponding militarization (involving the deployment of both official and private paramilitary forces) of the domestic sphere. This is consistent with the observation that "many governments in the face of economic hardships and social dislocations caused by neoliberal restructuring have adopted authoritarian measures and bolstered the state's capacity for repression."

The economic and political stagnation underlying this backlash is contrary to U.S. interests insofar as it (1) diminishes the prestige of American developmental initiatives and strategies, (2) complicates a U.S.-Mexico relationship already strained by issues of drugs, immigration, terrorism, and water, (3) makes hemispheric economic and trade integration less attractive to the other Latin nations, and (4) strengthens the hand of America's Asian and European competitors in the region. The aforementioned developments are, alternatively, contrary to Mexico's interests to the extent that such expressions of social, political, economic, and legal instability run the risk of diminishing the country's overall competitive advantage in the global order, thereby leading foreign investors to locate their commercial activities elsewhere.

The recent entry of China and Taiwan into the WTO could, in this connection, adversely impact Mexico's ability to attract and retain desperately needed foreign investment. The E-Mexico program, in tandem with the broad range of economic, social, political, and legal reforms undertaken over the past twenty years, presents an unique opportunity to overcome the systemic formalism, inefficiency, fraud, mistrust, and impunity that have long operated to preclude sustainable economic and substantive political development in Mexico. Assuming a timely and meaningful implementation, the E-Mexico program could improve the efficiency and certainty of commercial and governmental dealings and bolster Mexico's diminished faith in free markets and liberal democratic values. The accomplishment of these advances could, moreover, confirm Mexico's commitment to confronting the technological challenges of the future and protect its place in an increasingly competitive global economy. This progression, viewed from a long-term perspective, would be optimal insofar as history teaches that the strongest democracies are not those accomplished by fiat, but, rather, those that represent organic out growths of development.

Mexico's failure to take advantage of the developmental opportunities made possible by the Internet, considered in light of the cyclical nature of history in Latin America and the immediacy of the economic crisis produced by the terrorist attacks of September 11, 2001, will likely facilitate either a perpetuation of the status quo associated with the country's currently incomplete economic, political, and legal transformation or, in the worst case scenario, a partial or full return to previously discredited policies and perspectives.

E-Readiness: Challenges in Southern African Development Community (SADC)

ICT is a key weapon in the war against world poverty. When used properly, it offers huge potential to empower people in developing countries to overcome development obstacles, to address the most important social problems they face and to strengthen communities, democratic institutions, a free press and local economies. Yet, the reality of the digital divide is that a gulf exists between the potential of ICT and the actual levels of ICT use in developing countries.

World leaders in government, business and civil society are considering how best to harness the power of information and communications technology (ICT) for development. Current thinking on the topic often frames the discussion in terms of "e-readiness", or how ready a country is to gain the benefits offered by ICT generally in terms of policy, infrastructure and ground-level initiatives.

Three key factors motivate developing country decision-makers to improve e-readiness and promote the adoption of ICT in their countries:

— ICT promises enormous benefits as part of the solution to economic and social problems by empowering people in developing countries to help themselves.

— Countries face the threat of being left further behind if they do not address the growing digital divides both between and within countries. It is increasingly clear that ICT alone is notenough to solve long-standing imbalances, and can exacerbate existing inequalities if not appliedwisely.

— International leaders, foreign donors and lending agencies are increasingly requiring recipients to integrate ICT into their development and aid programmes.

Often developing country governments tackle e-readiness by focusing on either the need to improve the e-commerce capacity of the business sector or the need to improve access to ICT in disadvantaged communities. However, economic and social goals are interdependent and the relationship between them is complex. For example, social goals must incorporate business growth and the use of ICT as part of a larger vision, towards broader benefits for people.

However it is measured or approached, the broad range of factors that influence e-readiness are interconnected and the relationship between policy, infrastructure and ground-level initiatives are inextricable. Education is an excellent example of an issue that affects all areas. Education is central to the development of e-ready human capital, which is in turn an integral part of the growth of the local business sector and the implementation of programmes at ground-level. It is also a critical factor at the macroeconomic level, for instance where it influences foreign direct investment (FDI) decisions in developing countries.

Many developing country leaders are convinced that ICT use can be an engine for growth and development that will help their nations, and they are ready to drive the necessary changes to make that happen. However, translating a grand vision into practical steps that fit their local context is not a simple matter. They need to have a realistic appreciation for what ICT can - and cannot - do for their countries, and they must lead effectively and bolster public confidence in the path they take.

An e-readiness process based on an objective assessment that leads to sound e-strategies can offer a path for converting good intentions into planned action that brings real changes to people's lives.

E-Readiness in SADC Countries

There is no uniform level of e-readiness or economic and

social development within the SADC. Each SADC member state, and the region as a whole, must take its own path towards e-readiness, and any attempts to impose a single model would prove ineffective. Laws need to be tailor-made to address the unique policy, infrastructure and ground-level realities reflected within each state and the broader regional goals.

While most developed countries are regularly assessed, many developing countries, including some SADC countries, have had minimal or no assessment. Only eight of the SADC member states have been assessed. Most of these assessments are limited in content as they have been conducted through a short summary questionnaire or are merely comprised of non-explanatory statistical data.

South Africa has had six assessments, while Mauritius, Mozambique, Tanzania, and Zimbabwe have each been assessed twice. Botswana, the Democratic Republic f Congo (DRC) and Namibia have had only one assessment each, while Angola, Lesotho, Malawi, the Seychelles, Swaziland and Zambia have yet to be assessed.

Policy environment

There seems to be unanimous understanding among SADC governments about the benefits that telecommunications deregulation and liberalization can bring to the ICT industry, and the need for policy and market reforms. ICT policy reform processes have begun in almost all SADC member countries, but have not yet reached the implementation stage in all. Policy reforms to end monopolies in telecommunications are advanced in

Botswana, Lesotho, Mauritius, South Africa and Zambia.

Although an independent national regulator for telecommunications is still needed in the Seychelles, the telecoms network is fully privatized. For example, the second national operator is 51% foreign owned and has recently been licensed to provide fixed and mobile services.

The finance and banking sectors in most SADC countries are underdeveloped. Botswana, Mauritius, the Seychelles and South Africa, however, have advanced financial sectors, though these are also biased towards urban areas. Civil strife in Angola and the DRC continues to inhibit development in policy, infrastructure and ground-level projects.

Infrastructure development

SADC countries have unequal levels of infrastructure development. Overall, the existing ICT infrastructure is more developed in urban areas. Some countries, such as the DRC, have outdated and costly telecommunications infrastructure inherited from colonial times.

Aggressive infrastructure development is unfolding in Mauritius while Lesotho remains largely dependent on South Africa for electricity supply and transportation infrastructure. Transport infrastructure (roads, railways, harbours) development is uneven and the majority of rural highways are unpaved in most of the region. Large parts of the Angolan railway network are unusable due to landmines.

Ground-level projects

There are a number of initiatives under way at the ground level throughout the SADC region. World Links is working to train teachers and students in the use of technology to improve teaching and learning in South Africa, Mozambique, Botswana and Zimbabwe, with expansion to Swaziland and Tanzania anticipated in 2002.

A number of ICT access projects are run throughout the region by external development agencies such as the United States Agency for International Development (USAID), the World Bank and the Canadian International Development Agency (CIDA), as well as the public sector, such as the Microsoft Digital Villages initiative.

Projects to establish telecentres and other ICT access points are in place in most SADC countries. These efforts complement the initiatives launched by entrepreneurs and other market actors, providing goods and services on a commercial basis to thousands of subscribers.

The Southern Africa Regional Telecommunications Restructuring (SARTR) Project to help member states draft ICT policy reforms is in progress and significant advances have been made in Mauritius, South Africa and Swaziland.

Regional initiatives

Although each country has a unique development path to follow, broader initiatives have also been initiated at the regional level within the SADC. Organizations leading regional efforts in the SADC include Africa Connection, the coalition of Ministers of Communications in Africa, various NGOs and international bodies such as USAID and the International Development Research Center (IDRC).

In particular, a number of regional policy-making efforts are being launched, are under way, and have been completed with the aim to create a harmonized and coordinated approach to ICT policy reform. However, there are low levels of implementation at the national level to put regional agreements into effect. Moreover, some efforts are duplicative.

Regional agreements should be coordinated to ensure they do not duplicate efforts, and they should be implemented at the national level, their effectiveness evaluated, and the best practice lessons recorded for application in other developing countries.

Examples include:

— The SADC Human Resources Sector developed the SADC Protocol on Education and Training, signed in 1997. It promotes curriculum development and training, and coordinates policies, strategies and programmes promoting science and technology.

— The Southern African Transport and Telecommunications Commission (SATCC) formulated the Model Regulatory Framework for Telecommunications in 1998. Of the 14 member states 11 have established and have operating policies and autonomous regulatory authorities. Human resource development in this new field of regulation is a priority for the Telecommunications Regulatory Authority of Southern Africa (TRASA). In the remaining countries, progress in the application of the frameworks is in an advanced stage.

- The Southern African Telecommunications Association (SATA) obtained agreement on the GSM standard for SADC countries . SATA handles issues such as: technical standards, tariffs, sub-regional information infrastructure (SRII), cross-border investment (satellite technology) and public/private partnerships.
- TRASA has developed the Model Telecommunications Bill as well as regional guidelines on interconnection,tariffs and the frequency band plan. TRASA has also produced draft guidelines on universal access and services, licensing policy and implementation strategy in the SADC.
- TRASA has commissioned a project with the SADC and the Development Bank of Southern Africa (DBSA) to establish a database within the region. Information and performance indicators collated on a national level will be fed through to the SADC level to promote informed decision-making.
- Twelve .SADC governments have signed the SADC Protocol on Transport, Communication and Meteorology, published in March 1998. It details the need for a regional telecommunications policy and provides guidelines on issues from universal service, to technical standardization.
- The SADC drafted and adopted the Lusaka 1999 Theme Document: The Challenges and Opportunities of IT for SADC in the New Millennium, at the biannual Ministers meeting.
- The Common Market for Eastern and Southern Africa (COMESA) has drafted a Model Telecommunications Bill.

— Eight of the twenty-one COMESA member states hold dual membership in COMESA and SADC.

— SADC member countries have adopted at presidential level the policy guidelines on Making ICT a priority in turning SADC into an Information-Based Economy produced by SATCC.

SADC countries have three powerful means of directly improving e-readiness and harnessing ICT for social and economic advancement within the SADC region:

(1) establishing the policy framework for action,

(2) building the necessary infrastructure, and

(3) undertaking ground-level projects. Beyond direct interventions itself, the government can also act indirectly by creating a favourable environment for the private sector and NGOs to engage.

SADC governments are urged to promote ICT through dialogue with all stakeholders, and by setting a leadership example through e-government initiatives.A sound ICT policy framework creates a reliable environment within which business and social programmes can thrive.Key issues include: trade agreements and tariff standardization, enterprise and entrepreneurship development, e-commerce promotion and telecommunication liberalization.

ICT infrastructure is the broad foundation upon which business and social programmes are built.It includes basic infrastructure like electricity and transportation, and technical infrastructure like network connections and hardware. Key issues include: physical access to ICT, standards setting and interoperability, and country code top-level domains.Ground level initiatives spread the benefits of technology throughout society and provide a critical connection between policy considerations and the grassroots community.Ground-level initiatives are often driven by national policies, such as in the fields of education, entrepreneurship and healthcare. Key issues include: public access to ICT in disadvantaged and/or rural communities, e-government services, and local economic and enterprise development.

Policy Framework

Actions to promote e-readiness are affected by nearly all aspects of policy extending beyond specific ICT policy considerations, and ranging from digital signatures to collective bargaining to general macroeconomic policies. The relevant fields of policy to be considered can be generally grouped as follows:

— *Macroeconomic policies:* Fiscal stability, international coordination, customs standardization, tariffs and trade barriers, foreign direct investment, etc.

— *General industrial policies*: competition policy, taxation, defragmentation and free market considerations, labour policies, professional/vocational training, economic empowerment, collective bargaining and brain drain counter-measures

— *Sector specific policies*: e-commerce legislation, banking and financial sector structures, standards setting, telecommunications liberalization.

Macroeconomic policy issue: Trade agreements and tariffs standardization

(a) *Widely agreed policy recommendation*: Views on free trade agreements and tariff standardization vary depending on the economic context within which standardization is considered. Most countries generally perceive that standardization strengthens cooperation and unity of member states in trade areas; promotes the flow of trade and investments; protects members against unfair deals and exploitation by non-members in trade; and prevents competition between member states to avoid weakening the development community.

(b) *Key proponents of this recommendation*: ICT business community, Global Business Dialogue on e-commerce (GBDe), Organisation for Economic Co-operation and Development (OECD), World Bank, Telecommunication Service Providers, General Agreement on Trade and Tariffs (GATT), WTO (World Trade Organization).

(c) *Issues affecting application in developing countries*: By definition, tariff standardization will enable greater cooperation between SADC states. However, differences in local economic development levels and individual trade arrangements do not create an environment conducive to tariff standardization. Standardizing existing tariff agreements between South Africa and the European Union to include non-signatories of the agreement may be economically detrimental to the non-beneficiaries or smaller SADC members. Tariff standardization in regions of unequal economic development tends to favour the economically stronger states without fostering domestic growth in the economically weaker states in the region.

(d) *Recommended way forward*: Applying standard tariffs between unequal players tends to exacerbate existing inequalities and is unlikely to produce equitable outcomes. Emphasis should be placed on establishing coordinated political and economic fundamentals before applying standardized tariffs ultimately resulting in longer-term regional integration (as in the EU harmonization process). The SADC is struggling to establish and enforce acceptable political and economic basics among its members (political and/or economic turmoil in Angola, the DRC and Zimbabwe are examples). Tariff standardization should only be applied when common minimum levels of development are reached (these criteria should be debated and agreed upon by SADC states).

General industrial policy issue: Enterprise/ entrepreneur-ship development

(a) *Widely agreed policy recommendation*: The general view is that governments should promote a free enterprise economy, liberalize markets and pass supporting legislation that encourages the development of small, medium and micro enterprises (SMMEs). This is because fostering entrepreneurial activity helps boost economic development and sustainable job creation, and empowers local communities. Supporting training and skills development is required to ensure the sustainability and success of the entrepreneurial projects.

(b) *Key proponents of this recommendation*: Regional bodies (e.g. the SADC), international forums (e.g. World Economic Forum), private sector (e.g. Accenture) and academia (e.g. London Business School and University of Cape Town's Graduate School of Business).

(c) *Issues affecting application in developing countries*: Entrepreneurial activities in developing countries are hampered by high levels of unemployment and illiteracy, and an overall lack of basic skills, accompanied by a shortage of entrepreneurship support and capital. There is international expertise to be shared, but there are few linkages with communities and efforts at ground level to disseminate information in developing countries.

(d) *Recommended way forward*: Enterprise and entrepreneurship development programmes should be implemented to help advance ICT, to make ICT access and services affordable, provide employment and reduce poverty. Projects should run in conjunction with skills development programmes and public-private partnerships. Linkages should be established between policy-making and people at the grassroots level. Governments should create a favourable environment for the private sector, for instance by establishing well-designed ICT training and other projects, and introducing open standards for interoperability. Youth entrepreneurship and economic empowerment projects should be priorities.

Sector specific policy issue: Telecommunications liberalization

(a) *Widely agreed policy recommendation*: Telecom liberalization is widely accepted as the best way to reduce ICT prices and drive the widespread use of ICT for society's general benefit. This focuses on privatizing state-owned telecom agencies and making the transition to pro-competitive regulation that encourages new entrants to offer both basic and value added telecom services.

(b) *Key proponents of this recommendation*: ICT business community, GBDe, OECD, World Bank, telecommunication service providers, consumers of telecommunication services.

(c) *Issues affecting application in developing countries*: Telecom workers in developing countries whose jobs are threatened fail to see the longer-term benefits, so they support the telecommunications labour unions that oppose the liberalization of the sector. Governments are faced with the conflicting objectives of satisfying taxpayer (predominantly business community) demands on the one hand, and the demands of the voting majority and trade unions concerned with job security on the other hand. It is important to be aware of the depth of this issue within the national psyche, as many people in developing countries genuinely feel that natural resources (including things like telecommunications infrastructure) belong to the nation.

(d) *Recommended way forward*: Focus should be placed on overall employment gains through deregulation (within telecom services and in the broader ICT and

Internet sectors), to allay union concerns of job security. Retraining programmes are critical to ensure that workers are re-skilled for employment elsewhere. Governments further need to build widespread support for liberalization through public awareness campaigns to impart the positive impact of technology on people's lives.

Sector specific policy issue: E-commerce promotion

(a) *Widely agreed policy recommendation*: There are differing approaches to e-commerce policy with no general consensus, including on issues related to privacy, data protection, authentication, intellectual property, copyright, computer crime and security. One view generally supports regulation and enforcement by government; another view generally holds that the industry should self-regulate. An amalgamated third view is the preference for co-regulation over the two extremes of industry self-regulations and government-imposed regulation.

(b) *Key proponents of this recommendation*: Generally the US view supports the regulation of e-commerce related matters on a sector-by-sector basis, with sector-specific legal protections adopted solely in response to demonstrated cases of market failure. The EU view generally supports strong horizontal rules to prevent abuses and create a predictable legal and regulatory environment for electronic transactions. The amalgamation of these two views shows the recent tendency for government and the private sector to work together to come up with legislation that is both business-friendly and protects consumers, and is increasingly supported by international business and political leaders.

(c) *Issues affecting application in developing countries*: There is a real and perceived lack of trust by local populations towards government due to previous abuses of power and corruption. Concerns exist about government ability to safeguard electronic transactions. The AIDS crisis, for example, heightens fears of data insecurity and risks to personal privacy where medical records might be stored or exchanged electronically.

(d) *Recommended way forward*: Public discourse and broad consultation is needed to build trust. At this stage however, the key point for SADC countries is less about the choice between self-regulation and strict government regulation, than it is about the need to simply have a policy that is clear and enforceable. The adoption of either approach will improve the development of e-commerce. The task for developing country governments is to create an effective policy environment and dispel the uncertainty and lack of trust that is the biggest impediment to e-commerce and citizen use of electronic transactions. In the longer-term, the potential benefits to be had in co-regulation should be revisited.

Sector specific policy issue:Banking and financial sector development

(a) *Widely agreed policy recommendation:* A trusted and stable banking sector is necessary for participation in the e-economy, capable of providing reliable, secure and widely accessible payment systems and lines of credit for entrepreneurial ventures, both in the developing and developed world.

(b) *Key proponents of this recommendation*: International bodies such as the United Nations Commission on International Trade Law (UNCITRAL), the Bank for International Settlements (BIS), the International Chamber of Commerce (ICC), the WTO, business forums, finance departments, banks, financial sector companies.

(c) *Issues affecting application in developing countries*: Electronic transactions have speeded up the process but have brought the added dimension of cybercrime to the table. Developing countries need to be aware of the risks and precautions that go hand in hand with the advantages. In general, there are inadequate payment methods in the region by world standards. And SADC countries have the additional disadvantage that they face a lack of trust in the commercial sector, due to a strong perception that unaccountability and corruption exists in the region at higher levels than in the developed world, when this is plainly not the case.

(d) *Recommended way forward*: It is paramount that developing countries develop trusted and stable banking and financial sectors in order to fully participate in the international economy. Guidance should be sought from the international banking sectors on how to establish stronger local banking sectors, and governments should promote stringent and transparent financial sector guidelines drawn from international best practice and adapted to local conditions. Governments should also promote banking and other innovative initiatives to introduce payment products and options.

Infrastructure

Efforts to build infrastructure in the developing world, both by governments and development agencies, have focused predominantly on providing computer hardware, satellite connections and fibre-optic cabling. While these programmes are necessary, they must be supported by enabling infrastructure, such as adequate banking and transport facilities to enable growth and a continued development of basic infrastructure.

Affordable access to basic technology that is appropriate to local conditions best suits the developing world. Many of these substantive infrastructure considerations are affected by government policy and are influenced by policy prescriptions. Beyond the basic provision of telecommunications infrastructure, there are a number of complementary businesses and processes that need to be in place to allow the ICT sector to grow and to impact the rest of the economy. Governments must recognize that they are dealing with a complex system, and that they have to work in a broad fashion to support all of the actors that are involved in developing, using and exploiting ICT.

The relevant fields of infrastructure to be considered can be generally grouped as follows:

— *Availability of basic infrastructure*:Issues include the distribution of infrastructure along the rural-urban divide (using gross domestic product and poverty levels as indicators), basic electrification, transportation (e.g. road, rail, post), telephony and teledensity levels, universal access projects to ensure basic community access, computer density and available bandwidth.

— *Availability of technical infrastructure*:Issues include physical access and connecting infrastructure (e.g. T-1 lines, broadband access, satellite), hardware (e.g. personal computers, servers, routers), software (e.g. operating systems, applications), other (e.g. radio, television, handheld devices).

— *Access to enabling infrastructure*:Issues include the quality and diversity of service, the number of telecommunication operators, Internet service providers and Internet exchange points. It is unrealistic to expect that development aid, philanthropy or government subsidies will be enough to sustain infrastructure development, whether it comes in the form of donated computers or projects expanding telecommunications networks. At best, these projects can build constituencies for pro-competitive, market-opening policies in key areas (telecom regulation, foreign direct investment, etc.) and build critical mass for demand to support sustainable investment in ICT infrastructure. The implementation work may be undertaken by the public or private sectors or through combined public-private partnerships.

Basic infrastructure issue:Access to ICT

(a) *Widely agreed policy recommendation*:Increased globalization and the international information economy require ready access to ICT and global networks for information transfer and trade. In the developing world, mobile communication devices are regarded as a significant means to extend the information community.

(b) *Key proponents of this recommendation*:International business community, computer hardware and software providers, development agencies.

(c) *Issues affecting application in developing countries*:Given the impact of poverty and infrastructure limitations in rural settings, high computer penetration levels are often not feasible. Further, the whole process of introducing new technology and its cost in the context of social, cultural and technical aspects needs to be taken into account. In this regard, the developing world has shown a great affinity to the uptake of mobile ICT devices.

(d) *Recommended way forward*:Within disadvantaged communities, community-based access to computer resources is more realistic than individual access. Community access points providing desktop computing need to be supported by appropriate training programmes and relevant materials. Greater emphasis should be placed on mobile ICT devices that are increasingly more advanced and ubiquitous in terms of bandwidth, reach and utility. Research should be conducted to look at the potential of mobile devices to leapfrog preceding technologies. Projects to develop and deliver content via wireless applications should run concurrently.

Technical infrastructure issue:Standards setting and interoperability

(a) *Widely agreed policy recommendation*:The adoption of open ICT-related standards, as opposed to set standards, helps ensure the ease of communications and business transactions between countries, without tying countries to a particular solution. The openness and pace of change within the ICT sector mitigates against the effectiveness of set standard.

(b) *Key proponents of this recommendation*:ICT business community, international bodies (e.g. International Telecommunications Union and World Bank), users forums (e.g. International Telecommunications Users Group - INTUG), business forums (e.g. the Alliance for Global Business -AGB), commercial software and hardware providers.

(c) *Issues affecting application in developing countries*:Some view the implementation of a set standard as potentially costly and tightly controlled by developed world countries. Further, internationally accepted standards may exclude the needs of developing countries, as does the current "shortage" of Internet addresses. Others support the view that the adoption of standards can build and increase a common market for a specific technology in a developing country, allowing local or foreign producers to achieve the benefits of network effects and economies of scale in manufacturing.

(d) *Recommended way forward*:Standards setting and interoperability allow for ease of communications and participation in the international e-economy. In practice, however, very few standards exist. Emphasis should be placed on ensuring that technology is interoperable and that the preferred standard is open at least to the extent that it allows different networks/devices/technologies to work with each other. Regarding the "shortage" of Internet addresses, it is recommended that the African Regional Networking Centre (AFRINIC) be supported as the Regional Internet Registry. The Internet Protocol version 6 (IPv6) developed by the International Engineering Task Force (IETF) should be promoted. The strongly focused education of people in standards setting organizations and informed lobbying will ensure that the most optimal standards are adopted. The training of government officials making representations in the ITU is further recommended.

Technical infrastructure issue:Country code top-level domains

(a) *Widely agreed policy recommendation:*The efficient management and functioning of country code top-level domains (ccTLDs) support the adoption of growth of the Internet, bringing economic and social benefits to the region.

(b) *Key proponents of this recommendation:*ICANN, Internet Assigned Numbers Authority (IANA), Internet Society (ISOC), top level domain (TLD) administrators.

(c) *Issues affecting application in developing countries:*A significant percentage of ccTLDs are dysfunctional or non-functioning within Africa, hampering the growth of the Internet. The lack of sufficient data capturing techniques results in incorrect or missing service and information details in the IANA database. Developing countries also have to contend with the lack of an accepted standard for the appointment of TLD managers, and the degree of involvement of government agencies. Even in areas where the Internet is well established, the process of formalizing policy with regard to ccTLD administrations is not transparent or is incomplete.

(d) *Recommended way forward*: Research is required in the areas of ccTLD management. Developing countries must have ownership and manage their own domain names. There is potential for extending the lessons learned in the successful Kenyan ccTLD administration process to other developing countries. The DOT Force project has a focus point of assigning resources to people. It fosters people's participation in fora such as the Internet Corporation for Assigned Names and Numbers (ICANN). This project should be promoted, encouraged and expanded in the SADC region.

Ground-level Initiatives

While a supportive policy environment is essential, and infrastructure provides the necessary foundation for a country's use of technology, ICT must be applied on the ground for the country to realize its benefits in addressing traditional development concerns. Citizens must understand the value of ICT for their lives and be intrinsically aware of the potential for ICT to improve their lives. They must be involved in policy-making and development processes if their support for government reforms that may seem controversial is to be ensured. This will ensure the wide-scale economic and social advancement of the country. The approaches taken to improving e-readiness through ground-level initiatives are about as varied as the perspectives on the problem itself. A wide range of ground-level projects - both current and planned - aim at applying technology to the specific needs of people, from the provision of infrastructure to improving healthcare. The following broad categories represent the kinds of on-the-ground initiatives that should be considered:

— E-government initiatives

— Physical access providers

— Training programmes and e-awareness campaigns

— School computer learning programmes

— Distance education

— ICT support of basic education

— Locally relevant content generation

— Healthcare, particularly telemedicine and HIV/AIDs information dissemination

— Agriculture and sustainable development

Ground-level issue:Public access to ICT in disadvantaged and rural areas

(a) *Widely agreed action*:Experience in this field has shown the increasing necessity of having such access mechanisms made available to underserved communities, and that these services be financially sustainable.

(b) *Key proponents of this recommendation*:International organizations (e.g. ITU, UNESCO, World Bank), international donor organizations (e.g. IDRC), governments and private enterprises.

(c) *Issues affecting application in developing countries*:The sharp uptake of cellular telephone services in

Southern Africa is evidence of a strong desire for developing world societies to participate in the communication revolution. Further, cultures in rural settings are not adapted to the use of explicit, codified information. Programmes and pricing have to be adapted to reflect the usage and content realities of developing countries.

(d) *Recommended way forward*:Emphasis should be placed on sustainable development that will improve the communities ability to afford the services and ensure the viability of the initiative once the donor funding cycle ends. Interest in the services has already been seen. The provision of useful content in these centres will also ensure the higher prioritization of spending on communication services. This coupled with income generating information will help break the lack of sustainability cycle.

Ground-level issue: E-government services

(a) *Widely agreed action*:Best practice has shown that a citizen centric online government presence improves government efficiency and accountability to the population it serves.

(b) *Key proponents of this recommendation*:International organizations (e.g. UNCTAD) and civil society initiatives (e.g. Institute for Democracy in South Africa) support the introduction of government e-initiatives. Governments themselves are increasingly seeing e-government as a means to reach outlying communities.

(c) *Issues affecting application in developing countries*:A lack of existing infrastructure and levels of government corruption do not foster a general will towards e-initiatives. There is insufficient interaction between many of the smaller successful initiatives that take place at the subnational (municipal, state, region) level.

(d) *Recommended way forward*:E-government initiatives should be undertaken in conjunction with general government reforms and accountability initiatives in Southern Africa. Furthermore, e-government stands to make a greater impact in the developing world due to outlying and rural communities that will be reached. National policies should foster and integrate domestic initiatives, and provide them with standardized software only for those functions that are not already being successfully provided locally. Exchange of best practices and lessons learned should be promoted locally, regionally and internationally.

Ground-level issue: Local economic and enterprise development

(a) *Widely agreed action*:Private enterprise plays an important role in developing ICT capabilities and enabling economic and social growth. Access to finance and credit is fundamental for the creation of new enterprise, and the survival as well as growth of the existing ones. A fair and appropriate commercial law and property rights system encourages a trading environment and local wealth-creation. Other important enabling conditions are fair tax regimes, access to ICT products/services, and access to local, regional and global markets.

(b) *Key proponents of this recommendation*:International bodies (e.g. UNCITRAL, BIS, WTO), business forums (e.g. ICC), private sector (e.g. Accenture), finance departments, banks, financial sector companies.

(c) *Issues affecting application in developing countries*:A general view against this argument would come from the proponents of social welfare ideology who believe that service and access provision is a state responsibility.

(d) *Recommended way forward*:E-readiness development initiatives should be accompanied by entrepreneurship development, enterprise development policies and empowerment projects if they are to be sustainable. While it is widely agreed that service and access provision cannot in the long run be a state responsibility, renouncing all state stewardship of the process is equally untenable. Seed efforts (through measures such as fiscal incentives, terms of concessions in privatizations, etc.) have proven to be key components.

Delivering e-Readiness

Having outlined the specific recommendations without outlining a process for implementation would result in another e-readiness report, with concrete suggestions, that failed to effect changes in the lives of the people it sets out to help. This section outlines the practical "how to" process to be followed to implement actions based on locally specific e-readiness strategies. Most countries within the SADC have started along this path, while some still require an initial internal assessment and e-strategy development.

The process of moving from e-readiness to e-strategies to e-actions is harder and subtler than the highly publicized first (and often only) step of making the assessments. For most countries this process is well under way, including the World Economic Forum's broad-based international consultation that provides a forum for the exchange of expertise between and among members of the international community and the developing world.

First step: Do some homework (clarify goals, conduct an appropriate assessment)

Determining which e-readiness assessment tool is appropriate depends on the country's goals for ICT integration, so it is critical that the process begins with a clear understanding of where the country wants to go. There is no objective measure for e-readiness, and all assessment tools have an underlying standard of e-readiness that will necessarily shape the results. Comparisons between countries with analogous political, social and economic landscapes can provide useful benchmarks and clues for how to set appropriate goals. Plans that set unrealistic goals, or make unrealistic comparisons, are doomed to failure from the outset.

Second step:Draft a strategy

The action plan must outline concrete steps toward ICT integration goals, including specific policy measures, business initiatives and development programmes that are to be undertaken. It must consider who can implement them and how to engage the appropriate participants. It should also set a time frame for implementation, and determine the oversight and evaluation processes. It must include specific actions to address the needs and views of the relevant constituencies in a balanced way, such as consumer rights, business and labour. Critical success factors need to be clearly outlined, as well as checkpoints for measuring advances and making further informed decisions.

Third step:Implement your strategy with concrete actions

The implementation process is by far the most difficult step, and is also where the most help is needed, both in establishing the process and creating awareness. Yet there are relatively few resources offering advice and expertise to assist governments. While there is no universal method for achieving e-readiness, a few general principles and best practices are emerging that can help countries focus their efforts and effectively harness ICT in the long term.

Practices for achieving e-readiness

1 *Catalyse action throughout society*. Governments should realize that they do not have to carry the burden alone. Government has the unique ability to lead the way while facilitating others to expand the scope of activity and become involved in the process. Stakeholders in the private sector, academia, community organizations and in local government should be encouraged to get involved in the process

and start their own initiatives within the context of the national e-strategy, drawing on their own expertise and perspectives. Critical bottlenecks can be identified allowing for concerted and urgent action to remove them. If government, business and societal leaders champion the cause, their support can be cascaded down through the various levels beneath them. But to achieve this, these same individuals must fully understand the benefits and opportunities that ICT can offer.

2. *Seek public support for the e-readiness plan by helping citizens understand the potential benefits of ICT for their daily lives,and by involving the private sector.* Ground-level pilot projects can be used to explore the options for improving e-readiness, while demonstrating the value of ICT to citizens, winning public buy-in and gaining the participation of all stakeholders. It is important to establish relationships between the various groups that will foster technology use, facilitate productive local use of technology to generate demand for content and services developed and delivered through technology, and demonstrate this demand to the public and private sectors to cultivate a self-sustaining economic environment. Only with broad consultation can all levels of society benefit from the introduction of ICT. This will also ensure that the private sector is involved in addressing the digital opportunities presented, and involvement at the grassroots level will ensure public support for government policies.

3. *Establish links between on-the-ground efforts and policy-making processes.* Both ground-level initiatives and policy reform are necessary, and information flow

between them will make both approaches more effective. Many ground-level programmes are limited by the lack of a supportive legal and policy framework. Most policy-making processes related to ICT issues would benefit from a clearer understanding of how policy affects the technology end user at ground level. Unfortunately, there are few models that effectively bring the two together. Government, business, society and technology users must understand and acknowledge each other's position and responsibilities.

4. *Establish and continue a feedback process throughout implementation.* There must be an independent review of the process, and a continued dialogue between the various stakeholders to make sure their needs are being taken into account. Clear critical success factors and checkpoints identified in the e-strategy to measure advances will provide these feedback mechanisms.

5. *Coordinate and avoid duplication of efforts.* Efforts to improve e-readiness and narrow the divide must be coordinated nationally and internationally. It is difficult to estimate the number of governments, businesses and non-governmental organizations (NGOs) that are involved in these initiatives. The majority are involved unilaterally, and as a result there is duplication of effort and scarce resources are wasted. It is important to assess the picture as a whole and identify actions that will have a catalytic effect and greater spin-offs. Consider how elements interact with each other and focus on the initiatives with the greatest impact on transformation. For example, within Southern Africa, the great uptake of

mobile communications means that mobile initiatives will have a larger impact.

6. *Establish national vision and leadership at the highest levels of government.* This requires identification, through consultation between the government, industry, civil societies, communities and other stakeholders, of local and national priority areas of development, followed by a programme of action and clear plans on implementation (and delivery timetables), as well as evaluation and enforcement mechanisms.

7. *Identify levels of priority for urgent and longer-term actions.* On the basis of unequal resources and levels of development in each member state, it would be unrealistic if not imprudent for all countries to aim for a quantitatively uniform set of goals in a uniform space of time. Country-specific short-term, medium-term and long-term achievable goals should be identified. Programmes of action with enforcements and the regular evaluation of progress should be drawn up and carried out. Countries should adhere to the plan of action unless it needs improvement or revision.

8. *Strengthen institutional capacity.* This refers to state, business and private institutions. A stable political environment and the rule of law are the building blocks upon which institutional capacity can be built. Enabling commercial laws and economic policies (including tax, tariffs, import and export laws) are crucial for the success of business institutions. When e-assessments are conducted in the SADC, countries have rated low on human capital, which is significant for institutional capacity. Policy on and a culture of

regular training for employees and ICT professionals in institutions is needed. Regular research programmes on updating institutional capacity to modern innovations should become the norm.

9. *Collaborate regionally and harmonize regional policies especially in telecommunications infrastructure.* Without implying the application of model laws, member states should harmonize economic and trading policies, as well as minimum ICT development levels if they are to develop as a regional force. Bilateral agreements between countries can supplement SADC guidelines towards this end. Member states should also participate in efforts to share information, for example by participating in the TRASA project to develop a data bank for the SADC to support informed decision-making. If all states contributed regularly, the levels of policy implementation could be recorded and tracked in a dynamic manner that enhanced further regional cooperation. The SADC has the opportunity to draw upon lessons and expertise garnered in the developed countries. But it is paramount that these international developments are tailored to apply to domestic circumstances.

10. *Simultaneously address traditional development and e-readiness issues.* Traditional development initiatives and e-readiness can no longer be separated as an either-or situation. Both are required to ensure equitable and sustainable development in Southern Africa. Further, if harnessed effectively, ICT can bridge pre-existing divides along cultural, racial, gender and socio-economic lines. Emphasis on traditional development concerns of rural electrification, basic education, primary healthcare, access to transport routes and basic telephony will

ensure that governments do not attempt to create an e-ready society in a vacuum. It will help ensure that the developments are taken side by side. Attempts to create an e-ready society will be fruitless and ineffective otherwise.

11. *Form partnerships.* Broad consultation and cooperation between the public and private sectors and the formation of Public-Private Partnerships (PPPs) allows governments to take advantage of private sector skills and know-how, improve the efficiency of service delivery and gain access to finance for new investments. If well designed, PPPs can bring improvements in the quality, availability and cost effectiveness of services. Various successful public-private partnerships have already been instituted within the SADC to address substantive concerns within policy, infrastructure and ground-level initiatives, including:
    - SADC plans for regional economic development and integration stress strategies such as export-oriented industrialization and Spatial Development Initiatives (SDI). The SDI is a programme initiated in 1995 by the South African Department of Transport and Trade and Industry
    - A key to the implementation of SDIs is the formation of PPPs in order to finance infrastructure development. A most prominent example of such a PPP in the region took place in the Maputo Development Corridor (MDC). The MDC, with the MOZAL Project, a Mozambican PPP initiative to stimulate local economic development, is the most advanced SDI in Southern Africa. Lessons learned from this SDI are expected to lead the way and set

the tone for socio-economic development in Southern Africa and the African continent.

— A number of SADC states have started initiatives towards PPPs. This has been set against a backdrop of past policies that severely restricted the use of private sector resources, and many prejudices and misconceptions remain.

— In January 2001, the South African Department of Finance produced a Strategic Framework for Delivering Public Services through Public-Private Partnerships , set up a PPP Unit in the National Treasury and spearheaded a number of projects. On a national level, partnerships have included the Dolphin coast water concession and the building of national toll routes.

— The World Bank has published "Toolkits" intended to assist a state with preparation for PPPs.

12. *E-readiness is about more than adopting model laws.* Model laws are not enough - there is a need for local solutions, that a country will buy into and that meet local needs. Model laws are often instituted with the good intention of addressing a common problem faced by both the developed and developing world, or a problem specific to the developing world context. However, these are often inadequate because they simply are not aware of the existing laws, political tensions and economic environment of the country. Instead of model laws, guiding criteria for drafting tailor-made policies, including international best practices, and a clear path for implementing these policies will help meet the goals of delivering economic and social advancement.

Vision to Implementation

On Tuesday, June 18, 2002, the World Bank hosted a workshop on E-Government, focusing on implementation challenges. Several officials responsible for Canada's - well-known Government On-Line (GOL) initiative shared their practical experiences and insights, along with Bank staff and select representatives from IT companies working on e-government projects in developing countries. The workshop examined the characteristics of successful e-government applications (and identified potential pitfalls) for improving governance, service delivery, and economic competitiveness. The workshop was organized in partnership with The Knowledge Centre, E-Government Services Sector of Public Works and Government Services Canada. Synthesizes the lessons learned from the Canadian government experience and how these lessons relate to and differ from the experiences of developing countries.

Strategy for Online Government

The Canadian government embarked on e-government with an aim to improve public service for Canadian citizens. The Canadian government sought to enhance public services so that they could offer similar types of quality and efficiency that the private sector in Canada provide to Canadian citizens. The aim was to provide Canadian citizens with an additional avenue by which to interact with government at the time and place of their choosing and in the language of their choice - French or English. There are two targets are identified.

— The government seeks to put the most frequently used services online by 2005.

— The government aims to achieve a ten percent increase in service improvement and customer satisfaction by 2005.

While embarking on this action plan, the Canadian government assessed whether the government and the country was ready for such ambitious targets. The Canadian Government found that there a number of activities and policy frameworks that need to be in place to enable e-government. At a minimum, government should consider the following:

> Setting the course and establishing objectives: In the case of Canada, the objective was to improve citizen service and provide citizens with another channel in which to interact with the government. This differs substantially from other e-government goals, that primarily focus on cost savings.

Determining the state of readiness: The government found that while it needed to invest significantly in the government's ability to provide services online in terms of infrastructure, legal framework, and process re-engineering, the country was ready in terms of the network infrastructure to access services online. Canada is a highly networked country. Low cost telecommunications services has enabled the population to access Internet at an inexpensive cost relative to other countries, where costs have hindered the growth of ICT.

To be able to roll out e-government services, the Canadian prioritized its IT strategy to work on the following areas:

1. Common Secure infrastructure

2. PKI, privacy, and legal framework
3. Information policy that allows accessibility
4. Accountability mechanisms
5. Pathfinder Projects

Up front investment

The government has already invested about $ 280 million (Canadian Dollars) into government online projects with an additional $600 million planned expenditures by 2005 in creating a common infrastructure. The Canadian government spent $65 million on PKI infrastructure and creating a certification authority.

The Government of Canada was able to obtain political buy-in at the highest level. With the Prime Minister's support, the government was able to mobilize political leadership within the government, bring internal stakeholders together and select champions within the government that would raise awareness, sustain commitment, and help government accomplish its target.

Establishing the boundaries

The government delineated its target environment and decided to roll out e-government services at the national level with a national geographic reach. E-Government would not supplement existing capabilities, rather, it would complement them. The government also decided to structure is services around the services for Canadians, Canadian businesses and for non-Canadians needs. Organizing services through the lens of business and citizen needs would force agencies coordinate to provide services together. It would also require the government to think about how to join-up government from different jurisdictions and levels of government. Often, different services are provided by the national, provincial or local government, and it is up to the citizen to research which departments to contact.

The government proposed a government-wide business and technical architecture. They urged agencies to migrate to a common e-government infrastructure where possible. Agencies were encouraged to share networks and host common applications and incentives such as funding, were provided for joint application development and pilot projects. Shared management of the e-service was also encouraged. The government encouraged horizontal collaboration among stakeholders. Each agency was encouraged to build and govern web content using common look and feel standards. Each web area was assigned a champion. To sustain the culture of change, initiatives were rewarded and those affected by the change were protected. To receive feedback and review, stakeholders were consistently engaged in the process. Citizens were surveyed through focus groups to improve or change the service.

The government set up a new management framework to ensure that these processes were followed. Management working groups were set up according to the following hierarchical structures:

Policy Frameworks and Tools

The Canadian Government came up with the policy frameworks in various areas, including: Privacy, security, information management, service quality, and procurement. Tool kits for government agencies were also developed to provide guidance on common look and feel standards, business transformation, human resources, privacy impact assessment, GOL supply arrangement, and common measurement tool. A frequently used tool kit that has to be followed by all agencies is the Privacy Impact Assessment Policy (PIA): The PIA provides a consistent framework to identify and resolve privacy issues during design of redesign of programs and services. The PIAs are made publicly available. The government requires that an agency or department conduct a PIA in the following cases:

— Increased collection, use or disclosure of personal information

— Broadening of client populations

— Shift from direct to indirect collection of personal information

— New data matching or increased reuse or sharing of personal information

Public Private Partnerships

Government Telecommunications and Informatics Services (GTIS) Branch of Public Works and Government Services Canada (PWGSC), in collaboration with federal institutions have contracted with a large consortium primed by Bell Nexxia to complete the architecture, design and construction of the Government of Canada Secure Channel. Strategic direction and funding for the project is being provided by the CIO Branch of Treasury Board Secretariat (CIOB).

As delivery agent, PWGS is responsible for developing and implementing the Secure Channel. PWGSC will manage the contract with Team BCE, for the Secure Channel, and work cooperatively with them on its architecture development, design and implementation. Key early lessons learned to date for Secure Channel procurement between the public and private sector reflect many of the key successes and challenges in undertaking the management, communications, implementation and evaluation of this important initiative. Some of these lessons learned include the necessity for:

— strong leadership with a shared accountability framework for success of the initiative as a whole with a clear and consistent vision;

— an effective and multi-tiered governance framework, with understanding and trust between the parties, as an essential element during procurement which must be clearly set and planned so that the initiative is implemented efficiently and effectively;

— a business case and policy framework to guide strategic procurements and strategic initiatives

— designing and managing the procurement around clear and tangible outcomes and benefits to be achieved among government and industry;

— contracting at the tactical level which is both flexible and reflects tactical outcomes as success ultimately lies in satisfying tactical needs.

Key Lessons

The government found that clustering services to fit the needs of citizens and business was the appropriate starting point. This created a momentum and allowed for the creation of a culture of change. More importantly, the strategy faced process re-engineering issues head on and challenges dealing with providing integrated services were brought to the table. Many issues such as governance, partnerships, content management, service standards were addressed early on in the planning process. The government found that it is more important to spend time and money on developing back-end infrastructure before embarking on front-end services.

The Canadian government created a common measurement tool to evaluate service improvement. The Canadian government opted to employ public polling firms that would conduct surveys. The firms used a common baseline to measure public services by comparing them to services offered by banks or phone companies and the private sector in general. The government has not currently invested in finding out whether citizens have experienced any quantifiable time and money savings as a result of using government online services.

Cost savings

The Canadian government has not invested in e-government to reduce costs and spending on public services. However, they do envision that once services reach a critical mass, cost saving will be realized. The problem lies in reaching that critical mass. Although access is not a problem, Canadians have yet to embrace interacting with government online.

Usage

The Government of Canada's websites are being visited more regularly. For example, Neilsen Netratings in March 2002 has the Government of Canada and its' websites as one of the 10 most visited web properties in Canada - in the same space as well known sites such as Yahoo!, MSN and AOL. One example which illustrates the delivery of government services on-line is the Canadian Customs and Revenue Agency's (CCRA) NETFILE Project which provides Canadians with a convenient option for filing personal tax returns on-line. NETFILE often receives attention national and worldwide on its initial take-up rate.

Last year, for returns filed in 2001 for the 2000 taxation year, more than 1.4 million tax returns were received through the NETFILE service. This exceeded expectations of the initial take-up rate estimate of 1.2 million for the service. When the CCRA conducted an on-line survey, respondents indicated NETFILE was easy to use and said they would definitely recommend it to other Canadians. The service has proved to be very successful, and CCRA expects that, as electronic commerce grows in popularity, so will NETFILE, attracting more participants each year.

Obstacles

The Canadian government has found that the most difficult challenges are the following:

— Seizing transformation opportunities is difficult - it puts to the test partnerships and commitment to citizen-centered service; and

— That it must now move from information and services that are grouped together to those that fit together.

In summary, these are the critical elements to consider when strategizing e-government initiatives:

— Establishing E-Government national objective

— Building internal commitment and ownership

— Involving constituents and meeting their expectations

— Effecting change in the public sector environment

— Obtaining adequate funding

— Managing complexity, risk and costs

— Establishing an appropriate governance structure

Lessons From Developing Countries

The Canadian model sparked much debate about the experience and goals of Canada and how they relate to the needs and interests of the developing world. Unlike Canada, developing countries have different e-government objectives that are tied to economic development. India for example seeks to increase foreign direct investment, Yemen hopes to help the private sector develop and reduce the burdens placed on the private sector by the government, and other developing countries hope to increase government revenue through e-government.

Self service seems to be an important objective for Canada, while in the developing world, e-government has emerged an assisted model, where intermediaries help citizens interact with government online in public places rather than interacting online from home. In many developing countries, where there are limited channels available to interact with the government, sometimes e-government applications provide the only channel available to a citizen. While the Canadians invested first in reforming the back end processes, many developing countries start with the front-end first.

Since most back-end processes are manual and are difficult to change, the front is developed first to have quick impact and buy-in from officials to reform the back end process at a later stage. Transparency is often an important goal for developing countries, where corruption and lack of knowledge about the way government works has resulted in a poor image of the public sector. While it is not an explicitly stated goal, many e-government initiatives improve government transparency to citizens and enhance internal transparency. In some cases, corruption is reduced as well. E-government in the developing world, provides significant value added, even when only part of the process is automated. For example, publishing of information, such as a tender notice, creates transparency and build public confidence in the procurement process, which is often marred by secrecy and corruption in the developing world. The collaborative strategy, which has produced results for Canada, is comprised of 3 key areas: service improvement to citizens; modernization of the federal Public Service; and integrated service delivery across department and other levels of government. This required a governance model involving technology, service delivery and policy working committees to address cross-jurisdictional issues and identify workable solutions to ensure efficient and effective implementation of Canadian Government On-Line.

This implementation model may represent challenges for developing countries where due to political and infrastructure considerations, much of the initiative and interest for implementing e-government initiatives tends to reside at other levels of government, particularly at the state and municipal levels. While there is certainly a need for developing country governments to come up with a strategy at the central level, the strategy should encourage and not stifle innovation that comes from lower levels of government. In many cases, e-government processes are outsourced because governments do not have the human resource capacity and technical expertise to do everything in-house.

Many governments have outsourced training, data entry to change from manual to electronic processes, network design and maintenance. To ensure sustainability and internal buy-in, the change management and business process re-engineering are not outsourced.

The challenges that remain for the developing world are:

- *Comprehensive electronic reform:* do the developing world governments have the human and technical resources to re-engineer their process?
- *Raising awareness:* citizens need to be made aware and educated on how to interact with government through ICT networks
- Can enough change be accomplished in reforming the culture of public servants which is often tied to rent seeking for political offices and services?
- Pilot projects have successfully showcased the benefits that e-government can offer, but where do

countries go from there, and how do they achieve sustainability?

Centralizing IT departments sometimes creates obstacles in terms of equipment procurement and standardization. In many cases, central IT departments are unaware of the infrastructure challenges and diversity across the different levels of government. Most e-government projects have succeeded because of buy in from the government at the highest level and constant engagement of senior government officials in the different stages of development and implementation.

Bibliography

Asian Communication Handbook. 1998. Asian Mass Communication Research Information Centre, Singapore.

Bangemann Group, 1994. High Level Group on the Infor-mation Society, Europe and the Global Information Society, Recommendations to the European Council. Brussels, May.

Carty, W. 1997. *Challenges to Academic Networks in Latin America,* Infolac, Vol. 8, No. 2, pp. 39–42.

Cerf, V.; Kahn, R. 1974. *A Protocol for Packet Network Interconnection.* IEEE Transactions on Communications, May.

Freedom of Expression on the Internet. Human Rights Watch Special Report, December 1998.

ITU. 1998. Telecommunication Development Bureau. Internet Diffusion Trends. Geneva

Mason, A. 1997. Public Interest Objectives and the Law of Copyright. In: B. Sherman and J. Thomas (eds.), Defining the Public Domain, Special Issue of Journal of Law and Information Science.

Melody, W. H. 1996. "Toward a Framework for Designing Information Policies". *Telecommunications Policy,* Vol. 20, No. 4.

Munk Ris, A. 1997. The Information Welfare Society: An Assessment of Danish Government Initiatives Preparing for the Information Age. In: Brian Kahin and Ernest Wilson (eds.), *National Information Infrastructure Initiatives: Vision and Policy Design.* MIT Press, Cambridge, Mass.

OECD. 1997. Summary of the Telecommunications Act of 1996. Communications Outlook 1997. Vol. 2, Regulatory Annex.

Ondobo, C. 1998. AMIC Annual Conference: Information Technologies Must Complement Traditional Educational Methods. AMCB, Vol. 28, No. 3, May-June.

Proceedings, 1997. Third EU/EEC Information Society Forum. European Parliament, European Commission, Brussels.

Sharma, M. 1997. Communications Technologies in Open and Distance Learning in Asia: The Experience of the Asian Development Bank. Educational Technology 2000: Global vision for Open and Distance Learning, pp. 19–30. Conference papers, Singapore, 15–17 August 1988, Commonwealth of Learning, Vancouver, B.C.

Sixty-Fourth IFLA Council and General Conference, 1998. *Conference Proceedings,* 16–24 August, Amsterdam, Netherlands.

Squire S Anders and Dempsey, 1998. Study on Adapting the EU Telecommunications Regulatory Framework to the Developing Multimedia Environment. A Study for the European Commission. January.

The Digital Age. European Audiovisual Policy. 1998. Report from the High Level Group on Audiovisual Policy. European Commission, Brussels.

Ure J. (ed.). *Telecommunications in Asia: Policy, Planning and Development.* pp. 1 4 7 – 91. Hong Kong University Press, Hong Kong.

Von Euler, M.; Berg, D. 1998. *The Use of Electronic Media in Open and Distance Education*. UNESCO, Paris.

Index

INFORMATION TECHNOLOGY
A Revolutionary Change

INFORMATION TECHNOLOGY
A Revolutionary Change
(In 9 Volumes)

Volume 7
(Networking and Educating Multiculturally)

Editor
RAMESH CHANDRA
Vice-Chancellor, Bundelkhand University, Jhansi (U.P.)

KALPAZ PUBLICATIONS
DELHI–110052

INFORMATION TECHNOLOGY: A REVOLUTIONARY CHANGE

(Information Technology)

Rs. 8000 (Set)
Rs. 900 (Each Volume)

ISBN: 81-7835-201-X (Set)
ISBN: 81-7835-226-5 (Vol. 7)

Published in 2003 in India by
Kalpaz Publications
C–30, Satyawati Nagar
Delhi–110052
E-mail: kalpaz@hotmail.com

Laser Typesetting at: Varsha Graphics, Delhi
Printed at: Mehra Offset Printers, New Delhi

Contents

Preface

The information and communication technologies (ICTS) provides new resources and material for expanding education. The interactive dimension of new multimedia technology can potentially involve students more integrally into historical research and enhance moral understanding, thus providing powerful pedagogical tools to teach tolerance and promote a multicultural and an anti-racist curricula. A mechanistic and all-too-common reductive abstraction of teaching from human experience and multidisciplinary perspectives can be overcome in part through the use of new multimedia as teaching devices.

The net-based education can help access to lived experience, as well as dramatize and concretize basic historical facts and knowledge. Many current criticisms of the role of computer and multimedia technology in the school stem from an inability to grasp the nature and importance of computer literacy and to understand how new technologies can help revitalize education. This failure to embrace new technologies as a teaching device has been preceded by an uneven and never adequate use of film and television material in the classroom.

The use of the most advanced technologies for educational purposes, is beneficial to showing how new technologies can advance and revitalize education for today's student. Creative use of new technologies, of course, depends on those who implement them and how they are deployed. Effective use is nurtured by the convictions and sustained efforts that must accompany projects embodying imaginative teaching designs and programs to further multicultural education and teaching of events, otherwise hard to grasp. A democratic and multicultural reconstruction of education thus requires the commitment and critical intelligence-as well as hard work!-of teachers, in conjunction with the students who so desperately need these kinds of resources to truly learn about the world, and hence themselves and their place in it.

Many educators and critics thus denounce out-of-hand new computer technologies rather than embarking on serious studies of how such tools can be used to enhance education. In a similar vein, criticisms are also proliferating concerning student propensities toward employing the computer, Internet, and the World Wide Web to plagiarize and cheat on term paper assignments, rather than seriously investigating the ways that computers and multimedia could be productively used to advance research and education. Such criticism obscures the real kinds of epistemological and behavioral shifts that an expanding computer and media culture are producing and the need to develop literacies and pedagogies to make use of these technologies for educational purposes.

Editor

1

Networking in Higher Education

Notwithstanding the financial challenges faced by both educational institutions themselves and their suppliers over the last five years, the concept of higher education as a business sector has become firmly established. Indeed, one example of this is University Business's listing of 280 higher education consultants. The range of specialist services offered, including financial aid, marketing, minority issues, technology, management, book shop services, libraries and fund-raising, indicates the degree of 'unbundling' that has occurred within the education sector. A further indicator is that resistance to the business lexicon, has almost evaporated: university committees routinely debate 'product', 'brand', and 'strategic positioning' without irony or inverted commas. Much has been argued in relation to the potential of universities to supplement their income, and work with industry and business through tailoring of programmes and links with corporate training units. Certainly many institutions in the US, as elsewhere, are seeking such business with business.

> However, according to a Corporate Universities Xchange survey, universities have not become a major beneficiary of corporate university outsourcing. Rather, 37 per cent of contracts are with training vendors, which are more 'business-savvy' than universities, and more flexible; only 16 per cent of contracts involve universities.

This should not be surprising: not because universities are reluctant to engage with industry in providing short courses or degree programmes, indeed the evidence is to the contrary, but because so much of the company training market (estimated variously at US$ 66 billion to a low US$ 26.7 billion is simply new product training or low level IT upgrade training. Urdan and Huggen in fact that two-thirds of outsourced training in 1999 was in IT, and of this, only a quarter used technology-based delivery. A full 75 per cent of corporate training was still instructor-led in late 1999. The level of such training might be deduced from the largest expanding area of the for-profit sector: 28 per cent of two-year college programmes are now delivered in the for-profits, according to the Education Commission of the States.

One might observe that IT skills are more properly the preserve of the VET sector, andsome training is company specific. Online or video-delivered programmes arenevertheless a boon in such training, since they can reduce the costs of attendance atprogrammes, typically two-thirds of total training costs. Strategically-governed universities seeking to find alternate revenue sources via vocationally-oriented programmes are increasingly likely to focus on a niche market strategy, 'a selected vertical market', where the institution has a clear advantage through the reputation of a particular course, because so many for-profit providers have entered the market in generic products in narrow fields like business and IT, which were predicted to be the profitable areas.

The University of Pennsylvania's World Campus, for example, has decided on a select range of online programmes, based on its reputation in specific areas such as Adult Education, and Logistics; it also specialises in shorter Certificate level courses, in recognition of the greater attraction of brief commitments in continuing professional education. Carnegie Mellon has leveraged its reputation in electronic commerce. In Australia, some universities have already implemented this strategy, as the University of NSW has capitalised on its reputation in professional tax education and training, or as QUT's Faculty of Information Technology leverages its partnership with Cisco through the Cisco Networking Academy Program. Obviously, the advantage of the niche course approach is that it concentrates resources and staff, rather than dissipates energy and financial resources across the institution, which is the unfortunate effect of many Australian universities' 'flexible delivery' decisions. Alternately, a university could focus on a particular segment of the market, as UoP has captured the working adult with no pretensions to accessing an elite institution, and with the capacity to pay more for convenience. This appears to be an element of the strategy adopted by the Global University Alliance consortium in relation to its online MBA programme.

We observed that a number of e-learning portals has been established to direct potential students to universities on a commission basis. Dedicated commercial sites such as HungryMinds, Edupoint and Headlight have not prospered, partly because so many public sites now list distance education opportunities, and because, as we noted in relation to Western Governors, potential students can go directly to a provider institution's site. In the main, universities have now abandoned the use of portals to advertise and bring students to the institution; Penn State dropped Hungry Minds and other e-learning portals which link to enrolment information, because 'eyeballs do not convert to tuition dollars'. Instead, Penn State uses professional magazines and targeted advertising to professional groups. Often institutions prefer to offer a free introductory module of a programme, which does not attract a fee unless the student wishes to convert it to credit.

One potentially more promising model is the Monster.com launch of MonsterLearning. TMP Worldwide, formerly recruitment company Morgan and Banks, has developed an online resume service which now claims 74.5 millionusers, and a search tool which allows users to access a database of 15 000 awardand non-award online and class-based subjects in Accounting, It and Finance. MonsterLearning will develop a skills gap analysis feature that will then recommend subjects and programmes from its list to resume posters. Education providers pay membership fees of US$2000 to US$50 000 annually to advertise their wares. However, whether such a directive tool will convert into enrolments is a moot point. In any event, universities and colleges may be forced by such activities into spending even more on marketing, although the success of such marketing is not guaranteed, as the Hungry Minds experience demonstrates. Other business opportunities in educational services may emerge. E-learning infrastructure and testing companies have been encouraged by shifts in educational policy within the US and other countries towards a greater degree of accountability from individual institutions in terms of learning outcomes.

In many US states and school districts, mandated standardised testing at specified grade levels determines funding for schools. A national trend to standardised exit tests across higher education, calling into question the autonomy of current accreditation procedures, and the quality guarantees given by individual universities and departments. Since most of these tests are conducted by private companies, such as CTB/McGraw-Hill, profitability in this sector is expected to soar, according to most education analysts, with concomitant effects on the profitability of software companies supporting the data processing of results. There are clear synergies for publishers acquiring test instruments in textbook and online resource sales, as well as professional development programmes for teachers. For example, Harcourt, a subsidiary of Reed Elsevier plc, publishes the Stanford Achievement Test, the most widely used norm-referenced test in the US, at 15 million students annually. Harcourt has now purchased Classroom Connect, a K-12 provider of both online curriculum materials and professional development for teachers, demonstrating publishers' clear determination to cover the testing, publishing and continuing professional development education market.

> Although it is to be expected that moves to standardised testing will be resisted in the higher education sector, the pressure of high numbers in a mass education system has already increased the use of computerised assessment items, and the difficulties associated with constructing valid and complex tests in markable digital form, would

> suggest that such testing might become more centralised and 'corporatised' through outsourcing to specialist firms.
>
> Combined with corporate universities' activities in workplace education and training, and the trend already noted here for students to prefer short or non-award subjects directly relevant to their work, such activities might suggest that traditional universities may face difficulty in expanding continuing professional education enrolments.

Other business opportunities have emerged through the certification movement, which has strengthened the positions of testing companies, which can offer secure test premises and systems. National Computer Systems, for example, established Virtual Universities Enterprises Authorised Testing Centres, 700 in all, providing for certificated testing for Microsoft, IBM and Novell, among other clients. Companies specialising in test preparation for certification examinations have also spawned, an example being the National Pharmacy Technician Certification, and the public float of the Princeton Review, a test preparation company enrolling 100 000 students annually. The latter has not captured market favour since its June float. It too has diversified from its preparation role: in launching Review.com, it offers a portal to information on financial aid, along with links to its commercial activities. This diversification of business activity within such firms is an indication of the confusion regarding business models that many in the industry are suffering in consequence of the slamming of the door on the equity injections which sustained e-learning service companies until April 2000. Amongst the non-profit education service sector firms, the trend, as in non-profit universities, has been to the establishment of for-profit subsidiaries.

Educational Testing Service, which administers the SAT and Advanced Placement tests, has invested in College Board, which hopes to market recruitment and financial aid information services to students applying for tests via a revamped portal and organising software. Even the philanthropic Sloan Foundation, which had sponsored an online consortium of over 80 colleges and universities (including MIT) offering web-based programmes, tried to market these programmes through the for-profit EduPoint, an aggregator of courses for the corporate market. The latter has not however, been successful. The 'shake-out' predicted by Microsoft's Joe Powell in the BBE, was exacerbated not only by the effect of market forces expected in any emergent industry with excessive supply, but also by the 'irrational exuberance' associated with an over-supply of capital, and the hype of many analysts' predictions of profit in a fledgling industry.

> A strategy among the survivors is cross-ownership, substantial investment and partnerships, such as that between publisher Pearsons and netLibrary, to create (and on-license) digital versions of Pearsons' texts. Pearsons has itself customised the Blackboard platform for its CourseCompass digitised text venture. Yet, as analysts such as Urdan and Huggen point out, 'currently all the players appear to be partnering with each other', and 'part of the value of a partnership is its exclusivity'. The same observation could be made of the multiple partnerships entered into by universities themselves: Columbia's major venture in Fathom competes with its interest in Cardean University, for example, and it is difficult to see how both investments are sustainable.

Most programming in for-profit, corporate and online providers was in the areas of IT, and Business, and that 'soft skills' were difficult to translate into the online platform. Nevertheless, Urdan and Huggen, among others, consider that soft skills training will migrate increasingly to an internet environment. There is little indication of this at present. Two contra-indications in the business of education are the emergence of open source code for many of the functions currently offered by commercial vendors, and the slow emergence of resource banks of teaching materials online. The North Carolina State University My-Library Portal Project allows script downloads in PERL, which may reduce sales as more institutions note the business failures of their suppliers, and either choose to develop their own systems, or choose major suppliers.

The Java Special Interest Group, JA-SIG, a research consortium of major universities, develops and shares applications for use in portals amongst the group, but may distribute its software more widely. Of great interest is MIT's decision to develop OpenCourseWare, a course development and content project to place 2000 subject resources and curricula, including assignment topics, on the web. MIT will make these freely available for use or adaptation. The cost of the project is estimated at US$100 million over 10 years, with some funding coming from private sources. The decision was announced as an altruistic initiative designed to counter commercial exploitation of the internet, in which MIT had a more than passing interest as a result of its research and application in online technologies. Although staff had been widely consulted via a long sequence of seminars on the issues involved, not all staff are convinced of the value of placing materials online, and copyright issues have risen as a concern. However, it is clear that since this is a university-wide initiative, and staff will be employed to assist academics to place their materials online, 'co-ownership' principles will be adopted.

The issue is less pertinent at MIT than elsewhere because there is no intention to profit commercially from the venture. Participation is voluntary, but all staff would be expected to progressively move their materials online, and the ten-year time frame seems likely to make this feasible. Analysts' reactions to this venture are intriguing: Newman (2001) doubts it will dent the commercial content providers' business, since simply posting content does not ensure learning, nor develop the necessary learning community needed to ensure student retention and motivation. Such observations are in distinct contrast to their enthusiasm for stand-alone generic vendor products. A further project, the Open Knowledge Initiative, is being led from MIT, in a consortium of Stanford, Harvard, Wisconsin, Pennsylvania, North Carolina, Dartmouth, and IMS, as well as Cambridge. The intention is to develop a learner management system in open source code for Internet. Interestingly, OpenCourseWare is not committed to using the OKI platform.

The MIT initiative has not prevented MIT from entering other for-profit online ventures, such as its arrangement with the PBS Business Channel to offer Certificates of Completion (not award programmes) in web-based subjects, Internet Commerce and Supply Chain. The subjects consist of two hours per week of streamed video or video satellite delivery, with an additional four hours per week of assignments, over six weeks. Student support is built in, with email discussion groups and telephone tutoring. At the University of Maryland, the Faculty Online Technology Training Consortium has assembled a professional development programme to prepare staff to use online technologies, and to share their teaching and learning materials. The course is freely available.

The organisation is growing rapidly after a slow start. As the responses to AAHESGIT's proposed Open Source Professional Development Environment make clear (AAHESGIT-121: 3/10/01), the financial and cultural challenges posed by open source shared resources are immense. At the same time, 'the spirit of the internet' as a vehicle for freely shared research has been asserted by university and public agency research communities. For physicists, mathematicians and computer scientists, the Los Alamos E-Print Archive has long operated as a free posting and retrieval service for original papers, many already submitted to peer-reviewed journals. Those associated with the database note its altruistic motive, since two-thirds of its 'visits' are from outside the US, and it is considered an essential resource for developing country scientists, where the costs of journals are increasingly prohibitive.

The founder of the archive intends to take the database to Cornell University, and to expand its offerings into other disciplines: Paul Ginsbarg believes that ultimately, the web could function as a first source, 'raw data' archive, freely available, while research articles wind their way through peer review and commercial journal publication. Many academics are now attempting to challenge the commercial publishers' domination of discipline knowledge and the soaring prices of academic journals. One such challenge is an attempt to begin a series of low cost online social science journals which pay for peer review, but which also remain cheap for subscribers by virtue of their online-only distribution costs and CHE online edition, March 9, 2001.

Another is the launch of SPARC, Scholarly Publishing and Academic Resources Coalition, which distributes science journals to 180 libraries in four continents. SPARC began BioOne, a network which will publish 40 journals online. A UK initiative, the Public Library of Science, supported by scientists from 170 countries, declared a boycott of major publishers, especially Elsevier, starting September 1. Most publishers have refused the scientists' demands for free online access to full text journals within six months of hard copy publication. It will be interesting to observe the outcome.

> It is apparent that the imperatives of the business of education collide with the ethos of both the academic and the internet worlds; there is unlikely to be any short-term resolution to the struggle for academic principles of openness and speedy distribution of research and teaching resources, while so many in higher education see the potential for individual gain in their university-based endeavours.

What has become clearer since the 2000, is that quality online education programmes from 'brand name' institutions have not delivered cost savings at the institutional level. Staffing costs have increased, reflecting both the longer time teaching staff must spend in interactive teaching, and the expense of technical and administrative support systems. The University of Florida's online MBA students pay three times the on-campus tuition fee, reflecting higher delivery costs and a more intensive and interactive teaching strategy. Both Keller Graduate School of Management and UoP, as noted in the 2000, charge more for their online courses, although the profit margin is greater for their online programme.

> Clearly, universities seeking to profit from online programmes face difficult choices in terms of pricing, and pedagogic approach. The mass distribution model of simply putting resources online has not been adopted by reputable institutions, or has not

> been viable where it was used, and the teaching 'service' in the online environment remains the most expensive budget element. This is so even where for-profit organisations, such as UoPOnline and Keller, utilise casual tutor labour.

Some institutions, an extension of their student cohort as a result on online offerings, but numbers remain small. The University of Florida, for example, has a mere 40 students per year in its online MBA, while UMUCOnline 's MBA has 30 students.

> One pertinent observation on the education business supports the warning of Jim Mingle of SHEEO in the BBE, in his concern about market forces pressing on education provision: 'the market won't support research, except in the most applied way, the arts and sciences, small institutions, programmes and fields, and students who can't pay full price - low income students'. Sir James Watson, VC of Brighton University in the UK, in a paper on funding for the education sector, noted that in London particularly, 'universities with the most progressive social missions are beginning to look like market failures' as a consequence of low enrolments and students choosing 'better brands', as all institutions seek to increase enrolments in a declining market. A number of UK progressive universities whose focus has traditionally been on marginalised students, comprehensive programme offerings, supplementary learner support, and strong teaching profiles, are facing mergers or closure.

The Borderlessness of Education

The conditions that impelled predictions of a borderless education industry in the late 1990s have increased in intensity since our 2000 publication, notwithstanding the failures of many online eduction ventures. Twigg, that 63 per cent of all colleges and universities in the US are already engaged in distance and distributed eduction at some level, with another 31 per cent planning to do so. 'National' companies have become international in focus; international organisations such as the World Bank and the OECD have argued the case for online education and training as a developmental responsibility of donor countries; internet connections have increased even in developing economies; 'globalisation' has become a topical issue of concern to citizens and politicians as well as economists. Small scale examples of internationalisation by universities abound, although these are usually at the level of physical programmes: staff and student exchanges; curriculum 'export' to a partner institution; and physical 'branch campuses' as with Cornell's planned medical campus in Qatar at that country's expense; and Sylvan's purchase of several overseas institutions.

The National University of Singapore plans a 'reverse' move to the usual pattern: the establishment of a college specialising in IT in California's Silicon Valley, while the Indian government reportedly has committed US$14 million to MIT to co-develop Media Lab Asia, to develop technologies of benefit to the rural poor. Other ventures are in embryonic, even test-tube stage: Universitas21, as noted, has achieved its student and staff mobility aims, but remains in development mode; UoPOnline remains largely a continental American operation. However, higher education has far to go before it can boast of being a global industry, and attaining the level of internationalisation achieved by top US companies, which glean 30-65 percent of their revenues offshore. Yet there is no shortage of contenders for global education provision, with one of the most ambitious being the UK's proposed e-university. Further, the US university sector remains in the early stages of understanding globalising influences on higher education, as the Ford Foundation's 2000 sponsorship of The Futures Project: Policy for Higher Education in a Changing World at Brown University demonstrates. A booming economy, a large population, and low unemployment made inward-looking policies and complacency inevitable. However, the changing economic climate is forcing even non-profit institutions to look to expansion and an external clientele.

The US for-profit universities and the now privately-owned GATE remain the major lobbyists for faster resolution of the WTO 1994 agreement on recognising education as a tradeable commodity. There are complex regulatory and international issues involved, which go to the heart of national interests, quality regimes, and funding mechanisms to support the public subsidy of education. Professional associations such as accountants and architects are already smoothing different national accreditation requirements, and it may be that their moves, shaping as they do higher education curricula, will do more to standardise higher education provision and global education than the ongoing negotiations over GATS. Nevertheless, there remains strong opposition to global education at the labour level, with Education International, a confederation of 300 teacher unions recently reasserting their rejection of the WTO stance. Whatever the truth of statements such as Urdan and Heggens observation that 'The world is hungry for education made in America', there are few indications of a stampede to the trough. At Pennsylvania State

University, where its World Campus was launched to great fanfare in 1998, only 3 per cent of the 3500 annual student enrolments are international, with the great majority from the eight most populous states surrounding Pennsylvania, and one-third enrolled in a non-credit WebMaster Certificate level programme, WC's most popular programme.

World Campus also benefited from a US$982 000 grant from the Learning Anywhere Anytime Partnerships (LAAP) programme to develop their courses, with in-kind support from Apple and Sun. Indeed, it cannot be stressed enough how much technological initiatives in US universities have benefited from relatively enormous grants by Australian standards, and from the generosity of philanthropic foundations. The Alfred P. Sloan Foundation alone has provided over US$35 million in grant support for online education ventures since 1992, most of them using an interactive not independent learning model. While some education consultants continue to 'talk up' the potential of global markets in education, and organisations such as the World Bank promote the use of 'exported' educational products while insisting on at least partial local ownership of the 'distribution channels', or local learning centres, other observers are more cautious. Stokes (2001), for example, tellingly places a question mark in his assessment of the potential of a globalised education sector, and his list of 13 major global 'players' includes only one company whose core business is degree education, Apollo, owner of UoP. The others are publishers, or training/service companies such as SmartForce.

The challenges associated with global expansion should not be underestimated, notes Stokes, and include the difficulties of intellectual property developed through joint ventures with local companies in states where the legal system is yet to offer protection, repatriation of profits in some regions, as well as adaptation of curriculum. Stokes' summary does not consider the cultural, pedagogical and philosophical issues associated with distance education in many cultures, we believe these remain pertinent. One company has recognised some of the 'soft issues' involved in borderless education: Sylvan's international strategy is to focus not on its content divisions, but on its service operations, since these are 'exportable'. Whether they too are culture free is a moot point. The pull of a global presence in higher education makes membership of consortia of institutions with similar interests an attractive possibility for some in higher education. Consortia have been made possible by internet-based communication, and made necessary by the high cost of multimedia and web-enhanced teaching and learning.

Although the majority of these consortia are still national, there is an increasing trend, often led by institutions outside the US but including several US institutions, to international collaboration. One national example is JesuitNET, a three-year project of 25 US Jesuit institutions, including the long-established distance education Regis College. The Association of Jesuit Colleges and Universities has partnered with IBM to develop a software programme, which can record how students solve problems online, how it might assess online competency-based education (a particular strength at Regis). AJCU will jointly develop online subjects incorporating the particular emphases of Jesuit educational philosophy.

Although immediate benefits are expected for the

subscribing members in terms of sharing resources and increasing student numbers across the consortium, a longer-term strategy is commercialisation of the software. Blackboard is the platform used. Eleven British and US research institutions, including the Universities of Bristol, Manchester and Illinois at Urbana-Champaign, have formed the Worldwide Universities Network to bid for a portion of the UK e-university, but there are also plans for a web-based graduate school by 2002. Partnerships for teaching are another emerging feature, for example, the University of Pennsylvania's Wharton Business School has announced a partnership with France's INSEAD campuses in Fontainebleau and Singapore to expand their global continuing and executive education. Franchising and licensing of programmes are other strategic moves employed in the quest for global expansion. For example, Scottish Knowledge, part-owned by News Corporation, markets Heriot-Watt University's web-enhanced ScholarTutor university preparation programme. The latter has been adopted by the Open University of Malaysia for its foundation Science course.

Some interesting data are emerging regarding the likelihood of long-term interest in global university degree programmes. As many governments begin to respond to internationalisation and globalisation agendas, and students themselves become more mobile, student flows have increased. Although postgraduate study at centres of international excellence has long been a feature of tertiary education, especially for those intent on an academic career, directed mobility programmes are now attracting undergraduate students in larger numbers. UK student numbers in US institutions have steadily increased to over 8000 in 2000, half undergraduate. Johnson reveals that Science and Engineering postgraduates (including IT students) in both the UK and US are increasingly seeing research study as an entrée into the labour force of the host country, with, for example, no Irish students returning to Ireland within 12 months after completion of the doctoral degree, and in the US, low return rates for Indian and Chinese graduates. This may suggest a strategic motivation on the part of students seeking better employment prospects to seek migration via further studies.

This would militate against take-up of online degree programmes, leaving the field to the short coursework programmes also targeted by the corporate and for-profit providers. Moreover, a number of commentators are noting more determined moves by many countries to develop their own distance learning initiatives. China Central Radio and Television University, for example, with 1.5 million students and a synchronous broadcast model, is now training staff at the Open University of Hong Kong, in an effort to introduce more flexible delivery modes. However, online provision remains a challenge in China as in most developing countries, where computer access is a major inhibiting factor in mass education efforts. Following the January 2001 founding of the Arab Open University, which has links to the UKOU, Jordan's public Hashemite University recently announced plans for a US$20 million Arab American University for Distance Learning, to begin in late 2002, specifically catering for the Middle Eastern population as well as Arab expatriates; it is to provide a Muslim perspective but to specialise in IT.

Although Hashemite currently has only 7000 students, the Jordanian authorities predict the external university will enrol 10 000 students in its first year. Half of the money would come from a private Kuwaiti firm. This announcement of a 'virtual university' sponsored by the state echoes the comments made above in relation to state belief in the potential of virtual universities, with assistance from private partnership funding. Apart from Thomson's links with U21, there is little evidence of much enthusiasm from private equity partners for global education ventures. More countries are also imposing stricter controls over foreign distance programmes. South Africa has strict regulations in place for higher education institutions, and India is also in the process of demanding registration of all providers. Brazil has refused to recognise any foreign-sponsored qualifications. In Malaysia, tax breaks previously available to parents sending children abroad for education have been withdrawn, forcing more students to remain in country, and more to consider the distance programmes set up by government.

There are other cautionary signals in the take-up of global distance education provision. The first is the questionable demand for for-credit higher education in developed economies in an increasingly fragmented Knowledge Economy. The growth of the for-profit market in higher education was predicated on a population demographic of advanced economies that suggested that the baby boomer group, excluded from prior higher education, was increasingly recognising the value of higher education for its upwardly mobile aspirations. There were also predictions of higher education participation rates among the bulge of 'echo boomers', attracted by the 'private good returns' of further education and the increased access available in a mass education system as a result of heavy investment in the university system in the 1970s.

However, recent figures from the UK indicate that the early rush of mature age students to part-time programmes has declined as a result of the introduction of tuition fees, and a buoyant labour market. Goddard analyses a Funding Council, Supply and Demand in Higher Education, indicating that growth in full-time undergraduate enrolment had declined since 1993 despite a population growth in the school leaver cohort, that part-time undergraduate and sub-degree level enrolments had not achieved their targets in 2000, and mature age numbers fell 1995-2000, although enrolments have risen slightly in the new academic year 2001. In the later age group, Engineering and Technology courses enrolments dropped, along with numbers in the physical sciences, with only small growth in IT and medical studies. Non-traditional populations were still not seeking further education, notwithstanding the advent of new institutions and alternate pathways to higher education, and the expanded places in new institutions. Rather, expansion was placing pressure on old 'brand name' institutions.

The same decline in enrolments was seen in 2000 figures in further education, with drops in both school leaver and adult cohorts, down by 1.8 per cent. This does not, however, gainsay the demand in the developing world. The second factor is the limited take-up of exclusively online degree study, even from 'brand' institutions, as employers question the credibility of solely online programs for developing soft skills. 37 per cent of Human Resources officials were reluctant to accept online graduate degrees, prompting Cathy Gunn, the Director of the Illinois Virtual Campus, a broker for 62 state colleges and universities, to decry the public perception that e-learning is 'easier', and to initiate a massive marketing campaign for distance education.

The failure of a supply-driven model, at least in generic online products such as the MBA. At a national US level, online and distance programmes constitute only 2.5 per cent of total MBA enrolments in 2000, with more than half of these in UoP's programme, reflecting both the attraction of its brand in the convenience rather than prestige market, and UoP's superior focus on online delivery.

There are several elements in the credibility problem suffered by distance award programmes. The first relates to the perception that online education, like distance education more generally, is a poor experience:

> People have taken to the net quicker than any previous household technology. Still, e-education lags far behind other online activities, such as gathering travel or health information. The promise of e-learning is great; the barriers, beginning with public trust are as many.

The founder of smarthinking, the troubled online tutorial company, observed in an interview that 'some people thought it would be easier to change people's behaviour than it really is. The technology is there, but the economics, the organisation, and the behaviours of people take far longer to change.... Technology is the easy part.' Even in non-award programmes, and notwithstanding early claims of massive savings to corporations, few e-learning vendors have been able to verify purported ROI on investment in learning programmes. Indeed Chen in his Eduventures, on Return on Investment, argues that only one case was able to demonstrate convincing ROI for e-learning programmes, and only four companies, IBM Mindspan, Digital Think, Docent and Saba, were able to assist corporations in even evaluating ROI. In corporate America, the effectiveness of e-learning was still largely determined by take-up across the organisation, and reduced travel/accommodation costs, not insignificant measures, but hardly reflective of efficacy.

The second relates to online technology itself. BBE noted that notwithstanding the hype and boosterism attached to online distance education, videoconferencing, television broadcast with audio-response capacity, and teleconferencing remain popular forms of delivery for 'distributed' learning, because the nature of such distance modes does not challenge the 'comfort zone' of either staff or students, since it replicates the oral/visual lecture/tutorial format. It has been argued that the numbers involved in such delivery modes are higher than those in web-based only programmes. Shive and Dirr found that live interactive video remained the most popular delivery mode at the end of the century. Certainly the University of Maine's distance enrolments reflect a telecourse enrolment of four times its online enrolment numbers, though the latter are growing sharply. Other institutions are making the difficult decision to abandon 'old technology' and migrate their video segments to the web, but the demand remains, and the technology is reliable and cheap for those institutions which invested in it in the 1970s. One large education provider, Learning Tree International, insists that no successful business model for e-learning has emerged, with the result that it would remain in classroom-based provision.

BBE noted that non-credit certificate programmes were already emerging as the most likely form of education for the business market, with the promise of the internet for 'anytime, anywhere, any place' study being more attractive for acquiring workplace-related skills through non-credit short courses in the training sector. This observation is supported by the recent work of Cliff Adelman, of the US Department of Education, in his research on certification programmes offered by software and hardware companies through franchise or internal training programmes. One recent indication that online certification programmes may enter Australia outside the established Novell, Microsoft and Sun distribution channels, is the recent announcement by eWebUniversity, an e-learning platform and content provider, that it would partner with San Jose State University to deliver IT certification courses into Australia. Details are as yet very sketchy, but Australia's shortage of IT specialists has led to perceptions of an under-served market. This trend to certification is a reflection of the move to knowledge management within organisations, and measurable outcomes from training, although a gap remains between ascertaining that employees have in fact learned something via assessment of their capabilities, and the ROI on training. However, there may be signs that the certification of IT skills is plateauing as well.

The Information Technology Association of America in April released a study. The number of job vacancies in IT dropped 44 percent from 1999, although this still left an estimated 425 000 jobs unfilled because of a lack of qualified staff. The best job preparation for skills and knowledge in software engineering, database development and technical writing, though graduates of private technical schools offering certificates were preferred by employers for network design and digital media production. More significantly, non-IT companies preferred employees with a degree qualification, while IT companies (those developing IT) ranked certifications at least as highly as a degree. The ITAA pointed out that there are 300 000 more non-IT than IT companies in the US, indicating that the employment preferences of the majority of employers should be a greater guide to work preparation for most students. In summary, as recession looms in most economies in late 2001, it remains to be seen whether fear of unemployment will translate into a growth in education and training enrolments. Most educators and analysts suggest a surge as unemployed adults retrain, but increased personal contributions to tuition in major economies, and higher tuition costs, may well deter individuals, and as argued above, corporations have resorted to layoffs rather than retraining, and are likely to delay the new product development which drives most company training.

Staffing issues

In 2000, we noted the growth in the number of part-time and casual teaching staff within US higher education institutions. This trend has increased, with part-timers constituting 45 per cent of staff 1998-99, compared to 40 per cent in 1992-93 and salary gaps widening between private and public institutions, and between tenured and non-tenured staff. One US study found that 34 per cent of all undergraduate subjects were taught by graduate students. In reaction, Teaching Assistants, who are in most cases graduate students with high teaching loads, have begun to unionise at many campuses, for higher pay and lower contact hours, with some success. There is also a large increase in the number of institutions not offering tenured positions, from 8 per cent of institutions to 14 percent over the same period, reflecting the funding pressures on non-profit universities to alter employment conditions. In Australia, the casualisation of the workforce has also increased since the BBE, with nearly 90 percent of teaching-only staff designated as casual, and 18 per cent of all academic staff. Hence the contrast between 'traditional universities' and for-profit institutions in the 2000, has become less stark in relation to the use of part-time and casual teaching staff.

Meanwhile, in corporate universities, staff salaries account for a mere 31 per cent of operating costs, a significant difference from labour costs in more traditional institutions, and an indication that the proportion of institutional costs spent on staffing has some way to go before it reaches this industry level. The debate on the role of the teacher in higher education has intensified as online methods of delivery have become more embedded into standard programmes. As e-learning providers themselves concede the ineffectiveness of many of their earlier stand-alone and generic online courses, it is more widely recognised that quality internet-based learning requires more than 'information delivery', and depends on the interactive dimension provided by a participating teacher, who provides the dialogue that Laurillard has argued is essential for education.

Student Issues

'Convenience', 'student-centred service' and condensed programming are three significant lessons traditional universities have quickly learned from the new providers, as university administrators perceive that higher education is 'a consumer led market'. US research indicating an increased instrumentalist attitude to education, which might suggest even stronger growth in 'no frills' degree provision. Almost two years' worth of experience in student reactions to electronic teaching modes, distributed and online learning, and changes in on-campus attendance patterns. Three significant trends can be discerned.

The first is growing evidence of high attrition, at 60-80 per cent, in asynchronous non-award online generic programmes in IT and business, even where these are supported by employers, to the extent that the Masie Center and the American Society for Training and Development surveyed students and employers, and considered financial incentives might be necessary. Frankola, of NYUOnline, agrees; in her experience, some face-to-face sessions in the course are also vital for completion because of the value students perceive in proximal learning communities. This desire for social interaction may be particularly acute in work-related learning, as suggested by several commentators in the 2000.

Others argue that assessment of company training would increase completion. Both elements of course leach the cost savings that e-learning promised the corporate sector, and eliminate the own-time convenience of asynchronous learning. There is also a growing concern that virtual work-related learning is no panacea for either employer or employee simply because it is 'anytime, anywhere', and thus intrudes into already crowded work and domestic routines. However, were assessment attached to company training, it would increase the pressure on education providers to credit their company training into award programmes.

Second, attrition rates in for-credit programmes appear to be more promising: State's World Campus courses have a 95 per cent completion rate, while UCLA have improved their retention rate to 85-89 percent because of the high level of interactivity supported by the University, via both course managers and instructors, and the insistence of the University that instructors undergo five to six weeks of intensive training in preparation for online teaching, as well as a mandated online time of five days a week several times a day to respond to questions and guide discussion. At the associate degree level, the figures are not so encouraging: in California, the community college sector distance completion rates 13 per cent below those for on-campus programmes. Third, there is some evidence of the emergence of resistance in on-campus undergraduate courses to decreasing contact time, larger classes and lack of 'real' laboratory classes, the transactional aspects of education conceived as more than information delivery. Students, it appears, want the choice of flexible attendance, but are unhappy when face-to-face sessions are reduced.

Of critical interest to university funding agencies and managers in Australia is the issue of student response to online forms of learning, and student expectations of on-campus study. Flexible delivery of programmes, made possible by the new technologies, have combined with changing social attitudes and patterns of connection among school leavers to alter the nature of higher education. It is therefore difficult to extricate the extent to which online education provision, sometimes confused with flexible delivery, is a response to actual demand by students, or a supply-push mechanism by commercial vendors and university managers seeking supplementary income and reduced costs. Most likely, it is both, although as indicated, students in the main are concerned at the prospect of diminished choice in relation to on-campus classes.

Disengagement' from the campus experience consequent on increased paid work commitments, increasing access to digital resources, and flexible programming. McInnes warns against a simple response to 'student demand', which might abrogate university responsibility to determine optimal curriculum design and learning experiences at the undergraduate level. Yet universities must also resist the temptations to ignore the reality of student lives, and to persist with a 'romantic' vision of the ideal student experience. One might posit a shift in university attendance and engagement, which more closely mirrors that of the old apprenticeship model of blended work/study, particularly as universities themselves seek to incorporate more workplace-based training in their professional programmes. This may have the effect of establishing lifelong learning, conceived as a constant renewal of work work work work work skills, as a standard education 'system'

More immediately, it is also likely to extend the period of enrolment for undergraduate and postgraduate students, and increase administrative costs by spreading students over a longer time to graduation, unless units are reconceptualized via curriculum design to the short course, six-week UoP model. For McInnes, one implication of a lack of student engagement is the necessity to re-assert the value of a coherent and cohesive curriculum.

Intellectual property issues

The confusing and complex state of IP in US universities is well-exemplified in an interview with Kenneth Salomon in University Business. Salomon argues that academia is currently protected by exception from the work-for-hire rule that assigns copyright to the employer if the employee is tenured, or the digitisation of his/her knowledge is performed as part of expected work duties. However, the situation is vastly complicated by the input of other institutional employees into the digitisation process, as, for example, graphics illustrators, as well aBs the matter of students copying notes and then posting them for sale on the web. For educational institutions, the critical issue is to agree and implement a policy on ownership and/or use of materials, including the right to amend any future use of the materials, and right to use after the originator leaves the institution. Some universities such as the University of North Texas now have agreements allocating royalties to staff producing online materials, although the amount depends on how much assistance was provided by the university. We documented the Arthur Miller case at Harvard, where Arthur Miller produced teaching materials for another Law School, and Harvard objected. Salomon argues that this 'wasn't a copyright issue per se; it was a conflict of interest and conflict of commitment to Harvard', that should have been addressed in terms of employee exclusivity arrangements.

At the institutional level, a major breakthrough in digital copyright law has been achieved with the TEACH (Technology, Education and Copyright Harmonisation) Act. This allows only non-profit educational providers to digitise materials that would normally be used to support face-to-face classes for limited-time online access by bona fide students. For-profit providers will continue to pay for copyright, which is a further reason many are anxious to partner with e-publishers. The onus then is on individual universities to negotiate with employees regarding the 'ownership' of teaching materials. However, the broader issues associated with IP in borderless education remain a matter for caution.

Curriculum Issues

A number of commentators in the 2000, flagged the issue of curriculum control as critical to the future of public higher education as corporate, virtual and for-profit entities expanded, and as non-profit educational institutions struggled with falling public funding. Watkins (Council of Higher Education Associations, CHEA) and Mingle (SHEEO) noted that thus far, the community college sector was most susceptible to corporate influence on curriculum and pedagogical practice, since the mission at VET level is to be industry-responsive, but also because corporations could exercise direct financial pressure. However, there is now growing evidence of curriculum change within universities, both in response to student demand for incorporation of job-relevant certifications and of vendor deals, which provide equipment in return for use of their certification programmes. Hence proprietary, corporate or for-profit institutional online training programmes are incorporated into accredited degree programmes, as the California State University has agreed to do for a networking training programme developed by Alcatel, in return for lab equipment and teaching staff from Alcatel. Other institutions, such as Colorado State and Georgia State, are incorporating such proprietary products as SkillSoft's web-based self-paced offerings, in their continuing education courses. The same trend is already present in Australia, in such programmes as Cisco certification as a component of the QUT IT degree. The President of one community college which welcomes NETg's free courseware distributed through Michigan Virtual University, recognises the issues this raises in terms of the integrity of curriculum, and accreditation:

> Colleges and universities must learn to adjust and make decisions about how to incorporate programmes like this into their credentialing processes. This is not an isolated incident. It's the dawn of a new age in high-quality, web-based curriculum that's commercially prepared.

Such deals raise the issue of quality and coherence of the curriculum, as well as who teaches these components, and flags the entry of more complex curriculum decision-making at departmental level, as staff consider whether what amounts to training leaches the cognitive capacities of students because of the performative performative performative performative performative emphasis of certification.

Administrators of online programs assume consumers want a bite-sized 'point and click' accumulation of facts rather than a more reflective, less easily measured search for knowledge. It's also wrong to assume that all student customers know entirely what they need in an education program and what kind of material will lead to the desired educational product.

Credit transfer, is a further challenge to curriculum integrity. UoP, that their incoming students have accrued as many as five unit equivalents from different institutions, and equivalence is determined at institutional, not faculty level. This would suggest that the previous reliance on individual academic expertise to ensure the quality of degree composition has been further eroded, and that we must seriously question the notion of what a degree in a particular discipline might mean. To date, little attention has been given to curriculum matters: O'Donoghue and Twigg are two of the few who note it as critical in the development of private/ public partnerships and consortia of providers. Certainly we can discern a major shift away from the traditional 'input measures' of quality such as qualifications of the faculty teaching subjects, and the number of books in the library. Further, the increase in global university consortia, agreeing on common core curricula, places further pressure on the academic preference for distinct and self-generated curricula within individual institutions. As memoranda on joint curricula are agreed at the institutional level, the 'not-invented-here syndrome' becomes increasingly harder to maintain at the individual academic level.

When curricula are shared between institutions, supported by major publishers, and the design and development component of academic work becomes more centralised (as in the for-profit institutions), greater attention will focus on the role of teaching as a central role for academics, and the issue of training for, and the accreditation of, teaching will gain greater prominence in the higher education context.

Technology Developments

Many of the technical problems associated with online

learning remain, notwithstanding predictions that interoperability of various platforms would be achieved quickly, and bandwidth would increase dramatically in response to demand. Where in 1999 and 2000, debate swirled about the efficacy of 'distributed' or distance education via new technologies, and whether or not cost efficiencies could be achieved, there is now growing recognition that quality education on the web will not significantly reduce costs, that hybrid modes are required for retention of students, and effective learning, and that early predictions of productivity gains, improved quality of learning outcomes, and cost reductions have proved difficult to demonstrate with any validity, when each is added to the ROI equation.

However, Urdan and Weggen, 14 per cent decline in interactive web-based training in 1999 over the previous year, indicating that as margins tightened in the e-learning market, vendors were reverting to static, generic and asynchronous uses of the web and the internet. The very aspects of online learning that promised to revolutionise learning, and that most experts recognise as fundamental to motivation and retention, such as live interactivity from a distance, customisation, streaming media and so on, have become prohibitive in terms of cost. The critical issue is that interactivity is thus far not scaleable. While the notion of '24/7' service has become standard rhetoric, the reality in most online programmes is somewhat different: certainly access to digital resources is common on a continuous basis at most institutions, but few have managed the resourcing necessary to enable day-long tutorial or technical assistance.

As indicated above, the major technological challenge for most institutions is integrating the various software programmes for different functional areas of their operations. It has certainly occupied far more administrative time and far more of the operational budget than tentative moves into online teaching, although media attention has focused on the more dramatic change signalled by e-learning. The Connecticut State University system, for example, is still struggling with implementation of a software programme that has consumed five years in development and implementation, and is several million dollars over budget. The costs of implementing administrative software remain huge: the University of British Columbia has spent C$12 million over five years to introduce PeopleSoft. Canadian universities entering the overseas market 'tectonic clashes' between electronic administrative systems designed for local markets being unable to incorporate international funds transfers, and student complaints regarding administrative systems outnumbering academic complaints by 10:1.

Furthermore, the range of services demanded by a 'client centred focus' in universities has changed, as students demand faster access to resources, the ability to transfer funds electronically, and the ability to access tuition aid programmes online. Administrative systems must be adapted to accommodate online teaching and learning, and this is proving difficult. Consequently, costs have increased because universities must maintain dual paper/digital systems. There are other difficulties of a cultural nature: Gartner Group Vice President Michael Zastrocky, that only 2 per cent of US non-profit education providers use an external host system for information systems because of continuing concern about security issues.

Although a number of analysts, for example Hambrecht and Co, predict the demise of the CDROM and video as delivery mechanisms, publishers do not seem to agree: core textbooks increasingly come as hybrid products of text and accompanying CDROM. Nor is there any indication of students spurning print text: indeed Prof. Shirley Alexander's current research at the University of Technology, Sydney, indicates a strong resistance to screen reading, and a strong desire to print any screen information. E-books, through deals with web publishing software makers such as Adobe Systems. Adobe's eBook University initiative of mid-2001 involves a partnership with nine institutions, including MIT's Sloan School of Management, the University of Maryland University College, and the University of Wisconsin (the latter two amongst the largest distance education providers in the US), to provide texts through Adobe's eBook Reader. Students will be able to download the Reader for free from publishers' websites, or a bookstore with an online purchase of the text. Adobe has secured agreement from all major publishers for the initiative, which promises cost savings on warehousing of physical texts and distribution costs. However, student acceptance of e-texts is not a foregone conclusion. At the same time, digital publishers are looking to for-profit providers to encourage e-books. Apollo has signed an exclusive agreement to use Microsoft Reader, and to ultimately offer all texts digitally.

Analysts suggest that the adoption of a proprietary reader platform is crucial to penetration. However, publisher-exclusive deals with one reader platform would seem business suicide. Over the last two years, new technological developments have focused on the programming of learning objects, and digital publishing. Both are in the early stages of standardisation and commercial application. A critical issue in the digitising of learning resources remains the cost factor, and 'legacy issues'. As museums and universities seek to make their rich resources available to a wider public, the costs of the process, and the maintenance of dual physical and virtual collections, along with the fact that there is no current solution to changing technical platforms and the preservation of current digitised resources, are proving major challenges.

One ironic footnote on technological developments might suggest some caution on the part of universities introducing wireless internet access on-campus. Two private US colleges, Bentley and Babson, have been obliged to block internet access to their lecture theatres during classes, because students were surfing and emailing rather than 'paying attention'. A further caution is the increasing tendency of US students to download huge video and music files, jamming servers, increasing university costs, and potentially opening the university to copyright breaches. Student demand has forced many universities such as the University of Denver to double bandwidth, install 'shapers' to limit entertainment downloads via peer-to-peer file-sharing.

Quality Assurance Issues

A major issue in the area of policy remains the issue of quality control of degree study as the internet makes cross-border provision of education relatively easy for dodgy providers. This is not an issue confined to Australia, but it is one that has thus far found no simple solution; Twigg describes online quality processes as 'chaos' from a student perspective. Contreras provides a brief update on the activities of some of the exposed diploma mills; for example, Columbia Pacific University was closed down in California, was re-established in Montana as Columbia Commonwealth University, and has also been 'accredited' in Malawi. Montana does not legislate private provision of higher education. Variations in state regulations allow questionable operators to locate in states such as Wyoming and Hawaii, which are lax in their regulatory environments. One institution, Preston University has a majority of its students in Pakistan, but is based in Wyoming.

Another previously fraudulent operator, La Salle University in Louisiana, was bought out and 'legitimised' in 1997 after nearly 10 years' operation. It established a sister provider, Orion College, which however, has attracted fewer than 100 students by end-2000, prompting its chief academic officer to note ruefully: 'When you go legitimate, the sad thing is that it is not a good thing for the money situation'. Not even the imprimatur of an accrediting agency in the US is guaranteed to provide consumer protection: The Chronicle of Higher Education lists three spurious accrediting committees, including the American Council of Private Colleges and Universities. It is evident that neither legal nor systemic regulatory systems have been able to keep pace with the rapid advances made in technology over the last decade. The Napster case is a prime example. The e-learning and for-profit education environment has demonstrated that current quality assurance systems are inadequate to deal not merely with unscrupulous providers, but more significantly, that they are not addressing the many different issues involved in distributed learning.

This has prompted organisations such as the Commonwealth of Learning and the Pew Learning and Technology Program to convene symposia to tackle the many issues involved in quality assurance. At the same time, the number of 'best practice guidelines' for online education provision has proliferated. Labour organisations such as the National Education Association and the American Federation of Teachers ('Distance Education Guidelines for Good Practice', have outlined their approaches, along with regional accrediting bodies (such as the Council of Regional Accrediting Committees), and WICHE. The Institute of Higher Education Policy has also published a commissioned study, 'Quality on the line: Benchmarks for success in internet-based distance eduction'. Ryan summarises some of these. What is clear is that traditional quality assurance systemic measures are no longer adequate for the new educational environment, with its blurred borders between informal and formal learning, online and on-campus provision, and a greater emphasis on outcomes-based assessment.

2

Trade Barriers

The GATS is the first ever set of multilateral rules covering international trade in services. Previous international trade agreements covered trade in products, but never services.

The GATS was negotiated in the Uruguay Round and came into effect in 1995. It is administered by the World Trade Organization (WTO) which is made up of 144 member countries.

The World Trade Organization (WTO) is the only global international organization dealing with the rules of trade between nations. At its heart are the WTO agreements, negotiated and signed by the majority of the world's trading nations and ratified in their parliaments.

The GATS is one of these key agreements and is a legally enforceable set of rules. The GATS has three parts. The first part is the framework that contains the general principles and rules. The second part consists of the national schedules that list a country's specific commitments on access to their domestic market by foreign providers. The third part consists of annexes which detail specific limitations for each sector can be attached to the schedule of commitments. This will be discussed in more detail later, but first it is essential to understand what kind of education services will be covered by GATS and what is meant by higher education services.

Modes of Trade in Services

The GATS defines four ways in which a service can be traded, known as 'modes of supply'. These four modes of trade apply to all service sectors in GATS.

Categories of education services

Trade in education is organized into five categories or sub-sectors of service. These categories are based on the United Nations Provisional Central Product Classification (CPC). The three categories that are most relevant to this report are 'higher', 'adult' and 'other'. The four modes of service described above apply to each of the categories. Critics of this classification system believe that it does not reflect the reality of today where non-traditional and private providers exist and alternate forms of delivery using new technologies are being used. However, countries are able to add their own qualifications or supplements to the UN CPC classification scheme and therefore, in principle, should not be limited by the scheme.

Key elements and rules of the GATS

The overall framework contains a number of general obligations applicable to all trade in services regardless of whether a country has made a specific commitment to sectors or not. These are called unconditional obligations. Fundamental to this discussion is the Most Favoured Nation (MFN) rule. Each WTO member lists in its national schedules those services for which it wishes to provide access to foreign providers. In addition to choosing which service sector/s will be committed, each country determines the extent of commitment by specifying the level of market access and the degree of national treatment they are prepared to guarantee.

Controversial Questions and issues related to higher education

The GATS is described as a voluntary agreement because countries can decide which sectors they will agree to cover under GATS rules. This is done through the preparation of their national schedules of commitments and through the 'request-offer' negotiation rounds. However, there are aspects of the agreement that question its voluntary nature, notably the built-in progressive liberalization agenda and other elements described in this section. Probably, the most controversial and critical issue related to the agreement is the meaning of Article 1.3. This article defines which services are covered or exempted. According to the WTO, the agreement is deemed to apply to all measures affecting services except "those services supplied in the exercise of governmental authority". But what does 'exercise of governmental authority' mean? GATS supporters maintain that education provided and funded by the government is therefore exempted. Sceptics question the broad interpretation of the clause and ask for more a detailed analysis.

The agreement states that "in the exercise of governmental authority" means the service is provided on a 'non-commercial basis' and 'not in competition' with other service suppliers. This begs the follow-up question - what is meant by non-commercial basis and not in competition? These issues are at the heart of much of the debate about which services are covered. Education critics of the GATS maintain that due to the wide-open interpretation of 'non-commercial' and 'not in competition' terms, the public sector/government service providers may not in fact be exempt.

The situation is especially complicated in those countries where there is a mixed public/private higher education system or where a significant amount of funding for public institutions in fact comes from the private sector. Another complicationis that a public education institution in an exporting country is often defined as private/commercial when it crosses the border and delivers in the importing country.

Therefore, one needs to question what 'non-commercial' really means in terms of higher education trade. The debate about what 'not in competition' means is fuelled by the fact that there does not appear to be any qualifications or limits on the term. For instance, if non-government providers (private non-profit or commercial) are delivering services, are they deemed to be in competition with government providers?

In this scenario, public providers may be defined as being 'in competition' by the mere existence of non-governmental providers. Does the method of delivery influence or limit the concept of 'in competition'? Does the term cover situations where there is a similar mode of delivery, or for instance, does this term mean that public providersusing traditional face-to-face classroom methods could be seen to be competing with foreign for-profit e-learning providers? There are many unanswered questions that need clarification.

Supporters of the GATS emphasize that education is to a large extent a government function and that the agreement does not seek to displace the public education systems and the right of government to regulate and meet domestic policy objectives. Others express concern that the whole question of the protection of public services is very uncertain and potentially at risk in view of the narrow interpretation of what governmental authority means and a wide-open interpretation of what 'not in competition' and non- commercial basis' mean.

Clearly, the question -which higher and adult education 'services exercised in governmental authority' are exempted from GATS - needs to be front and centre in the debate on the risks and opportunities associated with the agreement. What does the principle of progressive liberalization mean? GATS is not a neutral agreement. It aims to promote and enforce the liberalization of trade in services. The process of progressive liberalization involves two aspects- extending GATS coverage to more service sectors and decreasing the number and extent of measures that serve as impediments to increased trade.

Therefore, in spite of the right of each country to determine the extent of its commitments, with each new round of negotiations, countries are expected to add sectors or sub-sectors to their national schedules of commitments and to negotiate the further removal of limitations on market access and national treatment.

The intention of GATS is to facilitate and promote evermore opportunities for trade. Therefore, countries that are not interested in either the import or export of education services will most likely experience greater pressures to allow market access to foreign providers. GATS is a very new instrument and it is too soon to predict thereality or extent of these potential opportunities or risks.

At the 'request-offer' stage of the process, there are bilateral negotiations on market access and national treatment commitments. The key point at this step, is that sectors for which access is sought do not have to correspond to those for which requests are made. So country A may request of Country B greater access to transportation services. Country B can respond by requesting access to education services. It is up to each country as to where they are willing to make concessions on foreign access to domestic markets. This situation applies to all sectors and may be of greatest concern to countries, developing or developed, who have not made commitments to open up education services and might therefore consider their education service sector vulnerable to negotiating deals across sectors. These issues relate to the mechanics and legalities of the agreement itself. Each one raises questions that need further clarification and analysis and collectively they serve to wave the red flag that more attention needs to be given to these matters. There are other aspects of the GATS, such as the dispute mechanism, subsidies, treatment of monopolies which are controversial and apply to all sectors and which need further study.

Article 6.4, which addresses measures relating to qualification requirements and procedures, technical standards and licensing requirements may have serious implications for education and requires further clarification. It must be remembered that GATS is still anuntested agreement and a certain amount of confusion exists on how to interpret the major rules and obligations. It took many years to iron out the inconsistencies in the General Agreement on Tariffs and Trade (GATT) and the same will likely be true for GATS. While trade specialists and lawyers need to review the technical and legal aspects of the agreement, it is educators who need to study how the agreement applies to and impacts education services.

Commitments to Trade in Education Services

Extent of country commitments

The education sector is one of the least committed sectors. The reason is not clear, but perhaps it can be attributed to the need for countries to strike a balance between pursuing domestic education priorities and exploring ways in which trade in education services can be further liberalized. Or it could be linked to the fact that to date, education, in general, has taken a very low priority in the major bilateral agreements and rightly or wrongly, the same may be true for the GATS.

Only 44 of the 144 WTO Members have made commitments to education, and only 21 of these have included commitments to higher education. It is interesting to note that Congo, Lesotho, Jamaica and Sierra Leone have made full unconditional commitments in higher education, perhaps with the intent of encouraging foreign providers to help develop their educational systems.

Australia's commitment for higher education covers provision of private tertiary education services, including university level. The European Union has included higher education in their schedule with clear limitations on all modes of trade except 'consumption abroad', which generally means foreign tuition paying students. Only three (USA, New Zealand, Australia) of the 21 countries with higher education commitments have submitted a negotiating proposal outlining their interests and issues. The next section provides a brief summary of key elements of the three proposals.

Analysis of negotiating proposals

Role of government

It is clear that all three proposals acknowledge the central role government plays in higher education. Perhaps the controversy about which public services are exempted from the GATS has prompted this explicit recognition of the government role. Some are comforted and appeased by these statements. Others are even more concerned about the potential erosion of the role of government in higher education provision and the setting of domestic policy objectives. In some countries, education is decentralized from national to provincial or state governmental bodies. Private education, though nominally under state authority, may not be primarily governed or regulated by a government. These situations further illustrate the complexities involved in determining which services are exempted from GATS coverage and the very different impact GATS will have on individual countries.

Rationales and benefits

The rationales that drive further liberalization differ from country to country. Australia stresses greater access for students, New Zealand points to economic and social benefits and the USA focuses on opportunities for new knowledge and skills. Benefits are closely linked to rationales. Australia believes that the competition inherent in more trade will have flow-on benefits to students. New Zealand emphasizes that in addition to revenue generation there are benefits at the individual, institutional and societal level through academic exchange,technological transfer and cross-cultural linkages.

The USA highlights the contribution to global spread of the modern knowledge economy and improved competitiveness. It is not a surprise that the economic benefits are emphasized but it is noteworthy that social and academic value to individuals, institutions and society are not totally overlooked. More work is needed to understand and analyse the perceived rationale and benefits as this will lead to a clearer picture of what countries expect from increased import and export in education. Of course, expectations can be seen in terms of desirable or undesirable results. A better understanding of anticipated outcomes would assist in the development of policies to help achieve or prevent them. At the same time, it is equally important to be mindful of 'unintended consequences'.

Public/private mix

The public/private mix of higher and adult education provision is implicitly and explicitly recognized in the proposals. It is interesting to note that New Zealand suggests that education may be one of the least committed service sectors due to the recognition of its 'public good' element and the high degree of government involvement in its provision. The USA is more pointed when they state that private education co-exists with the public domain and will continue to supplement, not displace public education systems. There are mixed reactions to this statement and a great deal of uncertainty as to how the GATS will affect the balance of a mixed system, especially given the individualized nature of mixed systems.

Further analysis needed

Further analysis of the factors driving commitments or the lack of commitments in higher education is needed. There are diverse perspectives on the number and substance of commitments because countries have different national policy objectives and therefore different goals and expectations from trade in education services. For example, a consumer oriented rationale can be interpreted as the need to provide a wider range of opportunities to consumers, or the need to protect consumers by assuring appropriate levels of access and quality. The economic rationale can be understood as a way to increase trade revenues for exporting countries or seen as a means to attract additional investment for education for importing countries. Other see the economic rationale as sabotaging the social development goals of education, or even scientific enquiry and scholarship. Any number of issues can be used to illustrate the debate and the dichotomy of opinions on the rationales and benefits of increased trade in education. Differences exist between and within countries and certainly among education groups as well. Further debate and analysis is necessary so that an informed position is taken on why or why not trade liberalization is attractive to an individual country and how trade agreements help or hinder achieving national goals and global interests.

Developing country interests

The voices of developing countries need to be heard so that the benefits and risks associated with increased trade are clear and do not undermine national efforts to develop and enhance domestic higher education. However, the voices and interests of the developing countries differ. The opportunity to have foreign suppliers provide increased access to higher and adult education programs or to invest in the infrastructure for education provision is attractive to some. The threat of foreign dominance or exploitation of a national system and culture is expressed by others. Trade liberalization for whose benefit or at what cost are key questions. Quality and accreditation are at the heart of much debate.

The importance of frameworks for licensing, accreditation, qualification recognition and quality assurance are important for all countries, whether they are importing and exporting education services. Developing countries have expressed concern about their capacity to have such frameworks in place in light of the push toward trade liberalization and increased cross border delivery of education. The GATS is one of many factors and instruments encouraging greater mobility of professionals. Although the agreement focuses on temporary movement of the labour force, it may lead to and facilitate permanent migration as well.

The implications of increased mobility of teachers and researchers are particularly relevant to developing countries. It will be a major challenge to improve education systems if well-qualified professionals and graduates are attracted to positions in other countries. At the root of the impact of GATS on developing countries is the fundamental issue of capacity to participate effectively in the global trading system and to be equal members in the WTO. Strong feelings exist about the potential for trade rules to make poor countries poorer, instead of narrowing the gap between developed and developing countries. The perceived injustice that poor nations are expected to remove trade barriers while rich nations retain barriers on certain goods, contributes to the strong reactions of some developing countries about the impact of GATS in general.

Barriers

Identification of the barriers to trade in higher education services is fundamental because it is the elimination of these barriers which is the raison d être of GATS. There are some barriers that are applicable to all sectors. There are other impediments that are specific to the education services sector. The following two sections list some of the generic barriers and also those most relevant to the four modes of trade in education. The sources used to identify these barriers are the three negotiating proposals described above, reports by non-governmental organizations (NGOs) and intergovernmental bodies, and by the WTO itself. This is a comprehensive collection of perceived barriers, not a list of the most significant ones. There is no agreement or consensus on which barriers are the most critical as they are usually seen from a self-interest perspective.

The list is for illustrative purposes only. Attention needs to be given to whether the barriers are seen from the perspective an exporting or importing country. Finally, it is important to remember that what is perceived as a barrier by some countries is perceived as fundamental to the education system in another.

The majority of these generic barriers are from an exporter country's point of view and focus on supply modes one and three.

— lack of transparency of government regulatory, policy and funding frameworks·

— domestic laws and regulations are administered in an unfair manner

— subsidies are not made known in a clear and transparent manner

— when government approval is required long delays are encountered and when approval is denied, no reasons are given for the denial and no information is given on what must be done to obtain approval in the future

— tax treatment that discriminates against foreign suppliers

— foreign partners are treated less favourably than other organizations.

Of course, many of these barriers are not new or specific to the GATS, as they already impact the flow of education services across borders. However, the barriers are significant as they are seen by some as key elements of a public education system that need to be maintained, and by others as impediments to trade. Some of the barriers identified above affect internationalization initiatives, in other words, those activities that do not have an economic or for-profit motive.

For instance, mobility of students and teachers for academic exchange or research purposes are affected by many of the barriers noted for supply modes two and four. It is important to note that within a country's schedule of commitments, it is possible to list specific limitations to market access and national treatment. These are a type of barrier and must be honoured. For example, Mexico has telecom laws that restrict the use of national satellites and receiving dishes. This has potential impact on cross border delivery of education services.

It is hard to predict what future barriers, especially technological ones, could be applied in order to control the electronic movement of education services across borders.

For instance, the capacity to install electronic fences may have major repercussions on cross border e-education. Finally, it should be mentioned that countries that have not made any formal commitments to trade in higher education services are currently in the process of easing some of the identified barriers.

A good example of this is the number of countries who are changing visa and employment requirements to attract more international students to study in their country. This is happening irrespective of the GATS.

Policy Issues and Questions

Given the current interest and pressure toward increasing trade liberalization, what are the policy implications that the higher education sector needs to look at? It is a challenging task to examine policy implications as the impact of trade liberalization is firmly enmeshed with other issues and trends in higher education. These trends include:

— the increasing use of ICTs for domestic and cross border delivery of programs

— the growing number of private for-profit entities providing higher education domestically and internationally

— the increasing tuition fees and other costs faced by students of public (and private) institutions,

— the need for public providers to seek alternate sources of funding which sometimes means engaging in for-profit activities or seeking private sector sources of financial support.

— the ability of government to fund the increasing demand for higher and adult education.

These trends are with us today in both developed and to some extent, developing countries. How does the existence of the GATS relate to these trends? While the GATS may lead to expanded use of electronic or distance education and may contribute to more commercial or market oriented approaches to education, it cannot be held responsible for the emergence or existence of these trends. Supporters of more trade in education services can celebrate the existence of the GATS to maximize the benefits of these trends and opportunities. Critics, on the other hand, can emphasize the risks associated with increased trade, believing that it leads to more for-profit providers, to programs of questionable quality, and to a market oriented approach - all of which are seen to challenge the traditional 'public good' approach to higher education. However, the impact of trade liberalizationon education cannot be positioned as an 'either-or' question or answer; it is a multi-layered and complex set of issues.

Role of government

The changing role of government is a contentious issues. First, let it be said that in general, globalization and the new public management are challenging and changing roles of government and nation state. The movement toward more trade liberalization is yet another factor. With respect to education, the government usually plays a role in the funding, regulation, monitoring and delivery of higher education or at least, designating bodies to do so. This is true in countries where a public system dominates or where a mixed public/private system exists. The advent of increased cross border delivery by foreign education providers raises the following issues all of which impact on the role of government:

— licensing and regulation procedures for foreign providers

— quality assurance and accreditation for imported and exported education services

— funding protocols including operating grants, loans, subsidies and scholarships

— qualification recognition and credit transfer systems

These issues will be discussed in more detail in other sections but the role of government as an education provider needs to be examined. A combination of increased demand for public services and limited financial capacity is forcing governments to examine their priorities and options for service delivery. In higher education, this has prompted a number of new developments. These include:

— developing funding formulas which are placing more of the financial burden on students

— forcing publicly funded institutions to seek alternate and additional sources of funds through entrepreneurial or commercial activities at home and abroad

— individual institutions wanting increased autonomy from government regulation

— permitting new private providers (non-profit and for-profit) to deliver specific education and training programs

These developments are further complicated if and when

a) a foreign public or private education provider is interested in access to the domestic market; and

b) if a domestic public provider is interested in seeking markets in other countries.

Together these scenarios require the government to take a long term and macro perspective on the impact of increased foreign trade on their role in the provision of and regulation of higher education.

Student Access

Many governments and public education institutions have keenly felt the responsibility of ensuring broad access to higher education opportunities. In many, if not in most countries, this is a challenging issue as the demand for higher and adult education is steadily growing, often beyond the capacity of the country to provide it. This is one more reason why some students are interested in out-of-country education opportunities and providers are prepared to offer higher education services across borders. When increased trade liberalization is factored into this scenario, the question of access becomes complicated. Advocates of liberalized trade maintain that consumers/students can have greater access to a wider range of education opportunities at home and abroad. Non-supporters of trade believe that access may in fact be more limited as trade will commercialize education, escalate costs and perhaps lead to a two-tiered system. Trade is therefore often perceived by critics as a threat to the 'public good' nature of education services. This raises the question of the capacity and role of government with respect to providing access to higher education.

For instance, if education is seen as a public function, can private providers or foreign providers help to fulfil this public function? If so, would foreign for-profit providers be eligible for the same grants, subsidies and tax incentives as public providers under the national treatment obligation of the GATS? Would this in turn decrease the amount of financial support available to public universities if funds were distributed across a larger number of institutions? Different education models exist and must exist in order to respond to the needs, resources and priorities of individual countries.

Funding

Many of the same issues and arguments regarding access can also apply to funding. Some governments have limited budget capacity or at least lack the political will to allocate funds to meet the needs of higher education. Can international trade provide alternate funding sources or new providers? Or, because of the GATS obligations such as most favoured nation treatment and national treatment obligations, does it mean that public funding will be spread too thinly across a broader set of domestic and foreign providers? Furthermore, does the presence of foreign providers signal to government that they can decrease public funding for higher and adult education, thereby jeopardizing domestic publicly funded institutions. Does international trade in education advantage some countries, such as those with well-developed capacity for export, and disadvantage others in terms of funding or access? Once again, the impact of more liberalized trade can be a double-edged sword with respect to funding, whether public or private, higher education teaching/learning and research activities.

Regulation of foreign or cross border providers

As already noted, a regulatory framework is needed to deal with the diversity of providers and new cross border delivery modes, and becomes more urgent as international trade increases. In some countries, this may mean a broader approach to policy which involves licensing, regulating and monitoring both private (profit and non-profit) and foreign providers to ensure that national policy objectives are met and public interests protected. It may also involve a shift in government and public thinking- while higher education remains a "public good", both public and private providers can fulfil this public function. This in turn may introduce greater competition among providers and general confusion for the consumer. Hence a coherent and comprehensive regulatory framework is called for- to serve national interests and protect the interests of different stakeholders, especially students. More work is necessary to determine how national regulatory frameworks are compatible with, or part of, a larger international framework. Increased connectivity and interdependence among nations, as well as liberalized trade, will mean urge greater coherence between national frameworks. How can coherence between a national framework and an international framework actually strengthen national regulatory and policy functions, not weaken them? Clearly there are risks and opportunities associated with this issue but doing nothing is a risk in itself.

Recognition and transferability of credits

New types of education providers, new delivery modes, new cross border education initiatives, new levels of student mobility, new opportunities for trade in higher education- all this can spell further confusion for the recognition of qualifications and transfer of academic credits. This is not a new issue. Trade agreements are not responsible for increased confusion, but they add to the complexity and also make resolution more urgent. National and international recognition of qualifications and the transfer of credits have already been the subject of a substantial amount of work. The 'Lisbon Convention on the Recognition of Qualifications of Higher Education in the Europe Region', the 'European Credit Transfer

System', and 'University Mobility in Asia Pacific' are good examples of regional initiatives that could lead to a more international approach.

Quality assurance and accreditation

Increased cross border education delivery and a set of legal rules and obligations in trade agreements require that urgent attention be given to the question of quality assurance and accreditation of education providers. Not only is it important to have national mechanisms which have the capacity to address accreditation and quality assessment procedures for the academic programs of new private and foreign providers, it is equally important that attention be given to developing an international approach to quality assurance and accreditation.

There is growing awareness that in the world of cross border education trade, national quality assurance schemes are becoming challenged by the complexities of the international education environment. While there may be growing awareness, there is no acceptance or agreement that harmonization of national policies with an international approach to quality assessment and accreditation is needed. It is imperative that education specialists discuss and determine the appropriate regulating mechanisms at the national and international level and not leave these questions to the designers and arbitrators of trade agreements.

Another, potentially contentious issue is the application of quality assurance schemes to both domestic and foreign providers. It may well be that under certain conditions, the national treatment obligation requires that all providers, domestic and foreign, be subject to the same processes and criteria. In some countries this will not be a problem, in others it will be hotly debated. Quality assurance of higher education in some countries is regulated by the sector, and in others by the government to a greater or lesser degree.

The key point is that authority for quality assurance, regulation and accreditation of cross border delivery needs to be examined and guided by stakeholders and bodies related to the education sector and not left solely in the hands of the market.

Research and intellectual property rights

In the new economy that emphasizes knowledge production and trade, there is increasingly more value attributed to the creative and intellectual content inherent in both products and services. The 'Trade-Related Aspects of Intellectual Property Rights' (TRIPS) is another trade agreement, completely separate from the GATS, but which also addresses trade liberalization. TRIPS covers such things as patents, trademarks and copyright, all of which are salient to the research and teaching/learning functions of higher education. Careful monitoring of TRIPS is also necessary by the higher education sector.

A look at the potential implications of trade agreements on research and scholarly work reveals a number of issues. A consistent theme expressed by trade critics is a deep concern about the increased emphasis on commercialization and commodification of the production of knowledge. Sceptics believe that the highly valued trinity of teaching, research and service at traditional universities may be at risk. A more differentiated and niche oriented approach to higher education may be an unanticipated outcome of increased trade in education and the growing importance of agreements such as GATS and TRIPS.

Internationalization

Attention needs to be given to the impact of trade liberalization on non-profit internationalization activities. Will trade overshadow and dominate the international academic relations of countries and institutions, or enhance them? Many internationalization strategies might be jeopardized by a purely commercial approach. For example, participation in international development or technical assistance programs can lead to mutual benefits for all partners and important spin-off effects for research, curriculum development and teaching.

Will these programs have less or more importance when there is increased pressure for trade? Will revenue raised from commercial education activities be used to subsidize internationalization activities? What might happen to student exchange, internships, and other forms of academic mobility that do not have an income generation or for-profit motive? Will limited financial resources be directed to trade initiatives that have an economic return instead of internationalization activities which stress added academic value?

How can internationalization and trade activities complement each other? Will bilateral relationships and multilateral networks among institutions be shaped by trade opportunities at the expense of research, curriculum development and other academic endeavours? Effort is needed to profile the benefits and importance of non-profit internationalization and to direct resources to the implementation and sustainability of the international dimension of teaching, research and service.

Mobility of Professionals/ Labour Force

It has already been noted that the GATS may address the widespread unmet demand for skilled workers by facilitating the mobility of professionals. This impacts many of the service sectors and has particular implications for higher education. Not only is higher and adult education providing education and training programs to meet economic needs, the sector itself is affected by the mobility of its teachers and researchers. In many countries, the increasing shortage of teachers is resulting in active recruitment campaigns across borders. Since many teachers and researchers want to move to countries with more favourable working conditions and salaries, there is a real concern that the most developed countries will benefit disproportionately.

Culture and Acculturation

Last, but certainly not least, is the issue of cultural and indigenous traditions. Education is a process through which cultural assimilation takes place. In fact education is a fundamental vehicle for acculturation. Concern about the homogenization of culture through cross border supply of higher and adult education is expressed by critics of GATS. Advocates maintain that a positive hybridization and fusion of culture will evolve through increasing mobility and the influence of ICTs. In fact, some argue that this has been happening for decades and is contributing to new cultural exchanges and richness. Once again, the divergence of opinion shows that there are potential opportunities and threats to consider.

Institutional Level Issues

The emphasis of this section has been on macro policy issues. But the effect on individual institutions, \especially public higher education institutions, should not be ignored. The foremost issues are institutional autonomy, academic freedom and conditions of employment for academic staff. While these three issues are linked to trade liberalization, they are more closely associated with the larger issues of the commercialization and privatization of education in general, which many believe is advanced within as well as across borders.

Trade Dominates

Finally, it needs to be said that the question of trade liberalization, which most often is interpreted in economic terms, has the potential of dominating the agenda. There is a risk of 'trade creep' where education policy issues are increasingly framed in terms of trade. Even though domestic challenges in education provision are currently front and centre on the radar screen of most countries, the issue of international trade in education services will most likely increase in importance.

Supporters of freer trade applaud the fact that GATS is seen first and foremost as an economic agreement and that its purpose is to promote and expand free trade for economic reasons. Given that the market potential for trade in higher education is already significant and is predicted to increase, it is clear that GATS and other trade agreements will help to promote trade and further economic benefit. Critics of the trade agreements maintain that the domination of the trade agenda is at the expense of other key objectives and rationales for higher education such as social, cultural and scientific development and the role of education in promoting democracy and citizenship.

Moving Foreword

Actions and reactions of stakeholders. One of the prime objectives of this report is to get the issue of trade liberalization in higher education services on the agenda of university managers and higher education policy makers. Overall, there seems to have been little reaction to the issue. This does not dismiss, however, the work that has been done by some non-government organizations.

One of the more interesting initiatives is the 'Joint Declaration on Higher Education and the General Agreement on Trade in Services' developed and signed by four organizations: Association of Universities and Colleges of Canada (AUCC), American Council on Education (ACE), European University Association (EUA) and the Council for Higher education Accreditation (CHEA).

This declaration encourages countries to not make commitments in 'Higher Education Services' or in the related categories of 'Adult Education' and 'Other Education Services' in the GATS. Instead it supports the notion of reducing obstacles to international trade in higher education using conventions and agreements outside of a trade policy regime. Clearly there are supporters of the principles of the declaration, but there are also critics who feel that the protectionist position is rather self-serving, especially given the degree of exporting activity already in existence.

It is noteworthy that three of the signatories come from the USA and Europe, both of whom have made some commitments on education services in GATS. This is yet another sign of the heated debate, the complexities and the uncertainties related to GATS.

The most important role of the declaration is that it is drawing more attention to the issue. The declaration is the only internationally co-ordinated effort but there are many national level student, teacher and education organizations that are vocal in their questions and criticisms of the intent and impact of the agreement.

There are similar groups such as the 'National Committee for International trade in Education' (NCITE) in the US and other business organizations which are expressing support for freer trade in education services. At the intergovernmental level there appears to be some level of interest in the issues - primarily from the economic organizations such as APEC or OECD. At the same time, there are international non-government organizations such as Association of Commonwealth Universities that are trying to raise awareness about the broad issue of trade liberalization and the specifics of the GATS. But, this is only a beginning.

More work is needed to consult with the different education stakeholders so that their voices are heard in ongoing analysis and negotiations.

Important dates for WTO negotiations

The key dates to be aware of for the next phases of the GATS negotiations are:

— *June 30, 2002:* Countries will file initial requests asking trading partners to open their markets in service areas.

— *March 31, 2003*: Countries that were the subjects of requests will present offers too pen their markets in service areas. Trading partners will hold meetings and discussions. Overall, if insufficient agreement is reached regarding higher education. The sector could be part of new round of global negotiations after talks conclude in January 2005.

— *January 2005:* GATS negotiations will end.

This is a rather tight timetable and the next twelve months are key. By June 2002, the details of all education requests should be known. While it is important that the voice of the education sector is heard in the formulation of these requests, it may be even more important to influence the response to the requests. This involves working with the appropriate government officials and monitoring the offers made by one's own country in response to requests from other countries.

The second part is monitoring the offers that are being received by one's own country in response to the requests originally made to other countries. This is an important, but a rather daunting task due to the reality that education stakeholders hold differing perspectives on the extent and nature of the limitations on national treatment and market access and may or may not speak with one voice to government trade officials.

Complex and contentious. These two words sum up the current analysis and debate about the impact of GATS on higher education. Opinions on the risks and benefits are divided, if not polarized. They differ within and between countries.

Each country must undertake the very serious challenge of balancing opportunities and commitments to liberalize trade for exporting higher education services, with the possible impact, related to the same commitments, of the import of education services. This is not an easy task.

One can tend to be liberal while considering exporting opportunities and more protection is when analysing the implications of importing. At this stage, one is left with the impression that there are more questions than clear answers. The questions are complex as they deal with:

— technical/legal issues of the agreement itself

— education policy issues such as funding, access, accreditation, quality and intellectual property and,

— the larger more political/moral issues for society, such as the role and purpose of higher education, and the 'public good' or 'market commodity' approach.

The one certainty in this picture is the need for the higher education sector to study these questions and to consult stakeholders. At the same time it is necessary to be proactive and strategic in monitoring and influencing government negotiating positions for the request/offer stage of the GATS negotiations. This, of course, involves close communication with education departments and bodies in one's country. It is equally important not to lose sight of the need for international approaches and frameworks for the regulation of providers, quality assurance and qualification recognition. Finally, it is important not too ver state the impact of GATS. Trade in education was alive and well prior to and outside the purview of trade agreements. Yet, it is also critical not to understate the potential implications- risks and opportunities of GATS.

3

Education in a Knowledge Society

Two of the most important influences on educational planning today are what for want of an established name call all the futuristic business literature and the work coming out of cognitive science, broadly defined. There are, of course, many other influences, often from groups with a concern for some particular subject or aspect of schooling. But the two named are especially sweeping in their implications for educational change, each, in quite different ways, suggesting a reconceptualization of what schooling should be about. Yet each of these stops short of answering the question," What should it mean to be an educated person in the 21st century?" That is the kind of question that has motivated the development of liberal education and its periodic transformations.

The rise of the natural sciences led to the most profound transformation of liberal education. There were fears that it might not survive the transformation but it did, and no one would any longer conceive of an educated person who was ignorant of science. Now we are facing the possibility of a more radical transformation, one that does not involve so much the incorporation of new disciplines as a change in the way all disciplines are approached. Rumblings of such a transformation have been occurring throughout the past century, but the two new influences, along with the technologies they draw upon, may finally make it happen. Will it mean the end of liberal education or will liberal education re-emerge, strengthened through its renovation? Liberal education can be renewed, but it will take a careful synthesis of new ideas and enduring principles.

Liberal education is essentially enculturation. It is more than the handing on of a body of knowledge and wisdom, although that is a large part of it. That is the part that liberal education has in common with enculturation in all societies. What makes liberal education distinctive -what makes it 'liberal'-is its cosmopolitanism. Liberal education initiates the young into a culture that transcends the particularities of their social and ethnic backgrounds. A major concern of many advocates of liberal education is that cosmopolitanism itself is coming under attack. It has been more than adequately discussed. Instead, assume in the ensuing discussion that cosmopolitanism of some kind is an agreed-upon end of education. The liberal tradition, the new wave of economic globalization, and recent advances in the learning sciences all point in this direction. But how is such cosmopolitanism to be achieved when cultures are colliding and undergoing rapid, perhaps catastrophic change, when knowledge is expanding more rapidly than anyone can keep up with, and when the process of enculturation itself is subject to radical innovation?

The discussion begins by drawing out the contrasting educational implications of the futuristic business literature and of cognitive learning research the one emphasizing skills and personal qualities, the other emphasizing knowledge. Merging the two into lists of educational objectives, as is now common, does not begin to resolve underlying differences. The resolution propose depends upon taking seriously the idea of a knowledge society, a society organized around the production of knowledge in the same sense that an agrarian society is organized around agricultural production and an industrial society is organized around manufacture. The school should be a productive part of that society, a workshop for the generation of knowledge. Transforming schools into workshops for the production of knowledge mobilizes those skills and personal qualities valued by business futurists, putting them to work toward ends that are consistent with contemporary conceptions of learning and with the objectives of a modernized liberal education.

Two Views of Education for the 21st Century

By the 'futuristic business literature' refer to that flood of publications from organizational theorists, management consultants, economists, futurologists, and diverse social scientists that take as a backdrop the rapid rate of technological change, the rise of Asia Pacific economies, digitization, globalization, outsourcing, the shift from a manufacturing-based to a knowledge-based economy, and the need for constant innovation. This literature covers a great range in quality of ideas, which raises the twin dangers that policy makers may be influenced most by the lowest level and easiest to grasp ideas and that discriminating people will reject the whole literature, thereby ignoring ideas that provide a basis for well-reasoned new educational policies.

Some low-end educational ideas are that technology will revolutionize everything, that we don't need schools anymore, and that there is no use mastering any body of knowledge because it will soon be obsolete. The high-end educational ideas mainly flow from a recognition of the ascendant importance of knowledge: knowledge as a third factor in production, along with capital and labor; learning as the means for organizations to gain a competitive edge; finally, the idea of a social transformation going on that is as extreme as the 19th-century shift from an agrarian to an industrial society the shift to a knowledge society.

When it comes to formulating curriculum guidelines, however, the low-end and the high-end ideas seem to point in the same direction. They point to a set of personal qualities that must be cultivated if the education system is to produce people who can thrive in and contribute to the new order: imagination and creativity, ability to work in groups, communication skills, information-finding skills, problem solving abilities, technological literacy, and above all a continual readiness to learn. It is difficult to fault these, and they are now appearing conspicuously in curriculum guidelines and standards. But are they sufficient, and do they point educational planning in the right direction?

Cognitive science embraces an increasing range of approaches, addressing an increasing range of issues. It gains its strength from disciplined pursuit of the question," How does it work?" Cognitive learning research shares this wide-open character. There is no established 'cognitive approach' in education. Yet, for all its diversity, when the work of cognitive educational researchers is put alongside the futuristic business literature, the kinds of prescriptions for education in the 21st century suggested by these two bodies of work are seen to differ profoundly. The emphasis of the business literature is on process outcomes, on turning out students who function in such-and-such ways.

The current emphasis in cognitive learning research is on content, on turning out students with a genuine understanding of science, mathematics, and other school subjects. Educational reformers inspired by the futuristic business literature commonly minimize the value of content mastery. For instance, an announcement of Stanford University's "Just-In-Time Learning on Internet " project confidently proclaims," Traditional text books and traditional teaching methods requiring weeks of study are being made obsolete by the information explosion." The project leaders suggest that publishers might abandon their traditional bookish ways and start charging customers on a "pay-per-question" basis.

Are cognitive learning researchers, then, simply out of touch with the digital age? On the contrary, it seems that most of the business writers along with many educators, unfortunately are out of touch with progress in the understanding of learning. In the 1970s, cognitive learning research was where the futuristic literature is now, emphasizing cognitive strategies and learning-to-learn. For a combination of reasons, the emphasis has since shifted dramatically toward content learning. First there was the research on reading, which demonstrated that the overriding determinant of what one will get out of reading is what one already knows about the topic.

Then there was the accumulation of research on expertise, which showed that in all kinds of areas, practical as well as intellectual, expertise depends more on deep knowledge of one's domain, its problems and tools, than it does on general mental abilities. Perhaps most surprising was the research on misconceptions, which added up to the conclusion that students are passing through the schools having failed to grasp most of the ideas that constitute modern knowledge. Schools, it appears, are turning out graduates with pre Newtonian conceptions of physics, preDarwinian conceptions of biology, and preSmithian conceptions of economics. This ought at least to give some pause to futurists who imagine students at home in a postmodern world of quanta and dynamic systems.

Finally, however, the emphasis on content has been buoyed by the successes of new educational efforts aimed at learning with understanding. Once students start to get deeply into the pursuit of understanding, they begin to show spontaneously all the traits that the futuristic business literature urges: imagination, collaboration, problem-solving, communicative skill, and readiness to go on learning. A commonsense response to the differing implications of futuristic business literature and cognitive learning research would be," Let's have both". Why not teach both the general skills and dispositions urged by the former and the deep content knowledge stressed by the latter? In fact, that is what curriculum guidelines and standards are tending increasingly to propose. Attractive as this eclectic solution may be, its effect is to drain away the energy that might have produced something new and exciting out of the interaction of these two new forces.

A New Culture for Learning

The futuristic business literature does convey a revolutionary vision, but it is not to be found in the paragraphs on education. Those are, for the most part, a mixture of technological euphoria and run-of-the-mill school-bashing. The revolutionary vision has to do with knowledge-based organizations ones whose competitive advantage depends on cultivation and use of the organization's knowledge resources. Because those knowledge resources are generated out of (and to a large extent reside in) the work of everyone in the organization, maximizing them requires designing the organization so as to make everyone a contributor. That is the revolutionary part: abandoning bureaucratic structures in which a worker's responsibility is defined by routine tasks and where non routine problems are referred to a higher level, replacing them by mission-oriented team structures in which problems are solved and new knowledge is generated within the working groups. That vision has much in common with a new vision of education taking shape within cognitive learning research.

Early cognitive learning research was not only focused on cognitive strategies, it was also focused on the individual learner. Along with a shift toward content came a shift from trying to inculcate learning strategies in the individual student to trying to create classroom cultures that support inquiry and the pursuit of deeper understanding. Educational historians will probably give credit for this shift to a revival of Vygotsky's socio-cultural theory of development and to the theory of situated cognition, which came out of anthropology. These ideas found a ready audience, however, among cognitive learning researchers who had spent the previous decade trying to improve learning by teaching individual cognitive strategies, it was not that the strategies did not work or that they were too hard to teach. The results were often quite impressive in the short run. We seemed to be teaching a level of mental activity beyond anything required in normal schooling. It became evident, therefore, that any general upgrading of students' intellectual abilities and dispositions would require changing the prevailing culture of the classroom. Ordinary classroom life is organized around activities. This is true across the whole spectrum ranging from tightly controlled classrooms where the main activity is filling in workbook pages to child-centered classrooms where the activities are self-chosen and often self-initiated projects.

The new challenge has become to reorganize classroom life around the pursuit of knowledge. The shift from focus on individual cognitive strategies to classroom culture is clearly delineated in the influential work of Ann Brown. In the 1970s her research dealt with teaching memory strategies to mildly retarded children. By the 1980s individual strategy instruction had evolved into 'reciprocal teaching', in which children were organized into what might be characterized as rather highly structured support groups for reading comprehension. Reciprocal teaching then became assimilated into the more comprehensive 'communities of learners' in which the students became researchers and teachers of one another. Similar if not so clearly demarcated shifts occurred among many of the other cognitive learning researchers who had started out working with individual cognitive strategies.

The cultural shift that is implied in the new cognitive approaches remains poorly understood in the educational community, however the shift, that is, from classroom life organized around activities to classroom life organized around the pursuit of knowledge. Instead, reciprocal teaching, communities of learners, and other transformations of classroom culture are merely perceived as new activities to replace supplement old ones. The hottest innovations going in schooling today are 'project-based learning' and 'multiple intelligences.' The first is an old idea from the progressive education era brought back to life by new electronic media. The second is based on a theory of intelligence that has stimulated the invention of all kinds of new activities. New and more educative activities may indeed improve learning, but they short-circuit efforts to bring about the cultural shift that seems essential if schools are to play the role in knowledge development that cognitive research indicates they should.

This cultural shift must assume a more revolutionary form. Otherwise it will be continually reduced to "hands-on learning," "learner-centered education," or some other refurbishment of progressive education. Here is where the ideas about organizational transformation and knowledge work, prominent in the business literature, may be of service. Schools be reconstituted along the lines of other organizations whose function is to produce knowledge. Learning goes on in all organizations, but only some organizations have the function of producing knowledge. The learning that goes on in any organization, whether it is a shoe factory or a research laboratory, is internal to individual minds and to the developing practices of work groups and of the organization as a whole.

The excitement over the idea of a 'learning organization' reflects a growing appreciation of the value of this learning. It increases the competence of the organization to perform its functions; in these intensely competitive times, learning is one way for an organization to gain a competitive edge. Accordingly, we see efforts to promote learning that range from formal courses in company-run schools to coffee bars where employees may hang out and exchange instructive stories about their work. In addition, however, and quite apart from this internal betterment that we call learning, some organizations have the job of producing knowledge.

These include university research centers, independent laboratories, market research and opinion research companies, and research and design departments within larger organizations. Unfortunately, in the current learning organization lingo, this knowledge production is called learning, too, thus obscuring an important distinction. Of course, learning goes on in these knowledge-producing organizations as in all others -learning that develops the competence of the organization to do its work. But the work of the organization is not learning. It is producing knowledge. We accordingly refer to these as knowledge building organizations.

A research laboratory is a knowledge-building organization. A shoe factory is not, although it may contain a research group that is. Schools today are not knowledge building organizations. That is a radical cultural shift. The school becomes a workshop for the production of knowledge. The students are workers. They are learners, too, of course; and because of the nature of their work they may be expected to learn a great deal. But learning is not their job. Their job is producing knowledge. It is meaningful work, because what they are producing is something for their own use, and so their work has that quality, so rare in the industrial age, that comes with building one's own house or raising one's own food.

Many educators would endorse this proposal in the belief that it is what they are already doing. Yet very little of so-called 'constructivist' pedagogy that have observed or read about is actually concerned with the production of knowledge. Instead, it is concerned with the carrying out of projects that use knowledge but have some other objective than its production. Students may plan a trip to Mars or the building of a station on the moon, they may draw up an environmental or a business plan, or they may play a game or even create a game. At their best, such projects may generate a considerable amount of learning, but it is important to realize the difference between them and authentic knowledge creation.

In the course of studying ocean habitats, elementary school students were set to work creating educational computer games related to the ocean theme. Community of Learners and CSILE as 'project-based' approaches. While that is an accurate categorization, it reflects the common weakness in elementary education for elevating a procedural characteristic to the status of a pedagogical philosophy. The authors then proceed to distinguish Learning Science Through Design from the other two approaches in that it is less structured and awards students a higher level of "creative control over the production of an artifact." Evidently the students did throw themselves energetically into creating the computer games; they collaborated, consulted experts, and discussed programming problems. So if the purpose was to teach software design and programming, the project would have to be considered a success.

A computer bulletin board was used for discussion, but, the discussions were about game design and programming, not about oceans. Incredibly, the one science question posted was rejected by the teacher, who told the student not to expect others to do his research for him! The authors are candid in concluding that "Learning Science Through Design "in this instance failed "to create a consistent context for a deeper level of subject inquiry," and they suggest that in the future their method might need" to structure the electronic exchanges around content more along the lines described by both Scardamalia and her colleagues in the CSILE project and Brown and her colleagues in the COL environment." This sounds like a minor modification in procedure, however, whereas doing so successfully that is, getting students truly engaged with problems of marine biology instead of being solely concerned with software design would involve a shift in focus so radical that the game-building activity might no longer be relevant.

Students in a Community of Learners classroom intensely engaged with the problem of how male sea otters are able to mark off a territory of clean as their own a problem that was not handed to them but that they hit upon themselves as an anomaly in information they had assembled. The same sort of thing occurred in a CSILE classroom when a group studying the Arctic biome could not reconcile the reasons they were given for why trees do not grow in the Arctic with information other groups were providing about trees growing in deserts and in tropical rainforests. The issue here is not only the learning of science content. It is also learning about knowledge: learning that it is more than stuff sitting in textbooks to be used for answering quiz questions. Even more, it is a matter of gaining experience of what take to be the essence of life in a knowledge building organization the experience of producing knowledge of real value to someone.

But the extreme prominence given to them in modern pedagogy suggests to me an underlying belief that students have to be lured into learning, that they cannot be expected to pursue knowledge in its own right. No one says this openly, however, for belief in children's natural curiosity as the driving force in learning is one of the pillars of child-centered education.

However, is something even less savory. Educators examples of students 'genuine, sustained efforts to construct real knowledge, someone almost always remarks," That's fine for students who are motivated, but what about..." and there follows one of those shrugs or evasive mumbles that are meant to convey that we all know what kind of kids we are talking about although it is no longer safe to label them. The unrealistic part of the child-centered faith is the belief that each child's natural curiosity should be sufficient to sustain knowledge-seeking six or more hours a day for 12 or more years. Those of us who are trying to change classroom culture are not banking on that. Rather, the expectation is that if the production of usable knowledge gets established as the classroom's collective task, then ordinary motives of conformity and citizenship will suffice to keep students engaged when curiosity flags. There may be situations where establishing the classroom as a knowledge production workshop proves impossible, but it is certainly a more attainable objective than keeping the curiosity of 30 individual students constantly aroused.

Knowledge Construction in the Classroom

The idea of schools as workshops for the construction of knowledge wins ready assent from educators. The difficulty is in getting them to see that this is anything different from students planning space missions: It is all "project-based learning" or playing at being scientists. In discussing adult organizations earlier, it was easy to distinguish learning from knowledge building. Everyone learns, and progressive organizations do much to promote learning, but learning is not what people are employed for. Creating or adding value to knowledge, by contrast, is the purpose of an increasing number of jobs. Learning is the reason we send children to school, however, and knowledge building is only going to be valued insofar as students learn from doing it. But that does not make the distinction between learning and knowledge building any the less important. Students currently engage in all kinds of schoolwork, from doing sheets of arithmetic exercises to producing elaborate multimedia presentations, most of which is far removed from any kind of work that goes on in a knowledge society.

Since students need to do some kind of work in order to learn, why not let that work be the construction of knowledge. The reason we need a distinction between learning and knowledge building is in order for a statement like that to make sense. One major prejudice must be overcome if knowledge building, as real productive work similar to what goes on in industrial laboratories and university research centers, is to find a foothold in educational policy. This is the prejudice that bestows credit only on the first person to come forth with an idea. Although this may be a perfectly reasonable principle in patent law, when generalized it virtually denies the possibility of children's being real creators of knowledge; for rarely if ever will a child produce knowledge that is new to the world. But originality is always relative to context. If it should turn out that there are intelligent beings on another planet and that everything scientists on earth have discovered is already old hat to them, would that mean that Newton and Darwin were not scientists after all?

Furthermore, an original theory or explanation is only one kind of knowledge product, albeit an exceptionally important one. Other worthwhile products of knowledge building are interpretations of theories, criticisms, translations of them into simpler terms, analyses of their implications or applications in some context of interest, descriptions of phenomema which the theory does or does not explain, experimental demonstrations, simulations, and historical accounts. Many adults pursue respectable careers producing knowledge of these kinds, often demonstrating creativity and depth of insight in the process. There is no reason to deny students credit when they do likewise.

A student in a CSILE class enters a note asking what keeps gravity from leaving the earth. Later another student, she has read that gravity is a force between things and therefore not something contained within things. Several students seize on this as making sense of the idea they have heard that gravity is everywhere. As we adults read these notes we conclude that a genuine advance in knowledge has occurred, helped along as much by the first student's naive question as by the second student's important finding. We do not know how much has been learned that is, how much individual students in the class will carry away from this episode. Undoubtedly it will vary. What we do know is that knowledge has been produced, not of news-making or prize-winning calibre, but as important to the intellectual world that the students live in as the discoveries of a leading-edge university research team are to the intellectual world they live in. That is really all we need to allow in order to accept knowledge building by students as genuine productive work rather than merely a learning activity.

The preceding example combines remarks made by various students when asked to tell about their class's work. It is very similar to what one might get on dropping in on a university research group and asking how their work was going. The knowledge that the students have constructed is of course of a different order, but their unsolved problems are indeed unsolved in the world at large. They can legitimately claim membership in the communities of people who are working on such problems. They are, in short, doing real knowledge building, not playing pretend. Over the span of the school years, the job of students in the knowledge workshop is to construct an understanding of the whole world. Only today's students may go at it with more help and with improved tools and resources.

The achievement of such a unified and comprehensive understanding has traditionally been the highest aim of liberal education. However, in the past it has been seen as largely a matter of gaining possession of an existing understanding of the known world, such as Aristotle's or those of the medieval Summae or later the enlightenment project of Diderot's Encyclopedie. There were, of course, students who went beyond these fixed understandings to construct knowledge of their own, but in doing so they went well beyond the expectations of the curriculum and perhaps even beyond its allowable limits. The proposal to make knowledge building the principal activity in schooling would mean enlarging liberal education so as to encompass both the grasping of what others have already understood and the sustained, collective effort to extend the boundaries of what is known.

Multiculturalists, Marxist critics, and advocates of liberal education are alike in regarding schooling as a form of enculturation. "What should it mean to be an educated person in the 21st century?" we have to consider what kind of culture is foreseen and how schooling should relate to it. There is much more to this issue. The uncertainties of prediction and the alarming nature of many trends in contemporary culture are daunting. One social prediction seems much less risky than others, however, and that is the expectation of a continuing rise in the importance of knowledge and knowledge work. The only way this prediction could prove wrong would be if knowledge and technology stopped advancing, and barring worldwide suppression that could not occur. We do not know what the social consequences will be for employment, equity, quality of life, and so on -no matter how confidently pundits may extrapolate current trends. What we can say is that knowledge will be an increasingly salient part of the environment. You will not know your way around in tomorrow's world unless you know your way around knowledge.

A statement like the preceding can, however, mean next to nothing in a discussion of educational policy. To many people these days it will mean knowing your way around on the Internet, knowing how to do searches for Worldwide Web documents. The Web does, in fact, nicely epitomize a world overrun with knowledge; and so amazed to keep encountering writers on the Web proclaiming the centrality of information search skills as an educational objective for the knowledge age. The skills needed to do web searches can be learned in a few hours (less, if you know a bit of Boolean algebra). But years of subject-matter learning must come to the fore if you are to avoid retrieving thousands of documents none of which contains the information you were hoping to find.

Knowing around the Worldwide Web really means being on familiar terms with world knowledge in its manifold aspects. The more you know the greater your chance of learning something new. That is the real excitement of the new knowledge resources, yet it seems scarcely to be appreciated at all by the information media enthusiasts presuming to lead? education into the knowledge age. If it were appreciated, it would go some way toward re-establishing the importance of liberal education. The trouble, lies in a folk psychology which conceives of the mind as a storehouse of items of information, along with a set of mental abilities and skills for working with those items.

With this conception, it is very difficult to think of knowledge as the principal basis for finding or acquiring new knowledge, just as it is difficult to think of knowledge production as distinct from learning. We need a broader conception of knowledge. We must be able to treat it as a part of the world -along with computers, CD players, backpacks, and street people that students become enculturated into. Without that, schooling will remain lodged in an earlier and more primitive age, no matter how many computers line the walls, and will little prepare students for the world that exists on the other side of the modem. Working out a vision for education in a knowledge society minimally requires taking account of knowledge in two quite distinct senses: first, knowledge as something that people acquire and that becomes a part of them; second, knowledge as something that they work with and that in some sense takes in a life of its own.

The knowledge building classroom, as characterizing it, embodies this dual conception of knowledge. It thus presents a miniature of the knowledge society into which students are to become enculturated. Common sense of course recognizes this dual character of knowledge. When we talk about a child 'knowing (or not knowing) the Pythagorean theorem 'we simultaneously refer to knowledge as an attribute of the child's mental state and to the Pythagorean theorem as a piece of knowledge in its own right -as something created by a mathematician in ancient times and surviving to this day as a worthwhile thing-to-be-known. But in order to carry on a serious discussion about knowledge in education, we need distinguishing labels. Which can be quite useful so long as we are careful not to encumber them with excess meaning. The labels come from his metaphor of three worlds. World 1, the physical world, need not concern us at this point.

The important distinction is between Worlds 2 and 3. World 2 is the subjective world, comprising the knowledge in people's heads. (Without doing violence to Popper's concept, we can expand World 2 to include situated knowledge as well knowledge that is implicit in the practices of communities and not assignable to individual minds.) World 3 is, roughly speaking, the world of ideas. It consists of immaterial knowledge objects that can be discussed, modified, replaced, and so on.

The Pythagorean theorem is an object in World 1, the child's knowledge of the Pythagorean theorem is part of the child's World 1, the distinction thus coincides with the distinction have been making between knowledge building and learning. Knowledge building is work carried out to produce changes in World 3. Learning consists of changes in World 2. From an educational standpoint, what is especially attractive about the World 3 idea is that it encompasses both the traditional idea of a fund of accumulated knowledge that is passed on to the young and the more dynamic idea of knowledge advancing through people's creative efforts. We may think of World 3 as a workspace in which there are knowledge objects in various stages of development.

Some are finished to the extent that no one bothers to tinker with them anymore. Some, like phlogiston theory, are of no current value and are preserved for historical interest only. Others are under current development and are the subjects of research, criticism, controversy, repair operations, and novel conjecture. The Pythagorean theorem is one of the finished objects of World 3. But when students produce explanations of the theorem or intuitive proofs or examples of application, these are World 3 objects as well and the activity that produces them is work in World 3, just as was the work of Pythagoras. This conception of World 3 as a realm of activity stretches Popper's concept, but not very much.

Translating it into an educational prescription leads naturally to thinking of World 3 as a workspace and of education as providing entree to it. Accordingly, we may define the role of schools in the knowledge age as follows: It is to enculturate students into World 3. Enculturation into World 3 entails much more than mastering a body of established knowledge. Indeed, it leaves open such questions as what constitutes established knowledge and what needs to be mastered and in what ways. It implies, rather, that those perennial curriculum issues should be considered within the context of students' active participation in the world where such issues matter.

Enculturation into any world means becoming familiar with what is there, learning how to act, becoming involved in what is going on, and generally coming to feel at home in it. At a deeper level, enculturation implies that artifacts and activities will come to have a meaning for the newcomer that is consistent with the meaning they have for others in that world. This does not mean that one becomes the same as everyone else, but it does mean that the world is no longer exotic, bewildering, or forbidding.

In short, a whole epistemology is represented here, an epistemology sophisticated enough for the knowledge age and something far beyond what educators speak of as 'cooperative learning,'' problem-based learning,' 'constructivist learning,' or ((groan)' learner-centered education.' It is knowledge-centered education; and Mendel gets into the picture, not as a dead white male with the authority of the scientific establishment behind him but as someone with a contribution to make to a current knowledge problem. For Popper, as a philosopher of science, World 3 consisted primarily of discussible propositions or declarative knowledge—theories, conjectures, problem formulations, historical accounts, interpretations, proofs, criticisms, and the like.

However, he saw these as cultural objects existing in a larger world that includes other cultural objects such as poems, sonatas, folktales, food recipes, rituals, and monuments. Liberal education is enculturation into this larger world of cultural objects. World 3 is and always has been an important part of the world for liberal education. The world of cultural objects is quite different for a liberally educated Indonesian, for instance, from what it is for a liberally educated Italian. To be sure, both would probably score better on a test of cultural literacy than would the average American student for whom it was designed; but in the art, literature, music, and history with which they are intimately familiar, there will be profound differences.

These differences are valuable; cultures are kept alive by people who cherish and live on intimate terms with the objects of their cultures, and this is much of what gives richness to life. But it is important to recognize that things are different with the objects of World 3. Multiculturalists to the contrary, there are not culture-specific sciences, mathematics, literary or historical theories.

There are cultural differences, just as there are individual differences, in how people think about these things; but they are not differences that preclude constructive criticism and collaborative knowledge building. Or if they are, then something is wrong that education needs to set right. The boundaries of World 3 are approximately the boundaries of what can be profitably argued about in general terms. Liberal education, has the dual task of expanding those boundaries and of equipping students to engage in the argument. Not that arguing is all one does with World 3 objects; there is finding implications and applications, explaining, comparing, revising, and so on. But if a proposition is not arguable it is generally not amenable to these other operations either, and if people do not understand a World 3 object well enough to argue constructively about it they are probably not competent to do much else with it.

Liberal education today is embroiled in serious controversy about what cultural objects, representing whose culture, are to figure in the curriculum. This is an important controversy, accentuated by the increasing cultural divisions to be found within modern societies. But the largest cultural divide, cutting across the whole world with great consequence, is that which separates people who are at home in World 3 from those who are not. Any decision about enculturation that excludes students from enculturation into a cosmopolitan World 3 is a serious denial of children's rights to education.

Exclusion from World 3 could come in the form of an educational program so intent on preserving indigenous culture or ethnic pride that it relegates World 3 to the status of a foreign culture. This is what is happening when educators start referring to 'Eurocentric science,' for instance. Or exclusion could take the form of an educational program so child-centered or so intent on learning objectives that there is no participation in any larger intellectual world. Much of what is going on in education seems to be exclusionary in one or more of these ways. It seems that the education system itself is on the wrong side of the cultural divide, ill-disposed to treat knowledge as a focus of productive work. Better models of schooling are available, models that are compatible with the needs of a knowledge-based economy, with the best of cognitive learning research, and with enduring values of liberal education. Variations on project-based learning or whatever new method comes to the fore. In order to move to the other side of the divide, in order to find their place in a knowledge society, schools must undergo a much more radical transformation. Only by becoming knowledge building organizations themselves, can schools hope to provide students with a way into the life of a knowledge society.

4

Background of Multicultural Education

Cultures are the linguistic, religious, artistic, and mythological ways in which groups of the species *homo sapiens* express their originality. Of course, cultures can seem like stronger divisions than that: Cultural differences can become the fault lines in a society that offer pretenses for mistreatment, discrimination against, and oppression of one group by another.

Multicultural education came into being where fair-minded people sought ways to respond constructively to the challenge of members of different cultural groups sharing the same society. Although social action for justice may begin in other domains— laws and policies, hiring practices, housing, or access to health care, for example—sooner or later, schools must be involved in the effort. That is because progress in social arrangements ultimately requires that citizens adopt new attitudes, which in turn need new knowledge and experiences. A new education is needed by people on both sides of the cultural divide. Children of groups who have been oppressed need bolstering; and children of privileged groups need to broaden their perspective to take into account the views of children from other groups.

Multicultural education, then, is a movement in schools to promote awareness, mutual appreciation, and harmony among people of different cultural groups—usually with the ultimate goal of achieving social justice and social cohesion.

Those who pay serious attention to what happens in schools know that schooling has a formal and an informal side. On the formal or explicit side are the objectives of the state curriculum and the content of school books and lectures, as measured by examinations.

On the informal or hidden side are power relationships and implicit expectations for behavior: For example, do we succeed by cooperating or competing? Do students share responsibility for the classroom or only take orders? Also part of the informal side are attitudes toward one sex or one cultural group as opposed to another.

This aspect of the informal or hidden curriculum is often evidenced in what is *not* included in the formal curriculum: Whose pictures do not hang in the hallways, or are not seen in books? Whose stories are not told? Whose contributions to society are not chronicled?

Teachers who approach multicultural education often begin with the formal curriculum—with the content that is taught. Some, however, attempt to change the implicit aspects of schooling, too—to make aspects of schooling like power-sharing and interaction among students more supportive of students from all cultural groups and ultimately of the goal of social change.

A Model of Prejudice and Multicultural Education

Attitudes are not learned cognitively like facts and dates. How does multicultural education affect attitudes and outlooks toward cultures—one's own and others? The answer lies in the interaction between concepts and experience. Let us look, first, at how this interaction affects members of the dominant group.

> In their early years, members of Group Y begin to hear disparaging remarks said about members of Group X. They may hear these remarks, and detect the attitude they convey, before those members of Group Y have any real experience with members of Group X. The prejudicial remarks predispose them to have negative experiences with members of Group X when they eventually meet one: Members of Group Y will be willing to interpret virtually anything the Group X person says or does as evidence of their ________ or their _______ (whatever negative attribute they have learned to associate with members of that group). When that happens, they are now likely assume that our negative view of members of Group X is based on direct experience! They know that members of Group X have these negative attributes, because they have seen them with their own eyes!
>
> Unfortunately, this phenomenon may affect members of Group X as well, if all majority of the cultural reminders they see in public either ignore Group X—or worse, portray them in a negative light—members of Group X may, at best, conclude that they are not very important, that they don't really belong in the school or in the community; and at worst, that they really do possess the negative features that members of Group Y have ascribed to them.

These gloomy processes can be prevented from happening, however. Cognitive psychologists tell us, just as the model suggested, that we tend to notice what we know about: A person who knows her wild flowers will have an altogether different experience of a walk through a field than a person who knows nothing about wild flowers. Similarly, if in school, children from Group Y are taught many fascinating features of the culture of Group X, as well as many features that Group Y has in common with that group, then their personal experience with members of that group will no longer automatically lead them to form negative conclusions about them. Similarly, if members of Group X see people like themselves reflected in the school curriculum, and begin to see positive features and accomplishments of their group *validated in the school,* they will feel less alienated and more encouraged by their school experiences.

Both of the examples given above together have been called the *window and mirror* effects of multicultural education (Simms Bishop, 1996). Multicultural education provides a *window* into the cultures of minority children, through which children from majority groups can see them accurately. It also provides a *mirror* of their own culture, to children from minority groups, who heretofore may have seen only negative reflections of themselves, or no reflection at all, in the school curriculum.

Admittedly, a few widely scattered exercises in cultural awareness will not go very far to combat years of prejudicial attitudes that have been absorbed at home or in the neighborhood. That is why many experts in multicultural education argue for the infusion of multicultural influences throughout the curriculum and throughout the school day, week, and year. In fact, approaches that have been taken to multicultural education can be plotted along a continuum from occasional topic lessons to a transformation of the school.

Models of Multicultural Education

In the most straightforward of venues, multicultural education is limited to discussions of school curriculum. From a practical standpoint, this translates into using materials such as children's books, or projects such as oral histories, to increase awareness and understanding of the various cultural perspectives of the students in the school or classroom. The idea is that the content connects to the child and hence, each child will see himself or herself reflected in the daily curriculum and studies that take place in the classroom. Further, that the class will see itself as a collective made up of different experiences, all of which are equally important and valid, and by doing so will increase the understanding of each child of the other.

In other contexts, such as the political arena, multicultural education takes on a much broader scope and has been defined as "any set of processes by which schools work with rather than against oppressed groups." The most inclusive definitions suggest that multicultural education is a transformational process that permeates and impacts every aspect of the operation of an educational system, including government policy, staffing, curriculum, disciplinary policy, student involvement, parent and community involvement, pedagogy, assessment, and funding.

One of the underlying premises of multicultural education as transformation is "that as schools go so goes the nation," At the practical level, multicultural education then becomes a venue for social and political reform. Discussions of oppression, social inequality, power dynamics, race and ethnicity, as well as the role of the dominant culture, in the shaping of society's basic assumption about what constitutes school knowledge, appropriate social behavior, and national identity, is all part of the multicultural education discourse.

Regardless of where practice comes down on the definitional continuum, researchers, architects, and practitioners of multicultural education hold certain goals and assumptions in common.

Multicultural education assumes that pluralism is a good thing and that race, ethnicity, cultural and social class are all salient parts of a pluralistic society. Participation in a variety of ethnic experiences ultimately enriches one's understanding of the human experience and leads to a more fulfilling life.

A central goal of multicultural education is to help individuals live more productively in a pluralistic society. This is accomplished in two ways:

— Individuals gain a greater understanding of themselves by seeing themselves through the lens of other cultures.

— Individuals gain the necessary skills, knowledge, and attitudes needed to function within their ethnic culture and within and across other ethnic cultures.

Multicultural education is premised on the need for accuracy. In order for individuals to get a true picture of historical and social events, which have shaped national identity, they need to listen to multiple voices and understand multiple perspectives. It is not a matter of leaving out one version of events in favor of another; rather it is about re-envisioning history using an inclusive model that more accurately portrays events as they happened.

Multicultural education is a commitment to helping all students master the essential academic and social skills to become knowledgeable, caring, and active citizens in an increasingly polarized and troubled world.

Models of Multicultural Education Programs: Theory Into Practice

Regardless of how individuals view the multicultural education movement, there are some general models and specific areas of research that offer educators and policy makers a road map for program development. The two most often cited general modes are offered by Banks and by Sleeter and Gran These models differ from one another but are not mutually exclusive.

Other researchers such as Nieto, Delpit, and Ladson-Billings focus on particular areas of multicultural program development and offer suggestions relating to pedagogy, curriculum, and structure. Ladson-Billings, for example, focuses on the specifics of successful literacy education for African American students. Delpit is concerned with power relations in a classroom that can exist when minority children are taught by teachers of the dominant culture. Nieto is focused on institutional reform and student achievement.

When discussing theoretical models, how they actually look and operate in a classroom or school is often left out of the conversation. In that regard, Burnett suggests a third model that combines Banks, Sleeter, current research with an overview of actual programs as they are currently underway in the United States. Burnett's typology is particularly useful in that it reflects the translation of theory into practice and divides programs into three general categories according to program emphasis.

Content-Oriented Programs

Content-oriented programs are the most easily recognizable and hence the most common form of multicultural education. Content-oriented programs are committed to the inclusion of material that reflects the cultural make-up of the class or the school. The primary goal of these programs is to make students more knowledgeable about cultures within their schools or their communities.

Content-oriented programs come in various levels of engagement and infusion of the curriculum. In its simplest form, "this type of program gives a multicultural patina to the standard curriculum" by incorporating a few readings and the celebration of heroes and holidays of diverse groups. It gives only a cursory nod to multicultural education by focusing solely on "heroes and holiday." Students would read books, do projects, and learn about a variety of holidays but through the lens of the standard canon. At this stage, multicultural education is an add-on or tangential to current curriculum without changing the actual focus. More sophisticated and complex programs, however, set out to actually transform the curriculum. These programs have three goals:

— to develop multicultural content across the disciplines

— to incorporate a variety of different viewpoints and perspectives in the curriculum

— to transform the canon, ultimately developing a new paradigm for the curriculum

These programs can come in many forms, but often the most common is a single group study, such as women's studies, ethnic studies, etc. These programs can be the focus of the whole school, as in the examples of Afrocentric and single sex schools, or only portions of the curriculum.

Student-Oriented Programs

Student-oriented programs address the academic and learning needs of carefully defined groups of students, most specifically minority students. The goal of these programs is often to raise the academic achievement of these groups. Research in learning styles, language use and development, etc. often forms the basis of these programs.

Since the goal of student-oriented programs is to improve the academic success of specific groups and thereby make it possible for them to enter the mainstream, they are often seen as compensatory in nature. Further, there is no particular guarantee that student-oriented programs will be done in conjunction with content oriented programs. In fact, it is entirely possible to have one without the other. Again Banks suggests four broad program categories:

— programs that use research into culturally-based learning styles in order to match teaching styles to a specific group of students

— bi-lingual education or language/cultural immersion

— special math and science programs for groups, such as females and minorities that are seen as underachieving in these areas.

— Language programs and cultural programs specific to minority group

Socially-Oriented Programs

Socially-oriented programs are generally the most inclusive and broad-based. They are also often controversial and as a consequence less common. Programs such as these attempt to reform "both the schooling and the cultural and political contexts of schooling". The over-arching goal of socially-oriented programs is to increase cultural and racial tolerance and reduce bias as well as rearrange the social structure to reinforce and support this new paradigm.

In order to accomplish this, socially-oriented programs have a number of distinguishing characteristics:

— They seek to revise and transform the curriculum to create a new canon that is reflective of the current society.

— They seek to use current educational research to discover new ways to engage students in the educational enterprise in order that they may be academically successful, regardless of ethnicity and class.

- — They use the instruments and strategies of social activism and community organization to accomplish these goals.
- — They focus on the outcome of preparing students to be socially - active citizens and agents of change.

Sleeter and Grant have described socially-oriented programs as about human relations in all its many forms. As a consequence, such programs use a variety of approaches borrowed from disciplines as diverse as philosophy, ecology, and psychology. Some programs emphasize critical thinking and critical discourse, collaborative learning and multilingualism. Other programs focus on the use of the ecological model to enhance understanding of social structures and the diffusion of change, still other programs focus on the nature of inclusion and consensus and how best to translate those concepts into practice, not only at the classroom level but at the school and community level as well.

There is a danger in multicultural education programming of letting the political rhetoric and the academic research agenda overshadow the benefits of designing and implementing interesting and lively opportunities for children to learn. In fact, the reasons to use a multicultural approach in schools are simple and compelling.

- — A multicultural approach makes learning more interesting and relevant to children's lives.
- — A multicultural approach gives all students a forum in which to share information about who they are, how they live, what is important to them and their families.

— A multicultural approach gives students another lens through which to view history and society.

— A multicultural approach encourages tolerance and respect and supports notions of social reform and community cohesion.

Oral Histories

It is often the case that when a teacher says the word "history" to a group of youngsters there is a collective groan as eyes roll back and students brace for the worst. History can evoke images of dusty books, dimly lit libraries, and the tedious memorization of names and dates that take a long time to learn and a short time to forget. Fortunately, oral histories have none of those characteristics.

The broadest and simplest definition of an oral history is the reminiscences and recollections of living people concerning the past. These recollections can be passed down orally from generation to generation or may be the oral memories of an individual who was present at a specific time and event.

The only caveat is that the story is "collected" by an interviewer and then transcribed into text with some accompanying narrative or explanation that fleshes out the background of the storyteller and the particular situation. The topic is fairly irrelevant as long as it is about an actual memory or incident. Topics can be virtually anything from surviving a flood, putting food by, building a boat, memories of school days, tales of courage and moments of sheer hilarity and electrifying suspense.

The elements of a good oral history are the same as the elements of a good story. There are vibrant and fully realized characters such as; an eccentric aunt, Uncle so and so who was captured by pirates, the strongest man in the village or the lady across the street who loved cats. Each one of these people has a role in the tale and, most importantly, exists or existed in real life. There are problems to be solved. They can range from the grave to the mundane such as; harvesting food in a year with no rain, surviving the great depression, building a dyke against a flood or how to fix a roof, make a quilt or build a house without using nails.

The solutions to these problems or, in literary terms, the resolution, often illustrate everything from outstanding resourcefulness to blatant stupidity. The voice or the point of view of the oral history is that of the person telling the story.

The researcher acts as the invisible narrator who only adds those things, which help enhance or illuminate the dark corners of the tale that may be opaque to the reader. Finally the language or tone that the oral history takes is, and should be, true to the "teller". It is not the job of the oral historian to change the person's syntax and make them more or less educated, sophisticated or different from who they are. An oral history is not an exercise in creative writing but an exercise in telling the truth as someone else knows it.

Oral histories can be turned into books, articles, displays, and even videos. They are also a perfect venue for developing multicultural curriculum in schools. There is a compelling quote from the poet Rilke that ultimately summarizes what oral histories actually do.. *"Who ever tells the story shapes the world" The* oral history is the story, what a teacher does with it can shape the world.

The Steps in an Oral History Project

What follows is an abbreviated outline of the steps in an oral history project. For more complete information please see *Telling stories, writing lives: a guide to using oral history folklore and folklife.*

Getting started

The hardest part of an oral history is to decide on the topic. As students and teachers think about topics, perhaps the most salient question to answer is " will it make a good story". Think about events and people in a community that are pivotal. Wars, floods, and desperate times are natural starting points and usually come instantly to mind.

Another avenue to explore is memorable moments in people's lives such as weddings, births, chance meetings, and significant life choices. . These projects can result in stories of humor and grace that are informative as well as interesting. Families are full of these stories and they run the gamut from the serious to the romantic. How grandparents came to live where they do is a good start for an oral history on immigration.

How uncles and aunts learned their professions or met one another are opportunities for oral history around work and romance. How great aunt so and so learned to ride a horse or make a quilt or won a special prize at school are all part of the significant fabric of people's lives and are good choices for oral histories. The point to remember is that the stuff of life is the stuff of oral histories.

Where to go, who to interview and how

Once teachers and students have settled on a topic, the next hurdle in an oral history project is gathering information. This entails finding people to talk to, convincing them that that is a good idea, and finally, figuring out what to say. Gaining access is a term that refers to identifying and locating individuals that know about the topic. The interview is made up of a series of questions that encourages the speaker to tell his or her story. The most common mistakes that students make are to

a) pick topics that on the surface sound great but are in reality too difficult,

b) not find the right people to interview and

c) structure a weak interview.

The only real way to avoid making these mistakes is to practice. It is important to practice writing and doing interviews, as well as picking topics and designing projects that have a reasonable comfort level. For example, it would be unwise for students to decide to do an oral history project that requires them to travel great distances, or only interview very famous people. The likely-hood of failure would be high.

Interview guides are available and are helpful for the first time oral historian. When it comes to format and structure, there is no reason to reinvent the wheel. A good commercial interview guide can save students and teachers time and headaches as it provides useful suggestions and gives a solid structure from which to work.

The most accessible and fertile ground for oral history projects are in students' families and communities. Family and community oral history projects are very meaningful to students as they represent a celebration of easily recognizable individual and collective experience. Everyone loves to "know the hero" of the tale and local projects allow that to happen.

A gold mine of information exists in the elderly people in a community. What was life like fifty years ago is a wonderful place to start especially for school age children. Elderly people are usually interested in youngsters and generally enjoy their company. They are also often available for school visits and can become a real asset to any educational program but particularly one that is using oral history as part of a multicultural endeavor. Intergenerational perspectives are powerful and even more so when they include stories from diverse ethnic, racial and social groups.

Writing it up

Once students have collected stories and information the next step is to "write it up". The writing workshop is a perfect way to get lively and interesting pieces written. Important aspects of this process are talk and collaborative work. Students need time to assemble information and talk with one another about what they have and what they might do with it. Besides interviews, students can use photographs, souvenirs, news clippings and other artifacts relevant to the topic that they are researching. The most difficult part of the project comes when students must synthesize the information and "tell the story" in a voice that is true to the experience and to the person.

Finished products are only limited by the imagination and energy of the students. Oral history projects can be made into videos, displays, books for adults, books for children. They can be part of local celebrations as well as the focus for local and regional publications.

Oral History Projects

Oral history projects are about visibility. When students embark on a project those pieces of lived experience that have been in the shadows of families and communities come to light. What had once been invisible suddenly takes center stage. In a multicultural program this is particularly important as the experience of marginalized groups gets the same attention as the dominant group. Hero and heroines, problems and solutions emerge in the most unlikely places.

As a consequence, students and teachers have opportunities for discussions around such topics as courage, resourcefulness, fairness and opportunity but through the multicultural lens and anchored in the experience of students. This is a prime example of Simms Bishop's model of windows and mirrors. Oral histories can allow teachers and students to change the content of the curriculum as well as the way students gather information and understand each other.

Oral history projects reduce the distance between the student and the subject matter. It is one thing for students to learn about and discuss events and concepts from a theoretical perspective. It is a whole different matter to discuss the same events and concepts but anchored in the lived experiences of family and community members. From the perspective of Banks model, oral history projects offer teachers and students access to changing the structure of the curriculum by changing, in part, how some of the information is obtained and studied.

Oral history projects require a collaborative and inclusive working style. It is virtually impossible for students to carry out individual projects because there is too much involved; hence students need to work together. Furthermore oral history project are a bridge between the classroom and the community. It is essential that students go out into the community and it is equally essential the community come into the classroom. For students of minorities, this may be one of the first opportunities that their families can participate in a school-based activity as experts in a particular topic.

Oral history projects can illuminate social issues and problems and give students and teachers a forum for discussion, decision making and action. As students study their communities and listen to the stories of family members they see how those experiences highlight a need for action and social change. For example, an oral history project conducted in a small town in Connecticut focused on the plight of Portuguese fisherman, which ultimately resulted in new legislation in the fishing industry.

This is not to say that oral history projects can or should be the centerpiece of a multicultural program. However, these types of projects are a logical and interesting place to begin the discussion. They are not technically difficult to execute nor are they particularly expensive. They are worth doing if for no other reason than oral histories help us to see and to remember those pieces of the ordinary human experience that would be lost as it is in our stories that our lives have meaning.

Multicultural Publishing Projects

Publishing projects to support multicultural education projects can vary in a number of ways.

— *The authors* of multicultural publications can be the students in a classroom, selected students from a school, a group of young people recruited in the community for this purpose, teachers, or professional adult writers.

— *The audiences* can be the other students in a classroom, a whole school, students from different regions of the country (by means of exchanges), people in the immediate community, or even a national readership, if the works are published professionally.

— *The forms* the materials might take include a wall or hallway-mounted collage of texts, illustrations, and photographs. Or they might be a newsletter, a magazine, a handmade book, or a commercially printed book.

— *The genres and patterns* which organize the publications can take on interesting variety, also.

Patterns and Genres of Multicultural Publications

Readers expect patterns in the texts they read; but inexperienced writers often have difficulty finding a design and sticking to it. What are some useful patterns for works written for children?

The first set of patterns introduced below might be used by children who are writing their own books, or by adults writing for children. These ideas were collected by Sylvia Vardell.

— *Alphabet books.* (Animals, names, or objects presented from A to Z).

— *Counting books.* (Numbers from 0 to 10, 1 to 20; sets of 5 or 10; addition problems; telling time; counting money).

— *Predictable pattern books.* (This is... AI wish.. I like... Someday...)

— *Rhymes, songs, and poems.* (Anthologies, or one book containing a single poem)

— *Riddles, proverbs, jokes* (old favorites, ones collected in the community, new creations)

— *Retellings of traditional tales or religious stories* (including stories that were collected from sources in the community)

— *Personal narratives.* (First person accounts of individual experiences; or first person accounts told to the writer by a community person)

— *Vocabulary to learn or rules to demonstrate.* (A personal dictionary or guidebook for carrying out a procedure)

— *Biography or history.* (Based on interviews or research)

— *Autobiography of journals.* (Me, my family, my feelings)

— *Nonfiction or informational books* (about a favorite topic)

— *Concept books.* (Simple concept with examples given: colors, animals, senses).
— *How to do books.* (Clear instructions on how to build or create or do something).
— *Cookbooks.* (Anthologies or individual creations).
— *Word less picture books.* (In which a story is told entirely through pictures.
— *Favorite book formula.* (Imitate or innovate on the pattern of a favorite book).
— *Favorite character book.* (Make up a new adventure of a favorite character).
— *Original imaginative stories.* (Fictional characters or fantasy characters).
— *Art books.* (Single or mixed media collections of artwork with titles, captions, or stories).
— *Class anthologies.* (A mixture of all literary types).
— *Movable/pop-up books.* (Three dimension; moveable parts)
— *Shape books.* (Books in the physical shape of the topic, like letters, numbers, or shoes).
— *Bilingual books.* (Romanian/Romani, etc.)
— *Words/sounds.* (Featuring idioms, expressions, or initial consonants or vowel sounds, or syllables)

Longer Narrative Patterns

For more extended texts, narrative patterns are often used. There are a range of patterns around which narratives can be arranged some of them quite obvious, but a few of them less so.

1. *Sequential patterns.* The trappings of a traditional wedding could be highlighted as follows: At the start of the wedding feast, I ate a plum tart. But the bride still had not danced. By two o'clock I had eaten a plum tart and two hot crossed buns. But the bride still had not danced. By half past three I had eaten a plum tart, two hot crossed buns, and ________and so on.
2. *Amazing Grace.* In Carolyn Bench's book, Amazing Grace, a young girl growing up in a modern city is having a crisis of confidence over the school play. Her aunt from her native island inspires her with the confidence of her roots, and the girl eventually triumphs. Children in other cultures could use a similar message.
3. *The tension between traditional culture and modern culture.* In Sharon Bell Mathis' The 100 Penny Box, a hundred year-old grandmother keeps a penny from every year of her life and tells a story to go with each one to her young great-grandson, with whom she lives in a cramped urban apartment. The boy's mother has no use for the old woman's tales; and the boy is caught in between. This pattern bears recycling
4. *Plots that stem from characters and their problems.* Good stories can be developed by thinking of a character in her setting, wishing what a person would typically wish for in that place. The story is further developed as opposing forces or characters are brought into play.

Standards of Writing for Young People

As the patterns of writing grow more complex, writers must work hard to handle them well. Many professional writers say that good writing is revising. Many published authors seek out the company of writers' groups so they may share their works and receive suggestions. At many such workshops we have conducted, the suggestions writers offer each other tend to boil down to a fairly small set of recommendations. Suggestions such as the following are useful when writing fiction for children and young people:

— *Write within a genre*: If the story is realistic, don't have trees talking!

— Make it sound natural, but *write in patterns*.

— Create a *beginning* (in which characters are introduced and a problem is posed), a *middle* (in which the story is developed, and attempts are made to solve the problem), and an *end* (in which the problem is resolved and the characters' new circumstances are presented).

— Put the *Main Dramatic Question* close to the beginning.

— *Use words the way poets do*: for sound, meaning, and suggestion.

— *Put the child in the driver's* seat: That is, give the child a leading role in solving the problem.

— *Tell the truth:* don't offer unrealistic solutions to real problems.

— *Have the work be about something, but don't preach.* The most satisfying works seem on reflection to make some point. However, stories can teach by themselves without heavy-handed moralizing by the writer.

— *Show, don't tell* (Make the reader see, hear, smell, feel).

— *Trust the reader.* Don't explain everything.

— *Surprise your readers.*

— However realistic or even grim the characters' circumstances may be, *leave a ray of hope in your works.*

Writers' Workshops

There is a widely held belief that only certain gifted individuals can write anything worthwhile. Those who are not inherently gifted only embarrass themselves by attempting to write. Yet when one gazes on the portraits of those gifted individuals, hanging high on the walls of school classrooms, one perceives a curious pattern: They are all well dressed! They are all men! They are all white! (And they are almost all dead!). Perhaps it is not talent for writing that is in limited supply, but the expectation that many people, even young people, might have interesting things to say, in print.

Indeed, the multicultural writers' workshop movement has found and nurtured many fine writers who would not otherwise have been published. One of the most pleasing realizations that followed this effort in the United States was that these writers really had quite a lot to say: and, once published, they have stayed in print through their own popularity.

Even in schools, writers' workshop movements have encouraged personal authorship among students, and have had very positive results: (1) They nurture the students' self-expression and develop their self-esteem, and (2) they open other students' eyes to the experiences and ideas of their classmates from every neighborhood and from every ethnicity. (The mirror and window phenomenon again). Teachers also like the fact that personal authorship leads students to identify more closely with professional authors, and look more seriously at the author's craft.

Without denying that some people have more gifts for writing than others, we can say confidently that virtually any student can be helped to unleash what he or she wants to say on paper. What is needed are *permission to write about things that matter to the writer, real audiences who will receive the writing for what it says, frequent opportunities to write,* and *models and demonstrations of the process of writing.* The process of writing referred to in the last sentence has come to be understood to be something like the following:

The Writing Process

Is there one process that all writers go through to produce a finished piece? Surely not. But there is one description of the writing process that seems to come the closest to what most writers do when they compose. This is the writing process model put forward by Donald Murray and Donald Graves. This model has proved useful for organizing writing instruction, too.

The writing process provides a means by which a student begins with an idea, and gradually shapes that idea on the page to the point that it successfully communicates to the readers, and builds connections between the readers and the writer around the theme developed by the author out of the original idea. It is a step-by-step process through which students become credible authors, and writing becomes a vehicle for clarifying and expressing ideas.

According to the model of the writing process we will use here, most thoughtful pieces of writing go through three steps: rehearsing, drafting, and revising. Those that are to be published go through two more: editing and publishing. Does every piece of writing go through these steps, in this order? Again, of course not. It's very likely that young people will move back and forth through these steps, though they will most commonly use that order. In the pages that follow, we will explain each of these steps, and pause to show activities that help young people learn at each one. Again, it should be said that the writing process described here may be used in all subject areas, although special applications to the disciplines will be shared later in this guide.

Rehearsing. Rehearsing is the act of gathering information and collecting our thoughts. We survey the ideas we have available to us on a topic, and begin to plan a way into writing about it.

Drafting. Drafting is the act of setting ideas out on paper. Drafting is tentative, experimental. We write down our ideas so we can see what we have to say about out topic. Once they are there, we can make them clearer, even elegant.

When we are drafting, it is no time to be critical with our ideas, their form, or their spelling and handwriting: the time for all that will come later.

Most young writers (indeed, most writers) don't have the habit of writing more than one version of a paper. Proficient writers do. "Writing is rewriting," they say. We'll need to encourage students to think of writing as drafting.

Revising. After our paper is written in draft form, we can start to make it better. We'll improve the paper in two careful stages. At the revising stage, we want to see what we had to say, and decide how it can be said better. We are concerned that our ideas be clear, and that they be presented in the right form. We are still not worrying about spelling, handwriting, or grammatical correctness at this stage, although of course they are important: These issues will be dealt with in the next stage: the proof-reading or editing stage.

Editing. Once a paper has been drafted and revised, it is ready for editing. Editing is the final polishing a undergoes before it goes public. Editing is held off for last, because paragraphs or even pages may have been cut or added in the revising stage. After the piece is in final form, but before it is widely shared, is the time for editing.

The habit of editing must be taught. The habit consists of three things:

— caring that the paper be correct;

— being aware of errors;

— knowing how to set them straight.

Publishing: Publishing is the final stage of the writing process, and in important ways publishing drives the whole enterprise. The prospect of sharing what they have to say with an audience makes many students want to write, and rewrite, and smooth out and refine—especially if they've seen other students' work received with appreciation and delight. Publishing also lets students see what each other is doing. A good idea is contagious; and anything from an interesting topic, to a plot structure, to a way to use dialogue, to the habit of taking risks with spelling may be shared through the process of publishing.

A Demonstration Writing Workshop

Tied to the above description of the writing process, of what effective writers do in order to produce a viable work, is a strategy for teaching the process: The *writing workshop.* Writing workshops can be done in classroom, even primary grade classrooms; or they may be offered for adult groups. Perhaps the best way to visualize what a writing workshop looks like is to consider this Ascript@ for a very first writing workshop, as it is introduced in the Reading & Writing for Critical Thinking Project. The instructions are written for the person directing the workshop.

PREPARE FIVE TOPICS. You will need to have prepared in advance four or five topics about subjects that are lively and important to you just now. Take care that these are topics from "the human carnival," describing events and feelings that you are likely to have in common with the people in your workshop.

DISPLAY THE TOPICS. Begin by writing those topics on a sheet of newsprint, or overhead transparency. Explain that you (and they) will be writing short papers in this session about things that matter to you. You have thought of these topics as possibilities, and would like their help in choosing one of them to write about.

OTHERS INTERVIEW YOU. Request that they interview you about each topic, asking questions such as, "What interests you most about this topic?' "Tell us more about _______." "Why did you choose this topic?" Answer their questions, and as you do, make it clear why one particular topic stands out to you from the others—perhaps for its freshness, vividness, or poignancy; perhaps for its manageable scope. (Take time to point out that topics that are too abstract, too ambitious, or that you don't have enough information about are better left for another day).

OTHERS LIST TOPICS. Now ask them to do the same: make a list of four or five possible topics that matter to them, that they might like to write a short piece about.

OTHERS INTERVIEW EACH OTHER ABOUT THEIR TOPICS. After everyone has had four or five minutes to make a list, ask people to pair up and share their lists. Partners should then interview each other about their topics, just as they interviewed you, so that each person can be helped to identify the one topic that seems most interesting to other people, and to herself.

MAKE A CLUSTER. Now make a cluster of details about your topic. Write your topic in a circle in the center of the page, then write subtopics as "satellites" around your main topic, and add subtopics to each of those.

OTHERS INTERVIEW YOU ABOUT YOUR CLUSTER. Invite the participants to ask you about the details you listed, and the ways they go together. In short, have them help you "find your story." Mark prominently on your cluster the part you will write about.

OTHERS MAKE CLUSTERS AND INTERVIEW EACH OTHER. Now invite the participants to think through the topics they chose in the previous step, and make a cluster for the ideas they associate with it. After they have had seven or eight minutes to do so, ask them to stop and interview each other about their clusters, in order to "find their stories." They may have listed more details than they can work into a short paper; so after discussing the details with a partner, they should now mark the most interesting and relevant parts of their clusters.

EVERYONE WRITE FOR AN INTERVAL. Explain that you will all be writing drafts that can be changed before they are shared. The important thing is for people to get their ideas out on paper. They should write without stopping or going back for the allotted period of time (allow about 20 minutes for this). Be sure to tell them to write on every other line. You write, too, either on an overhead or on chart paper.

SHOW A PAPER THAT COMMUNICATES, BUT THAT CAN BE IMPROVED IN SOME RESPECT. You may need to prepare this ahead of time, but you should have a paper that conveys real ideas, but that also has something about it that could use revision— such as flat, colorless language that "tells" rather than "shows." Display the paper (either on newsprint or on an overhead) and ask the participants to say first what they find pleasing about it, and then to help you make it communicate better. Presumably they will call attention to the flat language, and you can then ask volunteers for suggestions for more vivid wording for each dull spot.

Take a moment now to talk about the difference between positive, constructive comments that help us make our writing better, and negative comments that discourage us. Positive comments include naming specific parts we liked—those that are most aptly described, most vivid, most surprising, most enjoyable—and saying what we liked about them. They also include asking about parts that are confusing to us or ambiguous, or where we would like more information.

Also, make a point about ownership: the idea that the ultimate responsibility for the paper rests with the writer. Others can tell us their reactions, and those are valuable to writers, but the decision of whether to change something change it always rests with the writer.

OTHERS READ PAPERS TO PARTNERS, FOR COMMENTS AND CRITIQUES. They should now take turns sharing their papers, and first comment on the meaning of the paper, and name what they liked about the paper. Later they can see if there are parts that could be made clearer or more vivid—just as they helped you do with your own. Writers should put in any additions or clarifications on their papers in the lines they left for that purpose.

WRITE REFINED DRAFTS OF YOUR PAPERS. Now everyone writes again for fifteen minutes or so, creating a new draft that improves on the previous one—we hope with the benefits of the conferring that just occurred.

READ TO THE WALL. Before the participants take the last step of sharing their papers with the larger group, ask each person to read his or her paper aloud to the wall, and listen for words that can be changed, unclear parts that can be improved, and unnecessary words or phases that can be omitted.

ASK VOLUNTEERS TO READ FROM THE "AUTHOR'S CHAIR." Designate a chair at "center stage" in the room, from which a volunteer will read his or her paper to the whole group. Remind the others ahead of time that after the reading, they will be asked to find one thing that they liked about the paper, and also ask the writer one question. Share four or five papers with the whole group in this way.

IN RETROSPECT, NOTE THESE GENERAL POINTS:

— The teacher served as a model, treating writing as a "studio craft," analogous to the ways he or she might teach a class in pottery making, or painting.

— The topics came from everyone's own interests and experiences, rather than from assignments.

— The thrust of the whole exercise was to communicate to a real audience something that interested the writer

— Peers helped each other communicate their messages more elegantly, instead of teachers receiving the papers for purposes of grading.

THE ESSENTIAL NEEDS OF A WRITING CLASSROOM: TIME, OWNERSHIP, AND DEMONSTRATION.

— *Time*: Writing workshops should be scheduled at regular intervals so that students know when they will have opportunities to write, get help with, and share their ideas.

— *Ownership*: Students should have opportunities to choose their own topics, or at least their own approach to topics. When conferences are conducted to help students improve writing, their "ownership" of the work must still be respected, with freedom left for them to choose which advice to follow.

— *Demonstration*: Teaching writing, as we said, is a "studio craft," with attention to the process of creating well written works. The teacher should demonstrate every phase of the process so students will know how effective writing is done.

The Dynamics of Illustrating Books for Children.

When we have conducted workshops with the intention of producing professionally published materials, we have often given an orientation to potential illustrators of the books, too. Picture books create unique challenges and opportunities to illustrators, since they sustain the same narrative over 16, 32, or 64 pages, and require many illustrations that reflect both the continuity of the text and the changing dramatic contours. The following are some points we often make with illustrators.

— *Characterization* (How does the illustrator makes us know each character by appearance? How are parts of a character used to denote him or her?)

— *Perspective and positioning* (Where is the central character positioned? From what perspective do we view the action? In what direction are things moving? It is said that a character seen on the left hand side of the page may appear to be more in control of things than a character seen on the right. The same is true of a character seen higher on the page, and larger).

— *Lay-out* (Double-page spreads can suggest expansiveness or serenity; whereas single page spreads move the story along more quickly. If the character is seen in several pictures on the same page, this often suggests that things are moving too quickly for him, and he might soon lose control).

— *Borders* (Borders contain the action. When actions spread out across the borders, it appears too large or powerful to contain).

— *Page turns* (There is a drama of the turning page, which creates suspense on the right- hand page before the turn, and resolves it on the left hand page after the turn).

— *The last page* (The last page often serves as a visual commentary, denouement, or punch line.)

— *The interaction of picture and text* (Good artists create a complementarity: What is stated in the text need not be illustrated, and vice versa).

5

Challenges of International Education

The impact of intensified globalization is possibly the most often cited challenge facing the field of comparative and international education at this point in time. Somewhat paradoxically, interest in globalization has attracted many new scholars and professionals to comparative and international research-but, at the same time, it has generated critiques of traditionally accepted modes of operation and frameworks of analysis.

At the heart of this are challenges to the prominence of the nation-state as the primary unit of analysis in so much work carried out within the field. Global forces, it is argued, are dramatically changing the role of the state in education, and demanding increased attention to be paid to factors operating beyond the national level.

The mechanisms and processes driving globalization are thus prioritized for examination, as is the increased significance of multi-lateral agencies in shaping global policy debates and agendas. However, recognition of the fact that the effects of globalization differ from place to place, draws attention back to the nature and implications of such differential effects-even at the national level.

Few empirically grounded studies have compared these differences in any sustained way to date- and those that have been carried out have largely focused upon Western industrial societies or the newly industrialized economies of East Asia.

The impact of globalization on the poorer, post-colonial societies of the "South" has received much less attention, despite the dramatic implications for development processes in such contexts. Here there is much urgent work for the field of comparative and international education in the future.

The challenges posed by globalization, however, also pull in other directions reflecting what Arnove and Torres have usefully characterized as the "dialectic of the global and the local". To cite Giddens, globalization is a complex set of processes, not a single one. And these operate in a contradictory or oppositional fashion. Most people think of it as simply 'pulling away' power or influence from local communities and nations into the global arena. And indeed this is one of its consequences. Nations do lose some of the economic power they once had. However, it is also has an opposite effect. Globalization not only pulls upwards, it pushes downwards, creating new pressures for local autonomy.

This draws attention to the fact that national and local cultures can and do play a significant role in mediating global influences. From this perspective, units of analysis that pay attention to the local effects of globalization are also prioritized. This, in turn, adds renewed legitimacy to qualitative modes of research that emphasize grassroots fieldwork, ethnography and the interpretive/hermeneutic paradigms that emphasize micro-level studies of education in context. While much more can be said about the challenges posed by globalization, it is argued that, despite its pervasive influence, numerous other challenges also face the field, and demand attention in their own right.

Related to the latter methodological issues, for example, are very significant paradigmatic and epistemological implications raised by increased sensitivity to culture and context. This is reflected in the impact on the field of post-structural scholarship, and of the application and critique of post-modernist and post-colonial theoretical frameworks.

In many respects post-colonial frameworks also draw attention to the challenges generated by dramatically changed geopolitical realities; from the decline of colonialism; from attention to culture and identity; and from the turbulent latter years of the 20th century.

This is reflected in the field's heightened awareness of the dangers of ethnocentrism, and its recognition of the problematic use of distinctions and terminology relating to, for example, "developed" and "developing" countries, and the "North" and the "South".

For the present writer, the methodological challenges of such developments point most strongly to the need for new forms of international relationships in terms of comparative and international research; to the importance of collaborative research and partnerships between "insiders" and "outsiders"; to research and development work that is more sensitive to local, social constructions of reality; and to strategies that facilitate the strengthening of research capacity within the South.

In many respects, the rational for this is related to efforts to help "bridge" the gap between educational research and its potential to improve policy and practice. This is, in itself, one of the most prominent challenges faced by educational research communities world-wide.

The widening constituency of policy-makers and practitioners who have taken renewed interest in comparative and international research are certainly looking for findings that will be of use to them in their professional activities. While this is a complex arena in which there are few simple answers, the challenges raised by such diversity of audiences are of considerable and renewed significance for the field. Relatedly, the intensification of international competition, spurred on by globalization, neo-liberalism and marketization, has major implications for cross-national studies of educational achievement.

If the funding of research is increasingly linked to commercial interests, for example, the potential for critical theory, or for alternative cultural perspectives to influence the construction of new knowledge, may be increasingly challenged-even in, paradoxically, the new "knowledge" economy. So questions of power and "whose knowledge counts?" in the process of development arise, perhaps, more strongly than ever before.

To this we could add the challenges raised by rapid advances in information and communications technology (ICT). As many have pointed out, these are many and varied-but it is argued that their implications arise most strongly in cross-cultural contexts, where the "digital divide" is greatest, and both their potential benefits and problems deserve urgent attention.

Growing tensions between the global, the national and the local, thus, so fundamentally underpin all aspects of contemporary society and development, that a similarly fundamental reconceptualization of the field of comparative and international education is required, if we are to more effectively address such issues.

The international on-line debate stimulated by the present publication, will also, helpfully, keep dialogue very much alive and make an ongoing contribution. Returning to the issues raised in the two special numbers of Comparative Education, and to the writer's earlier work, the following themes emerge most strongly. Firstly, it is argued that it is the comparative and international research focus that is at the forefront of the resurgence of interest in the field - and it is to ways of reconceptualizing research that we must increasingly look in the future. This includes theoretical, methodological, substantive and organizational dimensions. Work such as that by Bray and Thomas on multi-levels of analysis helps to point one way forward by acknowledging the potential of many different units of analysis. Other pointers may come from pioneering efforts to promote more genuinely collaborative international teams-especially linking different "territories" such as the North and the South, or policy and practice. Such organizational possibilities then have major implications for the theoretical and methodological frameworks that we might employ.

Sensitive to the differences between various theoretical discourses, Cowen, however, wisely cautions against a search for the one "right" mode- and celebrates the diversity of comparative educations. Writing within the second "response" special number of Comparative Education, Kazamias makes an impassioned plea for closer linkages between the humanities and the social sciences within the multi-disciplinary field. For Kazamias, the reclamation of the historical dimension of the field would counterbalance its post-World War II dehumanization, and represent a priority direction for the future. Whatever position we might adopt with regard to the role of history, there is certainly much to be gained from a more effective bridging with the best of past scholarship within the field, even as we look towards the future.

6

Strategies of Multicultural Education

School librarians are faced with the challenge of linking students from widely varying backgrounds to information sources and drawing them into patterns of regular library use. By creating a positive climate, the school library can provide English as a second language (ESL) students with a place for learning, sharing, and personal growth.

The ESL students were introduced to the library at a time when no other classes were there. Each student was given a diagram of the library, then walked through each area beginning at the entrance. Hands-on activities were provided, such as practice in using the copy machine.

Thereafter, students returned to the library on an individual basis, or in pairs, with a specific request to the librarian; at this time, individual explanations and demonstrations were given of the various areas and their uses.

Eventually, students were sent to the librarian with individual assignments. By this time, students were familiar with the library staff and did not hesitate to approach them for help. Students were encouraged to use the library before school, after school, and during study hall periods. As a result, the ESL students found the library to be a safe and welcoming place and became frequent users.

To draw ESL students into a pattern of regular library use, the library established a collection of reading materials in their first languages. To meet the full range of interests and reading abilities, collections of fiction and non-fiction books in Spanish, Arabic, and Portuguese were borrowed for extended periods through Interlibrary Loan. With school library funds, a small collection of Portuguese books, a weekly Portuguese newspaper, a Spanish newspaper, and foreign language dictionaries were purchased. Spanish magazines were contributed by the Spanish language teacher.

High-interest, low-reading-level paperbacks in English were borrowed from a local public library's literacy collection. At the request of the ESL teacher, these books were housed in the ESL classroom for easy access during classroom times. A listening station with a cassette player and headphone and a collection of read-along books in English were made available in the library conference room. Most books were classics that are required reading for high school students. In addition, a collection of wordless books was borrowed from several public libraries.

Many elementary school ESL teachers report multiple uses of these books, including promotion of oral language and conversation skills, development of sequence and prediction skills, and development of vocabulary skills.

For all students, but especially for ESL students, the optimal learning process involves connecting new ideas with old knowledge. To provide materials required for this, the librarian introduced the use of advanced organizers, an essential instructional strategy proposed by Ausubel to enhance classroom learning. That the information-processing system of humans is a set of ideas that provides anchors for new information or ideas, that in turn provides a storehouse when new meanings are acquired.

Central to enhancing the learning process for students with language needs is the technique of building learning upon prior learning and knowledge. Based on this view of how learners process information, and the realization that much of the material to be learned by ESL students is completely new and unrelated to anything they know, the librarian created opportunities for ESL students to gain essential prior knowledge through the use of advance organizers.

Collaboration between the librarian and the ESL teacher resulted in a list of key themes and subject areas related to the ESL text and curriculum. Appropriate materials were acquired, borrowed, and collected by the librarian for use in both the media center and in the ESL classroom. Because this strategy relies heavily on visuals and pictorial materials, a picture file was developed for advance organizers. To collect materials suitable for use as advance organizers, the librarian used references for collecting visuals with pictures of all kinds, especially designed for second language learners, a directory of resource organizations, and various bibliographies.

The school library organized a program with speakers on occupations, career choices, and vocational and education options for the ESL students through the local community college. Representing the college were an admissions officer, a Spanish-speaking counselor from Access to Opportunity (a counseling and mentor program for ESL, at-risk, low-income, and disadvantaged students), and a Spanish-speaking counselor from the Education Opportunity Center (a pre-admission center for ESL students needing counseling in language competency, financial aid, admission requirements, GED information, etc.).

The program was held in Spanish and English in the school library with an interpreter for the Portuguese students. Follow-up appointments were made and the counselor from the Educational Opportunity Center returned weekly to the school library for individual counseling.

The school library has a unique role in the integration of cultural differences within the school community. Because library services are essential to all segments of the school population and school activities, the librarian holds a strategic position as an integrator, coordinator, negotiator, unifier, and equalizer.

While a class of English-speaking students was researching Christmas customs around the world, the ESL class was researching Christmas traditions in the United States. The librarian offered to co-ordinate an intercultural program between the two classes to exchange Christmas customs and traditions. When the ESL students were researching the history and foods of Thanksgiving, the librarian proposed the preparation of a Thanksgiving dinner. Ultimately, the ESL teacher had a

Thanksgiving dinner brought into her class for her students.

One literacy activity took shape when the school librarian observed that senior students were assigned to the high school library for Spanish IV Independent Study. It seemed that there were opportunities for these students to improve their Spanish literacy if Spanish-speaking students could be in the library at the same time. This would help the Spanish-speaking students improve their English literacy skills and would help to promote multicultural understanding.

By consulting with the ESL teacher, Spanish-speaking ESL students were identified and an examination of their schedules showed that some of them could be scheduled into the library for the same period as the Spanish IV students. Alliances were formed with the Spanish and ESL teachers, and two student literacy groups were formed. Students were informed by the teachers of the purpose of the groups, and that they would be graded by the librarian for effort and participation. Spanish/English dictionaries were available at each meeting.

Initial sessions were centered around oral communication in Spanish and English. Because the students were strangers to each other, the flow of conversation of these early sessions was directed by the librarian.

In the beginning, there were periods of silence. However, as the meetings progressed, barriers were overcome and the project took on a life of its own. Conversation became natural and comfortable. Students began requesting a non-directed format of conversation.

Spanish was spoken during half of the period, and English was spoken during the other half. At times, conversations and discussions would alternate between Spanish-speaking students speaking in English, while English-speaking students responded in Spanish. At other times, the order would be reversed.

Culture-specific dialogues were created. For example, when teenage culture in Mexico and the United States was explored, recognition of similarities and differences clarified false assumptions and generalizations. As English-speaking students sought knowledge and information about the social, cultural, economic, and political issues of Mexico, the Spanish-speaking students became information givers, thus gaining a new status.

Following the oral communicative stage, the group moved on to reading in both Spanish and English. Following the reading of each article, students translated the article in their own words, then each student provided an individual interpretation of the article in English and Spanish.

The writing segment of this literacy activity began with students agreeing to be ethnographers by observing what was happening in and outside of class, at school functions, and in interactions between ESL students and native-English-speaking students. Students agreed to keep a journal to record their observations of differences and to reflect on whether these differences were cultural. This served as a springboard to multicultural understanding.

Finally, journal writing was introduced between students in both languages. Through journal writing, a sense of developing friendships was observed.

Noticeable, also, was the interaction of these students as they met between classes and in the hallways.

Although initiated as a literacy activity, these group meetings also produced a greater appreciation and understanding of cultural diversity, empowered students, and provided an opportunity for friendships to form. The English-speaking students began to acknowledge the expertise of the Spanish-speaking students and sought help from them more often than from the dictionary. In turn, the Spanish-speaking students developed new friends and were empowered by their new helping role.

In short, the development of skills in using the library and its resources is an essential part of learning English. Non-native English speakers may have an even greater need for library skills than native speakers. Although they may not have achieved the English proficiency necessary for expressing their learning needs, they may need information that native speakers take for granted. ESL students must be given the tools that will enable them to succeed in the American education system.

7

Strategies of Learning Development

The 1992, the National Education Commission reconfirmed the commitment of His Majesty's Government to achieve universal primary education and to improve the quality of education in line with the Jomtien Declaration of Education for All (1990) and the summit goals of the United Nations Convention on the Rights of the Child (1990). The 1992 Commission endorsed most of the policy and programmatic recommendations contained in the Basic and Primary Education Master Plan. The new democratic government gave top priority to primary and basic education as a means of promoting basic human rights and as a strategy for poverty alleviation. Among other priorities, the 1992 Commission emphasised the urgent need to address the educational needs of different linguistic groups and ethnic minorities, and to bring about the long overdue quality improvement of the education system.

The Basic and Primary Education Project (BPEP) was designed to identify efficient management structures, to expand and enhance access and learning conditions, and to improve the quality of primary and basic education. BPEP was implemented in a phased manner, covering 19 districts in the year 1992/93, adding six districts in 1993/94, and extending to another 15 districts in 1994/95 (thus totalling 40 of the 75 districts in the country). It was executed with the financial assistance of DANIDA (US$ 16.28 million), UNICEF (US$ 4.64 million), JICA (US$ 15.73 million) and IDA (loan of US$ 30.60 million). The external assistance amounted to 26% of the total BPEP expenditure and the remaining 74% (NRs. 10,976 million) was borne by His Majesty's Government.

BPEP adopted a management structure which led to the efficient delivery of project inputs on one hand, and which facilitated the development of programmes and materials on the other.

BPEP has made a significant contribution in programme development of different components, including:

— development of the new primary education curriculum;

— revision of textbooks, teachers guides and development of supplementary materials;

— development of schools and Resource Centres;

— development of teachers training packages;

— development of management training programmes;

— development of non-formal education packages;

— development of the special education programme; and

— development of the women's education programme

BPEP implemented several activities in order to improve the quality of primary education in the project districts. A summary of the activities is presented in Table 1.

Table 1.

Achievement Status of BPEP Activities in Quality Improvement

Quality Improvement	*Achievement*
Implementation of primary education curriculum (Grades 1 to 5)	Nation-wide
Distribution of textbooks and teachers guides (Grades 1 to 5)	Nation-wide
Distribution of supplementary materials (districts)	40
Teacher training (teachers)	
— 2.5 months	8,511
— Grade Teaching	994
— Multi-Grade Teaching	3,943
— Extra-curricular	1,448
— Whole School Approach	37,690
— Resource Centre (RC)	
— Resource Centres	669
— Resource Persons on duty	569
— Basic RP management training	834
— Advanced RP management training	482

BPEP adopted a strategy mix of constructing additional classrooms, promoting non-formal programmes, and gradual introduction of compulsory primary education. The achievements made toward promoting equitable access to the basic and primary education are summarised in Table 2.

Table 2.

Promoting Equitable Access: Achievement for 1992-1998.

Improvement Physical Facilities	*Achievement*
New classroom construction	14,112
Classroom rehabilitation	7,522
Furniture for classrooms	11,646
RC building construction and furnishing	306
DEO buildings	19
Distribution of manuals for school building maintenance (sets)	7,690
Maintenance training	7,152
Maintenance tools (sets)	7.152
Non-Formal Education Programme	
Out-of-School Programme I	114.197
Out-of-School Programme II	336,156
Out-of-School Programme III	1,500
Women's Education Programme I	204,397
Women's Education Programme II	56,416
Women's Education Programme III	11,049
Adult Education Programme I	39,505
Adult Education Programme II	6,154
New Literacy Programme I	265
Chelibeti Programme	19,818
Women Education Programme	
Recruitment of female teachers	4,151
Training for female teachers	3,588
Special Education Programme	
District Disability Survey	15
Scholarships for disabled children	2,700
Early Childhood Development (ECD)	
Training of ECD teachers	2,232
Establishment of ECD classes	1,200
Compulsory Primary Education (CPE)	
CPE initiated in districts	5

BPEP also institutionalised several measures to strengthen the management of basic and primary education at different levels. On the basis of the positive experiences from BPEP implementation, HMG has made the following policy decisions:

— Adoption of the Resource Centre structure and provision of School Management Committees as a tier of educational management

— Government decision to provide at least 10 days of recurrent training to every teacher each year

— Placement of at least one female teacher in each primary school

— Inclusion of ECD component in the regular structure of the MOE

— Decision to introduce the coupon system instead of the reimbursement policy for receiving free textbooks from dealers in the districts

— Inclusion of parents and representatives from disadvantaged communities on School Management Committees

— Gradual introduction of Compulsory Primary Education (CPE) in all 75 districts

The Primary Education Development Project

The Primary Education Development Project (PEDP) was implemented in 1993 as a complement to BPEP with focus on the development and consolidation of the teacher training system. PEDP was financed with an ADB loan of US$ 20 million. The most significant contribution of PEDP was establishment of a network of nine primary teacher-training centres. Specific details of PEDP's contribution toward improving the quality of the basic and primary education are outlined below.

— The National Centre for Educational Development has been established as an apex body of primary teacher training with the responsibility of planning, programming and managing primary teacher training, as well as training school supervisors, Headmasters and education management personnel. The infrastructure of NCED has been built in Sanothimi, Bhaktapur.

— Nine Primary Teacher Training Centres have been established in Bhojpur, Sunsari, Janakpur, Kavre, Bara, Tanahun, Rupandehi, Surkhet and Doti Districts to provide long-term training for untrained primary school teachers and school management training for the primary school Headmasters of 75 districts.

— Six District Education Office buildings have been completed.

— The project has succeeded in providing training for 22,141 teachers, 4,659 Headmasters, 264 supervisors and 115 education management personnel.

— 1,495 schools have been built and 1,425 schools have been provided with furniture out of 1,500 targeted schools. Toilets and drinking water have been provided to 950 out of 1,000 targeted schools.

— The project has supported the improvement of physical facilities (rehabilitation and educational materials) of the Faculties of Education of Birgunj

Campus and Sanothimi Campus and provided fund for producing qualified manpower for primary education (B.Ed. in primary education).

Promising strategies

The 1990s have remained a decade of development and consolidation efforts in the primary and basic education area of Nepal. Experiences gained and lessons learned from these efforts point to some promising strategies that could make a difference in optimising the quality and efficiency of the primary and basic education system. Some of the promising strategies are:

— co-operative and participatory planning processes at the central, district and community levels;

— establishment of Resource Centres and provision of Resource Persons (each for about 15-25 schools) to create a training, supervision and support system for the qualitative improvement of the primary and basic education;

— integration of special education programmes with primary and basic education;

— encouragement and recognition of local quality improvement efforts such as development of the RC as a community resource, and development and use of teaching/learning materials at the school level;

— management and use of educational information at the school and RC levels; and

— nutrition (afternoon food) programme for children in the rural areas as motivation to enrol and complete primary education.

A number of high-level government documents guide the development of curricula. They include the Secondary Education Perspective Plan (1996-2011), the Secondary Education Action Plan (1997-2002) and a recent High-Level Education Commission Report (1998).

Organisational Structure and Mechanisms in Curriculum Reform

The curriculum planned at the central level is modified by all the processes leading to its adoption. In the classroom at the secondary level most institutionalized activity is centrally controlled.

Ministry of education

The task of initiating educational activities throughout Nepal lies with the Ministry of Education (MOE). The Ministry is responsible for educational planning and management, as well as in improving service delivery systems across the country. MOE is composed of three divisions: Planning; General Administration; and Educational Administration.

Educational programmes and services are prepared by: the Curriculum Development Centre;

— the Secondary Education Development Centre; the Distance Education Centre;

— the Office of the Controller of Examinations;

— the National Centre for Educational Development;

— the regional education directorates and district education offices.

From July 1999 a new structure will be implemented with the formation of a Department of Secondary, Education, containing a Primary and Basic Education Division and a Secondary and Higher Secondary Division. This will separate policy making from executive actions.

A high-level National Curriculum Council (NCC), chaired by the Minister of Education, approves all curricula and guides the detailed developmental work of the Curriculum Development Centre (CDC) by setting operational and administrative policy.

The NCC forms ad-hoc technical committees when additional advice is required. Matters concerning the relevance of curricula drafted by CDC may be referred to such a technical committee if the NCC feels additional advice is necessary.

The CDC is responsible for the maintenance, transmission and renewal of the school-level curriculum and is also concerned with pre-primary education. (See below for further discussion of CDC).

The Secondary Leaving Certificate Board sets policies and makes decisions relating to the School-Leaving Certificate (SLC), which are then implemented by the Office of the Controller of Examinations (OCE).

A reformed SLC, with single subject certification is planned for July 2001. The courses leading to this examination are to be implemented from grade 9, beginning in July 1999.

The Secondary Education Development Centre

The Secondary Education Development Centre (SEDEC) is responsible for a range of in-service training activities at the secondary level. SEDEC operates through twenty-five secondary education development units at locations, which allow for national coverage.

The training activities also support the work of the Curriculum Development Centre and the OCE.

Janak Educational Materials Centre

The Janak Educational Materials Centre (JEMC), operating as a public limited company, produces and distributes school textbooks throughout Nepal. JEMC's Board of Directors is comprised of representatives from concerned ministries and organizations.

The Curriculum Development Centre

The CDC is responsible for the maintenance, transmission and renewal of the school education curriculum. The wide-ranging activities of the centre include developing, revising and disseminating textbooks and teacher's support materials.

A programme of seminars and workshops supports these activities. CDC's development and monitoring work is carried out by specialized curriculum subject units, advised by curriculum subject specialist committees. Subject units cover languages, science and maths, social studies, health and physical education.

To support CDC's activities, various studies and surveys are conducted on curriculum-related issues and problems. The activities of CDC give rise to a wide range of relationships with other institutions.

The most important of these is with the teachers and student in schools, who are the immediate end-users of the centre's products. CDC also incorporates a publishing unit.

The Publishing Unit (PU)

The PU (in collaboration with subject specialist units, their advisory subject specialist committees, subject advisers and consultants) sets textbook specifications. According to prescribed procedures, the PU also selects textbook writers on the basis of: subject knowledge, classroom experience and sample materials reviewed by teachers/ subject experts.

A PU staff member serves as the managing editor, and is responsible for briefing contracted writers and liaising closely with them to ensure quality and schedule controls, until the camera-ready copy goes to the printers.

The PU manager also arranges distribution of the draft materials to be tested in schools and validated by teacher groups. The managing editor, unit specialist, subject committee members, advisers and specialists all visit schools to collect comments which are subsequently relayed to the writers.

Subject Advisory Committees

The role of these committees is to advise on the preparation and revision of the curriculum, and the preparation, revision and evaluation of textbooks and teachers guides.

The Curriculum Officers, as members of the committees, also participate in these activities and provide the secretariat that promotes the committee's work. Subcommittees are established to carry out specialist developmental inputs. The subject committees cover Nepali, English, science, mathematics, social studies, and health, population and environment (HPE).

Task Committees

Like the publishing unit, the task committees cut across the boundaries of the various specialist units. Examples are the formative assessment committee and the dissemination committee. Task committees are formed to advise the cross-boundary projects managing officer on policy and operational matters.

Implementation and Follow-up of Curriculum Reform

The general aims of secondary education are to: produce healthy citizens who are: familiar with the national tradition, culture, social environment, democratic values; able to use language effectively in daily life; aware of scientific issues; creative, cooperative, industrious; able to contribute to economic development.

The secondary curriculum

The lower secondary curriculum (grades 6, 7 and 8) and the secondary curriculum (grades 9 and 10) are constructed with core subjects and optional subjects. The five lower secondary core subjects are Nepali, English, math, science and social studies.

The six secondary core subjects are Nepali, English, math, science, social studies, health, population and environment (HPE).

A. Option 1 paper subjects (any one)

Languages: Nepali, Arabic, Avadhi, Bhojpuri, Bengalit, Chinese, Hindi, Japanese, Maithili, Sanskrit, Tibetan, Persian, Hebrew, Urdit, English, French, German, Greek, Latin, Russian, Spanish. (Other national languages of Nepal will be included in the curriculum, provided that grammar books, teaching materials, etc., are available.)

Humanities, Social Science: history, geography, civics, economics, sociology.

Optional mathematics

B. Option 2 Paper subjects (any one)

Interdisciplinary: agricultural education, food science, architectural education, industrial education, office management and accounting, auditing, typing and shorthand, computer science, home science, handicrafts painting, sewing and knitting, bamboo-work, dance, music, Ayurveda naturpathy, health and physical education, photography, journalism, instrumentation.

Secondary Education Development Project

The Secondary Education Development Project (SEDP)

began in 1993. SEDP originally aimed at improving and reinforcing three subjects (English, science, mathematics). In 1997, support to Nepali and social studies was added. SEDP also has the goal of reforming the examination system and providing materials and equipment to selected secondary schools. The project has been providing support services through the Secondary Education Development Centre and the twenty-five training centres.

Accomplishments

As of July 1998, CDC had produced ten curriculum booklets outlining the lower secondary curriculum (grades 6-8) and the secondary curriculum (grades 9 and 10) and covering all core subjects therein. The curriculum and textbooks for grades 6 (1996), 7 (1997) and 8 have been printed and distributed (1998). The lower secondary curriculum is being prepared for publication. However, English is the only subject in which teacher's guides have so far been produced.

In July 1998, the National Curriculum Council (NCC) decided to restructure the curriculum of grades 9 and 10, to allow for the inclusion of a new sixth core subject, health, population and environment (HPE). This reduced English, Nepali, mathematics and science from six to five periods each week. The curriculum was adjusted in line with the reduction of periods. The grade 9 production schedule for textbooks and teacher's guides has now been separated from that of grade 10. The grade 9 textbooks for the six core subjects were scheduled for printing by the end of March 1999, while completion of grade 9 teacher's guides was foreseen for the end of April 1999.

CDC has formulated a seven-stage dissemination strategy for the grades 9 and 10 curriculum. The first stage (approval) was completed in November 1998. Included in the strategy are: detailed planning, package development, training of master facilitators and facilitators, training of head-teachers, cluster-based and school-based workshops. The full programme will be completed by the end of July 1999.

The Publishing Unit's first textbooks are clearly of a better quality than previous CDC/SEDP outputs. The unit has also produced a four-page CDC bulletin of a high standard (February 1998) to publicize its activities, as well as a leaflet in English and Nepali. Textbooks have been monitored for gender, socioeconomic and regional equity.

National goals of education

The National Goals of Education frame all the detailed technical work of curriculum development and should be reflected in all documents and materials developed by the Curriculum Development Centre.

The national education goals are to:

— nurture and develop the personalities and inherent talents in each person;

— instill respect for human values and the will to safeguard national and social beliefs so as to help develop a healthy social unity;

— help the individual to socialize, enhancing social unity;

— help the individual keep his or her identity in the national and international context and to help him/her lead a socially harmonious life in the modern world;

— assist the modernization of the country by creating able manpower for its development;

— teach the thoughtful protection and wise use of Nepal's natural resources;

— bring those who are underprivileged into the mainstream of the nation.

Developments and Challenges in the Design, Implementation and follow-up of Curriculum Reform

While the capacity of CDC to handle complex tasks is clearly improving, the capacity to plan and to develop human resources has certain constraints due to the rate of staff changeovers. This makes the institutionalization of curriculum development design processes very difficult. These staff changes are at all professional and administrative levels of the organization.

The same changes create problems of continuity and liaison with other organizations connected with the implementation process. These institutions 'District Education Offices, Regional Education Offices, OCE and SEDEC—also have high staff instability.

There are very few formalized follow-up activities, except by the SEDP BME Unit. These are mainly concerned with project evaluation.

Reforming the Curriculum with special emphasis on social studies

As described earlier all core curricula and many optional subjects have been changed in recent years. In the development of all core curricula there has been tension between traditionalists and modernists, as well as between nationalists and those in favour of globalisation or wider horizons—those who speak for 'our values' and those who speak of 'global values'.

Balancing these diverse views is a problem for all curriculum developers. No curriculum subject can avoid these controversies. While in science and mathematics the debate is narrower, in English and Nepali there are different dimensions due to the source of each individual language. Both of the two newer subjects—social studies and HPE—have proved to be controversial in different ways.

Translating the goals, general objectives and specific objectives of the social studies curriculum into a useful textbook proved difficult. Although there are many dimensions to the discussion, the fundamental debate concerns whether education is about passing knowledge or learning skills—or what is the balance between the two. Members of the subject committee did not always agree with those who set the framework for developing the new textbook, creating what is hopefully a creative tension.

Those setting the framework for developing the new textbook felt that the following factors are all important in the writing of a new style textbook:

— These will include not only factual information for knowledge and understanding, but specific skills such as interpreting a bar chart, locating places of historical importance, presenting an argument in favour of a certain course of action and collecting local data.

— The earlier textbooks mostly contained only factual information, followed by recall questions. The new textbook must present information in different forms (text, statistics, pictures, photographs, diagrams, graphs and charts, maps, newspaper items, source documents) and provide challenging questions to help students understand, interpret, analyse and evaluate the information.

— The textbook must include many project-related activities, starting with simple tasks, and moving towards longer projects. This will mean that most of the work studied has a local component and thus is of genuine relevance to the students. It will also mean that students can experience research activities, gaining practical investigation and analytical skills, and learning to present their findings. It will also help them to work together cooperatively.

— The students should be able to see what skills they are learning in each chapter and gain a sense of achievement and progress towards the school-leaving certificate (SLC). This may be done with a summary of chapters or topics. The exercises given in the textbook will not only test knowledge and understanding, but will expect analysis and evaluation of the information, and well-thought-out answers. They will also need to encourage the practice of practical skills and abilities. This will provide practice for new SLC-type questions.

Social studies curriculum

Objectives

There are twenty-eight general objectives listed in the grades 9 and 10 social studies curricula. Highly specific objectives are listed for grade 9 (twenty-seven objectives) and grade 10 (twenty-nine objectives).

Abilities

On achieving the course objectives, students will be able to demonstrate a wide range of abilities. Some examples of the abilities associated with knowledge and understanding and practical abilities are as follows:

Ability 1: Knowledge and understanding.

1. Describing projects in different zones and development regions;
2. Describing achievements of Nepal in fields of education, health, transportation, telecommunications, electricity and water supply;
3. Discussing the role of skilled manpower in the development of the infrastructure of Nepal;
4. Stating the role of international organizations in solving social problems;
5. Explaining different climates and the elements that affect them;
6. Giving a short introduction to the geo-economic activities of continents;
7. Identifying the problems created by population growth and migration and finding out ways to participate in solving them;

8. Describing the physical features of the Earth;
9. Examining the impact of landslides on the physical features of Nepal and participating in the task of avoiding them;
10. Listing the agricultural products grown in the various geographical areas.

Ability 2: Practical abilities.

1. Maintaining national dignity;
2. Drawing a map of Nepal and filling in the main industrial centres and roads;
3. Demonstrating models in class;
4. Analysing the data presented in charts;
5. Locating historical sites on a map;
6. Investigating the problems of population growth;
7. Appreciating the contributions of our national heroes;
8. Applying the knowledge of social studies for the good of society;
9. Drawing a picture of the Himalayan region;
10. Recording the maximum rainfall of the month;
11. Designing a research proposal to find out about social evils.

Criteria

The new-style social studies textbook must be developed so that students can be thoroughly prepared to take the new SLC examination. The textbook must help them not only to understand the content of the course, but also to develop the necessary skills and ability to think critically about the different topics. Thus, each chapter should have clearly thought-out learning outcomes. These will include not only factual information for knowledge and understanding, but will also include specific skills such as those outlined in the previous section. After studying this lesson the student will be able to:

— interpret a bar chart;

— locate places of historical importance;

— present an argument in favour of a certain course of action;

— collect local data.

The earlier textbooks contained only factual information, followed by recall questions. To prepare for the new SLC examination, the new textbooks must present information in different forms (text, statistics, pictures, photographs, diagrams, graphs and charts, maps, newspaper items, source documents) and provide challenging questions to help students understand, interpret, analyse and evaluate the information. As 30% of the new SLC marks will be given for project-style work to be carried out during the year, the textbook must include many such activities; starting with simple tasks, and evolving to longer projects. This will mean that most of the material studied has a local component and thus is of relevance to the students.

Global Trends in Learning Materials

The World Declaration on Education for All does not contain the words 'textbook' or 'learning materials' and there is only passing reference to such materials in the guidelines for implementation that accompanied the Declaration. Much more attention is given to the potential of technologies newer than print' television, radio and computers. This is not surprising, any more than that a policy declaration on transportation might omit reference to oil or one on television might omit reference to electricity. Schoolbooks have long been considered an essential educational commodity but one that can be turned on or off in supply, much like chalk or desks. It is only in the past decade that the complexities of developing the sustainable provision of books and other learning materials have come to be recognized by funding agencies and, to a lesser extent, by governments. It is only in the 1990s, too, that the importance of all links in the book chain to the sustainable provision of learning materials has come to be appreciated. The value of books, on the other hand, has long been recognized. As early as 1978, Heyneman et al. reported that:

From the evidence we have so far, the availability of books appears to be the single most consistently positive school factor in predicting academic achievement. In fifteen of the eighteen statistics, it is positive; this is, for example, more favourable than the thirteen out of twenty-four recently reported for teacher training.

In both Nicaragua and the Philippines, for example, testing in the early 1980s found that students with textbooks scored significantly higher, by about one-third of a standard deviation, than students without those resources. In many countries of the developing world, the textbook is the major, if not the only, medium of instruction. It is the main resource for teachers, setting out the general guidelines of the syllabus in concrete form, providing a guide and foundation to the content, order and pacing of instruction, supplying exercises and assignments for students to practise what they have learned. It is both a source of essential information and the basis for examination and appraisal.

The textbook retains its primacy because, in comparison to other educational technologies, books are inexpensive, easy to use, easily portable, and familiar. They can be used in districts where there is no reliable supply of electricity or communication. They can be of particular assistance to the tens of thousands of underqualified and undertrained teachers who have been pressed into service to meet the demands of increasing enrolments throughout the global South. Textbooks, moreover, may be the only introduction to reading for students who come from homes without books. They may be a young persons only exposure to reading in villages so remote that there are no newspapers, magazines or even shop signs. They are essential to teaching literacy in the many parts of the world where book hunger' even book famine' is endemic, where teaching is by rote and memorization of information, not always accurate and seldom up to date. As one expert has remarked, 'on the verge of the second millennium, education transmitted through oracy rather than literacy is inadequate in educating the labour force of a country [Ethiopia] with sixty million people'.

Books are, in short, essential to achieving the goal of Education for All. In large numbers of the world's primary and secondary schools, however, pupils and students have only limited access to them, despite millions of dollars that have been spent on programmes of book provision.

Textbooks cannot stand alone. To be effective, they must be supported by a variety of other educational materials. Each textbook should ideally be accompanied by a teacher's guide to using it.

Such guides may outline innovative ways of teaching a particular lesson, suggest class activities to reinforce the content, and provide examples of exercises and assignments. They are particularly important when a new curriculum or new teaching strategies are being introduced and at all times for inadequately trained teachers.

Supplementary materials expand upon the information in the textbook. They may range from chalk and blackboards to educational television and interactive computerized lessons. Those that are printed reinforce the lessons of literacy taught in the classroom, develop children's ability to read, expand their vocabulary, train them in retrieving and using information, encourage independent reading and may instil a lifelong love of reading and learning.

This survey defines supplementary materials as including work books, reading programmes or schemes, children's fiction (easy readers, stories, plays and anthologies), children's nonfiction, audio tapes, video tapes, multimedia learning packages, science kits, reference books such as dictionaries and atlases, magazines, comics, posters, wall charts and maps.

Most attention will be paid to the supplementary reading materials that may be located in school libraries. When printed supplementary materials are in short supply, as is often the case, it may be assumed that access to electronic materials is even scarcer.

Book provision in 1990

Both the World Declaration on Education for All and its accompanying Framework for Action are concerned with broad policy goals and targets, in only some of which the provision of school books and learning materials play a part.

With respect to that provision, the Framework for Action sets out the following principles:

> 'Addressing the basic learning needs of all means . . . capitalizing on the use of traditional and modern information media and technologies . . . [both of which] need to be designed to ensure equitable access, sustained participation, and effective learning achievement.'
>
> National and subnational planning should cover, among other subjects, 'the basic learning needs to be met . . . the languages to be used in education . . . modalities to mobilize family and local community support; the required capital and recurrent resources . . . possible measures for cost effectiveness, targets and specific objectives, and indicators and procedures to be used to for monitor progress in reaching the targets.'
>
> Attention should be paid to 'reduction of inefficiency in the public sector and exploitative practices in the private sector; provision of improved training for public administrators and of incentives to retain qualified women and men in public service; and provision of

> measures to encourage wider participation in the design and implementation of basic education programmes.'
>
> 'Efficiency in basic education does not mean providing eduction at the lowest cost, but rather the most effective use of all resources (human, organizational, and financial) to produce the desired levels of access and of necessary learning achievement.'
>
> 'Pre- and in-service training programmes for key personnel should be initiated, or strengthened where they do exist.' [In this context, curriculum developers are mentioned, but not publishing professionalism.]
>
> 'The quality and delivery of basic education can be enhanced through the judicious use of instructional technologies . . . (educational radio and television, computers, and audiovisual instructional devices) [which over time will] become less expensive and more adaptable to a range of environments.'
>
> 'Existing regional partnerships will need to be strengthened and provided with the resources necessary for their effective functioning in helping countries meet the basic learning needs of their populations.'

Textbook availability Most governments, and most educators, would like to provide every pupil with a complete set of school books in every subject, free of charge.

That, at least, is the ideal target' a text-book: pupil ratio of 1:1. In fact, it is a target imported from the industrialized nations that may be unnecessarily expensive.

An often-quoted experiment in the Philippines suggests that when school books are the property of the school and are not taken home, there is only a marginal difference between ratios of 1:1 and 1:2, and some experts have suggested that a ratio of 1:3 should be regarded as satisfactory.

Very few countries outside the industrialized North could afford to reach even the lowest of these targets in 1990. Instead, as a result of global recession and rising enrolments, the standard of textbook provision deteriorated during the late 1970s and the 1980s throughout Africa and in much of Latin America and Asia. It was well below the ideal as the decade came to a close.

A survey in 1990-91 of Bolivia, Colombia, Chile, Ecuador, Panama, Peru and Venezuela found that only 32 per cent of pupils between Grades 1 and 5 had textbooks; variations between countries ranged from 64 per cent in Chile to 20 per cent or less in Ecuador, Peru and Venezuela.

In Mexico, the figure rose to 75 per cent thanks to a national textbook programme; in Brazil, it was estimated at about 33 per cent. The national averages mask serious variations.

In general, book provision was much better in the cities and towns than in rural areas, and areas that were difficult to reach had the fewest books' sometimes none. The pattern of rural deprivation has been most clearly documented in Africa.

A summary of book sector studies in eight African countries found satisfactory to good ratios in the elite schools in important urban areas, but generally low levels of textbook provision at the primary level. Angola, Kenya, Nigeria and the United Republic of Tanzania recorded primary- level textbook:pupil ratios of 2:3 or better in urban areas, but 1:20 or worse elsewhere.

In Nigeria, the situation grew notably worse as one travelled northwards; in the majority of schools visited during a book sector study, the text-book: pupil ratio was 1:10 and sometimes 1:100. In the United Republic of Tanzania, a primary-level mathematics book that was available at a 1:3 ratio in the Southern Highlands plummeted to 1:700 in the Lake zone.

Only Sierra Leone had achieved a broad equity of supply between rural and urban areas, at a ratio of 1:3, as a result of an externally funded text-book project that paid particular attention to distribution networks. (Before the project, the ratio in Sierra Leone was close to 1:1,000.)

At the secondary level, few books were available in Angola, the United Republic of Tanzania or Zambia; in Kenya, Nigeria and Sierra Leone the ratios were between 1:10 and 1:28, implying only one to four textbooks per class.

Elite secondary schools, once again, were likely to have more textbooks. Most of the textbooks in the secondary schools had been repaired and maintained for fifteen to twenty years.

Variations between subjects and grades have also been noted. In Burundi, books were available only for language arts subjects in French and Kirundi.

The SECAB survey of Grades 1 to 5 in six South American countries found that while 70 per cent of the students had textbooks in Spanish language, only 30 per cent had textbooks in mathematics and fewer than 10 per cent had them in science and social science.

Where books were provided free of charge, those for a particular subject or grade were often unavailable when needed because of delays in printing and distribution. Where books were sold, variations reflected parental priorities and incomes. Parents were more likely to buy books in subjects that would contribute to their child's future financial success. In provinces of China where rural schools had little in the way of state-provided learning resources and parents bought books, teachers in the poorest areas sometimes bought books for children from their own salaries.

At the tertiary level, textbooks in Africa and many other countries were in chronically short supply. A great majority were imported and had become prohibitively expensive, despite schemes sponsored by the British and French governments to supply special low-cost editions. Shortages were more serious in teacher training and vocational institutes than in universities.

The translation of broad curriculum outlines to a concrete book is no simple task. The book must be written at a level of concept, content and vocabulary that is appropriate for the majority of pupils at the grade level and in a way that, ideally, will interest and motivate them. It must be consistent in approach, method and explanation. It should be of use to the less-qualified teacher but allow the good teacher to expand upon its content. Writing a good textbook requires the skills of a subject specialist, a curriculum expert, a good teacher with classroom experience and an imaginative author; the writing of such books is increasingly a team effort.

In 1990 there was ample evidence that the books used in schools in many parts of the world fell below these standards. They suffered from poor instructional design, particularly in the scope and sequence of material. A study of textbooks for Grades 1, 3, and 5 in fifteen countries found that for the earlier grades the material in mathematics and reading was too difficult; in Grade 5, the mathematics books were also too difficult but the reading books would have been more suitable for students in Grades 2 and 3. Textbooks in Pakistan were characterized by poor language grading from one level to another and even between subjects at the same level; teachers said the books were overly difficult for their students. Difficult books in the early grades were seen as contributing to the high early dropout rate in many countries. A study of textbooks in Mozambique found that, while they followed the established curriculum, they were generally too theoretical and lacked sufficient linkages to the everyday experiences of the target users. Neumann quoted a Deputy Minister of Education in the Philippines as saying that textbooks in his country should be aimed towards the schools in poor villages; nevertheless, most of the officially approved school books in the 1980s catered for the urban élite.

Textbooks also suffered from errors in fact and grammar, inappropriate illustrations and a poor choice of language or script. In many of the African countries, books were written in English, French or Portuguese, even though in any one country fewer than 20 per cent of the population was likely to be literate in any one of these metropolitan languages. Textbooks in the republics of the former Union of Soviet Socialist Republics were in Russian, ignoring local languages such as Azeri, Turkmen, Kazakh, Uzbek and Kyrgyz. In Pakistan, children could not read fluently the Arabic-style Nasakh script favoured by the curriculum developers and textbook writers, and as a result depended on their teachers to read the books for them and summarize the lessons.

In text and illustration, the books tended to reinforce traditional views of men and women. Lockheed and Verspoor et al., cite various studies showing girls or women in passive roles. A primary-school book in Swaziland depicted a boy happily playing ball and a girl shying away from a snake. In the twenty-nine most widely used primary textbooks in Peru, three-quarters of all references to and illustrations of people were of men. Similar discrepancies characterized the representation of men and women in school books from Costa Rica, Egypt, Kuwait, Lebanon, Qatar, Saudi Arabia, Tunisia, Yemen and Zambia. There were signs of change. In Costa Rica, after new books were produced with support from the United States Agency for International Co-operation (USAID), the proportion of women and girls in illustrations rose from 25 per cent to 31 per cent; female figures no longer were shown as less independent and more often in stereotypically male roles; males were sometimes shown as caring for children or undertaking domestic tasks.

To an increasing extent, even in former colonial countries, text-books were being written by local experts. European books were no longer being adapted, and even transnational publishers were using local authors with local teaching experience. If the books were less perfect pedagogically than their Northern counterparts, they were less Eurocentric and thus more related to the experience of pupils. In most countries, the physical quality of the books was well below Northern standards. Imported paper was expensive, binding facilities limited, and machinery old and in need of repair. As a result, books were too often poorly printed on low-grade paper, inadequately bound by the adhesive ('perfect') method, and used only black and white illustrations of varying quality. Such books could not stand up to the rigours of rainy climates, when pupils often had to walk long distances between home and school. Everywhere, the perfect-bound books were apt to fall apart. Externally funded textbook projects often used better paper and their products could be expected to last three years or more. Some incorporated four-colour printing, a feature that might be difficult to retain after the project closed. The number of subjects, and therefore the number of textbooks, was increasing in some countries. This trend was evident in Africa, where it was increasing strains on budgets and teachers.

In most cases, however, only core subjects were actually available, and some countries were reversing the trend. Mozambique, for example, had decided to concentrate on six core subjects for Grade 5 as opposed to the eleven subjects then taught in The United Republic of Tanzania. Ethiopia had decided to teach three subjects (natural and exact sciences, and geography) as environmental studies, with a single textbook.

Statistics of textbook provision are notoriously unreliable. Books that are reported to have been produced do not always reach the schools. They may be damaged in transit, pilfered or, more commonly, held up in district storehouses for lack of resources to carry them further. Those that reach the schools, moreover, may not be used in the classroom. This was apparently often the case in 1990.

The reasons for non-use varied. In some countries, government regulations made ill-paid teachers responsible for replacing lost and damaged books, and as a result teachers kept the books locked up. Teachers were not trained in the methods of new textbooks and therefore hesitated to use them or were reluctant to use them because their interests and experiences, and those of their students, were not reflected in the content. Some teachers felt threatened by new textbooks, and there was some evidence that less experienced teachers, who might be expected to benefit most from a carefully prepared textbook, were less likely to use them than were their more experienced colleagues.

Teachers' guides were seldom available in developing countries. Lockheed and Verspoor cite various studies: schools in Guinea-Bissau had guides only for Grade 1; in Malawi, fewer than 15 per cent of teachers had received a guide for a subject other than English; in rural Brazil, only 44 per cent of teachers had received teachers' guides. Where textbooks were bought by parents rather than provided by the state, teachers' guides were apt to be in particularly short supply. Moreover, many guides were unrelated to the ability of the average classroom teacher and were often designed without consideration of the teacher's reading fluency or the conditions under which the guides would be read; small type, for example, was ill-suited to be read in the poor lighting of rural communities.

Where textbooks were in short supply, supplementary materials might be expected to be even more scarce. In many countries school libraries either did not exist or had fallen into disrepair at the primary and secondary levels, except in elite public or private schools. Book stocks were outdated, and very often Eurocentric. At the tertiary level, textbooks and reference works were so scarce that students resorted to wholesale photocopying of library titles, if not to theft or mutilation. Even university libraries that had been well stocked in the past had been unable to buy many new books or journals for some years. Public libraries, a resource for school children, also deteriorated, although Mexico was remarkable in creating some 3,500 new public libraries in the period 1982-92 in a national system that served 71 million readers stretching from the capital to remote villages isolated by mountains, rivers and jungle.

In nine African countries surveyed in book sector studies, libraries and supplementary materials were seriously underfunded as governments channelled scarce resources primarily into textbooks. The majority of primary and secondary schoolchildren had no access to books or other reading materials apart from textbooks. Most books that were available were European in origin and inappropriate in content. There were not enough books about African history, geography, literature or cultures. Teachers and principals were not trained in the maintenance and use of school libraries. At secondary level, school libraries were disintegrating in terms of stock, buildings, furniture and trained staff. In some countries, governments distributed supplementary reading materials to the schools but did not develop the infrastructure to store and use them. Sierra Leone, however, did take that important basic step and, as a result, supplementary materials it had distributed to the schools five years earlier were still in place.

Schools that did have supplementary materials performed better than those that did not. The Escuela Nueva programme in Colombia used a variety of instructional materials, including school libraries, to great effect.

High achieving schools in Thailand benefited from community support for the purchase of supplementary text materials. Supplementary materials were also reported to have been used successfully at the Gonakelle school in Sri Lanka and in adult literacy programmes in Nepal.

Methods of textbook provision

Pupils in public systems of education received textbooks in one of three ways.

1. *Provided free of charge by the state.* This was the method followed in many countries of Asia, Africa, Latin America and the socialist republics of eastern Europe and western Asia. Free provision was more common in primary schools than at the secondary level. Books might be produced cheaply and given to the pupils each year for them to keep (as in the soviet republics) or given to the schools and lent to the pupils for their use during the school year on the understanding that they would be returned.

The provision of free books was intended to ensure equity in availability (although it did not) and responded to a viewpoint expressed by one Mexican expert that' if a government says that elementary education becomes an obligation for every citizen, then the government should provide the facilities for such education.' Remarkably, in some African countries university students were given free tuition and free books but primary school students were expected to pay for books, thus reinforcing an elite at the expense of the broader population.

2. *Sold through commercial channels.* Parents or students bought books, usually through retail outlets. The price of books might be subsidized by the state, sometimes with external assistance. Textbooks were sold at the primary level in some countries of Africa, Asia, and Latin America and the Caribbean. In the newly industrialized countries of Asia, textbooks were generally published by privately owned companies that worked closely with the educational authorities but usually received only limited assistance or subsidy from the government. Practices could vary within a single country: in Nigeria, primary-level textbooks were free in the Northern states but sold in the Southern and Eastern states.

Selling the book inevitably led to inequities. First, bookstores were located primarily in the urban centres, although text-books (a short-term investment with rapid turnover) might be sold at the beginning of the school year in stationery shops and other small retail outlets elsewhere. In the primarily rural Northwest Frontier Province of Pakistan, for example, text-books produced by the provincial textbook board were sold through a network of wholesale distributors and retailers that stretched from the provincial capital into the villages. Second, not all parents could afford to buy textbooks for their children. In Côte d'Ivoire, a textbook cost about one-tenth of the monthly salary of the head of an average family. Where books were in particularly short supply, as in Angola, a black market operated with high markups. Third, textbooks might not be available when needed because of inef-9 Thematic Studies Textbooks and Learning Materials 1990-99. Efficient ordering by the retailers or delays in shipping, which could be especially serious in a country or region with many islands, such as the Philippines or eastern Caribbean.

3. *Book rental.* Under this method, a school bought or was given class sets or part class sets of books and issued the books to the pupils in return for an annual fee. The books would be returned at the end of the year for reuse. The fee was set to recover part or all of the cost of replacing the books and to that end the rental income was placed in a revolving fund. This method allowed educational authorities to amortize the cost of books over a three- to five-year period, depending on the anticipated life of the textbook, and thus reduce the annual cost to the pupils or their parents. Such a system had been operating successfully in Lesotho for eight years, despite some problems, including delinquency in payments and inaccurate projections of needs. The government was planning, however, to supplement rental fees with an annual allocation to cover the costs of distribution and administratio. Rental schemes were seen as particularly desirable at the secondary level, but could operate in primary and tertiary institutions. In a variation on such schemes, parents might be required to supplement government allocations. In

Fiji, for example, because a flat grant from the Ministry of Education for each enrolled pupil was not large enough to cover full operating costs, some school committees charged parents a small sum for the purchase of textbooks, library books, and other materials.

In private schools, students would normally be expected to buy textbooks, which might or might not be the same as those used in the public system.

Production of textbooks

Historically, the provision of textbooks in developing countries followed three stages. Initially, the countries imported existing books from the North, usually from the colonial or former colonial power. Next, they began using adapted versions of foreign books, modified to meet local needs and experience, and often published by transnational companies based in the former colonial power. In the third stage, books were written and produced locally, often by the state.

By 1990 most countries had achieved local production, at least of primary-school textbooks, although specialized secondary-school textbooks were more likely to be adapted and tertiary texts often were imported. Typically, each country sought to produce its own books, sometimes without taking advantage of possible adaptations that would benefit from investments already made by other publishers in developing instructional methods. International trade in textbooks, either as licensing of adaptations or as imports of finished books, generally followed the path of North to South from the metropolitan countries of Europe and North America . To support local production, some countries imposed regulatory barriers. Zimbabwe, which secured its books entirely from the private sector, required local reprinting of foreign-originated books that sold more than 5,000 copies, and indeed began exporting text-books to neighbouring countries.

Local production was common even in sub-Saharan Africa, where large-scale book production was still relatively new and where the shortage of books was so acute that Hans Zell, the principal chronicler of African publishing, could exclaim that 'The picture of Africa at the end of the 1980s is largely that of a bookless society.'

In English-speaking sub-Saharan Africa, British transnationals (notably Macmillan, Heinemann, Oxford and Longman) had established sales offices which, in the more populated countries, functioned as regional publishers. As a result of the economic recession of the 1980s, many of these transnational branches closed, leaving behind trained editors and other staff who were ready to begin their own enterprises. By 1990 several branches had passed to private local ownership or control (for example, in Kenya and Nigeria). Elsewhere, foreign publishers entered into joint ventures with locally owned publishers of textbooks, which were often parastatal organizations in which the state retained a controlling share. Namibia, unlike other English-speaking countries of Africa, still depended primarily on imports, in its case from South Africa.

The countries of French-speaking Africa still imported large quantities of textbooks from France. In 1987, French-speaking Africa, excluding the Magreb, represented 13 per cent of the export market for French books, even though prices there averaged 44 per cent more than those in other French export markets that benefited from cheaper insurance and shipping, and lower risk. In 1990, ten countries of French-speaking Africa imported FF 163.7 million worth of books from France; in six of the ten, textbooks accounted for almost two-thirds of the total book imports; in the other four, where Arabic was a significant language, the textbook proportion shrank to 36 per cent. French publishers also had stakes in locally controlled textbook publishing houses. Local print runs could be substantial: le Centre d'édition et distribution africain (CEDA), owned jointly by the government of Côte d'Ivoire and the French publisher Hatier, printed 250,000 copies of one textbook.

Regional co-operation in publishing was rare. The ministries of education of eight French-speaking countries of sub-Saharan Africa, however, began the process in 1988 by identifying core subjects, such as French, mathematics and science, in which they could develop common curricula and textbooks. By 1990 they were well under way to producing the first books in mathematics.

In both English- and French-speaking Africa, state-owned and parastatal publishers benefited from hidden subsidies (for example, rent and staff costs that did not need to be recovered from sales, tax exemptions on supplies, subsidized state-owned or parastatal printing). Locally owned private publishers occasionally ventured into the school market, but for the most part they were marginalized by the much larger transactional, foreign, state-owned or parastatal textbook publishing operations.

In virtually every country of the world, the state is involved to some extent in the provision of learning materials' at the very least by establishing the curricula on which school books are based and, even in the freest of markets, by buying some or all of the materials used in the public system. In most of the world outside Western Europe and North America, the state played a much greater role than that in 1990. In many countries, the same Ministry of Education unit that defined the curriculum was also responsible for writing the books to support it. School books were printed in plants that were owned by governments or parastatals. Books were published by the Ministry or by parastatals under its control. Distribution also was often the responsibility of the Ministry or a parastatal. In some countries, particularly those with communist or strongly socialist governments, the entire process' from writing to use in the schools' was carried out by government ministries or agencies. In the former USSR, for example, all curricular materials were designed, controlled, manufactured and distributed free of charge, in sufficient quantities, by the state; the republics all had a uniform supply of such materials and followed the same curricula. In other countries the private sector might be involved in one stage or more of textbook provision. However, even in some countries with large commercial publishing industries, such as India, the state might retain responsibility for publishing textbooks for the public system. Searle listed possible combinations of private and state engagement and showed how functional responsibilities were divided in twenty-five countries where the World Bank had financed projects that had textbook provision as a component. Almost all the projects were in four regions: Eastern Africa, Western Africa, Latin America and the Caribbean, and East Asia and the Pacific. The diversity of patterns was remarkable. For the twenty-five countries examined, there were nineteen different patterns or arrangements of the four aspects of textbook provision considered. Only two patterns recurred.

State predominance was more evident in the ten African countries surveyed by Brunswic and Hajjar (1992). In most of the countries of French-speaking Africa, a specialized institution (commonly called l'Institut pédagogique national) was responsible for developing editorial guidelines, preparing manuscripts, and commissioning, publishing, printing and/or approving textbooks. In Senegal and Togo, the Ministry of Education had direct responsibility.

In some countries, state involvement in the provision of learning materials, as in other parts of the economy, was a matter of ideology. In others it began as a response to perceived necessity. With independence, former colonies had no indigenous source of school books. Foreign publishers who had supplied textbooks in the past were suspect as agents of colonialism and were themselves wary of investing in or extending credit to the newly independent countries. Yet there was an immediate need, not only in the former colonies but everywhere in the developing world, for cheap books to educate growing populations in curricula that had been revised to meet new national conditions and aspirations, and at the higher level to meet the demand for trained professionals and public servants. The private sector of most countries did not have the infrastructure or the capital to meet this challenge, and most families did not have the money to buy commercially produced books at full cost. Very small countries, such as the island states of the South Pacific, had no alternative to state responsibility. The task was taken on by government, if not from political belief, by default.

Tabel 2: Functional responsibilities in ten African countries with respect to textbooks

	Ministry of education or other government agency	*State and private*	*Private sector*
Writing	8	1	1
Production	6	3	1
Distribution	6	1	3
Financing	2	4	4

State involvement was seen as a means of controlling the use of scarce resources and subsidies. It was believed to be economical because it eliminated the markups and profit of commercial printing, publishing and bookselling. The Ministry could determine quantities and schedules, and ensure they were met. Those transnational publishers who continued to do business in developing countries were not averse to working with governments, particularly if in that way they could secure a monopoly or dominant position in providing textbooks. The World Bank and other major bilateral donors also worked with governments as a matter of policy, and in two early large projects in the Philippines and Indonesia (and in others later) encouraged the development of a central agency to develop, produce and distribute textbooks. A study sponsored by the World Bank concluded that:

Developing sustainable capacity for creating, testing, producing, and distributing student learning materials' as well as teacher guides and in-service training materials' requires a significant commitment of the central ministry's resources. Experience in Bangladesh, China, Ethiopia, and the Philippines suggests that textbook agencies, whether autonomous or divisions of the (national or federal) eduction ministry, are essential to establishing and sustaining a program of materials development. . . . Even small countries, where publishing industries are relatively weak because the market for textbooks is small, may have to set up a clearly defined unit for developing instructional materials, carrying out the design, development, and testing necessary to achieve high quality, and managing the storage and distribution of materials.

The dominance of the state impeded the development of private-sector educational publishing, and thus perpetuated the need for state involvement in countries where it existed. It also nurtured a 'state provider' mentality that proved difficult to dislodge.

Problems commonly ascribed to government bureaucracies arose. Policies changed and so did ministers. One major textbook project dealt with eight ministers of education in four years, each with a new approach to policy. Civil servants were often poorly motivated to seek economies and usually inexperienced in publishing practices. In many countries they were posted in and out of positions without regard to continuity, at the sacrifice of institutional memory. There was wastage and inefficiency, and some corruption' unsurprising when civil service wages fell far below the cost of living. There was inadequate co-ordination among the various functions of writing, production and distribution. An adviser to the World Bank warned that when government agencies produced textbook manuscripts for publication, the procedure was fraught with political implications and conflict of interest. Some of these problems bedeviled similar experiments everywhere. In Sweden, for example, a huge state-owned publishing house had collapsed under the weight of a large bureaucracy and great financial losses.

Separate state-owned companies, or parastatals, were created in an effort to retain government control without some of the constraints of government personnel policies. They were given considerable managerial and financial autonomy but received funds and sometimes direction from the government. It was expected that they would be managed more in line with commercial publishing practices. Some parastatals were joint ventures between the government and one or more foreign commercial publishers. CEDA, previously mentioned, in which the Ivorian government held 51 per cent, was one such venture, as was Nouvelles éditions africaines, which, before its breakup into three national companies in 1988, was owned jointly by the governments of Senegal, Côte d'Ivoire and Togo (60 per cent), and a consortium of French firms, and became a major force in publishing with a long list of titles. In English-speaking Africa, British publishers entered into joint ventures with parastatals in Ghana, the United Republic of Tanzania and Uganda, experiments which Buchan characterized as 'interesting and desirable . . . but too often the interests of overseas commercial publisher and local state enterprise were too divergent for them to stay together.'

In countries where the government dominated the writing and publishing of learning materials, there was normally only one textbook for each subject/level. This was the case in countries that required a massive effort simply to produce the single text in sufficient numbers, such as the Philippines and Indonesia, in the socialist countries of Asia and eastern Europe, in the USSR, and in many countries of Africa. In countries that permitted private-sector educational publishing, there might be a choice among competing textbooks, although in some cases the market was dominated by a single publishing house, local or foreign-owned. Zimbabwe and Nigeria were among the few African nations that permitted multiple choice in an open market in which schools chose the texts they would use from a list of government-approved titles.

Constraints in provision

Educational publishers, whether state-controlled or privately owned, faced serious constraints in 1990. The most important were in financing, production, distribution, information and human resources.

Financing. Book publishing of any kind, but especially the publishing of textbooks, is a capital-intensive business. It typically takes three years to identify authors, plan and write a textbook, edit it, pretest it in classrooms, prepare it for printing, print and bind it, and deliver it to the schools. With luck, the process may take less time, but more often it takes longer. During this time, staff and office expenses must be paid, paper and other materials bought and printers paid. A competitive textbook market involves additional expenses for marketing and promotion. If the books are to be sold, it may take two to three years more to recoup the capital investment.

The global recession of the 1980s and the policies of structural adjustment had a devastating effect on government budgets for education, especially on non-salary items such as books. Between 1985 and 1990, real public expenditure per pupil fell at the primary level in seven of nine Latin American countries for which data were available and in thirteen of twenty in Africa; it also fell at the secondary level in Africa. Budgets for classroom resources (books, teaching aids, furniture and other equipment) were already low.

When industrial countries were allocating 14 per cent of primary-school recurrent costs to classroom resources and 86 per cent to salaries, Asian countries were allocating 9 per cent to classroom resources and African countries only 4 per cent. Expenditures on learning materials and other non-salary recurrent expenses fell in countries suffering from recession, sometimes to close to zero. Supplementary materials were the first to be affected, then textbooks. The reduction in learning material procurement may have slowed after the middle of the decade, but only because by then salaries accounted for almost all recurrent expenditures. The trend was felt most strongly in sub-Saharan Africa. There, expenditure on educational materials represented about 1 per cent of the recurrent primary school budget in 1983, the equivalent of about US$0.60 per pupil. Given the unequal distribution of books, rural areas suffered disproportionately.

Within this restricted market, educational publishers in the private sector faced an additional hurdle: finding credit to capitalize textbook projects. Interest rates rose under structural adjustment, in some countries to 40 per cent or more. Banks, moreover, were reluctant to lend money to entrepreneurs in a high-risk, low-profit industry, or to recognize books in the warehouse or work in progress as collateral. Paper ceases to be collateral as soon as it is printed upon.

Under the stringency of falling export revenues, devaluation, inflation, and structural adjustment, African governments increased efforts to achieve partial or full recovery of costs in textbooks. Lesotho's success has already been mentioned. Ethiopia began charging for textbooks lent for the school year, with 45 per cent of the revenue being retained for printing more books and the balance shared between the schools and the regional offices; the latter was expected to use its share for expanding school library facilities. Angola and Mozambique sold textbooks but subsidized the price substantially. Uganda experimented with a subsidized rental fee.

Partial cost recovery, of course, did no more than reduce the problem of budget shortages. It did not make a nation's educational publishing programme financially self-sustaining. In Ghana, for example, a long-established system of partial cost recovery collapsed because revenue was insufficient to maintain supply. Under new guidelines issued in 1987, textbooks were to be rented for a fee that was based on the cost of production and the expected life span of the books.

For many countries, cost recovery was a new approach beset with problems. In Paraguay, for example, a government scheme to sell textbooks for profit through its Internal Revenue Service offices foundered and 90 per cent of the books were unsold. More commonly, books were unknowingly sold below true cost because of inadequate bookkeeping in Ministry or parastatal offices. In 1986 a World Bank publication suggested a radically different approach' one that would be relatively easy to administer if politically difficult' for cost recovery in one sector to benefit another.

The authors proposed that governments eliminate the free tuition and living allowances then commonly paid to African university students (a practice that reinforced an already existing elite) and invest the money thus saved in primary education. They calculated that if twelve African countries were to eliminate living allowances, the public resources thus freed would allow, on average, an 18 per cent expansion in the yearly budget for primary education. Nationally, the figure ranged from just under 3 per cent in Sudan to more than 40 per cent in Togo. If fees were introduced to cover all the operating costs of higher education, an additional expansion of 22.5 per cent in primary education would be possible.

Single most expensive item in book production costs, representing between 45 and 70 per cent of the cost of manufacture. Most of the paper suitable for books was produced in the North, and prices were set by demand from the prime user, the United States. Countries that had developed their own paper-making capacity often protected it with high tariffs, even for educational purposes, and locally produced paper was sometimes more expensive than superior stock produced overseas.

Book printing is specialized work, different in its requirements from printing newspapers, magazines or other commercial products. Capacity was limited by the number of book printers in most countries and by the quality of their equipment. Costs were driven up when presses and other machinery were old and ill-maintained, occasioning frequent need for repairs and consequent down time. Paper was misappropriated, damaged in transit, or used inefficiently because of mismatches between available sheet sizes and the printer's press size. A publisher in one developing country suggested that paper wastage from mismatching could reach as high as 50 per cent. Books were also delayed by mismatches in equipment' most commonly between new high-speed presses and outdated binding technology. The shortage of thread-binding equipment forced dependence on adhesive binding and resulted in books that fell apart. Printing and binding machinery, spare parts and materials were subject to high duties and sales taxes. Under such conditions, quality suffered, as did prices and schedules.

Local control of publishing does not require local printing. Commercial publishers in the North commonly crossed oceans in search of the most cost-effective printing. Many governments in the South, however, insisted that books be printed at home, often in state-owned or parastatal plants, regardless of efficiency or cost. In three of nine African countries surveyed in book sector studies, local printing prices were higher than could be obtained outside the country. Donated printing equipment not infrequently sat gathering dust for lack of trained operators or because there was no local service agency to repair it. Some equipment stood idle for much of the year because its capacity was far greater than needed.

Distribution. Geography impedes distribution in much of the global South. Some countries are archipelagos' there are 10,000 islands in Indonesia and 7,000 in the Philippines' or are themselves islands, separated by ocean from their neighbours. Transport is impeded by rivers, mountains, deserts and jungles. Roads are poor and trucking often inadequate. Tens of thousands of schools are hours from the nearest road and books for them must be delivered by canoe, head porterage or pack animal. State-supported distribution systems generally depended on teachers, parents or the community to carry learning materials from district depots to isolated schools. Even that system was seen to be breaking down as teachers' salaries dropped in real terms and were paid less reliably.

Where the state was responsible for distribution, books typically were gathered in a central warehouse and shipped to district depots, whence they were directed to schools. In some countries there was an additional step, books going first to regional depots, to be divided there for transshipment to districts and thence to schools. At each stage, there was the possibility of failure. District offices often lacked the funds to pay forwarders, sometimes because the money had not been provided, sometimes because they had never accounted properly for the previous year's advance for that purpose. Packaging and storage were often inadequate to protect the books against water, insects, mould and vermin. In one instance during the rainy season in 1984, new books were delivered to a regional store in Ghana that had no roof; within days the books were soaked and useless.

Books could be delayed by erratic shipping schedules or by the pursuit of economies. In order to ship books efficiently orders were often consolidated, in which case the total order could be held up until the last title was delivered by the printer or publisher. Sometimes distribution costs were unnecessarily high: in the scattered islands of the eastern Caribbean, for example, textbooks were sometimes delivered by freighter or even more expensive air freight, despite the presence of a regular, reliable and inexpensive domestic service that provided baking flour to the islands by boat.

Efficient, economical distribution was further impeded by a lack of adequate information from the schools. Depot storekeepers were untrained in inventory control and maintenance. Books were damaged, lost or stolen. A combination of delays, from development through to distribution, could result in books being delivered a year, or even three years, behind schedule.

In most countries where books were sold through retail outlets, bookstores were scarce in the urban centres and almost unknown outside the cities. Distribution depended on an informal network of suppliers.

Information. Efficient provision requires accurate and timely information on which to project enrolments, and therefore textbook needs, by school, grade and subject. Central planners need data on the number, size and type of schools; current enrolments by grade, school, sex and age; historical and projected rates of change in enrolment; numbers of teachers; numbers of school libraries; and so on. This kind of information was difficult to accumulate in countries where communication by telephone or mail was unreliable. Data were incomplete, sometimes false, more often outdated and pitted with errors created during collation at several steps up the ladder to the central office.

Human resources. Ministry of Education staff were rarely familiar with printing and publishing practices. Curriculum developers were often expected to make major decisions with little or no idea about the implications in cost or time involved. Costs were inflated by ill-informed decisions about book length, illustrations, colours and format.

Government, parastatal and private-sector publishers all suffered from a lack of trained personnel' authors, editors, evaluators, designers, production co-ordinators, distribution and warehouse supervisors, financial and publishing managers. Some publishing institutions obtained training through partnership with overseas commercial publishers. Others sent staff to short-term training courses within Africa or for long-term training abroad, but these resources in 1990 were still relatively limited.

To fund the growing needs of education, governments looked for international help. The World Bank expanded its mandate from project-related vocational training to provide support for school buildings, textbooks, curriculum development and institutional development. The proportion of education projects with textbook components grew steadily, from about 6 per cent before 1974 to 32 per cent in 1979-83 to almost 65 per cent by 1990. In northeast Brazil, a Bank project tripled the number of students receiving textbooks; in the Philippines, a massive effort was funded to reduce the textbook:pupil ratio from 1:10 to 1:2. In three projects alone, in the Philippines, Indonesia, and Ethiopia, more than 350 million textbooks were produced. The process was not without growing pains, however, as Barbara Searle recognized in a review of the Bank's educational projects over the previous ten years. She identified serious shortcomings:

> This review makes it clear that at least some of the projects approved early in this decade recognized that textbook publishing is complex and highly technical; that it requires professional competence in many specialties; and that developing a good textbook takes time, three years at a minimum. Yet, even with this recognition, projects underestimated the difficulties. Of the nine projects surveyed, only

> three . . . left behind functioning textbook provision schemes. Beyond this, the completed projects provide evidence for shortfalls in every aspect of textbook provision: poor quality books, inadequate distribution systems, inability to establish and maintain production schedules, inadequate procedures for handling paper procurement, teacher training activities out of phase with book publication, poor co-ordination between curriculum and manuscript development, and, above all, failure to establish institutions that can continue to provide good quality books after project completion.

Some 90 per cent of the forty-eight projects she reviewed financed the purchase or printing of textbooks, but fewer than half included teacher training, monitoring and evaluation, or dealt with policy changes. Only half the projects that provided books also financed manuscript development and book distribution, and only half of those (eleven projects) also financed teacher training. Only ten projects explicitly dealt with the institutional structure of the textbook provision system and modified it in some way. She concluded that:

> the likelihood of a textbook component attaining its objectives is directly related to the extent to which the project design addresses all aspects of the textbook provision system. It is not crucial that a project finance every component. However, the analysis of the system that is undertaken during preparation and appraisal must include all aspects to make sure that the entire supporting system is in place and functioning well.

The World Bank was the leading, but not the only international, agency supporting textbook provision. The British Overseas Development Administration had textbook programmes in Sierra, Leone, Jamaica and

Jordan. Its three-year project in Sierra Leone, where there was no publishing capacity when financing began in 1984, extended beyond book provision to creation of school storage and a school management system, teacher training in a new curriculum and use of textbooks, warehouse improvement and training of publishing staff. In French-speaking Africa, l'Agence de coopération culturelle et technique (ACCT), supported by France, Canada and Belgium, distributed dictionaries and reading materials to schools and in 1990 was organizing a training programme in printing, publishing, book distribution and bookstore management. Scandinavian governments were notable for their support of book development. The Swedish International Development Co-operation Agency (Sida) was active in Bangladesh, Cambodia, Ethiopia, Guinea-Bissau, Mozambique, the United Republic of Tanzania and Zambia; the Finnish International Development Agency (FINNIDA), in Namibia and Zambia; and Danish International Development Assistance (Danida), in Burkina Faso, Nepal, Uganda, the United Republic of Tanzania, and Zimbabwe. Non-governmental organizations, often with funding from their national government's aid agency, played a small but increasing role as well. The Canadian Organization for Development through Education (CODE), for example, supplied paper and distributed supplementary materials, and several book-related organizations in Europe organized short training courses.

The smaller contributions were generally ad hoc, uncoordinated, and short-term. Individual agencies had their own agendas, political or altruistic. Several projects involved the supply of paper, a short-term solution to immediate needs that could have the longer-term effect of distorting the market. (Unless the equivalent cost of the donated paper was recognized when it was used, book prices would rise abruptly when the supply ended and paper had again to be bought on the market. Then fiscal allocations for textbooks would have to be increased or, more often, textbook provision sharply reduced.) Equipment was too often supplied without spare parts or technical support for maintenance and repair. One-time seminars and workshops were held for writers, editors, publishers, printers and booksellers, but with little or no follow-up, and funding agencies were sometimes disappointed to find that people, once trained, moved from school book publishing to better paying jobs. Funders complained that they had difficulty in identifying all the links in the publishing chain and in understanding the broad concerns that underlay what might seem a simple project. The impact of much of the effort was short-lived and local.

One major exception was a loan guarantee scheme started in Kenya by the Dag Hammarskjøld Foundation, with support from the Ford Foundation of US$300,000. The Foundation negotiated with local banks to guarantee credit extended to local publishers in a normal way. Kenya was chosen because it had a well-developed book market, but one then dominated by transnational publishers. Eleven applications for loans were accepted under the scheme. There were problems in communication' the banks initially expected to be repaid as soon as books were published, not understanding that it takes time to recover publishing costs through sales' and some of the borrowers ran into difficulty because of financial or marketing inexperience. Nevertheless, only three publishers failed to repay their loans and had to be rescued by the guarantee. The scheme was significant in assisting the indigenization of Heinemann Kenya which now, as East African Educational Publishers Limited, is one of the strongest publishing houses on the continent. The project showed that small publishers who are able to gain access to commercial credit and who manage their finances carefully can succeed, even with interest rates as high as 30 to 40 per cent.

Major funders generally were more interested in institutional development than in supplying learning materials. They believed that direct support to pupils and teachers would be less efficient than funding central units for teacher training, curriculum development and educational planning that could increase the effectiveness of the entire system. Books and instructional materials received only a small percentage of total donor aid to education.

Major textbook projects, moreover, were directed to short-term gains to overcome immediate and urgent shortages. Typically, they lasted three to five years and gave little attention to building local publishing capacity. The size, urgency and complexity of the projects precluded local publishers from participating. That responsibility devolved on ministries and parastatals which were themselves ill-prepared and which, outside the project's funding, were at the mercy of legislative budget allocations and government policy changes. There was no long-term approach, among funders or governments, to the sustainable provision of learning materials.

There was, however, a growing interest in co-operation among donors and funding agencies. They met together, formally or informally, to discuss possible joint projects or to exchange information. Some donors preferred that these meetings be held only at the invitation of, and with full participation by, the potential recipients of aid; others were satisfied to meet as a donor group and offer a package of assistance. Some recipients saw the second approach as unfair 'ganging up' on recipients. Donors for African Education, which had been started during the 1980s as a donors' club to promote collaboration in educational projects and programmes in Africa, and thereby avoid competition and duplication, eventually expanded its membership in response to such concerns and, to emphasize partnership over assistance, changed its name to the Association for the Development of Education in Africa (ADEA). Its Working Group on Books and Learning Materials, established in 1989, included African ministries of education as well as development agencies concerned with book development and procurement.

Global trends

The provision of learning materials has been affected, like so many other sectors of society, by the political and economic changes of the decade since Jomtien. Worldwide, the principal trends were towards decentralization of selection and procurement, economic liberalization with a greater role for the private sector and cost recovery to achieve systemic sustainability. The first two trends marched hand in hand, although the balance between them could vary: the state might still dominate in a nominally privatized economy and commercial publishers might be active under centralized state procurement. The third trend, the drive for sustainability, was both a response to budgetary shortfalls in a period of rising demands and rising costs, and a recognition that learning materials are a recurrent expense that cannot practically be financed by continual infusions of external loans and grants.

Change was not always welcomed or rapid. As the authors of a World Bank review observed:

> In all countries entrenched ways of operating and vested interests will make change difficult. Education is intensely political: it affects the majority of citizens, involves all levels of government, almost always makes up the single largest component of public spending in developing countries and involves public subsidies that are biased in favour of the elite. Prevailing systems of education spending and management often protect the interests of teachers' unions, university students, elites, and the central government rather than those of parents, communities, and the poor.

Decentralization

The trend towards decentralization in education had two motivations. One was the democratic belief that all stakeholders should be involved in a function so important to the community' that the wishes of teachers, parents, students, parent-teacher groups and non-governmental organizations should be heard and that some of these groups might be involved in decision-making. In its ultimate expression, responsibility would lodge in the schools, which would be able to decide for themselves how to use substantial portions of their allotted resources, sometimes with the advice of ad hoc committees of teachers, parents, and/or students. The second motivation in many countries was the growing recognition that the existing system didn't work, and one reason was the cost and inertia of swollen bureaucracies.

In the Philippines, for example, a Congressional Commission on Education complained that the Department of Education was 'highly centralized . . . and its complex procedures in asset management have resulted in loss and waste.' It recommended that many responsibilities, including the procurement and distribution of textbooks and other essential materials, be devolved to the country's 126 divisional offices, bypassing entirely the 14 regional offices that lay between the divisions and Manila. Brickhill and Priestley found that 'as a general principle, the further the decision-making process is from the actual user of the material, the less efficiently the funds are used.'

For one reason or the other, governments decentralized the procurement of textbooks and/or their selection if there was a choice. The Russian Federation delegated responsibility for educational funding to the country's oblasts (provinces) in the early 1990s and gave teachers freedom of choice in textbooks. In the economically advanced post-communist countries of Eastern Europe as well, schools or local boards were given their own budgets and allowed to choose their own textbooks. The United Republic of Tanzania announced a policy in 1991 that would lead to selection at the district level and eventually in the schools.

Mexico was to have completed decentralization by the end of 1997, at which time each of the thirty-two provinces would be in control of its schools, teachers and budgets. Colombia devolved selection to the districts and schools, as did Kenya, Uganda, Zimbabwe and some provinces of South Africa. By the end of the decade, India had almost completed devolving the publication of textbooks, teachers' guides and work books to the state governments, which were expected to produce books at a more affordable price than the private sector had been able to achieve.

Not all governments by any means followed the trend or followed it all the way. In Singapore, for example, textbooks were published commercially but the writing of them remained with the Curriculum Development Institute. In Mexico, the government devolved administrative responsibility but not choice; it was reluctant to abandon the idea of 'a single textbook, written and produced by an official body, because it has long been the means of conveying the government's desired message to the population and . . . the record of national history'. In Bangladesh, the National Curriculum and Textbook Board (NCTB) continued to develop the curriculum, write the textbooks and produce the finished books, which it sold at a profit to the Directorate of Primary Education. NCTB opposed any change to the system and, despite proposals by a consortium of funding agencies, the government also showed little active interest in reform.

Decentralization is seen to have several advantages. It encourages the involvement of parents and others in the community. It may give teachers more responsibility and status and, especially in large schools, develop their sense of collegiality. Most important, decisions can be taken in the light of local conditions and to meet local needs. They are no longer made by bureaucrats in a central office, divorced from the realities of the underfunded, often isolated, classroom. Local decision-making is particularly important for rural communities and for minority groups whose concerns, needs, and beliefs have often been ignored in educational books published in' and with examples from' large urban centres.

The transition is not without difficulties, however. Financial decentralization raises concern about money lost through incompetence, misappropriation or corruption. Administratively, there may be confusion if the division of responsibilities is not clearly spelled out. There are often delays in the transfer of funds from the central to subordinate offices. Personnel at all the levels that are given new responsibilities, down to the school, require training in financial accounting, management of supplies, selection of books and other administrative tasks' a massive task. In a strongly hierarchical system, teachers and others are apt to be influenced in their decisions by superior officers, undermining the intent of decentralization. If procurement as well as selection of textbooks is decentralized, retail outlets may not be easily accessible or may be late in obtaining the books for school use.

Liberalization

At the same time as they were moving responsibilities downwards, national governments were withdrawing from the business of providing textbooks and other learning materials. Government departments that wrote and produced text-books as monopolies were turned into parastatal organizations and monopoly publishing parastatals were sold, in part or all, to private owners. Commercial publishers were allowed to compete for textbook adoptions, against one another and, not infrequently, against a parastatal. State-owned printing plants were turned into parastatals and expected to run on strictly commercial lines; parastatal printers were privatized.

The government often retained distribution of school books but, especially in the more liberalized economies, this function too might be given to the publishers. Liberalization was implemented in many patterns, but always in the expectation that commercially oriented enterprises would be more efficient than government and more responsive to educational needs, especially if there were competition in a multi-textbook system. Donors and governments had come to recognize that state monopolies rarely met the need for learning materials and that large-scale subsidies did nothing to encourage reinvestment in publishing development.

In some countries, including Zimbabwe and Jamaica, learning materials had long been supplied by commercial publishers. In others that had had communist governments, commercial production and competition were new concepts to an entire generation. The transition could be abrupt. In the Philippines, a group of commercial textbook publishers and agents, who had been supplying the 5 per cent of the student population in private schools, lobbied the Congress successfully in 1995 to achieve privatization of supply to the much larger and more scattered public system. The state was to get out of textbook writing, production and distribution entirely within three years. The time allowed was inadequate, particularly when implementation was delayed by government inaction and arguments between the public and private sectors, and numerous abuses of the new system in its first year were reported. Other countries approached the transition more cautiously and many were still in the early stages at the decade's end.

The United Republic of Tanzania was one that took a deliberate approach. In 1991 it adopted a policy of transforming the state-managed provision of textbooks into a completely commercial system with minimal government involvement and decentralized selection. A Pilot Project for Publishing (PPP) was established with external support to advise and assist publishers and ministries on an orderly transition. The change was not without its difficulties, but by 1997 commercial publishers had produced 21 titles (1.75 million books) and another 28 titles were in progress.

The first manuscripts were written in the The United Republic of Tanzania Institute of Education, but in 1996 the Institute was restricted to curriculum-related activities. The Ministry of Education continued to be responsible for procurement and distribution. The duration of the transition period has not been defined and will depend on how fast the actors can cope with new responsibilities, and some commercial publishers and booksellers feel the government should move faster in devolving spending power so as to allow full competition.

The beneficial effects of liberalization were to be seen in several countries. In Kenya, which already had a well established publishing industry with significant local ownership, schools were allowed to select the books they would use from up to six titles authorized for each subject/level by the Textbook Approvals Board. The new policies had resulted by 1997 in from three to five competing series in each of five primary-level subjects and comparable choice in subjects at the secondary level except in physics, chemistry and biology, for which books were mainly imported from the United Kingdom.

In other countries progress was slow' outstandingly so in Ghana, where the government had entered into an agreement (heralded as a 'unique, first-of-its-kind effort in all Africa') with five local publishers to co-publish thirty selected primary-school textbooks in 1984 but did not implement it until 1990. It was only three years later that the national publishers' association met for the first time with the Minister of Education to ask for more involvement. Since then the syllabuses, once restricted, have become more publicly available and in 1998 Ghana announced a more open textbook production after consultation with funding agencies, publishers, printers, booksellers, writers and teachers.

In Mongolia, the transition has been hampered by attitudes. The country has experienced and skilled people working in book production, but the business aspects of publishing are not fully understood, and publishers and printers are still primarily looking for funding and not for business opportunities.

Of seventeen countries of sub-Saharan Africa surveyed in 1997, eight apparently continued to use the single textbook system in the publishing of primary-school materials.

One, however, allowed a choice between state-published and privately published titles in some subjects, and three were in transition towards open markets and liberalized textbook publishing. Three countries offered a choice of parallel titles in every subject. Five countries gave limited opportunities for alternative titles in some subjects but not all. There was greater choice at the secondary level. Only Ethiopia and Mozambique apparently restricted schools to single textbooks; other countries had either parallel or, the majority, multiple choice.

At the end of 1998, however, relatively entrepreneurial Cameroon moved away from multiple choice. It signed an agreement granting a newly privatized company, CEPER, S.A., the exclusive right to conceive, produce and distribute all primary and nursery school textbooks in the country. It also exempted CEPER from all taxes on machines, spare parts, paper and ink. CEPER is the successor to the state-owned Centre d'edition et de production pour l'enseignment et recherche which had specialized in educational materials but shared the market with commercial companies, including the well-established Editions CLE. For the most part, the state kept some functions and turned others over to the private sector. In Zambia, manuscripts prepared under the Curriculum Development Institute were tendered to the private sector; the finished books were still being bought centrally in 1996 but there were plans to delegate that responsibility to school management boards. In Lebanon also, a state institution wrote the textbooks, which were then produced and distributed by private publishers. Several Eastern European countries have retained distribution as a governmental function, even though books may be produced in a free market. Occasionally the government has reclaimed responsibilities: Jamaica, which had previously allowed individual secondary schools to order books from their supplier of choice, is moving towards centralization of procurement in order to reduce costs.

In small countries, and in those with languages spoken by only a small population, a continuing state presence was inevitable. Commercial publishers cannot be expected to mount a sales force in countries as small as Niue, which has two schools, or Tokelau, which has three. In those Pacific island countries, central procurement remains the only feasible option. Mauritania encouraged private-sector involvement in publishing but the market was so unattractively small, as a result of population size and poverty, that the state was obliged to write, print and distribute textbooks; even an attempt to involve commercial booksellers in distribution failed. In other small nations, state involvement was by choice. Guyana, with a population of roughly 800,000 and English as a language of instruction, might have used some textbooks produced commercially elsewhere but instead secured external support to write and produce its own primary- and secondary-level textbooks in a government centre.

Where state-owned or parastatal organizations had been forced give up monopoly positions, they frequently continued to dominate the market. As Brickhill has noted, it is difficult to break up a monopoly and establish a level playing field when books are needed immediately and not in two or three years or more. The former monopolists benefited moreover from the conservatism of procurement officers and teachers who hesitated to stray from the former official textbooks. Some parastatals, while autonomous and commercial, still received government funding or hidden benefits such as the use of state-subsidized printing plants. The new publishers did not always prosper. Following liberalization in Kazakhstan, 150 private publishers registered for business in competition with 14 state-owned publishers, but soon after only 12 had survived and only 5 or 6 were effectively functioning.

Funding

In a time of rising enrolments and financial austerity, no

developing country was allocating more than 1 per cent of its primary education budget to textbooks, even though an increase of only 1 or 2 per cent in most countries would have ensured a textbook:pupil ratio of 1:1. Public recurrent expenditures in education were swallowed by teachers' salaries. In a survey of sub-Saharan Africa, only a handful of countries reported what proportion of recurrent educational expenditure was spent on learning materials in 1995 or 1996, but those statistics are gloomy. In primary education, only Mali, at 14.9 per cent, was shown as devoting more than one-tenth of annual recurrent educational expenditures to learning materials; from there the proportion dropped to 8.4 per cent in Comoros, 5.1 per cent in Gambia,1.7 per cent in Seychelles and so on down to 0.2 per cent in Uganda. The reported statistics for secondary education were somewhat higher: from 28.3 per cent to Mali and 8.5 per cent in Togo down to 2.4 per cent in Gambia and 1.4 per cent in Mauritania. Ministries of education were apt to find their legislative masters allocating only a portion of the budget that had been requested to meet stated objectives of free or subsidized text-book provision.

In Indonesia, the books needed to achieve a textbook-to-student ratio of 1:1 in Grades 1 to 9 would have cost an estimated US$380 million in 1995, when the economy was still buoyant; the amount actually spent amounted to US$36 million budgeted by the government and about US$43 million paid by parents' a shortfall of almost 80 per cent (ADEA/UNESCO survey 1999). One respondent with widespread experience observed that the shortage of textbooks is not so much a book famine as a money famine: there are many good quality textbooks available in most subjects in many countries but no funds to buy them and classrooms are generally short of everything but students. Governments admittedly must make difficult choices. Another respondent, this time from the Philippines, recalled that the chair of a congressional committee asked publishers appearing before it: 'How can we even think of books when people are hungry and dying"

In countries that were moving from state or parastatal publishing to private-sector publishing of textbooks, there could be uncomfortable surprises. In principle private enterprise is more efficient than government and should be able to produce text-books more cheaply. But privately owned publishers must recover from sales all their overhead costs' most significantly, wages, premises, office expenses, manuscript development, marketing and interest charges on loans' as well as the costs of production and a reasonable return to shareholders. Ministries that were engaged in publishing normally included only production costs and perhaps some wages in calculating the cost of school books, but they did not always account for those expenses in full and sometimes enjoyed the privilege of state-subsidized printing or tax-exempt paper. Parastatals did not always pay full market costs either. In asking for budgetary allocations, ministries and parastatals used their own calculations to project the annual cost to the government of learning materials.

Those that sold books also often simply charged only the production cost. In contrast, commercial publishers who enjoyed none of the hidden subsidies usually multiplied the cost of production (paper, printing and binding) by three or more to set a retail price that would give them a profit and allow a markup for booksellers. The markup for booksellers could be waived for central procurement by the government, but the price per copy was still likely to be more than double what the Ministry had been accustomed to allowing in its budget estimates. The fiscal allocation would then have to be doubled or more to maintain the same level of provision. If the legislature rejected that option, the number of books that could be bought by the state would be reduced by half or more. Savings could be realized only if the transition to the private sector were accompanied by the appropriate reduction in the civil service establishment, including any senior staff who were writing textbooks or managing publication.

Despite financial stringency, some countries continued to provide textbooks without charge, even if in reduced numbers. Sri Lanka, Nepal, Bhutan and Bangladesh, for example, all provided free textbooks to primary schools, and respondents to the ADEA/ UNESCO survey from those countries reported no book shortages. In countries where an international funding agency was subsidizing textbooks for specific areas (for example, the poorest provinces) or specific groups (girls or indigenous minorities), free distribution was sometimes maintained generally because it was felt inappropriate, if not illegal, to provide textbooks to the rest of the country under less advantageous conditions. It seems likely that free provision will gradually grow less common.

Bhutan is gradually withdrawing support for textbooks and stationery from the economically better-off areas because of rising costs. The Cambodian government is considering selling books for Grade 10 (basic education ends with Grade 9) and may legitimize the sale of core textbooks in lower grades to undermine the black market. Bulgaria suddenly accelerated the introduction of total cost recovery from parents after a World Bank-funded programme ended; what had previously been regarded as politically unacceptable and unaf-fordable suddenly became policy from economic necessity. In the short and medium term, however, governments continue to bear most of the burden of supplying books.

Where textbooks are produced commercially and sold on the open market, there should, of course, be full cost recovery with enough profit to encourage reinvestment in further manuscript development and revision. If necessary, the government may subsidize the publishers.

Where books are not sold, there has been growing attention to at least partial cost recovery through textbook rental. Book banks of this type were established at all levels of education, from primary to tertiary.

There is some evidence that parents prize education so highly as a long-term investment in the family that household demand for education is relatively price-inelastic. That is, enrolment does not drop in proportion to increases in private costs. On the other hand, the elimination of school fees in Uganda led to an increase in enrolment of more than 2 million students. In Samoa, parents grumble at paying school fees of 3 to 5 tala per term, less than the cost of one packet of cigarettes there, and schools, which have difficulty collecting that amount, hesitate to charge more (UNESCO/Danida case-studies: Samoa). Unquestionably, when textbooks are added to the direct costs of education' which may also include exercise books, pencils, uniforms and transportation, even when the schooling itself is free' children from the poorest families are going to be discouraged from attending. In many countries, girls are more likely to be affected than boys, for a variety of reasons: a cultural belief that girls do not need as much schooling as boys because they will spend their lives in domestic tasks, dependence on girls to help with household chores and, the extra cost of clothing for girls.

To compensate, various demand-side support programmes have been devised to encourage attendance by girls, including free textbooks and stipends that can be paid to parents to compensate them for direct costs and for the loss of their daughters' time. Such projects have been undertaken, for example, in Bangladesh, Egypt, Guatemala, Mali, Morocco, Peru, Tunisia and Yemen.

In the Pakistani state of Balochistan, funding for the purchase of textbooks has been part of a rural programme based on community support for schools. In Armenia, where schools operate book rental schemes with a four-year amortization, funds were provided for subsidies to the neediest 10 per cent of students, identified by the school community. A similar scheme has been under way in Guinea

There the book rental fee of approximately US$1.40 per year can be waived if, in the opinion of the school management committee, a student cannot afford to pay it. Funding agencies have also targeted their subsidies to education by directing loans to the most disadvantaged areas of the recipient country. World Bank projects of this kind include support of primary-level textbook development and publishing in six provinces and autonomous regions of China and in ten states of Mexico, both involving the development and publishing of textbooks and other learning materials in indigenous languages that had previously been underserved.

In private schools, textbooks have always been bought by students or families at market rates. The number of private schools varies from country to country and probably reflects to some degree the perception of the public system and the quality of its education. They sometimes play a prominent role. In the Dominican Republic, they have served about 20 per cent of all primary students and 30 per cent of lower-secondary students. In Colombia, private secondary schools outnumbered public ones almost two to one in the eighty-seven municipalities covered by a World Bank project. Private schools normally were located in urban centres and catered to the elite or at least well-to-do. In the second half of the 1990s, the World Bank and other funding agencies began financing projects to increase access to the private system. One method was to issue vouchers for tuition and incidental expenses to needy students. Another was direct funding of private schools serving poor children, as in the Dominican Republic, or serving primary-age girls, as in the Northwest Frontier Province of Pakistan.

Table 1. Projected in enrolment worldwide (in millions)

	1992	*2000*	*Increase (%)*
Primary	522	589	13
Secondary	227	269	19
Post-secondary	32	40	25

Availability of school books

Despite public statements and funders' support, and advances in some countries, it does not appear that textbooks are much more available globally ten years after the World Declaration on Education for All than they were before. Quantitative evidence is scarce, but qualitative reports suggest that, if anything, the situation in many countries has got worse. School enrolments have risen, a result of the demographic curve and national attempts to achieve universal primary education. The number of students attending school worldwide increased by some 50 million between 1990 and 1995, and some 60 million additional children were expected to enter the primary school age group during the next five years. The projected enrolment increases spread across the three educational levels (Table 1) and were expected to be sharpest in sub-Saharan Africa, the Arab States and Southern Asia. At the same time, funding for education has declined as a result of economic slowdown, the cost of servicing foreign debt, devaluation, policies of structural adjustment and competing social needs. Following the collapse of communism, education systems in Eastern Europe and Western Asia have fallen into disarray. In countries with large populations and a history of external textbook support, such as the Philippines and Bangladesh, the international banks are restricting educational loans to the most disadvantaged areas, leaving the majority of the school population to the vagaries of national legislative funding.

In a survey that covered 26 countries of Africa, all but 9 of 103 respondents considered that the book famine in their country was serious, and 87 per cent said there was a serious shortage of textbooks. Respondents to the same questionnaire elsewhere reported serious shortages of textbooks in some grades in Cambodia, for the new curriculum in Mongolia, and more generally in Afghanistan, Indonesia, Lebanon, Pakistan and the

Philippines. There was not total unanimity, however. The respondents from Lebanon and Pakistan differed among themselves, half saying there was in fact no shortage of textbooks.

Such differences of opinion underline the difficulty of judging availability when reliable data are scarce. J. Oliveira said that: Of the 93 countries responding to UNESCO inquiries on the topic, roughly 60 per cent of them (about 57 countries) report that they have a sufficient supply of books; however, several of this group, including Paraguay, Burkina Faso, and Colombia, in fact suffer from a major scarcity of textbooks. This finding not only illustrates that data are not reliable; it also shows that different countries have different opinions about what amount of textbook coverage is sufficient.

Moreover, the numbers given above usually only refer to delivery of textbooks to warehouses, not to what is actually available in school-houses in dense urban periphery neighbourhoods or remote rural villages. According to these same figures, twelve countries report that less than 30 per cent of their schools are supplied with textbooks. In addition, there is extensive evidence that the data regarding textbook use supplied by these and by many other countries are unreliable. Data from other sources . . . are hardly more reliable, since ultimately, they came from the same informants who supplied UNESCO with their education statistics: the Ministries of Education. Askerud concluded that during the last twenty years the ratios of books per pupil had fallen in most developing countries and that for the majority of the world's pupils and students, access to basic tools of learning is so limited as to constitute a major crisis.

A pilot survey of schooling conditions in fourteen of the least developed countries of Africa and Asia, conducted by UNESCO and UNICEF, found that half the pupils had no textbooks.

The survey paints a dismal picture of how classrooms are equipped, making it difficult to imagine how learning can take place. Rural schools generally fare worse than urban ones for learning materials. Final grades tend to be better equipped than the early ones, although conditions are far from adequate. The study found that half of the children have no textbooks. In none of the countries surveyed does every classroom have a usable chalkboard. Very few countries have a world map. No country has all classrooms equipped with a teacher chair and table. Not all children have something with which to write. Ten out of the 14 countries had virtually no supplementary readers, and most countries have no classroom library. These findings give a picture of the gap between official requirements and the actual situation. Most countries have a ministerial norm that there should be one chalkboard, a teacher's chair and a table in each classroom, but these norms were rarely met by more than a small number of schools.

There were pockets of advance, or at least stasis. In Cambodia, for example, the situation improved as a result of external support for the production and free distribution of textbooks for Grades 1 to 9 in the four core subjects: Khmer language, mathematics, science and social studies. Books for Grades 10 to 12 were also being developed and produced in a five-year project. Textbook:pupil ratios were gradually increasing to the target of 1:1 throughout the basic grades. In

Mozambique, too, it was possible for every primary school pupil to have his or her own books as a result of a World Bank loan and subsidies from the Netherlands and Sweden. It was uncertain, however, whether that situation would continue. In an isolated barangay of the central Philippines, 7 km from the nearest town, reached by an unpaved narrow road over hills, visitors to a two-room multi-grade school found an adequate supply of books for the different grades, although they were old and worn. In Egypt, the Ministry of Education gave students one textbook and one activity book each year to keep, reprinting each year to meet new demand.

Kazakhstan almost tripled its annual expenditure on textbooks between 1996 and 1999. As a result, 83 per cent of children in Grade 1 and 70 per cent of children in Grade 2 are reported to have been supplied with a new generation of textbooks that follow post-communist child-centred methods of education. Samplings suggest comparable provision at some other grades. In some areas rural schools are better supplied than urban ones. Textbooks are provided on payment of an annual rental fee from Grades 1 to 9, except for the Grade 1 alphabet book, which is free. The rental fees average about 3 per cent of a monthly family budget, and are waived for needy families. Students in Grade 10 and 11 must buy their books. There is a plan to sell textbooks in the future through the retail market, but needy families would still obtain them without charge.

A survey of six sub-Saharan African countries produced what appear to be favourable relations between target and actual textbook:pupil ratios but the authors describe the data as dubious, because there were rarely any statistics or systematic recording of the situation in schools; they suggest that the most reliable number is that from Zimbabwe, where all textbooks are published commercially and the Ministry has no vested interest in estimating distribution. At mid-decade, spending on education in most sub-Saharan countries had regressed and the shortage of textbooks was said to have reached crisis proportions. In Zambia, the schools had been without sufficient new books for seventeen years. In Ghana, books that had been purchased for the government for free distribution were found in the marketplace, but losses through theft were not unique to that country. In many, textbooks were stolen from government stores or taken from the printers. In Ethiopia, textbooks sometimes reached remote schools before urban schools' an unexpected reversal of the norm' because shipments for the urban schools had been diverted to the black market. UNESCO/Danida case-studies in three African countries also found a continuing shortage of textbooks. In Senegal, the Ministry of Education decided in 1992 to stop the free provision of books and now makes textbooks available to children at comparatively low cost; efforts are made to keep the price lower than commercially produced books.

The textbook:pupil ratio in the schools surveyed ranged from 1:2 to 1:10 for the French reader and from 1:5 to 1:10 for mathematics. Textbooks in science, history and geography were only negligibly available. In general, girls had fewer books than boys. In the United Republic of Tanzania, book shortages were reported in all subjects in the schools surveyed. Books were given free, lent by the school or bought from shops that might be 50 km or more from the school. Schools received books at varying times, most often after the beginning of the school year.

In two urban schools, a text-book: pupil ratio of 1:1 was reported in mathematics, science and English, but in another school there were no Grade 1 text-books. In Grade 4, the ratios ranged from 1:1 to 1:20. Some schools had no books in the national languages. Books were most scarce in the rural schools. Guinea introduced a book rental scheme in 1997, after an unsatisfactory experiment with private- sector provision. Rental schemes are administered by local five-member committees. The distribution of books is not always timely and some of the books are inappropriate for the pupils concerned. Many parents, moreover, are reluctant to rent textbooks for their children because they do not want to incur the possible cost of replacing any that are lost or damaged. Of textbooks that are available in the four core subjects, only a fraction were found to be actually in use. In one school, for example, only 39 per cent of the available textbooks in French were rented, 44 per cent in science, 41 per cent in mathematics and 26 per cent in civic education.

Table 2. Number of subjects and textbook-to-pupil ratios in some sub-Saharan African countries

	Primary education			*Secondary education*		
	No. core subjects	*Text book Planned*	*pupil ratio actual*	*No. core subjects*	*Text book Planned*	*pupil ratio actual*
Botswana	5	1:1	1:1	10	1:1-1:6	1:1-1:6
Ethiopia	4	1:2,1:3	1:2,1:3		1:2-1:3	1:2-1:3
Togo	4	1:1	1:1	5	-	1:10
United Republic of Tanzania	-	1:3	-		1:1	-
Zambia	5	1:2	1:4	5	1:1	1:2
Zimbabwe	5	-	1:7	8	-	-

In Latin America, educational spending emphasized higher education and quality education for a few at the expense of primary education, and especially primary education for the urban poor and the rural population. In the early years of the decade, textbook coverage was reported to average 32 per cent in Chile, Colombia, Bolivia, Ecuador, Panama, Peru and Venezuela. About 76 per cent of pupils in Grades 1 to 3 had one primary or language/art book; about 30 per cent had a mathematics book; and less than 10 per cent had a third book. For Grades 4 and 5 the numbers dropped by 20 per cent. Columbia, Ecuador and Guatemala presented an even bleaker picture. Even middle-income countries such as Brazil, Uruguay and Venezuela had failed to maintain a consistent supply of textbooks. By the end of the decade, however, textbook distribution had improved in some countries at least. In Chile it was universal at both primary and secondary levels as a result of World Bank assistance, successful international competitive bidding and negotiations with publishers in Spain and Mexico as well as Chile. Students had low-cost textbooks, 200 to 300 pages in length, with colour illustrations and good paper, at an average cost of US$3.

In a country as large as India, as might be expected, conditions varied greatly, as exemplified by three UNESCO/Danida case-studies. In a survey of Grades 1 and 5 in nine primary schools in Delhi, the capital, 100 per cent of the pupils were reported as having textbooks, although books were in short supply in one of the schools in Grade 4. Books were supplied free of charge in six schools in lower economic districts, and to 70 per cent of the poorer children in a seventh school. Other children bought their books. Teachers were not provided with textbooks, however, and normally borrowed a copy from a student during classes. In the state of Orissa, in contrast, learning materials were inadequate in all nine of the schools surveyed. Books were supplied free to pupils from Scheduled Castes and Scheduled Tribes, but in quantities well below enrolment. General students bought books on the open market, mostly from teachers who obtained them from outgoing students. Only two of the schools had science kits, and in most schools library books were locked up except during school inspections. Only one of the schools had a lavatory or urinal for children, and only one had even part-year access to safe drinking water. In the state of Maharastra, the State Textbook Bureau provides textbooks, but in practice much of the demand is met by private publishers. Supplies are adequate in urban schools and in schools that are considered average to good. In schools that are considered weak, and in schools in rural areas, there are substantially fewer books. The State policy is to supply books without charge to children in the most disadvantaged groups, but books are provided only to selected classes each year and often arrive more than one month after the beginning of the school year. Illiterate parents often are sold books that are unsuitable for their children's age-group.

In Central Asia, the shortages ranged from significant to critical. Supply was impeded by lack of funding, bureaucratic inertia, inexperience in operating under the post-communist economy, reliance on imports for raw materials and outdated printing equipment. Totally new textbooks were required in the light of revisions of the curriculum to suit new political and social realities and the displacement of Russian as the official language of instruction. In Central and Eastern Europe the situation varied from country to country. In some, new books were scarce and Russian books from before 1990 were still in use. Estimates of the current textbook shortage in the Russian Federation itself begin at 100 million copies and go up from there.

In 1996, the working document prepared for the Mid-Decade Meeting of the International Consultative Forum on Education for All could report that:

> The majority of developing nations have responded to the challenge of the Jomtien Conference by taking various actions to: evaluate their existing education systems; design policies to improve basic education; strengthen the capacities of people and institutions to manage education; create a more supportive policy environment; broaden partnerships and diversify the resource base; and explore ways to use traditional and modern channels of information and communication to provide basic education.

But at the end of the decade, a survey by Oxfam International was less positive in its finding:

> The limited progress towards basic education achieved during the 1990s points to a wide discrepancy between international declarations of intent and substantive planning for change. In the five years after Jomtien, over 100 'education for all' strategies were drawn up by governments, often in co-operation with donors. At the same time, the World Summit for Children, the Social Summit, and the Beijing Conference on Women all generated their own national planning exercises. Some success has been achieved. For instance, the national plans of action drawn up after the World Summit for Children have resulted in major advances in the areas of child and maternal health. In education, by contrast, national planning has generated limited progress. All too often, it has been characterised by vague statements of intent, empty promises, and a

> failure to mobilize resources. A senior official of the World Bank remarked more succinctly that it was 'particularly distressing to see how easy it is for governments to articulate a policy as an objective and not fulfil it'

Quality and use

The quality of textbooks continues to vary. It remains difficult in most countries to find good authors and many books continue to be written by subject specialists or curriculum developers in the Ministry of Education or one of its agencies. Many such authors were still oblivious or indifferent to the experience and abilities of the intended users. A respondent to the ADEA/UNESCO survey described the government-produced textbooks in Pakistan as by and large pedagogically unsound, sometimes filled with mistakes and usually very unattractive, in contrast to the books published by transnationals that are used in the private schools. Another said that student performance in that country in science and social studies is generally low because of the shortage of good books.

In systems with multiple choice of textbooks, there have been complaints, probably inevitable, about the process of evaluation and approval. In Kenya, the government was accused of favouring the former state publishing house. In Romania, officials in the educational system are free to become authors of competing textbooks, leading to concerns about conflict of interest and influence over subordinates. In the Philippines, publishers complained about inconsistency in appraisal: according to one, some books won conditional approval, even though they did not cover all the required curriculum, while others were rejected over an illustration or exercise. During the rapid adoption of new curricula and textbooks after the change of government in South Africa, textbooks, teachers' guides and work books were sometimes evaluated separately and a teachers' guide might be approved while its companion books were rejected.

At the end of the decade, physical quality of textbooks was still poor where printing equipment was outdated and in need of repair, as in Mexico and much of Central Asia, or where paper of good quality was scarce or expensive. Adhesive binding continued to give way and books fell apart. Printed appearance improved in many countries with the spread of computer-assisted composition (also called desktop publishing or DTP) and offset lithographic presses. In replacing traditional forms of typesetting, DTP also speeded the development of new textbooks and the revision of existing ones, although in the hands of undertrained operators it also opened the way to poor typographic design and illustration.

Increasing attention was paid to gender balance, but stereotyping persisted. A science textbook in Pakistan had a page illustrating the functions of various parts of the body: the function of the head, a woman's, was to carry a water pot. A survey in Mozambique, Zambia, and Zimbabwe found that women were under-represented in all the strategic points of textbook publishing and provision' that is, in writing, commissioning, and publishing manuscripts, school procurement and bookshop stocking. In all three countries the authors found evidence in textbooks of gender stereotyping, especially in the portrayal of adults. In Zimbabwe where, unlike the other two countries, textbooks were produced entirely in the private sector, they found 'a continuous thread' of 'gender stereotyping and prejudice against women in virtually any roles outside the home.' Efforts had been made in Zambia at role reversal, role balance and assertiveness of female role models, but stereotyping still appeared in illustrations through order of appearance, role representation, and size, voice and posture.

In the Amman Affirmation adopted by the Mid-Decade Meeting in June 1996, the International Consultative Forum on Education for All acknowledged that progress towards closing the gender gap in education had been excruciatingly slow. It also stressed the essential role of the mother tongue for initial instruction and in that respect, at least, some progress was being made. In Ethiopia, eleven national languages were used in instruction at the national level. In Bolivia, classrooms were allocated books in Quechua, Aymara and Guarini as well as Spanish. In Mexico, an ambitious educational project in ten of the poorest southern states included bilingual textbooks and learning materials for indigenous schools. Textbooks in South Africa are published in eleven official languages. There a large commercial house, Juta, launched an innovative series of learners' resource books, activity books and teachers' resource books in five African languages and were developing them in four more, using stories, folk tales and incidents common to the readers' experience. In the South Pacific, the difficulties of providing learning materials in local languages for small populations was being overcome through regional cooperation.

But the colonial languages have proved tenacious. In the Sahel countries of Burkina Faso, Benin, Niger and Senegal, the state distributed free textbooks in French, bought on a large scale through international competitive bidding, and the national languages were taught only at an experimental level, with no systematic production of materials in them. Indeed, in Burkina Faso there had been a step backwards; the national language was the sole language of instruction until 1985, when the government changed, and only since 1995 has it been gradually reintroduced. Publication in national languages can prove difficult, even controversial, if there is no agreement on orthography. In South Africa, where approval of textbooks is under provincial jurisdiction, a book in Zulu, for example, might be approved in one province and rejected in another because of its spelling.

European experiences and values also persisted. In first grade in Thailand, pupils learned that 'Ama took an apple to school', even though the only apples were expensive imports. In Nepal, 'Sushilla took a bus to the zoo' in fifth grade, although 60 per cent of children living in the mountains had never seen a wheel. In Côte d'Ivoire, primary-school texts were full of French markets and 'my time in Paris'. Such curricula alienated the majority of children from their culture and communities.

There was still no guarantee that teachers would use the books that were available, or use them effectively. Teachers did not always have an accompanying teachers' guide. Sometimes they did not know how to teach when every student had his or her own book; sometimes they were overly protective of the books; sometimes they felt the books provided were not appropriate or relevant to the needs of their pupils. In the increasing number of systems where parents were expected to buy textbooks, some families could not afford the expense, although some countries had programmes to assist their poorest communities. In systems with free distribution, teachers might still be personally responsible for replacing any textbooks that were lost or damaged, and therefore kept them locked up. On the other hand, even when such a policy changed, as in the Philippines, many teachers apparently did not believe that they would not be held responsible for losses or simply were not told of the new directive. Where multiple choice was a new concept after generations of single textbooks, teachers proved unexpectedly resistant to the idea of changing their habits. In Romania, both teachers and parents interpreted the new alternative textbooks as auxiliary to the old 'official' one, and some feared that alternative textbooks would create chaos in the classroom.

Educational materials

In most schools, the textbook and chalkboard were still the primary educational aids. Teachers relied heavily on the textbook, especially in science and mathematics, subjects in which they themselves were apt to be weak. In some jurisdictions, teachers were given lesson plans that they were expected to follow, leaving little scope for creativity or innovation. In the eight countries surveyed in the UNESCO/Danida case-studies, only schools in India and Jamaica reported the availability of electronic aids such as television, tape recorders and computers. All other schools depended on charts, chalk-boards, slates, mathematics sets, books or aids made by the teachers themselves. India began a country-wide programme in 1986 to provide schools with a list of materials, including maps, globes, science kits and flannel boards, but not all the listed materials were received. Classes visited in India under the UNESCO/Danida case-studies were typical of many in developing countries in that:

— teachers read aloud to the class from the textbook;

— teachers asked a few good students to read aloud; teachers asked questions related to what was read aloud, but answered the questions themselves;

— teachers wrote material on the chalkboard for children to copy;

— children copied what was written on the blackboard; and

— children did sums on their slates.

In one class, the teacher was unaware that the children could not find the correct page in their textbook.

In a sample of Jamaican schools, most materials used in the classroom were made by the teachers themselves. Most teachers were trained to use the materials and about 80 per cent of those observed used them appropriately. About three-quarters of the teachers included teaching aids in their lesson plans, and in all but a very few classes the children understood the materials. The materials were more likely to be used if they could be stored in cupboards in the classroom. Most, however, were kept in the head teacher's office.

The use of educational materials was part of pre-service teacher training in all eight countries in the UNESCO case-study survey, but only in Jamaica did teachers feel satisfied that the training was adequate. In Kazakhstan, teachers were receiving intensive training in the use of a new generation of textbooks from teams with expertise in personal and social psychology, educational theory, and curriculum and textbook practices. Authors played a crucial role in the process, visiting schools and demonstrating activities (UNESCO/Danida case-studies:

Kazakhstan). In another country, in contrast, there was no provision for training in the use of educational materials to teach a revised curriculum, the responsibility being left to school inspectors and the Institute of Education.

In some rural schools, pupils were encouraged to collect seeds, grain stalks, match sticks and other items that could be used as teaching aids in mathematics. Children also helped to make aids such as word cards, picture cards, number plates, abacuses, clock faces, balls and pots. Girls generally were more eager to engage in these activities than boys except in Jamaica, where the reverse was true, and in the United Republic of Tanzania, where there was no obvious difference between the genders. In other schools, teaching aids were either completely absent or inadequate in quality and quantity. In some cases they were simply decoration, usually placed above the students' eye level.

A village teacher in Maharastra, India, provided an example of innovative use of low-cost teaching materials. Vaishali Pawar has conscientiously attended in-service training offered to rural teachers in her area by a non-governmental organization. Her classroom has low blackboards on which the pupils can practise handwriting or draw pictures. A few pictorial charts hang at the children's eye level. To supplement reading materials, Vaishali has drawn charts that are large replicas of pages in the Grade 1 language book. Her drawing is not the best, but the charts have child-appeal and she has found that beginners who have problems with the size of the text in their primers are encouraged to read on the big pages. To teach mathematics in her multi-grade class, she uses graded work cards. While she teaches the Grade 1 children, the Grade 2 pupils use the cards individually or in pairs to practise newly learned skills. They thus become actively involved in learning and develop independent study habits.

Some countries were already actively exploring the potential of computers for education early in the 1990s. By 1991, Argentina, Belize, Brazil, Chile, Colombia, Grenada, India, the Republic of Korea, Malaysia, Mexico, Peru, the Philippines, Senegal, Sri Lanka, Swaziland, Thailand, and Trinidad and Tobago had attempted to use computers in at least some schools. India, Mexico and Tunisia were teaching computer literacy at the primary-school level and Argentina, Brazil, Kenya and Senegal were using computers to develop critical thinking, creativity and problem-solving. Costa Rica promised to put computers in half of all primary schools.

Well-designed computer programs had been proven effective: a test in the Philippines found that in 100 hours Grade 1 pupils could learn to read and write English at a level achieved by only a fraction of children in conventional classes at the same school. However, research in North America had already concluded that computers were less cost-effective than other equally effective methods of teaching. In any event, countries that could not afford to provide text-books were hard pressed to find the money for computers or simpler electronic equipment such as videorecorders. And at the end of the decade many' perhaps most' of the schools in Africa and South Asia still lacked reliable electric power to run computers, much less the telephone lines to connect with the Internet. Fewer than 10 per cent of schools in Central Asia had computers. Even in Eastern Europe, where computers were somewhat more common, most were old and could not support CD-ROM or Internet applications.

In a positive contrast, Barbados gave national priority status to installing multimedia facilities in all its schools and was considering including software among the materials available under its well-established textbook rental programme.

Supplementary reading and libraries

In general, supplementary reading materials continued to be scarcer than textbooks. As the decade came to a close, school libraries were said to have the lowest of priorities in educational spending. The majority of schools possessed no library. Where some semblance of a school library did exist, it was often no more than a few shelves of outdated and worn out material, inadequately staffed. A respondent in Bangladesh reported: 'Most of the students do not read books other than prescribed books. The curriculum and learning process in primary education do not encourage students to read or consult books other than the textbooks. There are no libraries attached to the schools or near them'

A study in Samoa found that in nine of the ten schools examined there were few books of any kind, whether instructional or recreational readers, textbooks or teachers' guides. The books that were there tended to be library books donated from overseas (many of them outdated or inappropriate to local culture), instructional readers from New Zealand and a small number of readers produced locally in the early 1990s. It appeared that the few available books were rarely used. Books were found on staff room shelves, in locked cupboards and still in packing boxes. Many were kept in the principal's office and access to them was not easy. Teachers relied instead on the blackboard, charts they had prepared themselves and self-produced books. Children sat on woven mats and read together as the teacher pointed to each word. The rural schools had grid wire windows and on wet, windy days learning material on the walls was ruined.

In southern Africa, better-than-average libraries were usually in secondary schools and heavily reliant on parental support. In Mali, a school library might consist of only 50 to 100 books, including textbooks, in a cupboard in the principal's office; most secondary schools had libraries but lacked suitable premises and budgets for them. In South Africa, the Department of Education and Training, which was responsible for the education of black Africans, did not officially acknowledge the role of school libraries until 1983. In 1997, the Education Foundation found that only 17 per cent of schools in South Africa had libraries and they were concentrated in white and Indian and, to lesser extent coloured, schools. In countries such as Mozambique and Cambodia, schools were destroyed and with them any libraries they had. In Ethiopia, librarians were held directly responsible for any loss of books and were accordingly reluctant to lend them.

School libraries and supplementary reading materials received growing attention during the decade, however. As the post-Jomtien era opened, the World Bank had at least fourteen projects involving primary or secondary school library development and at least five more at the tertiary level. Indonesia had 117,000 school libraries with a total collection of about 106 million books, an average of 900 per school. In the course of the decade small school libraries were centrally procured and distributed in Bolivia, Chile and Peru. In Egypt, a survey of 14 urban and rural schools of varying standards found that students were encouraged to use the school library and learning materials, and most of the schools had a computer and several software programs. The Carnegie Foundation was about to seek opportunities for strengthening libraries in selected African countries.

Cambodia, whose education system had been ravaged by civil war, was developing supplementary materials for the schools, often with support from non-governmental organizations and other international agencies. Up to 100 titles were involved, but some were simply copies of international children's books with Khmer translations pasted in by hand, and distribution tended to be concentrated in core schools in certain provinces. Reference books were almost nonexistent. Two educational magazines aimed at children were fairly widely available in the schools and at bookstalls in Phnom Penh, however, and a few schools had small libraries, especially at the upper secondary level.

A study of African school libraries reported three significant forms of initiative:

> Mali began a 'library in every school' campaign with initial support from the French Co-operation Mission. The pilot project involved 10 schools, with 20 more to follow out of the nearly some 250 public schools that offered nine years of education. For each library, the local community was required to provide appropriate premises, 20 chairs, 2 reading tables, and 2 sets of shelves, and to nominate a teacher to act as librarian. The government would then train the librarian and provide 225 books. Local communities could buy additional books, possibly by raising

money in the cities. The government co-ordinated the network of libraries.

The READ Trust in South Africa, founded in 1979 by a small group of volunteers, had grown to a significant trainer and supplier of materials. The Trust trained teachers in librarianship and in ways to encourage literacy and writing skills. It produced attractive, illustrated books, posters and theme packs designed to dovetail with the curriculum. It put together and distributed classroom libraries of about sixty books' colourful and exciting fiction, non-fiction related to the curriculum and a few reference books such as a dictionary and atlas' stored in a lockable wooden box that doubled as a display cabinet. The libraries could be replenished annually. Students were encouraged to use the books, first in silent reading lessons, then in any free time during school hours, and eventually to take home and share with the family. In reading and writing, children in

READ-equipped classes outperformed control school counterparts by as much as 189 per cent, and were ahead by 18 months in reading scores and two years in writing scores. An average of fifteen boxes per school cost about 20,000 rand (US$4,700), far less than provision of a formal school library.

Box-book libraries were distributed in Mozambique to reinforce understanding of Portuguese, the country's official language but for most people their second one. The project was funded by the Canadian Organization for Development through Education (CODE), but reported to the Cabo Delgado provincial director of the Ministry of Education and was managed by a local non-governmental organization, Progresso. Books bought in

Maputo were sent to the provincial directorate, where they were packed in boxes produced locally and sent to district education officers, who forwarded them to the schools. The initial plan was to create libraries of 150 books (15 titles, each in 10 copies), but by the end 46 titles had been bought, à total of 166,663 volumes. In the first year, all books were imported from Brazil, but locally published books were bought starting in Year 2 and by Year 5 all new purchases were locally produced. Training was incorporated after a midterm evaluation found that many teachers were poorly prepared to teach the early stages of reading and writing. Over five years, about 110,000 pupils were served in 550 schools at a total cost of US$303,117' an average of US$527 per box and US$2.75 per pupil.

In Thailand and the Lao People's Democratic Republic, UNICEF provided more than 400 book-box libraries each year to new graduates of teacher-training colleges and had them carry them to their schools throughout the countries.

Community resource centres' designed to serve an entire community, although often located in schools and used mostly by students and teachers' were appearing in most African countries. The Ghana Book Trust, supported by CODE, bought about US$45,000 worth of books in the mid-1990s, all of them written and published by Ghanaians, and distributed them to community libraries throughout the country. Teachers' resource centres were also established throughout Africa, each of them intended to serve a number of schools with a collection of textbooks, reference materials and classroom sets.

Jamaica was the only country in the UNESCO case-study survey to provide a substantial annual allocation for school libraries and its Library Service is a model for the Caribbean region in its philosophy, structure and systems. The Library Service's mandate includes ensuring that every school has a library. It distributes library books to schools and encourages inter-library loans from the main library to the schools. Schools are encouraged to accept gifts of books but the Library Service assesses whether they are appropriate and up to date. In order to improve school libraries, it runs annual training sessions for principals, teacher/librarians and other staff members. Its effectiveness is constrained, however, by the fact that many schools do not have the room for a library and by the high mobility of professional librarians (UNESCO/Danida case-studies: Jamaica). Commercial publishers, civil society organizations and international agencies took an increasingly active part in the provision of supplementary reading material for children. (Civil society organization is a broad term that includes non-governmental organizations, religious organizations, youth groups, trade unions and other bodies.)

In order to relieve the shortage of children's literature in Kenya, East African Educational Publishers inaugurated a Junior Readers Series in 1988 with 10 books. Ten years later there were 127 titles in the series, some acquired from publishers in other African countries, and with average sales of 3,000 copies the series was the fastest growing section of the publishing house. CODE sponsored a Children's Book Project in the United Republic of Tanzania that assisted the publication of selected titles and bought 3,000 copies of each for distribution to rural libraries and primary schools, with the understanding that the publisher would place at least 2,000 more copies in the open market.

The buy-back ensured that publishers would recover their initial investment, with profit to be made from sales through bookshops. CODE ran a similar, but less ambitious, project in Guyana. In 1997 UNESCO and the African Publishers' Network (APNET) launched a pan-African publishing initiative to produce popular books in science for young adults that would address Africa's energy crisis. Six books are being developed by teams from several countries and will appear in English, French,and Portuguese from local publishers in a series called Science for Africa/KAWI' kawi being Kiswahili for energy. The books will describe alternative energy sources, such as solar energy and biogas, in a context of African experience and folklore, and practical exercises. In Pakistan, the government and donor agencies brought international and local professionals together to produce Urdu fiction and non-fiction books for middle school students. More than 150 titles were produced and placed in 5,000 schools of the Punjab. These and other projects have had to deal with the scarcity of retail book outlets in many countries, and with the reluctance of most booksellers to stock many supplementary readers, which have a less certain sale than textbooks.

Donated books became an important addition to public, school and university libraries. Book Aid International, a British non-governmental organization, sent more half a million books each year to libraries and institutions, responding to profiles of interest submitted by the recipients. It also supported the Inter-African Book Support Scheme, in which selected books from African publishers were bought and sent to African libraries. That programme, and a similar book distribution programme operated by CODE, were found to work best when they were demand-driven' that is, when the books were sent to meet stated needs of the recipients and not as an offloading of unsaleable volumes.

Production of textbooks

Local production of learning materials probably increased during the 1990s, although it is difficult to determine by how much. National interest encouraged the development of local publishing in order to achieve self-reliance, nurture a cultural identity, create local employment and use local printing capacity. On the other hand, the national economy could not always support a local industry, nor could the immediate demands for large numbers of textbooks always be met by national publishers or printers who lacked capital, capacity and experience. At a time of structural adjustment, fiscal stringency, devaluation and inflation in developing countries, foreign publishers had the advantages of sufficient capital, stable currencies and low freight rates. Their branches in developing countries could attract better staff, buy paper and print with the leverage of a large customer, draw for adaptation on the textbooks published by the parent company and sister branches, and benefit from the profit on dictionaries, atlases and other reference works published by the parent organization.

For French publishers in particular, the African textbook market continued to be attractive. Its potential for growth was greater than that of industrialized countries because of demographic curves and efforts to increase net enrolments. Furthermore, the distribution of the world's French-speaking people was shifting away from Europe, towards 50 per cent living in Africa. French publishers invested in African companies, as in Côte d'Ivoire, and the large French publisher Hachette had a subsidiary, EDICEF, specifically to publish textbooks for markets outside France.

British transnationals continued to be active throughout the English-speaking world, although in some places, as in Jamaica, their attempts to establish branches failed and in others they had sold their interests to local publishers, many of whom they had trained. Some British publishers adopted a policy of decentralization, in which autonomous branches operated as regional publishers. Macmillan Kenya, for example, had a local managing director and a fully local staff, published what was appropriate for Kenya without interference from a head office, ran its own in-house training programmes, traded with other African countries regardless of whether they had a Macmillan office of their own, and retained all profits for new projects in Kenya. Macmillan had a more traditional operation in Swaziland, where it assisted in the writing of the textbooks used in the schools and enjoyed a monopoly over their publication. Between 1989 and 1994, British book exports to sub-Saharan Africa increased from just under '39 million to almost'57.5 million. At the end of the decade, however, a British consultant reported that publishers were growing less interested in new initiatives in developing countries because the return on investment was so uncertain.

Book exports were not all from North to South. India, a publishing superstate in its region, was exporting textbooks and other books for children to Southeast Asia and Africa. Malawi met an urgent need for textbooks by inviting publishers from other members of the SADC region to tender titles for it to buy with funding from Danida. The LIMUSA Publishing Company of Mexico published secondary school books for use in Chile, textbooks in primary mathematics for El Salvador, in a variety of subjects for bilingual education in Guatemala, in social science for Nicaragua, and in mathematics and Spanish for Venezuela. Its international success was all the more remarkable in that it was achieved despite state domination of its own domestic text-book market.

Of special importance was a growing tendency towards publishing partnerships between local and non-local firms. Such agreements assumed that textbooks would be sold commercially and envisaged a long-term relationship involving sharing of costs and revenue as well as the transfer of knowledge to the local partner. For example, a Canadian publisher, Irwin, co-operated with Ian Randle Publishers of Jamaica in the development of textbooks for the Caribbean. Another Canadian firm, Fraternité Matin, joined with Jamana in Mali to produce two grammar books. Both partnerships were assisted by a Canadian government initiative, International Publishing Partnership, which provided administrative, informational and financial support. In Cameroon, the French publisher EDICEF worked with a local partner, Editions CLE, to develop textbooks and work books in mathematics and French after the country's externally supported monopoly publisher collapsed. The new books were cheaper than the old ones and were bought by almost 50 per cent of the students in the first year they were available; subsequently the European Union subsidized copies for students in disadvantaged areas.

In what is still a relatively rare example of co-operation between publishers in neighbouring countries,

Fountain Publishers of Uganda was able, with local authors, to adapt text-books in science that had originated with East African Educational Publishers in Kenya. In general, however, regional cross-border trade in educational publishing was impeded by differences in language and syllabuses, trade barriers and difficulties in communication. International agencies played an active part in some joint ventures. UNESCO was involved in a UNDP-funded project to produce a new English course in China. Foreign publishers were invited to tender for the project in co-operation with the People's Education Press, the largest educational publisher in China. The project involved considerable counterpart training. The books continue to be sold, at very low prices, at a rate of more than 40 million copies per year, but the foreign publisher, who was paid a flat fee, barely broke even, making it doubtful whether the venture could be repeated.

Constraints in textbook provision

The constraints that public- and private-sector publishers faced at the end of the decade were little changed from those they faced in 1990, although the increasing role of the private sector and concern about cost recovery resulted in some reconfigurations. Inconsistencies or weaknesses in government were more significant, for example, to private publishers than to a public institution that might be part of the problem. The route towards liberalization had many roadblocks.

Government. Government policy was often inconsistent' not only because of changes in leadership but because of conflicts between government departments. Publishers had to deal with several departments, few of them directly concerned with textbooks. The Ministry of Education normally had the leading role, but the Ministry of Industry might be concerned with protecting domestic printing and manufacture; the Ministry of Trade might be regulating the import and export of paper, machinery and books; the Ministry of Finance possibly regulated the availability of foreign currency, and imposed taxes and tariffs; the Ministry of Agriculture might have some say in the importation of raw materials; and the Ministry of Culture might set language policies, and regulate publishing and printing. Some countries, among them Ghana and Zambia, waived taxes on imported printing goods meant for book publishing, but in other countries local printers and publishers had to pay tax and duties on imported raw materials such as paper at the same time as competitive foreign-produced books were imported duty-free.

More fundamentally, few countries in the developing world had coherent policies for publishing development or the provision of learning materials. Askerud found that lack of funding is often exaggerated as a cause for failure in providing basic learning materials and that other problems are more fundamental. Textbooks did not get the attention they required. Few decision-makers or managers understood publishing or even the difference between publishing and printing, and few gave proper recognition to those in the civil service, or outside it, who did have publishing expertise.

As a result, the design of programmes was left to educators who had little awareness of the professional skills required to produce and distribute quality learning materials successfully, of possible institutional needs for reorganization, staffing and budgeting, of the economics of educational publishing or of the difficulties of marrying educational concerns with the concerns of commercial publishing. From ignorance of the totality and complexity of the book chain, textbooks were treated as simple commodities and planners concentrated only on manuscript development and production. Furthermore, some consultants who had been retained to advise on textbook projects had no interest in seeing local publishing industries develop and ministries were often reluctant to surrender control of textbook provision even when the need was pointed out. Others have also pointed to such problems.

In those countries that were in transition from public to private provision of learning materials, inconsistency and unprofessionalism were apt to be compounded by confusion. Few countries made five- or ten-year plans for the change. Some failed to spell out clearly the roles of the players, the timing of change or the operational details of each phase. The capacity of the private sector was not always taken into account or the need to rebuild publishing skills that had atrophied under state monopoly. If local publishers could not respond to an abrupt transition, the way was opened to foreign ones. In Zambia, for example, the failure of the state monopoly and rapid liberalization led to a renewal of British transnational domination of the market.

Educational statistics remained unreliable and usually outdated. Under such circumstances it was difficult for governments to project requirements or for publishers to determine print runs. Data available from the United Republic of Tanzania indicate the discrepancies in supply and demand that can occur as a result of inadequate information, in this case in a period of increasing private-sector publication and continuing centralized public procurement. Variations of this magnitude can be financially disastrous to commercial publishers. So can unexpected cuts to education budgets by national legislatures. In the Philippines, for example, publishers who had lobbied for privatization were dismayed when they discovered how small the annual funding would be in comparison with the anticipated market. Failures in communication within government further hindered efforts to improve the availability of learning materials. Policies might be communicated so imprecisely that recipients were uncertain what they were expected to do, and as a result did not implement new policies or did so incorrectly. Even clearly-worded policies did not reach the schools, or were not believed when they did arrive. In Mozambique, another kind of failure in communication appeared.

That country had three separate book-box library projects between 1982 and 1996, but there was little exchange of information among them and lessons learned from one project were not transmitted to the next.

Few government officers appreciated the time it takes to write, edit, test and print textbooks. As a result many contracts allowed unrealistically short times from signing to delivery. The resulting textbooks were apt to suffer in quality or would have to be brought in from outside the country.

Political instability, authoritarian governments and war weakened or destroyed both educational and publishing facilities in the most unfortunate countries.

Finance. As devaluation and inflation drove up the cost of imported raw materials, the commercial school book publishers who were being encouraged by the new policies of liberalization and decentralization continued to have great difficulty in finding capital and credit. Investors found publishing unattractive because of low returns and high risk. Banks were reluctant to extend loans because sales revenue in publishing was notoriously unpredictable and few publishers had sufficient collateral or assets. Concessional credit from the World Bank and other international and regional finance institutions, available for agriculture and some other industries, was not extended to book publishing. If loans could be negotiated, interest rates throughout most of the developing world were high' commonly, from 23 to 40 per cent per year. One bank in Ghana did offer loans to publishers but none took up the opportunity because the annual interest rate was 45 per cent. If publishers were able to borrow money at lower rates abroad, they faced the further possible hazard of devaluation. Some in the United Republic of Tanzania went bankrupt after devaluation of the shilling, when the loans they had negotiated in foreign currency had to be repaid.

On a positive note, Nigeria established an Education Trust Fund, analogous to its long-established agricultural development banks, to provide soft loans not only to institutions but to publishers, printers, artists, and others involved in producing learning materials. Payment for textbooks was nearly always slow. Publishers might wait six months or a year for their money, making it even more difficult for them to produce books for the new school year. In Nigeria, the state and federal governments owed publishers considerable amounts of money for books delivered, in some cases, in the previous decade. Governments occasionally discriminated against local publishers, in effect depreciating what capital the publishers had. In Romania, international publishers were invited to bid on text-book provision and guaranteed payment in hard currency.

Local publishers, in contrast, were paid in local currency in the amount established at the time of contract, regardless of any decline in value of the currency by the time books were delivered and payment was finally made. One publisher calculated that his loss from currency instability amounted to 60 per cent in the case of a civics textbook. Joint ventures between local and foreign publishers were discouraged because the foreign partner would receive its share only in local currency. The Ministry of Education further hampered liberalization by establishing unrealistic times for printing and delivery and for teachers to assess competing books.

The capital required to bid on major projects restricted the ability of local companies to participate in major projects funded by the international banks. In Indonesia, private companies were allowed to publish books in a number of fields formerly reserved for the government-owned Balai Pustaka. In practice, only large firms were able to compete. The government issued an invitation in 1999 for bids for textbooks and teachers' guides at the junior secondary level in biology, physics and English. Publishers had to pay 1.5 million rupiahs (about US$220) per subject to obtain the bidding documents. They had further to demonstrate their financial soundness and resources, and prove that they had been operating for at least four years with an important part of their business being the publishing and/or distribution of educational books. This was a year after the collapse of the Indonesian economy and only the biggest of publishers were able to qualify.

In a similar instance two or three years earlier, a West African distributor found it impossible to participate in a World Bank project that involved four textbooks and teachers' guides for the following reasons. It had to find CFA 50,000 (about US$100) to acquire the tender documents, a bank guarantee of 2.5 per cent of the value of the tender and a staff housing tax clearance equal to 1.5 per cent of the salary of each member of the staff. If successful, it would have had to provide CFA 9.8 million (about US$20,000), about 5 per cent of the value of the contract, in guarantees. The company would also have had to demonstrate that it had been financially healthy for some years and had assets worth at least four times the value of the contract sum. The government would advance 30 per cent of the contract price, but only subject to a bank's guarantee. The requirements in this case, coming from both the government and the Bank, effectively doubled the guarantees normally required by the World Bank.

Market size. Not every country was large enough to support a competitive publishing industry. This was evidently true of small island nations, such as those of the Pacific and Caribbean. It was equally true of many other countries. Of the thirty-seven in sub-Saharan Africa, only two or three were thought to have a domestic market large enough to support a book industry, even in primary-level textbooks. In Central and Eastern Europe, the Soros Foundation considered a country in which 7 million people spoke the same language to be a large publishing market, but only ten of the twenty-two former communist countries in which the foundation was active met that criterion. In the other countries print runs and talent pools were smaller and the cost per copy higher. Even the relatively successful book industries of Kenya and Zimbabwe together could draw on a market that was only about one-twentieth of a small European country such as Norway, Denmark or the Netherlands' countries that had a single language and a much better infrastructure.

Local markets were further reduced by photocopying and pirated editions. In most countries, families had limited disposable income for books, including textbooks.

Markets could be expanded by export where there was a common language, as in Latin America. Elsewhere, the barriers mentioned previously worked to restrict publishers to their own countries.

Distribution. It was no easier to reach isolated rural schools at the end of the decade than at its beginning. In the United Republic of Tanzania, for example, official figures in 1994 indicated that more than 16 million textbooks had been delivered to district storerooms over the previous five years. Had all reached the schools, that should have resulted in a textbook:pupil ratio of 1:3 or 1:4. A trial survey that year found that the true ratio was closer to 1:9, with extreme variations between schools and districts. Many books didn't reach the schools, and some that did were kept in school storerooms 'due to uncertainty over supply'. Some books produced by the state were being bought by parents in the market.

Liberalization simply increased the problem if the state was not undertaking responsibility for distribution.

Bookstores were scarce outside the main centres and in many countries even well-established religious or family retail bookstore chains were diversifying, with books as only a minor item. In Latin America, it was said, no publishing house had a distribution network capable of delivering books to every school in every corner of the country, and in many instances books bought by the government simply remained in government warehouses. Kenya sought to resolve the problem by consolidating school orders for textbooks at the district level and then ordering the books from local booksellers, thereby strengthening the retail sector of the book trade and reducing the discrepancies that occurred under central procurement.

Production. Paper remained the principal expense. Some countries, such as Mozambique, had to depend on foreign printing for lack of domestic capacity. In general, the constraints previously noted prevailed.

Human resources. The lack of professionally trained staff continued to hamper state and private publishers in most countries. Large publishing companies did a certain amount of training in-house, however, as did transnationals. In general, the greatest need was in publishing management and marketing, although more training was also needed in textbook development, editing, design and evaluation. A study undertaken by Sida towards the end of the decade drew particular attention to the shortage of well-trained staff at the middle level.

Training received new attention in the 1990s and a number of initiatives were taken. The most ambitious was the African Publishing Institute, a training wing of APNET, which was established in 1992 with the help of several funding agencies, both governmental and non-governmental organizations. The Institute held occasional workshops in its early years. In 1999 it was scheduled to run twenty-two national and regional training workshops throughout the continent, on a variety of topics, and in English, French or Portuguese depending on the country. Workshops are held in co-operation with national publishing associations, using local trainers in accord with a comprehensive syllabus in book publishing and management.

The Asian Cultural Center for UNESCO, supported by the Japanese Ministry of Education and the Japan Book Publishers Association, organized annual courses in various aspects of publishing and book promotion for publishing staff in Asia and Oceania, as it had since 1967. El Centro Regional para el Fomento del Libro en Latina y el Caribe (CERLALC), an international organization created under an agreement between the government of Colombia and UNESCO, offered training courses in book-related topics and published training hand-books for book professionals. UNESCO sponsored training workshops in other countries and, through the International Institute for Educational Planning (IIEP), supported the development and publication of a series of training modules in text-book planning and publishing in Spanish, French, English and Arabic, available in print and for a time as an interactive course on the Internet.

A sampling of other initiatives' and it is only a sampling' illustrates the interest of governments and civil society organizations in publishing training.

The United Kingdom's Department for International Development (DFID, formerly the Overseas Development Administration) sponsored a number of programmes in the Commonwealth and the Arab States. The British Council offered training courses in China, India, Indonesia, Ukraine, the United Republic of Tanzania and Zimbabwe. The Services français pour la coopération bilatéral et multilatérale French Ministry of Co-operation organized training in Africa and France for librarians, publishers, booksellers, authors and illustrators. The Deutsche Stiftung für Internationale Entwicklung (DSE) organized short-and medium-term training courses and workshops in the development of materials, including several concerned with the writing, editing and publishing of textbooks in national languages in French-speaking West Africa. Sida and the Finnish Ministry of Foreign Affairs supported training in Mozambique, the United Republic of Tanzania, and Zambia.

Among non-governmental organizations, the Afro-Asian Book Council organized workshops on author development in Nigeria, Pakistan, Kenya, Ethiopia, and Malaysia. Two German non-governmental organizations offered training internationally, the Deutsche Gesellschaft für Technische Zusammenar-beit (GTZ) and the Ausstellungs und Messe GmbH. The latter turned its training attention from Asia and Africa in the 1990s and ran workshops, with support from the German government, in Central and Eastern Europe. The Centre africain de formation à l'édition et à la diffusion (CAFED), with headquarters in Tunis, offered initial, advanced, and refresher training courses and internships in France for managerial and technical staff.

Coopération par l'éducation et la culture (CEC), a Belgian civil society organization, ran workshops for authors and illustrators of textbooks and children's books in Niger, Tunisia and Zaire. CODE ran training programmes in children's literature, illustration and design in East Africa, and in editing and book design in Guyana. A Norwegian agency, International Movement towards Educational Change (IMTEC), organized a series of workshops on evaluation, editing, illustration and financial controls for textbook publishers of Pakistan. In the 1990s, it organized exchange visits of educational publishers of the Baltic countries and Western Europe. The International Network for the Availability of Scientific Publications (INASP) organized workshops on journal production and management for editors and publishers in Southeast Asia and Africa, and commissioned a reference handbook on book marketing and promotion.

PUBWATCH, a non-governmental organization based in New York, conducted professional workshops, seminars and training schools throughout Central and Eastern Europe and the former Soviet Union, published a quarterly newsletter describing assistance programmes, and sponsored the translation and co-publication of Western guidebooks on book publishing.

The Open Society Institute's Centre for Publishing Development in Budapest created a Web site with material that can be used for training in electronic publishing. The Publishing Training Centre (formerly Book House Training Centre) in London ran courses in Latin America, Central and Southeast Asia, and Central and East Europe, and developed distance learning packages in proofreading, editing and copyright.

Formal education for publishers was also available at universities in a number of countries, although many of the courses were more academic than practical.

Donors and funding agencies

At least 150 agencies' international and regional banks, governments and civil society organizations' had an interest in book development during the 1990s. The breadth of their interest in the development and provision of learning materials is evident in the foregoing pages. Although sustainability was a long-term goal, it was clear, as costs rose and national economies languished, that dependence on external aid would continue for many years. Five trends were significant. Funding. Six years after Jomtiem, the International Consultative Forum on Education for All reported that since 1990 there had been an overall increase in governments' financial commitments and disbursements to basic education. But the decade in general was one of financial belt-tightening in most countries, and as Northern governments reduced their budgets for overseas development, the textbook/learning materials components of educational programmes inevitably were affected. Even so well-established an agency as the Asia/ Pacific Cultural Centre for UNESCO announced in 1997 that it would have reduce its activities as a result of the downturn in the Japanese economy. Some bilateral development agencies announced that they would concentrate their activities on a few countries and/or core curriculum subjects.

Non-governmental organizations' local and non-local' had been well represented at Jomtien and were increasingly active, often in innovative ways, in supporting book provision. Many of the non-local ones operated with financial assistance from their governments. CODE, for example, received substantial funding from the Canadian International Development

Agency (CIDA), although the agency itself played little direct part in book provision. Civil society organizations too were affected by global recession, suffering either in government funding or in their fundraising efforts with individuals and corporations. Of particular importance in this context were local civil society organizations associated with the book trade. Among the most important were associations of writers, printers, publishers, booksellers and librarians, who could respond to local conditions and seek common solutions to problems.

Geographic concentration. At the beginning of the decade funding still focused on Africa, the continent most in need of educational assistance. As the educational legacy of communist governments collapsed, attention' from large-scale projects financed by the World Bank and the Asian Development Bank to complementary initiatives by some non-governmental organizations, including the Soros Foundation and PUBWATCH' turned increasingly to countries of East and Central Europe and Central and West Asia. However, the development and provision of textbooks and learning materials, particularly in indigenous languages, continued to be supported by loans and grants in other regions of the world.

Donor co-ordination. From the 1960s to the 1980s, there was little co-ordination among donors: some supported curriculum design, others production, others distribution. During the 1990s there was increasing attention to inter-agency discussion leading to a more coherent approach and an efficient, integrated system for book provision. Towards the end of the decade there was increasing interest in sector-wide support. In this approach, led by Sida, funding agencies meet together with government agencies to work out a plan under which as many parts of the book sector as possible receive the help they need.

The Working Group on Books and Learning Materials of the Association for the Development of Education in Africa (ADEA) provides a forum on book-sector issues for African ministries of education, development agencies and civil society organizations. It encourages the sharing of ideas and experiences among funding agencies, finances research into key areas of book policy; publishes the results of that research and books of practical publishing advice in its series, Perspectives on African Book Development; works with the UNESCO/Danida Initiative on Basic Learning Materials by encouraging collaboration among developing countries in specialized areas of national book development; helps national governments bring together the public and private sectors in book provision; and works with other ADEA working groups to promote education.

The Bellagio Publishing Network is an informal association of donors, African publishers, non-governmental organizations and individuals committed to strengthening indigenous publishing and book development in Africa. The participants meet from time to time to discuss common issues. The Network also publishes a newsletter and a book series that have become an important source of information about publishing development. The group evolved from an international conference on publishing and development organized by the Obor Foundation and held at the Rockefeller Center in Bellagio, Italy, in 1991.

One of the first indirect results of that conference was the formation in 1992 of APNET, which brings together national publishing associations from all sub-Saharan Africa, Enlish-speaking, French-speaking, and Portuguese-speaking. It has been assisted by several government agencies and non-governmental organizations in its work in networking, training, and trade promotion. The Asia-Pacific Cooperative Programme for Reading Promotion and Book Development (APPREB) is a UNESCO-sponsored and supported network of regional institutions and organisations which promote books and reading in Asia and the Pacific region. It was launched in December 1991 in Kuala Lumpur, at UNESCO's initiative, in an attempt to redress the publishing imbalance in the region' one in which many countries have made considerable advances in book development while others remained at an early stage.

The need for further co-ordination remains, however, and conflicts have occasionally arisen between funding agencies. At mid-decade in the Northwest Frontier Province of Pakistan, for example, half a dozen agencies were funding separate projects in curriculum reform and textbook provision. In Cambodia in 1993, an Educational Donors Group had thirty-five members, but about fifteen more operated independently. In Guyana, two funding agencies supported textbook production with DTP technology, with the result that in one room the small nation was learning how to operate separate technologies for primary and secondary level books, one IBM-based, the other Macintosh-based.

In Mozambique, the Netherlands and Swedish governments were supporting Caixa Escolar (the School

Fund), under which consumer subsidies were channeled from the Ministry of Education to district offices for the purchase of textbooks by the schools. The World Bank indicated an interest in the Caixa Escolar scheme in 1993, but eventually funded a parallel system under which books were printed outside the country and distributed free of charge. The Bank's project counteracted the Caixa Escolar system and the newly liberalized Mozambican school policy.

A more fundamental division between funders was in their approach to liberalization. One camp wanted to free production as quickly as possible. The other sought a phased development of capacity. The first was intended to meet immediate needs and often led to involvement, if not dominance, of the market by transnational companies with deep pockets and long-established lists that could be adapted quickly to national needs. The other was intended to provide for an orderly transition and nurture indigenous publishing. Demand-side financing. In the last half of the decade, agencies increasingly rejected the concept of providing printing paper and books as commodities to meet short-term needs for textbooks and learning materials.

More attention was paid to developing a viable system of provision, with concern for all links in the book chain. Sida, for example, decided to change its funding for textbooks, in countries that had begun decentralizing procurement, from the direct support of production processes to support for the development of competence and the local (district or school level) purchase of materials. The World Bank funded a number of educational projects involving demand-side mechanisms such as stipends and vouchers, and targeted subsidies to disadvantaged and minority groups. World Bank policies.

The World Bank was by far the single largest external source of finance for education. Between 1963 and 1997, it was involved in 560 projects in 112 countries, and at the end of that period was still involved in 202 education projects in 88 countries. Its projects ranged from very small countries such as Sao Tome and Principe, with 100,000 people, to China. Between 1980 and 1995, its total volume of lending for education tripled, and education's share in overall Bank lending doubled. Between 1994 and 1997 it lent US$550 million for text-books alone, the greater part for books at the primary level.

Bank funding in 1995 accounted for about one-quarter of all aid to education. Even though that massive assistance represented only about one half of 1 per cent of the total spending in developing countries on education, the Bank's policies were of extraordinary significance. The fact that regional banks marched more or less in step with the World Bank added to the latter's importance.

The World Bank's bank policies were not without critics, in par-ticular its insistence in opening textbooks to international competitive bidding in any contracts above a set threshold. Although the policy was questioned most often in discussions about Africa, in part because of the vigorous advocacy of APNET, that is not the only continent on which the issue has arisen. In the Philippines, international competitive bidding came into open conflict with national law, which required text-books used in the public system to be published by companies that were totally locally owned. The Bank has a general policy of encouraging awards through bidding to the 'lowest evalu-ated bid', a phrase that implies concern for quality and in specific projects has shown some flexibility in implementing competitive bidding' for example, by agreeing to weight bids with price as only a minor factor' but its officers have not been consistent. Regional banks have been somewhat more flexible in requiring international competitive bidding. Despite, or because of, the criticisms, local publishers in both Nigeria and Mali have won competitions for textbooks under World Bank projects against foreign-owned firms.

In 1997, the Bank organized a seminar at which stakeholders from different part of the book chain and from different parts of the world gathered to share their experiences. The proceed-ings of that seminar (Sosale, 1999), frequently quoted in this survey, comprise the most significant published examination of external funding to publishing development since the proceedings of the Bellagio conference at the beginning of the decade.

The seminar itself was part of a policy re-evaluation by the Bank. On the final day, one senior staff member wondered aloud whether the Bank should reconsider its insistence on the 'extraordinarily complex' rules of international competitive bidding for textbooks and look at appropriate national or local competitive bidding or other sorts of supply-side or demand-side financing.

A new Bank policy on textbook provision, released for discussion in draft in 1999, indicates a greater interest in articulating educational publishing with general publishing on the one hand and with educational outcomes on the other. It recognizes the importance of textbooks to a viable publishing industry and the importance of a viable publishing industry to the sustainable provision of learning materials' relationships that will be discussed further in Part V. The Bank's priorities, as set out in the document, are: (a) support to good classroom teaching and learning practice, including a coherent programme for the provision of teachers' guides and teacher training; (b) adherence to legal and other measures for the protection of copyright and other intellectual property rights; (c) articulation of agreed roles of the public and private sectors in the development, production and equitable distribution of textbooks and reading materials; (d) maintenance of transparent and competitive processes in the selection or purchase of books for educational use or for contracting publishing or printing services; and (e) commitment to longer-term financing of book development and provision.

Concerns remain among publishers, nevertheless. The new policy does not address procedural details that were raised at a meeting of West African publishers in 1998. They include high deposits for bidding, inadequate information, complex bidding documents, cumbersome procedures, low advance payments to the winning publisher and delivery periods so short that indigenous publishers cannot hope to meet them.

8

Transforming Technologies in Education

Technology in education has two faces: one of transformation and one of hype. The printing press revolutionized access to education, and in the process an explosion in scientific inquiry was born. Teachers could finally produce and communicate content to a growing number of students entering an industrial revolution.

Classrooms emerged as a great solution to disseminate content and augment interaction with faculty and other students. Traditional apprenticeships with experts polished the student to perfection. Within a short period of time, the industrial workforce ballooned and with it the student body. The need to scale student to teacher interactions encouraged us to turn to other technologies: radio, television, computers, and the World Wide Web. Individually, these technologies couldn't increase the ratio of experts to novices, or significantly add to their real world experience. The "educational transformation" hype emerged around these technologies and they didn't deliver as their evangelists claimed.

Access to computers, especially ones that are connected to communities would have an impact on education. The transformative differentiator for the next generation is the programmability of our interconnected networks. With increases in software programmability, we increase interactivity, increase communication, increase learner adaptability, increase shared visualizations, increase shared laboratory access, and increase experiential learning.

In 20 years, we're going to see an impact equal to the printing press. This time we'll see a global, diverse, educated workforce deliver on dependable innovation, shared vision, and collaborative creativity. The sweet spot for the use of technology in education may clearly be that software personalizes the learning experience, connects all the components, and emancipates publication for targeted and effective interaction.

In the future, no one owns content as an end product. It is molecular at its origin. MIT will give away their content for free, other institutions will follow with interactivity innovations, and quality content will be consumed in chunks by whoever needs it. Through a filter of standards, tools and personalization templates we'll be able to aggregate learning content, the relationships between the content, and our context for using the content in such a way as it becomes part of our own personal value proposition when studying or working with others. The objective: obtain and create knowledge at the right time, in the right place, in the right way, on the right device, for the right person.

Let's imagine where technology will be in 20 years to help us set a vision for taking advantage of this new power for education. Such an exercise will allow us to visualize a roadmap for getting there. From the first few months of life, children play with toys that teach them various concepts. In 2020, toys begin capturing children's learning experiences by using embedded technology that records information about the child's habits, preferences and progress to provide parents with a better understanding of their child's development. Toys provide parents with the child's learning profile, sending private information to the parent's information appliance so they can use the information in the selection and purchase of additional toys that will enhance the child's motivation and experience.

Over the course of the preschool years, children increase their play in Learning 2020 by engaging in supportive virtual reality games in which they build on the psychomotor, reading, writing and math skills they learn in school. Interaction with other students and teachers in the environment helps identify learner strengths and deficiencies.

The environments individualize around the children's content preferences, and create classroom activities that encourage children to expand their abilities through problem solving environments, complete with on- line personalized mentoring by parents and teachers. The games build critical thinking skills using simulated, situational environments that engage other members of the family and community to play along.

Because the parent is more involved, the access to outside content is monitored and manual personalization of student interest can be adjusted accordingly during prescribed home activities as well. The technology objective is to construct a safe environment for the child while engaged in technology driven learning experiences.

For real world interactions, video playbacks of children engaged in learning activities are frequent and reviewed by student, teacher and parent.

Since many parents send their children to kindergarten and traditional K-8 schools, while others home school their children, Learning in 2020 focuses on creating learning environments that facilitate communication and collaboration. Technology networks kids together in groups to learn and practice their combined skills. Whether children are working on art or science, they work with embedded technology that measures their performance.

Capture technologies record student interactions, teacher guidance and parent profiles to provide individualized and group feedback. Continuous personalization ensures each participant brings something unique and cooperative to the group keeping membership optimal. Children communicate with ubiquitous devices that provide targeted feedback to each other while working in groups, identifying compatibilities and suggesting what questions to ask. Group communication is the core objective, with shared activities as the principal methodology.

Students use wearable technologies to exchange, collect, communicate and present information either posted to large screen displays, or holographic 3D environments. As they collect information, it automatically maps to the learning objectives for their skill group and displays cumulative data about the group's success in onscreen graphics for easy monitoring. Anonymity is crucial, as performance indicators supplant grades. The focus on learning is group accomplishment of tasks, with individual contributions sent to the teacher and the student. The environment queries the student when it doesn't receive adequate information and works to help students draw similar inferences that other kids drew during similar exercises. Videos are served up to the students when they don't understand how to do something.

Students complete most of their projects by designing reusable e-books rich with simulations to share their work with others, creating long-term digital portfolios to be shared throughout the years. Teachers help students enhance screen literacy skills by building interactive multimedia for reuse among other learning populations worldwide. Sharing is the key objective, and working in diverse populations is preferred.

Teachers share their activities, thoughts, and technology ideas with a virtual team of experts in business, higher education and other institutions. A strong focus on integrating workflow and student activities throughout the community is enhanced by technology communication systems and easy to use large screen displays that encourage teachers to work together in distances to align industry, institution and schools together in real time knowledge construction and practice.

Teachers are mentors, still using their nurturing techniques in the learning spaces to socialize children. In addition, each child has their own virtual mentor that can be accessed anytime. The mentor follows the children's activities on- line, suggesting new ideas and dialoguing interactively to understand the student's emotions and competencies. When children go on-line, the experience is secure and private. On-line content is filtered by the virtual mentor, who constantly reports noteworthy events to the parents, teachers and other interested parties. Embedded assessment is constantly sent to the teacher, parent and mentor. The virtual mentor consistently maps to performance goals and adjusts student activities to keep kids more focused on learning rather than relying on test taking. Parents can participate in their children's activities wherever they are via wireless mobile video computing and emerging communication technologies.

Learning in 2020 combines the student personalization with the virtual mentor and sends the information out to coordinated work projects designed for community learning. Secured broadband video conferencing appears on every device, digital cameras capture visual content, workspaces grow more complex, and collaboration tools are linked directly to personalized digital libraries. These libraries stay with a learner for life. Digital highlighting, digital conversations, group note-taking and other personal annotations make the asset active throughout the individual's life and can be shared with colleagues at any time.

Since students are working more often in distributed groups, they need to be able to get information more effectively. Students work in groups and ask questions aloud, receiving information through earpieces that feed constant information and personalized entertainment upon request.

As the students work on an experiment trying to figure out how electromagnetism works, for example, they talk through their devices to ask for definitions of words, or ask for a simulation to show them how something like Faraday's law works. Sometimes explanations don't work, so calling up a simulation can help them grasp a concept better. Once they think they understand, they apply the principle to the design and ask for feedback from teachers and co-workers.

Teachers can listen into conversations as well, and they control input when necessary for group messaging or for helping students stay on task. Centralized visualized displays are constantly updated to project student progress, tasks to be performed, and provide guided instructions for learning more about a topic and to help with task completion. Experts are available on-line to evaluate the engineering quality of the students' projects. They are also available to students when they are presenting results, so they can help them deliver their results more effectively. If students are buying materials for their products, the transactions are integrated into their digital financial records, approved by the appropriate person and delivered to the laboratories immediately.

Voice recognition is the standard method of both input and output, occurring mostly outside the classroom where students spend much more time. Students work in laboratories communicating with devices that record student interactions, record hypothesis, previous student engagements, and direct communication links to communities that specialize in the use of the equipment and in the history of effective construction.

Underlying the user's experience is a ubiquitous interface that launches content based on what the student is working on. The interface is a 3D visual bar that can be visually refined to map to the user's experience. For example, if a student begins studying Computer Science, the visual bar identifies his learning objective, his location, his tools, his co-workers, his relevant e- mails, his notifications, the videos, related lectures and text, the experiments, the simulations, the top 10 reading lists, the polls, and the alerts for participating class members. Underneath, likes an assessment tool that reminds the students where to focus attention.

Students work in sophisticated visual environments deconstructing and constructing objects on the screen allowing them to question why things work the way they do. Imagine students using intelligent reusable visual components to build a plane that flies, a bridge that spans a ravine, or an electronic device that can actually be built by another team. As students work in simulated environments with smart learning objects, they begin to understand the underlying scientific principles, and each principle is measured and displayed to allow students to know where they are and what they need to work on next. Force feedback devices provide input that simulates real world instrumentation. Students develop a reason to learn math, and they enhance their communication skills by documenting and annotating their work for review by others.

As students work in collaborative environments, the learning objects adapt immediately to their learning styles in 2020. The tools model the user throughout their learning career. It maps their preexisting knowledge to the kinds of learning objects that are useful to them for rapid learning, much like the toys they used as preschoolers. Now, in this stage of their learning careers, their emotional responses are being tracked to help the m refine their ability to interact even more effectively with others. So many automated processes have been built in for them: inquiry style, learning style, personalized activity selection, multimedia preferences, physical requirements, and favorite hardware devices. For example, if the student is in research mode, natural dialogue inquiry and social filtering tools configure a working environment for asking questions and validating hypotheses. If students like rich multimedia and are working in astronomy, they automatically connected to the Sky Server which accesses all the telescopic pictures of the stars, introduces an on-line expert talking about the individual constellations, and pulls up a chatting environment with other students who are looking at the same environment.

If the student is struggling with a concept, the intelligent tutoring services turn on automatically. If the student needs to practice a psychomotor skill or is restricted because of physical limitations, hardware devices are immediately recommended to assist the student, and locations at various schools nearby are identified for the student to use the equipment. If the student is having difficulty with complex processes or principles either assisted or augmented reality is initiated and the student jumps into a virtual world scenario that gives them an enhanced perspective of the problem and allows them to play the actor solving problems. This is especially useful in engineering and scientific solutions because they also reveal the math behind the phenomena, giving the student real world examples, with the theoretical supporting math. Discovering the visualizations of math can be highly contagious.

The goal of technology, and especially information technology, must be to create an environment where every learner will have a series of resources and teachers in different discipline expertise and in different locations, with a teacher/mentor to help organize the information, and help the student pursue some areas in depth. This is currently too expensive, but there is hope that several upcoming technologies listed below can be deployed in the future. The motivation of the learner is the most important factor in learning. Hence the question becomes - how can technology help and facilitate motivation during the process of learning? We do not advocate replacing the human teacher with the technology!

Future technology must live in a symbiotic relationship amongst teachers, students, parents and society at large. We view the technology as an enabler in a number of ways:

1. Help organize and provide structure for the teacher's material to students
2. Help students, teachers and parents interact, in order to follow progress of learning in a given subject
3. Facilitate and assist in the authentication, search and prioritization of the digital material available on the web, which in this case serves as a world wide encyclopedia
4. Simulate and visualize structures and processes which are the result of physical, chemical, biological and engineering models and to interact in real time with them
5. Help in learning history, and /or future trends because technology can reconstruct life and, hence facilitate visualization of going back and forth in time.
6. A tool for the handicapped population. Technology can serve as an extension and enhancer for their missing capabilities, being either perceptual, physical or cognitive, so that they can equally receive the delivered information for a given subject, just as the

normal population. Several examples might be, for the visually impaired, one can have brail lettered terminals and input/output devices.

For paraplegic subjects there are several robotic customized devices for interacting with teaching material. For the cognitively impaired population, the teaching material must be adapted properly. Here the software enabler mentioned in example1 will be of use This technology can be of great help among the multilingual population, with automated translators available both to teachers, students and parents.

The above enablers depend mostly on subjects which are sufficiently conceptualized and can be delivered through media, such as television or computer screens. Here the information is textual, verbal or pictorial. However, there are skills to be learned that require physical interaction with the world, and/or carrying out an experiment. Here again, the ideal situation would be for each student to have their own experimental setup. However, in many cases this is not possible for a variety of reasons, not the least of which is the cost involved.

In order to have access to expensive laboratories and facilities, one can deploy tele -robotic technologies. With these tele -robots, students can interact with the physical experiment. They can see, hear and feel the affects of the interaction and ask "what if " questions. These kinds of interactions not only help students to understand and embody the knowledge, but it also keeps student's engagement active, which helps them to be motivated.

The most advanced and most desirable technology is the creation of a tele -immersive environment for teaching and learning. This is a three dimensional virtual space, which mimics the real space both visually, aurally and tactually. It is one in which both the student/ apprentice and teacher/master can meet and interact. This technology does not exist yet but it is very feasible from what we know today. The advantages of such an environment are many. First, the students and teachers do not have to be physically collocated. Secondly, the teacher can advise/coach several students and yet the student would feel that he/she is the only one getting the teacher's full attention.

This technology would facilitate demonstration/ coaching of physical and/or mechanical skills (such as surgery, operating complex machinery, etc.), which require true spatio-temporal observations of the master. In turn the master can make the same spatio-temporal observations of the students and give not only verbal but also mechanical feedback. This feedback is critical for the apprentice since it will give him/her a sense of being in direct touch with reality, of being able to control events and get the perceptual feedback concerning how he/she is doing. Finally, we can speculate on multi-site tele - immersive environments which may be needed for the teaching and training of cooperative activities, such as playing in an orchestra, dancing in an ensemble, coordinated war games, coordinated manufacturing and their like. It is not too difficult to extrapolate the one teacher/student scenario to multi-students and one director scenario by deploying the distributed tele-immersive environments.

All of this technology will never be used unless there is sustained and substantial investment into the necessary infrastructure covering not only schools, but libraries and homes, similar to the investment that was made in the past in electrification and later in telephone infrastructure. It is no more amazing now than electricity or the telephone was for us at the very beginning of the third millennium.

The very notion of Internet is disappearing for you because a world without it is simply unthinkable." "Most certainly, but what sort of challenges did you face as an educator in earlier days and how were they overcome?" asks the young teacher. "At the time," continues the veteran, "hardware and awkward user interfaces seemed the formidable foes. "Broadband access to information, wired or wireless, for the consuming public, was neither reliable nor affordable.

Once technological and political barriers were broken, machinery and access costs dropped and the flood of information began to rush in. The challenge was, and remains today, designing technical solutions that, however wondrous, contain a sustainable, scalable economic model and encompass easily used interfaces to access all the features of this rich information environment. Now, about two thirds of the world's eight billion people have anytime, anywhere, anyhow access at an affordable price.

For about 2 billion people today, the Internet is not a reality; it is yet a distant dream or perhaps entirely unknown. Electricity is still unknown or unavailable or unreliable. Sanitation, housing, food, water and education are in limited supply.

For those parts of our global society, Internet and its benefits seem far beyond reach. We must not give up pursuit, however idealistic, of access for all. "Running closely with these challenges was the whole notion of the proper training and use of content.

Learning how to use technology turned out to be at least as challenging as building it. The first computers and online access arrived in the old style classroom back in the mid 1990's. We were all entranced: teachers, administrators, parents. In a decade or two, three complementary interfaces will shape how people learn:

— The familiar "world to the desk top" interface, providing access to distant experts and archives, enabling collaborations, mentoring relationships, and virtual communities-of-practice. This interface is evolving through initiatives such as Internet.

— Interfaces for "ubiquitous computing," in which portable wireless devices infuse virtual resources as we move through the real world. The early stages of "augmented reality" interfaces are characterized by research on the role of "smart objects" and "intelligent contexts" in learning and doing.

— "Alice-in-Wonderland" multi-user virtual environments interfaces, in which participants' avatars interact with computer-based agents and digital artifacts in virtual contexts. The initial stages of studies on shared virtual environments are characterized by advances in Internet games and work in virtual reality.

The important issue in effectiveness for learning is not the sophistication of the technologies, but the ways in which their capabilities aid and motivate users.

Life Long Learning

Computing has already enriched and enhanced people's lives in countless ways, but we've only begun to see how it will transform our businesses, our governments and our communities. In the next few years - in the "digital decade" - we'll see computing become a much more significant and indispensable part of all our lives.

The pace of innovation is accelerating in all the core technologies of computing - from processing power to storage to network bandwidth - making it possible for computers to become better connected, easier and more intuitive to use, even less costly, and capable of handling all kinds of information. While this will create countless opportunities for business, entertainment and communication, the application of these technologies to the way people learn is the most important - and exciting.

By giving students access to a new world of information, sparking creativity, and facilitating rich communication and collaboration across vast distances, computers have long been a powerful tool for education. At the same time, the Internet has brought an unprecedented level of great educational content to a wide audience, encouraging teachers to share curriculums and resources worldwide.

E- mail has facilitated improved communication among administrators, teachers, students, parents and educational researchers, and emerging Web services technologies will create further opportunities for collaborative learning. Increased industry and government funding in learning science promises to vastly improve the ways technology is applied to learning.

In the years ahead, a whole generation of kids will leave college and enter the workforce with a broad understanding of the ways they can use technology effectively in their jobs. But we've still got a long way to go before we see how much technology can really do - particularly in education. Solving business problems with computers looks easy when compared to the often complex and little-understood process of learning. And technology is only part of the solution. All the computers in the world won't make a difference without enthusiastic students, skilled and committed teachers, involved and informed parents, and a society that underscores the value of lifelong learning. Finding effective ways to use technology to enhance learning is a challenge that educators, academics, policymakers and the technology industry must work together to solve.

Simulation Technologies

Simulation technologies and powerful sensor technologies provide scaleable models for engaging in the learning by doing. Simulations allow students the opportunity to build integrated environments with objects in one environment that serve similar purposes in another environment. This level of programmability across multiple visual environments is the metric for successful development. As students move from the visual world to the real world, sensors in laboratories provide students with feedback as they reconstruct and deconstruct various objects in real time, with real materials.

Intelligent Laboratory Objects

Embedded technology now designs learning into any object used in education. Students receive physical components that instruct the student how to design, test, and connect them together. Students build robots frequently to perform various functions to prove their concepts. If the student fails to create a solution, he automatically remediates to a visual environment for practice and better visualization of key concepts. If the student still struggles with the content and actions, he is sent back to the original set of instruction and exercises through an on- line video conferencing environment. Internet based laboratories are the norm where students are able to run laboratory experiments wherever they find them, meaning that not all schools don't have to budget to build exactly the same capabilities. Instrumentation is managed remotely and students work together in laboratory groups to learn how to use equipment effectively.

Project Management

Students write more software in 2020, not least because all scientific disciplines require increasing amounts of computing sophistication. So, they must be taught to identify opportunities and customers, manage their requirements, provide effective documentation, and manage source code, release management, testing and usability. Students manage several projects with outside customers through internet interfaces, virtual conferences, and shared workspaces. Task analysis software is personalized and everyone who is responsible for an action item is automatically notified, as well as all the related collaborators.

Voice technology eases communication as students wear technology in their clothing allowing them to access both content and people wherever they are. Students are finally getting a grip on how to program software, teach programming to their coworkers or team members, and manage software projects.

Paying games to learn complex skills

The military medic and the civilian Emergency Medical Technician (EMT) must be prepared to perform difficult, life-saving procedures, often in the face of traumatic injury and danger. These challenges have been increased with the emergence of Weapons of Mass Destruction (WMD), and the realization that civilian healthcare personnel in the United States may have to cope with mass casualties requiring prompt and effective medical care under difficult environmental conditions.

Like playing a musical instrument or flying a plane, medical procedures involve both cognitive and technical skills that demand frequent rehearsal for proper execution. Treating a patient in crisis with the added burden imposed by dangerous settings such as the combat battlefield may produce a stressful experience for the medic, sometimes leading to faulty decisions and medical errors. Unfortunately, skills such as Cardiopulmonary Resuscitation (CPR) are easily forgotten, and there is little opportunity for medics and other healthcare personnel to refresh their skills through practice on real patients in settings that approximate the dangers of the battlefield or the mass casualty event.

Computer-based simulation has been used extensively in the airline industry and in the military for effective training of cognitive, perceptual and motor skills. More recently, simulators have been used for training medical personnel in procedures using manikins and virtual reality systems.

Medical simulators may include both three-dimensional (3D) models of human anatomy displayed on a computer monitor coupled with a "haptics" device that conveys a sense of touch to the user. Thus, a paramedic inserting a chest tube or a surgeon cutting into a 'virtual' patient can visualize anatomy and feel the forces associated with the actual procedure using a force feedback device similar to the controllers used in computer gaming.

In addition to the value provided by simulators for skill training, these systems can also provide an ongoing assessment of the performance of the trainee, including metrics such as judgment, timing, sequencing of procedural steps, spatial accuracy, errors, etc. In medicine, the development of performance metrics and the objective assessment of performance is a difficult and complex process, because it requires decomposing the medical procedures into their elemental parts using a process called task analysis, depends on 'buy-in' from experts in the medical community, and requires validation using rigorous scientific methods. The performance can be displayed to the user in a debriefing session, and compared to the user's past performance and to the performance of other users. When properly configured and validated, computer-based simulators can provide objective assessment of performance to be used for certification in medicine, as they have been used for certification in aviation.

One approach for refreshing and sustaining technical skills is to allow the medic and other healthcare personnel to practice procedures in simulated environments that reproduce many of the difficulties found in real world, emergency settings. An advantage offered by simulation in all domains is the ability to expose personnel to unusual settings and situations where practice improves performance and reduces error in real world tasks.

The ideal medic training system would provide refresher training both in the field and at dedicated training centers, be deployable on a variety of hardware platforms, ranging from PDAs and laptops to full-blown immersive virtual reality training systems, be networked into larger simulations such as wargames and into hospital information systems to provide updated medical information, allow for retrieval of the user's past performance in relevant patient cases including replay of video, and be available for testing and skills certification.

However, in the short term, an optimal simulation game for medic training should at the very least, encompass the latest in learning technologies within the constraints imposed by medical training. The goal is to embed skills, judgment and knowledge so deeply into the central nervous system of the medic that diagnosis and therapy are promptly and effectively executed for point-of-wounding care even in the most dire and stressful of circumstances.

Patient case-based scenarios are a common tool for differential diagnosis and therapy in medicine. Providing the medic with a choice of case studies, retrieved by user input or automatically as part of the learning process, greatly enhances the training value of the simulation. Thus, if the simulation determines that that the student is having trouble placing an intravenous line, additional cases are called up from the database for training in venous access. In some cases, the trainee should be able to successfully perform the medical procedure by any number of alternate, valid pathways. This is often critical in medicine, since many procedures can be successfully performed using different approaches, many of which may arise as a consequence of the specific complications, anatomical anomalies, or combination of procedural elements that are

1. Automated patient case scenario retrieval based on the location, training need and circumstances as indicated by the user, or generated from the software program, including automated reach back functionality to select appropriate cases for training;
2. Recording of student state for on-the-fly adjustment of training resources;
3. Intelligent tutoring that can track the performance of each individual's progress during instruction and encourage trainees to formulate questions when they're confused, providing context -sensitive answers when appropriate, and summon human instructors when needed;
4. Performance assessment based metrics validated by the medical community, resulting in automated debriefing providing interpretation of cognitive skills and technical skills as part of the After Action Review (AAR).
5. Scalable training with SCORM (Shareable Courseware Object Reference Model)-compliant content modules, including different versions for field and training center applications;
6. Competitive and engaging computer graphics-based game environments, allowing trainees to compete

against each other and expert users, including single player and career modes, in the context of appropriate combat settings including specific ground warfare sites;

7. Distributed, networked capabilities supporting multi-player including team training capabilities and allowing interface with other systems;

8. Learning Management System, including event recorder and common administration database containing user performance ratings; Support for hardware interfaces and functionalities, including compatibility with laptop delivery platform, video capabilities for student state recording and playback modes, and extensions to immersive virtual reality devices presented by the specific patient case. The simulation should not only be able to track the student's progress through the content, it should also be able to determine the cognitive and emotional state of the student, determined by how the user behavior in the simulation, or by more direct physiologic measures of the student state such as EMG or video analysis, and adapt the instructional content to suit the needs of the trainee. Intelligent tutors, programmed into the simulation, or available as live experts accessible online, should provide remedial help when needed. Automated debriefing can list and score the correct and incorrect choices, for review by the trainee and his/her superiors.

Although great progress is being made in the development of computer simulation for skills training, the next generation of medical simulators will greatly extend the benefits of this approach through advances in technology. Today, we can envision the value of simulation training by providing medics with the opportunity to refresh their skills with engaging gameplay and validated medical content. In the next few years, not only will visually realistic simulators run on the desktop, they will also support sophisticated functions such as the integration of physiology to create realistic "breathing and bleeding" human simulations, predictive human models that can integrate diagnostic image data and laboratory tests to forecast disease within specific patients, simulations that can serve as testbeds for new therapies, drugs and interventions, and simulated surrogates that substitute for actual humans in dangerous settings.

The eventual goal of research and development efforts will be the development of a coordinated "Digital Human", consisting of models, simulations and databases spanning molecule to organism. The challenge posed by this work is that a valid and accurate model of human structure and function can be built to serve as the standard for medical diagnostics, therapeutics and education.

Given an aggressive investment and skillful management, technologies achievable by the year 2020 could transform learning - making it more productive, more personalized and more compelling for learners of any age and with any background. These technologies will make it possible to implement a range of powerful new instructional strategies long recommended by experts in cognition, but which were previously unaffordable. The instructional strategies enabled by these new technologies will more closely resemble some of the earliest forms of instruction based on tutors and apprenticeships than today's factory-like classrooms. For example, new tools will permit learners to explore and test their skills in simulated environments unaffordable or unattainable in any previous learning system. These new learning systems will change the process of learning, redefine the role played by the teachers, and create an enormous range of challenging new teaching occupations. What they will not do is replace the need for human teachers, tutors and counselors who can provide expert instruction, provide inspiration, encouragement and discipline, and serve as exemplars of the kinds of expertise a learner can aspire to achieve. Teaching and other related occupations in education and training systems will become much more like other "knowledge economy" professions, having more opportunities for professional growth and more support from technology and specialists.

In many sectors of economy, skillful use of technology has resulted in an increase in the quality of products and services, greater personalization of services, increased efficiency and reduced costs. Realizing these benefits required coupling information technology with careful rethinking of the processes, management structures and job descriptions of the people and institutions involved. There is no reason to believe that education will be any different. Consider what has happened in medicine. As little as a generation ago the occupations in medicine were largely limited to family doctors and nurses. But today, modern physicians can draw on an enormous array of medical professionals to provide specialized expertise, develop and maintain sophisticated medical equipment and software, and perform elaborate testing. It would be down right frightening if your medical care was limited to what your family physician could perform in his office - but that is largely the situation teachers find themselves in today.

By the year 2020, teachers will routinely work with teams of people with expertise in many different areas and draw upon a variety of learning products and services. New learning systems will enable teachers to create challenging assignments that can close the gap between the world of instruction and the world of work and tailor instruction to increase the efficiency of learning. New learning systems will make more productive use of both the teacher's and learner's time and talents and provide useful, multi-dimensional assessments of each learner's expertise and ability to accomplish complex tasks. For example:

· The process of learning will dramatically extend from "teacher push" to "learner pull." With future learning systems, human instructors and a robust array of software tools will shape the instructional path in ways that can be most efficient and most motivating for each individual. In the right time and place, lectures will still be critical, but current learning environments too often consist of sitting passively in a room with a hundred people and little expectation of being an active participant.

Next generation learning systems will allow learners to access live and recorded lectures from multiple sources. Performance-based assignments will allow learners and small groups to demonstrate levels of expertise in tasks where they are strongly motivated to succeed. Learning systems will be built from a set of powerful tools allowing instructional designers to go from concept to operational systems quickly. They will also permit continuous upgrades and improvements as problems are discovered and new concepts are proposed and tested. The tools will include systems for: continuously evaluating the learner's approach to expertise in critical areas; providing quick, context-sensitive, individualized responses to questions by dispatching questions to automated systems and human tutors and experts; rapidly building networks of learners and teachers; monitoring a user's level of interest, anxiety and motivation; adapting to specific learners (language of instruction, cultural background, learning abilities); and systems for building simulations reflecting the state-of-the-art in science, engineering and other fields.

Robust simulations will make possible assignments in which learners learn and test their expertise in addressing compelling assignments and problems. Coursework could include being turned loose in a virtual representation of Renaissance Venice and asked to find the secret behind the legendary blue coloring of their glass, engineering and building a (virtual) bridge over a (virtual) Mississippi River, navigating the interior of a (virtual) pancreatic cell to determine why signals reaching it do not stimulate insulin, or being given a broken (virtual) avionics system from a Boeing 777 and asked to repair it.

Teachers and learners will be able to call on a variety human tutors, counselors and experts and summon a variety of automated help systems for addressing routine questions. Learners will work face-to-face with teachers and tutors and be able to call on a worldwide network of subject-matter experts and other specialists when interesting questions arise. Sophisticated tools will help diagnose sources of confusion and suggest new learning strategies based on analysis of the experience of large numbers of learners facing similar situations.

A combination of automated monitoring tools, tutors and other specialists will make it possible to continuously adjust the pace, nature and style of the learning process to ensure a learning experience optimized for each learner. Instead of being forced to move all learners forward at a uniform rate, teachers will be able to move each individual forward at a rate consistent with his or her measured performance in each area. No one will be forced forward before demonstrating comfort and confidence in the concepts being learned. This combination of automated and human observers will enable continuous measures of competence integral to the learning process that can help teachers work more effectively with individuals and leave a record of competence that is useful and informative to learners, future teachers and employers.

As in every other sector of the economy that learned to make effective use of new information tools, these gains will require dramatic changes in the organizationa l structures and management systems of the institutions that deliver education and training services. Education and training institutions and their supporting industries must dramatically improve the way they invest in innovation, manage innovation, invest in capital equipment and assign responsibilities to different occupations. These changes will reshape the nature of employment in education in a number of ways:

— Teaching will become much more personalized because teachers will be able to spend much more time in dialogues with individuals and small groups.

— The roles bundled in the job of today's teachers are likely to be "unbundled" (lecturer, tutor, counselor, subject-matter expert, administrator, disciplinarian, record keeper, evaluator, curriculum designer) with many tasks performed by experts or automated systems with specialized expertise.

— As a consequence, teachers and tutors working directly with learners will work as a part of sophisticated and continuously changing team involving specialists and specialty firms. Professionals may specialize as subject-matter experts, expert teachers, instructional designers, courseware developers, applications designers, or a variety of other occupations, and they may concentrate on the roles at which they excel and find most rewarding. Individuals may undertake several roles simultaneously and are likely to move between jobs for career advancement or because an inspired opportunity defines a business opportunity.

— The new supporting industries will generate an enormous number of new occupational opportunities. Many of these will be in firms that produce tools and services sold to a large number of education and training institutions (and in some cases to individuals) worldwide. Since many of the skills involved will be required by other businesses, movement into and out of education professions is likely - a process that will ensure that education takes full value of innovations occurring throughout the economy. Online instruction will make it much easier for individuals to build new skills that would allow individuals to change specialties during the course of their careers.

— Professionals at all levels will need to continuously upgrade their skills and use an array of tools for professional development throughout their careers.

> This can include keeping abreast of developments in the field being taught, understanding advances in the theory of cognition, pedagogy and assessment, and understanding innovations in software design, standards and communications.

Fortunately teachers and other professionals will work in an environment allowing easy access to high quality instruction in all areas-sometimes using tools they themselves have developed. Demonstrations of expert teaching will be readily available over the high-speed internet, and the new information tools can let teachers see discussions on how other teachers have approached a subject or dealt with a difficult situation and facilitate dialogues with their colleagues as they struggle with similar issues.

The improvements in teaching and learning just described will require a major national investment in research and skillful management of these innovations by education and training institutions. The needed research will require large, persistent, well-managed research programs and partnerships drawing on industry, government, foundations, universities and schools.

New learning systems will only be affordable if these research insights are used to build robust, reliable, well-evaluated tools that allow investments to be amortized over a large number of users. It may, for example, cost several million dollars to build a powerful biomedical simulation, but the investment can be returned quickly if the product and interaction model can be used by hundreds of thousands of course designers and teachers worldwide. It may seem expensive to employ specialists in specific types of learning disabilities, but if the specialists can work online to quickly diagnose and advise teachers and learners in a large region the amortized cost will be affordable. Making effective use of these tools and redefining the roles of teachers and other professionals needed to use them to achieve real gains in learning will require creative management by education and training institutions and supporting industries.

The challenging new occupations of teaching, tool building and support services will give education occupations the same respect, and same remuneration, enjoyed by other knowledge professionals. There will be much more room for professional growth and mobility, and more time to learn from colleagues and specialists. Society will need to make a choice about whether the efficiency gains will be used to cut the cost of delivering high quality education and training or whether to use it to deliver more and better education and training services to more people. We suspect that both will happen and that markets and political leaders will recognize that increased investment in professionally delivered learning services is a key to a prosperous and just society.

Future jobs

These jobs may be performed onsite or offsite and the services may be provided by the institution or purchased from other providers Notes Gifted lecturers and experts in various fields capable of giving outstanding and unique presentations that can motivate and inspire Some individuals may be some superstars used widely by teachers and learners Teachers and tutors gifted in working closely with individual learners may work face-to-face with learners or exchanges may be via online exchanges.

Counselors sensitive to the individual needs, interests, abilities, and cultural background of each learner may do site visits but generally will work with learners online

Learning specialists who have specialized expertise in assisting learners with particular learning difficulties and disabilities may do site visits but generally will work with learners online.

Subject-matter experts who define instructional requirements for courses and propose strategies to evaluate whether appropriate expertise has been reached will work with professional societies, certification organizations and employers

Curriculum designers who work as part of a design team to translate objectives into creative courses of instruction.

Competing firms may specialize in instructional modules or entire suites of instruction Simulation and virtual environments engineers who build and maintain the components for synthetic environments, including specialized scientific software, e.g. a digital human that can be used for a variety of learning situations. Specialists in building the components of simulated towns, instruments, landscapes, biological systems, or physical phenomena.

Software engineers who work in teams to develop and maintain systems that can track individual learner progress, help provide accurate automated answers and summon instructors.

Developers of tools for continuous evaluation of a learner's expertise, "user models" of motivation, state of confusion, diagnose confusion and take approximate action.

Evaluation and certification experts who ensure that the knowledge and expertise measured match instructional goals Independent measures of expertise or certification of embedded assessments.

Management and support occupations that provide a variety of services including record keeping, IP management, repair, MIS systems, micropayments, etc. may be provided by the institution or services and software tools may be purchased or licensed from specialty firms.

Classroom Model for 2020

A new paradigm for K-12 education will evolve over the next 20 years as innovative information technology and pedagogy are integrated into the learning environment. This process is being fueled by two factors: broadband Internet capability and the emergence of immersive technologies. When these technologies are combined, the Internet as we know it today will be transformed from a low fidelity medium for browsing information to a high fidelity medium that delivers rich and immersive experiences. These new remote immersion systems will bring interactive and stimulating classroom experiences to all student populations - regardless of location. Classroom boundaries will fade as students and teachers are brought together by high-resolution video and immersive 3D shared environments that allow natural discussion, collaboration, and interaction among physically distant participants.

With remote immersion, students and teachers will investigate, play, explore, and learn together in an environment that dynamically adapts to the content - from a biology laboratory to a visit to the aquarium. The transformation of the Internet into a system for rich experiences will bring about the creation of massive distributed online archives of past lectures, interactive presentations, simulations, proficiency testing, and problem presentations. This new content, designed specifically for these new technologies, will replace current textbooks and workbooks with a national resource of high-production and content quality materials, cross-indexed and customized for individuals or classes. Once created, the archives will be updated and further improved by continuous contributions and links from teachers, production groups, and authors anywhere.

Advances in information management technology will be integrated with both the delivery and content creation technologies to address the critical need for meaningful learning assessment. Rather than relying on current periodic testing results, automated tracking of students' progress will provide statistical models of presentation sequences and paths, providing instant feedback to the student, the instructors, and administrators on progress or problems in the curriculum and its presentation. There is a great need within the education community for such innovations and the pressure to make changes is being felt by schools at all levels. While information and digital media technology has been progressing at breakneck speeds over the past decade, unfortunately little has changed in the delivery and the design of the curriculum.

The majority of efforts involving technology in education have focused on CD-ROMs or web sites containing little more than digitized versions of textbooks, or broadcast lectures with poor quality audio and video. Little has been done to design the content to take advantage of the potential of new delivery mechanisms.

Technology up to now has been viewed as a way of reaching a larger audience, and not as the enabler of new learning paradigms. We envision a new partnership evolving between technology and pedagogy-a partnership that will result in a new education paradigm. Teachers and students might be thousands of miles apart, yet they will appear and sound to each other as if they are in the same classroom.

Facilitated by unobtrusive picture and sound display devices, the infrastructure will give them a strong sense of presence, as if they are actually in the room together. Students will be able to "touch" objects in a faraway museum or "feel" forces in a virtual physics experiment through the use of haptics (touch-based technology).

Teachers will be able to search for past lectures that best suit the needs of the session at this time. Data acquired automatically from the student's interactions in this immersive environment will be captured and used to optimize the lesson progression.

The term interactivity will be transformed from mouse-clicking and instant messaging to realistic, life-sized representations of teachers and classmates sitting next to you and talking. Imagine students interacting with avatars of James Watson and Francis Crick tutoring and guiding them on the discovery of the DNA structure. Imagine students immersed in a role playing experience at the Continental Congress during the Revolutionary War era. This is what remote immersion can do for education. As appealing as this vision may sound, the truly revolutionary transformation will take place at the core-the dramatic reformation of our teaching methods themselves.

New approaches will be developed for content authoring and modeling for simulation and for creating models of learning and assessment to measure the progress of students and guide them through the learning and problem-solving process. Students will interact with content material, explore challenges and perform inquiry-driven collaborative investigations, using an array of virtual laboratory tools and simulations. This new education environment will incorporate 3D computer animation and graphics, real-time image rendering, multichannel immersive audio, video, text, and haptics. Techniques that promote a high degree of student attention, goal attainment motivation, and satisfaction will be adapted from approaches already much better understood and employed by the gaming industry.

New multimedia and Internet technologies are creating novel ways to teach and learn through this very process of creating new ways to see, hear, and touch. From an educational viewpoint, the use of sensory immersion has never been investigated. There is evidence from learning and psychology research indicating that memory is significantly enhanced by spatial associations. For example, optimal recall is achieved when an experience is not only captured as a set of sound and image streams, but when these are reproduced in such a fashion that the replay experience preserves the spatial relationships among the various elements. How will this paradigm of bringing remote teachers and students together improve our standard classroom where the teacher and students are already in one place? It extends the classroom, opening it up to a vast treasure trove of educational experiences beyond the physical room walls and delivered in specific ways designed and crafted to enhance learning and understanding. Clearly, when the teachers and students are physically in the same classroom, the technology will still deliver experiences and materials in a way that enhances learning. This will also open the door to consistent and continued education for children with disabilities, or those in medical institutions, or those with difficulties traveling to a classroom. The new paradigm of K-12 education we envision will evolve steadily over the next decade. As the technologies are introduced, we also envision the transformation of society in countless other ways, including the ways we communicate socially, conduct business, produce goods, and entertain ourselves.

Broad dynamic content will feed future education technologies. We will integrate motion and haptic interfaces, display and sound sciences, computer simulation breakthroughs, and next-level communication and information technologies. The vast possibilities created by these merging technologies make it crucial to bring together great minds from every discipline to begin building a foundation for the development of massive amounts of evolving content simultaneously and in collaboration with the design of next-generation education technology.

Future education process

The future of education will be profoundly affected by forthcoming information technology. But even more importantly, it will be affected by how educators and students use the technology to prepare for lifelong learning in the face of unrelenting change. Human beings have been slowly evolving along with their tools for millennia, but we have now entered an age in which revolutionary transformations take place every few years. This makes it difficult for most people to even imagine what technology will be available in two decades, let alone for institutions to plan its effective use.

Exponential change presents the danger that people will be swept away by an irresistible flood of new technologies that supplant all that they have learned, making them irrelevant to society and incapable of contributing to it. However, in the hands of skillful and dedicated teachers, new information technologies have the potential to greatly improve the educational process. People of any age with access to them may learn to embrace change as an exhilarating part of life and adapt as rapidly as the world about them transforms. The responsibility for determining whether technology overwhelms or elevates future students belongs to everyone, not just the developers and marketers of products. More than ever, the joint efforts of concerned teachers and involved parents will be needed to ensure the proper use of technology in the classroom so that education becomes an integral part of living.

Extrapolating from historical advances in electronics, we can roughly predict some of the tools that will be available in 20 years:

— Hand-held (or wearable) computers will be able to calculate 10,000 times faster than they can today, and will thus begin to rival the data processing capability of the human brain. They will be the hubs of digital assistants that could store more textual information than a human could read in 10 lifetimes. Such assistants will combine the present functions of telephones, web browsers, and recorders and players of both audio and video. Through wireless web access, they will be able to download far more video information than a human could watch in a lifetime.

— Digital assistants may be capable of real conversation, responding to verbal requests with questions to clarify the requester's intent. A third party wouldn't be able to tell if a person is conversing with his or her digital assistant or with another person, using the assistant as a telephone.

— Display technology will also have advanced tremendously. In 20 years, we'll have eyeglass displays that will be able to project virtual or recorded images that the wearer will perceive as immersive three-dimensional reality. Such glasses will be able to overlay or blend telemetry, virtual images and the real world almost seamlessly. A person will be able to see someone seated across a table, and - in the next "seat" - another person physically located halfway around the globe.

If we accept these projections, what can we guess about the future of education and learning? We can imagine two extreme scenarios following from present trends: the first a distinctly bleak but all too possible future and the second a vision in which teachers and technology work together to help students realize their full potential.

A blind acceptance and inexpert use of information technology in future classrooms could lead to a generation of people with no ability to interact with each other or with the unpredictable surprises and accidents that occur in everyday life. Judging from the way in which computers are often used in schools today - by teachers who don't understand technology or are intimidated by it - we can easily envision a future in which teachers in elementary school use immersive technology as digital Ritalin, to keep young students quiet and docile.

The students themselves could become addicted to the virtual worlds they are presented and prefer them to the real world. This scenario projects that children in the future will have very little contact directly with each other and would become social misfits. This is not all that far-fetched, since all too often today young children come home from school to turn on their computers rather than going out to play with each other. It could also mean that tomorrow's students will have too little experience of the real world: if they are given a steady diet of prepared scenarios and virtual models, they will be totally unprepared and unable to deal with new problems that arise. A model can only have built into it the types of behaviors that people understand or have already experienced; however, Murphy is a lot smarter than any programmer, so a student brought up on canned solutions to problems may be completely overwhelmed by a unique experience or interaction.

Furthermore, if education software is an extension of current computer games, then all children will have homogenized backgrounds and will react to the same stimulus in the same fashion. Technology used in this improper fashion has the capacity to crush the creativity out of young people and turn them into obliging responders to prepackaged stimuli, such as advertisements or political propaganda. Does that mean that children under a certain age should be banned from using computers, rather like today's youth are denied cigarettes? That's not a desirable (nor practical) objective, since highly capable computers can and should be used to encourage and enhance the creativity of a person. However, teachers and parents must carefully consider how to introduce and stage students' work with computers as one component of their educational experience. In the optimistic scenario, new technologies properly utilized in the classroom have the potential for encouraging differentiation and creativity.

Very few people have the skill with a brush to craft a great painting or the facility with the musical scales to compose a symphony. But with appropriate technology and software, it should be possible to digitally create any image or sound that a person can imagine. This possibility dramatically expands the range of assignments that young learners can tackle and the ways in which they can express themselves. They key is that the tools are used as an extension to creativity, not a set of fixed restrictions on what a student can do.

Traditional classroom learning involves experiencing new material at least five times: previewing a textbook, listening to a lecture, reading the text for comprehension, performing directed problem solving and reviewing the information (usually for an examination that is intended to gauge how well the student mastered the material). This paradigm can be adapted for highly capable digital assistants, where new material is introduced gradually over a period of time by presenting it within meaningful contexts, the lecture could be a recording of a great master teacher, the reading for comprehension could be done with an active tutor that senses when the learner is having difficulties, etc.

All of this presupposes that real people with a strong sense of social responsibility become involved in creating the software and the environments that are used in the learning experience. This will require that we better comprehend human cognition and use that improved understanding in designing our tools to establish a sound pedagogy. Thus, improved technology provides greater imperatives for performing research in areas that will help us to be more aware of ourselves. The daily experiences of teachers must be incorporated into any new approach to curricula, so that they will work with digital assistants to customize lessons according each pupil's aptitudes and interests.

Above all, we must understand that there can be no substitute for direct human contact, even with all of the imperfections and misunderstandings that can arise. People have always learned best through their mistakes or the mistakes of others, and no technology will change that. Given these considerations - the need to use technology appropriately and not attempt to substitute it for human interaction or experience with the real world - future technology could provide qualitatively new types of learning.

The human aural system is similar to a serial communications channel, which is greatly afflicted by noise and transmission errors. Normal human writing and reading emulates this serial process. However, vision is inherently a parallel information communication system. People with sight can see everything within a two-dimensional frame simultaneously, and, moreover, that frame can be updated frequently. That means learning and comprehension may benefit greatly from the development of a universal visual language. Such a language is in a sense already developing - it appears in a wide variety of media and it is also evolving through viewgraph presentations, where a presenter can mix aural and visual stimuli to convey large amounts of complex information in a short time.

Future book equivalents may actually be written in a visual language, in which more information-rich symbols are used, perhaps something like hieroglyphics as clip art. A U.S. student studying South Africa could not only attend lectures and discussions, read books, listen to music, see the art and cultural artifacts, watch TV and films, and access a wealth of factual information on the Internet, he or she could also meet and communicate in a universal language directly with a South African student studying the U.S. to appreciate different perspectives and world-views.

In short, tomorrow's educational environment should be greatly enhanced by future information technology, which can engage more of the senses in the learning experience for vastly improved comprehension. The ubiquitous availability of information could abolish the constraints of time and place for education, which should become a part of the fabric of everyday life. And everyone should have equal access and be able to contribute to the continual flow of new information, which in turn must be verifiable or subject to review and rebuttal! This approach to education recalls the universal truth attributed to both Chinese and Native American wisdom: "Tell me and I'll forget. Show me and I may remember. Involve me and I'll understand." We must all become involved, not only in understanding future technologies but the ways in which those technologies will be put to use. Technology can never be a substitute for excellent teachers and involved parents, but it can enable a more enriching and effective educational experience for those fortunate enough to be in an environment where it is used properly. The future begins today.

In theory, technology offers endless possibilities to enhance the educational experience. Educational technology can offer students expanded academic opportunities as well as critical employment skills necessary for entering the workforce of the global economy. Technology may have the potential to transform from a goal to a reality the ideal that every child will succeed academically. In practice, however, what we do in the present will define our future. And, as in space travel and medicine, technological advances in education will require major national commitment and resources.

By the next decade, technology could bring students to exciting new worlds, enhance teaching and learning strategies, and facilitate effective parental involvement. Twenty-four hour access and pervasive technology will be the norm. Students will require both technological fluency, and whole new levels of media literacy skills. Educational employees will have a vast array of tools to tap the potential of every child, but will also face the significant challenge of managing these new responsibilities.

Bibliography

Bare, J., and Meek, A. 1998. *Internet Access in Public Schools* (NCES 98-031). U.S. Depart-ment of Education, National Center for Education Statistics. Washington, DC: U.S. Government Printing Office.

Heaviside S., Riggins, T., and Farris, E. 1997. *Advanced Telecommunications in U.S. Public Elementary and Secondary Schools,* Fall 1996 (NCES 97-944). U.S. Department of Education, National Center for Education Statistics. Washington, DC: U.S. Government Printing Office.

Heaviside, S., and Farris, E. 1997. *Advanced Telecommunications in U.S. Private Schools, K-12,* Fall 1995 (NCES 97-394). U.S. Depart-ment of Education, National Center for Education Statistics. Washington, DC: U.S. Government Printing Office.

Heaviside, S., Farris, E., and Malitz, G. 1995. *Advanced Telecommunications in U.S. Public Schools,* K-12 (NCES 95-731). U.S. Depart-ment of Education, National Center for Education Statistics. Washington, DC: U.S.Government Printing Office.

Heaviside, S., Rowand, C., Hurst, D., and McArthur, E. 2000. *What Are the Barriers to the Use of Advanced Telecommunications for Students with Disabilities in Public Schools?* (NCES 2000-042). U.S. Department of Education, National Center for Education Statistics. Washington, DC: U.S. Government Printing Office.

Levin, D., Hurst, D., and Burns, S. 2000. *Computer and Internet Access in U.S. Private Schools and Classrooms: 1995 and 1998*

(NCES 2000-044). U.S. Department of Education, National Center for Education Statistics. Washington, DC: U.S. Government Printing Office.

Lytras, M. D. and G. I. Doukidis (2001). *'E-Learning Pedagogy: Define the Value'. Technology in Education International Conference & Exposition* (TechEd 2001), March 26-29, 2001 Southern California ,USA .

Lytras, M. D. and H. Odman (2001). *Fulfilling organizational learning on concurrent enterprises: The Multidimensional Dynamic Learning model for knowledge management exploitation.* 7th International Conference on Concurrent Enterprising (ICE 2001), June 26-27, 2001, Bremen, Germany.

Riley, R., Holleman, F., and Roberts, L. 2000. *eLearning: Putting a World-Class Education at the Fingertips of All Children.U.S. Department of Education,* Office of Educational Technology. This document is available online (http://www.ed.gov/Technology/elearning/e-learning.pdf).

Rowand, C. 1999. *Internet Access in Public Schools and Classrooms: 1994-98* (NCES 1999-017). U.S. Department of Education, National Center for Education Statistics. Washington, DC: U.S. Government Printing Office.

Ryan, M. (1995). *Human resource management and the politics of knowledge:linking the essential knowledge base of the organization to strategic decision making.* Leadership and Organizational Development Journal Vol. 16(No. 5).

Shuell, T. J. (1992). *Designing instructional computing systems for meaningful learning.* In M. Jones & P. H. Winne (Eds.), Adaptive learning environments: Foundations and frontiers, New York: Springer- Verlag, pp.19-54.

Smerdon, B., Cronen, S., Lanahan, L., Anderson, J., Iannotti, N., and Angeles, J. 2000. *Teachers' Tools for the 21st Century: A Report on Teachers' Use of Technology* (NCES 2000-102). U.S. Department of Education, National Center for Education Statistics. Washington, DC: U.S. Government Printing Office. Williams, C. 2000. Internet Access in Public Schools and Classrooms: 1994-99 (NCES 2000-086). U.S. Department of Education,

Index

INFORMATION TECHNOLOGY
A Revolutionary Change

INFORMATION TECHNOLOGY
A Revolutionary Change
(In 9 Volumes)

Volume 8
(On the Road to Electronic Environment)

Editor
RAMESH CHANDRA
Vice-Chancellor, Bundelkhand University, Jhansi (U.P.)

KALPAZ PUBLICATIONS
DELHI–110052

INFORMATION TECHNOLOGY: A REVOLUTIONARY CHANGE
(Information Technology)

Rs. 8000 (Set)
Rs. 900 (Each Volume)

ISBN: 81-7835-201-X (Set)
ISBN: 81-7835-227-3 (Vol. 8)

Published in 2003 in India by
Kalpaz Publications
C-30, Satyawati Nagar
Delhi-110052
E-mail: kalpaz@hotmail.com

Laser Typesetting at: Varsha Graphics, Delhi
Printed at: Mehra Offset Printers, New Delhi

Contents

Preface

Today, computers and other electronic devices increasingly communicate and interact directly with other devices over a variety of networks, such as the Internet. The information and communication technologies (ICT) are central to the creation of the emerging global knowledge-based economy and can play an important role in accelerating growth, in promoting sustainable development and eradicating poverty in developing countries as well as countries with economies in transition and in facilitating their effective integration into the global economy.

The new technologies can shape and enhance a wide range of development applications —from e-commerce to access to financial markets; from generating employment to providing opportunities for investment to entrepreneurs, in particular small and medium-sized enterprises; from improved agricultural and manufacturing productivity to the empowerment of all sections of society; from long-distance education to tele-medicine; from environmental management and monitoring to prevention and management of disasters. Access to information and knowledge-sharing is largely determined by education, capabilities, including resources, transparent societies, capacity to generate and utilize knowledge, connectivity and the availability of diverse content and applications, and the policy and legal/regulatory framework. Efforts to achieve universal connectivity, particularly at the lower income levels, in all countries and especially in developing countries, will require innovative approaches and partnerships, including group and community connectivity and private-sector investment. In this regard, the establishment of integrated multipurpose and multimedia community information centres will be important.

Effective and meaningful collaborative efforts are required, involving Governments, multilateral development institutions, bilateral donors, the private sector, civil society and other relevant stakeholders, to enhance the developmental impact of ICT. Such efforts should include transfer of technology to developing countries on concessional and preferential terms, as mutually agreed, especially technology related to knowledge-based sectors, the mobilization of resources from all sources, public and private, at the national and international levels, and promoting capacity-building.

Editor

1

Technology in Electronic Environment

Today, computers and other electronic devices increasingly communicate and interact directly with other devices over a variety of networks, such as the Internet. Consumers and businesses have been particularly quick to recognize the potential and realize the benefits of adopting new computer-enabled networks. Consumers now routinely use computer networks to identify sellers, evaluate products and services, compare prices, and exert market leverage.

Businesses use networks even more extensively to conduct and re-engineer production processes, streamline procurement processes, reach new customers, and manage internal operations. This electronic revolution in economy is spurring additional investments in facilities, hardware, software, services, and human capital. Ultimately, it may change the structure and performance of the American economy as much as the introduction of the computer a generation ago. While the burgeoning use of electronic devices in economy is widely acknowledged and discussed, it remains largely undefined and unrecognized in official economic statistics.

Telecommunication Revolution

Telecommunications is a growth industry and also will be moving towards a horizontal structure. The greatest opportunities for established carriers are likely to be in providing network outsourcing services. The changes required to exploit these opportunities will be major, and it is very likely that there will be huge bankruptcies and writedowns. However, the telecom industry, as measured by revenues, is likely to grow, as it has in the past. There will be greater diversity in available communication services, which should provide for a more resilient infrastructure, even when individual companies restructure.

The telecom crash that started in the year 2000 has been brutal to the traditional long distance carriers and devastating to the new carriers, whether in local or long distance segments of the market. The telecom crash was a crash only for the telecom suppliers, the result of an unsustainable explosion in capital expenditures. Total revenues of service providers have been growing all along at rates of 5 to 10% a year for the whole sector, with some companies going out of business, while others boom. That rate of growth is very respectable, and, following historical precedent, faster than the growth rate of the economy as a whole.

The crash occurred because even this fast growth rate was simply not sufficient to sustain the boom in capital expenditures. The growth of the entire telecom pie allows for relatively gentle transformations. In particular, new services can grow without destroying old ones. That has been the historical pattern, and can be seen today. There is much public concern about the slow spread of broadband in the US. Yet, with the number of households with DSL or cable modems about tripling in 2001, that rate is quite fast, certainly by comparison with the spread of cell phones.

Some countries have experienced much faster broadband penetration, but then their prices have been much lower. For a service that costs $40-50 a month, the US is not doing too badly in speed of broadband adoption. Lower price would certainly increase US penetration, but this price sensitivity just reinforces the point that the perceived utility of broadband is not all that great, at least not yet. At a low enough price, people will buy just to get a modestly improved performance with email. At the higher price that prevails in the US, consumers have to be convinced that the higher bandwidth and the always-on capability provide real value, and that takes time.

Of course, in a low marginal cost business such as telecommunications, even a drop of 8% is noticeable, and would surely be reflected in stock market valuation of the companies. The main issue is whether some compensating sources of revenues can be developed in the meantime. New technologies, such as wavelength switching, are on the horizon, and will surely transform the industry. However, that will take time.

The telecommunications industry is extremely complex. What is beyond dispute, though, is that most of the costs are at the edges of the network. Furthermore, technology over the last two decades has been shifting the balance of costs even further towards the edges than before. The main reason the established long distance carriers have been suffering is that their consumer voice business is not viable. When the Bell System was broken up, long distance transport was still expensive.

However, for several years now wholesale prices for long distance voice calls in the US have been under a penny a minute. Those costs and a competitive marketplace are not compatible in the long run with consumer prices that are 10 times as high. It was inevitable that for ordinary customers, long distance was eventually going to be provided by their local carriers on a flat rate basis. The decline in long distance transport costs that doomed consumer long distance voice carriers predated the Internet.

However, the Internet helped speed up the transformation we are witnessing by leading to the wild overbuilding of long distance transport and by accelerating technical advances. The costs on the Internet are even more heavily concentrated at the edges, especially if one considers the Internet as just a component of the entire IT infrastructure. The electronics have been getting less expensive, but the labor has not, and in particular the costs of the final few hundred feet of a connection to the network have been remarkably stable and remarkably high.

After all, most households do have three separate communication systems, the copper-based one from their ILEC, a coax-based one from their cable TV provider, and a cell phone from a wireless carrier. Thus a much deeper look is needed to understand what is going on. A key factor is that change is slow but inevitable. Hence a static analysis of technology choices, without taking account how quickly consumer are likely to move, is bound to be inadequate. In particular, whether DSL or cable is better technically is not overwhelmingly important. Both are capable of speeds in the hundreds of megabits per second in both directions over short distances.

Further, the relevant distances will be getting smaller as fiber is pulled closer and closer to the home by both cable and DSL carriers. Eventually fiber will go all the way into the home. Whoever manages to accomplish this, will then likely have a true natural monopoly, with the ability to increase the bandwidth of the connection at low cost. Victory in this race to bring fiber to the home will likely depend mostly on the strategies and tactics of the competing players, and not so much on technology.

The cell phone industry has been making capital expenditures of around $1,000 per subscriber, while copper or coax connections to add additional subscribers run about twice as high. In the financial markets, wireless carriers are valued at about $2,000 per subscriber. ILECs are valued at $2,000 to $3,000 per line, while cable TV networks are valued at $4,000 to $5,000 per subscriber.

In 1996, the US passed the Telecommunications Reform Act that was expected to create vigorous competition in all segments of communications. Six years later, after the telecom boom and bust, the entrenched ILECs appear to be even more securely entrenched, apparently the sole winners to emerge from all the turmoil. The reformers are beginning to concede that the "first mile" is a natural monopoly, and are being driven to consider remedies such as separating the ILECs into monopoly wholesale providers of basic network connectivity and retail service providers that alternative carriers might have a hope of competing with.

However, given the long lead times that US legislative and judicial systems operate on, especially where drastic changes are involved, there is very little hope of any such transformation being forced through in less than 5 years, and potentially it could take much longer. Even without any ILEC separation, though, we are likely to see several serious challenges to the ILEC monopoly emerge in the next half a dozen years.

The main challenge is likely to come from diversion of voice traffic to cell phones. Already a substantial fraction of the population regards cell phones as their primary communication tool, and that fraction is likely to increase. Policy makers who are interested in promoting competition could help this move along by forcing those ILECs that have not yet done so to completely sever their ties with cellular carriers. Competition from cellular carriers for voice is likely to force ILECs to concentrate on exploiting their natural advantage in bandwidth, and to emphasize Internet access. ILECs will also be forced to emphasize broadband by competition from cable TV companies.

For broadband communication, wireless distribution inside the house is especially attractive, given the costs of alternatives. Depending on how issues of scaling and business models are resolved, this approach could extend to a much wider communication network. So far wireless data communication has been a great disappointment, and 802.11 standards are the first ones that appear to be gaining wide acceptance. As wireless data spreads, and especially as voice transport capability is provided, we might see it offering serious competition to DSL and cable modem systems. What is especially attractive about wireless communication is that at least potentially it scales with the size of the population that is served, and so avoids the huge upfront costs of wireline infrastructure.

The traditional model for the telecom industry has been that of a carrier that provides all the equipment and systems and sells a service. This model has been fading for a long time, with customers buying their own phone sets, fax machines, and PBXs. A comparison with the computer industry is likely to be productive, especially since communication, information, and computation are becoming increasingly interrelated.

The general trend in the modern economy has been away from vertical integration and towards horizontal integration. This trend is consistent with what one would expect in view of Coase's theory of the firm, as improved communication makes it possible to use market mechanisms between different layers, and at the same time makes coordination easier.

Among the main advantages of a division into horizontal layers, with separate companies operating in each layer, is that it provides a method handling complexity and rapid change. It is worth noting that such separation was already visible inside the vertically integrated enterprises.

For example, in telecommunications, the wireline carriers have for quite a long time had essentially separate divisions handling the optical network and the voice and data networks that rode on top of it and were the only ones visible to most customers.

The computer industry is a prime example of the trend away from vertically integrated enterprises. A standard example of such an enterprise was IBM in the 1960s through much of the 1980s. It developed and produced its own processors, memories, hard disks, operating systems, application software, and so on. The current paradigm is that of horizontal players, in which Micron produces memory chips, Intel microprocessors,

Microsoft the operating system and basic applications, Dell assembles the components and sells them, etc. The most successful player in this game is Microsoft.

In the computer industry, everybody wants to be Microsoft, but there is only one Microsoft, and there cannot be too many Microsofts. Microsoft has annual revenues approaching $30 billion, after-tax profits approaching $12 billion, $38 billion in cash, and a stock market valuation of $330 billion. It has attained this enviable financial position by dominating the desktop software market, and appropriating the lion's share of the profits in PC software.

In communications, the trend towards a horizontal structure of the industry also appears inevitable. Who will adopt to it best is uncertain. The natural division would seem to be into providers of physical connectivity, providers of basic data transport, and outsourcers, who manage customer networks. The established long distance carriers, with their expertise in serving large enterprise customers, would seem to be best positioned to dominate in basic data transport and outsourcing. On the negative side, they have heavy debt loads and also the legacy of the consumer long distance business as a burden.

The ILECs have the financial resources to attempt moving into outsourcing, but lack the expertise, and would require a wrenching cultural change to adapt. Their natural niche seems to be in providing physical access and basic data transport, although even there, one could have separation into several layers.

Some parts of the telecom world appear destined for commoditization, especially long distance transport. The Internet at its core is a "stupid network," as David

Isenberg has called it. With technological progress and the fierce competition created by the massive overinvestment in that area, backbone transport is not and will not be all that big a piece of the telecom pie.

Local access is likely to be a large part of the industry. The costs are going to remain high, and economies of scale will limit competition. Hence revenues are going to be large, and profits are likely to be substantial. However, the potential for exorbitant profits will be slim, both because of regulation and growing competition. The greatest growth opportunities in telecommunications are likely to lie in services. As was mentioned above, the "stupid network" metaphor for the Internet ignores the huge costs at the edges of the network, costs that are often not explicit, since they involve time and aggravation for the customers. This again mirrors what happened in the computer industry.

It again brings up the example of IBM, a company that is in the process of transforming itself from a vertically integrated producer of computer systems to a service company, running other companies' IT operations. IBM has about three times the revenues of Microsoft, two thirds of the profits, a lower growth rate, and a stock market valuation about 55% that of Microsoft. However, it is regarded as a remarkable success story, and its stock price has not been devastated to the extent that shares of most of the other computer companies have been.

Definitions of Cyber-terms

The terms Internet, electronic commerce, electronic business, and cybertrade are used often. However, they are used interchangeably and with no common understanding of their scope or relationships. Establishing terms that clearly and consistently describe the growing and dynamic networked economy is a critical first step toward developing useful statistics about it. The definitions are used for the electronic revolution taking place in the economy, and must recognize that these changes take place in a larger economic context. For example, global competition, interest rates, laws and regulations, social concerns, industry traditions, and consumer preferences are all part of the broader "environment" which can affect all business activities.

Similarly, electronic and non-electronic businesses share an infrastructure of available economic resources, including natural resources, utilities, structures, equipment, telecommunication and other services, employees, and workforce skills. It is useful to think of the electronic economy as having three primary components—supporting infrastructure, electronic business processes, and electronic commerce transactions.

A common feature of both electronic business processes and electronic commerce transactions is reliance on the use of computer-mediated networks. It is reliance on the use of computer networks, and the benefits this can provide, that is the "bottom line" difference between electronic and other kinds of business.

There are three primary components of US electronic economy, and the feature shared by two of them, are defined below. Each definition includes examples of its scope and content. The definitions are intentionally broad to provide an inclusive framework for planning statistical measures, and to allow flexibility to incorporate continuing changes in the electronic economy.

E-business infrastructure

E-business infrastructure is the share of total economic infrastructure used to support electronic business processes and conduct electronic commerce transactions. It includes hardware, software, telecommunication networks, support services, and human capital used in electronic business and commerce. Examples of e-business infrastructure are:

— Computers, routers, and other hardware

— Satellite, wire, and optical communications and network channels

— System and applications software

— Support services, such as web site development and hosting, consulting, electronic payment, and certification services.

— Human capital, such as programmers.

Electronic business

Electronic business is any process that a business organization conducts over a computer-mediated network. Business organizations include any for-profit, governmental, or nonprofit entity. Their processes include production-, customer-, and internal or management-focused business processes. Examples of electronic business processes are:

— *Production*: focused processes include procurement, ordering, automated stock replenishment, payment processing and other electronic links with suppliers, as well as production control and processes more directly related to the production process.

— *Customer*: focused processes include marketing, electronic selling, processing of customers orders and payments, and customer management and support

— *Internal or management*: focused processes include automated employee services, training, information sharing, video conferencing, and recruiting.

Electronic commerce

Electronic commerce is any transaction completed over a computer-mediated network that involves the transfer of ownership or rights to use goods or services. Transactions occur within selected e-business processes and are "completed" when agreement is reached between the buyer and seller to transfer the ownership or rights to use goods or services. Completed transactions may have a zero price.

Computer-mediated networks

Computer-mediated networks are electronically linked devices that communicate interactively over network channels. Generally, both electronic devices will be computer-enabled, but at a minimum at least one device must be computer-enabled as in the case of a typical telephone linking with an computer-enabled interactive telephone system.

Typically, the interactive link involves minimal human intervention though someone activates the electronic devices, accesses the network, and may even assist with the process or transaction. For example, many e-commerce businesses are providing shoppers with the on-line capability of "chatting" with customer support representatives or even speaking with them through the use of internet telephony software. Examples of devices and networks are:

— Linked electronic devices such as computers, personal digital assistants, webTV,

— Internet-enabled cellular phones, and telephones linked with interactive telephone systems.

— Networks such as the Internet, intranets, extranets, Electronic Data Interchange (EDI) networks, and telecommunication networks. Networks may be either open or closed.

E-commerce transactions

Following are the examples of e-commerce transactions are:

— An individual purchases a book on the Internet.

— A government employee reserves a hotel room over the Internet.

— A business calls a toll free number and orders a computer using the seller's interactive telephone system.

— A business buys office supplies on-line or through an electronic auction.

— A retailer orders merchandise using an EDI network or a supplier's extranet.

— A manufacturing plant orders electronic components from another plant within the company using the company's intranet.

— An individual withdraws funds from an automatic teller machine (ATM).

Identifying e-commerce transactions often is not as straight forward as the previous examples may make it appear. An e-commerce transaction since agreement occurred over computer-mediated networks. In contrast, the purchase of a pre-packaged music CD from a computerized kiosk would not be considered an e-commerce transaction. Identifying and measuring e-commerce transactions is new for statistical agencies and it can be complicated. The simple example of an on-line retail book purchase illustrates some of these complexities and points out some of the measurement issues that remain to be addressed.

While comprehensive measures of e-commerce may be wanted to profile all of these transactions, such detailed business statistics coverage would be unprecedented. In addition, the value of e-commerce transactions, like their brick and mortar counterparts, are aggregated and presented by the industry of the business entity selling the goods or services so the industry classification system will impose additional measurement constraints.

For example, Bigbook would be classified in North American Industry Classification System (NAICS) retail industry 454110, Electronic Shopping and Mail-Order Houses along with traditional catalog stores. Data on employment, total sales, or e-commerce sales would be provided for the industry as whole; information would not be broken out between electronic shopping and mail order houses. Understanding the industry classification system and its implications for e-commerce and e-business measures is a must for all prospective data users. Moreover, classifying emerging and rapidly evolving businesses engaged in e-commerce activities will remain a challenge for statistical agencies. An additional complexity is that the transactions relating to John Doe's simple book purchase involve many parties and some play multiple roles.

The business-to-consumer transaction will involve a larger number of related business-to-business transactions. This transactions multiplier effect is not unique to e-business; however, its expected growth and continued change will add to the challenge of measuring e-business and e-commerce. Growth in transactions is expected because as e-commerce expands related business-to-business transactions will become more fragmented; participants will concentrate on performing their highest valued-activities and rely increasingly on third parties for lower-value added activities.

The measurement challenges of this growth include accounting for the increased volumes, identifying the new e-business players, maintaining up-to-date information for the known players, and avoiding double counting the value of related transactions. Change in the scope and nature of e-commerce transactions is expected because electronic business methods permit the players to change their roles relatively easily and they increasingly will do so. Examples of changes in roles are today seen in manufacturers and wholesalers who now sell directly to consumers, and in the "virtual" integration of firms through informal alliances that link firms electronically.

These new arrangements impose additional measurement challenges including identifying the new players and their roles, maintaining up-to-date information on them and how their roles are changing, and updating data collection methods. E-business is any process that a business organization conducts over a computer-mediated network. E-commerce is any transaction completed over a computer-mediated network that involves the transfer of ownership or rights to use goods or services. The definition includes both monetary and non monetary transactions.

Some transactions may have a zero price (for example, the download of free software) while other transactions may be paid in-kind or through barter. E-business infrastructure is the share of total economic infrastructure used to support processes and conduct e-commerce transactions. The definition includes hardware, software, telecommunication networks, support services, and human capital along with associated examples.

Network channels

Network channels include the Internet, intranets within organizations, extranets and Electronic Data Interchange networks linking trading partners, and telecommunication networks. Electronic linked devices include computers, personal digital assistants, webTV, Internet-enabled phones, and interactive telephone systems.

While the e-commerce examples also include a computer-enabled kiosk and an ATM as linked electronic devices, in the definition people have chosen to go with a short, rather than a long list of electronic devices to minimize possible reporting confusion. Fax machines, while clearly electronic devices that can link over network channels, were excluded because they do not communicate interactively.

Electronic gas pumps often are linked interactively over network channels with other electronic devices. The device, the electronic pump, can be activated in a number of different ways. ATM machine or a computer-enabled kiosk, once the device is activated the consumer can specify the transaction and complete the transaction.

The electronic pumps also support a number of E-business processes including tracking sales and gallons sold, with links to automated inventory replenishment systems to name a few. The functionality embedded in pumps is expected to grow. For example, BP Amoco PLC is planning to introduce even more sophisticated pumps that will include Web browsers and Windows CE operating system that will even permit the gas purchaser to order fast food at the pump.

Communication Revolution through E-mail

E-mail is the most important, unique method for communicating and developing relationships. It is easy to use. People also find it familiar and safe because it is similar in many respects to writing letters - minus the annoyances of addressing envelopes, licking stamps, and trips to the mail box. Of all the methods for developing relationships on the internet, it is the most common - and perhaps the most powerful. Although friendships and romances may indeed begin in text-driven chat rooms, MOOs, MUDs, or the newer multimedia chat environments, these relationships almost always progress to e-mail as a way to deepen the communication. It is a more private, more reliable, less chaotic way to talk.

Even when other methods improve greatly by becoming more effectively visual and auditory - as in video teleconferencing - e-mail will not disappear. Many people will prefer it BECAUSE it is a non-visual and non-auditory form of communication. After all, we don't see people rushing out to buy video equipment to accessorize their telephone - even though that technology has been available for some time. E-mail is not just electronic mail sent via the internet. E-mail communication creates a psychological space in which pairs of people - or groups of people - interact.

People type words to communicate via e-mail. More technologically sophisticated methods enable you to incorporate pictures and sounds into the message, but that's a more complicated process that destroys the simplicity and ease of use that attracts many people to e-mailing. On the other hand, some people may not be attracted to e-mail BECAUSE it involves typing.

While everyone knows how to talk, not everyone knows how to type. Some people also may not feel comfortable or skilled in expressing themselves through writing. The typing/writing barrier filters some people out of the e-mail world. For those who love to write, e-mail is heaven.

In the typed text of e-mail, you can't see other people's faces or hear them speak. All those subtle voice and body language cues are lost, which can make the nuances of communicating more difficult. But humans are creative beings. Avid e-mailers have developed all sorts of innovative strategies for expressing themselves through typed text.

A skilled writer may be able to communicate considerable depth and subtlety in the deceptively simple written word. Despite the lack of face-to-face cues, conversing via e-mail has evolved into a sophisticated, expressive art form. People may not know who you are or where you are when you send them an e-mail. If you want, you can use a pseudonym in the message. And the return address contains only general information about where you are. The average user doesn't know how to track down the origin and identity of a mysterious message.

If someone is determined to remain hidden, they can send their mail through an anonymous mailer service that will strip away all identifying information from the e-mail. This potential for anonymity in e-mailing disinhibits some people. They say things they wouldn't ordinarily say. The lack of face-to-face cues amplifies this disinhibiting effect. In some cases the result may be people who speak in an aggressive, antisocial manner. Sometimes it encourages people to be more open, honest, and affectionate. Anonymity isn't intrinsically a "good" or "bad" thing. It cuts both ways. E-mail conversations do not occur in "real time." You and your partner do not have to be sitting at the computer at the same moment in order to talk.

Unlike face-to-face encounters, which are synchronous, e-mail discussions do not require you to respond on-the-spot to what they other has said. You have time to think, evaluate, and compose your reply. Some people take advantage of this convenient "zone for reflection." Some do not. Because e-mail communication is asynchronous, the rate at which you converse is maneuverable. A conversation may occur over the course of minutes, days, weeks, or months. Interactive time can be shortened or stretched, as needed. Changes in the pacing of the e-mail exchange between two people reflects the dynamics of their relationship.

Most e-mail programs allow you to cc people or create a mailing list. These features make it very easy to expand a dyad conversation into a group discussion. Large groups of dozens or more people can be managed through such programs as "listserv." The membership boundary of the e-mail interactive space is as flexible as its members want it to be. Sometimes the boundaries are hidden: people can be dropped from a discussion without their even knowing it.

Spam - Inevitably, e-mail users are subjected to the "spam" of unrequested messages designed to sell an idea or a product. Junk mail. To internet oldtimers, spam is anathema. It's the apocalyptic sign of the commercialization of cyberspace. People subjectively experience e-mail as a personal space in which they interact with friends and colleagues. Spam is the commercial that pops up in your face, intruding on that private zone.

In the list of incoming mail, it stands out like a wart. One of the very few good things about spam is that it reminds you of how e-mail is NOT a totally private space. Unwelcomed others can inject their irrelevance. And although it rarely happens, technically clever sociopathic and other nosy people can secretly listen in on your conversations.

Today, almost everyone is using e-mail, not everyone is using it to the same extent. One way to classify people is by the frequency and intensity of their e-mail use. People in each category tend to behave a bit differently in their e-mail relationships than people in other categories.

The impact e-mail has on your interpersonal life increases as you become more avidly involved. It becomes an upward spiraling process: the more you e-mail, the more relationships you develop, the more you need to continue e-mailing in order to stay connected to your colleagues and friends. With that ever-expanding e-mail life comes increased skill in composing and reading e-mail.

You become sensitized to the nuances of e-mail relationships, which makes that interpersonal world even more enticing, challenging, and rewarding. For avid e-mail users, the computer is a major feature of their interpersonal and/or professional life, including dyad relationships and group memberships. Their online world has become deeply ingrained into their psyche and e-mail is an extremely important pathway for psychologically maintaining the integrity of that world.

They check their e-mail at least once a day, often several times a day. It's one of very first things they do in the morning and may be the last thing they do before bedtime. E-mailmay receive a hundred or more messages - the bulk of those messages coming from the group lists to which they belong.

Some avid users may have their e-mail programs set to automatically download at regular intervals, while even more hardcore users check each message as soon as it comes in. For the avid user, a technical failure resulting in a loss of e-mail capability is a catastrophe. You feel cut off, out of the loop.

Many avid users have some type of back-up system to counteract such disasters - for example, a second or third e-mail account, or a second e-mail capable computer (e.g., a computer at the office and at home). Avid users almost always have at least one online buddy who acts as an emergency intermediary. When the user's e-mail capability goes down, he or she contacts the buddy who relays news of the user's predicament to their online friends and colleagues. Regular e-mail users check and write e-mail a few times each week, often at at a prescribed time.

Their internet relationships can become a very significant feature of their lives, as with the avid user - although their e-mail worlds do not take on the same intensity as with avid users. Technical failures resulting in disconnection also doesn't stir up the same degree of anxiety. The casual e-mail user does e-mail sporadically, maybe once a week, or less than that. For these users, e-mail is a curiosity, a toy to play with, an amusement for leisure time. They may enjoy tinkering with this form of communication - and may even establish some friends and colleagues through it.

But e-mail has not become an important feature of their interpersonal world. Difficulties may arise when regular users - and especially avid users - begin e-mailing with casual users. There is a disparity in the perceived importance of developing the relationship via e-mail. The avid or regular user may be expecting more frequent exchanges, but does not receive them. Experienced users quickly recognize this disparity and adjust accordingly. E-mail usually is one of the first things a new internet user attempts. So the newbie e-mail user usually has just entered the world of cyberspace They don't understand the rules of the road or how things work. They may breach etiquette, like typing in caps, which is the text-talk equivalent of shouting. They don't fully understand the depth and complexity of the e-mail world. They don't yet appreciate its potential for developing relationships. Essentially, they don't know what they are getting into.

Avid users often can spot a newbie very quickly. Some of these more experienced users enjoy taking the newbie under their wing. Other undesirable types may toy with or try to take advantage of the naive newbie.

A person's ability to communicate effectively via e-mail depends highly on his or her writing skills. People who hate to write probably will not become consistent e-mail users. Regular and avid users usually enjoy writing. Some even report that they PREFER writing as a way to express themselves. They take delight in words, sentence structure, and the opportunity to craft exactly how they wish to express their thoughts and moods.

They enjoy that "zone of reflection" where they can ponder and self-reflect before expressing themselves. As such, e-mail usually is a less spontaneous form of communicating than speech. Unlike verbal conversation - where words issue forth and immediately evaporate - writing places one's thoughts in a more visible, permanent, concrete, and objective format. An e-mail message is a tiny packet of self-representation that is launched off into cyberspace. Some even experience it as a creative work, a gift sent to one's internet pal. It's a piece of oneself that experienced e-mail users enjoy constructing. The quality of the relationship between e-mail correspondents rests on their writing skills. The better people can express themselves through writing, the more the relationship can develop and deepen.

Poor writing can result in misunderstandings and possibly conflicts. In the absence of an accurate perception of what the other is trying to say, people tend to project their own expectations, anxieties, and fantasies onto the other. A disparity in writing ability between e-mail partners also can be problematic. The equivalent in in-person encounters would be one person who is very eloquent and forthcoming, talking to another who speaks awkwardly and minimally.

The loquacious one eventually may resent putting so much effort into the relationship and taking all the risks of self-disclosure. The quiet one may feel controlled, ignored, and misunderstood. We tend to think of writing abilities as a fixed skill - a tool for expressing oneself that is either sophisticated or not. It's also possible that the quality of one's writing is affected by the quality of the relationship with the other.

As an e-mail relationship deepens - and trust develops - a person may open up to more expressive forms of writing. They are more willing to experiment, take risks - not just in what specific thoughts or emotions they express, but also in the words and composition used. Spelling and grammar conjure up all sorts of memories and emotions from the school years of one's childhood. Your self-concept may ride on those memories. In the course of an e-mail relationship, those issues from the past may be stirred up. Writing isn't just a tool for developing the e-mail relationship.

Writing affects the relationship, and the relationship influences the quality of the writing. Writing effectiveness changes as a result of what is happening in the ongoing e-mail encounter. Composition advances when people feel safe and are ready to explore; it regresses when they feel threatened, hurt, or angry. Those changes reflect the developmental changes in the relationship. In addition to writing skill, writing STYLE also affects the e-mail relationship and is in turn affected by it. Concrete, emotional and abstract expression, complexity of vocabulary and sentence structure, the organization and flow of thought - all reflect one's cognitive/personality style and influence how the other reacts to you.

Compulsive people may construct highly organized, intellectualized messages with little emotional revelation. Histrionic people may show less concern about organization and much more for the emotions they express. Narcissists may write extremely long, rambling blocks of paragraphs. Schizoids may produce very short but penetrating messages. Different writing/personality styles may be compatible, incompatible, or complementary to other styles.

There are seven components for E-mail messages:

(1) the sender's name as indicated in your incoming mailbox,

(2) the subject line, as indicated in your incoming mailbox,

(3) the greeting that introduces the body of the message,

(4) the body of message, including quoted text,

(5) the sign-off line and name, and,

(6) the signature block. The body of the message is what most people consider the actual "message" itself.

However, the other components of the message also can be tiny gems of communication. Much meaning can be packed into those little nuggets. How those deceptively simple components of the message change over time may signal important changes in the relationship.

The Sender's Name reflects the ongoing identity that one wishes to present online. The name chosen usually is one's real name, a pseudonym, or a combined name.

Using one's real name indicates a wish to simply be oneself. It's a straightforward, "honest" presentation. Pseudonyms are more mysterious, playful approaches. "Can you guess who I am?" They express some hidden aspect of the person's self-concept. They reveal unconscious motivating fantasies and wishes about one's identity.

A combined name is a "letting it be known" that you have a partner - that the two of you are sharing the e-mail program and may BOTH be reading all the mail. When people change the username setting in their e-mail program, it reflects an important change in how they wish to present their ongoing, online identity. Moving from a pseudonym to one's real name expresses the wish to drop the "mask". Changing the combined name to a single name is a move towards separation and individuation that invites more private, one-on-one dialogue.

The subject line is a tiny microcosm unto itself. Most often it's used to simply summarize or introduce the major idea/s contained in the body of the message. But experienced e-mail users understand the more subtle techniques for communicating meaning and emotion in the titles they bestow to their e-mail. The subject line can lead into, highlight, or elaborate a particular idea in the message. It can ask a definitive question, shoot back a definitive answer, joke, tease, prod, berate, shout, whisper, or emote.

Sometimes it's meaning may blatantly or discreetly contradict the sentiment expressed in the body of the message. A creative application of caps, commas, slashes, parentheses, and other keyboard characters adds emphasis and complexity to the thoughts and emotions expressed in the subject line. In an e-mail archive, examining the list of subject lines across the development of the relationship is like perusing the headlines of a newspaper over the course of months or years.

It reflects the flow of important themes in the history of the e-mail encounter. These patterns or trends over time might reveal hidden or unconscious elements in relationship between the two people. For example, one interesting feature is the use of "re:" as a prefix to the subject line. The use of "re:" versus creating a new subject line can be an interesting dynamic interchange between e-mail partners. Creating a new line is a bit like taking the lead in the relationship by introducing a new title for the interaction - like creating a headline for the little "story" that is the ongoing dialogue. It's an attempt to conceptualize, summarize, and highlight what the person perceives as the most important feature of the conversation.

Creating a new subject line calls into play the "observing ego" - that ability to step back and reflect on what is happening. It shows a sense of responsibility and ownership for the dialogue - in some cases maybe even an attempt to control the dialogue. In this fashion, some e-mail partners "duel" with each other via the subject line. Simply clicking on reply without creating a new message title may indicate less of an observing ego and more of a spontaneous reaction. Some people chronically fail to create a new subject line and persistently use "re:" They may be a bit passive in the relationship, or lazy. They may not feel that sense of responsibility, ownership, or control. If this isn't true, their partner may still perceive them as being that way. Spammers will try to exploit the dynamics of a subject line in order to trick you into opening the message.

Beware of subject headings written all in caps, embellished with asterisks and exclamation points, or containing overly friendly or seductive messages—especially when you don't recognize the sender's name. If it looks and smells like spam, it's spam.

Similar to writing letters or meeting someone on the street, the conversation usually begins with a greeting of some sort. Different greetings convey slightly different emotional tones and levels of intimacy. It sets the mood for the rest of the message. Over the course of a batch of messages, the back-and-forth changes in the greeting can become a revealing little dance - sometimes playful, sometimes competitive. No greeting at all is an interesting phenomenon that cuts both ways.

In some cases, it may reveal that the sender is lazy, passive, or how he/she lacks any personal connection to you. In an ongoing, back-and-forth dialogue, there may be no greetings at all throughout a string of exchanged e-mails. In the face-to-face world, you don't say "hello" in the midst of a energetic discussion. In cyberspace, the same principle holds. Although each e-mail message LOOKS like a letter that traditionally starts off with a greeting, it actually isn't. It's a segment of an ongoing conversation. The body of the message is the most complex component of the e-mail.

Messages can vary widely in length, organization, the flow of ideas, the use of quoted text, spelling errors, grammar sophistication, the use of caps, tabs, smileys and other unique keyboard characters, the spacing of paragraphs, and the overall visual "feel" of the message. The structure of the e-mail body reflects the cognitive and personality style of the individual who creates it. People who are compulsive may strive for well organized and logically constructed messages with few, if any, spelling or grammatical errors.

Those with a histrionic flair may offer a more dramatic presentation, where neatness plays a back seat to the expressive use of spacing, caps, unique keyboard characters, and colorful language. People with schizoid tendencies may be pithy, while those who are more impulsive may dash off a disorganized, spelling-challenged message with emotional phrases highlighted in shouted caps.

Empathic people will specifically respond to what their e-mail partners have said. They ask their partners questions about themselves and their lives. But they also construct their messages anticipating what it will be like for the recipient to read it. They write in a style that is both engaging and readily understood. With appropriate use of spacing, paragraph breaks, and various keyboard characters to serve as highlights and dividers, they visually construct the message so that it is easy and pleasing to read. Essentially, they are good writers who pay attention to the needs of their audience. This is quite unlike people with narcissistic tendencies, who have difficulty putting themselves into the shoes of the recipient. They may produce lengthy blocks of unbroken text, expecting that their partner will sustain an interest in scrolling, reading, scrolling, reading, for seemingly endless screens of long-winded descriptions of what the sender thinks and feels.

Paradoxically, the narcissistic person's need to be heard and admired may result in the recipient hitting the delete key out of boredom. A carefully, empathically constructed e-mail sometimes can lack spontaneity. It is possible to over-think and micro-manage the message to the point where it sounds a bit contrived. Perhaps the most effective message is one that strikes a balance between spontaneity and carefully planned organization. Also, short messages with some obvious spelling errors, glitches, or a slightly chaotic visual appearance can be a sincere expression of affection and friendship - as if the person is willing to let you see how they look hanging around the house, wearing an old t-shirt and jeans. Or such a message can be a genuine expression of the person's state of mind at that moment. In the course of an ongoing e-mail relationship, there will be a engaging rhythm of spontaneous and carefully thought out messages that parallels the ebb and flow of the relationship itself.

Experienced e-mailers have developed a variety of keyboard techniques to overcome some of the limitations of typed text - techniques that almost lend a vocal and kinesthetic quality to the message. They attempt to make e-mail conversations less like postal letters and more like a face-to-face encounter. Thoughts and feelings placed in parentheses or brackets are a kind of subvocal muttering to oneself - as if one is thinking outloud, tipping one's hand, allowing the other to peek inside one's head. There's an honest or even vulnerable quality to this parenthetical expression because you're letting the other person in on something that otherwise could be kept hidden.

Actions placed in parentheses indicate body language - an attempt to convey some of the face-to-face cues that are missing in typed text encounters. Options range from a simple standard grin [g] to more complex, personally tailored descriptions. Of course, people have much more conscious control over these parenthetical actions than they do over body language in the in-person world. Voice accentuation can be accomplished using caps, asterisks, underlining, and other keyboard characters. Exclamation points add to the effect. It's an attempt to mimic the changes in voice emphasis that you might hear in face-to-face world as well as the emotions that accompany that emphasis.

A series of dots - "trailers" - can be used creatively in a variety of ways. Usually they mimic a pause in one's speaking. That pause might be used dramatically, to lead the person into or psychologically prepare them for your next idea - sometimes even a "you might want to sit down for this" warning. Or the trailer indicates a pause to breath, a transition in your thinking, or a temporary lapse or faltering in your train of thought. The addition of the "um" and "uh" in that last example helps simulate the sense of hesitation and confusion in that faltering thought process. As the term "emoticons" suggests, these keyboard faces are tagged onto the end of a sentence to enhance emotional expression. Including the smiley, the frown, and the winky, they may amplify the feeling expressed in the sentence, add a subtle affective spin to the sentence, or even contradict its sentiment. The smiley often is used to clarify a friendly feeling when otherwise the tone of your sentence might be ambiguous. It also can reflect benign assertiveness, an attempt to undo hostility, subtle denial or sarcasm, self-consciousness, and apologetic anxiety. The winky is like elbowing your e-mail partner, implying that you both know something that doesn't need to be said outloud.

The ubiquitous LOL (laughing out loud) - which originated in chat rooms - is very handy tool for responding to something funny without having to actually say "Oh, that's funny!" It's feels more natural and spontaneous - more like the way you would respond in a face-to-face situation. The sequence of acronyms listed above indicate increasing levels of mirth - beginning with the weak, perhaps even perfunctory "lol" and moving toward the unrestrained "rolling on floor laughing" and raucous "laughing my ass off."

How and when to use exclamation points is a bit of an art form. Unless the sentiment of the sentence is clearly negative, they tend to lighten up the mood. But like spice in cooking, there are dangers of excess as well as omissions. Leaving out exclamation points entirely - as in the first example above - may result in a message that appears bland or ambiguous.

Without even a hint of enthusiasm, some people might wonder if the sender is suppressing some hostility. On the other extreme, too many exclamation points - as in the third example above - may result in a message mood that seems contrived, shallow, or even uncomfortably manic. A message peppered lightly with exclamations, at just the right spots, can give the message a varying texture of energy that emphasizes what needs to be emphasized.

An advantage of e-mail conversations over face-to-face ones is that you have the ability to quote parts or all of what your partner said in his previous message. Hitting "reply" and then tacking your response to the top or bottom of the e-mail is a quick and easy rejoinder. In some cases it's a very appropriate strategy - especially when your partner's message was short, which makes it obvious what you are replying to. However, inserting a reply at the top or bottom of an entire quoted message which is LONG may be perceived by your partner as laziness or indifference on your part - as if you simply hit the reply button, typed your response, and clicked on "send." The person may not be sure exactly what part of the message you are responding to. You also force your partner to download an unnecessarily long file. Sticking a reply at the end of the lengthy quoted message can be particularly annoying because it forces the person to scroll and scroll and scroll, looking for the reply.

The alternative to quoting the whole message is to select out and respond individually to SEGMENTS of it. The arrow marks may appear at the beginning of each line of quoted text, or the sender may place them a the beginning and end of the quoted segment.

Some people use [snip] to indicate that what follows is quoted text. It takes more time and effort to quote segments rather than the whole message, but there are several advantages. People may appreciate the fact that you put that time and effort into your response. It makes your message clearer, more to the point, easier to read. It may convey to your partner a kind of empathic attentiveness because you are responding to specific things that she said. You are letting the person know exactly what from their message stood out in your mind. Replying to several segments can result in an entertaining and intriguingly rich e-mail in which there are several threads of conversation occurring at the same time, each with a different content and emotional tone.

In one multilevel e-mail, you may be joking, explaining, questioning, recalling a past event, and anticipating a future one. For continuity and clarity, several back-and-forth exchanges can be captured by embedding quoted segments. There is a downside to quoting segments. In flame wars, you often see people citing more and more of what the opponent said, using it as ammunition to launch counterattacks.

A contrast between the greeting and the sign-off may be significant - as if writing the e-mail altered the person's attitudes and feelings. Across a series of messages, the sign-off lines may be a string of repartees between the partners that amplifies, highlights or adds nuance to their dialogue in the message bodies. The progression of exchanged sign-off lines may itself become an encapsulated, Morse-code dialogue between the partners. "Sincerely," "Regards" or other similar sign-offs are rather safe, all-purpose tools borrowed from the world of postal mail. They are formal, polite ways to exit. Some avid e-mailer users use them sparingly because they suggest a snail-mail mentality and a lack of appreciation for the creatively conversational quality of e-mail. Almost invariably, the sender's name follows the sign-off line. Simply typing your real name is the easiest, most straightforward tactic. If the e-mail partners both belong to the same online community, they may have to make a conscious choice about whether to use their real names or their online usernames. The online name can be entertaining and revealing, but changing from that imaginary handle to your real name may be a gesture of honestly and intimacy - a kind of "coming out."

Creatively playing with your sign-off name can be an another effective way to express your state of mind, some aspect of your identity, or your relationship to your e-mail partner. Usually this type of play only feels appropriate with friends, or it indicates that one wishes to be friendly, loose, and imaginative. Proclaiming their identification with net culture, people sometimes apply the common cyberspace practice of fusing two capitalized words to create a "neologistic name" for themselves. Leaving out the sign-off line and/or name may be an omission with meaning. It might suggest a curt, efficient, formal, impersonal, or even angry attitude about the conversation.

The ending could appear especially bureaucratic or impersonal if the person inserts his signature block and nothing else. On the other hand, friends may leave out a sign-off line and name as a gesture of informality and familiarity. "You know it's me." They may assume that the conversation is ongoing - as in a face-to-face talk - so there's no need to type anything that suggests a good-bye. Many e-mail programs offer the option of creating a signature file or "block" that automatically will be placed at the bottom of your message.

People usually place factual or identifying information into that file - such as their full name, title, e-mail address, postal address, institutional affiliation, phone number, etc. It's a prepackaged stamp indicating "who and where I am." What a person puts into that file reflects what they hold dear to their public identity. Some programs offer the feature of writing alternative signature files, which gives the person the opportunity to create several different fingerprints—each one tailored for a specific purpose. For example, one may be formal and factual, another more casual and playful. Each one is a slightly different slice of the person's identity. Because all signature blocks have a non-spontaneous, "prepackaged" feeling to them, friends often make a conscious effort to turn it off when writing to a cyberspace pal. In a sense, you are dropping your status and title while also assuming the person knows your e-mail address, phone number, etc.

The message in which the sig block is first dropped probably reflects the sender's move towards feeling more friendly and casual in the relationship. As with the sign-off line and name, a change in a person's sig block reflects a shift in their identity or in how they wish to present their identity.

Like any subculture, the world of e-mailing has developed a unique language. Having its own novel terms and expressions that outsiders don't understand gives any group a sense of distinctive identity. To be in the group is to be in the know. If you appropriately use the parlance, you are demonstrating your knowledge of and belonging to the subculture. The unique language also evolves for purely practical reasons. It makes communication more efficient.

In the world of avid e-mail users, a variety of acronyms and abbreviations have developed. Many of these were borrowed from chat lingo. A private language also may develop between two people or among a small group of people who e-mail each other frequently.

It may include unique acronyms, expressions, character symbols and words (neologisms) that only those people understand. The evolution of that private language reflects the evolving identity, cohesion, and intimacy of the dyad or group. Usually the language crystallizes around issues that are discussed frequently and therefore personally important to the e-mail partners.

Because e-mail has an adjustable conversing speed, the pacing of message exchanges will vary over the course of an e-mail relationship. The excitement of getting to know each other - and enjoying each others company - will result in an increasing pace that eventually plateaus into a rate of exchange that feels comfortable to both partners. As a general rule, the more frequently people e-mail each other, the more important and intimate the relationship feels to them.

Some people e-mail each other every day, or several times a day. Bursts in the intensity of the pace occur when "hot" topics are being discussed, when recent events in one's life need to be explained, or when work needs to be done. These bursts may reflect a sudden deepening of the intimacy in the relationship.

Declines in the pace may indicate a temporary or longterm weakening of the bonds between the couple - either due to a growing disinterest in the relationship or distractions from other sectors of one's life. Significant changes in the cadence always indicates a significant change in feelings, attitudes, or commitment. When people become enthused about e-mail, they may expect that their partners will respond at a pace as intense as their own enthusiasm. They may even unconsciously experience the interaction as if it is a face-to-face encounter - and so, perhaps unconsciously, they are expecting an almost immediate reply. Experienced e-mail users understand that different people have different paces. Some do e-mail every day; some two or three times a week; some once a week or less. Even avid and regular users have slightly different rhythms. You adjust yourself accordingly. You settle into a tempo that is right for each relationship. You accept that tempo as a meaningful indication of what that relationship is about. Drastic drops in the pace, or an apparent failure of the partner to respond at all, throws you into the "black hole" experience.

The partner's silence may be a sign of anger, indifference, stubborn withdrawal, punishment, laziness, preoccupation with other things... But you don't know for sure. The ambiguity inherent in the no-reply easily can become a blank screen onto which we project our own expectations, emotions, and anxieties.

Without hearing a person's voice - or seeing body language and facial expressions - you may not be exactly sure what the person means. This ambiguity enhances the tendency to project your own expectations, wishes, and anxieties unto the somewhat shadowy figure sitting at the other end of the internet - what is called a "transference reaction."

As an e-mail relationship develops over time, there may be ebbs and flows in the transferential feelings and attitudes towards the other person. When you first connect through e-mail, they tend to be minimal since you do not know the other person and have little psychological investment in the relationship.

Transference reactions are more likely to surface when emotional attachments begin to form but you still do not have a good "feel" for the person due to that lack of f2f cues. Other peak moments occur when emotional topics come up but you are unable to pinpoint exactly where the other person stands on the issue. Under ideal conditions, as we spend more and more time conversing with an e-mail partner, we begin to understand and work through those transference reactions so that we can see the other person as he/she really is.

However, even under the best of circumstances, there often is some aspect of our mental image of the other person that is based more on our own expectations and needs than on the reality of the other person. It may be the way we think he looks, her voice sounds, or some aspect of his personality. We may not even be consciously aware that we've formed that impression until we meet the person f2f and discover, much to our surprise, that they are - in some way - very different than what we expected.

Generally speaking, transference reactions are unconscious. We don't see them coming, and don't fully realize how they are steering our behavior. That's why they can get lead us astray and into trouble. Some incoming e-mail may be prepackaged with transference even though the person is a complete stranger to us. If you have a web site - or other information about you is available on the internet - people can form inaccurate impressions which they launch your way in the form of an e-mail. They may idealize you, detest you, or anything inbetween.

These kind of transference reactions often are deeply ingrained, prepared responses in the person that are ready to leap out at any opportune moment. Leaning towards passive dependency, they are operating at a rather immature interpersonal level. They see others in terms of their own needs rather than as separate people with needs of their own. The spoon-feeder also might be a good example of transference towards one's computer that carries over into transference towards other people. Unfortunately, another common transference reaction is the "chip on my shoulder" e-mail.

People who have antagonistic conflicts with authority figures may feel free to send a flaming e-mail to someone they perceive as an parental figure. The sometimes extreme hostility in such a message reflects the depth and intensity of the transference reaction. Anyone who has a web site that in any way presents themselves as an authority on some topic may be subjected to the "chip on my shoulder" e-mail.

A big advantage of e-mail encounters over f2f ones is that you can keep an exact record of what was said. At your leisure you can reread and reflect on the exchanges between you and your e-mail partner. If two people only know each other via e-mail - and at least one of them saves all of the exchanges messages - we could even make the argument that the "relationship" has been preserved in its entirety. Often, however, a person only saves some of the messages, probably those that are especially meaningful - emotional high points, moments of intimacy, important personal information, or other milestones in the relationship. Comparing the messages saved by one person to those saved by the partner could reveal similarities and discrepancies in what each of them finds most important about the relationship.

One person might savor humor, practical information, personal self-disclosures, emotional recollections, or intellectual debate - while the other may not. Saving mostly one's own messages, or mostly the other person's messages, may reflect a difference in focus on either self or other. The area of significant overlap in saved messages reflects the common ground of interest and attitude that holds the relationship together. It's very possible that there might be a significant difference between partners in the number of saved messages. The person who saves less - or maybe none at all - may have a lower investment in the relationship. Or they may not be as self-reflective about relationships as people who wish to reread and think about what was said. On the other hand, that person may simply have less of a need to capture, preserve, or control the relationship.

There are several stages in the development of an e-mail relationship. First, the people must come in contact with each other. That may seem like a serendipitous or uneventful occurrence - they just "happened" to run into each other on the internet, or that first round of e-mail involved some "simple" request for information. But often there is more going on below the surface. Although, theoretically, people can connect with everyone else on the internet, they don't. They establish ongoing relationships with only a handful of people. Consciously - and often unconsciously - we filter through the hundreds and thousands of names that scroll down our monitor and select out those people that have similar interests to ours, those that address our psychological and emotional needs those that fit our transference dynamics. When reflecting on one of your ongoing e-mail relationships, it's interesting to open your archive and look up those first few messages that were exchanged. Those first few messages can reveal the needs and emotional dynamics that sparked the relationship. As in all relationships, the momentum begins with those sparked dynamics and evolves from there.

The people gradually reveal more about themselves to each other, which adds more layers of complexity onto the core dynamics that drew them together. The lack of face-to-face cues encourages them to discuss thoughts and feelings that they otherwise might not reveal - which helps solidify the bond between them. But filling in for that lack of face-to-face cues also deepens the relationship. Because cyberspace easily can be a world isolated from one's "real" life - a world where you can remain anonymous or take on an imaginative identity - revealing your ACTUAL identity is taken as a sign of intimacy and commitment. The more people start to share that kind of real-world information in their e-mail, the more the relationship is deepening. The developmental path in e-mail relationships is one that leads towards becoming more and more real to the other person. For the relationship to move beyond a certain point, the couple will want and need to have more real-time and face-to-face contact. They might try meeting in online chat, which can make the other person's "presence" seem more powerful and thereby enhance the feeling of actually "being together" in real time. It also tests each other's commitment to the relationship, because you both have to be there at a specific time. If they have the technical skills, they might try communicating with video or audio streaming. They might attach pictures of themselves to their e-mail.

An even bigger move forward is to step outside the sometimes invisible psychological boundary that "we are ONLINE friends." You break the cyberspace barrier by sending letters, photos, and gifts via postal mail.... or telephone the other person... or you take the final, inevitable step of actually meeting your friend in-person. Each of these moves towards becoming more real to the e-mail partner is a significant turning point in the relationship.

The thoughts and feelings that are discussed during and after each of these more intimate contacts builds new dimensions to the relationship. This is especially true of taking that big step forward by meeting your e-mail companion in-person. Both of you are taking that decisive step OUT of cyberspace and into the face-to-face encounter. It can be a bit anxiety-provoking. Some experienced online people feel they can suspend any expectations about what others will actually be like when they meet in-person. They claim that they are rarely surprised by that real world encounter. Others say that got to know someone so well through e-mail that meeting in person seemed very smooth and natural. In many cases, however, finally standing toe to toe with the other person can be a real eye-opener. The companion is not exactly what you expected. They look or talk differently than you had imagined. Some aspect of their personality is very different than you had imagined.

Due to the lack of f2f cues, people do not act the same in e-mail as they do in-person - and that difference may be striking when you meet. On the other hand, the contrast in how they appear on and offline may be the result of the false impression you had formed of them. Standing toe to toe, you have the opportunity to test out the image of your companion that you had created in your mind. You may have wanted or needed the person to be a certain way. Steered by your past intimate relationships, you may have EXPECTED them to be a certain way. Or you may have completely overlooked something in the e-mail that couldn't be ignored in the f2f encounter. Stated in a nutshell, meeting the person gives you the opportunity to understand and work through your transference reactions. Meeting in-person often will deepen the relationship. Afterwards the couple discuss, assimilate, reminisce, and cherish the encounter. They build on it. They share the ways in which the meeting confirmed and altered their perceptions of each other.

As such, ideally, they help each other understand and work through their transference reactions. But the in-person meeting doesn't always enhance the relationship. People may be disappointed after the meeting. The companion was not what they had hoped for. This unfortunate outcome may indicate that transference wishes were strong but off target. Some e-mail companions may not have the opportunity to meet each other. In some cases, the relationship still thrives - though there may be periods when the conversation dwindles. In other cases, the e-mail contact fades away for good. A face-to-face meeting may have been needed to energize the relationship, or perhaps it was inevitable that the relationship would evaporate. Some people choose NOT to phone or meet in-person their e-mail companion, even though such meetings could be arranged. They prefer to limit the relationship to cyberspace.

Perhaps they fear that their expectations and hopes will be dashed, or they feel more safe and comfortable with the relative anonymity of e-mail contact. They may be relishing the online fantasy they have created for themselves. Or they simply enjoy the e-mail relationship as it is and have no desire the develop the relationship any further. In all cases, choosing not to increase face-to-face contact with the e-mail partner is a choice not to make the relationship more intimate, well-rounded, or reality-based.

Experienced e-mailers often have friends and colleagues with whom they converse in-person and via e-mail on a regular basis. These dual relationships can be tricky. Sometimes the two realms become a bit dissociated from each other. The relationship starts to operate on two different psychological levels. Due to the lack of f2f cues in e-mail, thoughts and feelings that are difficult to express in-person may surface online. Those disclosures may occur consciously or unconsciously. Unless those disclosures are quickly brought into the f2f relationship, a gap starts to develop between the online encounters and the in-person meetings. It may become more and more difficult to speak in-person about what was said online.

The f2f relationship may become uncomfortable, or feel stiff and shallow. It's best to prevent this uneasy situation before it starts. Even under the most benign of circumstances, you may experience a tiny psychological hurdle that needs to be jumped in order to bring the online encounter into the f2f encounter, and vice versa. But do jump it. The most rewarding outcome is an integrated in-person and e-mail relationship. The beauty of e-mail is that you have the opportunity to contact people from around the world.

2

Internet: Learning to Live Together

The Internet has been growing at unprecedented rates. Because it is versatile and penetrates deeply into the economy, it is affecting all of society, and therefore has attracted inordinate amounts of public attention. The growth rates of the Internet into the proper context by providing comparisons with other communications services. The overwhelmingly predominant view has been that Internet traffic doubles every three or four months. Such unprecedented rates did prevail during the crucial two-year period of 1995 and 1996, when the Internet first burst onto the scene as a major new factor with the potential to transform the economy.

The Internet traffic is about doubling each year. The evidence was always plentiful, and the only thing lacking was the interest in investigating the question. By the year 2000, though, the myth of Internet traffic doubling every three or four months was getting hard to accept. Very simple arithmetic shows that such growth rates, had they been sustained throughout the period from 1995 to the end of 2000, would have produced absurdly high traffic volumes. For example, at the end of 1994, traffic on the NSFNet backbone, which was well instrumented, came to about 15 TB/month. Had just that traffic grown at 1,500% per year, by the end of 2000, there would have been about 250,000,000 TB/month of backbone traffic in the US. Assume 150 million Internet users in the U.S., that would produce a data flow of about 5 Mb/s for each user around the clock.

The assumption of a doubling of traffic every four months produces traffic volumes which are only slighly less absurd. Table 1 shows estimates for traffic on the Internet. The data for 1990 through 1994 is that for the NSFNet backbone, and so is very precise. It is incomplete only to the extent of neglecting what is thought to have been small fractions of traffic that went completely through other backbones. The data for 1996 through 2000 are estimates, and the wide ranges reflect the uncertainties caused by the lack of comprehensive data.

The voice network still dominated, but was likely to be surpassed by the public Internet within a year or two. In terms of bandwidth, the Internet is already dominant. However, it is hard to obtain good figures, since, as discuss later, the bandwidth of Internet backbones jumps erratically. In terms of dollars, though, voice still provides the lion's share of total revenues.

The growth rates in Internet traffic, as measured in bytes. For many purposes, it is the other measures, namely bandwidth and revenues, that are more important. The reason look at traffic is that more regularity there, and in the long run, there will be direct relations between traffic and the other measures. In particular, based on what observed so far, expect capacity to grow somewhat faster than traffic.

Table 1

Traffic on Internet backbones in US. For each year, shows estimated traffic in terabytes during December of that year

year	*TB/month*
1990	1.0
1991	2.0
1992	4.4
1993	8.3
1994	16.3
1995	?
1996	1,500
1997	2,500 - 4,000
1998	5,000 - 8,000
1999	10,000 - 16,000
2000	20,000 - 35,000

The proposal of a new form of Moore's Law, namely that a doubling of Internet traffic each year is a natural growth rate. This hypothesis is supported by the estimates of Table 1, as well as by evidence presented in of many institutions whose data traffic has been growing at about that rate for many years. It is not a law of nature, but rather, like the Moore's Law for semiconductors, a reflection of the complicated interactions of technology, economics, and sociology. Whether this 'law' continues to hold or not will have important implications for the fiber optic transmission industry. Yet more evidence of how often popular perception and subsequent technology and investment decisions are colored by myths that are easy to disprove, but which nobody had bothered to disprove for an astonishingly long time. The historical growth rates of various communication services, and how they compare to the much higher growth rate of the Internet.

Some of the various types of growth rates that are relevant in different contexts. The evidence about Internet traffic growth rates have been able to assemble. The conventional 'Moore's Law' and the analog are proposing for data traffic. A way of thinking about data traffic growth, based on an analogy with the computer industry.

Internet growth is an unusual subject, in that it has been attracting enormous attention but very little serious study. In particular, the general consensus has been that Internet traffic is doubling every three or four months. Yet no real evidence of that astronomical rate of growth was ever presented. Internet traffic did grow at such rates in 1995 and 1996, but before and since it has been about doubling each year.

Telecommunications has been a growth industry for centuries, but growth rates have generally been modest, except for a few episodes, such as the beginnings of the electric telegraph. For example, the number of pieces of mail delivered in the US grew by a factor of over 50,000 between 1800 and 2000, but that was a growth rate of about 5.6% per year. The number of phone calls in the US grew by a factor of over 230 between 1900 and 2000, for a compound annual growth rate of 5.6%. Long distance calls grew faster, about 12% per year between 1930 and 2000, and transatlantic calls faster yet. One communications industry that has been growing very rapidly recently is wireless communication.

In many other countries, wireless communication has developed faster and plays a bigger role than it does in the U.S. Still, even in the U.S., at the end of 2000, there were close to 100 million cell phones in use, and the rate of growth was far higher than for traditional wired voice services.

The cell phone example is worth keeping in mind, since it shows that volume of traffic or even the number of users has only a slight correlation to value. In the US (unlike several other countries), there were more Internet users than cell phone subscribers at the end of 2000 (around 150 million vs. about 100 million). However, the revenues of the cell phone industry were far higher than those of the Internet. Take a rough estimate of 60 million residential Internet users, and assume they pay an average of $20 per month (both slight overestimates), the total revenues from this segment come to about $15 billion. Business customers, with dedicated connections to the Internet, pay considerably less than that. For example, the 2000 revenues from business Internet connections of WorldCom (whose UUNet unit has the largest backbone in the world, often thought to carry over 30% of the total backbone traffic) were just $2.5 billion. Even in the U.S., basic Internet transport revenues are less than half those of cell phones. Yet volumes of traffic are far higher on the Internet.

The average daily time spent by a subscriber on a cell phone in the US is about 8 minutes. If count wireless communication as taking 8 Kb/s (since compression is used), the total volume of traffic generated by cell phone users in the US at the end of 2000 was only about 1,500 TB/month, a tiny fraction of the 20,000 to 35,000 TB/month traffic on US Internet backbones. The comparison of revenues from Internet connectivity to those of the cell phone industry leads naturally to the next topic, namely a comparison with the entire phone industry. Internet revenues were under $25 billion in the U.S. in 2000.

On the other hand, the revenues of the entire telephone industry (including wireless communication and data services such as private lines leased by corporations) were around $300 billion that year. Thus in terms of revenues, the Internet is still small. Furthermore, it is so intimately tied to the phone industry that it is difficult to see what its role is. The basic technologies that are used for Internet transport were developed initially for voice telephony, but were easily adopted for data. At the transport level, voice has been carried as bits for a long time. What happened is that during the late 1990s, the long distance telecommunications infrastructure has changed. It used to be dominated by the demands of voice transport, and data was a small part of what it carried. Now, however, its development is driven by data, especially Internet. For quite a long time, the volume of data was extremely small, so that even though the growth rate was higher than for voice, this did not affect the overall growth rate of the infrastructure. That was one reason the telecommunications industry has repeatedly been surprised by the demand for bandwidth in the 1990s.

Moreover, the transition from voice to data domination was complicated by the presence of several types of data, with substantially different growth rates. Another reason that the recent upsurge in demand for bandwidth was a surprise is that there had been several previous false predictions that data traffic was about to explode. The excitement of the early 1990s about the 'telecommunications superhighway' and '500 channels to the home,' to be accomplished through technologies such as hybrid fiber-coax, certainly led to large financial losses and serious disappointments. However, there were even earlier periods of extremely rapid growth followed by sudden deceleration. For example, the number of modems in the U.S. grew between 1965 and 1970 at about 60% per year, to over 150,000 at the end of that period. Had that growth rate been maintained, about 200 billion modems in the U.S. by the end of 2000, clearly an absurd number. Instead, it appears that growth in the 1970s followed the projections made around 1970, which predicted annual increases of 25 to 30%.

It is interesting to read the speculations in about the supposedly rosy prospects for electronic cash, distance education, and other data services that were supposed to power the growth of networks. In general, predicting what communications services society will accept, and how it will use them, has been very hard. In particular, even recent history is littered with technologies that seemed extremely promising at one point, such as ISDN or SMDS (Switched Multimegabit Data Services—a high speed packet switched WAN tecnology), but never attained more than a marginal role. There are two aspects of the inability to forecast the prospects of communications technologies that are worth discussing at greater length. One goes back to the earlier discussion of wireless telephony, and how the mobility offered by cell phones appears to be more important for many people than broadband Internet access.

Sometimes, though, higher bandwidth did prevail. In the early days of telephony, there was widespread lack of appreciation of how attractive it would eventually prove to be. The telephone was used primarily for business purposes, and the telegraph appeared to be adequate for that to many. Yet it was the phone that won, even though it appeared to use bandwith very wastefully when compared to the telegraph, and even though it encouraged what was often dismissed as 'idle chatter.' The attractions of instantaneous personal interactions turned out to be crucial in leading to an almost universal penetration of the telephone in industrialized countries. In the last four decades of the 20th century, though, the telecommunications industry several times attempted to extend its success with the voice telephone by introducing videotelephony. This service appeared to offer the attraction of an even deeper level of communication than voice. Yet prospective users have not only not embraced it, but have in many cases treated it with hostility. There is a growth of videoconferencing, but even that is far slower than its proponents had forecasted. For a variety of reasons that have not been completely explained, videotelephony does not appeal to people for person-to-person communication. On the other hand, mobile narrowband voice flourishes. The other aspect of the dismal record in forecasting the prospects of communications technologies that now consider is that of the nature of traffic carried.

Data networks, which in commercial settings go back about four decades, have spent essentially all this time in the shadow of the much larger voice telephone network. It was therefore natural for networking experts to continuously think of voice traffic, and in particular of the possibility of eventually carrying it as data. Looking further out, to a stage where the progress of technology appeared to offer the possibility of data networks becoming much larger than the phone networks, it was also natural to think of enriching the communications medium through the addition of video. Later the huge volume of broadcast data offered further possibilities for traffic that could be carried on data networks. The key point is what was seen as eventually filling data network was streaming multimedia traffic.

The Internet's rise to dominance was a surprise for many reasons, but one of the main ones was that it did not fit this model. Although much current work on Internet technologies is devoted to streaming multimedia, there are good reasons, why such traffic is not likely to dominate. Although it has proven hard to forecast which technologies will be widely adopted, once a service had been successfully introduced, it often showed regular growth rates for extended periods of time. The approximately 30% annual growth rate that had been projected in 1970 for data transmission appears to have held not just in the 1970s, but in the 1980s and most of the 1990s as well. There are no comprehensive statistics. However, there are a few pieces of evidence supporting those growth rates around 1980 in.

Those same growth rates appeared to also hold for long distance private line transmission in the mid 1990s, and for local data bandwidth in the late 1980s and most of the 1990s. The comprehensive data summarized in is especially interesting. During that period, installed computer power came close to doubling each year, and the new 'Information Economy' was taking root, but this was not reflected in the volume of data traffic. This low rate of growth in data transmission may have come from the high cost and poor quality of data transmission, of from other causes, such as lack of uniform standards that would enable easy data communication between companies. It may also have been caused to a large extent by the slow rate at which computation and communication technologies were adopted. Whatever the reasons, this low growth rate of approximately 30% a year in data transmission was higher than that of voice networks. Hence by the mid-1990s, the bandwidth of long distance data networks was already comparable to that of the voice network. The Internet has historically had a growth rate of close to 100% per year in the traffic it carried. It was growing with striking regularity in the early 1990s at this rate. Then it experienced a period of astronomical growth in 1995 and 1996, and then reverted to an approximate doubling each year in 1997, and has continued growing at about that rate through the end of 2000. The big question is how fast it will grow in the future. While the overwhelming preponderance of opinion all through the end of 2000 was that Internet traffic was doubling every three or four months, by early 2001 the consensus started changing. Some analysts even began projecting declines in the growth rates to the 50% per year range by around 2005. And indeed, some sources of growth did dry up. With the crash of telecom stocks, investments slowed, and many dot-coms that had been busily filling transmission pipes with their content disappeared. In a related development, corporate managements started asking for detailed justifications for new data networking expenditures, instead of rushing to endorse any proposals that came along.

At various enterprises, the growth rates of data traffic, which had been close to doubling every year in the late 1990s, began to slow down towards doubling every 18 or 24 months. It is not inconceivable that overall data traffic growth may be moving back to its historical rate of around 30% per year. At this point just remark that the dominant role of the Internet in communications, whether in terms of bandwidth of networks, or popular consciousness, is a fairly recent phenomenon. There had been extensive discussions of the 'Information Superhighway' and the 'National Information Infrastructure' for a long time. Leading thinkers foresaw the possibilities for much improved communication offered by new technologies, and there was tremendous effort devoted to various systems. However, the general expectation was that the 'Information Superhighway' would be composed of a very heterogeneous collection of networks. This was true even as late as the beginnings of the Clinton presidency, in 1993 and 1994. It was only in the mid to late 1990s that the Internet was perceived as evolving towards the all-encompassing network, carrying all types of traffic.

The past 5-10 years have witnessed not only an explosion of activity, but the creation of entirely new sectors within the optical industry. As the concept of WDM began to emerge, many new companies developing WDM transport equipment came into existence. The newer enterprises pushed the older established equipment vendors to more aggressive deployment schedules and a constant downward trend for the corresponding prices of WDM transport equipment followed. In what appeared to be an almost insatiable demand for more bandwidth, a situation arose that allowed the creation of the new companies and the accompanying innovation.

Not only did new equipment vendors emerge, but also new national scale carriers were created. This trend is continuing as the concept of optical layering/networking is gaining acceptance and new optical equipment companies are being formed on a regular basis. They deal not only with 'traditional' WDM transport equipment, but also with terrestrial ultra long haul systems, regional and metro optimized systems, and various incarnations of optical cross connects. There were hundreds of developments and contributions enabling this burst of activity.

When one now speaks of the Internet, it is usually described as an evolution from ARPANET to NSFNET, and finally to the commercial Internet that now exists. Arguably, the phenomenal growth of the Internet started in 1986 with NSFNet. However, the path was very complicated and full of many twists and turns in its roughly 40 year history. From the very early research in packet switching, academia, industry, and the US government have been intertwined as partners. Ironically, the beginnings of the Internet can trace itself back to the Cold War and specifically to the launch of Sputnik in 1957. The US government formed the Advanced Research Agency (ARPA—the name was later changed to DARPA, Defense Advanced Research programme Agency, and later back to ARPA) the year after the launch with the stated goal of establishing a US lead in technology and science. As ARPA was establishing itself, there were several pivotal works in the early 1960s on packet switching and computer communications. These works and the efforts they spawned laid many of the foundations that enabled the deployment of distributed packet networks. Generically speaking, this idea is not much different from what today's Internet has become. Concurrently the National Physical Laboratory (NPL) in England deployed an experimental network called the NPL Network making use of packet switching. It utilized 768 kb/s lines. A year before the Moon landing, in 1968, the first ARPANET requests for proposals were sent out, and the first ARPANET contracts were awarded. Two of the earliest contracts went to UCLA to develop the Network Measurement Center, and to Bolt, Beranek and Newman (BBN) for the Packet Switch contract (to construct the Interface Message Processors or IMPs—effectively the routers).

One of the next major innovations for the fledgling Internet (i.e., ARPANET) was the introduction of the first host-to-host protocol called Network Control Protocal or NCP, which was first used in ARPANET in 1970. By 1972 all of the ARPANET sites had finished implementing NCP. Hence the users of ARPANET could finally begin to focus on the development of applications—another paramount driver for the phenomenal growth and sustained growth of the internet. It was also in 1970 that the first cross-country link was established for ARPANET by AT&T between UCLA and BBN. By 1971, the ARPANET had grown to 15 nodes and had 23 hosts. However, perhaps the most influential work that year was the creation of an email programme that could send messages across a distributed network.

Although there was already considerable work being done on packet networks outside the US, the first international connections to the ARPANET took place in 1973. To put the time frame in perspective this was the same year that Robert Metcalfe did his PhD which described his idea for Ethernet. Also during this year the number of ARPANET 'users' was estimated to be 2000 and that 75% of all the ARPANET traffic (in terms of bytes) was email. One needs to note that in only 1-2 years from its introduction onto the Internet email became the predominant type traffic. The same behaviour took place several years later for HTML, and to a somewhat lesser degree, this was seen for Napster—like traffic within many networks a few years later.

Several other key developments began to take place in the mid 1970s. The initial design specification for TCP published by Vint Cerf and Bob Kahn in 1974. The NCP protocol which was being utilized at the time, tended to act like a device driver, whereas the future TCP (later

TCP/IP) would be much more like a communications protocol. The evolution from ARPANET's NCP protocol to TCP (which in 1978 was split into TCP and IP) was critical in allowing the future growth and scalability of today's Internet. DARPA had three contracts to implement TCP/IP (at the time still called TCP), at Stanford (led by Cerf), BBN (led by Ray Tomlinson) and UCLA (led by Kirsten). Stan-ford produced the detailed specification and within a year there were 3 independent implementations of TCP that could interoperate. It is say that the basic reasons that led to the separation of TCP (which guaranteed reliable delivery) from IP actually came out of work that was done trying to encode and transport voice through a packet switch. It was found that a tremendous amount of buffering was needed, in order to allow for the appropriate reassembly after transmission was completed. This in turn led to trying to find a way to deliver the packets without requiring a guaranteed level of reliability.

In essence, the UDP was created to allow users to make use of IP. In addition, it was also in 1978 that the first commercial version of ARPANET came into existence as BBN opened Telenet. In 1981-82 the first plans were being made to 'migrate' from NCP to TCP. It is claimed by some that it was this event (TCP was established as THE protocol suite for ARPANET) was truly the birth of the Internet—defined as a connected set of networks, specifically those with TCP/IP. A few years later another major development occurred, which later enabled the Internet to scale with the 'explosive' growth and popularity of the future Internet. This was the development of the name server. The name server was developed at the University of Wisconsin. This made it easy for people to use the network since hosts were assigned names and it was not necessary to remember numeric addresses. Much of the credit for the invention of the DNS (domain name server) is credited to Paul Mockapetris of USC/ISI. The year 1983 was also the date for two other key developments on ARPANET.

The first one was the cutover from NCP to TCP on the ARPANET. Secondly, ARPANET was split into ARPANET and MILNET. Although the road was convoluted, this split was one of the key bifurcations points that later allowed NSFNET to come into existence. Soon thereafter the number of hosts on the ARPANET had grown to 1000, and in 1985 the first registered domain was assigned in March. In 1985 NSFNET was created with a backbone speed of 56 kb/s. Initially there were 5 supercomputing centers that were interconnected. One of the paramount benefits of this was that it allowed an explosion of connections to take place. Two years later in 1987, NSF agreed to work with MERIT Network to manage the NSFNet backbone. In 1987 the number of hosts on the Internet broke the 10,000 number. Two year later in 1989 this had grown to around 100,000, and 3 years after that in 1992 it reached the 1,000,000 value. It is noted that if look at how the number of hosts had been growing from 1984 to 1992 that it was still pretty much tracking a growth curve that was less than tripling each year.

In the 1985-86 time frame key decision was made that had very long term impact: that TCP/IP would be mandatory for the NSFNet programme. In the 1988-1990 time frame a conscious decision was made to connect the Internet to electronic mail carriers, and by 1992 most of the commercial email carriers in the US were 'like the Internet'. This was still another development that cemented email as the single most important application to take advantage of the Internet. In 1990 the ARPANET ceased to exist, and arguably NSFNet was the essence of the Internet. Commercial Internet Service Providers began to emerge (PSI, ANS, Sprint Link, to name a few) and the Commercial Internet Xchange (CIX) was organized in 1991 by commercial ISPs to provided transfer points for traffic. NSF's lifting the restriction on the commercial use of the Net was again one of the pivotal decisions. This was again a key bifurcation point, in that this helped set the stage for the complete commercialization of the Net that would follow only a few years later.

In 1991 the upgrading of the NSFNet backbone continued as the work to upgrade to a T3 (i.e., 45 Mb/s links) began. It also interesting to note that it was the next year than the term 'surfing the Internet' was first coined by Jean Armour Polly, only two years before the ARPAnet/Internet celebrated its 25th anniversary. It was in the 1993-1995 time period that several major events seemed to emerge which fueled an almost explosive growth in the popularity of the Internet. One of the key ones was the introduction of 'browsers' most notable Mosaic. This led to the creation of Netscape that went public in 1995. Even as early as 1994 WWW (i.e., predominantly html) traffic was increasing in volume on the Net. By then it was the second most popular type of traffic, surpassed only by ftp traffic. However, in 1995 WWW traffic surpassed ftp as the greatest amount of traffic. In addition the traditional online dial up systems such as AOL, Prodigy and Compuserve began to provide Internet access. In 1996 the net truly became public with the NSFNet being phased out. Soon thereafter major infrastructure improvements were made within the transport part of the Internet.

The Internet is very hard to describe. By comparison, even the voice phone system, which is a huge enterprise, far larger in terms of revenues than the Internet, is much simpler. In the phone system, the basic service is well defined and simple to describe. The users have only limited ability to interact with the system. The Internet is completely different. Users interact with the system in a multiplicity of ways, on wildy different time scales, and there are many complicated feedback loops. The problems that arise in attempting to simulate the Internet. The problems of measuring the Internet are also formidable.

There are many different measures that are relevant. For the optical fiber telecommunications industry, it is capacity that is most relevant. Unfortunately there are numerous problems in measuring capacity. Much of the fiber is not lit, and even when it is lit, often only a few wavelengths are lit. Finally, much of potential capacity is used for restoration, through SONET or other methods. In addition, even at the levels of links used for providing IP traffic, it is hard to obtain accurate capacity measurements, since few carriers provide detailed data. Further, this type of capacity has a tendency to jump suddenly, as bandwidth is usually increased in large steps such as going from OC3 to OC12, and then OC48, a phenomenon that contributes to the low utilization of data links. Thus there is little regularity in capacity growth figures. On the other hand, do find astonoshing regularity in traffic growth, which leads us to propose that a form of 'Moore's Law' applies. In the long run, expect that capacity will grow slightly faster than traffic. For many purposes other measures are important, such as the number of users, how they spend their time, how many and what types of commercial transactions they engage in, and so on.

Whether Internet traffic doubles every three months or just once a year has huge consequences for network design as well as the telecommunications equipment industry. Much of the excitement about and funding for novel technologies appear to be based on expectations of unrealistically high growth rates. The comparison of the international bandwidth for Australia and China is instructive. In December 2000, Telstra had about 1,000 Mb/s to the rest of the world, about a third of Chinese bandwidth. Thus, making allowances for other Australian carriers, can speculate that Australia may be exchanging half as much traffic with international destinations as China does, even though the latter has over 60 times the population.

The data for the first two sources (ISPs and exchange points) is not nearly as complete nor reliable as only a few years ago. However, much better data is available for the 'stable sources', and several are examined in much more detail later. Traffic that averages 100 Mb/s is equivalent to about 30 TB/month. Unfortunately the largest ISPs do not release reliable statistics. This situation was better even a couple of years ago. Much of the older data was used in previous studies. For example, MCI used to publish precise data about the traffic volumes on their Internet backbone. Even though they were among the first ISPs to stop providing official network maps, one could obtain good estimates of the MCI Internet backbone capacity from public presentations. These sources dried up when MCI was acquired by WorldCom, and the backbone was sold to Cable &Wireless.

The traffic growth rate for that backbone had been in the range of 100% a year before the change. Today, one can obtain some idea of the sizes (but not traffic) of various ISP networks. The average utilizations of the links in the AboveNet long-haul backbone during those four months were 18%, 16%, 29%, 12%, 11%, and 10%, respectively. If one just adds up the volumes for each link separately, one finds that between March 1999 and April 2001, the total volumes of traffic increased at an annual growth rate of about 200%. However, this figure has to be treated with caution, as actual traffic almost surely increased less than 200%. During this period, AboveNet expanded geographically, with links to Japan and Europe, so that at the end it probably carried packets over more hops than before. Since, interested in end-to-end traffic as seen by customers (which can be thought of as the ingress and/or egress traffic into and/or out of 'the network'), deflate the sum of traffic volumes seen on separate backbone links by the average number of hops that a packet makes over the backbones. Even when there is reliable data for a single carrier, such as AboveNet, some of the growth seen may be coming from gains in market share, both from gains within a geographical region, and from greater geographical reach, and not from general growth in the market.

Internet exchange points: When the NSF Internet backbone was phased out in early 1995, it was widely claimed that most of the Internet backbone traffic was going through the Network Access Points or NAPs, which tended to provide decent statistics on their traffic. Currently it is thought that only a small fraction of backbone traffic goes through the NAPs, while most goes through private peering connections. Furthermore, NAP statistics are either no longer available, or not as reliable. This is in sharp contrast to the situation in 1998. As documented elsewhere, there is very little that can be reliably concluded about current growth rates of Internet traffic by examining the statistics of the public NAPs in the US. However, the situation was slightly better examined a large number of international exchange points. These included LINX (the London Internet exchange), AMS-IX (the Amsterdam Internet exchange), the Slovak Internet exchange, HKIX (a commercial exchange created by the Chinese University of Hong Kong, BNIX (located in Belgium), the INEX (an Irish exchange), and FICX (the Finish exchange). Some of these show growth rates of only about doubling per year while others show much faster growth rates. Traffic interchange statistics are hard to interpret, unless one has data for most exchanges, which is virtually impossible to obtain.

Much of the growth one sees can come from ISPs moving from one exchange to another, moving their traffic from one exchange to another, or else coming to an exchange in preference to buying transit from another ISP. Consider the specific case of LINX. A large part of its growth is almost surely caused by more ISPs exchanging their traffic there. Between March 1999, and March 2000, the ranks of ISPs that are members of LINX have grown by about two thirds, based on the data on the LINX home page. Hence the average per-member traffic through LINX may have increased only around 120% during that year. The traffic from residential U.S. customers will probably begin to increase at a faster rate in the near future. The growth in the number of users is likely to diminish. However, broadband access, in the shape of cable modems and DSL (and to a lesser extent fixed wireless links) will stimulate usage.

The evidence so far is that users who switch to cable modem or DSL access increase their time online by 50 to 100%, and the total volume of data they download per month by factors of 5 to 10. A 5 or 10-fold growth in data traffic would correspond to a doubling of traffic every four months if everyone were to switch to such broadband access in a year. However, that is not going to happen. At the end of 1999, there were about 3 million households in the US with broadband access. The most ambitious projections for cable modem and DSL access call for about 13 million households to have such links in 2003, and between 50-60 million in the year 2007. That is approximately a doubling each year. The traffic from a typical residential broadband customer is likely to grow beyond the level see today, as more content becomes available, and especially as more content that requires high bandwidth is produced.

Still, it is hard to see average traffic per customer among those with broadband connections growing at more than 50% a year, say. Together with a doubling in the ranks of such customers, this might produce a tripling of traffic from this source. Since the ranks of customers with regular modems are unlikely to decrease much, if any, and since their traffic dominates, it appears that the most likely scenario will be for the total residential customer traffic growing no faster than 200% per year, and probably closer to 100% per year. Traffic at various stable institutions, corporate, academic, and governmental. Growth in traffic can be broken down into growth in the number of traffic sources, and growth in traffic per source. For LINX, much of the increase in traffic may be coming from an increase in member ISPs. For individual ISPs, much of the increase in traffic may also be coming from new customers. Yet in the end, that kind of growth is limited, as the market gets saturated.

Consider growth in traffic from large institutions that are already well wired, such as corporations and universities. Most corporations do not publicize information about their network traffic, and many do not even collect it. However, there are some exceptions. Internal corporate traffic appears to be growing much more slowly than the public Internet traffic. Data for retail private lines as well as for Frame Relay and ATM services show aggregate growth in bandwidth in a range of 30-40% per year. The growth is slow for retail private lines, and fast for Frame Relay and ATM. These rates are remarkably close to the growth rate observed in the late 1970s in the US, which was around 30% per year. Thus, it is the corporate traffic to the public Internet that is growing at 100% per year. It is also important to note that in the year 2000 over two thirds of the volume on the public Internet appeared to be business to business.

Thus, the acceleration on the overall growth rate of data traffic to about 100% per year from the old 30% or so a year appears to be a consequence of the advantages of the Internet, with its open standards and any-to-any connectivity.

The spread of Napster through universities is a good example of the last point. Napster and related tools, such as Gnutella and Wrapster, are just the forerunners of other programs for sharing of general information, and not just for disseminating pirated MP3 files. As explained elsewhere, there is already much more digital data on hard disks alone than shows up on today's Internet. Further, this situation is likely to continue.

The arrival of Napster led many institutions to either ban its use or else limit traffic rates to some parts of the campus (typically student dormitories). Push technologies were stifled at least partially because enterprise network administrators blocked them at their firewalls. Email often has size restrictions that block large attachments.

Teleconferencing is only slowly being experimented with on corporate intranets, and even packetized voice sees very limited (although growing) use. Similar constraints apply to most of the content seen on the Web. As long as a large fraction of potential users have limited bandwidth, such as through dial modems, managers of Web servers will have an incentive to keep individual pages moderate in size. Thus, one can see that Internet traffic is subject to a variety of constraints at different levels.

Some are applied by network managers, others by individual users, and the interaction of these constraints with the rising demands is fundamental what produces the growth rates observed. The ability to sustain the high growth rate of Internet traffic will require the creation of new applications that will generate huge traffic of volumes. At current growth rates, by 2005 there will be 8 times as much Internet as voice traffic (on the US long haul networks). If voice were packetized, in all likelihood the voice traffic would only account for about 3% of the Internet traffic. Thus, voice traffic will not fill the pipes that are likely to exit, and neither will traditional Web surfing. This will create a dilemma for service providers, network administrators, and equipment suppliers: to sustain the growth rates that the industry has come to depend on, and to accommodate the progress in technology, new technologies are needed. Such applications will appear disruptive to network operations today, and as such they often have to be controlled. However, tin the long run, they must be encouraged.

It is often said that everything changes so rapidly on the Internet that it is impossible to forecast far into the future. The next 'killer app' could disrupt any plans that one makes. Yet there have been just two 'killer apps' in the history of the Internet: email and the Web. Many other technologies that had been widely touted as the next 'killer app,' such as Push technology, have fizzled. Furthermore, only the Web can be said to have been truly disruptive. From the first release of the Mosaic visual browser around the middle of 1993, it apparently took under 18 months before Web traffic became dominant on Internet backbones. It appears overwhelmingly likely that it was the appearance of browsers that then led, in combination with other developments, to that abnormal spurt of a doubling of Internet traffic every three or four months in 1995 and 1996. The text-based transmissions of those services, which probably averaged only a few hundred bits per second per connected user, were replaced by the graphics-rich content of the Web, so transmission rates increased to a few thousand bits per second. Finally, flat rate access plans led to a tripling of the time that individual users spent online, as well as faster growth in number of users.

The Internet was able to support this explosion in use because it was utilizing the existing infrastructure of the telephone network. At that time, the Internet was tiny compared to the voice network. It is likely that the data network that handles control and billing for the AT&T long distance voice services by itself was carrying more traffic than the NSF Internet backbone did at its peak at the end of 1994. Today, by contrast, the public Internet is rapidly moving towards being the main network, so quantum jumps in traffic cannot be tolerated so easily. In late 1999, a new application, Napster appeared that attracted extensive attention and led to many predictions that network traffic would see a major impact. However, upon close examination this does not appear to be completely accurate, and the use of Napster has not increased growth rates much beyond the annual doubling or tripling rates, even within university environments, where Napster is most popular. That is not to say that is has not resulted in huge amounts of traffic, nor that it has not had serious impact on several major networks.

Napster provides software that enables users connected to the Internet to exchange and/or download MP3 music files. The Napster (web) site matches users seeking certain music files with other users who have those files on their computer. The Napster system preferentially uses as sources of files machines that have high bandwidth connections. This means that universities are the primary sources, since other organizations with fast dedicated links, mainly corporations, do not allow such traffic. The result is that although college students are often cited as the greatest users of MP3 files, it is the traffic from universities that gets boosted the most. Regular modem users are usually not affected, since their connections are too slow. However, the proliferation of cable modems and DSL connections that have 'always-on' high bandwidth connectivity is leading to problems for some residential users, especially since the uplink is the one that invariably has the more limited bandwidth. A key reason that Napster is of great interest to us is that similar types of sharing applications effectively turn consumers of information into providers of information. These applications will effectively turn the traditional consumer PCs into Internet servers which will output large amounts of traffic to other users.

In Napster's case this has been predominantly MP3 music files, but other programs, such as Gnutella, work with more general data. It is highly probable that such applications could be one of the key applications that fuel the continued annual doubling or tripling of data traffic.

Napster first became noticeable in the summer of 1999. Its share of the total Internet traffic on many of the university networks has grown from essentially nothing to around 25% of the total traffic by mid to late 2000. In the traffic generated by Napster and its impact on various networks was examined. The amount of Napster traffic that is by several university networks range from around 20% at some to as high as 50%. However, the numbers are often very preliminary, and in some cases they compare Napster traffic to total traffic, while in others it appears that the high values may represent a comparison only to the out traffic. In any event this is a phenomenal growth rate for any single application.

Since it started from zero and data only goes out to about a year from that time, it is risky to extrapolate this initial explosion out indefinitely. In most cases Napster has had a noticeable effect on the growth rate of traffic on this campus, but not an outlandish one. Several networks, such as that of the University of Wisconsin-Madison that Napster traffic making up as much as 30% of the total are not doing anything to limit Napster since they claim that they still have plenty of bandwidth. Others have imposed limits on the total bandwidth available to the dormitories.

The approximate doubling of transmission capacity of each fiber that as described in is analogous to the famous 'Moore's Law' in the semiconductor industry. In 1965, Gordon E. Moore, then in charge of R&D at Fairchild Semiconductor, made a simple extrapolation from three data points in his company's product history. He predicted that the number of transistors per chip would about double each year for the next 10 years. This prediction was fulfilled, but when Moore revisited the subject in 1975, he modified his projection for further progress by predicting that the doubling period would be closer to 18 months. Remarkably enough, this growth rate has been sustained over the following 25 years. There have been many predictions that progress was about to come to a screeching halt , but the most that can be said is that there may have been some slight slowdown recently, the number of transistors in leading-edge microprocessors doubles every 2.2 years.

Experts in the semiconductor area are confident that Moore's 1975 prediction for rate of improvement can be fulfilled for at least most of the next decade. Predictions similar to Moore's had been made before in other areas, and in they were made for the entire spectrum of computing and communications. However, it is Moore's Law that has entered the vernacular as a description of the steady and predictable progress of technology that improves at an exponential rate. Moore's Law results from a complex interaction of technology, sociology, and economics. No new laws of nature had to be discovered, and there have been no dramatic breakthroughs.

On the other hand, an enormous amount of research had to be carried out to overcome the numerous obstacles that were encountered. It may have been incremental research, but it required increasing ranks of very clever people to undertake it. Further, huge investments in manufacturing capacity had to be made to produce the hardware. Perhaps even more important, the resulting products had to be integrated into work and life styles of the institutions and individuals using them. For further discussions of the genesis, operations, and prospects of Moore's Law. The key point is that Moore's Law is not a natural law, but depends on a variety of factors. Still, it has held with remarkable regularity over many decades. While Moore's Law does apply to a wide variety of technologies, the actual rates of progress vary tremendously among different areas. For example, battery storage is progressing at a snail's pace, compared to microprocessor improvements. This has significant implications for mobile Internet access, limiting processor power and display quality. Display advances are more rapid than those in power storage, but nowhere near fast enough to replace paper as the preferred technology for general reading, at least not at any time in the next decade. DRAMs are growing in size in accordance with Moore's Law, but their speeds are improving slowly.

Microprocessors are rapidly increasing their speed and size, but memory buses are improving slowly. For some quantitative figures on recent progress. From the standpoint of a decade ago, had tidal waves of just about everything: processing power, main memory, disk storage, and so on. For a typical user, the details of the PC on the desktop do not matter too much. It is generally assumed that in a couple of years a new and much more powerful machine will be required to run the new applications, and that it will be bought for about the same price as the current one. In the meantime, the average utilization of the processor is low, compression is not used, and wasteful encodings of information are used.

The stress is not on optimizing the utilization of the PC's resources, but on making life easy for the user. To make life easy for the end user, though, clever engineering is employed. Because the tidal waves of different technologies are advancing at different rates, optimizing user experience requires careful architectural decisions. In particular, since processing power and storage capacity are growing the fastest, while communication within a PC is improving much more slowly, elaborate memory hierarchies are built. They start with magnetic hard disks, and proceed through several levels of caches, invisibly to the user. The resulting architecture has several interesting implications, explored in. For example, mirroring disks is becoming preferable to RAID fault tolerant schemes that are far more efficient but slower.

The density of magnetic disk storage increased at about 30% per year from 1956 to 1991, doubling every two and a half years. In the 1990s, the growth rate accelerated, and in the late 1990s increased yet again. By some accounts, the densities in disk drives are about doubling each year. For purposes, the most relevant figure will be total storage of disk drives. However, that study was prepared in 1998, and since then IDC has revised upwards its estimates for disk storage systems towards a continuation of the doubling trend. It seems safest to assume that total magnetic disk storage capacity will be doubling each year for the next decade. However, even if there is a slowdown, say to a 70% annual growth rate, this will not affect arguments too much. The key point is that storage capacity is likely to grow at rates not much slower than those of network capacity. Furthermore, total installed storage is already immense.

An interesting estimate of the volume of information in the world is presented in. It shows that already in the year 1997 on the threshold of being able to store all data that has ever been generated in digital format on hard disks. By now well past that threshold, so future growth in disk capacities will have be devoted to other types of data that we have not dealt with before. Some of that capacity will surely be devoted to duplicate storage. Most of the storage, though, will have to be filled by new types of data. The same process that is yielding faster processors and larger memories is also leading to improved cameras and sensors. These will yield huge amounts of new data, that had not been available before. It appears impossible to predict precisely what type of data this will be. Much is likely to be video storage, from cameras set up as security measures, or else ones that record every movement. There could also be huge amounts of data from medical sensors on bodies. What is clear, though, is that 'the typical piece of information will never be looked at by a human being'. There will simply not be enough of the traditional 'content', nor even of the less formal type of 'content' that individuals will be generating on their own. Huge amounts of data that is machine generated for machine use suggests that data networks will also be dominated by transfers of such data.

There will surely be an increase in the raw volume of streaming real-time traffic, as applications such as videoconferencing move onto the Internet. However, as a fraction of total traffic, such transmissions will not only decrease eventually, but may not grow much at all even in the intermediate future. The huge imbalance in volume of storage and capacities of long distance data networks means that even the majority of traditional 'content' will be transmitted as files, and not in streaming form. For more detailed arguments supporting this prediction. This development is already making its appearance with MP3, Napster, and related programs. The huge hard disk storage volumes also mean that most data will have to be generated locally. There will surely also be much duplication (such as operating systems, movies, and so on that would be stored on millions of computers). Aside from that, there will surely be huge volumes of locally generated data (such as from security cameras and medical sensors) that will be used (if at all) only in highly digested form.

A 'Moore's Law' for data traffic is different from those in other areas, since it depends in a much more direct way on user behavior. In semiconductors, consumer willingness to pay drives the research, development, and investment decisions of the industry, but the effects are indirect. In data traffic, though, changes can potentially be much faster. A residential customer with dial modem access to the Internet could increase the volume of data transfer by a factor of about five very quickly. All it would take would be installation of one of the software packages that prefetch Web sites that are of potential interest, and which fill in the slack between transmissions initiated by the user. Similarly, a university's T3 connection to the Internet could potentially be filled by a single workstation sending data to another institution. Thus any 'Moore's Law' for data traffic is by nature much more fragile than the standard 'Moore's Law' for semiconductors, for example. Thus it is remarkable that so much regularity in growth rates of data transfers.

Links to the public Internet are usually the most expensive parts of a network, and are regarded as key choke points. They are where congestion is seen most frequently at institutional networks. Yet the mere annual doubling of data traffic even at institutions that have plenty of spare capacity on their Internet links means that there are other barriers that matter. The obvious one is the public Internet itself. It is often (some would say usually) congested. A terabit pipe does not help if it is hooked up to a megabit link, and so providing a lightly utilized link to the Internet does not guarantee good end-to-end performance. Yet that is not the entire explanation either, since corporate Intranets, which tend to have adequate bandwidth, and seldom run into congestion, tend to grow no faster than a doubling of traffic each year.

There are other obstructions, such as servers, middleware, and, perhaps most important, services and user interfaces. People do not care about getting many bits. What they care about is the applications. However, applications take time to be developed, deployed, and adopted. 'Internet time,' where everything changes in 18 months, has a grain of truth, but is largely a myth. Except for the ascendancy of browsers, most substantial changes take 5 to 10 years. As an example, it is at least four years since voice over IP was first acclaimed as the "next big thing." Yet its impact so far has been surprisingly modest. It is coming, but it is not here today, and it won't be here tomorrow.

What is perhaps most remarkable is that even at institutions with congested links to the Internet, traffic doubles or almost doubles each year. Users appear to find the Internet attractive enough that they exert pressure on their administration to increase the capacity of the connection.

Existing constraints, such as those on email attachments, or on packetized voice, or video, as well as the basic constraint of limited bandwidth, are gradually loosened. Note that this is similar to the process that produces the standard Moore's Law for PCs. Intel, Micron, Toshiba, and the rest of the computer industry would surely produce faster advances if users bought new PCs every year. Instead, a typical PC is used for three to four years. On one hand there is pressure to keep expenditures on new equipment and software under control, and also to minimize the complexity of the computing and communications support job. On the other hand, there is pressure to upgrade, either to better support existing applications, or to introduce new ones.

Over the last three decades, the conflict between these two pressures has produced a steady progress in computers. Similar pressures appear to be in operation in data networking. In conclusion, cannot be certain that Internet traffic will continue doubling each year. The historically it has tended to double each year. Still, trends in both transmission and in other information technologies appear to provide both the demand and the supply that will allow a continuing doubling each year. Since betting against such 'Moore's laws' in other areas has been a loser's game for the last few decades, it appears safest to assume that data traffic will indeed follow the same pattern, and grow at close to 100% per year.

Much of the almost hyperactivity within the optical fiber telecommunications industry over the past few years can be traced to the perceived and real growth of the traffic on the Internet. The overall growth rate of the Internet for most of its existence was remarkably close to "doubling every year", and anticipate that this rate will continue into the foreseeable future. In effect see a type of Moore's law associated with the growth of data traffic. This type of growth rate is in sharp contrast to the historical growth rates of various methods of communications that tended to be no greater than about 10% per year. Still, even though a doubling each year represents very fast growth, it is only comparable to the rate of progress in transmission capacity. Hence we are unlikely to see the huge increases in spending on optical communication that many business plans had been based on.

Throughout the history of the Internet there have only been two 'killer applications': email and the Web. Several events conspired which allowed an unprecedented explosion in Internet traffic in the 1995-1996 time frame, and the Internet was able to handle this since it made use of the existing telephone industry infrastructure. Since the Internet is quickly approaching the point at which it is the predominant network it is very unlikely that such huge growth rates could be so easily supported in the future. It also appears that, aside from short-range perturbations, there will be neither a 'bandwidth glut' nor a 'bandwidth shortage' going into the foreseeable future, in that supply and demand will be growing at comparable rates.

IP Addressing

Today, the Internet has entered the public consciousness as the world's largest public data network, doubling in size every nine months. This is reflected in the tremendous popularity of the World Wide Web (WWW), the opportunities that businesses see in reaching customers from virtual storefronts, and the emergence of new types and methods of doing business. It is clear that expanding business and social awareness will continue to increase public demand for access to resources on the Internet. There is a direct relationship between the value of the Internet and the number of sites connected to the Internet. As the Internet grows, the value of each site's connection to the Internet increases because it provides the organization with access to an ever expanding user/

customer population. Over the past few years, the Internet has experienced two major scaling issues as it has struggled to provide continuous and uninterrupted growth:

— The eventual exhaustion of the IPv4 address space

— The ability to route traffic between the ever increasing number of networks that comprise the Internet.

The first problem is concerned with the eventual depletion of the IP address space. The current version of IP, IP version 4 (IPv4), defines a 32-bit address which means that there are only 2^{32} (4,294,967,296) IPv4 addresses available. This might seem like a large number of addresses, but as new markets open and a significant portion of the world's population becomes candidates for IP addresses, the finite number of IP addresses will eventually be exhausted. The address shortage problem is aggravated by the fact that portions of the IP address space have not been efficiently allocated. Also, the traditional model of classful addressing does not allow the address space to be used to its maximum potential.

The Address Lifetime Expectancy (ALE) Working Group of the IETF has expressed concerns that if the current address allocation policies are not modified, the Internet will experience a near to medium term exhaustion of its unallocated address pool. If the Internet's address supply problem is not solved, new users may be unable to connect to the global Internet! The second problem is caused by the rapid growth in the size of the Internet routing tables.

Internet backbone routers are required to maintain complete routing information for the Internet. Over recent years, routing tables have experienced exponential growth as increasing numbers of organizations connect to the Internet—in December 1990 there were 2,190 routes, in December 1992 there were 8,500 routes, and in December 1995 there were 30,000+ routes. Unfortunately, the routing problem cannot be solved by simply installing more router memory and increasing the size of the routing tables.

Other factors related to the capacity problem include the growing demand for CPU horsepower to compute routing table/topology changes, the increasingly dynamic nature of WWW connections and their effect on router forwarding caches, and the sheer volume of information that needs to be managed by people and machines. If the number of entries in the global routing table is allowed to increase without bounds, core routers will be forced to drop routes and portions of the Internet will become unreachable! The long term solution to these problems can be found in the widespread deployment of IP Next Generation (IPng or IPv6) towards the turn of the century. However, while the Internet community waits for IPng, IPv4 will need to be patched and modified so that the Internet can continue to provide the universal connectivity have come to expect. This patching process may cause a tremendous amount of pain and may alter some of fundamental concepts about the Internet.

When IP was first standardized in September 1981, the specification required that each system attached to an IP-based internet be assigned a unique, 32-bit Internet address value. Some systems, such as routers which have interfaces to more than one network, must be assigned a unique IP address for each network interface. The first part of an Internet address identifies the network on which the host resides, while the second part identifies the particular host on the given network.

In recent years, the network-number field has been referred to as the 'network-prefix' because the leading portion of each IP address identifies the network number. All hosts on a given network share the same network-prefix but must have a unique host-number. Similarly, any two hosts on different networks must have different network-prefixes but may have the same host-number.

Primary Address Classes

In order to provide the flexibility required to support different size networks, the designers decided that the IP address space should be divided into three different address classes—Class A, Class B, and Class C. This is often referred to as 'classful' addressing because the address space is split into three predefined classes, groupings, or categories. Each class fixes the boundary between the network-prefix and the host-number at a different point within the 32-bit address.

One of the fundamental features of classful IP addressing is that each address contains a self-encoding key that identifies the dividing point between the network-prefix and the host-number. For example, if the first two bits of an IP address are 1-0, the dividing point falls between the 15th and 16th bits. This simplified the routing system during the early years of the Internet because the original routing protocols did not supply a 'deciphering key' or 'mask' with each route to identify the length of the network-prefix.

Class A Networks (/8 Prefixes): Each Class A network address has an 8-bit network-prefix with the highest order bit set to 0 and a seven-bit network number, followed by a 24-bit host-number.

Today, it is no longer considered 'modern' to refer to a Class A network. Class A networks are now referred to as '/8s' (pronounced 'slash eight' or just 'eights') since they have an 8-bit network-prefix. A maximum of 126 (2^7-2) /8 networks can be defined. The calculation requires that the 2 is subtracted because the /8 network 0.0.0.0 is reserved for use as the default route and the /8 network 127.0.0.0 (also written 127/8 or 127.0.0.0/8) has been reserved for the 'loopback' function. Each /8 supports a maximum of 16,777,214 (2^{24}-2) hosts per network. The host calculation requires that 2 is subtracted because the all-0s ('this network') and all-1s ('broadcast') host-numbers may not be assigned to individual hosts. Since the /8 address block contains 2^{31} (2,147,483,648) individual addresses and the IPv4 address space contains a maximum of 2^{32} (4, 294, 967, 296) addresses, the /8 address space is 50% of the total IPv4 unicast address space.

Class B Networks (/16 Prefixes): Each Class B network address has a 16-bit network-prefix with the two highest order bits set to 1-0 and a 14-bit network number, followed by a 16-bit host-number. Class B networks are now referred to as"/16s" since they have a 16-bit network-prefix. A maximum of 16,384 (2^{14}) /16 networks can be defined with up to 65,534 (2^{16} -2) hosts per network. Since the entire /16 address block contains 2^{30} (1,073,741,824) addresses, it represents 25% of the total IPv4 unicast address space.

Class C Networks (/24 Prefixes): Each Class C network address has a 24-bit network-prefix with the three highest order bits set to 1-1-0 and a 21-bit network number, followed by an 8-bit host-number. Class C networks are now referred to as "/24s" since they have a 24-bit network-prefix. A maximum of 2,097,152 (2^{21}) /24 networks can be defined with up to 254 (2^8 -2) hosts per network. Since the entire /24 address block contains 2^{29} (536,870,912) addresses, it represents 12.5% (or 1/8th) of the total IPv4 unicast address space.

In addition to the three most popular classes, there are two additional classes. Class D addresses have their leading four-bits set to 1-1-1-0 and are used to support IP Multicasting. Class E addresses have their leading four-bits set to 1-1-1-1 and are reserved for experimental use.

Dotted-decimal notation

To make Internet addresses easier for human users to read and write, IP addresses are often expressed as four decimal numbers, each separated by a dot. This format is called 'dotted-decimal notation.' Dotted-decimal notation divides the 32-bit Internet address into four 8-bit (byte) fields and specifies the value of each field independently as a decimal number with the fields separated by dots. Table 2 displays the range of dotted-decimal values that can be assigned to each of the three principle address classes. The "xxx" represents the host-number field of the address which is assigned by the local network administrator.

Table 2: Dotted-decimal ranges for each address class

Address class	*Dotted-decimal notation ranges*
A (/8 prefixes)	1.xxx.xxx.xxx through 126.xxx.xxx.xxx
B (/16 prefixes)	128.0.xxx.xxx through 191.255.xxx.xxx
C (/24 prefixes)	192.0.0.xxx through 223.255.255.xxx

The original designers never envisioned that the Internet would grow into what it has become today. Many of the problems that the Internet is facing today can be traced back to the early decisions that were made during its formative years. During the early days of the Internet, the seemingly unlimited address space allowed IP addresses to be allocated to an organization based on its request rather than its actual need. As a result, addresses were freely assigned to those who asked for them without concerns about the eventual depletion of the IP address space. The decision to standardize on a 32-bit address space meant that there were only 2^{32} (4, 294, 967, 296) IPv4 addresses available.

A decision to support a slightly larger address space would have exponentially increased the number of addresses thus eliminating the current address shortage problem. The classful A, B, and C octet boundaries were easy to understand and implement, but they did not foster the efficient allocation of a finite address space. Problems resulted from the lack of a network class that was designed to support medium-sized organizations. A /24, which supports 254 hosts, is too small while a /16, which supports 65,534 hosts, is too large.

In the past, the Internet has assigned sites with several hundred hosts a single /16 address instead of a couple of /24s addresses. Unfortunately, this has resulted in a premature depletion of the /16 network address space. The only readily available addresses for medium-size organizations are /24s which have the potentially negative impact of increasing the size of the global Internet's routing table. The subsequent history of Internet addressing is focused on a series of steps that overcome these addressing issues and have supported the growth of the global Internet.

Subnetting

In 1985, RFC 950 defined a standard procedure to support the subnetting, or division, of a single Class A, B, or C network number into smaller pieces. Subnetting was introduced to overcome some of the problems that parts of the Internet were beginning to experience with the classful two-level addressing hierarchy:

— Internet routing tables were beginning to grow.

— Local administrators had to request another network number from the Internet before a new network could be installed at their site.

Both of these problems were attacked by adding another level of hierarchy to the IP addressing structure. Instead of the classful two-level hierarchy, subnetting supports a three-level hierarchy.Subnetting attacked the expanding routing table problem by ensuring that the subnet structure of a network is never visible outside of the organization's private network. The route from the Internet to any subnet of a given IP address is the same, no matter which subnet the destination host is on. This is because all subnets of a given network number use the same network-prefix but different subnet numbers. The routers within the private organization need to differentiate between the individual subnets, but as far as the Internet routers are concerned, all of the subnets in the organization are collected into a single routing table entry. This allows the local administrator to introduce arbitrary complexity into the private network without affecting the size of the Internet's routing tables. Subnetting overcame the registered number issue by assigning each organization one (or at most a few) network number(s) from the IPv4 address space.

The organization was then free to assign a distinct subnetwork number for each of its internal networks. This allows the organization to deploy additional subnets without needing to obtain a new network number from the Internet. A site with several logical networks uses subnet addressing to cover them with a single /16 (Class B) network address. The router accepts all traffic from the Internet addressed to network 130.5.0.0, and forwards traffic to the interior subnetworks based on the third octet of the classful address. The deployment of subnetting within the private network provides several benefits:

— The size of the global Internet routing table does not grow because the site administrator does not need to obtain additional address space and the routing advertisements for all of the subnets are combined into a single routing table entry.

— The local administrator has the flexibility to deploy additional subnets without obtaining a new network number from the Internet.

— Route flapping (i.e., the rapid changing of routes) within the private network does not affect the Internet routing table since Internet routers do not know about the reachability of the individual subnets—they just know about the reachability of the parent network number.

Extended-Network-Prefix

Internet routers use only the network-prefix of the destination address to route traffic to a subnetted environment. Routers within the subnetted environment use the extended-network-prefix to route traffic between the individual subnets. The extended-network-prefix is composed of the classful network-prefix and the subnet-number. The extended-network-prefix has traditionally been identified by the subnet mask.

For example, the /16 address of 130.5.0.0 and want to use the entire third octet to represent the subnet-number, need to specify a subnet mask of 255.255.255.0. The bits in the subnet mask and the Internet address have a one-to-one correspondence. The bits of the subnet mask are set to one if the system examining the address should treat the corresponding bit in the IP address as part of the extended-network-prefix. The bits in the mask are set to 0 if the system should treat the bit as part of the host-number.

The standards describing modern routing protocols often refer to the extended-network-prefix-length rather than the subnet mask. The prefix length is equal to the number of contiguous one-bits in the traditional subnet mask. This means that specifying the network address 130.5.5.25 with a subnet mask of 255.255.255.0 can also be expressed as 130.5.5.25/24. The /<prefix-length> notation is more compact and easier to understand than writing out the mask in its traditional dotted-decimal format.

However, it is important to note that modern routing protocols still carry the subnet mask. There are no Internet standard routing protocols that have a one-byte field in their header that contains the number of bits in the extended-network prefix. Rather, each routing protocol is still required to carry the complete four-octet subnet mask.

The final step is to make sure that the organization's address allocation provides enough bits to deploy the required subnet addressing plan. For example, if the organization has a single /16, it could easily deploy 4-bits for the subnet-number and 6-bits for the host number. However, if the organization has several /24s and it needs to deploy 9 subnets, it may be required to subnet each of its /24s into four subnets (using 2 bits) and then build the internet by combining the subnets of 3 different /24 network numbers. An alternative solution, would be to deploy network numbers from the private address space (RFC 1918) for internal connectivity and use a Network Address Translator (NAT) to provide external Internet access.

Defining the Subnet Mask

The first step is to determine the number of bits required to define the six subnets. Since a network address can only be subnetted along binary boundaries, subnets must be created in blocks of powers of two [2 (2^1), 4 (2^2), 8 (2^3), 16 (2^4), etc.]. Thus, it is impossible to define an IP address block such that it contains exactly six subnets. For this example, the network administrator must define a block of 8 (2^3) and have two unused subnets that can be reserved for future growth. Since $8 = 2^3$, three bits are required to enumerate the eight subnets in the block. In this example, the organization is subnetting a /24 so it will need three more bits, or a /27, as the extended-network-prefix. A 27-bit extended-network-prefix can be expressed in dotted-decimal notation as 255.255.255.224. This means that each subnetwork with a 27-bit prefix represents a contiguous block of 2^5 (32) individual IP addresses. However, since the all-0s and all-1s host addresses cannot be allocated, there are 30 (2^5 -2) assignable host addresses on each subnet.

The eight subnets will be numbered 0 through 7. The XXX_2 notation indicates the binary representation of the number. The 3-bit binary representation of the decimal values 0 through 7 are: 0 (000_2),1 (001_2),2 (010_2),3 (011_2),4 (100_2),5 (101_2),6 (110_2), and 7 (111_2). In general, to define Subnet #n, the network administrator places the binary representation of n into the bits of the subnet-number field. For example, to define Subnet #6, the network administrator simply places the binary representation of 6 (110_2) into the 3-bits of the subnet-number field.

When subnetting was first defined in RFC 950, it prohibited the use of the all-0s and the all-1s subnet. The reason for this restriction was to eliminate situations that could potentially confuse a classful router. Note that today a router can be both classless and classful at the same time—it could be running RIP-1 (a classful protocol) and BGP-4 (a classless protocol) at the same time. With respect to the all-0s subnet, a router requires that each routing table update include the route/<prefix-length> pair to differentiate between a route to the all-0s subnet and a route to the entire network. For example, when using RIP-1 which does not supply a mask or prefix-length with each route, the routing advertisements for subnet 193.1.1.0/27 and for network 193.1.1.0/24 are identical - 193.1.1.0. Without somehow knowing the prefix-length or mask, a router cannot tell the difference between a route to the all-0s subnet and the route to the entire network! Regarding the all-1s subnet, a router requires that each routing table entry include the prefix-length so that it can determine if a broadcast (directed or all-subnets) should be sent only to the all-1s subnet or to the entire network. For example, when the routing table does not contain a mask or prefix-length for each route, confusion can occur because the same broadcast address (193.1.1.255) is used for both for the entire network 193.1.1.0/24 and the all-1s subnet 193.1.1.224/27. NETBuilder software permits the forwarding of traffic to a directed broadcast address but does not forward traffic to the all-subnets broadcast address.

With the development of routing protocols that supply the mask or prefix-length with each route, the address space defined by the all-0s and all-1s subnets is once again usable despite the cautions in RFC 950. As a result, vendors have begun to accommodate user demand and permit the configuration of the all-0s and all-1s subnets on router interfaces. There are three factors that determine when these subnets can be used with NETBuilder software.

— The interior gateway protocol (IGP)

— The version number of the NETBuilder software release

— The capabilities of other routers in the organization's network.

To support the deployment of the all-0s and all-1s subnets, the IGP must either carry extended-network-prefixes or have a mechanism to map each route to its extended-network-prefix. Both OSPF and I-IS-IS carry extended-network-prefixes, so they support the deployment of the all-0s and all-1s subnets in arbitrarily complex topologies.

NETBuilder software has taken a phased approach in its support for the deployment of the all-0s and all-1s subnets. Table 3 shows the NETBuilder software version number that first implemented the various features that support the deployment of these subnets. Finally, the other routers in the organization's network need to be able to correctly interpret, learn, and forward traffic to other subnetworks with all-0s and all-1s in their subnet number field.

Table 3: NETBuilder Software Features Supporting the All-0s and All-1s Subnets

Release	*Feature supported*
6.2	Permits a router interface to be configured with all-0s in the subnet field
7.0.0.6	Permits a router interface to be configured with all-1s in the subnet field
7.1	Correctly learns and forwards to routes with all-0s in the subnet field
8.3.0.2 7.2.1	Correctly learns and forwards to routes with all 1s in the subnet field

Variable Length Subnet Masks (VLSM)

In 1987, RFC 1009 specified how a subnetted network could use more than one subnet mask. When an IP network is assigned more than one subnet mask, it is considered a network with 'variable length subnet masks' since the extended-network-prefixes have different lengths. When using RIP-1, subnet masks have to be uniform across the entire network-prefix. RIP-1 allows only a single subnet mask to be used within each network number because it does not provide subnet mask information as part of its routing table update messages. In the absence of this information, RIP-1 is forced to make very simple assumptions about the mask that should be applied to any of its learned routes. How does a RIP-1 based router know what mask to apply to a route when it learns a new route from a neighbor? If the router has a subnet of the same network number assigned to a local interface, it assumes that the learned subnetwork was defined using the same mask as the locally configured interface.

However, if the router does not have a subnet of the learned network number assigned to a local interface, the router has to assume that the network is not subnetted and applies the route's natural classful mask. Assuming that Port 1 of a router has been assigned the IP address 130.24.13.1/24 and that Port 2 has been assigned the IP address 200.14.13.2/24.

If the router learns about network 130.24.36.0 from a neighbor, it applies a /24 mask since Port 1 is configured with another subnet of the 130.24.0.0 network. However, when the router learns about network 131.25.0.0 from a neighbor, it assumes a "natural" /16 mask since it has no other masking information available.

For these reasons, RIP-1 is limited to only a single subnet mask for each network number. However, there are several advantages to be gained if more than one subnet mask can be assigned to a given IP network number:

— Multiple subnet masks permit more efficient use of an organization's assigned IP address space.

— Multiple subnet masks permit route aggregation which can significantly reduce the amount of routing information at the "backbone" level within an organization's routing domain.

VLSM supports more efficient use of an organization's assigned IP address space. One of the major problems with the earlier limitation of supporting only a single subnet mask across a given network-prefix was that once the mask was selected, it locked the organization into a fixed-number of fixed-sized subnets. For example, assume that a network administrator decided to configure the 130.5.0.0/16 network with a /22 extended-network-prefix. Since a subnetted network could have only a single mask, the network administrator was still required to assign the 20 or 30 hosts to a subnet with a 22-bit prefix.

This assignment would waste approximately 1,000 IP host addresses for each small subnet deployed! Limiting the association of a network number with a single mask did not encourage the flexible and efficient use of an organization's address space. One solution to this problem was to allow a subnetted network to be assigned more than one subnet mask. Assume that in the previous example, the network administrator is also allowed to configure the 130.5.0.0/16 network with a /26 extended-network-prefix. A /16 network address with a /26 extended-network prefix permits 1024 subnets (2^{10}), each of which supports a maximum of 62 hosts (2^6 -2). The /26 prefix would be ideal for small subnets with less than 60 hosts, while the /22 prefix is well suited for larger subnets containing up to 1000 hosts.

VLSM also allows the recursive division of an organization's address space so that it can be reassembled and aggregated to reduce the amount of routing information at the top level. Conceptually, a network is first divided into subnets, some of the subnets are further divided into sub-subnets, and some of the sub-subnets are divided into sub 2-subnets. This allows the detailed structure of routing information for one subnet group to be hidden from routers in another subnet group.

The 11.1.0.0/16 subnet is then configured with a /24 extended-network-prefix and the 11.253.0.0/16 subnet is configured with a /19 extended-network-prefix. The recursive process does not require that the same extended-network-prefix be assigned at each level of the recursion. Also, the recursive sub-division of the organization's address space can be carried out as far as the network administrator needs to take it.

When developing a VLSM design, the network designer must recursively ask the same set of questions as for a traditional subnet design. At each level, the design team must make sure that they have enough extra bits to support the required number of sub-entities in the next and further levels of recursion. Assume that a network is spread out over a number of sites. For example, if an organization has three campuses today it probably needs 3-bits of subnetting ($2^3 = 8$) to allow the addition of more campuses in the future. Now, within each campus, there is likely to be a secondary level of subnetting to identify each building. Finally, within each building, a third level of subnetting might identify each of the individual workgroups. Following this hierarchical model, the top level is determined by the number of campuses, the mid-level is based on the number of buildings at each site, and the lowest level is determined by the 'maximum number of subnets/maximum number of users per subnet' in each building.

The deployment of a hierarchical subnetting scheme requires careful planning. It is essential that the network designers recursively work their way down through their addressing plan until they get to the bottom level. At the bottom level, they must make sure that the leaf subnets are large enough to support the required number of hosts. When the addressing plan is deployed, the addresses from each site will be aggregable into a single address block that keeps the backbone routing tables from becoming too large.

The successful deployment of VLSM has three prerequisites:

— The routing protocols must carry extended-network-prefix information with each route advertisement.

— All routers must implement a consistent forwarding algorithm based on the 'longest match.'

— For route aggregation to occur, addresses must be assigned so that they have topological significance.

Since OSPF and I-IS-IS convey the extended-network-prefix information with each route, the VLSM subnets can be scattered throughout an organization's topology. However, to support hierarchical routing and reduce the size of an organization's routing tables, addresses should be assigned so that they are topologically significant. Hierarchical routing requires that addresses be assigned to reflect the actual network topology. This reduces the amount of routing information by taking the set of addresses assigned to a particular region of the topology, and aggregating them into a single routing advertisement for the entire set.

Classless Inter-Domain Routing (CIDR)

By 1992, the exponential growth of the Internet was beginning to raise serious concerns among members of the IETF about the ability of the Internet's routing system to scale and support future growth. These problems were related to:

— The near-term exhaustion of the Class B network address space

— The rapid growth in the size of the global Internet's routing tables

The eventual exhaustion of the 32-bit IPv4 address space Projected Internet growth figures made it clear that the first two problems were likely to become critical by 1994 or 1995. The response to these immediate challenges was the development of the concept of Supernetting or Classless Inter-Domain Routing (CIDR). The third problem, which is of a more long-term nature, is currently being explored by the IP Next Generation (IPng or IPv6) working group of the IETF. CIDR was officially documented in September 1993 in RFC 1517, 1518, 1519, and 1520. CIDR supports two important features that benefit the global Internet routing system:

— CIDR eliminates the traditional concept of Class A, Class B, and Class C network addresses. This enables the efficient allocation of the IPv4 address space which will allow the continued growth of the Internet until IPv6 is deployed.

— CIDR supports route aggregation where a single routing table entry can represent the address space of perhaps thousands of traditional classful routes. This allows a single routing table entry to specify how to route traffic to many individual network addresses. Route aggregation helps control the amount of routing information in the Internet's backbone routers, reduces route flapping (rapid changes in route availability), and eases the local administrative burden of updating external routing information.

CIDR eliminates the traditional concept of Class A, Class B, and Class C network addresses and replaces them with the generalized concept of a 'network-prefix.' Routers use the network-prefix, rather than the first 3 bits of the IP address, to determine the dividing point between the network number and the host number. As a result, CIDR supports the deployment of arbitrarily sized networks rather than the standard 8-bit, 16-bit, or 24-bit network numbers associated with classful addressing. In the CIDR model, each piece of routing information is advertised with a bit mask (or prefix-length). The prefix-length is a way of specifying the number of leftmost contiguous bits in the network-portion of each routing table entry. For example, a network with 20 bits of network-number and 12-bits of host-number would be advertised with a 20-bit prefix length (a /20). The clever thing is that the IP address advertised with the /20 prefix could be a former Class A, Class B, or Class C. Routers that support CIDR do not make assumptions based on the first 3-bits of the address, they rely on the prefix-length information provided with the route. In a classless environment, prefixes are viewed as bitwise contiguous blocks of the IP address space. For example, all prefixes with a /20 prefix represent the same amount of address space (2 12 or 4,096 host addresses). Furthermore, a /20 prefix can be assigned to a traditional Class A, Class B, or Class C network number.

It is important to note that there may be severe host implications when deploy CIDR based networks. Since many hosts are classful, their user interface will not permit them to be configured with a mask that is shorter than the "natural" mask for a traditional classful address. For example, potential problems could exist if wanted to deploy 200.25.16.0 as a /20 to define a network capable of supporting 4,094 (2^{12} -2) hosts. The software executing on each end station might not allow a traditional Class C (200.25.16.0) to be configured with a 20-bit mask since the natural mask for a Class C network is a 24-bit mask. If the host software supports CIDR, it will permit shorter masks to be configured. However, there will be no host problems if were to deploy the 200.25.16.0/20 (a traditional Class C) allocation as a block of 16 /24s since non-CIDR hosts will interpret their local /24 as a Class C. Likewise, 130.14.0.0/16 (a traditional Class B) could be deployed as a block of 255 /24s since the hosts will interpret the /24s as subnets of a /16. If host software supports the configuration of shorter than expected masks, the network manager has tremendous flexibility in network design and address allocation.

In a classful environment, an Internet Service Provider (ISP) can only allocate /8, /16, or /24 addresses. In a CIDR environment, the ISP can carve out a block of its registered address space that specifically meets the needs of each client, provides additional room for growth, and does not waste a scarce resource. Assume that an ISP has been assigned the address block 206.0.64.0/18. This block represents 16,384 (2^{14}) IP addresses which can be interpreted as 64 /24s. If a client requires 800 host addresses, rather than assigning a Class B (and wasting ~64,700 addresses) or four individual Class Cs (and introducing 4 new routes into the global Internet routing tables), the ISP could assign the client the address block 206.0.68.0/22, a block of 1,024 (2^{10}) IP addresses (4 contiguous /24s). However, in a classless environment, the ISP is free to cut up the pie any way it wants. It could slice up the original pie into 2 pieces (each ½ of the address space) and assign one portion to Organization A, then cut the other half into 2 pieces (each ¼ of the address space) and assign one piece to Organization B, and finally slice the remaining fourth into 2 pieces (each 1/8 of the address space) and assign it to Organization C and Organization D. Each of the individual organizations is free to allocate the address space within its "Intranetwork" as it sees fit.

If CIDR appears to have the familiar look and feel of VLSM. CIDR and VLSM are essentially the same thing since they both allow a portion of the IP address space to be recursively divided into subsequently smaller pieces. The difference is that with VLSM, the recursion is performed on the address space previously assigned to an organization and is invisible to the global Internet. CIDR, on the other hand, permits the recursive allocation of an address block by an Internet Registry to a high-level ISP, to a mid-level ISP, to a low-level ISP, and finally to a private organization's network. Just like VLSM, the successful deployment of CIDR has three prerequisites:

— The routing protocols must carry network-prefix information with each route advertisement.

— All routers must implement a consistent forwarding algorithm based on the "longest match."

— For route aggregation to occur, addresses must be assigned so that they are topologically significant.

Another important benefit of CIDR is that it plays an important role in controlling the growth of the Internet's routing tables. The reduction of routing information requires that the Internet be divided into addressing domains. Within a domain, detailed information is available about all of the networks that reside in the domain. Outside of an addressing domain, only the common network prefix is advertised.

Routing in a classless environment

The "best" thing for the size of the Internet's routing tables would be to have Organization A obtain a block of ISP #2's address space and renumber. This would allow the eight networks assigned to Organization A to be hidden behind the aggregate routing advertisement of ISP #2. Unfortunately, renumbering is a labor-intensive task which could be very difficult, if not impossible, for Organization A. The "best" thing for Organization A is to retain ownership of its address space and have ISP #2 advertise an "exception" (more specific) route into the Internet. The exception route allows all traffic for 200.25.0.0/16 to be sent to ISP #1, with the exception of the traffic to 200.25.16.0/21. This is accomplished by having ISP #2 advertise, in addition to its own 199.30.0.0/16 block, a route for 200.25.16.0/21. Using the "longest match" forwarding algorithm, Internet routers will route traffic addressed to host 200.25.17.25 to ISP #2 which will in turn route the traffic to Organization A.

NETBuilder support for CIDR

— Support for CIDR has been implemented on the NET.Builder:

— NETBuilder software implements BGP-4. Support for CIDR is a significant part of the improvements made to BGP-4.

— NETBuilder software uses a routing table structure that understands a network number advertised with a prefix that is shorter than the natural mask. The NETBuilder's routing table and forwarding process ignore the traditional IP address Class and are capable of accepting any network/mask combination that it receives.

— NETBuilder software is capable of performing aggregation by way of BGP-4 configuration parameters. Also, the OSPF AreaRange parameter allows VLSM-based aggregation to be performed within an autonomous system. The network administrator may specify exactly what network numbers and masks are advertised outside of each area or domain.

Scaling the Internet Address Space

The turn of the century, the problems of IPv4 address shortages and expanding Internet routing tables are still with us. The good news is that CIDR is working. The bad news is that recent growth trends indicate that the number of Internet routes is beginning to, once again, increase at an exponential rate. The Internet must find a way to keep the routing table growth linear. The IETF is continuing its efforts to develop solutions that will overcome these problems, enabling the continued growth and scalability of the Internet.

RFC 1917 requests that the Internet community return unused address blocks to the Internet Assigned Numbers Authority (IANA) for redistribution. This includes unused network numbers, addresses for networks that will never be connected to the global

Internet for security reasons, and sites that are using a small percentage of their address space. RFC 1917 also petitions ISPs to return unused network-prefixes that are outside of their assigned address blocks. It will be interesting to see how the Internet community responds since many organizations with unused addresses don't want to return them because they are viewed as an asset.

RFC 1918 requests that organizations make use of the private Internet address space for hosts that require IP connectivity within their enterprise network, but do not require external connections to the global Internet. For this purpose, the IANA has reserved the following three address blocks for private internets:

10.0.0.0 - 10.255.255.255	(10/8 prefix)
172.16.0.0 - 172.31.255.255	(172.16/12 prefix)
192.168.0.0 - 192.168.255.255	(192.168/16 prefix)

Any organization that elects to use addresses from these reserved blocks can do so without contacting the IANA or an Internet registry. Since these addresses are never injected into the global Internet routing system, the address space can simultaneously be used by many different organizations. The disadvantage to this addressing scheme is that it requires an organization to use a Network Address Translator (NAT) for global Internet access. However, the use of the private address space and a NAT make it much easier for clients to change their ISP without the need to renumber or 'punch holes' in a previously aggregated advertisement. The benefits of this addressing scheme to the Internet is that it reduces the demand for IP addresses so large organizations may require only a small block of the globally unique IPv4 address space.

An Internet draft, "Observations on the use of Components of the Class A Address Space within the Internet" <draft-ietf-cidrd-classa-01.txt>, explores the allocation of the upper-half of the currently reserved Class A address space through delegated registries. As the demand for IP addresses continues to grow, it appears that it may be necessary to eventually allocate the 64.0.0.0/2 address space. Note that the 64.0.0.0/2 address block is huge and represents 25% of the IPv4 unicast address space.

Implications of address allocation policies

An Internet draft , "Implications of Various Address Allocation Policies for Internet Routing" <draft-ietf-cidrd-addr-ownership-07.txt>, discusses the fundamental issues that must be considered as the Internet develops a new unicast address allocation and management policies. The draft compares the benefits and limitations of an "address ownership" policy with an "address lending" policy. 'Address ownership' means that when an address block is assigned to an organization, it remains allocated to that organization for as long as the organization wants to keep it. This means that the address block is 'portable' and that the organization would be able to use it to gain access to the Internet no matter where the organization connects to the Internet. On the other hand, 'address lending' means that an organization obtains its address block on a 'loan' basis. If the loan ends, the organization can no longer use the borrowed address block, must obtain new addresses, and renumber before using them.

Hierarchical routing requires that addresses reflect the network topology in order to permit route aggregation. The draft argues that there are two fundamental problems that break the hierarchical addressing and routing model supported by CIDR:

— The continued existence of pre-CIDR routes that cannot be aggregated.

— Organizations that switch ISPs and continue to use addresses from their previous ISP's address block. The new ISP cannot aggregate the old address block as part of its aggregation, so it must inject an exception route into the Internet. If the number of exception routes continues to increases, they will erode the benefits of CIDR and prevent the scalability of the Internet's routing system.

The draft concludes with the recommendation that large providers, which can express their destinations with a single prefix, be assigned address blocks following the 'address ownership' model. However, all allocations from these providers to a downstream clients should follow the 'address lending' model. This means that if an organization changes its provider, the loan is canceled and the client will be required to renumber. This draft has generated a tremendous amount of discussion within the Internet community about the concept of address ownership and what it means in the context of global routing. The authors present a strong argument that the Internet has to make a choice between either address ownership for all or a routable Internet—it can't have both! Smaller organizations that want to own their addresses have concerns about the difficulty of renumbering and their lack of self-determination if their provider or their provider's upstream provider changes its provider.

Procedures for Internet/Enterprise Renumbering (PIER) In the face of the 'address ownership' vs. 'address lending' debate, it is clear that renumbering may become a critical issue in the late 1990s. Procedures for Internet/ Enterprise Renumbering (PIER) is a working group of the IETF charged with the task of developing a renumbering strategy. RFC 1916 is a request by PIER for the Internet community to provide assistance in the development of a series of documents describing how an organization might proceed to renumber its network. The ultimate goal of these documents is to provide education and practical experience to the Internet community.

An Internet draft ,"Suggestions for Market-Based Allocation of IP Address Blocks" <draft-ietf-cidrd-blocks-00.txt>, is a proposal to make IPv4 address assignments transferable and condones the exchange of money as part of the transfer procedure. It suggests that the Internet community embrace the profit motive as an incentive to motivate organizations to act in ways that will improve resource use. This proposal goes hand-in-hand with another proposal to introduce financial incentives for route aggregation.

3

Marketing on Net

The term "E-commerce" has been in wide and somewhat indiscriminate use for a number of years, electronic commerce is such a broad concept that it is difficult to be dogmatic about what should be included in the scope. Many are discovering just how international the Internet really is, processing orders not only from the next town or state, but from the next continent, too. That presents new challenges to sellers who have never shipped overseas and may have little experience with the taxes, duties and customs laws involved.

The United States and 28 other countries, working together as members of the Organization for Economic Cooperation and Development, have signed on to new guidelines. The guidelines: set out principles for voluntary "codes of conduct" for businesses involved in electronic commerce; offer guidance to governments in evaluating their consumer protection laws regarding electronic commerce; and, give consumers advice about what to expect and what to look for when shopping online. The goal is to build consumer confidence in the global electronic marketplace by working to ensure that consumers are just as safe when shopping online as when shopping offline-no matter where they live or where the company they do business with is based. E-Businesses that adhere to the guidelines:

— *Use fair business, advertising and marketing practices*: They provide truthful, accurate and complete information to consumers, and avoid deceptive, misleading or unfair claims, omissions or practices. The businesses can back up all claims, such as claims about how well a product works or how quickly a product will arrive.

— *Provide accurate, clear and easily accessible information about the company and the goods or services it offers:* They disclose the information consumers need to understand whom they're dealing with and what they're buying. These businesses post the company's name, its physical address, including the country, and an email address or telephone number consumers can use if they have questions or problems. They also provide a clear, complete description of the product or service being offered.

— *Disclose full information about the terms, conditions and costs of the transaction*: They provide consumers a full, itemized list of costs involved in the transaction, designating the currency involved, as well as terms of delivery or performance, and terms, conditions and methods of payment. If applicable and appropriate to a transaction, these businesses also include information about restrictions, limitations or conditions of the purchase; instructions for proper use of the product and any safety and health care warnings; warranties and guarantees; cancellation or refund policies; and whether after-sale service is available. If it's possible to carry out a transaction in more than one language, they make available all important terms and conditions in each language.

— *Ensure that consumers know they are making a commitment to buy before closing the deal*: These businesses take steps to protect consumers who are merely "surfing" the 'Net from unknowingly entering into a sales contract. They give the consumer a chance to change the order before committing to the purchase or to cancel it altogether. They also allow consumers to keep a record of the transaction.

— *Provide an easy-to-use and secure method for online payments*: They adopt security measures appropriate to the transactions to make sure that personal information is less vulnerable to hackers.

— *Protect consumer privacy during electronic commerce transactions*: They disclose their privacy policies or information practice statements prominently on their websites, and offer people choices about how their personal information is used. They give consumers the opportunity to refuse having their personal information shared with others or used for promotional purposes.

— *Address consumer complaints and difficulties*: They have policies and procedures to address consumer problems quickly and fairly, and without excessive cost or inconvenience to the consumer. They also take advantage of alternative dispute resolution mechanisms.

— *Adopt fair, effective and easy to understand self-regulatory policies and procedures*: They extend to electronic commerce the same basic level of protections that cover other forms of commerce. The agreement encourages businesses to work with consumer representatives to develop policies and procedures that give consumers the tools they need to make informed decisions and to resolve complaints.

— *Help educate consumers about electronic commerce*: They are helping create a consumer-friendly electronic marketplace. These businesses work with governments and consumer representatives to ensure that consumers understand their rights and responsibilities when participating in online commerce.

Advanced Technology Program (ATP) provides competitive, cost-shared awards for industry to develop high-risk, enabling technologies with broad-based economic benefits. The ATP seeks to help industry fill the gap between basic research and product development, and to invest in technology that wouldn't be developed in a competitive time frame without government cost sharing.

Opportunity for the ATP to make a major difference by supporting work that is unique or complementary to other industrial and government efforts, that offers timely and significant acceleration of research progress, and that requires a critical mass of funding. Because a large number of technology ideas have been submitted to the ATP in the area of electronic commerce, specifically internet commerce, the ATP is seeking industry's input to determine whether a focused program in electronic commerce is warranted. ATP has funded projects related to electronic commerce through General Competitions and through Focused Program competitions in Inform ation Infrastructure for Healthcare, Component-Based

Software, and Technologies for the Integration of Manufacturing Applications. Each project is cost-shared between industry and government, and ATP's average contribution is approximately one million dollars per year. The ATP is a unique partnership between government and private industry to accelerate the development of high-risk technologies that promise significant commercial payoffs and widespread benefits for the economy.

Electronic Data Interchange

Using electronic channels in ordering is no new phenomenon. Electronic commerce between companies existed long before the e-business boom seen the recent half decade. At that time, prior to the Internet's breakthrough, focus was on one-to-one relations, primary in form of EDI (Electronic Data Interchange). While EDI is mainly used to send orders and invoices between pairs of companies, the Internet based e-business expands these possibilities with low-costs, global access, aggregated information, customer support capabilities, searchable product information etc. One of the major disadvantages with EDI has been the cost related to implementation and maintenance of the systems. Due to this, the EDI electronic commerce is not suitable in many-to-many or one-to-many situations. However, already implemented EDI-connections that, for example, handle automatically generated transactions based on inventory replenishment rules from an ERP-system can be very efficient and therefore profitable. When the Internet began to be widely used, some companies started to set up web sites where their customers could browse and, in some cases, buy products.

The first adopters were companies with a manageable sales channel conflict and technology-friendly customers. Still today, most companies only use the web as a marketing channel and only 15 percent of the companies having a web site are able to accept orders via their sites. Some companies have developed the idea of marketing via the Internet and have begun to form virtual hubs, often called electronic marketplaces, where buyers and sellers can meet. At these hubs, products and services from a wide range of supply units can be offered as well as a total assortment from one individual supplier. In some cases the hubs also can support the business processes before, during and after the order. Two years ago the barber said since he couldn't ship haircuts in the mail and his customers couldn't FedEx their heads, the Internet was useless for him. As a few months ago, he is ordering replacements supplies online and accepting appointments via e-mail".

Marketplaces have always played a central role when conducting business. The marketplace, electronic or not, has three major tasks: to match sellers and buyers, to facilitate transactions between the seller and the buyer and to provide an infrastructure including a legal and regulatory framework. The electronic marketplaces can facilitate these functions by offering lower search costs for the sellers and buyers to find each other and by setting standards for how purchases should be accomplished. How the electronic marketplaces will make the information transactions easier and more effective, which makes it possible for the suppliers to customize their offerings depending upon knowledge about the customer. Furthermore, for products that can be distributed electronically, e.g. software, music and texts, the electronic marketplaces can act as stores where the customers can pick their products off the shelf and have them delivered at once.

Electronic marketplace

There are various definitions of what an electronic marketplace or emarketplace really is. An e-marketplace is a site on the Internet where goods and services can be bought from a wide range of suppliers by several buyers. Net Market Makers adds in their definition that the participants should be able to conduct business "without compromising individual processes and relationships among the participants". More general and argue that it is a meeting-point where suppliers and buyers can interact online, i.e. not only on the Internet. An emarketplace can consist of one single producer selling its goods and services to its customers, which is different from the one stated above since the previous definition demands several sellers. Several authors claim that there are different ways by which the emarketplace could be managed. Different authors use the electronic marketplace notation in different ways. Consider that an emarketplace is an electronic hub on an Intranet, an Extranet or the Internet where one or more different sellers and buyers can interact.

This implicates think that an emarketplace can be used within one single business group or a supply chain as well as between different companies in different industries. However, this use of the concept is not concordant with all other authors' usage of the notation even though most authors seem to agree that the emarketplace concept is broad without clear borders. The notation where an emarketplace must include several sellers and several buyers is a subgroup to electronic hub concept. To avoid misunderstandings use electronic hub explicit mean emarketplaces which are within one single company.

Electronic hubs within a single company

A growing concept today is electronic hubs as internal trading-places on companies' Intranets, sometimes called private e-hubs or private emarketplaces. These are most common in large business groups, where different business units interact in a similar way as on the external market. The private e-hub can be used to make companies' processes more efficient, cut lead times and to support an increased information flow. The private e-hub is very similar to an external emarketplace. In both cases, participators are using the e-hub to exchange information and products. While the public emarketplace may have products from numerous different companies the private variant may have products and services from different units within the same company.

Electronic hubs

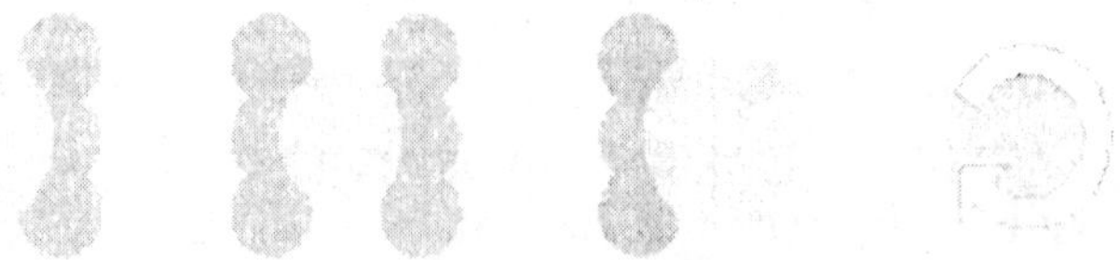

Figure 1: Electronic hub as a superior notation of all types ofemarketplaces

The same holds for the buyer side where the private e-hub might interconnect sales companies at different markets with the supplying part of the parent company. The main differences between emarketplaces within a single business group and those where different companies interact are:

— Level of existing business relationships. Private e-hubs consist of established networks of supply chain partners, while public emarketplaces often are more focused on new customers and partners.

— Level of information exchange. Private e-hubs tend to have a more detailed planning and information exchange than public emarketplaces.

Private e-hub

Private Network of supply chain partners

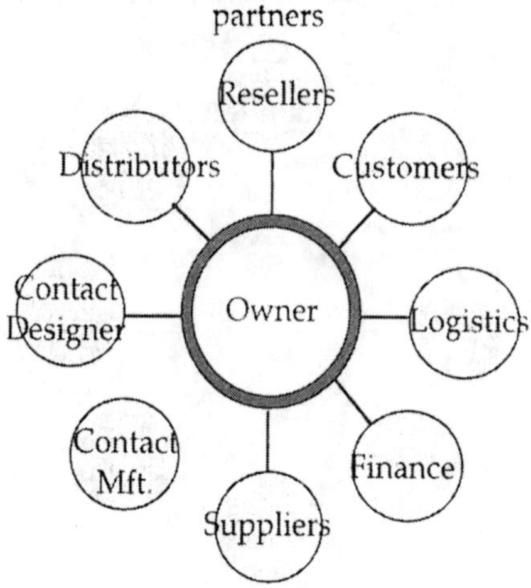

Another difference between the two concepts is the ownership. The private e-hub is governed by one of the parties within the company or the supply chain, for example a logistics department. On other hand, an external company can govern the public emarketplace. However, the purpose and functions of private and public emarketplaces are very similar. Both are meant to be a point where suppliers and sellers can meet to conduct business. They should simplify transactions and decrease the influence from distance between the interacting units. In addition to this, many of the private e-hubs as well as the public electronic marketplaces have supplementary functions as logistics, finance etc. to provide a complete offer. Therefore, believe that most of the theories, which were originally developed for public emarketplaces, can be used when discussing private e-hubs as well.

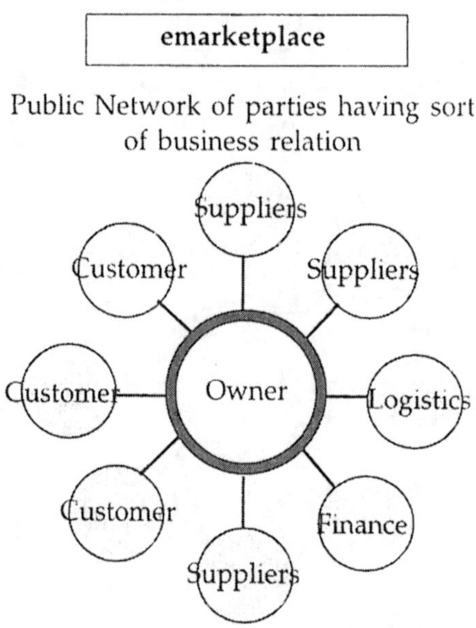

Figure 2: The private hub and the emarketplace concepts are very similar.

Categorization of emarketplaces

The emarketplaces can be categorized in several ways. In different types of emarketplaces classified by ownership, focus, pricing mechanism and how the customers buy. A natural classification of emarketplaces is by whom the marketplace is owned or controlled; this is irrespective of whether the emarketplace acts in the internal supply chain or at the public market. Many authors describe three major types of emarketplaces divided by this aspect as presented below.

emarketplaces controlled by suppliers

The first model in this categorization is the emarketplaces controlled by suppliers. According to Net Market Makers this type of emarketplaces was the first ones. They are often developed when one or more suppliers begin to use the Internet as a new sales or distribution channel, hoping that this will lead to a more efficient order or payment process. Companies using this model are often well established with a dominant market share or companies serving a fragmented market with many small customers. Kaplan & Sawhney also mention that these types of emarketplaces can serve as a forward aggregator that collects many orders from small customers so that larger orders can be sent to the sub-suppliers. An example of an often-quoted supplier-controlled emarketplace is the one handled by Cisco. That marketplace enables buyers to configure their networks, check order status and lead times, confer with technical experts, etc. At the same time as that marketplace facilitates the buying process for Cisco's customers, Cisco has managed to increase its turnover substantially with the same sales force.

Buyer-controlled marketplaces

This model is the opposite of the supplier-controlled emarketplaces. Buyer-controlled emarketplaces are set up by one or more buyers to gain advantages in form of reduced prices, smoother logistics, lower administrative costs, a more efficient procurement process, etc. The suppliers are getting requests to publish their product catalog and prices on these marketplaces. If the buyers do not have enough purchasing power, it is common that the emarketplace involves some sort of intermediary. These intermediaries act as agents or aggregators trying to find the best conditions for its owners. Sometimes this type of marketplace can be compared to reverse auctions with one or only a few buyers but a large number of sellers trying to bid under each other. Many of the buyer-controlled emarketplaces are private and inside the firewall of the buyer. However, there are also public buyer-controlled emarketplaces to which new buyers can affiliate that makes the emarketplace grow. A famous example of this type of emarketplace is Covisint. This emarketplace is set up a number of companies in the automotive industry in order to fulfill the needs of manufacturing input from their suppliers.

Neutral marketplaces

The third model in this categorization is emarketplaces independent from both suppliers and buyers. Instead a third part, a market maker, owns the marketplace and invites participators. This model can sound attractive since neither the buyer's nor the supplier's side has the control, a fact that could lead to a more efficient market. However, there are obstacles that the market maker has to overcome. One problem is the "chicken and egg" dilemma; no sellers want to participate unless a sufficient number of customers are affiliated to the emarketplace and vice versa. The fact that the sellers often join these emarketplaces at the expense of their traditional sales channel forces the market makers to prove that the pros will exceed the cons for the supplier. The market maker can earn money from the emarketplaces in numerous ways. A few examples are: transaction fees, subscription fees, advertising and data mining.

The neutral emarketplace has the best odds for success in a market that is fragmented on both the supplier's and buyer's side. At these markets the neutral marketplace can reduce transaction costs by aggregating order and supply as well as improving matching. Markets that are only fragmented on one side are more suitable for biased emarketplaces, i.e. an emarketplace controlled by a party with certain interests, for example buyers and suppliers. An example is be Band-X.com where telecom operators can sell and purchase. telecommunications capacity.

Focus of the emarketplace

Depending on what goods and services sold at the emarketplace it can be categorized by its focus. There are two major groupings described by various authors: based on products and on industries.

Product-focused

The emarketplaces focused on products, sometimes called horizontal emarketplaces, serve several industries with the same products. The perhaps most well-known emarketplaces with this focus are the many emarketplaces set up to handle MRO (Maintenance, Repair and Operation), i.e. products that companies do not need in their core business but as support. However, the product-focused emarketplaces can also include services. One of these emarketplaces is Ericsson's Click-to-Buy where employees can order non-production materials such as office supplies and consultant services online. This type of focused emarketplaces can bring value to both suppliers and buyers if the market is fragmented and if the cost of conducting purchase is high compared to the value of the goods and services.

Industry-focused

The second kind of emarketplaces in this categorization is the ones focused on a particular industry, sometimes called vertical emarketplaces. These emarketplaces can for example be focused on serving the telecom industry by selling products unique for this industry. Companies get involved in these emarketplaces to buy and sell products that are strategic for their business. There are several reasons to have an emarketplace focusing on a particular type of industry. One reason is to create a critical mass of key suppliers and buyers interested in the products processed at the marketplace. Others are to disseminate knowledge within the industry and to remove inefficiencies in the existing supply chain.

The pricing mechanism used can also categorize the emarketplaces. There are four different classes of price mechanisms that emarketplaces can use:

Catalog model: This model consists of product catalogs presented on the emarketplace. The model creates value for the participants by aggregating fragmented suppliers and buyers who transact often for relatively cheap products. Most preferable, the participants should be pre-qualified and have predefined business rules.

Auction models: This model is the one if non-standard, used or non-saleable returned products should be bought or sold at a market where the perceptions of the product's value differ among the participants. Another application is when there are only a few copies of a product.

Exchange models: Marketplaces with this model work as stock exchanges. A real-time bid-ask matching process is necessary as well as marketwide price determination. To gain high liquidity it is important that the products sold are standardized without need for customization. The model suits best for markets where the prices are rather volatile.

Barter models: Barter has traditionally been used in inflationary economics with shortage of a stable currency. Today emarketplaces can be set up for bartering manufacturing or transportation capacity.

The four classes of price mechanisms they presented another way to categorize emarketplaces combining the pricing mechanism with the focus of the emarketplace. This gives an interesting framework for deciding which type of price mechanism should be used. In an article in Harvard Business Review Kaplan & Sawhney presented a classification that starts from how businesses buy and what they buy. The purchases can be classified into manufacturing and operational inputs. Manufacturing inputs consist of products that go directly into the production while operational input is not industry specific but the same products for several industries. The authors acknowledge that manufacturing inputs normally are traded on an industry-focused marketplace while operational input is more likely to traded on a product-focused marketplace.

A second distinction make is to differentiate between how the products are bought, systematic or spot sourcing. Systematic sourcing involves negotiated long-term contracts with chosen opponents and close relationships while spot sourcing is characterized by a goal to fulfill an immediate need at the lowest possible cost. These two distinctions form the B2B Matrix where emarketplaces can be placed depending on their properties.

MRO Hubs: Emarketplaces in this category are horizontal markets where products are sold with a catalog pricing mechanism. The goods tend to be low-value products with relatively high transaction costs.

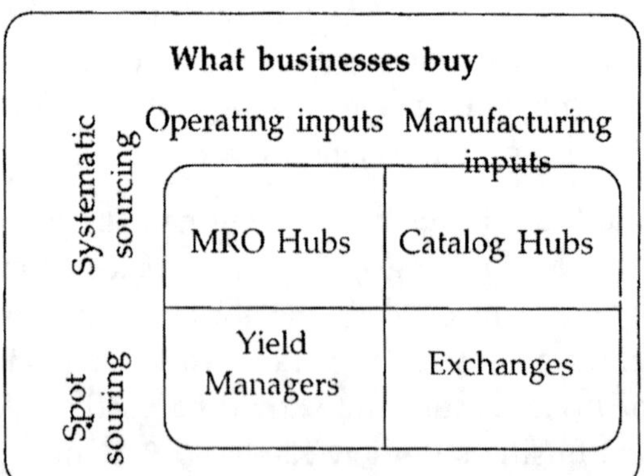

Figure 3: The B2B Matrix

Catalog Hubs: The difference between emarketplaces in this category and those in the past one, is that emarketplaces that are Catalog Hubs are vertical. The products are often more valuable but are still sold at list prices and within pre-negotiated contracts.

Yield Managers: These emarketplaces are horizontal and provide common operating resources like transportation and manufacturing capacity, which enable companies to manage temporary workload peaks. Also buying and selling of excess capacity such as general manpower is included.

Exchanges: Exchanges maintain relationships with the business participators so that they can conduct business without negotiating contracts or conditions. The goods and services handled by these emarketplaces are manufacturing inputs and the pricing mechanism is as the exchange model described earlier.

Functions supported by an emarketplace

To attract customers to an emarketplace, the emarketplace must create enough value for the customer in order to make a change from the traditional channel advantageous. In industries where it is hard for an emarketplace to compete with price, the additional services to the core products are important. The additional services which promote a deeper cooperation between companies will be of substantial importance for the emarketplaces, something that holds for public as well as for private emarketplaces. However, there is a risk when adding too many additional services to an emarketplace, especially to a vertical one. The added services have to be adapted for the customers and they have to be services which the customers demand. Besides, there is always a balancing between the cost of implementing a certain function and the added value for the participators. An emarketplace with too many additional services and products can be hard to navigate and it can be difficult to manage and gain profit from a too diversified marketplace. Strategies like supporting all customers in all processes are receipts for failure.

Furthermore, some activities such as demonstration, testing and persuasion might be handled less efficiently at an emarketplace than by for example a physical sales force. Some activities that might be handled at an emarketplace are mapped according to their business impact and ease of implementation. Functions like ordering, order status, pricing, online configuration etc. are functions which affect the companies' businesses substantially and, at the same time, are comparatively effortless to implement.

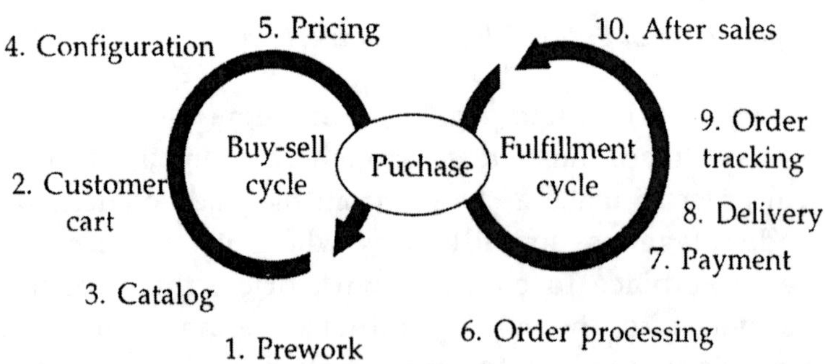

Figure 4: Activities in Internet purchase divided into two cycles

The ordering is one of the best functions suited to handle online. The companies can save a considerable amount of resources in their order processes if these processes are handled by an emarketplace. Even in the best companies up to 20 percent of all orders and invoices contain at least one error, a figure that can decrease down to less than one percent with help of online logistics. Besides, the author states, lead-times in the distribution process typically drop significantly.

Important functions in order to add value for the participating parties Gartner Group has developed a trade model of how purchases are conducted on the Internet. The model is divided into two parts. The first part is a buy-sell cycle in which the customers find products that meet their needs. The buy-sell cycle culminates in a purchase and is followed by a fulfillment cycle which includes activities from order processing and payment to delivery and after sales. In order to provide an online purchase service valuable for the customers, as many as possible of these activities have to be covered by the service.

Content Manager

To facilitate selection of product and supplier the emarketplace has to show the products and services sold in a way that lets the customer search by product, price, capacity etc. Since the data in the product catalog changes continuously, routines for updating have to be settled as well. If several suppliers are tied to the marketplace different strategies for displaying the goods and services might have to be used. For example, some suppliers might not want all customers to see all products or prices, suppliers might want to have their product catalog behind their own network's firewalls etc.

Configurators

If the customer decides to buy a product, the customer might need help to get the right version of the product etc. In order to be able to deliver more sophisticated and customized products and services than MRO commodities online, organizations have to implement some sorts of configurators. Any business segment in which internal expertise is used to make product and solutions recommendations may have advantages from configuration tools.

Aberdeen presents a division of the configurators based upon the primary users of the configurator. While the product configurators are used by the in-house engineering and manufacturing departments in order to ensure that the components in a product are compatible with each other, sales and external sales configurators are used later in the products flow.

A well functioning sales or external sales configurator may help the sales organizations or even the end-customers to place correct orders that fulfill the end-customers' needs.

Requisition routing and approval

After the customers have chosen and configured products, the fulfillment cycle as presented in Figure 4 starts. The first activity is order processing. Most companies have certain policies for which roles are allowed to process orders. When starting with e-business there might be a risk that more employees begin to order products themselves instead of via the traditional internal channels. Emarketplaces with functionality to route requisitions to the appropriate managers for their approval can have advantages since they support the customers in their purchasing process and force the user to follow correct purchasing routines.

Settlement

The emarketplaces have to handle the payment in some way. This can be solved by letting a third party take care of this function, by implementing a standardized payment solution or by building proprietary routines within the company.

Fulfillment

The fulfillment is the most complicated part for an emarketplace to handle, but also the part where the largest savings can be found. After the order has been matched with one of the previously described price mechanisms, a complex series of events set off which lead to delivery of the product. Mainly about physical goods and the consequences they lead to. The hard part is to handle all exceptions that can occur, for example out of stock, incorrect orders etc. The customers want the ability to track orders as well as seeing information about inventory, delivery times and production capacity and they want to have this information in real time.

Many emarketplaces send orders to the suppliers and leave the remainder of the fulfillment to the trading parties, which often handle these parts of the purchase offline. This is due to the fact that the emarketplaces usually are not integrated tightly enough with the supplier's back-office systems and the fact that these systems normally are not built with online ordering in mind and demand human interaction for handling incorrect orders and other exceptions.

It is of substantial importance that the emarketplace adds value for the participating parties. If not, it will be much harder to overcome the critical mass of participators needed to run the emarketplace. This might be particularly true in case of internal marketplaces. The added value can come in form of cut lead-times, lowered costs, better support, more information about the customer etc.

However, when reading about how the different types of e-business models add value to the participants, one must know what the authors have as a reference point. Is the point of reference an isolated company which only communicates with mail or is it a well functioning sales network with an efficient usage of information systems? Several of the below quoted authors, believe, compare with companies which, today, are not using information systems that coordinate them with the other participants in their network.

Added value for buyers

The substantial advantages buyers can get from e-business in form of price transparency, lowered search costs, wider selection etc. For example, buyers can use emarketplaces to focus their purchases of indirect material on preferred suppliers which they have pre-defined agreements with, or to take advantage of dynamic pricing mechanisms such as auction or exchange models.

- *Lower administrative costs:* With faster approvals and easier communication the cost of processing a purchase order can decrease substantially.
- *Control of maverick buying:* By channeling all approvals and funding through the procurement software buyers can control the maverick buying, e.g. buying outside permission or contracts.
- *End-to-end procurement cycle:* The electronic connections make it possible to tie the different parties' system together. For example, buyers can look in their suppliers systems to see inventory etc.
- *Buying consortiums:* By cooperating through an emarketplace small buyers can obtain the same price advantages that earlier was reserved for the large buyers. Furthermore, large companies with decentralized purchasing departments can benefit from coordinating their procurement to take advantage of their corporate purchasing power. In conclusion, the advantages for the buyers can be summarized into possibilities as lower costs for administration and supervising, increased control over the purchasing process and lower prices.

Added value for suppliers

The sellers are the most vulnerable participants on emarketplaces. There is a risk that the sellers have to compete on a more transparent market where the customers only search for low prices. Therefore, the strategy for the sellers is to set up seller-controlled emarketplaces unless the company gains substantially from lowered transaction costs or increased reach from joining a buyer-controlled or a neutral emarketplace.

However, sellers with their own emarketplace may have to open up their web site and invite competitors or at least complementors even if this means a decrease in sales in order to retain the control of the marketplace.

The substantial advantages may be found for sellers if the emarketplace ventures are handled correct. Possible advantages are for example:

— *Lower coordination costs:* As business partners move online, a potential exists to streamline the entire supply chain. Companies connecting with their customers and suppliers through an emarketplace can save costs and efforts by better coordination along the supply chain caused by better and faster information transmission.

— *Higher availability:* The supplier can increase the value experienced by the customer by increasing the availability.

— *Lower customer acquisition costs:* Suppliers can find new customers at a lower cost than earlier.

— *Lower selling cost:* Fewer errors, faster handling and lower inventory levels are possible effects of an emarketplace venture.

— *Some sellers will see higher prices:* Suppliers selling used goods or products with short life span can use emarketplaces with auction models and have a chance to get increased revenues for certain products. This since more interested buyers can be reached and that buyers willing to pay high prices can be found. In addition to constituting an additional sales channel, the emarketplaces, as seen above, may offer the supplier lower administrative cost, better coordination and the possibility to give the customer better support in form of faster supply handling and better information.

Choosing the right way to interact online

As seen during the explanation of different types of electronic hubs or emarketplaces, the choice of type differs depending on market position, overall strategy, market structure etc. In this section will briefly describe some additional factors that should help to decide the appropriate emarketplace strategy.

Berryman et al have compiled four questions companies should ask before they determine which strategy they should adopt. Are there transactions saving or benefits to be realized? Since cost reductions and increased process efficiency are two major reasons to join or start an emarketplace companies should conduct a detailed analysis of their current sales process.

If the most significant improvements are internal, the company should consider starting an internal e-hub to facilitate the processes. Apart from process improvements distribution of printed documents, product development, information management and wider reach might be categories where costs can be reduced or benefits found.

If there are substantial savings or benefits with an emarketplace for a certain product, the competitors are likely to set up own emarketplaces. This pressure from the surroundings can drive the company to an early presence, thus the competition can help the company getting out of the starting blocks. The developing speed of a market depends on the inefficiency of the current transactions and on how sophisticated the buyers are. Customer sophistication can be measured by their ability to place correct orders, understanding the differences between vendors, knowledge about the product etc.

This question is asked to determine which marketplace model that would be most effective. If the company's product is strongly branded and different from its competitors, the company might have better success opportunities if the product is sold from an own e-hub.

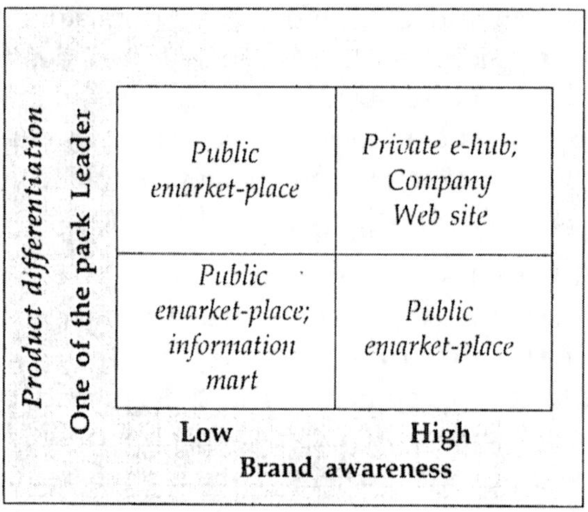

Figure 5: Choosing the right marketplace

Companies selling weaker products or selling products to a market with lower brand awareness should consider joining one or several external emarketplaces. Would a neutral intermediary be beneficial? Involving a third party in the emarketplace venture will, of course, lead to that the eventual profits have to be shared with an additional partaker. However, involving a neutral intermediary can bring positive effects such as more transactions, better service, more information about the customers and their purchase behavior and experience of earlier emarketplace ventures, advantages that might outweigh the drawbacks.

The two most important questions to be answered before deciding if and how emarketplaces should be used is first how the company should manage the change from traditional channels and, second, with which partners the company should get in alliance.

The second of these two questions is closely related to the last of the questions compiled by Berryman et al, while the first concerns something not covered by Berryman's et al questions. Finally, many authors state that traditional sales representatives even in the future will be the key to the buying process. Most suppliers will use emarketplaces as a complement to the traditional channels, rather then as a replacement for them. This because some product segments demand a detailed explanation, deep competence, and negotiation before a purchase. These products may be sold with direct sales contacts and then fulfilled via the emarketplace.

An e-hub is a comprehensive concept which includes public emarketplaces with numerous suppliers and buyers as well as internal marketplaces within a single company aimed to facilitate that company's processes. It is not totally clear what all authors include in their definition of emarketplaces and will therefore use the term electronic hub when talking about internal emarketplaces.

An important point of origin for companies at all times has been their relation to other companies. The individual firm is only a part of a more widespread network of suppliers, intermediaries, distributors and companies selling competing or complementing products and services. This makes it hard to study a company or unit within a company without looking at the company as a part of a larger network. In today's ever increasing competitive environment companies have to prove their right to exist by adding value with their products and services in an effective way. The companies have to focus on continuous improvements and customer satisfaction in order to keep their network position.

To be competitive and profitable over time all the company's value-added activities have to be efficient and coordinated. In 1985 Porter presented a model that segregates the company into a number of activities.The value-adding activities can, according to Porter, be divided into primary activities that are involved in the creation, sales and transfer of the product and support activities that supports the primary ones.

To make the activities as efficient as possible it is important to build linkages between them, both horizontal linkages between primary activities and vertical connections between primary and the supporting activities. For example, the inbound logistics department and the operations department could use a common information system in order to get the purchases done just in time. Linkages also exist between companies, the individual value chain is only a link in a wider value system. How suppliers or buyers perform their activities affect the performance and cost of the activities within the particular firm. By coordinating the suppliers' and the buyers' activities with the ones inside the own firm, all parties can gain considerable advantages.

Virtual value chain

The value chain can be extended in a number of ways. The complement Porter's value chain with a virtual one. While the traditional value chain treats information as a supporting element the virtual value chain model sees information as a source that can add value. That companies should create value by gathering, organizing, selecting, synthesizing and finally distributing the information to the customers.

By doing these five steps the company can create new markets, products and services. Thus, using the virtual value chain highlights the fact that information adds value for the customer. Besides, by collecting and sharing information with the adjacent actors the company can tie tighter relationships and achieve better coordination.

Value networks

The value chain is an important tool in order to break up the individual company into its activities. This is vital since participants conducting the independent activities they are best at ideally form a network. The companies within the networks build more or less tight relationship to each other. Hammarkvist et al have categorized these into: technical relationships, relationships in terms of time, knowledge relationships, social relationships, economical relationships and legal relationships. The bonds facilitate sharing of information within the network and give the participating companies a stability that can lead to a common ambition of development. Areas where networks supported by different forms of information technology add substantial advantages such as

Coverage: The customers can be offered all products and services they need from one single source. This source can coordinate the other participants in the network in a way that shapes an entirety for the customer.

Focusing: By being a part of a network that can offer a wide range of products and services the individual firm can focus on the things they are doing best. If every company in the network focus on their core business the network as a whole can be more efficient.

Process efficiency: To keep their place in the network the companies have to focus on continuously improving their processes. These individual improvements often benefit the whole network.

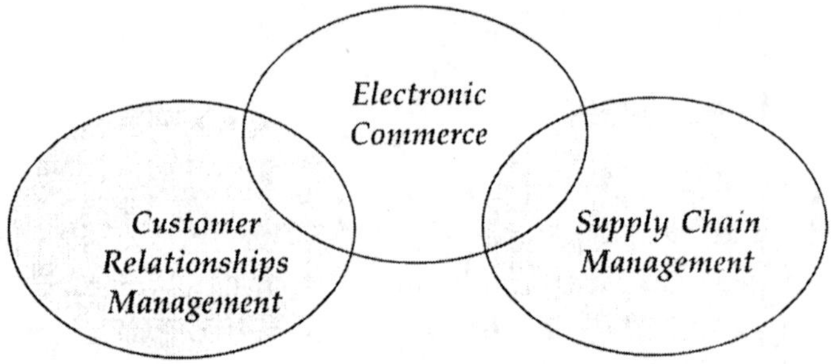

There are three different aspects that companies should focus on in order to improve their networks' positions. These aspects are:

Customer Relationship Management (CRM), Electronic Commerce and Supply Chain Management (SCM): These three areas can, in one way or another, help companies tighten their relations and increase the value of their network positions. The three aspects overlay each other and can be hard to distinguish from each other. For example, both Supply Chain Management and Customer Relationship management have been strongly affected and improved by electronic commerce. Electronic commerce can help joining supply chain management and customer relationship management to an entirety beneficial for the whole business network.

Supply chain management

Even if the definition of Supply Chain Management differs slightly among authors, most authors seem to agree that the concept considers the economic functions of the entire supply chain, from the suppliers of raw materials to the end-customers. Starting with the needs of its customers, a company must analyze how its supply chain is enabling or hindering its efforts to meet those needs. Firms must identify high-value opportunities for improvement through partnership, value-managed relationships or vertical integration. The differences between Supply Chain Management and other channel relationship theories are for example the amount of mutual sharing and monitoring of information and the amount of coordination of multiple levels in the channel.

The Internet is not only simplifying the distribution of information and the possibilities for a closer relationship with the customers and the suppliers. It also highlights the whole supply chain. Suddenly, all participants can see what the different links in the chain are doing and what they are costing. This will lead to that some middlemen disappear while others, who are doing the job better, appear. The supply chain will be reworked in many industries and become more Internet driven.

Three major issues that need to be considered when analyzing supply chain problems are: The flow of products. It is important to map the supply chain as far as to the end-customer. This because it is the end-customer with its purchase process that starts the activities in the supply chain. Moreover, it is possible that difficulties for the final customer may arise between the last organization in the chain and the actual use of the product.

The information flows: Many authors describe the flow of information as the critical key to effective supply chain operations. Thus, the entire channel can be managed more efficiently if its members have access to information relevant for the conduction of their business. However, it is not necessary that all chain members have the same information, as long as they get the information needed for them to conduct their own business better. By having an effective information flow within the supply chain the flow of material through the supply chain can be considerably smoother.

The organization and structure of the supply chain. It is of significant importance that the relationships within the supply chain serve as value adders and do not deteriorate the flow of products or information. There are several strategies for which channels that should be used to reach the end-customers. Whichever chosen the value-adding aspect has to be taken in consideration.

Customer Relationship Management

While Supply Chain Management focus on flows, Customer Relationship Management presents a distinctive relationship perspective. The term is widely used and there is no common definition but roughly all activities for coordinating, consolidating and integrating an enterprise's points of contact with their customers, partners and suppliers can be called Customer Relationship Management. Companies knowing their customers and their preferences can design offers where products, services and sales channels are adjusted to suit the particular customer or segment of customers.

Marketing, sales and service are three main areas for CRM. In each of these three areas companies have to develop different specific CRM capabilities such as 'measuring marketing effectiveness' and 'executing effective marketing plans' in marketing. In sales 'developing and executing an effective channel strategy,' and 'measuring sales effectiveness' are two important capabilities and finally in service and after-sale activities 'understanding customer profitability and cost to serve,' and 'developing differentiated/tiered customer service' are activities the companies should be able to handle. A study by Andersen Consulting showed that companies with specific CRM strategies enjoy better financial performance, similar evidences. To build the foundation for profitability it is important that the whole supply chain focuses on and supports activities to maintain long-term relations with the customers. The use of information technology has increased the possibilities for sharing customer information among channel partners.

The information technology has also made companies move away from market and product centricity towards a complete realignment of business processes in order to integrate with customer processes, which creates additional value to the customer and finally leads to lasting customer relations. In order to achieve this, many companies have begun to build their organizations around customer service and markets instead of around products or divisions. In a presentation of CRM, the maximization of customer value is about understanding the chain that builds a long-term customer relationship. Their model consists of four phases that the customer goes through during a purchase and activities that the selling company can perform to support this.

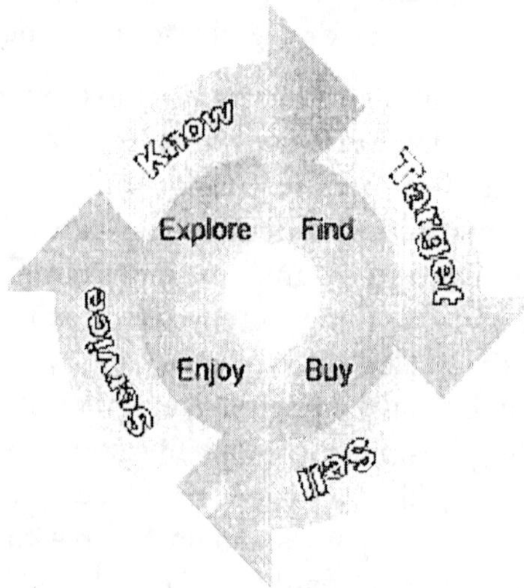

Figure 6: Activities for building a long customer relationship

During the explore phase the customer expresses a need and search for a suitable product. The more the selling company knows about their customer the better information can be presented to the customer. In the following find phase the customer finds and evaluates the product, here the selling company can differentiate their offer so it suits the customer. When this phase is concluded the customer hopefully buys the product. If the sales channel is designed in a suitable way this chance increases. Finally the customer enjoys the purchase and wants adequate service and support.

To support this process the different parties have to get suitable aids. In the following section assisting entities which support the activities in the process will be presented shortly.

Know: Information from databases with customer data, market analysis etc.

Target: For example electronic presence on the Internet designed in a way that makes it possible for the customers to adjust products and services according to their needs.

Sell: Effective sales and distribution channels designed to suit if not all so at least the most important customers.

Service: Order routines, saved information about the customers' earlier questions, systems and buys.

Channel Management

Much work has been done to enhance internal operations while the channels themselves have been somewhat neglected. This implies that managing the supply channels in a beneficiary way should be an excellent way to increase profits and competitiveness. The rapid information technology developments have given channel evolution a valuable boost. The Internet will challenge the present middle role between manufacturer and customer in the channel. However, as many authors claim this does not automatically lead to the death of the middlemen. Instead many new opportunities arise for intermediaries in the new information era. Moreover, using the Internet does not necessarily mean that all other channels will be abandoned. Many of the channels will coexist since they in many cases fulfill different customer needs.

The identified strategies for companies to reach their customers with help from the Internet. Three of these are:

Augment existing channels

Internet can enable companies to sell on markets or to customers that their existing channels are missing. With the augment existing channels strategy companies use the Internet as a new channel which complements their existing channels. The customers addressed by the Internet channel are not the same as them the existing channels address. The term virtualization and means that the additions to the channels mainly should serve well-informed and perceptive customers. However, this does not mean that intermediaries are cut out, merely that information is passed on more effectively in the supply chain. By using the Internet, companies can reach markets that are too fragmented and expensive to serve with a traditional outside sales force.

Enable existing channels for e-commerce

For many companies with existing sales channels, it can be hard to replace them with new electronic channels. Moreover, for many companies their customers are best served with their existing sales channels. The existing sales force has valuable information about the customers, support and configuration etc. Companies using this enabling strategy try to implement an e-commerce solution which affects the entire channel all the way to the end-customer, although not overriding it. The solution should support the sales process and information processes all through the channel. A similar strategy when they present their 'providing value-added services'-strategy. In this strategy, retailers act more like information or service brokers. Their focus shift from distribution to information gathering. This will make them vital in the supply chain again even after the traditional distribution role has become commoditized.

Disintermediate the channel

A technology forecaster at the Institute for the Future explains disintermediation such as "...networks and information systems [that] will allow buyer and seller to interact directly, thereby eliminating intermediaries and radically shortening value chains". They claim that it is about redefining or unbundling the channel partners' roles. More clear definition; they argue that disintermediation is when a certain stage in the supply chain is overridden. Companies that initiate this strategy will have problems with their existing channels since this strategy's aim is to eliminate the middlemen.

Today many companies' intermediaries have substantial control over the customer since they traditionally have had all contact with the customers and have lot of information about the buyer's needs and preferences. Meeker & Phillips believe that there are a number of factors that have to be considered before overriding an intermediary step in the supply chain. There is a difference between service and manufacturing industry. While the producers of physical products always will have to deal with shipment and inventory problems, the service industry does not suffer from these difficulties.

The implies that intermediaries in the service industry are the ones that most likely will be disintermediated. The more digitizable the product is the greater the possibilities for disintermediation are. However, the financial services sector has shown that IT alone will not automatically lead to disintermediation. The several other important factors, such as the current strength of the middlemen that will affect the possibilities for disintermediation. However, if the company succeeds with eliminating companies in the supply chain that do not add value, large savings can be achieved and considerable knowledge about the customers might be obtained.

Strategic channel phases

There is a general trend towards reintermediation. They do not identify this as an actual strategy, it is a development on the market. Reintermediation is when the group of previously disintermediated organizations are able to come back in the supply chain. The Internet will lead to a market development in a number of different phases. Before Internets breakthrough in an industry, very few middlemen only using the Internet to reach its customers exist.

As the industry mature, more intermediaries use only e-commerce in their sales, which leads to a disintermediation phase where the traditional intermediaries are losing the majority of the market they are serving to the ones using Internet as a sales tool. It is possible for the traditional intermediaries to take back parts of the market share lost to the e-commerce-only middlemen by becoming e-commerce-able intermediaries, i.e. able to perform electronic commerce themselves, perhaps on markets previously not served by them. It is not necessarily the samē company as the one that has been disintermediated that retakes market share from the e-commerce-only companies. Moreover, traditional intermediaries can also benefit from the reintermediation phase by providing new value-adding services, unrelated to their previous core business. New companies can also benefit from the reintermediation phase and, for example, become information brokers. The e-commerce-only intermediaries can also gain profits from becoming a technology provider to the existing companies, something that might be more profitable than being intermediaries themselves. Some of the factors explain reintermediation are:

Ownership of co-specialized assets: The area-specific expertise, installed customer base and supplier relationships enhance the existing companies chances to implement a successful new strategy. It is more unlikely that an e-commerce only intermediary, i.e. only doing business online, will have these competitive advantages than a traditional intermediary will.

Economies of scale: E-commerce only intermediaries have to build up a large amount of customers from scratch while the traditional companies already have a large customer base. While new intermediaries have to work hard in order to get the necessary economies of scale, traditional companies start off ahead with, hopefully, enough customers to begin with. The overall goal is to minimize the transaction cost per customer something that might be very costly for new intermediaries. However, these companies will have a first mover competitive advantage, which might be crucial in order to get support from the market.

The different strategic phases because it is not obvious that they consider it possible for a company to use many different channels. Although a certain channel, e.g. a channel serving a specific segment of the customers, might reach the reintermediation phase other channels, served by the same company, might continue to stay in the intermediation or disintermediation phase in the foreseeable future. Furthermore, point out that there still is a possibility for new intermediaries to continue to enter the business arena with the help of the Internet as a part of the reintermediation phase. The group of traditional intermediaries will have the dominant market share, but perhaps not where their traditional core business has been.

Channel Conflicts

Channel conflicts usually occur when two or more intermediaries try to reach parts of the same customer segment. However, this is not necessarily a bad thing since it can force non-rational intermediaries to change or leave the channel. Dangerous conflicts for the producer on the other hand typically occur when one effective channel targets a segment already served by another effective intermediary in another of the company's distribution channels. It is important to point out that channel conflicts are not exclusively between companies, different channels within a single business group may cannibalize on each other as well as on external channels. Made a framework for analyzing when channel conflicts are potentially dangerous and what decisions to make given certain situations. If a dangerous channel conflict has developed, much attention must be devoted to it in order to resolve the crisis.

Lambe states that there are four strategies for resolving channel conflicts:

Negotiation: Discussions aimed at resolving the crisis. The negotiating parties can either bargain with each other or focus on problem solving. There are two types of negotiation strategies that the parties can choose which will affect the relationship in the channel in very different ways:

Predatory: Channel members using this strategy assume that there is a fixed economic value between the companies where the channel conflict occurs, i.e. only one company can benefit from the negotiation. Therefore this player does not care about the other party's needs.

Symbiotic: Channel members using this strategy believe that there are economic benefits from cooperation, i.e. both companies might end up better off. Consequently, these organizations try to help the other party too. This is a problematic situation since both parties benefit the most when being predatory if the other party is using the symbiotic strategy. However, the predatory-predatory situation is the worst possible scenario for both companies, although the superior strength of a company might make this strategy the easiest to adopt and carry through.

Persuasive mechanism: One channel member influences the other participant's behavior. This requires a great deal of trust between the two parties since it is usually very hard to convince a hostile opponent to take view.

Legal remedies: Use of legal methods, e.g. contracts or laws, to persuade the channel member to convert to the organization's view. This should only be used as a last resort since using legal remedies generally is one of the best ways to destroy business relationships.

Climate management: The interactions of boundary personnel over an extended period of time determine the channel climate. Climate management is in essence to prevent conflicts by developing a positive channel climate over time. Conflicts do not normally appear overnight and much effort can be spared if it is detected and prevented at an early stage. Relationship marketing ethics will help people in the value chain to implement a positive channel climate.

The channel conflict is inevitable but that it is not always as dangerous as one thinks. Therefore, it is necessary to analyze the conflicts in order to find out which ones are dangerous and worth concentrating on. Channel conflicts often are good since they force the participants in the channel to improve their business in order to retain their positions. However, if the channel's participants begin to fight for accounts, the result can be a price war between the internal units in the channel which seldom is good for any channel member.

Buying and selling digital products

The Internet has opened new possibilities for distribution of digital products such as software, articles, music or images to customers over the whole world at a very low cost. The Internet plays the role of distribution medium in the case of digital products and he thinks that the range of digital products will expand substantially with the growth of e-business.

There are several differences between digital and physical products. The maybe most significant difference concerns properties that determine how the products are produced and distributed. The fact that the variable cost of producing another copy of a digital product does not increase, even if the number of copies is very large, is unique. Other special properties are:

The digital products are costly to produce but cheap to reproduce: When the first copy is produced, most costs are sunk costs. There are no natural capacity limits or bottlenecks in the reproduction apart from cheap reproduction, distribution of digital products is also inexpensive. A strategic implication of low reproduction and distribution costs is that it makes it possible to give away product samples at zero or to a relatively small extra cost. However, then one has to face the problem of controlling what the customer can try without having to charge them. Selling a bundle of many distinct information goods for a single price often yields higher profits and greater efficiency than selling the same goods separately. The reasons are for example that the bundled products can be tested to work together, the price taken for the bundled package can be higher than the average price when selling the products separately, a reduction in buyer diversity can decrease the development costs etc. Furthermore, concluded that product bundling is controlled by different relative costs as follows:

Production cost: The margin cost of producing another unit which is incorporated in the bundle.

Transaction and distribution cost: The total costs of shipping including administrative work and costs related to the payments attached with the bundle. Binding cost. The cost of setting up the bundle i.e. making changes in format to facilitate the distribution of the items as a bundle.

Menu cost: The cost of handling a multitude of prices. The choice of items in the bundle may be very large making the number of possible bundles even larger that may all be priced differently. However, bundling may also reduce the possibilities for different prices by reducing the total amount of product offerings. The primary reason for bundling is to increase the total revenues from the sales instead of having a cost focus. This is mainly connected to the dispersion in perceived customer value, the perceived value of the bundle often is less diverse than the perceived value of the individual products. This could instead imply that bundling will increase in the future.

Selling digital products online

A framework for deciding which products are most suitable for electronic commerce given a certain business type. The authors state that digital products and services together have the greatest market potential and the least business risk to be sold online. This is mainly explained by benefits gained from the logistical advantages of digital products. An explosive development of digital products and they forecast that the Internet will be the dominating market channel for these products. The reason for this depends not only on the smooth delivery but also of added value from interaction with the customer and new pricing models. Digital products can be bought in form of licenses or keys. For example, a company can buy the right to use Microsoft Excel at an additional computer on its network without having to buy the whole program but just a license. Furthermore, software or music can be bought for the particular time it is used by the customer. It is possible to buy the right to listen to a MP3 song once.

These ways of purchasing may lead to that the number of small purchases increases substantially. To keep the lead-times for this small, frequent buys at a decent level, selling them online with instant delivery might be the way most companies chose. Other authors are not as sure that the Internet is the only or best way of shipping information goods. Providers of proprietary information should keep existing direct channels in addition to an Internet presence. However, the number of steps between the production and delivery of especially digital goods and services will decrease since the producer now can distribute their products on the Internet in a much easier way. Instead of just measuring the suitableness of electronic commerce from the market potential and business risk/logistics importance, Brehmer classifies products into four dimensions. These four dimension do not cover market potential but judge how easy it is to sell the products online. The four dimensions are:

Information-intensity: How much information does the customer need to gather in the entire buying process?

Multisensory appeal: To what extent does the product evaluation require customers to engage the senses of smell, taste and touch?

Atmospherics: How important is the role of the physical store environment and the interaction with the salesperson in the purchase process?

Logistical efficiency: How efficiently can the product be packaged and shipped to individual customers?

Digital products excellently fulfill the last of these four dimensions. This since the products in many cases is produced, or reproduced, at the same time as they are ordered. Since buying digital products rarely demands that the buyer engages his/her senses, these products also seem to be suitable concerning the second dimension. However, digital products in the form of software is often very complex, much information might have to be transferred between the supplier and buyer in order to identify the customer's needs and to describe the product. This may speak against selling advanced software online or, at least, means that the supplier has to know the customer and its needs.

Procurement process

In order to sell and distribute products and services to its customer a company has to understand the customers' procurement processes. This is of course also valid for digital products. If consideration is not taken to how the customers are buying there is a substantial risk that new ventures will be unprofitable or at least less successful than predicted. This is especially significant when introducing new sales or distribution channels. Important things for the selling company to know are for example how purchasing decisions are made, how orders are coordinated and which persons that have to attest the orders. Depending on what author one reads, the definition of the procurement process can differ substantially. However, stages in the procurement process which many authors have in common are: define need, select product and supplier, order, transaction and payment.

The transaction phase, on which this thesis will focus, contains attest, order, order confirmation, delivery and payment. There are several ways in which e-commerce can simplify this second phase, for example by providing better information and a foundation for better supervision. The procurement process within a company can differ substantially depending on the product purchased. The procurement process into two dimensions, the complexity of the product and how often the product is bought. There are significant differences in buying behavior depending of these dimensions.

Buying complex products

When more complex products are bought, more persons from different hierarchical levels are involved as well as more company functions. There are three different roles involved in the purchase:

Executors: Take care of most activities to drive the process forward, office administrators can for example take responsibility for this role.

Determinators: Existing or potential users involved in key decision phases, the executors prepare the information needed while the determinators decide what to do. High level managers often have this role.

Gatekeepers: All categories of roles can serve as gatekeepers. However, only the executors are normally perceived by the selling company as gatekeepers. The gatekeepers act as interfaces for the customer towards the supplier. When buying complex products, the determinators are especially powerful during the first phases when the products are evaluated and a decision is made while the executors is doing the time-consuming following steps. The division of the tasks is due to the fact that the complexity of the products requires more time and knowledge than the determinators possibly can devote to every single product in Phase 2. The executors are often specialized on a certain product, which make them more suitable to handle the practical issues.

A consequence of this is that the executors become more powerful in the purchasing of complex products because of their knowledge and availability of time. However, that what is considered complex is highly personal and depends upon a number of factors such as experience and education. The main differences in activities are, when buying complex products more qualitative analysis and more technical negotiations are performed. The qualitative analysis contains an investigation of which customer needs that the product can fulfill. When less complex products are bought the specific needs are more obvious and a separate analysis is therefore unnecessary. For example, technical negotiations arise when the buyer has a problem and invites a supplier to discuss this problem. Sometimes the supplier can offer the customers unique products or solutions or can recommend products not known to the customer. These types of negotiations can be a necessity since the buyer in some cases does not have enough knowledge to determine what to order to fill the customers needs.

Selling complex products

Companies selling complex products must have routines for how support should be given to the buyers during the whole procurement process and not just in the decision phase. Moreover, the selling company has to know how to present information for the customers' decision-makers in an appropriate way since they often do not have detailed knowledge of differences between similar complex products. The appearance of the distribution channel between the suppliers and buyers is highly determined by product complexity. They argue that up until now, mainly simple products such as books and music CDs have been sold on electronic marketplaces. The authors mean that two factors, asset specificity and product complexity control what the structure between buyers and seller looks like.

Asset specificity: A list of seven types of asset specificities that should be considered when determining the products' properties. These are: site specificity, physical asset specificity, human asset specificity, dedicated assets, brand name capital, temporal specificity and finally time specificity.

Complexity of product description: Complexity of product description is defined as 'the amount of information needed to specify the attributes of a product in enough detail to allow potential buyers (whether producers acquiring production inputs or consumers acquiring goods) to make a selection'.

Products with low asset specificity and low product description complexity are likely to be sold at a traditional market with many buyers and sellers. However, if both factors are higher the authors claim that a single or a few sellers are likely instead of a market consisting of several sellers. Information technology can help to lower the complexity of the product description, but this is something that just recently has been learned by companies.

EDI has been used for decades, the aspects that might do the topic particularly interesting now is the decrease of cost for using electronic connections thanks to the expansion of the Internet. Other important developments from the pure EDI connections are that it has been easier to present information and to interact with other parties. More and more companies have begun to use the Internet in their purchase, sales and distribution. In order to increase volumes, find new markets or customers some companies have started electronic hubs where participators can interact online. These electronic marketplaces can either be private, inside an individual company, helping the units within the business group cooperate and be more effective, or public where many different companies can buy and sell products. The private ones are nearly exclusive for large global companies divided into different subsidiaries or units. Public electronic marketplaces on the other hand can help small companies reach a larger market or help large companies sell to small ones by aggregating orders. Whether private or not, several sellers and buyers interact on an electronic marketplace, even if these belong to the same business group in the private case.

In order to add value for the participating parties the emarketplaces must have more additional functions than just bringing buyers and suppliers together. Apart from being able to handle requisition routing, approval, fulfillment and settlement, it is important that the emarketplace can show the products and services sold in a way that makes it easy for the buyer to browse through the catalog as well as to search for specific properties. Other ways of providing added value are to have additional services, for example financing, credit, insurance and transportation.

The advantages of emarketplaces for the buyers can be summarized in lower costs for administration and supervising and better control over the purchasing process and in some cases lower prices. For the suppliers the emarketplaces can offer an additional sales channel, lower administration cost, better coordination and the possibility to offer the customer rapid order handling and better information. One must know the reference point when talking about the potential advantages with all e-business ventures. In this thesis, the point of reference is a company which is not using information systems that coordinate the company with the other participants in their network in an efficient way.

The emarketplaces can be categorized in a number of ways depending on ownership, focus etc. Different categories have their specific advantages and disadvantages. Depending on the market structure where the emarketplace will act, different categories of emarketplaces suit best.

Networks are considered increasingly important in today's economy. From Porters' original value chain model many discussions have arisen. One is the point of the virtual value chain where information is considered much more important than in the original model. The networks are built up in order to enhance business, this could be in form of coverage, focus or process efficiencies. Some authors believe that there are three components that companies should focus on to improve their networks: Supply Chain Management, electronic commerce and Customer Relationships Management. Supply Chain Management concerns all activities for delivering products to the end-customer as effectively as possible. That means that the company has to focus on activities around product flows, information flows and the organization that affect the companies supply chain.

The Internet has given many new possibilities for information sharing and lead to greater cost and information transparency throughout the supply chain.

Customer Relationship Management (CRM) on the other hand focuses on relationships instead of flows. There does not exist any unambiguous definition of CRM but many authors argue that it at least consist of marketing, sales and service. The Internet has made information sharing easier, which has led to possibilities for adapting the companies' processes to its customers' processes. This is important in order to maintain long and profitable relationships with customers, which is the goal of CRM. When using e-business at least three different channel strategies exist: augment existing channels, enable existing channels for e-commerce and disintermediate the channel, i.e. overriding existing channels.

The disintermediated channels will be reintermediated, i.e. formerly bypassed types of middlemen recover market share or take shares on markets previously not served by them. When channels are changing as drastically as it is expected that the Internet will force them to, there are risks of channel conflicts. However, not all channel conflicts are bad and therefore it is necessary to analyze what type of conflict really has occurred or will occur in order to judge what steps that are necessary to take. These steps are a mix of the possible strategies for resolving channel conflicts: negotiations, persuasive mechanisms, legal remedies and climate management.

Information goods in the frame of reference is that digital products indeed are different from other types of products. The key differences from physical products are:

The marginal production cost is zero, or close to zero: The distribution costs tend towards zero, at least the variable part of the costs These properties should be considered when strategies for marketing, selling and buying these products are developed. The product itself may consist of different components that are bundled together. Some authors believe bundling is the future of software products while other regards the Internet as something working against this phenomenon.

Buying can be separated into two dimensions: product complexity and how frequently the product is purchased. When buying complex products the actual purchaser, the so-called executor, becomes more important since that person has specific important knowledge about the products which people on higher positions do not posses. Therefore, larger companies which have specific departments dedicated to purchasing advanced products often can handle more of the purchase process themselves. Besides, the more technical competence the company possesses the easier the buying of complex products is.

Product complexity in two dimensions, asset specificity and complexity of product description. Furthermore, products that have low asset specificity and that are easy to describe are the most likely to be traded by many buyers and sellers on an open market. On the other hand, products with high asset specificity and complexity of description are more likely to be sold by one or a few sellers.

Advertising on the Internet

There are many rules that apply the forms of advertising on electronic marketing. These rules and guidelines protect businesses and consumers - and help maintain the credibility of the Internet as an advertising medium. The Federal Trade Commission (FTC) has prepared this guide to give you an overview of some of the laws it enforces. The Federal Trade Commission Act allows the FTC to act in the interest of all consumers to prevent deceptive and unfair acts or practices. In interpreting Section 5 of the Act, the Commission has determined that a representation, omission or practice is deceptive if it is likely to:

— mislead consumers and

— affect consumers' behavior or decisions about the product or service.

In addition, an act or practice is unfair if the injury it causes, or is likely to cause, is:

— substantial

— not outweighed by other benefits and

— not reasonably avoidable.

The FTC Act prohibits unfair or deceptive advertising in any medium. That is, advertising must tell the truth and not mislead consumers. A claim can be misleading if relevant information is left out or if the claim implies something that's not true. For example, a lease advertisement for an automobile that promotes "$0 Down" may be misleading if significant and undisclosed charges are due at lease signing. In addition, claims must be substantiated, especially when they concern health, safety, or performance. The type of evidence may depend on the product, the claims, and what experts believe necessary.

Sellers are responsible for claims they make about their products and services. Third parties - such as advertising agencies or website designers and catalog marketers - also may be liable for making or disseminating deceptive representations if they participate in the preparation or distribution of the advertising, or know about the deceptive claims. Advertising agencies or website designers are responsible for reviewing the information used to substantiate ad claims. They may not simply rely on an advertiser's assurance that the claims are substantiated.

In determining whether an ad agency should be held liable, the FTC looks at the extent of the agency's participation in the preparation of the challenged ad, and whether the agency knew or should have known that the ad included false or deceptive claims. To protect themselves, catalog marketers should ask for material to back up claims rather than repeat what the manufacturer says about the product. If the manufacturer doesn't come forward with proof or turns over proof that looks questionable, the catalog marketer should see a yellow "caution light" and proceed appropriately, especially when it comes to extravagant performance claims, health or weight loss promises, or earnings guarantees. In writing ad copy, catalogers should stick to claims that can be supported. Most important, catalog marketers should trust their instincts when a product sounds too good to be true.

Advertising directed to children raises special issues. That's because children may have greater difficulty evaluating advertising claims and understanding the nature of the information you provide. Sellers should take special care not to misrepresent a product or its performance when advertising to children.

The Children's Advertising Review Unit (CARU) of the Council of Better Business Bureaus has published specific guidelines for children's advertising that you may find helpful. The Internet provides unprecedented opportunities for the collection and sharing of information from and about consumers. But studies show that consumers have very strong concerns about the security and confidentiality of their personal information in the online marketplace. Many consumers also report being wary of engaging in online commerce, in part because they fear that their personal information can be misused. These consumer concerns present an opportunity for you to build on consumer trust by implementing effective voluntary industry-wide practices to protect consumers' information privacy.

The FTC has held a number of workshops for industry, consumer groups and privacy advocates to explore industry guidelines to protect consumers' privacy online. In June 1998, the FTC issued Online Privacy: A Report to Congress. The Report noted that while over 85 percent of all websites collected personal information from consumers, only 14 percent of the sites in the FTC's random sample of commercial websites provided any notice to consumers of the personal information they collect or how they use it.

While the 2000 survey showed significant improvement in the percent of websites that post at least some privacy disclosures, only 20 percent of the random sample sites were found to have implemented four fair information practices: notice, choice, access and security. Even when the survey looked at the percentage of sites implementing the two critical practices of notice and choice, only 41 percent of the random sample provided such privacy disclosures. The Children's Online Privacy Protection Act (COPPA) and the FTC's implementing Rule took effect April 21, 2000.

Commercial websites directed to children under 13 years old or general audience sites that have actual knowledge that they are collecting information from a child must obtain parental permission before collecting such information. Some FTC laws about specific marketing practices and the promotion of products and services in specific industries. The Franchise and Business Opportunity Rule requires franchise and business opportunity sellers to give consumers a detailed disclosure document at least 10 days before the consumer pays any money or legally commits to a purchase. The document must include:

— the names, addresses, and telephone numbers of other purchasers;

— a fully-audited financial statement of the seller;

— the background and experience of the business's key executives;

— the cost of starting and maintaining the business; and

— the responsibilities of the seller and purchaser once the purchase is made.

Multi-level marketing (MLM) also known as "network" or "matrix" marketing - is a way of selling goods and services through distributors. These plans typically promise that people who sign up as distributors will get commissions two ways - on their own sales and on the sales their recruits have made. Pyramid schemes - a form of multi-level marketing - involve paying commissions to distributors only for recruiting new distributors.

Pyramid schemes are illegal in most states because the plans inevitably collapse when no new distributors can be recruited. When a plan collapses, most people -

except those at the top of the pyramid - lose their money. MLMs should pay commissions for the retail sales of goods or services, not for recruiting new distributors. MLMs that involve the sale of business opportunities or franchises, as defined by the Franchise Rule, must comply with the Rule's requirements about disclosing the number and percentage of existing franchisees who have achieved the claimed results, as well as cautionary language.

The Truth in Lending Act requires creditors who deal with consumers to disclose information in writing about finance charges and related aspects of credit transactions, including finance charges expressed as an annual percentage rate. In addition, the Act establishes a three-day right of rescission in certain transactions involving the establishment of a security interest in the consumer's principal dwelling. The Act also establishes certain requirements for advertisers of credit terms. The Fair Credit Billing Act is important if you are a creditor billing customers for goods or services. The Act requires you to acknowledge consumer billing complaints promptly in writing and to investigate billing errors. The Act prohibits creditors from taking actions that adversely affect the consumer's credit standing until the investigation is completed, and affords other consumer protections during disputes. The Act also requires that creditors promptly post payments to the consumer's account, and either refund overpayments or credit them to the consumer's account. The Fair Credit Reporting Act requires that consumer reporting agencies (CRAs) - such as credit bureaus and resellers of consumer reports - that provide information to creditors, insurers, employers, and others, do so with due regard for the confidentiality, accuracy, and legitimate use of such data.

When those parties take adverse action on the basis of information in a credit report, they must identify the CRA that provided the report so that the consumer can learn how to get a copy to verify or contest its accuracy and completeness. Creditors and others may not knowingly provide false information to CRAs, which are required to maintain reasonable procedures to ensure the maximum possible accuracy of their data.

The Equal Credit Opportunity Act prohibits lenders from discriminating on the basis of race, color, religion, national origin, sex, marital status, age, receipt of public assistance income, or an applicant's good faith exercise of any rights under the Consumer Credit Protection Act. The ECOA requires creditors to provide applicants with the reasons credit was denied if the applicant asks. The Electronic Fund Transfer Act establishes the rights, liabilities, and responsibilities of participants in electronic fund transfer systems.

The EFTA requires participants to adopt certain practices when they deal with transaction accounting and preauthorized transfers and error resolution, and sets liability limits for losses caused by unauthorized transfers. The Consumer Leasing Act regulates personal property leases that exceed four months and are made to consumers for personal, family, or household purposes.

The statute requires that certain lease costs and terms be disclosed, imposes limitations on the size of penalties for delinquency or default and on the size of residual liabilities, and in some instances, requires certain disclosures in lease advertising. Advertisements promoting credit repair, promising loans for a fee in advance, or touting investment opportunities may trigger application of the FTC's Telemarketing Sales Rule if the ad allows consumers to order goods or services by telephone.

In general, this Rule does not apply to general media advertisements. If you're advertising credit repair, advance fee loans, or investment opportunities, or offering to recover money paid in previous telemarketing transactions, however, the Rule likely applies to you. Among other things, the Rule requires that certain disclosures be made before a customer pays for the goods or services. The Rule also prohibits material misrepresentations.

Testimonials and endorsements must reflect the typical experiences of consumers, unless the ad clearly and conspicuously states otherwise. A statement that not all consumers will get the same results is not enough to qualify a claim.

The Textile and Wool Acts require you to disclose country of origin information in catalogs and other mail order advertising and in Internet ads that sell textile and wool products. The description of each advertised item must include a statement that it was made in the U.S.A., imported or both. A general statement in your ads that all products are either made in the U.S.A. or imported is not adequate. Ads that say or imply anything about fiber content must disclose the generic fiber names in order of predominance by weight. This requirement applies to all ads, whether or not they solicit direct sales. The FTC works for the consumer to prevent fraudulent, deceptive and unfair business practices in the marketplace and to provide information to help consumers spot, stop and avoid them.

4

Electronic Cash Transactions

The emergence of electronic money (e-money) has prompted much research and study by both the public and private sectors. Although many have lauded the promise of these new payment methods for industry and government, less attention has been focused on the implications of e-money for consumers. Consumer acceptance in turn requires that consumers have confidence in the product; understand the benefits and risks of the new products; and believe that their concerns about the products have been considered and addressed.

The term 'e-money' encompasses a wide variety of existing and planned products designed to provide an alternative to traditional means of payment. This diversity of potential and existing e-money products makes it difficult to render a single description that encompasses all electronic money systems in terms of technological, market, or legal distinctions. For purposes of this programme, however, an 'e-money' or 'electronic stored-value' product is a prepaid balance of funds, or 'value,' recorded on a device controlled by the consumer, generally either a card or the consumer's personal computer. E-money can be used for point of sale or for

Internet-based purchases. The balance on the device is decreased, or debited, when the device is used for payment. A wide variety of card-based systems are possible, differing according to the technology used, whether the system is 'open' or 'closed,' whether transactions occur on-line to a central system or off-line, and whether the cards are disposable or reloadable. Card-based stored value has been in existence for many years. Early generations of card-based stored value, often known as pre-paid cards, involve recording a balance of funds on a magnetic stripe that is debited by the terminal after each use.

Although magnetic stripe technology provides a low-cost means to distribute stored value, it does not provide sufficient safety from tampering or counterfeiting to be applied to off-line systems in which relatively large amounts of value will be placed on the cards. In addition, options for reloading of magnetic cards are limited as is the ability to store transaction information. Smart cards, i.e., cards with an embedded microprocessor chip, provide features superior to those of magnetic stripe cards. The microprocessor chip can store and manipulate data according to pre-programmed functions on the chip and external instructions from a card-reading unit. Smart cards promise additional security by permitting sophisticated encryption technology to protect the value on the card from counterfeiting. In addition, smart cards may bundle various products on a single card, that could function as a credit card, a debit card, a stored value card, and a repository of personal information.

Many card-based systems presently in use are 'closed' systems—systems where the value is only redeemable in exchange for the issuer's goods or services. Most of these systems use magnetic stripe technology.

Common examples of closed systems include transportation systems in major metropolitan areas, photocopiers in public libraries, and long distance telephone cards. Utilities, laundry and parking facilities are also increasingly incorporating stored value systems. Other closed systems are multi-functional, and usually involve smart card technology. These systems generally involve a narrowly defined group of consumers, a small group of merchants, and a relatively small geographic area over which to install the necessary infrastructure. Such systems are also gaining in popularity. These semi-closed systems are most often seen on university and corporate campuses and surrounding environs, and on military installations. In truly open systems, on the other hand, e-money could be used with many merchants over an extended geographic area and function as a general medium of exchange.

Some stored-value card systems, such as pre-paid phone cards in the United States, interact with a central database system that maintains the records of funds associated with each card and require verification of every transaction on-line with the central system. However, most of the e-money systems envision that transactions will typically be off-line except for purposes of purchasing, reloading or redeeming the stored-value. Many of the current stored-value systems are reloadable, permitting consumers to add to the value on the cards through machines that accept currency or credit cards. Where cards are linked to the consumer's depository institution account, they can be reloaded through ATMs and in some cases through personal computers equipped with remote computer banking software and a card reader device.

A few e-money systems are designed primarily for Internet transactions, permitting consumers to use personal computers to make payments to other parties via Internet e-mail or other computer-to-computer communication methods. Consumers wishing to utilize these Internet systems must first install specialized software on their computers. In these systems, the device that stores the value is generally the consumer's personal computer rather than a card. The distinction between smart card and Internet based e-money systems appears to be diminishing as some providers of stored value cards are testing their systems internationally for Internet payments. Future systems may integrate these and other payment methods, possibly through the use of a smart card reader attached to the consumer's personal computer.

The Market for E-Money Products Consumers in the United States have a wide array of choices of payment mechanisms. They can use cash, checks, credit cards, debit cards, or money orders for many payments. Credit and debit cards are increasingly being accepted for smaller dollar payments—payments that traditionally were made in cash. Whether open e-money systems will succeed against this array of competing products in this market is unclear. Most retail payments in the US are made using one of six payment instruments: cash, checks, credit cards, debit cards, and Automated Clearing House ('ACH') debits and credits. The US has a predominantly paper-based payment system for retail transactions, relying on checks for 87 percent of noncash retail payments. The US is also the only developed country in which check use is increasing. Adoption of retail electronic payments has been relatively slow. However, there has been strong growth in electronic payments over the last several years as American consumers have become more familiar with these alternatives. For example, since 1990 consumers have increased their annual charge volume on bank credit cards by 128 percent. There has also been strong growth in the debit card market in recent years. Approximately 40 percent of financial consumers now use debit cards and the average number of monthly transactions grew from 4.7 to 7.3 in January of 1997. To date, e-money, whether card or Internet-based, remains a very minor player in the payments system.

E-money has been widely touted as an alternative to cash that provides consumers with added security and convenience for small-dollar transactions, while providing merchants greater efficiency in cash handling, and lower transaction fees. Although some have expressed doubts about the viability of e-money, these concerns have not stopped the proliferation of pilot programs worldwide. The major e-money sponsors are currently participating in pilot programs in Argentina, Australia, Brazil, Canada, Colombia, the Czech Republic, Hong Kong, Italy, Japan, Mexico, Norway, New Zealand, Poland, South Africa, Sweden, Switzerland and the United Kingdom. Additionally, Austria, China, Costa Rica, Greece, Israel, Korea, Malaysia, Moldova, the Netherlands, Saudi Arabia, and Singapore are also either presently or soon will be experimenting with domestic corporations' proprietary e-money products. Belgium, Denmark, Finland, France, Germany, Portugal, Spain, and Thailand have completed the experimentation stage and have begun implementing e-money systems nationwide. For example, Proton, founded by Banksys (a consortium of 60 banks), has issued 900,000 cards in Belgium alone, and more than 14 million cards worldwide. Several open e-money systems are currently in pilot phases in the United States. For example, over 1.7 million cards were produced at the 1996 Olympic Summer Games in Atlanta, and 200,000 transactions totaling about $1.1 million were conducted. Other pilot programmes currently underway in the US involve multipurpose multi-application smart cards that permit loyalty programs and ticketless airline travel.

One large-scale US pilot programme involving 50,000 consumers and over 500 merchants is currently underway on the Upper West Side of Manhattan. In this pilot, MasterCard and Mondex (in conjunction with Chase Manhattan Bank) and Visa (in conjunction with Citibank) in tandem are issuing their own products supported by interoperable readers capable of accepting value from either product. The results of these pilots to date indicate that consumer and merchant acceptance may be slower than initially thought. Internet-based e-money systems also promise consumers great convenience and security for Internet transactions. However, the development of the Secure Electronic Transactions protocol, encrypting consumer credit card numbers when used over the Internet, as well as the development of other security features for credit card transactions, may have satisfied consumers' desire for additional security in connection with an already-accepted payment mechanism. This development may cause Internet based e-money issuers to develop their product as a niche product for micro-payments, such as for purchases of information over the Internet. Additionally, as mentioned earlier, some stored value card issuers are exploring using their transaction protocols for Internet-based transactions.

Internet based e-money systems, however, have not yet been widely introduced or adopted by consumers or merchants. In fact, the three largest issuers of Internet payments products have conducted less than $3 million in transactions combined.

In addition to promising consumers greater convenience than cash, such products may also provide consumers greater physical security, particularly when consumers can add value to the cards at home using their personal computer. E-money will likely remain a minor segment of the US payments system for the near future. Consumers generally will not be compelled to use or accept e-money. Thus, issuers will face considerable market pressure to address factors that give rise to consumers' concerns in order to promote use of their products. Over time, advances in technology and decreasing costs in the storage of information should enable issuers to design stored value products with enhanced safety and security features that respond to consumers' demands. In addition, to promote use of their products, issuers will have an incentive to help consumers learn and become comfortable with the products through advertising, promotional campaigns, consumer education programmes.

E-money could also provide merchants the ability to reduce cash-handling costs, such as those resulting from employee theft. Additionally, some institutions with specialized needs are increasingly adopting stored value card systems. University campuses and their surrounding environs are one such specialized market. Universities, using smart card technology, can integrate payment capabilities with student identification cards, and provide students the convenience of only needing to carry one card. Other possible markets include corporate campuses, military installations and planned communities. For example, the US military is currently experimenting with stored value cards systems for their trainee's payroll. Government actions also may serve to help develop a larger market for e-money products. The Debt Collection Improvement Act of 1996 requires all federal government payments to be made via electronic means by 1999. The Financial Management Service currently anticipates delivering federal payments via direct deposit to all recipients with a deposit account at a financial institution.

Federal payment recipients who do not have a deposit account at a financial institution have the option of receiving electronic payments at an account established on their behalf by Treasury or if receiving an electronic deposit would be burdensome, recipients can exercise a hardship waiver and continue to receive paper checks by mail. Although e-money does not play an immediate role in the EFT' mandate, it may ultimately help eliminate government-issued, checks in the near future. Currently, traditional EFT payment mechanisms limit the government from making all payments electronically. For example, because direct deposit transactions require enrollment and authorization by the account holder well in advance of payment, the government must issue paper checks to individuals and businesses that require immediate payment.

E-money products could eliminate the necessity for paper checks in this situation by allowing the government to execute electronic payments immediately. Even now, some state governments are testing smart cards for the distribution of certain state administered benefits programs, such as food coupons and Women, Infants, and Children ("WIC") programs. Although the vast majority of these programs presently use on-line magnetic stripe cards, several states are exploring whether smart cards could be useful for the distribution of coupon-based benefit programs such as food stamps.

At the present time, the market for e-money is still developing, and it is difficult to predict its eventual structure. However, several important aspects of electronic money may affect the market's eventual development. E-money, like other electronic payment methods in use today, may display network characteristics, i.e. the value of the product to any user is increased as other potential users adopt the system. In particular, widespread e-money installation of point-of-sale devices capable of reading stored-value cards may be necessary to spur consumer demand while consumers may not demand stored value cards unless there are sufficient locations to use them. Conversely, merchants may lack the incentives to deploy terminals capable of accepting stored value cards unless consumers appear to be willing to use that payment mechanism.

Additionally, the technologies themselves often involve economies of scale. For these reasons, some believe that the e-money market will develop similarly to other network industries such as ATMs and credit cards. Initially, there will be a large number of products. However, due to many factors including economies of scale, the number of systems will decrease, resulting in a smaller number of large "branded networks" controlling a majority of the e-money transactions. In these networks, the network and its brand—not the individual issuer would have a strong retail presence and would be the foremost link in the consumer's mind. Although it is impossible to determine whether such a structure will develop in the US, evidence indicates that this may already have occurred for open systems, since there are only a limited number of dominant 'brands' of e-money emerging at this time.

Electronic money and electronic payments systems for retail transactions are commanding widespread attention. These systems, wherein neither legal tender, nor paper checks, nor credit-card numbers change hands at the time of purchase, have already started to spread across the globe. They offer significant and profitable opportunities for changing the way consumers pay for the widest possible range of goods and services. Hardly a month seems to pass without some announcement of another alliance of computer and financial services firms. Organizers' plans invariably envision a broad array of retail financial services and products available in an electronic or digital format.

The electronic transfer of funds is not a new phenomenon in the United States or, indeed, most of the developed world. Large scale and wholesale payment transactions in the United States and other nations have been conducted electronically for some time. What is new today is the expansion of electronic money technologv in financial transactions conducted by consumers and smaller, nonfinancial organizations. Electronic wholesale payments in the United States account for a much larger dollar volume of transactions than all retail transactions, but they take place among relatively few parties that have worked long, hard, and successfully at making these transactions secure. Retail transactions, the vast bulk of the number of transactions in the United States, take place among parties who are concerned about both the security and the privacy of those transactions. Developing systems that meet the variety of consumer and merchant needs during a period of evolving technology will be a challenge. Electronic money and the technology that makes it possible raise important questions about the continuing effectiveness of existing government tools and methods used to carry out traditional responsibilities in such areas as consumer protection and law enforcement. Further, in the United States, the operability of much electronic money technology and many electronic money systems for retail payments is largely untested, except in pilot projects and limited experiments.

At the same time, electronic money raises the possibility of actually reducing crime and increasing access for low and moderate income households. It is also quite possible that for competitive reasons private sector purveyors of this new technology will effectively address consumer, criminal, and other issues raised by the development and use of electronic money.

The basis of retail payments evolved gradually from physical coins to paper currency and checks and, more recently and rapidly, from there to debit and credit cards. In large-scale wholesale transactions, money has for decades been transactional information transmitted electronically over closed, wire transfer systems. Now, money in retail transactions is becoming electronic, transformed into information stored on a computer chip in a plastic card or on a personal computer so that it can be transmitted over open information systems, such as the Internet. There are two underlying developments.

Two forces in particular are responsible for pushing advanced economies around the globe into this next phase in the evolution of money. The first is the steep drop in the cost of computing power. The second is the continuing advance in the application of computer technologies to communications systems. Together, these forces are fundamentally changing the character of traditional money and related financial activities and are setting the stage for even greater changes in the years ahead.

The declining price of personal computers over the past decade has been dramatic. Despite reportedly thinning profit margins, that trend continues, while falling prices and enhanced performance also increasingly characterize computer peripherals such as hard drives, modems, and CD ROM drives.

The trend lines for consumer usage of electronic communication innovations are strongly upward. At the end of last year, 8.8 million Americans were connected to their offices by computer, an increase of almost 16 percent over 1994. In the last six years, host computers on the Internet increased by a staggering 4,700 percent. Some analysts have predicted that, by 1997, about six million Americans will be using some form of wireless communication-triple the number for 1995. At the same time, the capacity of communication channels is growing sharply, reducing the time needed to transmit text and graphics.

Those improvements in communication technologies are changing fundamentally the economics of conducting information-related business. As traditional barriers and costs to information-sharing fall, banks and others in the financial information business are better able to achieve economies of scale in storing and moving data. They can more comprehensively assimilate large quantities of financial data on their operations at a lower cost and in less time. They and their customers can have more direct and immediate access to each other, at lower cost. Most strikingly, perhaps, changes in communication and computer technologies also mean that banks and their customers no longer have to conduct their business face-to-face, and, consequently, no longer have to reside in the same country, state, county, or town. As the need for geographic proximity between financial institution and customer fades, so generally does the importance of geography-based procedures, practices, and rules that govern much of the financial services industry today.

New Retail Payments Systems

Advances in computers and communications technology have led to a change of some significance to policy-makers—the development and growth of new retail payments systems. The most noteworthy developments are electronic cash and engaging in financial transactions from home or elsewhere by personal computers.

Electronic Cash

Electronic cash is a claim on a party, most commonly, the issuer, stored in the form of computer code on a card about the size of a credit card or on the hard drive of a computer. Consumers purchase the claim with traditional money. Consumers exchange the claims for goods and services with merchants who are willing to accept the claim as payment. Cards representing such claims often go by the name 'stored value cards' (SVCs).

The technology for storing claims with which to make payments, and other information, on cards ranges from the magnetic strip common to all credit cards to computer chips that store and process information. Cards containing computer chips are called 'smart cards.' One convenient way to understand SVCs is to classify them as representing either 'closed' or 'open' systems. SVCs that are limited to just a few merchants regardless of location or to many merchants in a relatively small geographic area would represent a closed system.

SVCs that consumers could use at many different businesses over a large geographic area would represent an open system. The distinction between closed and open, however, is largely one of degree.

Closed-system SVCs: One example of a closed-system SVC is the system in which the card issuer and the seller of the goods and services are one and the same (the 'merchant-issuer' model). Examples of such cards include: the farecard used by riders of the subway system in Washington, D.C.; cards issued by a number of colleges and universities in the US to students and perhaps employees that holders may use to purchase a variety of goods and services supplied by the college or university; cards issued by public bodies; and cards issued by certain telephone companies to pay for telephone calls.

In these systems, the user buys a claim on the merchant-issuer with traditional money and receives electronic cash in return. When the user buys goods or services from the merchant-issuer, special point of sale (POS) devices record the transactions with the merchant, reducing the value of the electronic cash recorded on the card by the amount of the purchase. Although consumers make purchases in this system with electronic cash, the system is linked to the current payment system by the merchant-issuer's relationship with its bank.

Campus cards, and other such limited distribution cards, are examples of closed-system cards where the issuer and merchant are different parties. One such example is the 1995 Jacksonville Jaguar stadium card. In this case, one bank issued cards that fans could use at the stadium to buy food, drink, and souvenirs at football games. The transactions with these stored value cards work much the same as with the merchant-issuer. The special POS devices record the transaction for the merchant, altering the purchaser's stored value card to reflect the decreased value. The merchant later presents the electronic cash to the bank-issuer by downloading the payment information from the POS, receiving traditional funds in exchange, typically in the form of a deposit balance at the bank. The merchant's bank would then send the electronic cash through the traditional payment system in much the same manner as presenting a check. As with the merchant-issuer systems described above, bank-issued electronic cash in this somewhat more complex 'closed' system would commonly be closely linked to the traditional payments system.

Open-system SVCs: Examples of open-system SVCs exist today in several countries in Europe and the Far East, and to a more limited extent, in the US. They work essentially in the same manner as bank-issued SVCs in closed-systems, with the important exception that a greater variety of businesses over a relatively larger geographic area accept them. Technology, however, can support electronic cash regimes that could operate independently of banks and thus outside traditional payments systems. In these systems, users would buy electronic cash from issuers using traditional money. Users would 'spend' the electronic cash at a merchant, just as in the case of bank-issued electronic cash.

Merchants would then send the electronic cash to the issuer who would redeem it with some form of traditional money such as a check on a bank balance. In this system, the electronic cash would not 'clear' through the traditional payments system, but could circulate outside it. In expansive versions of either bank-issued or nonbank-issued electronic cash, such cash could circulate among users before presentment to merchants, in much the same manner as traditional cash.

Users would have their own special computer equipment enabling them to transfer electronic cash from one user's card to another. Such a transfer often goes by the name 'peer-to-peer' and can be accomplished with some electronic cash systems today. Peer-to-peer transfers of electronic cash would not clear through the traditional payments system, in contrast to peer-to-peer transfers involving paper checks. With such regimes, the only point of contact between the traditional payments system and electronic cash would be the initial purchase of electronic cash from the issuer with the use of traditional money and redemption of electronic cash by merchants.

PC Financial Transactions

The continued development of the personal computer (PC) has given many households the opportunity to conduct financial transactions from their homes, or indeed from any location where they can connect their portable computers to telephone networks. Through the use of special software and a modem, they can connect to the system used by their financial institution to examine accounts, issue orders to transfer funds among their own accounts, issue orders to transfer funds to the accounts of other parties (e.g., to pay bills or send funds to others), and apply for loans. In some cases, households dial a number that connects them directly with their financial institution. In other cases, households connect to their banks by using the Internet.

After gaining access to the World Wide Web portion of the Internet through their Internet service provider, households go to the Web page sponsored by their bank and conduct their business. Currently, most retail electronic banking involves transmission of information over relatively protected telephone networks or limited access networks of computers called intranets. To date, such systems have not given rise to significant security breaches. Even so, the widespread availability of powerful home computers poses the risk of financial crime, creating incentives for maintaining tight controls and security systems. Strong security systems will be especially important for successful banking and commerce over the more open Internet, where packets of information can pass through a number of computers, each one accessible to a large number of people, before reaching their final destination.

PC-based electronic cash: Technology permits the transmission of electronic cash over networks that link personal computers and the storage of electronic cash on the hard drives of personal computers. PC-based electronic cash is thus one means of paying for goods purchased over the Internet. The possible points of contact between PC-based electronic cash and the traditional payment system are functionally identical to those between SVCs and the payment system. So long as merchants regularly redeem such cash for traditional forms of money and there is little, if any, peer-to-peer transfers, PC-based electronic cash will be a simple adjunct to, not separate from the existing payments system. Regimes with peer-to peer transfers and little, if any, redemption of electronic cash for traditional money would offer the possibility of separate payments systems. As in the case of stored value cards, the popularity of such systems remains somewhat unclear for the immediate future.

Understanding the speed with which electronic money develops, and the actual systems that will be marketed and by whom, is key to the formulation of government policy. Notwithstanding a considerable amount of excitement over the development of electronic money in the press, the pace of moving from the analog world of retail payments to the digital world of electronic money is likely to be slower that many may think. Today, electronic banking is just beginning to become popular, electronic commerce and payments over the Internet are in their infancy, and principal use of SVCs in this country is in a relatively few closed systems. Nevertheless, financial and nonfinancial firms are spending billions of dollars to ensure the success of this market, and there is a clear public interest in these new products. As electronic money and banking products mature it may well turn out that many of the policy issues raised by these new technologies—money laundering, counterfeiting, fraud, consumer disclosure, access for low and moderate income households—will be resolved by the private sector. Beyond this, some policy issues—the loss of seignorage and the impact on monetary policy-only become important when there is widespread use of electronic cash.

Innovators will have ample incentive to introduce new products that will help solve many of the potential problems associated with electronic money. Inappropriate government intervention could delay, deny, or limit the quality of such improvements. Government will have to take care not to act in a manner that stifles innovation. At the same time, it is incumbent upon government to follow these developments carefully, in particular monitoring the pace of change, so that where there are emerging issues that can only be dealt with by government, they are in fact addressed. E-money participants may find that some regulation is necessary to assure consumer confidence and an acceptable environment for commerce develop.

Smart-card usage in the United States

Compared with several other countries, the United States has been slower to take up multi-user smart-card activity, although some usage has developed. The stadium card noted earlier is one example and the experiment conducted by VISA International during the 1996 Olympic Games in Atlanta, Georgia is another. The slow adoption of these systems in the United States may be explained by the abundance and convenience of other payment options. Many US consumers have access to cash, credit cards, checks, and debit cards, and for any purchase can select the payment option that best meets their needs. Another contributing factor may be the sheer size of the United States as compared to countries such as Belgium, Denmark, Finland, and Portugal where smart-card usage is more advanced. How long, then, will it take for US consumers to ultimately decide to embrace electronic money to any significant degree? Widespread electronic money use in the United States, particularly over open systems such as the Internet, seems to be at least two years away. The forces for change, however, are strong. There is considerable commercial interest in developing these new means of payment in the United States for both closed and open systems. As says that earlier there are growing applications of electronic cash technology to such arenas as transportation systems, college and university campuses, and even sports complexes.

Several firms such as VISA International, MasterCard, Mondex, and Proton in various alliances with banks are investing large sums of money into projects that will develop into open systems. Such ventures may need more than a few years to prove their merit. If consumer acceptance of electronic money parallels the history of automated teller machines (ATMs), direct deposit, the credit card, and banking by personal computer, growth in electronic money usage will be slow and limited for the first five years, but increasing dramatically thereafter.

Internet Commerce

Although the subject of much discussion, the actual level of Internet commerce remains modest by any standards. Scattered, unofficial estimates, the only ones available, suggest a level in the range of $100 million to $200 million in annual transactions. The growth of Internet commerce may increase the volume of Internet financial transactions, but will not necessarily guarantee the growth of electronic money. Some observers believe that efforts to reduce the cost of credit card transactions will be successful and that credit cards, one of the most ubiquitous substitutes for money payments in the United States, will become the dominant Internet payment vehicle. They cite the existence of a huge, familiar, and successful infrastructure currently supporting credit card purchases and clearings.

Despite the current level of electronic money activity in the United States, the forces stimulating faster growth in electronic money and commerce here are strong, and the pace of change could quicken. These forces include:

— Expanding electronic-based government payments The need for greater efficiency in government operations is perhaps stronger today than ever before. The question here is, 'How should the government use electronic money in its drive for greater efficiency?' Government has already begun to formulate its answer. The Debt Collection Act of 1996 and the electronic benefit transfer (EBT) initiative are but two examples of recent efforts to achieve greater efficiency. The implications of these and related measures on Treasury operations are substantial.

— *Debt Collection Act:* The Debt Collection Act of 1996 mandates government use of electronic funds transfers (EFT) for all government payments, except tax refunds, by 1999. This includes the payment of government benefits. The act has two effective dates. After July 26, 1996, every new recipient of government payments must accept them electronically, unless the recipient certifies that he or she does not have an account at a financial institution. After January 1, 1999, all payments made to individuals and businesses-including those to persons without accounts at a financial institution-must be made electronically. The Financial Management Service (FMS), a U.S. Department of the Treasury bureau, has adopted an interim rule as part of its plan for implementing the new law. The interim rule implements the requirements of the new law that became effective July 26, 1996, and establishes the responsibilities of federal agencies and federal payment recipients. Agency responsibilities. The interim rule requires all federal agencies to make payments electronically to individuals who, on or after July 26, 1996:

— apply for federal benefit payments;

— begin employment with a federal agency;

— apply for retirement benefits;

— enter into a contract or purchase order with the federal government; or

— file or renew a grant application.

Recipient responsibilities: The interim rule requires each recipient of a federal payment to designate a financial institution or authorized payment agent through which a federal payment may be made. If the individual does not have an account with a financial institution or an authorized payment agent, the individual must certify that in writing to the agency. Implementation of the new requirements by those paying and receiving benefits could help provide those without bank accounts better access to mainstream financial services.

EBT programmes: Even before passage of the Debt Collection Improvement Act, the federal government had taken some initial steps toward realizing the efficiencies promised by electronic money. One such step was the formation of a federal task force that would coordinate the development of EBT programs. Such programs substitute for benefit delivery systems used by both federal and state agencies. In one type of EBT program, the value of food stamps to an individual, and codes indicating the acceptable purchases that the individual could make with the electronic funds, would be encoded in the computer chip embedded in a stored value card. Benefit recipients use these cards in lieu coupons or vouchers to pay for goods and services at merchants and others equipped to receive this form of electronic payment.

Impact on Treasury operations: Conversion of Treasury payments, now running at about 800 million a year, to an all electronic format will bring changes permitting, for example, a consolidation of disbursing operations that currently produce checks. With regard to retail payments, the complete displacement of traditional cash is unlikely. About 18 billion in currency notes valued at approximately $400 billion circulate world wide, despite the growth in checks and wire transfers. Demand is especially strong outside the United States where about $270 billion circulates. There, among the less technologically advanced countries, cash is the principal means of payment, the dollar seems to be one of the currencies of choice, and the infrastructure that will support widespread use of electronic money seems many years away.

Impact on electronic money: The US government is the largest receiver and disburser of payments in the world, and as it makes ever increasing use of electronic payments it is likely to have an influence on operating standards for electronic payments systems. That is because it must ensure any system it uses meets its requirements for security, reliability, and accuracy. To the extent it adopts stored value technology, it will greatly affect interoperability standards. Thus, the pace at which the public sector seeks to implement electronic payments could have a significant effect on private-sector planning and related activity.

Greater efficiencies for businesses

Lower costs: Electronic money eliminates the costs of handling coin and currency. The estimated cash handling cost for US retailers and banks is over $60 billion annually, which includes costs associated with the processing and accounting of money, as well as storage, transport, and security. Electronic money brings greater efficiency to those tasks, offering substantial cost savings.

According to the National Automated Clearing House Association (NACHA), the cost savings to the banking industry alone flowing from the new requirement for federal EFT payments could be sizeable. For example, NACHA: 'Studies have shown that a financial institution saves between $.75 and $1.25 for each payment converted from a deposit made with a teller to Direct Deposit,' and consequently, 'annual costs savings to the banking industry as a result of these new electronic payments should run between $350 million and $500 million.'

Electronic money potentially provides merchants with cost savings resulting from: reduced collection and deposit float associated with coin, currency, and checks, and faster funds availability; increased sales due to faster throughput at checkout counters and consumer tendencies to spend more with stored value cards; and increased self-serve transactions. Acceptance of electronic money would allow merchants to move more commerce from the physical world to the Internet, which offers access to global markets at low cost. The continuing rapid decline in the cost of technology will increase the extent of these cost savings, enhance innovation, and further increase the attraction of electronic money and finance.

Reductions in some forms of fraud: While magnetic strip debit and credit cards can be overwritten or copied, smart cards are fitted with tamper-resistant chips and strong cryptographic protocols. Additionally, smart cards could be tied to biometric identification mechanisms, such as voice, hand, or retinal prints, to verify the identity of the user. To the extent electronic money displaces checks, moreover, check fraud may be reduced. The new systems will be, however, targets of criminal activity.

Greater safety and security: Another benefit electronic money offers merchants is increasing safety and security by eliminating some opportunities for theft. Electronic money could help curtail vandalism of vending machines, public phones, and the like, because there would be no coin or currency to steal. Similarly, owners and employees of retail establishments and other service providers who handle cash, such as taxicab drivers, could be much less vulnerable to robbery.

More value-added services: Electronic money technology-particularly smart card applications-could help sharpen merchants' offers of value-added services, strengthening customer relationships. For example, retailers could track customer activities (to an even greater extent than they currently do with credit cards) to discern buying patterns and offer buyer-specific discounts and loyalty programs. These targeted promotions, also known as 'micro-marketing,' are generally viewed as more efficient than the mass-marketing techniques currently used. Some hard-pressed communities may benefit. If merchants did not need to collect and store cash, they might be willing to locate in areas that they now see as unacceptably risky.

New choices for consumers

One of the biggest advantages of electronic money is that it is more convenient than other payment mechanisms for small-value purchases. It is faster and easier than exchanging cash and making change, writing a check, or getting a credit card authorization. For all micro-payments, including those on the Internet, sending a 10 cent digital coin for a small purchase of information could prove to be more convenient and less costly than using a credit card.

Obstacles to growth

Despite those benefits, uncertainties on the part of consumers and merchants about the underlying technology could slow widespread use and acceptance of electronic money systems. Some of these uncertainties focus on how well the technology secures personal transactions information over the Internet from theft and related forms of abuse such as false or non-authentic commitments. Other uncertainties arise from concerns about whether or not competing forms of electronic-money for use outside the Internet will require idiosyncratic computer hardware and software. Still others arise from the fact that innovation is often fast-paced, creating doubts about how long any particular technology will be at hand.

Internet security and authentication

Security: Many analysts believe that the use of electronic payments on the Internet will depend on the development of widely available systems that guarantee the security of credit card numbers and the various forms of electronic money. There are numerous mathematical formulas to code or encrypt such numbers, as well as electronic cash, in a way that seriously complicates the task of stealing them or interfering with the intended use. Experts tend to evaluate methods of encryption in terms of the difficulty knowledgeable parties would face in decoding or decrypting the information. There can be differences of opinion among experts on the strength of any particular form of encryption and such differences could contribute to consumer, and merchant, unease.

The availability and strength of encryption seems to be on the minds of some consumers: In informal surveys, consumers cite lack of security as the primary reason they are reluctant to purchase goods and services online. At the same time, consumers routinely send credit cards and credit card numbers through the postal system and over the phone to catalog merchants and offer them to anonymous clerks at retail counters. Such different results suggest that security per se may not be crucial to the success of electronic money on the Internet.

Encryption is not the only form of security of concern to consumers: Traditional cash and credit card transactions suggest that some consumers seem to value written verification of the basic facts of a retail transaction-the name of the seller, a description of the goods or services purchased, and the cost. The seller ordinarily offers the buyer a piece of paper containing those details. Consumers may want their use of electronic money, especially electronic cash, to create similar information. How issuers meet that need may determine the pace of electronic money growth.

Authentication: If consumers are to use electronic money over the Internet they must have confidence in the issuers of the electronic money and the merchants who accept it. Consumers may demand that a trusted third party certify or authenticate the legitimacy of both those parties. Confidence is particularly important for the development of Internet commerce with its virtual shopkeepers that consumers cannot see and evaluate in the traditional way.

Confidence is a two-way street: Merchants will want assurances that the consumers from whom they receive orders for goods and services are the consumers who really want them and that verified consumers will not refuse to meet their responsibilities as defined by law. A trustworthy and reliable system of authentication can provide comfort to merchants on both fronts. Merchants could require customers to sign orders with encrypted digital signatures that can be authenticated by trusted and reliable third parties. Such authentication would unambiguously identify the consumer and provide proof that the consumer requested the goods or service. Trustworthy authentication can also boost electronic communication among businesses, ranging from merchandise orders to contracts that bind all manner of business contracts. Authenticated digital signatures could, for example, substitute for the notary public of the analog world.

There is a growing concern among policy makers and consumer groups in Europe and the United States that individual privacy is greatly compromised by electronic commerce and electronic payments. Such concerns are of course not limited to recent developments regarding electronic money or payments, inasmuch as they apply to current use of credit cards. However, electronic money and payments are likely to materially increase the intensity of debate over these issues for several reasons. SVCs raise the possibility of tracking and recording virtually every payment an individual makes. Such extensive tracking and recording raise issues of extensive target-marketing, government surveillance, and even personal safety as patterns of behavior are mined from this potentially rich data.

In addition, the Internet raises serious concerns about the data being examined by unauthorized persons. Balanced against this is the potential for data created and stored in an electronic money environment to aid law enforcement authorities in preventing crimes and tracking criminals (and, indeed, some of the data may be essential for effective law enforcement efforts). As well, legitimate use of such data could help firms to be more efficient in their marketing efforts.

Interoperability: Most observers agree that electronic money will not find widespread use until technical experts solve the problem of interoperability. In the context of electronic money, the term interoperability captures the extent to which debit cards and stored value cards from different issuers use a common set of standards. These standards govern such issues as the size of the cards (length, thickness, and width) the location and size of the magnetic strip or computer chip, and the coding technology manufacturers use to store information on the magnetic strip or computer chip. They also cover other matters such as the design and workings of devices that "read" the cards. The greater the acceptance of common standards, the greater the degree of interoperability.

Large-scale interoperability would help promote acceptance of electronic money: Merchants generally would be more inclined to invest in card readers if one reader could service a variety of debit and stored value cards. Similarly, with large-scale interoperability consumers could be reasonably confident that many merchants would accept many forms of electronic money. In sum, the greater the number of merchants accepting electronic money the greater the inclination among consumers to use it; the greater the number of consumers using electronic money, the greater the number of merchants willing to accept. Interoperability made possible the success of credit cards and ATMs.

Technological change: Another potential problem is technical change itself. The march of technological innovation seems unending, offering opportunities for improving communications and computer capabilities. Such 'progress' can be disconcerting for consumers and merchants. It clouds, rather than clarifies, the future, creating incentives to wait for the next round of improvements, if not for the emergence of a technology that seems to be on its way toward winning widespread acceptance.

There is considerable debate about what role government should play in the transition to a digital world. Some argue that the government should play little, if any role and allow the private sector to resolve most of the issues. Others advise the government to go so far as to set all the standards for issuing and using electronic cash, if not be the exclusive issuer of electronic cash. Still others recommend approaches that fall between those two extremes. A look at the role of government in the analog world is helpful in considering the role of government in the digital world. In the analog world of finance, the private sector, through innovation and adjustments in practices, has solved many concerns government might have raised.

At the same time, both industry and the public have looked to government to set and enforce rules that provide a foundation for, among other things, consumer rights and responsibilities, law enforcement protections against financial crimes, and the conduct of money issuers. Given the increasing globalisation of finance, international agreements also come into play. At the same time, there are important differences between the development of electronic money, banking, and commerce today, and the development of other financial services products in the past that make it a bit less clear what the appropriate response of government should be. As says earlier, there is reason to believe that the private sector will work hard to resolve a number of potential policy issues that may emerge as the development of E-money proceeds, and use of E-money becomes more widespread. Moreover, developments are likely to unfold at a pace that allows careful study of potential issues. Accordingly, government must be careful not to overreact to, or stifle, new innovations that can greatly benefit the consumer and the American economy.

Government should take advantage of marketplace solutions to issues where appropriate. To do this, and at the same time to be in a position to act appropriately, it is important for government to maintain expertise in electronic money and payments developments, and to consider carefully major questions presented by these developments. In some areas, such as the issuance of electronic money, additional federal interpretations, rules or, perhaps, laws may be needed to provide an appropriate legal foundation for electronic money systems. In others, existing requirements are no longer relevant and need to be eliminated.

Consumer Issues

One important area of ambiguity in the law involves the rules (including mandatory disclosures) governing many of the financial transactions that are commonplace between consumers and financial firms. Transactional rules for electronic debit systems are relatively well-established, but those for electronic cash are not. The government must decide whether it is best that electronic cash transactional rules evolve by contract, whether it should apply rules and precedents developed for related areas to electronic cash, or if that is not appropriate, whether to develop new rules. A key consideration should be the ability of consumers and merchants to protect adequately their interests by negotiation.

The issue of protecting consumer interests has four parts: To what extent should consumers be liable for electronic cash that is lost, stolen or compromised by the insolvency of the issuer? How much information should an issuer of electronic money disclose to consumers? Will the privacy of electronic-money users be adequately protected? Should the government take steps to ensure that all consumers, including the poor, gain access to electronic money and banking services? Clearly, one issue common to those four questions is whether a given electronic money system is an electronic debit system that transfers value among deposit accounts or an electronic cash system. Since only chartered depositories can accept deposits, and since those firms are highly regulated, the existing statutory regime presents a ready framework within which to address issues raised by electronic debit systems. Electronic cash systems, however, may present significant challenges to policymakers. While most issuers of electronic cash, in all likelihood, will continue to be subject to some form of regulation, the application of existing laws to E-cash instruments is less clear. For some, the answer to these problems might be to restrict the issuance of electronic money to banks. Such a policy at the very beginnings of electronic money development could place unnecessary barriers in the way of competition and innovation, possibly delaying or denying public benefits.

Liability for losses

Most electronic cash holdings will not be insulated against certain kinds of losses, such as misplacement by the holder, theft, and insolvency of the issuer. Misplacement and theft are risks holders of traditional cash incur, but not loss due to the insolvency of the issuer. Some electronic cash issued by banks may have the protection of FDIC insurance, and some issuers may elect to provide holders with protections against loss and theft. Barring substantive changes in law, some electronic cash issued by nonbanks will not be insured by the government against a loss due to issuer insolvency, although state statutes governing money transmitters may reduce the risk of issuer insolvency. Electronic cash issued by banks, however, won't necessarily offer holders insurance against issuer insolvency, and the absence of such insurance would mark a sharp distinction between insured deposits and bank-issued electronic cash. Consumers may, therefore, be confused by the existence of visually indistinguishable electronic cash systems, and policymakers must decide whether this concern warrants legislative or regulatory action.

Disclosure

Existing federal rules governing transactions and disclosure may not extend to some electronic money activities. While the Electronic Fund Transfer Act and Regulation E, which is issued by the Federal Reserve, will apply to consumer electronic debit transactions, no comprehensive body of transactional rules defines the rights and obligations arising from electronic cash transactions. Similarly, detailed consumer disclosures for EFT transactions apply to debit systems, but not necessarily to electronic cash systems. There is likely to be some pressure from consumer groups and some market participants to extend current law to electronic cash systems, as those systems become more commonplace.

Privacy

Electronic commerce and finance creates new opportunities for unauthorized access to and manipulation of private information. Although the European Parliament has moved to address some of those issues, few federal laws address them. The extension of electronic debit and electronic cash systems to the Internet presents additional risks. Data traveling through the open network of the Internet is more susceptible to interception and can be copied or modified. The extent of the risk to privacy will depend on the design of the systems and the types of information traveling over the Internet. Protecting individual privacy in the digital world will be at least as complex as it is in the analog world. Finding the right balance between governmental needs for information to combat crime and individual needs for anonymity will be challenging. That is not the only hurdle.

Consumer data derived from financial transactions covers a broad spectrum of information, and consumers may be more concerned about the confidentiality of some types of information than others. For example, consumers may object strongly to the public release of data describing their income and net worth, but allow some information describing their spending patterns to be used by direct marketers.

Access

Judging the impact of electronic money on groups of consumers, especially the poor, is difficult. On the one hand, the application of advanced technology to finance and commerce could exacerbate current inequities in the access to financial services. The poor are much less able than others to afford computers or to have access to educational opportunities facilitating computer use. As the cost of computers and associated technologies continues to fall, the availability of financial services from traditional outlets such as branches, and perhaps even ATMs, will decline. That trend could also disadvantage those in rural areas where the infrastructure necessary for electronic money and banking is not now in place. On the other hand, not all PC developments need to disadvantage the poor. PC-based systems for banking services offer the potential for a community group or church to work as partners with a bank or other financial-services firm for the delivery of financial services at convenient and safe locations.

Additionally, the technological revolution holds the potential to enhance greatly the ability of the poor to have convenient access to financial services because of the advantages that are inherent to high-tech payments systems. The cost of low-value transactions-transactions most common to the poor-can be much lower in high-tech systems than in traditional payments systems centered, for example, on brick-and-mortar branches. High-tech systems have more flexibility than traditional systems in the delivery of financial services virtually. Evidence of this flexibility is available today in the form of electronic benefit transfer (EBT) systems, banking over the telephone, and to some degree in high-tech branches in supermarkets and convenience stores. Such flexibility provides added convenience, in that services can be available on virtually a 24-hour basis, and added safety, in that funds are less subject to theft. In the not-to-distant future, additional evidence may include the use of home television sets hooked up to cable systems that give access to banking and other services.

Law enforcement

Electronic cash could, depending on how it is developed, share an important attribute with traditional cash. Like cash, it could lead to anonymous transactions that do not leave a 'paper trail.' While those attributes give ordinary citizens privacy, they also make possible the commission of large-scale financial crimes with relatively low risk of apprehension. Should the use of electronic cash become pervasive, government may question the effectiveness of its regulatory provisions and investigative strategies and techniques in combating financial crimes.

Evaluations of those issues will necessarily depend on the particulars of electronic money and electronic cash product. For example, many smart-card systems abroad generate audit trails and limit the maximum 'value' that a card may hold at any time. Countries with such cards suggest that criminal interest in the cards is low. For the most part, the crimes in a world of electronic cash and digital commerce will be familiar: theft, fraud, counterfeiting, tax evasion, and money laundering. To ensure that law enforcement agencies have the necessary tools to combat financial crimes, government will have to determine the impact of electronic money systems on regulations and policies designed to control financial crime, and investigative strategies and techniques. Traditionally, law-enforcement agencies have relied on rules and regulations allowing them to see documents, hear information exchanges, and track or interdict goods in clearly defined jurisdictions in their fight against financial crimes. Such tangible evidence and the certainty of geography will erode in the digital world of electronic money.

Certain laws, such as the Bank Secrecy Act (BSA) and its implementing regulations, require consumers and businesses to provide information that enables the government to combat certain financial crimes. How such laws apply to new electronic payment systems is not clear. Historically, law enforcement and regulatory officials have relied upon banks and other types of financial institutions to provide data 'chokepoints' through which funds from criminal activities must pass.

The BSA, by requiring these institutions to keep records and file, on certain types of financial transactions provides a paper trail that enables law-enforcement officials to deter, detect, investigate, and prosecute illicit activity. Electronic money systems that allow large, unaccountable transactions have the potential, however, to undermine the effectiveness of the BSA. If such electronic money systems are not covered by BSA requirements, there is reasonable certainty that criminals will use them to evade the BSA 'chokepoints.' Electronic cash could lend itself to totally anonymous transactions without a paper trail, increasing the investigative hurdles faced by law-enforcement officials. The application of the BSA requirements to electronic money systems will depend upon whether the participants and products involved in those systems fall within certain definitions of the BSA.

Regulatory policy

Law enforcement and regulatory officials have mechanisms in place for tracking the flow of money derived from illegal activities based on laws and regulations applied to the financial system. With an open system such as the Internet or with electronic 'peer-to-peer' transactions, however, exchanges of financial value may occur that are not technically subject to the BSA. As electronic systems develop and government gains a greater understanding of the transactions conducted over these systems, government must identify what additional regulatory measures, if any, law-enforcement officials need to combat financial crimes.

Investigative techniques

With the advent of home banking and the development of new retail electronic payments systems, there will be fewer and fewer face-to-face financial transactions. Law enforcement agencies are particularly concerned about the ability of financial institutions to 'know their customers' in a potentially anonymous payment system. Further, government is concerned that paperless payment systems with anonymous users will present fewer opportunities to use traditional techniques such as analyses of financial documents, and surveillance of those suspected of financial crimes.

Decryption

Decryption is the reverse process of encryption. It refers to the decoding of messages that the sender altered-encrypted-in an attempt to keep the message secret from all parties except the one who was to receive it. There are many different encryption techniques, but they all revolve around a process of substituting a number, letter, or some other symbol for the true letter or number or symbol. Each process has its own rule for substituting a false symbol for the true one. Sometimes observers call this rule a 'key,' since knowledge of the rule or key will enable an interested party to 'unlock' or decode the encrypted message. Encryption provides the potential for security in the digital world, and in the minds of those with large financial stakes in the development of electronic commerce and money 'security is to the Internet what safety is to the airlines.' Within the last several years, the private sector has made significant strides in strengthening the commercially applicable encryption processes. These advances respond to consumer and business concerns about the authenticity, reliability, and security of buyers and sellers and of purchases and payments, whether transactions are conducted over the Internet or in the shop of a retail merchant. For the private sector, the stronger the encryption, the smaller the cause for concern.

Because of its law-enforcement responsibilities, government has as strong interest in its ability to decrypt encrypted messages and in the advances in encryption technologies. For the government, powerful, private-sector encryption technology can pose challenging issues. Undecipherable encryption could facilitate criminal activities and, potentially, expose the United States to national security risks. To manage those risks, the Administration has proposed development of a Key Management Infrastructure (KMI) that would, with court permission, give selected federal officials access to the "keys" that would unlock messages encrypted using private-sector technology. The debate on the advantages and disadvantages of this proposal is continuing.

Issuers of electronic money

Electronic money cuts across a wide spectrum of interest. Answers to the question have the potential to affect such activities as the regulation and supervision of issuers; and the management of both the payments system and monetary policy. For that reason they deserve discussion. By any measure, electronic money plays a minor role in the US economy and, as noted elsewhere, that role is not likely to increase any time soon. According to some estimates, "80 percent of all retail purchases in the United

States are settled in cash, the vast majority of them for less than $20." Debit cards, the biggest form of electronic money, accounts for about two percent of retail transactions, and credit cards, the most popular electronic payment option, accounts for only 5 percent.

If the government should find that the issuance of electronic cash involves the receipt of 'deposits,' federal laws precluding or restricting deposit-taking by nonbanks might be applied to nonbanks issuing electronic cash. The states could also limit the types of firms that can offer electronic money services.

In Europe, government officials favor banks as issuers of electronic money, reflecting, in part, the availability of a well-structured regulatory regime. In this country, there is a belief among a number of policy makers and knowledgeable private-sector parties that limiting the issuance of electronic cash to banks could stifle competition an innovation. Many also believe that appropriate regulation of the nonbank issuers can effectively resolve the problems they may pose. Designing the appropriate response will be a challenge. Some of the nondepositories may be affiliated with depositories and others may not be affiliated. Subjecting all nonbank electronic money issuers to the full panoply of depository regulation may not be appropriate. Although some requirements may well be appropriate, nonbank issuers, be they affiliated with depositories or not, may not warrant the same regulations regarding capital, asset diversification, and asset quality, for example, that now apply to depositories.

If and when the time for government action arrives, attention should focus on determining how different regulatory structures for depositories and nonaffiliated nondepositories will affect the competition between those two groups, including how consumers may value the regulatory structures. For example, depending upon whether electronic cash is found to be a 'deposit' under certain Federal Reserve rules, banks may incur costs of deposit reserve requirements that are not imposed on nonbank issuers. The government will also need to decide whether providing holders of electronic cash issued by both depositories and nondepositories with the kinds of protection available, for example, from the FDIC would be appropriate.

Payments system stability: Significant electronic money issuance, especially by those outside the traditional banking system, could also pose challenging problems. The operational failure or insolvency of a key issuer could create a widespread loss of confidence in other forms of electronic money, leading, perhaps, to additional insolvencies and a flight to legal tender. Conceivably, the orderly flow of the inter-bank clearing system could be at risk, to the extent that the ability of banks to meet their inter-bank payments depended upon the ability of electronic money issuers to redeem their obligations in traditional bank deposits. This would be of great concern to the Federal Reserve.

Monetary management: Electronic money, if successful, could gradually lead to shifts among different forms of money held by consumers, and thus potentially affect the behavior of the monetary aggregates. However, electronic money may be only one of a number of changes in financial markets in the years ahead. Some of these may require modifications in the details of how monetary policy is implemented, just as other financial innovations have required adjustments in the past. The Federal Reserve believes that it has the capability to adjust to these changing circumstances while continuing to meet its traditional responsibilities. In order to monitor the monetary aggregates, however, the Federal Reserve may need to obtain data on outstanding amounts of electronic money from issuers, similar to the situation with nonbank-issued travelers checks.

The government, as the exclusive issuer of currency, stands to lose revenue if privately issued electronic money significantly displaces the use of legal tender. Legal tender provides revenues in two ways.

— Signorage, the difference between the face value of coins and the cost of making them.

— Government interest payments are reduced to the extent that people hold currency instead of interest-bearing debt.

Some estimates suggest that the reduction in interest payments could be as much as $3.5 billion annually. As noted in the discussion of electronic money and Treasury operations, the likelihood that the adoption of E-money will lead to a significant reduction in avoided interest expenses for the Treasury is small.

International Cooperation

Electronic money systems operating over open systems such as the Internet can, for all intents and purposes, operate outside of clear geographic boundaries. Within the United States, this creates potential questions concerning the applicability of state laws to transactions that may be initiated by a consumer in one state who uses a financial institution headquartered in a second state to make payments to recipients located in still other states, by means of a computer at some unknown location. Those challenges are even greater at the international level. Nation states may find unilateral enforcement of electronic money related rules difficult. Laws such as those involving protection of personal privacy and entities permitted to issue electronic money may raise especially difficult problems, as will those dealing with tax collections. Sales over the Internet, for example, raise questions about the location of a transaction and consequently about which tax laws apply.

Because most electronic payments systems can operate internationally and in multiple currencies, resolving jurisdictional issues for financial crimes will be difficult. This erosion of national boundaries by retail electronic money and payments makes it even more critical for law enforcement and supervisory authorities in different countries to cooperate in their anti-crime activities and to adopt consistently strong law enforcement policies and standards.

Currently, the Financial Action Task Force (FATF), an international enforcement group with representatives from 26 countries, coordinates approaches to financial crimes and related areas. Recently, FATF adopted several recommendations for strengthening the ability of member countries to manage their crime-fighting efforts.

Electronic-money technology can generate and capture a great deal of payments information. This information has substantial value for both commercial and anti-crime purposes. Using such information for those purposes, however, can raise serious questions involving personal privacy. Recently, the European Union (EU) adopted a policy on personal privacy that provides protections that some believe may not be available in US law. Although the guidelines are extensive, they generally try to ensure that data on individuals are: collected for lawful purposes as specified in the directive and processed fairly and lawfully for purposes specified in the directive. Individuals have the right to see the data that pertain to them. The directive also requires those who hold and process personal information to notify individuals of releases of their personal data and, under certain circumstances, to obtain their consent for such release.

Electronic money systems are still in the relatively early stages of development, and the timing of many future developments is likely to be slower than some people expect, for there are many obstacles to growth. These include issues relating to interoperability, security and privacy, and transaction verification and authentication. The prospect of measured growth does not mean that government can simply sit back and wait for problems to develop. This is an area where major developments are taking place that could greatly alter the payments systems domestically and internationally. Policy makers will likely wrestle, sooner rather than later, with questions in four areas:

— Consumer issues-clarifying rights and responsibilities;

— Law enforcement-evaluating the effectiveness of traditional tools in combating financial crimes;

— Government payments-moving steadily toward the complete use of EFT technology; and

— International coordination-reinforcing the foundations of cooperative action across a wide range of issues.

Traditional government responsibility for areas such as payments system stability and monetary policy may require government action, if and when electronic money systems are more fully developed and commonplace, although the timing for that is likely to be well down the road. In acting upon the nearer-term issues, government can have an effect upon the removal of barriers to growth, a process in which the private sector has a considerable financial interest. Electronic payments and EBT initiatives can affect standards for interoperability. Law enforcement needs for information can affect privacy interests of consumers and merchants, as well as the technical standards that provide the security, transaction verification, and authentication of computerized messages. Specification of consumer rights and responsibilities can affect consumer confidence and acceptance of electronic money products.

Consequently, in meeting its responsibilities, government must combine patience with aggressive fact-finding, study, and coordination among government units both nationally and internationally. Premature action among government agencies or decisions based upon incomplete analysis could thwart innovation and its ensuing benefits, including, perhaps, the ability of US firms to compete effectively in global markets. For electronic money and banking, progress is best achieved through innovation by industry, and by government acting when markets are clearly unable to address concerns on their own.

5

Protection of Privacy in Electronic Era

Consumers are becoming increasingly concerned about how personally identifiable information is being used. This concern, if unaddressed, could have the potential to act as an impediment to widespread consumer acceptance of e-money. A significant barrier to the widespread usage of e-money will be lack of consumer trust or confidence in the privacy of the new payment systems. Both fair information practices and anonymous payments will help build that trust. The belief that systems should be developed to ensure consumer privacy and security, rather than having to add privacy protections later in response to demonstrated problems. Several openions are appropriate role for government is to set basic privacy principles to guide businesses as they build consumer privacy and security into their systems. The increase in data collection efficiency associated with e-money could provide merchants and other system participants with an increased ability to obtain personally identifiable consumer information.

Similarly, the diversity, quality, and quantity of information that is collected and the fact that there are multiple places it can be captured and stored, increase the privacy concerns that could arise with electronic money. The trend toward electronic money may eventually reduce a consumer's ability to use cash or other anonymous payment methods, whereas believed that the new technology could promote anonymous payment methods.

Similarly, several industry the use of encryption can enhance the technical security of products and provide greater privacy protection for consumers. The number of parties involved in new payment methods, including issuers, distributors and processors, could result in more people having access to consumer information. The potential for privacy invasions may be greater as cards become multifunctional because more information could be collected and stored in one place.

The consumers may not receive adequate disclosure of what personal data is being collected, who will receive that data, and how the data will be used. The information consumers voluntarily reveal to the issuer and information about their transactions with merchants would be transferred to the issuer's affiliates and to other parties. The self-regulatory actions, such as industry guidelines and privacy policies, do not provide any meaningful protections for consumers because they are largely unenforceable. Additionally, were concerned that the personal information collected through these new electronic payment methods may not be secure from illegal or unauthorized access and use.

The most consumers do not understand and will not be informed of the privacy implications of choosing different payment methods. There must be significant efforts to educate the public about information security and to seek fair information practices.

The governments should work with consumer organizations to help educate consumers about privacy considerations related to e-money. The governments should establish model disclosures and vocabulary to help consumers understand these products. The e-money would give governments greater access to consumers' financial information by eliminating their ability to make payments anonymously. The consumers may believe that auditable e-money systems will increase the government's ability to gain access to financial information. The belief that it is premature to prescribe a particular form of consumer disclosure about privacy, particularly when stored value products are in such an early stage of development and implementation.

The statutory and common law restricts third party access to many types of information. Some say that they currently provide consumers with general information about what information is being collected and the use of that information. Representatives of law enforcement expressed concerns that some of the new payment methods will diminish the government's ability to identify participants in financial transactions.

The use of encryption in e-money systems might make it more difficult for law enforcement authorities to identify, apprehend, and prosecute criminals who use encryption systems to facilitate money-laundering and counterfeiting. The existing constitutional and statutory provisions place many restrictions on governmental access to confidential information. The requiring that e-money issuers maintain detailed transaction records to facilitate law enforcement could chill product innovation and increase issuer costs, possibly hindering market acceptance of new payment products.

Privacy Issues

Consumer concerns about the privacy of their financial information extend beyond privacy in e-money transactions, and are varied and complex. Some consumers are extremely protective of their privacy and view any collection or use of personally identifiable information as an intrusion, while others are far less concerned about privacy-related matters. Although consumers' privacy thresholds are not uniform, consumers generally share certain key privacy concerns. First, consumers want to receive adequate information about an entity's information collection and use policies. Consumers also appear to be concerned about secondary use of information—the use of information for purposes other than the original transaction, either by the information collector or by a third-party to whom the information is sold or transferred (e.g., a third party processor). The potential for privacy intrusions seems to be at its greatest in these cases, where consumers may not be aware that their personal information is being put to new uses or have any control over those uses. Obtaining knowledge of an issuer's information use policies would allow consumers choice, i.e., so that they can make an informed decision about what e-money product is appropriate for their privacy needs. Additionally, disclosures could provide consumers with rights of redress should the issuer misuse their personal information in a way that is inconsistent with the disclosures or violated public policy.

Existing laws may limit access to, and use of, consumers' e-money information by issuers and third parties. However, unlike the nations of Western Europe, the United States does not have universal or omnibus privacy laws. A consumer's right to financial privacy has not been established as a fundamental right by the United States Supreme Court. Privacy protections in 80 the United States, have evolved on a sectoral basis (applying to certain sectors of society, e.g., banking industry or the public sector), reflecting in part how federal and state legislatures address competing policy objectives, including the prevention and prosecution of criminal acts. There are several existing privacy laws that may or may not apply to e-money.

Many openions expressed concern that consumers would not receive adequate information about an issuer's information practices. Some issuers will provide these disclosures, in an effort to distinguish their products from those of their competitors; however, market incentives may be insufficient to ensure that all consumers receive disclosures about an issuer's information policies. Moreover, existing legal requirements for disclosure of information policies may be inapplicable to most forms of e-money presently in the marketplace.

The Electronic Fund Transfer Act ('EFTA') and its implementing regulation, the Federal Reserve Board's Regulation E, establish the rights and liabilities of consumers who maintain an account at a financial institution and use electronic funds transfers ('EFTs') into or out of the account. Among other things, Regulation E requires financial institutions to document EFTs in writing and to disclose certain information to their customers. Among the disclosures financial institutions must provide to consumers is a description of the circumstances in the institution's 'ordinary course of business' in which it will disclose information about the consumer's account to third parties.

The FCRA enumerates the permissible purposes for obtaining a consumer programmes, including: where the consumer has given his or her written permission; in connection with a credit transaction or insurance underwriting; for employment purposes; and, if there is a legitimate business need, in connection with a business transaction initiated by the consumer. Information solely about transactions or experiences between a consumer and an entity, however, may be shared generally by the entity. Recent amendments to the FCRA expand the scope of permissible information-sharing among affiliates. Affiliated persons and entities are now permitted to share and use consumer information—including consumer programmes among themselves without becoming consumer programming agencies subject to the FCRA, provided the consumer receives notice and an opportunity before the consumer's information is shared to direct that the information not be shared ("opt-out").

Businesses may communicate their own transactional information about a consumer to a consumer reporting agency without notice to the consumer. To ensure the accuracy of this information, however, the FCRA amendments require that persons who furnish information to a consumer reporting agency avoid furnishing knowingly inaccurate information, correct and update information reported, and notify the consumer programming agency of disputes and account closures. It is uncertain whether consumer's e-money transaction information would fall under the protection of the FCRA for several reasons:

— e-money issuers may not be considered "consumer reporting agencies."

— the data collected-information on the consumer's spending patterns-may not fall within the definition of a "consumer report," for example, if the information is considered to be experience information.

However, e-money issuers that provided information to a consumer agency would be subject to the requirements of the FCRA regarding furnishers.

Several federal statutes may limit the government's access to consumers' e-money information. The Privacy Act of 1974 ('Privacy Act') controls the federal government's collection, use, and disclosure of information on individuals. It does not apply to state government agencies or the private sector. A federal agency may collect only such information about an individual as is relevant and necessary to accomplish a required agency function and the agency must provide a Privacy Act statement to each individual asked to supply information. The Privacy Act prohibits, with limited exceptions, a federal agency from disclosing any such record to any person or to another agency unless the individual to whom the record pertains has either requested the disclosure or consented to it in writing.

The Right to Financial Privacy Act ('RFPA') prohibits the federal government from accessing or obtaining information in a customer's financial records from a financial institution, and prohibits a financial institution from disclosing such information to the federal government, except pursuant to the customer's authorization, an administrative subpoena or summons, a search warrant, a judicial subpoena, or a formal written request. The RFPA defines a 'financial institution' as any office of a bank, savings bank, credit card issuer, industrial loan company, trust company, savings association, building and loan, homestead association, credit union, or consumer finance institution. The RFPA only covers 'financial records,' defined to include 'information known to have been derived from' a record pertaining to a customer's relationship with a financial institution. It is uncertain whether the RFPA would apply to a consumer's e-money transaction information for several reasons:

— the scope of institutions subject to the RFPA is limited, although many current e-money issuers would most likely fall within the RFPA's definition of 'financial institutions.'

— a consumer's e-money transaction information may not, in all instances, be considered to be a [financial record' relating to an 'account' for purposes of the RFPA.

Although the US has various sectoral privacy laws protecting some consumer financial information, it is uncertain whether these protections would extend to e-money. Accordingly, existing laws may not address consumer concerns about the collection and use of their e-money information, require issuers to disclose how information will be collected and used, provide consumers with the ability to control whether unaffiliated third parties can obtain the information, or generally limit government access to the information.

In US the Federal laws prohibiting unauthorized access to electronic communications may be applicable to the security of e-money payment information. The Electronic Communications Privacy Act ('ECPA') prohibits the unauthorized access or use of any facility through which an electronic communication service is provided or to intentionally exceed the authorization for accessing that facility. 'Electronic communications' is defined broadly and includes any transfer of signs, signals, writing, images, sounds, or intelligence of any nature transmitted by a wire, or electromagnetic or photo-electronic system, except electronic funds transfer information stored by a financial institution.

The ECPA also prohibits any person or entity from knowingly divulging to any person or entity the contents of an electronic communication while that communication is in transmission or in electronic storage. Again, it is unclear whether a consumer's e-money transaction information would fall within the ECPA's prohibition against disclosing electronic communications in transmission or storage.

Information on consumers and their preferences has important economic value to businesses and consumers. It can help businesses better allocate their resources, improve product quality, and assist consumers in product and service choice. Information can aid firms in the design and delivery of products and services, in marketing, and in inventory control. Although some information, such as mailing lists or product purchase patterns, has always been used for marketing purposes, technological advances of recent years have made that information easier to develop and cheaper to replicate.

Consequently, firms are able to make better use of existing information and to lower the costs of developing new information sources. Information resources can also generate their own independent source of revenue when replicated, sorted, and sold. In some cases, the revenue from direct sale of information might make the provision of primary services profitable. The development and use of consumers' information, however, also raises important questions about consumers' privacy.

The heightened public debate in recent years about privacy and electronic technology has begun to make financial industry participants more sensitive to issues surrounding the collection and dissemination of customer information. As in the financial services sector more generally, industry responses that could be relevant to e-money are continuing to evolve. For example, many products can be purchased on an anonymous basis, such as through vending machines. Similarly, the development of more anonymous e-money products is, itself, one market response that has the potential to provide consumers with new ways to enhance their privacy in financial transactions.

Industry responses based on new, more anonymous technologies may be constrained, however, by law enforcement concerns, which may constitute a significant barrier to the development of electronic money products with greater protections. Although it is too early to tell how many e-money products will ultimately develop, it is likely that more anonymous products will emerge if there is consumer demand for the products and law enforcement concerns can be accommodated. For example, consumer preferences might emerge for anonymous small dollar payments, which would not infringe on the important interests of government agencies to review suspicious large dollar transactions.

Current e-money technology is capable of delivering products with varying effects on privacy, ranging from fully anonymous, cash-like systems, in which no personally identifiable transaction records are created, to fully auditable systems that can identify and store every transaction conducted by every consumer.

As the technology evolves, new products will be developed. The extent to which new products will incorporate privacy protections will be influenced by several factors, including consumer preferences, law enforcement needs, and industry perceptions of the value of information. Consumers with a high degree of concern about the privacy of their transactions will likely favor cash or other cash-like payment products that preserve their anonymity. Other consumers are willing to surrender a degree of privacy in their consumer transactions in order to obtain consumer benefits available with auditable systems, such as convenience, error resolution, recovery of value for lost cards, purchase protection, and loyalty program awards. The majority of stored value systems in existence today involve some trade-off between these types of consumer benefits and privacy. Some e-money issuers claim that it is possible to combine some consumer benefits of an auditable system with the anonymity of a cash-like system, decreasing the need for this trade-off.

At the present time, whether consumers will demand e-money products that protect their privacy is uncertain. How widespread the existence of privacy protections will become may depend on the extent to which consumers tend to prefer products that offer these protections. Given the strong competing pressures from cash and other payment methods, issuers are more likely to face pressures to provide privacy protections, especially as consumer awareness over information collection and use rises and consumers increasingly seek such protections. Issuers in such an environment might see offering privacy protection as a way to differentiate their product, competing for customers on the basis of the privacy protections offered. Similarly, some issuers may then create a product for which consumers would, in effect, pay a premium in exchange for additional privacy protections. While there is reliable evidence that consumers are reluctant to commit to electronic commerce and e-money because of privacy concerns, a clear market demand for this 'privacy premium' product has yet to emerge.

Consumers that are not particularly concerned about the confidentiality of their purchases may not demand privacy protections or information about disclosure policies, as is currently the case for credit cards and similar payment vehicles. Market developments may in some respects address consumer concerns about privacy. Moreover, even if individual consumers do not demand specific protections—due to lack of knowledge or otherwise—implementation of privacy protections by individual firms could increase consumer confidence overall and thereby foster development of the e-money market. In addition, many financial industry participants, either individually or as part of industry groups, are exploring self-regulatory responses to consumer privacy concerns in the financial services industry more generally. Several groups have voluntarily established privacy policies or codes of fair information practices. Also, several industry groups are considering developing 'Acceptance' or 'Privacy' marks.

The SmartCard Forum's Privacy Guidelines encourage their members to: respect the privacy expectations of consumers; ensure that the data are as current, accurate, and complete as possible; promptly honor consumers' requests for information that a company has about them; enable consumers to correct inaccurate personally identifiable information; limit the use, collection, and retention of customer information; and apply appropriate security measures to protect consumer data. The SmartCard Forum principles also encourage their members to provide consumers the opportunity to opt-out before personally identifiable consumer information is to be provided to unaffiliated third parties for marketing or similar purposes. Third parties receiving the information from SmartCard members are encouraged to adhere to equivalent privacy standards with respect to that information.

Similarly, the guidelines suggest that service providers should implement policies and procedures to limit employee access to personally identifiable consumer information on a need-to-know basis, educate employees about the privacy guidelines and their responsibilities under the guidelines, and monitor employee compliance, taking appropriate disciplinary action where appropriate. In September 1997, the American Bankers Association ('ABA'), The Bankers Roundtable and its division, the Bank Information Technology Secretariat ('BITS'), the Consumer Bankers Association (CBA), and the Independent Bankers Association of America ('IBAA'), endorsed a common set of privacy principles ('Banking Industry Principles'). These principles provide that subscribing financial institutions should:

— recognize a consumer's expectation of privacy by making available privacy guidelines and/or providing a series of questions and answers about financial privacy to their customers;

— only collect, retain and use individual customer information where it would be useful (an ' allowed by law) to administer that organization's business and to provide products, services, and other opportunities to its customers;

— establish procedures to ensure customer information is accurate, current, and complete in accordance with reasonable commercial standards, including responding to requests to correct inaccuracies in a timely manner;

— limit employee access to personally identifiable information to those with a business reason for knowing such information, educate employees so that they will understand the importance of confidentiality and customer privacy, and take appropriate disciplinary measures to enforce employee privacy responsibilities;

— maintain appropriate security standards and procedures regarding unauthorized access to customer information;

— not reveal specific information about customer accounts or other personally identifiable information to unaffiliated third parties for their independent use, except for the exchange of information with reputable information reporting agencies to maximize the accuracy and security of such information or in the performance of bona fide corporate due diligence, unless 1) the information is provided to help complete a customer-initiated transaction, 2) the customer requests it, 3) the disclosure is required by/ or allowed by law or 4) the customer has been informed about the possibility of such disclosure for marketing or similar purposes through a prior communication and is given the opportunity to decline;

— if personally identifiable information is given to a third party, the financial institution should insist that the third party adhere to similar privacy principles that provide for keeping such information confidential;

— devise methods of providing a customer with an understanding of their privacy principles. In conjunction with the privacy principles, BITS is in the process of developing a plan for implementing the principles. Thus far, the BITS Board of Directors, made up of the Chairs of the largest banks in the United States, as well as representatives of the ABA, IBAA, and Bankers Roundtable, have approved and endorsed the 'Privacy Principles Implementation Plan.' This plan states that: a plan for implementing the privacy principles will be approved at the level of the Board of Directors or the Office of the Chair of the bank; bank policies related to customer privacy will be communicated to bank customers; employees will be informed and educated about the bank's plan to implement the privacy principles; banks will obtain agreements from third-party vendors on a case-by-case basis to comply with the bank's privacy principles; where a bank provides information to unaffiliated third parties for their independent use for marketing or similar purposes, the bank will notify customers of their right to opt-out from the information sharing; banks will establish and maintain procedures by which customers can correct inaccurate information, and banks will establish internal policies to ensure compliance with and to address breaches of a bank's privacy policy. These principles are more likely to address consumers' privacy concerns in a meaningful and effective manner if they involve a means to assure adherence by industry participants.

Certain industry self-regulatory initiatives include a compliance assurance mechanism. For example, the members of the Individual Reference Services Group ('IRSG') have agreed to self-regulatory principles that require an annual review by a 'reasonably qualified independent professional service' to assess whether the reference service is in compliance with the IRSG's principles. The results of this review must be made public. Also signatories to the principles have agreed only to sell information to reference service companies in compliance with the principles. Separately, a company's failure to honor its own stated privacy policy may also constitute a deceptive practice prohibited by the Federal Trade Commission Act ('FTCA') and state law.

The Federal Trade Commission Act prohibits any person or corporation from engaging in unfair and deceptive acts or practices in or affecting commerce. Even if any industry self-regulatory policies are not implemented through a formal mechanism for enforcement, the interplay of these practices with existing law may result in certain remedies being available to consumers.

— A court may find that the consumer's reliance on an issuer's stated privacy policy gave rise to a contractual relationship between the consumer and the issuer concerning the terms of the privacy policy. Thus, the issuer's failure to follow the terms of the policy statement could constitute a breach of contract.

— A consumer may argue that the issuer's failure to follow its privacy statement was a breach of warranty.

— Consumers may have actions in tort for negligent misrepresentation.

Both the SmartCard Forum guidelines and the Banking Industry Principles appear to generally address many consumer privacy concerns. Each set of guidelines appears to encourage practices that address certain concerns about the collection and use of information. However, neither set has yet developed a formal means to assure adherence by participants or other members of industry. The lack of a means to assure adherence may limit the effectiveness of these guidelines.

The consumers were concerned that e-money technology would enable issuers and merchants to obtain large amounts of information about them. Similarly, the consumers were concerned that they would not receive adequate disclosure about an issuer's information practices, and that issuers would be able to share a consumer's e-money transaction information with third parties without the consumer's consent. The increased efficiency of data collection methods associated with e-money may increase the potential for privacy intrusions.

The technology provides opportunities for increased privacy, and that different privacy policies and product characteristics may be appropriate for different consumers depending on their disparate individual preferences relating to privacy. Moreover, e-money is in an early stage of development, and there is not yet any indication that anonymous payment methods will not remain available. Additionally, existing laws and market responses may address some consumer concerns. Industry participants appear to have significant incentives to develop an e-money market for consumers especially concerned about privacy.

Privacy protections are essentially evolutionary in the United States, and there is little precedent for comprehensive government established privacy protections. Until e-money has had more time to develop, it is premature to assess whether and the degree to which it will present threats to privacy that would warrant government action. As the e-money industry changes and matures, the extent to which industry participants have effectively addressed consumer privacy interests through self-regulatory initiatives should be carefully monitored. The need for government action regarding privacy standards for e-money then can be reassessed based on the growth of e-money as a payment media and the success of e-money providers in implementing effective privacy principles and policies.

Privact Compliance and Enforcement Mechanisms

Privacy compliance and enforcement are different topics, but are interrelated. They are different, since compliance refers to the level of adherence to legal requirements, while enforcement refers to the mechanisms which can be used to compel such adherence and to protect the rights of data subjects when violations occur. At the same time, the two are closely interrelated, since the higher the level of compliance, the less need there is for enforcement, and a strong level of enforcement may motivate actors to adopt a higher level of compliance. This matter recognises the close interrelationship between these two topics, and thus deals with compliance and enforcement together, while still recognising the potential distinctions between them.

On March 12, 2002, a Questionnaire on Compliance with and Enforcement of Privacy Protection in the

Context of Business-to-Consumer Electronic Commerce was sent to OECD governments and private sector participants. It was developed as part of the work programme of the ICCP Working Party on Information Security and Privacy (WPISP) to fulfil the objectives of the OECD Ministerial Declaration on the Protection of Privacy on Global Networks issued at the OECD Ministerial Conference in Ottawa, Canada in October 1998. Responses were received from 20 member countries and three private organisations. In the Declaration, Ministers declared that they will take steps to ensure that effective enforcement mechanisms are available both to address non-compliance with privacy principles and policies and to ensure access to redress. Moreover, the Declaration calls on the OECD 'to promote user education and awareness about online privacy issues and the means at their disposal for protecting privacy on global networks.'

Compliance and enforcement have become central issues in privacy protection since the OECD Ministerial Conference was held. Considering the limitations of purely legalistic and regulatory approaches, both governments and the private sector have been developing alternative methods of compliance and enforcement which make use of self-regulation, market incentives, technological means, and other mechanisms which go beyond traditional regulatory approaches, and which can better cope with the borderless and fast-moving nature of electronic commerce. It was thus the appropriate time to take stock of compliance and enforcement mechanisms used in the OECD member countries and analyse whether they cope adequately with the requirements of electronic commerce. Respondents were requested to provide basic information rather than detailed analysis. Governments were requested to answer the questions with regard to any 'legal provisions', meaning any domestic laws or regulations, including court decisions (case law), or conventions, treaties or other international legal instruments.

Information was solicited both about governmental agencies (such as a government ministry) and independent privacy regulators (such as a data protection authority), the term 'government agency' refers to both types of entities. Input was also solicited from the private sector, since the private sector can provide practical experience, highlighting the process it undertakes when implementing privacy safeguards. Thus, private sector participants were requested, in addition to providing information on legal provisions they are familiar with as described above, also to provide information on any self-regulatory solutions which they are aware of, such as trustmarks, seal programmes, the use of corporate privacy officers, private sector enforcement programmes, and the like, as described further in the questionnaire.

Among the countries with omnibus privacy legislation are Australia, Austria, Belgium, the Czech Republic, Finland, France, Germany, Italy, Korea, Norway, the Slovak Republic, Sweden, Switzerland, and the United Kingdom. Countries without a single omnibus law include Japan, Mexico, Turkey, and the United States. Legislation is currently being considered in Japan and Turkey. Some countries have sector-specific laws as well. For instance, many European Union (EU) member States have sectoral legislation regarding telecommunications privacy, and Finland has laws on telecommunications, openness in government activities, employment privacy, police data files, and criminal records. The United States has laws that address privacy protection concerning various sectors, such as the privacy of children's information, and financial and medical information. Germany has specific acts relating to online services. Most respondents also have additional forms of legal regulation, such as decrees, ordinances, administrative rules, and case law (for instance, France, Germany, Italy, Sweden, and Switzerland have ordinances or decrees). Case law plays a differing role in various member countries: for example, in the United States it is a major source of law, while French law does not regard it as an independent source of law. In Japan there are various self-regulatory guidelines in place, while in the United Kingdom human rights legislation is of particular relevance. Administrative rules and regulations play an important role in the United States.

The member countries of the EU are all bound by the Data Protection Directive, and the various public law agreements and instruments which the European Commission has entered into (such as the Safe Harbour arrangement, and the model contracts for data transfer). Some European countries are also parties to other EU agreements that include data protection provisions, notably in the area of police co-operation. The same countries and others are also members of the Council of Europe (COE), and are bound by the Convention for the Protection of Individuals with regard to Automatic Processing of Personal Data. Mexico has signed an Economic Partnership, Political Consensus and Co-operation Agreement with the European Union and its member States which establishes commitments to promote the protection of personal data, among other aspects. The respondents also share a commitment to implement various other international instruments (such as the OECD Guidelines on the Protection of Privacy and

Transborder Flows of Personal Data (the OECD Privacy Guidelines), the United Nations Guidelines on Computerised Personal Data Files, and others). With regard specifically to model contracts for data transfer, the decisions of the European Commission on model contracts are applicable in the EU member States and have been implemented by them.

The Czech Republic recommends the use of model contracts. The USCIB has participated in the drafting of the alternative model contracts that the International Chamber of Commerce (ICC) and other business organisations have recently presented to the European Commission for approval. A set of model clauses has also been jointly published by the ICC, European Commission, and COE.

Most countries do not have government-endorsed codes of conduct. In Australia, some industry codes of practice have been lodged with the Privacy Commissioner for approval. In the Slovak Republic, all technological norms are endorsed by a governmental entity, while in Sweden industry organisations may submit codes of conduct to the Data Inspection Board for an opinion and the Board has, so far, issued opinions on two such codes. Japan has created a model for guidelines to be set up by business organisations, and a number of companies have set up guidelines in conformance with the model. In many countries (such as Austria, France, Mexico, and the United States) the use of codes of conduct for privacy protection is encouraged. The majority of respondents mentioned that they have private sector codes of conduct, best practices, seal or trustmark programmes that are either endorsed by a business federation, or widely used by the private sector either generally or in a specific sector. Most of the responses concerned codes of conduct, but some (Germany, Japan and the United States, for example) also mentioned that they had seal or trustmark programmes. The Korean Association of Information and Telecommunications mentioned that they award an 'ePrivacy Mark' to qualified Internet sites that satisfy stringent data protection criteria.

Nearly every respondent mentioned some form of government regulation applicable to the security of Web sites, although in many countries (e.g. Austria, Finland, France, Norway, and Sweden) there is no special legislation dealing solely with Web sites but general data protection or security legislation. In Japan private sector guidelines set forth security parameters for business, and guidelines have also been promulgated by governmental entities. In Mexico there are self-regulating measures in the financial sector that guarantee the security of online services. In the United States, a site's misrepresentation to consumers about its privacy and security practices could be a violation of federal consumer protection law. Additionally, there are statutory provisions and administrative rules on security safeguards applicable to the financial sector.

Respondents indicated that a wide variety of entities are consulted in their countries for information and advice on compliance with the norms identified above. Those with a public independent privacy authority (for instance, Australia, Austria, Belgium and the Czech Republic) indicated that they could be consulted. A number of respondents also mentioned private-sector lawyers and law firms (e.g. Finland). Some mentioned governmental bodies other than privacy commissioners: for instance, in Japan there are 'Information Security Advisers' at each Prefectural Police Headquarters (Local

Police Department) who give information and advice about 'Unauthorised Computer Access Law' and computer crime.

Respondents indicated that governmental authorities responsible for privacy protection can review privacy practices of businesses. This can be based on administrative procedures, reviews based on best practices, software tools, or other means for reviewing the privacy practices followed by businesses engaged in online activities, Japan indicated that there are standard practices in place (such as 'JIS Q 15001') which provide for regular business audits, as well as for a 'Privacy Mark System'. Switzerland mentioned that there is an initiative in the private sector for a labelling and auditing programmes for e-commerce. In the United Kingdom, the British Standards Institute has published an audit manual for self-audit, and has included data protection in its suite of software legal compliance tools. Similar initiatives have been promulgated by industry groups such as the World Wide Web Consortium (W3C); this was mentioned by the United States, which indicated that software tools can help companies translate their privacy policies into a Platform for Privacy Preferences (P3P) machine-readable format and can allow a company to inventory all features on its Web site so it can track and control its privacy risks.

In the German omnibus privacy act, there is a provision on privacy auditing which is to be implemented by more specific legislation. Australia and the United States indicated that they encourage companies to voluntarily engage in self-assessment of their privacy practices. It was noted that, in the particular case of the 'Safe Harbor' frameworks in the United States, participants must assess their practices, either by a third party or by self-assessment. In the Netherlands, the data protection authority has developed auditing tools in co-operation with private organisations (e.g. a self-evaluation method and a framework for privacy audits). In Mexico and Sweden, companies voluntarily engage in such self-assessment. Most countries indicated that self-assessments are not usually made publicly available, with the exception of the United States, where some (but not all) companies make them public. Only in the Slovak Republic is there a legal requirement for self-assessment.

In countries with governmental data protection agencies, such authorities are competent to oversee compliance with norms. Other governmental agencies may also monitor compliance with norms in specific sectors (for instance, in Finland the Finnish Communications Regulatory Authority together with telecommunications operators, the telecommunications equipment industry, and user associations promote privacy protection and information security in telecommunications). In those countries where private sector compliance systems are active (such as Japan and the United States), the entities that run such systems also monitor compliance with them, together with competent governmental agencies. The organisation and powers of governmental regulatory bodies are determined by appropriate legislation.

Private sector oversight entities are usually set up based on agreements entered into by the participants in the system. Governmental bodies have oversight powers as granted to them by law, which typically include carrying out audits, issuing warnings breaches to the appropriate authorities (as in France). Private sector entities tend to have similar powers, which can include responding to complaints and enquiries and expelling offending organisations from the scheme, without, of course, the full panoply of powers available to governmental entities.

Responses indicated that there is an increasing trend on the part of companies to appoint internal Data Protection Officers; in a few countries, there is a legal obligation to do so. The USCIB and United States government say that self-regulatory bodies can offer advice on policy and practices, that over 500 companies now have Chief Privacy Officers who are responsible for ensuring that their companies adhere to existing laws and follow sound privacy practices, and that there now exist umbrella organisations in the private sector to assist companies in developing practices and procedures. The United States also mentioned that entities covered under the Health Insurance Portability and Accountability Act will be required by law to appoint a privacy officer when the Act takes effect in April 2003. Also, in Korea, companies must appoint a company privacy officer who will safeguard information and deal with complaints from data subjects. In the Slovak Republic, if a controller of information systems employs more than five persons, he has to appoint a responsible person or several such persons to carry on the supervision of compliance with statutory provisions in personal data processing.

Finally, in Germany, public and private entities with more than four employees have to appoint a data protection officer. Almost none of the other respondents indicated the presence of a legal requirement for companies to appoint a privacy officer in charge of compliance. However, in Finland, the Data Protection Ombudsman has recommended that companies appoint a privacy officer, as do various self-regulatory programs in Japan and the data protection authorities in Norway,

Switzerland, and the United Kingdom. The law of some member countries (e.g. Germany, the Netherlands and Sweden) exempt companies that appoint a company privacy officer from certain legal obligations.

Notification of data processing to an oversight entity is mandatory in Austria, Belgium, the Czech Republic, Finland, France, Italy, Norway, the Slovak Republic, Sweden, Switzerland, and the United Kingdom. However, even in such countries, certain exceptions apply, or notification may apply only to certain situations. For instance, in Sweden notification is not required if a personal data representative has been appointed or if the processing takes place with the individual's consent. Also, in Japan the TRUSTe Japan seal programme requires the notification of processing to an oversight department. Notification of data processing by banks may be required in Mexico under certain circumstances.

Technological solutions to protect privacy are implemented to a limited extent only, although some member countries (such as Japan, the United Kingdom, and the United States) indicated that the use of technical standards (such as P3P) to ensure compliance is expanding. The UK Information Commissioner promotes the use of privacy enhancing technologies, while in the United States there are many such tools widely available on the Internet (including P3P) but it is unclear how many businesses or consumers take advantage of them. The German Ministry of Economy and Technology has a programme to encourage the anonymous use of online technology. The Netherlands indicated that the Dutch government has committed itself to the use of privacy-enhancing-technologies in new public data processing systems.

However, these initiatives remain exceptions. Otherwise, the use of technology to protect privacy was mentioned in the context of security. In Austria, as in other countries, the use of firewalls, anti-virus software and other safety precautions is standard, and the law requires certain data security measures but does not specify the exact techniques that are to be used. Finland indicated that the situation in companies varies to a great extent depending mainly on the size and partly on the field of the company. Japan stated that SSL and other encryption technologies are used to protect sensitive information such as credit card numbers, as is the case in Turkey.

Every OECD member country has at least one government authority, which can enforce privacy norms. Italy mentioned that under the law, data subjects can always turn to data controllers to exercise their rights in the event of a dispute. Japan, the United Kingdom, and the United States say that data subjects may also be able to turn to a self-regulatory scheme, in cases where one is applicable. Most respondents indicated the possibility of obtaining judicial or administrative relief based on a case brought in court or with governmental authorities, such as monetary compensation for damages, injunctive relief, erasure of data or blocking of processing. Austria say that most privacy claims against private entities must be brought before the courts, but that many claims regarding privacy issues are resolved through other legal instrumentse OECD member countries.

The United States say that the Federal Trade Commission (FTC) could sue companies who misrepresent their privacy policies, through administrative procedures or through the courts, and could obtain injunctions and monetary redress for complaints are brought before data protection or consumer protection authorities, which may then investigate the complaint and take appropriate action, which may include imposing penalties or referring the case to the courts or criminal authorities. In some countries (such as Italy) the data subject should first make an application to the data controller before applying for relief to the data protection authorities, whereas in others (Sweden, for example) the data subject may turn directly to the authorities or go first to the data controller. As Japan pointed out, self-regulatory bodies have their own procedures for handling complaints.

Online filing of complaints is possible in a number of member countries (for example, Australia, Austria, France, Germany, Japan, Sweden, and the United States). Norway indicated that, while online filing was not formally provided for, it was used in practice (i.e. data subjects would often send complaints or inquiries to data protection authorities by e-mail). The United Kingdom is working on an online filing system. Mexico specifically noted that the Federal Consumer Protection Agency (Profeco) takes part in an international programmes conducted within the framework of the International Marketing Supervision Network (IMSN) which has resulted in the establishment of a Web site to gather and share complaints about cross-border electronic commerce. In the United States, the FTC administers the IMSN website programme and also maintains its own agency Web site to allow consumers to criticise on privacy complaints, including those relating to Internet representations and e-commerce transactions.

Alternative dispute resolution (ADR) mechanisms for privacy-related disputes, such as arbitration and mediation, are in use in only a few countries, such as

Austria, Korea and the United States. France indicated that a number of such schemes are now being developed by the European Commission. Italy indicated that ADR schemes are used, but that they are not specifically focused on privacy disputes. Such mechanisms are now being developed in Japan. In Germany some trustmark providers may offer such schemes.

Only a few countries indicated that auditing of privacy practices is used as a method of enforcement. In Finland the Data Protection Ombudsman has the right to audit personal data registers and the Finnish Communications Regulatory Authority has the right to audit telecom operators' activities. The French Data Protection Authority (CNIL) has also used online surveys to inventory the practices of Web sites. Auditing by self-regulatory bodies is used in Japan and the United States, and voluntary audits are used in Mexico. Auditing may also be a kind of mandatory enforcement mechanism used by governmental agencies, for example in Sweden and the United States. Some of the local data protection authorities in Germany are presently using software tools to conduct audits of Web sites. Many respondents mentioned that security audits are often used to review the security of information systems and computer networks.

Most countries stated that the public or private sectors had undertaken campaigns to educate the public as to their privacy rights. Among the methods used are speeches and meetings; media interviews; disseminating copies of publications; information on the Web sites of privacy authorities, the publication of annual programmes by privacy authorities; the creation of online 'privacy toolboxes' by companies; and self-regulatory schemes which tell users how they can limit disclosure of their personal information, what choices they have about how such information is used and shared, and under what circumstances they can access it.

No respondents have specific legal requirements to post online privacy policies. However, in many member countries data controllers (including operators of Web sites) have legal obligations to inform the data subject of the processing of his data (including such matters as access rights etc), and this obligation can be satisfied through an online privacy policy. Many government and private sector schemes also encourage companies to post online privacy policies. When a privacy policy is posted, it may need to include certain mandatory information, such as the identity of the data controller and the purpose of the processing.

Intellectual Property Protection (IPP)

There has been a lot of controversy on the role of intellectual property protection (IPP) regime especially the patent system in fostering innovation, technology and industrial development of a country. IPP is expected to encourage innovation by rewarding the inventor with the grant of monopoly rights over the commercial exploitation of their inventions for a specified period. On the other hand, strong IPP regime may inhibit diffusion of knowledge and even technology development in the countries that are technology followers. The history suggests that countries have fine-tuned their IPP regimes as per their developmental requirements. Typically, countries in Asia and in other regions have had softer IPP regimes in the early stages of their development and these regimes have been strengthened as the countries developed and became significant producers of innovations and new technology themselves. In particular, some countries, such as India, have successfully developed cost-effective processes to produce life saving drugs with softer patent regimes. This enabled the national health system to provide affordable medicines to masses of poorer people. Against this backdrop, the on-going attempt to harmonize and strengthen the IPP regimes worldwide, as a part of the TRIPs Agreement, is widely seen to be adversely affecting the technological activity in developing countries by choking the knowledge spillovers from industrialized countries to developing countries. Furthermore, the implementation of the provisions of TRIPs Agreement threatens the access and affordability of poor people to lifesaving drugs by pushing up their prices. This has been highlighted by the recent controversy regarding the availability of AIDS drugs in South Africa.

The global technology generation or innovative activity is known to be highly concentrated in a handful of technologically advanced developed countries. The top ten countries account for as much as 84 per cent of global resources spent on R&D activity annually, they control 94 per cent of the technological output in terms of patents taken out in the US, and receive 91 per cent of global cross-border royalties and technology license fees. Hence, the concentration in terms of technological output is even more uneven than for technological inputs. The control over technology is reflected in their 74 per cent share of global FDI outflows. The relative position of countries in terms of different indicators varies. It is curious to find, for instance, that Japan accounts for 17-18 per cent of global R&D expenditure and US patents, but shares only 8.6 per cent of global technological receipts (and only 3 per cent of FDI outflows). Similarly, The Netherlands and Switzerland command a much higher proportion of global royalties than their share of R&D expenditure or patents. The discrepancy between the share in technological activity and returns in terms of royalties could be on account of different focus of the technological effort of different countries. The technological effort of Japanese corporations seems to be geared towards obtaining competitiveness of their products in domestic and export markets more than for supporting the transfer of technology and production.

However, the bulk of this 5.7 per cent share is accounted for Taiwan (which accounts for 2.54 %) and South Korea (with 1.86 %), although a few countries e.g. Israel, China, Hong Kong, Singapore, India are showing an increasing trend of patenting in the US. The rise of innovative activity in Taiwan and Korea is not only reflected in increasing number of US patents owned but also in emerging technology exports which are as yet small in value terms but have grown rapidly over the past few years. Therefore these countries together with Japan make important cases for analyzing the role played by IPRs in their technology development.

There are three ways that the strength of the IPR regime could affect economic growth indirectly: IPR regime may affect the innovative activity that in turn is the source of total factor productivity improvements and thus contributes to growth. The IPR regime could affect the inflows of FDI and technology transfers and which could impinge upon the growth. Given the international dimension of IPR regimes, there could be implications for international trade of countries, for instance, on the ability of countries to export certain goods. Finally, the changes in IPR regimes may imply some redistribution of income between the countries and between communities within the country.

There are a few studies that have addressed the issue of effect of IPR regime on growth directly. However, the observed effects could be subject to the causality problem as developed countries are likely to have stronger IPRs regime than the poorer ones. In other words, the level of development is likely to be a determinant for strength of IPR regime rather than the other way round. Ginarte and Park in a study covering 110 countries for the period 1960-90 corroborated that either the level of economic development or factors correlated with it e.g. the level of R&D activity, market environment, and international integration explain the strength of patent protection provided by countries.

Furthermore, Maskus and Penubarti find the relationship between IPR protection and level of development to be non-linear suggesting that patent protection tends to decline in strength as economies move beyond the poorest stage into a middle-income stage in which they have greater abilities to imitate new technologies. Therefore, the finding of Gould and Gruben that found a significant positive effect of the strength of patent protection on growth of 79 countries (after controlling for investment rates and human capital development) particularly for open economies could be subject to causality bias. The indirect nature of the possible effect of IPRs on growth is also confirmed by Park and Ginarte. Thompson and Rushing empirically observe that universally imposed minimum standards for patent protection are not likely to contribute to increased growth in developing countries. However, stronger patent protection could contribute to economic growth rates once a particular level of development has been achieved. In a further refinement to their earlier results, Thampson and Rushing find that patent protection could be positively associated with improvement in total factor productivity, and hence growth, in wealthy or developed countries. Therefore, the IPR regime could affect economic growth and development through other variables such as innovative activity, FDI inflows and technology transfers. In what follows the evidence on the effect of IPR regime on innovative activity and FDI and technology transfer and trade is reviewed.

The main argument offered in favour of tighter and more stringent laws to protect intellectual property and patent rights is to provide better conditions for appropriability of innovations. However, the existing empirical literature suggests that the effectiveness of patent protection varies from industry to industry and is most effective only in chemical and pharmaceutical industries. A study by Mansfield showed that around 65 per cent of pharmaceutical and 30 per cent of chemical inventions would not have taken place but for patent protection. In the case of most other industries patent protection was not important. In the case of most of the engineering industries, and in particular, electrical & electronic goods, and instruments etc. patent protection was not found to be essential for the introduction of inventions. This finding was confirmed by most of the subsequent studies. For instance, a survey conducted by Levin et al. showed that product patents were found to be highly effective as means of appropriating returns only in five of 130 narrowly defined lines of businesses. These five included drugs, organic chemicals, pesticides. Shankerman in an analysis of French patent renewal data for the period 1969-72, concludes that while patents may be a significant source of returns to innovative enterprises, they are not the major ones. The main reason for limited effectiveness of patents is the ability of competitors to legally 'invent around' patents.

Gallini finds that longer patent life pushes the rivals to invent around the patent inventions. Hence, optimal patent life are sufficiently short to discourage imitation. These studies also revealed that secrecy to be more effective than patents in protecting process innovations. Besides in the case of several high technology industries like aerospace and industrial machinery the complexity of the products made reverse engineering very costly and imitation difficult even without patent protection. Hall using a game theoretic model of a R&D race to analyze the effect of weakening patents has on the timing and profitability of R&D, found that in general, a second innovation (or inventing around) would occur later than it would have if the IPR policy had not been weakened. Scherer and Weisburst examined the impact of strengthening of pharmaceutical patent protection in Italy since 1978. They concluded that the regime change had little or no impact on the trend of inflation-adjusted R&D expenditures or on the introduction of new chemical entities. Hence, they expressed their scepticism on the prospect of the trend of lengthening of patent protection with TRIPs Agreement in significantly raising innovative activity especially in developing countries.

Cohen and Levinthal, in their comprehensive model explaining R&D intensity, considered technological opportunity as well as appropriability as determinants and also assessed the net impact of the spillovers of R&D. Technological opportunity is a function of technological and research output in that area as well as the output of other R&D units which the patent owners wish to protect by reducing the spillover effects. On the other hand the spillover effect is one of the notable inputs to R&D. The analysis showed that the positive absorption incentive associated with spillovers seemed to increase relative to the negative appropriability incentive in the case of many industries.

A more detailed analysis conducted to examine whether the spillovers on balance actually encouraged R&D in some industries found that in the case of chemicals and electrical and electronics, R&D intensities increased with spillovers. Therefore, the available evidence does not indicate that further tightening of patent laws would increase expenditures on R&D. On the contrary, strong patent laws could even hurt subsequent R&D effort by restricting spillovers.

In this context it might also be useful to recall that Schumpeter had argued for a short-term monopoly profits to encourage innovation and not for a legal institutionalized monopoly position. He had emphasized that monopoly offered no cushion to sleep on and hence the temporary state of monopoly resulting from the possession of a new technology. In the medium and long term the firm would be subject to the threat of competition and the advent of better or improved products from rivals. Hence, the need for the firm to safeguard its market position through continuous innovative activities. It was this process that prevented the original creator of a new technology from being complacent and prompted the monopolist to be constantly creative. A legal protection as provided by the patent system for a rather longer term of twenty years, therefore, erodes the threat of potential competition and hence, the need for continuous improvement.

The importance of foreign R&D spillovers as a determinant of R&D activity could be even more critical in developing countries where much of the R&D activity is of an adaptive nature. A number of studies have empirically demonstrated the ability of rather weaker intellectual property rights in stimulating domestic innovative activity in developing countries to absorb spillovers of foreign R&D. Fikkert in a study of Indian enterprises found evidence of their R&D activity absorbing considerable foreign R&D spillovers facilitated by weak Indian patent regime. He suggested that a 'weak patent regime may allow spillovers simultaneously to promote R&D and to have a positive direct effect on productivity' and concluded that the adoption of a 'stronger patent regime may not be optimal from either the short- or long-run perspectives'. Similarly, Kumar and Saqib found Indian chemical industry enterprises to be among the more innovative ones in the Indian industry. They attributed this to the weak patent laws viz. absence of product patents in India which enabled Indian enterprises to undertake alternative process development.

The importance of spillovers from innovative activity in developed countries for domestic technological effort in developing countries facilitated by softer IPRs has also been corroborated by other studies. Haksar estimated marginal products of R&D and technology imports and their spillover effects using the Reserve Bank of India data for 642 Indian firms distributed across 65 industries for 1975-1990 period. His finds both local R&D and disembodied technology imports generating positive spillovers. In the pharmaceutical industry the return to R&D were found to be particularly large and was explained in terms of highly successful adaptive R&D effort of Indian firms directed at development of alternative processes of known drugs made possible by the absence of patents on pharmaceutical products.

The above review of literature suggests that the evidence on the role of IPRs as a determinant of innovative activity is quite weak. In fact stronger IPRs may actually affect the innovative activity adversely by chocking the absorption of knowledge spillovers that are important determinants of innovative activity. Mazzoleni and Nelson is a survey of theoretical and empirical studies also conclude that 'there is reason for concern that the present movement towards stronger patent protection may hinder rather than stimulate technological and economic progress.'

Technology Licensing and Trade

There has been a considerable controversy on the role of intellectual property protection in determining inward FDI flows and their effect on technology licensing and trade. In the OLI theory of international operations of firm, exports, FDI and arm's length technology licensing are considered as alternative modes of servicing a foreign market by firms. Stronger protection increases the value or revenue productivity of a firm's intellectual property such as technology, brand and trade names. Stronger protection should help exporters by making imitation and counterfeiting more difficult. The favourable effect of stronger IPRs in foreign countries on exports has generally been confirmed empirically by a number of studies.

However the effect of IPR strength on FDI and licensing is not that straight forward. By reducing the transaction cost of transfer of knowledge by MNEs to foreign countries, stronger protection may encourage arm's length licensing of the knowledge and reduce the need for undertaking FDI. On the other hand, it has been argued that poor IPR regime tends to adversely affect the investment climate and hence the probability of MNE investments. Relatively little empirical verification of these contentions that has been made has generally shown an insignificant influence of the extent of IPP on inward FDI. Frischtak and Bosworth did not find a significant role of IPRs in influencing the pattern of FDI and technology transfers respectively. Ferrantino found no discernible impact of a country's adherence to IPR agreements on the arm's length exports or subsidiary sales (i.e. FDI) of US firms. But subsidiaries in countries adhering to IPRs had a greater chance of sourcing more components from the US than from the host countries.

The affiliates in countries belonging to the Paris Convention are also likely to have higher payments of royalties and licence fees than others. The greater dependence on parents for sourcing components also creates greater potential for transfer pricing. Since the 'U.S. is generally a low tax regime compared to LDCs, this suggests that strong international IPRs may indirectly cause a diversion of tax revenue from LDCs to the US treasury'. Kondo found no consistently significant relationship between the strength of patent laws in terms of four alternative indicators and the levels of and changes in US FDI in a sample of 33 countries over a 15 year period. Lee and Mansfield, on the other hand, in a sample of 14 countries (observations pooled over three years) find the perceived weakness of intellectual property protection adversely affecting the volume as well as the composition of US FDI inflows to the countries. However, given the small size of sample, a rather subjective measurement of intellectual property regime (based on firm's perception), and low t-values of the coefficients, the findings could be considered only as indicative unless replicated in larger samples. In a study covering 27 less developed countries for the period 1975-90, Sayoum finds that IPR factors to be significant in explaining variation in inward FDI and the effect was particularly strong for emerging countries. Mascus found that strength of patent protection had a negative effect on the sales and assets of affiliates of US MNEs, although only the coefficient was statistically significant only in the second case. However, the impact of patent protection affiliate sales and assets was positive and significant in the case of developing countries sub-sample.

The strength of patent protection in explaining the sales and value addition of affiliates of US and Japanese affiliates in 74 countries in seven broad branches of industry and at three points of time in the framework of an extended model of location of foreign production. The strength of patent protection regime although with a positive sign never had a statistically significant coefficient for affiliate sales or value added in the case of US MNEs. In the case of Japanese MNEs, the results were sensitive to inclusion of dummy variables identifying the two tiers of Asian NIEs. The coefficient of patent rights was not significantly different from zero in a full sample test when the regional dummies are not included. When the Asian NIEs are separated with the dummy variables, than the coefficient of patent rights becomes statistically significant with a positive sign. This suggests that Japanese MNEs have tended to overlook the relatively weaker IPR regime prevailing in the East and South East Asian countries for their outward investments. Outside East and Southeast Asia, Japanese investments are concentrated in the

European Union and North America-countries having stronger IPR regime. Hence, one gets a positive significant coefficient. In the sub-sample estimations for Japanese affiliate sales in developing countries, patent rights variable comes up with a significant coefficient with a negative sign. That could be explained in terms of high concentration of Japanese investment in developing countries in those countries that have weaker IPR regime.

The coefficient of the strength of patent protection is never significantly different from zero while explaining the value added of US and Japanese affiliates. The strength of patent regime does not appear to be a significant factor in determining the patterns of US or Japanese FDI. Some further analysis of the same data set at the level of seven broad sectors, currently in progress and reported in Kumar suggests that strength of patent protection does not influence the patterns of US affiliate sales in any of the seven branches of manufacturing except the miscellaneous industry where it had a significant but negative coefficient. Smith finds that foreign patent rights increase US affiliate sales (i.e. FDI) as well as licenses. However, the effect is larger in the case of arm' length licensing than for FDI. These conclusions are consistent with those of Yang and Mascus who find that patent rights promote arm's length trade and they have a less significant effect on internalized technology transfers viz. FDI.

The issue of IPR protection links more directly with R&D activity in the context of globalization of R&D activity of MNEs. MNEs may be apprehensive of locating their key R&D centres in countries with weak patent regimes. However, where the overseas R&D is directed to local adaptations and to providing other support to the local production of the MNE, and not directed to new product development, the patent regime may not be of much consequence to it. Kumar in a study explaining R&D intensity of affiliates of US MNEs in 54 countries in 1977, 1982, and 1989, found that strength of patent protection had a significant positive influence on R&D intensity of affiliates located in developed countries and has a negative coefficient in a developing country sub-sample which is not statistically significant.

Thus stronger patent protection does not appear to be a prerequisite even for R&D investments by MNEs in developing countries. Kumar provides case study evidence suggesting that MNEs have been locating R&D centres, R&D joint ventures and contracting research in India in the field of chemicals and pharmaceuticals despite the patent regime not recognizing product patents in these sectors. Therefore, availability of abundant trained low cost human resources and scale of ongoing R&D in their own fields appear to be more important considerations for location of R&D in developing countries than the strength of IPR regime.

These hypotheses were verified in a more recent study that explained R&D intensity of affiliates of US and Japanese MNEs in 74 countries in seven branches of industry and at three points of time, 1982, 1989, and 1994. This study found that the strength of patent protection offered by the country remained statistically insignificant in explaining R&D intensity of US and Japanese affiliates throughout. The bulk of the variation in R&D intensity was explained by the abundance of R&D manpower and its relative cost, scale of national technological effort and technological capability of the host country especially in the field of the affiliate.

It would appear from the above that the contention that stronger norms of IPR protection will facilitate greater inflows of FDI in the country is rather weak in either theoretical or empirical terms. The theory suggests that stronger IPRs may tilt the balance between exports, FDI, and licensing in favour of exports and arm's length licensing. The empirical evidence has been mixed generally supporting no strong effect of the strength of patent protection on FDI inflows, their composition and even overseas R&D activity of MNEs. As Mascus puts it, if strong IPRs were able to provide sufficient incentives for firms to invest in a country, 'recent FDI flows to developing economies would have gone mainly to sub-Saharan Africa and Eastern Europe. In contrast, China, Brazil and other high-growth, large-market developing economies with weak protection would not have attracted nearly as much FDI'.

IPRs in Asian countries

The rapid and sustained growth and development in the East Asian economies, viz. Japan; South Korea, Taiwan, Hong Kong and Singapore, Malaysia, Thailand, and Indonesia and China, generally termed as the 'East Asian Miracle', has attracted a large volume of literature. The growth rate of per capita income over the 1960-90 for these economies averaged over 5.5 per cent, making it the fastest growing region in the world sustaining such rates of growth over such a long span of time. Japan and Asian nies have been able to expand their share in world exports from 8 per cent in 1965 to 13 per cent in 1980 and 18 per cent in 1990, suggesting that their exports have expanded much faster than any other region's. Their share in world's manufactured exports has grown from 11 to 21 per cent over the same period. In particular rapid transformation of Korea and Taiwan from technologically backward and poor economies into affluent and relatively modern economies by early 1990s has been truly remarkable.

Some analysts have attempted to downplay the East Asian achievement as a result of factor accumulation along the production function. However, since then a number of studies have corroborated that a substantial proportion of East Asian growth was contributed by growth of total factor productivity (TFP) and it was not a result of merely factor accumulation. The total factor productivity growth in Japan, Korea, Taiwan, Hong Kong and Thailand has averaged between 2 to 4 per cent per year over 1960-89 thus contributing over a third of the growth of output!

A large volume of literature has also been concerned with the explanation of the rapid TFP growth in the East Asian countries. It is now widely accepted that the assimilation of foreign technology was a 'critical component of the Asian Miracle'. There seems to be a general consensus that the East Asian success owes a lot, in general, to their ability to imitate, absorb, assimilate and replicate foreign innovations. Kim highlights the role of 'duplicative imitation' in the Korean industries initially in the light industries such as textiles, toys, consumer electronics in the 1960s and in such heavy industries such as automobiles, steel, shipbuilding and machinery in the 1970s. Hobday provides case studies of firm level learning in Korea as well as other East Asian countries. Singh and Trieu provide econometric evidence suggesting that R&D expenditures in Japan, South Korea and Taiwan have contributed to TFP growth.

The existing evidence on the role of IPRs regime in promoting growth is largely anecdotal. Although the literature is not explicit in acknowledging its role, the soft intellectual property protection regime adopted by these countries in the period of duplicative imitation or reverse engineering has played and important role in facilitating the firm level technological learning. Below we attempt to put together some evidence for Japan, Korea and Taiwan on the role weak IPRs regime adopted by these countries have facilitated their technological and economic development.

Japan

Japan is known to have greatly benefited from intellectual property generated in other developed countries in the early stages its development. In fact the two international treaties on the IPRs viz. the Paris Convention for industrial property and the Berne Convention for copyrights "were negotiated, in part because of frustration over alleged infringements in the 'newly industrialising countries' of the day, such as the United States and Japan". Furthermore, in Japan the patent protection has been designed with an ultimate objective of contributing to the 'development of industry' and not as an end by itself. In tune with this objective it has contained several features that have helped the absorption of spillovers of foreign inventive activity by domestic enterprises. For instance, although Japanese Patent System (JPS) was established in 1885 by the Patent Monopoly Ordinance that was replaced by the Patent Ordinance of 1888, the food, beverage, pharmaceutical products and chemical compounds were excluded from the scope of patent protection until 1975 to facilitate the process innovations. In 1905 the Utility Model Law was introduced to provide protection to adaptations or improvements over the imported machinery or equipment by domestic inventors that were considered too minor to be patented primarily. As many as 99.9 per cent of utility models have been granted to Japanese nationals over the 1905- 79 period. Furthermore, the JPS provides for protection of industrial designs which only needed to demonstrate novelty and not inventiveness.

The utility models and industrial designs have allowed Japanese firms to receive protection on technologies that were 'only slightly modified from the original invention'. JPS also employs the first-to-file principle rather than the first-to-invent principle incorporated in the US law, pre-grant disclosure that lays open or publishes the patent applications for inspection or opposition for eighteen months, provides for compulsory license if a patent has not been worked (i.e. used in manufacture) in Japan continuously for more than three years or in public interest, and required the patent applications to be limited to a single narrow claim. All these features have been designed to favour adpatations by domestic enterprises. That they have been used to encourage technology adaptations by domestic entrepreneurs is clear from the fact that in 1980 Japan had awarded 49000 utility models to its nationals compared to just 533 to foreigners. Similarly Japanese nationals were granted 31000 industrial design patents vis-à-vis 600 to foreigners. There have also been complaints of discrimination by JPO and foreign applicants appear to face longer pendency periods than do domestic applicants in Japan.

Mascus and McDaniel in a systematic quantitative study have found that the above features namely utility models, design patents, compulsory licenses, first-to-apply, narrow claims, among others, that make JPS considerably weaker than the US patent system, for instance, have facilitated absorption, transfer and diffusion of technology by allowing reverse engineering and contributed to the TFP growth during the period 1960-93. The scope of patent system was expanded to cover chemical and pharmaceutical products only in 1975. Kotabe attributes the regime change to the growing international pressure. However, it was probably motivated by the realization that by 1970s, Japanese enterprises had developed their technological capability adequately and hence needed protection for their own innovative activity. In October 1970 the Japan Patent Association surveyed its member firms on whether they favoured introduction of chemical product patents. About 60 per cent of the respondents favoured product patents and only 9 per cent opposed. With this strong support from the industry, the Japanese government began the process of amending Japanese patent law to provide for product patents for chemicals and pharmaceuticals. The amendment was adopted by the Diet in May 1975 and became effective from January 1976.

South Korea

South Korea adopted the patent legislation only in 1961. The Korean patent law was amended in 1981 to conform with the Paris Convention that provided for multiple claims for related inventions in a single application. However, the scope of patenting did not cover patenting of products and processes to manufacture food products, chemical substances and pharmaceuticals. The US government initiated an investigation on Korea under Section 301 of the Trade Act threatening trade sanctions on Korean exports for its failure to provide protection to US products. That pushed Korea to strengthen its IPR regime. The revised patent, copyright, and software legislation was passed by the National Assembly on 31

December 1986 and became effective in July 1987. The new law extended product patent protection to new chemical and pharmaceutical products, adopted a comprehensive copyright law, and extended copyright protection to computer software.

The patent term was also extended from 12 to 15 years. Korea has also followed an IPR regime that facilitated adaptations and imitative duplication of foreign technologies by domestic enterprises through utility models and industrial designs. It is evident from the fact that 92 to 95 per cent of all utility models and industrial designs have been granted to its nationals. The delibrate softening of IPR regime by the government to facilitate imitation by domestic enterprises has been acknowledged in the literature on Korean technological capability. Lee, for instance, observes that during the imitation stage, the 'government tried to minimize IPR protection to help domestic firms use foreign intellectual property. Laws and regulations were formulated in such a way as to meet minimal international standards. Furthermore, enforcement of the law was less than strict'. Kim provides highly illustrative case studies of several industries documenting firm level successes in absorbing technology and other knowledge with the help of duplicative imitation or reverse engineering and gradually emerging as innovators in their own right. The softer patent regime adopted by the country facilitated this process of reverse engineering. La Croix and Kawaura in an event study of the effect of the new patent law on the market valuation of Korean pharmaceutical firms listed on the stock exchange found a cumulative decline of -74 per cent over the 14 months period. Korea's ability to absorb foreign innovative activity through duplicative imitation has helped it to grow rapidly during the 1960-1980s. The real

GDP expanded by 9.5 per cent per year during the 1965-1980 period and by 8.6 per cent during 1980-87 period. Despite the new Patents Act of 1986 according product patents for chemicals and pharmaceuticals, Korea continued on the priority watch list of the US government under Special 301 till 1993 for enforcement concerns. In February 1993 Korea launched a comprehensive new plan to strengthen IPRs protection and enforcement followed by a new Patent Act in 1995. Nevertheless, Korea has often been regarded as being weak in protecting IPRs.

In view of the role played by soft patent regime in Korea's development, Kim infers that current trend of strengthening of IPR protection will pre-empt duplicative imitation of foreign technologies by developing countries of today. Reverse engineering of foreign products for duplicative imitation will be more difficult and costly for developing countries than it was for Korea in the 1960s and 1970s. China, for instance, faces enormous pressure from the United States to honour IPRs which Japan, Korea and Taiwan did not face in their early industrialization stage'.

Taiwan

Taiwan has also employed a weak IPR policy to facilitate local absorption of foreign knowledge through reverse engineering on the lines of Japan and South Korea. In fact Taiwan's government seem to openly encourage counterfeiting as strategy to develop local industries. In the mid-1980s an estimated 60 per cent of world's pirated or counterfeit goods were allegedly originating in Taiwan. Wade documents a number of cases of government's tacit approval of counterfeiting. In a late 1970s case, several factories were found to be manufacturing circuit fuse breakers with forged Westinghouse and Mitsubishi labels. When Mitsubishi complained to the authorities, the firms were fined all of US$600.

The government publicly denied that this was a serious case, while privately saying that "political factors" made it impossible to take tough action. Those political factors were the adamant opposition of most Taiwan firms and industry associations to any signs of tough enforcement, since they saw themselves as handsome beneficiaries of non-enforcement. And the government itself tended to view counterfeiting as a shortcut to industrial success. As recently as 1983 an unattributed government document entitled "Intellectual Property Rights Protection, a Republic of China Perspective," said with remarkable candor, "The R.O.C. government has viewed imitation as a necessary process in the evolution of human civilization and believed that commercial counterfeiting is an inevitable phenomenon in most developing countries. Local officials were cognizant of the negative aspects of counterfeiting although they made little effort to accommodate overseas interests or enhance domestic enforcement efforts when such aspects were seen to be outweighed by the positive development of the industrial base.

Lax treatment of IPRs in Taiwan attracted the attention of the US government. In March 1983, the US government instituted bilateral consultations on IPRs with Taiwan. As a result of growing US pressure, Taiwan amended its copyright law in 1985 to strengthen penalties for piracy, provide criteria for recognizing foreign firms' standing before the Taiwanese judiciary in copyright cases, and extend protection specifically to new media, including software. This followed enactment of a new patent law in 1986 extending protection to chemicals and pharmaceutical products. However, these legislations and their enforcement were considered inadequate by the US government. Under heavy pressure from the US Taiwan promulgated its new Patent Law on January 21, 1994 that allows patents on food, beverages, micro-organisms, and new uses for products, all of which were previously excluded under the government's social policy. In addition the duration for new patents was extended from 15 years to 20 years.

Like Japan and Korea, Taiwan also provides for utility models (for 12 years duration under the new law) and design patents (term 10 years under new law). However, many concerns have continued to remain. These include elimination of imprisonment penalties for patent infringement while they continue for violations of utility models and design patents primarily held by Taiwan nationals. There is a provision for patent marking under which a patent owner who fails to mark the patent certificate number on the patented article or packaging cannot claim damages from infringement.

The East Asian countries viz. Japan, Korea and Taiwan have absorbed substantial amount of technological learning under weak IPR protection regime during the early phases. These patent regimes facilitated the absorption of innovation and knowledge generated abroad by their indigenous firms. They have also encouraged minor adaptations and incremental innovations on the foreign inventions by domestic enterprises and developed a patent culture through utility models and design patents. As the local technological capabilities matured and the domestic industry sought stronger protection for guarding their own inventions, the IPR regime was strengthened in Japan in mid-1970s. In the other two countries, the IPR regime had to be strengthened under US pressure.

In the chemicals and pharmaceuticals it did not prove a constraint as the process patents in the absence of product patents essentially served the purpose of encouraging process adaptive activity of domestic firms. As a result, the domestic chemicals and pharmaceutical industries have developed in their capabilities considerably over the past three decades. However, in the engineering industries and others, there was not a mechanism for encouraging minor adaptations of domestic firms. This difference could perhaps explain not so encouraging performance of Indian enterprises in other industries. Furthermore, IPR regime is only one of the determinants of the technological capability building. The domestic technological effort in absorbing the foreign technologies and innovations in East Asian countries has been vastly more substantive and has been sustained over a much longer period compared to India that attempted to build capabilities with softer patent regime only since the mid-1970s. Before this India's patent regime was comparable to those prevailing in the developed countries.

India

India had inherited The Patents and Designs Act 1911 from the colonial times that provided for protection of all inventions except those relating to atomic energy and a patent term of 16 years from the date of application. However, a few domestic chemical and pharmaceutical enterprises that tried to develop their own technology in the 1960s ran into trouble with foreign patent owners. A number of cases highlighted that foreign patent owners were neither using their patents for domestic manufacture nor allowing them to be used by local firms.

That led to a build-up of pressure in the late 1960s for a new patent law. Desai in a questionnaire survey of 53 firms conducted in 1969 found that by and large foreign firms were against any liberalization of patent laws, Indian firms were not against patents but wanted greater access to patented know-how especially when patent owners not allowing their patents to be used. The conflict of views was sharper in chemicals and pharmaceuticals where patents had been used to prevent entry of Indian firms. Therefore, a new Patents Act was adopted in 1970 that reduced the scope of patentability in food, chemicals and pharmaceuticals to only processes and not products. Since virtually any chemical compound can be made by a variety of processes, the scope of patent protection was greatly reduced. The term of process patents was reduced to 7 years in food, drugs and chemicals and to 14 years for other products. The compulsory licenses could be issued after three years. The Indian Patents Act of 1970 has continued to govern the IPR regime in India over the past 30 years except for recent amendments brought to provide for exclusive marketing rights (EMRs) in tune with India's obligations under WTO's TRIPs Agreement.

India joined the Paris Convention and the Patent Cooperation Treaty only in 1999. India has a ten years transition to provide product patents viz. till the end of 2004. It is by now widely recognized that the abolition of product patents in chemicals and pharmaceuticals has facilitated the development of local technological capability in chemicals and pharmaceutical industry by enabling the domestic firms in their process innovative activity. A number of quantitative studies have shown that the innovative activity of Indian domestic enterprises was facilitated by the softer patent regime under the 1970 Act. The gradual build up of technological capability of Indian enterprises is visible from a rising trend of residents in patent ownership in India.

Improved technological capability is also reflected in terms of the ability of India to raise her share in patents granted by the US patents office from 0.02 per cent in 1977-87 period to 0.06 per cent during 1996-2000. Although still having marginal share in the US patent grants, India has not fared badly compared to other developing countries. In 1998, it ranked seventh amongst all developing countries in terms of the magnitude of US patents obtained, behind Taiwan, South Korea and Israel-the three leading nations-but ahead of Brazil, China and Mexico. Interestingly, in the chemicals sector-which accounts for the bulk of all patents-and in biotechnology-one of the cutting edge sectors-India ranks fourth amongst developing countries. Moreover, in biotechnology, the gap between India and countries ahead of it is not large.

In particular, the rapid evolution of Indian pharmaceutical industry since the mid-1970s highlights the fact that weak IPRs regime could be instrumental in building local capabilities even in a poor country such as India. In what follows we take a look at some indicators of evolution of technological capability of Indian pharmaceutical enterprises. In 1970 much of the country's pharmaceutical consumption was met by imports and the bulk of domestic production of formulations was dominated by MNE subsidiaries. Of the top ten firms by retail sales in 1970 only two were domestic firms and the others were MNE subsidiaries. In 1996 six of the top ten firms in the industry are Indian firms. By 1991, domestic firms accounted for 70 per cent of the bulk drugs production and 80 per cent of formulations produced in the country.

The increasing technological capability is reflected in terms of rising exports of drugs and pharmaceuticals. With their cost effective process innovations, Indian companies have emerged as competitive suppliers in the world of a large number of generic drugs that are now outside the patent protection. That has resulted in a steady growth of India's exports of drugs and pharmaceuticals. Thus the industry has evolved from being one being highly import dependent to one that generates increasing export surplus for the country. The faster growth of pharmaceutical exports has resulted in their share in India's exports rising from 0.55 per cent in 1970-71 to over 4 per cent by the 1999/00. India ranks second after China among developing countries in export of pharmaceuticals and is ahead of such technologically advanced countries as Mexico, South Korea, Brazil, Israel.

Indian exports of pharmaceuticals received a boost in the late 1980s when a number of drugs went off the patents and Indian companies manufacturing them with cost-effective processes entered the international markets after obtaining FDA approval. Therefore, in the late 1980s, as much as 61 per cent of India's pharmaceutical exports comprised bulk drugs. However, subsequently some of the larger and more dynamic Indian enterprises such as Ranbaxy Laboratories, Dr Reddy's Labs, Cipla and Cadila, have started marketing their own formulations in different countries with the help of a growing network of overseas offices and subsidiaries set up in key international markets. USA is the biggest market for India's pharmaceutical exports accounting for 10-12 per cent of exports. The export basket of India includes generic drugs like Ibuprufen, Sulphamethoxazole, Metronidazole, Amoxycilline, Ampicilline, Mebendazole, Beta Ionone, Erythromycin, Pappain, Potassium Iodide, Brucine Salts,

Cephalexin, Ethambutol Hydrochloride, Trimethoprim etc.A study comparing the performance of MNE affiliates and domestic enterprises in Indian pharmaceutical industry over the 1990s based on a balanced sample of 76 firms (60 domestic and 16 MNE subsidiaries) found the domestic enterprises are more dynamic in terms of growth of investment and output, export-orientation, R&D activity, technology purchases from abroad and in terms of labour productivity (defined as the net value-added per rupee spent on labor). However, MNE affiliates enjoyed considerably higher profit margins because of their greater focus on more value adding formulations and their well-established brand names.

The development of process innovation capability of Indian enterprises has enabled them to introduce newer medicines within a short time lag. Most of the drugs could be introduced within 4-5 years of their introduction in the world market. The prices of these drugs in India have been much cheaper compared to rest of the world. For instance, Ranitidine, Famotidine, Astemizole, Ondansetron sell in the US market at about 50 times the Indian prices! The cheaper prices of drugs have made them affordable to the masses of poor in the country and thus have served an important social cause of providing access of modern medicine to poorer people.

The technological capabilities of Indian companies have grown to a point when leading MNEs have started to take note of it. For instance, Eli Lilly established a joint venture with Ranbaxy in the mid-1990s for development of a cost effective process for synthesis of Cefaclor, among other products, taking advantage of the latter's process development capabilities. Similarly, Bayer contracted Ranbaxy to develop single doses formulations of its proprietary Ciprofloxacine. A number of leading MNEs have also contracted Indian public funded R&D institutions for synthesis of new molecules and process development. These include Abbot Laboratories, Parke Davis, and Smith Kline and Beecham, among others, that have commissioned Indian Institute for Chemical Technologies, Hyderabad and National Chemical Laboratories, Pune. Astra (now Astra-Zeneca) has set up a full fledged R&D centre in Bangalore to draw upon trained manpower and research infrastructure available in the country, despite the fact that Indian patent regime does not provide product patents.

Thus the Indian pharmaceutical industry has evolved from one dependent upon imports and some formulation activity in the late sixties to one which is able to introduce some of the most sophisticated products indigenously produced within a relatively short lag and at a fraction of the cost, and export a growing proportion of its produce to emerge as a net foreign exchange earner. It is a remarkable.achievement especially because it has been accomplished within two decades of the change of patent regime. The case study of India, besides those of the East Asian countries, further highlights the critical importance of fine-tuning and calibrating the IPR regime to the level of development of the country.

TRIPs Regime for Developing Countries

The international environment with respect to intellectual property has changed considerably with the conclusion of the TRIPs Agreement. The TRIPs Agreement accommodates the demands of the industrialized countries for higher international standards of protection by mandating the extension of patentability to virtually all fields of technology recognized in developed country patent systems, by prolonging the patent protection for a uniform term of twenty years, and by providing legal recognition of the patentee's exclusive rights to import the patented products. The patent rights are enjoyable without discrimination as to the place of invention, the field of technology and whether products are imported or locally produced.

All the signatories to the trade negotiations are, therefore, obliged to harmonize their IPR regime and to provide product patents for pharmaceuticals and chemicals. The coverage of the patent protection has also been expanded by the provision for patents on micro-organisms and protection of plant varieties either by patents or by an effective sui generis system or by any combination thereof. The full implementation of the TRIPs Agreement is likely to have an important bearing on the patterns of development in developing countries. In what follows we briefly review some of the important dimensions of these effects.

a) Local Technological Capability Building

The strengthening and harmonization of IPR regimes worldwide has considerable implications for the process of acquisition of local technological capability by developing countries. The provision of product patents on chemical and pharmaceutical products, for instance, would adversely affect the process of innovative activity of the developing country enterprises in the manufacture of chemicals covered by patents. The development of new chemical compounds is generally beyond the capability of most developing country enterprises in view of the huge resources involved. Therefore, they focus attention on process innovations for the known chemicals and bulk drugs. This imitative duplication or reverse engineering activity is an important source of learning in developing countries. Indeed, most industrialized countries of today and newly industrialized countries encouraged local learning through soft patent laws and the absence of product patents in chemicals in the early stages of their development as highlighted earlier. It means that the poorer countries of today will not be able to benefit from an important source of total factor productivity growth (viz. absorption of spillovers of foreign inventions) that was available to countries that have developed already. In that respect the TRIPs Agreement is highly inequitable.

The probability of stronger IPR regime encouraging innovative activity in developing countries is very small. In fact the adoption of utility models or petty patents and design patents has a greater potential in encouraging local technological activity rather than implementation of the provisions of TRIPs in poorer countries.

b) Industrialization, Technology Transfers and Trade

Recent trends suggest a reversal of trend of the growing importance of arm's length licensing as a mode of technology transfer as MNEs prefer to internalize the technology transactions. The strengthening of IPRs regime may further limit the access of technology by developing country enterprises. Kim provides a number of examples of Korean corporations being denied technology licenses by patent holders in the Western world forcing them to reverse engineer the products. A number of local enterprises in developing countries will come under pressure to close down or form alliances with larger firms, resulting in a concentration of the industry. Dependence on imports may go up. Mascus and Penubarti for instance, find that TRIPs could affect import volumes significantly; e.g. in Mexico, the anticipated rise in manufactured imports could be of the magnitude of $ 6.3 billion, amounting to 9.4 per cent of its real manufactured imports in 1995.

c) *Prices of medicines and loss of consumer welfare*

A number of studies have examined the effect on prices of medicines after introduction of product patents and have simulated welfare losses for consumers in developing countries. It is widely believed that drug prices will go up upon introduction of product patents as happened in China which introduced them in 1993. Nogues finds the welfare losses to 6 developing countries (Argentina, Brazil, India, Mexico, Korea and Taiwan) from introduction of product patents to be between US$ 3.5 billion to $10.8 billion depending upon the assumptions. The gains to the patent owners from such introduction would range between $ 2.9 billion to $ 14.4 billion. The welfare loss to India could be between $ 1.4 billion to $ 4.2 billion in a year. Watal simulates the likely increase in pharmaceutical prices and decrease in welfare in India with the introduction of product patents in 22 existing pharmaceutical products and finds that weighted mean drug price in India could increase between 26 per cent (for a linear demand function) to 242 per cent (with a constant elasticity-type demand function). An earlier study by Subramanian had found the maximum price increase of 67 per cent for India following the introduction of product patents. Fink finds the range of price increase between 182 to 225 per cent.

That suggests that introduction of product patents would affect prices of medicines significantly and unless new drugs are more efficient, there will be a decline in the health levels of population. The recent case of huge differences between prices of HIV Aids drugs sold by patent holders in South Africa and their generic substitutes just provides an further evidence to the potential of price increases following the introduction of product patents. It may be argued that the vast majority of drugs are out of patent protection and hence will not be affected. Yet the AIDS drugs controversy shows that effective treatment for many of scourges of the day such as cancer, cardiac failures, renal problems, among others, may be affected.

d) Income transfers from developing countries

Given the near complete domination of developed countries on technology generation as evident from the 95 per cent ownership of US patents, the strengthening and harmonization of IPRs regime will lead to a substantial increase in flow of royalties and license fees from developing countries to developed countries. McCalman quantifies the impact of patent harmonization finds that it has the capacity to generate large transfers of income between countries, with US being the major beneficiary. World Bank updates the computations of McCalman and suggests that the net patent rents derived by the US (in 2000 US$) could add up to over $ 19 billion, to Germany $ 6.7 billion, and Japan $ 5.7 billion. Among the developing countries, China could see an outflow of patent rents of the order of $5.1 biliion, India $ 903 million, Israel $ 3.8 billion.

Furthermore, the extension of IPRs to plant varieties could further increase the outgo of royalties for the breeder lines of the seed companies even though the basic raw material for the development of these varieties, viz. genetic diversity which is largely found in developing countries and is supposedly the work of generations of farmers in these countries, is generally available to them free.

e) *Impact on global technological activity and availability of drugs*

One of the arguments in favour of a stronger IPR regime is based on the premise that expenditures on R&D were significantly determined by appropriability conditions. Hence, ensuring adequate appropriability with more stringent IPR protection was deemed to be a necessary condition for sustaining the pace of innovation in the global economy. The empirical literature, however, does not support this presumption as patent protection was found to be instrumental for only a small proportion of innovations.

On the other hand, studies show that spillover effects of R&D activity of other firms to be a lot more important in inducing firms to undertake R&D compared to appropriability. The R&D outputs of other firms form valuable inputs for the R&D efforts of these firms. Hence, tightening of IPRs is likely to affect innovative activity adversely by stifling these spillovers. Therefore, it is by no means clear that strengthening of IPRs will increase innovative activity even in the developed world especially for solving the problems and diseases faced by developing countries. As World Bank cautions 'there is now a risk of excessively strict IPRs adversely affecting follow-on innovations and actually slowing down the pace of (technological development)'. Furthermore, the research priorities of MNEs are determined by the purchasing power and very little R&D is currently done on tropical diseases. Unless some steps are taken by the international community, such as those discussed by the recent report of WHO's Commission on Macroeconomics and Health

(CMH), the pattern is not likely to change significantly in the future.

Issues for National and International Action

The preceding discussion suggests that the ongoing trend of strengthening and harmonization of IPR regime is going to affect the process of development of poorer countries in a significant manner by choking an important contributor of growth that has been variously described as imitative duplication, reverse engineering or knowledge spillovers from abroad. It is also likely to affect the prices of a large number of important drugs and thus affect the health systems in poorer countries. It would lead to income transfers from poorer to richer countries. It is likely to adversely affect the manufacturing activity in developing countries and may increase their imports but does not guarantee increased in FDI inflows, access to technology or R&D investments in tropical diseases. These challenges require a response at the national policy levels as well as a response from the international community. In what follows, we outline some of the policy responses that could help in moderating the adverse effects of TRIPs Agreement on developing countries.

Policy responses to be taken at the national level

a) Incorporating the Provisions of Compulsory Licensing in the IPR Legislation: Developing countries should build adequate provisions for compulsory licensing in their IPR legislation in order to safeguard them from possible abuses of monopoly power obtained by patent owners. The compulsory licenses are permitted under Article 31 of the TRIPs Agreement.

The Agreement does not limit the grounds upon whch compulsory licenses may be granted and only sets forth the conditions to be applied in the case of granting. This includes specification of grounds of compulsory licensing and the reasonable rates of licensing fees. Recent withdrawal of proceedings by the US against Brazil's compulsory licensing provisions show that intelligently crafted domestic patent laws can meet national objectives and yet be TRIPs compatible.

b) *Incorporating the Research Exception:* Developing countries could incorporate provisions allowing researchers to use a patented invention for research, in order to understand the invention more fully. Experimentation on a patented invention is clearly admissible as an exception to exclusive rights under Article 30.

c) *Early Working Exception or 'Bolar' Provision:* It is possible to make provision for allowing manufacturers of generic drugs to use the patented invention to obtain marketing approval without patent owner's permission and before the expiration of patent. This facilitates the generic manufacturers to market their products as soon as the patent expires. This provision is sometimes called the regulatory exception or Bolar provision under Article 8. The US, Canada, Australia, Israel and Argentina have adopted Bolar exception in their patent legislation.

d) *Resisting the Attempts to Evolve TRIPs Plus Regime and Ever-greening of Patents:* Developed countries are constantly putting pressure on developing countries to implement stricter patent legislation than required under TRIPs, exclude compulsory licensing, parallel imports provisions and include provisions that would result in increasing the life of the patent (ever-greening), as well as grant data exclusivity to them. The TRIPs Agreement however, is clear that a new use for an old formulation does not constitute an inventive step (Art. 27(1)). Therefore, member countries are within their rights not to permit the practice of ever-greening of patents.

e) *Allowing Parallel Imports or Grey-Market Imports:* Since 'exhaustion of rights' issue cannot be raised in the dispute settlement under TRIPs Agreement, developing countries should allow parallel imports or grey-market imports. The experience of several countries suggests that substantial costs savings could result from such imports because of differential pricing strategy practiced by MNEs depending upon the extent of competition in different markets.

f) *Competition Policy:* The patent system grants temporary monopolies to the firms that introduce innovations. The national competition or antitrust policies are needed to prevent the build up of excessive monopoly power of certain enterprises and to deal with possible abuse of monopoly power emanating from patent protection. The TRIPs Agreement (Articles 8 and 40, Section 8) explicitly provides for appropriate measures to prevent the abuse of IPRs or the resort to anti-competitive practices. Apparently in the US, 'compulsory licensing has been specified as a remedy in more than 100 anti-trust cases making available some 40,000 to 50,000 patents at reasonable or no royalties'.

g) *Incorporating Breeders Exceptions and Farmers Exceptions in sui generis Plant Variety Protection:* TRIPs Agreement allows flexibility to the member countries to exclude plant varieties from the scope of patent protection and instead opt for an effective sui generis system. In order to minimize the adverse effect on the plant breeding programmes and protecting small and marginal farmers from buying seeds who typically save them for the next crop, developing countries could build provisions for exceptions for farmers and plant breeders.

h) *Price Controls for Essential Drugs:* To protect the poor masses from the price increases following the introduction of product patents, governments may impose regulation of prices of essential drugs. To keep the price controls effective, transparent formula for evolving them could be made providing for a reasonable mark-up over the cost. Indian experience shows that price controls have proved to be effective means of keeping prices of life saving essential drugs under check. However, given the possibility of transfer pricing manipulation, there may be complications in administering price controls for imported drugs.

i) *Introduce Utility Models and Industrial Design Patents:* The experience of several East Asian countries suggests that petty patents and industrial design patents could be effective means of encouraging domestic enterprises to undertake minor adaptive innovations and foster a innovation based rivalry among them.

Policy responses at the international level

The recent controversy concerning the HIV AIDS drugs in South Africa, among other factors, has helped to focus attention of the international community on the possible adverse effects of the implementation of TRIPs Agreement on poorer countries. Over the past year a number of international initiatives have been taken to deal with the matter. These include establishment of the Commission on Macroeconomics and Health by the WHO and Commission on IPRs by the British Government. WHO and WTO organized a Workshop on Differential Pricing and Financing of Essential Drugs at Hosbjor, April 2001. The Fourth Ministerial Meeting in Doha in November 2001 adopted a Declaration on TRIPs Agreement and Public Health. UNDP's Human Development Report 2001 as well as World Bank's Global Economic Prospects 2002 reports focused on the IPRs and their impact for developing countries. However, these initiatives are yet to lead to a concrete outcome addressing the many problems that are raised by the TRIPs Agreement. In what follows we summarize a few avenues for possible international action.

a) *Moratorium on further strengthening of IPR regime:* There is tendency in some developed countries to treat provisions of TRIPs as the minimum standards and are constantly attempting to evolve stronger norms through unilateral or bilateral approaches. A consensus needs to be built on the need to put a moratorium on such approaches for the next couple of decades or so.

b) *Granting flexibility to developing countries in implementing the provisions of TRIPs:* Most of the adverse effects concerning TRIPs on poor countries arise not because of IPR regimes but from the attempt to harmonize them across the countries at different levels of development. Thhere is also a discussion whether TRIPs should fundamentally belong to

WTO. However, the least that could be done is allowing flexibility to developing countries to implement the provisions of the Agreement as and when their level of development has reached a certain stage. This could be achieved if a consensus among the developed countries is built on the differential need of developing countries for IPR regime 6 . A possible revision of TRIPs could incorporate a provision that grants to developing countries a flexibility to implement the TRIPs obligations until they reach a per capita income of the level of US$ 1000, for instance. Another possibility could be to shorten the term of product patents applicable to low income countries. This way the Agreement would have incorporated development dimension. The Commission's work could be instrumental in building such a consensus.

c) *Incorporating Specific Provisions for Transfer of Technology:* The TRIPs Agreement pays an inadequate attention to the transfer of technology. Access to technology is increasingly become difficult for developing countries, as observed earlier. There is need for defining conditions, norms and practices for facilitating transfers of technology for production of essential drugs and other critical inputs.

d) *International Funding R&D Activity in Low Income Countries:* One of the ways of compensating the low income countries for the adverse effects of strengthened IPR regime is to provide increased technical assistance and R&D funding to local enterprises to help them build local capabilities. One possibility in this -respect could be that developed countries donate (a substantial proportion of) technology license fees collected from low income countries to a fund created in the respective countries to assist inventive activities of domestic enterprises. Furthermore, there is need to address the issue of funding R&D on special problems and tropical diseases that concern low income countries. It has been widely acknowledged that global pharmaceutical industry has neglected research on tropical diseases. The CMH has recommended a donor commitment of $ 27 billion per annum for the health needs of low-income countries including $ 3 billion per annum for R&D for diseases of the poor. It is arguable that this funding of $ 3 billion could also help to moderate some adverse effects on the inventive activity in low-income countries if it is awarded to institutions and enterprises based in these countries. Therefore, an additional recommendation could be made in conjunction with those of CMH that the funds would allocated to eligible and competent institutions and companies of low income countries.

e) *Differential Pricing:* There has been a lot of discussion on the possibility of improving the access of poorer countries to patented medicines through differential pricing. There are a number of practical issues concerned with the differential pricing that need to be resolved.

Bibliography

Azarchs, Tanya (2000). *The Internet's Impact on Financial Services,* Standard & Poor's CreditWeek, Jan. 26.

Bank Network News (2000). *Virtual Banks Get Physical With ATMs* 18, 21, March 30.

Barth, James R., Daniel E. Nolle, and Tara N. Rice (2000). *Commercial Banking Structure, Regulation, and Performance: An International Comparison, in Modernizing Financial Systems,* edited by Dimitri B. Papadimitriou, St. Martin's Press, Inc.

Carlson, Tina (2000). *One CU's Secret: Lack of Technology,* The Credit Union Journal, March 6.

Costanzo, Chris, and Adriana Senior (1999). *Banks Opting for Discrete Web Units,* American Banker, December 6.

Couch, Karen, and Donna L. Parker (2000). *Net Interest' Grows as Banks Rush Online.*

Daudelin, Art (2000). *Wingspan Losing Altitude?* Bank Technology News 13, 1, January.

Day, Kathleen (2000). *Web-Only Banks Start to Get Real,* Washington Post, March 31.

Egland, Kori L., Karen Furst, Daniel E. Nolle, and Douglas Robertson (1998). *Banking Over the Internet,* Quarterly Journal 17, 4, Office of the Comptroller of the Currency, December.

Furst, Karen, William W. Lang, and Daniel E. Nolle (1998). *Technological Innovation in Banking and Payments: Industry Trends and Implications for Banks,* Quarterly Journal 17, 3, Office of the Comptroller of the Currency, December.

Hallerman, David (1999a). *Spinning a New Web of Online Banking,* Bank Technology News 12, 7, July.

Hitt, Lorin M., and Frances X. Frei (1999). Do Better Customers Utilize Electronic Distribution Channels? *The Case of PC Banking,* Wharton Financial Institutions Center, Working Paper Series No. 99-21, April.

Hitt, Lorin M., Frances X. Frei, and Patrick T. Harker (1999). *How Financial Firms Decide on Technology,* Brookings-Wharton Papers on Financial Services: 1999.

Horsfield, Richard (2000). *Shaping the future of online financial services,* The Banker, January.

Marks, James (1999). *The Impact of the Internet on Users and Suppliers of Financial Services,* Brookings-Wharton Papers on Financial Services: 1999.

Moody's Investors Service (2000a). *The Internet and U.S. Banks,"* January.

O'Sullivan, Orla (1998). *Technology Spending's Uncertain Payoff,* U.S. Banker, September.

Pizzani, Lori (1999). *Web Offerings Lure Small Businesses,* Bank Technology News 12, 3, March.

Radecki, Lawrence J., John Wenninger, and Daniel K. Orlow (1997) *'Industry Structure: Electronic Delivery's Potential Effects on Retail Banking,* Journal of Retail Banking Services, 19, 4, Winter.

Robertson, Douglas, Jim Cambruzzi, Kevin Jacques, Peter Nigro, Bill Pate, Hugh Rich, and Art Steele (2000). *Large Bank Retirement Services: A Comparative Practices Study.*

Timewell, Stephen and Kung Young (2000). "*Online surge blasts banks,"* The Banker, January.

Toonkel, Jessica (2000a). *Compubank, Failing to Excite Public, Eyes On-Line Service for Businesses,* American Banker, March 3.

United States General Accounting Office (1998). *Electronic Banking: Experiences Reported by Banks in Implementing On-line Banking,* GAO/GGD-98-34, January.

Index

INFORMATION TECHNOLOGY
A Revolutionary Change

INFORMATION TECHNOLOGY
A Revolutionary Change
(In 9 Volumes)

Volume 9
(Understanding the Information and Communication Society)

Editor
RAMESH CHANDRA
Vice-Chancellor, Bundelkhand University, Jhansi (U.P.)

KALPAZ PUBLICATIONS
DELHI–110052

INFORMATION TECHNOLOGY: A REVOLUTIONARY CHANGE

(Information Technology)

Rs. 8000 (Set)
Rs. 900 (Each Volume)

ISBN: 81-7835-201-X (Set)
ISBN: 81-7835-228-1 (Vol. 9)

Published in 2003 in India by
Kalpaz Publications
C–30, Satyawati Nagar
Delhi–110052
E-mail: kalpaz@hotmail.com

Laser Typesetting at: Varsha Graphics, Delhi
Printed at: Mehra Offset Printers, New Delhi

Contents

Preface

The emergence of the new online environment is part of a major transformation of our entire communications system. The second half of the 20th century has witnessed the global phenomenon of an information explosion. The development of different electronic technologies has made it possible for millions of people to have fast access to huge information resources stored in different places on the planet, to communicate with each other and to handle information presented in various forms.

Today's global networks create connections between people which span time and distance in ways the world has never before seen and with implications which are beginning to have major political, social, and economic implications. It also giving millions of people direct access to information in ways the world has never before seen. In today's 'reach out and touch someone' age, millions of people who would never put pen to paper to write a letter will spend evenings writing to dozens of people through their online connections. Electronic mail has given new life and new meaning to a profoundly traditional form of communication. Telecomputing may in fact be the last frontier of written literacy available which will incite students to traditional literacy skills.

If the information society is to be both open and universal it should develop along the principles embodied in the Universal Declaration of Human Rights. They are, among others, the right to freedom of expression, free access to information, the right to education and the right to participate in cultural life. Governments, industry and the civil society are seeking to apply these long accepted principles to the electronic information environment, but these efforts are hampered by major difficulties and challenges, including the critical issue of how to ensure fair conditions for developing countries, which are entering the digital age at a major disadvantage.

A number of international consultations are showing that clearer policy guidelines are needed in the increasingly open, interactive and global information environment. Such guidelines should cover all aspects of the global information networks—technological and economic, but also educational, scientific, cultural and social. Today, however, most national and international debate is concentrating on technological and economic aspects, because of their more immediately perceived impact, often to the detriment of other issues which will ultimately have a deeper, more fundamental significance in achieving an Information Society for All.

Editor

1

The Infotech Landscape

The emergence of the new online environment is part of a major transformation of our entire communications system. More than half of all Americans were hooked up to the Internet by the end of 2000, and within the next four years that number is expected to grow to 85 percent. Nearly nine out of ten American homes will soon be interactively wired. Most will connect through personal computers; but other devices, including digital TVs, game consoles, portable devices, and next-generation digital cable set-top boxes, will increasingly provide a link.

In many ways, teens are the defining users of this digital media culture. They are the first generation to grow up surrounded by and immersed in digital technologies. With nearly three-quarters of twelve-to-seventeen-year-olds online, teens surpass adults in their use of chat, instant messaging, and other forms of Internet communications. As is early adapters of these technologies, teens are as comfortable growing up with digital media as their parents generation was with the telephone and TV. This easy fluency among teens, in contrast to the typically greater hesitancy among adults, is shifting power relationships within the family.

Teenagers are not only helping their parents learn how to use a computer, they often guide their families purchases for computer-related products. Teens are also integrating interactive devices into their daily lives in unexpected, often inventive ways. Dubbed Webbersli or viewers by the media industry, many teens have already begun using the television and the computer simultaneously, far in advance of the so-called convergence of these two media. A host of new products is being created exclusively for teens, which may very well be the test market for the next generation of digital content and services. For example, teens desire to chat is spawning many new hand-held, wireless tech products that are designed primarily for instant messaging and chat, but which also feature interactive gaming, Internet access, digital picture and music storage, and personal information management.

The young people of today are also tomorrow's adults; how they consume and participate in new media will help determine the future shape and direction of the media system Teens are more than just consumers of media content; they are also active participants and creators of this new media culture, developing content themselves, designing personal Web sites, and launching their own online enterprises. As one trade publication observed, young people have not simply adopted digital media, they have internalized it. The behaviours, attitudes, and values that teens are embracing as part of their new-media experience could have significant impacts on the larger culture. New media technologies are making their way into American life at a time when teens have become a booming target market for advertisers and marketers. Spending among teenagers has increased steadily during the past several decades, rising dramatically in more recent years. Teen spending power doubled between the years 1960 and 1980, and tripled in the 90s. By 2000, 31.6 million teenagers spent an estimated $155 billion of their own money in the retail market. Teens not only spend money on themselves; they also wield tremendous influence over purchases made by their parents. The increase in families where both parents work, along with the aggressive marketing of adult products to children, have given teens much more power and responsibility in purchasing decisions of such big-ticket items as cars, family vacations, and furniture.

Indeed, the rise of teen digital media is part of a larger proliferation of new product categories and programs targeted at this valuable demographic group. This is a generation that has grown up in a marketplace that zeroes in on younger and younger audiences, employing synergy and cross-marketing among television and movie characters and products to create a ubiquitous commercial youth culture.

In the 1980s, children got their own TV networks, radio networks, magazines, newspapers, kids clothing brands, books, banking, and such high-ticket items as video games and other high-tech products. By 1995, notes market research expert James McNeal, virtually every consumer goods industry was somehow involved in marketing to children, either as a primary influence, or future market, or some combination of these.

Despite the rapid growth of this new digital culture, comparatively little public attention has been paid to it. When the spotlight has been cast on teens and new media, news coverage has tended to focus on the negative impacts. For example, after the 1999 shooting at Columbine High School, the world of cyberspace was seen as a dark and dangerous place that ensnared young people. News stories and congressional hearings occasionally provide frightening accounts of teens who have become unwitting victims of pornography or, even worse, of online predators who lurk in chat rooms.

Concerns about online pornography produced the Communications Decency Act in 1996, which was subsequently ruled unconstitutional, as well as two subsequent acts, which are currently facing court challenges. Dozens of filtering software products have flooded the market, promising to assuage parental concern by blocking out harmful content on the Internet.

But while parents, policymakers, and educators worry about pornography and predation, they also express optimism about the Internet's power to enhance educational opportunities and communication possibilities. Most Americans believe that children should enjoy equitable access to these powerful new technologies, prompting a range of public and private initiatives to wire the nation's schools and libraries in order to help bridge the ihdigital divide.

This contradictory discourse, with concerns about the hazards of the Internet on the one hand, and visions of its educational potential on the other, echoes earlier public attitudes over new media. Each new media technology brought with it great promise for social educational benefits and great concern for children's exposure to inappropriate and harmful content. As a consequence, even as this new medium is becoming a pervasive presence in teens' lives, it remains largely under the radar of parents, scholars, and policymakers alike.

The World Wide Web, as the centre of innovation and implementation for the new-media system. The Web sites, identifying the key features that characterize online content and activity for teens, and analysing the major industry trends that are influencing the design and direction of the new teen media culture.

Many research has documented a number of critical biological, cognitive, and emotional changes that take place during the transition period of adolescence. One of the most important is identity formation. As teens begin the exploration of their adult identities, they undergo a shift in self-perception. They begin thinking about their hypothetical future selves, often choosing from different possible identities, and trying some on for size. They also become intensely preoccupied with comparing themselves to others. As their self-identity undergoes these changes, teens are exposed to ever-greater levels of uncertainty and vulnerability.

Media have always played a role in this process. As teenagers spend less time with their families, outside influences become more important. The opinions of friends matter more; and diverse media, such as music, movies, magazines, and computers, become more powerful influences as well. Teens are active users of media, basing their choices on both interest and need. Because teen engagement with media usually intensifies just as parental influence is waning, the media can play a strong role in shaping teen attitudes, as well as their sense of self and the world.

The handful of studies that have been conducted on teens' use of new media suggest that accessing the Internet addresses many of the same needs served by traditional media such as entertainment, identity formation, high sensation, coping, and youth culture identification. However, the unique nature of the new digital environment presents an unprecedented array of possibilities for communication, interaction, and expression never before available.

No longer must teens serve strictly as consumers of one-way messages (as from television or radio). Online technologies offer new tools and new opportunities to become more actively involved in the exploration of identity, and to find expression for many different possible selves. Chat rooms, for example, allow teens to create personas quite distinct from their everyday identities, and to act them out in cyberspace.

The Internet and other digital media have created a new culture of simulation, is with profound implications for the development of identity. From scientists trying to create artificial life to children ,morphing through a series of virtual personae. But it is on the Internet that our confrontations with technology as it collides with our sense of human identity are fresh, even raw.

In the real-time communities of cyberspace, we are dwellers on the threshold between the real and virtual, unsure of our footing, inventing ourselves as we go along.

Electronic communication also relieves teens from typical gender role constraints that often influence face-to-face interactions. Susannah Stern's study of the home pages of adolescent girls concludes that home pages provide girls with greater opportunity to openly express thoughts, interests, and to create a public identity. Other studies have noted that young adolescent girls find the Internet particularly liberating because they are treated with a degree of respect missing in face-to-face conversations. For example, teen girls, who stereotypically are less talkative and assertive than boys, spoke freely and passionately in a computer-mediated forum. Scholars have also suggested that teens use the Internet not just to communicate with individual others, but also to participate in various online communities.

Particularly for those teens who feel uncomfortable or unaccepted in their (offline) lives, online communities provide extensive networks of like-minded others with whom teens can share their thoughts and experiences. For example, in a communications environment that feels anonymous, young people can reveal their fears and secrets.

Beyond the psycho-social concerns are a broader set of political and cultural issues. One that interests us is whether the Internet can contribute to greater civic and political engagement by youth. In his recent book, Bowling Alone, Harvard University political scientist Robert Putnam documents how each successive generation of Americans has been less inclined to vote than was its immediate predecessor. He worries that even with the proliferation of news sources in the mass media, young people today are substantially less knowledgeable about public affairs.

A 1999 study found, however, that although young people were in general much less likely to seek out political information than were older cohorts, they were more likely to use the Internet as their preferred means of access. And while voter turnout is lower among young adults, volunteering for community activities among adolescents is on the rise.

While a handful of notable youth media examples exist, much less is known about whether online political sites actually stimulates or serve merely as a virtual substitute for real civic engagement.

In focusing primarily on the content and services for teens on the World Wide Web, we acknowledge that the Internet is only one sector of a much larger new digital media system. However, that the technological innovation, experimentation, and evolving business practices that are taking place in the online context reveal a great deal about overall trends in the digital media. As more and more household appliances are connected to a digital hub, moreover, and as the use of portable wireless devices proliferates, the distinction between ionlinelo and inoffline will diminish accordingly. Thus we used the Internet as a lens through which we could take a snapshot of this evolving new-media culture.

The dynamic changes occurring on the Internet are part of a much broader set of economic, institutional, and technological forces that are shaping the entire digital landscape. Since we were interested in understanding these larger trends, we also conducted an analysis of the key factors that are influencing the design and direction of the new teen media culture, both on the Web and in other emerging media platforms such as wireless application protocol (WAP) portable devices and interactive television.

Web sites are being created under non-profit auspices and, in some cases, by teens themselves. In this arena, teens are engaging in community-building activities, volunteering for public service, and participating in various forms of political activism. Most of the research on how teens actually use the new media comes from the commercial market-research sector. Thus we investigated that sector, too, and obtained some of its findings through conferences and trade shows, as well as gleaning other pertinent data from trade publications.In the latter half of 2000, the economy of the Web plummeted, as venture capital quickly dried up amid projections of less-than-expected revenues.

New Trends and Future Directions

Computers are now capable of handling audio files with fidelity that rivals that of CDs, and the quality of streaming video, still in its early development, continues to improve. Televisions, in turn, are now being used to access the Internet, a trend that will grow with the introduction of new, more sophisticated cable set-top boxes.

Mobile phones, pagers, and personal digital assistants (PDAs) are now manufactured as Internet-ready devices, and videogame consoles are being designed as integrated home entertainment centres, with the ability to play movies and music as well as to surf the Web. And the Web itself will one day be bypassed, giving way to new forms of content and new means of delivery, including new ways to exploit the Internet. A study shows Internet's future pointed to four trends that were likely to usher in the post-Web world:

(1) the wireless revolution, with content tailored specifically for portable, mobile devices;

(2) peer-to-peer computing, featuring new software and services that will facilitate the exchange of data among PCs, including both collaborative projects from remote locations and distributed processing (harnessing several computers simultaneously across distances);

(3) instant messaging, expanded to include multimedia conversations across digital TV and wireless platforms; and

(4) machine-to-machine communications, automating tasks and undertaking negotiations on the user's behalf.

The Net is a platform around which we will build all sorts of really interesting products and services, explains Richard Newton, dean of the College of Engineering at the University of California at Berkeley.

Many of these new products and services will be delivered by a range of devices beyond the standard personal computer. Such appliances as personal video recorders (PVRs), third-generation (3G) mobile communications devices, and interactive television (ITV) via advanced set-top boxes will produce dramatic changes in the ways in which media content is produced, packaged, and disseminated and the ways in which revenues are derived in the process.

Not only is media content becoming accessible nearly everywhere, but the options concerning when, where, and how consumers access such programming are rapidly expanding. Rather than passively consuming the media in static and linear forms, consumers are already creating their own unique media experiences, using customizable PVR and ITV programming features, for example, or assembling personal music collections by downloading MP3 sound files from the Internet and in burning their own CDs.

The launch of the Digital Entertainment Network (DEN.net) in 1998 was accompanied by fanfare typical of the dot-com boom the television-like network was simply ahead of its time, before enough teens had access to high-speed broadband Internet service. And some industry observers concluded that the site self-destructed because of a weak business model, complicated by a scandal over lavish spending and other alleged improprieties.

Many experts view the recent fluctuations in the Internet economy as a period of readjustment in an over-hyped industry where venture capital has flowed in too often on the basis of rather shaky business plans. The Internet is undergoing a vast weeding- out, remarked one market research executive, noting that survivors are finding the right combination of business practices to enable them not only to stay afloat but to generate a profit.

But the starts and stops in the dot-com marketplace should not divert our attention from the inexorable movement of digital media into the lives of teens. This generation is growing up at the centre of the technological explosion that has transformed the media system. Their coming of age is occurring simultaneously with the growth and maturity of the new digital media culture. Their increased personal spending power, combined with their technological savvy, have made teens a particularly powerful target market for online businesses, generating a cornucopia of varied content and activities on the Web, tailored specifically to their interests.

Teenagers have embraced this new online world with great enthusiasm, responding eagerly to its invitation to share ideas, contribute content, and otherwise place their stamp on a media system that they themselves create and manage. Teens have also seized upon all manner of electronic gadgets from pagers to mobile phones to PDAs. And with the promise of Internet connectivity to all of these devices and others just around the corner, teens are marching into the future with the potential for unprecedented levels of communications and information retrieval at their fingertips.

The media world that teens inhabit departs in significant ways from the one their parents knew during their own adolescence. The digital media are challenging many of the conventions and institutions of the past, blurring or obliterating the boundaries between public and private, commercial and noncommercial, school and home, local and global.

The properties of the interactive media are particularly seductive to adolescents, tapping into many of their developmental needs, capturing their imaginations, and kindling their hopes and desires. Online communication tools enable instantaneous and constant contact with peers; personal home pages offer compelling opportunities for self-expression and identity exploration; and ubiquitous portable devices facilitate mobility and independence.

The Internet's extensive reach and its promise of anonymity create an environment that encourages information-seeking on a wide variety of topics inaccessible or taboo for earlier generations. Chat rooms and forums allow teens to engage in discussion and debate without fear of exposure. As the features and functions of this new digital online marketplace are being tested and refined, teens serve as subjects for continuous and pervasive market research, connected through electronic umbilical cords to a phalanx of companies that monitor their every online move.

As a consequence, a unique symbiosis has developed between the creators of this digital culture and its most avid users; today's teens are eager and willing partners in the design and implementation of an array of cultural products and practices. Their engagement with digital media is ushering in a new set of behaviours, values, and expectations that this generation has internalized and will carry with them into adulthood.

With the whirling pace of change in communication technologies as we move toward an increasingly converged media environment, it remains vital to keep abreast of these developments. There is an urgent need for further research on the role that new media are playing in the lives of youth. We find it very troubling that so much of what is known about how teens are interacting with the new digital media is confined to the proprietary domain of market research, where it is either completely off-limits to outsiders or priced so prohibitively as to be inaccessible to the public.

Except for a handful of scholars, the academic community has failed to respond in a timely or effective fashion to the dynamic changes in the media environment of young people. Conventions and constraints within academic institutions keep scholars far behind the rapid pace of change in the media. For example, traditional methods for studying mass media content do not lend themselves easily to analyses of Internet content and services. As a consequence, many scholars are hesitant to tackle the methodological risks of conducting such studies.

For example, with the variety of options available for plugging in, teens have adapted, in part, by developing the ability to engage in several activities simultaneously. But no one knows what this means for the depth of their processing or whether the high level of stimulation from a variety of media affects attention span, although these are concerns that have been raised among parents and educators. Additionally, the access to boundless information without leaving home is unique.

Adolescents are not a monolithic group, after all. There are not only personal differences, but income, ethnic, geographic, and sexual differences within this highly diverse group of young people. The way these various subgroups relate to the new media may differ sharply from what is known in the existing research literature.

Since so much of this new-media culture is rooted in very sophisticated technologies, we need to understand more fully the inherent properties and capabilities of these new digital tools, and how they can be harnessed most effectively to serve the needs of children and adolescents. We also need studies of the institutions that are creating this digital culture, both its commercial and its noncommercial sectors.

Multidisciplinary approaches are needed, combining the contributions of historians, sociologists, anthropologists, and economists, who can study new media in all of their dimensions. Although longitudinal studies of the impact of media are important, we also need focused, policy-relevant research that addresses specific issues and needs. Sometimes this research may not be entirely conclusive, and the fluid nature of the media system may pose methodological challenges to researchers. But the need for serious appraisals at this critical, early stage of the new media's development seems clear.

The new-media environment for teens is primarily commercial in nature, positioning youth as consumers of popular culture and as a market for a multitude of products and services. In some respects these trends are logical extensions of what has been happening throughout this century, with the increasing number of products and services created for and marketed to youth, fuelled by the rise in young people's spending power.

But the nature and extent of marketing in the online world is unprecedented, with the digital media intensifying many of the existing trends in the commercialization of children's lives. At every turn, from home to school to shopping mall, teens encounter various efforts to involve them in commercial transactions. By exploiting the interactive capacity of the online media to involve youth themselves (wittingly or not) in the marketing of various products, marketers have taken a qualitative leap in their use of sales tactics to shape and influence teen behaviour.

In addition to the merger of content and commerce, and the ease of buying products online through e-commerce (which will become even easier in new interactive TV implementations), the push toward impulse buying is made stronger.

The new media have spurred an alphabet soup of commerce, including e-commerce, t-commerce, and m-commerce (covering the worlds of the Internet, television, and mobile communications). In a culture that is already commercialized and market-driven, the ready availability of instant gratification (and delayed payment) online raises questions about the new media's impact on young people in particular and the quality of our culture in general.

Many teenagers work at after-school jobs, often to pay for the many consumer goods and services targeted directly to their demographic. These trends have raised concerns among parents and educators, as many high school students find it difficult to work and keep up with their schoolwork. Consumer groups note with alarm that credit card debt is rising among young people.

New digital marketing strategies will very likely compound these trends, as ubiquitous marketing tools on wireless devices, in wired classrooms, and through interactive televisions will target teens throughout the day and night with seductive appeals designed to encourage impulse buying, and with special digital credit devices to facilitate instantaneous purchases.

Consumer protection policies will be needed to ensure that teens are not unfairly taken advantage of in the digital marketplace.

Teens are the most avid participants in such programs, which pay them both to post a view bar or payball at the bottom of their screens while they surf the Web, and to recruit other into the program. The viewbar exhibits various advertisements and companies monitor the amount of time users spend on the Web (and thus, ideally, watch ads on the viewbar) and pay them an hourly rate.

Similar programs pay teens to use branded e-mail programs or to listen to streaming audio programming. Not only do teens take advantage of this easily way to make money online, but many become marketers themselves by posting entire pages that list pay-for-surf companies, as a means of generating additional payments for referrals. Although these are strictly voluntary programs, regulators should examine this form of marketing closely and consider possible policies against any unfair practices targeted at underage youth in the digital environment.

Teen privacy protection is a particularly urgent concern that merits public attention and consideration for policy formation. Often, the concept of teens' online safety is framed as protection from stalkers and insulation from online pornography or other inappropriate material. While these are legitimate causes for concern, the collection of personal data for commercial purposes is more pervasive. Thus we need to broaden the concept of online safety to include the maintenance of personal privacy.

Younger audiences (or even adult audiences, for that matter) may not understand that when they provide personal information online, they may be compromising the sanctity of their own personal privacy.

When a Web site such as Bolt or Thirsty prompts teens to share their names, addresses, and other information in the interest of incommunity, or when teens give in to the very natural adolescent tendency to share personal information as a means of expressing themselves and bonding with others, they stand to lose much more than they gain.

Coupled with other databases and profiles both online and off, the isolated bits of information that teens surrender in registering for site membership and contests, or in the course of online chats and discussions, may add up to a complete loss of privacy.

Market research also plays a role in this regard. Teenagers who freely discussed what they liked and disliked about the Ford Focus advertising campaign in the Ford-sponsored car section of Bolt may not have realized that their feedback (and quite possibly their names and other personal information) are now the property of Bolt. Such data can be sold to other market researchers who are a part of the $1.5 trillion industry of direct marketing and advertising databases.

Moreover, even if such Web sites post privacy policies that explain that they are, indeed, collecting teens' personal information to use as market research or sell to other companies, it is questionable whether teens will search for such policies.

Children under the age of 13 are currently protected under the Children's Online Privacy Protection Act (COPPA), which took effect in 2000. COPPA prohibits commercial Web sites and online services from collecting personal information from these children without parental consent and proper notification.

To date, however, teens are not afforded any privacy protections in the digital media. As content and services for teens continue to migrate to cell phones and other smart wireless devices with global positioning systems (GPS), threats to their privacy will grow.

Public concerns over privacy are already on the rise, prompting a proliferation of congressional hearings and a number of legislative proposals. A coalition of consumer groups formed this year to promote the need for privacy policies, especially for the digital media. The particular concerns of adolescents will need to be included in any legislative or regulatory remedies.

The central role that market research is playing in the digital teen culture is of special concern. Never before has there been a medium with the ability to tap into the needs, desires, interests, and behaviours of children and youth. Never before has there been such an intertwining of the machinations of the marketplace with the activities of young people.

Some of the market research practices such as the creation of online focus groups disguised as chat rooms may well be deceptive, a matter that the Federal Trade Commission (FTC) should investigate. Close attention should be paid to these online market research practices as well as those being developed for other digital technologies.

Parents, health professionals, and policymakers will need to be particularly vigilant as marketers continue to focus attention on younger and younger age groups, grooming the so-called for their role as teen consumers. The American Psychological Association has been looking into the questionable role played by some child psychologists who sell their services to market research firms, and is developing ethical guidelines for the profession.

While technologically savvy and comfortable with digital media, children and youth may not be as sophisticated as they need to be to protect themselves from manipulative and exploitative marketing and data collection practices in this new interactive world. Clearly, there is a need for comprehensive consumer education in the schools, with a curriculum that is sufficiently flexible to stay current in this rapidly changing marketplace.

The digital media also create unique opportunities to harness the power of technology as a positive force in the lives of children and youth. However, the full potential of the digital media will not be realized unless there are clear public and private policies to help guide their development. In order to achieve this goal, we need a new framework for thinking about the media and their relationship to children and youth.

For example, thousands of scientific studies (and considerable federal money), as well as countless articles in the popular press, have been devoted to assessing the relationship of televised violence to antisocial behaviour.

While these issues are important and will remain so in the future, the emergence of digital media provides an opportunity to define some new goals for the media system, and to take steps to ensure that these goals are realized.

On the one hand, the Internet has fostered many opportunities for community- building, participation, information-seeking, and collaboration. All of these activities can contribute to the development of the necessary attributes for citizenship. On the other hand, the rapid and pervasive commercialization of the digital media may be moving the culture in the opposite direction, encouraging values, attitudes, and behaviours that are aimed at grooming and consumers rather than effective citizens.

But there are a number of challenges that must be met if we are to see the emergence and survival of a healthy youth civic sector in the digital landscape. The dominance of the for- profit model on the Web raises serious questions about the continued viability of the truly noncommercial content and services that are integral to the authenticity of an alternative online culture.

As the Internet continues to make its transition to the next generations moving from slow, fixed dial-up connections to broadband access, interactive television, and wireless mobile devices the noncommercial civic media initiatives that are visible on today's Web may either be marginalized or may disappear altogether. Foundation grants, government support, and contributions from the private sector will all be needed to sustain non-profit, civic, and grassroots sites. Only with the effort of informed and active citizens, and with public policies that are conducive to the development of an online civic sector, will such support mechanisms be put in place.

A number of efforts in this regard are already underway, involving schools, libraries, public broadcasters, and other community organizations. Some of these projects (e.g., the Digital Promise) are concerned with identifying sources of funding for the production of noncommercial civic, educational, and cultural materials online.

Other projects are designed to test the online civic-sector concept at the community level. Still other projects (e.g., the Communitarian Network), primarily academic in nature, explore the philosophical underpinnings of the in common concept. What is missing in all of these efforts (and there are many others) is a means of coordinating them in some fashion, helping to create a critical mass of civic content online that will serve both local needs and national interests.

Finally, despite the rapid penetration of the Internet into American homes, there remains a troubling in digital divide that threatens to leave many youth behind in the technological revolution of the twenty-first century. Even though programs such as the the -rattler are making it easier for less-advantaged schools and libraries to gain affordable access to the Internet, the rapid introduction of broadband technologies may undercut the positive impact of these policies. More youth may have access as Internet penetration continues to grow, but the quality of that access may suffer in comparison to new premium services that are being introduced. As a result, a new digital divide might emerge, separating those with rudimentary, dial-up access from those who enjoy sophisticated, state-of-the art communications. The content of the new broadband universe, moreover, will reflect these inequities.

Such is the ambivalent picture that inevitably results from a serious appraisal of the new Web culture. Attractive in its ease of use, its ready access to seemingly boundless information, its open invitation to users to submit their own content, potentially even strengthening the bonds of community, the Web also raises serious concerns.

Fortunately, the digital age is still very much in formation, and the answers to these questions await our active participation in fashioning the kind of new media system that will serve the public interest as effectively as it generates private profits. We stand, in short, on the threshold of a new era. We have a unique window of opportunity to ensure that the potential benefits of the new media for teens and children are fully realized, while the harms and negative impacts are minimized. To achieve this goal, however, we will need a broad-based movement, enlisting all those who care about the quality of the media culture, both to explore and assess the system we have today, as well as to envision and enact a more promising system for tomorrow.

Building of Infotech Skills

The impact of the rapid creation and adoption of IT on the U.S. economy, describe the demand and supply trends for the core IT occupations and "Descriptions of Core Information Technology Professions" IT labour market. Over the past several years, the nature of America's information technology (IT) work force challenge has been the subject of much debate. There are many conflicting views of the challenge, and even among those who agree on the nature of the challenge, there are conflicting views of what the best solutions are. The perception of the challenge tends to be shaded by the perspective of the observer.

For the most part, industry sees the problem as a worker shortage. Companies believe that there simply aren't enough people in the IT occupations to meet the growing demand. Employee groups and advocates for employees, on the other hand, believe there are enough trained technical professionals in the United States, but industry has not tapped these existing labour pools.

And economists argue that the IT work force challenge is the expected result of the rising importance of IT in our economy and the consequent demand for highly-skilled core IT workers, and that, in the long run, market forces will fix the problem.

The Office of Technology Policy finds merit in each of the perspectives. However, it is our conclusion that the true nature of the challenge is more complex than any of these views individually, and that the challenge is driven by the unique nature of IT and its pervasiveness throughout the U.S. economy and our society. Two factors are chiefly responsible for creating the IT worker challenge. First, there has been sustained rapid growth in the demand for highly-skilled IT workers-demand that has accelerated in recent years. This demand is the product of the Information Age-virtually every segment of the American economy has embraced IT for the productivity improvements it brings to existing business functions, as well as for the new capabilities, products and services IT enables.

The ubiquity of IT can be seen almost everywhere: in the shift of business's equipment investment into information technologies, in the unprecedented emergence of the web as a venue for commerce and communication, and in the proliferation of computers in businesses and homes to name a few. As a result, demand for highly-skilled IT workers leads all other occupations and is expected to continue in the years ahead.

Second, the variety and complexity of software and hardware products and their applications, together with the unique business requirements of each industry, have created "spot" demand for workers with unique combinations of IT skills, experience and industry knowledge-expressed often by employers as needing "the right person, with the right skill, at the right time." The combination of time-sensitive competitive pressures and limited-time need for employees with unique combinations of technical skills, business skills, and hands-on experience has led many employers to pursue "buy" decisions in this labour market, rather than "make" decisions (to hire, then train for the task). Thus while there is a need to address the growing demand for highly-skilled IT workers, there is the additional challenge of meeting the unique demands of this niche labour market.

In a broad sense, the term "information worker" can be applied to data entry personnel, auto mechanics who use computer diagnostic equipment, medical technicians who operate CAT scan equipment, and loan officers who use computers to assess creditworthiness, as well as computer programmers, systems analysts, and computer scientists and engineers.

Office of Technology Policy analysis shows that the difficulty in meeting the national demand for IT workers is primarily for those with higher-end skills. The core IT occupations are differentiated, generally, from other IT and IT-related jobs by significantly higher skill and educational requirements.

The ability to conduct a quantitative analysis of IT employment is limited, to a large extent, by the availability of data, especially consistent longitudinal data that enables analysis of trends. Through its Occupational Employment Survey, the Department of Labour collects employment data on the four IT occupations that comprise our definition of core IT workers, and uses that data for its biennial ten-year projections of occupational and industry employment.

In addition, the Current Population Survey (CPS)-conducted jointly by the U.S. Department of Labour's Bureau of Labour Statistics (BLS) and the U.S. Department of Commerce's Census Bureau-provides data on core IT workers in two occupational categories: "computer systems analysts and scientists" and "computer programmers." While accounting for three of the core IT occupations, CPS data does not provide detailed information on the number of computer engineers.

The National Science Foundation does not consider computer programming as a science or engineering occupation, and therefore its Scientist and Engineer Statistical (SESTAT) data system does not fully account for the total number of computer programmers in the United States.

Computer scientists generally design computers and conduct research to improve their design or use, and develop and adapt principles for applying computers to new uses. They are distinguished from other computer professionals by the higher level of theoretical expertise and innovation they apply to complex problems and the creation or application of new technology.

Computer scientists employed by academic institutions work in areas ranging from theory, to hardware, to language design. Some work on multidisciplinary projects, such as developing and advancing uses for virtual reality. Computer scientists in private industry work in areas such as applying theory, developing specialized languages, or designing programming tools, knowledge-based systems, or computer games. Included in the "computer scientist" occupation are database administrators and computer support specialists.

Database administrators work with database management systems software, coordinating changes to, testing, and implementing computer databases. Since they also may be responsible for design implementation and system security, database administrators plan and coordinate security measures. Computer support specialists provide assistance and advice to users. They interpret problems and provide technical support for hardware, software, and systems. Support specialists may work within an organization or directly for a computer or software vendor.

Many others specialize in analysis, application, or design of a particular system or piece of the system. Network or systems administrators, for example, may install, configure, and support an organization's systems or portion of a system. Telecommunications specialists generally are involved with the interfacing of computer and communications equipment. Computer security specialists are responsible for planning, coordinating, and implementing an organization's information security measures.

Computer engineers work with the hardware and software aspects of systems design and development. Computer engineers may often work as part of a team that designs new computing devices or computer-related equipment. Software engineers design and develop both packaged and systems software.

Systems analysts use their knowledge and skills in a problem solving capacity, implementing the means for computer technology to meet the individual needs of an organization. They study business, scientific, or engineering data processing problems and design new solutions using computers.

This process may include planning and developing new computer systems or devising ways to apply existing systems to operations still completed manually or by some less efficient method.

Systems analysts may design entirely new systems, including both hardware and software, or add a single new software application to harness more of the computer's power. They work to help an organization realize the maximum benefit from its investment in equipment, personnel, and business processes.

Computer programmers write and maintain the detailed instructions, called "programs" or "software," that list in logical order the steps that computers must execute to perform their functions. In many large organizations, computer programmers follow descriptions prepared by systems analysts who have studied the task that the computer system is going to perform.

The transition from a mainframe to a primarily PC-based environment has blurred the once rigid distinction between the programmer and the user.

Increasingly adept users are taking over many of the tasks previously performed by computer programmers. A growing number of sophisticated software packages allow users and systems analysts to write programs.

The sweep of digital technologies and the transformation to a knowledge-based economy have created robust demand for workers highly skilled in the development and use of information technology. While there has been explosive employment growth in the U.S. software industry for more than a decade, the demand for workers who can create, apply and use information technology goes beyond the IT industry, cutting across manufacturing and services, transportation, health care, education and government.

Technology has contributed almost half of the Nation's long-term economic growth since World War II. And IT is the most important enabling technology in the world today. It is responsible for new products and services; creating new companies and industries; revitalizing existing products, services, and industries; providing new venues for commerce; enhancing our ability to manage information and to innovate; and improving our productivity, quality of life, and national standard of living. IT is changing the way we live and work, and transforming the economy at a fundamental level. The evidence is ubiquitous:

— Information technology's share of the U.S. economy nearly doubled between 1977 and 1998, growing from 4.2 percent to 8.2 percent. Information technologies contributed more than a third of real U.S. economic growth between 1995 and 1997.

— The cost of computing-measured in millions of instructions per second, or MIPS-fell 98.5 percent from $230 in 1991 to $3.42 in 1997. And the price per MIPS is expected to fall below a dollar this year, and to about one-fifth of a cent within a decade. This decline in computing costs is credited with reducing inflation by more than a full percentage point in 1997.

In 1994, three million people used the Internet. Year-end 1998 figures indicate more than 147 million people worldwide were accessing the Internet at least once a week from home or business. The number of Internet users is projected to grow to approximately 320 million by 2000, and to 720 million by 2005.

Traffic on the Internet is doubling every 100 days. This rapid growth in traffic is generating demand for both hardware and software, as well as for skilled IT workers to implement and manage these systems. Between 1998 and 2003, U.S. business-to-business commerce over the Internet is projected to grow from $48 billion to $1.3 trillion, with an additional $1.8 to $3.2 billion in global e-commerce; and U.S. consumer sales over the Internet are projected to rise from $3.9 billion to $108 billion.

For years, economists have expressed skepticism about IT's contribution to economic growth and productivity improvements. In recent years, many economists have come around. Today, one of the Nation's leading economists, Federal Reserve chairman Alan Greenspan, is an enthusiastic supporter of the vital role of IT in the U.S. economy.

The rapid acceleration of computer and telecommunications technologies is a major reason for the appreciable increase in their productivity in this expansion, and is likely to continue to be a significant force in expanding standards of living into the twenty-first century.

Ways in which employers tap the labour market, and the decisions they make about hiring and training investments, are affected by the business environment in which they operate. Today, the business environment for IT product and service producers is having a significant effect on employer approaches to the recruitment, retention, and training of highly-skilled IT workers.

In the decades following World War II, the U.S. high technology enterprise was dominated by government spending in defence and space. Dominant employers of highly-skilled technical workers resided in industries characterized by product life cycles measured in years, not months, such as the defence and aerospace industries.

Later, with the development of commercial computers, new IT industries began to play an important role in the labour markets for highly skilled technical workers, with the growth of computer hardware makers such as IBM, semiconductor manufacturers such as Texas Instruments and Intel, and service companies such as Electronic Data Systems. These large and stable firms had the time and incentive to serve as the training grounds for highly-skilled technical workers.

Many of these workers then brought their knowledge and skills to small and medium-sized high technology firms connected to these industries, and founded and staffed the new entrepreneurial firms that fuelled America's growing IT industry.

Today, the defence and aerospace industries have been downsized and are experiencing slow or no growth, and U.S. IT hardware manufacturers have globalized. At the same time, the computer and data processing services industry-consisting of software producers and IT consultants-has experienced a remarkable period of growth, with employment growing sixfold from 1976 to 1996.

The employment growth in this industry is a product of the phenomenal demand for IT related-products and services that not only enhance the productivity of current operations, but also create new products, services, and firm capabilities. Software and its applications are often the critical driver of these improvements. Today, the computer and data processing services industry is, by far, the largest employer of highly skilled core IT workers, employing more than a quarter of all workers in these professions; in 2006, the industry's share is projected to rise to nearly 40 percent.

Growth in science and engineering jobs is beginning to reflect this shift. Time is one of the most critical competitive factors for companies for whom IT is their core business. While product and technology life cycles have decreased markedly across all industry sectors, time pressures are most intense for these IT product and service producers. These companies confront life cycles or project deadlines that are measured in months or Internet years. For example, at Hewlett Packard, new products earn their greatest revenue in their first year on the market and, by their second year, revenues are already tapering off. Nearly two-thirds of the company's revenues are generated from products less than two years old. Moreover, early market entry provides a critical competitive edge. In many cases, the first competitors to the market with a new product are likely to capture most of the market share.

For example, in some key areas of packaged software-Internet browsers, word processing, spread sheet, page layout, and e-mail-two producers account for the lion's share of the market. Competitors who are among the first to the market capture the critical flow of funds generated by those markets that is needed to pay the costs of developing the next generation of technology and products.

Sometimes they become the de facto standard. If a company fails to reach the market in time, the lack of revenues to invest in development poses a serious risk that the company will eventually fall at the hands of more nimble competitors.

The pressures of time-based competition are often felt more acuteiy by smaller firms which may lack the buffers that larger firms have, such as a broader product portfolio from which to generate revenues or a larger staff available for retraining and deployment to projects.

In industry segments characterized by fast-paced creators or innovators of IT products and services, jobs and companies change rapidly, with a high rate of creative destruction. In this group, a few firms will grow into large, dominating competitors. Some will be acquired by other firms. Many will die in the creative destruction process. It is important to note that the development of software is highly labour-intensive.

A principal way to accelerate software development is to devote more human resources to the process. In addition, rapid technological change makes it more difficult for companies to predict future resource requirements and introduces greater uncertainty into the business environment. Therefore, companies may not be able to ascertain their specific skill needs very far into the future.

Another major competitive factor concerns the production of hardware versus the production and application of software.

Developing and producing high-tech hardware is highly capital intensive, requiring expensive manufacturing plants and other facilities. This is a relatively high barrier to entry into the business, a barrier that tends to limit the number of competitors. In contrast, software development and application can be carried out from a home basement, with a few computers and desks.

Both the pressures of time, and product and service proliferation, play an important role in the market for IT workers. The critical element of time argues for hiring workers who already possess the needed technical skills and experience, who can work productively at once. Otherwise, when faced with a six-month product life cycle, a training period as short as six weeks for a new IT worker or team represents one quarter of time-to-market.

In that scenario, an employer risks missing the market window altogether and, thus, the stream of revenues needed to keep the company in high-tech competition. Similarly, an extended breaking-in period for an employee increases the chance that a customer's project deadline will not be met. Product proliferation creates the need for IT workers specialized in particular technical skills and their application.

The information technology industry is advancing at a whirlwind pace; with product cycles and time-to-market periods shortening, and demands for continued innovation and productivity growing with each passing day. What we will offer next year has not been invented today.

Among employers of IT workers, some focus on the development of new IT-related products and services, or perform projects under contract to other firms. These employers, for which IT is the core business, are the ones that must often contend with very short product life cycles and intense competitive pressures, or pressure from customers to bring projects in on time and within budget. Often, these employers, such as those in the computer and data processing services industry, have a high level of IT worker intensity in the work force.

Other employers of IT workers focus on the application of information technologies to enhance their core businesses in other fields, such as in insurance, banking, retail, or manufacturing. These firms have lower IT worker intensity, and typically enjoy longer life cycles in their use of information technologies. These different types of IT employers confront different business challenges, which affect the way they recruit, retain, and invest in IT workers.

The mix of knowledge and skills required can vary significantly from one IT job to another, in terms of the specific technical skills needed, industry knowledge and experience, and other qualifications in areas such as project management, communications, and organizational skills. Thus IT workers qualified for one job may not qualify for another.

Certain technical skills may be in high demand or "hot," or be new skills-such as today's Java programmers, and computer security and e-commerce specialists-with employers having difficulty recruiting and retaining people with those skills. Also, IT is changing rapidly, which causes companies to frequently need different skill sets.

Today's IT labour market appears to be tighter at the high-end, with the competition for talent especially intense for workers with specific "hot" skill sets, often in combination with appropriate experience. Those with hot skills are seeing fast rising salaries and commanding a salary premium above those whose skills are in less demand, more dated, or more generic. Those with multiple hot skills and relevant industry experience are seeing especially fast rising compensation.

Many employers, especially those for whom IT is their core business, demand job candidates with exact skill fit, requiring no additional training. Faced with short product life cycles, customer deadlines, and competitive pressures that leave no time to spare, such employers want workers with the right skills and experience who can be productive right away.

With numerous combinations of technical skill sets and fields of experience, part of the IT labour market appears to operate as a series of niches requiring specialized, higher skill sets. Even if a company receives many resumes from which to choose to fill its job, the right candidate, with the right skills and experience may not be in the resume mix.

For example, one IT company had hired 1,000 engineers after receiving 22,000 resumes, or a selection rate of about 4 percent. A technical recruiter lamented that they had gotten 300 applicants at an IT job fair, yet did not find anyone qualified for the job for which they were recruiting.

As time has become an increasingly important factor of competitiveness for many employers of IT workers, the time available to retrain existing employees or train new employees in the skills needed for new projects has diminished. In its recent report on the supply of IT workers, the Computing Research Association (CRA) states that "companies are forced by short product life and short product development cycles to hire new employees or reassign existing workers in ways that do not require a lot of break-in training before they can be productive."

In this environment, many companies have concluded that they cannot afford the time penalty and the uncertainty associated with "making" the employees they need (through training or retraining). Many employers are, instead, pursuing a "buy" strategy, seeking the exact skills and experience they need for a particular project and paying a premium for that.

The CRA report acknowledges the need for looking outside the company to find the required technical skills, saying that the business environment "makes it difficult to retrain an existing employee for a significantly different job. Thus employers are sometimes forced, by competitive pressures, to lay off workers of one type and hire workers of another type. Or they may refuse to hire anyone who does not already possess the needed skills.

These employer practices receive harsh criticism at times from labour unions and some government officials, but to some degree this is a rational and perhaps necessary reaction to the realities of the marketplace. There is, of course, a time risk associated with seeking to recruit and hire the candidate with the exact skills and experience, especially in a tight labour market. Outside hires also lack important, company-specific knowledge, and may be less committed and loyal to the employer.

Companies also pursue buy decisions for other reasons. First, in fast-growth IT companies, often every core IT worker is deployed on current projects leaving none available for retraining. Second, in a dynamic, fast paced, highly competitive environment such as IT, the technology paths are often uncertain, making it very difficult to project future skill needs.

Though the "buy" strategy generally requires paying a premium for the requisite skills, companies are able to reduce the risks associated with the uncertainty about their future skill needs, while reducing or even eliminating the cost of training. At the same time, employers can be reasonably assured that new hires are able to hit the ground running.

As with other investments, companies generally invest in training because of the returns it brings through improved performance. However, the current IT business environment and its effect on the highly-skilled IT labour market increase the risk of training investments and reduce the likelihood of capturing an acceptable return on the investment.

The tight IT labour market-a function of both the rapid demand for core IT workers, generally, and the need to fill specific niches- has created an environment in which many companies seek to find the people they need by luring talented IT workers away from their current employers using a variety of mechanisms. These inducements encourage job-hopping among IT employees, creating another major disincentive for companies to train or retrain workers. Companies that invest in the training of employees to upgrade their IT skills may create an attractive target for poaching by other companies, putting at risk both the employees and the companies' training investment.

Employers who apply information technologies in support of their core businesses in other fields often have more stable employment environments and longer IT life cycles and, thus, have greater ability to "make" their skill base by investing in training. However, since they share the same labour pool with firms whose core business is IT, they are buffeted by the actions of others. They, too, risk poaching of their employees and may also have to pay premiums to acquire and retain certain IT skills, especially the ones most in demand.

In some companies, training and education are offered as benefits to employees (to attract or retain them) who understand they must keep their skills current if they are to remain viable in the IT labour market.

As many companies have turned to a buy strategy to gain the critical skills they need, they have undertaken a wide range of strategies to attract and retain workers-from the commonplace to the extraordinary. Unlike so many occupations in which job stability is a hallmark of success, the business environment in IT has created a labour market in which job hopping serves as a means to gain the vital technical skills needed for career opportunities. Acquiring new skills allows them to move within the entire IT work community for opportunities, rather than solely within a particular company.

The impact can be seen in how quickly IT workers move from one employer to the next, and how intensely they are recruited. The average job length is four years for IT staffers and five years for IT managers. More than two-thirds of IT professionals have been contacted by a headhunter in the past year-an average of three times each in just the past six months. The recruitment is even more intense for the hot skills. For example, three out of four staff members, and nine out of ten managers in data mining report being contacted by recruiters in the past year. And in super hot Silicon Valley, the average length of stay at a single job is 18 months, according to Digital Nation.

IT workers ranked "challenge of their job, responsibility" and "job atmosphere" ahead of "base pay" as what mattered the most to them about their jobs. Quality of working life issues, job stability, and having the opportunities to gain critical skills through job assignments dominated the responses. Still, monetary compensation ranks high among the tools used by companies to recruit and retain employees. Among the more common tools employed: signing/performance bonuses, salary premiums for hot skills, stock options, referral fees, royalty fees, child care, flexible hours, telecommuting, training and education, tuition reimbursement, time off/extra vacation time, gyms and exercise facilities.

A sutdy said about the reported high rates of vacancies in IT companies and other IT-worker intensive organizations. Vacancies are a normal part of business, the result of turnover and the time it takes to fill a job. In industries and occupations that are experiencing sustained, rapid growth, and relatively high rates of labour mobility, vacancies should not be surprising. If it takes between 35-70 days to fill different positions, and the company is experiencing rapid growth, and if a specialized type of employee is being sought, vacancies are to be expected. A tight labour market compounds the challenge.

Not all employers of IT workers enjoy a well-oiled and nimble human resources department, with sophisticated and creative recruitment methods, and a streamlined hiring process. Many small companies do not have human resource departments at all, and hiring functions may be performed by technical professionals who have little or no knowledge and experience in human resources practices.

Many companies contract with recruiting firms to fill their jobs, but many of these recruiters lack the technical knowledge to do much more than follow the technical specification the hiring firm provides.

Making the labour markets work better-in terms of effectively identifying the critically needed skills, rapid identification of potential candidates, and streamlining the internal hiring process-could help reduce the time it takes to staff operations and reduce vacancy rates. Finally, it should be noted that recruitment of skilled IT workers is not limited to companies. Many states see a highly-skilled IT work force as a major tool to encourage economic development.

The loss of skilled IT workers to others is also a concern of economic development officials. For example, the Hudson Valley, New York area is losing IT professionals to contract work for employers in other areas. It was noted at the Hudson Valley town meeting that the northern New Jersey market pays IT professionals 10 percent more and the New York City market pays 25 percent more.

Some people see information technology as a tool to keep the residents from moving to other states for job opportunities. U.S. Senator Kent Conrad expressed his concern about the isolation of small towns around the country stating, "There is a need to keep the best and brightest in North Dakota. This is the biggest concern of parents. IT is an opportunity to provide these jobs."

Some employers of IT workers are looking to foreign workers to meet their skill needs. Whether or not to allow larger numbers of skilled foreign workers to enter the country in order to meet employers' demands for new IT workers is a contentious issue.

The allowable number of H-1B visas, which allow skilled foreign workers to work in the United States for up to six years. Although H-1B visas are "non-immigrant" visas, they are often used as a stepping stone to permanent immigration. In some cases, foreign students enter the United States on a student visa, receive an H-1B visa after graduation, and then seek permanent employment-based immigration.

Nearly half of the people who become permanent employment-based immigrants convert from H-visa non-immigrant status. Prior to 1998, the number of H-1B visas had been capped at 65,000 workers per year. The IT industry has increasingly used H-1B visas. In 1995, only about a quarter of temporary skilled foreign workers were in IT-related fields; by 1997 about half were in IT fields. Largely due to the increased use by the IT industry, the H-1B cap was reached for the first time in August 1997.

The IT industry led a major effort to increase the H-1B visa cap. IT industry needs more skilled foreign workers to help meet skill shortages, an inability to find workers has limited growth in the IT industry and other parts of the economy that need IT workers, the IT industry needs an international work force to meet the needs of international markets, the IT industry needs to be able to attract the best and brightest workers from around the world, and the alternative to bringing foreign workers to the United States is to move work overseas.

H-1B workers cause wages in IT occupations to be lower than they would otherwise be, reducing the incentive for U.S. residents to enter, or stay in, these occupations; thus immigration can create a self-perpetuating demand for more immigration, and the H-1B program has been abused by firms, which have brought in foreign workers to work at less than the prevailing U.S. wages.

In late 1998, the Congress and the White House agreed to compromise legislation that would temporarily increase the H-1B cap and also attempt to curb abuses in the program. The law also provides for the collection of a $500 fee for each H-1B application in order to create a fund for low-income student scholarships and training programs.

The National Science Foundation will administer the newly established Computer Science, Engineering and Mathematics Scholarship Program, providing student scholarships to enable the achievement of higher education degrees in IT-related disciplines. The law also includes new provisions intended to prevent abuses of the program. For example, H-1B dependent employers must attest that they are not laying off U.S. workers for similar jobs and that they have made significant efforts to recruit U.S. workers.

In the midst of a tight labour market, there are numerous anecdotes of middle-age technical workers having difficulty finding IT jobs. Data from the National Science Foundation indicate, however, that the employment profile for computer and math scientists closely parallels that of the overall science and engineering work force.

The IT industry is young and fast growing compared to many other industries and, thus, has a younger worker demographic profile which may contribute to the perception that it is not a hospitable environment for mid-career workers. The difficulties faced by mid-career technical workers have been widely reported in IT magazines 26 and this issue was raised at several of the town meetings. There are a number of reasons mid-career technical workers may face barriers in the IT labour market. The IT industry is populated by many younger workers. Approximately 75 percent of computer systems analysts and scientists, and nearly 80 percent of computer programmers are under the age of 45.

Many managers in the IT industry are in their 20s and 30s, and may be uncomfortable hiring or managing older and more experienced workers. A Network World survey of 200 readers with some hiring responsibility showed that younger network managers are less likely to hire older workers than younger workers. Almost half of respondents 20 to 30 years of age had never hired a person over the age of 40.

Many IT companies have operating modes that require long and intense work hours, and mid-career workers, for example those with family obligations, may be assumed to be unwilling to work these long hours. Some employers may hold the perception that mid-career workers expect higher pay for doing the same work that younger workers do. There is a perception that mid-career workers may not be current with the latest skills, may not be as flexible in doing different kinds of work, and may be less innovative, compared to younger workers. Some employers may have concerns that mid-career workers will cost the company more in insurance premiums, due to age and higher likelihood of having covered family members. On the other hand, many mid-career workers have kept up with the latest skills (or could easily obtain them), are innovative, and are willing to work long hours for market pay rates. Many mid-career workers have a breadth of experience that could benefit many young IT companies.

Some mid-career unemployed and underemployed engineers may find difficulty in obtaining employment because they expect higher wages or, while they may be highly-skilled and experienced, they may not have the specific technical skills that employers want. On the other hand, it is likely that some mid-career engineers who have appropriate skills and are willing to work at market wages are overlooked because of the perception-not the reality-that older workers cannot do the job.

It should also be noted that many of the IT jobs that are the hardest to fill are those in non-IT industries, in government, and in schools. Many of these types of organizations do not seem to have the same youth-oriented culture that characterizes many entrepreneurial software companies, and would welcome mid-career technical workers.

The 1998 American Competitiveness and Workforce Improvement Act, which increased the number of skilled non-immigrant foreign workers allowed to work in the United States, requires the National Science Foundation to contract with the National Academy of Sciences to conduct a study assessing the status of older workers in the IT field, including a consideration of the existence and extent of age discrimination in the IT work place. Many mid-career workers have a breadth of experience that could benefit many young IT companies.

In an uncertain business environment, faced with rapid technological change, many employers seek flexible means of staffing their projects. Employers use independent contractors or temporary workers employed by staffing companies as a mechanism to meet their need for IT workers in this dynamic environment.

In the case of contract workers, the workers are not considered to be employees and are responsible for paying their own payroll taxes and unemployment insurance. In the case of temporary workers, the staffing companies are responsible for their employees' wages and legally required payroll deductions, and may provide some benefits as well. Using either independent contractors or temporary workers has advantages for the employer. Employers can get the specific skills they need for a temporary project without hiring people that might need to be laid off later. Employers can also check out people on a trial basis before deciding whether or not to hire them. And companies do not have to pay for expensive benefit packages. Contract or temporary work can also be advantageous to some employees.

Independent contractors with skills in high demand can get paid at a higher rate than most employees, and some workers desire the greater flexibility and variety that can come from temporary or contract work. Temporary work may also let employees gain work experience that may make them more marketable. On the other hand, many employees who accept such arrangements may prefer to have permanent employment. The IT industry has been expanding its use of various types of temporary workers.

According to the National Association of Temporary and Staffing Services, total wages paid for assigned technical workers (a category that includes computer programmers, computer systems analysts, designers, drafters, editors, engineers, and illustrators) grew from $1.9 billion in 1991 to $4.7 billion in 1998. The increasing use of temporary workers has implications for the training of IT workers. When a company uses temporary or contract workers, it is generally purchasing skills for immediate use, and has little or no motivation for investing in training for that worker.

The incentive and responsibility for investing in training lies clearly with the individual worker, and, to some extent, with the temp agency. Temp agencies do invest in training. A 1998 survey by the National Association of Temporary and Staffing Services indicated that staffing firms expended $720 million for skills training in 1997, training 4.8 million individuals.

The Court of Appeals panel held that workers who are employed by a temp agency can also be considered common-law employees of the company that directs their work, and, as such, are entitled to participate in company benefits. This ruling will clearly make long-term employment of workers through temp agencies more expensive and less attractive to employers, and is likely to slow the use of independent contractors and temporary workers.

Outsourcing technical skills should allow the proliferation of technical consulting companies and staffing operations that can offer a wider range of opportunities to individuals. These operations should also be able to capture a greater return on investments in training because they can provide better career paths for technical employees, focus their retention practices, and provide internal mobility, thereby reducing turnover.

As information technology has emerged as a fundamental driver of global business and economic growth, there has been explosive growth in the demand for IT professionals. For more than 15 years, employment in the core IT occupations- computer scientists, computer engineers, systems analysts and computer programmers- has grown at an astounding pace. The growth rate for computer scientists and systems analysts has even accelerated in recent years.

In addition, employment in the computer and data processing services industry 83 -which employs the largest number of IT workers and has the highest proportion of IT workers in its work force-has experienced rapid employment and revenue growth.

Current Population Survey (CPS)-a joint project of the U.S. Departments of Commerce and Labour-shows the number of "computer systems analysts and scientists"-which includes computer engineers- and "computer programmers" soared from 719,000 to 2,084,000, an increase of 190 percent, more than six times faster than the overall U.S. job growth rate of 30.4 percent. Computer systems analysts and scientists have shown the most rapid growth, 433 percent, during this period. In contrast, computer programmers grew by 38.4 percent, much closer to the overall U.S.

For more than 15 years, employment in the core IT occupations- computer scientists, computer engineers, systems analysts and computer programmers-has grown at an astounding pace. The growth rate for computer scientists and systems analysts has even accelerated in recent years.

Though the overall job growth rate for the country has remained steady, the core IT occupations have grown at an even faster rate in recent years than for the 15-year period. Annual average growth for computer systems analysts and scientists was 11.8 percent and 2.2 percent for computer programmers during the 1983-1998 period, according to CPS data. Between 1995 and 1998, computer systems analysts and scientists recorded an annual average job growth rate of 16.4 percent, while computer programmers scored a 3.7 percent annual average job growth. Thus employment growth for IT occupations seems to be even stronger in recent years than in the past.

There are three primary Federal government data sources for information about the U.S. information technology work force-the Current Population Survey (CPS), the Industry-Occupation Employment Matrix (I-O Matrix), and the National Science Foundation's Scientist and Engineer Statistics (SESTAT) data system. Each source uses different methodologies for collecting data and arriving at estimates of the number of these workers. Despite the different methodologies, there is general agreement that the size of the core IT work force in 1998 was approximately 2.1 million.

Some computer engineers are captured in "Computer Systems Analysts and Scientists" occupation, though others are captured under the occupational title "Electrical and Electronic Engineers." Computer systems managers are captured under the occupation "Managers and Administrators," of which 498,000 are engineering, science and computer systems managers.

The three fastest growing occupations in the 1996-2006 employment projections are core IT occupations. Computer scientists, computer engineers, and systems analysts are each projected to more than double during this period.

Compared to the other core IT occupations, computer programming has a slow projected growth rate over the ten-year projection period. Several causes have been cited as underlying factors in this relatively slow growth:

— *Offshore contracting of code writing*: Once the higher-level work involved in software development-design, identification of key variables, specification of program modules for manipulation of data, and determination of operation flows and linkages needed to carry out a set of desired tests-has been accomplished, lower-level coding work can be broken into many separate pieces and the work distributed. Increasingly this type of work is being outsourced to low-cost regions of the world, such as Bangalore, India.

— *Automation of code writing*: Tools such as CASE (Computer Aided Software Engineering), a collection of automated tools and methods, assist software engineers and reduce the need for programmers by increasing productivity through automation of manual tasks, improving quality through automated checks and reminders, incorporating standardization, and by providing complete and accessible documentation. In effect, this transfers the programmer function to higher-level software engineers.

— *Advanced programming languages/Object-oriented programming*: The transition from a mainframe environment to a PC environment blurred the distinction between programmers and users. As prepackaged software has found its way onto desktops around the country, end-users have become increasingly capable of performing many of the functions that previously resided in the sole domain of programmers.

Employers pursuing more bang for their salary buck are seeking employees from other IT or IT-related specialties-such as computer scientists, electrical engineers, and math majors-who also have strong programming skills. While they may not carry the title "programmer," programming is an essential, often core, part of their responsibilities.

In the IT core occupations, in particular, past BLS projections often have been on the low side, often significantly underestimating their growth. For example, in their 1994 to 2005 projections, BLS projected the number of new core IT workers needed for new jobs and to replace those exiting the profession to average approximately 95,000 a year. In their next round of projections, that average grew to approximately 138,000 a year-an increase of 45 percent, even though the 1996-2006 projections include nine of the years included in the previous projections.

BLS's projected annual average growth rate for core IT occupations between 1996 and 2006 is slightly lower than the actual growth rate in the preceding decade, despite the economy's growing reliance on information technology.

In US, although Current Population Survey (CPS) data are not directly comparable to OES-based data, CPS data show tremendous growth in IT occupations since 1996. According to CPS data, the increase in computer systems analysts and scientists/ computer programmers during the first two years of the projection period exceeded the average pace anticipated for the core IT occupations in the 1996-2006 projections by more than 50 percent. Viewed in terms of growth rates, CPS data indicate these occupations grew at a substantially higher annual average growth rate than BLS projected for core IT workers during the 1996-2006 period.

The service sector, in general, and the computer and data processing services (CDPS) industry, in particular, will lead growth in the core IT occupations according to BLS projections. The service sector 38 is expected to account for the lion's share of growth in the core IT occupations during the 1996-2006 period. By 2006, the service sector is projected to increase its employment of computer systems analysts, scientists, and engineers by 177 percent and computer programmers by 47 percent.

In contrast, the manufacturing sector is projected to experience comparatively slower growth in the number of computer scientists, computer engineers and systems analysts (approximately 44 percent), and a 20 percent decrease in the number of computer programmers.

IT occupational growth in the service sector will be led by the CDPS industry, according to BLS projections. CDPS is, by far, the largest employer of core IT workers. In all, the CDPS industry is projected to account for 55.8 percent of the total employment growth in IT occupations between 1996 and 2006. The CDPS industry also has the highest IT worker intensity of any industry. In 1996, more than one-in-three CDPS workers were in the core IT occupations, by 2006 that ratio is projected to grow to more than two-in-five.

IT worker intensity-defined as the percentage of an industry's work force composed of core IT occupations-provides a guide to which industries are most reliant on these workers and, by extension, which might be affected most by tight IT labour markets.

When IT worker intensity and size of the IT work force are taken together, a picture emerges as to which industries' competitive performance would be most adversely affected by difficulties in hiring highly skilled IT workers. The computer and data processing services industry stands out starkly as an industry with much at stake in the supply of IT workers. But not only is the CDPS industry affected by the supply of IT workers, the unique characteristics of the industry and its work environment significantly affect the national pool of IT workers from which all industries must draw.

The core IT work force has a much different demographic and educational composition than the civilian labour force as a whole. In particular, core IT workers have a much higher level of educational attainment, a higher proportion of male workers and are more likely to be employed in the service sector; the finance, insurance, and real estate industries; and manufacturing.

Most characteristically, core IT workers get their education from four-year colleges; however, there are a wide range of other education and training grounds for IT workers generally, including: two-year associate degree-granting community colleges, which provide grounding in applications as well as basic theory, and vocational technical education programs. Most jobs in the core IT occupations, however, require a four-year degree or equivalent skills.

There are approximately one million college graduates whose education has included significant preparation for IT work, most of them holding bachelor's level degrees or higher. Specifically, the analysis counts approximately 783,700 college graduates in the United States with bachelor's degrees or higher in information technology fields-computer and information sciences or computer engineering-through April 1997. It includes graduates with bachelor's degrees in electrical engineering that reported second majors or minors in computer science or related IT specialties. In addition, OTP estimates approximately 105,000 additional college graduates with IT degrees through June 1999.

The National Science Foundation's SESTAT database provides a window into the educational background of core IT workers who have a bachelor's degree or higher. An analysis of the recently released 1997 SESTAT data shows that 42 percent of the core IT work force with degrees has an IT degree, while another 4 percent completed an undergraduate minor or second major in computer science or computer engineering, for a total of 46 percent. An additional 40 percent hold a degree in another engineering, science, or mathematics discipline. The remaining degreed IT workers hold degrees in business and other disciplines.

Beyond its relationship with 1,900 commercial training companies, Microsoft is working with 1,000 academic institutions around the world to achieve this extensive training capacity. While approximately 900 of these academic institutions are located in the United States, Microsoft expects that the fastest growth in education partnerships in 1999 will be outside the United States.

Some study suggest that the combination of fast employment growth, rising compensation and low unemployment rates may signal a tight labour market. In contrast to the strong quantitative data showing the rapid growth of the core IT occupations, evidence of strong rising compensation for these occupations is mixed. While it seems clear, from both government and non-government data, that the compensation level for IT professionals is both high and rising, the question remains whether rising compensation is unique to these occupations and the result of a tight labour market, or whether it is part of a more general trend generated by a very prosperous U.S. economy.

Government experts suggest that the variance between the government and private wage surveys is generally the result of various factors including sample size and survey methodology (design of samples, use of well-constructed and tested questions, methods of obtaining higher rates of sample responses), concluding that the government data is likely to be significantly more accurate. Though there are mixed signals on compensation for the core IT occupations generally, analysis by the Commerce Department's Office of Technology Policy indicates a consensus in several areas:

— *IT worker salaries are high and rising*: Those with hot skills are seeing fast rising salaries and are commanding a salary premium above those whose skills are less hot, more dated or more generic. Those with combinations of multiple hot skills and relevant industry experience are seeing especially fast rising compensation.

— *Starting salaries are rising fast*: Food counter workers have benefited from a 6.4 percent average annual salary increase, driven in part by an increase in the minimum wage from $4.25 per hour to $5.15 per hour during this time period. The increase in the minimum wage also contributed to the overall work force's 3.0 percent average annual salary increase.

Computer systems analysts' and scientists' salary increase during this period was equal to that of the overall work force, but higher than professional specialty occupations as a whole, and lawyers, physicians, and teachers in particular. Computer programmers enjoyed an even greater increase in salary during this period, posting an average annual salary increase of 4.3 percent, despite the fact that demand for computer programmers has been, and is projected to be, much slower than for other core IT occupations.

However, the higher average annual salary increases for computer programmers are supportive of the Office of Technology Policy's conclusion that skills in the hot programming areas are in high demand and being rewarded accordingly. 1997 National Occupational

Employment and Wage Estimates, OES data does not allow for an analysis of wage trends because the OES survey only began collecting wage data in 1996. However, the information from OES provides a good snapshot of employment and wages for the core IT occupations.

The Institute of Electrical and Electronics Engineers-USA (IEEE-USA) 1999 Salary and Fringe Benefits Survey. IEEE-USA reports in its 1999 Salary and Fringe Benefits Survey that the purchasing power of its members has reached an all-time high, surpassing the previous high recorded in its previous biennial survey.

In particular, IEEE-USA's 1999 Salary and Fringe Benefits Survey finds that the primary income-base salaries, net earnings from self-employment, and commissions and bonuses-of IEEE members working full-time in their areas of professional competence rose 13.9 percent to $82,000 between 1997 and 1999, compared to a 3.3 percent increase in the Consumer Price Index in urban areas for the same period.

New entrants into the core IT occupations have benefited from high increases in starting salary offers during the past three years, according to the National Association of Colleges and Employers. NACE has collected data for many years on starting salary offers for bachelor's degree holders across a wide range of occupations, including three of the core IT occupations-computer scientists, computer engineers, and computer programmers.

NACE data provide a window into the long and short-term behaviour of starting salary offers. OTP analyzed starting salary offers for the IT professions and several other professional specialties-accounting (private), financial/treasury analysis, design and construction engineering, manufacturing and industrial engineering, and research and development-to identify longer term and more recent trends.

Compared to other professions, IT workers have enjoyed faster growth in average annual starting salary offers during both the short and longer term. In contrast, the national unemployment rate-which reached a 42 year low of 4.2 percent in March 1999-is still three times as high as the unemployment rate of the core IT occupations.

State and Regional Perspective on Supply, Demand and Salaries supply and demand conditions for different types of workers in each region, or whether they are due to differences in the kind of work performed in occupational categories among the regions.

The National Science Foundation's SESTAT database provides regional salary information on core IT workers for those with degrees in computer and information sciences (regardless of their occupation), as well as for those employed as computer and information scientists. The Pacific region has the highest median salary in both categories, $55,000 for those employed as computer and information scientists, $53,000 for those with degrees in computer and information sciences. The United States needs to do a better job at encouraging and preparing young people to enter technical education and careers.

Town meeting participants identified the image of the technical professional as an important factor in shaping young people's attitudes about careers in science and technology. Many people have a distorted, negative image of IT workers, scientists and engineers, perceiving them as highly intelligent, but socially inept or absent-minded "geeks" or "nerds." The media play an influential role in shaping these public perceptions.

Women and minorities are infrequently portrayed in technical roles; typically, scientists and technologists are portrayed by white males. The print media also perpetuate such images. Many children and adults embrace these stereotypical images, and have limited exposure to the wide variety of careers and people in the IT, science and engineering fields. In preparation for the IT Work Force Convocation, a group of students from Missouri in the sixth and ninth grades was asked to draw a picture of an IT worker. Prevalent among the images were bow ties and bald heads, pocket protectors, pants that were too short, and nearly all of the IT workers portrayed wore glasses. Of the 160 pictures of IT workers submitted by the students, only 16 of them portrayed women.

Television offers many examples of real life scientists and engineers. The PBS program NOVA features technical professionals from a wide range of disciplines. Natural scientists are frequently featured in programs about nature and animals. Today, many local television weather forecasters are meteorologists and offer snippets of information about meteorological science. Still, participants in the national dialogue suggested that efforts are needed to improve the image of the technical professions.

This would include explaining the important contributions science and technology make to our economy and quality of life. Identifying and highlighting role models could help young people and their parents learn that technical workers are normal people who perform a wide range of interesting and exciting jobs in science and technology. Participants also suggested that industry and government open a dialogue with the entertainment industry, as well as the national and local media to encourage these influential shapers of image to improve their depiction of technical professionals, and expand and improve the quality of national and local science and technology reporting.

Government and the private sector should work together to support and develop national information and advertising campaigns to improve the image of the technical professions, and communicate the portfolio of skills needed to thrive in the new economy. Information products in a variety of print, video, and digital media should be tailored to reach parents, students, teachers, and guidance counsellors. Messages should focus on the vital role science and technology play in the economy and our quality of life.

Materials could explain that most jobs in the future will require some technical skills, and that science, technology and IT work involves a broad array of exciting careers. The campaign could identify and highlight "normal" role models, including women and minorities, what they do, and their contributions to society.

Industry and government-at the Federal, state, and local levels-should establish a dialogue with those who heavily influence perceptions about people who make and use science and technology. At the national level, industry and government could establish a dialogue with the entertainment industry and the press to improve the image of technical professionals and the portrayal of their work in television, movies, and the printed media. State and local government officials could join regional businesses in establishing a dialogue with local media to encourage a more positive portrayal of technical workers, and expanded coverage of the community's science and technology activities and those who participate in them.

Technology-intensive companies and organizations could invite members of the community in which they reside to visit and see how such organizations work, how they use technology, their working environments, and their contributions to the economy and quality of life. The Federal government could expand its efforts to promote Federal scientists and engineers as role models, and publicize the exciting diversity and value of their work.

Prepearing Students for IT Carrers

For lack of knowledge and interest in such careers, students may fail to take the appropriate courses in math and science needed to help prepare them for a technology-intensive workplace in a rapidly changing economy. Young people form opinions about careers before they graduate from high school, and middle school is seen as a key decision-making point. Many students receive little information about the wide range of interesting and exciting careers in science and technology, the industries that develop and use science and technology, or the education and skills needed to pursue technical jobs. In recent testimony before the Senate Judiciary Committee, an academic expert said, "Currently, few students in high school are aware of what it is that computer scientists do, what academic skills are required, the challenges and activities on the job, and what the economic rewards are. "

Parents play one of the most important roles in influencing children's career choices. For example, a group of students in the third, sixth, ninth, and twelfth grades was asked: What or who has influenced your decision about what you want to do or be when you enter the work force. At every grade level, parents were identified as exerting the most influence over career choices. Yet, parents often lack information that would enable them to encourage their children to choose a career in science and technology.

Teachers and school counsellors are providers of career information, but may also lack knowledge about science and technology-based industries. A recent Harris Poll commissioned by the American Association of Engineering Societies confirmed a lack of public awareness of the technical professions. In the survey, 61 percent of Americans felt that they were not very well or not at all informed about engineering and engineers.

Due to a lack of career information and encouragement, and few positive role models, many students at an early age dismiss the notion of or never develop an interest in a science or technology career. Information on Careers and Industry. Company visits for middle school students were viewed as a good way to introduce them to technical careers and high-technology work settings. Maryland high-tech organizations sponsored a technology career fair to bring middle school students and their parents together with companies to discuss the kinds of careers that are available. An Arizona industry representative suggested that kiosks be placed in libraries which provide information about a region's industry clusters and the jobs in those clusters, so students and parents can become familiar with job titles and content.

Career planning tools include self assessment exercises, and other general career planning and management information and tools. Each Cornerstone Partner Society has developed a career web site with information on each field and current career options. The 3M Foundation and Minnesota State Colleges and Universities sponsored the development of the Technical Careers Tool Kit. The tool kit provides educational and motivational materials to promote awareness of career opportunities in technical fields and the importance of two-year post-secondary technical and career education.

The kit is now being marketed to employers and educators nationwide and is designed to help them work together to create cooperative programs that provide students with exposure to today's work-places and technologies. The kit contains video presentations and background materials. The videos show successful School-To-Work activities in action, including workplace visits, internship programs, and high-tech professionals in the classroom. The videos highlight successful school and business partnerships and demonstrate how such activities can trigger enthusiasm among employees.

TECH (Technical Teams Encouraging Career Horizons) is one of 3M's Science Encouragement Programs. Teams of women and men scientists visit junior and senior high schools to inform students-especially girls and minorities-of career opportunities in science and engineering, and of the need to maximize their career options by studying math and science in school. Each year up to 250 TECH volunteers reach 8,000-10,000 students. Most of the schools are in the St. Paul area, but TECH has recently expanded to involve the 3M Austin Centre in Texas and there are plans to set up TECH programs nationwide.

To make the route to high-technology careers more transparent, state and local governments, and educators could identify K-16 pathways to IT and other technical careers, highlighting career ladders, job market data, and skill requirements. Education and training opportunities could be identified or developed to help students move along these pathways that lead to careers. Businesses could sponsor/cooperate on work-focused IT, science, and engineering projects, at school or the company workplace, with projects focusing on the use of the computer. Schools could develop after-school and summer courses in IT, science, and technology, and encourage students to participate in the development and maintenance of school-based IT infrastructure. K-12 faculty and businesses could work together to create curriculum, and have technical professionals from local high-tech industries speak to students, or teach a class or short course.

The U.S. Department of Education makes a major investment in programs to strengthen math and science education, and to prepare Americans for technology-based careers. To improve math and science education, the Department focuses on improving teaching quality through teacher preparation and effective professional development, upgrading curricula by providing schools with good information and resources, providing learning support for students who need extra assistance, and building a research and evaluation base. The Department also is working to connect U.S. classrooms to the Internet, and ensure that all Americans will be technologically literate. Efforts involve helping ensure teachers are prepared to integrate technology into the curriculum, and use the new teaching and learning styles enabled by technology, as well as demonstrations of innovative uses of technology for education and training. The Department leads efforts to prepare students for high technology careers, for example through school to work programs, and to open the doors of college to more students through a range of financial mechanisms.

The growing use of computers on the job and the high growth in computer-related occupations have made computer skills an important component of most students' educational portfolio.

In many industries, the number of workers who use a computer at their job now ranges from 50 to 85 percent. IT is being widely deployed in the U.S. K-12 educational system. Today, there are about six students for each computer in K-12 schools, though student access varies.

Efforts are springing up to help build IT infrastructure in the K-12 education system. For example, U.S. Tech Corps is a national non-profit organization dedicated to improving K-12 education at the grassroots level through the effective integration of technology into the learning environment. TECH CORPS recruits, places, and supports volunteers from the technology community who advise and assist schools in the introduction and integration of new technologies into the educational system.

A student's own interest and skills are influential in career choice, and computer use in K-12 provides early exposure to IT and the opportunity for skill development. The development of students' computer skills is increasingly integrated into instruction, for example studying chemistry using spreadsheets and simulations.

According to the National Assessment of Education Progress, 54 percent of U.S. fourth grade math teachers use computers for math/learning games, and 27 percent of eighth grade math teachers use computers for simulations and applications. In the assessment, more Computer use in K-12 provides early exposure to IT and the opportunity for skill development.

There are a growing number of programs aimed at developing students' information technology skills. For example, in 1996, local community leaders in Omaha, Nebraska recognized that many young people were not obtaining the academic and cultural skills required to compete in the metro area's growing technical labour market. At the same time, local IT companies reported increasing difficulty in recruiting for many high skilled, high wage positions.

A number of efforts are designed to help develop teachers' computer skills. The International Technology Education Association (ITEA) is the professional organization of technology teachers which strengthens the profession through leadership, professional development, membership services, publications, and classroom activities.

ITEA conducts various professional development programs:

— The Technology Teacher, Technology and Children, The Journal of Technology Education, TTTe, Curriculum Brief, and a variety of other publications and videos provide teaching directions, instructional ideas and networking opportunities.

— Ten primary committees coordinate all aspects of technology education and sponsor dozens of meetings, conferences and exhibits each year.

— An active honours and awards program recognizes outstanding teachers and programs (K-12) from states, provinces and countries that are affiliated with the Association. ITEA also presents award certificates and supports other programs which recognize outstanding efforts in the technology teaching profession.

— A public policy program provides information to government agencies, associations and other special interest groups concerning technology education. The Association strives to provide an understanding of the importance of technology education to the future growth and wellbeing of all nations.

Steps to Improve Schools' Capacity for IT Skills Development:

— Expand technical education/IT infrastructure in schools:

— Businesses could donate IT equipment, software, and IT-related services to schools and keep them up to date.

— Strengthen teacher training in IT:

— Create and implement IT curricula in schools of education.

— School systems could reward liberal arts teachers who integrate IT into curriculum, as well as reward teachers who obtain IT certifications and remain in teaching.

— Businesses could work with schools to develop "teaching the teacher" programs in which high-technology industry's technical staff conduct training workshops for teachers.

Challenges in Preparing Post-Secondary Students for the Information Technology Work Force

There are number of challenges to better prepare college students for the high-tech work force, including: increasing student opportunities for relevant technical education and skills development, increasing faculty exposure to high-tech industry, ensuring that curricula are up-to-date and impart the knowledge and skills employers need, and ensuring adequate IT education and training infrastructure.

Students need greater knowledge of the work environments to which they will move after graduation. This would increase their understanding of the skills needed to play a productive role in the high-tech workplace, and help illustrate the relevancy of what they learn in the classroom.

A number of efforts to increase student exposure to the world of work were discussed. A large high-tech company in Washington state described an effort in which faculty would teach theory during the class and then software engineering students went to the company to work on a real project-with real software engineers and a real technical manager-applying what they learned in class.

For example, In US, the University of Maryland formed a partnership with a private IT school which created an intensive five-week training program to teach COBOL to students of all ages to address the year 2000 problem.

Businesses are recruited to sponsor students' training and to hire them upon completion of the program. Participating businesses also contribute to a scholarship fund. After a stint at the sponsor company, a student can draw from the scholarship fund to pay for up to four years of tuition toward a bachelor's degree.

There is concern that fewer college students will pursue graduate level IT studies, opting instead for lucrative job opportunities as IT workers in industry. The "seed corn" problem could result in insufficient numbers of faculty to train the next generation of students, as well as fewer U.S. master's and Ph.D. graduates for advanced, cutting edge IT work.

There are different steps to increase student Opportunities:

— *Expand student opportunities for technical education, training, and experience*: Businesses could provide funds for science and technology scholarships for high school students, college students, or current workers who commit to working for a contributing company or in states and regions where the private sector's need for IT workers is growing.

— *The business and education communities should develop more hands-on work-study opportunities*: The Federal government could work with community colleges and computer science/engineering schools, local business communities, and others to establish an IT/ e-commerce extension service in which students studying IT assist small and medium-sized firms with IT planning, implementation and problem solving.

— Barriers (i.e., recognizing class credits) to matriculating from two-year IT programs at community colleges to four-year IT programs at universities should be reduced.

The Global Wireless Education Consortium (GWEC) was established in 1997 to increase the quality and quantity of technicians, engineers, and IT specialists to meet the demands of an expanding wireless communications industry. Industry members work with colleges and university partners to develop up-to-date wireless technology curriculum. GWEC provides its members with industry/educator developed wireless curriculum packages for adaptation by two-year, four-year, or Master's level academic programs.

GWEC industry members also offer students pursuing wireless education in GWEC partnership schools the opportunity to compete for paid intern-ships and co-ops with GWEC member companies in the Practical Work Experience Program (PWE). The PWE program is developed by schools and industry members to enhance the wireless education of students pursuing computer science, engineering or technician related fields of study. Faculty attendance at industry sponsored training courses and training materials are also provided to member schools without cost. One hundred participants attended a faculty workshop held in the summer of 1998, and the number of participants is expected to double at the 1999 summer workshop.

The National Science Foundation is playing a leadership role in strengthening curriculum for technical skills development at the Nation's community colleges. The Advanced Technological Education (ATE) program promotes improvement in technician education delivered at the undergraduate and secondary school levels. Focused on both national and regional levels, it provides funding to support curriculum development and program improvement for technicians being educated for the high performance workplace of advanced technologies. Curriculum development encompasses the design and implementation of new curricula, courses, laboratories, and instructional materials. Students enrolled in ATE programs at two-year colleges typically earn an associate degree in a science or technology discipline qualifying them for employment or transfer to a four-year institution. Program improvement encompasses faculty and teacher development, student academic support, and formal cooperative arrangements among institutions and other partners, such as industrial internships and cooperative experiences.

One of the ATE Centres of Excellence is the Northwest Centre for Emerging Technologies (NWCET) in Washington state. NWCET has developed a set of skill standards for eight career clusters in information technology. Key in the retraining of incumbent workers is NWCET's participation in Washington State's Worker Retraining Program, a program that provides financial aid to those who have been laid off from their jobs which allows them to return to school to obtain marketable skills.

The National Science Foundation is playing a leadership role in strengthening curriculum for technical skills development at the Nation's community colleges. The Advanced Technological Education Program promotes improvement in technician education delivered at the undergraduate and secondary school levels.

Each year, NWCET helps to provide retraining to hundreds of individuals who continue on to successful careers in the IT industry. While industry needs the skills often produced in short-term intensive skills training programs, such programs may not provide enough emphasis on the underlying knowledge and problem-solving needed for a rapidly changing business and technological environment. If workers do not possess the underlying knowledge and skills, their specific technical skills will become outdated in a few years.

A growing number and wide variety of programs have been established to upgrade the skills of the current IT work force. These include internal company training programs, training programs provided by technology vendors, private training schools, community college and university-based programs, Federal and state programs, and others. Many of these programs focus on developing the skills of low to mid-level IT workers, and include certificate programs at community colleges in areas such as network technician and web design, as well as popular vendor certification programs, for example, those focused on Microsoft and Novell products. These programs provide a limited set of technical skills in a short duration, compared to the knowledge, skill development, and time commitment required for competency in high skill jobs such as computer scientists and computer engineers.

For highly skilled IT jobs-where job growth is the fastest, labour markets tightest, education and training pipeline the longest, and where employers are often exacting in the skills they need-many employers prefer to pay a premium to hire a worker who already fits a specific education and skill profile. Many employers want employees with experience, in addition to technical skills, making it difficult for workers who may acquire technical skills in demand, but lack experience in their application.

Since providing IT skills for the current work force requires educating for broad knowledge and skill, and training for specific technologies, educational providers need to examine ways to match the method of skill upgrading to the speed and depth of reskilling needed. IT workers also need information on technological trends, and the skill needs that will flow from them, so they can pursue options for keeping their skills relevant to the market place.

A representative of an IT professional society said "Internet-based learning networks offer a particularly effective, convenient, and potentially more affordable alternative to conventional classroom and laboratory-based instructional programs..." Some concern was raised about the ability to use Federal financial support for training from for-profit training providers.

To be eligible for certain kinds of Federal financial aid, including Pell grants and guaranteed student loans, an education and training provider must meet certain requirements, such as being accredited, being authorized to do business in the state where it offers education and training, having been in business for two years, having programs that result in a credential, and offering programs of some minimum length. These requirements follow provisions of the Higher Education Act, and exist in large part to help prevent fraud and abuse.

For-profit schools can and do meet these requirements, including some computer training programs that result in certificates. However, a substantial number of computer training programs are not currently eligible for Federal financial aid. They may not have been in business for two years, or they may not meet the instructional time requirements. Many schools have not tried to meet the standards, such as accreditation, required for Federal financial aid. In a hot area such as IT, schools that have enough students and are making ample money without access to financial aid may have little motivation to go through the steps required to qualify for the aid.

Some communities are implementing more comprehensive approaches to training workers, and linking them to potential employers. The Northern Virginia Regional Workforce Development Coordinating Centre acts as a regional information clearing-house for individuals seeking IT jobs and skills, as well as employers seeking assistance in finding qualified workers with critical IT skills. The centre works with employers to create education programs to produce qualified workers, as well as with potential employees to help them identify careers and training programs linked to current and future job openings in the IT field.

The web site provides a data base of technology training and education providers, a listing of links related to IT assessment and career development, listings of job vacancies, and information on financing IT training and education programs. As of May 1999, 1,109 students are receiving training at four regional colleges, 614 have completed IT training and 192 students have been placed in IT or IT-related positions. The Summer Technology Program which focuses on developing technology-related interest in middle school students in Northern Virginia had 230 student participants in 1998.

Specific skills include computer repair, computer-related design and drafting, and business machine repair. For dislocated workers who need new skills for jobs in demand, one-year retraining scholarships are provided through the JobLink program for individualized programs of education and training at colleges, technical colleges and training institutes. Between July 1997 and June 1998, the program filled 1,701 jobs with 1,144 employers.

Employers should establish and participate in consortia or collaborate in other ways to develop regional training infrastructure and provide worker training. This could be accomplished by businesses alone, or in partnership with the local and regional education community, and other stakeholders. The Federal government could provide matching funds to organize and facilitate cooperation among firms in developing these alliances, as well as participate in alliances as an employer in areas where IT workers are needed to fill government jobs.

To expand the size of the IT labour pool, there is growing interest in tapping nontraditional sources of labour, and training workers from these groups for IT jobs. A representative of an IT professional society suggested that the pool of workers available for IT jobs is broader and deeper than commonly thought. This includes college graduates with science and engineering degrees, college graduates with nontechnical degrees, downsized and older engineers, non-degreed technicians with the potential to increase their skills, and mid-career workers.

Microsoft is working to recruit and train those leaving the armed services, many who have acquired good technical skills during the course of their military training. The Microsoft Military IT Career Initiative-a partnership between Microsoft authorized training providers and career placement organizations-provides resources and guidance for those interested in pursuing a post-military career in IT. This includes: a skills assessment to determine what type of IT career a candidate might be suited for and what training would be needed, technical training programs, financial assistance, and job placement services.

There is also interest in moving highly-skilled, mid-career technical workers who have been displaced into the IT professions. For example, the Massachusetts Software Council Fellowship Program (SCFP) Inc. is a private non-profit corporation providing displaced, but highly skilled workers to the software industry through retraining and education. Initiated in 1993 under the sponsorship of the Massachusetts Software Council and the Commonwealth of Massachusetts, the SCFP provides a bridge for mature professionals who are making a transition from other technical industries to find careers in the software industry.

The integrated learning approach includes a five-month on-site company project experience and weekly seminars to keep the Fellows current on issues unique to the software industry. Classes start approximately every two months. More than 450 individuals have graduated from the program and have been placed in companies. Graduates earn a starting salary that is 93 percent of their previous wages and reach their previous salary or surpass it within a year's time. Positions into which graduates are placed include software engineers, quality engineers, customer support, marketing and sales, and technical documentation.

The underrepresentation of women and minorities in the professional IT work force stems partly from their underrepresentation in the technical education pipeline that leads to these jobs. Women leave high school about as well prepared in math and science as men. In computers, however, according to a report by the American Association of University Women's Educational Foundation, while 30 percent of high school boys take a computer science course, 25 percent of high school girls do.

Only 2 percent of high school girls take a computer applications course, compared to 6 percent of boys. While women earn more than half of all bachelor's degrees, they are less likely to earn degrees in science and engineering than men.

The science and engineering selection rate- those earning degrees in science and engineering as a percentage of the total bachelor's degrees awarded in all fields-is much lower for women, 29 percent, than for men, 41 percent. This suggests that increasing women's participation in the education pipeline that leads to many IT jobs may require efforts to get more college-bound women to choose science and engineering as a field of study, especially computer science and engineering disciplines.

There are many efforts underway to increase the awareness and interest of girls in science and technology careers. The Girl Scouts of the U.S.A. has a variety of programs to increase the interest of girls in science and technology by providing fun yet valuable hands-on learning experiences. Starting with the youngest program age level, girls can participate in projects and earn awards involving computers and technology. Older girls can interact with positive women role models who are active in science and technology careers. Some local Girl Scout councils sponsor career exploration and "Walk-A-Day in My Shoes" internships in which girls can find out what it is like to work in a professional career by spending time side-by-side with a mentor in a local company or organization. Local councils often collaborate and coordinate these type programs with the outreach activities of other organizations like the American Association of University Women.

Some of the underlying factors contributing to the underrepresentation of Black, Hispanic, and Native American students in the technical education pipeline are different than those for women. In 1996, large differences remained at all grade levels in the math and science achievement scores of Black and Hispanic students compared with Whites and Asians.

Native American students generally scored closer to the national average than did Black or Hispanic students. There are disparities in the types of math and science courses taken. Forty-four percent of Black, 46 percent of Hispanic, and 41 percent of Native American high school graduates have taken chemistry. Less than 20 percent of Hispanic and Black high school graduates have taken physics.

Racial and ethnic minority college freshmen declare science and engineering as a major at a rate equal to or greater than White college students. Black and Hispanic college students earn bachelor's degrees in science and engineering at rates roughly equal to White students but less than Asian students. There is some difference in the rate at which different ethnic and racial minorities earn engineering degrees, as a percent of all achelor's degrees awarded. Of racial and ethnic minorities who earn bachelor's degrees, Blacks and Hispanics earn them in computer science at rates equal to or greater than White or Native American students.

The High School Computer Competition is a mentoring program for minority high school students sponsored by local chapters of the National Black Data Processing Associates. There are more than 1,660 active student members. The goal of the program is to provide students with information about computer history, terminology, theory and programming and to provide hands-on experience in Visual Basic design, coding, documentation and testing. The program is targeted to students in the ninth through eleventh grades. Mentoring and educational assistance is provided to students at computer training camps during the winter and spring months of the school academic year.

In July 1998, the Office of Technology Policy launched a web site on the IT work force. Through the web site, which lists more than 200 resources, visitors can learn about high-tech work force initiatives across the country, tap valuable information resources, and network with other people who can offer insight and opportunities for collaboration.

For example, companies can explore ways that other companies have used to develop a skilled work force. Individuals can get information on scholarships, internships, training, and job banks. State and local government agencies can find out what other governments are doing to build a high-tech work force.

During the IT Work Force Convocation held in January 1998, the Education Department announced $6 million in grants to expand employer involvement in school-to-work programs. Among the awards since made has been a grant to a school-to-work project cooperatively sponsored by the National Alliance of Business, the Information Technology Association of America, and the

Education Development Centre, Inc. The goal of the project, the Techforce Initiative, is to highlight and expand IT employer involvement in School-to-Work or School-to-Careers activities nationwide by facilitating and supporting the efforts of individuals and organizations committed to building IT-focused School-to-Careers partnerships.

Major activities of the project include managing a Learning Network of Centres of Excellence for IT and School-to-Careers, organizing regional symposia for IT industry leaders and educators around the country, developing champions for IT School-to-Careers within the industry and educational communities, and widely marketing the great role and potential of IT School-to-Careers in addressing the IT workers/skills issue.

In Spring 1998, two Department of Labour supported information systems, America's Talent Bank and America's Job Bank, were integrated to create an $8 million nationwide network linking employers and job seekers into one Internet-based system. America's Job Bank's computerized network can now link state Employment Service offices to provide job seekers with the largest pool of active job opportunities available anywhere and nationwide exposure for their resumes. For employers it provides rapid, national exposure for job openings and an easily accessible pool of candidates.

In addition to the Internet, the job openings and resumes found in America's Job Bank are available on computer systems in public libraries, colleges and universities, high schools, shopping malls, transition offices on military bases worldwide and other places of public access. With the debut of Version 4.0 of America's Job Bank in April 1999, approximately eight to nine million individual job searches per month are being reported. In July 1998, the Labour Department awarded $7.7 million in grants for demonstration projects, in partnerships with employers and training providers, to train dislocated workers for technology-related occupations and industries. Awards were made to eleven organizations throughout the country, which will use the awards to retrain and prepare workers for careers requiring information technology and other advanced technology skills.

Under the terms of the American Competitiveness and Workforce Improvement Act of 1998, the Department of Labour has been authorized to support new innovative skill demonstration programs to solve labour shortages. Approximately half the revenues generated by the $500 fee that U.S. employers pay for each visa application under the H-1B nonimmigrant skilled worker program will be used to make awards to private industry councils, including regional skills alliances, to demonstrate cooperative industry/ community-based approaches to work force skills development.

The American Federal government is not only engaged in addressing the national IT work force challenge, but its own IT work force challenge as well. Viewed as a single employer, the Federal government is among the largest, if not the largest, employers of core IT workers. In 1996, the Federal government employed 67,857 core IT workers; by 2006, BLS projects the number to climb to 96,704. In addition, it is estimated that almost half the Federal IT work force may retire or otherwise leave the Federal service during this period.

Facing an expanding IT work force and the need to replace large numbers of its current work force, the

Federal government faces a daunting challenge in meeting its own IT work force needs. In 1998 the Federal Chief Information Officer's Council (CIO Council) established a multi-agency working group under its Education and Training Committee to help address this challenge by identifying ways to recruit, retain, and re-skill IT professionals, both technicians and managers. The Federal government's role as one of the largest employers of IT workers in the Nation means that its IT worker recruitment, retention, and re-skilling strategies can play a significant role in shaping the policies of other employers and, thus, indirectly contribute to meeting the national IT work force challenge.

2

The Internet Applications

The origin of the Internet in 1969 can be traced to cold war research. The United States Department of Defense Advanced Research Projects Agency (DARPA) set out to create a robust mechanism for computer-based communications. The original network was called ARPANET. Its objective was to construct a communications network able to withstand disruptions that would take place in the event of nuclear war.

The network was designed to allow multiple destination paths and to enable lower-level communications software to utilise alternative paths at will. In addition, the network offered a built-in mechanism for load balancing as well as the ability to bypass inactive circuits. Initially the Internet provided four basic network services: remote access (Telnet), file transfer (FTP), mail, and news. To promote education and research activities, access was generally free. The concept of a free public network, rather than a private, commercial one, was a clear part of the culture surrounding the network. Academics and students used the network to exchange information, to share software, and to discuss and debate issues. During the 1970s, other academic organisations around the world began to construct similar networks to ARPANET using the same software available in the United States. The military, in particular, realised that it would need to create a more secure network than the experimental ARPANET. The military wanted to maintain its own secure telecommunications system and also maintain links to the public networks. To make this possible, an *internetting* project was initiated to link together these networks; hence the name the Internet.

An inter-networking protocol was developed to work with the original transmission control protocol. This combination of transmission control and an Internet protocol, abbreviated to TCP/IP, is the dominant standard for computer-based communications today. The benefit of the TCP/IP standard is that it is supported by virtually every computer and software manufacturer in the world. Whether the intention is to publish material or services for world-wide access or to confine them to an organisational environment, a wide choice exists in hardware and software. By enabling a rich inter-connection of computing and communication environ-ments, TCP/IP offers a simple mechanism for communi-cating from both present and future information systems. By 1986, the National Science Foundation (NSF), an independent government agency established to promote science and engineering, had taken the lead role to put together a high speed backbone with a transmission rate of 1.5 Megabits per second (Mbps). It established a mechanism for regional and local commercial providers to offer access outside government and academic communities. Government subsidies helped to support the technology while demand grew. By 1989, backbone speeds were increased to 45Mbps.

In April 1995, NSF support for the Internet backbone was withdrawn and the Internet is now operating using commercial telecommunications providers. The level of traffic generated on the Internet has been growing rapidly. One of the most remarkable features of the Internet is the flat fee policy. In the flat-fee model, users are charged for the size of the 'pipe' or maximum rate of transmission rather than the actual amount of data transmitted. For modem users, of course, charges may be based on connect time. While allowing users open access to any site, the Internet enables world-wide communication without the overhead of a toll system similar to the long distance telephone network now in place. The institution of long distance charges on the Internet would be impractical, since it would be impossible for users to predict the charges resulting from a given connection.

The World Wide Web and the Internet are commonly considered to be synonymous. "In actuality, the Web is a collection of protocols and standards used to access the information on the Internet. On the other hand, the Internet is a physical medium used to transport the data. The World Wide Web defines and unifies the 'languages' used to retrieve data on the Internet." The World Wide Web was introduced in 1991. Developed at CERN, a particle physics research centre in Switzerland, the WWW is a distributed hypertext system that operates on a client/server model. Web servers store available documents as plain ASCII text. These documents contain markup tags and follow a standard known as Hypertext Markup Language (HTML). The hypertext feature of

HTML provides support for linkage instructions, or URLs (Universal Resource Locators), and allows direct access to pages on other Web servers. In contrast to earlier connection-based protocols, the Web permits a seamless connection to any Internet address. The client programs that run on the user's computer, providing access to the Web, are known as browsers. The Mosaic browser, written for graphical user interfaces, became the prototype for many imitators, such as Netscape Navigator. This software family supports a mixture of text, sound, graphics, images, video, animation and binary (executable) files.

The information provided to users by Web servers is not limited to static files. Several methods exist to forward requests to other server processes that are able to extract information from large database systems and format it for the user. This technique permits simple transaction processing and is the foundation for electronic commerce via the Internet. Software developers have been working to advance the capabilities of the Web by creating special viewers. For example, there are special viewers for *Postscript* documents or for executing multimedia presentations. Viewers are usually given away free by software developers, in hopes of marketing their development system. For the past two years, Sun Microsystems has been promoting an Internet development system called *Java*, that permits platform-independent software to be executed directly via the Web. More elaborate software tools, such as three-dimensional virtual reality generators, require far more bandwidth than the standard text-based Web page. With enhanced display features, the Internet is an attractive marketing medium with a wide global audience.

If the Internet becomes an effective means to distribute information, the viability of the technology will be a public concern. Current issues of concern to developers of Web sites include changes to the telecommunications infrastructure, security, copyright protection, and universal access. The evolution if not resolution of these issues will impact the future development of available information services and will have an impact on the appropriateness of this medium for government. The condition of international telecommunications infrastructure is a critical determinant of the viability and utility of government Internet-based services. It has therefore been the principal focus of state attention in deliberations about the Internet. Deregulation has been seen as a key tool in many countries seeking to upgrade their telecommunications infrastructure. However, a balance of state and market will still be required in many circumstances, though with the state taking a more promotional than regulatory role.

The experience of the United States is indicative of the political difficulty in balancing state and market. Due to the prior interests of Vice President Al Gore, the Clinton Administration was instrumental in focusing public attention on the idea of a future National Information Superhighway in 1994. The administration produced a *Strategic Planning Document* that placed the highest priority on information technology because "any nation that dominates information technology will be a leading superpower of the 21st century." The administration sees an active role for government, citing the prior success of the state in the development of a High Performance Computing and Communications (HPCC) programme, sponsored legislatively by then Senator Gore in 1986. This program was responsible for the development of the high speed (45Mbps) Internet backbones that are in place today. However, the continuing federal budget deficit combined with opposition from congressional Republicans to government interference in the free market process has limited activities to existing research projects. Although these projects involve US$2bn-worth of federal research funds, this is a scant commitment when applied to a nationwide communications infrastructure. In 1996, the US Congress passed The Telecommunications Act. The act attempted to reduce government regulation and control, recognising that communications technologies had advanced to the point where the transmission medium no longer defines the type of service. The act did not provide government funding for constructing an infrastructure.

By placing responsibility for managing the Internet backbone with telecommunications companies, the commercialisation of the Internet is likely to accelerate and a period of change and competition is underway. Of course, that is not a guarantee that competition will continue to be the norm. There is a high cost associated with building independent data networks that reach every household. The consolidation of competitors may restore local monopolies that restrict the range of services available to the public. The large infrastructure investments increase the likelihood that competitors will merge until several massive communication service providers dominate the industry. The providers might be far different from traditional communications providers, as the experience of television indicates. While AT&T dominated the telephone industry before its break-up in 1984, it controlled only the transmission medium, not the content. Broadcast television stations have, in effect, controlled the use of their channel license and in so doing have concentrated on the lowest common denominator for programming. Cable operators, although forced to provide limited public access on their systems, have followed a similar path and while many systems routinely advertise more that 100 channel capability, a large percentage of these channels are dedicated to pay per view and premium entertainment services.

The danger of entertainment-oriented system design is that it allows for a high speed channel in one direction only, thereby limiting information providers to those organisations who control the source of the high speed data stream. In the US, then, there has been a massive expansion of the telecommunications infrastructure, but the interaction of government and commerce remains an area for conflict, with a continuously shifting boundary of responsibilities. The same outcomes of conflict and shifting responsibilities are seen world-wide, and they will ultimately determine the extent to which an infrastructure exists to support government use of the Internet.

To support commercial and governmental transactions the Internet must offer a secure environment in which such transactions can take place. In a packet switched network the precise path from one site to another is unknown; therefore, the possibility exists for those packets to be examined, imitated, or diverted, resulting in the loss of personal information that may be used to commit fraud. The developers of Internet software have been working to construct secure transaction systems. However, public trust remains low, and some government agencies have also become involved. The development of secure network systems using large key cryptography has been opposed by law enforcement officials in a number of countries, notably the US. US government regulations, for example, have prohibited the export of cryptography technology since World War II. The fear is that if criminals obtain technology from which information cannot be decoded, it would be impossible for law enforcement officials to track their activities.

Government security agencies have asked that a second key be available that would permit the equivalent of government wiretapping. However, the global nature of the Internet makes it highly unlikely that a security system with a *back door* known only to the US government will be universally adopted. In addition to security, an increase in electronic commerce as well as other types of transactions raises concerns about privacy. The information collected about users in an all-digital environment is potentially immense and the ability to develop personal profiles from past transaction records could result in instances where life and health insurance are denied or employment is refused because of such profiles. The full impact of participating in an electronic marketplace that can be monitored and analysed has yet to be fully understood.

The ease with which digital information can be replicated has threatened the viability of conventional copyright laws. Information is no longer bound to a physical object such as a book or a vinyl disk that is difficult to reproduce. Digital information can be replicated with no loss of quality. Software tools can be used to modify or transform content from one form to another. The material may be transmitted quickly to any location on the network. At the same time, there needs to be a further clarification of what constitutes fair use. Fair use has traditionally allowed the transfer of material purchased and has allowed the purchaser some degree of ownership over the material. However, many software and content developers have taken the position that only the original purchaser has any right to use material and has no right to transfer it to others. If this concept had been applied to books, there would be no libraries, and books would have to be burned rather than sold or given to others.

If access to the Internet becomes essential for conducting ordinary day-to-day business, then it will be necessary to ensure that the average citizen has such access. The doctrine of universal access has, for example, been behind regulatory efforts to maintain low local phone rates at the expense of business users who pay the bulk of long distance charges. The strategy has been successful in a number of countries, with near universal access for phone services being achieved in many of the industrialised nations. At present, the costs of obtaining Internet access are too high to bring about universal access and the computer systems used are too difficult to set up and manage. The minimum functionality that will constitute access has been changing and will continue to do so. On the one hand, access is becoming easier, with options to use TV sets for display and alternate access methods such as satellite and coaxial cable. On the other hand, data transfer requirements continue to rise with the complexity of online materials. Universal access, therefore, is a moving target. Whilst access rates are likely to improve, universal access is still a long way off.

Before the advent of the Internet, collocation was a key success factor for rapid product development. When key team members from the various functions sit next to each other all day, information transfer is frequent and rich - very "high bandwidth". Formal meetings keep the project on track and establish goals and commitments, while informal meetings around the coffee pot allow people to build trust and teamwork and to discuss ideas or get help with problems.

Internet technologies allow remote, virtual collaboration in ways that were not possible just a few years ago. To use these tools successfully, product development teams must have a complementary IT infrastructure, matching tools, and the appropriate leadership, as well as the incentives and discipline to work together in a new way. These virtual teams - not "collocated" but "co-wired" - offer distinct advantages. For example: In a "co-wired" environment, people can also communicate frequently, both formally and informally. Formal meetings should be held regularly to keep the project on track and coordinate actions. In addition, informal communication channels, such as chat windows, should be very easy to learn and to use. The CAD design tools must be compatible among all team members, so that communicating design ideas and innovations is seamless. Most virtual collaboration software allows for automatic recording and tracking of the proceedings of meetings. Action items are written down and indexed. Repositories of knowledge are available that make the inventory of knowledge much more visible. Most virtual project teams have a knowledge manager position to care for this inventory. Collocated teams could take advantage of these same techniques, but few have the discipline to do so.

A co-wired product development team requires a communication infrastructure of two layers - a collaboration layer and a control layer. The collaboration environment includes areas for four levels of communication: project management, real-time design sharing, structured discussion and social and brainstorming spaces. The control layer builds and stores the knowledge inventory. The various design tools should smoothly connect these two layers. If they are properly organized and managed co-wired teams can develop products faster than collocated teams. Some types of communications, such as team building meetings, should be face-to-face or via video-conferencing, whereas other types such as technical exchanges can happen in real time or virtual time over the Internet, or by email. The meetings and communications should be "bandwidth-matched" to the needs at the time. Co-wired, virtual teams can take advantage of global expertise and diversity with very flexible capacity. The infrastructure and leadership of co-wired teams must provide for fast acknowledgement of communications, mutual understanding of each communication and a path for commitment and actions. The leader of a virtual, collaborative team should invest significant time in achieving the trust and social inclusion of all team members. The leader's goal is to align goals, processes, skills and tools across the team. Remote team members should be treated with the same respect and given the same promotional opportunities as collocated team members.

The next crest of the Internet wave will come from markets that are already well along the way with the most capacity for upside surprises, since their social structures and communications infrastructures offer few barriers. There are more adults with intentions of going online than there are adults with Internet access. Far from being dead, the Internet has a large growth potential everywhere, but progress is destined to be slower than its most enthusiastic advocates might have envisioned a few years ago. To expand the reach of the Web in developing countries, he says, public venues—libraries, schools, offices and Internet cafés—will have to play a more crucial role. The widespread availability is a long way off in the most populated areas of the world.

The Internet offers a unique opportunity to streamline the delivery of government services, enhance communication with its citizenry, and serve as a catalyst for empowering citizens to interact with government. The growth in popularity and ease of access to the Internet appears to coincide with pressures from public interest groups and some legislatures for more access to public information. The need for some governments to embrace this new technology is in part driven by the legislative mandate that all agencies provide public access to information. Meeting the requirements of this mandate often proves difficult using the *ad hoc* methods and controls of the past. Despite the passage of freedom of information legislation in many countries, there is still a resistance to sharing information by people within government who want to limit access to their data.

Development of the World Wide Web (WWW) has created a platform-independent mechanism for the transfer of documents, the ability to search large databases, to enter basic transactions, and even the ability to run applications. Governments are often frustrated in their efforts to co-ordinate and manage information by the wide variety of hardware and software platforms owned within the public sector. Internet technology offers a unifying platform on which the collection of data for internal and external use can be built. It has been adopted by hundreds of thousands of content providers and tens of millions of users.

The presence of a large user community makes a compelling case for the preparation of an information framework that takes advantage of this technology. In a very short period of time, many government officials will realise that the growth of Internet technologies will have a major impact not only on how information is presented to the public, but on how business is conducted among government agencies and the general public. Internet technology may set the stage for the online public services of the future.

Towards Electronic Democracy

In today's wired world, the interactive citizen is one of the fundamental cornerstones of change. The Internet has put new power into the hands of the citizen. Governments can no longer simply be dispensers of information, even in sophisticated forms being developed by many governments. But governments have not been passive observers and are rising to many of the challenges. New technologies are being used not only to deliver services to the public but also to enhance government administration and facilitate businesses. At this stage of development few governments have effectively been able to involve their citizenry electronically in the democratic process. Many governments have been effective dispensers of information, which often passes as a means of enhancing the democratic process. There are many government initiatives seeking to help citizens to get online, seek feedback on government reports online, and develop listservs and discussion groups to elicit the views of the citizens. There are also many groups actively participating in online activities in the hope of influencing government policies. But for the most part, governments are far behind the activities of citizens online around the world. Those actively engaged in online activities involving social or political change see the Internet as a medium to foster, enhance and change the way people have traditionally engaged in the democratic process.

Much of the enthusiasm and hope for new forms of democracy and citizen input into public issues, sound very like the gushing optimism expressed about the potential of television in its nascent years. It is not yet known if the potentials offered by the Internet will be met.

The Internet has been a tool of enrichment for large numbers of our populations. It has allowed diversity, the rise of the entrepreneur, the mushrooming of home businesses, the bringing together of family and friends through instant communications, the Internet has been a voice for many who for too long did not have the means to express themselves because prior mediums of the expression of communication have been controlled by the few.

The Internet has been many things to many people. New, advanced medical technologies and scientific breakthroughs have lengthened our average life span and brought us better health and lifestyles. On the Internet, there are pockets of dissent and discourse. there are many who use the new technologies for learning, to facilitate their businesses, to get a service, whether from government or business, play games with each other over long distances, keep in contact through email and a thousand and other good usages that can benefit the individual. We know the benefits, we know of the attempts of many professionals who seek to use the Internet to both gain knowledge and dispense and share knowledge. Perhaps, the most important feature of the Internet is that it has allowed individuals to communicate in ways not available before. This is an important new channel through which communication, ideas and knowledge can flow.

It can be persuasively argued that throughout history all new technologies have changed the way the world lives and operates as a society. Transportation brought the world together and television resulted in the global village that brought all of us on the planet closer together as a people. Now tourism is the world's second largest industry with millions of people on the move all around the world, experiencing and sharing in other cultures. Of course, these millions are mostly from the rich nations. It appears we see nothing wrong in going to exotic and culturally challenging parts of the world, in the quest for something new and exciting and the next best thing to experience, and then pay scant attention to the many more millions of poor. Ironically, many will argue that tourism brings needed dollars and helps these economies. But even this does not ring with the hallowed sound of truth as studies show that those who benefit most are the western multinational recreational chains and others who sell their wares globally to all and sundry. Whatever the opinions or views of individuals and governments in society it is evident that we need a far deeper debate and discourse over the impacts of technologies. There are concerns over ensuring all citizens have universal access to the Internet, there are serious, abiding anxieties about the digital divide that is occurring throughout the world.

Privacy laws, to protect people's information and endow on their certain rights over their own personal information, are spreading. But the implementation of such laws is but one small step. Articulation of these issues is just the start. We need deeper discourse. Ironically, it is this medium that affords the opportunity to bring such discourse forward. This is why online e-Democracy is so important as this activity represents the power of this technology and how it can be used to embrace democracy and involve people in the social, economic, cultural and political issues of the day. This is a tool that can give people, the individual citizen, the power to influence public policy.

Governments are slowly coming to realize that there is an undercurrent of democratic change going on in the world. The face of democracy is beginning to change and a few thousand at the moment are doing it. But this is a change that has the potential for growth. Many changes do occur in society when people speak out and spark debate. It is now time for such a discourse over the future of technology. We need to develop a philosophical base about all these new technologies so society drives technology and not technology drives us. Many governments are moving to electronic governance. In this context governance can be seen as both a means to using new technologies to deliver services to the citizen and ways in which to change and improve the efficient methods of administration within governments themselves. Another element looked at in this section is the means as whereby governments will increasingly be able to involve citizens in the democratic process of government. At this stage of development few governments have effectively been able to involve their citizenry electronically in the democratic process. For the most part, governments are far behind the activities of citizens online around the world, who see the Internet as a medium to foster, enhance and change the way people have traditionally engaged in the democratic process.

Governments tend simply to provide information on their web sites and use the Internet, and other technologies, to deliver services electronically. The prime example of this is the US White House site which is primarily an information tool and conduit to executive agency web sites. It was only in January 2000 that President Clinton announced that government had to be interactive with the citizen. The dispensing of information, without substantial input from the citizen, is not a real interactive transaction. Yet, the Internet in and of itself is an interactive medium. Individuals on the Internet understand this and, for growing legions of people, it is becoming a force that is changing the nature of democracy as we know it today. But this is just part of the wider picture of developments in electronic democracy. In fact, individuals and groups are coming together online around the world to influence policy. Politicians are also using the web. In the United States every Presidential candidate has a web site. There are also alternative web sites by interested citizens or groups who want to have their say about the candidates. There are also other groups who are offering sites which will present in-depth analysis of the issues in the upcoming presidential and congressional elections as well as elections at the local and state level.

The online world of democratic activism is growing around the world. This section looks at the emerging trends in electronic democracy, how citizens active online are changing the nature of democracy as we have understood it, and how governments are going to have to tap into this emerging trend. This section shows the distinction between online democracy, and what its participants are achieving, and electronic governance. In the wired world, the online citizen is increasingly playing more and more of a role in the democratic process. There are now hundreds of groups involved, from the community and local level to the national and international stage, in some way working to have an influence on government policies and programs, and on societal issues of our age. Because of these changes, the process of government will soon no longer be controlled from the top and micro-managed by a few when it comes to public policy. In the changing wired world, citizens are voicing their say. Governments may not necessarily be listening, but the thousands upon thousands of people engaging in discourse on the thousand and one issues of the day are certainly listening to each other. This is resulting in powerful currents of change which are only beginning to manifest themselves.

Electronic democracy is not about citizens voting on a multitude of referendums as laid out by governments. It is citizens engaging in the political process in means chosen by individuals. The new democracy we see surfacing is more the expression of individual voices that congeal into a collective whole over ideas that the society of peoples online develop into a consensus. And while a consensus might be formed on major issues, people are still in a position to express their individual thoughts and ideas (even if they range from the erudite to the opinionated). In this emerging world we see the evolution of a true populist democracy (albeit a small one at this point in time). Although people's ideas do not necessarily have to be acted upon individually, the means exist for individuals to communicate freely to an audience. That audience can be large or small, but it represents a freedom for the individual that has not existed up to this point in time. The mass media still hold the reigns of mass communication. It is still important to get that letter to the editor published so you can reach a wide readership. But with this new medium of the Internet you can write something and it will reach the level of interest in the audience out there. Because the Internet as a medium is becoming the tool through which the nature of democracy itself is changing and taking new shapes and forms, it is important that governments understand this phenomenon. Increasingly, public officials and elected politicians are going to be faced with not only an informed citizenry but a citizenry that wants to be engaged in the decision making process in some form or another. An analysis of the numerous groups springing up on the Internet on a multitude of issues illustrates that there are voices out there that governments are going to have to tap into.

In the wired world, individuals can now make their own choices as to which authorities and information sources they will accept. This is leading to a greater democratization of knowledge, empowerment of the individual, and the potential for more informed interactions between the citizenry and organizations, including government. Moreover, since individuals now have ready access to a variety of information resources, organizations have to adopt new proactive measures to compile and disseminate information in a competitive information environment.

A citizenry that is able to seek and obtain information and knowledge from any place in the world through the Internet will, in all likelihood, also expect more from government. One of the means that people can collectively work together to bring about change is through the strategic gathering, absorbing and using of information. Online groups and online activists, researchers and others involved as information professionals, instinctively understand this. It is the understanding of the nature of information and how it influences us as individuals that is going to bring the next big shift in society. As the Internet takes hold in our daily lives, and begins to take a new and ubiquitous shape and form, the need for governments to develop information policies to suit the changing nature of these technologies is becoming more evident. In much of the developed world, the Internet is a communications force that is growing.

According to NUA plc, a company in Ireland, that tracks the growth of the Internet and the implication of our growing information technology infrastructure, as of the end of the year 2000, 60% of the population in the United States and Canada will have some form of online access to the Internet. This can be in the office, the home, an educational institute or some public space, such as libraries, community halls, Internet cafes and other public venues. In the United Kingdom, over 50% of the population now enjoy some kind of Internet access. There, much of the growth of the Internet has been stimulated because many companies offer Internet access free. The citizen pays only for local calls.

In Europe, the whole question of measured rates is a serious issue, as many contend, this does impede not only access to the Internet, but, even if there is access, then the individual has to be careful about how long one is online. This is because the cost factor can act as an inhibitor to accessing the Internet and the amount of time spent online. However, despite these problems, there are now over 200 million people online around the world. We are now awash with information in our new cyber environments. There are currently billions of pages out on the world wide web. There is so much information that no single search engine can go out and suck up all the information an individual might be seeking. In fact, there is such a proliferation of information that many search engine companies now do not give total access to everything that is on the web. What some of the search engine companies are now doing is giving priority to companies who pay to have their company or organization show first on a search, when a given topic or key word is entered into their search engine.

When entering cyberspace, the challenges for the citizen who wants an open and accountable society, both from government and the private sector world, are now many. The success of our new information technology environments is going to depend on how much say and control citizens will have on information in the decade to come. Information is shaping our world. We now live in the Digital Age, in which information, in a global knowledge economy, has become the supreme commodity. Information is not only a piece of barter for the business world to use for competitive and commercial value. Information is now a precious commodity for the citizen. In our new Internet environments, citizens are increasingly demanding more privacy rights to protect their personal information. However, there is also a contradiction here, as at the moment, citizens are sharing and using personal and aggregate information more than ever before. But in a cyberspace environment, the citizen is becoming increasingly sophisticated in understanding the impact that information can have on one's life.

The Information Age appears to be bringing more demands for accountability. In the years to come, the public will come to expect more and more accountability, in the form of enlightening information, from private sector organizations. The Internet is an open network, which has created open environments. With this openness has come a demand for certain rights, to ensure the inherent democratic nature of the Internet is maintained. This idea is now spreading into society as a whole, resulting in demands for more and more accountability from all our public and private sector organizations. Thus, it appears that the next wave of information rights will spread out to the private sector. As the average citizen becomes armed with more knowledge, then it will be private sector organizations, along with governments, who are going to have to become more forthcoming about the information held in their organizations.

In an information-intensive society, citizens want more from both governments and the private sector alike. There are numerous ways that governments at the local, regional and national level can facilitate these new forms of democracy that are emerging. One is to take the example of Canada. The Canadian government, through their Community Access Program (CAP) has a goal to establish over 10,000 public access sites in rural and urban communities across Canada. Launched in 1994, CAP has already established over 4,200 sites in approximately 3,000 rural and remote communities and is a key component of the government's "Connecting Canadians" strategy - aimed at making Canada the world's most connected nation." The program is now being expanded to include urban centres with populations over 50,000. CAP matching funds of up to $17,000 per site are available to eligible applicants such as educational institutions, public libraries, community organizations, and municipal and territorial governments. The community funds can include cash or "in kind" contributions such as facilities, equipment and staffing of public access sites. This is a good model to be followed not only by national governments but international organizations.

If we are to handle the digital divide between those who have the opportunities to be online and the vast numbers of people who cannot necessarily afford the costs of going online, it is going to be essential to level the playing field. In any populist democracy it is important that initiatives embrace all the people. At the moment it is estimated there are only between 150 and 200 million people online. These are small numbers where our world population has exceeded 6 billion people. International organizations could also provide programs to educate people on usage of the Internet. Education then leads to individual usage. It will, naturally, vary from individual but through knowledge of how to use the Internet people can be participants in this new trend in democracy as they see fit. Such programs can embrace many peoples around the world and ensure that the users who most benefit are not just those in the affluent, industrialized countries.

3

ICTs and Media

ICTs have produced an unprecedented profusion and diversity of media. They have also opened up territory where the most powerful media are in cutthroat competition, and risk either crushing the weakest actors under their weight or leaving them jobless by the wayside. The reason is that the control and use of these new technologies require capital and capabilities of such enormous scale that, on the wealthiest of the consumer media markets, they inexorably lead to further concentration. However, is that this concentration is occurring just when thousands of new and independent media are bursting into disorderly life, in contrast with the previous era of one-party systems and the state-controlled monopoly of information.

In Africa in particular and in the countries of the former Soviet Union, the stranglehold of the state on the media has been broken, at least in the written press. There is a paradox within that paradox. In countries where until recently only one party predominated, the transition to democracy has been propitious for the media, whereas the return to democracy in the countries of the Southern Cone, and the end of apartheid in South Africa, have seen the disappearance of many titles that used to support the fight for freedom. It may be that periods of transition are more auspicious to pluralism and media diversity than the advent or return of democracy.

The transnationalization of media groups complicates the task of certain regimes that seek to hide the 'opposite point of view' from their people and merges together a number of cultural, political and journalistic models. Despite the fact that the new media in many countries have played the role of contradicting the party line, their globalization has not necessarily introduced the worldwide adoption of the values (human rights, freedom, tolerance) that their most ardent supporters believed they represented. Indeed, in certain countries, 'media interference' has, on the contrary, provoked even harsher reactions from authorities or countries with an identity crisis. While the objections of authoritarian regimes are fairly easy to overcome in the name of the principles of freedom, those put forward by democratic countries on the fundamental conception of freedom of expression - and above all on its limits - are worthy of particular attention.

The debate between the champions of free speech, based on the model of the First Amendment to the Constitution of the United States of America, and those who wish to impose stricter limits on the freedom of expression in the name of the struggle against racism, discrimination or war, lies at the heart of the information revolution. In this respect, technology has contingencies of its own, for the freedom of speech specific to one country is not necessarily that of other nations, who may define this notion by other norms. Freedom of expression is precisely one of the issues concerning labelling and filtering systems for Internet sites which are supposed to protect the public, and especially children, against inappropriate messages.

The Internet has a decisive role to play, because it escapes the technical and legal barriers set up by governments far more easily than the satellite television programmes picked up by dish antennas. The Internet is both a medium with its own audience, and a source of information for the other media. It is also a 'creator' of information flows, since it enables individuals and groups hitherto marginalized to become involved. Oppressed or isolated ethnic communities, underprivileged social groups, local social movements, banned political parties: all find in the Internet a means of entering onto the world stage, of presenting their situations in their own words, of expressing their claims independently of governments and the channels laid down by the large media groups. This role of the Internet is reinforced by e-mail, which also forms a new broadcasting medium. 'Virtual communities' have therefore become - a reality. The Internet also enables contact to be made with a new, younger audience, already prepared by experience with video game interactivity to plug into the cyberworld. These features have led some observers to the rather hasty conclusion that the Internet is the antidote to the dominant power of the media giants, the absolute weapon against state control and censorship, and the instrument of a new, more participatory form of citizenship.

New technology, however, does not eliminate conflictual relations or financial considerations. The large and most frequently visited Internet sites are already the prerogative of the established media groups. The communication giants present in the other media have purchased access providers or data banks. In most of the countries in transition, the costs of computer equipment and access subscriptions continue to be major obstacles which de facto exclude a large majority of the population from using the Internet.

Corresponding to this explosion in the scope of knowledge and scale of communication, are the new forms of state censorship. With limited success, governments have multiplied measures to prevent the media from crossing borders by banning dish antennas or foreign radio broadcasts. They even hope to dampen the liberating or contentious repercussions of the Internet by erasing 'hostile' sites using labelling and blocking systems, sanctioning access providers which tolerate them, and multiplying administrative or financial obstacles in order to limit the number of users. Democratic states are not necessarily the least repressive. The new media also offer new methods of information manipulation, which is the other face of censorship. Counselled by international public relations agencies, masters in the art of abusing information and communication techniques, authoritarian governments or large corporations with controversial business activities turn these new media around and use them against those who saw in them no more than an instrument of freedom. China has created its own site specializing in human rights.

In many countries, it is not the state which poses the greatest threat to the freedom of expression, but the 'new powers', non-governmental organizations which are taking over the work of state violence, either against it or with its connivance. In recent years, an increasing number of journalists have been the victims of mafia groups, paramilitary gangs and extremist religious factions. Increasing areas of the globe under the control of such groups have once again slipped out of range, thereby limiting the capacity for data collection at the source.

The new technologies are a poor weapon when armed gangs seal off an area and terrorize its people. More and more private individuals and public corporations are bringing court actions for slander or damages against even the most respectable programmes and publications, thereby attempting to intimidate them. Some of these lawsuits are legitimate, because freedom of speech must be balanced against other rights such as nondiscrimination, respect for privacy, or for a person's reputation and honour, but they are increasingly seen as a means of harassing the media and limiting public debate.

In the United States, they have been given the eloquent name of 'slapp', for strategic lawsuits against public participation. The privatization of censorship is also occurring at the distribution level. Closely supervised by self-appointed guardians of morality, or ethnic or religious groups, certain chain stores refuse to display and even sell certain books, videos or CDs. Internet access providers exclude sites deemed to be dangerous or harmful, and some public libraries, at the risk of blocking legitimate sites, have installed filtering software in order to prevent their younger customers from having access to obscene products. But the use of keywords enabling 'obscene' sites to be detected can just as easily block access to sites fighting pornography, defending the rights of women and children, or describing violations of human rights.

Technology in these instances is simply a new battlefield for groups which have always defended censorship in the name of morality, nationalism or religion. Now that the media have become commercialized, they worry about damage to their public image and try to avoid publicity which might keep them from being seen by general audiences. Censorship self-censorship - may therefore be the result of the supposed reactions of consumer groups or lobbies which are the noisiest and best organized. This situation also leads producers to steer clear of topics which are too sensitive or too controversial, thereby limiting the public space necessary for genuine debate and diversity. Hence a truly new paradox: just when technology is capable of pushing back the frontiers of censorship virtually to infinity, society is redefining the 'acceptable' limits of freedom of expression, through legislation or by adopting speech codes which are sometimes extremely strict, thus outlawing points of view which are deemed politically incorrect.

Public Service Broadcasting

In recent years, powerful media groups have grown still more powerful, not only in the countries of the North, but also in many countries of the South. The number of these media groups with their different levels of influence, ranging from global to regional, to national, to local, is in itself decreasing from year to year as a result of various mergers, takeovers and alliances. Concentration is horizontal, combining different media (the written press, television, etc.) and/or vertical (ranging from film studios to television channels and cinemas). It also sanctions a convergence of content (information and entertainment) and technology (the same content simultaneously supplies the written press, the audiovisual sector and the Internet). In certain countries, sometimes more than half the national circulation of daily newspapers is controlled by just one press group.

In most countries, local monopolies are the rule, and in these cases the newspapers are often part of powerful national or international groups, such as Gannett or Knight-Ridder in the United States or the Hersant group in France. Backed by their press power, these local enterprises usually extend business activities to the audiovisual sectors, as well as to publishing and advertising, and in so doing engulf neighbouring countries: instances include the German press in Austria, the French press in Belgium, and the Swedish press in the Baltic countries. Rupert Murdoch's News Corp. is an edifying example of the trend towards vertical and horizontal concentration, because the company is present in practically every media form, and covers the entire information chain: News Corp. has bought not only the exclusive rights for broadcasting sporting events, but also the subject of the information itself, i.e. the sports clubs, to ensure a more prestigious content and therefore a captive audience for its sports channels.

Mass media behaviour is to a considerable extent anchored in everyday events, in routine habits and customs. The relationship of the broadcasting media to viewers and listeners has become deeply rooted in their personality and behaviour. These are factors opposed to change, and they favor constancy and permanence. For this reason, the mass media of the future should be examined from the standpoint of constancy as much as from that of change and revolution. The radio and television media incorporate a large number of key elements which hardly alter or which change very slowly. On this basis, the forecasts which seek to see beyond the new media revolution can be founded upon assumptions that emphasize continuity.

A number of elements and success factors in the future of public service broadcasting are precisely of this kind and they are just as significant as are the opportunities for change. Many researchers regard television as a manifestation and symbol of so-called modernized Western society. They claim that television has replaced the traditional 'user interfaces' which included a variety of socio-societal structures such as place of residence, social class, religion and profession. For audiences in Western societies, radio and television have become a value- and culture-specific arena which reinforces personal identity. Radio and television channels broadcast programmes with elements of familiarity, belonging and continuity. They provide their audiences with identifiable points to which they can relate personal memories, common experiences of delight and pleasure or of anguish and sorrow.

The broadcasting media have thus become the single most important 'user interface' for personal identities and for experiencing what is perceived as being 'personal' in modern culture. In a recently published report, the Future Committee of the Finnish Parliament has stressed that experiencing something as one's own is one of the most important value bases of the information society.

Unless people find intellectual, community, environmental or material values with which they can identify in the networking and diversifying media, change is likely to lead to confusion and chaos rather than to the moral strengthening of the community. The strong influence of the broadcasting media on the everyday life of cosmopolitan societies is most probably based upon such feelings of personal recognition.

In modern communities, people are increasingly experiencing in their lives solidarity and events which are familiar to them through the mass media. This goes a long way to explaining why people from very different backgrounds, spheres and professions follow the same programmes and events at the same time. Viewing television and listening to radio, people manifest their solidarity and feel that they belong to a group. Today, this belonging often concerns national or regional cultures, but it can also relate to global togetherness. The principal broadcasting channels with a sense of responsibility must endeavour to meet the feeling and meaning of the audiences' common experience.

Critical tensions between various groups in societies are heightened when the programmes put out by the mass media channels do not provide a real response to the need of individuals to experience something as their own. Under these circumstances, feelings of alienation and of cultural and social discrimination are reinforced. Broadcasting programmes can thus be socially 'dysfunctional', as witnessed in some countries where people's power took over the public media, set up alternative media, or rejected the information put out by the official media. In 1990, when Gorbachev was seeking to keep Lithuania as part of the Soviet Union, the public proclaimed loudly that the country had been independent since 1921.

Pluralistic media are fundamental to the value systems of democratic societies. In order to exercise the basic values of freedom of speech and expression individuals must be able to obtain and acquire knowledge and information that is significant to them personally, created by the community itself and independent of those in power.

Public service broadcasting, as it originated in Europe, was created to serve these goals. Its ideal was to provide citizens with media that would be independent of both government and economic control. Public service broadcasting has thus always emphazised the significance of public control, reflected in the fact that it is accountable to the audience in a way in which the commercial media are not, even when they are popular. The principle of accountability implies that audiences can demand that the media provide programming that is important and significant to them on a personal level. The corollary is that public service broadcasting is also based upon the concept of an active, developing and self-fulfilling human being.

Public service broadcasting has traditionally been given the mandate to produce programming with informative, educative and also entertaining content. It has been expected to meet the needs of the various facets of the personality in a balanced way so as to provide a whole image of the individual. Broadcasting technology spread to Africa and Asia, often as a part of colonization. For this reason, public service radio, and later television, tended to serve the interests of the colonizing powers and later those of the newly independent national regimes, rather than those of the general public for whom they were originally established. Thus historically, in many of these countries, the public service mandate was often subservient to the whims and caprices of those in power, and was viewed as a primary tool for ensuring continuance in power.

In South Asia, one generally sees an entrenched government control over radio and television despite a colonial legacy of a BBC-type of public broadcasting code such as in India and Sri Lanka, along with a free press. But in other countries of the subcontinent, like Pakistan, Bangladesh and Nepal, one sees a situation similar to that in Eastern Europe, where some state broadcasters continue to work only as propaganda agents of governments despite the maturing of these democracies. In Nepal, in contrast, the government produced a communication policy paper in 1990, followed by a revised broadcasting act in 1992. Since then, several new FM stations have been granted a licence to broadcast, including Radio Sagarmatha, an independent station run by a consortium of NGOs. Their programmes do indeed reflect the community's concerns: environment, education, culture.

In view of the prospects opened up by developments in technology, it may be asked whether the ideals set up by public service broadcasting are still sustainable. This question arises because audiences today can use advanced communication technology to access those media contents which they think will best meet their various communication needs. Communicating via network media and the Internet, audiences now have unrestricted access to those sources of information that were previously beyond their reach, behind, inter alia, a variety of media gatekeepers. It may be argued that communication built upwards does away with the need for public service broadcasting which, despite everything, is always constructed by programming planners and gatekeepers.

It is true that in the network society the individual has an unprecedented opportunity to obtain access to virtually any source of information though this opportunity is not available equally to everyone. The Internet era has multiplied the individual's opportunity for accessing new, geographically distant sources of information which are not dependent on fixed-time programming schedules. The limits of time and space are disintegrating. In particular, the Internet has opened up the borders of the world to its users and promoted the unrestricted movement of information in a manner that is without parallel in world history. It has also facilitated genuine debate among people united by a common topic or interest.

Many information networks are complementing the diverse sources of news used by broadcasting. One of these is the International Freedom of Expression and Exchange Network (IFEX), and particularly noteworthy is the work of the Pacific Islands News Association, which issues news alerts concerning the media in this region.

The number of computers connected to the Internet is still growing rapidly. In July 1998, there were 36.7 million computers connected to the Internet worldwide. In Finland, there were 100.53 computers per 1,000 inhabitants connected to the Internet. However, the worldwide communication network and information gateways are, by their very existence, creating the need for the pendulum to swing the other way. As both the sources of information and the number of connections multiply, the need for meanings that unite also grows. One of the most important challenges of the information society, beyond making information available, is to enable analytical interpretation of it and to facilitate understanding.

In the networked information society, public service broadcasting should emphasize the contribution to its prestige made by the high level of interpretation and analysis which is part of its mission. Those working and communicating in the various networks need both knowledge and certainty about their own points of departure. Only a communicator who is certain about his or her own self can engage in a fully reciprocal communication process with others.

The elements of public service broadcasting that are emphasized in the information society are pluralism, independence, and, finally, communication, which strengthens identity and instills understanding about the meaning of citizenship. The sense of self and identity are reinforced when the members of a society and a culture are given the opportunity to obtain information that is relevant and important to them. The growth and vitality of this sense is often simulated by fictional material and storytelling: films, serials and series, music, entertainment and humour.

Public service broadcasting best carries out its mission in the information society when it provides all segments of the audience with cultural material to reinforce a positive sense of identity and self. Public service broadcasting must become more aware of this key characteristic and must emphasize it as a core element of its mission.

Boundaries are being broken down, the roles of states are changing, many operations are being globalized and contexts are becoming more complex. Decision-making in matters affecting citizens is becoming more distant and is, in many cases, no longer recognizable. Political citizenship generally means that people are capable of understanding matters affecting them and their relationship to such matters.

An integrating and globalizing world, where decision-making is often faceless, offers a particular challenge to the media. In order to enjoy full citizenship in the information society individuals must be able to obtain information on matters affecting them personally and to feel that they can influence such matters. This is quite a different matter from the consumers' opportunity to obtain the communication services which they require.

Citizenship in the information society also signifies that individuals can increasingly and naturally participate and do business electronically. Finland has sought to promote the conditions and opportunities for electronic public dealings and participation by citizens. The fulfilment of civil obligations, dealings with welfare services, study, library visits, relations with the authorities and other such matters will soon be managed remotely. Such forms of interactivity should also be promoted by public service broadcasting. In a democratic information society populated by active citizens, encouraging the ideals of citizenship and of civil duties and rights is particularly important and should therefore be a core element of the future mission of public service broadcasting.

Citizenship in the information society implies that individuals have the right to relevant and reliable information. Under these circumstances, the number of sources of information is less important than the reliability and relevance of the information to which citizens have access. Citizenship is closely tied to equality, and all members of the community must have an equal opportunity to obtain basic information service. On the eve of the information society, we should reassess what is meant by basic information services. For example, is equal access to communication networks one of the basic rights of the citizen of the information society? If so, how is it to be implemented? Can it be achieved only through relatively expensive hardware investments, or can equal connection and basic services be implemented by means already available to the overwhelming majority of the public?

As far as public service broadcasting is concerned, all these questions are significant. This raises the original question of whether the information society is for eveyone, or for only a few. In operational terms, the question is whether there are realistic and practical governmental and entrepreneurial policies and strategies to ensure that networks and services are expanded to reach all countries, or whether these polices and strategies are market driven and profit based. If profit is the sole or principal motivation, are decision-makers deliberately excluding large segments of the world's population by consciously employing a policy of social exclusion? This would undoubtedly run counter to the ideals and objectives of public service broadcasting and related media. Furthermore, such policies would be self-defeating since they negate the objective of universal access to information and communication media and are not even favourable to the new concept of global marketing!

Because digital broadcasting technology allows for new ways of registering and monitoring communication, it is all the more important that the privacy of individual citizens as communicators be respected. Individuals can be equal players in the public political arena only if they can be certain of respect for their privacy and integrity. Political systems must be able to guarantee this protection if they are to earn the trust of their citizens. In a multiple-source and increasingly complex situation, the ethics of communication should also require journalism to be firmly based on reliable and objective argumentation. In a multi-channel world, the prestige associated with reliability for all channels will increase and will also be subject to more critical exposure.

In recent years, public service broadcasting the world over has seen economic resources diminish. Nevertheless, over the next few years, digital technology will require appreciable financial investments in both technology and programme content. Even for many large companies, such expenditures present a difficult financial problem. In this context, it has been suggested that the public service broadcasting companies ought not to invest too much in digital technology, but rather focus for the time being on dealing with the basic analogue broadcasting media. This choice would nevertheless be fatal for both public service broadcasting and for society as a whole. Without the slightest doubt, the basic point of departure must be that public service broadcasting should not only enter the digital era, but should take the lead in exploring the new possibilities which the information society offers to all media.

Digital technology allows public service

broadcasting to carry out its mission more effectively and in a more focused way. Digital broadcasting technology can provide public service programming to several different audience groups simultaneously. Some countries are developing digital services in the belief that new digital channels targeting niche audiences will complement and enrich the programmes already offered by the basic channels, but will neither displace nor replace the full service programmes. For the cultural and value reasons discussed earlier, viewers and listeners will continue to feel the need for general channels in the future. At the same time, their demand for in-depth and even highly detailed information which can be supplied via special channels or via digital television user-oriented network services will increase.

Public service broadcasting companies should be involved increating a new audiovisual communication culture in which traditional broadcast products converge with new media and multimedia products. In the public service range, these products can be presented either in parallel or as specific elements of programmes. Audiences are expecting public service broadcasting to play a prominent and visible role in the new media. Several public service broadcasting companies have developed, inter alia, Internet services, and their success has been encouraging. For example, the BBC's Internet services are the most popular network services at the moment. The appeal of the public service companies 'Internet pages is based on the fact that the audience has an image of these companies which stresses reliability, diversity and quality. In the chaos of the media world, consumers are on the look out for organizations or 'portals' through which they can access reliable, interesting and significant sources of information.

The changes in both the content and programming structures of public service broadcasting represent a major operational challenge which will affect not only the operating and production methods within companies, where digitalizing production technology is creating new opportunities, but also the relationship to the content production sector operating outside radio and television. Public service broadcasting companies will survive the challenges of the digital era only if they are able to create collaborative networking with both the new media technology sector and the content production sector.

Many sectors of society can contribute more than can be imagined to content production for the digital broadcasting media. It is natural that in the past, education, social services or the science sector, for example, did not perceive themselves as being close to the audiovisual production sector. Today, however, they are already producing a variety of ambitious new-media audiovisual products, which could well form one part of the new broadcasting content.

The public service companies must now invite new organizations in society to cooperate in digital production. To a large extent this is a question of motivation and example, and public service broadcasting should take on a pioneering role particularly in the areas of culture, science, education and welfare. This role should also to extend to making information society services available to citizens and households.

One universal obstacle to the advancement of the information society is the reluctance of citizens to use the new electronic services and information technology in general, even though the benefits of such use are clear. The fears of and negative attitudes towards electronic information ought not to be underestimated. Public service broadcasting should, as a part of its information society role, provide new services that emphasize the citizens' point of view, and this in turn will encourage an adaptation of public service broadcasting to the environment of the future. Moreover, the image of reliability, independence and public accountability associated with public service broadcasting offers a good basis to start moving in this direction.

For many members of the broadcast audience, the transition to an information society is still an abstract, or even unacceptable, vision. They are concerned about the undermining of human interaction and about the possible increasing alienation of large, less affluent segments of our societies. In many countries, those retiring from active life in 1999 will live, on the average, for about twenty years in the emerging information society, and it may be asked whether their needs will have been taken properly into account. Others are concerned about the overemphasis on the commercial and marketing aspects of the digital future.

However, for many, the so-called information society represents new opportunities just for huge global businesses. Public service broadcasters will undoubtedly understand the importance of market revenue in developing new services. However, the value base of the information society - just as for any society of whatever period - should not be business oriented, and public service broadcasters should take an intellectual lead in the public debate on these matters. Such a debate should not be an abstract discussion of the objectives and structures of the information society, but should include concrete demonstrations of services which viewers and listeners can utilize every day in public service broadcasting programmes.

In providing a well-balanced and structured range of old and new services to the audiences, public service broadcasting should present an understandable and approachable view of what the information society means in the audience's everyday life. As is the case with existing public service broadcasting, it would be difficult - and even undesirable - to try to define in detail which concrete operations and services these new products should provide in the future. The public service mission is not a list of quantifiable tasks. A society defines what public service broadcasting means in each particular context and this is often expressed as a broadcasting law. The statement ratified by the member states of the Council of Europe defines public service broadcasting as an essential factor in pluralistic communication accessible to everyone and hence as a central factor of social cohesion in the information society. This guideline is also valid for the production of new digital and multimedia services.

4

Freedom of Expression on the Net

The Internet is uniquely decentralized, global, abundant, inexpensive, interactive and user-controlled. In US, the campaign finance laws were developed for the centralized, scarce, and expensive media of radio, television and print. The Internet supports a diverse range of content—text, graphics, audio and video; chat rooms, moderated and unmoderated email lists, and "newsgroups;" and World Wide Web sites endlessly and seamlessly linked on a global basis—much of it spontaneous and independent from campaign committees and the political parties. Initial efforts to apply the Federal Election Campaign Act (FECA) to these new and varied Internet communications have yielded troubling results, threatening to burden.

In US, the Internet fosters what the Supreme Court has called a "never-ending worldwide conversation." As such, the Court has held, expression on the Internet is entitled to the highest level of protection under the First Amendment. It would be worse than ironic if rules designed to deemphasize the unfair advantage of money, to broaden the diversity of groups that can have an impact on the election process and to "return our electoral process to the people" were applied to deter individuals from using the "electronic soapbox" of the Internet.

More recently, there has been a hint of change from the FEC, with bolder calls from some individual Commissioners for redefinition of the campaign finance law's application to the Internet. We support such calls, and we urge the Commission - to the maximum extent possible within the terms and exceptions of FECA - to recognize that a large portion of the political activity in cyberspace does not merit regulation. Ultimately, however, it will likely require a Congressional amendment to FECA to protect individual advocacy and remove any cloud from this most democratic, open and inexpensive of mass media.

In US, the Centre for Democracy and Technology is a public interest organization dedicated to developing and implementing public policies that protect and enhance civil liberties and democratic values in the new digital media. We are not experts in campaign finance law and we have not taken a position on legislative proposals concerning campaign finance. However, we have made it one of our priorities to defend freedom of expression on the Internet.

CDT staff were among the first to articulate the ways in which the architecture of the Internet serves core First Amendment values by increasing access to diverse information sources and minimizing the need for government content regulation.

CDT helped organize the Citizens Internet Empowerment Coalition, which challenged Congress' first attempt to control content on the Internet, the Communications Decency Act (CDA). We brought the

Internet into the courtroom in Philadelphia, demonstrating its unique features to the three judge panel hearing the CDA case. US user-controlled vision of the Internet proved central to the Supreme Court's landmark ruling in Reno v. ACLU, holding that the Internet was a unique medium entitled to the highest First Amendment protection. It is from that perspective that we have become concerned about the implications of the FEC's initial efforts to apply the campaign finance law to the Internet.

In evaluating the First Amendment standards applicable to any medium of communication, the Supreme Court has long recognized that "differences in the characteristics of new media justify differences in the First Amendment standards applied to them." The Supreme Court found that the Internet is a unique medium, distinct from broadcast, print, and cable. The Court described the speech outlets of the Internet as "vast democratic fora" and a "new marketplace of ideas," which "provides relatively unlimited, low-cost capacity for communication of all kinds," the growth of which "has been and continues to be phenomenal." The Court recognized that it is the very breadth and variety of speech over the Internet that gives the Internet its extraordinary communicative power:

This dynamic, multifaceted category of communication includes not only traditional print and news services, but also audio, video, and still images, as well as interactive, real-time dialogue. Through the use of chat rooms, any person with a phone line can become a town crier with a voice that resonates farther than it could from any soapbox. Through the use of Web pages, mail exploders, and newsgroups, the same individual can become a pamphleteer.

Characteristics of the Internet

Architectural and economic characteristics of the Internet make it a medium uniquely suited, if properly fostered, to achieving the marketplace of ideas which the First Amendment is intended to support and through which our democratic ideals can best be realized. These unique characteristics must guide the application of campaign finance rules to the Internet.

— *Decentralized*: Traditional mass media's system of limited distribution channels sets up a gatekeeper system controlled by a relatively small number of entities. In contrast, the Internet's architecture is decentralized and distributed. It is a network of networks consciously designed to function without gatekeepers.

— *Global*: The Internet provides immediate access to information from around the world. With simple email, it is as easy and inexpensive to send a message to another continent as to the building across the street. Search engines on the World Wide Web list local and foreign sites without distinction. Those wishing to avoid government regulation have shown the ability to quickly "mirror" content on servers outside the reach of censors.

— *Abundant*: The Internet can accommodate a virtually unlimited number of speakers. Thus, while the architecture of mass media creates scarcity, the Internet's architecture places little limit on the amount and diversity of information that can be made available. As the Supreme Court stated, "Unlike the conditions that prevailed when Congress first authorized regulation of the broadcast spectrum, the

Internet can hardly be considered a scarce expressive commodity. It provides relatively unlimited, low-cost capacity for communication of all kinds... ."

— *Inexpensive*: Existing campaign finance law reflects the economics of the mass media: speaking effectively is expensive. In contrast, on the Internet, "talk is cheap." The Internet sustains a level of speech among individuals and loosely organized groups unparalleled in other media. It is the first electronic medium to allow every user to be a publisher. Users can reach and create communities of interest despite geographic, social, and political barriers, enabling nearly everyone who wants to espouse political opinions to do so. Armed with an email account, an individual can send a mass emailing to hundreds of thousands of individuals with little expense. At one of the many portal services, individuals can create Web pages to discuss their likes, dislikes, wage a campaign against a corporation, flak products, or express their political views - for free.

— *Interactive*: Unlike the one-way transmissions typifying most radio and television, the Internet is bidirectional in nature. It allows responsive communications from one-to-one, from one-to-many, and from many-to-one.

— *User-controlled*: Unlike television and radio, which offer individuals little opportunity to make decisions about what information they receive, the Internet is a user-controlled medium. As the Supreme Court found in striking down the Communications Decency Act, individuals are not assaulted by information on the Internet but rather enjoy an unequalled ability to direct and control the information that they come in contact with.

In US, the 1996 presidential election witnessed the beginning of Internet-based political activity. Both the Clinton-Gore and the Dole-Kemp campaigns used Web sites to distribute information, solicit volunteers, and highlight campaign activities. What was more important, however, than the major political parties' adding the Internet to their campaign strategies was the way in which the Internet served as a platform for informal, unorganized, grassroots political discussions of a breadth and variety rarely witnessed in the off-line world.

The Internet provides individuals and informal organizations the ability to communicate inexpensively. From their virtual platforms, individuals and organizations are publishing newsletters, advertisements, voters guides and other election-related materials; creating dynamic forums that support issue-based organizing, interactive discussions, and political advocacy; and registering voters. The Internet can lower barriers to participation.

Small groups and minor parties, among the first to use the Internet, are currently engaged in long-term affiliation-building activities online. Foreshadowing the significant future role of the Internet in political campaigns and the national political dialogue, the Web has been credited as a decisive factor in recent.

In addition to broadening the number and diversity of speakers, the Internet creates opportunities for new forms of speech. Real-time dialogues can be hosted, creating a parallel to the town hall meeting without the time and expense. Conversations can be held outside of real-time, as postings on Web sites form "threaded" discussions on specific topics, which can be archived and returned to at any time.

The Internet also provides voters with an efficient and timely method to gather information about candidates. It has been suggested that many voters make uninformed choices or become frustrated and drop out of the process not because they do not care about the outcome of an election but because becoming informed takes too much effort.

The Internet has particular advantages in enabling voters to obtain information, compare candidates, review voting records, and hear from third-parties through easy-to-find resources. Voters can access information when they want it. 10% of voters have already used the Internet to gather information they used in a voting decision. Exit poll respondents said that the information they found on the Internet was simply not available in traditional mediums. They also highlighted the convenience of the Internet and the sheer volume of information available.

The Federal Election Campaign Act (FECA), adopted in 1971 and significantly amended in 1974, seeks to quantify the cost of political speech, limit the amount of money collected and spent on campaign-related activities, and enable public scrutiny of the impact of money on campaigns and elected officials through disclosure of the identity of contributors.

In general the law establishes:

— Contribution limits: Federal election law limits the amount of money individuals and groups can contribute to candidates, party committees, and political action committees (PACs). In particular, the law limits an individual's overall contributions at $25,000 per calendar year and sets caps on contributions: to a candidate at $1,000 per election; to a national party committee at $20,000 per calendar year; and to other political committees at $5,000 per calendar year. While "contributions" are thus limited, "independent expenditures" by individuals or groups are not·

— Prohibited contributions and expenditures: The law prohibits corporations, labour organizations, federal government contractors and foreign nationals from making any contributions and expenditures to influence federal elections. It also prohibits contributions to federal elections in another person's name and prohibits cash contributions in federal elections of more than $100.

— Disclosure requirements: Candidate committees, party committees and PACs must file periodic reports disclosing the money they raise and spend, and generally identifying the source of contributions. Candidates must disclose and attribute contributions from PACs and party committees and they must identify individuals who contribute more than $200 per year.

— Identification requirements: While "independent expenditures" by individuals or groups are unrestricted, where any expenditure finances communications expressly advocating the election or defeat of a clearly identified candidate or soliciting contributions through any general public political advertising, the communication must identify the party responsible by name and indicate whether or not it is authorized by the campaign.

Existing campaign finance law is based on several assumptions that reflect the nature of traditional mass media. First and foremost, the law assumes that speech is expensive and that therefore money inextricably determines the amount and impact of political speech.

In contrast, the Internet greatly reduces the cost of speech. Because the initial start-up costs of becoming a speaker on the Internet are relatively low and, once the investment is made, the difference between communicating to a single individual and communicating to masses of individuals is marginal, the effect of money is vastly diminished in the online environment.

In addition, the campaign finance law assumes that the content of political speech (at least the political speech that matters) will be conducted by a relatively small set of entities created to influence elections. The law assumes that there is a distinction between speakers and listeners, that the speakers will be the candidates (and their committees and parties), and that most citizens will participate in the campaign process not by speaking but by contributing money.

Under this traditional scenario, to the extent that individuals become involved in the political process as "volunteers," it is assumed they will not be speaking, but rather will be disseminating material (mainly printed material) produced by the campaign in the form of leaflets that volunteers will stuff into envelopes or deliver door-to-door. On Internet, in contrast, anybody can be a speaker. A "volunteer" can create a Web site as good as the campaign webmaster's.

There is another difference between the traditional mass media and the Internet, one having to do with the role of advertising. Television and radio work on the advertising model: advertisements pay for the content. By and large on television and radio, the content is not political in nature.

Most content providers on radio and television are studiously apolitical in their programming. To the extend there is content regarding politics, it is in the form of news, which is exempt from FECA. By and large, on television and radio, the only way that political speech is broadcast outside of the news is in the form of very expensive paid political advertisements.

On the Internet, the distinctions between content, news and advertisement are very different. There is a great deal of content not supported by any advertising. Some content on the Internet is supported by advertising, but it is different in two crucial ways, especially in the campaign context.

On the Internet, most political content is not in the form of paid political advertisements; it is in the form of freestanding Web pages. On the Internet, there is no disincentive for political content. By and large, candidates do not spend a lot of money on the Internet for paid political advertisement that support the content of others. Rather, to the extent that candidates "advertise" on the Internet, they do it the way everybody else does, with banner adds that do not carry content, but that try to attract viewers to click away from one content page to another content page (i.e., the candidate's).

One way to assess the application of campaign finance laws to the Internet is to try to map the asserted goals of campaign finance regulation onto the new medium. Doing so illustrates how the goals of campaign finance would be best achieved by not regulating much of the campaign and election-related activity on the Internet.

Supporters of campaign finance restrictions argue that the role of money in politics fosters inequality in our democratic system. The original supporters of FECA feared that well-financed political action groups thwart the one person, one vote principle. The goal of FECA was to "broaden the diversity of groups that can have an input on the election process" and to "return our electoral process to the people." Current campaign finance reformers share this goal.

The Internet is an inherently equalizing force for non-candidates and minor candidates to participate in campaign discussions in ways previously reserved to well-funded candidates. Because it is open and inexpensive, the Internet empowers all users with the ability to speak to a large audience. A single wired individual can be powerful: one man organized over 100 campus protests against the Republican Party's Contract with America from his basement computer.

The Internet is unlikely to reduce the amount campaigns spend on radio and television. But certainly, the Internet does not significantly increase the amount of money spent by campaigns, and does not impose large additional fund-raising demands on politicians and candidates.

Online, voters can easily check distorted candidate or organization statements. A search for a candidate name is sure to deliver not only the candidate's views on an issue but critiques and criticisms of the can did ate's position as well as other relevant information. Proponents of campaign finance reform often raise concerns about the expense and delay of responding to distorted claims made by incumbent candidates or moneyed interests in traditional media.

The expense of responding online is relatively low. Through linking and searching, opposing points of view and responses to a candidate's claim will be simultaneously available to the voter. Special interest groups can and will spend money on Internet political efforts, but individuals and smaller groups can inexpensively build Web sites responding to or critiquing candidate and interest group statements.

Given the global nature of the Internet, this is one goal that no amount of regulation can achieve. Restricting outside influence to local elections is probably made substantially more difficult by the Internet. Because the Internet is a global medium, an out-of-state voter or organization utilizing the Web for political advocacy is just as likely to influence an election as an in-state voter or organization. Web sites overseas will be beyond the reach of U.S. regulators.

The FEC has clearly established that disseminating information about federal elections through the Internet can be subject to regulation under the Federal Election Campaign Act. In 1995, the FEC ruled that a Web site distributing information, run by an independent, "virtual PAC" is a form of "general public political advertising." The FEC has found that an individual may have to report to the government in order to create a Web page expressing support for a candidate, that hyperlinks may constitute political contributions, and that providing free Web sites to all candidates is a prohibited corporate contribution.

Hypertext links form one of the distinguishing characteristics of the World Wide Web. In 1998, the FEC concluded that "links" constitute a thing of value and that a link on a corporate site constitutes an illegal corporate contribution.

The most important FEC ruling on nonpartisan online political activities is Advisory Opinion 1996. Online service provider CompuServe wanted to offer free Web sites and member accounts on a "nonpartisan basis" to all federal candidates in order to allow the posting of position papers and to facilitate responding to questions from voters via email. CompuServe told the Commission that it typically charged $9.95 per month for the service but provides free accounts to many journalists, schools, charities, government entities, and non-profit organizations.

In response, the FEC ruled that the free accounts would be considered prohibited corporate contributions to federal candidates. The Commission had previously permitted a cable television station to give free airtime to candidates. That fell under the exemption for news stories or commentary by media outlets, but CompuServe did not qualify for the media exemption. Neither CompuServe's contention that the Web sites would add value to the CompuServe service nor the fact that the accounts were similar to those given to other non-profit entities allowed CompuServe to escape the law against corporate contributions.

Financial information provider Bloomberg later asked the FEC to review its proposal to conduct electronic town meetings with federal candidates on its Web site. In the Bloomberg proposal, journalists were to moderate the discussions, which would be available for later broadcast on Bloomberg television.

The FEC ruled that Bloomberg was a "news and commentary provider via computer linkages" and was "performing a newspaper or periodical function for computer users." The Commission said that the

Bloomberg proposal differed from CompuServe's because the "means of presentation [were to be] controlled by a press entity." Because Bloomberg was only exempted as a "wire service," the question of whether any exclusively Internet-based company can be defined as a media company remains unanswered.

In Advisory Opinion 1997-16, the FEC made its first ruling on organizational activities on the Web. The Oregon Natural Resources Council Action (ONCRA) wanted to announce candidate endorsements of its affiliated PAC , Oregon Natural Resources Council Action Federal PAC (PAC), to its members on the ONCRA Web site instead of by mail. The FEC ruled that the group could not list its endorsements on the site unless it instituted a screening mechanism to ensure that it was only accessed by members. Corporations, including non-profits groups, can communicate endorsements to their members, but if they communicate to the general public it is considered an illegal corporate contribution. PACs on the other hand can make endorsements, contributions and expenditures with regard to Federal elections subject to the limits and disclosure requirements of FECA.

If the FEC determines that Exley or another Web user spent over $1,000 in support of a candidate, the user will have to register as a political committee. Those who are required to register must provide their name and address, appoint a custodian of books and a treasurer, and report all bank accounts and funds to be used for political activities. If any contribution to the political committee exceeds $200, such as a computer, the committee must also have records of the contributor's occupation and employer.

Similarly, if the FEC strictly enforces the election law's limits on association with the official campaign, many activities such as collecting information from campaigns for inclusion on a Web site, linking to the official campaign Web site, or other minimal communications between campaign staff and the outside individual or group may constitute associated efforts.

Since the FEC has concluded that links constitute in-kind contributions, candidates will probably also have to report the personal information of any Web site operator that links to the candidate Web site.

Web sites that announce the availability of linked images or html code for linking to their Web site could run into trouble when they are not informed that other sites have decided to link to their site.

The prohibition on links from corporate Web sites creates problems for any site linking to candidate Web sites. Additionally, if individuals and small groups register their advocacy sites with the FEC, linking to those Web sites may constitute reportable in-kind contributions to private political committees. This extra layer of potential reporting means that Web sites would never know whether with every hyperlink they are making a prohibited or reportable contribution.

If candidate Web sites are difficult for users to find, citizens will find the wealth of information on the Web overwhelming and cumbersome to navigate. Internet users are currently frustrated by the number of parodies and non-official sites that have taken the domain names where they expect to find the official Web site.

The Internet's way of solving for such problems without reducing the number of participants in the debate or closing down important efforts by third parties is to allow Web site operators to link to the official site. Citizen efforts, search engines, ISPs, non-profit groups, and individuals can point users to the official site while perhaps also providing links to their favourite independent efforts. Commentators have even suggested that the FEC provide links to candidate Web sites or free space on its server.

The FEC has not only refused to include these links on its Web site, it has erected barriers to others' linking to candidate Web sites. For online politics to truly become an important force in voter decision- making, links to official Web sites need to be encouraged, not discouraged. Ensuring that each candidate has a voice through free links might reduce the influence of money in politics; candidates would be able to buy banner ads on other sites but anyone who wanted to compare candidates could easily find all positions.

On the Internet, however, drawing the distinction between individual and corporate speech may be difficult. For example, is it a corporate contribution if an ISP or a provider of free Web site hosting allows the posting of statements supporting candidates on Web sites, chat rooms or bulletin boards, especially if the ISP or other service provider is not a common carrier but retains some control over the content of information? Another FECA distinction rendered obsolete by the Internet is the distinction between media and non-media. To meet the FEC's definition for the "media exemption," one must meet several requirements: the content must be a news story, editorial, or commentary from a qualified press entity using the press entity's routine means of distribution.

The Internet has fostered an explosion of alternative news providers, some of which become absorbed into the mainstream media, while many have only an online presence. The current definition of media assumes the model of traditional mass communicators. Even as governments around the world acknowledged the difficulties inherent in censoring the Internet, legislative proposals continued to threaten free speech. While human rights and civil liberties groups pointed out the global implications for the rights to privacy and free expression represented by such proposals, regulators around the world were quick to refine online monitoring, screening, and other controlling technologies. Arguing that national regulatory frameworks are not appropriate to the global nature of the Internet, industry leaders joined forces to create an international Internet content rating system to "protect children and free speech" on the Web. In May they formed the Internet Content Rating Association (ICRA) to facilitate the development of an integrated self-regulatory approach to dealing with "harmful and illegal" content on the Internet. Human Rights Watch, along with other members of the Global Internet Liberty Campaign (GILC), argued for more deliberate consideration of so-called self-regulatory approaches to Internet content control.

The Global Internet Liberty Campaign Member Statement further emphasized the danger that rating and filtering systems could, in fact, facilitate government censorship. The wide-scale deployment of rating and blocking systems could be used by regulators to stifle expression and marginalize any Web sites that failed to adopt ratings. The existence of a standardized rating system for Internet content-with the accompanying technical changes to facilitate blocking-would allow governments to require Internet service providers (ISPs) and other content access providers (public libraries, schools, etc.) to employ such regimes. Exemplifying this possibility, the Australian government on June 30, 1999 approved the Broadcasting Services Amendment (Online Services) Act, which would force Australian ISPs to remove objectionable material from Australian sites and to block access to similar sites overseas. Material suitable for blocking was to be identified based on existing national film and video classification standards. The new law placed sweeping restrictions on adults providing or gaining access to material deemed unsuitable for minors. In Bahrain, Iran, Saudi Arabia, the United Arab Emirates, and Yemen, ISPs-either under government orders or pressure-all blocked Web sites on the basis of their content.

At least in the first four of these countries, blocking extended to cultural and/or political content. Proxy servers such as the ones in place in the U.A.E. and Saudi Arabia could be used by authorities to track which computer terminals were accessing which Web sites and for how long. While U.A.E. authorities denied monitoring individual Web use, Saudi Arabian users who requested blocked sites received a message on their screens warning that all access attempts were logged. State-controlled or state-influenced ISPs in Tunisia, Iran and Bahrain blocked Web sites containing political or human rights criticism of their governments. Tunisia acknowledged blocking only those sites that offended moral values, but apparently this included the sites of various human rights organizations critical of the government. Videsh Sanchar Nigam Ltd. (owned by the Indian government) was the nation's largest Internet service provider and controlled the international Internet gateways used by ISPs in India. During the last week of June, at the height of the Kashmir crisis, Internet users in India could not reach the online news site of the Pakistan daily Dawn, which was known for its independent coverage of the crisis. Fearing that VSNL gateways blocked access to the newspaper site, other Web sites began posting information explaining how surfers from India could break the blockade, and a number of mailing lists began circulating articles from Dawn in text format. Radio B92, the leading independent radio station in Belgrade, Yugoslavia, was banned in March but continued to broadcast news on the Internet. Online users around the world were able to continue to access Radio B2-92's independent news via the Web as a daily digest with headline updates every hour. In late 1998 the United States Congress passed the Child Online Protection Act (COPA), making it a crime to publish "any communication for commercial purposes that includes any material that is harmful to minors, without restricting access to such material by minors." In April the U.S. Department of Justice appealed a federal appeals court ruling declaring the law unconstitutional, the result of a lawsuit brought by opponents of the COPA.

Governments rarely admit to "eavesdropping" on e-mail, and it is extremely hard to ascertain whether government monitoring is occurring when most information about monitoring mechanisms is classified. But during 1998 official disclosures in Europe and Australia provided a glimpse into one such system, a monitoring process referred to as ECHELON. According to a January 1998 report published by the Scientific and Technological Option Assessment (STOA) unit of the European Parliament, ECHELON formed part of the UKUSA spy system and wasdesigned for primarily nonmilitary targets: governments, organizations and businesses. The system operated in virtually every country and intercepted fax, e-mail and telephone messages routinely and indiscriminately. In Britain, the Home Office announced a number of proposals in a June 1999 consultation paper on the interception of communications. Future laws based on these proposals would require "communications service providers" to integrate government interception facilities into their networks, including the Internet, at their own expense. These proposals followed the specifications secretly agreed by European police officials in ENFOPOL plans revealed the previous year. (ENFOPOL was a standard European Commission classification for documents concerned with law enforcement matters.) The British consultation paper also argued that the maintenance of an interception capability was a basic requirement for providers of communication services in countries such as France, Germany, the Netherlands, Sweden, Canada, the United States and Australia. On April 2, the Second Chamber of the Dutch Parliament approved a new Telecommunications Act that included a chapter intended, among other things, to force ISPs to facilitate monitoring by the police and intelligence services. In April, an Internet service provider, Singnet of Singapore, apologized to its subscribers after scanning their computers without their knowledge. Singnet had asked the Home Affairs Ministry to check the computers of its 200,000 subscribers during a computer virus scare.

In Russia rules requiring ISPs to provide the security service with complete access to users' e-mail were challenged by an ISP based in Volgograd. The rules, known as System of Efficient Research Measures 2 (SORM-2), were written by the Russian Federal Security

Services and the State Communications Agency in 1998. In the Middle East and North Africa, where many governments routinely tapped the phones of potential dissidents, Internet users in many countries, including Bahrain and Tunisia, suspected that the right to privacy of correspondence was being violated by government surveillance of e-mail communications. One Bahraini spent more than a year in jail on suspicion of e-mailing "political" information to dissidents abroad. Under India's License Agreement Provision of Internet Service, ISPs had to maintain logs of all Internet users and the service they were using. These logs, as well as copies of all the packets originating from the customer premises equipment (CPE) of the ISP, had to be available in real time to the government telecom authority.

China continued its crackdown on Internet dissent by explicitly prohibiting the transmission or posting of what the government considered "anti-government propaganda." In January 1999, a computer technician, Lin Hai, was sentenced to two years' imprisonment by a Shanghai court for giving the e-mail addresses of 30,000 Chinese subscribers to a dissident site that published an online magazine from the United States. In a worrying development, Internet providers and telecommunications companies in many countries could be forced to build special data taps into their Internet servers to allow government security agencies real-time monitoring of every e-mail message and Web page sent to or from their servers. This could allow government agencies to circumvent national privacy laws, allowing them to rely on surveillance mechanisms in other countries. Citing national security concerns, governments continued to avoid releasing information on monitoring mechanisms.

The development of and freedom to use encryption software could provide substantial protection for the privacy of online users. Yet contrary to the spirit of international norms that recognize privacy as a fundamental human right, governments continued to use export controls or other national laws limiting the public's access to encryption technologies and inhibiting the development of new encryption products. In December 1998, the Wassenaar Arrangement announced, largely due to United States pressure, new guidelines that would authorize restrictions on the export of most commercial cryptography products above a fifty-six or sixty-four bit strength. But there were other, more encouraging developments in this area. In Germany, an export license was no longer required for the export of encryption products to third-country markets. Ireland, counter to the wishes of its E.U. neighbors, was willing to adopt policies that favored the use of strong encryption to encourage Internet trading. The French prime minister announced in January that due to the threat of electronic espionage and other dangers to privacy France would allow encryption strengths up to 128 bits, and would remove the compulsory or third-party escrow of encryption keys.As should be evident, the field of Internet regulation and surveillance was still very much in flux in 1999. It was clear, however, that the privacy and free expression rights of users of this global medium would be shaped by a multiplicity of regulations and policies, including self-regulatory approaches promoted by Internet industry leaders as well as myriad national and international rules on surveillance and encryption.

Privacy on the Net

As a mass medium, the Internet can enable anyone to receive and to disseminate alternatives to state-controlled information at a low cost. While few individuals and groups have the means to publish books or newspapers, make a film, or air a radio or television program, any person with access to a personal computer and modem can communicate with a huge international audience. A connection to the Internet can increase access to information in less-developed countries by putting within easy reach one of the world's great repositories of information, much of it free and continuously updated, and by making that information more easily manageable and transferable. Such benefits do not depend on a large number of persons having the means to purchase their own equipment and Internet accounts.

A government policy of making computers available to the public at libraries, schools or community centers, or the presence of privately run "Internet cafés" or "cybercafés, can help to democratize use of the Internet even in relatively poor countries. In light of the Internet's vast potential for empowering people to exercise the right to free expression, some have argued that governments have an affirmative obligation to facilitate Internet access for all segments of the population on terms of nondiscrimination. Some have also contended that the Internet can significantly assist governments in enabling citizens to exercise the right, under article 25(a) of the International Covenant on Civil and Political Rights, "to take part in the conduct of public affairs, directly or through freely chosen representatives." The exercise of this right is enhanced by providing citizens access to all draft and effective laws, transcripts of parliamentary debates, and other information relevant to civic affairs.

New communications technologies are providing developing countries with an unprecedented means to leapfrog antiquated communication networks. Limits on access are imposed by governments for a variety of reasons, including economic gain and political control. Some governments, including India and Saudi Arabia, have chosen to control the liberalizing effect of the Internet by denying access to entire segments of their populations, either through exorbitant charges or by confining access to select populations, such as universities. Rather than attempting to extend the Internet to a diverse group of citizens, these governments are striving to reap the economic benefits of Internet access without making it available to economically, socially, and politically disadvantaged groups, for whom it has the greatest potential for positive change. In some countries, such as Saudi Arabia, individuals who have Internet connections through foreign-owned corporations are able to elude these restrictions.

Privacy issues are closely related to the regulation of content and access. On-line communications are particularly susceptible to unauthorized scrutiny. Encryption technology is needed to ensure that individuals and groups may communicate without fear of eavesdropping. The Internet has the potential to be a tremendous force for development by providing quick and inexpensive information, by encouraging discussion rather than violence, and by empowering citizens, to cite but a few examples. But this potential can be realized only if it becomes a truly global effort. Policy makers must make every effort to ensure that internationally guaranteed rights to free expression are extended to on-line communication and call for the repeal of censorship legislation. Without such commitments, individuals face the danger of seeing their rights eroded by the very technologies they are embracing.

A government agency can violate the privacy of e-mail correspondence just as easily as it can tap a person's telephone in order to listen to conversations or intercept faxes. The equipment needed is neither costly nor complicated to operate. Authorities can monitor by tapping an individual phone line and intercepting data streams as they are sent and received. If a user has Internet access via a private ISP, employees of that ISP can open and read e-mail sent through it or allow police investigators to do so, unless special safeguards are put in place to protect privacy. If authorities have access to an ISP's server or the country's telecommunications network, they can capture e-mails while they are in transit. Authorities can read, block, or delete messages based on such criteria as the e-mail address of the sender or the recipient, the Internet Protocol addresses identifying the sending computer and the destination computer(s), or the presence of specified character strings in the body of the message--say, the words "Emir" and "corruption" in close proximity. Such a system is analogous to a postal delivery system in which all pieces of mail are first delivered to a single location, where officials can inspect items at will.

Although data is broken up and sent in "packets," each packet contains Internet Protocol (IP) addresses. Packets can easily be reassembled while en route with the aid of eavesdropping tools. An eavesdropper can generally identify the computer terminal that is sending or receiving data, but not the person who is typing on its keyboard. For this reason, some governments are uneasy about allowing computer terminals with Internet access in places where extra effort would be required to monitor who is using each terminal, for what, and when. A contract provided by Tunisia's state-run Agence

Tunisienne d'Internet (ATI) requires institutional Internet subscribers to refrain from offering anyone remote access via their computers without prior authorization, and to declare to the ATI the names of all persons having accounts on, or access to, the computers and to inform the agency of changes in the user list.

Expression via the Internet includes the use of means that are private and others that are public. E-mail is private in the sense that the sender specifies the persons and addresses to whom it will be sent. By contrast, launching an open-access web site or posting a comment in a public newsgroup are acts of public speech since they are viewable by anyone who wishes to visit the web site or newsgroup. Computer users have various means to protect their privacy and anonymity, some more effective than others. At the low-tech end, a user can try to avoid surveillance by using a computer terminal or e-mail account that is not being monitored, for example, one belonging to a friend. These techniques may help users escape identification if they are not already under surveillance, but they are no insurance against interception if a user's computer communication is being monitored. Experts agree that there are basically three methods that, for the time being at least, make surveillance extremely difficult: direct-to-satellite and other forms of wireless transmission, anonymous re-mailers, and encryption. Small dishes are available that enable users to transmit and receive data directly via satellite, bypassing the ground-based telecommunication system. These fit into a suitcase-sized carrying case and can be placed discreetly on a balcony while in use. They resemble in size the "pizza" dishes used to download satellite television broadcasts, but are capable of sending as well as receiving.

Some countries of the Middle East and North Africa either ban or require permits for direct-to-satellite dishes. Cost also puts this technology beyond the reach of most individuals and nongovernmental organizations in the region. But as they grow more affordable and widespread, wireless communications offer a potent means of evading government monitoring and censorship. Encryption, on the other hand, costs nothing or next to nothing. Strong and easy-to-use encryption software, such as the "Pretty Good Privacy" (PGP) program, can be downloaded for free from the World Wide Web and stored on a laptop or personal computer.

While experts using powerful computers have been able to break strong encryption codes, the process requires considerable resources and time and is impractical for routine monitoring. Users should nevertheless pay attention to developments in the field--as well as to local laws governing the use of encryption. The Global Internet Liberty Campaign maintains a country-by-country review of legislation. The right to encrypt messages is of particular importance to the protection of human rights. In many countries human rights organizations use PGP to protect the identity of witnesses and victims when sending data electronically. Rights groups in Guatemala, Ethiopia, Haiti, Mexico, South Africa, Hong Kong, and Turkey are among those that use encryption, according the GILC survey. Some groups use cryptographic techniques to digitally sign messages that they send over the Internet to ensure their integrity and authenticity, that is, to prove the messages are indeed coming from them and have not been altered in transmission. The power of encryption to foil monitoring has led a number of governments to impose restrictions on the use, sale, and export of encryption software. Tunisia, Saudi Arabia, and Israel are among those countries that ban the use of encryption without prior authorization. Encryption has an Achilles heel: it may effectively shield a message's contents from an eavesdropper but not the fact that something has been encoded. This alone may lead to harsh consequences if the authorities wish to punish the sender or recipient, or coerce them to disclose the message's contents or their "private keys." Upon obtaining the latter, authorities could then read every message encrypted with the user's "public key" or use the compromised private key to impersonate that user in corresponding with others.

One way to circumvent this danger is to camouflage encrypted messages by using steganography. This type of program hides one form of data inside another in such a way that makes it more likely to escape detection by interlopers. For example, a sensitive document proving that a police unit moonlighted as a death squad can be encrypted and embedded in a photograph of a soccer team, and then e-mailed to a person outside the country who has the means to extract the document. Steganography software can be downloaded for free from the World Wide Web. However, some experts warn that sophisticated eavesdroppers can detect when a file has something steganographically hidden in it. The third anti-surveillance strategy is to route communications via secure and trusted web-based re-mailing services that forward them to the designated recipient only after expunging the original address and other identifying data. To reduce traceability further, users can select re-mailers that keep no records of the addresses from which they receive, and to which they send, data. They can also program messages to pass through more than one re-mailer; some re-mailers do this automatically.

Protecting Freedom of Expression on the net

In 1948 proclamation of the international human right to freedom of expression, the citizens of the world have the ability to exercise that right on a truly global basis, "regardless of frontiers." With the advent of the Internet, methods of accessing and disseminating information have been fundamentally changed, with profound implications for individuals, civil society and governments.

Like no medium before it, the Internet permits any individual with a computer and a gateway to the Internet to communicate instantaneously with others worldwide. The Internet offers educational institutions, businesses, and non-profit organizations an opportunity to exchange ideas and promote scientific, cultural, and economic progress. Traditional forms of media can greatly expand their audiences at nominal cost.

The Internet is global in its reach. To a degree that no other technology can, it transcends national borders and eliminates barriers to the free flow of information. These unique features of this new technology, if properly supported, can foster the freedom of expression essential to democratic rule and civil society in ways previously impossible.

The Global Internet Liberty Campaign is a group of human rights and civil liberties organizations that advocate the following:

— Prohibiting prior censorship of on-line communication.

— Requiring that laws restricting the content of on-line speech distinguish between the liability of content providers and the liability of data carriers.

— Insisting that on-line free expression not be restricted by indirect means such as excessively restrictive governmental or private controls over computer hardware or software, telecommunications infrastructure, or other essential components of the Internet.

— Including citizens in the Global Information Infrastructure (GII) development process from countries that are currently unstable economically, have insufficient infrastructure, or lack sophisticated technology.

— Prohibiting discrimination on the basis of race, color, sex, language, religion, political or other opinion, national or social origin, property, birth or other status.

— Ensuring that personal information generated on the Internet for one purpose is not used for an unrelated purpose or disclosed without the person's informed consent and enabling individuals to review personal information on the Internet and to correct inaccurate information.

— Allowing on-line users to encrypt their communications and information without restriction..

Governments, however, have already begun to impose controls on the Internet, threatening the potential of this new medium. Some governments have enacted laws prohibiting certain content on the Internet and have sought to prosecute users and service providers. Others have tried to control access, by insisting on the installation of national "proxy servers" and requiring the blocking of targeted web sites.

And in other countries, governments have encouraged forms of "self-regulation" that are in fact intended to enlist service providers to control the behavior of their customers.

An increasingly well-established body of international law protects the right to freedom of expression. As we shall see, various human rights instruments are diluted by exceptions and may be difficult to enforce. Moreover, not all countries are parties to a binding human rights agreement.

But international human rights law undoubtedly has advanced the cause of free expression and undoubtedly applies to the Internet and other digital media. Given the broad language of international and regional human rights documents, there is no doubt that government measures to control the Internet are subject to challenge under international law.

The technology itself both demands and can support fuller protection of free expression: The borderless nature of the Internet requires that the phrase "regardless of frontiers," which appears in the key international human rights instruments, be applied with a fresh eye.

The concept of a right to "impart" information takes on new meaning when anyone can be a publisher. Since censorship in one country may constitute a direct infringement on the right of persons in other countries to "impart" information "without regard to frontiers," the traditional deference given to local norms should be less relevant to the Internet.

The decentralized nature of the Internet makes government controls less effective, because Internet users have numerous ways of circumventing them. At the same time, the user-controlled nature of the technology means that government controls are less necessary in some contexts.

Furthermore, given the essentially unlimited capacity of the Internet, there is less need for government intervention to ensure fairness or balance or to protect reputation. On the Internet, the marketplace of ideas can function with less regulation since good ideas can always achieve the space they deserve. Mistakes can be corrected and the right of reply can be effectuated instantaneously.

Under international law, necessity, proportionality, and efficacy are key concepts in judging the validity of restrictions on freedom of expression. If government regulation of content on the Internet is not likely to succeed and not necessary, then it becomes less supportable under international rules.

Applying international human rights principles to the Internet requires an appreciation of the fundamental characteristics of the digital on-line media. The unique qualities of the Internet justify according the strongest protection to free expression on-line and should prompt a new vision of the right to receive and impart information "regardless of frontiers."

The Internet is really a network of networks and is comprised of a number of different technologies and infrastructures. Viewed as a whole, it is uniquely:

— *Global* - The Internet provides immediate access to information from around the world. With simple e-mail, it is as easy to send a message to another continent as it is to the building next door. Through the World Wide Web, thousands of newspapers and tens of thousands of other information sources are available from around the world. While access is still not available to most of the world's population, the fastest rates of growth are in less developed countries.

— *Decentralized* - The Internet was designed by purpose to be decentralized, to work without gatekeepers, and to accommodate multiple, competitive access points. The absence of gatekeepers of the kind that exist in broadcasting, cable television, or satellite transmission, the availability of numerous hosting sites, and the irrelevance of geographic location mean that material can almost always be published outside the control of governments, monopolies or oligopolies.

— *Open* - The Internet has low barriers to access. Service can be priced very inexpensively. The costs of creating and disseminating content are extreme-ly low. Because of the Internet, anybody who has a computer and a modem can be a publisher - a digital Gutenberg.

— *Abundant* - The digitization of information and the ability to transmit it over the telephone network, combined with the decentralized nature of the Internet, mean that the Internet has essentially unlimited capacity to hold information. In economic terms, the marginal cost of adding another web site, sending another email message, or posting to a newsgroup is essentially zero.

— *Interactive* - The Internet is designed for bi-directional communication: All Internet users can be both speakers and listeners. The Internet allows responsive communication from one-to-one, from one-to-many, and from many-to-one.

— *User-Controlled* - The Internet allows users to exercise far more choice than even cable television or short wave radio. The user can skip from site to site in ways that are not dictated by the content providers or by the access provider. User can control what content reaches their computers.

— *Infrastructure independent* - The Internet is not linked to any infrastructure other than the telephone system. Dial-up access is available from any telephone that can make an international call. Access to the Internet can also be wireless and satellite based and therefore further removed from effective control of governments. Courts and other institutions that have considered in depth the question of Internet regulation have recognized these unique features.

A unique characteristic of the Internet is that it functions simultaneously as a medium for publishing and for communication. Unlike in the case of traditional media, the Internet supports a variety of communication modes: one-to-one, one-to-many, many-to-many.

An Internet user may "speak" or "listen" interchangeably. At any given time, a receiver can and does become content provider, of his own accord, or through "re-posting" of content by a third party. The Internet therefore is radically different from traditional broadcasting. It also differs radically from a traditional telecommunication service."

The United States Supreme Court, in ruling that the Communications Decency Act was unconstitutional and that the Internet merited the strongest protection of free expression, based its judgment on the conclusion that the Internet was "a unique and wholly new medium of worldwide human communication."

The Internet Promote Democracy

The vast new potential of the Internet for expanding access to information and participation in government and civil society has already begun to show itself with concrete contributions to democracy and human rights.

The bi-directional nature of the Internet has tremendous potential for fostering democratic participation, giving voice to the voiceless. The Internet could allow citizens to communicate with their government, to pose questions to their elected representatives, and to submit comments on pending issues. While many governments have been slow to take advantage of the democratic potential of the Internet, some harbingers of progress can be seen.

The Costa Rican government, to make voting more convenient, is working to shift to an electronic voting system. Taking advantage of a literacy rate of 94% and the fact that about 50% of grade schools have Internet-connected computers, Costa Rica hopes to run an entirely electronic balloting in 2002. International bodies also use the Internet to promote public participation in their activities. For example, last year the EU conducted an online forum regarding illegal or harmful content on the Internet. Grassroots organizations can use the Internet to mobilize voters to be active on issues.

One of the most important potential benefits of the Internet is the ability to provide rapid access to the full text of government documents. If a government is willing, it can provide its citizens access to enacted and proposed laws, regulations, government reports and statistics, transcripts of parliamentary debates, judicial decisions, all searchable by word or concept.

Information previously available only to experts, usually only in the capital city, and often only with great expenditure of time and money can now be made available to individuals in the smallest rural town and at public libraries in the poorest neighborhoods. This vast openness need not be the luxury of only wealthy nations.

Strengthening civil society through the building of networks among individuals The Internet has opened up new opportunities for discourse, on matters political, intellectual, and personal. The Internet's architecture allows for a diversity of views and exchange of information that is simply not possible in any other media. As of August 1998, one service identified 29,000 IRC (Internet Relay Chat) channels, 30,000 Usenet newsgroups, and 90,095 mailing lists - each one representing a network of individuals worldwide interested in a particular subject.

Among the first to use the Internet were human rights activists. In 1992, the International Freedom of Expression exchange (IFEX) was established to provide accurate and timely information regarding censorship and attacks on journalists. The primary method of transmitting information is by e-mail: whenever there is a serious threat to freedom of expression, the IFEX action alert network sends out detailed information on the case via e-mail to participating organizations and individuals, who in turn mount international protests from their own regions. The Internet has been at the forefront of democratic uprisings. In Indonesia, "Bypassing the government-controlled television and radio stations, dissidents shared information about protests by e-mail, inundated news groups with stories of President Suharto's corruption, and used chat groups to exchange tips about resisting troops."

The Web has become a place where there is ready access to newspapers and other publications. A wide range of print publications are available on-line, and many broadcast media now have on-line services that allow searching of past broadcasts, a capability previously available only to governments and a few research institutes.

Information is exchanged via a centrai computer located in Paris. AIM texts are available in Serbian, Croatian, Bosnian, and a choice of texts is available in English. Subscribers to AIM regularly receive the whole production of AIM via e-mail. The China News Digest makes available news from non-official sources. While the site is sometimes blocked by the Chinese government, users in China have found ways to access it. The service also uses e-mail to disseminate its news within China.

With the Internet, it is increasingly difficult for governments to control content. The Internet offers creative ways to disseminate information around the controls of censors. Once an issue is ready to be published, it is secretly delivered to the United States and then emailed back to China from an anonymous address.

The technology of the Internet frustrates control in other ways. Proxy servers purportedly block access to web sites known to contain objectionable content and thus preclude such content from being accessed. Such servers fail to achieve their goal, however, because:

1) web site operators whose sites are targeted as containing undesirable content can simply change their web site address; and

2) an Internet user in a country imposing controls can simply dial into a server outside the country and

access the desired information, thereby avoiding the proxy server altogether.

Given the global nature of the Internet, content can be published from anywhere in the world. When a government tries to prosecute a content provider or force the withdrawal of material, there are others around the world prepared to copy or mirror the information on their own sites, in countries where the information is legal.

Governments' Control on Internet content and Access

Despite the power of the Internet - or perhaps because of that very power - governments have sought to restrict it. Government actions infringing freedom of expression on the Internet take many forms:

— *Internet-specific laws*: Some governments have criminalized certain types of speech on the Internet. Such criminal penalties may come in the form of laws whose expressed intent is to protect minors from certain material regarded as "harmful." However, as the United States Supreme Court recently found, requiring that Internet speakers shield certain populations from their speech is effectively a total ban on that speech.

— *Application of existing laws*: Governments can act to restrict speech without specifically enacting laws targeting Internet-based speech. For example, German government action against CompuServe for providing access to material illegal under German law did not require enactment of new law, merely the assertion by government agents that certain Internet speech violated the existing laws.

— *Content-based license terms applied to Internet users and service providers*: Several countries have already established licensing systems that require Internet users and/or service providers to agree to refrain from certain kinds of speech, or block access to speech as a condition of having a license to use the Internet or provide access to the Net. China has issued rules requiring anyone with Internet access to refrain from proscribed speech. And the Singapore Broadcasting Authority requires all Internet Service Providers to abide by licensing terms demanding that they block access to foreign web sites and newsgroups deemed harmful to national morals.

— *Compelled use of filtering, rating or content labeling tools*: Blocking, filtering, and labeling techniques can prevent individuals from using the Internet to exchange information on topics that may be controversial or unpopular, enable the development of country profiles to facilitate a global/universal rating system desired by some governments, block access to content on entire domains, block access to Internet content available at any domain or page which contains a specific key word or character string in the address, and over-ride self-rating labels provided by content creators and providers. Where any such mechanisms are required by public authorities or otherwise forced on users, they constitute serious threats to human rights.

Over the past half-century, international human rights law has enshrined the rights to free expression, access to information, and privacy of communications, creating a strong presumption against governmental intrusions. These rights are reflected both in the provisions of numerous international and regional agreements and in decisions rendered by human rights tribunals. These human rights doctrines protecting freedom of expression are fully applicable to the Internet. Indeed, these protections may offer especially strong protection to the Internet, given its unique features. These human rights instruments have their limitations. The Universal Declaration has been accepted in effect by all 185 Member States of the United Nations, but not all of its provisions have become binding.

The International Covenant on Civil and Political Rights is binding, but its enforcement mechanisms are limited. While there are binding regional agreements for the Americas, for Europe, and for Africa, there are none for Asia or the Middle East. Enforcement mechanisms are available under these regional agreements, but they are limited too. Where individual review is available, the time required to pursue a case all the way to the international level may be substantial. Most importantly, these instruments, particularly the European Convention, are burdened with exceptions that have been seriously criticized as over-broad.

Nonetheless, these human rights agreements have served to expand freedom of expression worldwide, becoming part of international law and affecting the domestic laws of many nations. The numerous international and regional instruments discussed herein provide substantial evidence that the principle of free expression is a well-settled principle of international law.

The collection of treaties, agreements, and international tribunal decisions also evidences an international consensus on the scope of this right: it applies to all forms of media, it applies to the ability to receive and to impart information, and it is subject to only limited restrictions. The advent of the Internet raises the question of how these human rights instruments apply to the new communications media. The answers are in some respects encouraging: the instruments are drafted with very forward-looking language, with powerful implications for a medium that operates "regardless of frontiers."

The international community has stated its commitment to the right to free expression in a series of fundamental agreements, including the Universal Declaration of Human Rights, the International Covenant on Civil and Political Rights, and the International Covenant on Economic, Social and Cultural Rights. The right of free expression was first proclaimed an international norm by the then-members of the United Nations in the 1948 Universal Declaration of Human Rights. Taken together, Articles 19, 12, and 27 of the Universal Declaration constitute a blueprint for the protection of free expres-sion on the Internet. Article 19 of the Universal Declaration proclaims: "Everyone has the right to freedom of opinion and expression; this right includes freedom to hold opinions without interference and to seek, receive and impart information and ideas through any medium and regardless of frontiers."

Article 12 of the Universal Declaration provides: "No one shall be subjected to arbitrary interference with his privacy, family, home or correspondence." The language of this provision is broad enough to encompass all communications directed to an individual or group of individuals, including electronic mail and newsgroup communications. Finally, the right to seek, receive and impart information guaranteed in Article 19 of the Universal Declaration is reinforced by Article 27, which upholds the right of each individual "freely to participate in the cultural life of the community, to enjoy the arts and to share in scientific advancement and its benefits." Given that the Internet's roots are in the exchange of scientific information, Article 27 seems particularly apt to the protection of communications on the Internet. The foresightful language of Article 19 ("through any medium") makes it clearly applicable to expression via the Internet. The rights to "seek" and "impart" information seem particularly relevant to "surfing" the 'Net and posting information on Web sites for all to read, while the right to "receive" information encompasses the exchange of electronic mail and the downloading of information.

Article 29(2) provides: "In the exercise of his rights and freedoms, everyone shall be subject only to such limitations as are determined by law solely for the purpose of securing due recognition and respect for the rights and freedoms of others and of meeting the just requirements of morality, public order and the general welfare in a democratic society."The Universal Declaration is not a treaty. It was adopted by the United Nations General Assembly as a resolution having no force of law on its own. However, over time the Declaration has become a normative instrument that creates some legal obligations for Member States of the UN. Many of the principles established by the Universal Declaration have since entered the corpus of international law as evidenced by an overwhelming consensus of opinion and practice among states. This consensus is illustrated in subsequent international and regional treaties and agreements, decisions of international tribunals, and domestic constitutions and legislation. Further, the Declaration has served as an inspiration for other human rights agreements of more direct effect.

The United Nations Commission on Human Rights was created in 1946 under Article 68 of the UN Charter. States name representatives to the 53 member Commission, where they serve as instructed governmental delegates. The Commission prepares reports and coordinates an expansive network of working groups and rapporteurs with thematic or country mandates. It has been criticized for being politically motivated and selective in approach, but it serves as the principal UN forum for addressing charges of human rights violations and as a focal point for broadening the human rights agenda of the UN.

International Covenant on Civil and Political Rights The principles first enunciated in the Universal Declaration are reiterated and expanded upon in the 1966 International Covenant on Civil and Political Rights ("ICCPR"), which took effect in 1976 and has now been ratified by 140 nations. Article 19 of the ICCPR restates Article 19 of the Universal Declaration almost verbatim. It declares: "Everyone shall have the right to hold opinions without interference. ... Everyone shall have the right to freedom of expression... ." In words somewhat more expansive than the Universal Declaration, Article 19 of the ICCPR expressly states that the freedom of expression extends to all forms of media: "this right shall include freedom to seek, receive and impart information and ideas of all kinds, regardless of frontiers, either orally, in writing or in print, in the form of art, or through any other media of his choice." The ICCPR also reiterates the crux of Article 12 of the Universal Declaration: "No one shall be subjected to arbitrary or unlawful interference with his privacy, family, home or correspondence." The ICCPR defines the scope of limitations that could be imposed on the freedom of expression. Consistent with the law of most if not all nations, the ICCPR recognizes that freedom of expression may be curtailed under certain circumstances. The ICCPR requires, however, that restrictions on free speech be narrowly defined and not arbitrary. Article 19(3) of the ICCPR provides that restrictions on the freedom of expression are valid only where such restrictions are "provided by law and are necessary: a. For respect of the rights or reputation of others; [or] b. For the protection of national security or of public order, or of public health or morals."

The essence of applying the ICCPR involves interpreting this limitation. It has been urged that this provision means that laws restricting freedom of expression must be "accessible, unambiguous, drawn narrowly, and with precision." Moreover, the burden of demonstrating the validity of a restriction on free speech should lie with the government. The key hurdle for governments is the requirement that restrictions be "necessary;" this has generally been interpreted as a high standard. The ICCPR includes several other provisions relevant to freedom of expression. Article 17 provides, "No one shall be subjected... to unlawful attacks on his honour and reputation. ... Everyone has the right to the protection of the law against such... attacks." Article 20 states, "Any advocacy of national, racial, or religious hatred that constitutes incitement to discrimination, hostility or violence shall be prohibited by law."Under the Covenant, States Parties are required to submit reports every five years on the measures they have taken to protect and advance human rights. The Covenant established a Human Rights Committee, one of the principal functions of which is to examine these reports. The Committee makes conclusions on individual state reports and also issues general comments, which serve as advisory opinions on the Covenant. In 1976, an optional protocol went into force which enables private parties to file individual complaints against States Parties that have ratified the covenant. The protocol is itself a treaty, and therefore binds the states that have ratified it. Complainants must exhaust domestic remedies first. Once a complaint has been admitted as properly drawn, the Committee brings the matter to the attention of the state involved, which has six months to respond. The Committee, after considering all the written communications on the matter, issues its "views." The Committee has no power to enforce its findings, but it does require States Parties to indicate in their periodic reports what measures they have taken to give effect to the Committee's recommendations. "In particular, the State Party should indicate what remedy it has afforded the author of the communication whose rights the Committee has found to have been violated."

Restrictions on the Internet also implicate rights established by the International Covenant on Economic, Social, and Cultural Rights ("ICESCR"). Echoing Article 27 of the Universal Declaration, Article 15 of the ICESCR recognizes the important "benefits to be derived from the encouragement and development of international contacts and cooperation in the scientific and cultural fields." Accordingly, the 136 signatories pledge to "diffuse science and culture" and to "respect the freedom indispensable for scientific research and creative activity." These provisions articulate that free expression across borders must be respected to realize social, scientific, and cultural advancements. To take advantage of such progress, Article 15 of the ICESCR establishes that all individuals are entitled "to enjoy the benefits of scientific progress and its applications." One of the most effective means of doing so is through Internet communication, which enables people in distant and diverse countries to share valuable scientific research and social insights.The ICESCR does not establish any interstate or individual complaint system. It only requires the States Parties to submit "reports on the measures which they have adopted and the progress made in achieving the observance of the rights recognized herein." Art. 16(1). Regional human rights agreements in Europe, the Americas, and Africa establish the right of free expression for all individuals and privacy in their communications with others. Such freedoms are protected in all forms of media and "regardless of frontiers." These regional agreements are especially important because of the opportunities they offer for international judicial review of actions restricting free expression.

The European Convention for the Protection of Human Rights and Fundamental Freedoms ("European Convention") was adopted in 1950 by members of the Council of Europe. Article 10 states in full: "(1) Everyone has the right to freedom of expression. This right shall include freedom to hold opinions and to receive and impart information and ideas without interference by public authority and regardless of frontiers. This Article shall not prevent States from requiring licensing of broadcasting, television or cinema enterprises. "(2) The exercise of these freedoms, since it carries with it duties and responsibilities, may be subject to such formalities, conditions, restrictions or penalties as are prescribed by law and are necessary in a democratic society, in the interests of national security, territorial integrity or public safety, for the prevention of disorder or crime, for the protection of health or morals, for the protection of the reputation or rights of others, for preventing the disclosure of information received in confidence, or for maintaining the authority and impartiality of the judiciary." The European Convention thus establishes that the right of free expression pertains to cross-border communication, which naturally applies to much of the content available on the Internet. Closely linked to freedom of expression are additional rights in the European Convention: the right to respect for correspondence and privacy, contained in Article 8; [24] the right to freedom of peaceful assembly and freedom of association, contained in Article 11; and the right to manifest one's religion or belief, contained in Article 9. Article 10 is not stated in absolute terms. The second paragraph specifies that freedom of expression can be curtailed in furtherance of a series of enumerated interests.

It has been widely debated whether these exceptions are too broad. But even in the U.S. and other countries with constitutional free speech provisions, restrictions are permitted through judicial interpretation. Supporters of Article 10's approach argue that Article 10 is preferable because the catalogue of possible restrictions is limited and because Article 10 also establishes that any restriction on the exercise of the freedom of expression must be "prescribed by law" and "necessary in a democratic society" to serve one of the enumerated interests. In specific situations, it has been found that there was no violation of Article 10 in: the application of blasphemy laws to seize a film, the UK's ban on broadcasting interviews with representatives of the IRA, prohibitions on Nazi material, laws against obscenity, even state disciplinary measures against a lawyer who used aggressive or insulting language.Article 10 must be interpreted in light of other Articles, notably Article 17, which states that nothing in the Convention creates a right to engage in activities "aimed at the destruction of any of the rights or freedoms set forth in the convention." Article 17, it has been held, was intended "to prevent totalitarian groups from exploiting, in their own interests, the principles enunciated in the convention." Accordingly, for example, the Court has concluded that it was not a violation of the Convention for the Netherlands to convict extremist right-wing Dutch politicians for distributing racist leaflets. Other provisions affecting the freedom of expression include Article 6, which guarantees the right to a fair trial, and the right to personal privacy in Article 8, which protects a person's honor and reputation against attack, both of which concepts are also reflected in Article 10(2) itself.

Most European countries that are party to the Convention have made it part of their national law, meaning that it can be invoked in the national courts. For many years, the UK declined to do this, but the Convention will be fully incorporated in UK law when the Human Rights Bill 1998 is enacted. The European Convention has an explicit enforcement mechanism based on judicial review by an independent regional tribunal, the European Court of Human Rights, located in Strasbourg. The most important feature of the Court's jurisdiction is that individuals can bring complaints against Contracting States alleging violations of the Convention. It is sufficient to note that individuals may bring their cases before the Court after exhausting local remedies and that an application must first be presented to the European Commission on Human Rights. The Commission decides on the admissibility of the complaint. Article 10 has a potential role in connection with competition law and rules on the free movement of goods and services. In addition, in its legislative capacity, the Council of the European Union has referred to Article 10 as a relevant norm for EU legislation. The Court's judgments on the merits are binding but declaratory in nature. The Court has no power to quash the impugned decisions of the national authorities. The Court may, however, award "just satisfaction" in the form of financial compensation. In most cases, States have been reasonably swift to make the changes in their laws and practices necessary to bring them into conformity with the Court's decision.

The European countries manifested their commitment to free speech in the Council of Europe's 1982 Declaration on the Freedom of Expression and Information. This Declaration reaffirms Article 10 of the European Convention and proclaims that the freedom of expression is "a fundamental element [of] the principles of genuine democracy, the rule of law and respect for human rights." The Declaration also provides that the freedom of expression and information is "necessary for the social, economic, cultural and political development of every human being, and constitutes a condition for the harmonious progress of social and cultural groups, nations and the international community." The Council of Europe Declaration thus recognizes that the freedom of expression serves not only an individual interest, but the interests of nation states and the international community as well. Significant in the context of Internet communication, the Council of Europe Declaration recognizes that "the continued development of information and communication technology should serve to further that right, regardless of frontiers, to express, seek, to receive and to impart information and ideas, whatever their source." To achieve this high level of protection, the Council of Europe member states agreed to the following objectives:

— "absence of censorship or any arbitrary controls or constraints on participants in the information process, on media content or on the transmission and dissemination of information;

— "the availability and access on reasonable terms to adequate facilities for the domestic and international transmission and dissemination of information and ideas; [and]

— "to ensure that new information and communication techniques and services, where available, are effectively used to broaden the scope of freedom of expression and information."

The 55-member Organization for Security and Co-operation in Europe ("OSCE"), formerly known as the Conference on Security and Co-operation in Europe, sponsored the 1990 Charter of Paris for a New Europe. Signed by 31 countries from Europe, Russia, Canada, and the United States, the Charter proclaims: "We affirm that, without discrimination, every individual has the right to freedom of thought, conscience and religion or belief, [and] freedom of expression." The OSCE's 1994 Budapest Summit Declaration, "Towards a Genuine Partnership in a New Era," complements the Charter by asserting that participating members "take as their guiding principle that they will safeguard" the right to freedom of expression and recognize that "independent and pluralistic media are essential to a free and open society." The Internet is the most "independent and pluralistic" of all media; it should therefore benefit from the strongest protection against restrictions on the free flow of information.OSCE member states also have committed to making "efforts to facilitate the freer and wider dissemination of information of all kinds [and] to encourage co-operation in the field of information." In accordance with this commitment, and in recognition of commitments made under the Universal Declaration and the ICCPR, the OSCE declared that its member states "will ensure that individuals can freely choose their sources of information."Finally, countries of the OSCE reaffirmed the ICCPR's limitations on the scope of permissible restrictions on the right of free expression. The 1990 Conference on the Human Dimension concluded that any restrictions on fundamental rights and freedoms must be (1) provided by law; (2) consistent with obligations under international law, particularly those made pursuant to the ICCPR and the Universal Declaration; and (3) must relate to one of the objectives of the applicable law and be strictly proportionate to the aim of that law.

Regional agreements from the Americas also explicitly embrace the freedom of expression. The American Declaration of the Rights and Duties of Man was the first international human rights instrument, predating even the Universal Declaration. Article IV of the American Declaration states: "Every person has the right to freedom of... expression and dissemination of ideas, by any medium whatsoever."The American Convention on Human Rights ("American Convention") was adopted in 1969 and entered into force in 1978. It is worth quoting in full, for several of its provisions are of particular relevance to current debates concerning the Internet:

"1. Everyone has the right to freedom of thought and expression. This right includes freedom to seek, receive, and impart information and ideas of all kinds, regardless of frontiers, either orally, in writing, in print, in the form of art, or through any other medium of one's choice.

"2. The exercise of the right provided for in the foregoing paragraph shall not be subject to prior censorship but shall be subject to subsequent imposition of liability, which shall be expressly established by law to the extent necessary to ensure:

a. respect for the rights or reputations of others; or

b. the protection of national security, public order, or public health or morals.

"3. The right of expression may not be restricted by indirect methods or means, such as the abuse of government or private controls over newsprint, radio broadcasting frequencies, or equipment used in the dissemination of information, or by any other means tending to impede the communication and circulation of ideas and opinions.

"4. Notwithstanding the provisions of paragraph 2 above, public entertainments may be subject by law to prior censorship for the sole purpose of regulating access to them for the moral protection of childhood and adolescence.

"5. Any propaganda for war and any advocacy of national, racial, or religious hatred that constitute incitements to lawless violence or to any other similar action against any person or group of persons on any grounds including those of race, color, religion,

> language, or national origin shall be considered as offenses punishable by law." As is the case with the international and European counterparts to these agreements, the plain language of the American Convention is clearly applicable to the Internet.

The American Convention has several features that go beyond other human rights instruments. For one, the American Convention explicitly states that the exercise of the right of freedom of expression "shall not be subject to prior censorship." The rule against prior censorship is also reinforced by Article 14, which provides for a right of reply by anyone inured by inaccurate or offensive statements or ideas disseminated to the general public. In a provision that may be relevant to the problems posed by Internet "self-regulation," the American Convention applies to private action and makes it clear that the right of expression may not be restricted by indirect methods or means. Article 13(3) provides that the "right of expression may not be restricted by indirect means, such as the abuse of government or private controls over newsprint, radio broadcasting frequencies, or equipment used in the dissemination of information, or by another means tending to impede the communication and circulation of ideas and opinions."

The American Convention, in language identical to the ICCPR, sets forth a list of permitted grounds for restriction, a list narrower than that in the European Convention: restrictions on speech must be "expressly established by law to the extent necessary to ensure [either] [r]espect for the rights or reputation of others... or [t]he protection of national security, public order, or public health or morals." Article 11 of the American Convention, like other international agreements, protects the privacy of personal communications: "No one may be the object of arbitrary or abusive interference with his private life, his family, his home, or his correspondence."

Undertaking a judicial case in order to advance the cause of human rights is always a risky business. It requires careful selection of the complainant, the respondent, and the forum. It calls for a clear-eyed weighing of the chances of success. A poorly conceived case can yield an adverse decision that represents a set back for the cause of liberty. Mindful of these concerns, it is clear that the international human rights instruments offer opportunities to NGOs seeking to challenge governmental regulation of Internet content and access. In some cases, the most promising venues may be under the regional agreements.

Under human rights principles, expression on the Internet will still be subject to restriction, but without the "margin of appreciation" that has supported restrictions in so many cases. The Internet requires the adoption of a true international standard of review, one that must look to consensus rules generally. The rise of the Internet also requires a reexamination of the meaning of the concept to "seek and receive" and to "impart" information. National restrictions on local speech have a direct and negative impact on the ability of Internet users around the world to "seek and receive" information and ideas, as well as their right to "impart" information. For example, if citizens of one country are prohibited from discussing political issues critically online, then not only are their rights infringed upon, but also the right of others around the world to "seek and receive" that information is directly implicated. Internet Service Providers (ISPs) play a special role in the operation of the Internet. While ISPs differ in nature from country to country, most people most of the time access the Internet through an ISP. The crucial role ISPs play in providing access to the Internet has made them the target of some governments' efforts to regulate content on the Internet. Those countries have assumed that if they can control ISPs, they can control content on the Internet. ISPs do not fit any of the existing media paradigms. They are very distinct from broadcasters. For this reason, it is not legitimate to subject them to regulatory structures designed for other technologies. There are two sets of arguments against making ISPs responsible for content they do not create. First, trying to make ISPs responsible for information that flows over their systems (but which they did not create) would fundamentally change the nature of the Internet and could destroy its power. Second, there is growing recognition that ISPs cannot technically assume responsibility for content they did not create. The task of sifting information is impossible. It would be so easy to encrypt content, to change addresses, to send images by email.

Technical factors prevent a service provider from blocking the free flow of information on the Internet. First, an Internet service provider cannot easily stop the incoming flow of material. No one can monitor the enormous quantity of network traffic, which may consist of hundreds of thousands of emails, newsgroup messages, files, and Web pages that pass through in dozens of text and binary formats, some of them readable only by particular proprietary tools. A number of countries have recognized, after considerable study and debate, that ISPs should not be liable for content they did not create. This reflects a judgment that while ISPs ought to provide law enforcement reasonable assistance in investigating criminal activity, confusing the role of private companies and police authorities risks substantial violation of individual civil liberties. In 1997, Germany adopted a Multimedia Law which provides that access providers are not responsible for any third-party content to which they only provide access. Providers also are not responsible for "any third-party content which they make available for use unless they have knowledge of such content and are technically able and can reasonably be expected to block the use of such content." In the United States, section 230 of the Communications Act, 47 United States Code sec.230, states "No Provider or user of an interactive computer service shall be treated as the publisher or speaker of any information provided by another information content provider." In adopting this provision, Congress specifically found that "the Internet and other interactive computer services offer a forum for a true diversity of political discourse, unique opportunities for cultural development, and myriad avenues for intellectual activity," and it said that its goal was "to promote the continued development of the Internet." In the EU and in a number of other countries, "self-regulation" has been offered as a viable alternative to governmental control of Internet content.

The use of the term "self-regulation" is a misnomer in the context of controlling speech on the Internet. In the normal sense of the phrase, "self-regulation" is when a group of people or companies decide that, in their own best interest, they should themselves regulate how they go about their joint interests. However, what is being suggested by the term "self-regulation" as applied to the Internet is not that ISPs as a group should regulate their own behavior, but rather that ISPs should regulate the behavior of their customers by taking down offensive websites or blocking offensive content. Under international law, privatized control may be harder to challenge. However, in a number of cases, it may be clear that the ISP is acting under pressure from the government and has, in essence become the agent of the government for carrying out a government policy. What is often promoted as Internet "self-regulation" is actually "privatized censorship." It is consistent with the fairly common occurrence of having a formerly direct government function turned over to a private business. The backing is still state power and government threat, but the actual implementation and mechanics of the suppression of material is delegated to a trade group. When ISPs come together to self-regulate certain classes of content in exchange for some limit on their liability for that content, the overwhelming tendency will be to censor more material, rather than less, in an effort by the ISPs to be certain that they have removed any material that might be illegal. Where ISPs are dependent on government grants of liability limitations, their "self-regulating" actions must satisfy the perceived demands of law enforcement, even if this results in removal of legal, protected speech.

5

Global ICT Scenario

Information and communication technologies (ICT) pursue two main goals: processing information (i.e. presenting it in various forms, storing it, searching for it, reproducing it, etc.) and transmitting information from one geographical point to another, from one person to another, to a group of people or to the whole community. So in a certain sense the development of ICTs reflects the development of human beings throughout history.

The second half of this century has witnessed the global phenomenon of an information explosion. The development of different electronic technologies has made it possible for millions of people to have fast access to huge information resources stored in different places on the planet, to communicate with each other and to handle information presented in various forms (text, graphics, video, sound, etc.).

Yet for the great majority of people in the world, traditional information technologies (postal services, press, radio and television) are still playing and no doubt will continue to play in the near future a much more important role than the ICTs such as electronic mail, multimedia and global computer networks. There are two main reasons for this : on the one hand, the use of these ICTs requires certain investments (the purchase of a computer, for instance) that still are too high in relation to average incomes in poor countries and, on the other hand, the ICTs need an adequate communication infrastructure, including telephone lines in sufficient number and quality.

The relations between the various technologies are complex. Postal services, for example, provide a channel for press distribution, in the same way that telecommunications channels provide an infrastructure for digital networks. Some technologies are more concerned with transporting information, while others are more concerned with its production.

Radio and television simultaneously produce and convey information, and are therefore of a different nature. The Persians were the first to establish a formal network to transmit messages across their empire, so the postal service is an ancient working technology.

It also plays an important role in the life of contemporary society because it is not only a media for a person-to-person communication, but also a media for the distribution of printed materials (newspapers, journals, magazines, advertising material, etc.). Clearly, the significance of postal service as a means of person-to-person communication is steadily declining, since contemporary technology offers much faster, more reliable and cheaper solutions.

For example, it takes only a few hours, or even just minutes, to deliver an e-mail message over the ocean, and it costs a few cents. Sending the same message to the same address by postal service takes days and costs dollars. The mail function of the postal service will, nevertheless, continue to play an important role at least in the near future, even in highly industrialized societies, as it is the only communication technology which can ensure the delivery of originals documents. Of course, modern Internet technologies also offer some solutions in this area, such as the delivery by e-mail of digitally signed messages, but these solutions are yet to be legally recognized by the great majority of countries.

The second function of the postal service as a means to distribute newspapers and other printed material in a community will no doubt survive, despite the development of modern technologies. Even the most devoted Internet users can hardly imagine themselves at the breakfast table looking at a computer monitor, rather than a newspaper, for a news item. One of the main indicators of the state of the postal services in a given region is the number of letter-post items posted per capita.

The exponential development of ICTs in industrialized countries has had practically no effect on the domestic postal service: the number of letter-post items posted per capita by the domestic services in industrialized countries has been growing steadily since 1985. However, the slight reduction in the number of international post items in industrialized countries could be a consequence of the development of Internet mailing and fax messaging.

A sharp disproportion between industrialized and developing countries in the availability of postal services. This could be the result of a whole group of factors, one of which is the higher illiteracy rate in some developing countries. The economic importance of the postal service should not be underestimated. As a public service, it has been considered for many years to be a state monopoly. However, the recent development of private delivery services has certainly created an entirely new situation, which puts strong pressure on traditional services.

The printed press is quite another type of information technology. Whereas the postal service is primarily used for of person-to-person communication, the main goal of the press is to deliver information to a large group of people, such as the population of a town or country.

Daily newspapers may be considered as a most significant part of the press, because they offer the latest information. The publishing of daily newspapers requires a highly-qualified staff of journalists and editors, as well as important infrastructures for the quick printing of a huge quantity of material, and fast and reliable delivery services. For this reason, the number of titles of daily newspapers as well as figures for their total circulation are good indicators of the situation of the press in the various regions of the world.

Today, telecommunications are one of the most important of the contemporary ICTs. They include wired and wireless telephony; different mobile services, such as cellular telephones and paging; voice and data transmission; and Integrated Services Digital Networks (ISDN), which provide a very high quality of voice as well as high data communication rates. Existing telephone networks are now also used as a compiement to computer networks, including the Internet and other wide area networks (WAN).

Yet since their very origins at the beginning of this century, the main goal of telecommunications has remained that of providing better, faster and more reliable person-to-person communication. This is why radio paging is usually considered to be a telecommunications service, in contrast to videotext for example, which is considered by many experts to be a television service. Telecommunications are a rapidly developing and highly profitable business.

International Telecommunication Union (ITU), in 1996 the world total telecommunication investment was about $109,670 million, whereas the world total telecommunication revenue was about $515,490 million. Telecommunications revenues are generated mainly by two sources: equipment trading and communication charges.

According to the International Trade Centre data, the top ten major world exporters (manufacturers) of telecommunications equipment are: the United States, Japan, Germany, the United Kingdom, Sweden, Singapore, France, China, the Republic of Korea and Canada. It may be noted that the list of the top ten major exporters and importers of telecommunications equipment is identical, except for Hong Kong, which replaces Sweden in the list of the top ten main importers.

The development of the global situation concerning the availability of telecommunication services may be characterized by the growth in the number of telephone lines (both main and cellular) per capita in different geographical regions. Cellular telephony is becoming more and more popular throughout the world, mostly in the developed countries.

In 1997 according to data from Ericsson, one of the world's leading manufacturers of telecommunication equipment, the total number of cellular subscribers in the world increased from 70 million to 207 million. Among them more than 112 million are subscribers to digital cellular networks and about 9 5 million are subscribers to analog cellular networks. The highest number of cellular networks subscribers is in North America, with about 60 million, followed by Western Europe with 57 million, Asia and the Pacific with 40 million, Japan with 29 million and Latin America with 13 million. The rest of the world numbers 8 million subscribers.

There will be 830 million subscribers to cellular networks by 2003, and an average annual growth rate between 1998 and 2003 of 27%. By the end of 2003 nearly 15% of the world's population will subscribe to cellular telephone networks. Among them will be almost 60% of the population of Japan, more than 50% of the population of North America and about 50% of the population of Western Europe.

Another popular mobile telecommunication service is radio paging. It is cheaper than mobile telephones, which usually include a radio paging mode. Radio paging is most popular in Asian countries. In 1996, according to the ITU data in 1996 Singapore and the Republic of Korea had the highest number of radio paging subscribers per 100 inhabitants - 35 and 28 respectively.

In comparison, for Hungary which has the highest number in Europe. It is interesting to note that the ITU data show that normally in those countries where figures of cellular subscribers per 100 inhabitants are high, the corresponding figures for radio paging ·subscribers are relatively small, and vice versa. The situation in the European countries confirms this observation. Cellular telephones and other mobile services are now a top advantage of telecommunication technology.

Integrated services digital networks (ISDN) are another leader. As with cellular telephones, the use of ISDN in a given region reflects the state of development of the most contemporary telecommunications technologies.

There are 22% are in the United States and 3% in the rest of the world. The world leader in the number of ISDN channels and subscribers, in 1996, was Germany, with 5,150,000 channels and 1,945,000 subscribers. There is very slight development in the rest of the world, and a sharp disproportion between industrialised and developing countries in the availability of telecommunication services, even such traditional ones as wired telephony. However, the example of China shows that some developing countries have great potential in manufacturing telecommunication equipment, and are thus capable of improving the availability of telecommunication services. The development of telecommunication services in a given region has a vital impact on the development of the Internet for which they provide the necessary infrastructure, as they do for other wide area networks (WANs).

The Internet and other Networks

Digital networks include the Internet, intranets and WANs and share several features including the large amount of data transmitted, the high speed of transmission and the use of digital technologies and data transmission protocols. While these features make digital networks different from the other telecommunication networks, they are not isolated from them. For instance, the 'last mile' by which a user reaches the Internet is often the common telephone wire.

Furthermore, it is convenient to distinguish the Internet, which is based on the TCP/IP protocol, from other WANs, which are most often based on other protocols such as X.25 or the asynchronous transmission protocol (ATM). There are also gateways among the networks. For instance, a subscriber to America On Line (AOL), which is a private commercial WAN, can access the Internet, and conversely Internet users can, under certain conditions, access various other WANs. Private WANs based on TCP/IP protocol are called intranets and can also be linked to the Internet and other WANs.

In an international market forecast published in 1997, the International Data Corporation estimated that the total compound annual growth rate of the purchase of products and services related to the use of Internet between 1996 and 2000 would be 49.5%. Other sources give different estimates for the Internet turnover in 1996: the total varies from $9,000 million to $10,000 million, including from $500 million to $530 million for retail trade, about $600 million for business-to-business trade, $200 million for information and the same figure for financial services.

The main indicators of the Internet and other WAN development appear to demonstrate extremely high annual growth rates, but the divergence between industrialized countries and the rest of the world still remains significant. According to various sources, the Internet is little by little becoming less exclusive.

Radio and Television

Both radio and television produce and distribute informations via their own channels. In both, although ICT production is technically separated from distribution, the two processes do coexist in these media. It may be that the educational levels of radio and television audiences are lower in comparison with those of newspaper readers or Internet users: a subscriber to a newspaper cannot be illiterate, in contrast to a radio listener or television viewer. It is also true that listening to the radio or watching television is less costly than subscribing to a newspaper or using the Internet.

Radio, for which it is sufficient to make a fairly small investment only once, is the cheapest. Finally, poor communities need not invest in their own radio or television industry since they may listen to radio or watch television programmes produced by other countries. All these considerations explain the fact that radio and television are the most available and widespread ICTs in the world, both in developing and developed countries with radio in first place.

The difference between the developed and developing countries in the availability of radio is not so sharp as in the case of printed press. Moreover, the share of developing countries in the list of the top ten world manufacturers of television receivers and radio receivers is quite large. The top ten television exporters are Mexico, the Republic of Korea, Malaysia, Japan, the United Kingdom, Singapore, Thailand, France, Germany and Spain; the top ten radio receiver exporters are Malaysia, China, Singapore, Japan, Mexico, the United States, the Netherlands, Portugal, Germany, Belgium-Luxembourg.

According to BIPE Conseil data, in the European Union Countries, television and other home appliances such as VCRs and camcorders still represent about 58% of expenditures on hardware equipment for home use, whereas expenditure on special hardware for multimedia is only 1%. This implies that multimedia per se is of very little interest for the population of this region and is more commonly used with computer equipment.

Since multimedia is basically a form of representing information, this situation is not surprising. In addition, expenditures on personal computers for use in the home are only slightly less than expenditures on television sets. This seems to indicate that the home software industry and home use of the Internet have a bright future in industrialized countries. Radio and television are clearly the most available ICTs in the world, and their development still has good prospects in both industrialized and developing countries.

Sub Saharan Africa

The sub-Saharan countries are often divided into the socio-geographic groups of East, West, Central and Southern Africa, of which West Africa is the most populous. There are also many other country groupings around areas of common interest. The most important of these are the Economic Community of West African States (ECOWAS), Common Market for Eastern and Southern Africa (COMESA), Southern African Development Corporation (SADC), Central African Customs and Economic Union (UDEAC), East African Co-operation, the Customs Union of the Southern Africa, L'Agence de la Franco-phonie, the Commonwealth and the Lomé Convention African Caribbean and Pacific (ACP) countries.

The region's population was estimated at 636 million people for 1998 - about 9% of the total world population of 5.7 billion. Nigeria has by far the largest number of people at 122 million. Ten countries have populations above 15 million, with the five largest countries comprising 50% of the subcontinent's total population. Growing at 3% annually, an additional 20 million people a year are being added to the subcontinent. Population density is relatively low - only 24 people per square kilometer - compared to a world average of 43 and an Asian average of 110. At the same time, the degree of urbanization is low - only 32% of the region's people live in cities, as compared with 78% for high-income countries.

There is a high level of ethnic and linguistic diversity: several thousand identifiable ethnic groups and about 1,300 distinct spoken languages characterize this region. The national boundaries of most of the countries were imposed by the colonial powers and as a result language groups overflow them.

Information and use of communication tools in SSA have until very recently been almost entirely in the hands of state monopolies. Now that the trend towards democracy and more liberal market-oriented policies has become established on the continent, there has been a marked improvement in the availability and diversity of information and communication channels. Rates of telephone line growth are at their highest levels ever, hundreds of new media outlets in print, radio and television have emerged in the last couple of years and in 1998 the Internet was locally available in the capital of every country in Africa. These changes coincide with an estimated average 4.7% growth in Gross Domestic Product (GDP) in 1998.

After years of stagnation, these growth levels are close to those in Asia, and in the wake of the Asian financial turmoil, it is likely that Africa may even surpass Asia as the fastest growing region in the world. The information revolution is often said to be Africa's 'last chance to catch up' and it is already clear that a number of African countries have committed themselves to joining the Global Information Society.

Most of the advances have taken place only in the latter half of this decade and are not yet reflected in many of the official statistics available, for which 1995 is the latest year published. As a result, the degree of change is not been as evident as it should be. This has in part given rise to efforts by progressive African leaders such as Presidents Museveni and Mandela to declare an 'African Renaissance' which, if present trends continue, suggests a degree of optimism for the future of the African public that is unsurpassed in recent history. Nevertheless, change is occurring from an extremely low base, and the subcontinent has a daunting degree of transformation to effect before living standards come even close to world averages. The region has 33 of the 48 countries classified as 'least developed'.

There are no 'high-income' countries and the only countries classified as 'upper-middle income' are Gabon, Mauritius, Reunion, Seychelles, and South Africa. There are six lower-middle income countries (Botswana, Cap Verde, Djibouti, Namibia, Senegal, and Swaziland) and by far the majority of countries in the region - 39 of the 48 nations - are classified by the World Bank as 'low income'. Development statistics for the region often include South Africa and North Africa and as these are much more developed areas, their inclusion can obscure the true extent of the development gap.

ICT Infrastructure

Although encouraging trends have emerged in the last few years, the differences between the development levels of SSA and the rest of the world are even wider in the area of ICTs than they are when more traditional measures of development are used. The majority of the population has never even made a telephone call, only 2.5% of the world's televisions are on the subcontinent, and just one person in 9,000 has access to the Internet compared to a world average of one in 38. Irregular or nonexistent electricity supplies are a common feature of the sub-Saharan landscape and a major barrier to an increased use of ICTs, especially outside the major towns.

Many countries have extremely limited power distribution networks, which do not penetrate significantly into rural areas, and power sharing (regular power outages for many hours) is a regular occurrence, even in some capital cities such as Accra and Dar es Salaam. Furthermore, most tax regimes still treat ICTs as luxury items, which m a kes these almost exclusively imported commodities all the more expensive, and thus unobtainable by the majority. It is not therefore surprising that radio is still by far the most dominant mass medium in Africa with ownership of radio sets being far higher than for any other electronic device. In 1995, radio ownership was estimated by UNESCO at close to 18% of the population. It should also be noted that many people listen to the same radio or watch a television at the same time.

In fact, large scale sharing of information resources is a dominant feature of the African media landscape - readership of newspapers is often above 10 and it is not uncommon to find most of a small village crowded around the only TV set, often powered by a car-battery or small generator. It has been estimated that over 60% of the population of the subcontinent are reached by existing radio transmitter networks, while national television coverage is largely confined to major towns.

Some countries still do not have their own national television service. Following liberalization of the sector in many countries, an increasing number of commercial stations are being established. However, the news and information output of these commercialisation is usually either a re-broadcast of the national (state-controlled) news, or that of an international broadcasting service or news agency.

Local news and current affairs, especially that focusing on events outside the capital, is rarely broadcast. Community radio has been slow to take off in the region. Genuine community radios are often seen by governments as a threat. Pressure is also being put on community radios - usually by the donor organizations which helped to create them in the first place - to become financially sustainable. Among the multinational broadcasters, the BBC World Service radio programming is the most widespread, redistributing its signal locally on FM and AM bands in 25 countries and 46 towns in the sub-Sahara.

The BBC's coverage is followed by that of Radio France International (RFI) and the Voice of America, all three of which are actively competing for the African radio listener via terrestrial re-broadcasting. The battle is being carried to the satellite television market as well, with the BBC and Canal+ focussing an Anglophone and Francophone audiences respectively. Portuguese colonial history is similarly reflected in services of the national television, RTP, being re-broadcast in the Lusophone countries.

For many years the South African company MultiChoice has been distributing its South African subscriber channels (M-Net) through local terrestrial broadcasters in 39 countries in SSA. Its recently launched music channel, Channel O, claims to be the most watched television station in Africa.

In 1995 M-Net launched the world's first digital direct-to-home subscriber satellite service called DSTV which carries over 30 video channels and 40 audio programmes on C-band to the whole of Africa and on low-cost KU-band to Southern Africa south of Lusaka. This year the South Africa public broadcasting Corporation (SABC) launched Channel Africa, a new satellite-based news and entertainment channel aimed at the subcontinent.

However, the audience for satellite broadcasts are confined to the elite who can afford the equipment and subscription fees. In 1998 some parts of northern sub-Sahara started receiving DTH Television broadcasts from Nilesat, the continent's first locally owned geostationary satellite, operated by the Egyptian Radio and Television Union (ERTU). World-Space has finalized its digital radio service, which began broadcasts in early 1999 and will make a suite of five audio channels available to anyone on the continent who can afford $200 for the special digital radio that has been manufactured.

In most sub-Saharan countries the telecommunication networks are being expanded and modified, with the number of main lines growing at about 10% a year. Nevertheless, the overall teledensity in 1996 was still only about one telephone line per 100 inhabitants. In addition, much of the telecommunication network is analogue and many sections are operating at saturated capacity or are highly unreliable, especially during rainy seasons.

On a worldwide basis, the sub-Saharan countries can be seen to have by far the least developed infrastructure. In 1996 the region contained almost 10% of the world's population, but only 0.4% of the world's telephone lines. The penetration of phone lines on the subcontinent is five times worse than for the average low-income country. However, there is a high level of variability among countries in the state of their existing telephone networks.

Some such as Botswana and Rwanda have made telecommunications a priority and are installing digital switches with fibre optic intercity backbones and the newest cellular and mobile technology. At the other end of the scale, countries like Madagascar and Uganda have largely unreliable analogue telephone systems and poor national links between urban centres. Surprisingly, the proportion of digital lines on the subcontinent in 1996 was 69%, close to the world average of 79%.

On a sub-regional level, the countries of the Sahel and Central Africa, such as Mali, the Niger and the Democratic Republic of the Congo have less than 2 telephone lines for every 1,000 people. North Africa and South Africa have a teledensity of around 35 per 1,000, West and East African coastal countries have densities of between 2.5 and 10 per 1,000. A much smaller proportion of the population can actually afford their own telephone: the cost of renting a connection averaged almost 20% of the 1995 GDP per capita, as compared with a world average of 9% and only 1% in high income countries.

In 1996 the average sub-Saharan business connection cost $112 to install, $6 a month to rent and $0.11 per 3-minute local call. But installation charges were above $200 in some countries, line rentals ranged from $0.8 to $20 a month, and call charges varied from $0.60 an hour to over $5 an hour. Local call tariffs in some countries have increased even further, to over $10 an hour, making extensive residential use of the World Wide Web (WWW) in these countries unaffordable to all but a tiny elite. Because of high tariffs and the large number of international calls, telecommunications operators enjoy above-average profits on their lines.

Mobile cellular telephony has experienced very rapid growth in the SSA. As well as providing an alternative to the limited public telecommunications networks, the cellular market has usually involved the private sector which has been able to institute more aggressive start-up plans. Cellular services are now available in 38 countries, supplied by over 65 operators who provide access mainly in the capital cities but also in some secondary towns and along major trunk routes.

The number of cellular subscribers in 1997 was estimated by the International Telecommunications Union (ITU) at over 225,000 outside of South Africa, where the cellular market outpaced all expectations, reaching over 2 million in 1998. Traditional data communication services based on X.25 are available in half the countries, most prevalently among those which are francophone where the use of the Minitel was adopted before the Internet became available.

SITA, the airline co-operative, has by far the largest X.25 network in Africa. SITA's commercial division, SCITOR (recently renamed Equant), which was formed to service the non-airline market, now operates dialup points of presence in 39 SSA countries. These are used by a variety of multinational organizations.

Subscribers to Internet service providers (ISP) in Europe and North America who are members of IPASS (a group of ISPs, including SITA, who share their points of presence, or POPs) can also access their home ISPs via these points of presence for about $0.22 a minute. X.25 packet-switched based services were in the past the most popular method of establishing wide-area data networks in Africa, but because of their high-cost, traffic-based tariffs, they are now mainly used by banks and other large corporations requiring secure real-time low-volume data transactions such as credit-card verification.

By contrast, the Internet has spread rapidly through the region over the last two years: at the end of 1996 only eleven countries had local access; but by the end of 1998, according to ITU, all African countries had some access to the Internet. But Internet services are still largely confined to the capitals and major towns.

To address this situation ten countries have made the decision to provide local call Internet access across the whole country using a specific area code. A few countries (Angola, Benin, Botswana, Ghana, Kenya, Namibia and the United Republic of Tanzania) do have POPs in some of the secondary towns, and South Africa has POPs in about 70 locations.

Most African capitals have more than one Internet Service Provider (ISP), and in mid-1998 there were over 265 ISPs across the region.

The total number of computers connected to the Internet in the sub-Sahara excluding South Africa was estimated at just over 5,000 in mid-1998, but the figure may be closer to 6,000 or 7,000 due to the measurement technique, which does not count hosts which are not fully referenced in domain name servers. Africa's share of Internet host sites worldwide was only 0.025% in 1997, and this had fallen to 0.022% by the beginning of 1998 due to Internet growth worldwide.

The opening up of the Nigerian Internet market will probably change the picture as the national telecommunications operator (Nitel) has big plans to provide Internet countrywide. With a fifth of sub-Sahara's population, until mid 1998 Nigeria, which has been one of the slumbering giants of the African Internet world, had only a few dialup e-mail providers and a couple of full ISPs operating on very low bandwidth links.

The rapidity with which most African public telecommunication operators (PTOs), have established Internet services is noteworthy. In the last three years PTOs have brought full Internet services on stream in 31 countries, and similar moves are afoot in three others.

The Mauritian government has a strong commitment to increase the use of ICTs and has made a number of efforts in addressing the regulatory and legal framework for ICTs. Several bills have already been drafted, and with the passing of the Copyright Bill at the National Assembly in July 1997, the legal challenges posed by the use of ICTs will be reduced significantly.

The National Computer Board (NCB) was established by government in late 1996 as a parastatal institution whose aim is to assist in the diffusion of ICTs in the various socio-economic sectors of the country. One of the NCB's major areas of activity is the use of the Internet in government, as well as the more general issues of privacy, security and intellectual property.

The NCB has established an extensive web site which acts as the home site for information on other government ministries. NCB is the programme manager for the National IT Strategy Plan (NITSP) which is currently under active development as part of the Mauritian government's strategic objectives to move the country toward an information-age economy.

In Mauritias, Government Information Infrastructure (GII), will provide the electronic mail and publishing facilities for the Government to create a responsive and 'paperless' environment. It will also aim to provide information and services to the public round-the-clock via the Internet. Over time, the GII is also expected to evolve into an electronic backbone and infrastructure to meet the future public sector connectivity needs.

The telecommunications sector is regulated by the Mauritius Telecommunications Authority (MTA) and will be advised by a newly-created Telecommunications Advisory Council (TAC). The Public Telecommunication Operator (PTO), Mauritel/ MTS, is currently a monopoly but is engaged in a slow process of liberalization and tariff rebalancing which is expected to be completed by the end of 2004 when the entire sector will be opened up for competition as outlined in the recently published Telecommunications White Paper.

Mauritius has a far better telecommunications infrastructure than most other countries in Africa. As part of its national strategy to become the 'Singapore of Africa', it has made telecommunications and data services a high national priority for some time now, and this is reflected in the availability of ISDN services in some areas, relatively short waiting times for the installation of new telephone lines (especially for businesses) and a rapidly emerging range of data communications services such as Internet, X.25 and EDI.

Three SDH fibre optic rings have been built in Mauritius to improve the local telecom infrastructure and to provide a high-bandwidth connection to the main groundstation in Port Louis. Mauritius will be connected by fibre optic cable to the global backbone in 1999 when South Africa's Far-East (SAFE) project links Cape Town to Kuala Lumpur and Singapore via submarine cable.

Few of the countries outside of South Africa had international Internet links larger than 64Kbps until last year, but 128Kps connections are now becoming increasingly common. More than 256Kbps of international bandwidth is currently present in only eleven countries. Most of the international connections are carried via satellite. The exceptions to this are the marine optic fibre link from South Africa to the cross-Atlantic hub in the Canaries, and Djibouti which has access to the SEA-ME-WEA cable. By far the majority of international Internet circuits in the region connect to the United States, with a few to the United Kingdom and France.

Generally, ISPs must pay the entire cost of the connection to Europe or the US, which effectively gives the developed country ISPs free access to the continent's network and further increases the costs of ISPs in Africa. The United Nations Development Programme (UNDP) and the Agence de la Francophonie. They adopted a project to install a regional register for Internet addresses, AFRINIC, similar to those existing in other regions. Reflecting the high telecommunication costs and the small markets, often supplied by a single operator, ISP charges for dialup access are generally higher in Africa than elsewhere: the average cost of using the Internet for five hours a month in Africa comes to about $60 per month.

In response to the high cost of full Internet-based services, and also because of the overriding importance of electronic mail, the e-mail-only store and forward services with dialup connections to the Internet are generally continuing to attract subscribers. There is also growing interest in telecentres, kiosks, cybercafes and other forms of public Internet access, such as adding PCs to community phone-shops, schools, police stations and clinics, which can share the cost of equipment and access among a larger number of users.

Computers and data processing

Demand for various services on the Internet is expected to increase only when there is a broader penetration of computers and data processing equipment on the subcontinent. Although the limited levels of equipment penetration are readily apparent, accurate estimates of the quantity of this equipment in use are notoriously hard to gather.

There have been few effective centralized systems of monitoring, and high duties and sales taxes in many countries discourage the declaration of imports and other transactions. In addition, convergence and rapid change in the technologies makes the categorization of equipment types even more difficult. Most recent estimates for the number of PCs in the sub-Sahara put the average at about 3 per 1,000 people in 1996.

However some studies, such as the 1995 survey carried out by the Agence de cooperation culturelle et technique (ACCT), indicate that this figure may be between 3 and 6 times too high, making the average closer to less than 1 per 1,000. Some countries such as Botswana, Mauritius and South Africa have significantly higher levels of penetration, at least 5 per 1,000, perhaps to 20 per 1,000. At the same time, account should also be taken of the number of users sharing a single computer, which is much greater than in more developed regions.

Generally, the penetration of computers is much lower in the public sector, with by far the majority of PC equipment being used by the private sector for accounting and word processing. Spreadsheets are used to some extent for forecasting or as a simple database application. The small number of database systems often use Microsoft Access, but many national documentation centres and archives, as well as small university and NGO libraries, use the UNESCO-developed micro CDS/ISIS package for bibliographic data, or the functionally similar package of International Development Research Centre (IDRC). Geographic Information Systems (GIS) and digitization facilities are beginning to be installed by planning departments and municipalities.

Outside of South Africa, there are only a handful of mini- and mainframe computers, and most of these are confined to Ministries of Finance for government payroll, and a few of the larger parastatal organizations, telecom operators, banks and insurance companies. The Millennium Bug, or 'Y2K problem', has gained significant attention across the subcontinent, especially because there are large numbers of older machines in use and very limited resources or skills to ensure their compliance.

The vast majority of people in the sub-region rely almost exclusively on radio for information, with smaller and more elite groups in the cities and towns also making use of television and newspapers. There were about 175 daily papers and 300 weekly or monthly general news journals in the SSA in 1996, but this number is thought to have increased substantially in the last two years.

As mentioned earlier, the majority of Africans have not yet made a phone call. But interestingly, the use of international lines is much higher than the world average, partly reflecting the large size of the African Diaspora and the arbitrary borders within the region.

In 1996 the SSA average for international outgoing calls was 233 minutes per line per year, compared to a world average of 93, and 113 for high-income countries. Current estimates put the number of sub-Saharan Internet users at about 870,000. Most of these are in South Africa leaving only about 70,000 among the remaining the 638 million people on the subcontinent.

South Africa's Internet community is 3 0 times larger than any other in Africa, being among the top 20 countries in the world when ranked by the number of Internet nodes. The definition of a 'user' or 'subscriber' may vary, however, since the number of accounts being shared in Africa may be much greater than in more developed regions.

A recent study by the UN Economic Commission for Africa (UNECA) found on average that there were 3 users for each computer with an Internet or e-mail connection. This could mean that the number of e-mail users outside South Africa is over 200,000.

The French-speaking SSA countries have a far higher profile on the World Wide Web and greater institutional connectivity than the non-French speaking countries. This is due to the strong assistance provided by the various francophone support agencies and the Canadian and French governments, which are concerned about the dominance of English on the Internet. As a result, the anglophone and lusophone countries have considerable 'catching up' to do to reach the same levels of connectivity and representation.

On a sub-regional basis, Southern Africa is the most advanced region in terms of use of ICTs, followed by East and West Africa, with Central Africa lagging furthest behind. The Library was chosen in part for its long standing experience with e-mail access and CD-ROM use, the latter which has in part been assisted by the sub-Saharan African Program of the American Association for the Advancement of Science (AAAS).

Support for the GNICC has been widespread, including from government, with participation from the ministries of environment, science and technology, education, information, transport and communication. The Ghana Government has indicated its support for promoting access to ICTs in all segments of society, particularly in the educational system. The Minister of Finance in his 1997 budget statement made the following declaration: 'In view of the positive effects of the application of information technology on development,

Government will ensure that key institutions of state machinery are linked to the Internet.

All the science resource centres will be connected to the network as and when they are commissioned. The program to link the Universities together and to the Internet will also be pursued.' UNESCO has since agreed to fund the $250,000 project, with the primary local partners being the Ministry of Environment, Science and Technology and the Ministry of Transport and Communication. One of the initial goals will be the establishment of the Ghana Academic and Research Network (GARNET). The government has requested the Bank for Institutional Development Fund to implement a network to connect the Office of the President, Parliament, the Ministry of Information and some other key ministries.

The technical subcommittee of the GNCIC has been charged with designing the specifications of a national networking backbone. Within the context of the GNICC/ GARNET project it was originally envisaged that the University of Ghana would form the hub for GARNET's Internet links to the other Universities and research centres.

The university is installing a fibre optic campus network with support from the Danish International Development Agency (DANIDA). It is located about 12 km from the centre of Accra, using a wireless link to the local Internet hub operated by NCS.

With the emergence of NCS's national Internet backbone with POPs in three cities, along with its active support for academic networking, and furthermore Gilat's interest, a joint private/public sector networking project may emerge. The Ministry of Transport and

Communications (MOTC) established the Accelerated Development Programme (ADP) for telecommunications in 1995 to address the stagnant growth in the sector. The ADP is a reform program involving the establishment of a centralized regulatory body, the National Communications Authority (NCA), as the agency responsible for regulation of the telecommunications sector.

At the same time Ghana Telecom (GT) was separated as a commercial entity from the Ministry of Posts and Telecommunications, with a 30% stake sold to a Malaysian consortium for $38 million and the availability of a second national operator's license was announced. The license was subsequently awarded to a consortium proposing a $10 million investment headed by the Ghana National Petroleum Corporation (GNPC), with the African Communications Group and Western Wireless. GNPC is working with the Israeli company Gilat to deploy a VSAT-based telephone network around the country.

The MOTC plans to divest a further 21% of Ghana Telecom. It also hopes to exploit Ghana's strategic location at the centre of the ECOWAS region and intends to position the country as a hub for trade and commerce-driven telecommunications services. Currently, Ghana's telephone network still reflects a poor state of development, but it is undergoing a process of rapid modernization. Many of the exchanges in Accra are now digitized, providing advanced services such as password, abbreviated dialing, call transfer, three-way conference, wake-up and call waiting.

Although there are a few notable government Web sites, such as those of Angola, Mauritius, Mozambique,

Senegal and Zambia, there is as yet relatively little government use of the Internet for existing administrative purposes. E-mail is used for general correspondence and document exchange, technical advice, managing projects, arranging meetings, and exchanging research ideas, although its use is still limited for accessing formal information resources.

Across the continent, users report that e-mail has increased efficiency and reduced the cost of communication, but as yet is used almost exclusively for contacting individuals in other regions, and the Web is still a relatively under-utilized resource. In the area of local content development, the SSA Web-space is expanding rapidly, and almost all countries have some form of local or internationally-hosted Web server unofficially or officially representing the country with varying degrees of comprehensiveness.

However, still relatively few institutions are well represented on the Web. While increasing numbers of organizations have a Web site with basic content and descriptive information, many are hosted by international development agency sites and very few sites actually use the Web for their activities.

There are about 120 electronic mailing lists and UseNet newsgroups on the Internet (almost entirely hosted off-continent) which discuss issues related to SSA. There is a list for almost every country as well as others on more general topics ranging from African Cinema to Post Colonialism. Two web search engines specializing on Africa have emerged over the last year: Woyaa and Orientation Africa. As with other similar services elsewhere, these are run by commercial companies which generate revenue through advertising.

The news media are now relatively well represented on the Web. The African Studies department of Columbia University in the United States has identified over 115 different newspapers and news magazines in the region that are now available on the Internet, of which over 60% are published on the subcontinent, in about half of the countries. Also of note are the efforts of the ISP Africa Online to host daily newspapers on their web sites.

There are two major continent-wide African news agencies, both of which extensively use electronic media: Inter Press Service (IPS) and the Pan African News Agency (PANA). Sub-regionally, Southern Africa has the only active news agencies using ICTs, the Southern African Broadcasters Association (SA BA) and the Media Institute of Southern Africa (MISA).

In other regions use of ICTs among the media is much lower, but in West Africa, WANAD (West African News Media and Development Centre) is assisting journalists and media outlets to adopt the use of ICTs. Of course international news correspondents in SSA are heavily dependant on ICTs to deliver material to their operations in the United States and Europe.

Cable News Network (CNN) and the other international television news companies regularly rent temporary space segments all over Africa with the local representatives of IntelSat and PanamSat to deliver reports and live coverage. Radio journalists (even freelancers) are now sending edited sound files by e-mail to agencies such as the BBC World Service. Across the subcontinent, there are as yet few locally-developed electronic information repositories of national or sub-regional significance, and none of the existing ones are currently available on the Internet. This is partly because national archive and library systems are extremely poorly resourced and many have had little opportunity to obtain ICT skills or equipment.

Although statistics-gathering operations are also at a very low level due to insufficient support, many statistical offices are now using common standards and new tools. With the help of e-mail and fax, the collection of statistical information is no longer confined to the largest urban centres. The number of studies aiming at better knowledge of the structure and functioning of the socio-economic sectors is growing and price indices now cover rural areas.

There has been a gradual wave of restructuring in telecommunication and broadcasting sectors in sub-Sahara over the past five years. Ten countries, including Cote d'Ivoire, Ghana, Guinea, Senegal, South Africa and Uganda have partially privatized national telecommunications operators and fifteen more, including Cameroon, Madagascar, Malawi and the United Republic of Tanzania, intend to do so shortly. The cellular sector, which is almost completely private, already comprises about 20% of the market. World Trade Organization (WTO) Multilateral Trade Negotiation commitments have been made by Cote d'Ivoire, Ghana, Mauritius, Senegal and South Africa.

By the beginning of 1998, twenty African countries had established independent or quasi-independent regulatory bodies for the telecommunication sector.

The liberalization of the sectors in some of the countries will undoubtedly improve the prospects for increased investment in ICTs over the next few years. However, many governments still see the media as an organ of the state and the telecommunications sector as an important part of their general revenue base. This means that public network operators are not free to reinvest their profits in network development.

Furthermore, much of the existing revenue for telecommunication operators comes as a result of the existing accounting rate system, which currently channels significant sums of international telecommunications revenue to African PTOs. The pending reform of the accounting rate system could deprive PTOs and/or their governments of vital investment capital just when they most need it.

However, the international telecommunication industry is waking up to the fact that Africa is the world's largest untapped market, and with governments desperate for ways to radically modernize telecommunications systems, new alliances are being forged between the private and public sectors.

There are nevertheless concerns that little consideration is being given to the medium- and long-term implications, more particularly because when it comes to deregulation of the telecommunication sector, the assumption of many governments is that liberalization models, which have worked in the North, can simply be applied wholesale to the South.

Moreover, commercialization of broadcasting, without adequate reform of the public broadcasting sector, has done little to promote plurality and diversity on the airwaves. Given the extent of rural poverty, profit-driven entrepreneurs have little or no interest in broadcasting to these more marginalized communities. The establishment of commercial broadcasting.

The urban-based broadcasters have then been granted re-broadcast licences to other heavily-populated areas, which increases the stations' appeal to advertisers, but contributes little to the diversification of broadcasting in the country. These new commercial broadcasters have tended to be either owned by the ruling party or by staunch supporters of that party. These public broadcasters are also increasingly under pressure to make a profit in order to save on already overstretched national budgets. In order to compete with newly-established commercial stations, public broadcasters have little choice but to act and think commercially.

Sub-regional collaboration between countries in the development of strong regulators and legislation may be one important means of addressing some of these issues. To this end the Southern African grouping of thirteen SADC countries have agreed to a legally binding Protocol on Communications which includes commitments to Universal Service and adopting the model policy and telecommunications legislation that has been developed.

ICTs are at a critical strategic entry point for development in SSA. The infrastructure is steadily improving, but not fast enough to accommodate the growth in demand for the multitude of services now available. In particular, the need for high bandwidth infrastructure for the Internet creates serious pressures on the telecommunications networks in Africa. But the Internet is just one of a number of forces that will have an impact on telecommunications operators in the region.

There are many others, such as international pressures on regulating accounting rates charges, and the growing presence of callback technology. The challenges in this area focus on issues such as expansion of the local network and tariff rebalancing (for national operators); the erosion of international revenues (through, for example, callback systems, the Internet and the breakdown of the accounting-rate system); regulatory weaknesses that need to be addressed to ensure a level playing field and to attract investment; the need to provide rural services; the shortage of skilled personnel; and the need for customer focus in terms of quality, service coverage and price.

In telecommunications alone, investments totalling at least $6,000-8,000 million would be required in SSA over the next four years to add an additional 4.5 million lines. This would improve the teledensity in a significant way, even though it will remain the lowest in the world. There have nevertheless been an increasing number of indications that the sub-region's decision-makers are committed to achieving substantial change.

One of the most important events, which helped to accelerate moves toward increased adoption of ICTs in Africa, was the Addis Abeba Symposium on Telematics for Development, organized by UNESCO in April 1995. This meeting brought together almost all of the major forces in international computer networking development projects. One of the results of this Conference was the development of a framework document entitled the African Information Society Initiative (AISI), which was adopted at the subsequent meeting of the Conference of African Ministers in May 1996.

AISI calls for the formulation and development of a National Information and Communication Infrastructure (NICI) plan in every African country, driven by national development priorities, and proposes co-operation, linkage and partnership among African countries to share successful experiences. The countries that have so far begun the process for developing in-depth national information infrastructure and communication development plans are Benin, Burkina Faso, Cameroon, Comoros, Ethiopia, Lesotho, Namibia, Mozambique, Rwanda, South Africa and Uganda.

In conjunction with efforts to built new infrastructures and improve the existing facilities, there are innovative efforts to improve accessibility to services through the use of shared public access facilities, which exploit the convergence of technologies to provide cost effective services in under-serviced and isolated areas.

Commonly called community tele-centres, the concept has received considerable support from the ITU and other members of the international community, as well as a number of national governments and PTOs. This has resulted in over 20 pilot telecentres across the subcontinent set up to test different models, means of implementation and mechanisms for sustainability.

International and Regional Co-operation and Development Assistance Related to ICT

With the worldwide recognition of the importance of ICTs in accelerating development, a number of recent international development assistance initiatives have improved the prospects for wider access to information and communication networks on the continent.

In relation to the AISI initiative described above, a study on future information infrastructure-building activities in Africa was conducted through a collaboration between IDRC, BellaNet, UNECA, UNESCO and the ITU, called the African Network Initiative (ANI).

To address the growing need for co-ordination, donors and implementing agencies involved in ICTs in Africa have agreed to establish an ongoing forum for information exchange on such projects called Partnerships for ICTs in Africa (Picta).

The overall funding coming from international and regional co-operation and related to ICT shows the importance that the international community attributes to this sector. But in Africa as in the rest of the world, the development of adequate infrastructure is only the first step in the right direction. Adequate policies should ensure that such progress will not widen the gap between the information-rich and the information-poor. The risk may be greater in Africa than in other parts of the world, since the initial situation is more critical than anywhere else.

The Status of ICT in Arab Countries

The Arab countries are are also struggling to meet the challenge of ICT's multiple impact on the social, economic, cultural and political aspects of life. The first striking feature in the Arab region is the wide variation among countries in terms of population, gross national product (GNP) per capita, education and use of ICT.

The total population is over 260 million, according to 1997 estimates. The population of individual countries ranges from 0.6 to 62.5 million, with four countries numbering over 20 million inhabitants and one country, Egypt, more than 60 million. Nine countries - Bahrain, Djibouti, Kuwait, Lebanon, Mauritania, Oman, Palestine, Qatar, United Arab Emirates - are below 5 million. Three of them are found in the Gulf area and have populations below 1 million. In the period between 1970 and 1995, annual population growth rate in the region ranged from 0.8% to 9.6%. Lebanon's rate was the lowest, but this is expected to rise after the civil war has ended.

By contrast, in Qatar and the United Arab Emirates, the annual population growth rate was very high, 6.6% and 9.65% respectively, due to the large number of immigrants needed to improve the quantity and quality of the labour force in these two oil-producing countries. Growth is expected to decline between 1995 and 2015 in all countries except Lebanon.

In such an environment, where literacy levels are also low, the new communication technologies, including television, can be very useful. Illiteracy remains a challenge for some Arab countries in spite of the campaigns which have been launched in the last few decades.

In schools, the gender balance is somewhat better. The high enrolment rate in primary education suggests that literacy rates could improve dramatically over the next generation, provided the high number of dropouts were reduced. The total enrolment rate ranges from 38% to 116%. It was above 80% in all but six countries in 1995, and higher than 90% in nine countries. The percentage of females to males is over 80% except for two countries. In secondary schools, enrolment rates decrease. In a few countries they never exceed 25% of the registration achieved in primary education.

In order to organize the presentation of ICT in the Arab countries, we have adopted the model proposed by Kobayashi which suggests five main categories. The first category, called 'human interface', covers the technologies involving interaction between the machine and human beings, such as radio, television, the telephone, personal computers (PCs) and connections to the Internet.

The second category refers to all ICT networks, including broadcasting, telecommunications and computer networks. The third category deals with ICTs used in government and administration, and the fourth concerning those found in education and research. The last group deals with information and knowledge services, such as decision support systems, the world wide web and all printed - or 'typographical' - information as it is called by Kobayashi.

In the human interface technologies, radio shows the highest penetration rates. Five countries show over 400 radio sets per 1,000 inhabitants, and four of these rise above 450 radios per 1,000 inhabitants. Only three countries are below 150 sets per 1,000. Television is the second most common communication technology, with a range of 13 to 457 sets per 1,000 inhabitants. Seven countries show a penetration rate above 250 sets per 1,000 inhabitants, and eight are below 100. Telephone lines are expanding. In 1997, these ranged from less than 1 line for 100 inhabitants in Somalia to more than 35 lines per 100 inhabitants in the United Arab Emirates.

The personal computer is the most important terminal used with a human interface: it allows for a high level of interaction, and makes it possible to do co-operative work online. It may include the use of a CD-ROM, as well as general Internet connectivity including e-mail and many other functions. Data on the penetration rate for personal computers are limited, but those available show that the level of 50 PCs per 1,000 inhabitants has been reached in two countries in the Gulf.

In many countries the number decreased, yet in one country, the United Arab Emirates, the number increased dramatically. The total number of Internet users almost doubled in most countries during the six-month period extending from July to December 1997. In the Arab countries, 98% of the Internet users are men, which is a disturbing figure. Users are evenlysplit among those who use the Internet at home and those who use it from their place of work.

Regarding electronic commerce, a survey conducted in 1998 by the magazine Internet Arab World, published by Dubai Information Technology, showed that only 4% of users in Arab countries made a purchase through the Internet during the year.

Among the factors affecting the penetration of electronic commerce, one can mention the fact that this kind of commerce is relatively new in the region, that it lacks a critical mass of consumers and has to overcome a conservative attitude regarding the security of electronic transactions. However, Arabic software companies expect to generate 33% of their sales through the Internet in the next two or three years. Some observers expect electronic commerce to grow by 100% over the next 12 months. The fax machine is complementary to the telephone, whether it is used directly on the telephone line or through a PC. As the Internet expands, e-mail may rapidly replace fax since it is more user-friendly and supports multimedia message delivery.

Available radio frequencies have reached the saturation point in most Arab countries in the last decade. On the other hand, TV channels and telecommunications have expanded greatly with the creation in 1967 of ARABSAT, the Arab Satellite

Communications Organization. The purpose of this enterprise is to invest in and operate the Arab space sector; arrange and secure extended communication of telephone, faxes, telexes, and pictures; arrange radio and TV broadcasting; offer paid consulting services in the area of satellite communication; and encourage Arab industries to invest in satellite communication.

The first satellite was launched in 1985. The available channels were used by Arab information ministries (broadcasting and TV) as well as telecommunication ministries and in co-ordination with the ground networks. ARABSAT worked as a business organization and was able to finance all successive projects. During this first generation experience it manufactured three satellites and bought two more (in orbit) to meet the increasing demand. Then it launched two second-generation satellites to expand the area covered. The first satellite of the third generation was launched on 27 February 1999 and will cover both the Arab region and Europe.

As for the cellular mobile telephone, ITU data show the total percentage increase between 1995 and 1997 in Arab countries to be 62.8%, probably due to the privatization of this service. The Egyptian satellite NILE SAT was launched in April 1998 to provide digital TV and radio broadcasting, Internet services, and distance education at different levels and in different languages. It covers the Middle East region from Baghdad to Rabat, and parts of southern and northern Europe. Several Arab countries such as Bahrain, Kuwait, Iraq, the Libyan Arab Jamahiriya, Oman, and Tunisia are channel providers.

With respect to computer networks, many organizations are moving away from centralized information systems or local area networks (LANs), a change which often implies the revision of administrative structure. Some large organizations have started thinking of establishing Intranets based on the Transmission Control Protocol/Internet Protocol (TCP/IP).

Heavy demand for telecommunication networking pushed some countries like Egypt to begin privatizing this sector. Public data networks are being enhanced from the X.25 standard to Frame Relay and Asynchronous Transmission Mode (ATM). Internet connectivity uses a variety of methods, whether through satellite links or optical fibre.

Total channel capacity to access the Global Internet has reached around 12 Mbps, of which 2.5 Mbps are used by the Egyptian Universities Network. This capacity also serves various governmental sectors, and more than 40 Internet Service Providers (ISPs) are distributed among 16 governorates.

Some of the remote ISPs in upper Egypt use very small aperture terminals (VSATs) for their local connections. A regional communication network, RITSENET, has been planned by the Egyptian government, but implementation is still in progress. Efforts to link Algeria, Morocco, Tunisia, Mauritania and the Libyan Arab Jamahiriya to the network have begun.

In most Arab countries, attempts to computerize government offices began during the mid-1980s. Since then, the building of data bases and networks within different departments and local organizations has continued to grow. Because of the non-latin alphabet of the Arab language, fax communication, introduced more than two decades ago, is still widely used despite the spread of e-mail.

The classical applications known as clerical automation and management information systems (MIS) have now matured and include accounting, inventory control, financial information, personnel and planning. The Arab League ICT Regional Arabic Institutes have tried to stimulated these countries' interest in adopting ICT through studies, workshops and conferences organized at the national level.

Geographical Information Systems (GIS) were introduced in Egypt in 1996. The systems were designed with a long-term perspective that would allow progressive implementation and continuous monitoring. Priority was given to environmental applications, infrastructure building, municipal administration, socio-economic studies, and information and mass communication.

With support from the Islamic Bank, efforts are underway to improve productivity and strengthen industrialization in the field of electronics, informatics and communication, by linking data input, operations research, modelling and implementation. Decision Support Systems (DSS) have been installed in different Arab countries since the mid-1980s. An Egyptian centre for DSS was set up in 1985 and is expanding its activities to include training and other services.

Arabization, however, is a critical factor in developing information systems, but with the increasing investment in ICT and the increase in the number of users, companies are also responding faster. Microsoft introduced an Arabic version of Windows 98 in October 1998 in Dubai, just five months after introduction of the English version. Each year there are also conferences and exhibitions in different Arab countries which address particular issues such as expert systems, modelling, virtual reality, but it is too early to evaluate the results. Finally, the number of businesses in this field is expanding and the number of software companies linked to multinational firms, or specialized foreign companies in the same sectors, such as GIS or banking, is also increasing. A high percentage of systems are designed and implemented by foreign companies.

With regard to management and administration, many national services in the Arab countries have been automated and are improving: from customs, taxes and licenses, to reservations, check payments and, to some extent, information retrieval.

National activities that have direct relation with international facilities such as airports, maritime ports and financial service cards are the most advanced in this respect since they require only a single node to be linked to a global network. National identification numbers similar to the social security number in western countries will soon facilitate the collection of statistics and improve interactions between government and the population.

Within the research community, ICT is becoming an essential tool, particularly with respect to the retrieval of scientific information. Moreover, specialized institutions involved in informatics are being established. In some cases, they participate in supervising the dissemination of scientific knowledge at the national level.

In Saudi Arabia, for example, King Abdul Aziz City of Science and Technology is supervising the introduction of Internet connectivity in Saudi Arabia. It has licensed 37 companies to provide Internet access, and 85,000 subscribers are expected by the end of 1999.

In Egypt, the Academy of Scientific Research and Technology is facilitating the access to scientific library material and patent databases. The Egyptian Universities Network is serving Egypt's top-level national administrators. The Information and Decision Support Centre (IDSC) is supervising the introduction of Internet services to the governmental sectors and also licensing Internet access to the private ISPs.

The electronic Research Institute in Cairo and the Mubarak City of Science and Technology have established special departments for dealing with Informatics. Similar examples can be found in Algeria, Morocco and Tunisia. As for university education, the task of co-ordinating information among Arab institutions is being undertaken by the Union of Arab Universities. Almost all Arab universities are connected to the Internet, although there is not yet an Arab Backbone Network.

In some countries, universities are all connected to a single network. For example, Egypt's twelve universities are linked through the Egyptian Universities Network, together with Al-Azhar and the American University. Since Tunisia, Kuwait and Egypt were the first Arab countries to have Internet connectivity, they have accumulated more experience in using this technology in the university context. Nevertheless, the United Arab Emirates and Lebanon have recently witnessed a sharp increase in Internet penetration.

Many universities already have separate departments for computer engineering and computer science. In some cases, separate colleges for Information and Computer Science have been established. Distance learning is becoming more important as pilot projects are being implemented using ARABSAT and NILESAT. For precollege education, four types of computer applications can be identified. The first type concerns the introduction of computers at schools to let students, teachers, and administrators grasp the fundamentals of information technology. The second type is the use of computers in a multimedia environment to support the teaching of different subjects and to experiment with new methods of cognitive-based education and learning. The third type is the use of Internet as a means of enhancing collaboration between Arab students and their fellows all over the world, and also to experiment with Web- based education and learning. The fourth type concerns teacher-training and the support of education administrators through the use of videoconferencing networks.

For instance, all the regional teacher-training centres in all the governorates of Egypt are linked to the main centre at the Ministry of Education through a videoconferencing network. Prototype multimedia-based educational material is being tested in Saudi Arabia and Egypt.

However, it should be emphasized that computer penetration is still low in Arab countries, and more funding and teacher training are essential. Additional efforts are required to produce educational material in the Arabic language and which reflects the cultural values of the region.

Printed products - books, newspapers, magazines, scientific periodicals, dictionaries and encyclopaedias, black and white pictures or coloured images - still represent a basic tool for diffusing information, knowledge, and news. The interaction between printing and ICT is quite strong. For instance, it is now possible to receive news on-line and in real time from all over the world, to store it, to communicate it worldwide and to make it accessible on demand. Editors and publishers can now revise in parallel with the authoring process, saving precious time.

Authors and writers now have at their disposal a number of timesaving tools for retrieving information and data, or to assist them during writing. A great number of journals are accessible on the Internet. A number of encyclopedias and dictionaries are in electronic form, some of them as hand-held devices. ICT paved the ground for remote printing, allowing newspapers, journals, and periodicals to be on time all over the world and in the form required. Libraries are also automated and equipped with CD-ROMs. The era of the electronic library is on the way. All these changes are also taking place in the Arab region.

Most of the Arab countries also import a number of magazines and newspapers from abroad, although their distribution is limited to a small number of cities. There is also a union for distributors of Arab newspapers and an Arab union of journalists, founded in 1964. The latter contributes quite actively to upgrading the profession, through a number of courses and seminars including, lately, the use of modern technology and the Internet.

Arab civilization has been closely linked with the production of books and other printed matter. Historically, its efforts in translation have been instrumental in transmitting the works of ancient writers, and Arab contributions in many fields of knowledge are well known. Today, the publishing situation is different and the basic production is translated from western sources. Most of the textbooks used at university level in certain faculties are in English or French, even if the original is Russian or Japanese.

The Arab region appears to favour the simultaneous promotion of industrialization and communication technologies. However, there seems to be more focus on ICT. ICT systems are being upgraded at many levels, but this is especially apparent in efforts to increase efficiency and thus improve productivity. Some of the countries, however, are only just now becoming familiar with ICT. Nevertheless, education at all levels is a top priority throughout the region, and computers and modern communication technologies are considered key tools in preparing all countries for the 21st century.

Below the strategic level, some organizations are studying the newly introduced data warehousing platforms, together with some data mining techniques that sometimes use expert-system methodologies. There is also an urgent need to support the creation of public information systems and to make them accessible to the general public. The launching of the last ARABSAT satellite will greatly contribute to the improvement of telecommunication, broadcasting and access to information.

Local wireless loop services may be developed as a complement. The satellite will also facilitate broadcasting news about events of common interest to Arab and Islamic countries, whether conferences, cultural events, or sports. NILESAT-2 is also expected to be launched at the end of 1999. Finally, an internal expansion of telephone subscribers is taking place in most countries of the region.

In spite of globalization, it is generally acknowledged that governments and their associated institutions have a key role to play in formulating and implementing ICT strategies. There are fundamental and complex issues that have to be addressed, and the benefits that some countries have obtained from this successful experience should be considered. Increasingly, ICTs are an integral part of the overall national strategy and this interdependence between them both is a precondition for their common success.

Arab countries rank ICTs as a high priority within their development objectives. They are seen as an essential element in education, communication, and technology transfer.

The strategic plans have to become more systematic in order to develop integrated information systems that would support greater co-operation between enterprises at different levels across the country. But in order to achieve positive results and increase efficiency, the quality of the data, their definition, and the agencies responsible for their collection and validation must also improve.

Network technologies are to be applied not only for data and information, but across the board. Some of the programmes for ICT at the European Union could be used as a model for the Arab countries. The type of co-operation that is already taking place for broadcasting should be extended. ICT is making radical changes in teaching and learning in higher education, both on campus and in distance education.

The Open University is just starting in the Arab region, but provides a model that should help modernize other sectors and promote continuous learning. Electronic commerce is new in the region and consumer resistance can be overcome gradually with appropriate information campaigns. The integration of ICT into the different activities will help ensure a positive outcome.

The Asia Crisis and ICTs

The current 'Asia Crisis' has had a negative impact on economic and social life in most of Southeast and East Asia. It has jeopardized the human development gains made in the health and education sectors in recent years. It has also brought to the fore new concerns relating to ethnic tensions, social unrest, an increased lack of peace and security, women's rights, poor health conditions and hunger as countries slip into rampant unemployment and inflation pushes millions of households back into poverty.

Despite the crisis, the use of electronic media, telecommunications and Internet are continuing to increase throughout the region as a result of globalization. Governments and business are expanding their activities in radio and television, satellite broadcasting, telecommunications and digital production, while individuals and organizations are making their own decisions about investing in various information technologies.

The prognosis is that bandwidth and new communications technologies are becoming cheaper as governments gradually liberalize their telecommunication sectors. Consequently, the foundation for distance education and open-learning systems in the 21st century will already be in place, and within the next two decades even remote Asian villages will be linked to the global communications network.

Electronic communication and programmes brought via networked media systems and instructional technology in community centres and Internet kiosks will be the new channels for educating, informing and training those in the rural and urban areas.

Since 1997, Bhutan, Papua New Guinea, Laos, Cambodia, and Viet Nam have been wired into the Internet for the first time. Apart from Myanmar, most countries in the region now have some form of presence in this global network.

India has been the largest democracy in the world since its independence in 1947. Today it is a country undergoing a massive transition with far-reaching consequences not only for its more than 900 million citizens, but for the entire globe. After a delay of nearly three years, and mired in litigation and controversy for over a year, the long-awaited ISP Policy has been announced and the process of issuing licenses has begun with gusto.

On 22 November 1998, Prime Minister Atal Bihari Vajpayee inaugurated Satyam Online, the first private-sector Internet access service in Hyderabad, and at the same time the first phase of the Hi-Tec City project near Hyderabad. The highlight of the ISP policy is that licences will be issued for 15 years and there will be no licence fee or any limit on the number of licences awarded.

The railways, state electricity boards and the National Power Grid Corporation are all allowed to provide Internet backbone services. ISPs can set up their own international gateways but require a security clearance from an inter-ministerial committee. The norms for security clearance have not yet been worked out.

India currently has an installed base of only 2 million PCs and less than 500,000 Internet users. The demand for PCs and Internet connections is expected to increase significantly due to the new services being launched. While Internet is not new in the country thanks to the efforts of the Education Research Network (ERNET) and UNDP, it has been limited to those associated with educational institutes or R&D organizations. Previously, access was highly controlled and restricted, which limited its reach.

In August 1995, Videsh Sanchar Nigam Limited (VSNL), a public-sector undertaking and the international telecom carrier, launched the first public Internet service in six major cities, which has today expanded to 42 cities and is expected to reach 70 cities by year-end. There is also a move to enable routing of calls at local-call rates from any of the 800 cities that have STD/ISD (long-distance calling) capability. Instead of setting up a local point of presence (POPs) in all cities, calls to the number 17222 will be directed to the closest Internet POP at no additional charge.

In the first year, 50,000 customers went online on VSNL's Gateway Internet Access Service (GIAS) and today the number exceeds 150,000. New Delhi and Mumbai constitute half the customers. The target is to reach one million users by the year 2000, but that seems unlikely even with the entry of private ISPs.

One of the major factors limiting the expansion of Internet in the country is poor infrastructure, with problems such as the non-availability of telephone lines and an overloading of telephone circuits that were designed for voice communication. To partially overcome this problem, VSNL has installed routers at various telephone exchanges and linked them on dedicated 2Mbps circuits, thus bypassing the congestion.

In the last five years the Department of Telecommunications (DoT) has successfully undertaken a mammoth job of converting telephone exchanges to digital/electronic exchanges and shifting to an optical fibre backbone. This has resulted in very good quality and stable connections, and a huge number of new phone connections. However, many more connections will be needed as India has achieved a teledensity of only 1%.

One of the greatest challenges India now faces is to improve penetration and broaden the access base. If the target of one million Internet subscribers is to be achieved, the entire infrastructure, especially data communication and telecommunications, will need to be overhauled. Another challenge in the short term will be a lack of expertise and talented workforce to handle ISP operations. A sizeable number of people are attracted to the field by world-wide growth figures and are thus jumping onto the ISP bandwagon, but they are often unfamiliar with the dynamics of the business.

India's software business, which relies heavily on computer networks for international operations, is reportedly poised to attain revenues of $6,000 million by the turn of the century. Exports would account for about $4,000 million of the total. Improved availability of the Internet will have a very positive impact on the software industry.

The installation of such a network throughout the region will depend on a number of factors: the regulatory approaches of governments, the number of Internet Service Providers (ISP) or web hosts and approaches to providing infrastructure. The only constant is that every country in the region carries out these activities differently and is at a different stage of development. Consider these examples. In Singapore, one of the most 'wired' countries in the region, there are only three ISPs, yet across the water in the Philippines there is a more relaxed approach to regulation that has spawned some 145 ISPs and countless walk-in access centres.

In Cambodia, the government has allowed the two ISPs to offer a full range of Internet services and has no plans to censor content, but over the border in Viet Nam the authorities have implemented a firewall that intentionally blocks access to selected sites and unintentionally has caused numerous others to become unavailable because of technical problems.

Further to the North, Laos has only just allowed its citizens to access the web after first experimenting with an e-mail-only connection. In the Himalayas, Nepal has a burgeoning Internet industry and some interesting local content programmes, while near-neighbour Bhutan is implementing an internal system · intranet - with only e-mail access to the outside world.

In Mongolia, the locals are using their high levels of literacy and technical education to create an innovative network using whatever means possible: satellite, xDSL modems, radio modem and some creative fund-raising schemes.

The list goes on throughout the region. This same diversity is present when it comes to telecommunications, broadcasting and print media, and runs parallel to developments for the Internet. The Singapore government, for example, owns the two broadcasting companies, the Television Corporation of Singapore and Singapore Television.

Competition is limited in telecommunications, which is dominated by Singapore Telecom, and there is only one print media outlet, the Singapore Press Holdings. By contrast, in the Philippines there are some 17 newspaper organizations, more than 100 television stations, and telecommunications have been opened up to foreign competition. Laos and Viet Nam, which have tried to prevent the inflow of certain content from the Internet, have similar policies for broadcasting and other media, whereas Mongolia opened up its media just before the arrival of the Internet - with the result that there are a flourishing number of print publications and satellite television channels now available in many parts of the country.

Despite this diversity, it is possible to categorize many of the countries into three broad groups. At one end are those that are moving to some form of broadband access and encouraging the use of high-bandwidth applications such as interactive multimedia and e-commerce.

A second tier of countries have a well-established presence on the Internet and a diversified number of access providers, content providers and users. This group would include the Philippines, Indonesia, Thailand, Sri Lanka, China, India, Pakistan and Nepal. Finally, there are those countries that have only recently joined the Internet community. These third-tier countries have a very limited number of ISPs, few examples of local content, and access is confined to one or perhaps two main cities rather than throughout the country. Included in this group are Viet Nam, Bhutan, Laos, Papua New

Guinea (PNG) and Cambodia. Existing media structures, broadcasting facilities, telecommunications infrastructures and regulatory environments tend to conform to this classification of Internet connectivity.

Nevertheless, some countries do not fit neatly into one of the three tiers, and even when they do, diversity is still the key feature, with each country taking its own culturally specific route to enter the information age.

Viet Nam, Bhutan, Laos, Papua New Guinea and Cambodia are all characterized by monopoly telecommunications carriers, low telephone densities, and government regulators who take a dim view of foreign ownership and outside influences. Because of this strict regulatory regime, there have been no private sector initiatives to connect to the Internet until recently. Even the academic sector - one of the catalysts for Internet access in the West and more developed Asian countries - has been slow to act. By contrast, the development sector has been very active.

Four of the five countries mentioned - Viet Nam, Bhutan, Laos and Cambodia - all received support to connect to the Internet from Canada's International Development Research Center (IDRC) under a programme called Pa n Asia Networking (PAN). The programme was launched in 1994 to promote South-South and North-South Internet networking. In the case of Papua New Guinea, the government started by opening up Internet access provision to the private sector.

The most recent entrant to the Internet, Bhutan, is not surprisingly the country that is perhaps the least open to the outside world. Bhutan has long had a policy of limiting tourism and has only allowed television transmission since 1997. The adoption of Internet is following this cautious approach, with the first connections allowing only e-mail access to the outside world and web access restricted to local sites.

All telecommunications services in Bhutan are operated and maintained by the Ministry of Communications' Division of Telecommunications. The current telecommunication network is digital and is capable of supporting data communications and other non-voice services without major problems. Laos also took a tentative approach to the Internet and started with e-mail-only services. More recently, GlobeNet, a subsidiary of Philippines-based satellite provider Globecom, has started to provide full Internet access in conjunction with the Ministry of Information and Culture.

A massive effort in training and in technology transfer is needed to develop a self-sustainable Laotian IT industry. Although such help is readily available in the Lao expatriate and resident IT communities, it does not seem to be readily accessed. There has been some urgency for Laos to adopt some effective means of mass communication, particularly as the offices of the Association of Southeast Asian Nations (ASEAN) have adopted the Internet as the standard means of communication.

Nevertheless each of the countries has a limited number of Internet service providers and coverage. Full Internet services arrived in Cambodia in May 1997 with the establishment of CamNet, a joint venture between the Ministry of Posts and Telecommunications of Cambodia (MPTC) and IDRC. Shortly after, a second ISP, Big Pond Cambodia, a subsidiary of the Australian carrier Telstra in co-operation with MPTC, entered the market. As part of the license agreement with Telstra, MPTC is not allowing new ISP players until 2002. MPTC is both the telecommunications operator and the regulatory body.

At present, there are no specific laws in the country relating to the Internet. The number of users hooked up to the two main e-mail-only servers, Open Forum Information Exchange and WorldMail, is low, numbering about 2,000. However, like other countries in the region, walk-in access centres are becoming a feature and will allow more widespread use in future.

CamNet operates two public Internet centres, one to serve Cambodian research organizations and another aimed at expatriates and tourists. CamNet is working with various Cambodian organizations to publish their own material on the Internet.

Viet Nam first allowed commercial Internet services in late 1997, following more than eighteen months of indecision. An Internet Steering Committee has been set up, headed by the Minister of Science, Technology and Environment and representatives from the Ministries of Security, Culture and Information, Education and Training as well as the Directorate General of Posts and Telecommunication.

Four companies were awarded licences to become Internet Service Providers: NetNam, Viet Nam Data Communications (VDC), Financing and Promoting Technology (FTP) Corporation and the Saigon Post Company. The ISPs must go through the monopoly gateway operator, VDC (a subsidiary of the country's monopoly carrier VNPT) for international connections and are not allowed to lease their own lines. A PAN project is also currently underway to help develop Vietnamese content and is being co-ordinated by NetNam in collaboration with organisations such as the National Centre for Scientific and Technological Information and Documentation (NACESTID) and the Ministry of Culture and Information.

Like other countries in Asia, a significant problem in presenting local information on the world wide web is the lack of a unified coding standard for the local character set. NetNam has designed a utility that recognizes the various codes in use to display Vietnamese text. The utility can detect the six (out of about ten) most common formats that are in use.

In many areas, the final link is provided by High Frequency (HF) radio which can be unreliable for data transmission. The Pacific Islands offer a complete contrast to the vast majority of Asian countries. Despite high levels of aid, the Pacific Islands region has experienced low growth and economic stagnation. This problem is attributed to high population growth, rural-urban migration, the restricted economic conditions of atoll life combined with the need to import a large number of goods and, finally, to high vulnerability to natural and economic disasters.

Government is the major customer, employer and supplier of services in the islands, maintaining in many cases a monopoly. Given the unique geographical dispersion of theses countries, Information and Communication Technologies, particularly telecommunications, offer a real opportunity to diminish the adverse effects of isolation.

The physical infrastructure for telecommunications seems well established. Three satellites can be accessed from every country, while other systems, such as telex and data transmission, cover only some of them. With the exception of emerging arrangements in mobile markets, telecommunication services are provided under state monopoly. But operations seem often to be inefficient. Coverage is poor in remote areas and consumer dissatisfaction is high. Teledensities are relatively low, with large differences between urban and rural areas.

One of the largest potential user communities for Internet is within the university sector. The University of Papua New Guinea (UPNG) and the University of Technology have recently commissioned fibre-optic campus networks that support Internet/Intranet services. In 1998, IDRC and the South Pacific Centre for Communication and Information in Development at the UPNG launched a project to establish a country-level information server that will carry PNG content from many PNG partner institutions.

One country that has recently made the transition from state-controlled and restricted media, broadcasting and information technology to a more liberalized communications policy is Mongolia. While infrastructure in rural areas is still limited and competition in telecommunications not quite a reality, the country has made great strides in providing informations technology to its people in recent years. In 1990, Mongolia switched from a communist state- E-mail services are popular with business customers and the extended family networks resulting from significant population movements.

Every Pacific Island country receives international radio. Some of them also have local radio stations. Most countries produce local television content, although in many countries this is limited to a few hours per day. The penetration rate for personal computers may vary between 1 and 30 personal computers per 1,000 inhabitants, with the exception of Niue, which has almost reached a rate of 80/1,000. There are no statistics for Fiji, the Federated States of Micronesia, Nauru and Palau. The University of the South Pacific provides distance education services using dedicated leased lines.

Additional sites are planned in Kiribati and Samoa. But the limited communication infrastructure means that visual content cannot be distributed. Pacific Islands consumers pay high prices for international and domestic phone services, leased lines and Integrated Services Digital Network (ISDN) services. The monopoly situation and/or the small margins impose prices which are 25% to 58% higher than those prevailing in other environments.

There is an overwhelming consensus in multilateral agencies and regional political groupings to endorse liberalization of telecommunications in order to attain better pricing, service quality and access. Benefits would extend to both public and private institutions as well as the general public.

Sixteen independent states located in the Pacific Ocean are grouped in the South Pacific Forum, an intergovernmental organization which includes the thirteen island states described in this box in addition to Australia, New Zealand and Papua-New Guinea. In addition to the regular budget made up of assessed contributions, eight developed countries and the European Union provide funding for operational assistance controlled economy to a democratic, market-based economy. Since then, the government has liberalized many sectors of the economy including data communications and the media. For a country that until recently had a heavily regulated media, the number of publications and available television stations in the country in 1999 is quite extraordinary.

In information technology as well Mongolia has made great progress in catching up with other countries in the region. At the end of 1996, through assistance from IDRC's PAN programme and a government loan, the local networking company Datacom Ltd set up a satellite earth station and initiated the country's first Internet connection. Since then, a number of projects have seen Internet's reach extend in terms of coverage, usage and the amount of local content.

For example, Datacom has been connecting Mongolian institutes and universities to the Internet through high speed radio modem links. Secondary schools are also being connected via satellite, with support from an IDRC grant. Part of this project will be an Educational Web Centre and an experimental information broadcasting network for provincial schools.

The Philippines and Thailand are examples of other countries that have a wide range of projects that aim to make greater use of information technology and to expand its reach to the general population. However, each country is achieving this end by different means. In the Philippines, where there has been a very open media sector and a dynamic private sector, it is not surprising that the government has taken a hands-off approach to the Internet.

As a result, the private sector is the dominant force when it comes to providing Internet access, and unlike many countries in the region, it has been given a relatively free hand in establishing services and initiating international connections.

The result is some 145 Internet access providers, many of which have countrywide points of presence, a burgeoning array of cheap, walk-in access centres, and some vibrant local content. This situation mirrors what can be seen in the print, broadcasting and telecommunications industries. There are 45 private telecommunications organizations as opposed to 7 public organizations; 86 private television stations compared with 33 government-owned stations; 466 commercial radio stations; and more than 20 daily newspapers.

The Philippines came to the Internet by a traditional route, with the initial connection being a product of the academic sector. The country's first Internet network, PHNET, was initiated in 1994 by the Department of Science and Technology and a consortium of Philippine universities and institutions. It is still the main academic backbone in the country and most recently is proposing to expand its coverage to 2,000 schools by the end of 2000. The resulting network will become the Philippine Science Academic and Research Network (RP-SARNET). In the long run, Internet in the Philippines is expected to be structured around several national backbones - one for government, one for schools and one commercial - each of which will be connected to the other.

In Thailand, the government has played a more direct role in providing access to information technologies within the country. National IT initiatives are formulated within the IT-2000 plan, which was put forward by the National IT Committee and approved by the National Economic and Social Development Board as part of its eighth national development plan.

The three broad aims of IT-2000 are to build an equitable national infrastructure, invest in people and enhance government services and the information industry. National projects such as the academic Internet backbone, a government information network, and a proposed Thailand Software Park are all part of the IT-2000 plan.

Similarly, the government dominates Thailand's broadcasting industry, controlling nearly all radio and television stations, while telecommunications is split between two main government carriers (Telephone Organization of Thailand (TOT) and Communication Authority of Thailand (CAT)) and two private carriers.

The monarchy also plays a major part in the country's development, and in accordance with a long historical tradition a number of IT projects have been initiated by the king and other members of the royal family. Indonesia has traditionally also taken a government-led approach to communications, but has suffered most from the economic crisis owing to internal political unrest and a devastated economy.

Extending telecommunications to all 27 provinces and each main island is a daunting task, yet one which Indonesia has traditionally embraced as a means of creating national cohesion. This recognition of the need for communications for development and modernization occurred more than twenty years ago, in 1976, with the launch of Indonesia's domestic satellite, PALAPA. Indonesia's national information infrastructure is being created under a programme known as Nusantara 21 which calls for all major islands and cities to be linked either by submarine and terrestrial cable, or by satellite, by the year 2001.

However, the current economic crisis has added a level of uncertainty to this project and to many government and business initiatives. The education sector in Indonesia is active in information technology and has suffered less from the economic fallout. More than half of the country's universities are connected to the Internet exchange of the Institute of Technology Bandung, which is connected via a 1.55 Mb/s link to the Asia Pacific AI3 backbone. Despite government backing for Internet and other information technologies, the second-tier countries are still held back to varying degrees by regulatory provisions. These provisions are designed to protect monopoly telecommunications interests and lessen government fears about the impact of the Internet and other outside media. This approach can be seen in countries as diverse as Nepal, Bangladesh, Pakistan, India, China and Sri Lanka.

In nearly all of these cases, Internet access must go through a monopoly carrier or designated gateway, resulting in increased costs to both ISPs and, ultimately, users. The situation is compounded by the lack of telephone lines that can be supplied by monopoly providers. For example, in Bangladesh, a country with only 0.4 telephone lines per hundred people, ISP networks are saturated due to a lack of access lines - and this is in the capital city, Dhaka. Trying to provide services to most remote villages is presently impossible owing to a lack of infrastructure.

A fibre-optic communications network owned and run by the Bangladesh state railway has been viewed by some ISPs as a possible means of gaining widespread connectivity. The transmission lines run alongside the major rail corridors and connect most major centres in the country, but its capacity is underutilized. However, the railway authority has been reluctant to let others use its dormant capacity.

In Sri Lanka, the government imposes a licence fee of Rs3 million, which ensures that ISPs are operated only by large organizations. Many local observers have suggested that this prevents smaller niche players from providing services, many of whom would be able to start in smaller areas that are ignored by the larger organizations. There are currently eight licensed Internet Service providers in Sri Lanka and many more value-added resellers, although with only an estimated 12,000 users by June 1998.

Despite these regulatory impositions, there are signs that countries in this second category are gradually liberalizing telecommunications, broadcasting, and media - albeit slower than many in the private sector would like.

In Nepal, for example, the government has recently allowed the private sector to operate its own satellite facilities rather than go through the monopoly provider, Nepal Telecommunications Corporation (NTC). This follows the setting up of an independent regulator, the Nepal Telecommunication Authority (NTA), in April 1998. One of the first decisions of the NTA was to open the market for very small aperture terminal (VSAT) satellite facilities, which will allow ISPs to obtain their own international bandwidth at a cost well below that offered by NTC.

The regulator has indicated that other aspects of telecommunications will also be opened up to competition in the next two years, although there is no indication that broadcasting will also be liberalized.

Nepal's four television stations and seven radio stations are all government-owned. By contrast, the Internet in Nepal was first introduced by the private sector, in 1993, and has flourished without any sort of public assistance.

While there are only three ISPs, there are literally hundreds of walk-in access centres, a pattern that has previously been established for telephone and fax services, where Public Call Offices (PCOs) offer walk-in services. A group of more than 30 Nepali research organizations is also networking together to provide local research and development information on NepalNet, a PAN project.

In most of the countries mentioned, there are indications that telecommunications and the media are slowly being liberalized, with governments in the process of overhauling their regulatory structures to make way for the new information environment.

In Bangladesh, control over regulatory matters was recently moved away from the state-controlled Bangladesh Telephone and Telegraph Board (BTTB); China has recently restructured and merged its regulatory environment; India has removed the monopoly for providing Internet services enjoyed by the state-owned carrier, VSNL; Pakistan is privatizing its telecommunications carrier, and the list goes on. While some governments are slower than many in the private sector would like, the momentum to liberalize will certainly continue, in a manner deemed appropriate by each country.

It is not surprising that those countries moving to broadband infrastructure based on technologies such as ATM (asynchronous transfer mode) networks · which allow for the convergence of voice, data, video, and

Internet - are also moving at a more rapid rate towards the full deregulation of the media, telecommunications, and the Internet.

The economies in this category - Australia, New Zealand, Singapore, Malaysia, Hong Kong, South Korea, and Japan - are also the most developed and prosperous in the region and have well-developed infrastructures and well-educated technical work forces. Each of these countries is also vying to become a regional hub for broadcasting and information technology, a fact which seems to further encourage liberalization and investment in infrastructure and services.

In recent years, Japan, Australia, and New Zealand have opened up their markets for telecom- munications services, while in Singapore, Malaysia, Taiwan (China), Hong Kong and the Republic of Korea this process is well underway and in some cases has been accelerated. In terms of Internet access, Japan, Australia and New Zealand are all in the top tier of nations globally. When the ratio of host computers is compared to GDP, New Zealand is the second most wired nation in the world, behind Finland.

The New Zealand city of Wellington, according to the January 1998 survey by United States-based Network Wizards, is the world's most Internet-connected city, with 4,70 2 Internet-connected computers per 100,000 people. In Australia, according to the latest figures from the Bureau of Statistics, almost a third of Australian adults, or 4.2 million people, use the Internet, while the number of households with access to the Internet increased by 46% last year to almost 1.25 million (18% of households), giving it one of the highest Internet penetration rates in the world. This increase is backed up by the number of

Internet hosts, which has been consistently among the top five nations, even though the population base is a mere 18 million.

In Japan, there were some 2,600 registered ISPs and 13 million users as of October 1998. In the year 2000 the number of users is expected to rise to 20 million. One feature of the Internet in Japan has been its spread into virtually all areas of the countryside through a multitude of small niche-market providers. Similarly, Japan's media and telecommunications industries are notable for the array of choices and the number of small players.

For example, there are 121 daily newspapers in circulation as well as 291 community papers and 528 town papers, while in telecommunications there are some 4,726 providers of varying sizes and descriptions.

In Singapore, Malaysia, Taiwan (China) and the Republic of Korea the government has historically taken a prominent role in guiding the use and spread of broadcasting and media for both political and economic reasons. The introduction of Internet has followed this pattern, although there are increasing signs that these governments recognize the need to open up more than in the past.

Nevertheless, the public sector is still instrumental in propelling these countries towards an information society. For example, Malaysia has made a number of well-publicized initiatives aimed at placing itself at the forefront of the global information economy, particularly through its Multimedia Super Corridor (MSC) project. The MSC is Malaysia's hope for becoming a knowledge-based society having developed country status by the year 2020.

MSC incorporates two 'smart cities', an advanced telecommunications infrastructure and seven flagship application areas in government, education, medicine, finance, manufacturing, R&D and marketing. As part of its efforts to attract electronic commerce projects to the MSC, it is in the process of introducing cyberlaws that aim to create a regulatory framework for information and e-commerce services. Malaysia has approximately 205,000 Internet users.

Malaysia has partially deregulated its media and telecommunications industries but government influence is still strongly felt in all sectors. In telecommunications, deregulation has been limited to a handful of large players, while in broadcasting a number of private radio and television stations have emerged, although the government stations are still in the majority. In 1996, Malaysia launched its own satellite, the Malaysian East Asian Satellite (MEASAT).

Malaysians can receive satellite transmissions only through this domestic service, rather than from other sources as an open policy would permit. In Singapore, IT 2000: a vision of an intelligent island' is a masterplan for the introduction of IT into every aspect of Singaporean society. Initiatives such as the Singapore ONE broadband network are part of IT 2000 and are aimed at turning the country into an IT and broadcasting hub. The backbone of this network uses state-of-the-art asynchronous transfer mode (ATM) switches connected via fibre optic trunks that thread through the central business districts and residential neighbourhoods.

Access to the network for individual users will be via asymmetric digital subscriber line (ADSL) modems and hybrid fibre-coaxial (HFC) cable modems, both of which can deliver Internet access at bandwidths of 2 Mbps or better. Once implemented, the network will be available to 90% of all homes. The total number of Internet users in 1998 was estimated at more than 400,000. In keeping with its approach to media in general, the government of Singapore has taken a hands-on approach to the regulation of Internet content.

The Singapore Broadcasting Authority (SBA) regulates both ISPs and Internet Content Providers through the Internet Class Licence Scheme, which requires all providers and resellers to follow the SBA's Internet Code of Practice. Under the obligations of the code, Internet access providers are required to deny access to sites that have been prohibited by SBA.

In the Republic of Korea, the IT and electronics industries have been a successful part of the economy with many large high-tech manufacturers and exporters. The government is also involved in building capacity through the Korea Information Infrastructure (KII). The KII is intended as a broadband infrastructure and comprises two networks: a public network for the private sector and a government network for government or public institutions.

The Ministry of Communications and Information plans to put this broadband infrastructure in place by 2010 through a combination of private and public sector investment. The number of Internet users was 2.5 million at the end of 1997. In advertising, there are approximately ten active companies and many others preparing to enter online activities. In publishing, book stores are opening cyber facilities, while data communications companies are also opening cyber bookstores as part of cyber shopping-mall initiatives. In the media, 'Internet only' journals that do not publish regular paper journals are also beginning to appear.

Basic telecommunications infrastructure in Taiwan (China) is well advanced and dominated by Chunghwa Telecom Co., which is in the process of being privatized. There are over 9 million telephone sets, extensive microwave radio relay trunk systems on the east and west coasts for domestic connections, satellite earth stations and submarine cables to Japan, Philippines, Guam, Singapore, Hong Kong, Indonesia, Australia, the Middle East and Western Europe.

Currently, there are over 500,000 users from around 400 academic institutions, colleges and universities in the island who benefit from the Taiwan Academic Network's free services to promote academic research. The island's National Information Infrastructure (NII) plan was introduced in 1994 with the following priorities: network construction, education and training, electronic government, electronic commerce, social welfare, life long learning, Chinese culturalrelics online, the study and revision of related laws and regulations and internationalization of Chinese networks.

Today, libraries must redefine their roles if they are to survive and prosper in the new age of information-based societies. The dramatic capacity increase of digital media, the convergence of telecommunication and broadcasting, and the availability of information resources accessible through the Internet have driven home the realization that libraries must reposition themselves. The new vision sees libraries as part of networked environments, and the promotion of IT is an integral part of library services in meeting the changing information needs of users.

Thus, the focus has been on developing the digital library, which includes identifying repositories of multimedia digital information resources and integrating the country's libraries and knowledge-based institutions through networking; establishing information resource networks or 'libraries without walls'; creating local content or databases - text (reports, publications, bibliographic databases), audio, video, maps, pictures, graphics - in digitized form, using image processing and character recognition among the technologies employed; making information resources accessible on the Internet; marketing library services through web pages; and providing Internet facilities and stimulating an Internet culture among the public.

Satellite television is one of the obvious areas of regional activity and its reach and influence has been dramatic. In recent years a large number of local, regional and multinational satellite television companies have been set up in Asia. Prominent among these is Hong Kong-based Star TV, which beams programmes to 220 million households in the Asia-Pacific region.

Increasingly, many of the programmes and channels are localized and broadcast in a variety of Asian languages. However, the use of such regional services varies from country to country, with some, such as India and Japan, welcome foreign programmes while others, including China, Malaysia and Singapore, restrict the entry of foreign programming.

In terms of telecommunications, satellite facilities are also providing regional coverage, most notably through regional systems such as AsiaSat, Apstar, as well as through international systems such as PanAmSat, Intelsat and the forthcoming Iridium and similar low-earth orbit

(LEO) schemes. Taiwan (China) and Singapore have also co-operated to launch the ST-1 telecommunications satellite in 1998.

Telecommunications networks using fibre-optic cable are also coming to the fore. Prominent among these are Fiber Optic Link around the Globe (FLAG), which links the rest of the world with countries including Korea, Singapore, Hong Kong and China, and SEA- M E - W E 3 , which in Asia connects Singapore, Australia, Korea and Japan. Another regional telecommunications project known as ACASIA comes from ASEAN countries. It is aimed at providing multinational corporations with cross-country private network services.

Development agencies have been instrumental in helping developing countries in Asia adopt information technologies. IDRC's PAN programme, mentioned earlier, promotes South-South and North-South Internet linkages, while the UNDP also implements numerous technical co-operation programmes throughout the region. The UNDP's Asia Pacific Development Information Programme (APDIP) based in Kuala Lumpur, Malaysia, promotes the use of IT in the region and also focuses on Internet governance issues.

Another regional body involved with Internet governance and infrastructure issues is the Singapore-China, officially the People's Republic of China, is the world's third largest country by area and the largest by population. Covering a total area of 9,596,960 square kilometres, China encompasses a diversity of landscapes extending from the Tibetan Plateau at the southwest extremity to the deserts in the Mongolian borderland of north central China and to the sub-tropical fertile plains of the Canton Delta to the south.

China's population density is relatively high. Distribution, however, is uneven: the coastal areas in the east are densely populated, with more than 400 people per square kilometre, while the plateau areas in the west are sparsely populated, with fewer than 10 people per square kilometre. Telecommunication is one of the fastest growing industries in China.

Domestic and international telecommunication services are increasingly available for private use. By the end of 1997, the number of telephone lines had expanded to 120 million, with 9.55 telephones per hundred persons. The domestic system serves principal cities, industrial centres, most townships and is fast reaching villages. By 1997, 55.6% of China's villages were connected to the public telephone system.

By 1997, 14 inter-provincial fibre-optic trunk lines had been installed, while mobile communication networks and international services have been expanding rapidly. The Chinese government encourages the development of Chinese software and formatted fonts facilitate the use of Chinese characters for digital communication. It is estimated that Internet users in China will exceed 2 million by the end of 1998 and reach 5 million in the year 2000.

Yet considering China's population of 1.2 billion, the percentage of people accessing the Internet is and will be very small. For the whole nation to become 'wired', the geographic, professional, gender and economic obstacles to accessing the Internet would need to be addressed. In China, major metropolitan cities and economically more advanced regions tend to have the best network facilities and therefore it is not surprising that most Internet users are based in Beijing, Shanghai and Guangzhou. Beijing also has the most ISPs.

Ordinary people are still not very aware of the Internet, and current users are mostly in computer-related professions or have higher education qualifications. The average user is young - 80% are between 21 and 35 - and 88% of Internet users in China are male. Placing great emphasis on the strategic importance of information/communication technologies to the modernization of China's economy, the Chinese government has made it a priority to build the national information infrastructure (NII), especially national economic computer network projects in the country's Ninth Five-Year Construction Plan (1996-2000).

The government supports the expansion of Internet into China, though it maintains close control over content. While foreign ownership of any Chinese telecommunications and information infrastructure is strictly prohibited, the government actively seeks foreign investments to fund the rapid development of China's information infrastructure. The four major Internet backbone networks are all government sponsored and must use China Telecom links to connect to Internet sites in other countries. All ISPs must register with the police.

The Temporary Provisions of Internet Administration of the Computer Information Communication network of the P.R.China'. This mandated that the four established Internet networks - ChinaNet, CHINAGBN, CERnet and CASnet - should be separately administered by the Ministry of Posts and Telecommunications, the Ministry of Electronics Industry, the State Committee of Education, and the Science Institute of China.

In June 1998, the government restructured its information and telecommunications authorities. The

Ministry of Information Industry (MII) was established by merging the Ministry of Electronic Industry and the Ministry of Post and Telecommunications.

The new ministry is responsible for invigorating the manufacture of information products, telecommunications and software; formulating sectoral programmes, policies and legal codes; mapping out an overall plan for telecommunications trunk networks (including local and long-distance telecommunications networks), broadcast and television networks (including radio and cable television networks), and special-use telecommunications networks for military and other departments.

At the opening of the 7th Annual Conference of the Asian Media Information and Communication Centre in May 1998, UNESCO's representative Mr Claude Ondobo observed that in education, information technologies must better respond to the different learning and training needs of society; in culture, multimedia technologies must promote cultural and linguistic pluralism; and in science, information highways must improve both access to scientific information and the sharing of research facilities on a large scale and in a more interactive way. This Asia-Pacific ICT report card seems to demonstrate these ICT goals.

ICT and Central and Eastern European Countries

All Central and Eastern Europe (CEE) countries are undergoing a process of fundamental political and economic transformation that interacts with changes in social structure and, in many cases with the need to redefine territorial and cultural boundaries. Economic policy has focused on social, economic and labour problems resulting from the crises provoked by the collapse of the old system and the accompanying need to dismantle and/or modernize inefficient and unproductive industries. Consequently, little attention has been paid to promoting forward-looking policies in information and communications technology (ICT) and progress has been slow.

Central and Eastern European countries entered the 1990s with broadcasting and telecommunications infrastructures inherited from the communist era when they were underdeveloped and tightly controlled. Now, however, big changes are underway.

The direction and the pace of change differ greatly from country to country, depending on the general political and economic context. In some of the more advanced countries, a dual system of private and public broadcasting is already operating in ways similar to the pattern prevailing in Western Europe. Elsewhere, the state monopoly of broadcasting has been preserved to all intents and purposes, with the old state broadcaster still operating and dominating the scene.

Central and Eastern European countries represent a wide variety of social and political environments, as well as different levels of economic and technological advancement. Reliable data for some of them are very hard to obtain. The following overview, therefore, cannot claim to be complete. In some cases, data from several sources and for different years have been used to provide as full a description as possible. More detailed information is generally available for Central European countries, and therefore much of the attention will be focused on them.

Progress in new information and communication technologies is determined to a very large extent by the level of economic and technological development, as well as the size of the market and the purchasing power of the population. Therefore, discussion of ICTs in Central and Eastern Europe would be incomplete without at least a cursory examination of these structural factors.

In low-income countries, the volume is insignificant, indicating that telecommunications are not yet an important part of the economy. There are also clear differences in the level of telecommunications revenue and investment between more and less advanced countries in the other income brackets.

To take one example, Lithuania is one of many CEE countries where the existing quality of local communications does not satisfy the users' requirements. Therefore, plans call for replacing analogue telephone centres with digital ones - to be completed by 2015 - and for setting up of a telephone subscriber information system, with the gradual introduction of special equipment, such as voice simulation, automatic system control, and communication with other countries' systems. By 2000, existing coin-box telephones will be replaced by card-operated ones; card telephone control and diagnostics centres will be established in all branches of Lithuanian Telecom.

Rapid development of the fibre-optic cable line network is planned. In 1996, a fibre-optic line from Kaunas to Klaipëda via Panevëpys and Diauliai was introduced, with digital 155 Mb/s multiplexing systems. Lithuanian telecommunications will be provided with a second international communication line via Latvia; it will be possible to connect twelve Lithuanian cities by means of a high-capacity transmission system. The same fibre-optic lines will be used for the setting up of a national public data network.

At the 1996 Central and East European Information Society Forum it was pointed out that penetration targets for fixed telephone lines set for the year 2000 range from 18.9% for Romania to 50.0% for Latvia. To meet those targets, CEE telecommunications would need to install new lines that are at least 50% faster over the next five years.

The total investment required in all ten CEE countries together to achieve those targets would be about $20,000 million, or $4,000 million per annum. Those targets are high compared with an annual investment rate of $1,600 million for the four years up to 1995 during which the three International Financial Institutions (IFIs) provided at most $440 million per annum.

In some countries, pay television is available and spreading. As with cable, reception of Direct to Home (DTH) satellite television and VCRs, the appearance and development of pay television is determined by the size of the market and living standards (including discretionary purchasing power) prevalent in a particular country. For this reason, pay television can be found mostly in Central European countries.

Spending on hardware, software and services is another important difference between the less and the more advanced countries. The country-level markets of Central and Eastern Europe remain heavily oriented towards personal computers and PC-related technologies. These accounted for the largest percentage of IT hardware spending during the 1996-1997 period.

By contrast, in the Czech Republic, personal computers and related hardware represent less than 35% of IT spending, with the remainder being shifted to implementation services, networking applications, development and support. Elsewhere, the low-end office equipment market, local area network (LAN) hardware and the LAN server market have experienced considerable growth over the last several years. However, the computer systems segment (mainframes, servers, workstations) has stagnated in several countries due to reductions in funding for public IT projects.

Particularly strong growth is being seen in the market for packaged software, such as PC applications software, enterprise resource planning (ERP) applications, and application tools for database development and management. Demand for basic services such as IT consulting, contract programming and software design is also strong. Most growth in the software and services sector is derived from large-scale projects in banking, financial services, government administration, telecommunications and industry. Local firms play a role of growing importance as system integrators, value-added resellers, software developers and training centres.

New information and telecommunication technologies are gradually being introduced into all spheres of life in Central and Eastern Europe. In Estonia, for example, a national school computerization programme, known as 'Tiger Leap', has been launched. In 1997, 25% of all schools were connected to the Internet. By the year 2000, all the schools are scheduled to be on the Internet.

A similar project, School-Net, was inaugurated in 1996 in Hungary, with a view to providing direct access to the Internet for about one thousand schools by 1 September 1998. As a result of this project, schools are being equipped with computer laboratories incorporating 6 to 18 multimedia computers per laboratory.

In Estonia, computer workplaces installed in national public administration authorities (PAAs) were expected to achieve an average of almost 90% by the end of 1997. Some branches were expected to reach 100%. Local area networks (LANs) are rapidly being adopted in Estonian PAAs. In 1993 there were only 15 networks in operation and 23 uninstalled network kits; by the end of 1997 the estimated number of LANs was expected to reach 431. However, the LANs used in these administrations are usually not large. The average number of workstations connected into a public administration LAN is 14.5, including 56 in networks of supporting structures, 17 in ministry networks, 12 in national board networks, 6 in inspectorates and 15 in county government networks.

In Lithuania, due to the limited funding available from the state budget in 1993-1995, only the most important technology projects were selected for investments. These included the integration of computer networks for public institutions, the state register system and geographical information systems, and networks for local authorities and customs. Altogether, 46 institutions were united into the Public Institutions Computer Network (VIKT): the Seimas (Parliament), the Government, the Ministries of Economics, Finance, Communications and Informatics, Foreign Affairs and Internal Affairs, the Customs and Statistics Departments, the Vilnius Municipal Office and similar bodies. They were also provided the opportunity of connecting to the

Internet. LITNET, a Lithuanian science network, has been an official member of the Internet since 1994.

LITNET allows the multimedia exchange of texts, graphs, signals, static and moving images among subscribers from 173 countries of the world. The network's services are used by 10 universities and academies, 14 research institutes, and about 140 other schools, libraries, public institutions, and healthcare establishments. LITNET consists of over 2,000 computers and the number of users exceeds 10,000 people.

There is a co-ordinated effort to develop computerized information systems (IS) that help manage government departments like the Ministry of Internal Affairs, the State Control Department, the Ministry of Finance, and the Ministry of Social Security and Labour. An X.25-standard data communication network, Vilniaus DATAPAK, with 240 connection ports, is operated by Lithuanian Telecom. It is used by the Customs IS and the Bank IS. The examples of Estonia and Lithuania illustrate the increasing use of ICT in Central and Eastern European countries, where they are among the most developed in the region.

Broadcasting monopolies are a thing of the past in Central and Eastern Europe, but political and economic circumstances in individual countries have shaped broadcasting systems differently. In most Central European countries, a dual system of public and private broadcasting is operating at the national and also, in some cases, at the sub-national level.

In the Commonwealth of Independent States (CIS), the situation is different. In these countries the private sector is non-existent: there are, in most cases, no independent or commercial stations at the national level, and 'authorities have retained control over important state-owned media. If they have not outlawed independent or opposition altogether . . . they have retained important levers: they may withdraw subsidies, increase the rent of editorial premises, refuse to print or distribute a paper, delay registration, deny a licence or frequency to a broadcaster, increase tariffs, restrict access to information or file libel suits'.

Economic factors also weigh heavily on growth prospects for the media in most CEE countries. Larger or more buoyant markets attract foreign investors and generate relatively high volumes of spending on advertising. On the other hand, underdeveloped and stagnant economies are not capable of sustaining extensive media growth: there is neither start-up capital, nor sufficient advertising to finance such activity.

Central European states resulting from the demonopolization of television at the national level. Practically everywhere in CEE countries cable television is in private hands, with foreign companies sometimes holding a majority stake. Progress is also being made, albeit at a slower pace in some countries, towards the liberalization of telecommunications. No doubt this is aided by the fact that many Central European states aspire to membership in the European Union (EU) which requires policies in harmony with those of the EU.

In traditional telecommunications services, the market in many cases is still closed, or open only to limited competition. Even where telecommunication companies have been privatized, many of them have been given exclusive long-term licences. Full liberalization will come only when these licences have expired. As far as new services - Global System for

Mobile Communication (GSM), Nordic Mobile Telephone System (NMT) 40, Digital Cellular System (DCS) 1800, satellite communications, radio paging, data transmission, Internet service provision - are concerned, the market is open in most cases and they have been launched from the start by private companies, many with significant foreign shareholders.

Bulgaria and Romania have yet to liberalize their telecommunications. Poland has begun a process of privatization of Polish Telecom (TP S.A.) by selling a part of its shares on the stock exchange. A strategic partner is to be chosen in 1999. Several countries have decided to choose international operators as strategic investors by partially privatizing their telephone companies. Several local telephone operators have been licensed. New services are provided by private companies, many with foreign shareholders.

The Estonian government sold 49% of Esti Telefon to a Scandinavian consortium. The private investors have been given management control with a 25-year concession to operate the national network, as well as an exclusivity period of eight years to provide long-distance service.

Hungary at first sold 30% of its national operator MATÁV to a consortium of Deutsche Telecom and Ameritech. MATÁV obtained the right to operate long-distance and international services as well as two-thirds of the local areas with an exclusivity period of eight years for public telephone services. Later, Hungary sold a further 37% of MATÁV's shares to Deutsche Telecom and Ameritech.

The government's share holding is now down to 25% so that the foreign consortium has both majority ownership and full management control. The remaining local areas have been sold to several smaller operators under similar conditions. The private investors have management control with an 8-year concession.

Latvia sold a 49% stake of Lettelkom to a consortium led by Finland Telecom and Cable & Wireless, with a 10% equity stake bought by the International Finance Corporation. Lettelcom has a 20- year concession to provide domestic and international telecommunication services.

In Lithuania, the market is theoretically open, but in most areas there is only one operator, Lietuvos Telekomas (LT). It is foreseen that a new telecommunications law will grant LT exclusive right to provide some services until 2003. The Czech government allowed SPT Telecom A/S to increase its capital by creating new shares which were sold to Tel Source. This consortium, which includes the Dutch telecommunication and postal group (KPN) and Swiss Telecom, owns 34% of SPT and has management control. The arrangement helps finance the company's modernization plans.

Central and Eastern European countries which are associated with the European Union have been able to benefit from the Phare Fund. This Fund is available for upgrading the knowledge and practical experience of staff who handle the operational and regulatory aspects of improved telecommunications systems.

Other projects have concentrated on facilitating investments, on providing aid for setting up independent telecommunications regulatory authorities and on developing licensing guidelines and expanding services. Additional funding has been earmarked for restructuring the transport, energy and telecommunications sectors in

CEE countries to help them play a larger role in a market economy.

For example, assistance has gone towards eliminating bottlenecks at some of the important border crossings and towards developing a more rational and efficient use of resources. The old system's artificially low prices for energy had encouraged inefficient production techniques and high consumption, which in turn led to serious environmental degradation. To address these problems, the European Union has supported the setting up of commercial companies to manage energy production, telecommunications services, privatization of road transport, restructuring of rail companies and the preparation of a regulatory framework for both the telecommunications and transport systems.

Since 1995, the European Commission has organized annual European Union/Central and Eastern European countries (EU/CEEC) Information Society forums whose goal is to integrate candidate CEE countries into European and international efforts towards the Global Information Society. Policies and strategies for implementation have been developed through a series of meetings.

In 1996 the second Forum created four panels which dealt with strategy and policy formulation for the Information Society; implementation of demonstrations, pilot projects and other actions; education and training for the Information Society; and the application of information and communications technologies in public administration. At the same Forum, an Action Plan for Information Society pilot projects in CEE countries was adopted. It was based on the conviction that 'for the CEE countries, the information society is a top priority in order to improve competitiveness and enhance the efficiency of public administration.

Even though some important political decisions have yet to be made, and the financial resources available are severely limited, it is still crucial to send positive signals about the information society in order to raise public awareness. For this reason, this set of ideas has been put forward in the form of an action plan. . . . The action plan has identified thirty themes covering the areas where pilot projects will be particularly effective.'

The 'informatization' of Central and Eastern European societies has been both a top-down and a bottom-up process. It began only after 1989 when political and administrative constraints on access to, and use of, information and telecommunication technologies were lifted. Considering these inauspicious beginnings, CEE societies have indeed made great strides in the past decade.

Nevertheless, it is clear that Central and Eastern European countries are only at the beginning of their journey towards the Information Society. In 1996, Panel A, Financing of Infrastructure, of the Central and East European Information Society Forum, concluded that 'in most cases, the governments of CEECs are not organized in such a way as to enable them to monitor the evolution of the "Information Society" as an economic sector [and] specific new responsibilities are needed.

To be effective, such responsibilities would have to operate across the boundaries of existing government ministries and other agencies'. Even more importantly, many of those governments have yet to focus fully on the issue of the Information Society, preoccupied as they are with the job of creating a market economy and dismantling the legacy of the centralized economic system. For many, economic underdevelopment and crisis/stagnation have created immediate and pressing challenges which direct attention away from the promise of the Information Society.

Nevertheless, a number of countries have adopted action programmes oriented towards laying the groundwork for the creation of the Information Society. In Hungary, a National Information Infrastructure Development Programme had been operating for more than ten years in 1997. Hungary has established a Governmental Committee on Information and Telecommunication Technology and has developed a 'National Informatics Strategy'.

In Lithuania, the task of the Ministry of Communications and Informatics is to form and to implement the Lithuanian communications and informatics strategy, to organize postal, telecommunications and informatics activities, and to co-ordinate the operation of public telegraph, telephone, data transmission, information, radio and television facilities and networks belonging to enterprises, institutions, organizations and individuals. The Ministry of Communications and Informatics co-ordinates the development of the national data transmission networks and state databases, registers and information systems.

In Estonia, a development plan for Estonian informatics has been adopted. It includes a package of documents describing Estonia's information policy: 'Fundamentals of the Estonian Information Policy', an 'Action Plan' and 'Proposals to the Government of the Republic'. Similar documents developed in the past have had little impact.

By the year 2005, the plan calls for extending the information infrastructure to the countryside and for advancing informatics in Romania to the level required for integration into the European information society. The Polish government has adopted a 'Telecommunications

Development Policy' and has before it a number of draft documents concerning ways of moving towards the Information Society. The third EU/CEEC Information Society Forum (1997) invited CEE governments to ensure that their national Information Society strategy and related action plan contain chapters specifically devoted to such important areas as national budgetary provision, the pro-active role of government, protection of personal data, information security and cryptography, education for the Information Society, promotion of cultural and linguistic diversity and international co-operation in statistics.

Impact of ICT in Latin America and Caribbean

The situation of information centres and libraries and the networks being set up within Latin America and the Caribbean to link them together, with the support of the Organization of American States (OAS) and the Hemisphere Wide Inter-University Scientific and Technological Information Network (RedHUCyT). Thirdly, we shall consider communications, touching briefly on the situation of mass print media, and referring to the extraordinary growth of telecommunications in the region.

The worldwide expansion rate of Information Technologies has been increasing rapidly, and the Latin America and Caribbean region is no exception to this trend, although the regional growth rate is generally below that of the developed countries and of the world as a whole.

In the Information Society Index (ISI) designed by International Data Corporation, the region ranks close to the world average for a number of social criteria (freedom of the press, civil liberties and secondary education), for one computing infrastructure criterion (percentage of PCs in networks) and for one information infrastructure criterion. For the remaining factors, it is below the world average, and far below the position of developed countries such as the United States.

The Latin American and Caribbean region contains approximately 6% of world population and accounts for 3% of world IT investment, whereas North America, with 5% of the population, accounts for 45% of world IT investment. The relative position of the region in this respect is similar to that of Africa/Middle East. All other regions outstrip Latin America, with the exception of Asia and the Pacific (excluding Japan).

The Latin American IT market represents 3% of the world market, but growth in Latin America is above the world average, being twice as high in the period 1995-1996, and almost twice as high in 1996-1997. For the period 1997-2002, growth in the Latin American market is forecast to be 51% higher than the world average.

Information and Library Services

In general, libraries in Latin America and the Caribbean have sought to adapt to new technological developments, while their efforts have been concentrated on meeting local needs. Traditionally, however, co-operation initiatives, which are a top priority for modern information services, have been few and far between.

Institutions such as the OAS and UNESCO have been supporting the creation of networks between libraries in the region, as a way for these to cater for the growing demand for information services in spite of increasingly tight budgets. As a result, there has been progress in setting up local, national and regional consortia to develop library tools and thereby meet more of the requirements that have been created by the Information Age.

Academic and research libraries have been the most successful in entering into co- operation networks and they have received the most international support. It is on the basis of these networks that other libraries will be seeking to create networks among themselves. Consequently, we shall concentrate here on academic and research libraries.

Although the idea of co-operation between libraries was frequently discussed in the 1960s and 1970s, it was a long time before it became a reality in the region, owing to poor telecommunications infrastructure and to restrictions on computer imports in certain countries. These negative factors managed to overwhelm the strong common regional heritage of language, religion and history, which had created a territorial situation probably unique in the world.

The Costa Rican National Research Network (CRNet), supported by the RedHUCyT, is the mainstay of the trunk network which will link up the networks of the Central America region. The first connection was made in November 1996: Costa Rica and Nicaragua were interconnected directly by digital link. Since then, the other countries have also been interconnected. RedHUCyT is supporting the process and providing technical consultancy services to El Salvador, Honduras, Nicaragua and Panama. In March 1997, an agreement was signed with the University of Costa Rica to provide technical assistance to other countries in Central America and the Caribbean.

With the process of creating a trunk network thus under way, Internet use has gained momentum, and this has been reflected in the substantial rise in the number of hosts since 1996. Even so, the number of hosts per capita has remained very far below the regional average, and is falling farther behind all the time. Cellular telephony has always been below the regional average, and is likewise dropping ever farther behind. As regards the number of personal computers (PCs) per capita, the gap with the region is very large indeed, although there could be some uncertainty about this as our source does not have data for certain Central American countries.

In the process of setting up co-operation mechanisms, a number of information networks have emerged, with many of them relying on the CDS/ISIS software distributed by UNESCO which was prepared especially for developing countries.

Among the new fields of operational information there are networks for public administration (CLAD), social sciences (CLACSO), health sciences (BIREME), education (REDUC), planning (INFOPLAN and CARISPLAN), and Major contacts and arrangements are currently being made to connect the Universidad Estadual Minas Gerais and other institutions to the Internet with the support of the RedHUCyT project. This network was one of the joint sponsors and organizers of the First Network Forum in Latin America, together with the National Research Council/National Research Network (CNPq/RNP).

Although progress of this kind had already been achieved before the Internet boom of recent years, the extraordinary growth of Internet use is definitely strengthening co-operation among libraries in these countries.

The Inter-University Network

With the new opportunities generated by the Internet have come new initiatives to support the creation of Latin American information networks that can provide the basis for greater co-operation among libraries in the region. Of these initiatives, particular mention should be made of the RedHUCyT project (Hemisphere Wide Inter-University Scientific and Technological Information Network), launched by the OAS, which began in 1991.

Its main objective is to 'connect Member States to the Internet, forming an electronic network for the exchange of scientific and technological information. The project provides high-tech equipment and technical support, and sponsors technical workshops and seminars in the region to prepare technical projects, improve skills, share technical knowledge and train network managers in the countries'.

The importance of this type of information infrastructure was recognized by the 34 American heads of State at the Summit of the Americas held in Miami in 1994. The Plan of Action signed by them emphasizes the importance of telecommunications and information infrastructure, an entire chapter being devoted to the subject. They state: 'The telecommunications, information technology and broadcasting infrastructure of a country is an essential component of political, economic, social and cultural development.

The Governments of the Americas propose to meet these needs by undertaking a wide range of actions,' in which it is stated, and highlighted in bold, that Governments 'will urge the main universities, libraries, hospitals and governmental organizations to link up to these networks by taking advantage of the OAS Hemisphere Wide Inter-University Scientific and Technological Information Network'. Again, the RedHUCyT has received the backing of Ministers of Science and Technology who, at their Cartagena Meeting in 1996, undertook that their respective countries would 'Promote active participation by the countries of the region in the construction, design and standardization of the Global Information Infrastructure, and encourage them to link up through regional networks such as RedHUCyT'.

In turn, the General Assembly of OAS, meeting in Panama on 3 June 1996, once again stressed the importance of RedHUCyT, with the participants resolving to 'Strengthen regional networks such as the Hemisphere Wide Inter-University Scientific and Technological Information Network (RedHUCyT)'. As a result of the undertakings and support provided on these various occasions, more and more countries in Latin America and the Caribbean have come to participate in the RedHUCyT, constructing their own national networks and connecting them to others.

With this ongoing support and encouragement, the RedHUCyT has been carrying out important activities. During the first stage of the project, the focus was on setting up the basic infrastructure needed to provide academic institutions in the region with access to the Internet. Many of these connections are made via the PAS-1 satellite operated by the Panamerican Corporation of Florida, which provides a direct link-up to the NSF node in Florida. Latin America and the Caribbean 251 for the following countries: Argentina, Costa Rica, Ecuador, Honduras, Paraguay, Peru and Venezuela. The other countries of the region make the connection through operating companies.

The following objectives were set for the second stage of the RedHUCyT project, here quoted verbatim:

— International expansion of Member States' intercommunication and value added networks: the new and increasingly large applications being introduced into electronic networks require high communication speeds. Immediate action is needed on this, as numerous requests for support have already been received.

— Increase in the number of connections and points of presence available nationally for the electronic networks currently in use in member countries. Although most of the countries in the region have some kind of electronic network connectivity, there is a need to create or expand national backbones so that a greater number of institutions can be interconnected. Likewise, local networks within institutions need to be expanded so that a greater number of final users can be reached.

— Assistance for other non-academic sectors, such as: government agencies, particularly those that have databases of interest to the scientific community, and other sectors such as trade, promotion of democracy, human rights, environment and others.

Compuserve Global Data Communication to connect up to the OCLC (Online Computer Library Center) Network. As the RedHUCyT project advances, increasing use will be made of OCLC services in the future. Now that OCLC is using Internet TCP/IP, replacing the proprietary communication protocols with which it began when it was set up in 1970, it is easier and easier to gain low-cost access to libraries connected to the Internet.

Information Services and Libraries in Latin America and the Caribbean will turn this advantage to increasingly good effect. Thus, WorldCat (the OCLC online union catalogue), the Inter-Library Loan System and the FindSearch service, which have yielded such good results in the United States, will be used more and more in the region.

The tide of democracy in Latin America and the Caribbean has generated hopes and expectations of greater freedom of expression and an expansion of the press, radio, TV and other mass media. Although the fall of dictatorships and the emergence of governments elected by popular suffrage do not necessarily guarantee adequate press freedom - as is illustrated, for example, by what has been seen in Guatemala, Peru and Venezuela - they do open the way for a process leading to greater social, political and economic openness, which will gradually foster greater press freedom and freer speech through the media.

Privatization, deregulation and a growing influx of outside capital are acting as catalysts in the process that the tide of democratization made possible and set in train. They are also bringing the countries of the region into the globalization process, which is providing the underpinning for greater expansion of the media and for greater interaction between them and the rest of the world. A good image of this rapid progress towards greater openness to the world may be observed in the juxtaposition of the 150-metre high Entel Tower which dominates the Avenida Bernardo O'Higgins in Santiago, Chile, just two blocks away from the 400-year-old La Moneda Palace. This tower is the voice of the capital; with its satellite and microwave links, and with its data, video and audio communications network, it connects the capital with the rest of the country and with the world beyond the Andes and the Pacific, the geographical barriers that kept Chile isolated in the past. Something similar is happening, rather slowly perhaps, but steadily, throughout Latin America and the Caribbean.

The rapid development of the mass media in recent years has not diminished the great differences and contrasts found in this sector, and may indeed have increased them. What has come out of this process appears to be an intermixing of the First and Third Worlds. On the one hand, there are the multimedia conglomerates typical of the First World, thriving printed newspapers and magazines, television networks and production companies that export television serials and other material. These large corporations have little reason to envy their northern counterparts. The Industria de Medios Latinoamericana owns two of the world's largest and most profitable television networks.

On the other hand, there are newspapers with very

low circulation and rural areas that are sometimes served by just a single primitive radio set. Notwithstanding this contrast, the rise of the communications media would appear to be helping small firms that are effective and efficient to grow, while causing less efficient ones to perish or to be absorbed by better-performing ones.

Consequently, the trends appear to be very promising; this at least is the opinion of a number of authors who have researched the media situation in Latin America. Print media in Latin America and the Caribbean do not appear to have grown significantly in the last two decades.

Some countries, such as Argentina and Chile, have taken firm steps in the right direction; in others, such as Brazil, Colombia, Mexico, Peru and Venezuela significant progress is being made, but prospects are somewhat uncertain and the future is unpredictable enough to discourage the big operating companies from committing greater resources.

However, the great potential of Latin America is attracting more and more attention from operators willing to run the risks involved. Long-term strategies are beginning to take precedence over short-term profits. For example, Robert Meyer, the business development manager for Latin America of BellSouth International, has claimed that 'to be successful here (in Latin America) you need to have patience, and partners that understand the region'.

Two of the main factors driving growth in the telecommunications industry in the world as a whole, and in the Latin America and Caribbean region in particular, are Internet plus mobile computing technologies and wireless communications. These two areas of technology are enjoying the most rapidly accelerating growth in the telecommunications industry. The growth of cellular telephony is remarkable, particularly in developing countries like those of the region, since it is being used as a substitute for traditional telephony, whereas in developed ones it is being used to complement it. The underdevelopment of traditional telephony in developing countries, and the inadequacy of the infrastructure used to provide this service, have led to growth in cellular telephony that is as extraordinary as it is unexpected.

The use of Internet/Intranet/Extranet-related technologies is growing at an extraordinary pace in the region. Corporate spending in this area was $18,000 million in 1997, and in 1998 it increased substantially, according to the 1998 Latin American Corporate Internet Strategy and Adoption Report produced by the International Data Corporation (IDC).

Latin American corporations, however, do not yet have significant plans for electronic commerce, although 45% stated that they had electronic commerce applications. Latin American executives gave two main reasons for this, namely: the problem of security, and a perception that electronic commerce is not particularly profitable, at least for the time being. Security is an issue that has attracted a great deal of attention from Latin American corporations, as a result of which major investments are being made in firewalls and other security mechanisms.

In fact, 40% stated that they were using firewalls in their Web sites and 23% that they were using them in their Intranets. More than 95% stated that they were using some type of Internet/Intranet security mechanism.

Growth in the number of hosts in Latin America and the Caribbean is exponential, as it is in the rest of the world.

Although what has been said so far is equally applicable to Latin America and the Caribbean, except where we have referred explicitly to Latin America alone, we believe it would be useful to make some specific reference to the Caribbean subregion.

Association of National Telecommunication Organizations (CANTO) have been gradually furthering the development of telecommunications and computing in the subregion. The mission of CANTO is to promote and facilitate co-operation and integration in the development of telecommunications in the Caribbean. Its ambition is to become the backbone of the Caribbean family with its focus on human and economic development, through telecommunications.

Its aims are to exchange information, know-how and experience in the area of telecommunications; to help generate the inputs needed for orderly growth and for the formulation of appropriate policies; to consider aspects that are of mutual interest to the Caribbean countries; to develop telecommunications links between those countries; and to promote technical and economic co-operation between them.

CANTO seeks to achieve these aims by providing technical, financial and administrative advisory services, facilitating human resources training, keeping member organization in formed and aware of developments, carrying our out strategic planning, identifying and designing projects of interest and organizing conferences, seminars and exhibitions in the subregion. CANTO held its fifteenth Annual Conference and Trade Exhibition in Aruba from 16 to 20 May 1999. The Organization of Eastern Caribbean States (OECS), whose membership is made up of nine island countries of the Eastern Caribbean, has the objective of making these countries attractive to electronic equipment manufacturers, information processing companies, tourist development companies and agribusiness.

To that end they have set up the Eastern Caribbean Investment Promotion Service (ECIPS) which has recently been giving priority to its efforts in the areas of computing and telecommunications. They hope to turn the Caribbean into a major artery in the information superhighway. Their objective is gradually to build up the advantages of the Eastern Caribbean countries so that foreign companies will site their information processing operations there.

Most of the Caribbean countries now have access to the Internet. Connections to the outside are made through telephone companies. RedHUCyT has also helped arrange two important subregional seminars and financed a number of consultancy operations. In a second phase, the OAS is providing significant funding for the purchase of communications equipment, technical assistance and training, to help enable a greater number of academic, scientific and governmental institutions to connect to the Internet.

In cellular telephony they were slightly above this average until 1996. The apparent decline since then is not a real one, as several Caribbean countries have not reported data. In personal computing, the Caribbean is well below the region; in fact, together with Central America, it has the lowest values for this indicator. A number of Caribbean countries did not provide data in 1996 or 1997, which accounts for the irregular pattern of those years.

Latin America and the Caribbean aim to secure these advantages by providing member countries, which are geographically close to North America, with good-quality and reasonably priced telecommunications services, an efficient labour force with a good command of English, tax incentives, a peaceful and stable environment and pro-business governments.

These efforts are beginning to yield some initial returns. The World Bank has given the OECS countries support in building up telecommunications. Amendments to the laws governing this sector of industry have considerably improved pricing. The Cable and Wireless company is implementing major investments and technological improvements in the OECS countries, including the installation of fibre optic networks. Jamaica has just granted a licence to Globalstar Caribbean Ltd. to provide mobile and wireless communication services, both in Jamaica and in the Caribbean generally. The wireless communication services of this company are based on 48 Globalstar satellites, which send and receive signals to and from regions that are not covered by terrestrial cellular telephony.

ICTs and Western Europe and North America

De regulation of the telecommunications sector, the emergence of global markets and the convergence of media and developments in telecommunications and information technology have forced countries all over the world to face up to new challenges.

It will be less and less easy to separate telecommunications from networked computer-based communications (i.e. the Internet, electronic commerce, Internet-telephony, etc.) and electronic media and content (broadcasting, multimedia, on-line services). The convergence of electronic networks and services is a global phenomenon which transcends national boundaries and increases international competition. Furthermore, unemployment and its harmful effects on society increase the pressure to seize the new economic opportunities offered by the emerging Information society.

These developments represent a political challenge. Experts say that sustainable economic growth and prosperity can be supported by making more efficient use of telecommunications and information technology, by increasing productivity and the development of new products and services.

The development potential of new services such as digital television and the Internet offer huge scope for services that are either completely new or designed to complement existing ones. However, the process of technical convergence brought about by digitization and the merging of previously distinct areas should not lead to the assumption that future developments will be dominated solely by technical issues. Initially we are 'merely' talking in terms of technical potential.

The extent to which this potential is realized and utilized in the countries of Western Europe and North America will depend primarily on infrastructural penetration, usage rates with corresponding added value in work and daily life, and last but not least on political initiatives for the emerging information society.

The worldwide ICT market grew from 910,000 million euros to 1,225,000 million euros between 1994 and 1997, an increase of around 35%. Europe takes second place with 371,000 million euros (30%), followed by Japan with 171,000 million euros (14%). The combined total for all other countries amounted to 259,000 million euros (21%), with growth rates in Asia and Latin America being mainly responsible for the disproportionate increase in this category.

A comparison of national ICT expenditure in 1997 shows that in the United States, it reached 7.0% of GDP and exceeded 6% in the United Kingdom, Sweden, Switzerland and Ireland. In Western Europe ICT technology averaged a direct proportion of 4.9% of GDP in 1997. However, the extraordinary financial significance of information and communications technologies to competitiveness is not only illustrated by the increasing proportion of turnover that this sector represents. More important still is the fact that ICTs are an innovative interdisciplinary technology for other products (e.g. in the fields of mechanical engineering, equipment manufacturing and automotive engineering) and services (e.g. electronic commerce) and represent a high proportion of the potential added value creation of these markets.

At the same time, the extensive digitalization of content, services, networks and terminals is reinforcing the trend towards convergence in the fields of information technology, telecommunications and media (broadcasting, publishing etc.), leading to increased process and product innovation in the value-added chain of the developing multimedia markets. The ongoing process of convergence in the information technology, telecommunications and media sectors serves to reinforce the increasing significance of multimedia-related markets for overall economic development.

In Western Europe, the annual expenditure in these converging fields increased by around 21% between 1993 and 1996 from 743,000 million euros to 897,000 million euros. However, information and communication technologies continue to be the driving force for ongoing growth in the converging sectors.

A study carried out by Booz, Allen and Hamilton on multimedia-related ICT markets (content, networks, components and terminals) in the G7 countries reported a total expenditure of around $1,344,000 million for 1996. The growth rates in these markets have been approximately 10.4% each year since 1992, with the content sector (software, games, multimedia, TV/Pay-TV), which is to a large extent dependent on the software and ICT service market, showing the highest growth rate.

Basic Indicators of ICT

One of the main factors determining a country's competitiveness, its ability to develop innovative new services and content and provide equal access to the new multimedia-related markets for all, lies in the creation of an ICT infrastructure that allows these new services to be distributed among and used by large sections of the population. From a sociopolitical point of view, the problem of ensuring equal access to these markets calls for particular vigilance, because the new media, services and content on offer in an emerging information society represent much more than mere commercial products or sources of market information.

The development of multimedia is in itself a significant cultural issue and serves to express cultural identity. Therefore the extension of technological infrastructures in ICTs and multimedia is one of the main pillars for developing economic and cultural prosperity. However, willingness to invest in information and communications technology - and the financial capacity to do so - varies greatly inside Europe and between Europe and North America.

The lowest per capita ICT investment is found in Greece, Italy, Portugal and Spain. Access to electronic information and services can only be provided where the country in question possesses a network infrastructure that allows the user to connect to the various information and communications services at areas on able price. This infrastructure includes analogue and digital telephone lines, mobile telephone networks and cable and satellite Television connections.

Unlike in Africa, where there are only 2 main telephone lines for every 100 inhabitants on the average, the widespread availability of telephone lines is almost taken for granted in Western Europe and North America. In addition to individual telephony, a telephone line used in connection with the appropriate hardware provides extra functions and services (telephone answering, fax services), which are increasing in importance for both personal and business use. Furthermore, the combination of a telephone line, a personal computer (PC) and modem is currently the most important gateway to the Internet network, which is expanding very rapidly all over the world.

The United States and Canada are again among the leaders, with over 60 lines for every 100 inhabitants.

Germany is the overall international leader in this field, with 4.4 integrated service digital network (ISDN) lines per 100 inhabitants in 1997. By comparison the United States is a long way behind, with around 0.5 ISDN lines per 100 inhabitants.

However, ISDN will face increased competition from other digital transmission technologies in the future, such as Asymmetric Digital Subscriber Line (ADSL), which can multiply the transmission capacity of ISDN using the digitized telephone network. The same applies for the multifunctional application of cable and satellite television, which is currently used almost exclusively for the reception of radio and television programmes, but which will also be used for new multimedia services in the near future.

Within Western Europe, cable and satellite penetration stands at almost 100% of television households, particularly in the Benelux countries. Following close behind with over 90% penetration are Denmark, Switzerland and, with a slightly lower penetration, Germany. However, terrestrial television is still of great importance in Europe and in individual countries such as France, Italy, Portugal, Spain and the United Kingdom.

With around 66 million cable television connections in the United States and 8 million connections in Canada, North America has a very high level of cable penetration. Its lead in relation to the total figure for Western Europe of 42.5 million cable television households is considerable, despite the fact that individual countries in Europe had a higher cable penetration in 1997 than Canada and the United States.

In Western Europe 24.5 million television households received their television and radio programmes via satellite at the end of 1997, representing 16.6% of all television households. Europe is therefore a long way ahead of North America in terms of satellite penetration.

The commercial significance of digital television using broadband transmission via cable and satellite will increase in the future. The interlinking of new television services with new interactive services (Internet access, Online shopping, e-mail by television, electronic commerce, etc.) is particularly important in opening up new economic opportunities for the multimedia-related ICT industry and the media sector. The decisive advantage of digital transmission systems is that, by using compression techniques, the data quantities to be transmitted can be greatly increased, and the frequencies released in the process can be used for new multimedia services.

The current trend within the digital market in European countries shows that the countries that have traditionally been pay-television countries, such as France and Spain, have the highest digital television penetration. France, with the digital television providers Canal+ and the Television par Satellite consortium, and Spain with the providers Canal Satellite Digital and ViaDigital, are currently the only digital television markets in Europe in which there is any noteworthy level of competition.

Digital television is to be launched over the American cable networks this year after a long experimental phase, with the largest cable network operators such as TCI, Time Warner and Comcast having already ordered several million Set Top Boxes for digital reception. The software company Microsoft has also prepared itself for this development, investing around $1,000 million in the cable network operator Comcast in 1997.

This involvement should speed up the development of data and video services available via the Comcast cable network and promote the merging of PCs and televisions , as will the takeover of Web-TV, a company involved in the provision of Internet services and Internet navigation systems via the television set. In the Canadian market, two digital satellite systems have been available since the end of 1997, Expressvu, which has 30,000 customers, and Star Choice, with 50,000 subscribers.

The digital mobile telephone sector is one of the few other areas of the telecommunication sector apart from ISDN development in which Western Europe holds an edge over North America in terms of its position in the world market. This applies both to the production of hardware (e.g. Nokia, Siemens, Ericsson), the development of Global System for Mobile Communications standards (GSM) and in terms of the usage figures for mobile telephone subscribers. The Nordic states of Finland, Norway, Sweden and Denmark in particular surged ahead of North America in the number of lines.

Growth rates in the mobile telephone sector from 1993 to 1997 are impressive. The boom is particularly pronounced in those countries that had previously occupied a mid-range position, with the number of subscribers increasing between five- and tenfold in the last four years. Increasing competition, the integration of tariffs with the fixed network and new services will lead to an increase in the number of mobile telephone subscribers.

In addition, new digital network developments in the mobile telephone sector such as Universal Mobile Telecommunications Systems (UMTS), which have transmission capacities far in advance of those that can be achieved using ISDN, will promote further growth.

In the Southern countries of Europe, on the other hand, only one in ten inhabitants possesses a PC. Penetration is most advanced in North America (United States and Canada), where almost one out of two inhabitants possesses a PC.

At the heart of the multimedia-related ICT revolution is the Internet, the most dynamic market of the future from a financial point of view (electronic commerce, Internet telephony, Internet broadcasting, on-line shopping, etc.). According to figures from the Fachverband Informationstechnik (FVIT), around 89 million people used the Internet or online services on a regular basis in 1997. It is extremely difficult to measure the number of Internet users directly, because individual accounts are sometimes used by several people, and figures from Internet Service Providers (ISP) and on-line services cannot be verified with any certainty.

In both Canada and the United States almost one in four inhabitants was using the Internet at the beginning of 1998. Within Western Europe a very mixed picture emerged with large variations. In the Nordic countries of Europe, Internet use is very advanced, but in the Southern countries (Spain, Italy, Portugal, Greece) at the beginning of the year only around 3% of the population had access to the Internet.

Internet hosts are computers that are permanently connected to the Internet via a fixed Internet Protocol (IP) number and through which access can be gained to the

Internet at any time using the IP. Computers that have access to the Internet only at certain times (e.g. using telephones with alternating IP numbers) are not considered here.

The percentage distribution of Internet hosts illustrates even more clearly the large lead that the Scandinavian countries have gained over other European countries, with Finland having overtaken even the United States. The great variations within Europe have very different causes.

On the one hand, due to their economic weakness, the ability and willingness of Southern European countries to invest is much lower than that of countries with stronger economies and higher incomes.

Cost structures for Internet access are also very varied within Europe and disproportionately high in comparison with North America. The liberalization of the European telecommunications market has been an important factor in causing telecommunications costs to fall within Europe, thus reducing the costs of Internet access. This indicates that the growth rate for Internet use will increase more rapidly in countries where Internet use has previously been at a lower level than in those countries that already have relatively high Internet penetration.

For most governments, the availability of infrastructures for electronically transferring and accessing information is perceived as essential for the realization of the economic, social and cultural benefits and competitive advantages for the economy.

The well known metaphor 'Information Superhighway' is very attractive to the American public.

From the beginning, the NII initiative emphasized benefits for all Americans and stressed a broad concept of universal service and public access. The administration therefore received strong support from public-interest groups. Furthermore the Information Infrastructure Task Force (IITF), set up to co-ordinate the United States Federal Government's activities, developed at an early stage a specific programme aimed at promoting non-commercial applications for the public and non-profit sectors, called the Telecommunications and Information Infrastructure Assistance Programme (TIIAP), which serves the public interest.

In contrast the TELEMATIC application programme in Europe is not limited to the non-profit sector but also supports commercial projects to promote the competitiveness of the European Union. Western Europe and North America 273 The reform of the United States telecommunications law dating back to 1934 took place, when President Clinton signed the Telecommuications Act in February 1996.

This act primarily pre-empts state laws that prohibit entry into local telephone services; establishes the conditions for competition for local telephone services; eliminates restrictions that prevent cable and telephone companies from entering each others' business; gives the Federal Communications Commission (FCC) broad authority; requires the FCC to continue to update the definition of universal service, and to provide discounted service to schools and libraries; and makes the transmission of obscene or indecent communications to minors illegal.

As far as online communication is concerned, legal provisions of the 1996 Telecommunications Act outlaw the transmission of indecent or patently offensive material to minors over PC networks. But the Supreme Court ruled that this Commmunication Decency Act would be unconstitutional as it breaches freedom of speech protected under the First Amendment of the United States Constitution.

In a speech at the International Telecommunications Union (ITU) in 1994, Vice President Gore argued for world wide co-operation to extend the project of the NII to a Global Information Infrastructure (GII). This proposal was later endorsed at a 1995 meeting of ministers from the G7 group of leading industrialized countries. This G7 ministerial conference in Brussels was the first large international conference devoted to the information society, and bringing together political leaders on that subject.

The G7 conference outlined common principles for the worldwide information society and common guidelines for co-operation. The principles outlined were to promote dynamic competition; encourage private investment; define a regulatory framework that can change with the times; ensure open access to networks; guarantee universal supply of and access to services; promote equal opportunity for all citizens; promote diversity of content, including cultural and linguistic diversity; and recognize the need for global co-operation by paying particular attention to the least-developed countries.

This agreement was important as a means of facilitating multinational efforts to co-ordinate the work of global bodies like the World Trade Organisation (WTO), the World Intellectual Property Organization (WIPO) and the International Telecommunication Union

(ITU). The GII is regarded as a key element of economic development and industrial policy in many developed countries as it creates opportunities for reaching international markets.

The United States Administration's major programme for supporting research and development related to the NII is the $1,10 0 million High-Performance Computing and Communications (HPCC) initiative.

Since 1993 the scope of the programme has been expanded to include support for the NII applications and technologies. In October 1996, President Clinton announced the Next Generation Internet (NGI) initiative that will support universities and national laboratories with networks that are much faster than today's Internet.

The Canadian Information Highway

The Canadian Information Highway proposed three main objectives for Canadian strategies, which were to create jobs through innovation and investment, reinforce Canadian sovereignty and cultural identity, and ensure universal access at reasonable cost.

To reach these goals and to provide advice and recommendations to the Minister of Industry the Information Highway Advisory Council (IHAC), with representatives from industry, education, research, labour, consumer and public interest groups, was established at the beginning of 1994. In September. 274 1995, the Advisory Council released its final report Connection, Community, Content: The Challenge of the Information Highway, which contains some 300 recommendations for government action.

In May 1996, the Government of Canada unveiled its plan for building the Information Highway in a report, which underlined four strategic thrusts with the following policies and initiatives:

— building Canada's Information Highway by creating a competitive, consumer-driven policy and regulatory environment that is in accord with the Canadian public interest and that is conducive to innovation and investment by Canadian industry in new services on the Information Highway.

— growing Canadian content on the Information Highway, thereby strengthening the ongoing national cultural dialogue and creating economic growth and jobs.

— realizing the economic and social benefits for all Canadians of the Information Highway and allowing them to participate fully in the emerging information society.

— getting government right by ensuring better services and more affordable, accessible and responsive government and making government a model user and a catalyst for Information Highway development across Canada.

The government also expressed the intention - where market forces fail - to ensure affordable access to essential Information Highway services for all Canadians, regardless of their income or geographic location. In September, 1997, the IHAC published its second final report of its mandate to encourage continuing action with regard to these commitments.

The IHAC concentrated on two tasks, namely advancing the public policy agenda by advising the government on outstanding issues and concerns related to the Information Highway, and reporting on Canada's progress in the transition to an information society and a knowledge-based economy. The IHAC emphasized that technology-neutrality must be the central principle of policy and regulation for the Information Highway, so that no obstacles remain to using the best technology for a given application or purpose.

Access for all Canadians and Canadian quality content are seen as most important imperatives to ensure Canada's future as a knowledge society. The government instructed the Canadian Radio-Television and Telecommunication Commission (CRTC) early in 1995 to conduct public hearings on regulatory changes required as a result of the convergence of broadcasting and telecommunications.

In 1997 the CRTC adopted measures to fully liberalize Canada's telecommunication market by January 1998 and to encourage convergence between telecommunication and broadcasting. New telecommunication entrants were allowed to offer local services in 1998. As regards convergence, cable television operators were immediately allowed to offer local telecommunication services, while telecommunication companies were entitled to apply for broadcasting licenses to enter the market in 1998.

These decisions reflected the policy objectives included in the 1993 Telecommunications Act and the 1991 Broadcasting Act and, last but not least, the priority that the Canadian government has placed on the development of a competitive communications environment. The CRTC is an independent federal agency and is responsible for the supervision and regulation of telecommunications and broadcasting in Canada. The Telecommunication Act gives the CRTC a broad range of powers, including the regulation of telecommunication rates and conditions of service, approval of interconnection agreements, and quality of service standards.

In Canada, a wide range of social and cultural approaches built upon the Canadian tradition of a mixed public/private system (e.g. broadcasting) to the. Western Europe and North America NII have emerged during recent years. In order to develop the new information infrastructure, public policy promotes a new hybrid model of communication, which combines the social and cultural objectives of both broadcasting and telecommunications, and provides new regulatory mechanisms.

Information Policy for European Union

Since the early 1990s the European Union has recognized the need to act quickly to develop an Information Society in Europe. The pace of globalization is picking up and Europeans fear that they will lose ground to the United States, Japan and the new emerging industrial nations in the Far East and South-East Asia. An analysis of the policies of the European Community reveals a gradual shift taking place in strategy. In the 1980s, the emphasis was on promoting information technology. Due to its multifunctionality and cross-sector significance, information technology was designated a 'key technology' and computer manufacturing was elevated to a 'key industry sector'. The key role given to information technology was illustrated in particular by the efforts made by the EU to set up the European Strategic Programme for Research and Development in Information Technology (ESPRIT) in 1984 and the increases in budget allocation for this area in subsequent Framework Programmes. This period was followed by measures aimed at improving the communications infrastructure and accompanied by the deregulation of the telecommunications sector.

By creating a comprehensive telecommunications infrastructure the idea was to offer, by simple, cost-effective means, opportunities to companies, authorities and citizens to share multimedia information (in the form of data, text, voice, still and moving images) to a high technical standard and with no constraints of distance. The creation of a European telecommunications infrastructure featuring narrow- and broad-band networks began with the Research and Development in Advanced Communications Technologies (RACE) and continued with its successor, the Advanced Communications Technologies and Services (ACTS). Within the framework of European policy on promoting the information society, increased assistance was given in the early 1990s towards establishing a trans-European network. To help accelerate and finance this expansion of the technical infrastructure, the European community has adopted deregulation and liberalization of the telecommunications sector as a key pillar of policy with some basic rules: an important precondition in this process is the need to safeguard a universal service and maintain interconnection and interoperability in a manner which ensures open and fair competition.

The liberalization of the European telecommunications market was largely completed at the beginning of 1998. The next step was to place greater emphasis on business matters relating to new services and content in the information society (information as a commodity and factor of production markets). This issue came to the fore, mainly because of the increasing convergence between telecommunications, computing and broadcasting/media sectors. These considerations led among other things to the setting up of the Telematics research programme.

The programme placed greater emphasis on demonstration projects (i.e. in the area of transport, education, health and administration) that reflected market needs and provided assistance for products and multimedia applications likely to prove successful in the marketplace. In this context the problems facing small and medium-sized enterprises (SMEs) were given greater attention within the European assistance programmes. The 'information economy' was seen as the key area which will determine future growth and prosperity.

In December 1993, the European Council entrusted a high-level group, later known as the Bangemann group, with drafting a report. The report by the Bangemann group underscored that the private sector should be given a leading role in developing the European Information Society. In July 1994, the European Commission published a communication entitled Europe's Way to the Information Society: An Action Plan that underlined issues such as the legal and regulatory setting as well as services, applications, content and social and cultural aspects. Since the mid-1990s, new approaches in European information policy, particularly in the area of education and training, pointed to the need to consider the social repercussions of the information society. This change in approach grew from the realization that the upheavals taking place in society and business needed to be underpinned by a social framework. It was also understood that if such a social dimension were to be overlooked, growing problems of acceptance could jeopardize further progress.

The High Level Group of Experts on Social and Societal Aspects of the Information Society, set up in April 1995, and the Information Society Forum (ISF) in July 1995 focused more attention on the social aspects of the information society. However, it can be seen that from the beginning the United States gave more prominence than Europe did to the notion of supporting the non-profit-sector and of improving the ways in which democracy functions and achieving higher levels of political codetermination with the help of online technology. One of the main problems with the European approach of concentrating on individual aspects of the information society one after the other is an inability to anticipate well in advance the cross-sectoral repercussions of the various actions for society, business, law and technology, along with accompanying structural changes. Only with the Green Paper on convergence of December 1997 has the European Commission launched a public discussion regarding a more comprehensive regulatory approach in the field of telecommunications, media and information technology.

Bibliography

A. Friedlander, *Natural Monopoly and Universal Service: Telephones and Telegraphs in the U. S. Communications Infrastructure*, 1837-1940, Corp. for National Research Initiatives, 1995.

A. R. Bennett, *The Telephone Systems of the Continent of Europe*, Longmans, Green, and Co., 1895.

Anonymous, *Distributing music over telephone lines, Telephony*, vol. 18, no. 25 (Dec. 18, 1909), pp. 699-701.

B. Klopfenstein, *Problems and potential of forecasting the adoption of new media*, pp. 21-41

D. Blair, *Impact of the Internet on core switching network*, presented at ENPW '98, March 1998, Les Arcs, France.

D. Cressy, *Coming Over: Migration and Communication between England and New England in the Seventeenth Century*, Cambridge Univ. Press, 1987.

D. Gabel, *The Evolution of a Market: The Emergence of Regulation in the Telephone Industry of Wisconin*, 1893-1917, Ph.D. Dissertation, University of Wisconsin-Madison, 1987.

D. R. Irvin, *Modeling the cost of data communication for multi-node computer networks oper-ating in the United States*, IBM J. Res. Develop. vol. 37 (1993), pp. 537-546.

E. Baark, *Lightning Wires: The Telegraph and China's Technological Modernization*, 1860- 1890, Greenwood Press, 1997.

F. Cairncross, *The Death of Distance: How the Communications is Revolution will Change our Lives*, Harvard Business School Press, 1997.

F. J. Brown, *The Cable and Wireless Communications of the World*, Pitman, 1927.

H. S. Dordick, The *Information Society: A Retrospective View*, Sage, 1993.

J. Ahvenainen, *The Far Eastern Telegraphs: The History of Telegraphic Communica-tion between the Far East, Europe and America before the First World War*, Ann. Acad. Scien. Fennicae #216, Helsinki, 1981.

J. Altmann, B. Rupp, and P. Varaiya, *Internet demand under different pricing schemes,* in Proc. ACM Conference on Electronic Commerce (EC-99), ACM, 1999, pp. 9-14.

M. Blondheim, *News Over the Wires: The Telegraph and the Flow of Public Information in America, 1844-1897*, Harvard Univ. Press, 1994.

M. Castells, *The Rise of the Network Society*, Blackwell, 1996.

M. S. Baratz, *The Econonrics of the Postal Service*, Public Affairs Press, 1962.

P. Flichy, *Dynamics of Modern Communication: The Shaping and Impact of New Communi-cation Technologies*, Sage, 1995. Original French version published in 1991.

R. R. John, *Recasting the information infrastructure for the Industrial Age*, pp. 55-105 in A Nation Transformed by Information: How Information has Shaped the United States from Colonial Times to the Present, A. D. Chandler, Jr., and J. W. Cortada, eds., Oxford Univ. Press, 2000.

Index